PATRICIA BROOKS is the author of 13 books on food and travel and the coauthor of a guidebook on Spain. She has written many articles about Spain for *Travel & Leisure, Bon Appétit,* and other magazines, and has lived in Spain and visits it frequently.

TOM BURNS, a resident of Madrid since 1974, has been the Spain correspondent for *Newsweek* and the *Washington Post* and is a regular contributor to the *London Financial Times*. He is also an associate editor of *Lookout,* an English-language travel and leisure magazine published in Spain.

GERRY DAWES lived in Spain for eight years and studied at the University of Seville. He now lives in New York, where he works in the wine trade. He is a regular contributor to the *Wine Enthusiast* and the *Wine News*. He has lectured on Spain at the Smithsonian Institution and travels in Spain frequently.

ELLEN HOFFMAN is a freelance writer whose work has appeared in the *Washington Post* and the *Los Angeles Times,* among other publications. She received a prize from the Spanish government for her writing about the country.

CARLA HUNT is a freelance writer and contributor of articles to North American and international newspapers and magazines. She travels regularly on the Iberian Peninsula.

MIKE JACKSON, based in New York, is a writer-producer of television documentaries who has travelled much of the world, from South America to South Africa to Europe, Eastern Europe, the Pacific, and the Far East, but Spain, especially northern Spain, is where he returns every chance he gets.

ROBERT LEVINE, a New York–based music and travel writer, has contributed to the travel sections of the *San Francisco Examiner* and the *Denver Post,* and to *Pulse!* and *Fanfare* magazines, among other publications. He visits Spain several times each year.

STEPHEN O'SHEA is a writer and journalist who has covered France and Spain for many years. He is a contributor to *The Berlitz Travellers Guide to France* and currently lives in New York City.

ROBERT PACKARD has written many articles about Spain. His work has been published in the travel sections of *The New York Times* and the *Philadelphia Inquirer* and in *Connoisseur* and *Travel & Leisure* magazines. His latest book, *Refractions:*

Writers and Places, includes chapters on Cervantes and La Mancha and Irving and the Alhambra. A professor of the humanities, he visits Spain frequently.

FRANK SHIELL, a New York writer, is a graduate of the University of Madrid. He is fluent in Spanish and travels frequently throughout Spain.

THE BERLITZ
TRAVELLERS GUIDES

THE AMERICAN SOUTHWEST

AUSTRALIA

BERLIN

CANADA

THE CARIBBEAN

COSTA RICA

ENGLAND & WALES

FRANCE

GERMANY

GREECE

HAWAII

IRELAND

LONDON

MEXICO

NEW ENGLAND

NEW YORK CITY

NORTHERN ITALY AND ROME

PORTUGAL

SAN FRANCISCO &
NORTHERN CALIFORNIA

SOUTHERN ITALY AND ROME

SPAIN

TURKEY

THE BERLITZ TRAVELLERS GUIDE TO SPAIN

Fifth Edition

ALAN TUCKER
General Editor

BERLITZ PUBLISHING COMPANY, INC.
New York, New York

BERLITZ PUBLISHING COMPANY LTD.
Oxford, England

THE BERLITZ TRAVELLERS GUIDE
TO SPAIN
Fifth Edition

Berlitz Trademark Reg U.S. Patent and Trademark Office
and other countries—Marca Registrada

Published by Berlitz Publishing Company, Inc.
257 Park Avenue South, New York, New York 10010, U.S.A.

Distributed in the United States by
the Macmillan Publishing Group

Distributed elsewhere by Berlitz Publishing Company Ltd.
Berlitz House, Peterley Road, Horspath, Oxford OX4 2TX, England

ISBN 2-8315-1720-6
ISSN 1057-4638

Designed by Beth Tondreau Design
Cover design by Dan Miller Design
Cover photograph by Joan Kramer & Associates, Inc.
Maps by Diane McCaffery
Illustrations by Bill Russell
Fact-checked by Claire Vossbrink,
Charles Pappas, and John Immediato
Edited by Amy K. Hughes

Printed in the United States of America
1   3   5   7   9   10   8   6   4   2

THIS GUIDEBOOK

The Berlitz Travellers Guides are designed for experienced travellers in search of exceptional information that will enhance the enjoyment of the trips they take.

Where, for example, are the interesting, out-of-the-way, fun, charming, or romantic places to stay? The hotels described by our expert writers are some of the special places, in all price ranges except for the very lowest—not just the run-of-the-mill, heavily marketed places in advertised airline and travel-wholesaler packages.

We are *highly* selective in our choices of accommodations, concentrating on what our insider contributors think are the most interesting or rewarding places, and why. Readers who want to review exhaustive lists of hotel and resort choices as well, and who feel they need detailed descriptions of each property, can supplement the *Berlitz Travellers Guide* with tourism industry publications or one of the many directory-type guidebooks on the market.

We indicate the approximate price level of each accommodation in our description of it (no indication means it is moderate in local, relative terms), and at the end of every chapter we supply more detailed hotel rates as well as contact information so that you can get precise, up-to-the-minute rates and make reservations.

The Berlitz Travellers Guide to Spain highlights the more rewarding parts of the country so that you can quickly and efficiently home in on a good itinerary.

Of course, this guidebook does far more than just help you choose a hotel and plan your trip. *The Berlitz Travellers Guide to Spain* is designed for use *in* Spain. Our writers, each of whom is an experienced travel journalist who either lives in or regularly tours the city or region of Spain he or she covers, tell you what you really need to know, what you can't find out so easily on your own. They identify and describe the truly out-of-the-ordinary restaurants, shops, activities, and sights, and tell you the best way to "do" your destination.

Our writers are highly selective. They bring out the significance of the places they *do* cover, capturing the personality and the underlying cultural and historical resonances of a city or region—making clear its special appeal.

The Berlitz Travellers Guide to Spain is full of reliable information. We would like to know if you think we've left out some very special place. Although we make every effort to provide the most current information available about every destination described in this book, it is possible too that changes have occurred before you arrive. If you do have an experience that is contrary to what you were led to expect by our description, we would like to hear from you about it.

A guidebook is no substitute for common sense when you are travelling. Always pack the clothing, footwear, and other items appropriate for the destination, and make the necessary accommodation for such variables as altitude, weather, and local rules and customs. Of course, once on the scene you should avoid situations that are in your own judgment potentially hazardous, even if they have to do with something mentioned in a guidebook. Half the fun of travelling is exploring, but explore with care.

ALAN TUCKER
General Editor
Berlitz Travellers Guides

Root Publishing Company
350 West Hubbard Street
Suite 440
Chicago, Illinois 60610

CONTENTS

This Guidebook	vii
Overview	5
Useful Facts	25
Bibliography	36
Madrid	47
Getting Around	89
Accommodations	92
Dining	97
Nightlife	114
Shops and Shopping	118
Side Trips from Madrid	126
El Escorial	131
Avila	135
Segovia	141
Pedraza de la Sierra	148
Alcalá de Henares	149
Aranjuez	150
Chinchón	152
Old Castile	155
Asturias and Galicia	261
Cantabria	304
The Basque Country	326
La Rioja	365
Navarra	392
Aragón	424
Barcelona	445
Getting Around	476
Accommodations	478
Dining	482
Cafés, Bars, Nightlife	490
Shops and Shopping	493

Catalonia   498

The Balearic Islands   535
   Minorca   541
   Majorca   557
   Ibiza   574

Valencia   587

La Mancha   615

Extremadura   647

Andalusia   674

The Canary Islands   785

Historical Chronology   817

Index   835

MAPS

Spain   2
Madrid   48
Palacio Real to the Prado   60
Madrid Environs   128
Old Castile   156
Salamanca Area   178
León Area   196
Valladolid-Palencia Area   216
Aranda de Duero-Burgos Area   230
Asturias and Galicia   262
Cantabria   305
The Basque Country   328
La Rioja   366
Navarra   394
Aragón   425
Barcelona   446
Las Ramblas and Barri Gòtic   452
Catalonia   500
Minorca   542
Ibiza and Majorca   558

Valencia/Alicante	588
City of Valencia	596
La Mancha	616
Toledo	622
Extremadura	648
Andalusia	675
Seville	688
Córdoba	711
The Costa de la Luz and the Costa del Sol	742
Canary Islands	786
Grand Canary and Lanzarote	791
Tenerife	798

THE
BERLITZ
TRAVELLERS
GUIDE
TO
SPAIN

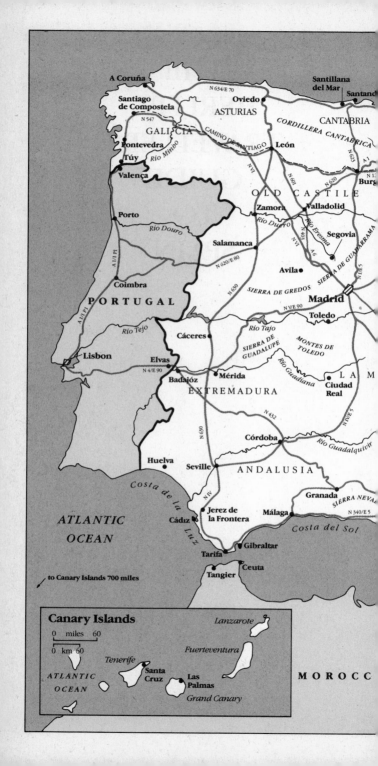

OVERVIEW

By Patricia Brooks

Patricia Brooks is the author of 14 books on food and travel, and the coauthor of a guidebook on Spain. She has written many articles about the country for Travel & Leisure, Bon Appétit, *and other national magazines, and visits it frequently.*

Spain is a country that evokes strong emotions.

The landscape—ranging within short distances from mountain highs to sea level, from tableland to marshland, with dramatic visual changes often occurring within a single mile—demands them. Few visitors who travel the country's length and breadth are unmoved by the experience, the scale, the scope, and, yes, the grandeur of the terrain and the effect it has had on the people who inhabit it.

Writers and artists are among those with the strongest proprietary feelings about Spain. Ernest Hemingway's fascination with the country is well known; yet Virginia Woolf, a writer of very dissimilar sensibilities, wrote this about Spain in one of her essays: "It is the light of course; a million razor-blades have shaved off the bark and the dust, and out pours pure colour: whiteness from fig trees, red and green and again white from the enormous, the humped, the everlasting landscape."

If ever a landscape affected its inhabitants and shaped their character, their lives, their destiny, that landscape is Spain's. One of the pleasures awaiting a visitor to Spain is the opportunity to discover its many regions with their different personalities and distinctive cultures.

Spain is not a single, ethnically unified country but a mix of many ethnic groups sharing what is (if you include the Balearic and Canary islands) the third-largest land mass in Europe, after Russia and France. It is the diversity of all these regions, the fresh experiences and encounters as you move from one to another, that may turn you from a onetime visitor to Spain into a lifelong pilgrim and aficionado. Visiting Spain is like eating peanuts; it is almost impossible to stop with just one.

This is why those of us who have been nibbling at Spain for decades recommend that you do the same, savoring the country a region at a time. While a once-over-lightly tour may show you specific sights—the Alhambra in Granada, the Prado in Madrid, the Giralda in Seville—it will barely touch the cultural, physical, and political differences that exist from region to region, sometimes even from town to town.

Every region has its proponents. Those who love the languid air and matching lifestyle of Andalusia, with its gentle rolling fields and sunstruck all-white villages, look askance at others equally enamored of the craggy, dry terrain and fierce, clear light of Castile, or of the apple-green Galician northwest, or of the Pyrenean villages of Catalonia, where Romanesque church towers loom suddenly into sight around the tortuous turns of the mountain roads.

Geographical Layout

To understand Spain, turn back to the land. The Pyrenees, Spain's natural Maginot Line in the north, have separated the country from much, but not all, of the savaging that has beset the rest of Europe for centuries. As Harold Livermore wrote in *A History of Spain,* "The Pyrenees rose like a wall to mark it off from the rest of the continent, and its coast was clear and economical. In early times men were struck by the sharpness of its outline: Strabo compared it to a stretched ox-hide, and the metaphor of a rough, tawny surface lying taut and dry in the strong sun is an apt one."

At its southern extreme Spain is farther south than Greece and just nine miles from the tip of Africa, another geographic accident with cataclysmic effects on the country's history and cultural and political life. Spain's western edge, Extremadura, melts into eastern Portugal, and the history of the two countries that share the Iberian Peninsula has often intersected through the centuries. Spain's eastern coast, from the edge of France south to Gibraltar, has endured the same seafaring conquerors, traders, and adventurers as other lands washed by the Mediterranean.

Much of Spain's history has been shaped by its high mountains and its life-giving rivers. Next to Switzerland, Spain has the highest average land altitude in Europe. The Meseta, a massive plateau that dominates the country's interior, with Madrid at its center, has an average height of 2,000 feet and is crisscrossed by several mountain ranges. Three rivers flowing west into Portugal—the Duero in the north, the Tajo (Tagus) and the Guadiana farther south—have etched deep valleys into the Meseta. Between the Duero and the Tajo are the stark ridges, some more than 8,000 feet high, of the Sierra de Gredos and the Sierra de Guadarrama; and between the Tajo and the Guadiana rise the peaks of the Sierra de Guadalupe and the Montes de Toledo.

Dominating the northwestern corner of the country is the Cordillera Cantábrica, whose highest peaks, the Picos de Europa, reach 8,688 feet in altitude. Northeast of the Meseta and the plains of Aragón, which are drained by the Río Ebro, the Pyrenees rise up along the French border, with Spain's Pico de Aneto reaching 11,168 feet.

The highest mountain in continental Spain, Mulhacén (11,411 feet above sea level), crowns the Sierra Nevada, which lies far to the south, near Granada, in Andalusia. Andalusia's most important river is the Guadalquivir, which starts east of Córdoba, flows through Seville, and empties into the Golfo de Cádiz at Sanlúcar de Barrameda. Many of the caravels and galleons heavy with gold and silver from the New World sailed into Seville along this waterway, which has since greatly silted up.

The varied terrain accounts for sharp climatic changes from region to region as well, with the northern provinces of Galicia, Asturias, Cantabria, and the Basque Country, all bordering the Atlantic Ocean, being green and fertile, while the central Meseta—Madrid and Castile—is swept by frigid winds in winter and suffers a dry, scorching, airless heat in summer. The east-coast regions of Catalonia and Valencia and Andalusia's Costa del Sol share the humid summers and mild winters common to areas bordering the Mediterranean. Inland Andalusia can be bone-chillingly cold in winter and extremely humid in summer.

History and Culture

Although Spain's protected peninsular location shielded it from many sweeping invasions and petty territorial border wars, that doesn't mean that all was perennially tranquil south of the Pyrenean border—quite the contrary, as a matter of fact.

EARLY SETTLERS

The earliest known settlers in what we now know as Spain were Paleolithic people who left their colorful graffiti in the cave paintings of the Altamira Caves, near Santillana del Mar, on the north coast in Cantabria, and in eerie, Stonehenge-like monuments called talayots on Minorca in the Balearics. Much later, Celtic tribes arrived in the north and west, and the so-called Iberians, a people believed to have originated in North Africa, settled in the south and east. No one knows for certain the origins of the Basques, who are believed to antedate the Iberians.

Greek writers of the third century B.C. called inhabitants of the Meseta Celtiberians. The most famous lasting monument left by these early settlers is *La Dama de Elche,* the mysterious stone portrait found in Elche, on the southeastern coast, now displayed in the Museo Arqueológico Nacional in Madrid. Phoenicians established colonies (most prominently at Cádiz), as did the Greeks; but it was Carthage, an African colony itself established by the Phoenicians, that subdued most of the peninsula by the third century B.C.

THE ROMANS

Romanization came after the end of the second Punic War with Carthage (201 B.C.) and lasted through the fifth century A.D., during which time the country, like Gaul, was divided into three parts: the provinces of Tarraconensis (north, northwest, and central), Baetica (mostly southern Spain), and Lusitania (principally Portugal). Testaments to the endurance of Roman building skills exist most dramatically in the aqueduct in Segovia, the Roman bridge at Córdoba, the amphitheater and the aqueduct in Tarragona, and the theater and amphitheater in Mérida. But Roman ruins are almost commonplace throughout Spain, with notable excavations in Mérida, in Extremadura; Empúries, north of Barcelona; Itálica, outside Seville (where two Roman emperors, Trajan and Hadrian, were born); and Baelo Claudio, near Tarifa, at Spain's southern tip.

The origin of Christianity in Spain is undocumented but is believed to date back to the first century A.D. Records of the time indicate that there were Christian communities in Almería, Granada, and elsewhere in Andalusia. Later, as Christianity became an official faith of the Roman Empire, it spread north to Galicia and Asturias and throughout Spain.

LATER INVADERS

The collapse of the Roman Empire in Spain was followed by consecutive invasions by the Germanic Suevi (Swabians), Vandals (who gave their name to Andalusia), and Visigoths. These last, who assumed control of part of the land around A.D. 484, were a mere 250,000 or so in a population of some six to nine million. Their legacy was small, most evident today in the church of San Román in Toledo, which was their capital. The Visigoths were easily defeated in the first Moorish invasion of 711, when a Muslim army, under Tariq, marched up Roman roads to defeat Roderick, the last

Visigothic king, near Arcos de la Frontera in Andalusia. The Moors subsequently took control of almost all of Spain, all but erasing traces of Visigothic influence.

The surviving Visigoths fled north to their strongholds in Asturias and the Pyrenees, skirting Basque territory, which even then was fiercely independent. It was Pelayo, a local Asturian hero, who held the charge and held the Visigothic line against a Muslim invasion of the Picos de Europa at Covadonga around the year 720. From then on the Moors steered clear of this mountainous area with its perilously narrow valleys, and the Neo-Gothic kingdom of Asturias was left alone to survive, prosper, and join forces with Galicia in the west and Cantabria in the east.

THE MOORISH OCCUPATION

For centuries thereafter, Spain's history is checkered by big battles and little wars between various Muslim caliphates and Christian kingdoms. The Moors touched every region of Spain but made their biggest impact in Andalusia, where they brought a more advanced culture and technology. Centers of Arabic learning flourished in Córdoba, Seville, and, farther north, Toledo.

Moorish architecture and art had enormous influence in Spain, as evidenced in the use of glazed *azulejos* (decorative ceramic tiles), calligraphy, carved plaster work, ornamental brickwork, mosaics, pierced marble screens, fretted woodwork, and wooden inlaid ceilings (*artesonado*). The legacy can be seen all over Andalusia, even in the smallest white town (as the tiny whitewashed Moorish villages are called), and, sometimes surprisingly, throughout Castile, most dominantly in Toledo, Segovia, and Tordesillas. One can't imagine Spain today without its great Moorish monuments—the Mezquita (mosque) of Córdoba, the Giralda tower of Seville, the Alhambra of Granada, and the myriad Arabic horseshoe arches in evidence throughout Andalusia, Castile, Aragón, and parts of Catalonia.

As politics became more complex, with Moors subduing Christians and Christians subduing Moors in territorial games of give-and-take that lasted for centuries, the artistic legacies blurred. In response, artistic terms were created to refer to two unique sets of circumstances: *Mudejar* refers to Muslim work produced by Muslims living under Christian rule, such as the Gothic-Mudejar cathedral of Teruel and the Alcázar of Seville; *Mozarabic*, conversely, signifies Muslim-influenced work by Christians living in Muslim-dominated areas.

As for the literary and philosophical culture of the Muslim world, its importance to the development of medieval philosophy and theology (especially Scholasticism) and its seminal role in the subsequent rise of humanism in the Christian world of Western Europe—via Spain in particular—cannot be overestimated, least of all in its transmission of the thought of ancient Greece and especially the works of Aristotle.

CHRISTIAN ARTS AND CULTURE

Meanwhile, on the Christian side of the frontier, the Catholic Church was the torchbearer of the arts as well as philosophy, as churches, monasteries, convents, and hermitages were built and embellished with paintings, sculpture, and interior decorations.

The eighth- and ninth-century pre-Romanesque style of Asturian churches, such as Santa María del Naranco near Oviedo, led in time to the Romanesque, which was introduced first in Catalonia, through that region's link with France and Italy, and then in the north by French religious orders and pilgrims following the renowned Camino de Santiago, the pilgrims' route along Spain's northern tier from France west to Galicia. It was epitomized by the inner façade and the Pórtico de la Gloria of the cathedral at Santiago de Compostela, the pilgrims' goal.

Romanesque slowly gave way to Gothic, another French innovation, in such major Gothic triumphs as the cathedrals of Burgos, León, Toledo, and, much later, Seville. Gothic acquired a particular Spanish coloration in a unique style of elaborate stone ornamentation known as Isabelline, introduced during the reign of Isabella la Católica (1474–1504) and shown at its most beautiful in the façade and patio of the Colegio de San Gregorio, now the Museo Nacional de Escultura, in Valladolid. Isabelline evolved into Plateresque (from the word *platero,* "silversmith"), a lacelike carving of entire façades, so intricate they are reminiscent of silver filigree. The finest Plateresque work can be seen in the Patio de las Escuelas in Salamanca.

The Renaissance in Spain left many monuments, most prominently the monastery-palace El Escorial, northwest of Madrid, and the palace of Charles V at the Alhambra in Granada. When Baroque appeared in the 17th and 18th centuries, it too added an indigenous element: the exuberant flourishes known as Churrigueresque (named after the three Churriguera brothers of Salamanca), which is visible all over Spain. Salamanca's convent of San Esteban and the Palacio del Marqués de Dos Aguas in Valencia are two prime examples.

THE RECONQUEST
AND THE GOLDEN AGE

It was not until the rulers of two powerful Christian kingdoms, Ferdinand of Aragón and Isabella of Castile, joined forces (in matrimony and battle) that the Moors were finally and forever banished from the peninsula. The last battle, over Granada, was in 1492, a significant date in Spain for two other reasons as well: the expulsion of the Jews from Spain and Columbus's voyage to the New World.

The farsightedness, resourcefulness, and perhaps just plain luck of Isabella in financing Columbus's expedition to the Indies led to Spain's unusual new role as one of the prominent players on the world stage and to a long period of cultural and artistic flowering known as Spain's Golden Age. This era began during the reigns of Holy Roman Emperor Charles V (who was also Spain's King Carlos I), Ferdinand and Isabella's grandson, and of his son, Philip II. As Queen Elizabeth I's reign in England fused conquest with culture, much the same occurred in Spain during the 16th and 17th centuries. There was a flourishing of the arts: the written works of Fray Luis de León, Saint Teresa, Saint John of the Cross, Miguel de Cervantes, Lope de Vega, Tirso de Molina, Pedro Calderón de la Barca, Francisco Gómez de Quevedo, and others; the architectural achievements of Pedro Machuca, Juan de Herrera, Alonso de Covarrubias, Bartolomé Bustamante, Rodrigo Gil de Hontañón, Enrique de Egas, Andrés de Vandaelvira, and the Churrigueras; the paintings of Pedro Berruguete, El Greco, Francisco Zurbarán, Bartolomé Esteban Murillo, Valdés Leal, José Ribera, and Diego Velázquez; and sculpture by Alonso Berruguete, Diego de Siloé, Gil de Siloé, Rodrigo Alemán, Juan de Juni, Alonso Cano, Pedro de Mena, Juan Martínez Montañés, and others.

Through the marriage of Juana la Loca, the daughter of Ferdinand and Isabella, to Philip of Burgundy in 1496, Spain acquired claim to Philip's lands, including the Low Countries. In 1519 the Hapsburg Charles V was elected emperor of the Holy Roman Empire; he annexed Milan and Naples, then solidified Spain's claims to Burgundy and the Netherlands, making them Spanish provinces—and thus bit off far more than his successors could chew. For a while, Spain was the dominant country in Europe, successful, expansionist, and extravagant, living overconfidently on the riches that spouted like La Granja's fountains from the Spanish colonies in the Americas. Under Philip II Portugal became a part of Spain, losing its independence for the first time since the 12th century. And the battle of Lepanto (1517) against the Turks gave Spain control of the Mediterranean.

SPAIN'S DECLINE
Eventually the bills came due. The Netherlands bubbled with political unrest and won its freedom. The Inquisition, having reached a nadir with the expulsion of Jews and

Moors, continued to fester, isolating Spain intellectually from much of Europe. With the brilliance of hindsight, historians date the beginning of Spain's decline to the defeat by the British of the Armada in 1588, which demolished the Spanish navy and led to Spain's downfall as a major maritime power. But in many ways Spain spent the next few centuries being nibbled to death by minnows: the Thirty Years War here, the War of the Spanish Succession there, the loss of a profitable colony here, there, and everywhere.

Spain's decline was helped along by a series of inept, ill-trained, spendthrift rulers. When Carlos II, the last Hapsburg, died in 1700 without an heir, the throne went to Philip, duke of Anjou, grandson of Louis XIV of France and María Teresa. This was the beginning of the reign of the Bourbons. It led immediately, from 1701 to 1714, to the War of the Spanish Succession, which was primarily a power struggle between Bourbon France and Hapsburg Austria, with a little help from their various friends and enemies. The result was that Philip V was formally recognized as king of Spain. He and succeeding Bourbons seemed intent on making the Spanish court as much a Frenchified home away from home as possible and proved ineffectual in leading the country, which remained forever alien to them.

THE 19TH CENTURY

The 19th century began ignominiously for Spain, with the weak Carlos IV on the throne, and his domineering, dissolute wife, María Luisa, and her advisor, Manuel de Godoy, behind it. A series of misadventures followed: the Aranjuez revolt, Napoleon's installation of his brother, Joseph, as king of Spain, and finally the War of Independence (or Peninsular War), in which the British under the duke of Wellington helped the Spanish repel the French. France's occupation was the first by a foreign power since the Moors had left in 1492. When the French departed, they carried off as much booty as possible, stripping churches and cathedrals of innumerable treasures. The wonder is that there is still so much left. Francisco de Goya's etchings *Desastres de la Guerra* (Disasters of War), displayed in the Prado, evoke the horrors of the period more effectively than any words. And his Prado paintings of the supercilious Carlos IV, his foolish wife, and Godoy are mercilessly revealing of their frivolities.

The War of Independence left Spain in control of its own destiny, but only in a manner of speaking. Spain's American colonies used the war to their own advantage, and by 1825 most of them had gained their independence. For the remainder of the 19th century Spain underwent a series of tumultuous revolts, uprisings, and civil wars, fueled by the spirit of liberty that fanned much of Europe and also by the weaknesses of an inept, self-indulgent monarchy. The coup de grâce to Spain's image as a colonial power came in the Spanish-American War of 1898, in which Cuba, Puerto Rico, and the Philippines were irrevocably lost. What followed was a long period during which much of the literary and intellectual energy in Spain was directed toward somehow coming to grips with the clear reality of the country's decline from eminence; writer-philosopher Miguel de Unamuno's *The Tragic Sense of Life in Men and Nations* was an example, as was his emphasis on the quixotic elements in the Spanish character. This national crisis of spirit, as so often happens, produced a cultural renaissance, if not a political one. In one respect, though, Spain was fortunate: It remained neutral during the carnage of World War I.

THE 20TH CENTURY

Much of the 20th century has nonetheless been unkind to Spain. General Miguel Primo de Rivera's dictatorship (1923–1930) and Alfonso XIII's abdication in 1931 led to a republic: A Popular Front government of Republicans, Socialists, Syndicalists, and Communists was elected in 1936. Then the assassination of Monarchist leader Calvo Sotelo triggered a military revolt led by Francisco Franco in Spanish Morocco that quickly spread to the Spanish mainland. There Franco joined with the forces of the Movimiento Nacional, and the Spanish Civil War began. After three bloody years in which family fought family and region fought region, the war ended with the Republican loss of its last three strongholds: Barcelona, Valencia, and Madrid. Franco's forces, much assisted by the Axis powers of Germany and Italy, were victorious, and Franco became head of state. Considering the decimated, impoverished condition of the country, it might be said nobody won—but Spain surely lost.

The Franco years (1939 to 1975) were tranquil on the surface. As the old saying goes, the trains ran on time (and still do) and the streets were safe for wandering till 3:00 A.M. (no such guarantees today). Though the government of Spain was sympathetic to the Axis powers during World War II, the country remained nonbelligerent.

Franco died in 1975, and the grandson of Alfonso XIII, Don Juan Carlos de Borbón, Franco's designated successor, became king. Three years later a new democratic constitution was passed, establishing Spain as a constitutional monarchy. The country is now governed by an elected parliament, the Congreso de Diputados (commonly called the Cortes), and a prime minister. In 1981 Juan Carlos proved himself a hero and solidified his popularity by helping to undercut an attempted military coup.

SPAIN TODAY

The country became a member of the European Community in 1986 and a full economic partner in 1992. That year represented an apotheosis of sorts for 20th-century Spain on several levels: In addition to the full fruits of European Community membership, the country pulled out all the stops in commemorating the 500th anniversary of Columbus's voyage to the Americas, with a major celebration in Seville (Expo '92). On March 31, 1992, in Madrid's Bet Yaakov synagogue, King Juan Carlos signed a royal decree symbolically nullifying the Edict of Expulsion, which 500 years earlier had sent thousands of Jews out of the country. And Spain received worldwide attention when it hosted the Summer Olympics in Barcelona.

Socially, today's Spain is not a place a visitor from the 1950s or 1960s would recognize. Freedom has brought its excesses, as elsewhere: pornography, drugs, disruption of family life, and street crime in the larger cities. It is no longer advisable to leave your car unlocked, even in smaller cities, or to keep anything of value in it even if it is locked.

But for the most part democracy is alive and well here, and most Spaniards revel in it. Economically, Spain has leapfrogged in a couple of decades from one of the more sickly economies of Europe to one of the most robust. You have only to drive through Extremadura now and compare it to what it was 20 years ago, steeped in feudal poverty, when donkeys laden with fagots were more common on the roads than cars. Historically Spain's poorest province, from which so many *conquistadores* escaped to make their fortunes (or so they hoped) in the New World, even Extremadura now boasts wide new highways and new factories. A donkey is a rare sight there today.

The Arts

Culturally, Spain is not just alive and well but, freed from the fetters of Franco's censorship, positively blooming in all the arts—from the arresting films of Pedro Almodóvar and the vitality of opera (spurred on by the success of superstars José Carreras, Montserrat Caballé, Plácido Domingo, Teresa Berganza, and others), music, dance, and the visual arts, to the hyperproductive literary scene. In the past ten years the number of books by Spanish authors has quintupled. Spanish novelist Camilo José Cela, recipient of the Nobel Prize in literature in 1990, is one of many making names for themselves in Spain and throughout Europe. Many Spanish authors have not yet been translated into English, but names to be aware of include Daniel Múgica (who at age 22 received the respected Seville Ateneo prize for his second novel, *Going Crazy*), poet Rafael Alberti, Eduardo Mendoza (au-

thor of the award-winning *The City of Marvels*), Antonio
Muñoz Molina, Juan José Millas, Miguel Delibes, Juan Benet,
Juan Goytisolo, Javier Marias, Soledad Puértolas, and the
venerable Spanish Civil War survivor Gonzalo Torrente
Ballester, whose *Nightingale of My Sorrow* won the major
Planeta prize in 1989.

It's obvious Spain does more than merely persevere.
Nowadays it positively prospers. An ever-expanding middle
class has created a demand for better clothes and shops, new
restaurants, and a better lifestyle. Life in Spain's largest cities
is increasingly similar to life in other major capitals of the
world. The difference is that Spaniards seem to have a knack
for enjoying it.

Yet the amazing thing is that despite the prosperity and
the desire to catch up with the 20th century after decades of
isolation, so much of Spain retains its sense of place and of
history.

Spain for Travellers

For most visitors in this age of the jumbo jet, Spain begins in
Madrid. In truth, all roads (and most air and rail routes) lead
from the capital, whether you head north, south, east, or
west. However, here we ignore the logistic realities and
begin our discussion in the north and, while tending to
move in brushstrokes from east to west, work our way south
to Andalusia and then up along the Mediterranean coast to
Barcelona—followed by the Balearic Islands in the Mediterranean and the Canaries in the Atlantic off Africa. Our chapters unfold in a slightly different manner: There we begin in
Madrid and then cover the regions north of the capital,
generally west to east, then the regions south of the capital
in a more-or-less east to west sweep.

The first thing to keep in mind about Spain is not to be
greedy. Resign yourself to the fact that in a country as vast as
this one you can't see it all, learn it all, or understand more
than a bit of it in the usual time frame of a short vacation.
Relax, choose a landscape, a climate, a region—and experience it. Next time, try another.

PARADORES

Spain's marvelous network of government-run hostelries,
known as paradores, can help give a framework to your
exploration of the country. In 1928, in an effort to promote
tourism, the Spanish government opened its first parador in
the Sierra de Gredos, west of Madrid. The idea was to
preserve historic buildings—castles, palaces, monasteries—
and in the process provide attractive accommodations in
remote places and offbeat locales that travellers might not

otherwise visit because of a dearth of adequate facilities. The subsequent popularity of the paradores is one of Spain's major touristic success stories. Today there are 86, with two more near completion. In many regions you can plan an entire trip using paradores as the overnight framework of your journey.

Paradores are no longer installed only in historic buildings; many are new, built in traditional regional styles to blend with their landscape. A few are even located in popular tourist places, such as Córdoba, Toledo, and Pontevedra (in Galicia, in the northeastern corner of Spain), where other decent accommodations do exist. For most travellers a parador serves as a recognizable beacon of civility in what is often a difficult landscape. In some places—Trujillo in Extremadura and Vic in the Catalan Pyrenees, for instance— a parador is a reasonable alternative to a characterless hotel; in small towns such as Almagro (in La Mancha) and Chinchón (southeast of Madrid) the parador is virtually the only recommendable place to stay.

In all the paradores, whether old and historic or new, regional cuisine, antiques, and indigenous crafts are the common threads. In the parador in Granada, for instance, the traditional Granada weaving is much in evidence in draperies and bedspreads, and the blue-and-green pomegranate motif of Grenadine pottery can be seen in decorative fruit bowls and flowerpots. Local lacework and the distinctive multicolored ceramics of nearby Talavera de la Reina and El Puente del Arzobispo are in evidence in the Parador Villey de Toledo, at Oropesa. The stunningly modern parador at Segovia retains its "Spanishness" by virtue of its dramatic abstract paintings by contemporary Spanish artists and stylized terra-cotta pots rooted in the Castilian tradition. (See Useful Facts, below, for parador booking information.)

NORTHERN SPAIN

The Basque Country

Just over the border from France is the Basque Country, for many visitors the first encounter with Spain. The Basques, with their rosy cheeks, high cheekbones, dark hair, and enigmatic language (thought to be a pre-Indo-European tongue, unique in Europe), are known as the gastronomes of Spain. Whether you stop in the little fishing villages in the inlets below the steep cliffs facing the Bay of Biscay or in the fashionable coastal resort of San Sebastián, you will eat well in the Basque Country, where tables are set with such dishes as *bacalao al pil-pil* (cod with garlic and red pepper), *el marmitako* (a tuna-and-potato stew), roasted fresh sardines, grilled *besugo* (sea bream), *merluza con salsa verde* (hake in an herb sauce), and the Basque goat cheese *idiazabal,* washed down with the refreshing white wine of the region, *chacolí* (*txakolí* in the Basque language). For epicures, **San Sebastián** is the center of culinary gravity, and much time can be spent sampling the city's numerous award-winning (and expensive) restaurants.

San Sebastián is graced by one of the most beautiful beaches in Spain, Bahía de la Concha, strung like a half-moon between Monte Igueldo to the west and Monte Urgull on the east, and edged by a handsome beachfront promenade. Military hobbyists might climb Monte Urgull to the old fort, Castillo de Santa Cruz de la Mota, where Napoleon's troops were holed up during a British-Portuguese attack during the War of Independence.

Just east of San Sebastián are the delightful little towns of Pasajes de San Juan, where Victor Hugo lived briefly, and Fuenterrabía, with a comfortable parador ensconced in an old castle and a peekaboo view right into France.

Following the coast west will lead you to the Basque Country's major industrial center, Bilbao, which is of considerable importance to Spain's economic well-being. It also has the notable Museo de Bellas Artes and numerous restaurants. Vitoria (in Basque, Gasteiz) is another modern industrial mammoth, but its old section, the Campillo, is a worthwhile stop for a glance at its old mansions, narrow streets, and several exceptional churches.

Cantabria

Just to the west are Cantabria and its main city, **Santander**, which is also a smart and popular Atlantic resort in a prize location on the U-shaped Bahía de Santander. The city is distinguished by its many glass-fronted balconies, wide boulevards, plazas, flower-dotted parks, and an impressive beach, El Sardinero. Several fine hotels, stylish shops and art galleries, and good restaurants add vivacity to life in Santander. Cantabria's kitchens rely on the sea and the charms of *rabas* (fried chopped squid), anchovy pie, fresh tuna, sea bream, hake, and salmon, the last often served as *arroz santanderino* (salmon, rice, and milk). Desserts, especially pastries made of milk and eggs, are a regional specialty: *los sobaos pasiegos* (a rich egg-and-butter pastry), *quesada pasiego* (made with honey, cheese, and butter), *leche frita* (fried milk), and *arroz con leche* (rice pudding).

Cantabria is a sweet land of sailors and also of shepherds, whose flocks can be seen chewing up the steep emerald-green hillsides. West of Santander is the medieval village of **Santillana del Mar**, which has tawny homes roofed with red tiles, rows of manorial houses with imposing stone crests on their façades, a first-rate parador, and a lovely 12th-century Romanesque church, the Colegiata. Just a mile from the village are the **Altamira Caves**, with their extraordinarily vivid paintings done more than 10,000 years ago by Paleolithic people.

Continuing west on the coast brings you to two beautiful little coastal villages with fine beaches, Comillas, which has a hilltop location and a pavilion designed by Antoni Gaudí, and San Vicente de la Barquera, a small port with a photogenic castle ruin and notable church. Moving inland, you will come to the rugged **Picos de Europa**, among the most spectacular mountain scenery to be found in Spain.

Asturias

Still farther west along Spain's northern tier is the province of Asturias. This is a terrain that combines a cliff-hung coastline with inland valleys bursting with apple orchards, rough mountain passes, mines, and an industrial base. Although the area attracts fewer visitors than most of the rest of Spain, there are worthy sights, especially in the history-rich capital, **Oviedo**, with its Flamboyant Gothic cathedral, and in the scenic seaport of Gijón. Covadonga, a mist-layered hill town in the Picos de Europa, is steeped in myth and history.

Asturian food is highlighted by *fabada* (a uniquely Asturian stew of white beans, ham, pork, bacon, *longaniza* sausage, and *morcilla,* blood sausage); a regional light, sour, hard cider known as *sidra; cabrales* (goat cheese); and *chorizo* (sausage) or *merluza* cooked in *sidra.*

Galicia

Spain's northwestern corner belongs to Galicia, one of the most beautiful provinces and certainly the greenest, flagged by vineyards and tiered fields dotted with granaries and stone crosses. Galicia hugs Spain's northern and western coasts; its southern end meets northern Portugal. The coast is scored by a series of *rías* (firths), lagoons, gorgeous beaches, rock formations, sandy coves, and picturesque marinas. Proximity to the sea has formed Galicia's cuisine, which dotes on *angulas* (baby eels), *vieiras* (scallops), oysters, *percebes* (goose barnacles—an expensive delicacy), and lobster, but other dishes prevail as well, most notably *caldo gallego* (a stew of cabbage, potatoes, beans, *chorizo,* and ham; *gallego* means "Galician"), *empanada* (pie filled with a variety of succulent ingredients), a delicate almond cake called Santiago, *filloas* (sweet pancakes), and *rosquillas* (biscuits). The best-known Galician wine is Ribeiro, which doesn't travel well, so enjoy it in its natural habitat.

Galicia's star is **Santiago de Compostela**, a medieval city studded with churches, monasteries, university buildings, a stunning, historic parador, one of the most splendid cathedrals in Spain, and a monumental square, the Plaza del Obradoiro. The city is a feast of Romanesque and Gothic architecture, a textured tapestry of sand-hued limestone buildings and terra-cotta-tiled rooftops.

You may choose to travel to Santiago along the pilgrims' ancient **Camino de Santiago**, and we discuss some places along that route below. But there are other points of interest in Galicia: Pontevedra is a coastal city of quiet charm and many monuments; Lugo is a fortress of stone, with splendid walls, gates, and watchtowers; A Coruña (La Coruña) boasts a fine harbor and the only Roman lighthouse still in use; peaceful Túy faces Portugal across the Río Miño.

Navarra

If you follow the Camino de Santiago—and such a plan provides an excellent raison d'être for a northern journey— you will begin in the eastern province of Navarra, in the border town of Roncesvalles (you may cross into Spain from France here), site of one of the most celebrated ambushes of medieval times. The major Navarrese city is **Pamplona**, which has a cathedral, boulevards, parks, and a notable *ayuntamiento* (town hall) to recommend it, though its main fame comes from its annual *encierro,* the running of the bulls at the Fiestas de San Fermín, July 7 to 14.

Navarra stretches from the Basque Country and the French border in the north, south to **Tudela**, a city laced with Moorish, Jewish, and medieval memories, west to Logroño, the beginning of La Rioja, and east to Aragón. Navarra's vast plains and mountains are a haven for quail, partridge, and rabbit, which, along with trout from the sparkling-clear mountain streams, anchor the Navarrese cuisine. Puente la Reina, Los Arcos, and Torres del Río highlight the Camino de Santiago pilgrims' route here with their fine Romanesque churches and monasteries.

La Rioja

Logroño, major city of the wine region of La Rioja (and a good home base for winery hopping), is braced along a plain on the south bank of the Río Ebro, southwest of Navarra and east of Burgos. You might combine a sampling tour of the complex and fine Rioja wines and the robust regional cooking with exploring such Camino de Santiago towns and villages as Laguardia, Nájera (with its monastery of Santa María la Real), and Santo Domingo de la Calzada. Visiting Romanesque and Gothic churches and monasteries, followed by wine tastings and meals of roasted lamb chops and stuffed peppers, can make for a rewarding day.

CENTRAL SPAIN

Old Castile

An irregular stretch of vast plains, steep mountains, and valleys west of La Rioja and north and northwest of Madrid, pierced by the Río Duero and dappled with castles guarding hilltops, is the large province of Castilla y León, a rough-hewn playing field for many major episodes in Spanish history, and which we call Old Castile. Major stops are **Burgos** and, farther west on the main east–west road that was part of the Camino de Santiago, **León**, both cities deserving considerable attention from a visitor. Both have splendid Gothic cathedrals, but Burgos rings with echoes of El Cid, while León is the most conspicuously French of all Spanish cities.

Castilian cities, each showing a proud, stern hilltop profile against the cloudless blue sky, share the same amber limestone in their sturdy, fortresslike buildings, but each city differs, too. **Zamora**, on the Río Duero, reveals its treasures slowly. The most spectacular are the elaborate, well-preserved 15th-century tapestries in its cathedral museum. **Salamanca** basks in a glow of golden lights, its two cathedrals serving as beacons in this comfortable university center. Underappreciated **Valladolid**, noisy and confusing at first acquaintance, deserves the effort you must make to find its core; one of its rewards is the wonderful Museo Nacional de Escultura. The Valladolid area, and east along the Duero to Aranda de Duero, is another wine-producing region to rival La Rioja. **Aranda de Duero**, straddling the Río Duero, boasts the beautiful Gothic church of Santa María, with its Isabelline doorway, and the best roast lamb in Castile. **Segovia**, rising above a hillside surrounded by the Eresma and Clamores rivers, quickly reveals its treasures: its highly visible Roman aqueduct, its cathedral, and the turreted Alcázar. (We cover Segovia in the chapter Side Trips from Madrid.)

Castile's smaller towns are also of interest to the visitor: Tordesillas, where Juana la Loca was imprisoned much of her life; Ciudad Rodrigo, a bastion for centuries, its medieval ramparts intact; Pedraza de la Sierra (covered in Side Trips from Madrid), a classic, fortified Castilian hill town.

Madrid and Environs

And sitting majestically in the center of the Spanish universe is Madrid, the capital and a relatively new city by Spanish standards, basking in its own glow. It takes the magic of evening, when the city's café life begins to unfold, fountains are lighted, and lights twinkle throughout the old city, for most first-time visitors to begin to understand Madrid's allure. This is the time of day when Madrid's sociability rises to a crescendo in the old city's many *tapas* bars and *tabernas,* where people of all classes gather to snack on *tapas* and sip Sherry, red wine, or beer.

Circling Madrid are its satellites, easily visited on short excursions from the city (and covered in Side Trips from Madrid). The monastery-palace **El Escorial**, to the northwest, suggests the most stern and forbidding elements of the Spanish soul, an austerity echoed in the grim walled city of **Avila** (farther west), where Saint Teresa began her life's work, while **Aranjuez**, south of Madrid, reveals the Bourbons' pleasure-loving ways. In **Chinchón**, to the east of Aranjuez, you will find one of Spain's innumerable surprises, a bullfighting ring that doubles as the town's central plaza.

Aragón

East of Castilla y León is Aragón, a harsh and forbidding land at first sight that nonetheless unfolds, little by little, some of the most dramatically beautiful scenery in Spain. Aragón is home to **Zaragoza**, with its eclectic but fascinating Seo (cathedral), the Moorish-accented town of Teruel, and the tiny walled Moorish village of Albaraccín.

La Mancha

Spain's largest, most diverse, and most geographically puzzling province is La Mancha (officially called Castilla–La Mancha), which sweeps in a band to the south of Madrid from fortresslike Oropesa on the west to Cuenca on the east, northeast to the hill town of Sigüenza, and as far southeast as Albacete. Towns as disparate as the touristic "must" **Toledo**, with its abundance of Muslim, Jewish, and Christian monuments and memories, and the harmoniously medieval but "undiscovered" **Almagro**, with its gemlike 16th-century theater, are just two of the many treasures to be uncovered throughout this windmill-marked land of Don Quixote. **Ciudad Real**, once a major thoroughfare, is not quite the "dull, one-horse little place" author Gerald Brenan has called it, but we have nonetheless minimized it in our coverage of the region.

Extremadura

Your thoughts invariably turn to the *conquistadores* when exploring little-travelled Extremadura, whose parched land was home to so many of those brave adventurers. From Madrid, your route should lead you southwest to the austerely beautiful towns of **Trujillo** and **Cáceres**, enhanced by palaces and churches built with some of the treasure of the Andes. A detour is recommended to the imposing shrine of

Guadalupe, with its lode of Zurbarán paintings. Farther south is **Mérida**, whose Roman past seems omnipresent, and finally there is Zafra, one of Hernán Cortés's last stops on his way to the New World.

SOUTHERN SPAIN

Andalusia

Another broad sweep of territory encompasses Andalusia, whose profile has formed so many foreigners' images of Spain. Most visibly charming and seductive is that golden triangle of cities, **Granada, Córdoba**, and **Seville**, with their imagery of flamenco, Gypsies, bullfights, and a languid lifestyle. Food and Sherry are a big part of Andalusian life, and you'll want to try the flavorful *jamón de Jabugo,* which many consider the best ham in Spain, the famous *pescaito frito* (deep-fried fish), and, of course, the many versions of gazpacho. In Seville especially you'll want to sample *tapas,* those tasty tidbits nibbled on with wine or beer before lunch and dinner that were reputedly invented in Seville and are particularly relished here.

But Andalusia in itself is too large and diverse to consume in a single gulp, including as it does **Málaga** and the lotus-eaters' playgrounds of Torremolinos and Marbella on the development-saturated **Costa del Sol**, the dazzling white hill town of Ronda in the region's interior, the Renaissance and Gothic town of Ubeda at the region's northern tip, and the Sherry-producing bodegas of **Jerez de la Frontera** and its neighbor Sanlúcar de Barrameda, both near the port of Cádiz on Andalusia's western, Atlantic coast. The little-visited eastern end of the Costa del Sol, near the unprepossessing city of Almería, has spectacular coastal scenery—and the not inconsiderable attraction of being somewhat removed from the rest of Andalusia.

You might choose to follow in the footsteps of the *conquistadores,* tracing a route to Andalusia's western extremes, to the gleaming whiteness of Moguer and Palos de la Frontera, former ports (now silted up) from which many of the 15th-century explorers, including Christopher Columbus on his seminal journey, set sail. A few miles west is Huelva, an industrial city to be passed through quickly en route to the Portuguese border.

THE MEDITERRANEAN COAST

Murcia

A tiny bite has been taken out of the Andalusian landscape along the Mediterranean coast east of the Costa del Sol and south of Valencia by the region of Murcia. It has treasures of its own, especially in its capital, also called Murcia, with its magnificent cathedral and museum, and in the often over-looked port of Cartagena as well. We cover Murcia in the Valencia chapter, as it ties in well with a visit to that region.

Valencia

Valencia city is the capital of the Costa del Azahar, north of Murcia on the Mediterranean, and the region called Comunidad Valenciana, which shows still another face of the Spanish landscape—level marshland, voluminously productive. This is the land of *paella valenciana* and other rice dishes, *horchata* (a refreshing drink with the consistency of a milk shake), artichokes, almonds, and oranges. The city of Valencia takes most of our time here; don't rush it. Just outside Valencia is Manises, where a special blue-and-white pottery (and other colors as well) has been made for centuries. To the south of Valencia is **Alicante**, with its palm-lined promenade, the Explanada, and an easygoing air. Side trips from Alicante will lead you to Elche, Alcoy, Jijona, famous for its nougatlike *turrón,* and Orihuela, a lovely town with many architectural delights.

Catalonia and Barcelona

Continuing up the Mediterranean coast north of Valencia brings you to Catalonia, a triangular area that is, like most other places in Spain, full of different possibilities for the visitor. For the traveller interested in wine, one trip might center on the southernmost area of Catalonia, where the vineyards and wineries of the Penedès vie for attention with the coastal charms of the town of **Tarragona** and the resorts along the Costa Daurada, as well as the monasteries of Poblet and Santes Creus. On the road farther west is Lleida (Lérida), an industrial city whose monumental cathedral is slowly being restored.

Our major focal point in Catalonia is **Barcelona**, capital of the region, and a strategic point from which to make excursions into the surrounding area. Barcelona's signatures—creative cookery, first-rate music, rich museums, and avant-garde art and design—are there to be enjoyed in a setting graced with lingering fin-de-siècle architectural landmarks, including the most renowned works of Antoni Gaudí, that look as fresh as new. Don't let the Catalan reputation for business and commerce and the hustle and bustle on the streets fool you; when they aren't working, Barcelonans know how to enjoy life to the brim. Catalan food is among the best and most imaginative in Spain, as you'll discover in such dishes as *escudella* (a Catalan stew), *butifarra* (sausage), *suquet de peix* (a fish soup), and the famous dessert *crema catalana* (a richer version of flan). Local white wines and sparkling *cavas* are superb, too.

Barcelona is currently in the midst of a building boom. The 1992 Olympics led the city to expand its hotel space, clean the façades of many of its Modernist buildings, and take its rightful place as one of Europe's most cosmopolitan cities.

From Barcelona you can move northeast up the rugged **Costa Brava,** with its many irresistible seaside villages and its scalloped, rough-cut coastline, darting inland to visit the ancient cities of Girona, with its Roman, Arabic, and Jewish echoes, and Figueres, near the French border, home to the unusual Salvador Dalí museum and two notable restaurants. From the latter two cities or from Barcelona, art and architecture fans might make a foray into the Catalan Pyrenees to visit the many tiny, remote mountain villages, as locked in time as their landmark Romanesque churches are.

SPAIN'S ISLANDS

The Balearic Islands

The Catalan coast is the springboard to the Balearic Islands. You will probably choose just one of the Balearics for a visit, and temperament often dictates choice. Those intrigued by history, botanical variety, and the romance of the George Sand–Chopin dalliance in **Majorca** will perhaps be lured there; **Ibiza**'s visual beauty, its stark whiteness, and its on-the-go international community seem to attract the artistically inclined; **Minorca**'s appeal, apart from its English connections, is as a getaway.

The Canary Islands

Spain's other island group, the Canary Islands, is just as diverse, with considerable topographical variety. Relatively few North Americans find their way to Tenerife, Grand Canary, or Lanzarote, the major islands of this group off the Atlantic coast of Africa, which are magnets for European and Middle Eastern sunseekers, especially in winter. Beach lovers may head for the profligately long stretches of sand on Fuerteventura, and solitude seekers may wish to bask in the seclusion of the islands of Gomera, Hierro, or La Palma.

'Where did you go?" a first-time visitor who had spent ten days in Spain was asked. "Everywhere!" was the exuberant reply. Everywhere? In Spain? Ten days? Impossible! Think of a first trip as an introduction. Then expect to spend a lifetime going back for more.

USEFUL FACTS

When to Go

There is no single season that is ideal all across the country; Spain is too large and topographically diverse for that. Generally speaking, late spring and fall are excellent almost everywhere and there are fewer tourists then to obstruct your view of *Las Meninas* in the Prado. In spring you can expect rain in Galicia, in the northwest (indeed, throughout much of the year), but elsewhere the weather is usually well behaved, with sunny days and refreshingly cool nights. You'll find the fields of Castile, Andalusia, Extremadura, Aragón, and Catalonia smothered in colorful wildflowers and the hillsides dappled with new lambs. The pageantry of Semana Santa (Holy Week) makes spring a compelling time for a visit, although in cities known for their spectacular processions (Seville, Málaga, Cuenca) hotels are booked as much as a year ahead. Barcelona and the Costa Brava are at their most tranquil then, before the French tourists arrive, and the weather is warm and breezy, as it is in the Balearic Islands.

The dry, merciless heat of Madrid and Castile and the humidity of Valencia and other southern cities can be suffocating in July and August, and in August many of Madrid's best restaurants close. Yet summer is the best time for the Cantabrian and Basque beaches of the north and also, if you can tolerate the mobs of European sunseekers, for swimming along the Mediterranean's Costa del Sol. It is also the season, especially during August, to see the very best flamenco in that triangle of musical cities: Seville, Jerez de la Frontera, and Cádiz.

Fall lingers lovingly in most of Spain, especially on the coasts, turning grape leaves golden in the ubiquitous vineyards. Winter in Spain, especially in Castile and the northern regions, can be bone-chillingly cold, but skiers head happily for the resorts of the Catalan Pyrenees and the Picos de Europa in Asturias and Cantabria. Winter is meant for Canary Islands sunshine (and swimming) and for Barcelona, which, of all major Spanish cities, usually manages to remain balmy throughout most of the chilly season, warmed by its coastal waters. Despite the sunshine that prevails, Andalusian winters can be quite cold; you might stroll along the beaches of the Costa del Sol, but the water's not for swimming.

In fall, winter, and spring, cultural life in Barcelona and Madrid blossoms, and the theater, music, and art scenes there are at their liveliest. While the Christmas holidays are quiet family times throughout Spain, January 6, Three Kings Day (Epiphany), is celebrated with parades, fireworks, and pageantry almost everywhere. Fiestas know no seasonal restraints in Spain, so whatever the time of your visit, something lively and interesting is almost guaranteed to be happening somewhere.

Entry Documents

Citizens of the United Kingdom and other EC member countries need only present their identification card to enter Spain. Canadian, Australian, New Zealand, and U.S. citizens need a valid passport. Visas are required only for those staying longer than six months. Customs procedures are usually quick and easy.

Arrival at Major Gateways by Air

Flying from the United States. From the United States, Iberia has daily nonstop flights from New York to Madrid (two on Mondays and Thursdays) and two nonstop flights a week to Barcelona (Mondays and Thursdays). (Note: In airline lingo *nonstop* means just that, but *direct* means a stop en route, though no change of plane.) Iberia also flies daily nonstop from Miami to Madrid and twice a week from Los Angeles to Madrid (Wednesdays and Sundays). TWA flies daily nonstop from New York to Madrid and daily direct to Barcelona. United Airlines flies daily nonstop from Washington, D.C., to Madrid; American Airlines has daily nonstop flights from Dallas–Fort Worth and from Miami to Madrid. Continental flies daily to Madrid from Newark, New Jersey, and from Houston. Delta has a daily direct flight from Atlanta to Barcelona with a stop in Madrid. British Airways also offers daily service from New York to Madrid and to Barcelona, via London, as well as service from 16 other U.S. cities, all requiring a change of plane.

Flying from the United Kingdom. From the United Kingdom, British Airways offers six nonstop flights a day from London to Madrid, three a day to Barcelona, two a day (three a day weekends) to Málaga, and one a day to Bilbao (in the Basque Country). Iberia has three or four direct flights from London to Madrid and to Barcelona, two to Málaga, and daily flights to Seville, Bilbao, Valencia, Alicante (on the Costa Blanca, south of Valencia), and Santiago de Compostela (in Galicia). There is a daily flight from London to Murcia (on the Mediterranean coast north of the Costa del Sol), Granada, and Almería (Costa del Sol), all via Barcelona, as well as daily flights (with more in summer) from London to the Canary islands of Tenerife and Grand Canary, via Madrid or Barcelona. Iberia also offers one flight a week from London to Vigo (in southeastern Galicia, near the Portuguese border) by way of London and frequent flights to the island of Majorca.

Flying from Canada and Australia. From Canada, Iberia flies from Toronto to Montreal and then nonstop to Madrid twice a week (Fridays and Sundays), and then on to Barcelona. British Airways has service from Montreal, Toronto, and Vancouver, in Canada, and from Brisbane, Sydney, Melbourne, Perth, and Adelaide, in Australia.

Arriving in Madrid. In Madrid, planes touch down at the Aeropuerto de Barajas, which is 16 km (10 miles) northeast of the city. You can reach the city by airport bus, which picks you up in front of the terminal and deposits you at Plaza de Colón, for 300 pesetas. From the plaza you can taxi to your hotel, or you can taxi directly from the airport for about 1,200 to 1,500 pesetas, depending on the traffic. The drive, normally half an hour, can take 50 minutes during peak traffic hours.

Arriving in Barcelona. The international airport of El Prat de Llobregat is 14 km (9 miles) south of Barcelona, a 20-minute taxi ride (at 1,400 to 1,800 pesetas) to the city center. Less expensive, but cumbersome if you have much luggage, is the airport train, which leaves every half hour from 6:00 A.M. to 11:00 P.M. and deposits you 15 minutes later at the central Sants train station, from which you can take a taxi to your hotel.

Arrival by Train

There is fast, comfortable, direct train service to Madrid from both Paris and Lisbon, and to Barcelona from Paris, Zürich, Geneva, and Milan, aboard the excellent, modern International **Talgo** (Tren Articulado Ligero Goicoechea y Oriol). From Paris the train leaves Austerlitz station at 8:00 P.M., arriving the following morning in Madrid's Chamartín station at 8:32 A.M. (In contrast, the older Puerta del Sol overnight express leaves Paris at 6:05 P.M. and arrives the next day at 9:50 A.M.) There is a daytime high-speed TGV train that leaves Paris (Montparnasse station) at 7:00 A.M., but passengers change to a slower train at the border, and don't arrive in Madrid until 10:00 P.M.

From Lisbon the daytime train, the Luiz de Camões, leaves Lisbon at 12:15 P.M. and arrives at Chamartín station about 9:30 the same night. The deluxe Pablo Casals International Talgo departs from Zürich at 7:33 P.M., stops in Geneva at 10:46 P.M., and reaches the Sants station in Barcelona at 9:10 A.M. the following day. A section of the same train leaves Milan at 8:00 P.M. and joins the Zürich–Geneva train at Chambéry, France, for the ride to Barcelona.

To travel by International Talgo you need seat or sleeping-cabin reservations in addition to your rail ticket. International Talgo tickets can be purchased in the countries in which the trains originate; reservations should be made months ahead. Europe Train Tours handles International Talgo reservations if they are made as part of a tour package, along with hotel reservations. In U.S. and Canada, Tel: (800) 551-2085 or (914) 698-9426; Fax: (914) 698-9516.

For information on train service throughout Europe, call Rail Europe; in U.S. and Canada, Tel: (800) 438-7245 or (914) 682-2999.

Arrival by Sea

From Britain, there is twice-weekly Brittany car ferry service from Plymouth to Santander (Cantabria); alternatives are available from Sealink Car Ferry Centre, Grosvenor Gardens, London SW1. From France, the Algérienne car-ferry line runs from Marseilles to Palma de Majorca (Canary Islands); other possibilities are available through French Railways, 179 Piccadilly, London W1. Ferries from Morocco leave Tangier, Ceuta, and Melilla for Algeciras, in the south of Spain near Gibraltar. There is also hydrofoil service between Algeciras and Tangier six days a week; tickets are available through Transmediterránea, Tel: (9-56) 66-52-00.

Arrival by Car

You can drive into Spain from France, Portugal, and Gibraltar. There are 17 border crossings from France; the most commonly used are those between Perpignan and Girona/Barcelona and between Bayonne and the Basque provinces. From Portugal there are also 17 crossing points; the most travelled routes are those from Valença to Túy (Galicia) in the north and from Elvas to Badajoz in Extremadura. A new bridge crosses the Río Guadiana from Vila Real de Santo António, Portugal, to Ayamonte, in southwestern Spain. (There is also a car ferry, which takes just ten minutes.) From Gibraltar there is only one road through the checkpoint at La Línea de la Concepción, and it can be slow and choked with traffic. Most other crossings are relatively painless.

Around Spain by Air

Spain's two domestic airlines, Iberia and Aviaco, have offices in all major cities and serve more than 36 cities and towns. Flights from Madrid to many Spanish cities are one hour or less. The problem with domestic air travel is that you often can't fly between two smaller cities: You have to return first to Madrid and depart from there. And while many domestic airports are only a few miles from town, the airports at Málaga and Murcia, to cite two of the extremes, are both 32 miles away; if your time is limited, this can be a problem.

If you fly Iberia to Spain from the United States you are

eligible to buy a City Plus pass, which allows you to visit any one of 24 destinations in Spain for an additional $50 ($80 to include the Canary Islands). A Visit Spain airpass costs $249 and provides four vouchers for air travel anywhere in Spain, including the Balearic Islands ($299 includes the Canaries).

Around Spain by Train

Spain's well-developed 8,125-mile rail network is operated by the state railway RENFE (Red Nacional de los Ferro-carriles Españoles), and generally excellent trains link the entire country. Train travel is clean, comfortable, and reliable and, depending on the type of service and your destination, can be the least expensive means of transportation available, except for bus. (Discount fares are discussed in detail further below.)

Standard Train Service. The Talgo trains are speedy, deluxe, and air-conditioned, and they provide express service between Madrid and other major cities: Barcelona, Bilbao, Cádiz, Málaga, Seville, Valencia, and Zaragoza. The diesel Ter and Electrotren, which also have first-rate accommodations, make more stops, are a bit slower, and serve various parts of the country. Sleepers, couchettes, and coach seats are available in both first and second class, depending on the destination.

In 1992 a brand-new high-speed train known as AVE (Tren de Alta Velocidad Española) began service between Madrid and Seville. Reaching speeds up to 186 miles an hour, AVE cuts the travel time between the two cities from six hours to two hours, 45 minutes. There are five to six departures a day in both directions, from Atocha station in Madrid to Santa Justa station in Seville. Reservations are required in all three classes: Club, Preferente, and Turista. There is a RENFE office in Madrid's Aeropuerto de Barajas, so reservations can be made upon arrival in Spain. RENFE also has a reservations number in Madrid; Tel: (9-1) 563-0202.

Special Excursions. RENFE offers a number of special excursions on a beautifully refurbished 1920s luxury train, the **Andalusian Express** (Al-Andaluz in Spanish), which accommodates a maximum of 72 passengers. Al-Andaluz follows two itineraries, a six-day trip from March through June and September and October that goes from Madrid or Seville to Córdoba, Granada, Ronda, Jerez, and back to Seville. At Christmas time Al-Andaluz follows a three-day itinerary from Madrid or Seville to Córdoba and back to Seville or Madrid. For reservations or further information in Spain, contact C/ Capitán Haya, 55, 28020 Madrid; Tel: (9-1) 571-5815; Fax: (9-1) 571-1417. In the U.S., the U.K., Canada, or Australia, contact the Tourist Office of Spain; see "For Further Information," below.

Another special excursion train is **El Transcantábrico**, which travels through the beautiful terrain of northern Spain. RENFE also offers half a dozen or more one-day excursions on *trenes turísticos,* such as the Tren de la Fresa (Strawberry Train) to Aranjuez, the Ciudad Encantada de Cuenca (Enchanted City of Cuenca), the Muralles de Avila (Walls of Avila), and the Monasterio de Piedra (Monastery of Stone), through the natural wonderland of Aragón. There are also overnight weekend excursion-train tours from Madrid to Palencia, Santiago de Compostela, Zamora, and Burgos. Tickets for these excursion trains, which run on weekends from spring to fall, may be purchased in Spain at a travel agency or RENFE ticket office.

Schedules and Fares. RENFE schedules, fares, and supplements are somewhat complicated. It is advisable, if you plan much train travel, to pick up a free copy of *Como Viajar Barato en España,* a 52-page booklet published in Spanish by the Secretaría de General de Turismo, available at RENFE ticket offices. This booklet is full of information about special discounts and rates on Spanish railroads, airlines, and ships and provides a calendar of Blue Days, when reduced rates pertain.

Two types of rail passes—a Spain Rail Pass (similar in concept to the Eurail Pass) and a Flexipass—can be purchased in advance outside Spain through Rail Europe; in the United States and Canada, Tel: (800) 438-7245. The Spain Rail Pass is available in increments of eight, 15, and 21 days, for either first or second class, and is good for unlimited travel on any regular RENFE train inside Spain (starting with the day the first train ride begins) excluding the AVE. The Flexipass offers two possibilities: four days of unlimited travel within a 15-day period or nine days of unlimited travel within a 21-day period. Both the Spain Rail Pass and the Flexipass are a good value if you are planning frequent and/or extensive travel, but are not necessarily a bargain if your plans include only a single trip from, say, Madrid to Barcelona.

Several other cost-saving options are available at RENFE offices *within Spain only.* These include youth passes, children's passes, family passes, senior-citizen discounts, round-trip fares, and special discounts on Blue Days.

Around Spain by Bus

Spain's cities and towns are linked by numerous small bus companies; there is no national bus company. While buses are generally inexpensive, much time can be wasted waiting for connections from town to town. For schedules and information check the telephone directory, or inquire at a travel agency or the local tourist office.

Renting a Car and Driving

If you plan to drive in Spain, you must be at least 18 years old and have a valid U.S., Canadian, British, or international driver's license. There are major car-rental agencies, such as Avis, Hertz, Godfrey Davis, Budget, Europcar (National), and Atesa (the least expensive), in all large cities and airports. Rental fee includes basic public liability and property-damage insurance, oil, and maintenance. Full vehicle-damage insurance adds an extra daily charge. The high cost of gasoline in Spain and the narrow streets in many small cities are strong arguments for choosing a small car, and security concerns suggest one with a closed trunk, not a hatchback, where your visible belongings might tempt thieves.

Spanish Roadways. Driving in Spain is the best way to see the smaller towns, villages, and countryside. Spanish roads range from *autopistas* (superhighways), which charge high pay-by-distance fees, to pockmarked, weathered country lanes. But the norm is a two- or three-lane asphalt road, well maintained and surfaced, with well-posted international highway symbols. Gas stations are few and far between in the countryside, so plan ahead. Spanish drivers are generally courteous, and truckers are known for signaling you to pass when the road ahead is clear.

A few caveats: Seat belts are mandatory outside city limits; even on a country road you might be stopped, ticketed, and fined if you are unhitched. Also, radar zones shouldn't be taken lightly; you may receive a ticket forwarded to your home address, if you aren't tagged on the spot. Parking places even in small cities can be difficult to find; head for the big blue signs marked with a large white "P" for parking or areas with machines from which you purchase a ticket to display in your window.

City Driving. If your visit is limited to large cities you will be much better off if you get there by air or train and then rely on local transportation. Fast traffic, a surfeit of one-way streets, and narrow, labyrinthine passageways make city driving hazardous. Parking is a problem, too, and tickets and tow-aways are standard operating procedures for city police. To cope with Madrid's traffic jams, fines for traffic violations in the city have been raised to as much as $900 for the more serious offenses (speeding, running red lights) and as many as six years in jail for drunken driving. The lowest fine is $150—for double parking.

Accommodations

The Spanish government has a national rating system for accommodations by which it classifies each accommodation according to specific criteria and then assigns it a number of stars, ranging from one to five. Every hotel has a blue plaque outside its door with an "H" (for hotel) and its starred classification on it. The criteria for assigning ratings include the number of lounges, bars, elevators, telephones, hygiene and service facilities (such as beauty salons, laundry service), rooms with private baths, suites, and the square footage of rooms and public areas. In broad terms, the more amenities a hotel has, the higher its government rating and, usually, the higher its prices.

In addition to the H (for hotel) rating, there are "Hs" (for *hostal,* meaning a modest hotel with or without restaurant), "HR" (*hostal residencia,* essentially a bed and breakfast), and "P" (*pensión,* cheap lodgings, with meals taken with the family). A very few five-star hotels bear "GL" on their plaque, which signifies *gran lujo*—the *crème de la crème* of deluxe hotels. The Hotel Ritz, Hotel Villa Magna, and Hotel Santo Mauro in Madrid, the Hotel Alfonso XIII in Seville, and the government-run Hostal de los Reyes Católicos in Santiago de Compostela and Hostal de San Marcos in León are among the few with this top listing.

The flaw in the government rating system is that it doesn't take into account such amorphous things as "character," "charm," or "ambience," and often it is these very, admittedly subjective, qualities that may make an old, historic four-star hotel more appealing than a modern, well-equipped, five-star high-rise. In our recommendations we have generally opted more for ambience than mere modernity. For example, the Hostal del Cardenal in Toledo is listed by the government system as a three-star HR, though it is an 18th-century archbishop's palace, with a delightful garden and a first-rate restaurant, and is well maintained. The rooms are small and basic (which probably accounts for the rating), but its overall charm can greatly enhance a Toledo visit.

Paradores. Paradores (government-run hostelries) are extremely popular and, because of the limited number of rooms available, should be booked ahead. This can be done directly with each parador (see each chapter's Accommodations Reference information) or, in the United States and Canada, through **Marketing Ahead**, 433 Fifth Avenue, New York, NY 10016; Tel: (212) 686-9213 or (800) 223-1356; Fax: (212) 686-0271. This reservation organization also represents 100 of the more exclusive hotels in Spain.

Rates. The hotel and parador rates listed in this book are projected rates for 1994, for double room, double occupancy. These are projections; prices may vary considerably, due to changes in the economy and other factors. Nevertheless, they should give some idea of the *price ranges* of different accommodations. We strongly recommend that you confirm the price when making reservations.

Telephoning

The country code for Spain is 34. Area codes for major cities are: Madrid 1, Barcelona 3, Seville 5, Valencia 6. When making a call from within Spain to another area code, you must dial "9" before the area code. Throughout this book, we include the "9" in telephone numbers; drop the "9" if you are calling from outside the country. If you want to make an international call from Spain, dial "07" before the country code.

Public telephones in Spain take 5-, 25-, 50-, and 100-peseta coins. Instructions are usually printed inside the booths in several languages.

Local Time

Mainland Spain is six hours ahead of New York, Toronto, and other areas on eastern standard time (five hours ahead from April to October during daylight saving time), one hour ahead of Greenwich mean time, and eight hours behind Sydney, Australia. The Canary Islands, five hours ahead of eastern standard time (four hours during daylight saving time), are on the same time as the United Kingdom, except during daylight saving time, when the Canaries are one hour behind.

Currency

The peseta is Spain's basic monetary unit. Bank notes are issued in 1,000-, 2,000-, 5,000-, and 10,000-peseta denominations. Coins are 1, 5, 25, 50, 100, 200, and 500 pesetas. Caution: The 100-peseta coin is similar in size to the 25-peseta coin, so inspect each carefully before disbursing. There are both old and new coins in circulation, so there are, for the time being, three different 1-peseta coins, two 5-peseta coins, and so on.

Exchanging Money. Money can be exchanged at banks, *cambios* (exchange offices), and hotels; the rates are best at banks, second best at hotels. Rates change almost daily these days, so check listings at major banks or in the *International Herald Tribune* or other daily newspapers.

Checks and Credit Cards. Major traveller's checks are accepted widely throughout Spain, as are such credit cards as

American Express, MasterCard, Visa, Diners Club, and Carte Blanche. Many hotels, restaurants, and shops have decals on their front windows indicating which cards are accepted; the Eurocard is equivalent to MasterCard. Some shops will add an extra charge for credit-card payments. Relatively few hotels and restaurants will accept personal checks.

Electric Current

Common voltage is 220, but in some places, especially newer hotels, 110 is available in the bathrooms. Even so, the 110-volt outlets customarily require a Continental two-pin, round-prong plug, not the North American flat-blade plug. The best solution is to carry an adapter. If you take a North American standard radio or cassette player with you, remember to bring batteries: The 50-cycle Spanish current won't match 60-cycle equipment.

Business Hours

Banks, Shops, and Businesses. Banking hours are from 9:00 A.M. to 1:00 or 2:00 P.M. weekdays, 9:00 A.M. to 12:30 P.M. Saturdays. Most other businesses, shops, and boutiques are open from 9:00 or 10:00 A.M. to 1:00 or 2:00 P.M., then from 4:00 or 5:00 to 8:00 P.M., Monday through Friday. Many shops and businesses are open Saturdays as well, from 9:00 A.M. to 1:00 P.M. Department store hours are 9:30 or 10:00 A.M. to 8:00 P.M., Monday through Saturday.

Restaurants and Bars. Restaurant hours are generally from 1:00 to 4:00 P.M. for lunch, 9:00 or 9:30 to 11:30 P.M. or midnight for dinner (though in major cities, some restaurants, especially those in hotels, accommodate hungry tourists by opening at 8:30 P.M.). Many restaurants and other businesses close for vacation part or all of the month of August. Bars and discos often stay open all night in summer, and until 3:00 or 4:00 A.M. in winter.

Museums and Churches. Museums, monuments, and churches, especially in smaller towns and villages, often operate on schedules that seem to be known only to themselves. In general, the hours are from 10:00 A.M. to 1:00 or 2:00 P.M., Tuesday through Sunday, with certain institutions open weekday afternoons from 4:00 to 7:00 P.M. as well. To further complicate the picture, there are summer and winter hours at many museums. Most are closed Mondays and on major holidays.

Theater and Sporting Events. Hours for theaters and movies are usually 7:00 and 10:00 or 10:30 P.M. weeknights and Saturdays, and about 4:30 P.M. on Sundays and holidays.

Bullfights begin around 5:00 P.M. Sunday afternoons from March through mid-October. Soccer matches begin around 5:00 P.M. in smaller cities and towns, a little later in major cities, September through June.

Holidays

On the 14 official national holidays observed throughout Spain, banks, offices, shops, and some restaurants are closed. These holidays are January 1 (New Year's Day), January 6 (Epiphany or Three Kings Day), March 19 (Saint Joseph's feast day), Holy (or Maundy) Thursday, Good Friday, Easter Monday, May 1 (May Day), Corpus Christi (a movable feast, usually in late June), July 25 (feast of Santiago, Spain's patron saint), August 15 (Assumption of the Virgin), October 12 (National Day), November 1 (All Saints' Day), December 8 (Immaculate Conception), and December 25 (Christmas).

Easter is a *five-day* holiday in Spain, beginning Holy Thursday and lasting through Easter Monday, during which time many restaurants, shops, and museums are closed. In addition, in many towns and cities the feast day of Saint Peter and Saint Paul (June 29) is celebrated, and the day honoring the local patron saint is also a local holiday, with many shops, offices, and museums closed.

Safety

The precautions you would take in a large city in the United States, Canada, or Britain should be applied in Spain's major cities as well. Madrid, Barcelona, and especially Seville, along with coastal tourist centers such as Málaga and Torremolinos, are the cities where thieves operate most freely. In Seville, it is wise to leave passports and any unnecessary valuables safely locked up in your hotel and to avoid empty streets during the siesta hours. Smaller cities, towns, and villages are relatively crime-free, though a prudent traveller always safeguards his or her wallet, passport, and other valuables.

In any town or city lock your car when you leave it, and do not leave anything visible inside. In fact, it is unwise to leave luggage and other valuables even in the trunk, and *never* overnight. As a precaution against pickpockets and motorbike thieves who snatch and ride away, do not carry a camera on a strap around your neck or a shoulder-strap handbag; the straps are easily cut. Some experienced travellers wear a money belt or "fanny pack" around the waist, or a jacket with zippered or inside pockets, in which they can carry a minimal amount of essential cash.

Some of the scams that have been operating internationally have made their way to Spain. Be especially wary if someone spills something on you and another person rushes up to "help" (and lift your wallet), or if a passing motorist signals you to pull over (so he or she can steal your belongings).

For Further Information

The Tourist Office of Spain has offices in London, Toronto, Sydney, New York, Chicago, Miami, and Beverly Hills, with many brochures available to anyone planning a trip to Spain. The addresses of the major offices are: 57–58 St. James's Street, *London* SW1 A1LD, Tel: (071) 499-1169; 102 Bloor Street West, 14th Floor, *Toronto,* Ontario M5S 1M8, Tel: (416) 961-3131; 203 Castlekeogh Street, Suite 21A, *Sydney,* NSW 2000, Australia, Tel: (612) 264-7966; 665 Fifth Avenue, *New York,* NY 10022, Tel: (212) 759-8822; Water Tower Place, 845 North Michigan Avenue, Suite 915E, *Chicago,* IL 60611, Tel: (312) 642-1992; 1221 Brickell Avenue, Suite 1850, *Miami,* FL 33131, Tel: (305) 358-1992; San Vicente Plaza Building, 8383 Wilshire Boulevard, Suite 960, *Beverly Hills,* CA 90211, Tel: (213) 658-7188.

A new nationwide tourist information line has been put into effect in Spain. It gives information about accommodations, transportation, festivals, cultural events, museums, and many other things in French, English, and Spanish, from 10:00 A.M. to 8:00 P.M. every day. From anyplace in Spain outside Catalonia, Tel: (9-01) 30-06-00; in Catalonia, Tel: (9-00) 30-03-03.

—Patricia Brooks

BIBLIOGRAPHY

Marcel Acier, editor, *From Spanish Trenches* (1937). Letters, newspaper accounts, and journal entries from participants and observers in the Spanish Civil War.

Dawn Ades, *Dalí and Surrealism* (1982). A detailed study of Dalí's work in context with the main currents of 20th-century art, enhanced by photographs.

James M. Anderson, *Spain: 1001 Sights* (1992). This unique archaeological guide covers sites (*not* sights) from prehistoric Spain through the Islamic conquest, with drawings, photographs, maps, and suggested routes. Strong on dolmens, cave drawings, necropoli, tumuli, and the entire Roman period; scattershot treatment of Islamic period.

Homero Aridjis, *1492, The Life and Times of Juan Cabezón of Castile* (1991). A Mexican novel emphasizing that Spain's year of discovery was also one of Inquisitional persecution of Jews, Muslims, and *conversos* (converts to Christianity).

Francisco Ayala, *Usurpers* (1987). Seven tales on the corrupting force of power, recalling different historical events of medieval and Golden Age Spain, by a master of Spanish prose who won the National Prize for Literature in 1983.

PETER BESAS, *Behind the Spanish Lens: Spanish Cinema Under Fascism and Democracy* (1985). The history of Spanish films through the early 1980s.

BERNARD BEVAN, *Spanish Architecture* (1938). A survey of Spanish architecture that includes styles indigenous to Spain, such as early-16th-century Plateresque and 18th-century Churrigueresque.

ANTHONY BLUNT, *Picasso's Guernica* (1969). An art expert's view of Picasso's controversial painting.

JOSÉ CABELLERO BONALD, *Andalusian Dances* (1959). A standard text, with photographs, that examines the origins and development of *jondo* and flamenco dances. This historical survey of song and dance in Andalusia traces the Gypsy and Arabic influences to their earliest sources.

GEORGE BORROW, *The Bible in Spain* (1843). After a century and a half, still an English-language classic on travel in Spain. Spirited, opinionated, engaging. "Unlike most books acclaimed by contemporary critics as unmistakable works of genius, *The Bible in Spain* is as impressive today as when it left the publisher's hands," writes Peter Quennell in the introduction.

YVES BOTTINEAU, *The Wonders of Spain* (1962). A collection of photographs that provides a sense of Spain's geographic and cultural range.

CLAUDE G. BOWERS, *The Spanish Adventures of Washington Irving* (1940). A former American ambassador to Spain writes knowledgeably and sympathetically of Irving's two decades in Spain.

ALASTAIR BOYD, *The Companion Guide to Madrid and Central Spain* (1974). An erudite, stone-by-stone guide to much of Castile, with special insights for careful readers. His *The Essence of Catalonia: Barcelona and its Regions* is invaluable as well.

GERALD BRENAN, *The Face of Spain* (1951). Memorable, especially for his account of his search for the burial place of Federico García Lorca.

————, *The Literature of the Spanish People* (1965). A thorough, scholarly, yet eminently readable discussion of Spanish literature from Roman times to the present. Admirable in its scope and engrossing analysis.

————, *South from Granada* (1957). A close and informed look at Andalusia's wild Alpujarras range.

————, *The Spanish Labyrinth* (1950). An examination of the social and political background of the Spanish Civil War, as well as a searching look at the war itself.

VINCENT BROME, *The International Brigades: Spain 1936–1939* (1965). A historical assessment of 40,000 men, a "modern crusade," who came from other countries to fight in the Spanish Civil War.

JONATHAN BROWN, *Diego de Velázquez, Painter and Courtier* (1986). An exceptional biography of the painter's remarkable life by a professor of fine arts at New York University.

PETER BUCKLEY, *Matador* (1958). Twenty-four hours in the lives of three fictional matadors. The more than 100 photographs by the author constitute a pictorial narrative of a bullfight.

TITUS BURCKHARDT, *Moorish Culture in Spain* (1972). An almost indispensable analysis of the culture of the Moors in Spain, with line drawings and photographs. Readable, scholarly, and something of a classic.

WILLIAM BYRON, *Cervantes: A Biography* (1978). The definitive biography of Cervantes, and an impeccably researched and well-written portrait of his age.

PEDRO CALDERON DE LA BARCA, *Life Is a Dream* (1635). The prolific 17th-century dramatist's most frequently produced comedy, with tragic overtones, which advocates the necessity of order, however painful, against the terror of chaos: Life is a dream, but it must not be lived irresponsibly.

A. C. CALVERT, *Southern Spain* (1908). A travel book on Andalusia, stressing its historical and artistic heritage. Outdated touristically but still of interest aesthetically.

JEAN CANAVAGGIO, *Cervantes* (1977). An expert on Spain's Golden Age, Canavaggio has written a lively and reliable book (winner of the 1987 Prix Goncourt for biography in France) reminding us "that each new century reinterprets *Don Quixote* according to its own values and concerns."

PENELOPE CASAS, *Discovering Spain: An Uncommon Guide* (1992). An "unabashedly personal guidebook" that combines social history and culture with a highly individual guide for touring, lodging, and savoring gastronomic Spain. A pleasure to read and to own.

————, *The Foods and Wines of Spain* (1982). That rare cookbook that is informative, literate, entertaining, and decidedly practical, by an expert on Spanish cuisine.

————, *Tapas* (1985). A definitive look at "the little dishes of Spain." Recipes, menus, and recommended *tapas* bars in Spain. Her high standards in writing and research prevail.

AMERICO CASTRO, *The Structure of Spanish History* (1954). Perhaps the best scholarly analysis of Spanish thought and history. "This history is viewed and organized from within," Castro writes, "and not as a result of natural or economic causes, or of the operation of abstract ideas allegedly valid above time and space."

MIGUEL DE CERVANTES, *Don Quixote* (1605). La Mancha's Don Quixote and Sancho Panza ride forth in one of the world's great novels.

GILBERT CHASE, *The Music of Spain* (1959). A survey of Spanish music emphasizing its diversity of cultural influences and the qualities that make it unique.

J. M. COHEN, EDITOR, *The Penguin Book of Spanish Verse* (1956). A splendid chronological anthology of Spanish poetry, with biographical notes and Cohen's prose translation of each poem.

PETER COLLINS, *The Arab Conquest of Spain: 710–797* (1990). The first of three volumes on Moorish Spain, in which Collins's infectious skepticism regarding historical assumptions permeates a learned book full of brilliant ideas.

VALENTINE CUNNINGHAM, EDITOR, *Spanish Front: Writers on the Civil War* (1986). An anthology of famous writers' letters, essays, and poetry on the Spanish Civil War. Includes much hitherto unfamiliar (and fascinating) material by Simone Weil, Stephen Spender, Herbert Read, Virginia Woolf, and Evelyn Waugh, among others.

REINHART DOZY, *Spanish Islam* (1972). A history of the Muslims in Spain through the 11th century. Translated by Francis Griffin Stokes.

HUBRECHT DUIJKER, *The Wines of Rioja* (1987). A lively and informative work on the greatest red-wine region of Spain.

HAVELOCK ELLIS, *The Soul of Spain* (1908). The eminent psychologist chooses Spain as an analysand.

EBERHARD FISCH, *Guernica by Picasso* (1988). A short, clear, explicit historical and critical look at Picasso's seminal painting.

JAMES FITZMAURICE-KELLY, *Lope de Vega and the Spanish Drama* (1902). A survey that follows the course of Spanish theater up to 1900.

RICHARD FLETCHER, *The Quest for El Cid* (1990). With verve and sensitivity, the author offers a comprehensive reassessment of Rodrigo Díaz, born in the mid-1040s and the hero of Spain's great medieval epic.

RICHARD FORD, *A Hand-book for Travellers in Spain* (1845). A classic that "takes its place among the best books of travel, humor and history—social, literary, political, and artistic, in the English language," wrote Sir William Sterling-Maxwell.

FEDERICO GARCIA LORCA, *The House of Bernarda Alba* (1936). In what is perhaps his most famous play, Lorca fuses powerful imagery and an almost surrealistic design in a theme of sterility and frustrated love. Many critics consider him Spain's finest poet-playwright since Lope de Vega.

IAN GIBSON, *Federico García Lorca: A Life* (1989). After 20 years of research, Gibson, now a Spanish citizen, offers what seems likely to be the definitive treatment of the life and art of García Lorca. A model biography: accurate, thorough, sensitive, penetrating.

DAVID C. GOODMAN, *Power and Penury* (1988). The relationship among government, technology, and science in Philip II's Spain, a subject consistently overlooked until now by historians of science.

CLIVE GRIFFIN, *The Crombergers of Seville: The History of a Printing and Merchant Dynasty* (1990). An account of an entrepreneurial 16th-century German family in Spain whose commercial interests in printing, mines, and ranches encompassed both Spain and Mexico.

JOSE GUIDOL, *Goya* (1989). The text and illustrations illuminate Goya's chronological development in becoming what many believe to be Spain's greatest artist.

MARIANNE HARASZTI-TAKACS, *Spanish Masters* (1966). A surprising look, through text and reproductions, at the rarely exhibited Spanish paintings in the collection of the Budapest Museum of Fine Art. El Greco, Zurbarán, Ribera, Murillo, Velázquez, and Goya are among the artists.

RICHARD J. HARRISON, *Spain at the Dawn of History: Iberians, Phoenicians and Greeks* (1988). A prehistorian's view of recent excavations in Spain, with emphasis on the Iberians between 1000 and 200 B.C.

ERNEST HEMINGWAY, *The Dangerous Summer* (1960). An account (with an introduction by James A. Michener) of a visit to Spain in the summer of 1959 that highlights the rivalry between the bullfighters Antonio Ordóñez and Luis Miguel Dominguin.

————, *Death in the Afternoon* (1932). Many consider this the definitive book on bullfighting, written by an aficionado.

————, *For Whom the Bell Tolls* (1940). His classic novel about the Spanish Civil War, starring the lovers Robert and Maria, the indomitable Pilar, and the moving earth.

————, *The Sun Also Rises* (1926). His first and, many critics think, his best novel. Pamplona, Madrid, and a Spain that is more heterodox than historical.

THOMAS HINDE, *Spain* (1963). Quotations from a wide variety of writers on various aspects of Spanish life, tied together by the author's observations. Photographs.

JOHN HOOPER, *The Spaniards: A Portrait of the New Spain* (1986). An excellent account by a British journalist of the changes in Spain after Franco, with insights into sociological, political, economic, and regional developments.

DAVID HOWARTH, *The Voyage of the Armada* (1981). An account of the Armada's ill-fated voyage to England, told from the Spanish perspective. Draws on 16th-century documents and letters discovered in the royal archives.

ROBERT HUGHES, *Barcelona* (1992). A mammoth (571 pages) best-selling sweep (1,500 years) of Barcelona's rocky political and cultural history, enriched by Hughes's uncompromising, iconoclastic style and his talents as a critic of art and architecture. *Barcelona* scants the Spanish Civil War but the chapter on Gaudí is brilliant.

PIERRE IRVING, *The Life and Letters of Washington Irving* (1973). Irving's nephew devotes much of this detailed biography to his uncle's stay in Spain. Many hitherto unpublished letters.

WASHINGTON IRVING, *Tales of the Alhambra* (1832). The book that many think is responsible for both the recognition and the condition of the Alhambra today.

MICHAEL JACOBS, *A Guide to Andalusia* (1990). The author's dauntingly comprehensive grasp of the history, traditions, literature, and contemporary bar life of southern Spain makes for a stimulating and refreshing guide. The book includes a "gazetteer" that highlights locations with respect to art, architecture, crafts, beaches, bars, archaeological sites, and lodgings.

GOTTHARD JEDLICKA, *Spanish Painting* (1964). A critical study with excellent reproductions of the works of seven great Spanish painters: Valdés Leal, Goya, Ribera, Zurbarán, Murillo, Velázquez, and El Greco.

JULIAN JEFFS, *Sherry* (1970). The authoritative work on Sherry, the distinctive wine of Jerez, and how it is made.

HUGH JOHNSON, *Hugh Johnson's Modern Encyclopedia of Wine* (1987). Sections on La Rioja, Jerez, and Catalonia are a must for anyone with a keen interest in the wines of these regions.

SIMON J. KEAY, *Roman Spain* (1980). A thorough account, plus excellent pictures and maps, of the 600-year Roman occupation of Spain, with an emphasis on archaeology.

GEORGIANA GODDARD KING, *Heart of Spain* (1941). A Bryn Mawr professor examines the art, architecture, and literature of "Old and New Castile." Writing early in this century, King remains an acknowledged expert in the field.

NORMAN LEWIS, *Voices of the Old Sea* (1986). The three-year metamorphosis of a post–World War II Catalonian fishing village into a garish tourist resort, written by an Englishman who worked locally as a fisherman.

DAVID LOTH, *Philip II of Spain* (1932). The history of the man who ruled Spain at the height of her power and prosperity, and at the beginning of her downfall.

PAUL MACKENDRICK, *The Iberian Stones Speak* (1969). A reconstruction of cultural history based on the study of archaeological remains in the Iberian Peninsula from 12,000 B.C. to A.D. 350.

GARRETT MATTINGLY, *The Armada* (1959). An engaging and informative report of Spain's naval encounter with the British fleet in 1588.

THOMAS A. MCGANN, EDITOR, *Portrait of Spain* (1963). A collage of British and American accounts of Spain in the 19th and 20th centuries.

JOAN MELLEN, EDITOR, *The World of Luis Buñuel* (1978). Forty essays by international writers and film critics on Buñuel's films and career.

ROGER B. MERRIMAN, *The Rise of the Spanish Empire in the Old World and in the New* (1934). A history that covers the period from Ferdinand and Isabella to Philip II.

JAMES A. MICHENER, *Iberia* (1968). The author gives Spain his usual exhaustive, often rewarding treatment.

TOWNSEND MILLER, *The Castles and the Crown* and *Henry IV of Castile*. These two eminently readable histories capture the spirit of 15th- and 16th-century Castile.

SAMUEL ELIOT MORISON, *Admiral of the Ocean Sea* (1942). Morison's classic two-volume history of the events and adventures surrounding Columbus and his voyages.

JAMES MORRIS, *The Presence of Spain* (1964). The culture, history, and people of Spain as seen by possibly the best travel writer of our time. Photographs by Evelyn Hofer.

————, *Spain* (1979). A revised, updated text of the previously listed book by the author as Jan Morris. Now without photographs, this contemporary edition has a darker tone.

H. V. MORTON, *A Stranger in Spain* (1986). A very personal look at Spain through sympathetic and perceptive eyes.

EDWIN MULLINS, *The Pilgrimage to Santiago* (1974). An entertaining guide to the Camino de Santiago with a number of amusing, and sometimes piquant, observations.

HENRY MYHILL, *The Spanish Pyrenees* (1966). A thorough and engrossing discussion of the Basque, Aragonese, and Catalan Pyrenees, with maps and photographs.

MARTIN NOZICK, *Miguel de Unamuno: The Agony of Belief* (1982). A penetrating critical and biographical study of Unamuno, highlighted by the "Myth of Don Quixote" analysis. Nozick writes of Unamuno's philosophy and his role as a member of the innovative "Generation of 1898" with uncommon tact and evenhandedness.

JOSE ORTEGA Y GASSET, *Meditations on Quixote* (1914). Never translated during his lifetime, Ortega's first book on "the consciousness of circumstances" heralded a career that led to Albert Camus's encomium: "Ortega y Gasset, after Nietzsche, is perhaps the greatest European writer."

————, *Revolt of the Masses* (1932). A critique of modern society by a writer whom many regard as the foremost Spanish thinker of the 20th century.

GEORGE ORWELL, *Homage to Catalonia* (1937). Orwell describes his experiences fighting on the side of the Republicans in the Spanish Civil War.

ELLIOT PAUL, *The Life and Death of a Spanish Town* (1939). An expatriate resident of Santa Eulalia del Río on Ibiza describes how the onset of the Spanish Civil War tore the town apart.

ROBERT PAYNE, EDITOR, *The Civil War in Spain, 1936–1939* (1962). Some 50 firsthand accounts by journalists, letter writers, soldiers, and observers of the war that ravaged the Spanish nation.

F. ALLISON PEERS, *Catalonia Infelix* (1936). The political and cultural history of Catalonia from the 12th century through the Spanish Civil War.

JOSEPH PLA AND CHRISTIAN SARRAMON, *Seeing Catalonia* (1985). Text and photographs tell the story of Catalonia, its history, its culture, and its attractions for the traveller.

D. E. POHREN, *Adventures in Taste: The Wines and Folk Food of Spain* (1972). This idiosyncratic, privately published classic describes encounters with artisan wine makers.

WILLIAM H. PRESCOTT, *History of the Reign of Ferdinand and Isabella the Catholic* (1838). After a century and a half, Prescott's three-volume history of the Catholic monarchs, Columbus, and the dawn of the Golden Age remains one of the most complete and most readable accounts in English.

V. S. PRITCHETT, *Marching Spain* (1928). A 300-mile walk in 1927 from Badajoz to León in a Spain that no longer exists, yet is instantly recognizable. Pritchett later described this book as "juvenile," but it offers the reader an invigorating ride high in the rhetorical saddle.

————, *The Spanish Temper* (1954). Pritchett once again proves himself a masterly writer on Spain, this time in the early 1950s, when the country was "poor in body, stunned in mind, but not . . . fundamentally changed."

JAN READ, *The Moors in Spain and Portugal* (1975). A broad historical narrative incorporating accounts of cultural and sociological development over the 800 years the Moors were in the Iberian Peninsula.

————, *The Wines of Spain* (1986). This book, or any of the four others by the reigning English-language authority on Spanish wines, is informative and engaging.

ARTHUR STANLEY RIGGS, *The Spanish Pageant* (1928). A search for the "real Spain . . . somewhere between the spattery sunshine of two-weeks tourists and the gray textures of historians." This book, though dated, remains a pleasure to read.

CEDRIC SALTER, *Try-Out in Spain* (1943). A history of the Spanish Civil War based on the theory that it was in fact the beginning of World War II.

GEORGE SAND, *Winter in Majorca* (1956). Her account of a less-than-idyllic winter sojourn with Chopin in Valldemossa, a Majorcan town that has never quite recovered. Robert Graves, who spent much of his life in nearby Deya, translated.

MARIA JOSE SEVILLA, *Life and Food in the Basque Country* (1989). A captivating, loving look at the gastronomic aspects of Basque life—and the rare book in English with any insights on the subject. With recipes.

SACHEVERELL SITWELL, *Spain* (1951). A rather eccentric and often perceptive view of Spain 40 years ago; Sitwell responds to Spain like an itinerant hummingbird in search of exotic Iberian pollen.

RHEA MARSH SMITH, *Spain* (1965). A detailed but occasionally plodding history that begins with the Visigoths and ends in the 1960s.

WALTER STARKIE, *The Road to Santiago* (1965). De rigueur reading for those with a serious interest in the Camino de Santiago. Engagingly written by one of the greatest Hispanophiles of all time.

JAMES JOSEPH SWEENEY AND JOSEP LLUIS SERT, *Antoni Gaudí* (1970). A comprehensive study of Gaudí's art and architecture, supplemented by hundreds of photographs and drawings.

A. W. TAYLOR, *Wild Flowers in Spain and Portugal* (1981). A definitive guide to Spain's wildflowers, from mountainous regions to the Meseta.

F. JAY TAYLOR, *The United States and the Spanish Civil War* (1956). American attitudes toward, and participation in, Spain's Civil War, with an analysis of domestic political considerations.

TERESA OF AVILA, *The Life of Saint Teresa* (1611). The autobiography of Avila's Carmelite Renaissance nun, said to be the most widely read prose classic in Spain.

HUGH THOMAS, *The Spanish Civil War* (1961). A thorough, penetrating account of the Civil War, with appendices on its economics, casualties, and foreign intervention.

MARIMAR TORRES, *The Spanish Table: The Cuisines and Wines of Spain* (1980). Useful basic information on wines by a member of one of Spain's most successful wine families.

MIGUEL DE UNAMUNO, *The Tragic Sense of Life* (1913). The philosopher's passionate advocacy of his view of existentialism.

W. MONTGOMERY WATT, *A History of Islamic Spain* (1967). That rare book on Islamic Spain written by an expert on Islam who perceives the 800-year Moorish occupation of Spain in a global context. Sharp, succinct, scholarly, but unstuffy.

F. J. Wiseman, *Roman Spain* (1956). A comprehensive study of Roman antiquities in Spain and Portugal.

Nicholas Wollaston, *Tilting at Don Quixote* (1990). Part travel-adventure (the author follows Don Quixote's erratic trail through La Mancha), part autobiography, and wholly enjoyable.

—*Robert Packard*

MADRID

By Tom Burns with Patricia Brooks

Tom Burns was born in London and read modern history at Oxford University. He was posted to Madrid in 1974 by Reuters and is currently a director of Spanish Trends, *a Madrid-based business monthly, and an associate editor of* Lookout, *a magazine for English-speaking residents in Spain. He contributes frequently to the* London Financial Times. *Patricia Brooks contributes to other sections of this guidebook.*

All main roads in Spain lead to Madrid. Wherever you are on the national highways, the red-topped kilometer markings will tell you how far you are from the Spanish capital. Madrid was designated Spain's capital city more than 400 years ago because it was as near the center of the Iberian Peninsula as it was possible to be. At the Puerta del Sol, the Spanish version of Piccadilly Circus, in the heart of Madrid, you can stand on the flagstone that marks kilometer 0.

George Borrow, who was Britain's Bible Society agent in Spain midway through the last century and who earned fame with his account of his peninsular exploits in *The Bible in Spain,* travelled every one of the Spanish highways several times, and most of the byways as well. He never quite got over his first impressions of Madrid. "I have visited most of the principal capitals of the world," wrote the engaging Borrow, "but upon the whole none has ever interested me as this city of Madrid, in which I now find myself."

Borrow understood exactly what the city is about. What amazed the much-travelled author was Madrid's people: "Within a mud wall scarcely one league and a half in circuit, are contained two hundred thousand human beings, certainly forming the most extraordinary vital mass to be found in the entire world."

With a current population of slightly more than four million, Madrid has grown twenty-fold since Borrow's time, and the mud wall has long since vanished. But the zest for

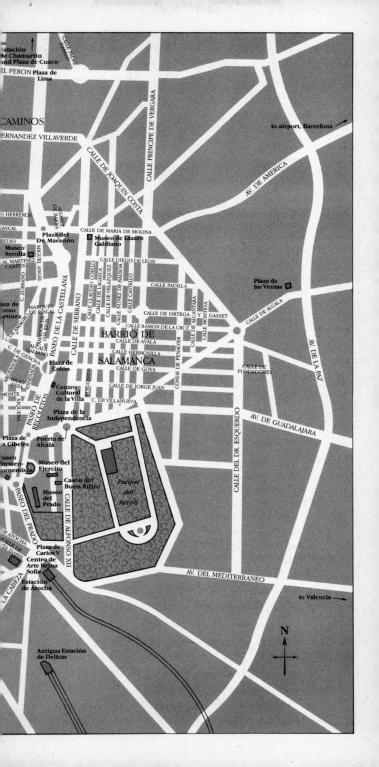

life remains. Madrid, where all the national highways converge, remains the teeming melting pot of Spain. It draws all the peninsula's vitality toward it and shakes the peoples of Spain into a sparkling cocktail.

MAJOR INTEREST

Hapsburg and Bourbon history and architecture
Fine art collections
Hanging out in *tapas* bars, tavernas, and sidewalk
    cafés
Fine dining, especially at seafood restaurants
Shopping for antiques, crafts, and custom-made items

The Prado Area

Museo del Prado: El Greco, Zurbarán, Velázquez,
    Goya
Parque del Retiro
Museo Nacional Centro de Arte Reina Sofía: Picasso's
    Guernica
Museo Thyssen-Bornemisza's international painting
    collection

Old Madrid

Puerta del Sol, the center of Madrid
Real Academia de Bellas Artes de San Fernando:
    Goya paintings
Plaza Mayor, the center of Hapsburg Madrid
Old *tabernas* and *tapas* bars
Plaza de la Villa's 17th-century architecture
Typical Old Madrid restaurants in the Puerta de
    Moros area
El Rastro flea market

The Palacio Real Area

The Bourbon Palacio Real and Royal Armory
Ermita de San Antonio, Goya's burial place
Convento de la Encarnación's 17th-century art collection
Real Monasterio de la Descalzas Reales: Hapsburg
    family portrait collection

Northwestern Madrid

Museo Cerralbo: Spanish masters and archaeological
    finds

Northeastern Madrid

Sidewalk cafés on the Castellana
Museo Arqueológico Nacional
Barrio de Salamanca for shopping, galleries, and
    dining

Madrid's fizz can hit you head on. The city sits on Spain's central tableland in the shelter of the Sierra de Guadarrama, nearly 2,300 feet above sea level; the city's altitude may help create its effervescence. In *Death in the Afternoon,* Ernest Hemingway described the Madrid of the 1930s as a "mountain city with a mountain climate." This was, of course, before smog—the city began to acquire a large industrial belt in the 1950s—and Hemingway waxed lyrical about Madrid's environment: "It has the high cloudless Spanish sky that makes the Italian sky seem sentimental and it has air that is actively pleasurable to breathe."

There are still many days—more than you might expect—when the skies that Diego Velázquez loved to paint make you gasp in admiration, and there are mornings when you gratefully gulp the gusts of air that sweep down from the Sierra. On certain evenings, if you time it right, as you walk up the Gran Vía from the Plaza de la Cibeles you can see the sun, looking every inch the fiery red ball it is supposed to be, dip over the brow of the busy thoroughfare. In essence, Madrid has not changed that much.

Certainly the joyousness, the boisterousness of Madrid that entranced Hemingway and Borrow, remains in place. "Nobody goes to bed in Madrid until they have killed the night," noted Hemingway. "In no other town I have lived in, except Constantinople during the period of Allied occupation, is there less going to bed for sleeping purposes."

Coming from the author who lauded Paris as a moveable feast, such observations are praise indeed. They are also relevant. Madrid today has appalling traffic problems, a good number of hideous buildings that have replaced elegant palaces and mansions, and a sprawl of unsightly suburbs—but fun it undeniably remains.

The History of Madrid

MADRID'S ORIGINS

Back in prehistory a river ran down what is today's Paseo de la Castellana, modern Madrid's main north–south axis, and mammoths grazed on its banks. Stone Age people grunted their way along the grassy edges of the river; evidence of their Paleolithic settlements has been found deep below the present-day sewers. The Romans and the Visigoths also came and went (traces of their fleeting presence in the Madrid area are exhibited in the city's Museo Arqueológico Nacional).

The founder of the city is nevertheless generally agreed to be Omeya, the fifth emir of the independent caliphate of Córdoba, who in the middle of the ninth century raised a watchtower near where the Palacio Real now stands. He named the location Mayrit (running waters). The Moorish occupation was to last some 200 years, but no real vestige of it remains today.

THE MIDDLE AGES

In 1085 Alfonso VI, monarch of the kingdoms of Castile and León, razed Omeya's watchtower and established Christian control over Mayrit's 12,000-odd souls. Alfonso was not particularly interested in the new property he had added to his domain, and later that year his troops marched quickly on to take the far bigger prize of Toledo, a city soon to achieve the status of capital of the two kingdoms.

Madrid had to wait until 1202 and the reign of Alfonso VIII before it was granted a *fuero* (charter of rights), and it was not until 1346 and the reign of Peter the Cruel that it acquired that other status symbol of the Middle Ages, a proper castle. Peter's *alcázar* (fortress) was built on the site of the original watchtower, overlooking Río Manzanares, which is now occupied by the Palacio Real. The city failed, however, to acquire a lasting medieval accolade by way of a decent cathedral. It was not then important enough for that.

British author Alastair Boyd (*The Companion Guide to Madrid and Central Spain*) makes the point that Madrid backed the losing side every time medieval Spain erupted into civil wars. The people of Madrid vainly supported Peter the Cruel when everybody else, fed up by his despotism, had abandoned him. (He had murdered, among others, a Granada caliph and 37 of his courtiers whom he had invited to a banquet, an archbishop, several cousins, and even his own queen.) Eventually, in the midst of a see-saw civil war, he was stabbed to death in his tent by his half-brother Henry II, the founder of the new dynasty of Trastamara. More than a century and a half passed before the city was back in royal favor: under Henry IV, who resided occasionally in Peter's *alcázar* and died there.

THE REIGN OF THE REYES CATOLICOS

Upon the death of Henry IV, known as the Impotent, the city unwisely decided to back the claims to the throne of his purported daughter Juana, a young girl who was popularly known as La Beltraneja (because her real father was reckoned to be the royal favorite Don Alvaro Beltrán de la Cueva). Ranged against little Juana was her ultimately victorious aunt, Henry's sister, the redoubtable Isabella—who was crowned queen of Castile in Segovia in 1474 and who was to go down in history as La Reina Católica.

There is a monument to Isabella set in pleasant gardens that look out on Paseo de la Castellana, at the foot of a small hill that leads up to the Museo de Ciencias Naturales (natural history museum). But in fact the Reyes Católicos, Isabella and her no less formidable husband, Ferdinand of Aragón, effectively bypassed Madrid during an epoch-making reign that saw the conquest of Granada, the creation of modern-day Spain, and Columbus's voyage to the New World. Such were the follies of backing the wrong side. It was Philip II, Isabella's great-grandson, who finally put Madrid on the map.

THE HAPSBURG DYNASTY

Madrid is not an old European capital in the sense that London and Paris are, and, compared with Spain's historical cities, it is very much a newcomer. It was not until 1561 that Philip II had the court moved permanently to Madrid, then a small town of some 20,000 inhabitants. Toledo and Seville at that time had quadruple Madrid's population, and even Valladolid had more than double. It was an odd move given Madrid's insignificance in the 16th century, but the monarch had his reasons.

Philip, an all-powerful ruler (whose beard Francis Drake boasted he had singed after successfully attacking the Invincible Armada when it was being assembled in Cádiz) who is known to Spaniards as the Prudent King, disliked the powerful clergy of Toledo, which was where his father, Emperor Charles V, had set down the court. He was worried about heresy in Valladolid, which had served as Spain's capital in the reign of his great-grandparents Ferdinand and Isabella. Other factors were Madrid's proximity to El Escorial, the monastery-cum-palace-cum-royal pantheon he had ordered to be built at the foot of the Sierra de Guadarrama, and the good boar hunting in the woods that surrounded the city. But most of all Philip liked Madrid because it was central. The monarch thought it right that "so great a monarchy should have a city fulfilling the function of a heart located in the middle of the body," wrote his biographer Luis Cabrera de Córdoba, as cited by Hugh Thomas. Madrid thus finally came into its own through this royal decision, and it never looked back.

Expansion of Hapsburg Madrid

The immediate consequence of Philip's move to Madrid was the rapid growth of the population. By 1597, less than 40 years after the king's decision, the number of the city's inhabitants had more than tripled, growing from around 20,000 to 65,000. Over the next 40 years the population almost tripled again; in 1630, during the reign of Philip's grandson, Philip IV, it stood at 175,000, making Madrid the fifth-largest city in Europe, after Constantinople, Naples, London, and Paris.

The population boom was the direct result of the installation in Madrid of the massive bureaucracy—the chanceries, councils, secretariats, and law courts—that was created by the Spanish Hapsburgs. Along with the army of bureaucrats came an even greater multitude of camp followers. The new capital attracted, according to Federico Sainz de Robles's *Brief History of Madrid,* "litigators, eternal students, sophists, retired soldiers, friars founding branches of their order, people looking for official jobs and contracts, bawds with their whores, fairground and market tricksters, purveyors of potions and the occult arts, strumpets who hang about the corners and under the arcades, back door smugglers here today and gone tomorrow."

Philip II and his Hapsburg successors built up the area of Madrid centered on the Plaza Mayor. The architect Juan de Herrera, who completed the construction of El Escorial, and his pupil Juan Gómez de Mora were the architects of choice. Herrera stamped his personality so clearly on the period that the Spanish Hapsburg architectural style has come to be known as the *estilo herreriano.* For a rapid acquaintance with the period's architectural style head for the **Plaza Mayor**, built according to Herrera's designs by Mora. The obvious feature of Herrera's style is its sobriety: The buildings are solid and somber to the point of being gaunt, and sport spires and dormer windows. Their façades are granite and red brick, and the roofs are usually covered with slate.

THE BOURBON EMPIRE

Philip IV's son, the impotent and half-mad Carlos II, known as Carlos the Bewitched, represented a sad, freakish end product of the Hapsburg intermarriage policy. His death plunged Europe into the War of the Spanish Succession, which led to the arrival in Spain in 1700 of the Bourbon dynasty in the person of Philip V, the grandson of Louis XIV, the Sun King.

The Bourbons soon stamped their personality on Madrid. The *estilo herreriano* meant little to them, nor did the new dynasty favor the cautious drift toward Baroque ornateness that was favored by some late-17th-century Spanish architects, notably by the Churriguera brothers, José Benito, Alberto, and Joaquín, whose main achievement was the Plaza Mayor of Salamanca. With the Bourbons came a pronounced Classical style, with all its columns and cupolas. Italian architects were much in vogue due to the good offices of Philip V's two Italian wives, María Luisa of Savoy and Isabella Farnese, and they continued to be in the forefront during the reign of Carlos III (son of Philip and Isabella Farnese), who was king of Naples before he was crowned king of Spain.

Expansion of Bourbon Madrid

A fire that burned down Peter the Cruel's original *alcázar* in 1734 (the building had been much restored and extended in the intervening centuries) provided Philip V with the perfect excuse to build a wholly new palace according to the new Bourbon taste. The Italian architect Filippo Giuvarra and his pupil Giovanni Sacchetti accordingly designed the massive Palacio Real (royal palace). Philip V sponsored other major landmarks in Madrid, such as the domed church of San Francisco el Grande, just south of the Palacio Real. But it was left to his son, Carlos III, to promote the finest of the 18th-century Bourbon buildings in the city, as he worked to bring Madrid up to the architectural standards of rival European capitals.

Carlos commissioned Francesco Sabatini, another Italian architect, to build the wonderfully measured Puerta de Alcalá and design the building that today houses the treasury, just off the Puerta del Sol on Calle de Alcalá. Juan de Villanueva, a Spaniard who was also much favored by Carlos and who successfully adopted the Classical style, designed the building that now houses the Prado and the nearby pavilions of the Jardín Botánico.

Carlos, an enlightened ruler who assembled a talented and efficient government, is a readily recognizable figure: He posed frequently for Goya. You need look no farther than the Goya canvases that hang in the Prado and in such other city museums as the Real Academia de Bellas Artes de San Fernando to recapture those heady late-18th-century days. His paintings of the aristocracy dancing and picnicking in the broad hats and long cloaks of the popular classes at fiestas and *ferias* along the Río Manzanares offer faithful records of the era. There could be no more explicit diarist of a period's foibles and fantasies, its decorum and its disasters.

The Decline of the Bourbons

The royal court itself was a somewhat similar mix of grandeur and decadence. In 1788, the year before the storming of the Bastille in Paris, Carlos IV succeeded his father, Carlos III; unfortunately, however, he inherited none of his parent's intelligence. The façade of royal power remained, but the edifice was crumbling. A handsome young guards captain, Manuel de Godoy, became the royal favorite (and the queen's lover), and the cuckolded Carlos showered him with honors. Godoy, who became prime minister and was awarded the title of Prince of Peace, polarized opinions both in and out of the court. Goya was clearly conscious that a storm was gathering. When really bad times came and Napoleon's troops took over the city, the Madrileños rose up heroically against the invaders, and Goya faithfully recorded the change, the valor, and the tragedy of the patriotic populace.

Finding the Real Madrid

The historian Hugh Thomas rightly cautions in *Madrid, A Travellers Companion,* that "the charm of Madrid is elusive." Richard Ford, a contemporary of Borrow and author of the classic *Hand-book for Travellers in Spain,* never had time for the city—"the more Madrid is known, the less it will be liked"—and even Hemingway, who was to become such an aficionado of Madrid, conceded: "I do not believe anyone likes it much when he first goes there." But the traveller who takes the time to search out the real Madrid, and to find the city's essence, will be greatly rewarded.

Madrid, as befits the capital city of an old nation, has its fair share of places of historical interest. If you know where to look you can virtually touch a medieval world, smell its odors, and hear its sounds. You will certainly come across the Madrid that the Hapsburgs built and also the one that the succeeding Bourbon dynasty created. There are palaces, churches, and convents, triumphal arches, ornamental gardens, and sturdy bridges. As the home of Velázquez, whose patrons were the Hapsburgs, and of Goya, who painted the Bourbons, Madrid is assured its place in the cultural firmament, with the Museo del Prado as its high temple.

Madrid has, when all is said and done, been it all and seen it all. It became the capital of Spain overnight because Philip II decided to make it so at a time when Spanish might was at its 16th-century zenith. But 100 years later Madrid's extravagantly Baroque exterior could scarcely mask the fact that it was the headquarters of a fast-decaying empire. Home of the court and of the bureaucracy, Madrid spent much of its time battling to hold Spain together and trying to make ends meet.

Francisco Goya, in the late 18th and early 19th centuries, and novelist Benito Pérez Galdós, many years later, depicted a city of heroism and intrigue that was graceful and bawdy by turns—and scarcely knew the difference between the two. The atrocious behavior of Napoleon's troops, the turmoil of the 19th century, the fierce siege the city endured during the Spanish Civil War, and the hungry years that followed its surrender to Franco—nothing succeeded in dampening Madrid's spirit.

THE MADRILEÑOS

But you will only partly understand Madrid by visiting its monuments and treasures. To gain the full experience of the city you must also turn your observations to its inhabitants:

to the *ambiente* (ambience) and the *alegría* (joy), to the atmosphere and the joie de vivre that the Madrileños can, and do, create.

The Madrileños have a lot of swaggering style to them. Bumper stickers proclaim that Madrid is the "Gateway to Heaven." But the assertiveness is tempered by a self-deprecating, street-smart humor. Ramón Gómez de la Serna, a witty between-the-wars chronicler of the city's virtues and vices, said that Madrid was "putting your hands in your pockets better than anywhere else in the world." This would imply insolence were it not for the innate decency and humanity of the Madrileño.

The people of Madrid, Spaniards to the hilt as they are, have undoubted flair. There is no English equivalent for the Spanish verb *estrenar,* which means to use or to show off for the first time, much in the sense of "to premiere." Consumption-conscious Spaniards, and in particular Madrileños, are constantly *estrenando* (premiering) everything from their new clothes to their new cars. Nor is there an exact Spanish equivalent for such English words as eavesdrop or overhear. In Spain it is unnecessary to eavesdrop in the usual sly sense of the word because people simply speak too loudly. The noise level in Madrid, as in all of Spain, is several decibels above what might be acceptable elsewhere. Everything is convivial and loud, and that applies to acquaintances meeting on a street corner as well as to groups gathered in a bar and to drivers honking their horns in gridlocked traffic.

DOING THE CITY

You can take Madrid in an orderly way, progressing from one specific interest point to another. That way of approaching it is by no means to be sneered at. Be warned, however, that Madrid is neither obviously grand nor stylish nor historical in the way that London, Paris, and Rome are.

Another approach is just to let Madrid rush at you and to take you over, to let it infect you with its peculiar pace. Experience the *terrazas* (sidewalk cafés) of Paseo de la Castellana from June to September, when they are in full swing long after the midnight hour. Stroll the Parque del Retiro on any Sunday morning, when the gardens are crammed with musicians, puppeteers, and mimes. Join the bullfight throng of the San Isidro *feria* (festival) in May. Dress up at Carnival time. Dance along at the neighborhood street parties during August and September.

Be part of the crowd that shops at Christmastime for Nativity figures from the street vendors in the Plaza Mayor. Form part of the tidal wave of humanity that invades El Rastro flea market on weekends. Have long lunches and longer dinners. Go *tapas* hopping from old bar to older tavern, nibbling a wealth of snacks and drinking cold beer—served in the small, narrow glasses called *cañas*—or Valde-peñas wine, served in the smaller, stumpier glasses called *chatos*.

But the city's pace can be an exhausting one. The streets appear permanently crowded and the stranger may well wonder when anyone ever works—or sleeps. People seem to spend their lives in cafés and restaurants, and meals last for hours. But the visitor who joins them will find a Madrid not described in guidebooks or listed on itineraries: the Madrid of today.

Madrid does not have obvious identity marks like the mix of Modernism and Mediterranean that you find in Barcelona. It does not have the southern sensuality of Seville, nor does it offer breathtaking silhouettes of ages past as Salamanca, Segovia, and Toledo do. That said, a visitor to Madrid is honor bound to give the city a chance to produce the kaleidoscope of sensations that it has evolved over the centuries.

We begin our coverage of Madrid in the southeastern quadrant of the city center, at the Plaza de la Cibeles, one of the city's main plazas. We then proceed south to the Museo del Prado, Madrid's most important attraction and a fine introduction to the Hapsburgs and Bourbons who molded the city. Two other important art museums are in the vicinity: the renovated Museo Nacional Centro de Arte Reina Sofía, now home of Picasso's *Guernica,* and the brand-new Museo Thyssen-Bornemisza, the most important private collection of paintings in the world.

After the Prado area we explore Old Madrid, centered on the Plaza Mayor, and its mainly Hapsburg historical and architectural sites. The Palacio Real area, built up by the Bourbons to the west of Old Madrid along the Río Manza-nares, follows. East of the Palacio and north of the Plaza Mayor we visit two convent-museums with fine collections, and then several museums in the northwestern section of Madrid center.

Finally we work our way eastward to the Castellana, Ma-drid's grand boulevard, and the elegant Barrio de Salamanca on its eastern bank. Museums in this area include the fasci-nating Museo Arqueológico Nacional.

THE PRADO AREA

Plaza de la Cibeles

Positioned in the northwestern corner of the Prado area—
which encompasses the southeastern quadrant of central
Madrid—the Plaza de la Cibeles provides a fine entryway to
a tour of the city. Madrid's best-loved landmark, the **Fuente
de la Cibeles**, a fountain-monument honoring the mythological queen of the sea built in the reign of the Bourbon king
Carlos III, is the focal point of the plaza. Surrounding the
lovely Cibeles and her lion-borne chariot are three centers
of modern might: communications, cash, and that ultimate
power broker, the military. The Palacio de Communica-
ciones, a fantastic edifice built in 1904 that now serves as
Spain's main post office, sits on the east side of the plaza; the
Banco de España, a large, Neoclassical mid-19th-century
bank building, holds down the southwestern corner; and the
Spanish army's general staff headquarters in the Palacio de
Vistahermosa, guarded by soldiers and surrounded by gardens, stretches up to the northwest.

The meeting place of two main streets of Madrid, the
Paseo de la Castellana and the Calle de Alcalá, the Plaza de la
Cibeles serves in effect as a hub for central Madrid's neighborhoods, and is a good place to get your bearings before
you head south to the Prado.

PASEO DE LA CASTELLANA
The Paseo de la Castellana, a broad boulevard shaded by
acacia trees, runs north–south and serves to divide the city
into an east side and a west side. As a rule of thumb, modern
Madrid, including the upscale Barrio de Salamanca, is on the
east side, while Old Madrid—an effervescent mix of bohe-
mianism, trendiness, and classless popularity—can be found
on the west side. Although it is commonly called the
Castellana along its entire length, the boulevard is actually
named the Paseo de Recoletos in the stretch from Plaza de
Colón south to Plaza de la Cibeles, and the Paseo del Prado
south of that.

CALLE DE ALCALA
Calle de Alcalá runs east–west and crosses the Castellana at
the Plaza de la Cibeles, effectively dividing the city into an
uptown and a downtown. Developed by the Bourbon king
Carlos III, Calle de Alcalá meets the Parque del Retiro to the
east at the triumphal Puerta de Alcalá, one of the most
impressive monuments built during Carlos III's reign, and

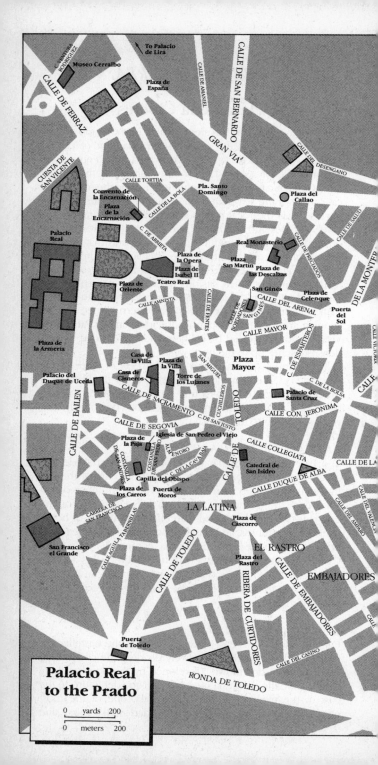

Palacio Real to the Prado

0   yards   200

0   meters   200

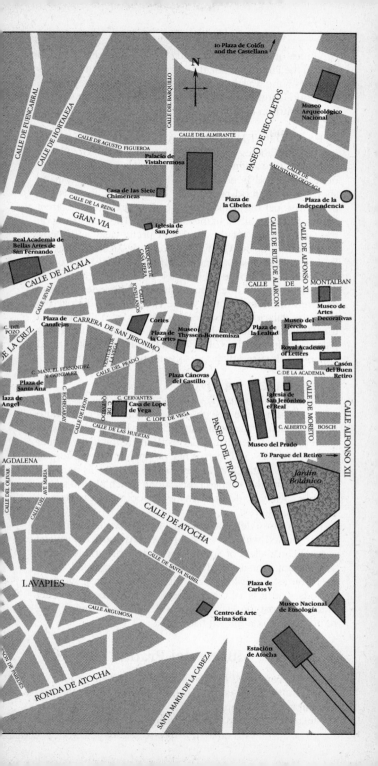

continues on out of town. Going westward, it climbs uphill toward the Puerta del Sol, the heart of old Hapsburg Madrid, passing on the way the Real Academia de Bellas Artes de San Fernando, another of the treasures bestowed upon the city by the Bourbon king.

WEST OF THE PLAZA DE LA CIBELES

Just west of Cibeles the Calle de Alcalá meets the Gran Vía, a grand city thoroughfare that was once Madrid's main business center and is now lined with movie houses, touristy shops, and fast-food restaurants. Nevertheless, there is still the occasional big bank or merchant house, and the street has a lot of style, albeit of the fading kind. The side streets off the Gran Vía are for the most part pretty tacky and seedy.

At the foot of the Gran Vía, at Calle de Alcalá 43, sits the **Iglesia de San José**, a fine example of Spanish Baroque, designed by Pedro de Ribera. Just to the north by way of Calle del Barquillo, the **Casa de las Siete Chimeneas** (House of Seven Chimneys), sitting in the Plaza del Rey right across from the Palacio del Vistahermosa, dates from the reign of the Hapsburg ruler Philip II and is typical of the private palaces built near the Calle de Alcalá during the city's rapid expansion. It currently houses the ministry of culture.

PASEO DEL PRADO

Downtown from the Plaza de la Cibeles, the Castellana extends south as the Paseo del Prado. This leafier and more sedate stretch of the boulevard echoes with the elegance of earlier ages of true leisure. Carlos III inaugurated the monument to Cibeles and that of her companion, Neptune, just south at the Plaza Cánovas del Castillo in 1790, as part of a plan to create this refined *paseo* along which Madrid's fashionable society could promenade on foot or in carriages to display themselves.

Today's Paseo del Prado, lined with *terrazas* in summer, is just as packed with the look-at-me crowd and has inspired current chroniclers of Spanish mores to write about Madrid as a vibrant capital that throbs with the unexpected and is every bit as astonishing as it was during its most glorious periods. And it is, of course, the location of the Museo del Prado, just past the Plaza Cánovas del Castillo (to which we return, below) on the left-hand side.

Museo del Prado

Originally conceived by Carlos III and his architect Juan de Villanueva as a museum of natural history, the Prado was inaugurated as a museum of painting and sculpture by Ferdinand VII, Carlos's grandson, in 1819. It is ironic that

Ferdinand, an arrogant and small-minded individual who has had rough treatment from historians and from artists (Goya painted him looking incredibly oafish), should have been responsible for this high temple of culture. The Prado alone makes a visit to Madrid worthwhile, or, put more exactly, the Prado is far and away the main reason for coming to Madrid. To get the most out of a trip, a visitor should spend much more time in the Prado than in all of the city's other cultural venues put together. This is why we devote a relatively large amount of space to it here.

The Prado opened as a museum shortly after the Louvre and before London's National Gallery. Clearly it has strengths, such as the Velázquez and Goya holdings, that put it well ahead of its two peers, in the same way that it has deficiencies. It is, however, different from both in one curious respect: Everything in the Prado was either paid for or acquired through donations; there is not a single example of war booty.

A second general point is that it is primarily a royal collection. In this sense the Prado reflects the tastes of the Spanish monarchs. Their standards were generally high, and in certain cases, notably that of Philip IV, the sensibility toward art was peerless. In addition, the ramifications of the Hapsburg family power being what they were, the Spanish royal collection, as it was built up in the 16th and 17th centuries, was able to draw on the Flemish, German, and Italian schools that flourished, as it were, in the back yards of the Madrid court.

The collection of the Prado is probably best approached chronologically, moving from the early Flemish and German masters on to the Italians and finally on to the museum's tour-de-force troika: El Greco, Velázquez, and Goya. The effect of the collection, as is true of all really first-class galleries, is exhausting, and the museum's pleasant cafeteria is the ideal place to take a break.

The Prado is open from 9:00 A.M. to 7:00 P.M. Tuesday through Saturday; from 9:00 A.M. to 2:00 P.M. Sundays and holidays; closed Mondays.

EARLY FLEMISH AND RENAISSANCE PAINTERS

A host of paintings in the Prado have been familiar companions for years. This is certainly the case with Dürer's astonishingly contemporary self-portrait, which bears the legend: "I was 26 years old and I painted this picture of my face." The picture used to belong to Charles I of England; it was acquired—after his execution—by the discriminating Philip IV. Dürer's portraits of Adam and of Eve were presented to Philip by Queen Christina of Sweden. Tradition has it that Carlos III (that admirable monarch, who had, nonetheless, a prudish streak) would have had them burned for indecency had Rafael Mengs, one of his court painters, not taken them away from the royal collection and hidden them in the Real Academia de Bellas Artes de San Fernando, where they remained until late last century.

Rogier Van der Weyden's showpiece in the Prado, *The Descent from the Cross,* is arguably one of the greatest Gothic paintings. It belonged to Queen María of Hungary, the sister of Emperor Charles V, and was so admired by her nephew Philip II that he commissioned Michel Croxie to reproduce it. The copy, which is remarkable, now hangs in El Escorial; the original eventually came into Philip's possession after his aunt died. Critic Juan Gómez Soubrier contrasts it with the message of peace and hope expressed in Fra Angélico's *Annunciation,* which is yet another of the Prado's treasures.

The Garden of Earthly Delights, by Hieronymus Bosch, known in Spain as El Bosco, is another of the highly familiar paintings in this section. It was bought by Philip II in 1593, five years before his death, and he kept it in his private apartments in El Escorial. Philip's final days, gout ridden and disease wracked, were frightful, and few ventured near him on account of the stench. Bosch's extraordinary evocation of short-lived sensual pleasures may have suited his mood.

THE ITALIAN PAINTERS

One of the highlights of this section, Andrea Mantegna's *Death of the Virgin,* also belonged to Charles I, and was bought by the judicious Philip IV when Cromwell auctioned off the beheaded monarch's pictures. Other paintings here that once belonged to Charles include Veronese's *Jesus Disputing with the Doctors* and Tintoretto's huge *Lavatorio.* At least two other Tintorettos, *The Medianite Virgins* and the *Episode in a Battle between Christians and Turks,* were bought by Velázquez, who toured Italy scouting for artworks for Philip IV—and picking up brush-stroke and lighting skills in the process.

Raphael's *The Cardinal* is an arresting canvas. Art historian Alfonso Pérez Sánchez, the Prado's director, recommends it for prolonged viewing: "All the scornful intelligence, the implacable coldness and the refined sensuality which we imagine in the Renaissance prototype, bloom with an amazing intensity in this profound, sober portrait." Works by Fra Angélico, Botticelli (illustrating a grisly tale from *The Decameron*), Andrea del Sarto, and Il Giorgione also hang in this section.

Close attention is also demanded by Titian's fabulous equestrian portrait of Charles V, *Emperor at the Battle of*

Mühlberg. The suit of armor that Charles wore in the picture, and in the actual battle, is exhibited in the Palacio Real's *armería* (see below). The full range of Titian's astonishing output, from religious commissions to such outpourings of pagan sensuality as *Bacchanal,* is superbly represented in the Prado, topped off by his magnificent self-portrait, painted when he was in his 80s after a life of good living. One historically interesting Titian picture is his portrait of a dashing young Philip II; it was packed off to London, where it won the heart, as was the intention, of Mary Tudor. Philip, who was then a prince and heir to his father, Charles V, disliked the picture and wrote to his aunt, María of Austria, "If there were more time I would have him [Titian] do it again," but the diplomatic advantages of marriage to the English queen outweighed his vanity.

Mary's return portrait to Philip, painted by Anton Van Dashorst, who was known as Sir Anthony More in England and as Antonio Moro in Spain, hangs among the Prado's Flemish pictures. It shows Mary looking distinctly shrewish and spinsterish. At 38, she was 11 years older than Philip, and he cannot have been enraptured by her likeness. Mary was the second of Philip's four wives; their marriage lasted from 1554 until her death in 1558.

EL GRECO

Doménikos Theotokópoulos, El Greco (1541–1614), can best be appreciated in Toledo, which is an essential side trip for every serious visitor to Madrid. The Prado's collection of El Grecos, however, is far greater than that possessed by any other national art collection, and, more than being merely an appetizer for the Toledo trip, it is indispensable viewing.

The great religious themes to which El Greco devoted his art—the Nativity, the Crucifixion, and the Resurrection—are all well represented in the Prado. So are all the elongated figures, the purples and the greens, the zigzags and the whole Mannerist bag of tricks that the Cretan-born genius evolved. *The Adoration of the Shepherds* is compelling because of the power that emerges from the absurdly tiny child. As the dead Christ in *The Trinity,* the same Savior is huge and heavy, suspended by a compassionate, pain-stricken father and weighted down toward earth. The Prado also boasts the intriguing portrait called *The Cavalier,* the subject of which has his hand on his chest; this gesture and the searching eyes that El Greco gave his subject are haunting in the extreme. Professor Diego Angulo suggests that this unknown *caballero,* who shows only his right arm, is Miguel de Cervantes, who lost his left arm in the battle of Lepanto.

ZURBARAN

The best introduction to the Prado's strong collection of works by Francisco Zurbarán (1598–1664) is the canvas that depicts Saint Luke as a painter positioned before Christ on the Cross: Zurbarán painted himself, palette in hand, as the saint. The Zurbarán in the portrait is evidently both resolute and reflective, not at all flashy, but quite aware of his value as an artist.

From here you move on to the religious works that kept Zurbarán gainfully employed, to the series depicting the life of Hercules that he painted for the Palacio del Buen Retiro and that gained him royal recognition, and to the still life, or *bodegón,* of a collection of pots that assured him enduring fame.

Zurbarán is worth taking some trouble over for he hands you straight over to Velázquez. "[Zurbarán's] work, while excellent, is still slightly claustrophobic," notes British author Alastair Boyd. "There is no air round his figures; they are substantial but they do not breathe—that comes with Velázquez."

VELAZQUEZ

It is hard to decide whether the Prado belongs more to Diego Rodríguez de Silva Velázquez or to Francisco José de Goya y Lucientes. Goya means more to contemporary man, but perhaps Velázquez wins by a hair's breadth because he was, as well as every bit a consummate artist, the court painter of Philip IV, who was the museum's greatest patron. The Prado is, without a doubt, the only place in the world where you can gain a close acquaintanceship with both Velázquez and Goya.

Philip IV doted on the Sevillian-born Velázquez (1599–1660), just as his great-grandfather, Charles V, had on Titian. For an interesting contrast, compare Velázquez's portrait of the great-grandson with Titian's rendering of victor Charles V in *Emperor at the Battle of Mühlberg* (discussed above). Velázquez's Philip IV is exceedingly sober, bereft of armor, spurs, and lances; a shy, sensitive, and questioning man who had a special relationship with his painter.

Velázquez's masterpiece, *Las Meninas* (The Maids-in-Waiting), one of the most visited of all the Prado's pictures, is an extraordinary composition, a masterful exploitation of spatial depth and lighting effects. Velázquez himself appears in the painting, bearing the red cross of the noble order of Santiago, which, tradition has it, was painted on not by the artist but by Philip IV (Velázquez did not become a knight of Santiago until two years after completing the painting). The key element of this giant work is the delightful Infanta Margarita, who, attended by her maids of honor and two

dwarfs, is visiting the artist's studio, where her parents, the
king and queen, are sitting for a formal portrait. The artist
paints himself at work on the royal portrait, while the infanta
and her entourage look on. The king and queen are mere
reflections in a mirror in the background of the composition. The painting's depth of field, the players standing as if
upon a stage, the self-possessed child, and the murky faces
of the royals make this a masterpiece to contemplate.

Las Meninas is in the hall dedicated to Velázquez's main
portraits of the royal family. Another painting there is the
arresting equestrian picture of the conde duque de Olivares,
Velázquez's earliest patron and the powerful prime minister
during the first half of Philip IV's reign. There can be few
more exact renderings of confident megalomania than this
portrait of Olivares, a contemporary and rival of France's
Cardinal Richelieu. This hall, and the adjoining one dedicated to the buffoons, gives you the whole world picture that
surrounds *Las Meninas*. Pay close attention to *Las Hilan-
deras* (The Spinners); it was in this canvas that Velázquez
solved many of the problems of depth and light that he later
applied to his masterpiece.

Surrender of Breda (popularly known as *Las Lanzas*—
The Lances) is another of the hugely famous Velázquez
paintings. What is most remarkable about it, seen close up, is
not so much the civility and courtesy of the surrender but
the humor and the laid-back attitudes, roguishly picaresque
and typical of 17th-century Madrid, that are painted into the
pike-bearers of the left foreground.

Velázquez knew all about decorum, for he was every inch
a court painter and, as displayed in the astonishing portrait
of the conde duque de Olivares, he knew all about political
ambition and power, too. But he also knew how to portray
real people, such as the ones drinking with Bacchus in *Los
Borrachos* (The Drunkards). The god in his painting *Mars* is
not a fierce and proud warrior but a tired, flaccid soldier
who looks as if he may have had one too many. There is
nothing mythological about the workers in his *Vulcan's
Forge,* either.

17TH-CENTURY SPANISH AND FLEMISH PAINTERS

Bartolomé Esteban Murillo, a sugary Sevillian contemporary
of Velázquez, suffers by being so close to the master. His
work is nevertheless highly indicative of the popular Catholicism of 17th-century Spain just as much as it marks general
Hapsburg exhaustion and a decline in Spanish taste that was
not to be properly righted until Goya appeared on the
scene. Juan Carreño, who became court painter after Velázquez's death in 1660, offers some insight into the Hapsburg

decline with his portrait of Philip IV's aging widow, Mariana of Austria, and of the unfortunate product of that marriage, Carlos II (the Bewitched). Mariana was never attractive, as Velázquez's portrait of her when she was 19 and newly married shows all too well.

The Spanish Hapsburgs by no means confined themselves to the domestic art scene, for they were nothing if not a multinational royal family. Jan Brueghel and Peter Paul Rubens became known to Philip II by way of their patron, the archduke Albert of Austria, who married the monarch's beloved daughter, the Infanta Isabella Clara Eugenia. The two, together with other late Flemish school painters, are more than well represented in the Prado—too well, perhaps, in the case of Rubens; there is almost an overexposure of his fat matrons posing as nymphs.

The real highlights of this collection are the excellent oval portrait that Van Dyck painted of himself with Sir Endymion Porter and a very revealing Rembrandt self-portrait that displays, as Alastair Boyd notes, "a frankly lascivious nature." There is also a Rembrandt rendering of Artemis in which the artist used his new wife, Saskia, as the model. You might compare this canvas to Rembrandt's portrait of Saskia that hangs in the city's Museo de Lázaro Galdiano. Both the Prado Rembrandts were added to the royal collection by Carlos III.

GOYA

Goya's genius lays bare his life and times. You move from the delightful cartoons, painted for tapestry weavers, which show a people at peace, at work, and at play, to the horrors of the Napoleonic invasion. The etchings of the *Desastres de la Guerra* (Disasters of War) series are like an album of war photography and constitute a searing antiwar manifesto. You are treated to his women—the nude and the dressed Maja, who legend has it was the duchess of Alba—and, in the series known as the *Disparates* and the *Caprichos,* you share the keen, critical intelligence of a man of the Enlightenment. But Francisco José de Goya y Lucientes (1746–1828) is much more than a magnificent recorder. In the *Milkmaid from Bordeaux,* for example, which he painted when he was 80, Velázquez and Renoir are present in the same canvas.

The Third of May, 1808, a giant canvas also called *Shootings in Moncloa,* is either the greatest of all protest pictures or is a close second to Picasso's *Guernica.* There are other terrifying Goyas in the Prado, from the "black" paintings of sabbaths and witches to the strange picture of a dog buried up to its neck in sand and the beastliness of two men, up to their knees in a bog, flaying themselves to death in the *Duelo a Garrotazos;* these paintings continue to disturb you long after you first see them.

You also meet a very uninspiring court presided over by the cuckold Carlos IV and his toothless and brainless queen, María Luisa. The whole royal group in the *Family of Carlos IV,* according to Goya expert Javier Sánchez Canton, is "looking at [Manuel de] Godoy who, from the royal guard, had come through the royal bedchamber to control the destiny of Spain." The young prince whose hand the queen holds is the spitting image of Godoy, who was reputed to be his father. Goya lost his job as court painter as a result of this group canvas.

Goya can overpower a Prado visitor. "Velázquez, Rembrandt, and Nature are my only masters," he once stated. In his self-portrait Goya, open-collared and tough-looking, appears arrogant and sure of himself, but his troubled eyes reveal a very complex mind.

Around the Prado

The Prado's annex, the Casón del Buen Retiro, is a five-minute walk from the museum. On the way, glance down Calle de Ruiz de Alarcón, the street that runs behind the Prado, to see the **Iglesia de San Jerónimo el Real**, a much-restored 16th-century church that is the scene of many society weddings, including royal ones.

The Casón del Buen Retiro formed part of the grand out-of-town royal residence called the Real Sitio del Buen Retiro, built in 1638 by Alonso Carbonell and used by the later Hapsburgs and the early Bourbons until the completion of the Palacio Real in 1764. Little remains of the palace, which was undoubtedly the showpiece of Hapsburg Madrid. The building that houses the Museo del Ejército was one of the palace's wings, and the Casón del Buen Retiro was an outbuilding. Most of the large Velázquez canvases in the Prado, such as *Surrender of Breda,* used to hang in the palace.

CASON DEL BUEN RETIRO
From 1981 to 1992 Picasso's masterpiece, *Guernica,* hung in the Casón del Buen Retiro, until it was moved to the overhauled Museo Nacional Centro de Arte Reina Sofía, down the Paseo del Prado. Shorn of its prized and short-lived possession, the Casón risks returning to its former life as one of Madrid's under-visited museums. It now houses a wholly academic and not particularly distinguished collection of 19th-century Spanish art, which is nonetheless of interest for the images of Spain represented. Numerous historical pictures portray different events of the nation's history, and a wealth of romantic genre pictures exaggeratedly displays the Spain of matadors, bandits, and sultry women that so entranced 19th-century travellers. The mu-

seum's main hall, which used to be one of the palace's main reception areas, has ceiling frescoes by Luca Giordano, known in Spain as Lucas Jordán, whose work peppers El Escorial. Here Giordano painted an allegory of the Order of the Golden Fleece, the senior class in Spanish chivalry.

MUSEO DEL EJERCITO
Standing just north of the Casón del Buen Retiro on Calle Méndez Núñez, the Museo del Ejército (army museum) has a series of menacing cannons and field guns occupying its terrace. Inside there is an astonishing array of weapons of the ages: case upon case of crossbows, muskets, swords, rifles, and every other conceivable war implement. The Spaniards are second to none when it comes to fighting and conquering, and the latter-day exhibits deal with the Spanish Civil War, when they set upon each other.

MUSEO DE ARTES DECORATIVAS
A block or two north of the Museo del Ejército (walk up Calle de Alfonso XII, which runs along the Parque del Retiro's western limits), at Calle de Montalbán 12, is the Museo de Artes Decorativas (Museum of Decorative Arts), a pleasing collection of Spanish furnishings and handiworks of the past 400 years. There are three floors of well-planned exhibits of lacework and leatherwork, jewelry, ceramics, and glass. One of the most charming areas of the museum contains its collection of little Nativity figures. These elaborate stagings of Bethlehem have a place of honor in Spanish households during Christmas; if you happen to be in Madrid in December, you will find such figures on sale at special stalls set up in the Plaza Mayor.

Parque del Retiro

The Parque del Retiro, the enormous expanse of greenery to the east of the Museo del Prado, is a people's park. On Sunday mornings the park is teeming with quick-portrait artists, musicians, and fortune-tellers—and of course Madrileños out for a stroll. A fine entrance to the park is via the **Plaza de la Independencia**, in the northwestern corner, just a few blocks north of the Museo de Artes Decorativas. The triumphal archway in the middle of the park, the **Puerta de Alcalá**, is a magnificent legacy of the reign of Carlos III, the well-loved Bourbon monarch.

El Retiro was originally a 17th-century Hapsburg hunting park and formed the private estate of the Real Sitio del Buen Retiro, of which only the Casón del Buen Retiro and the building that houses the Museo del Ejército remain. During the 17th-century reign of Philip IV, masked balls, concerts, fireworks displays, and even mock sea battles on the boating lake were staged in the park. In 1868 the gardens were opened to the general public.

This is a big park—300 acres—with numerous attractions: a very beautiful rose garden, a lake for boating, gorgeous leafy avenues, countrified landscapes, and carefully laid out flower beds and box hedgerows according to the French ornamental garden tradition. Of the park's numerous landmarks, the Monumento al Angel Caído (Monument to the Fallen Angel), erected in 1878, deserves special mention. Standing near the rose garden, it depicts Satan as an athletic, good-looking youth, crashing down to earth.

El Retiro is well stocked with gazebos on whose terraces you can sip aperitifs, and there are a number of hansom cabs in the summer to take you around in comfort. If you are so inclined you can take advantage of the park's jogging course. Just inside the Plaza de la Independencia entrance to the park are a bandstand, where Sunday concerts are given, and a theater, where puppet shows are performed, also on Sundays. In the center of the park are two exhibition halls, the **Palacio de Cristal** and the **Palacio de Velázquez**, that feature changing displays. Run by the ministry of culture, they were both built in the 1880s and lie near a lovely, weeping-willow–rimmed pond. The Palacio de Cristal is a reproduction, on a smaller scale, of the Crystal Palace that was erected in London for the Great Exhibition of 1851.

South of the Prado

The **Jardín Botánico**, just south of the Prado, is a lovely place to breathe some fresh air after a morning of museum-going. The pavilions in the garden's eastern side were built by Juan de Villanueva, the architect of the Prado.

MUSEO NACIONAL CENTRO DE ARTE REINA SOFIA

Midway through 1992, Pablo Picasso's *Guernica* was transferred from the Casón del Buen Retiro, where it had hung for ten years, to the Museo Nacional Centro de Arte Reina Sofía, popularly known as the Sofidú, in reference to Paris's Pompidou Center, which it tries to emulate. Located at the southern end of the Paseo del Prado, at Calle de Santa Isabel 52, just off the huge Plaza de Carlos V, the Reina Sofía underwent extensive renovation before and after the *Guernica* transfer and is now a major 20th-century art museum. It is housed in a very large, solid, four-story stone edifice that once served as Madrid's main hospital. The severe 18th-century façade has been lightened by two outsized lifts that career up and down the outside of the building, lending it an ultramodern touch.

Picasso's celebrated masterpiece, commemorating the blanket bombing of the Basque town of Guernica during the Spanish Civil War, is exhibited together with 63 preliminary sketches and is the museum's premier crowd-puller. Other Picasso work in the collection is unremarkable. Although born in Málaga (in Andalusia) and raised in Barcelona, the genius of 20th-century art lived in France and never set foot in Spain after Franco's Civil War victory. Consequently, there is little depth to exhibitions of Picasso's work in his home country (aside from those at the Museu Picasso in Barcelona).

The Sofidú does, however, boast big representations of the other two giants of 20th-century Spanish art, Salvador Dalí and Joan Miró, both of whom donated major collections of their work to the nation. The Dalí legacy includes Surrealist landmarks such as the *Great Masturbator*. The Miró collection is weighted toward later work, in which Miró's maturity as an artist enhanced the childlike innocence of his vision. On a more reduced scale, Juan Gris, Picasso's fellow Cubist painter and Parisian neighbor, is also represented. He was the final member of the fabulous Spanish modern-art foursome, but his early death probably denied him the stature achieved by his long-lived compatriots.

Also represented in the Reina Sofía's collections are 20th-century Spanish artists who are not well known abroad. Among them are the turn-of-the-century Catalan Modernists who influenced the adolescent Picasso in Barcelona, including Isidro Nonell, Ramón Casas, and Santiago Rusiñol; José Gutierrez Solana, a representative of the between-the-wars Madrid school of expressionist realism; and Basque figurative painter Ignacio Zuloaga. The works of such postwar Spanish artists as Antoni Tàpies, Rafael Gordillo, Rafael Canogar, and Antonio Saura indicate that the Spanish art scene is still vital.

PLAZA DE CARLOS V

Across from the Reina Sofía, and dominating the Plaza de Carlos V, is the huge wrought-iron and glass Estación de Atocha, one of Madrid's two main railway stations. Opposite the station's eastern flank, just south of the Ministry of Agriculture building, is the **Museo Nacional de Etnología** (National Ethnology Museum), at Calle de Alfonso XII 68. This minor anthropological and ethnological collection was inaugurated in 1875 and is in a somewhat dilapidated state. Its library, however, is highly regarded by specialists.

The Plaza de Cánovas
del Castillo Area

The Plaza de Cánovas del Castillo, between Plaza de Carlos V and the Plaza de la Cibeles, is anchored by the late-18th-century, Classical-style **Fuente de Neptuno**, the Neptune fountain. Just to the northeast is the **Plaza de la Lealtad**, upon which sits the venerable ▶ **Hotel Ritz**, a fine place for a drink, if you aren't lucky enough to be staying there (see the Accommodations and Nightlife sections, below). The Monumento al Soldado Desconocido, in the center of the plaza's half-circle, commemorates Madrid's unknown soldier.

MUSEO THYSSEN-BORNEMISZA

On the other side of Plaza de Cánovas, in the northwestern corner, the Palacio de Villahermosa, an elegant red-brick and granite town mansion that dates from the late 18th century, now houses the Museo Thyssen-Bornemisza, which opened in 1992. This 800-strong picture collection, owned by Germany's Baron Heinrich-Hans Thyssen-Bornemisza, is magnificent as a self-contained unit, but gains immeasurably from its new stately and luxurious location (it was formerly exhibited in Switzerland), just a five-minute walk from the Prado and fifteen minutes from the Reina Sofía. The Thyssen-Bornemisza collection both complements the two public museums and plugs their gaps.

Visitors to the museum will see the collection to its best advantage by starting on the second floor and working forward chronologically. The second-floor exhibitions include primitive Italian, Flemish, and German masters and a fine Renaissance showing. The combination of Madrid's strong natural light, subtly softened by glass and blinds, and the marble floors imported from Verona creates the effect of the 14th-century Tuscan mansions and churches in which many of these paintings originally hung.

On the first floor the visitor will find a strong representation of Flemish art, including Hans Holbein's remarkable *Henry VIII,* a penetrating full-length psychological study of the English monarch who had six queens, two of whom were beheaded. Other first-floor rooms are dedicated to 18th- and 19th-century American, French, and British art. The 20th-century holdings include a stunning *Auvers Landscape* by Vincent van Gogh, an extremely impressionistic *Portrait of a Peasant* by Paul Cézanne, Pablo Picasso's *Harlequin with a Mirror,* and Edward Hopper's *Hotel Room.* The Palacio's ground floor is set aside for the Thyssen-Bornemisza collection of the post-Cubist, abstract, and vanguard genres, and the basement galleries, immediately beneath the art forms of the day before yesterday, are reserved for special exhibitions of art that is yet to be created.

WEST OF PLAZA DE CANOVAS

Plaza de las Cortes, just to the west of the Museo Thyssen-Bornemisza, is adorned by the **Palacio de las Cortes**, home of the Spanish parliament, and the ▶ **Palace Hotel**, the other of Madrid's reputable dowagers and a lively place for a drink amongst the city's politicians and journalists (see also the Accommodations and Nightlife sections, below).

The network of narrow streets just behind the Palace Hotel to the west has been referred to as Madrid's Parnassus because several of the literary giants of Spain's Golden Age lived in the area at one time or another. Luis de Góngora (1561–1627), who made fashionable a flowing, lyrical literary style, and the satirist Francisco de Quevedo (1580–1645) both lived on the corner of Calle de Quevedo and Calle Lope de Vega. Miguel de Cervantes (1547–1616) died in a house that stood at the corner of Calle de Cervantes and Calle de León.

The only one of these original dwellings to have survived is the house that was occupied by Félix Lope de Vega at Calle de Cervantes 11 (at the corner of Calle de San Augustín, just two blocks southwest of the Palace Hotel), now the **Casa de Lope de Vega**. Lope de Vega (1562–1635) is reputed to have written more than 1,800 plays—and still to have found time to serve in the Invincible Armada and to have had a legendary love life. His home is now essentially a period re-creation of a modest 17th-century Madrid household.

OLD MADRID

Carrera de San Jerónimo leads west out of plazas de Cánovas and las Cortes, through Plaza de Canalejas, to Puerta del Sol. The area west of Puerta del Sol is old Hapsburg Madrid. Its main axis is Calle Mayor, which runs west out of Puerta del Sol to Calle de Bailén. Plaza Mayor, the area's centerpiece, lies off Calle Mayor to the south.

To get a more or less accurate picture of who was where in Hapsburg Madrid, keep in mind that the court and the wealthy occupied the area near Calle Mayor. This street was suitably close to the *alcázar*, Peter the Cruel's fortress, which stood on the site now occupied by the 18th-century Bourbon Palacio Real, across Calle de Bailén. The solid buildings at the western end of Calle Mayor, around the Plaza de la Villa and between Calle Mayor and Calle de Sacramento, to its south, were the 16th century's prime real estate. The majority of the people lived south of Calle de

Sacramento. Artisan Madrid, the popular Madrid of the picaresque genre, extended from here southward to Puerta de
Moros, which in early Hapsburg times marked the southern
limits of the city. Some of these areas still retain the feel of
old popular quarters.

Puerta del Sol

The Puerta del Sol is the heart of Madrid and of Spain. On
the sidewalk in front of the building housing Madrid's regional government, on the south side of the square, is the
marker for kilometer 0 on the national highway system; the
kilometer markers on all of Spain's national highways mark
the distance from this point.

The Puerta del Sol is also a good starting point for some
favorite Spanish pursuits: eating, drinking, and shopping.
Calle Victoria, a small street just before the entrance to
Puerta del Sol off Carrera de San Jerónimo, and the alleyways leading off it, is lined with bars, and this block constitutes what is arguably the best *tapas*-hopping area in the city.
(See the Dining and Nightlife sections, below, for more on
Madrid's eating and drinking establishments.) Calle Victoria
has always been favored by the bullfight crowd, and you can
buy bullfight tickets at booths set up along the street during
the season.

If you want to combine modern-day shopping with cultural touring, look in on **Calle de Preciados**, a pedestrian
precinct leading northwest out of Puerta del Sol and linking it with the Gran Vía. Two branches of Spain's rival
department-store chains, El Corte Inglés and Galerías Preciados, stand conveniently close to each other on this
street. (Shops and Shopping, below, lists many more of
Madrid's shopping venues.)

REAL ACADEMIA DE BELLAS ARTES DE SAN FERNANDO

Before plunging into the heart of old Hapsburg Madrid,
which is concentrated mainly south and west of Puerta del
Sol, we suggest a quick walk to the east to Madrid's academy of fine arts just off the square at Calle de Alcalá 13.
This is a quiet place to pursue the study of Goya, the great
chronicler of late-18th-century Bourbon Spain.

The academy's collection includes a good number of old
masters confiscated from the Jesuits when the order was
expelled from Spain by Carlos III, but Goya, who was for a
time the academy's director, provides the highlights. There
is the bright side of the artist in his canvas of the carnival
called *Burial of the Sardine,* and there is the tormented side
in his study of a madhouse. The critical, politically commit-

ted Goya emerges in his scenes of the Inquisition, an institution that he also lampooned brilliantly in a series of etchings that hang in the Prado.

There are portraits of people he liked and admired, such as the liberal literary lion Leandro Fernández de Moratín and the architect Juan de Villanueva, who redesigned the academy building along Neoclassical lines. And there are portraits of people he did not like at all, such as Godoy, the guardsman turned prime minister, and Ferdinand VII, the despotic son of Carlos IV. Goya's true feelings toward the woman known as La Tirana, whose large portrait also hangs here, are less clear. She was a well-known courtesan who was allegedly exceptionally severe to her admirers. To round out its Goya collection, the academy possesses a self-portrait similar to the one at the Prado.

The academy's shop is well worth a browse; it sells reasonably priced prints by Goya and others from original plates.

Plaza Mayor

Madrid's Plaza Mayor is exactly what an arcaded plaza in Castile should be. There are larger and more artistically impressive *plazas mayores* in central Spain, such as the one in Salamanca, and there are a host of smaller, more intimate ones, because every largish village and small town required such a center point for communal activities. Madrid's Plaza Mayor, however, is not only well up to the best architectural standards, but is also more historic than any other. Perfectly harmonious in its proportions and in its 17th-century style, the square was designed by Juan de Herrera under the auspices of Philip II and completed in the subsequent reign of Philip III by Herrera's pupil Juan Gómez de Mora. The bronze equestrian statue in the center of the square honors Philip III.

In centuries past important executions were held here, bloodcurdling autos-da-fé were organized with operatic grandeur by the Inquisition, and on major holidays the whole square was converted into a giant bullring. Edward Hyde, the first earl of Clarendon, saw a bullfight here in 1650 and described, with evident pride, how when the bull became too unruly "the King [Philip IV] calls, as a last resort, for the English mastives." The royal family used to occupy the balconies of the stuccoed Casa de la Panadería, on the north side of the square, during such spectacles.

The Plaza Mayor, which is home to several restaurants that have tables out on the plaza as well as inside, is a pedestrians-only precinct and is within comfortable walking distance of most of Hapsburg Madrid's other major landmarks. Leaving the square by its southwest corner, through the **Arco de Cuchilleros**, you enter Madrid's oldest quarter. This area is ideal for those who like simply to "lose" themselves among taverns and artisan shops. You might aim for the cathedral of San Isidro, to the south, and then amble westward to the Capilla del Obispo in Plaza de la Paja and from there to El Rastro (all of these sights are discussed below). One block southeast of Plaza Mayor is the **Palacio de Santa Cruz**, which houses the foreign ministry and is one of the remaining great Hapsburg edifices.

Plaza de la Villa

Plaza de la Villa lies just west of Plaza Mayor and opens onto Calle Mayor. The **Casa de la Villa**, Madrid's city hall, occupies the western façade of the plaza. Designed in 1644 by Juan Gómez de Mora, the Casa de la Villa originally imitated the severe lines of the *estilo herreriano,* introduced by Gómez's teacher, Juan de Herrera, in El Escorial and Madrid's Plaza Mayor. The severity was later toned down when the building was extended by the Bourbon architects Teodoro Ardemáns, who built La Granja near Segovia for Philip V, and Juan de Villanueva.

The building at the south end of the plaza linked to the Casa de la Villa by a covered bridge is the **Casa de Cisneros**, built in the 1530s by a nephew of the famous 15th-century churchman Cardinal Cisneros. Its chief interest lies in the Plateresque façade at the rear of the building, on Calle de Sacramento; this is one of the very few examples in Madrid of that ornate Spanish Renaissance style that is so common in Salamanca and Toledo. The building facing the Casa de la Villa is the **Torre de los Lujanes**, which dates from the mid-15th century—a rare survivor, though much restored, of pre-Hapsburg Madrid. Francis I of France was imprisoned briefly in the tower in 1525 after he was defeated and captured by Emperor Charles V at the battle of Pavia.

From the Plaza de la Villa a short walk west takes you to the **Palacio del Duque de Uceda**, now the military headquarters but once a great Hapsburg building. The *palacio* sits at the intersection of Calle Mayor and Calle de Bailén, on the other side of which is the Palacio Real.

Plaza de la Paja Area

A short walk south of the Palacio del Duque de Uceda (take Calle de Bailén one block south to Calle de Segovia, then go east and turn south into Plaza de la Paja) stands the **Capilla del Obispo** (Bishop's Chapel), on the corner of the Plaza de la Paja and Costanilla de San Andrés. The chapel was built in the 1520s, and its combination of Gothic vaulting and Renaissance or, more exactly, Plateresque decorations shows off the transition between the two styles. The altarpiece, by Francisco Giralta, a pupil of Alonso Berruguete, deserves close inspection. The domed **Capilla de San Andrés**, next door, contained the remains of San Isidro, Madrid's patron saint, until they were transferred to the cathedral of San Isidro (see below). A third old church in the immediate vicinity (a short walk from San Andrés up Costanilla de San Pedro) is the **Iglesia de San Pedro el Viejo**. Built in 1354 over an old mosque, the brick Mudejar-style tower is all that remains of the original church; the main building, which has a Renaissance air to it, dates from 1525.

CATEDRAL DE SAN ISIDRO
Just a couple of sinuous blocks east of San Pedro, the Catedral de San Isidro, on Calle de Toledo just south of Calle de Sacramento and due south of Plaza Mayor, was temporarily Madrid's cathedral while the permanent one, La Catedral de Nuestra Señora de la Almudena, was being built alongside the Palacio Real on Calle de Bailén.

San Isidro is chiefly important for being the home of the uncorrupted remains of Madrid's patron saint, Isidro, an amiable and pious medieval farm laborer. Tradition has it that angels descended to drive his plow when he was either having a siesta or attending mass. The basilica, completed in a low-key Baroque style in 1661 to serve as a Jesuit college, and converted into a cathedral when the Jesuits were expelled from Spain in the following century, was modeled after the Roman church Il Gesù.

The Puerta de Moros Area

Plaza de los Carros, south of Plaza de la Paja, is named for the *carros* (carts) that parked in this square when its gate, the Puerta de Moros, served as one of the original entry points to the old medieval city of Madrid. There are two main reasons for exploring the Puerta de Moros area: typical old restaurants and the medieval atmosphere in such quarters as El Rastro flea market.

Calle de la Cava Baja, the narrow street that leads northeast off Puerta de Moros to Puerta Cerrada (a small square at the end of Calle de San Justo), has two excellent eating houses: **El Chotis**, at number 11, and **Casa Lucio**, a bit farther on at number 35. At Puerta Cerrada (if you are in the Plaza Mayor, you reach this busy little square by leaving the plaza through the Arco de Cuchilleros) there is a third superb tavern: **Casa Paco**, at number 11.

EL RASTRO

To capture the atmosphere of the city 300 and more years ago, as it bulged with a rapidly increasing population, head east out of Puerta de Moros to Plaza de Cascorro, the northern edge of the flea-market area, El Rastro. This part of Old Madrid is still alive with the same "camp-follower" humanity as in the Madrid of the 17th century, which gave birth to the picaresque genre. To this day the somewhat slummy areas of Old Madrid, such as La Latina, Embajadores, and Lavapiés, with their taverns, stall holders, and tricksters, remain picaresque rather than picturesque.

The area occupied now by El Rastro was built up in the late 18th century as the city continued to expand southward, but it still exhibits the bustle of Madrid's popular quarters as recorded by Hapsburg writers. On Saturdays and Sundays a huge crowd assembles around the stalls that occupy both sides of the broad **Ribera de Curtidores**, which runs down from the Plaza de Cascorro. It is a noisy, boisterous scene as people haggle over prices, tout all kinds of products, and fill the bars. All humanity is on this particular stage—including pickpockets and drug pushers.

THE PALACIO REAL AREA

The Bourbon dynasty, arriving in Spain at the beginning of the 18th century when the Spanish Hapsburgs died out, oversaw the expansion of Madrid beyond the immediate confines of the Plaza Mayor and the Calle Mayor axis. The Bourbon mark on the city is most prominent to the west of the original 16th- and 17th-century center along Calle de Bailén, on which stands the Palacio Real. From El Rastro it is possible to loop through this Bourbon area by starting at Puenta del Toledo, then heading up Calle de Bailén to take in the church of San Francisco el Grande and then the palace and its surroundings.

PUERTA DE TOLEDO

The Puerta de Toledo, a triumphal arch built by the Bourbons, sits at the southern end of Calle de Toledo (where it meets Ronda de Toledo), surrounded by an architectural wasteland. This arch lacks the grace and the surroundings of the Puerta de Alcalá, but it is an interesting reminder of Madrid's—and Spain's—ups and downs. It was originally designed in honor of Napoleon, then it was hoped that it would be inaugurated by the patriotic liberal members of the Cádiz parliament, and it finally served to mark the arrival of the returning Bourbon, Ferdinand VII, who tore up the liberal constitution and exiled those who framed it. A designer and boutique shopping mall, **Mercado de la Puerta de Toledo**, has opened here, incongruously close to El Rastro's flea market at Ronda de Toledo 1, on the site of what used to be Madrid's main fish market.

SAN FRANCISCO EL GRANDE

It's just a few blocks up the Gran Vía de San Francisco (the southern extension of Calle de Bailén) from Puerta de Toledo to the large, domed church of San Francisco el Grande, which bears the stamp of the Bourbon monarch Carlos III's Neoclassical ambitions for Madrid. He commissioned Sabatini to create the main façade in that style in 1776, at a time when work that had begun on the church 15 years earlier was at a standstill. Joseph Bonaparte, Napoleon's brother, who was briefly king of Spain during the French occupation (1808), wanted to turn the church into a parliament, and midway through the 19th century it became a military barracks. Today it is a museum, housing an early work by Goya, a set of apostles by José Ribera, and a host of mostly nondescript paintings by minor 19th-century artists. The Renaissance choir stalls stood originally in the Monasterio del Paular, nestled in the Sierra de Guadarrama.

NORTH TO THE PALACIO REAL

To reach the Palacio Real, head north on San Francisco el Grande along Calle de Bailén and across the towering viaduct that looks down on Calle de Segovia. The **Puente de Segovia**, to the west, was the first stone bridge across the Río Manzanares, commissioned by Hapsburg king Philip II in 1584. It is still in use today, and not much changed, a testimony to the talents of its architect, Juan de Herrera, who was to achieve fame and glory with the royal commission to finish El Escorial, Philip's massive monastery-palace.

The Río Manzanares is of less interest than its bridge, however, and has earned little praise. It was put in its place by no less an authority than Cervantes, who termed it an "apprentice river." Until recent channeling improved the situation, it used to dry up in summer. It has been said that Madrid ought to either sell its fine bridges or buy itself a proper river. The playwright Lope de Vega, a contemporary of Cervantes, remarked that Philip II's Puente de Segovia was "hoping for a river."

Palacio Real

Continue north on Calle de Bailén, past the Calle Mayor intersection, to reach the Palacio Real, a grand, rectangular 18th-century palace built around an internal courtyard. The eastern façade of the royal palace, all 460 feet of it, looks across Calle de Bailén at the Plaza de Oriente and the Teatro Real opera house. The more imposing façade, however, is the western one, which looms over the Río Manzanares and the parklands of the Casa de Campo on the western bank.

Construction of the palace commenced in 1738, in the reign of Philip V, four years after the old *alcázar* that stood on the site burned to the ground in a fortuitous fire. Chief architect Filippo Giuvarra designed a palace four times bigger than the one that was finally completed. His successor, Giovanni Sachetti, rescaled the plans, and the palace was finally completed in 1764, five years after Carlos III, Philip V's son, had ascended the throne. The Doric columns and the general sumptuousness of the palace mark a distinct break with the severe brickwork and the slate tiling that were favored by the Hapsburg architectural pacesetters Herrera and Mora.

Entrance to the Palacio Real is gained through the parade ground, called the **Plaza de la Armería**, which lies at the southern end, between the palace and the new cathedral of Nuestra Señora de la Almudena. The palace is run by the Patrimonio Nacional, Spain's national trust, which is in charge of most royal foundations. The trust conducts guided tours every quarter of an hour or so from the parade-ground entry lobby (there are English-speaking guides). The tour rushes you through more than 50 rooms, some of them huge and all of them overflowing with objets d'art, in about two hours, while the guides ply you with statistics about what you are seeing. The sumptuous Sala de Gasparini, with a lovely chinoiserie stucco ceiling, and the Sala de Porcelana, the china room, both part of Carlos III's chambers (visited in the early part of the tour), are particularly intriguing. The state dining room is also impressive, with its ceilings painted by Francisco Bayeu, Goya's brother-in-law, and by Rafael Mengs, Goya's rival as court painter; the music room has a magnificent clock collection that was started by Carlos III; and the private rooms of Alfonso XIII give interesting insights into the personality of the failed monarch of the interwar years—he favored the clublike atmosphere of a regimental officers' mess, and he had the hooves of his favorite horses turned into paperweights.

Carlos III, the first king to occupy the palace (he died here in 1788), and Alfonso XIII, the last monarch to use it as a permanent home, are the two monarchs whose presence is most strongly felt. Alfonso and his family occupied the apartments that look out onto the Plaza de Oriente, until he was forced to leave the palace for exile in 1931, when the Spanish republic was proclaimed. Carlos III lived on the western side, overlooking the Campo de Moro.

The palace is now used only for official receptions. The

present monarch, Juan Carlos, Alfonso's grandson, prefers the intimacy of the Palacio de la Zarzuela, a former hunting lodge that lies beyond the Casa de Campo to the west in the middle of a large deer park.

THE ROYAL ARMORY

The **Armería Real**, adjoining the Palacio Real and also entered by the Plaza de la Armería, is great fun. When you have viewed the 44 suits of armor made for and worn by Charles V—one of the greatest figures in the history of Europe, who was both Holy Roman Emperor Charles V and Spain's King Carlos I— you feel you know quite a bit about the man who battled his way across the continent to keep hold of both the Holy Roman Empire and the Spanish one. It seems all the more odd that such a warrior should have chosen to abdicate in favor of his son, Philip II, in 1556 and to retire to the Monasterio de Yuste, hidden away in the wilds of western Spain (northern Extremadura). Among the wealth of historic military hardware here are the swords that belonged to *conquistadores* Hernán Cortés and Francisco Pizarro.

North and West of the Palace

CAMPO DE MORO

The Campo de Moro, the royal gardens extending west of the Palacio Real, provide the best views of the palace. (If you want to visit the Campo de Moro without going through the palace, enter on Cuesta de San Vicente, the street bordering the northern edge of the complex.) The park's impeccably kept avenues, decorative fountains, and yews, cedars, and poplars provide a lovely retreat. On the western edge sits the **Museo de Carruajes**, featuring the elaborate carriages of Spain's bygone royals.

CASA DE CAMPO

To the west of the Campo de Moro is the Casa de Campo, a vast forested park with a well-equipped amusement park and a scenic, well-stocked city zoo. King Carlos III, whose apartments looked over the Campo, went hunting here virtually every day. Goya painted engaging portraits of the weather-beaten monarch, musket in hand, among the oaks of the Casa de Campo, with the Sierra de Guadarrama on the horizon.

ERMITA DE SAN ANTONIO
DE LA FLORIDA

This late-18th-century hermitage dedicated to Saint Anthony of Padua is on Paseo de la Florida, a healthy stroll northwest of the Palacio Real and the Campo de Moro along the Río Manzanares. This is hallowed Goya ground. He is buried here—or, more exactly, the trunk of his body is, because mystery surrounds the whereabouts of his head. The hermitage's domed ceiling, which Carlos IV commissioned Goya to decorate in 1798, shows the artist in top form. What was intended to be a religious fresco depicting the appearance of Saint Anthony before the people of Lisbon becomes, with Goya, a bold and very secular celebration of the Madrid of his time.

Plaza de Oriente Area

The Plaza de Oriente, facing the Palacio Real across Calle de Bailén, is adorned with an equestrian statue of Philip IV as well as 44 statues of Spanish royals that were too heavy to embellish the Palacio Real, for which they were commissioned. On the east side of Plaza de Oriente is the **Teatro Real**, Madrid's opera house. The nearby **Café de Oriente** has a pleasant outdoor terrace for an alfresco drink. Behind the Teatro Real are the Plaza de la Opera and the Plaza de Isabel II. In the vicinity of Plaza de Oriente, caught up in the giant orbit that the Spanish Bourbons created around the Palacio Real, are two of Hapsburg Madrid's treasures, the Convento de la Encarnación and the Real Monasterio de las Descalzas Reales.

CONVENTO DE LA ENCARNACION

Just northeast of Plaza de Oriente on Calle de la Bola is **Plaza de la Encarnación**, a pleasant spot graced by a statue honoring Golden Age playwright Lope de Vega. **Alambique** is an interesting culinary-equipment store and cooking school on the plaza. **La Bola**, a popular bistro at Calle de la Bola 5, is a reliable lunch spot.

The Convento de la Encarnación was founded by Margaret of Austria, wife of Philip III, and built by the ubiquitous Juan Gómez de Mora, who completed the Plaza Mayor for her husband. It has a museum attached to it, run by the Patrimonio Nacional, which contains 17th-century artwork (Francisco Pacheco, Juan Carreño, and Ribera, among others) that is somewhat less impressive than the collection in the nearby Descalzas Reales (see below). The church's exterior is suitably severe, but its interior is somewhat overdone, due perhaps to excessive royal patronage. The organ, which is played at 10:30 A.M. during Sunday mass, is arguably its best feature. A few of the convent's private rooms (La Encarnación remains a cloistered institution) are open to view and preserve intact the atmosphere of the 17th century.

EAST OF THE PLAZA DE ORIENTE

Calle del Arenal leads off Plaza de Isabel II and runs to the
Puerta del Sol. The neighborhood to the south of this old
artery (north of Calle Mayor and west of Puerta del Sol) is a
pleasant old quarter of narrow streets with a 17th-century
flavor that properly belongs to Hapsburg Madrid. The 17th-
century **Iglesia de San Ginés**, at Calle del Arenal and Calle de
Bordadores, is the church in which Lope de Vega was married and the satirist Francisco de Quevedo was baptized.
Quevedo tore into the later Hapsburgs with much the same
effect that Alexander Pope and Jonathan Swift had on the
Hanoverians.

REAL MONASTERIO DE LAS DESCALZAS REALES

Madrid is a busy city in which the hustle and bustle is
occasionally tempered by unexpected places where you
can retreat into silence and contemplation. The convent-
museum of the royal "barefoot" nuns, the Real Monasterio
de las Descalzas Reales, set between Puerta del Sol and the
Gran Vía, is one such place.

From San Ginés (or Plaza Mayor) it is just a block or two
north on Calle de Bordadores and across Calle del Arenal to
Plaza de las Descalzas, where the convent occupies the
whole façade of the square. (From the Convento de la
Encarnación, take Calle de Arrieta southeast to Plaza de la
Opera and Plaza de Isabel II, at which point you can go left
on Calle del Arenal and head east to Calle de Bordadores.)

The Real Monasterio was founded by Juana, Emperor
Charles V's youngest daughter, the widow of Prince Henry of
Portugal and the mother of Portugal's ill-fated king Sebastian, who died campaigning in North Africa. Juana was later
joined in the convent by her sister María, widow of the
emperor Maximilian, and the institution was even more
richly endowed by Isabella Clara Eugenia, Philip II's daughter. Hapsburg family portraits are as numerous in the museum part of the Real Monasterio as religious artworks are in
the chapels of the convent area. The monastery rivals the
Prado in the number of portraits of the relatives of Charles V
and Philip II—and offers a considerably more intimate look
at them.

The building, which still houses a small community of
nuns, is in the stern, austere mold that was favored by
Philip II. A former mansion that housed Charles V's treasurer, Alonso Gutiérrez, it was adapted to serve as a monastery by Juan Bautista de Toledo, the architect who began
designing El Escorial before Herrera took over the monumental work. The convent-museum is owned by the Patrimonio Nacional, and accordingly visitors have to join

conducted tours that are herded through the different apartments. Some of the guides speak English.

NORTHWESTERN MADRID

Walk north from the Real Monasterio to the Gran Vía and continue northwest to the **Plaza de España**, a large, pretty square with a massive monument to Miguel de Cervantes that overlooks the rolling expanse of the Casa de Campo across the river.

MUSEO CERRALBO

Just northwest of Plaza de España on the corner of Calle Ventura Rodríguez and Calle de Ferraz (the northern extension of Calle de Bailén), is the Museo Cerralbo, housed in the 19th-century town mansion of the aristocratic Cerralbo family. Its impressive art collection was built up by the 17th marqués of Cerralbo, who donated it to the nation in 1924. The collection includes works by El Greco, Ribera, and Zurbarán, and there are also extensive archaeological exhibits thanks to the numerous digs that the marqués financed in Rome, Greece, and the Middle East. The mansion itself is decorated in the grand style; the visitor is swept into a world of stuccoed ceilings, chandeliers, and mirrors.

PALACIO DE LIRIA

Occupying a whole block on Calle de la Princesa, the street that leads out of the Plaza de España's northeastern corner (from the Museo Cerralbo simply take Calle Ventura Rodríguez northeast to Calle de la Princesa), and hidden behind its extensive front gardens, the 18th-century Palacio de Liria is the Madrid home of the dukes of Alba and contains one of the best private collections of old masters in the world. It is very much a private residence, but *occasionally,* and by prior appointment, groups of visitors are allowed in for conducted tours. Ask at the gatehouse—you may just be lucky—or write in advance to obtain permission (provide your passport number): Patronato de la Fundación Casa de Alba, Calle de la Princesa 20, 28008 Madrid.

CIUDAD UNIVERSITARIA

Calle de la Princesa continues north from the Palacio de Liria to the Ciudad Universitaria, most of which was built in the Franco years—and looks it. The **Museo de América** is in Ciudad Universitaria, off Avenida de los Reyes Católicos, which meets Calle de la Princesa across from the Parque del Oeste. Currently closed and undergoing extensive restoration, the museum has a strong collection of pre-Columbian art, including the gold hoard called the Treasure of the Quimbayas that was presented to Spain in the last century by the government of Colombia. The museum stands near a large and pretentious arch that was erected by Franco to mark his Spanish Civil War victory.

NORTHEASTERN MADRID

The area north of the center of Old Madrid, a dozen blocks east of the Palacio de Liria and north of the Gran Vía, is a warren of small, narrow, and often labyrinthine streets with two fine museums.

The Plaza de Santa Bárbara Area

The Plaza de Santa Bárbara, just off Calle de Génova about six blocks west of the Plaza de Colón and the Castellana, is a good place to enjoy a slice of life in this old quarter. The **Cervecería Santa Bárbara**, one of Madrid's best beer halls, is very popular with students and is a good stop for a beer and a ration of prawns.

MUSEO ROMANTICO
Head out the far southern end of Plaza de Santa Bárbara and down Calle San Mateo to reach the Museo Romántico, a charming but undervisited museum at number 13, housed in the late-18th-century mansion of the marqués de la Vega Inclán. A cultured and energetic aristocrat, Inclán's initiatives at the turn of the century included the creation of the Casa y Museo de El Greco in Toledo and the opening of a parador in the Sierra de Gredos, the first of today's large network of state-run hotels.

The strength of the museum is in the atmosphere it creates of the Madrid, or at least of the upper-class Madrid, of 100 years ago. Its collection, left to the nation by Inclán in 1920, is a jumble of paintings, furniture, and assorted objects that run the gamut from dueling pistols to dollhouses. Nothing is particularly outstanding, but the whole is extremely pleasing and in a sense romantic.

MUSEO MUNICIPAL
Just around the corner (take Calle San Mateo to Calle de Fuencarral and turn right) is the Museo Municipal. The not very interesting 19th-century building (the former Hospicio de San Fernando) that houses the museum is made special by an amazing and original Baroque extravaganza encasing its main entrance (Calle de Fuencarral 78) that was carved by Pedro de Ribera in the early 18th century. It is a rare

example of this florid, extravagant style in Madrid. The museum within, containing prints and models, presents a very clear picture of the growth of Madrid and the city's changing styles. There is a detailed town plan dating from 1656, the earliest extant, and a charming model of the city that was constructed in 1830. This being a Madrid museum, Goya could not be absent, and his painting *Dos de Mayo* (Second of May) has pride of place.

Plaza de Colón

Several blocks east of the Museos Romántico and Municipal, Plaza de Colón punctuates the Paseo de la Castellana, north of the Plaza de la Cibeles. A large garden covers the plaza's eastern side, under which is the **Centro Cultural de la Villa**, city hall's arts center. You enter it behind the long waterfall that lines the Castellana side of the garden. In addition to art exhibitions, the center has several venues for concerts, plays, and lectures, and a very good coffee shop. The bus station serving the airport is also under this square.

The massive building flanking the garden on the south is the home of the national library, which you can enter from the Castellana, and the Museo Arqueológico Nacional. But if you need a break from serious sightseeing, head down the Castellano, called the Paseo de Recoletos here, to **Café Gijón**, at number 21, the fabled temple of Madrid's café society. (You can also reach Gijón directly from the Museo Municipal or Romántico by heading south on Calle de Fuencarral, then left on Calle de Augusto Figueroa, left again on Calle de Barquillo, and right onto Calle de Almirante, a very upwardly mobile street packed with fashion shops. When you emerge on the Castellana, you will be right near the café.)

MUSEO ARQUEOLOGICO NACIONAL

The Museo Arqueológico Nacional (National Archaeological Museum), with its entrance at Calle de Serrano 13, one block east of the Castellana, is Madrid's most important museum after the Prado, and contains by far the most comprehensive archaeological collection in Spain. Its showpiece is the mysterious bust, possibly representing a Carthaginian goddess, called **La Dama de Elche**. The *Dama* (lady), unearthed in the southeastern coast town of Elche, is exhibited in the Iberian art section. Few remain unmoved in her presence; she has astonishingly modern looks and an attractive, distinctive personality.

The museum will provide an interested student or visitor with a strong understanding of the tapestry of cultures that make up Spain. There is a better exhibition on the Roman

Empire in Mérida; Granada and Córdoba display more Islamic treasures; and there are astounding Romanesque art exhibits in Barcelona—but Madrid's museum has examples of all three influences, with a broad collection stretching well back into the Bronze Age. In the gardens a special exhibit reproduces those treasures of the dawn of Western art, the Altamira cave drawings (the originals can be found near Santillana del Mar in Cantabria).

Barrio de Salamanca

The orderly grid of streets east of the Castellana and north of the Parque del Retiro and Calle de Alcalá constitutes Madrid's ritzy, east-side Barrio de Salamanca. Named for the marqués de Salamanca, the mid-19th-century real-estate tycoon who developed it (and modeled it on the Parisian grid system) the Barrio de Salamanca is now a fashionable residential and shopping district. The **Calle de Serrano**, running north–south, one block east of the Castellana, is the emblem of Barrio de Salamanca elegance and serves as modern Madrid's Bond Street. The area is packed with stylish shops and trendy restaurants, many of which are discussed in our Dining and Shops and Shopping sections below.

CULTURAL INSTITUTIONS

The **Fundación Caja de Pensiones**, an art gallery financed by a bank, lies midway along Calle de Serrano, at number 60, near the Calle Ramón de la Cruz intersection. Its exhibitions generally deal with 20th-century art and are usually outstanding. Not far away, the **Fundación Juan March**, Calle Castelló 77, lies on a street running parallel to and five blocks east of Calle de Serrano, in the heart of the *barrio*. Standing at the intersection of Calles de Padilla and Castelló, this cultural center is named after the founder of one of Spain's wealthiest banking families. The temporary home of some of the world's top contemporary picture collections, the Fundación Juan March also stages free lunchtime concerts and evening lectures. It boasts a good art shop on the premises that sells reasonably priced contemporary prints.

MUSEO LAZARO GALDIANO

The Museo Lázaro Galdiano, at Calle de Serrano 122, a large, turn-of-the-century mansion close to where the Serrano crosses Calle de María de Molina (the city's main access to the airport and to N II, the Barcelona highway), houses a very rich art collection amassed by financier Lázaro Galdiano and bequeathed to the nation on his death in 1947.

Galdiano was an astonishing collector who cast his discriminating net very widely indeed. The collection of ivories and enamels is quite inclusive, with, for example, magnificent Limoges exhibits. The religious plate gold and silver work, the glassware treasures, and the array of bronze work that goes all the way from early Iberian clasps and buckles to Renaissance candlesticks are also outstanding. There is even a collection of ladies' fans through the ages.

Pictorial art here is just as all-embracing, ranging from anonymous primitive triptychs to a Constable landscape with Salisbury Cathedral's spire in the distance. Rembrandt's portrait of his wife, Saskia, as herself instead of as a model for Artemis as in the Prado, hangs here, and there is a good representation of the Spanish greats: El Greco, Zurbarán, Velázquez, and Goya.

North along the Castellana

MUSEO SOROLLA

North of the Plaza de Colón is the Plaza del Dr. Marañón, to the west of which, in an elegant 19th-century quarter, is the Museo Sorolla, just off Calle Miguel Angel, at Calle General Martínez Campos 37 (across the Castellana from the Museo Lázaro Galdiano). Set in the former home and studio of Joaquín Sorolla (1863–1923), a highly successful society painter, the museum houses a mix of the artist's belongings, including a collection of baptismal fonts, which now stand in the garden, and of his output—a nostalgic celebration of sunny holidays, happy harvests, ruddy peasants, and fashionable young ladies wearing big hats.

NORTHERN MADRID

Straight up the Castellana lies fast-paced northern Madrid, where the city has seen rapid growth in the last 20 years. The expansion of the business area can be seen in the increasing number of tall buildings on the city's northern skyline—of which Madrileños are rather proud.

After Plaza del Dr. Marañón, the Castellana is punctuated by Plazas de Lima, de Cuzco, and de Castilla, respectively. These areas, while offering little in the way of sightseeing, do have hotels, restaurants, and nightclubs (the area west of the Plaza de Cuzco has a lively night scene), some of which are mentioned in our Accommodations, Dining, and Nightlife sections, below.

GETTING AROUND

Arrival by Air

Most international travellers arrive in Spain at the **Aeropuerto de Barajas**, 12 km (7½ miles) northeast of town and just off the Madrid–Barcelona highway, N II. If the traffic is flowing easily—most times it's not—the trip to downtown Madrid takes about half an hour. If you are catching or meeting a plane early in the morning, at lunchtime, or in the early evening, give yourself a good hour to reach Barajas.

There is an airport bus service that runs between the airport terminal and the Plaza de Colón, on the Castellana, the next big intersection north of Plaza de la Cibeles. An alternative is to take a taxi, which will have a fixed extra charge for trips to and from the airport. Check on the extra charge when you get in the cab (it is printed on a sheet that ought to be visible to the passenger), and make sure that the taxi driver has his meter running as he drives off. A normal run into town should cost less than 2,000 pesetas.

Renting a Car

Most major car-rental companies operate in Madrid; at the Aeropuerto de Barajas cars may be booked with Avis, Hertz, and Europcar. In general, rates are cheaper, often considerably so, if you book the car before travelling to Spain. There is little point in using a car in central Madrid. Local driving habits are daunting for the uninitiated, and parking is horrendous (and new traffic penalties could run you up to $900). For trips out of town, however, a car is an obvious bonus.

Arrival by Train

Madrid's two main railway stations are Chamartín and Atocha. Chamartín stands in the north of the city, off the northern limits of the Castellana, and Atocha is at the very southern end of the same boulevard. An underground rail line that runs all the way along the Castellana links the two stations and has intermediary stations at Nuevos Ministerios, in the northern zone of the Castellana, and at Paseo de Recoletos, close to the Plaza de Colón and the airport bus depot.

Atocha station came back into service in 1992 after extensive renovation, and now serves western, southern, and southeastern Spain: Extremadura, Andalusia, and the Levante coastline (the area between Valencia and Alicante on the east coast). Chamartín handles Barcelona, San Sebastián, and all other rail traffic north of Madrid.

Taxis

Both Atocha and Chamartín stations are on the Metro line, but travellers arriving at either station may opt for taxis. Again, there is a fixed extra fee for such pickups, so check the meter. There are extra charges for night service and for luggage as well, and these again are on the printed form that every cab driver possesses. Every taxi carries a complaint book and has its driver's license number clearly displayed; trouble should be reported to the nearest municipal policeman or to the Patronato Municipal de Turismo, at Calle Mayor 69.

Taxis are a sure way of getting around Madrid. They are relatively cheap, and the cabbies are normally pleasant. Tip 25 pesetas, as a rule, for a normal ride. The area around the historic center of Madrid, the Plaza Mayor and its Hapsburg offshoots, should be explored on foot. Distances here are comparatively short, and taxis are a waste of time.

Public Transportation

Traffic can be frightful in Madrid, and buses, which have special lanes on such thoroughfares as the Castellana, are usually a faster means of transportation than taxis. The Madrid Metro, the subway, is even faster, and is clean, safe, and easy to use.

City buses have a fixed rate; buy your ticket from the driver as you board. You can also obtain a discount voucher for ten rides—called a *bono bus*—from the major bus stations, such as the one on the Castellana close to the Prado, and also from most newspaper kiosks. You insert the voucher, a cardboard strip, into a punching machine near the driver. There are helpful signs at every bus stop indicating the route and the stops of each bus. The Metro operates on a similar flat fee for all destinations. You can also buy a ten-ticket discount voucher (*bono metro*) at subway-station ticket offices. Bus route and Metro maps are available from travel agencies and from the Patronato Municipal de Turismo, at Calle Mayor 69. The subway maps are particularly well laid out and easy to use.

Roads out of Madrid

The national highways fan out of Madrid like the spokes from a wheel's hub. They are the symbol of the Spanish capital's exalted heliocentric status; the rest of the nation should—or at least that is the theory—revolve around the Madrileño sun. The highway network was built up methodically in the 18th and 19th centuries by the elite corps of state road engineers; its job was to transform into reality a royal policy that sought uniformity throughout the unruly patchwork of provinces, regions, and nationalities that together made up Spain, and to extend royal power to the farthest corners of the kingdom.

The Carretera Nacional I (N I) leads north across Castile to Burgos, on to San Sebastián, and to the French border at Irún-Hendaye. N II travels northeast to Zaragoza, to Barcelona, and to the French border at Perpignan. Running east out of the city, the N III reaches the Mediterranean at

Valencia, and the N IV travels south through the La Mancha tableland to Córdoba, Seville, and Cádiz, near the Strait of Gibraltar, which separates Spain from North Africa. The N V leads directly west to the *conquistador* country of Extremadura and to Badajoz, on the frontier with Portugal. The final spoke, N VI, travels northwest to A Coruña (La Coruña) in Spain's misty, Celtic province of Galicia.

The Castellana axis serves N I at its northern end and N III and N IV at its southern one. Halfway down the Castellana, at the Plaza del Dr. Marañón intersection, N II, which also leads to Barajas airport, enters Madrid along Calle de María de Molina, and N VI enters through Calle José Abascal. To get onto N V from the city center, take Calle de Alcalá and the Gran Vía northwest from Plaza de la Cibeles to Plaza de España. Madrid's ring road, M 30, encircles the city and feeds traffic onto N I, N II, N III, N IV, and N V.

ACCOMMODATIONS

Most of Madrid's hotels are situated either on or very close to Paseo de la Castellana, the main north–south boulevard that slices through the city and acts as its main reference point. The modern northern end of the Castellana is now Madrid's main business area; the south, closer to the historic sites and the Prado, is considerably more casual. (Although the boulevard is called Paseo de Recoletos and Paseo del Prado in its southern reaches, it is familiarly known as the Castellana along its entire length.) The farther away from the Castellana, the cheaper the accommodations are likely to be.

Cut-price accommodations for backpack travellers means resorting on the whole to *pensiones;* the best of these can be found on the Castellana's downtown "west bank," on the Calle de Alcalá as it moves into Puerta del Sol, and off Carrera de San Jerónimo, a parallel thoroughfare that likewise heads toward Puerta del Sol.

The hotel rates listed below are projected rates for 1994, for double room, double occupancy, in pesetas. We strongly recommend that you confirm the price when making reservations.

Madrid's area code for telephoning from within Spain is 9-1. When calling from outside the country, drop the 9.

Downtown Castellana

Madrid's utterly sumptuous ► **Hotel Ritz** is a splendid Belle Epoque building on Plaza de la Lealtad, a stone's throw north of the Prado. Across the square, facing it almost like a mirror image, stands the Palace Hotel, another wedding-cake slab of turn-of-the-century elegance. The Ritz oozes gentility and is stiff on protocol: It has a tradition of turning away film actors, and no one without a tie gets through its revolving doors. You sink into the carpets as you enter, and you'll feel obliged to speak in hushed tones, aware that you are paying exorbitantly for every breath you take. Exquisite chamber orchestra concerts are staged beneath its chandeliers, and, in summer, candlelit dinners are served in its gardens. Among its numerous extras, the Ritz has a special long-weekend program during the partridge-shooting season—sportsmen are ferried to a shooting estate, and their nonsporty companions are indulged in a cultural tour.

Plaza de la Lealtad 5, 28014 Madrid. Tel: 521-2857; Fax: 532-8776. 49,000 pts.

The ▶ **Palace Hotel** is no poor relation of the Ritz. A recent face-lift has created a dazzling, mural-encased lobby: Trompe l'oeil walls and ceilings make you believe you are entering a Florentine villa where Giotto has stayed as a houseguest. The Palace also costs a pretty penny, but it has a considerably more relaxed atmosphere than its rival across the square. Stockbrokers make their presentations at the Ritz, and publishers launch their books at the Palace: It's a question of what sort of company you prefer. The Palace bar, which is where Jake and Lady Brett drank a lot of martinis together in the closing stages of Hemingway's *The Sun Also Rises,* has changed considerably, but it remains the chatty rendezvous for journalists and politicians (the parliament building, the Cortes, lies just across the road). "How did you know about the plot?" a young rightwinger was asked by a judge in the aftermath of a failed putsch attempt during the time of the Spanish Republic of the 1930s. "I heard about it in the bar of the Palace," he replied, and was acquitted without further ado.

Plaza de las Cortes 7, 28014 Madrid. Tel: 429-7551; Fax: 429-8266; in U.S., Tel: (800) 223-6800 or (212) 838-3110. 37,000 pts.

The turn-of-the-century façade of the ▶ **Hotel Villa Real** belies the fact that it is one of Madrid's newer hotels. Inside, the hotel is modern, and what it misses in elegance it makes up for in efficiency. Its location, 100 yards from the Cortes and just up the street from the Prado, is its greatest asset. It also helps business to be a stone's throw from the Palace Hotel; the Villa Real usually takes in the overflow from its long-established neighbor.

Plaza de las Cortes 10, 28014 Madrid. Tel: 420-3767; Fax: 420-2547. 31,000 pts.

Calle del Prado (a separate street from Paseo del Prado) leads southwest from the Palace Hotel up a hill lined with antiques shops to the boisterous Plaza de Santa Ana and the ▶ **Hotel Reina Victoria**. The hotel's refurbished elegance is complemented by efficient service. Manuel Rodríguez ("Manolete"), the legendary matador who was gored to death by a Miura bull in 1947, used to patronize the Victoria, and the

Plaza de Santa Ana boasts a good beer hall that attracts the bullfighting crowd. The whole area is packed with taverns and flamenco joints, revelers and actors (the Teatro Español, Madrid's national theater, is also on the Plaza de Santa Ana).

Plaza de Santa Ana 14, 28012 Madrid. Tel: 531-4500; Fax: 522-0307. 22,950 pts.

Locked in between Calle de Alcalá and Carrera de San Jerónimo near where the Gran Vía begins, the ► **Hotel Suecia** is quiet, sedate, and popular among Madrid's culture connoisseurs. It backs on the **Círculo de Bellas Artes**, a turn-of-the-century arts center on Calle de Alcalá that welcomes everyone to its exhibitions, poetry recitals, and bars, and lies close to the Teatro de la Zarzuela, the home of the *zarzuela* operetta genre. Perhaps this is why literary travellers tend to patronize it. The only *sueco* (Swedish) element to the hotel is its smorgasbord restaurant, Bellman (described below, in Dining).

Calle Marqués de Casa Riera 4, 28014 Madrid. Tel: 531-6900; Fax: 521-7141; in U.S., Tel: (800) 528-1234. 16,536–21,146 pts.

A smallish, idiosyncratic hotel (with possibly the tiniest elevator in the world), ► **Hotel Arosa** has a dandy location just south of the Gran Vía (and north of Puerta del Sol) and handsomely decorated guest rooms with double-glazed windows and helpful concierges. Its extensive breakfast buffet is a real treat.

Calle de la Salud 21, 28013 Madrid. Tel: 532-1600; Fax 531-3127; in U.S., Tel: (800) 223-1356; Fax: (212) 686-0271. 18,000–23,000 pts.

Midtown Castellana

The ► **Hotel Villa Magna**, at the intersection of the Castellana and Calle de Ortega y Gasset (north of Plaza de Colón) is, like the Ritz, one of Madrid's genuinely deluxe hotels. It hosts international bankers and upper-bracket business travellers who value first-class communications more than antique carpets, chandeliers, and murals. Movie stars are also welcome. You'll pay a lot for discreet and ultra-efficient service, but you get your money's worth. The hotel is extremely handy for Calle de Serrano shopping—you can afford everything in the street's classy boutiques if you can afford to stay at the Villa Magna—and its rear door leads straight to a branch of the Galerías Preciados department-store chain. (For the Villa Magna's excellent *nueva cocina* restaurant, see Dining, below.)

Paseo de la Castellana 22, 28046 Madrid. Tel: 576-7500; Fax: 575-9504. 55,000 pts.

Located in an elegant residential back street west of the Castellana, the recently opened ► **Hotel Santo Mauro** is

Madrid's last word on exclusive gracious living. Set in its own gardens, the building was the town mansion of the duques de Santo Mauro, and the hotel's extensive refurbishment has maintained the character of a stately home. It has just 36 rooms, with prices ranging from more than $350 for a single bed for the night to around $2,000 for 24 hours in the Presidential Suite. The hotel's restaurant, **Belagua** (see Dining), is among the city's most elegant. One of its private dining rooms is set in what was the Santo Mauro family's private chapel. The garden buffet, which opens in summer, is more relaxing and, with the evening's candlelight, more romantic.

Calle de Zurbano 36, 28010 Madrid. Tel: 319-6900; Fax: 308-5477. 52,800 pts.

The ▶ **Castellana Inter-Continental**, on the corner of Calle García de Paredes and the Castellana, close to the Plaza del Dr. Marañón, was Madrid's Hilton until it was absorbed by the Inter-Continental chain. It has the sort of service you would expect, with the added bonus of a lot of style accrued over the years. Once the most modern of Madrid's hotels, in the three decades plus of its existence it has become almost part of the city's antique furniture. It is odd to think that when it was built it was virtually on Madrid's northern outskirts. American expatriates and embassy staff patronize the bar.

Paseo de la Castellana 49, 28046 Madrid. Tel: 310-0200; Fax: 319-5853; in U.S., Tel: (800) 327-0200. 37,100–48,200 pts.

The ▶ **Hotel Miguel Angel**, just off the Castellana's Plaza del Dr. Marañón at the intersection of Calle José Abascal and Calle de Miguel Angel, is functional, yet retains a certain classiness. Older and cheaper than the Villa Magna, younger than the Inter-Continental, it has good facilities for business travellers as well as an indoor swimming pool.

Calle de Miguel Angel 31, 28010 Madrid. Tel: 442-8199; Fax: 442-5320. 48,500 pts.

The ▶ **Hotel Wellington** has a period charm to it. It is also the place to be during the mid-May to mid-June San Isidro bullfight *feria,* because this is where the top matadors change into their suits-of-light (the colorful, tight-fitting costume) before the *corrida,* and where the top aficionados gather for the postmortems when the fight is over. At the intersection of Calle de Velázquez and Calle de Jorge Juan, three blocks east of Calle de Serrano and just north of the Parque del Retiro, the hotel is strategically placed in Madrid's grid-patterned residential and shopping quarter, the Barrio de Salamanca.

Calle de Velázquez 8, 28001 Madrid. Tel: 575-4400; Fax: 576-4164. 30,500 pts.

On Calle de Zurbano, at its intersection with Calle Bretón de los Herreros, the smallish ▶ **NH Zurbano** offers extremely good service and doesn't burn holes in your credit-card statement. It lies just west of the Castellana, also near the Plaza del Dr. Marañón, in a quiet residential area. The Zurbano belongs to a Spanish-owned chain of moderately priced hotels that has several other strategically placed establishments in Madrid; if the Zurbano cannot fit you in, the chain, NH Hoteles, should be able to find you a room at another of its properties.

Calle de Zurbano 79, 28003 Madrid. Tel: 441-4500; Fax: 441-3224. 21,600 pts.

Uptown Castellana

Among the high rises in the northern stretch of the Castellana, off the Plaza de Cuzco intersection, the ▶ Hotel Eurobuilding stands on the corner of Calle del Padre Damián and Avenida de Alberto Alcocer. It has its own mini shopping mall, several bars, coffee shops, and restaurants. It offers a full range of services and has an open-air swimming pool. This business rendezvous of modern Madrid is permanently busy.

Calle del Padre Damián 23, 28036 Madrid. Tel: 345-4500; Fax: 345-4576. 31,500 pts.

The ▶ Hotel Meliá Castilla is another huge, modern hotel complex catering essentially to expense-account executives and built with the convention market in mind. It stands on Calle del Capitán Haya, an uptown street that runs one block west of and parallel to the Castellana, at its intersection with Calle Rosario del Pino. This area, just off the Castellana's intersections with Plaza de Cuzco and Plaza de Castilla, has a fast-paced nightlife. People cruise around its clubs and discotheques until the wee hours.

Calle del Capitán Haya 43, 28020 Madrid. Tel: 571-2211; Fax: 571-2210; in U.S., Tel: (800) 336-3542. 28,600 pts.

One of the city's newer hotels, the ▶ Holiday Inn Madrid was launched in 1985 and offers the usual standards and facilities of the American chain. It stands just to the west of the Castellana's intersection with Plaza de Lima among the towering office blocks that changed Madrid's skyline during the 1980s.

Plaza Carlos Triás Beltrán 4, 28020 Madrid. Tel: 597-0102; Fax: 597-0292; in U.S., Tel: (800) 465-4329. 19,500–31,000 pts.

Budget Hotels

The large lobby and the high hallways of the ▶ Hotel Asturias are a reminder of better times. No longer grand, the hotel represents value for money. It stands a block away from the Puerta del Sol on a short but busy street that links Calle de Alcalá with Carrera de San Jerónimo.

Calle Sevilla 2, 28014 Madrid. Tel: 429-6676; Fax: 429-4036. 9,650 pts.

The two Madrid hotels operated by the Tryp chain are efficiently run and moderately priced:

▶ **Hotel Tryp Rex**. Gran Vía 43, 28013 Madrid. Tel: 547-4800; Fax: 547-1238. 14,500 pts.

▶ **Hotel Tryp Washington**. Gran Vía 74, 28013 Madrid. Tel: 541-7227; Fax: 547-5199. 14,500 pts.

The plain, simple ▶ **Hotel Puerta de Toledo** has small rooms but is only a ten-minute walk south of Plaza Mayor. This is a good budget hotel, and the staff is very accommodating.

Glorieta Puerta de Toledo 4, 28005 Madrid. Tel: 474-7100; Fax: 474-0747. 10,800 pts.

The ▶ **Hostal Delfina**, two blocks up from the Gran Vía's start at its intersection with Calle de Alcalá, is typical of the cheap but mostly clean boarding houses that are either on or just off Madrid's "Broadway." If they cannot accommodate you, take their advice on the next-best choice.

Gran Vía 12, 28013 Madrid. Tel: 522-6423. 3,900–4,100 pts.

▶ **Hotel Carlos V**, just off the Gran Vía, is small and quiet and handy to the major department stores.

Calle Maestro Vitoria 5, 28013 Madrid. Tel: 531-4100; Fax: 531-3761. 11,200 pts.

Just off the Castellana, near Plaza de Colón, is the convenient and moderately priced ▶ **Galiano Residencia**.

Calle Alcalá Galiano 6, 28010 Madrid. Tel: 319-2000; Fax: 319-9914. 14,000 pts.

—*Tom Burns*

DINING

Back in the frugal 1950s there were just two premier restaurants in Madrid, the Jockey Club and Horcher, both of which specialized in Continental cuisine. Now there are more than 4,000 restaurants in the city, with a wide range of cooking styles including *nueva cocina española* (a nouvelle approach to Spanish cooking), traditional Spanish, and regional Spanish, as well as French, Middle Eastern, Asian, even American—a sign of how Madrid has changed, prospered, and expanded its gastronomic horizons.

The Cuisine

The regional cuisines of Spain predominate in Madrid restaurants. The center of Spain geographically, Madrid is also the country's psychic center. Here you'll find restaurants from every region guaranteed to assuage any provincial Spaniard's homesickness. The most predominant of the regional cuisines in Madrid, aside from Castilian, is Basque. So respected is Basque cuisine here that it is sometimes said, only half facetiously, that behind every successful restaurant, no matter what the cuisine, stands a Basque chef.

On every menu in almost every restaurant, seafood occu-

pies center stage. In many countries you might hesitate
before ordering fish hundreds of miles inland, but in Spain
geography does not hinder the freshness of the seafood.
Truck drivers race by night to rush the day's bounty from the
Atlantic and the Mediterranean to Madrid's markets. You
have only to visit the Mercado de San Miguel, near the Plaza
Mayor, early in the morning to see the freshness and diversity of the seafood.

The variety boggles the mind: shrimp, oysters, clams,
scallops, sole, turbot, cod, and fish unknown to most North
Americans, such as *besugo* (sea bream), *merluza* (hake),
salmonete (red mullet), and *rape* (anglerfish). Then there
are *angulas* (baby eels), the astonishingly expensive *percebes* (edible goose barnacles that look like prehistoric
denizens of the deep), *berberechos* (tiny clams), *nécoras*
(small crabs), *bígaros* (minuscule black snails), *navajas*
(reedlike shellfish), and such variations of crustaceans as
gambas, langostinos, and *carabineros* (all types of prawns),
cigalas and *santiaguinos* (types of lobsters), and other
varieties of fish and shellfish unknown elsewhere.

Choosing a Restaurant

One of the things to consider when choosing a restaurant in
Madrid is how fancy or trendy you want to be. The fashionable new restaurants, mostly located in the Barrio de
Salamanca and farther uptown, are expensive (5,000 to
10,000 pesetas per person), but are comparable to their chic
counterparts in New York or London. There are also many
fine restaurants in the 3,000- to 5,000-peseta (per person)
range, and many rustic old-time restaurants serve hearty,
unsophisticated fare for approximately 2,000 to 2,500 pesetas per person. Neighborhood *tascas* (small cafés) and
rough-cut *tabernas* (taverns or bars) charge even less, 1,000
to 1,500 pesetas. Almost all restaurants, regardless of price
category, offer a menu of the day (usually posted outside)
that provides three courses and often includes a drink, at a
price that is usually substantially lower than the à la carte
menu. This is a great opportunity for sampling some of the
city's best restaurants.

Madrid also has its share of inexpensive fast-food places
where savings are even greater. An alternative to a sit-down
meal is to go "*tapas* hopping" from bar to bar, trying a
variety of appetizers accompanied by a few glasses of house
wine, for less than 1,000 pesetas at each stop. Several department stores have inexpensive dining rooms that make convenient lunch stops, especially since you can then shop while
everything else in town is closed. The Museo del Prado and
Museo Nacional Centro de Arte Reina Sofía both have cafés.

Dining Customs

Madrileños thrive on eating out. In fact, they probably spend more time at meals away from home than any other Europeans. Although Madrid authorities have tried to shorten lunch hours and eliminate the siesta, centuries-old habits die hard. While the siesta itself may be dying, the customs of preprandial drinks and the long lunch hour persist. As most tourist attractions and many shops (except department stores) are closed during the lengthy afternoon break (from 1:30 to 4:30 or 5:00 P.M.), *la comida* (the midday or main meal) is a long repast. Relax and enjoy it: It's the wise foreigner who follows the crowd and makes lunch the main meal of the day, then has *la cena* (a light dinner) at 10:00 P.M. or later.

After work, which for most people ends at 8:00 P.M., Madrid really comes alive. In warm weather the sidewalk cafés throb with life and high-decibel conversation. Even in chilly weather people are on the streets and avenues, enjoying a *paseo* or dropping by a favorite bar to nibble *tapas* (tidbits or appetizers) with Sherry or wine before dinner. It's not until 10:00 or 10:30 P.M. that thoughts finally turn to the evening meal.

Reservations are expected at fashionable restaurants, and—as many places are closed on Saturdays and/or Sundays and for the entire month of August—it's always wise to call ahead. The telephone area code for Madrid is 9-1 (drop the 9 if you are dialing from outside the country). Some restaurants do not accept credit cards, and most add a service charge to the bill, although an additional 5 to 10 percent tip is considered proper.

—*Patricia Brooks*

The Wines of Madrid

The wine-growing area of the autonomous community of Madrid is a *denominación específica* (specific denomination), made up of three areas south of the capital—Navalcarnero, San Martín de Valdeiglesias, and Arganda—that produce more than 13 million gallons of wine per year. From the white grape known locally as Malvar, Madrid produces some very nice white wines—young, fresh, fruity, and medium bodied. Local vintners also make good *rosados* (rosés) and some excellent red wines from Tempranillo and Tinto de Madrid grapes, especially in the charming Arganda towns of Colmenar de Oreja and Chinchón. If you visit the picturesque town of Chinchón (covered in our chapter Side Trips from Madrid), which is also famous for one of Spain's best liqueurs, *anís,* don't fail to try the excellent red wines of Jesús Díaz from Colmenar de Oreja.

—*Gerry Dawes*

Tapas

The Spanish custom of *el tapeo*—indulging in *tapas*—is at its liveliest in Madrid, though Sevillanos claim to have invented this pursuit. Its name is derived from the verb *tapar* (to cover); a *tapa* is a small, saucer-size dish containing an appetizer—as simple as ripe olives, salted almonds, a few chunks of *queso manchego* (cheese), a slice of *tortilla española* (omelet), or slivers of *jamón serrano* or *jamón de Jabugo* (cured ham)—served along with a *chato* (small glass) of *tinto* (red) house wine or *fino* (pale dry Sherry), or a *caña* (glass) of draft beer. Small portions of *tapas* are called *pinchos;* large servings are *raciones.*

The practice of *tapas* hopping—moving from bar to bar, usually within a single neighborhood, to have a drink and sample the bar's special *tapas*—is a deeply ingrained tradition in Madrid. It takes place daily from about noon to 2:00 P.M., before lunch, then from 8:00 to 10:00 P.M., before dinner. Because of the *tapas* tradition, most Spaniards are ready to order dinner immediately, without a preliminary cocktail, when they finally sit down at a restaurant table.

Each *tapas* bar has its specialties, running the gamut from marinated mussels to grilled *setas* (mushrooms) to sautéed squid to shrimp boiled in their shells. Today *tapas,* reflecting Spain's new prosperity, have become more elaborate: béchamel-coated mussels with cured ham, small servings of casserole dishes, bits of pickled quail, lobster salad, creamed kidney and onions. *Tapas* hopping is an enjoyable and inexpensive way to dine, the Spanish equivalent of "grazing." Never mind dinner later. With enough *tapas,* you won't need it.

Tapas Bars. Some of the coziest bars for *tapas* are on the tiny streets of Old Madrid off the Plaza Mayor and Puerta del Sol (especially along Calle de la Victoria, which runs south off Carrera de San Jerónimo) and around the Plaza de Santa Ana (especially Calle de Echegaray, a short street east of the plaza), reached by taking Calle del Prado southwest from Plaza de las Cortes. Many of these *tapas* places also have full-fledged, if casual, restaurants—often in the rear or upstairs.

At **El Gallego**, adjacent to the Plaza Mayor, the businesspeople who crowd in after work find 25 or more varieties of *tapas* to choose from, including shellfish pie and sliced octopus marinated in olive oil. (A restaurant with "Gallego" in its name is almost a guarantee of the fresh seafood that is a trademark of Galician cooking.)

La Toja, outside an arch leading from Calle Mayor into the Plaza Mayor, serves the classic *gambas al ajillo* (prawns in garlic and hot oil) in a terra-cotta dish and an elegant *salpicón de mariscos* (a mélange of seafood with a vinaigrette of onions and green peppers), among other delicacies. Across the plaza and through the Botoneras arch is **Mesón los Gallegos,** a *tasca* where *chopitos* (fried baby squid) are a specialty; consider staying for a dinner of Galician seafood. Calle Cava de San Miguel, just west of Plaza Mayor, is lined with wonderful *tapas* bars, such as **Rincón de la Cava, Mesón de la Guitarra,** and **Mesón de Champiñón** (this last devoted, as you would expect, to mushrooms). At **Bar Gallego,** on the Plaza de Puerta Cerrada, in the same area, you'll find such Galician specialties as steamed mussels (best eaten with Ribeira, a Galician white wine). **Calle de Cuchilleros** is also wall-to-wall *tapas* bars, each with a single specialty. At **La Chata,** farther along on Calle de la Cava Baja, a specialty is *jamón de bellota* (cured ham from acorn-fed pigs). **Casa Palacios,** on the same street, is known for its snails and grilled mushrooms, among other *tapas* choices.

A great favorite with local *toreros* is **Vista Alegre,** Calle del Pozo 2, a tiny street just east of Calle Victoria, parallel with Carrera de San Jerónimo. A one-time Hemingway watering hole was **Cervecería Alemana,** Plaza de Santa Ana 6, and it's still going strong, its stand-up *tapas* crowd spilling out onto the street on warm evenings. *Cerveza* (beer) is the drink of choice here, as it is two doors down at **Cervecería Natur Bier** (at number 9). This newish place is Madrid's only pub that brews its own; German-style lager is made on the premises in huge, gleaming copper vats, as you sit at rustic tables munching *tapas* or bratwurst and sipping the house *rubia.* There are tables outside during the summer. Next door at number 10 is another pub, **Cervecería Santa Ana,** also with outdoor tables, making this small plaza with its pocket park something of a Beer Row. Nearby, just northeast of Plaza de Santa Ana at Calle Manuel Fernández y González 7, is the popular **Café Viva Madrid,** easy to find because of the colorful tilework on its façade. **La Trucha,** at number 3 on the same street (with a branch of the same name at Calle Núñez de Arce 6), is another local favorite whose specialty is trout. Also handy are **Los Gabrieles,** at Calle de Echegaray 17, an old tavern with tiles and *tapas,* and **Lerranz,** serving first-rate *tapas* and desserts down the block at number 26.

Restaurants in Old Madrid

The area around Plaza Mayor is where you'll find most of the old Castilian *mesones* (rustic inns or taverns) and *tascas,* many of which are relatively inexpensive.

Prevalent throughout Castile, *tascas* are very much a part of Madrid's dining scene. They began in the 19th century as simple taverns, so rough-edged that the heavy wine of La Mancha would be served from the goat skins in which it was stored. Before long, some taverns began serving plain, homespun meals. Roast suckling pig and baby lamb were the mainstays, as well as, on specified days, a typical Madrid boiled meat-and-vegetable dinner known as *cocido madrileño*. Traditionally, *tascas* have been egalitarian places where workers and aristocrats rub elbows at the bar. Today, as Spain becomes increasingly Europeanized, *tascas* are more popular with Madrileños than ever—nostalgia, no doubt, for an identifiable but disappearing past.

South of Plaza Mayor. High on most visitors' agenda is a visit to **Antigua Casa Sobrino de Botín**, better known as Casa Botín or just Botín, located at Calle de Cuchilleros 17, on one of the oldest streets in Madrid, just below the southwestern corner of the Plaza Mayor, which has several *tascas* and considerable character of its own. Popularized for English speakers by Hemingway ("We lunched upstairs at Botín's . . . we had roast young suckling pig and drank rioja alta."), Botín's has been going strong since 1725 (the *Guinness Book of World Records* calls it the oldest restaurant in the world). Surprisingly, despite its long run and a massive overdose of tourists, its food remains excellent and a fine value; it would be hard to find better roast suckling pig anywhere in town. The pig and the roast baby lamb are prepared in *hornos* (ovens) fired with *encina* (oak) and are then shoveled with wooden paddles onto big wooden platters. Enjoy your roast with a big ceramic pitcher of the house wine, a red Valdepeñas. Although Botín's is always busy, for both lunch and dinner, it avoids the feel of herd feeding because its five cozy dining rooms—decorated with blue-and-white tiles, small windows with mullioned glass panes, and low ceilings with rustic exposed beams—are spread out over three floors. Tel: 366-4217.

Unusually chic for a Castilian *tasca,* and perennially popular with upscale Madrileños, is **Casa Lucio**, at Calle de la Cava Baja 35, a continuation (southward) of Calle de Cuchilleros. Even King Juan Carlos is a regular (more or less incognito), and the tables at dinner look like a Who's Who of local politicos, actors, and other celebrities. Located below Plaza Mayor in the oldest part of the city, the restaurant looks from the outside like an ordinary *tasca.* Don't be deceived. Inside, past a bar where rows of *jamón de Jabugo* hang from exposed beams, there are two floors of whitewashed dining rooms with ceramic floors, wood-beamed ceilings, and brick arches. The menu is classic Castilian: Begin with a starter of razor-thin slivers of *jamón de Jabugo,* followed by shrimp in garlic sauce, then baby lamb chops or *churrasco de la casa,* a thick, one-pound steak served on a sizzling platter. Tel: 365-3252.

Another Castilian classic, **Posada de la Villa**, just down the street from Lucio, at Calle de la Cava Baja 9, has even more atmosphere. An old inn restored and converted to a new restaurant in 1982, the Posada has the air of a country *mesón,* with an arched vaulted ceiling and a huge rounded beehive oven and open hearth. You can watch the suckling pigs and baby lambs being removed from the oven while you savor the wood scent. Whet your appetite on the wide variety of *tapas* and round loaves of delicious hearth bread displayed on the long bar. Tel: 366-1860.

Casa Julián de Tolosa is a third popular roasting house on the same street, at Calle de la Cava Baja 18. The menu of this attractive restaurant is small, featuring just a few starters and such entrées as grilled lamb and pork chops, enhanced by spicy peppers that are a house specialty. The high quality of the meat draws the crowds to Casa Julián. Tel: 365-8210.

North of Plaza Mayor. Not all the restaurants in the older part of Madrid are traditional. Light-years away in style is **Café de Oriente**, in a fin-de-siècle setting at the edge of the peaceful Plaza de Oriente (at number 2), across from the Palacio Real. The cuisine here is classic Spanish and *haute* French, with *haute* prices to match. Fresh Rascafría trout and roast suckling pig are among many specialties. This is a pleasant place to drop by for afternoon tea or coffee. A less expensive, and first-rate, meal can be had in the basement grill, **Horno de San Gil**. The proprietor is a priest, Father Luis de Lezama, who also has four other restaurants, all called Taberna del Alabardero, in Madrid (just to the northeast at Calle Felipe V), Marbella, Seville, and Washington, D.C. For both, Tel: 541-3974.

East of Plaza Mayor. Casa Ciriaco, Calle Mayor 84, just southwest of Puerta del Sol, is a favorite of Madrid artists, writers, and celebrities. The old-style food is always reliable, especially the chicken dishes. Tel: 548-0620.

Just east of the Puerta del Sol, at Carrera de San Jerónimo 8, is **Lhardy**, a long-standing Madrid restaurant, though not in the *tasca* mode. Lhardy opened in 1839 and was going strong as the city's only temple of *haute cuisine* by the time Dumas dropped by in 1846. It is still a custom, especially among the over-50s, to stop by Lhardy's ground floor for a pick-me-up cup of consommé served from a massive silver samovar, paper-thin tea sandwiches, *tapas,* and Sherry before lunchtime. Meals in three high-ceilinged, aged Belle Epoque upstairs dining rooms, with well-polished parquet floors and tooled-leather wall coverings, still yield gustatory if pricey dividends, but you must choose carefully to avoid the mundane. A hearty *cocido madrileño* (chick-pea stew), tripe in a succulent garlicky tomato-and-onion wine sauce, and a *soufflé sorpresa* (baked Alaska) are among Lhardy's reliable preparations. Tel: 522-2207.

About four blocks east of Lhardy is **Luarqués**, at Ventura de la Vega 16 (a street that runs south from San Jerónimo to Calle del Prado). This unobtrusive, minimally decorated Asturian restaurant is one of the best values in Madrid and is extremely convenient for visitors staying at the Palace Hotel (just three blocks away). Local businessmen flock here for grilled salmon and other fish, *setas y angulas* (mushrooms and baby eels), *arroz con leche* (rice pudding), *fabada asturiana* (Asturian bean stew), and other Asturian dishes. Portions are huge, prices moderate. Unfortunately, Luarques does not take reservations, so it is smart to go early (about 1:30 P.M.) for lunch. (Although the restaurant is open for dinner, it is liveliest at lunch.) Tel: 429-6174.

In recent years, several chic *nueva cocina* restaurants have opened in the older part of town. Relatively new and trendy, and attracting Madrid's most elegant diners, is **El Cenador del Prado**, at Calle del Prado 4, near Plaza de Santa Ana. Among the prettiest, most romantic restaurants in the city, it has two tiny dining rooms, one in shades of apricot, the other in tones of yellow. Chef Tomás Herranz worked for years in New York, and his menu is a Spanish interpretation of nouvelle cooking with many imaginative variations. While some dishes are bland, many are winners, such as cream of eggplant soup with a flan of basil-accented tomato floating in the center, cheese-flavored semolina gnocchi with brains over a spinach purée, and duck leg in a caramelized prune sauce. Tel: 429-1561.

Another newish *nueva cocina* restaurant in Old Madrid is **La Basílica**, at Calle de la Bolsa 12 (just east of Plazas Mayor and Santa Cruz). Located in a former Baroque church, this high-style restaurant has a domed ceiling, high-backed wooden chairs suggesting stylized choir stalls, white and gold trim, and elegant food to match. Tel: 521-6160.

The latest hot spot, especially for the politicos and government officials who work a block away at the Cortes, is **Paradís Madrid**, at Calle Marqués de Cubas 14 (north off Carrera de San Jerónimo), a *nueva cocina catalana* offshoot of a Barcelona restaurant (which also has a New York branch). The lovely understated decor includes finely grained wood walls and marble restrooms. The restaurant specializes in Mediterranean and seafood dishes, but various mushroom preparations—especially *hojaldre de setas gratinade* (mushrooms in a puff pastry), rice dishes, and heavenly desserts (such as *tarta de fruta seca*, dried-fruit tart) are also memorable. Tel: 429-7303.

A favorite of the culinary cognoscenti is **Irizar**, a Basque restaurant at which chefs from other restaurants dine on their evenings off. It's directly across the street from the Teatro de la Zarzuela, at Calle Jovellanos 3, a tiny street behind the northwest corner of the Cortes (which faces Carrera de San Jerónimo). Its brass sign is small and discreet, and the sparkling, all-white dining room is upstairs. Crepes of *bacalao* (cod) with pimiento sauce are just one of Irizar's innovations. The pear tart with chocolate sauce is delicious, as are the Basque cheese *idiazabal* and the Basque white wine *chacolí* (known as *txakolí* in Basque Country). Chef Irizar's creativity does not come cheap. Tel: 531-4593.

Paseo del Prado Area

East of Paseo del Prado on the western edge of Parque del Retiro are two of Madrid's most distinguished restaurants. **Horcher**, located at Calle de Alfonso XII 6, across from the park, is one of the city's oldest shining stars (founded in Berlin in 1903, moved to Madrid in 1943 to escape the Allied bombings). While it has lost a bit of its luster in recent up-and-down years, it still maintains fine service (such as placing an embroidered cushion under each female diner's feet) and offers an excellent classic German menu strong on game. Venison is a longtime favorite, and the Viennese desserts are luscious. Tel: 522-0731.

One of the most promising of Madrid's *nueva cocina* restaurants, **La Gamella** (The Feeding Trough), is on the same block at the ground floor of a 19th-century mansion in which philosopher José Ortega y Gasset was born (Calle de Alfonso XII 4, next door to Sotheby's and directly across from the Parque del Retiro). Chef-owner Richard Stephens, a friendly American expatriate from Decatur, Illinois, came to Madrid as a choreographer in 1964 and fell for the lifestyle. There's nothing Middle American about La Gamella's food or decor, which uses Matisse-like prints on tablecloths and banquette covers. After a lunch of creamy almond-garlic gazpacho, red mullet stuffed with Spanish blue cheese in olive sauce, or sea bream fillet encrusted with toasted garlic and hazelnuts, a brisk stroll through the park is more than just a good idea; it's almost a necessity. Tel: 532-4509.

A star among Madrid's hotel dining rooms is the one at the **Hotel Ritz**, Plaza de la Lealtad 5, just north of the Prado. Now under the guidance of a young French chef du cuisine, Patrick Buret, the Ritz has been beautifully renovated and has diversified its French menu with such Spanish classics as *jamón de Jabugo,* smoked Asturian salmon, Galician mussels simmered in saffron, Aragonese lamb roasted with thyme, and a superlative veal liver in a honey-*tomillo* sauce. The Ritz serves *cocido madrileño* every Thursday for lunch, in honor of King Alfonso XIII, who always had this gargantuan and robust dish on

Thursdays, then retired for such a long siesta that his schedule was cancelled for the rest of the day. It's all pricey, but superb. Tel: 521-2857.

The **Grill Neptuno**, the handsome restaurant in the Palace Hotel, on the other side of Plaza de Cánovas del Castillo at Plaza de las Cortes 7, has also become locally popular again, thanks to such dishes as terrine of smoked salmon in anchovy butter. The setting and the fine service add up to a memorable dining experience. Tel: 429-7551.

Barrio de Salamanca

Many of Madrid's most stylish and new restaurants can be found in this fashionable neighborhood east of the Castellana. The food is very good at **El Amparo**, but it is the restaurant's romantic ambience that makes it so popular with Madrid trendsetters. Tucked into an alley, at Callejón de Puigcerdà 8, near the corner of Calle de Jorge Juan (even taxi drivers have trouble finding it), the Basque-accented restaurant looks like an abandoned warehouse from the outside. The inside has three levels and resembles a loft, with huge rough-hewn beams, posts, and a skylight. Beige, fabric-covered walls complement the elegant pink linen and oversize china. If the food doesn't always live up to the dramatic decor, it is usually interesting, occasionally inspired, often worth the rarefied prices charged. Among some of the better dishes here are *bisque de marisco armagnac* (seafood bisque), duck with vinegar and honey, lobster salad, mango and apricot sorbets, and a superlative dessert of poached pear in puff pastry with *crème anglaise* laced with Pear William eau de vie. The *menú de degustación* (tasting menu) is usually a good option for a first visit. Tel: 431-6456.

Many of the restaurants located in the Barrio de Salamanca and farther uptown are more expensive than those in and around Old Madrid, but there are some moderately priced old-time establishments, as well as coffee shops, cafeterias (more like cafés than self-serve cafeterias), fast-food places, and department-store restaurants. One old reliable is **Alkalde**, Calle de Jorge Juan 10 (between Calles de Lagasca and Velázquez), where Basque dishes are served in rustic, barrel-vaulted rooms. It isn't cheap, but you won't have to mortgage your house, either. Try the stuffed peppers or sea bream Basque style. You can also make a meal out of the *tapas* in the large bar, which is hung with cured hams. Tel: 576-3359.

Viridiána, which moved recently to a more chic location at Juan de Mena 14, is a stylish newcomer with an enthusiastic clientele and a very personal approach to *nueva cocina,* all managed in tiny rusticated quarters. Crêpes with blood pudding in a pimiento sauce and rice pudding with a mango sauce are among the specialties. Tel: 523-4478.

A current rage is **Teatriz**, Calle de Hermosilla 15 (entrance on the corner of Calle de Claudio Coello), a popular late-night spot with a dramatic and romantic mood. You enter through a cool minimalist bar to a theatrically exuberant dining room (the work of French interior designer Philippe Starck and Valencian designer-artist Javier Mariscal), with high-backed chairs and tables facing a luminously lighted barlike stage. The menu is *cucina nuova* Italian, with various pastas, carpaccios of beef, salmon, and sole, osso buco, and other delights. Tel: 577-5379.

As part of its major renovations, the Hotel Villa Magna (Paseo de la Castellana 22, at Calle de José Ortega y Gasset) has moved its dining room from the basement to the ground floor, making it accessible from both the lobby and the street. Renamed **Restaurante Berceo**, it is ensconced in the handsome wood-paneled space (now slightly enlarged) that used to be the bar. An outdoor terrace garden has been added for warm-weather dining. Grilled sole with béarnaise sauce and *mille-feuille* of salmon and turbot in a white Vermouth sauce are two outstanding offerings on a *nueva cocina* menu that excels in seafood and stunning presentations. Tel: 575-3377.

El Pescador, right down the street at Calle de José Ortega y Gasset 75 (between Calles de Alcántara and Montesa), has a smart address in the Barrio de Salamanca, but a rustic and simple setting. Savvy locals head here for the stunning abundance of fresh fish and shellfish. On any given day as many as 30 varieties of seafood (many flown in from Galicia) are on view in the glass cases. It's best to order your fish here *a la plancha* (grilled) with a slice of lemon. The delicious house fish soup is also a good choice. Tel: 402-1290.

Many of Madrid's stylish newer restaurants feature *nueva cocina española,* the new Spanish cuisine. It has been especially well interpreted by the Basques, perhaps because their traditional cuisine has a light touch and relies on fresh, light sauces. Basque chefs are acknowledged, even by rival Catalans, as creative masters. It's not surprising then that many of the fashionable *nueva cocina* restaurants that have sprouted like wild *setas* in recent years in uptown Madrid have Basque origins.

A case in point is the city's premier gastronomic temple, **Zalacaín**. Aficionados have known for years that this Basque-owned restaurant, located at Alvarez de Baena 4 (a quiet, fashionable street off bustling Calle de María de Molina, at the very northern tip of the Barrio de Salamanca), is the best in the city—in fact, in most views, the best in the country.

What makes it so is absolutely seamless perfection, from the polished brass nameplate by the front steps to the warm farewell by staffers as you leave. The salmon-hued walls, fresh flowers, paintings, and elegant china and silver service plates are a backdrop for intriguing variations on Basque-Navarrese classics and original creations by the Basque chef Benjamín Urdain. Owner Jesús María Oyarbide describes the food as "modern *haute* cuisine with a Spanish flavor." It is all that and more. Fresh foods, mainly from Spain, such as fish and game, Guadalajara truffles, and olive oils, are augmented by a vast cellar of mostly Spanish wines. Since Oyarbide opened his doors in 1973, Zalacaín has set new standards and spawned imitators all over Spain. For a first visit, the *menú de degustación* is recommended for a sense of the breadth and depth of the restaurant's capabilities. Expensive but memorable. Tel: 561-4840.

West of the Castellana

The area opposite the Barrio de Salamanca on the "west bank" of the Paseo de la Castellana has its share of Madrid's finest and most popular restaurants.

A worthy place to eat in the heart of the new avant-garde fashion district that has arisen west of the Castellana (where you're likely to see the rising designer stars of this scene at nearby tables) is the well-named **El Mentidero de la Villa** (The Gossiping Place), Calle Santo Tomé 6, just south and west of Plaza de Colón by way of Calle Bárbara de Braganza. The decor in the two tiny dining rooms revolves around large wooden horses (like those seen on carousels, but stripped to the natural wood), and the menu is exquisite *nueva cocina* with a delicate Japanese accent and presentation. Ken Sato, the chef and co-owner, is Japanese and once had a restaurant in London (The Secret Garden, on Old Brompton Road). Tel: 308-1285.

Still one of Madrid's most elegant restaurants, **Lúculo**, Calle de Génova 19 (near the corner of Calle de Zurbano), is another of the places Madrileños go to dine and be seen. Approached through an office building atrium, the restaurant unfolds in a series of tiny rooms, one of which overlooks a small garden. Although not new, Lúculo is currently a "hot ticket," known for its *nueva cocina* style, evidenced in such dishes as salmon carpaccio with clams and scallops in virgin olive oil and pheasant and cabbage in puff pastry. There is an unusual cheese selection (for Spain), with many choices imported from Androuet in Paris. Tel: 319-4029.

So many new restaurants have opened in recent years that it's easy to forget **Jockey**, Calle Amador de los Ríos 6, just northwest of Plaza de Colón, off Calle Alcalá Galiano. Yet this longtime favorite of local movers and shakers has been serving consistently fine classical food since it opened in 1945. The background is understated, with wood paneling, banquettes, and soft lights. The Continental specialties are predictable—Chateaubriand with béarnaise sauce, veal kidneys tarragon flambée, and the like—but nobody does them better. There are a few surprises, such as an appetizer of smoked eel mousse and turbot flambée with Pernod. To avoid the fate that occasionally befalls the first-time foreign visitor, ask for a corner table when making a reservation. Otherwise you may find yourself at the vortex of a whirlpool of waiters hurrying to and from the kitchen. Tel: 319-1003.

Another of the city's fine hotel dining rooms is the **Belagua**, at the elegant new Hotel Santo Mauro, Calle de Zurbano 36 (corner of Calle de Caracas). The entrance to the restaurant is through mirrored doors in the hotel lounge. Beyond is a second dining room called **La Biblioteca** (The Library), intimate and romantic. The food is distinctive *nueva cocina,* with a good mix of seafood and meat dishes. Fish carpaccio with pimientos, scallop ragout, and hake with *kokotxas* (fish "cheeks"—a Basque specialty that's a current Madrid rage) are standouts. Tel: 319-6900.

Near the Villa Magna is another of Madrid's most beautiful (and pricey) new restaurants, **Fortuny**, in a handsome old mansion with a garden setting at Calle de Fortuny 34 (between Calle de Rafael Calvo and Paseo General Martínez Campos), one block west of the Castellana. Surrounded by Champagne-colored brocaded walls and attended by impeccable service, you'll dine on such delights as artichokes stuffed with foie gras, grilled sole, and fresh fruit tarts. In summer you can dine outdoors on the terrace. Tel: 308-3267.

Northern Madrid

The high-rise neighborhoods of northern Madrid have welcomed many new and elegant restaurants in recent years.

Seafood is fresh and wonderful, if expensive, in almost any Madrid restaurant, but at **La Dorada**, Calle de Orense 64, it is often a work of art. Located in an uptown, residential neighborhood two long blocks west of the Castellana (just south of Avenida del General Perón near the Urbanización Azca), this is a branch of a similar and equally fashionable restaurant in Seville. It specializes in authentic Andalusian dishes such as *fritura especial malagueña* (a mix of tiny Mediterranean fish lightly and crisply fried), *coquinas* (tiny clams) in a parsley-and-wine sauce, and *dorada a la sal,* giltfish (similar to red snapper) baked in a heavy overcoat of rock salt that retains the juices but leaves no saltiness on the moist, flavorful fish once it is chipped off. Seafood is flown to Dorada from Andalusia by private plane daily. Tel: 570-2004.

While some restaurants overwhelm you with their decor, the extravagances at the Galician restaurant **O'Pazo** come in the seafood displays, known as *joyerías* (jewelers' windows). These lavish piles of expensive shellfish invite conspicuous consumption (and heart failure when the bill is presented). The variety is mouth-watering, with lobsters, king crab, scallops, oysters, shrimp, and prawns as stellar attractions. You're best off here ordering your fish grilled or sautéed and your shellfish steamed or grilled, and avoiding dishes with more elaborate sauces, which are sometimes prepared with a heavy hand. Located at Calle de Reina Mercedes 20 (a short street one block south of Avenida del General Perón, between Calle de Orense and Calle de Dulcinea), O'Pazo's slightly glitzy *moderne* decor shouldn't distract you from the superb seafood. Tel: 553-2333.

A well-respected Navarrese-Basque restaurant is the up-scale **Señorío de Bertiz**, whose chef and manager came from Zalacaín. What better provenance? The specialty is seafood; the hake *al pil-pil* (with garlic and chili peppers) is outstanding. The restaurant is just west of O'Paza, at Calle Comandante Zorita 6. Tel: 533-2757.

One of the most popular of northern Madrid's restaurants is **Príncipe de Viana**, at Manuel de Falla 5, a short street off the Castellana just north of Plaza de Lima. The first restaurant of Jesús María Oyarbide (before Zalacaín), it is now run by his son, and is as popular with chic Madrileños as ever—although its mystique eludes many nonregulars. Certainly you can't fault the service or the comfortably luxurious decor, but while most dishes look elegant and are skillfully prepared, many lack intensity, and few are done with the flair of those at Zalacaín, although prices are almost comparable. Tel: 457-1549.

Fish is the draw at **Cabo Mayor**, Calle de Juan Ramón Jiménez 37, at the corner of Calle Juan Hurtado de Mendoza (a block north of Plaza de Cuzco in a smart post–World War II neighborhood), whose late owner, Victor Merino, from Santander, was a pioneer in the new Spanish kitchen. A *nueva cocina* flair for light, creative dishes and pleasing presentations of seafood prepared the northern, Cantabrian way characterize this charming nautical-themed establishment, which is located below street level. The stylized shiplike interior of one dining room even has portholes, allowing diners, most of them too sophisticated to bother, to peer into the pristine kitchen, where such delights as *besugo estofado al tomillo* (sea bream stewed with thyme), red mullet sautéed with mint, and a salad of oyster and sea bass drizzled with lemon, olive oil, and fresh dill are being prepared. Tel: 350-8776.

Nearby, at Calle Juan Hurtado de Mendoza 11, is **Sacha**, a very "in" Parisian-style bistro with good Galician fish dishes, such as anglerfish *a la jacobina* and marinated oysters, and a fine house Rioja. Try the *filloas,* dessert pancakes filled with jam, a typical Galician dessert. Tel: 345-5952.

Finding a good Valencian restaurant in Madrid wasn't easy until **La Albufera** opened at the Hotel Meliá Castilla, Calle del Capitán Haya 43 (on the corner of Calle de Rosario Pino, one block west of the Castellana). The specialty here, as you might expect, is *paella,* prepared in a variety of ways. The most notable is the *paella de mariscos* (with shellfish). Tel: 579-6374.

Foreign Restaurants

Another sign of changing times in Madrid is the recent popularity of restaurants serving foreign cuisine. A mainstay for some years has been **Al-Mounia**, at Calle Recoletos 5, just east of Paseo de Recoletos. Related to restaurants of the same name in Casablanca and Paris, Madrid's Al-Mounia is a fiesta of Moorish tiles, fabric-covered banquettes, horseshoe arches, and Moroccan accoutrements. A ewer is brought to your couch for hand washing before dinner; a glass of mint tea is served at meal's end. Big brass trays deliver a first-rate couscous, *tajine aux amandes* (lamb with almonds), and other authentic Moroccan delicacies—all an excellent value. A dessert cart, wheeled to your table, carries wonderful pastries, including the delicious *cigarillos* filled with marzipan and sprinkled with sesame seeds. Lunch or dinner here is a delightful experience. Tel: 575-0173.

De Funy, Calle de Serrano 213, on the corner of Infanta María Teresa, specializes in Lebanese dishes and has live piano music and belly dancing in the late evenings. Order the *mezze:* ten different appetizer tidbits served with chunks of pita bread. Squash stuffed with rice and lamb is an unusual, tasty specialty, as is *kharous-ousi* (lamb with rice, almonds, and spices). Tel: 457-6915.

Another well-established Middle Eastern restaurant, not too pricey but out of the way for many visitors, is **Sayat Nova**, Calle Costa Rica 13 (an extension of Avenida de Alberto Alcocer), off Plaza de Cuzco, in the northeastern commercial section of the city. Well-seasoned shish kebab is a signature dish. Tel: 350-8755.

Among the newer foreign restaurants is a very good Indian restaurant, **Annapurna**, centrally situated at Calle de Zurbano 5, a few blocks west of Paseo de la Castellana, in a residential area full of art galleries and boutiques. The carpet and walls, painted a terra-cotta color, and the Mogul arches, brassware, and a tease of a garden create a tranquil Eastern ambience for such delicious dishes as the lamb-based *rogan josh, pulao arasta, murgh karabi,* and other Indian and Pakistani specialties. Tel: 319-8716 or 308-3249.

On Calle Jovellanos, a short street behind the Cortes and opposite the Teatro de la Zarzuela, are several restaurants, including the aforementioned Irizar and the longtime favorite **Edelweiss**, at number 7. The moderately priced food here has a German accent, but such dishes as *paella* are also on the menu. Tel: 532-3383. For authentic Persian cuisine try **Restaurante Teheran**, Calle de Ayala 113, in the Barrio de Salamanca; Tel: 401-2096. **Bellman**, the restaurant in Hotel Suecia, at Calle Marqués de Casa Riera 4 (just south of Calle de Alcalá), features an authentic Swedish smorgasbord with an emphasis on salmon dishes every Thursday, Friday, and Saturday at lunch. Tel: 531-6900.

Robata, a handsome Japanese restaurant on two floors, with tatami rooms, a sushi-sashimi bar, and a step-back-into-old-Japan look, has recently opened at Calle de la Reina 31, one block north of the Gran Vía (between Calles Clavel and Victor Hugo). Tel: 521-8528. **Los Galetos**, with an inviting blue-tiled interior, is a moderately priced Brazilian restaurant (one of four branches) at Calle Veneras 3, off Calle de Preciados (south of the Gran Vía). Tel: 559-1729.

Quick Meals

It is increasingly easy to find inexpensive places to eat in Madrid that are attractive and don't require a two- or three-hour time commitment. Among them is **Mallorca**, a delicatessen chain with counter seating, offering quick lunches or snacks. High-quality sandwiches, quiches, cheeses, and sausages are among the choices. There are five branches, but the one at Calle de Velázquez 59, in the Barrio de Salamanca, is especially appealing (and handy for shoppers). **La Plaza**, a new self-serve restaurant in La Galería del Prado (next to the Palace Hotel, on Plaza de las Cortes), is also handy for a quick lunch before or after a visit to the Prado. Pick from the numerous choices at separate salad, hot food, pastry, and beverage bars, then retreat to a table in an airy alcove away from the central bars. **Embassy**, on the Castellana north of Plaza de Colón (corner of Calle de Ayala), combines a first-rate gourmet food shop with a small tearoom in the rear (whose walls are hung with amusing Dalí prints) and a proper restaurant upstairs that serves lunch. Light meals (the Welsh rarebit is delicious), cookies and cakes, and freshly brewed tea make the tearoom a favorite with foreign and local residents. Tel: 576-4877 or 435-9480.

Churros, Coffee, and Tea

Imbibing in *churros con chocolate* is a Madrid institution. Squiggles of "raked" dough the size of breadsticks, deep-fried and served hot, *churros* (and the thicker *porras*) are eaten sprinkled with granulated sugar and/or dunked into a cup of thick, rich hot chocolate. The most popular place in Madrid for *churros* is **Chocolatería San Ginés**, located at Traversía del Arenal 18, between Calles del Arenal and Mayor in Old Madrid. This century-old *churrería* is pipe-rack plain and totally unprepossessing—and that's the way Madrileños like it. Go in the early morning hours (it opens around 4:00 A.M. and closes at 10:30 A.M., reopening from 5:00 to 10:00 P.M.), when it jumps with people. Stopping by a *churrería* after a nightlong revel of *tasca* hopping is the Madrid equivalent of having a predawn bowl of onion soup in the old Les Halles in Paris.

A mid-morning coffee break is de rigueur in Spain. An appealing place for it (and for snacks, light meals, and terrific *tapas*) is the Belle Epoque **Café Espejo**, Paseo de Recoletos 31 (west side, between Calle Bárbara de Braganza and Plaza de Colón). Across from it on the promenade is a sister café, **El Pabellón del Espejo**, large, new, but also with a vintage air. **Café Gijón**, at number 21, is Madrid's art and literary hangout. **Café Castellana**, uptown at Paseo de la Castellana 8, has *churros,* buns, and coffee in the morning, and *tapas,* snacks, salads, and light meals later in the day and evening.

Currently very "in" is **Petrosiam Café**, Calle Amnistía 10, a block south of the Teatro Real in Old Madrid. A handsome Art Deco bar with banquettes, it serves a bargain-priced Continental breakfast with freshly squeezed orange juice—a welcome alternative to a costly hotel breakfast. At **Café Viena**, Calle Luisa Fernanda 23 (just off Calle de Ferraz, a northern extension of Calle de Bailén, across from Jardines Cuartel de la Montaña), there is a choice of 22 different coffees.

A longtime favorite for tea and light meals is **Embassy** (see Quick Meals, above). Another tea or coffee (or cocktail) stop might be at **Café Círculo de Bellas Artes**, an arts center at Calle de Alcalá 42 (at the intersection of Gran Vía). In its grand high-ceilinged *sala,* hung with crystal chandeliers, is a bustling bar where you can sip Sherry, hot chocolate, or *café con leche* while watching the avenue action from the café's huge front windows; in summer there are tables outdoors in front. Also lively is **Café de Oriente** (see Old Madrid, above), especially its open terrace in summertime.

In the late hours, a relaxing place for coffee uptown is the **Café Bar El Globo**, Calle Esteban Terradas 3 (near Plaza de Castilla), while the **Gaviria Palace**, at Calle Arenal 9 in Old Madrid, is a late-night scene with concerts, art exhibits, and conversation to accompany coffee and drinks.

—*Patricia Brooks*

NIGHTLIFE AND ENTERTAINMENT

Bars and Cafés

The **Café Gijón**, which stands at number 21 on the strip of the Castellana called Paseo de Recoletos, is the most famous of Madrid's old-style bars and cafés; you will find people here from breakfast time until very late at night. It is the home of the *tertulia,* an old Spanish ritual that consists of regular meetings among like-minded friends to exchange news and discuss everything under the sun. You are likely to find a famous author holding court here. Meals are served at lunchtime on the marble-topped tables, and in summer the Gijón's outside terrace is one of the most popular on the Castellana.

The **Café Comercial** is another *tertulia* haunt with marble-topped tables and wood-paneled walls. It lies on Glorieta de Bilbao, a plaza at the intersection of Calle de Carranza and Calle de Sagasta, reached by taking Calle de Génova northwest out of Plaza de Colón. The Comercial is nowadays particularly popular with younger people, who meet here to map out their evening: There are lots of cinemas and cheap restaurants on and around Calle Luchana, which leads into the Glorieta de Bilbao from the north, and immediately south of the plaza lies the narrow-streeted neighborhood of Malasaña, which is packed with disco bars. Malasaña can be rough late at night as police search out drug pushers.

Different sorts drink in different parts of town: A very distinct crowd of people—literati, theater people, hangers-on, and poseurs—congregates at the **Círculo de las Bellas Artes**, at Calle de Alcalá 42, just up from Plaza de la Cibeles, west toward Puerta del Sol. The Círculo stages experimental drama and photography exhibitions and has a very lively bar, **La Pecera**, where this crowd ends up in the evenings. Later on these same people tend to cross over Calle de Alcalá to the Gran Vía and on to a narrow street, Calle de la Reina, that runs parallel to and north of the Gran Vía. At **Cock**, Calle de la Reina 16, drinking and chatting continue until the early hours.

Young professionals and fashion models follow their own evening itinerary. You will find them at the **Hispano**, Paseo de la Castellana 78, just north of the Plaza del Dr. Marañón intersection, or farther uptown, east of the Castellana's Plaza de Cuzco intersection, at **El Balneario**, Calle de Juan Ramón Jiménez 37, which is full of potted plants. You'll find the same sort of crowd at the similarly decorated **El Sur**, Calle Alberto Bosch 14, near the Parque del Retiro.

Totally unpretentious people, students of both the real and the eternal kind, flock to Plaza de Santa Ana in the evening and stay in that area most of the night. The plaza, flanked by the Teatro Español and the Hotel Reina Victoria, lies close to the Palace Hotel, up Calle del Prado. There is a group of bullfighting aficionados in the **Cervecería Alemana**, a beer hall on Plaza de Santa Ana, that acts as if Hemingway had just walked out of the door (he did often drink there), and there is also a big crowd at **Café Viva Madrid**, another beer tavern, which lies on Calle Manuel Fernández y González at Calle de Príncipe, where it leads into the plaza.

For serious drinkers there is nothing to beat **Balmoral**, except perhaps the bar of the Palace Hotel (see below), which is where the Balmoral's chief barman learned to shake cocktails. The Balmoral has an English club atmosphere—hushed conversation, oak panels, and hunting trophies. It is located at Calle de Hermosilla 10, between Calle de Serrano and Paseo de la Castellana, just north of the Plaza de Colón intersection. On the corner of Calle de Ayala, the next street north, and the Castellana, the **Embassy** bar serves superlative Champagne cocktails and also extremely good English teas with wafer-thin sandwiches. The Embassy's founder, a Mrs. Taylor, set up the business after she grew tired of being a governess.

Finally, a quick rundown of some of the finest drinking digs in the city: hotel bars. The bar of the **Palace Hotel** (Plaza de las Cortes 7), where politicians leak to journalists and writers quibble with their publishers, is the most animated among the hotel drinking spots as far as the city's networkers are concerned. The bar at the **Hotel Villa Magna** (Paseo de la Castellana 22) is strictly for mega dealmakers; the bar at the **Hotel Ritz** (Plaza de la Lealtad 5) is for snobs; and the bar at the **Hotel Meliá Castilla** (Calle del Capitán Haya 43) is for singles. The **Castellana Inter-Continental** bar (Paseo de la Castellana 49) is allegedly an international-spy hangout, which means that there probably isn't one within a dozen blocks, but the bar is snug enough.

Nightclubs

Archy, housed in an elegant mansion west of the Paseo de la Castellana, about halfway between Plazas de Colón and del Dr. Marañón, at Calle Marqués de Riscal 11, is the current "in" spot. Although it is essentially a discotheque where celebrities like to be seen, it also serves lunch and has a bar that is open from midday on. **Joy Eslava**, between Puerta del Sol and Plaza de Oriente, at Calle del Arenal 11, in a building that used to be a theater, was the top spot until Archy came along, and it still retains a faithful following. Arguably the best of the bunch among the student discos, **Cats**, on the edge of Madrid's Complutense university campus (Calle Julián Romea 4), is young and noisy, and, if you happen to be both, it could be memorable. Open till 3:30 A.M.; the later you arrive, the more crowded (and fun) it will be.

The best jazz is usually to be heard at the **Café Central**, Plaza del Angel 10, just alongside Plaza de Santa Ana's drinking venues. There is a good cabaret at the **Café Maravillas**, Calle de San Vicente Ferrer 33, four blocks south of Glorieta de Bilbao, in the heart of the sometimes rough Malasaña neighborhood, and there is folk music at **Elígeme**, down the street at number 23.

For big international-type shows you have to go to **Scala Meliá Castilla**, at Calle del Capitán Haya 43, which is part of the Meliá Castilla hotel complex. Flamenco is performed very professionally at **Zambra**, at Calle de Velázquez 8, in the Barrio de Salamanca, and at the **Café de Chinitas**, at Calle Torija 7, a small, narrow street south of the Gran Vía near the Convento de la Encarnación; Chinitas also has a restaurant; Tel: (9-1) 248-5135. Most visitors have more fun at flamenco clubs in which they can participate as well as watch; if you want to join in, try **Al Andalus**, at Calle del Capitán Haya 19, one block west of the Castellana, just north of its intersection with Plaza de Cuzco.

Classical Music, Dance, and Theater

A serious music and theater fan arriving in Madrid should check the programs at the **Auditorio Nacional de Música**, Calle Príncipe de Vergara 146, Tel: (9-1) 337-0100, the home of Spain's national orchestra; the **Teatro Lírico Nacional de la Zarzuela**, Calle Jovellanos 4, Tel: (9-1) 429-8225, Madrid's opera house and its main ballet venue; and the **Compañía Nacional de Teatro Clásico**, a publicly funded drama company that performs at three different venues: the **Teatro Nacional María Guererro**, Calle Tamayo y Baus, Tel: (9-1) 319-4769; the **Teatro de la Comédia**, Calle Príncipe 14, Tel: (9-1) 521-4931; and the **Teatro Español**, Calle Príncipe 25, Tel: (9-1) 429-9193.

Madrid's brief annual opera seasons are in April and September. Occasionally one of Spain's top opera stars—Plácido Domingo, Montserrat Caballé, José Carreras, Teresa Berganza, Juan Pons—will put in an appearance. Tickets are hard to come by, but the porters at such luxury hotels as the Ritz and the Palace can sometimes come through—at a price. At other times, and particularly in the summer, *zarzuelas,* the name given to Spain's charming operettas, are performed at the **Centro Cultural de la Villa**, an underground arts complex beneath the Plaza de Colón, Tel: (9-1) 575-6080, and at the Teatro Lirico Nacional de la Zarzuela (see above). *Zarzuelas* are Gilbert and Sullivan–type productions with Latin picaresque and *bel canto* enhancements that have remained highly popular since the middle of the last century.

In the fall and winter the Compañía Nacional de Teatro

Clásico usually stages three or four new productions at one of its venues. This is a good opportunity to see highly professional renderings of the works of Golden Age dramatists Lope de Vega, Tirso de Molina, and Calderón de la Barca, who were the precursors of the French classical trio Moliére, Beaumarchais, and Racine.

The national orchestra's season normally extends from September to May, during which they perform every Friday, Saturday, and Sunday, and often midweek as well. The theater presents a full program of visiting orchestras during the summer. The Auditorio Nacional, which was inaugurated in 1990, is architecturally uninteresting but is a state-of-the-art edifice when it comes to acoustics, sight lines, and well-positioned Champagne bars.

Spain's national ballet company usually takes over the Teatro de la Zarzuela for a brief season in late September. Visiting classical dance companies use the theater for special performances at other times of the year. In July and August both the Spanish company and visiting ones often give open-air performances late at night at the large central patio of the **Cuartel Conde Duque**, Calle Conde Duque 9–11, Tel: (9-1) 588-5285, an 18th-century infantry barracks near the Plaza de España that has been converted into an attractive and popular venue for exhibitions and performances. In summer the center's several bars stay open long into the night, and, if a major ballet is not scheduled at the main central patio, there are likely to be flamenco or experimental theater performances in one of the smaller patios.

La Corrida

Madrid's bullring, the **Plaza de las Ventas**, northwest of Parque del Retiro at Calle Alcalá 237, seating some 23,000 *aficionados,* is the largest in the world after the one in Mexico City and is considered the "cathedral" of *la corrida* (the bullfight). It is here that reputations are made or broken. The Feria de San Isidro, which starts on May 15 in honor of Madrid's patron saint and normally comprises daily bullfights until mid-June, draws the top stars and bull breeders and is the high point of the season. There is a mini-*feria* with about five fights in mid-September that serves to promote reputations for the following season. Otherwise, there are fights every Sunday from early March until midway through October. These occasionally launch a star, but usually they pitch second-rate matadors against extremely difficult bulls that the stars refuse to fight.

Getting Tickets. Tickets for the San Isidro and the September *corridas* are expensive and hard to obtain, as a high proportion of the ring's seats are held by season ticket holders.

Tickets go on sale the day before the fight and, if any are left, the day of the fight at 9:00 A.M. at the ticket offices by the bullring and at the booths on Calle Victoria. Be prepared to pay at least $30 for a moderately good ticket. (There are also booths selling tickets at a 10 percent markup as well as scalpers who will sell to the highest bidder.) Tickets are cheaper and easier to obtain for the non-*feria* fights. The tickets in the *sol* (sun) are cheaper—with good reason, as you will find out sitting in the full glare of afternoon. You pay more for the privilege of *sombra* (shade).

Bullfight Hangouts. Those in Madrid during the Feria de San Isidro should visit the **Venta del Batán** bullpens in the Casa de Campo (take the Metro to Batán), where the bulls are kept in a dozen corrals until the morning of their fight. There these magnificent, highly bred animals can be examined at close quarters. The Venta del Batán's open-air restaurant is not the least of the attractions here. The **Hotel Wellington**, at Calle de Velázquez 8, is another gathering spot for *aficionados* during the *feria,* where a before-lunch drink at a bullfight bar set up for the *feria* is de rigueur. Between sips of Sherry you can watch videos of the previous day's fight and listen to passionate discussion about what went on. Top matadors usually stay at the Wellington, and their managers are invariably at the bar.

—*Tom Burns*

SHOPS AND SHOPPING

You might expect to find every product made in Spain available in Madrid, and you probably would—if you had the time, interest, and energy to search the city's 50,000 or more shops. But it's far better, if your travels take you elsewhere in Spain, to buy the locally made products in their natural habitat. If Madrid is your only Spanish stop, there are special things to look for and certain places to find them. In general, the best shopping is concentrated in two areas of the city, both of which can be covered on foot.

Madrid's most fashionable shopping is in the **Barrio de Salamanca** (Salamanca district), along the 15 blocks of Calle de Serrano that stretch from Plaza de la Independencia and Calle de Alcalá at the south end north to Calle de María de Molina. Cross streets, such as Calles de Jorge Juan, José Ortega y Gasset, and Diego de León, form a grid in between, and parallel streets—Calles Claudio Coello, de Lagasca, and de Velázquez in particular—are lined with boutiques, clothing and shoe shops, bookstores, *perfumerías,* art galleries, and restaurants favored by Madrid's chic and fashionable.

In this area you'll find many international names—Yves Saint Laurent, Giorgio Armani, Hermès, Jaeger, Ted Lapidus, and Christian Dior, among others—and along Calle de Serrano the many quality designer-clothing shops include Camper, Acosta, Farrutx, Stephane Kelian, Geltra, Bravo, and Yanko. For imaginative children's clothes try **Friki**, at Calle de Velázquez 35, or **Nancy Niños**, at Calle Diego de León 25. **Cat**, Calle Claudio Coello 7, sells high-quality avant-garde jewelry; and **Tres Zetas**, Calle de José Ortega y Gasset 15, features innovative high-fashion Spanish designer clothes.

A second prime area for shopping runs from Carrera de San Jerónimo near the Palace Hotel to the streets between Gran Vía and Puerta del Sol, as well as a honeycomb of streets around Plaza Mayor. There you'll find custom crafts, antiques, and specialty shops, as well as two of Madrid's major department stores.

Many hot new fashion boutiques are clustered in a new shopping area west of Plaza de Colón and south of Calle de Génova. Look along Calle de Almirante (just west of Paseo de Recoletos) and nearby Calle de Xiquena (perpendicular to Almirante), Calle Piamonte (perpendicular to Xiquena), and Calle Argensola (parallel to Xiquena).

In general, Madrid offers good buys in crafts, custom-made items, leather goods, high fashion, contemporary art, and antiques. Certain French perfumes and liqueurs are actually made in Spain and cost less here than if bought elsewhere in Europe.

Shop hours are generally from 10:00 A.M. to 2:00 P.M. and from 5:00 to 8:00 P.M. weekdays and from 10:00 A.M. to 1:30 P.M. Saturdays. Department stores are open from 10:00 A.M. to 9:00 P.M. Monday through Saturday.

Crafts

For a good selection of Spanish crafts and made-in-Spain household accessories, try the government-run **Artespaña** shops. Prices are competitive, and the range of goods is extensive, displaying the finest workmanship from all over Spain. Furthermore, the shops will pack and ship overseas.

There are three Artespaña shops in Madrid: Calle de Hermosilla 14 (east of the Castellana, one block north of Plaza de Colón); Calle D. Ramón de la Cruz 33 (at the corner of Calle de Castelló in the Barrio de Salamanca); and in La Vaguada shopping center in the northern part of Madrid. The largest and best, at Calle de Hermosilla 14, specializes in furniture, rugs, and ceramics.

If you can't visit the town of Talavera de la Reina, you'll find the famous decorated Talavera ceramics at **La Cerámica de Talavera**, Calle de Lagasca 44 (two blocks east of Calle de Serrano, near Calle de Goya). **La Tierra**, at Calle de Almirante 28, just west of Paseo de Recoletos, specializes in antique and modern ceramics, as well as some other crafts.

The much-collected Lladró porcelain figures may be bought at **Lladró**, the company's Madrid showroom, at Calle de Quintana 2, just west of Calle de la Princesa (an extension of the Gran Vía). Lladró figures are also available at the department store Galerías Preciados (see the section on department stores below).

El Arco de los Cuchilleros, at Plaza Mayor 9, has unusual contemporary ceramics, jewelry, and other crafts. The **Museo Nacional Centro de Arte Reina Sofía** has an excellent small gift shop with contemporary home accessories, many of which are by internationally known artists and designers such as Isamu Noguchi and Alvas Alto.

Traditional Spanish Clothes and Objects

Time was when Madrid was a center for custom-made clothes, shoes, linens, furniture, and accessories of various kinds. That era is fast passing, but it is still possible to find some exquisite handmade goods in Old Madrid, on streets radiating from the Plaza Mayor.

Leather Goods. For fine made-to-order leather boots, all kinds of people—from Franklin Roosevelt, Ernest Hemingway, and Anthony Quinn to horsemen from Argentina to Zambia—have made the trek to the minuscule workshop of **Hijos de García Tenorio**, at Calle de la Bolsa 9, not far from the Palacio de Santa Cruz. Carrying on a 150-year-old tradition, the García brothers make every boot by hand from a pattern drawn to the purchaser's foot. Each pair takes about three months to make and may last forever. The patterns are kept on file for future orders.

Fine leatherwork is a Spanish tradition, and it is almost synonymous with the name **Loewe**. Loewe suede and leather coats, suits, jackets, handbags, gloves, wallets, and accessories can be bought at three main shops in Madrid: numbers 8 and 26 on Calle de Serrano, and Gran Vía 8, as well as in 15 branches throughout the rest of Spain. Another much-respected place for leather and suede clothes, handbags, and the like is **Herrera y Ollero**, Calle de Almirante 9. **Acosta**, known for leather bags, shoes, belts, and accessories, has seven shops in Madrid; the handiest are at Calle Princesa 60 and Calle Claudio Coello 95.

Accessories. If you fancy a dashing Spanish cape, the place to have it made is **Seseña Capas**, Calle de la Cruz 23. They've been selling their seductively warm wool capes to the rich, famous, and beautiful since 1901. **Trea**, at Calle Don Ramón de la Cruz 14, is known for fine linens, lingerie, and men's underclothing.

Fans have become popular again in Spain with women *and* men, and **Casa de Diego**, Puerta del Sol 12, is the place to buy them, as well as gentlemen's walking sticks. At **Casa Yustas**, Plaza Mayor 30, you'll find every imaginable kind of men's hat or cap (fedoras, *kepis,* military, ambassadorial, and sports caps, even the Royalist red beret), as well as military buttons, belt buckles, and insignia. **Ramírez**, Calle Concepción Jerónima 2 (south of Plaza Mayor), sells top-quality classical and flamenco guitars, as does **Félix Manzanero**, Calle Santa Ana 12 (south of Plaza de Cascorro). Bookbinder **Antolín Palomino Olalla**, at Calle de Conde Duque 11 (northwest of Plaza de España), does beautiful work.

Haute Couture. Spanish couturiers have been turning out elegant clothes for generations. Among today's hot names are three in the Barrio de Salamanca: **Purificación García**, Calle de Velázquez 55; **Adolfo Domínguez**, at Calle de Ayala 24, Calle de José Ortega y Gasset 4, and Calle de Serrano 96; and **Sybilla**, Calle de Jorge Juan 12. Other stars are **Francis Montesinos**, Calle Argensola 8; and **Agata Ruiz de la Prada**, Calle Marqués de Riscal 8, west of the Castellana. Longtime favorites include **Manuel Pertegaz**, Calle Maestro Ripoll 8, just east of the Castellana; **Elio Berhanyer**, G. Mena 25 (boutique) and Calle de Ayala 124 (atelier); and **Antonio Nieto**, Calle del Prado 22, in central Madrid. Many consider **Angél Collado**, Calle de Almirante 21, the best men's tailor in town, a view reputedly shared by King Juan Carlos. **El Corte Inglés** department store features clothes by name designers Guy Laroche, Balenciaga, Pierre Balmain, Roberto Verinno, Paco Casado, Nacho Ruiz, and Georges Rech. Look for avant-garde clothes and designers on Calle de Almirante at **Ararat** and **Berlin**, both at number 10; **Puente Aéreo**, Calle Conde de Xiquena 11; and **Ekseption**, Calle de Velázquez 28.

Antiques

When shopping for antiques in Madrid, keep in mind that bargaining or negotiating the price is practiced in Madrid antiques shops as much as anywhere else—unless an object is marked P.V.P. (*precio venta público,* or fixed price).

Two streets on which numerous antiques shops are clustered are Carrera de San Jerónimo and nearby Calle del Prado (which leads off San Jerónimo). One of the oldest and largest shops, **Abelardo Linares**, Plaza de las Cortes 11, at the corner of San Jerónimo, sells age-burnished Talavera plates, gilded Baroque wooden angels, *santos,* and vintage furniture.

Many visitors do their antiquing on a Sunday visit to El Rastro (see Markets, below), but keep in mind that 40 percent of the antiques shops in the Rastro area are open daily. Serious buyers should visit them on weekdays, when they are far less frenzied. Three galleries—modified malls with 30 or so shops in each—are located on Calle Ribera de Curtidores: **Nuevas Galerías** at number 12, **Galerías Ribera** at number 15, and **Galerías Piquer** at number 20.

More than 50 antiques and art galleries fill the **Centro de Arte y Antiqüedades,** housed in a handsomely restored building from the 1850s at Calle de Serrano 5. **Centro de Anticuarios Lagasca,** Calle de Lagasca 36, is an "umbrella" for 11 or so dealers under a single roof.

Antique jewelry is still relatively underpriced in Spain. In Madrid, look for it at **Sala Fabergé** (which doubles as an auction house), on the Gran Vía; **L'Ermitage,** Calle de Villanueva 27 (in the Barrio de Salamanca); and at **Monte de Piedad,** Plaza de Celenque 2 (just northwest of Puerta del Sol), where there are monthly auctions.

Rare books can be found at **Luis Bardon Mesa,** at Plaza San Martín 3, and also at **Ramón Montero,** Callejón de Preciados 4, both near Puerta del Sol in the old city.

Art and Design

Anyone interested in reproductions of furniture designed by Gaudí and other Modernist designers, as well as contemporary pieces, should try **BD Madrid** (a branch of the avantgarde Barcelona store BD Ediciones de Diseño) at Calle de Esteban Collantes 32.

Contemporary Spanish art, especially paintings and graphics, has been an excellent value since the late 1960s. Most Madrid galleries are located on small streets east and west of Paseo de la Castellana. A few of special interest are Galería Theo, Calle Marqués de la Ensenada 2, and Galería Celini, Calle Bárbara de Braganza 8, both west of Plaza de Colón; Fernando Vijande, Calle Núñez de Balboa 65, east of the Castellana; and the galleries along Calle de Villanueva, such as Juana Mordó (at number 7) and Galería Egam (number 29). For good prices on original prints try the **Fundación March,** Calle Castelló 77, near the corner of Calle de Juan Bravo, and **Estiarte,** Calle de Almagro 44.

A helpful booklet, *Arte y Exposiciones,* is available free at most art galleries. Published three times a year, it lists all Madrid galleries and exhibitions and has an invaluable artist index, telling where each artist exhibits on a regular basis. Look also for major art and antiques auctions. **Sotheby's,** Plaza de la Independencia 8, holds four or five important ones a year, with art featured at the Hotel Ritz and decorative objects at the Castellana Inter-Continental. There are monthly auctions at **Durán,** Calle de Serrano 8, known to have the largest and most varied collection in Spain.

Books

One of the best selections of foreign-language books (and books on Spain and Spanish culture) is at **Turner Librería**, Calle de Génova 3–5 (off Plaza de Colón). Turner's bulletin board is a great source of info swapping (for apartments, Spanish lessons, and jobs). **La Casa del Libro**, Gran Vía 29, stocks more than 300,000 books and is the best general-interest bookstore in town. For the inveterate bibliophile, there's endless browsing at the secondhand-book stalls along Cuesta de Moyano, near Atocha station.

Department Stores

Travellers in a hurry can solve many of their gift problems with a stop at one of Madrid's numerous department stores. The two major stores and their main locations are **Galerías Preciados**, Plaza del Callao, off the Gran Vía; and **El Corte Inglés**, Calle de Preciados, off Puerta del Sol. El Corte Inglés has the widest selection of high-quality goods, and its best branch store is at Calle Raimundo Fernández Villaverde 63, at the intersection with Calle de Orense (just west of the Castellana). Its other Madrid branches are at Calle de Goya 76 and Calle de la Princesa 56 (near the corner of Avenida de Alberto Aguilera). Galerías Preciados has four branches in Madrid: Calle de Goya 87, Calle de Serrano 47 (behind the Hotel Villa Magna), Calle Arapiles 10–11 (near the Glorieta de Quevedo intersection), and La Vaguada (see Markets, below). To cure a touch of homesickness, Brits can gravitate to **Marks & Spencer**, located at Calle de Serrano 52.

Markets

Madrid's famous flea market, operating only on Sundays, is **El Rastro**, as much a sight as a source. Its stalls sprawl along Calle Ribera de Curtidores (below the cathedral of San Isidro), from the north end of Plaza de Cascorro south to Ronda de Toledo. Morning is the time to visit; by noon you can barely move through the crush of people, and by 2:00 P.M. the crowd thins out to head for *tapas* or lunch. El Rastro is made to order for pickpockets, so be careful. There's more trash than treasure, but the panorama of people makes a visit a must.

A stamp-and-coin market is held each Sunday from 10:00 A.M. to 2:00 P.M. under the covered arcades of Plaza Mayor. Even if you're not a collector, it's worth going for the people-watching. **Filatelia Casa del Sello**, Calle Mayor 29, is a stamp-and-coin shop in the same area. There's a modest hippie-style jewelry market every Saturday afternoon at Plaza de Santa Ana.

New in 1989, the **Mercado de la Puerta de Toledo**, located below Plaza Mayor southwest of Madrid center, is a modern four-story brick complex built on the site of the old central fish market, using the market's cyclops-eye tower as a symbol. The new market is home to some 150 stylish shops and the **Café del Mercado**, which has live jazz in the evenings. For the visitor with limited time, the market is a précis of Madrid antiques, crafts, books, boutique clothes, and shoes. The most imaginative one-of-a-kind items are on the fourth floor. Especially noteworthy are **Tafetán Taller Textil**, with unusual handwoven stoles, rugs, and towels; **Jesús Riano** for witty, original adult toys; **Cristina de J'osh** for vintage and modern dolls. Madrid designers with shops there include Angela Arregui, Sara Navarro, Susan Unger, and Cristina Fernández.

Shopping complexes are now a fact of Madrid life. César Manrique, an artist from the Canary Islands, designed the most unusual one: **La Vaguada** (also called Madrid-2), at Barrio del Pilár in the north end of the city, reachable by the Metro line. It's a three-story complex almost two blocks long, with some 300 shops, including an Artespaña, a branch of Galerías Preciados, C & A department store, several inexpensive restaurants, nine cinemas, a bowling alley, and an open-air park on the roof. It's out of the way for most visitors but worth seeing if you're in the neighborhood. New and stylish is **La Galería del Prado**, with 38 fashionable, upscale shops located on two floors, reached through the Palace Hotel or off Plaza Cánovas de Castillo. Among the shops there are: Don Carlos, Zocco, Lucia Romani (lingerie), iOh Que Luna! (linens), Godiva (chocolates), Atico (gifts), and Campos de Ibiza (swim gear). Newest of the shopping centers is **Moda Shopping**, at Avenida del General Perón 40 (off the Castellana at Plaza de Lima), a large commercial center with banks, restaurants, cafés, and three floors of fashionable shops and boutiques.

Food and Culinary Shops

The sub-basement of El Corte Inglés's main store on Calle de Preciados has an impressive *supermercado* (supermarket) and is an excellent stop for anyone contemplating a picnic in the country or searching for Spanish specialty foods. The cheese, pâté, and sausage sections are especially impressive. Extra-virgin olive oil is now available in easily transportable plastic bottles, and various types of nuts, capers, and saffron are also enticing. The store's Club de Gourmet section in its branch at Calle Raimundo Fernández Villaverde 63 also has a fine cheese and pâté selection.

Choose from the wonderful array of Spanish cheeses at **Cuenllas**, at Calle de Ferraz 1, an extension of Calle de Bailén (north of the Palacio Real, across from Plaza de España). Even handier is **Ferpal**, Calle del Arenal 7, one block west of Puerta del Sol, where you will find great cheeses, Spain's excellent regional hams, sausages, *turrón* (nougat), and other foods. If you don't have time for a proper lunch, buy a *bocadillo* (small sandwich) and a glass of beer and eat stand-up style as the regulars do. **Charlot**, at Calle José Ortega y Gasset 8, is a food shop with great varieties of goodies. **Mallorca,** a chain of six top-drawer delis (Calle de Serrano 6, Calle de Velázquez 59, Calle Bravo Murillo 7, Calle de Comandante Zorita 39, Calle Pérez Zuñiga 24, and Avenida de Alberto Alcocer 48), has terrific cheese and charcuterie sections. The **Museo del Jamón**, at Carrera de San Jerónimo 6, has a tempting selection of hams, cured meats, and cheeses. **Del Pozo**, Calle del Pozo 9 (one block south of Carrera de San Jerónimo), is known for its *hojaldres* (puff pastries) and *empanadas* (turnovers), as well as its vintage 1830 charm. Uptown, at Calle de Capitán Haya 23, is a well-stocked branch of the wonderful Barcelona food shop **Semón**.

Casa Mira, circa 1855, at Carrera de San Jerónimo 30, has the best *turrón* in Spain behind its handsome wood-paneled exterior. You can buy it (as well as many other candies and sugared almonds) by the slab, cut to order on a marble countertop. Up the street is **La Violeta**, Plaza de Canalejas 6, a tiny shop known for its violet candies and other *bombones*.

Madrid's best-known cookware shop, **Alambique**, Plaza de la Encarnación 2, near the Palacio Real, sells all kinds of kitchen accessories, cookware, and china. Alambique also offers cooking classes, sometimes in English. Tel: (9-1) 547-8827.

—Patricia Brooks

SIDE TRIPS FROM MADRID

EL ESCORIAL, AVILA, SEGOVIA, ARANJUEZ

By Patricia Brooks

Few capitals are as well situated as Madrid for visitors who want to see as much of a country as they can in a limited amount of time. Madrid's geographic location dead-center in Spain helps, but it is the wealth of historic and cultural sights in the nearby towns that makes the capital's position ideal. Many of the Castilian cities encircling Madrid are far older and richer in monuments and memorabilia than it is.

In this chapter we cover the part of Castile in the immediate vicinity of Madrid. We cover Castile to the north and west of Madrid, beyond Segovia and Avila, in a separate chapter, later in the book, called Old Castile.

Around Madrid are such Castilian treasure towns as El Escorial, Avila, Segovia, Pedraza de la Sierra, Alcalá de Henares, and Aranjuez. The old university town of Alcalá, just east of Madrid, and historic Aranjuez, with its royal palace, to the south, are easy day trips. The massive monastery-palace of El Escorial, northwest of Madrid, can also be a day trip, or it can be part of a longer side trip to Avila, to its west, and Segovia, to the north. Spend a full day in El Escorial, then drive west to the impressive medieval walled city of Avila for the first night. Enjoy a day there exploring the walls and the Romanesque churches and following the trail of Saint Teresa before heading northeast to Segovia for a minimum of one night, but ideally two or three. You'll want to see Segovia's sights—its Roman aqueduct, Gothic cathedral, and fortress-castle—then use the city as a base for excursions to surrounding towns: Riofrío, La Granja, Rascafría, and the well-preserved medieval hill town of Pedraza de la Sierra (which can also be visited on a day trip from Madrid).

In your explorations you will enjoy a hearty helping of Castilian art, history, cultural life, and cuisine. You will also discover the crosscurrents of Moorish, Jewish, Castilian, and Germanic cultures that have enriched Spain over the centuries. And you will experience some soul-stirring scenery that takes you from scraggy, rock-encrusted, surreal landscapes to pine forests and soaring mountaintops (north and west of Madrid are the Guadarrama mountains, popular with hunters, fishermen, and skiers).

Toledo, south of Madrid, is another possible day trip from the capital; we cover it (and the rest of Castilla–La Mancha) in the La Mancha chapter, later in the book.

MAJOR INTEREST

Castles, Gothic cathedrals, and Romanesque churches
Moorish architectural elements
Hearty Castilian cuisine, especially roast lamb and
    suckling pig

El Escorial

Philip II's monumental monastery-palace
Tour of the royal apartments
Works by Velázquez, Titian, Dürer, and others in the
    new museums
Side trip to the Valle de los Caídos, Franco's monument to Civil War dead

Avila

Well-preserved medieval walls
Trail of Saint Teresa of Avila
Fine Romanesque churches
Cathedral's graceful interior

Segovia

Spectacular Acueducto Romano
Moorish traces in the old city
Gothic cathedral
Fairy-tale Alcázar

Around Segovia

Typical Spanish castle at Coca
Riofrío's royal hunting lodge
Philip V's palace-farm at La Granja de San Ildefonso
Rascafría's historic Monasterio del Paular

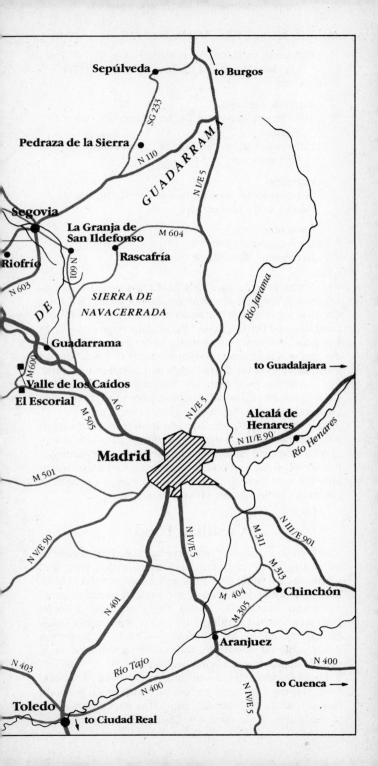

Pedraza de la Sierra, medieval hill town with charming Plaza Mayor and traditional Castilian restaurants

Alcalá de Henares
16th-century university: former intellectual center of Spain
Plateresque architecture of the Colegio Mayor de San Ildefonso

Aranjuez
Seasonal foods: strawberries and white asparagus
Palacio Real's lush gardens

Chinchón
Dining at lovely parador
Picturesque Plaza Mayor

For centuries Castile was a battlefield, fought over by competing armies: Visigoths versus Moors, Moors versus Christians, Christian kings against one another. From the death of Ferdinand III (Saint Ferdinand) in 1252 until the reign of the Reyes Católicos, Ferdinand and Isabella, in the early 16th century, the region was in almost continuous turmoil. It was hard on the inhabitants of the towns caught in the endless tug-of-war, but it probably built character. That may explain why even today Castilians are known to be tough, stoical, wryly independent, indomitable. They've had a lot of experience.

The very name "Castile" derives from those centuries of interminable warfare. It signifies *castillo*—castle—the mountainous landscape having been stippled with castle-fortresses that served as lookout posts and garrisons for various rulers. Mile for mile there are probably more castles or shells of castles in Castile than anywhere else in Spain.

Castilian Food

Castile's robust cuisine, reflecting its rugged, mountainous terrain, is strong on game, such as partridge, hare, and rabbit, and on fresh river trout and *trucha plateada* (silver trout). Its dishes are as hearty and straightforward as *queso manchego* (ewe's-milk cheese). This is the land of *cochinillo asado* (roast suckling pig) and *cordero asado* (roast lamb), roasted in wood-burning ovens to a perfection rarely achieved elsewhere, with crackling skin and juicy, succulent meat that can be cut with a fork.

Cocido madrileño—a well-simmered stew of beef, pork, fowl, *chorizo* (sausage), garbanzos (chick-peas), potatoes, onions, carrots, and cabbage, with other ingredients added at the whim of the cook—is Castile's most famous dish.

Traditionally, it is a complete meal, its constituents served in consecutive courses: first the soup, then the vegetables on one platter and the meats on another.

Other standbys to be found throughout the area are *sopa de ajo* (garlic soup), *tortilla español* (Spanish omelet, made with potatoes and often served cold on picnics and in cubes as *tapas* with cocktails), and *leche flan,* the rich caramel-enveloped custard that is popular throughout Spain.

For the wines of the area, see the Dining section in the Madrid chapter.

EL ESCORIAL

Few edifices evoke the presence of past rulers as tangibly as El Escorial speaks of Philip II, son of the Hapsburg emperor Charles V (King Carlos I) and great-grandson of Ferdinand and Isabella. Among them, these four rulers were responsible for the creation of Spain as a nation and as the international power that dominated Europe for decades—decades that shaped the country's image for centuries. It is no small legacy.

Philip II, the most complex and least understood of this great foursome, has fared poorly in recorded history, especially in Anglo-American history. A proud, publicly austere, formal man (who was privately jolly, amusing, and warm-hearted), he presided over Spain's Golden Age in the second half of the 16th century and also, because of the misfortunes of the Armada, the beginning of his country's long decline.

El Escorial owes its existence to two vows Philip made: one to his father to build a royal mausoleum and the second to Saint Lawrence just before Spanish troops launched an attack on the French at St. Quentin in Flanders. It was August 10, 1557, Saint Lawrence's Day, and Philip pledged to the saint that if the Spaniards won, a monastery would be built in thanks. They did and it was. The king chose as his site a small, isolated, scruffy village on a foothill between ridges of the Sierra de Guadarrama and called the complex he built there El Real Sitio (the royal seat) de San Lorenzo el Real del Escorial.

THE BUILDING OF EL ESCORIAL

It is understandable how the remote (at that time) setting must have appealed to this ascetic monarch, who from 1562 lavished 21 years on this monumental building project. All the while Philip fussed over the plans, altering and blue-penciling, climbing over scaffolding to view the progress: Much of the final effect should be credited to him. Philip's first architect, Juan Bautista de Toledo, had worked with Michelangelo on St. Peter's in Rome but died while work on El Escorial was in progress; an assistant, Juan de Herrera, completed it. In his orders to Herrera, the king requested "simplicity in the construction, severity in the whole, nobility without arrogance, majesty without ostentation." Ultimately that was translated into a massive, gray-granite parallelogram, with slate roofs and turrets, towers at each of the four corners (reminiscent of those in Madrid's Plaza Mayor), and an elevated central section in the form of a grid with higher towers and the church dome. There are simple Doric elements in the courtyards (16 in all), doorways, and architectural detailing, developed as a reaction against the Plateresque flourishes of the preceding period. As you approach from a distance, the complex looks more like a fortress—some say a prison—than a palace, with its rows of windows overshadowed by the somber gray walls. Of the four elements the king desired, severity seems to have won out.

Philip was so satisfied with the buildings that he spent the last 14 years of his life at El Escorial, boasting that from the foot of a mountain he ruled the world. He dwelled in relative austerity in the palace, which was attached to the monastery, housing Hieronymite monks (it is home now to Augustinians). His intention was to keep things simple, but simple here is as royalty does: Philip hired artists from Italy and northern Europe to do paintings and frescoes for the walls, amassed one of the world's great collections of rare manuscripts and books for the library, and provided the church with paintings and gold and silver vessels. Later rulers carried the decoration and enlargement of the place even further, though fire (in 1671) and plunder (by French troops in 1808) created some havoc, both inside and outside. After the death of Ferdinand VII in 1833 most of the finest art was taken to Madrid, and in 1861 El Escorial ceased to be a royal residence altogether.

THE MONASTERY-PALACE

The first surprise in store at El Escorial is how vast the monastery-palace complex is. The second surprise may be the discovery that it doesn't exist in a vacuum in the middle of nowhere but is in the center of a flat but lively, bustling provincial town, 50 km (31 miles) northwest of Madrid on M 505, in the shadow of Mount Abantos. During your lunch break (when the palace complex shuts down), you can enjoy a leisurely meal (see below) and take a walk around a bit of the town, which developed as a resort for Madrid aristocrats during the period when the palace was used as a residence. Today, Madrileños enjoy driving here for a Sunday outing.

The complex consists of the royal apartments, the church

(built in the shape of a Greek cross), the royal pantheon (where all but three of the Spanish rulers from Charles V to the present have been buried, in 26 identical Baroque sarcophagi), the new museums, chapter houses, library, monastery, and king's courtyard. A single ticket, obtained at either the north or west entrance, admits you to all sections except the monastery and to two 18th-century royal lodges outside the grounds, the Casita del Príncipe and the Casita de Arriba. Connoisseurs of fine woodworking can purchase an extra ticket to the Habitaciones de Maderas Finas (fine woods), a small, choice suite in the Palacio Real with exquisite marquetry on furniture, doors, windows, and floors, dating from the reign of Carlos IV at the turn of the 19th century. No ticket is needed to visit the church.

Touring the Palace

As you will soon discover, all this is too much to see in a single day, except in the most superficial way. To compound the problem, you lose a little time waiting for the requisite conducted tour. This tour leads you almost in lockstep through the royal apartments, but then, mercifully, the guide pretty much leaves you on your own for the more compelling (at least to art lovers) new museums, where you can wander at your leisure. In doing so, though, keep in mind the other aforementioned treats still to be seen along the way. Even so, the new museums are a top priority.

Considering the monumental size of this gridlike complex and its formidable exterior, the interior is on a more human scale than you would expect, as royal palaces go. Some of the most pleasing rooms of the **royal apartments** are the small ones that you enter first, hung with tapestries made from cartoons by Goya, David Teniers, Francisco Bayeu (Goya's brother-in-law), and others. Especially evocative is Philip II's cell-like bedroom, which contains the litter on which he was carried on his last painful, gout-ridden journey from Madrid. This room adjoins his simple audience room, with whitewashed walls, Talavera tiling, and two 16th-century Brussels tapestries.

Much of El Escorial's extraordinary art collection was collected by Philip himself. In the series of connecting vaulted galleries called the **new museums**, followed by several subsidiary galleries, you are left to your own pace to savor Gerard David's *Descent from the Cross,* Velázquez's luminous *Joseph's Tunic,* Hieronymus Bosch's satiric *Los Improperios* (The Mocking of Christ), and works by Titian, Veronese, Tintoretto, Dürer, Van der Weyden, El Greco, and many others.

Continuing your tour, you won't want to miss Benvenuto Cellini's white marble Christ sculpture and Juan de Her-

rera's tabernacle and massive marble, jasper, and onyx
retable above the main altar in the church; the curious
pudridero (rotting place), a vault outside the royal pantheon
where the regal bodies were preserved for ten years before
being placed in the royal pantheon; the paintings by José
Ribera, Daniel Seghers, and others in the chapter houses;
and the remarkable **library**, with vaulted ceiling, marble
floor, Herrera's gracefully designed Doric bookcases, Philip
II's globe, and some 40,000 books, including Saint Teresa's
diary and prayer books belonging to Charles V, Ferdinand
and Isabella, and Philip II.

The Casitas

The **Casita del Príncipe** is nearby in the Jardines del
Príncipe, just 2 km (1¼ miles) east of the Escorial complex.
Its finest paintings have been removed to the Prado, but
you'll still be able to enjoy all the 18th-century French and
Spanish furniture, carpets, clocks, and *objets*. This miniature
palace, designed by Juan de Villanueva, was built for the
inept Carlos IV in 1772, when he was still a prince, in the
style of the Casa del Labrador at Aranjuez. Villanueva's even
more petite and slightly less ornate palace, **Casita de Arriba**,
is 2 km (1¼ miles) southwest of town on Paseo de Carlos III,
the Avila road. It was home in the early 1970s to Spain's
present-day king, Juan Carlos, when he was a prince. If you
turn left off the *paseo* at the sign for the Herrería Club de
Golf (before the *casita*), you'll come to the Silla de Felipe II,
the rock formation on which Philip II sat to watch the
construction of El Escorial. It offers a fantastic view.

DINING AND STAYING
IN EL ESCORIAL

A simple but zesty lunch, washed down with a house wine
from Cebreros, can be had at the **Café del Teatro Carlos III**,
inside the Real Coliseo, across from El Escorial on Calle
Floridablanca; Tel: (9-1) 890-3662. The food is good, but star
billing goes to the place itself, part of a skillfully restored,
beautifully decorated 18th-century royal theater built for
Carlos III. Scores of distinguished guests have visited the
theater, including Goya, Manuel de Godoy, and, most recently, Queen Sofía.

Also handy and very upscale is **Charolés**, Calle Floridablanca 24 (on the next block), a favorite with Madrileños
who come out on weekends for the grilled meats, steaks,
and *nueva cocina* specialties, such as duck breast in a
strawberry vinaigrette and pear sorbet in Champagne sauce,
served in a cozy, intimate setting; Tel: (9-1) 890-5975. An
equally compelling lunch or dinner choice is **La Cueva**,
nearby at Calle de San Antón 4. Not at all cave-like, despite

the name, the restaurant, its *taberna,* and lively *tapas* bar occupy three floors of an 18th-century house attractively outfitted with blue-and-white-tile wainscoting and exposed-beam ceilings. Grilled meats are the specialty. Tel: (9-1) 890-1516.

If you opt for spending the night in El Escorial, the ▶ **Victoria Palace Hotel,** just a short walk up the main thoroughfare, Calle Juan de Toledo, the road that leads north out of town, is the place to do it. As its name implies, this is a huge, old-fashioned establishment, comfortable but not fancy, with big rooms, wide porches, terraces, gardens, ample grounds, a swimming pool, and a central location.

VALLE DE LOS CAIDOS

Before you head back to Madrid from El Escorial, or continue on to Avila or Segovia, you might wish to pay a brief visit to Valle de los Caídos (Valley of the Fallen), some 9 km (5½ miles) north of El Escorial, near the village of Guadarrama. This grandiose memorial to the Spanish Civil War casualties of both sides may be interpreted by the cynical as Francisco Franco's monument to himself and to Falangist martyr José Antonio Primo de Rivera. Unquestionably, Franco chose a glorious site, a stark and awesome mountain-ringed valley. Marking the spot is an enormous reinforced-concrete cross faced with stone. The stated intention was to erase the scars of the devastating 1936–1939 struggle, even though political prisoners were used to work on the memorial; the result, with its pompous theatricality, may have the opposite effect. Franco himself is buried behind the main altar of the Capilla del Sepulcro, and Primo de Rivera is under the cupola of the overblown, subterranean basilica. Juxtaposed with the monastery of El Escorial, Franco's monument seems almost trivial, massive though it is.

AVILA

At 3,711 feet above sea level, Avila is Spain's highest provincial capital. It is also the coldest—fair warning if you're planning a winter visit. Avila is 111 km (69 miles) northwest of Madrid on the way to Salamanca, via A 6 north and N 110 west. From El Escorial, take the twisting M 505 (63 km/39 miles) or return to A 6 by way of the Valle de los Caídos road and take A 6 to N 110 (70 km/44 miles). A particularly beautiful and varied drive, though not a day trip from Madrid, is from Toledo to Avila on N 403.

THE CITY WALLS

Avila's most memorable and significant sight, its encircling medieval walls, accentuates the city's closed-in-upon-itself austerity. Even in summer, this sense of gravity or sobriety is almost tangible, although in warm weather the walls are lighted at night, and the luminosity makes them seem less oppressive than they do in daylight. The best view of the walls is from a *mirador* (scenic lookout) at **Los Cuatro Postes**, just north of Avila on the road to Salamanca (N 501). You can pause for a drink and the vista at **Hotel Cuatro Postes**.

The walls are unusual in Europe for their completeness and are the oldest and best-preserved circumferential walls in Spain. Ten feet thick and an average of 33 feet high, they make a bold, dramatic statement from any direction. Depending on the time of day and amount of sunlight, they can reflect gold, gray, lavender, or deep purple. From the rear garden of the Parador Raimundo de Borgoña (described further below), just inside the north walls, you can climb the walls for views of the city and the rolling countryside. (It's the *only* place you can gain entry to walk around on the walls.) "Parador" signs will lead you through a gate right to it.

Avila's walls would be a remarkable engineering feat in any era. In 1088, when Count Raymond of Burgundy, son-in-law of the ruler Alfonso VI, undertook construction, the project must have seemed nearly impossible. It took three years to encircle the city. Completed with 88 cylindrical towers and bastions and nine gateways into town, the walls gave Avila, well situated as it was on a wide ridge that slopes west to the Río Adaja, a commanding view of the approach to the pass between the Sierra de Gredos and Sierra de Guadarrama and the junction of two major roads. Small wonder that from the time the walls were completed, the city remained a Christian stronghold, successfully keeping the Moors at bay. Later, in the 12th century, the crenellated apse of the transitional Romanesque-Gothic cathedral was incorporated into the walls.

SEEING AVILA

Inside the walls, Avila is a medieval hill town of narrow, cobbled streets and passageways, difficult for driving but very walkable (if you don't mind steep inclines). The major sights are mostly centered in the north, south, and east, hugging the walls inside or sprawled a few blocks outside. For the sights inside the walls, a car is a hindrance, but outside the walls parking is easier, and you can make faster time driving from sight to sight. We cover first the life of Saint Teresa of Avila and the many sights associated with her, both inside and outside the walls. We then tour some fine churches outside the walls and finally the sights within the walls.

SAINT TERESA OF AVILA

Avila, or Avila de los Caballeros, to state its full, if rarely used, name, is a city of churches. Its focused asceticism has long been attributed to a remarkable woman known as Santa Teresa de Jesús or Saint Teresa of Avila, one of the great mystics of the Catholic Church. To get the most out of a visit to Avila, you'll want to follow Teresa's trail throughout the city, both inside and outside the walls. A map provided at the tourist information office, on the Plaza de la Catedral, across from the cathedral, will help you pinpoint the sights.

The daughter of an affluent Avila family, Teresa Sánchez de Cepeda y Ahumanda became a Carmelite nun at age 18, in 1534, a time of turmoil in Europe. The new Reformation was gaining ground and the Catholic Church was increasingly criticized for the laxity and softness of its monastic orders. Teresa was in her forties before she found her mission in life, reforming a religious order that had grown rich with time but lazy and dissolute. She managed to convert many nuns to a back-to-basics Spartan life in a new order called the Descalzas Carmelitas (Barefoot Carmelites). She personally founded 17 convents, preached throughout Spain, and wrote extensively. Somerset Maugham called her autobiography one of the greatest ever written. Her letters to her spiritual advisor, Saint John of the Cross, himself a poet of stature who also lived in Avila, became famous. (Unlike Teresa, he left few traces—except for his writings.)

Teresa's life in her native city is well documented, and the traveller can visit many places associated with her: the Baroque **Convento de Santa Teresa**, built on the site of her family home near the Puerta de Santa Teresa, in the south of the city just inside the walls; the **Iglesia de San Juan**, on the Plaza de la Victoria (two blocks northeast), where she was baptized (and which contains the tomb of Sancho Dávila, Philip II's brilliant commander); the **Convento de Nuestra Señora de Gracia**, just outside the southeastern wall (exit through Puerta del Alcázar and make a sharp right), where she was educated; the **Convento de la Encarnación**, just north of town (follow Calle de la Encarnación, off Avenida de Madrid), where she lived her first 20 years as a nun, before beginning her reforms, and which maintains a kitchen and typical nuns' cells as they were during her stay (there's a great view of the walls from the convent's wide plaza); and the **Convento de San José**, four blocks northeast of the Puerta del Alcázar, the first convent she founded (1562) and now a small museum with her artifacts, relics, and a replica of her nun's cell.

OUTSIDE THE WALLS

For fanciers of Romanesque art and architecture, Avila is a diminutive feast. If you have time for just one Romanesque church, it should be the **Basílica de San Vicente**, in the northeastern corner of town, diagonally across from the Puerta de San Vicente, one of Avila's oldest gates and a main entrance point to the city. The church was founded in 1307 on the site where Saint Vincent and his sisters, Cristeta and Sabina, were martyred around 304. The saint's ornately carved Romanesque sarcophagus (ca. 1180) has graphic renderings of the three martyrs stretched on the rack, their skulls being crushed by boulders. The Gothic canopy over the sarcophagus was a later (1465) addition. The church's style evolved from 12th-century Romanesque to 14th-century Gothic before it was finished. The most notable elements are the well-carved southern portico and a western façade with a double doorway bordered by sculpted Romanesque figures.

Avila's other Romanesque churches are all outside the walls, forming a wide arc north to south on the east side of town. Most are not open unless a service is in progress. **San Andrés**, just north of San Vicente, has a 12th-century apse and fine southern and western doorways. Going clockwise to the Puerta del Alcázar, the southeastern gate to the city, you'll find the **Iglesia de San Pedro**, facing the vast, spacious Plaza de Santa Teresa, on which autos-da-fé were once held. San Pedro is an 11th- to 13th-century gem with a lovely rose window, a Romanesque apse, and a 16th-century retable. The **Iglesia de Santiago**, southwest of San Pedro, and the **Iglesia de San Nicolás**, farther southwest still, near the road to Toledo (N 403), a few blocks south of the Puerta de Rastro, are both restored but still appealing.

Circling the city to its northwestern corner brings you to one more Romanesque church, the **Ermita de San Segundo**, sitting just below the ramparts. Although much of its Romanesque interior was altered in the 16th century, it still has finely carved capitals in the apse. The statue on the tomb of Segundo, Avila's first bishop, who achieved fame by tossing a Moorish chief from the walls above the church, was carved by Juan de Juni in 1572.

One other church outside the walls is worth a visit. Drive southeast of the Plaza de Santa Teresa along Avenida del Alférez Provisional to the Gothic **Real Monasterio de Santo Tomás** (built 1482–1493), which Ferdinand and Isabella founded. In front of the main altar their only son, Prince Juan, who died at age 19, is buried inside an imposing white marble tomb. The tomb of another famous (or infamous) personage buried here is no longer in the convent: Grand Inquisitor Tomás de Torquemada was buried in the chapter room, but 19th-century revolutionaries destroyed his tomb.

Torquemada reportedly condemned some 8,000 Castilians to death from 1485 to 1498. A simple slab now marks his burial site in the sacristy. The convent also contains a masterly retable by Pedro Berruguete depicting the life of Saint Thomas Aquinas; three richly decorated Gothic cloisters; the royal quarters where the Reyes Católicos stayed on their frequent visits; and a modest display of Asian art collected by the missionary monks.

INSIDE THE WALLS

Return to the Puerta de San Vicente to enter the walled city. Once inside, an immediate left turn will lead you along Calle del Tostado ("the Swarthy," named for Alfonso de Madrigal, a 15th-century bishop) to the **cathedral**, attached to the eastern wall. The cathedral's interior, far more graceful than its formidable fortresslike exterior suggests, contains many treasures. Especially notable are the three-tiered main altar retable depicting events in Christ's life painted by Pedro Berruguete (court painter to Ferdinand and Isabella), Juan de Borgoña (his successor), and Santos Cruz; a silver monstrance made in 1571 by Juan de Arfe, a Renaissance artisan, in the sacristy; the well-carved *sillería* (choir stalls) by the Dutchman Cornelis; a painting of San Andrés by Ribera; many fine Gothic paintings in the sacristy; and Romanesque and Gothic sculptures throughout the church.

Having seen the sights, you might spend some time strolling the hilly side streets of Avila, enjoying the façades of some of the 15th- and 16th-century Renaissance palaces. A number of them, notably the palace of the Dávilas and the mansions of the Polentinos, Superunda, Almarza, and Núñez Vela families, are snuggled close to the south walls, near the convent of Saint Teresa. You might pause in your walk at **La Flor Valenciana**, a *turronería* and *heladería* just south of the cathedral at the corner of Plaza de Calvo Sotelo and Calle Cruz Vieja, for ice cream or a sweet. For craft shopping try **Barros**, Calle San Segundo 19, north of Plaza de Santa Teresa.

STAYING AND DINING IN AVILA

On the Plaza de la Catedral, at number 9, is a four-star hotel built inside a 15th-century bishop's palace, the ▶ **Palacio Valderrábanos**. Decorated with Spanish provincial furnishings and handicrafts, the hotel has all the desired modern accoutrements, and its location across from the cathedral is very convenient. Its spacious lounges with comfortable couches are great for mid-afternoon tea or drinks.

Another good overnight choice is the ▶ **Parador Raimundo de Borgoña**, a modernized, somewhat enclosed version of a 15th-century palace in the northern part of town with a garden that gives onto the walls.

As befits a place devoted to spiritual matters, you might expect Avila to lay no special claim to the pleasures of the table. That was once true, but recently things have improved. Just east of the Plaza de Santa Teresa, outside the east walls, is **Copacabana** (Calle San Millán 9), whose specialties are *pimientos rellenos* (stuffed peppers) and a dish made with the famous Avila white beans, *judías del Barco con chorizo*. Tel: (9-20) 21-31-15. **El Fogón de Santa Teresa**, in the Palacio Valderrábanos, also serves local dishes in pleasant surroundings, at somewhat higher prices. Tel: (9-20) 21-10-23. Also convenient, if a bit mundane, is the dining room of the Parador Raimundo de Borgoña, which emphasizes regional dishes. This is a good place to try the local sweet, *yemas de Santa Teresa,* made with lots of egg yolks. For a lively *tapas* scene, drop by **Piquio**, at Estrada 4, just north of Plaza de Santa Teresa; Tel: (9-20) 21-14-18.

The current "in" dining spot for locals is **El Molino de la Losa**, set in a charming, rusticated 15th-century mill on the Río Adaja that faces the hermitage of San Segundo across the river. It's especially nice in warm weather, when you can dine outside. The *sepia al ali-oli* (cuttlefish with garlic mayonnaise) and roasted meat dishes are strong suits. At Bajada de la Losa 12, it's rather hard to find; take the first right off Puente de Ajada on the Carretera de Salamanca. Tel: (9-20) 21-11-01. Just before the turn onto the side road to El Molino is **El Almacén** (Carretera de Salamanca 6), another newish restaurant that also serves good food, along with wide-angle views of San Segundo and the city walls. Tel: (9-20) 25-44-55.

Don't look to Avila for the sparkling café life of Andalusia, though it has its moments. This is, after all, a Castilian town, and an unusually reserved one at that. Experience it for what it is: a chance to step back, at least in atmosphere, to the spirit of the Middle Ages.

EXCURSIONS FROM AVILA

If you are driving to Segovia or Valladolid and have time for a diversion, consider **Arévalo** (about 32 km/20 miles due north of Avila), a tiny town with a number of Romanesque churches and a large, cobbled Plaza Mayor lined on three sides with unusual arcades of wood (and some stone) columns supporting medieval timbered houses. West from Arevalo on C 605 is **Madrigal de las Altas Torres**, another minute-size town, whose **Convento de las Agustinas** contains the remains of the royal palace where Isabella la Católica was born. The convent is cloistered, but if you ring the bell, a nun will conduct you on a tour (in Spanish) of the lovely cloister, refectory, and many beautifully restored palace rooms with handsome furnishings and paintings. In the **Iglesia de San Nicolás de Bari**, on the main plaza (Plaza del

Generalísimo), you'll see the large stone font where Isabella was baptized, a fine *artesonado* (wooden-coffered) ceiling, Romanesque sculptures, and other artifacts.

SEGOVIA

The 88-km (55-mile) drive from Madrid along A 6 and N 603 northwest through the Sierra de Guadarrama to Segovia is a beauty, passing through hunting and fishing country, with grand vistas on both sides of the road and an ever-escalating landscape dotted with pines and brilliant yellow gorse. From Avila the drive northeast along N 110 is 66 km (41 miles).

Like other Castilian hill towns, Segovia surprises the first-time viewer with its dramatic profile of golden buildings with red-tile roofs, roosting on a rocky spur some 3,250 feet high, with two little rivers, the Eresma and the Clamores, forming a necklace, or natural moat, around the base. The land is shaped like a ship, with the stern on the east and the prow, where the *alcázar* commands the view, facing west, with deep valleys on either side. Unlike most towns its size (about 50,000 inhabitants), Segovia doesn't have just one major attraction—it has three, each part of the stunning Segovia skyline and each a testament to a different period in the city's history.

THE ROMAN AQUEDUCT

Most spectacular of Segovia's attractions is the **Acueducto Romano**, whose 165 gray-granite arches extend almost half a mile southeast from the city, marching like rows of massive stone soldiers between two hills. In the **Plaza del Azoguejo**, where the major roads enter the city, in the lower, eastern, part of town, the arches rise to just 96 feet, but elsewhere, depending on the contours of the land, they are as high as 422 feet. All the massive cut stones were carefully fitted together without cement and lifted into place by huge pincers (you can still see the slots in the stones where the pincers gripped).

The Romans came to this area on the northern side of the Sierra de Guadarrama in 80 B.C. and renamed the small existing Iberian village Segobriga, but it wasn't until Trajan's reign (first and second centuries A.D.) that the aqueduct was built. Considered the finest Roman structure extant in Spain, this masterpiece of engineering was used steadily, *más o menos,* until a few decades ago. Despite the rush of religiosity in 1520 that substituted statues of the Madonna and Saint Sebastian for Hercules in the highest niches, the aqueduct remains nearly unchanged. It is almost surreal in the timeless way it dominates the landscape.

SEEING THE OLD TOWN

Walking is really the *only* way to savor Segovia (this applies to the old part of every Castilian city). If you arrive by car, the natural place to park is around the **Plaza del Azoguejo**. (A convenient parking spot in the upper town is at the Plaza de la Merced, west of the cathedral. Follow Calle San Juan, a sharp right turn uphill off Carretera de Bocequillas—the main highway outside of town—just before the aqueduct.) From there you can stroll about town, noting especially evidence of the Moors, who inhabited Segovia from the eighth to the eleventh century and left many traces here in doors, gates, archways, foundations, and façades decorated with Mudejar designs.

Walk up Calle de Cervantes from the Plaza del Azoguejo past the **Casa de los Picos**, a 14th-century mansion whose unusual façade is armored with protruding pointed stones (*picos*), to Calle Juan Bravo, the main street, facing the Plaza de San Juan. Dominating the plaza is the bronze statue of Juan Bravo, a local hero who led the revolt of the *comuneros* against Charles V in 1519–1520, and the old 16th-century Lozoya tower with its fine Renaissance galleries. Just beyond, to the west on Calle Juan Bravo, is the 12th-century Romanesque **Iglesia de San Martín**, with sculpture-ornamented porticos and an eclectic interior, one of numerous Romanesque churches in town, all of which are much restored. You may note a Moorish legacy in this area in the pastel (pink, lemon, avocado, and pale blue) buildings with decorative designs incised into their façades. This incision work is a Segovia signature.

THE CATHEDRAL

From the rear of San Martín, Calle de Infanta Isabella, lined with pastry shops and bars, leads to the Plaza Mayor, a big, bustling square (with the tourist office located at the southeastern corner), full of sidewalk cafés and small hotels, facing the cathedral, the highest point in town and the second of the city's great treasures.

Segovia's cathedral, completed in 1590, was the last Gothic cathedral built in Spain. It was the work of Juan Gil de Hontañón and his son Rodrigo, who followed up the success of their Catedral Nueva in Salamanca (see the Old Castile chapter) by repeating a similar design here, using the stellar vaulting learned in Germany and beautiful golden stones that give the exterior a tawny glow. Although it lacks the treasures of some Spanish cathedrals, its wide aisles and richly detailed vaulting give Segovia's cathedral a sense of space and elegance. Look particularly for the 16th-century Flemish stained glass by Pierre de Chiberry, the 1571 retable by Juan de Juni in the **Capilla de la Piedad**, and the graceful 15th-century Gothic

cloister transported from an earlier, demolished cathedral. In the **sala capitular** (chapter house) are 17th-century Flemish tapestries from Rubens's cartoons and an *artesonado* ceiling.

AROUND THE CATHEDRAL

There are several 12th- and 13th-century Romanesque churches clustered near each other northeast of the cathedral: the **Iglesia de San Esteban**, on Plaza de San Esteban, has a five-story, galleried Romanesque tower; the **Iglesia de San Quirce**, just east on Calle San Quirce, has a rich portal, though the church is now a university building; and the **Iglesia de la Trinidad**, also nearby on Calle Trinidad, has an ungainly, squat tower but pure Romanesque columns and capitals on its porch, and well-preserved, sculpted capitals with many fine details inside.

THE ALCAZAR

Segovia's third major sight is the *alcázar,* perched on the western edge of the old town, dominating its hilltop as a well-planned fortress-castle should. Turrets, towers, and slate roofs crown the golden-hued stone walls: It is a fortress straight out of the *Arabian Nights.* The *alcázar* is so perfect, so much a fairy-tale castle, that it comes as a surprise to discover that it isn't what it seems. The *alcázar's* origins are obscure; the roots may have been Roman, but it later became a fortified Moorish palace. (The word *alcázar* is Arabic for fortress, castle, or royal palace.) By the mid-14th century, when the Christians got around to building their own fortress, there weren't many Moorish elements left here, only the foundation, parts of some walls, and the name—all of which they co-opted, adding Gothic elements and Muslim-style decorations. Extensive additions were made in the first half of the 15th century by Catherine of Lancaster and her son, Juan II. Isabella was crowned queen here in 1474. England's Charles I, as a prince, dined here in 1623 on "certain trouts of extraordinary greatness." A fire gutted the building in 1862 (when it was being used as an artillery school), and the 1882 rebuilding added the present Romantic arabesques and turrets.

If you climb the 162 steps of the circular staircase inside the building to the top of the crenellated Mudejar-style tower, your reward will be some spectacular views of the city, the *meseta* (plateau), and the verdant valley along the twists of both the Eresma and Clamores rivers. Inside, you'll want to see the **royal chapel**, with a fine wooden Moorish-influenced ceiling inlaid with stars, and the **hall of armor**, with much medieval weaponry.

OUTSIDE THE WALLS

It is a ten-minute hike (or drive) downhill from the *alcázar*, across the Río Eresma, and just west of town to **La Vera Cruz**, a tiny 13th-century Romanesque chapel. This 12-sided building with three apses was built of tawny limestone by the Knights Templar. If you climb the 52 steps up the tower, you'll have thrilling upward views of the *alcázar* and of Segovia's profile.

Just east of La Vera Cruz, north of the city, off the *ronda* (the circular road around Segovia), is the 15th-century **Monasterio del Parral**. Once a mammoth monastery, now a still-splendid but deteriorating home to a mere ten monks, it harbors many treasures: a Flamboyant Gothic portal at the entrance, 15th-century stained-glass windows in the apse, Gothic and Plateresque tombs, and a fine 16th-century retable by Juan Rodríguez. In the tranquil garden there is a grand view across the river of the *alcázar*—this is a good place from which to photograph it without getting the telephone wires that spoil so many pictures.

If you have time, return to the lower part of Segovia, southwest of the Plaza de Azoguejo by way of Avenida Fernández Ladreda, to see the tenth-century **Iglesia de San Millán**. Though much restored, San Millán is a visual delight, with its triple apse, exterior arcades, and carved capitals.

DINING, STAYING, AND SHOPPING IN SEGOVIA

The most famous restaurant in Segovia is **Mesón de Cándido**, Plaza del Azoguejo 5, in the shadow of the aqueduct in a three-story 15th-century building. Although atmospheric, with smoked hams hanging overhead, fireplaces, and many cheerful whitewashed rooms with exposed beams, the place is so crammed with tourists that service can be hurried and even rude on occasion. If you decide to brave the crowds, noise, and erratic service, the roast suckling pig and lamb are satisfying, washed down with a sturdy red house wine from La Mancha. Try the Segovian dessert *tarta de ponche,* a marzipan, rum, and egg-yolk concoction. Tel: (9-21) 42-59-11.

More ingratiating, and just as colorful, is **Duque**, Calle de Cervantes 12, just up the hill from the aqueduct, whose *asados* (roast pork, lamb, and chicken) are very tasty indeed. As a grand finale you'll be offered a huge (ten inches in diameter) brandy snifter with the house escutcheon on it. The waiter warms it with hot water, empties it, then fills it with brandy sufficient for twice the number at your table. Tel: (9-21) 43-05-37.

Another agreeable spot is **Mesón José María** (Cronista Lecea 11, just north of the Plaza Mayor), a good place to try *judiones del Real Sitio* (the huge white beans of La Granja with *chorizo*). The bar in front of the dining room is the liveliest *tapas* scene in town, with many agreeable choices. Tel: (9-21) 43-44-84.

If you're surfeited with folklore, the restrained, modern dining room in the ▶ **Parador de Segovia**, 3 km (2 miles) northeast of town, on the *carretera* (highway) to Valladolid (N 601), is also appealing. The succulent *cochinillo asado* almost measures up to the exhilarating views of the city across the river. This is one of the most up-to-date paradores in the country, furnished in contemporary style, with modern Spanish paintings on the walls. All the rooms have balconies and stunning city views, and there are heated swimming pools indoors and outdoors.

Right in town is ▶ **Hotel Las Sirenas**, on Calle Juan Bravo, with compact but nicely appointed guest rooms and an attractive lobby. (Ask for a room facing the rear.)

Shoppers might look in at El Pajaro Azul, at Calle Herrería 22, a short street across from the entrance to San Martín. This small shop has many sophisticated gift items, wooden stand-up puzzles in the shape of Groucho Marx and Charlie Chaplin, adult toys, unusual ceramics, and leather bags. **Paradiso**, at Plaza de la Merced 1 (the corner of Calle de Marqués del Arco), specializes in ethnic art, such as African and other naïve sculpture. In **Artesania**, a small shop at the Convento de Santo Domingo, at Calle Capuchinas Altos 2, you'll find Baroque-style religious plaques and replicas of *santos*.

AROUND SEGOVIA
Northwest of Segovia

Two small towns to the northwest of Segovia can be the destination of a leisurely day trip. Some 35 km (22 miles) northwest of the city on C 605 is the town of **Santa María la Real de Nieva**. Stop to visit its church of Santa María la Real, founded by Catherine of Lancaster in 1393, which has a lovely Gothic cloister. Sixteen kilometers (10 miles) farther, along SG 341, is **Coca**, reached through an imposing medieval town gate called Arco de la Villa. The presumed birthplace of Roman emperor Theodosius, Coca has a 15th-century castle that epitomizes the proverbial Spanish castle. Adorned with battlements, turrets, and polygonal watchtowers and surrounded by a dry moat, it was built by the powerful Fonseca family (the dukes of Alba) and is considered Spain's finest example of Mudejar military construction. It has been restored and is now used as a vocational training school, but is open to visitors; don't miss the

Romanesque wood carvings in the chapel. Coca's church of Santa María has an unusual 14-sided sanctuary and four 16th-century Fonseca family tombs.

South of Segovia

RIOFRÍO
A quick and enjoyable day trip can be made to Riofrío (which means "cold river"), just 11 km (7 miles) south of Segovia via N 110, the least known of the many *real sitios* (royal seats) near Madrid. This one has an opulent Italianate palace built in 1752 for King Philip V's Italian-born wife, Isabel Farnese, with a small hunting museum within. For years it served as a royal hunting lodge, though a less rustic one than most—with a classical courtyard and staircase, luxurious furnishings and tapestries, and paintings by Goya, Velázquez, and others illustrating the history of the hunt. It is fitting that you'll probably encounter deer on the wooded grounds.

LA GRANJA DE SAN ILDEFONSO
On your way back to Madrid or as a day trip from Segovia you can take in La Granja de San Ildefonso (the farm of San Ildefonso), usually called just La Granja, about 11 km (7 miles) southeast of Segovia on N 601. More of a *petit palais* than the farm Philip V dubbed it, La Granja must have reminded the king of his French roots. A sweeping carriageway lined with chestnut trees leads to a French-style palace (which 19th-century English traveller Richard Ford called "a theatrical French château, the antithesis of the proud, gloomy Escorial, on which it turns its back") and formal French gardens. La Granja's furnishings are sparse because of a disastrous fire in 1918 that gutted most of the royal apartments, but the splendid tapestry collection, which includes examples brought from Brussels by Emperor Charles V and others made from Goya cartoons, remains.

What truly distinguishes La Granja, however, are its tiered fountains, some 26 of them, spouting from various levels along floral walkways, designed in an elaborate plan similar to that at Versailles. The water isn't always running, but three times a year (May 30, July 25, and August 25) there's a maximum flow, and the resulting cascades, sprays, spurts, spirals, and waterfalls are a sight to behold. The village of La Granja itself is a quiet, understated summer resort in which Ernest Hemingway set some of the action in *For Whom the Bell Tolls*.

For a small place, La Granja has had more than its share of historic events, having been the site where Philip V abdicated in January 1724 (only to return the following August) and where Queen María Luisa's inept advisor, Manuel de Godoy, signed the treaty in 1795 that effectively put Spain into France's pocket, thus opening the door to the Napoleonic invasion. A perhaps even more dramatic event occurred here in 1836 when another hapless Bourbon, Queen Regent Cristina, deferred to mutinous soldiers and agreed to restore the 1812 constitution.

RASCAFRIA

Farther afield, tucked into the curves of the Navacerrada mountains between Segovia and Madrid, off C 604, is Rascafría. From La Granja, Rascafría is a 40-km (25-mile) drive south on N 601 and northeast on M 604. Rascafría's claim to fame is the **Monasterio de El Paular**, a Carthusian monastery established in 1390. The monks were expelled in 1836 and their buildings confiscated by the government in a burst of anticlericalism. In 1954 Benedictines were invited to take over the property, and since then a comfortable détente has existed between church and state. (There is a small irony in the fact that filmmaker Luis Buñuel once spent a peaceful month here writing his virulently anticlerical movie *Viridiána*.)

The government has built a modern hotel within the monastery, but the few monks still in residence go about their business making and selling their Pau Gor cheese (in a shop next to the church), cultivating their trout ponds, and giving tours of **San Bruno**, a tiny church on the grounds that is a *fantasía* of Flamboyant Gothic, exalted Baroque, and a dash of the Churrigueresque (with a restful Gothic courtyard). Like a small bandbox, it contains some lovely things: a lavish 15th-century Gothic retable with Last Supper and Resurrection scenes; a *reja* (grille) by Juan Francés dating to 1500, as delicate and intricate as embroidery; and the exuberant Baroque Chapel of the Tabernacle created in 1719–1724 by Francisco Hurtado.

Lunch or dinner in the monastery's restaurants, **Mesón Trasta María** (open only on weekends), which overlooks a cobblestone patio, or **Dom Lope** (open every day), can be a delight. Choose the hearty *cocido* and grilled sea bream—or trout from the pond on the grounds—and, for dessert, almond ring filled with a creamy custard. A solid wine list, strong in Riojas, features several well-priced house brands. Tel: (9-1) 869-1011. The government-owned ▶ **Hostal Santa María de El Paular**, installed in the monastery structure, is thoroughly modern, with tennis, a heated pool, an equestrian center, winter sports facilities—and mountain views.

To return to Madrid (about 80 km/50 miles) from Rascafría, take M 604 back to N 601, and N 601 south to A 6.

Northeast of Segovia

PEDRAZA DE LA SIERRA

A favorite day trip for Madrileños, who love any excursion that combines a small bit of sightseeing with a larger helping of lunch, is Pedraza de la Sierra, 125 km (78 miles) north of the city via superfast E 5 and N 110. One of the most pristine medieval hill towns in Castile, a designated treasure town preserved "as is," Pedraza is also a pleasant trip from Segovia, which is about 35 km (22 miles) to its southwest via N 110.

Your first view of Pedraza is of the castle guarding the hilltop, seemingly welded to solid rock. The buildings inside the town gate, beige stone with red-tile rooftops, are typically Castilian. It is best to park near the gate and then wander on foot through the twisting medieval lanes, most of which eventually end up in the **Plaza Mayor**. This is one of Castile's most charming main squares, ringed with arcaded stone and wood buildings, many with heraldic crests. Since the days when the painter Ignacio Zuloaga (1870–1945) had a studio in the castle (which once held as prisoners the sons of France's Renaissance king Francis I), Pedraza has become something of an artists' colony, and part of the fun of a visit is in stopping by the various pottery workshops and studios.

Dining, Staying, and Shopping in Pedraza

Aside from its feudal countenance and harmonious architecture, the town's main draw is its restaurants, with signs proclaiming *hornos de asar* (roasting ovens) to tempt you inside for traditional Castilian dishes, especially *cordero asado* and *cochinillo asado*. One of the best places to lunch is **El Yantar de Pedraza**, whose windows overlook the Plaza Mayor. This cozy restaurant features some of the best Castilian food in town; Tel: (9-21) 50-98-42. Roast lamb is the specialty at **Hostería Pintor Zuloaga**, Calle Matadero 1, a government-run hilltop building, the former Casa de la Inquisición, with a toasty fireplace on chilly days and sweeping views of the valley below; Tel: (9-21) 50-98-35.

La Olma, at Plaza del Ganado 1, a block from the Plaza Mayor, is a brand-new, delightful country-style restaurant inside an old house, with beamed ceilings, fireplace, and terra-cotta tile floors, where you can dine on the expected *cordero asado*. Tel: (9-21) 50-99-81. Also new to Pedraza is a comfortable place to overnight, the small, cheerful, flower-accented ▶ **La Posada de Don Mariano**, which has the charm and handcrafted accoutrements of a miniature parador.

A few steps down the street from the Hostería Zuloaga is **De Natura**, one of the most attractive shops in Castile, with three floors in an ample country house filled with handmade accessories you may find nowhere else in Spain: baskets, mirrors, glassware, candles, and pottery, as well as sophisticated country furniture. Next door is **Muebles Artesanos**, a shop selling rustic furniture and antiques.

SEPULVEDA

Some 21 km (13 miles) north of Pedraza on SG 233 is Sepúlveda, another Castilian hill town, still relatively unspoiled. It boasts several Romanesque churches: San Bartolomé; San Justo, with 12th-century crypt carvings and a Mudejar *artesonado* ceiling; and, best of all, San Salvador, with a galleried portico, a belfry, and a lateral door dating to 1093.

ALCALA DE HENARES

Just 31 km (20 miles) east of Madrid on N II/E 90, heading into the northeastern part of Castilla–La Mancha, is the lively once-and-future university city of Alcalá, on the north bank of the Río Henares. In many ways the town is more interesting for what it *was* than what it is. (Note that most of Alcalá's public monuments are closed Mondays.)

It was, for three centuries, the intellectual heart of Spain, until the university was moved to Madrid and became the University of Madrid. Queen Isabella's confessor and later regent of Spain, the ambitious Cardinal Francisco Jiménez de Cisneros, founded the university in 1508, dedicating it to humanistic studies. The Complutensian Polyglot Bible, a masterwork in Hebrew, Greek, Chaldean, and Latin, was produced here in the early years of the 16th century. Don Juan of Austria studied here and, during Spain's Golden Age, playwright Lope de Vega and many poets were in residence for a time, as were assorted philosophers, humanists, scholars, and, in the university's heyday, 10,000 students.

Miguel de Cervantes Saavedra was born in Alcalá in 1547, and his bronze statue, bearing sword and pen, dominates the tree-sheltered **Plaza de Cervantes**, the central square of the old quarter. Catherine of Aragón, Ferdinand and Isabella's daughter and the first wife of England's Henry VIII, was also born in Alcalá, but no traces of her time here remain.

Alcalá is once again a university town, with its own branch of the University of Madrid, though now it is also a bustling industrial center. The tree-shaded streets in the old university area are usually crowded with students. The most imposing of the many fine old buildings centered in this area is the **Colegio Mayor de San Ildefonso**, facing the pretty little Plaza de San Diego (just east of the Plaza de Cervantes, down Calle Bustamante), with its statue of the all-powerful Cisneros modestly garbed as a friar. The major building of the old university, the *colegio* was begun in 1498 by Pedro Gumiel and augmented in 1543–1583 by Rodrigo Gil de Hontañón. Extensive bombing during the Spanish Civil War wreaked havoc on it, as on many of Alcalá's finest architectural treasures, but much of the building has been restored. A beautiful Plateresque façade embroidered with stone *cisnes* (swans, Cisneros's emblem) opens onto a series of splendid patios, each unfolding episodically like a picaresque novel. First and most spectacular is the three-story Renaissance Patio Mayor, bordered by 96 Neoclassical columns. All four sides of the stone well in the center bear a swan in bas-relief. From the third patio, El Trilingüe (Three Languages)—in whose surrounding rooms were the schools of Greek, Hebrew, and Latin—you enter the Paraninfo (Great Hall), now being restored, with delicate Plateresque galleries and a colorful red, blue, and gold *artesonado* ceiling decorated with six-pointed stars.

El Trilingüe also leads into the bar of **Hostería Nacional del Estudiante**, located in the old college of Saint Jerome. Now rusticated and decorated with vintage Castilian furniture, it is the best lunch stop in town (try the cream of asparagus and clam soup, the *pisto manchego,* a dish similar to ratatouille, or the *cochinillo asado*). The restaurant's main entrance is at Calle de Colegios 3; Tel: (9-1) 888-0330.

SOUTH OF MADRID
Aranjuez

Foreigners visit Aranjuez (Ah-rahn-HWAYTH), just 46 km (29 miles) south of Madrid on superhighway N IV down into La Mancha, any time of year, but to Spaniards the best times to go are late spring, when the prized white asparagus (*espárrago*) is in season, and midsummer, for the tiny wild strawberries (*fresas*) that are sold with cream at roadside stands on the way. (Toledo is only about 44 km/27 miles southwest of Aranjuez; see the La Mancha chapter.)

Aranjuez's proximity to Madrid and its oasislike greenness, a rarity on the Castilian plains, make it seem like nirvana in summer to sweltering Madrileños. But when Spaniards think of Aranjuez, their thoughts may turn to March 1808, the time of the infamous Motín (revolt) de Aranjuez. The less-than-regal family of Carlos IV and María Luisa (captured so well in Goya's purse-lipped portraits) were in the summer palace, planning their escape to America, a decision that had been made on the advice of the foolish and venal Godoy (Goya got him right, too). The people, angered at Godoy's "neutrality," which gave the French army free passage to Portugal through Spain, attacked Godoy's palace. Carlos panicked and abdicated in favor of his son, Ferdinand VII, for all the good it did; Napoleon soon named his own brother, Joseph, king of Spain.

TRENA DE LA FRESA

It was Queen Isabella II, ever the hedonist, who began the custom of the Trena de la Fresa (Strawberry Train) in 1851, leaving sweltering Madrid for a weekend of cool river breezes and emerald greenness at the royal seat in Aranjuez. Other Madrileños followed suit, and the Trena de la Fresa soon became a regular summer happening. The custom has recently been revived, with a special excursion train, complete with attendants in Victorian costumes serving baskets of berries en route, making the 75-minute trip every Saturday, Sunday, and holiday from late spring through early fall, excluding August (see Getting Around, below).

THE ROYAL PALACE

Although the town was the site of a summer residence in Ferdinand and Isabella's day and was a shooting preserve for Charles V, it was Philip II who ordered the architects of his monastery-palace, El Escorial, to create a true palace here. Two catastrophic fires, in 1660 and in 1665, led to an 18th-century reconstruction of the palace by Philip V, grandson of France's Louis XIV, and later reconstructions by subsequent Bourbon kings, in what became something of an exercise in nostalgia for the glories of France.

The location of the palace couldn't be better, at the confluence of the Jarama and Tajo rivers. The gardens, following the Tajo's serpentine twists and bends, are the primary reason for a visit to Aranjuez. They are at their best in spring and summer, still providing a cool escape from Madrid's heat. Off-season, especially in winter, the flat chessboard of a town seems lifeless, and the palace and grounds are bleak.

The **Palacio Real** is a sumptuous if rather sterile showcase of 18th- and 19th-century opulence, left much as it was at the end of the last century, with a plethora of Brussels tapestries, porcelains, mirrors, the ornate bed of Isabella II, and gifts from other monarchs to the Bourbons. One wing, the central section, and the first floor are open to view. In addition, you can stroll the many walks and avenues of the parterre, the formal French garden, with its heroic statuary, magnolia trees, boxwood hedges, and ornamental fountains along the willow-shaded Río Tajo (the mouth of which is at Lisbon). In the romantic Jardín de la Isla, across from the Cascade of the Castanets, on the opposite side of the river from the palace, listen for the nightingales, permanent residents of Aranjuez.

THE JARDIN DEL PRINCIPE
Visitors to the Jardín del Príncipe, a 300-acre park northeast of the palace between the Tajo and Calle de la Reina, can tour the 1803–1805 **Casa del Labrador** (House of the Worker), built in the Petit Trianon style. Here Carlos IV and his entourage played farmer amid frescoed Pompeian ceilings, embroidered silk hangings, and such furnishings as a green malachite table and chair (a gift from Prince Demidoff of Russia).

DINING IN ARANJUEZ
If you want to sample the local asparagus and strawberries in season, **Casa Pablo**, Calle Almíbar 42, not far east of the palace in the tree-shaded town, is the place of choice; you may also want to try its roast suckling pig, local pheasant, and a bottle from its excellent wine cellar; Tel: (9-1) 891-1451. Facing a twist in the river, **La Rana Verde** (The Green Frog), Calle de la Reina 1, is known for its fish, game, and, of course, frog legs; Tel: (9-1) 891-3238.

Chinchón

It is possible to visit Aranjuez and Chinchón, nearby to the northeast (take N IV north to M 404 east; 20 km/12 miles), on the same one-day trip; from Chinchón it is just 52 km (32 miles) back to Madrid. The contrast between the two towns is dramatic, as you drive from the languid riverside greenery of Aranjuez over the dusty La Mancha hills and plains to Chinchón, a study in ochre and red-tiled roofs nestled against a hillside.

PARADOR DE CHINCHON
With an early start from Madrid to Aranjuez, you can arrive in Chinchón in time for a very late lunch at the handsomely restored ▶ **Parador de Chinchón**, one of the most appealing and sprightly paradores in Spain, just off the main road into town. There you can sample the local anise-scented *aguardiente* (an eau-de-vie) called Chinchón, which is distilled in the old castle atop the town, and enjoy the parador's restful garden, with its towering cypress trees and tinkling fountain. You might even have a refreshing dip in the pool. The parador also offers accommodations, if you should decide to spend the night. This old brick convent was impeccably restored in 1982, and the guest rooms are sim-

ple but delightful, with hand-painted alcoves, modern tapestries, and hangings that tie in with the building's religious heritage.

PLAZA MAYOR

There should still be plenty of time for a look at Chinchón's chief attraction, the colonnaded Plaza Mayor, the most level part of a town that spirals upward with a number of steep streets and inclines. This prettified and much restored half-oval, half-rectangular plaza is ringed with bright green wooden balconies, from which spectators watch bullfights when the plaza doubles as a bullring on summer weekends. If the plaza looks familiar, it probably is: It has been used as a location in many movies. On the balcony of **Mesón de la Virreina**, right on the plaza at number 28, you can dine on *perdiz escabechada* (marinated partridge), *judías con chorizo* (beans with sausage), and other Castilian and Manchego specialties, and if there's a bullfight in progress you'll have a ringside seat; Tel: (9-1) 894-0015.

GETTING AROUND

The recommended way to visit the area around Madrid is by car. The roads range from good to excellent, with *autopistas* (toll superhighways) from Madrid going almost all the way to El Escorial, much of the way to Avila and Segovia (A 6), and directly to Alcalá de Henares (N II/E 90) and Aranjuez (N IV).

From Madrid there are 15 trains daily to Avila, via El Escorial, and 20 or more trains (from Atocha or Chamartín stations) and four buses (Metro Moncloa or Herranz, Paseo Moret 7) directly to El Escorial. From Madrid to Segovia there are 12 trains daily (from Atocha) and four buses (Metro Norte or La Sepúlvedana, Paseo de la Florida 11). The train station in El Escorial is just two blocks from the Casita del Príncipe and about 2 km (1¼ miles) from the monastery-palace. In Avila the station is about a ten-minute cab ride from the old town. Segovia's station, at the eastern edge of the new town, is a five- to ten-minute cab ride from the base of the aqueduct.

Buses (from Metro América, Avenida América 18) and trains (from Atocha or Chamartín) run every few minutes each day from Madrid to Alcalá de Henares, which is practically a suburb. Aranjuez is a major railroad junction, and trains from Madrid's Atocha depart for it every 15 minutes daily.

RENFE (the Spanish national railway system) offers a number of special tours by train from Madrid to outlying areas. Among them are the **Trena de la Fresa**, a daylong tour to Aranjuez on Saturdays, Sundays, and holidays, usually from late spring to early fall, excluding August; and a one-day trip to Avila called **Muralles de Avila** (Walls of Avila), Sundays only. Information is available from RENFE ticket offices or travel agents in Spain.

ACCOMMODATIONS REFERENCE
The hotel rates listed below are projected rates for 1994, for double room, double occupancy, in pesetas. We strongly recommend that you confirm the price when making reservations.

When dialing telephone numbers in Spain from outside the country, drop the 9 in the area code.

▶ **Hostal Santa María de El Paular.** El Paular, **Rascafría,** 28741 Madrid. Tel: (9-1) 869-1011; Fax: 869-1006; in U.S., Tel: (800) 221-2340; in Canada, Tel: (800) 955-2442. 14,500–18,000 pts.

▶ **Hotel Las Sirenas.** Calle Juan Bravo 30, 40001 **Segovia.** Tel: (9-21) 43-40-11; Fax: 43-06-33. 7,500 pts.

▶ **Palacio Valderrábanos.** Plaza de la Catedral 9, 05001 **Avila.** Tel: (9-20) 21-10-23; Fax: 25-16-91; in U.S. and Canada, Tel: (800) 223-1356 or (212) 686-9215; Fax: (212) 686-0271. 13,500 pts.

▶ **Parador de Chinchón.** Avenida Generalísimo 1, **Chinchón,** 28370 Madrid. Tel: (9-1) 894-0836; Fax: 894-0908. 14,000 pts.

▶ **Parador Raimundo de Borgoña.** Marqués de Canales y Chozas 2, 05001 **Avila.** Tel: (9-20) 21-13-40; Fax: 22-61-66. 9,500–11,000 pts.

▶ **Parador de Segovia.** Carretera Valisario, Apartado de Correos 106, 40000 **Segovia.** Tel: (9-21) 44-37-37; Fax: 43-73-62. 14,500 pts.

▶ **La Posada de Don Mariano.** Calle Mayor 14, 40172 **Pedraza de la Sierra.** Tel: (9-21) 50-98-86. 11,000 pts.

▶ **Victoria Palace Hotel.** Calle Juan de Toledo 4, **San Lorenzo de El Escorial,** 28200 Madrid. Tel: (9-1) 890-1511; Fax: 890-1248. 13,750 pts.

OLD CASTILE

*By Mike Jackson and Gerry Dawes,
with Robert Levine*

*Mike Jackson, who has contributed the introduction and the
sections on Salamanca, Zamora, and León for this chapter,
is also the contributor for the subsequent chapters on Asturias and Galicia and on Cantabria.*

*Gerry Dawes, the contributor for the sections here on
Valladolid, Palencia, and Burgos, has also written the chapters on the Basque Country, Navarra, and La Rioja, and the
sections on regional wines throughout the book.*

There is no Old Castile as such. Over the centuries Castile
has existed more as a state of mind, an agglomeration of
attitudes, than as a political entity. With the ejection of the
Moors from Spain, starting in the eighth century, Castilians
began deciding who was in and who was out. For several
hundred years they were busy building all those *castillos*
(castles) to ensure the Reconquest. Once Spain was back in
Spanish hands the Castilian gentleman's elegant speech
patterns—the "Castilian" dialect, with its "*th*" sound that
makes *España* come forth as "Eth-pan-ya" or *castillos* as
"cath-tee-yooth"—began to emerge as proper Spanish, sepa-
rating the elite from commoners. This speech technique is
practiced, even after 400 years, by only about one-third of
the nation. Spain overall, though, seems to have readily
accepted the Castilian gentleman's definition of the Spanish
personality.

The low mountains of the Sierra de Guadarrama, just
north of Madrid, form a natural buffer between New and Old
Castile. New Castile constitutes the urban, more industrial
Spain of Madrid, Toledo, Cuenca, Albacete, and Ciudad Real,
south of the Guadarrama, recast in recent years as the
Madrid/Castile–La Mancha region. To the north is Old Cas-
tile, keeper of the flame of the rural, remote, aloof Spain:
Valladolid, Segovia, Salamanca, Zamora, Avila, Burgos, Palen-

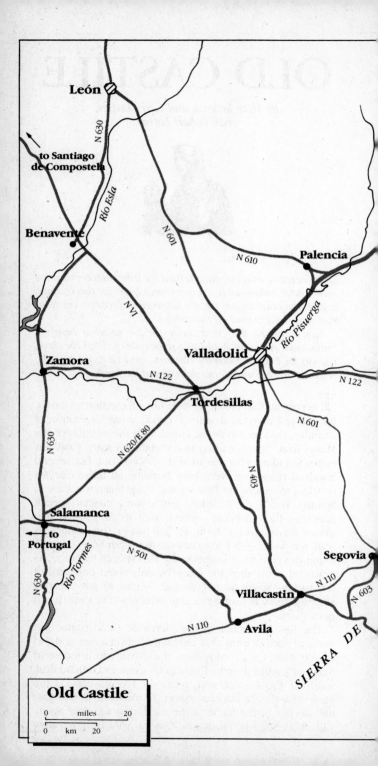

Old Castile

miles 20

km 20

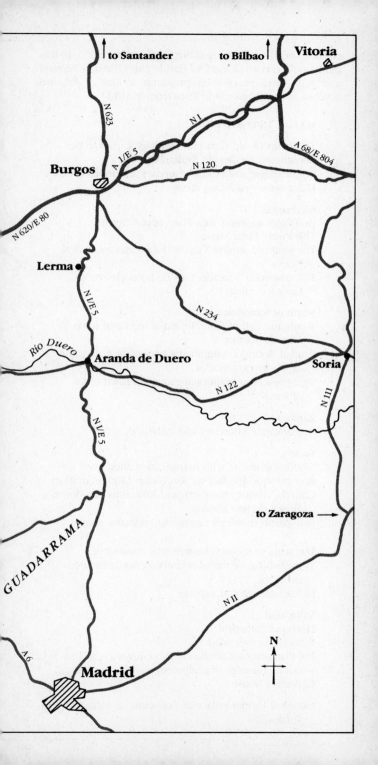

cia, and León, now known as the Castile-León region. In this guidebook, certain of the Old Castile cities, such as Segovia and Avila, because of their proximity to the capital, are covered in the chapter Side Trips from Madrid.

MAJOR INTEREST

The heart of old Christian Spain as it used to be
Roman and medieval Castilian cities
Romanesque and Gothic churches and monasteries
Major wine-producing areas

Salamanca
Buildings adorned with Plateresque façades
The lovely Plaza Mayor
The simple Catedral Vieja and the ornate Catedral Nueva
The university's façade, Luis de León classroom, Gallego ceiling

South of Salamanca
Tomb and cell of Saint Teresa at medieval town of Alba de Tormes
Ciudad Rodrigo: magnificent encircling wall, cathedral, fortress-parador
Well-preserved traditional mountain town of La Alberca

Zamora
Romanesque churches and cathedral

León
Gothic cathedral, with marvelous stained glass
Romanesque Basílica de San Isidoro and its treasury
Church, cloister, museum, and luxurious parador at Hostal de San Marcos
San Martín quarter's taverns and artisans' shops

Day trips to medieval towns and monasteries
Trout fishing, beautiful scenery in northern León province
La Maragatería countryside

Valladolid
Herreran cathedral
Baroque Universidad
Pre-Plateresque Colegio de San Gregorio (and national museum of sculpture)
Cervantes house

Medieval former palace at Convento de Santa Clara in Tordesillas

Rueda wine country
Peñafiel and the Ribera del Duero red-wine villages
Castles

The Palencia Area
Palencia city's cathedral and Romanesque churches
Seldom-visited medieval towns and churches on the
    Camino de Santiago
Seventh-century Visigothic church of San Juan de
    Baños

Aranda de Duero and Southern Burgos Province
Asador restaurants for roast lamb in Aranda
Ribera de Burgos wine country
Covarrubias and other well-preserved medieval towns
Romanesque monastery of Santo Domingo de Silos
    and ruins of the monastery of San Pedro de
    Arlanza

Burgos
Historical traces of El Cid
Medieval ambience
Great Gothic cathedral

Medieval monasteries outside of Burgos
Romanesque hospices and churches along the Ca-
    mino de Santiago

La Meseta

La Meseta is the great central plateau of Spain that begins not
far from the Mediterranean, spreads to the Portuguese border, and rises to an occasional height of 3,000 feet before
being dominated by the mountains of Europe's largest wilderness area, the Cordillera Cantábrica, to the north. To
speak of La Meseta is to speak in superlatives: the country's
largest chunk of geology—accounting for two-thirds, in fact,
of the Iberian land mass; generator of Spain's coldest winters and hottest summers; battleground of Spain's bloodiest
history, both civil and foreign; harshest forger of the Spanish
soul, capable of branding even the indifferent visitor. V. S.
Pritchett, upon sighting "that strange, moon-like tableland,"
declared, "I might almost say, without being guilty of rheto-
ric, that the sight of the landscape of Castile changed my
life."

The moon-like aspect can be attributed in part to the
erosion caused by many centuries of grazing sheep. Iberians, the first settlers of this part of Spain, are thought to have
come from North Africa some 4,000 years ago, bringing their
sheep with them. Herders, seeking protection for their
flocks from the scorching summer heat of southern Spain,

began an annual trek to the cool pastures of the north, establishing the famous sheep walks that continued for hundreds of years. A loosely organized sheep-owners' cooperative, called Mesta, whose name probably derived from the word for "mixed" (as in many flocks of sheep with many owners banding together for convenience and protection), controlled the sheepways and guaranteed equal rights to all sheep owners (some of whom, interestingly, were women).

The growing awareness of the value of a newly discovered wool on the back of the North African merino sheep late in the Middle Ages changed all that. The advent of the merino (overlooked until then, perhaps because the merino makes good wool but bad lamb chops) increased the number of passing sheep manyfold. By the late 13th century the Castilian crown, recognizing a good thing, assumed control over Mesta, formalized the group, and accomplished two goals: It permitted trafficking in merino sheep only to those individuals authorized by the crown (merino wool quickly attracted royal attention by its rapid rise as a solid earner of foreign exchange); and it provided a source of income to needy knights, home from the Crusades, for whom dirty hands were anathema—thumbs down for farming, thumbs up for sheep. Eventually the gentlemen shepherds limited Mesta participation to aristocrats, and the crown gave sheep the right of way over any and all lands, a right still in force today.

Merino wool quickly became the most valued wool in the world, and for 500 years Mesta moved as many as 4 million sheep per year up and down the sheep walks of La Meseta, until Mesta's decline in the 19th century. Spain paid a stiff price, though: The arable land of central Spain was exhausted. Because farmland was, by decree, sheepland first, agriculture never developed on any unified, meaningful basis. All raw wool was exported, so not even a milling industry to make finished cloth (and provide jobs and foreign income) ever developed. (The Italians did see the possibilities, and milling became the underpinning for several Italian fortunes, including that of the Medici.)

La Meseta's sometimes forbidding face may be why late spring, with its wildflowers of red, purple, blue, and yellow, seems especially beautiful. Vast carpets of bright green, burgeoning wheat and barley show why southern Old Castile is nicknamed "Spain's Breadbasket." (The northern sector is known as "Spain's Vineyard.") There is little rainfall in the region, and irrigation from several rivers, especially the mighty Río Duero, is needed to put that bright green tint on the fields. Spring sees Old Castile on its best behavior, with autumn a close second. Summer and winter are about equally uncomfortable, too hot and too cold, respectively.

The cities and towns that have grown up in this section of

La Meseta offer much diversity to explore and enjoy. Medieval **Salamanca**, called the "golden city" for the way the afternoon light tones its old buildings, has two cathedrals and a university that was founded just 50 years after Oxford, in the days when universities were as much centers of political power as centers of learning. Within 50 years the Western world's four most powerful universities were those at Oxford, Paris, Bologna, and Salamanca. The southwestern corner of the region has remote mountains and villages, including **Ciudad Rodrigo**, with its lovely plazas, cathedral, commanding view of the surrounding countryside, and a remarkable wall that encircles this 12th-century border fort.

León has the great cathedral and a sumptuous hotel in what surely is one of the handsomest buildings in Spain, the 16th-century Hostal de San Marcos. In **La Maragatería**, the rough country west of León, reminders exist of the Camino de Santiago (Way of Saint James), the passage trod by pilgrims to Santiago de Compostela, in Galicia. The pilgrims had travelled a long way in supplication to Spain's revered religious figure and they still had a long and arduous way to go. In northern León province the tableland turns to an alpine range (Spain's overall elevation is second in Europe only to Switzerland's) threaded by white-water rivers and spectacular ravines.

Valladolid has a fine cathedral, a handsome university, and the wonderful pre-Plateresque Colegio de San Gregorio, housing distinctly Spanish polychrome wood sculptures in its National Museum of Sculpture. The surrounding countryside is dotted with wine towns and castles. Quiet **Palencia province** offers medieval villages and ancient Visigothic churches, while its eponymous capital city has a lovely Gothic cathedral.

Southern **Burgos province**, especially Aranda de Duero, is the place for typical Castilian roast houses, with brick ovens and rustic crockery. **Ribera de Burgos** is picturesque wine country with bodegas and wine villages. **Santo Domingo de Silos**, to the north, is a beautiful Romanesque monastery, and nearby **Covarrubias** is a well-preserved ancient village.

The great city of **Burgos** has much to offer the visitor: echoes of El Cid, a lively, picturesque old quarter, and a resplendent cathedral. Outside of town are ancient monasteries of great historical and artistic importance.

The Food of Old Castile

Old Castile is the land of roasts, and here that means exceptional lamb and pork, including suckling lamb, *lechazo,* and suckling pig, *cochinillo.* A meal in a Castilian *asador* (roast house) may consist only of a quarter of suckling lamb or pig roasted in a brick oven, or a pile of baby lamb chops, some potatoes, a simple salad of lettuce, tomato, and onion, and a pitcher of local wine, but people from Madrid think nothing of driving 100 or 150 miles on a Sunday to have this experience.

Sopa castellana or *sopa de ajo,* with garlic, bread, and an egg floating on top, is the classic soup of Castile. The ewe's-milk cheeses, *cecina* (cured beef), and *morcilla con arroz* (blood pudding with rice) of Burgos are justly famous, while *revueltos* (scrambled eggs with wild mushrooms, shrimp, *jamón serrano*—mountain-cured ham—or asparagus) are on every menu. *Cangrejos de río* (river crayfish), partridge, rabbit, venison, and quail are offered in many restaurants. Other dishes native to the area include *gazpacho serrano,* a cold soup of boiled eggs, onions, garlic, parsley, vinegar, oil, and bread; *picadillo,* tasty chopped beef or pork cooked with vegetables, garlic, paprika, and eggs; and *chanfaina,* a rice dish with diced chicken and sausage. *Menestra* (a mixed vegetable dish), artichokes with ham, and white asparagus are also staples on many menus here. Except in fancy restaurants, dessert choices are fairly limited, but *postre de abuela* (Burgos cheese served with honey and nuts) and *cuajada* (sheep's- or cow's-milk curd with honey or sugar) are superb.

— *Gerry Dawes and Robert Levine*

The Wines of Castile-León

Old Castile's **Ribera del Duero**—the Duero river valley, which in Portugal is the Douro, the fabled Port river—is the home of Spain's most expensive wine, the mysterious and exotic Vega Sicilia, until recently the only winery to receive any real notoriety beyond the region's borders. In 1982 the Ribera del Duero was granted DO (*denominación de origen,* or classified region) status, and a number of new wineries, notably Pesquera, Viña Pedrosa, Victor Balbás, and Torremilanos, in this section of historic Old Castile (now known as the region of Castile-León) began to receive justly deserved critical acclaim. The best red wines from Ribera del Duero are a beautiful black-raspberry color, have nice perfumed noses laced with oak, are often loaded with rich fruit, but are well balanced and age beautifully.

Before Pesquera and Viña Pedrosa emerged as quality producers, only Vega Sicilia and Bodega Ribera Duero (the cooperative at Peñafiel, producer of Protos) made really noteworthy wines in the region. Almost every village had its cooperative (sometimes two), with epoxy-lined cement tanks whose temperature during fermentation was controlled by nature. If the fermentation season was cool and the tanks were clean, some stupendous house wines could end up in the pitchers of the region's wonderful roast lamb restaurants, and a few cooperatives even made bottled *reservas* that acquired an underground reputation with some Castilian wine aficionados.

The major grape here is the Tinto del País (known as Tempranillo in La Rioja), a superb varietal that may well be a long-acclimated clone of Pinot Noir, probably brought here in the 12th century by the Cistercians, the same monastic order that founded Clos de Vougeot in Burgundy (and Santa María de Valbuena near Vega Sicilia as well). Garnacha Tinta (Grenache) is also authorized, as are limited plantings of Cabernet Sauvignon, Merlot, and Malbec.

The Ribera del Duero continues to be dominated by the two great superstars, Vega Sicilia and Pesquera—the former priced in the stratosphere, the latter still reasonable, given its quality. Although not as widely distributed as the two big guns, Viña Pedrosa and Victor Balbás also produce excellent wines. Torremilanos, Bodega Ribera Duero, Bodegas Valduero, and the newly modernized and revitalized Bodegas Ismael Arroyo, which produces Mesoneros de Castilla and the first-rate Valsotillo Reserva, all make solid, reasonably priced, well-made wines that are available in many stores and restaurants here.

In the past decade, **Rueda** (Valladolid, Avila, Segovia), located northwest of Madrid between Medina del Campo and Tordesillas, has begun producing excellent dry white wines from the Verdejo grape by cold-fermenting the musts and giving them little or no time in wood. The permitted grape varietals are Verdejo, Palomino Fino (the main grape of Jerez), and Viura. The wines labeled Rueda Superior (12½ percent alcohol) are crisp, fresh, balanced, medium-bodied, with good fruit and texture. Marqués de Griñon, Marqués de Riscal, Cuatro Rayas, Castilla la Vieja, Martivillí, and the exceptional Martinsancho are fine examples of white Rueda.

Toro (Zamora, Valladolid) is one of Spain's newest official *denominaciones*. Toro literally means "bull" in Spanish, and most Toro wines live up to their name, attaining alcohol levels of 15 percent, but the trend is toward a more modern style—wines that are still big, rich, and concentrated, but with more finesse and less alcohol. Several Toro wines, notably the excellent Colegiata from Bodegas Fariña and Tío Babu and Valdevi from Bodegas Luis Mateos, reflect this style. (Toro wines should not be confused with Torres Sangre de Toro, a wine from Penedès, Catalonia.)

A new *denominación de origen,* **El Bierzo**, officially became DO number 34 in early 1989. The red wines show promise, especially the well-made Valdeobispo and Señorío del Bierzo, both made from the highly prized local grape Mencia.

Granted *denominación de origen* status in 1991, **Cigales**, located just north of Valladolid, is renowned in the region and, increasingly, in the rest of Spain for its dry Tinto Fino and Garnacha *rosados,* which have improved greatly in recent years because of modern vinification techniques. Try Carrosantos and Torrecigales.

—Gerry Dawes

We cover Old Castile in two segments, both of which begin north of Avila and Segovia, (covered in the Side Trips from Madrid chapter). The first segment begins at the *western* side of Old Castile, closer to Portugal, with the city of Salamanca and then points to the south, including Ciudad Rodrigo and the countryside around it. From there we move north to Zamora and then to the city of León—an important stop on the old Camino de Santiago pilgrimage route and the north-westernmost city of Old Castile—beyond which lies the green northwestern corner of Spain: Asturias and Galicia (covered in a separate chapter).

The second segment covers the part of Old Castile *east* of the first half, due north of Avila and Segovia. We start at Valladolid and its surrounding wine country, then move north to Palencia, east to Aranda de Duero and its vineyards, and finally north to the great city of Burgos, another stop on the Camino de Santiago and the gateway to the Basque Country to the northeast and to Cantabria on the north coast.

OLD CASTILE WEST

SALAMANCA

Looming over the Río Tormes, Salamanca occupies the high ground at 2,600 feet above sea level, a value seized upon by Hannibal in the third century B.C., when Salamanca was already a good-sized prize to be snatched. Hannibal remarked favorably about the citizenry, and you probably will, too, as the people here are unfailingly courteous to the traveller seeking aid. Hannibal doubtless travelled in an elephantine way, but you can reach Salamanca over excellent roads northwest from Madrid, a 207-km (128-mile) drive on M 505 and N 501 by way of Avila, or southwest from Burgos, 240 km (149 miles), via Valladolid, on N 620/E 80 all the way. Remember that a high steppe, which is just what

Salamanca sits on, means that even in mid-May temperatures on the Plaza Mayor on a bright, breezy day may reach only about 50 degrees Fahrenheit. (July's another story.)

Salamanca's past is a fusion of the cerebral, the spiritual, and the bloody. After Hannibal, the Romans moved in, followed by the Moors, who were finally driven out late in the 11th century. Salamanca stepped into the sun in the 12th century with the founding of its *universidad,* which rose to fame and glory. Its reputation grew on its excellence in mathematics and science, and its skill as tutor and interpreter of Arab philosophy (and Aristotle) to the rest of the Western world. A medieval Salamancan far from his home in this golden city on the Río Tormes needed say only, "I am from Salamanca," to be taken for a scholar. The city paid homage to its good fortunes with the building of the Romanesque Catedral Vieja (old cathedral) in the 12th century and the Gothic Catedral Nueva (new cathedral) in the 16th century.

In 1808 Napoleon installed his brother Joseph as king of Spain. The golden city had fallen on dark days, as had all of Spain, intensified here by the cumulative destruction of the university's reputation and its near demise. The steadfast duke of Wellington forced the French out of Salamanca in 1812, pushed on to Madrid, and eventually into southern France. The university's recovery began late in the 19th century and was accelerated under the great Basque philosopher and educator Miguel de Unamuno in the early 20th century. Today the university, if not quite up to its pinnacle of the past, is respected both domestically and internationally and has a modern-day student population of 16,000. Salamanca's genuflection to conservatism, akin to the deep bow of Valladolid, its neighbor to the northeast, is reflected in the city's role as capital for the rightist insurgents during the 1936 Civil War. Salamanca is now a successful small industrial city of nearly 170,000 sprawled around the old town that houses its distinguished heritage.

It was sun and time burnishing the sandstone buildings for six or seven centuries that turned Salamanca's old town to old gold, as manifested in the cathedrals, the Palacio de Monterrey, and other buildings hard by the handsome and inviting Plaza Mayor, truly the heart and spirit of Salamanca. This is the home of some of the country's finest examples of Plateresque, the intricate, elaborate workings in soft stone, direct descendants of Queen Isabella's love of the ornate, that express an odd amalgam of Gothic, Renaissance, and Moorish leftovers. Plateresque is seen here on an especially wonderful façade of the medieval university building as well as on the Catedral Vieja, the Palacio de Monterrey, and the Convento de San Esteban. There are good restaurants and good hotels in town, including an excellent parador whose exterior suffers as an ugly duckling but whose service, dining room, and views of the golden city put it in the swan class.

PARKING IN SALAMANCA

Salamanca's old town extends in a loose bell shape to the north from the bank of the Río Tormes. If you're driving in from the east or the Madrid area on N 501 along the Tormes, the towers of old Salamanca will appear to your right and a right turn onto the second bridge, the Puente de Enrique Esteban, will lead you straight into the old town. Once there, park your car and proceed on foot. You can park on the street; some areas have the kind of meter that requires pesetas and issues time-stamped tickets, which you then place under your windshield wiper; you'll see, also, the occasional parking garage along the perimeter of the old town. You can also park at the Parador de Salamanca (described below), perched on a bluff to the left, on the opposite bank of the river, overlooking the river and N 501, just a short way beyond the Puente de Enrique Esteban. Call for a taxi from the parador or make the 20-minute walk down the slope and across the narrow, pedestrians-only **Puente Romano** (Roman Bridge).

The Old Town

There's nothing like going straight to the heart, and as the Plaza Mayor is the heart, geographically as well as metaphorically, of old Salamanca we start—and end—our tour there, fanning out to the cathedrals old and new, the Casa de las Conchas (House of Shells), the *universidad,* with its amazing Plateresque façade and the tranquil *claustro* (cloister) of the Escuelas Menores (lesser schools), the Palacio de Monterrey, the Puente Romano, and streets off the Plaza Mayor and neighboring Plaza Mercado for shopping and dining. You will find a local map handy, available at news kiosks, as well as a small pair of binoculars, useful not only for appreciating the details of, say, the Virgen de la Vega high overhead in the Cathedral Vieja, but for bringing into focus the name of that street whose sign is dusty and just beyond clarity.

PLAZA MAYOR

It was James Michener, a lifelong Hispanophile, who adjudged Salamanca's Plaza Mayor "the finest in Spain and one of the four best in the world," confirming the view of most Spaniards and putting it right up there, in Michener's view, with the main squares of Venice, Mexico City, and Samarkand. Alberto Churriguera gets the credit for his 1728 plan that unified the huge square with buildings of like design executed by the Churriguera brothers and others over the next 30 years.

The Churriguera name is heard often in reference to Spanish design and architecture. The Churriguera brothers, José (1665–1725), Alberto (1676–1750), and Joaquín (1674–1724), initiated this style, which can best be described as exuberant Baroque and was widely imitated throughout Spain. Churrigueresque architecture is characterized by the use of sculptured lines and curves, exaggerated reliefs, and motifs drawn from nature and blended with the architecture to decorate façades, altarpieces, and so forth. Magnificent examples of Churrigueresque can be seen throughout Salamanca.

The renovated Plaza Mayor, requiring the approval of Philip V, was needed to serve a burgeoning Salamanca with its multiplying shops of craftsmen and tradesmen and the nearby manses being built by noble families. The buildings on the eastern and northern sides of the plaza were funded by local authorities, and those on the west and south sides—beginning with the Pabellon Real (Royal Pavilion)—by private initiative.

Churriguera's design of arched supports is quite simple, almost plain, except for a relatively ornate three-story, tiered front along the north wall that frames the *ayuntamiento* (town hall) and is capped by a clock and a cupola of three bells. A balustrade supports carved figures from Spanish history. There are archways on the north and south walls, with the principal entrance to the square beneath the bell tower. An arcade, once a market, wraps around four walls of shops, small restaurants, and bars with a border of tables and chairs offering café, *bebidos* (drinks), and snacks.

In this companionable, attractive atmosphere, all mingle. As is the Spanish custom, class distinctions crumble and all manner of elbows are rubbed when an opportunity for pleasure crops up—good *tapas,* say, in a convivial bar or *taberna*. The Spanish can seem severe, even forbidding, but not here, where all join in animated talk and laughter and appreciative applause for *la tuna,* the strolling groups of student minstrels in red-slashed, black Renaissance velvet who play and sing the songs of old Spain. The plaza serves as a stage for occasional music recitals, and in the early evening a Punch-and-Judy puppet stage may be set up under the clock tower, drawing enthusiastic *niños,* even the occasional *adulto*. Plaza Mayor is a good place to start your tour of old Salamanca and a good one to find respite and refreshment at the end of the day. Its easy-going display of Spain past integrated with Spain present sets the stage for the visitor's appreciation of this old, alive city.

AROUND THE PLAZA MAYOR

Salamanca draws attention because of its profusion of architecturally interesting old buildings in good repair, of which it may have more than any other city of comparable size in Spain. The sites of primary interest lie in a fan shape to the west and south of the Plaza Mayor toward the river.

West of the Plaza Mayor

Out the south side of the plaza and to the right a short distance, just across Calle del Prior, is the majestic **Palacio de Monterrey**, a fine example of Spanish Renaissance architecture. The original 1639 design envisioned a truly grandiose (not to say monstrous) palace three times bigger than the one completed. Even so, the Monterrey is an imposing building with a superior example of Plateresque sculpture on the top gallery.

A couple of blocks west of the Palacio along Calle Ramón y Cajal is the **Colegio del Arzobispo M. Fonseca**, named in 1521 for its founder, the archbishop of Salamanca, and sometimes referred to as the Colegio de los Irlandeses (College of the Irish) for its Irish students. It housed novices in pursuit of the priesthood, to which end the young novitiates were reportedly required to spend eight years, rise daily at 4:30 A.M., and forgo vacations. The *colegio* now serves as a residence for university lecturers. There is an elegant Plateresque door, and the patio is one of the most beautiful examples of Spanish Renaissance architecture, with capitals and medallions.

South of the Plaza Mayor

There are two principal streets leading south from Plaza del Poeta Iglesias, just south of Plaza Mayor: Rúa Mayor and Calle de San Pablo, which continues nearly to the river. Head south along Rúa Mayor to a favorite building in Salamanca, the **Casa de las Conchas** (House of Shells), built by Dr. Talavera Maldonado, a knight of Santiago and counselor to Queen Isabella. There's a lovely patio, and the outside of the house is decorated with 400 scallop shells, Dr. Maldonado's tribute to the religious symbol of pilgrims on their way to Santiago de Compostela. The 15th-century building has emerged essentially unscathed from a recent renovation. Michener, ever profuse with words, used quite a few to illustrate his pleasure at the progression of sunlight across the shells in the early afternoon: It can be compelling.

Also on Rúa Mayor, just below Plaza del Poeta Iglesias, is **IMBIS**, whose sign over the entrance states: "*cevecería, cafetería, freiduría* [fried-fish store], *platos combinados*." IMBIS is a big, noisy room where you can get a sandwich or a typical *plato de la casa* of Hungarian steak, salad, mushrooms, and fried potatoes. It's a cheerful place, where over-achiever sits alongside ditch-digger, folks from the neighborhood bring their children, and the waiters are moving all the time.

A block to the east of Rúa Mayor (take Calle Felipe Espino Miñagustín, turn right and right again) on Calle de San Pablo is the **Palacio de la Salina** or the Palacio de Fonseca, sometimes simply called La Salina. Built in 1519, it now houses the provincial government and has the most harmonious façade of all the 16th-century buildings in the city. Just across the street is a quiet, green park, Plaza de Colón, a nice spot if you are in need of a time-out. Continue along the north edge of the park to the corner of Calle del Consuelo and Calle Calderos to see the **Torre del Clavero**, an old castle keep (mid-15th century) with a headband of eight small, overhanging turrets that looms above other buildings. It is the local home of Radio Nacional España, so if you see signs for that institution you're on the right track. You are not allowed to go up to the top of the *torre* for a sentry's view of the city, but there is a museum of local interests in its base.

SOUTHEASTERN SALAMANCA

Closer to the river, in the southeastern corner of the old town, are more of Salamanca's architectural treasures. From the Torre del Clavero, proceed south along Calle del Consuelo, go left onto Calle Juan de la Fuente, and head across the Gran Vía to Calle Rosario. At the corner of Calle Escoto stands the **Colegio de Calatrava**, currently the School for Theological Studies but originally the college for the military order of Calatrava, founded by Charles V in 1522. The Baroque building (1717) was designed by Joaquín Churriguera; many of the original decorative figures of the façade were ordered removed in 1790.

The 16th-century **Convento de San Esteban**, adjacent to the Colegio de Calatrava, has a wonderful Plateresque façade that competes in quality with the wall of the main entrance to the *universidad*. This Dominican monastery houses one of the most intimate churches anywhere. From a distance the sandstone façade looks as if it were carved from marzipan. Inside, golden columns support altars topped by arches of gold. Wood-layered floors serve as a nice contrast and give it warmth.

Heading west toward the cathedrals, you may want to stop first at the **Colegio de Anaya**, located right across the Plaza de Anaya from them. The *colegio,* named after Diego de Anaya Maldonado, owner of the building and a cleric who was active in politics, was founded in 1411, but the Neoclassical building standing now dates from the 1760s. Currently, philology, geography, and history are taught here. The lobby has on display four Roman tablets that were found during the building's construction—the three on top are fake, the bottom one is genuine. In the courtyard, on the staircase landing, there is an imposing bust of Unamuno by Victor Macho. On the upper floor is the impressive *aula magna* (great lecture hall), containing carved wooden medallions and portraits of Spain's kings and queens. The old chapel, by Alberto Churriguera, dates to 1731 and is known as the Iglesia de San Sebastián.

THE CATHEDRALS

We have saved the best for last: the Catedral Vieja and the Catedral Nueva, and the Universidad. If your time in Salamanca is limited, and you want to see something of the old town, you must see these institutions, which are clumped more or less together due south of Plaza Mayor along either side of Rúa Mayor, relatively close to the river (look for several stork nests in the towers and cupolas of the 17th-century Clerecía at the intersection of Calle Jesús and Calle San Isidoro). From the Convento de San Esteban, heading down along Calle Buenaventura to Plaza de Carvajal brings you to the rear of the Catedral Nueva.

Vaulted Gothic cathedrals tend, upon initial entry, to overwhelm. The **Catedral Nueva** (New Cathedral) of Salamanca is no exception. The Catedral Nueva was begun in 1513 (the same year Machiavelli turned 44), during that post-Isabella, so-called Golden Age of Spain when largesse was flowing in from the New World. The initial architects were Juan Gil de Hontañón, his son, Rodrigo, Juan de Alava, and Juan Gil de Mozo. In the early 18th century finishing touches of Baroque were added—choir stalls, the retrochoir, and the organ loft—by the seemingly omnificent brothers Churriguera.

Some people apparently feel compelled to put up tall, imposing buildings. The Catedral Nueva had the added assignment of holding up the **Catedral Vieja** (Old Cathedral), weakened by 400 years of aging, tectonic meandering, possibly even faulty construction. The obliging Catedral Nueva looms above and nearly around the Catedral Vieja. The two are literally joined at the hip; one side of the Vieja was removed and the Nueva added on and, in fact, the public entrance to the Catedral Vieja is via that common wall. There is an admission fee for the Vieja, payable at the small box office to the right upon entering the Nueva. (On Saturdays, though, there is a stream of wedding ceremonies being performed in the Old Cathedral, using the wide door to the right of the main entrance of the Nueva to gain access; you can do the same for the aesthetic of stepping directly from the street into a cathedral interior that seeks to embrace rather than overwhelm.)

The Catedral Nueva is all massive grandeur. The Catedral Vieja, in contrast, is almost intimate, with a simple, quiet elegance. You'll see why the Vieja is regarded by some as one of Spain's most interesting Romanesque churches. Dedicated to Santa María and dating from the 12th century, the Vieja was built on the site of an earlier church that commemorated the expulsion of the Moors from Salamanca in 1055.

A popular drawing card in the cathedral is the Virgen de la Vega, midway up the retable. The statue, which overlooks the central altarpiece, is a 12th-century Romanesque wooden sculpture, exquisitely decorated with gilding and Limoges enamel. Its wealth of detail and depth of feeling have led some to call it Spain's finest work of art. You'll need your binoculars if you want a close view of the detail. The altarpiece, by Nicolás Florentino, was completed inside the cathedral itself in 1445. Two chapels are to the right of the altar: The Capilla de Santa Bárbara (1314) contains a 15th-century fresco by Fernando Gallego and the tomb of the late Bishop Lucerno of the 14th century; and the Capilla de San Bartolomé, donated by Bishop Diego de Anaya in 1422, houses his alabaster sepulcher. The organ, dating from 1380, is one of Europe's oldest. The cloister was rebuilt after earthquakes in 1755 (which largely destroyed Lisbon).

On your way out look to the left of the apse in the Catedral Nueva for the Capilla de San Expedito, Patrón de los Grados Pasajeros (Saint Expeditious, Patron of Passing Grades), who receives offerings in a small box attached to the bars of the chapel's entry under a sign that reads: "*San Expedito . . . Peticiones y Favores*" ("petitions and favors"). For several hundred years now the way to San Expedito has been heavily trammeled at examination time by suddenly devout students of the *universidad*.

There are graffiti from long ago in bull's blood and oil on buildings throughout the area—names of victorious candidates for degrees, dashed off by students as they raced in celebration through the streets of the town. Opposite the Catedral Nueva there's quite a clear one in the entryway between the two pairs of very high doors (between the entry to the Colegio de Anaya and its cloister).

THE UNIVERSIDAD

The **Universidad de Salamanca** is scattered around the city, but its heart and soul—and glory—reside in a few buildings from the 15th and 16th centuries on either side of Calle Libreros (booksellers street) just west of the cathedrals and Plaza de Anaya. From the Plaza Mayor go south along the Rúa Mayor, make a slight right at the Clerecía (with its storks' nests), and left onto Calle Libreros, a quiet cobblestone street. On your right, at number 4, is **La Luna**, a student hangout with a few outdoor tables in the correct weather, a dark, small, but pleasant bar downstairs and a *comedor* (dining room) upstairs. Breakfast and lunch are available here, *platos combinados,* as well as dinner. You can tell it's a student hangout because the customers are young and burdened and the music is defeatist British rock.

Farther along Libreros you will see, on your left, the 16th-century façade of the *universidad,* a wonderment three stories high, possibly the finest example of Plateresque in all of Spain. Afternoon light best shows the medallions of Ferdinand and Isabella and other monarchs surrounded by a mad company of figures—pagan, literary, and religious—a writhing, tangled, three-dimensional tapestry in stone. Plateresque (*Plateresco,* from *platero,* or silversmith) pays tribute to the mineral that makes such brittle delicacy possible. The technique, pioneered in Salamanca and peculiar to Spain, uses a stone that is soft and workable in the manner of silver when quarried; exposure to air eventually hardens it. Stand back from the façade and look up to just below the roofline at the first row of recognizable figures; count left three columns, and there beneath the large head of a sad woman is a small skull with a frog sitting atop—sighting skull and frog is the other talisman students seek out at examination time (they then make a beeline from here straight to the embrace of San Expedito). Skull and frog are displayed in replica in Salamanca souvenir shops.

Through the Plateresque entryway is the **cloister**, three floors high, with the chapel and lecture rooms at ground level. This is the core of a university founded in 1218 by Alfonso IX, king of Castile. Most of the existing buildings date from the 15th century, with a few 14th-century vestiges. For 400 years, embracing the rise and decline of Spain's Golden Age, this was one of the preeminent places of learning in the Western world, a renowned province of mathematics and science, international law, an explicator of Arab philosophy. Columbus came here to study Copernican astronomy at a time when there was real risk attached to taking up that heretical world view. "La Latina," Beatriz de Galindo, considered the western world's first woman professor, taught Latin to the young Isabella. Scholars here questioned the legal posture of the *conquistadores* of the New World—Cortés, Pizarro, and others—which surely contributed to the travails of that most venerated figure of the university, Luis de León.

The **Paraninfo de Luis de León,** Fray Luis's lecture room, is third to the left, along the *claustro* walkway, looking, with the exception of the windows, quite as it did when it was his *sanctum* in the mid-16th century. Arched beams, dark in a white plaster ceiling, suggest the ribs of some giant Viking ship. There's room for perhaps 200 students on narrow rough-hewn slabs of wood (a railroad tie would be about as comfortable, but the benches were a step up for students accustomed to sitting on stone floors). Their tables, nearly as narrow, are covered by a lattice-work of initials carved over the last several centuries. At the rear wall is the lecturer's rostrum. The ceiling, the ancient benches, the small windows, and the dim light collectively give the feel of a ship.

In the shadowy confines of this ancient hall, little is required to conjure up Fray Luis de León, university professor, lyric poet, theologian (*De los Nombres de Cristo,* a Platonic dialogue on the nature of Christ), and master classicist. Just released by the Inquisition from "detainment" in 1576 (at age 50), he is said to have stepped beyond the reality of a five-year persecution, up to the rostrum in this very room, and looked out upon what surely was a most attentive body of students. He began the new day: "As we were saying yesterday...."

Michener relates a more recent ordeal, that of "distinguished philosopher-poet Miguel de Unamuno," born in the Basque Country, rector of the university. In 1936 the political climate in Spain was not dissimilar to that which had fostered the Inquisition. One autumn day, in the hall next to that once occupied by Fray Luis, Unamuno, old and ill, entered into debate with a hero-general of the Franco government risen to national fame through military exploits in North Africa. The subject, raised by Professor Unamuno, concerned General Millán Astray's personal battle cry, "Long live death!" which had been eagerly taken up by his countrymen. Unamuno questioned the logic of such a slogan. General Astray, waving his remaining arm, screamed at Unamuno, "Down with intelligence! *Viva la muerte!*" Neither would relent. The incident was subsequently reported to Generalísimo Franco, whereupon that worthy reportedly said of Spain's "leading intellectual": "If necessary, shoot him." Unamuno saved Franco the bullet by dying a few months later.

Leading up from the lecture halls is a grand stone staircase with a Plateresque balustrade that changes theme at each level, from *dueñas* and jesters to jousts and bull-baiting. The third-floor ceiling is a striking *artesonado* (coffered or caissoned), in wood, carved in geometric patterns in the Mudejar style. Also on the third floor is the library of more than 50,000 volumes, including 4,000 pre-Gutenberg, handwritten manuscripts.

Outside, across the street from the Plateresque façade, are the **Patio de las Escuelas** and a statue of Luis de León; at the rear of the patio is the entrance to the **Escuelas Menores** (lesser schools). On the far side of the cloister is a small museum with one outstanding attribute: half of its ceiling is a wonderful painting by Fernando Gallego, a major Hispanic-Flemish artist of the late 15th century, composed of gilded symbols of the Zodiac and constellations—charioteer, snake, centaur, crab. The rest of the museum is essentially standard-issue 18th-century clerics' robes of gold damask brocade, so, upon entering, look up for your reward. To complement these grounds of the Escuelas Menores, there were once Escuelas Mayores (greater schools), several colleges reserved for the aristocracy.

Since its glory days the university has had a roller-coaster ride more or less down, reaching a nadir early in the 19th century when the student population dwindled to 300. Currently, without the help of Fray Luis de León or Miguel de Unamuno, Salamanca's *universidad* has gained international respect, particularly for its depth in Spanish language, culture, and history, with foreign students making up a large proportion of the present student body of 16,000. For these venerable buildings the glory never faded, and to walk the cobblestones of Calle Libreros is to be in step with an honorable past.

THE PUENTE ROMANO

If you're on foot and want to head for the parador, continue on along Calle Libreros down the hill to the Río Tormes and across the Puente Romano (Roman Bridge), sufficient once for chariots and ox carts but now confined to pedestrians. The original 15 of its 26 arches date from the post-Hannibal Roman occupation, and the bridge has been rebuilt several times, most recently in the 16th and 17th centuries. Today the *puente* is a popular *paseo*.

If you are driving from the old town, you can reach the bridge by turning right along an old stone road that parallels N 501 just *before* crossing the Puente de Enrique Esteban. You'll find parking along this road near the Roman Bridge.

Staying in Salamanca

The ▶ **Parador de Salamanca** may look from the Puente Romano like a design-by-committee habitat at a low-energy world's fair, but then the forced conjunction with the mellow beauty of medieval Salamanca doesn't help. Inside, the parador makes up for any exterior lack with a competent staff; dramatic views of the city, particularly in early evening; a good *comedor,* with an excellent breakfast buffet; and comfortable rooms with great showers.

Salamanca's other major hotels are within easy walking

distance of the Plaza Mayor. The 100-room ► **Gran Hotel** is just south of the Plaza Mayor at Plaza del Poeta Iglesias 5. The Gran Hotel, with classic decor and a good bar and restaurant, may not be quite worth the rates charged, but it is at the heart of things. Its sister, the ► **Hotel Monterrey**, 89 rooms on Calle del Azafranal 21, is elegant in a slightly faded, Old World way; it is northeast of Plaza Mayor a few blocks.

Dining in Salamanca

Salamanca is off Spain's well-beaten tourist track, and as it is not in one of the coastal regions, its fare tends toward meat rather than fish. The traditional roast suckling pig and lamb are staples of the local restaurants.

This is a university town, so there are plenty of student hangouts, such as those in **Plaza del Mercado**, the square on the Plaza Mayor's east side, that serve local (and somewhat muscular) *tinto* (red wine), *farinatos* (sausages), and regional cheeses. *La tuna* strolls here, too, as in Plaza Mayor, serenading wedding parties certainly, young women preferably, with songs about Spain, the town, the school, and, oh yes, love. *You* get to join in with a shout of "¡bravo!" or "¡olé!"

Working up the food chain from the steely-stomached student, try **El Candil Viejo**, founded in 1940, which is off Plaza del Mercado at Calle Ventura Ruiz Aguilera 10; Tel: (9-23) 21-72-39. Viejo has a barroom at the entry and a dining room beyond. The bar is a crowded, noisy, friendly place, with parents showing off their children to friends; good *tapas* served by efficient, brusque bartenders. Both restaurants have white-tablecloth decor, and their cuisine is typically Castilian, with such dishes as *tostón* and *lechazo pierna asado* (two variations of suckling pig), *truchas del Tormes* (trout from the Río Tormes), and *sopa de rabo de buey* (oxtail soup). Service in both places is efficient and somewhat aloof, as often befits success, so make reservations.

For seafood try **Albatros**, Calle Obispo Jarrín 10–12, east of Plaza del Mercado. Panelled walls, glass cases of wine bottles, and tanks of large lobsters and crabs all befit a seafood restaurant—although there are also the haunches of dried pigs hanging from hooks over the small bar. Albatros serves a very flavorful *sopa de marisco* (seafood soup) and a delicious *lubina de Cantábrica con hinojo* (grilled Cantabrian sea bass with fennel). It has the dignity common to good Spanish restaurants; tasty dining in quiet, pleasant, low-key circumstances; Tel: (9-23) 26-93-87.

If you simply can't wait until 9:00 P.M. for dinner without having a *tapas* or two, there are a couple of bars near the Albatros on Calle Obispo Jarrín where, on a weekend evening, people from the neighborhood will be cheering—or hissing—*futbol* on TV. Sometimes, for whatever reason, everybody leaves one bar and flows lemming-like to the other one. If you'd like to be in the flow, try either **The Big Apple** (number 11) or, right across the street next to the Albatros, **Don Sancho** (number 18).

King of the Salamanca dining mountain, though, is unquestionably **Chez Victor**, which, despite the name, is not limited to French cuisine. It gets a star from stingy Michelin, which is significant because there is only a handful of restaurants so sanctified in all of northwestern Spain. Just west of Plaza Mayor at Calle Espoz y Mina 26, Chez Victor reflects the union of Salamanca-born chef Victor and his French-born wife, Marguerite. It is difficult to go wrong here whatever you order; just bring an appetite—and money. Tel: (9-23) 21-31-23.

Shopping in Salamanca

North of Plaza Mayor and Plaza del Mercado is a network of small shops, many selling shoes and handbags, along Calle Pozo Amarillo. **Venus Droguería & Perfumería**, at Calle Pozo Amarillo 12, sells fancy gifts and gadgets, such as folding knives, clippers, clocks, necklaces, and perfumes. The pedestrian street Calle Ventura Ruiz Aguilera is lined with *tapas* bars, pizzerias, and cafés, such as **El Caudillo Rosa**, at number 8. Perhaps you'll encounter the one-man band, a talented fellow with exuberant mustachios, playing a silver trumpet while accompanying himself on a Yamaha keyboard with amplifier ensconced in a wheelbarrow.

Salamanca has a strong tradition of leathercraft and garment making. Some shops that carry leather and fur goods are: **Armino**, Corral de Villaverde 4, a kilometer northeast of Plaza Mayor near Plaza de España; **Abolengo**, on Plaza Mayor at number 6; and **Campero**, Plaza del Corillo 5, south of Plaza Mayor and adjacent to Plaza del Poeta Iglesias.

Beautiful jewelry, with the delicate gold and silver filigree work that is part of the traditional Salamancan costume, is also crafted in the Plaza Mayor area. Rings, earrings, and key rings are readily available in jewelers' and souvenir shops. Jewelers and other shops can also be found in the **Multiplaza**, a general shopping mall located off the Plaza Mayor.

There are excellent hunting and fishing areas in this region of Spain, and outfitters in Salamanca include **Sky**, Avenida Portugal 48, due north from Plaza Mayor along Calle de Zamora and right on Avenida Portugal to Calle los Ovalles; and **Esterra**, southeast of Plaza Mayor near the Torre del Clavero at Calle del Consuelo 16.

Excursions from Salamanca

SOUTHEAST OF SALAMANCA

Alba de Tormes

Route C 510 picks up the trail of Saint Teresa of Avila at Alba de Tormes, 23 km (14 miles) southeast of Salamanca. This medieval town was once the domain of the duke of Alba, whose ancient castle still stands over all. Alba has several interesting churches: the Romanesque-Mudejar San Miguel, the church of Santiago, the church of San Pedro, and the 12th-century San Juan. A medieval bridge with 22 arches spans the Río Tormes, on one side of which stands the convent of **Las Carmelitas Descalzas**, founded by Saint Teresa in 1571. The body of Saint Teresa is preserved in a tomb in the main altar of the church, and the cell in which she died in 1582 has been reconstructed. (If you want to continue on the trail of Saint Teresa, head southeast on route N 501 to Avila, 98 km/60 miles from Salamanca. See our Side Trips from Madrid chapter.)

You can have a saddle made in Alba de Tormes, and beautiful leather boots in the towns of **Alaraz** or **Macotera**, both to the east. Continue southeast from Alba de Tormes to Valdecarres, then turn left (north) onto SA 113 for Macotera, or continue straight ahead for Alaraz. From Alaraz, C 610 goes north through Macotera and joins N 501 at Peñaranda de Bracamonte; turn left at that junction to return to Salamanca.

SOUTHWEST OF SALAMANCA

Another day can be spent southwest of Salamanca at **Robliza de Cojos**, about 31 km (18 miles) on N 620, where the local cattle ranches produce some of Spain's finest bulls—and bull barons, who, come September fiesta, will don native dress and attempt to take over Salamanca (they draw a crowd, so book early for a September visit). You'll find more leather-crafters—saddles, boots—in **Martín de Yeltes**, another 25 km (15 miles) southwest, and in **Villar de Ciervo**, **Lumbrales**, and **La Bouza**, all west of Martín de Yeltes.

CIUDAD RODRIGO

Some 90 km (54 miles) southwest from Salamanca on N 620 is Ciudad Rodrigo, with its majestic wall (40 feet thick and nearly a mile and a half long) around a small and relaxed

PORTUGAL

Emblase de Almendra

Lumbrales

La Bouza

Villavieja

Villar de Ciervo

Martín de Yeltes

C 517

C 525

N 620/E 80

SA 322

Tamames

to Portugal

C 515

Ciudad Rodrigo

SIERRA DE

La Alberca

Fuenteguinaldo

Mogarraz

C 526

N

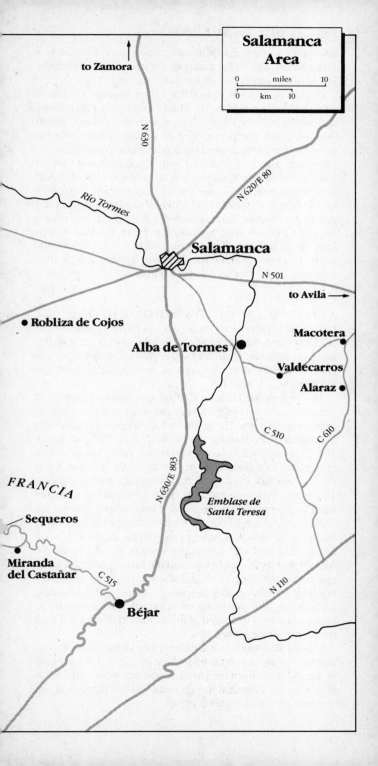

Salamanca Area

0 miles 10

0 km 10

to Zamora

N 630

N 620/E 80

Río Tormes

Salamanca

N 501

to Avila →

● **Robliza de Cojos**

Alba de Tormes ●

Macotera ●

Valdecarros

Alaraz ●

C 510

C 610

N 630/E 803

FRANCIA

Sequeros

Miranda del Castañar

C 515

Emblase de Santa Teresa

N 110

● **Béjar**

town with a graceful Gothic cathedral, a good parador in a 14th-century castle (for lunch or for overnight), and small, lovely plazas ideally suited for quiet strolling.

Ciudad Rodrigo is named for Count Rodrigo González, who took the town from the Moors in the mid-12th century and began reorganizing it into a bulwark of the Castilian frontier. From the perspective of a mile or two away, its appeal to the military mind becomes instantly evident, as the fortress is astride a high cliff with a commanding view of many miles. Arthur Wellesley saw it—and took it for his own in a surprise attack on the French early in 1812, enabling him to be a grandee of Spain, duke of Ciudad Rodrigo, even before he became duke of Wellington. You can see what a sentry might have seen by walking the wall. A series of steps lead up to the top of the wall, which was built with the angles of a many-pointed star. This wall is one of the pleasurable reasons for visiting Ciudad Rodrigo.

AROUND IN CIUDAD RODRIGO

Walking about Ciudad Rodrigo is a joy. There's a relaxed feel of being "far from the capital." The old town is the interesting part, as usual, small and self-contained, and the pace is easy, especially if you're coming here directly from the hurly-burly of a large city.

The ▶ **Parador Enrique II**, Plaza del Castillo 1, is a good rendezvous—you can park your car and lunch there before exploring the town. The menu includes regional dishes such as *alberjas blancos de la Nate* (stewed beans with partridge). The 27-room parador is a 15th-century castle covered with enough ivy to make an Ivy Leaguer feel right at home. If you elect to stay, ask for a room that overlooks the Río Agueda. These rooms have small balconies overlooking a formal garden of geometric hedges and stately juniper cones. One of the more agreeable things to do in this part of Spain is to sit on one of those balconies of an evening and look down at the garden and out across the ancient tile roofs, to the Agueda and its Roman bridge and the broad plain beyond— and not *do* anything. Just watch the sun go down. Observe a hundred starlings as they desperately wheel and dive against a deepening sky, practicing evasion tactics while they try to figure out who's in charge of the formation. It's a good cool spot for morning coffee, too.

Ciudad Rodrigo is not a difficult city to find your way in, and wandering around is part of the pleasure. Ask for a map of the old town from the parador desk and walk to the Plaza Mayor or the cathedral through tree-shaded plazas and under balconies with hanging plants.

The Cathedral

Ciudad Rodrigo's magnificent cathedral, east of the Plaza Mayor through Plaza de San Salvador, was begun by Ferdinand II in 1190 (Ferdinand also added greatly to the fortifications) and was continued in the 13th and 14th centuries. The apse was designed by Rodrigo Gil de Hontañón in the 16th century, and the choir stalls (1503) are by Rodrigo de Alemán, who is best known for dotting the Spanish countryside with parish churches whose choir stalls are covered with pagan-inspired designs like the ones you'll find here. The Renaissance altar features a breathtaking alabaster *Descent from the Cross,* and the Capilla de Cerralbo houses a painting by José Ribera.

The Plaza Mayor

Ciudad Rodrigo's Plaza Mayor is a mix of the ancient with active commercial enterprise on a wide cobblestone street with shops, stores, cafés, and banks with cash machines. The *ayuntamiento* (town hall), once the court and prison of the town, is a lovely Renaissance mansion at the east end of the plaza. Take a coffee break at **Don Julián**, Calle de la Colada 3, at the west end of Plaza Mayor. Cool and dark inside, the Don Julián serves tasty *tapas* such as *huevo relleno* (a hard-boiled egg inside a flaky, tasty crust) and has outside tables on the plaza that, when the sun has retreated a bit, make a congenial place to observe evening plaza life. Nearby, for lunch or dinner, is **Restaurant Mayton**, Calle de la Colada 9, which includes regional dishes on its menu. Dinner reservations are advisable; Tel: (9-23) 46-07-20. **El Rodeo**, at the other end of the plaza on Calle Gigantes 6, is a secluded, small bar with many pictures of matadors in action and repose. It has a small *comedor* and good *tapas*. If a picnic is your pleasure, you can be well outfitted at **Supermercado Tandy**, Calle Diez Taravilla 9, the second street west of the plaza, where you will find everything from bread to booze.

If you've been travelling about the region and listening to the musical (maybe) clank (certainly) of *ciseros* (cowbells), and want one for your very own, visit **Casa Juvenal**, the tiny workshop of Jesús Castaño Aparicio, Rúa del Sol 27, at the east end of Plaza Mayor. Señor Garzón, spirited but courteous, accepts commissions for crafting medals and trophies in gold when he's not welding tractor frames or plow blades. Some of his handsome cow and goat bells can rightly be termed *objets d'art*.

Ciudad Rodrigo's annual carnival of the *toro* is the local version of Mardi Gras, during which a wild time is had by all as bulls run through the streets and tourists try to stay out of the way.

SOUTH FROM CIUDAD RODRIGO

About an hour's drive southwest of Ciudad Rodrigo are the rugged and beautiful mountains of the **Sierra de la Peña de Francia** (named, it is believed, in honor of 11th-century French colonists) and the quite remote mountain village of La Alberca, where life continues much as it probably was 500 years ago. La Alberca carries lightly the weight of its role as a national monument, meaning no stone may be turned without government approval. Nearby, equally steeped in time, is **Miranda del Castañar**, still two steps ahead of monumentalization. Past La Alberca, down the flank of the Sierra de la Peña de Francia, quiet and remote, winding and twisting, down and down a dozen kilometers or so (7 or 8 miles), lies the pleasant green valley of Las Batuecas, right on the Extremadura border.

From Ciudad Rodrigo follow C 515, a narrow secondary road with a decent surface, through rolling farmland where the brilliant yellow of new wheat shines against green seas of grass, olive trees toss in the wind like dancers in abandon, and fields of poppies spring up periodically. At the southern end of the hamlet of El Maillo (about 30 km/19 miles from Ciudad Rodrigo) you have a choice of continuing straight ahead on C 515 to Sequeros and, eventually, Béjar, or turning right onto SA 202 at the sign to La Alberca, 11 km (6½ miles) distant. Farther south on C 515 at El Cabaco there is another access to La Alberca: SA 202, rougher, twistier, but more interesting scenically, is currently being upgraded, which has both good and bad aspects, as a better road will surely draw more traffic. Just beyond a one-lane bridge over the Río Francia, and just short of La Alberca, there is a campground for tents and caravans, ▶ **Camping Al-bereka**, a new facility with a small café and a gracious hostess.

La Alberca

When small Spanish villages are converted into national monuments, there is always a trade-off, and La Alberca is no exception. The villagers gain some economic relief in return for the inevitable invasion, while the visitor may not see quite precisely the village of old but does get, in the case of this village at least, a reasonable approximation and some creature comforts as well. Walk past the vendors (as yet unjaded, eager to please) displaying their objects of woven straw, a typical product of the region, past the kids playing soccer on the cobblestones, and you will see a pretty place of Moorish origination, much as it has been for five centuries. A sour old farmer slouched over a shaggy white mule, with saddle bags of gaily-colored straw, taking up the middle of the street is still *típico* of town life.

On the main street, among the gift shops, there is the **Fábrica de Muebles**, a furniture maker displaying small, heavy wood chests and armchairs, crafted in the Spanish style, and huge copper pans. Up the hill is the ▶ **Hotel Las Batuecas**, in an attractive, squarish, stone building with a big comfortable lounge area, cool and dark, and a good-sized *comedor* for lunch or dinner. And the pleasant young woman behind the reception desk speaks better English than she thinks she does.

AROUND LA ALBERCA

Due south of La Alberca, S 201 climbs the peak of El Portillo, 4,000 feet high, then descends into hairpin hell, down into the green valleys of **Las Batuecas**, which until the 17th century were believed to be populated by fiendishly evil spirits—fears theoretically allayed when a Carmelite monastery was erected nearby in 1599.

East from La Alberca S 202 leads to **Mogarraz**, Miranda del Castañar, and **Béjar**—all excellent sources for regional leather and jewelry products. From Béjar, you can pick up N 630/E 803 and head straight on up to Salamanca, 73 km (43 miles) north.

ZAMORA

Zamora, rising prettily from the north bank of the Río Duero 62 km (38 miles) north of Salamanca (by way of N 630) and about 250 km (155 miles) from Madrid, is capital of the province of Zamora—and of its own destiny, if one accepts the city's motto, *"Zamora no se ganó en una hora"* ("Zamora was not won in an hour").

Zamora was a stronghold in the revolt of *los comunidades* (the cities), the general uprising by *los comuneros* (the commoners). The protest, which spanned Castile, grew out of the demands of the first Hapsburg in Spain, Carlos I, king of Castile, soon elected (1519) Holy Roman Emperor, as Charles V. Prior to Carlos I, Spain was divided into many separate kingdoms and principalities, not unlike Germany in the very early 19th century. Castilian towns and cities had a tradition of independence and self-determination dating to the Romans, a tradition not surrendered lightly to Carlos's drive to take power. The *comuneros* attempted to band together in defiance of Carlos but rapidly degenerated into class strife, but a unified, centrally controlled Spain gradually came into being.

Around in Zamora

The first conde (count) de Alba y Aliste built a palace in Zamora in 1459; it was rebuilt by the fourth count of that title after Zamora was retaken from the *comuneros*. That palace is now the handsome ▶ **Parador de Turismo Condes de Alba y Aliste**, which you can find by following the signs for *centro ciudad* to Plaza de Viriato 5, off Calle de Ramos Carrión. Zamora is a small city with a population of 60,000, but it has a quiet, small-town feel, and the 27-room parador is at the center of what you will most likely care to see. Inside this *palacio* is a patio whose four sides, rather than being open, are huge windows, two-story walls, in fact, of multipaned glass in stout wooden frames—quite striking. Its grand staircase (watched over by a knight and horse in armor) is a stunning example of Leonese-Castilian architecture. Each of the patio's columns has a crowning medallion depicting a historical or mythological figure; the family tree of the original owners of the palace appears as well.

THE CHURCHES OF ZAMORA

If you like old churches, Zamora could be your town, for there is a remarkable array of Romanesque examples with Byzantine overtones dating from as early as the 11th century. Just next door to the parador, on Calle Ramos Carrión, is the **Iglesia de San Cipriano**, which was begun in 1025. It is a rather squat building with fine exterior carvings; inside is a handsome 15th-century Madonna.

A block farther west (after Ramos Carrión has become Rúa de los Francos) is **Iglesia de la Magdalena**, a 13th-century church with only one aisle. It has rose windows worthy of note, an arched doorway carved with flora and fauna, and a pair of canopied tombs within. Diagonally across the street from La Magdalena is the **Iglesia de San Ildefonso**. Built in the 11th century and rebuilt several times since, this church boasts a tower from 1719 by the flashy Joaquín Churriguera. Inside, behind seven locks, are said to be the relics of the town's patron saints. There is also a fine triptych by an unidentified master.

THE CATHEDRAL

Rúa de los Francos turns into Rúa de los Notarios on its way westward to the cathedral, a 10- or 12-minute walk from the parador near the edge of the city. Still partially surrounded by ancient walls, the cathedral is looked over by the ruins of a 12th-century castle. The first thing you notice is its great dome: While it is properly Romanesque, having been completed in 1174, the dome's style is decidedly Byzantine. Within Zamora province you can find a sprinkling of other examples of this style—but you will not find anything like it anywhere else in Spain. The dome is surrounded by four smaller, rounded towers with points, and the whole effect, with flat, overlapping stones, is Turkish in flavor. The entire structure is gigantic, and its square tower only adds to the architecturally entertaining hodgepodge. Within are great doors, huge columns, and painted, twisted ribs supporting the grand dome.

Architecture aside, there are treasures to be found in the cathedral. The choir stalls, behind an exquisitely intricate wrought-iron grille (there are several such grilles here), are carved with figures of saints and biblical personages, each with a sympathetic face. On the undersides of the seats and on the armrests are carvings of dragons and other beasts in odd positions, and comparably zany scenes from the lives of monks. These last were meant as satires, and during the 16th century the seats were nailed down by church officials so they couldn't be seen. In a side altar on the left you can see the sculpted 13th-century *Virgen de la Calva,* painted in the 16th century. A silver monstrance from 1515 is also on display.

The cathedral's cloister is unexceptional, but leading off it, up a small staircase, is a **museum** with a fine collection of Flemish tapestries given to the church by the sixth count of Alba y Aliste in 1608. The ones depicting the Trojan War are particularly vivid.

After exiting the cathedral, cross the plaza and walk to the right along the network of tree-shaded little streets that parallel the hustle and bustle of the larger streets. The river curves ever inward, and you are soon back near the parador.

DINING IN ZAMORA

Turn right from the door of the parador to get to the **Plaza Mayor,** a few minutes' walk northeast. For lunch or *tapas* try **Serafín**: Walk under the arcade of the *ayuntamiento viejo* (old town hall) on the south side of the plaza, bear right at the fork just beyond to Plaza Sagasta, to the right of which is Serafín, at Plaza Maestro Haedo 10; Tel: (9-80) 53-14-22. It's a sunny, pleasant, low-key place with a very long bar (and a courteous barman), and tables next to the windows. The tasty *tapas* offered include *boquerones* (dried anchovies, not overly salty); *arroz con chorizo* (rice with sausage), and *calamare* (squid). There's also a dining room for the lustier appetite. For fancy (and expensive) dining, try **Rey Don Sancho,** Parque de la Marina Española 2, serving regional cuisine in a garden and on an outdoor terrace. Dinner reservations are a good idea here; Tel (9-80) 52-60-54. Parque de la Marina Española is a 20- or 25-minute walk east (in the same direction as Serafín) from the parador or the Plaza Mayor.

San Pedro de la Nave

An interesting side trip from Zamora is to the **Iglesia de San Pedro de la Nave**, 20 km (12 miles) northwest of Zamora. Take N 122 west for 12 km (7½ miles), then turn right onto a narrow, poorly paved road, following signs to the town of **El Campillo**. When you enter town, ask how to see San Pedro; it isn't always open, but someone will be glad to show you around. The simple church dates from the end of the seventh century and contains some marvelous examples of pre-Moorish Christian carvings, mostly of scenes from the Old Testament.

LEON

The city of León lies largely along the east bank of the Río Benesga, 320 km (198 miles) northwest of Madrid, 198 km (123 miles) north of Salamanca, 136 km (85 miles) north of Zamora, and 216 km (134 miles) west of Burgos. Around the time of the birth of Christ, Augustus sent Rome's Seventh Legion here as a bulwark against Asturians raiding out of the mountains to the north of León. By the tenth century the kings of León *were* Asturians and ruled a vast section of Spain: south through present-day Valladolid, Zamora, and Salamanca; Asturias, Cantabria, and Galacia to the north and west; even northern Portugal before that country achieved independence in 1140. Two hundred years later Peter the Cruel of León, allying himself with the Black Prince of England against France, initiated the city's decline by moving his court to Seville, only to lose at the battle of Montiel, in 1369, and be murdered in the French commander's tent. León was left to be ruled from afar.

León continued to administer to pilgrims seeking Santiago but, absented from political power, gradually dissolved into the decay noted by English travellers of the 19th century. More recently León has experienced new energy (quite literally, as a broker of the surplus of hydroelectric power enjoyed by northern Spain) and a renaissance, partly as a result of nearby iron and coal mining, and has become a successful industrial city.

Today León, with a population slightly more than 130,000, has the feeling of a well-managed city pulled by two dynamics: its rich heritage and its current role of boom town. The old district, epitomized by the Plaza Mayor and nearby small ancient streets (and still, essentially, surrounded by walls), is nestled right beside modern buildings along ample streets and thoroughfares. Somehow, it works. (Or it *would* work, were it not for the street signs. Spain, in the course of its urban updating, seems determined to rip the old street labels from corner buildings and replace them with some obscure obeisance to designers that is probably fine with the locals, but can be hell for the uninitiated.)

Parador Hostal de San Marcos

Penetrating León from any direction means threading through traffic throngs past modern-day buildings and other unremarkable evidences of the late 20th century. Stay with it though, think thoughts of the ▶ **Parador Hostal de San Marcos**, Plaza de San Marcos 7, the parador—and paragon—of León. Follow the *centro urbano* signs around beautiful fountain plazas, and purity and pluck will surely lead you to this quite extraordinary church, cloister, museum, and opulent hotel—all under one remarkable, 300-foot-long roof—standing with grand ease on the east bank of the Bernesga. (Coming from the south on N 630, go left after crossing the river, halfway around the Plaza de Toros onto Avenida de la Facultad de Veterinaria, and parallel the river to Plaza de San Marcos.)

Successful cities, cities with pride, usually have some unifying symbol. León's proud pennant has surely been, for several centuries, its cathedral, joined, more recently, by the Parador Hostal de San Marcos. Even if you're day-tripping or staying at another hotel, the hostal is a good beginning and ending point for a tour of León's other attractions, most of which are in a loose cluster in the old town, a 20- to 25-minute walk, or a 10-minute taxi ride, to the east.

It was the idea of Doña Sancha (the wife of Ferdinand II) late in the 12th century to build a church and hospital near the bridge that carried the main road—and thus thousands of pilgrims—out of León toward Santiago. Shortly thereafter the canons and friars of San Loyo, a military order, took over. Under the auspices of Ferdinand II they formed the military order of Santiago of the Sword in 1173, with the purpose of protecting pilgrims en route to Santiago from highwaymen and bandits, providing lodging in their inns, medical care in their hospitals, and, when necessary, burial in their cemeteries. Nothing of that original building remains.

In 1513 the Order of Santiago began the construction of a lavish new building to house their ever-growing activities and staff. Construction was supervised over the centuries by many important figures in Spanish art and architecture. Construction went on and on, finally ending in the 18th century with an addition to the main façade.

As you face the complex, the hotel entrance is on the left and the church is on the right. The cloisters are in the rear of the church and can be reached via the north end of the transept (the cloisters are frequently closed but can be seen through enormous glass windows from the hotel). The Museo Arqueológico—small but important—can be reached through either the hotel lobby or the right end of the transept; it occupies the sacristy designed by Juan de Badajoz in 1549, and two adjacent rooms.

The structure itself is remarkable. The exterior of the building has an enormous Plateresque façade, extravagant with statues, pillars, medallions, scallop shells (symbol of the Camino de Santiago), and visages of famous Spaniards. Above the main door is a figure of Santiago (Saint James) on horseback, and this entire section of the façade is in the shape of a Spanish lady's coiffure or hat. To stand at a slight distance in front of the Parador Hostal de San Marcos in the morning light is to be dazzled. The building's proportion of extreme width to moderate height seems an ideal shape that is simultaneously grand and simple. A border of cheerful pansies looks impertinent beneath the towering Plateresque façade.

THE CHURCH AND MUSEUM

The church of San Marcos is a fine piece of work, with extraordinary choir stalls on the upper level. The intricate wood carvings depict the Apostles in the upper row and biblical characters in the lower. The cloister was built in three stages during the 16th, 17th, and 18th centuries. Stop to see the large relief by Juan de Juni depicting the Nativity.

The **Museo Arqueológico** is notable for its Romanesque capitals, Iberian artifacts, and Roman mosaics and sarcophagi, but its real treasures are two crosses: the 11th-century ivory crucifix known as *Cristo de Carrizo,* which is unforgettable for the penetrating gaze, braided hair, and tunic of its Christ figure, which suggest Byzantine influences; and the tenth-century Mozarabic *Cruz de Penalba.*

THE HOTEL

The choice rooms (some of them grandiloquent suites) in the Parador Hostal San Marcos are those in the original monastery facing the plaza. The walls of the old monastery's rooms are three feet thick, offering plenty of privacy. Many of the rooms are decorated with works of art dating back as far as 1027. Tapestries cover the walls in some rooms, and you might find that your bed has a hand-carved headboard. Other rooms have four-poster beds or handwoven rugs. The hotel offers a bridal suite, or you might prefer a suite in the tower, where the ceilings are 20 feet high. Some of the suites have canopied beds and marble bathtubs.

The Parador Hostal de San Marcos is a place for people who want to feel the ambience of centuries of history—all in comfort, with television and minibar, of course. Considering world deluxe hotel prices, this one is a rather astonishing bargain (possibly matched only by the parador at Santiago de Compostela, Hostal de los Reyes Católicos). While the rooms in the newer wing are nothing to sneer at—those looking out onto the Bernesga and its medieval bridge, especially late in the day as the river turns to dusky gold, are quite lovely—if you want a taste of past grandeur, make certain to specify reservations in the original building. Parking in the rear is protected by fence and guarded entry.

The San Marcos's restaurant, the **Rey Don Sancho**, is excellent, and the grilled trout is a regional specialty. If for some reason you can't stay at the San Marcos, at the very least visit the grand, Moorish-style bar in the lobby—everyone in León, dressed up or dressed down, eventually stops by for a drink.

(If you are unable to get a room at the Parador Hostal San Marcos, try the ▶ **Hotel Riosol**, Avenida de Palencia 3, on the west side of the river across the bridge—guarded by two stone lions—from the Plaza Glorieta de Guzmán El Bueno.)

Around in the Old Town

From the San Marcos you can take a very pleasant walk under the trees of the Paseo Condesa de Sagasta along the river. Buy a city map from the news kiosk across from the hotel on the *paseo* and you can ponder as you amble. This route is a bit out of the way, but it is a pretty park and does put off the plunge into the commercial area. In the evening, its role as *paseo* expands as people walk dogs, lovers stroll, philosophers take issue. There's a footbridge across the Bernesga halfway along to the Plaza Glorieta de Guzmán El Bueno; turn away from the river at the plaza (with its extraordinary fountain, one of many around the city, reflective of the superabundance of water in northern Spain) and go east along Avenida de Ordoño II (named for a tenth-century king of León; his father, Alfonso III, gave him Galicia), a busy commercial and shopping thoroughfare lined with banks, clothing stores, jewelers, drugstores, and services. The women's clothing store **Novedades EDI**, on the north side of Ordoño II, sells the traditional embroidered stole called *mantón de Manilla;* **San José Optica y Radio**, Avenida de Ordoño II 19, has many types of photographic film as well as audio supplies. There's an excellent Telefonica office, lime green and marked by a large *T,* where you can make domestic or international calls, on Calle Burgo Nuevo 15, which is a block south and parallel to Avenida de Ordoño II.

THE PLAZA DE SANTO DOMINGO — PLAZA DE SAN MARCELO AREA

Avenida de Ordoño II becomes Calle Generalísimo Franco at the Plaza de Santo Domingo, with its rather prosaic fountain. Grouped nearby are the 16th-century Palacio de los Guzmanes, at right angles to the late-19th-century Casa de los Botines, designed by Antoni Gaudí, which is across the Plaza de San Marcelo from the 1585 *ayuntamiento* (town hall). After seeing these diverse buildings you might enjoy exploring this lovely little square as well, which has three restaurant-bars grouped next to each other at its east end.

Casa de los Botines

On the north side of the plaza, across Calle Generalísimo Franco, is Casa de los Botines, built in 1894. It may not be great Gaudí, but to the *aficionado* a little Gaudí is better than none at all. This one resembles a child's idea of a medieval castle, with stone-inlaid towers at each corner that seem straight from a small boy's dream of knights of old. Over the main entrance, Saint James on horseback and in full armor keeps a crocodile from molesting any of the customers entering the Caja España's branch office on the ground floor. Each window in the five-story building is different: your basic Gaudí effect. (Gaudí's palace for a bishop is in Astorga, 46 km/28 miles west of León.)

Palacio de los Guzmanes

The Palacio de los Guzmanes (the Guzmanes were a family of wealthy noblemen) is at the corner of Calles Generalísimo Franco and El Cid. Begun in 1559, this old building, now housing the *diputación* (county council), has stone tablets in front that display the family arms; note the beautifully preserved Renaissance patio inside with Doric columns and oculi punctuating the arcade. The building also has the distinction of having a doorway located off-center, making the entire façade appear a bit wobbly.

The Ayuntamiento

The *ayuntamiento* (town hall), at the east end of Plaza de San Marcelo, is a handsome Renaissance building. The imperial coat of arms of León crowns the façade, and the building houses historical documents as well as a collection of full-length portraits of all of León's monarchs, from the beginning to the 20th century.

At this end of the plaza, in a spring morning's soft light, there is a feel of old Spain. A lone shade tree stands in front of the *ayuntamiento*. A few young guardhouse soldiers may be weeding flower beds, raking leaves, sweeping, working out minor infractions under the eye of a guard their own age, who will perhaps be sharing a cigarette with one of his prisoners. There is a pleasant hustle-bustle of people on missions in and out of the *ayuntamiento*. If you have to conduct business with the city, this certainly is an attractive circumstance in which to do it.

Bars and Restaurants around the Ayuntamiento

At lunchtime many people repair to **Bar los Pelayos**, directly across from the entry to the *ayuntamiento* (Pelayo was the legendary Asturian chieftain who, in the eighth century, led the first uprising against the Moors). This is primarily a stand-up bar with sandwiches and *tapas*. Things are usually jumping in this busy place with a mix of lawyers, artists, intellectuals, laborers, and young workers from the *ayuntamiento,* who all come to drink beer or wine or coffee and interject an animated opinion. It's a good stop if you want just a quick snack before moving on. Next door is **Casa Pozo**, at Plaza de San Marcelo 15, more of a sit-down restaurant, open for lunch and quite popular for dinner. It has full-course dinners with wine starting at 2,500 pesetas, in addition to an à la carte menu; Tel: (9-87) 22-30-39 or 23-71-03. (The owner's brother has his own establishment, **Adonias**, at Santa Nonia 16, in the new part of town. This moderately priced restaurant features terrific food and is decorated with Spanish ceramics; Tel: 9-87/20-67-68.) Next to Casa Pozo is **Principal**, closer to Bar los Pelayos in ambition but without the clientele—maybe because the *tapas* are too oily.

Basílica de San Isidoro

A long block north of Plaza de San Marcelo, along Rúa de Salazar, is the Basílica de San Isidoro, a Romanesque structure built on the ruins of an ancient temple, subsequently dedicated to Saint John the Baptist, that was destroyed by Almanzor's troops in the tenth century. Alfonso V built a modest church here shortly thereafter. Ferdinand I, the first king of León and Castile, began to build a new church in honor of San Isidoro on the site in 1063, when he ordered the saint's remains transferred to León from southern Spain. Ferdinand died in the structure five days after the remains arrived, and now only the pantheon remains from Ferdinand's reign. His daughter, Queen Urraca, had the building expanded from the pantheon later that century, and Alfonso VIII completed the right nave in the second half of the 12th century. This is the structure we see today.

THE LIBRARY AND MUSEUM

The route through the basilica to the royal crypt takes you through the library, museum, and treasury. The library includes a Bible that dates from 960. The museum is located in a spacious hallway and houses many interesting Roman pieces, including stone tablets found during excavations in the kitchen garden of the old monastery. Many of the objects bear the seal of the Seventh Legion of Rome.

THE TREASURY

But it is the treasury that could very well take your breath away. In an 11th-century wood-and-silver casket are the remains of San Isidoro. Born in 570, Isidoro was an important figure in early Spanish history when the country was undergoing the transition from Roman rule to the autonomy of individual regions. He was known as "Doctor de las Españas" (note the plural). As the bishop of Seville, in 619 he presided over the second Council of Seville and in 636 (the year of his death), the fourth Council of Toledo, at which ecclesiastical laws were reviewed and rewritten to strengthen the Church in its dealings with the changing political scene.

Another notable item in the treasury collection is a tenth-century ivory piece carved in the shape of a coiled dragon. There is also a casket containing the remains of San Pelayo and Saint John the Baptist, a gift from Ferdinand II and his queen, Doña Sancha, inlaid with 26 pieces of ivory. Another casket is a 12th-century enameled piece from Limoges. There is a chalice made of onyx mounted on gold and surrounded by precious gems. The treasury also contains a priceless collection of medieval tapestries, including two 12th-century stoles said to have been designed by the noblewoman Leonore Plantagenet.

THE ROYAL PANTHEON

In the royal pantheon are the remains of many early Spanish monarchs and other royal personages: 11 kings, 12 queens, 21 princes, and various nobles. The crypt is adorned with many fine Romanesque works. The magnificent ceiling of the mausoleum has earned the basilica the sobriquet "the Sistine Chapel of Romanesque Art"; the almost completely preserved Romanesque frescoes date from the reign of Ferdinand II (1157–1188). They depict Christ enthroned, biblical figures, themes from the Apocalypse, the first complete Nativity scene in all of Spain, the constellations, and themes from everyday life—all in ochers, violets, blues, yellows, and grays.

The Cathedral

The basilica is more a quiet, peaceful place of worship than is the cathedral, the so-called "jewel of León," a five-minute walk southeast along Calle Fernando Reguera, past Plaza Omana, and left on Calle Damisco Merino. Arguably the finest Spanish Gothic cathedral, it has been described as "Spain's simplest and purest Gothic building." Begun in 1258 and finished in the 14th century, the church is distinctive for its shape and sheen, seeming to be made of golden sandstone.

THE WINDOWS

Be prepared for glass—a *lot* of glass—composing more than half of the cathedral. The initial reaction usually is: How does this building remain standing? The everyday, run-of-the-mill cathedral makes do with half a dozen or so windows; the "jewel" here has 125 windows plus quite a few circles (oculi) and three enormous roses. These are not just squinty little apertures, either, but 40-foot expanses filled with stained glass, some of which goes back to the 13th century and is arranged in three themes: The lowest level represents the flora of León; the next level is drawn from heraldic themes; and the upper windows represent saints, prophets, martyrs, monarchs, and other important figures. The rose window above the south portal is, especially, an astounding work of art.

AROUND IN THE CATHEDRAL

"The windows *are* the cathedral," the locals insist, but while the stained glass is by far the most stunning feature of the cathedral, it certainly is not the only one. Nice detail can be seen in many of the doorjambs, displaying figures from legend. The Locus Appelation, the place where the supreme court of justice in ancient León met to settle disputes, is in the cathedral, dominated by a statue representing Justice.

The diocese of León makes imaginative use of its splendid cathedral with occasional exhibits, such as the recent Ages of Man, which followed the development of Western music using the church's organ and bells and objects from the Museo Diocesano (see below) to illustrate its theme. You may want to make advance inquiries about the special-events schedule during your visit—the organ festival is in September and October, and there are music festivals in May and June.

THE MUSEO DIOCESANO

Across the street in the Seminario Mayor, the museum comprises three separate galleries. The first houses a collection of paintings, including *The Adoration of the Three Kings* by Pedro Campana and *La Inmaculada* by Eugenio de Cajes. There is also a Mozarabic Bible, considered to be the oldest existing Romance-language document in Spain. The second room of the museum houses a cupboard in the Mudejar style, a style much in evidence in León. The third gallery of the museum houses many old stone tablets and statues of Roman origin.

THE LIGHTING OF THE CATHEDRAL

Standing inside the jewel of León is a little like standing inside a kaleidoscope. If you're lucky enough to be present at the right moment *outside* the cathedral, however, there's an even more dazzling sight. That moment is at night with only the building's dark bulk before you. Suddenly the interior lights flash on. The enormous building seems to disappear. All the windows, huge against the night sky, are magically suspended in space. James Michener, on having the good fortune to behold this spectacle, wrote: "It is a rare sight, and if I were in Madrid and someone proposed, 'Let's drive up to León to see the cathedral lit from within,' I would not hesitate to make the journey, for to see this thing is to see something so different as to illuminate a lifetime of travel."

South to San Martín

West of the cathedral, back along Calle Damisco Merino, is the moderately voguish Calle de Cervantes. **Bellas Artes**, at number 15, where Calle de Cervantes meets Calle de Lopez Castillón, is both a well-stocked artists' materials store and a *sala de exposiciones* (art gallery) owned by the low-keyed José Manuel Juárez Pérez; it's a good source for the travelling artist in need. At Calle de Cervantes 9 is **El Gran Café**, a spacious bar-restaurant with a wonderfully long marble-top bar and good-sized tables. It's a late-afternoon favorite of upmarket, slightly self-conscious young folks. Calle de Cervantes ends at busy Calle Generalísimo Franco; nearby, at number 25, is the traditional (it's a hundred years old—it has to be traditional) **Café Victoria**.

South of the cathedral, across Calle Generalísimo Franco, old León continues with a jumble of angled streets interesting in their own right. Calle Mariano Domínguez Berrueta leads to and borders the somewhat scruffy Plaza Mayor, beyond which is the popular Plaza de San Martín. Just off Plaza Mayor is **Mercería Guerrero**, Calle Plegaría 7, nominally a dry-goods store but also a good source for traditional workingman's berets, run by Señor Guerrero, a courteous, energetic, and knowledgeable retailer.

PLAZA DE SAN MARTIN

Plaza de San Martín, the core (perhaps "spirit" would be more precise), of the old quarter, is chockablock with small bars and cafés lining both sides of the street. Take your choice for late-afternoon or early-evening *tapas* and *bebidos.* Tiny **Bar Chivani** serves thick, crusty halved baguettes stuffed with *calamare* and with sardines just out of hot oil. Around 10:00 P.M., though, the plaza comes alive, and by midnight the barroom floors are ankle-deep in *servellitas,* those little twists of paper that accompany drinks, a disheveled tribute to a successful evening. That's when people are two or three deep at the bars of **El Rancho Chico, La Bicha, El Racimo de Oro, El Tizón,** and **El Ruedo**. If you've had enough for one day, you're only ten minutes by taxi from Hostal de San Marcos, or most other hotels.

EXCURSIONS FROM LEON

The southern sector of the province of León is a continuation of La Meseta, while in the northern and northwestern areas begin the mountains that meant hard going for the millions of pilgrims plodding the Camino de Santiago from France to Santiago de Compostela. The source of one person's pain can be another person's pleasure: Hunters, fishermen, and outdoorsmen from Spain and the rest of Europe are drawn to these same mountains for deer, stag, ibex, and wild boar; for rivers and streams (1,800 miles worth) that teem with trout and with salmon homeward bound from the Atlantic; and for winter skiing in several mountain passes. Others seek only the remote solitude and scenic beauty of Europe's last great wilderness.

West of León

When *los peregrinos* (the pilgrims) left behind the hospitality and protection of León, they knew they were on the last third of their seven-month journey along the Camino de Santiago. They also knew that it was the journey's most difficult section. The Camino de Santiago carefully skirted the alpine wilderness of the Cordillera Cantábrica, some of whose peaks never lose their crowns of snow. But the Montes de León now lay across the pilgrims' path; while difficult enough in summer, the León mountains in winter can be as snow-choked and forbidding as the Cordillera.

Today you can still get a sense of the pilgrims' path on a day trip west of León. The old trail parallels the public road quite closely as it winds through a necklace of small villages. This region is known as La Maragatería, home of an ancient

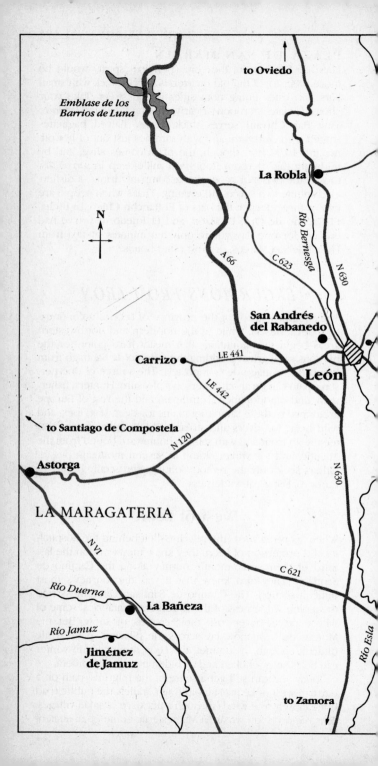

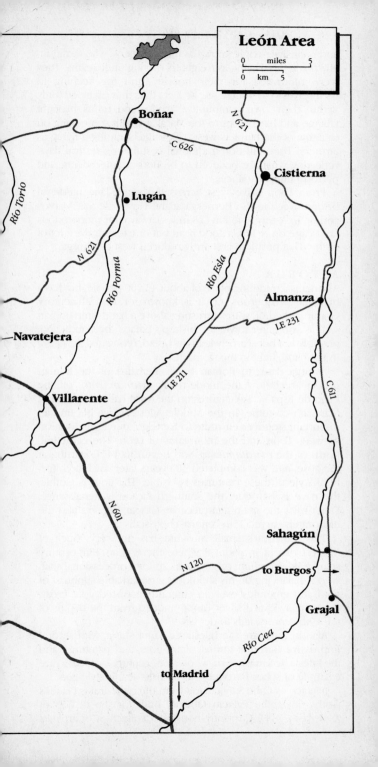

and reclusive people known as the Maragatos, who traditionally made their living as freighters driving mule teams. They were renowned for their honesty, and for keeping to themselves—so much so, in fact, that they married only within their own community. Trucks and trains brought change and hard times to the Maragatos, but some hang on in a few of the hamlets west of Astorga, scraping a living as farmers. They still don traditional costume on festival days, reflecting what are believed to be Berber antecedents, and perform unusual dances.

From León drive west across the single-lane medieval bridge over the Río Bernesga at the Hostal de San Marcos and on to Astorga, 46 km (28 miles) away over monotonous landscape on N 120, a good road but one that draws a lot of traffic. That problem is sharply reduced west of Astorga.

ASTORGA

Astorga is a middling place of about 13,000 people, but has a bustling, prosperous air. It is known for its 15th-century Gothic cathedral, spires thrusting above a handsome Roman wall as you enter town; its "bishop's palace" by Gaudí; and, possibly last but scarcely least, its bread, renowned as "heavy in the hand, light in the stomach."

Astorga dates to Roman times. Remains of the Roman prison are below the modern-day *ayuntamiento,* off the Plaza de España. Two figures on the town hall's clock are in Maragato costume. In the Middle Ages Astorga became an important stopover en route to Santiago, due to its location between León and the mountains of León. The **cathedral**, north of the *ayuntamiento,* was begun in 1471, starting at the apse, and was completed 300 years later. Each architectural style of these centuries is visible: The apse is Gothic, the nave is Baroque, the southern façade is Renaissance. Don't miss the main altarpiece by Gaspar Beçerra and the elaborately carved 15th-century choir stalls.

The cathedral's small museum has not very much of interest except in room 8 where there is an 18th-century small gold seraphim, originally a cap for a processional staff, who is balancing on his shoulders a remarkable sunburst of gold and emeralds over an emerald-encrusted gold cross. Even the awkward silver canopy, added from the depths of the 19th century, fails to detract.

Also in town are the **Iglesia de Santa María**, with several impressive Baroque tombs, altarpieces, and paintings, and the **Iglesia de San Esteban**, whose 16th-century façade is a rare example of sober Baroque—as no-frills as this style gets.

Just across Calle Santa Marta from the cathedral is Gaudí's Gothic joke, the **Palacio Obispo,** built for the bishop of Astorga in 1889. Currently housing a collection of artifacts from the pilgrimages to Santiago, it gets mixed reviews. One assessor has termed its interior tilework "gaudy Gaudí."

Nearby, practically in the cathedral's front yard, is the ► **Hotel Gaudí**, Plaza Ingeniero Eduardo de Castro 6. The hotel has a *comedor* and a large, paneled barroom with a long bar serving *tapas,* and comfortable leather armchairs and tables—a trifle clubby, maybe, but pleasantly cool and dark and just fine on a hot day. It's a perfectly adequate spot for lunch, dinner, or an overnight stay.

West of Astorga is where the flat, featureless landscape of La Meseta finally surrenders to the Montes de León. There are a couple of simple lunch possibilities along the way, but this is also good picnic country. You can gather ingredients in Astorga. There's a line of shops along **Calle de León**: a *pesca* and *fruta* (fish and fruit) shop at number 75; a *carnicería* at number 79, where the butcher will slice some *chorizo* (spicy sausage), or whatever your pleasure; as well as a *farmacía* at number 73. In the other direction down Calle de León, at number 56, is a *panadería* with particularly tasty examples of the Astorga specialty, and sandwiches! ¡Con fruta! ¡Y vino! And don't go off without a bottle of water.

WEST INTO LA MARAGATERIA AND THE MONTES DE LEON

At the north end of Astorga, N 120 converges with N VI, which continues on to Ponferrada. Just before the junction of the two highways is the LE 142 to La Maragatería, a narrow secondary road. If you make this drive in the morning and return in the late afternoon, the sun will be out of your eyes and on the landscape, making the scenery look good and you less cranky. Just a few kilometers west of Astorga is the entrance to **Castillo de los Polvazares**, an expensively, faithfully restored little village of red brick and stone—a great deal of stone—with fresh green doors and green shutters, unquestionably a nice place to live. The local brochures say it is "the most beautiful village in La Maragatería." Perhaps so, but you have to like stone. The main street is particularly lumpy. The local gentry gather at **Mesón la Magdelana**, halfway along the *calle principal,* for lunch or a drink or to overthrow the town government. The restoration process, pure Maragato, helps the Maragatos survive.

LE 142 is a quiet road. The Camino de Santiago parallels close by, and occasionally they are one and the same, with the pilgrim's path so marked by a small iron cross or a stone rendering of a scallop shell, for centuries the symbol of the pilgrim who has completed the journey to Santiago. Most who seek Santiago do so by modern transport, but there is still the occasional pilgrim who treks all the way from France or even more distant points. A few thousand each year qualify for a certificate from church authorities in Santiago by hiking or biking the last 125 miles.

At **Santa Catalina de Somoza** the picture-taking begins: a large tree in the foreground overhanging a stone wall, the snowcaps of the Montes de León in the background. It's a nice picnic spot, too. At El Ganso the road narrows even more, although the surface remains sound, and begins to climb through rough, shaggy country with rocky soil intermittently covered by a gray thatch looking more suited to goats than the occasional flock of sheep. Little villages that existed on offering hospitality to pilgrims, and on the skills of the Maragatos, are now tumbling down. The few people you might encounter are quite likely to respond to a friendly wave or smile, unlike their city cousins, perhaps because hospitality is ingrained and they don't see very many travellers these days. There are thatched-roof structures in El Ganso and Rabanal del Camino (*rabanal* means "radish" but is also a disparaging term meaning "insignificant"), where there is a Romanesque church and artifacts from an outpost of the Knights Templar, the military-oriented religious order that grew out of the Crusades and protected pilgrims along the Camino del Santiago.

The drive continues, with more scenic vistas, small explosions of wildflowers: poppies, daisies, and purple *uce* towering over all. You'll pass the occasional hiker or cyclist in incongruous Day-Glo Lycra, and the rusty sign for Foncebadon, which has bullet holes through it. Just beyond that, about 30 km (19 miles) west of Astorga, there is a giant pylon of stones with a simple iron cross set atop. This is the **Cruz de Ferro**, where a pilgrim paid penance by adding the largest stone he or she could carry. A few kilometers farther along, military radio towers mark a high point of 1,500 meters (4,950 feet), and a dozen hawks relax in a thermal column rising out of the valley below. This is another good picnic spot.

Acebo is a pretty village rather more intact than the others, with slate roofs and balconies that hang over the street. At Acebo's edge, about 42 km (25 miles) west of Astorga, turn left at the sign for Compludo, a village 5 km (3 miles) down a breathtaking road that twists and drops into the valley far below. Tiny wildflowers pepper the roadsides, and there are more purple *uce* and yellow *tujo,* a kind of gorse. Deep chasms groove the slopes. On the far slope a zipper of lime green, brilliant against the gray-brown, traces a small stream to the valley floor. At the bottom the road makes a sharp angle and reveals the source of the lime green, the Río Mahuelo, more stream than river, creating a cool park of aspen. There are good picnic sites all along here, such as a grassy bluff overhanging the road with a grove of half a dozen oaks of enormous girth.

Shortly, across the Mahuelo again, is **Compludo**, which isn't much, we are happy to report, except some farmers' houses and **El Bodegón** (taproom), where there is a dark bar with a shy barmaid, and dining al fresco with three or four big tree stumps for tables and little tree stumps for chairs. If you want to supplement your picnic, the shy barmaid will serve your choice of *jamón, lomo* (pork loin), *cecina* (beef jerky), *chorizo, tortilla de patata* (potato omelet), and *vino* or *cerveza*. Then, over *café de puchero* (coffee from the pot), you can sit and assess the commerce of Compludo: a trout fisherman working the stream, an elderly woman carrying laundry, a farmer leading two cows yoked together like a team of oxen (cows do double duty here).

The hardest part of this day trip may be making the decision to take the road back up the mountain to the real world, where left is to Ponferrada and right is to Astorga and León.

SOUTH OF ASTORGA

South of Astorga is **Jiménez de Jamuz**, 23 km (14 miles) by way of N VI, a little town of potters. There is currently a revival of interest in their distinctively glazed ceramics, which are peculiar to the region and highly appreciated by collectors. You might also want to take a look at the town's 16th-century church.

East of León

An excursion east of León can take you back in time to the Romans and the Moors and leave you in the Moorish city of Sahagún, a fine jumping-off point for a trip into the eastern part of Old Castile.

Just two miles northeast of León, on the banks of the Río Torio, is **Navatejera**, where the ruins of a Roman villa have been discovered. The villa dates to approximately the fourth century, and some mosaics from that period survive here.

If you take N 601 some 12 km (7½ miles) southeast of León, near the town of Villarente you'll come to the monastery of **Santa María de Sandoval**, founded in 1167 by Cistercian monks. Much of this building is in the Mozarabic style, particularly the entrance to the church on the left side. The setting is lovely, too—the monastery sits where the Porma and Esla rivers flow together.

From Villarente, head south on N 601 to LE 211, then follow that northeast to LE 231, which will take you east to **Almanza** (a 46-km/28-mile drive), whose name means "lookout" in Arabic. Located on the Río Cea on the boundary between the kingdoms of Castile and León, Almanza was fortified in the 13th century. Take note of the old gate, the Arco de la Villa, that was the portal to the old walled quarter.

Sahagún

Sahagún, an outstanding provincial city and one of the most important in León province, at least from a historical point of view (it was an important stop on the pilgrims' trek to Santiago, and it's a natural stop if you're coming from or going to Burgos), makes a worthwhile half-day trip from León. Take N 601 south from León 40 km (25 miles) and then take highway LE 911 for about 28 km (17 miles) east into Sahagún. If you are coming from Almanza, Sahagún is due south on route C 611, 34 km (21 miles).

AROUND IN SAHAGUN

Although Sahagún has all but fallen apart, it is being slowly rebuilt and is worth seeing. The Moorish influence is evident here; Sahagún was an important center of Mudejar art, and there are many 12th- and 13th-century churches here in this style. On Calle San Francisco (probably the first main street you'll spot) are the remains of a Benedictine **monastery**. This was the richest monastery in León province in the 12th century; it was destroyed late in the 19th century, but what is left of the main façade can be seen as an entry arch.

Directly across the street is the 12th-century **Iglesia de San Tirso**, one of the first and most notable examples of Romanesque-Mudejar style in Spain. The church has three naves, a transept, a trapezoidal main chapel with half-circle apses, and a magnificent tower over the main chapel. Farther southeast, across this small town (five minutes on foot), is the Plaza de San Lorenzo, on which stands the church of the same name. Dating from the 13th century, the **Iglesia de San Lorenzo** is flawless Romanesque. It is made of brick and has three naves and three beautifully decorated apses. The tower over the main chapel is worth a close look.

SOUTH OF SAHAGUN

About 5 km (3 miles) south of Sahagún, on C 611, lies the **Monasterio de San Pedro de las Dueñas**. This 12th-century Benedictine monastery will bring to mind León's Basílica de San Isidoro. Note the delicate early-17th-century carvings on the capitals and the crucifix by Gregorio Fernández. (If the church is closed, the woman in the last house to its left will open it for you.) Nearby is the ancient town of **Grajal**, which houses a Renaissance palace in excellent condition.

North of León

To the north lie trout streams, mountain hiking, hunting, and, at the recently completed reservoir at Riaño, water sports as well. Go north from León on N 621 over rolling land lent a rough prettiness by purple and yellow gorse. At about 30 km (19 miles) the snowcaps of the Cordillera Cantábrica spread themselves across the horizon, still 25 miles in the distance, already impressive. The road makes an abrupt left turn here, near Barrio de Nuestra Señora, to accommodate the Río Porma, where, during the season, you will see an occasional trout fisherman. There's a pretty view of the town of Lugán dropping away to the right on the east bank of the Porma as the road begins to climb, and there are good picnic sites just north of Lugán. Also near here is a sign, next to the road, from the Communidad de Castilla y León, with a map that shows fishing limits and towns on this section of the Porma.

There is not much in the way of overnight accommodations along here until **Boñar**, 44 km (27 miles) north of León, and the small ▶ **Hostal Inés**, Avenida de la Constitución, a simple, pleasant, quite new place with a bar and a cheerful *señora* who does the cooking and serves it in an equally cheerful dining room with green-checked tablecloths. The Ines caters to banquets, weddings, fishermen, and, rest assured, travellers.

NORTH TO RIAÑO

From Boñar take Calle Escuelas east through Grandoso, which is not very, and other relatively prosperous small towns, noting the open-face coal mining near Sotillos. About 20 km (12 miles) from Boñar make another required left turn at Santa Olaja de la Varga, along the Río Esla; the mountains begin to look more serious here. Another 34 km (21 miles) up N 621 is the **Embalse de Riaño** (Riaño Dam), an enormous complex of dam and new lake caught between two huge, white, granite alpine thrusts, very rough, craggy, dramatic-looking things. The old town of Riaño lies beneath many fathoms of lake, and the replacement town is approached by a stunning new bridge over the dam that is at least a kilometer long. The new Embalse de Riaño lives to serve: water buffs, swimmers, sailors, windsurfers, hikers, campers, fishermen, hunters—name your *deporte,* they'll figure it out. If you overdo it and have need of medical services, there is a **Centro de Salud** (health center) on the far side of the town of Riaño, near the river.

There are new condos and at least one new hotel in Riaño, the ▶ **Hotel Presa**, Avenida de Valcayo, the first left turn after exiting the main road. Slick, modern, efficient, the

Presa seems to embody the New Spain in action. It may be plastic, but it has a big, comfortable bar and a decent *comedor*. And there is nothing plastic about the views of those giant alpine shoulders sloping down to the lake and looking two-dimensional and magical in the hazy, foggy blue of late afternoon.

NORTH TOWARD LOS PICOS DE EUROPA

North of Riaño spectacular grandeur begins—and little valleys with quiet streams and carpets of wild daffodils peering out of thick grasses in boggy meadows. Just north of Portilla de la Reina, about 20 km (12 miles) north of Riaño on N 621, there's a lovely spot for a picnic near an old stone bridge crossing the Río Yuso. Near Llaneves de Reina, just a few kilometers farther, on the Río del Naranco, there's an amazing blanket of lichen of many colors and shades on towering rock walls that continue for two or three kilometers and are so close to the road you should keep your elbows in. Just beyond, near kilometer marker 119 on N 621, is a striking spread of alpine peak and slope and meadow. If you're a photographer or painter, don't leave home without camera or canvas.

OLD CASTILE EAST

East of the Salamanca and León regions is the Valladolid-Burgos segment of Old Castile. We begin our coverage of that area with Valladolid, which is east of Zamora, and move generally northeast through the wine-growing areas of Rueda, Duero, and Ribera de Burgos to the city of Burgos itself.

VALLADOLID

Valladolid (whose name derives from the Arabic Belad-Walid, "Land of the Governor") is a large provincial capital with a population of about 330,000. The city, located 193 km (120 miles) northwest of Madrid and 90 km (55 miles) east of Zamora, sits surrounded by wheat fields on a high plain more than 2,100 feet above sea level at the confluence of the Ríos Pisuerga and Esgueva. The area is in the middle of the Castilian plateau, the Meseta Central, which means that the climate of Valladolid is subject to the same extremes—bitterly cold in winter, blazing hot in summer—as the rest of Castile.

Compared to many other Spanish, and even Old Castilian cities, Valladolid, founded by Count Pedro de Ansurez in 1084, one year before Toledo was recaptured from the Moors, is a latecomer. For centuries this area, down to the valley of the Duero, was a no-man's-land, a buffer between the warring Moorish and Christian forces. But this former capital of Old Castile was the site of a number of important events in Spanish history, including the wedding of Ferdinand and Isabella; the death of Christopher Columbus; the births of Philip II, Philip IV, and Anne of Austria (mother of Louis XIV of France); and a three-year sojourn by Cervantes. It had the unfortunate distinction of having served as Napoleon's headquarters during the War of Independence (Peninsular War). During its glory days, in the 15th and 16th centuries, Valladolid proved fertile ground for a number of Spain's most important artists and architects.

In addition to being the center of Castile's vital agricultural region—the breadbasket and wine pitcher of this part of Spain—and a major university town, in recent years Valladolid has become highly industrialized. As new factories have been built, such as the giant Renault plant, the population of the city has grown apace.

Valladolid today is crowded, and its less-than-visionary traffic patterns can make it very difficult to get around in, but even before the unbridled growth of the last decade or so Valladolid was no favorite of travellers. William Byron, author of a splendid biography of Cervantes, tells of a 16th-century Dutchman who claimed that the city was full of *"picaros, putas, pleytos, polvos, piedras, puercos, perros, piojos, pulgas"*—rogues, whores, lawsuits, dust, stones, swine, dogs, lice, and fleas. And 20th-century wayfarers have not helped to upgrade the city's reputation much. Greek writer Nikos Kazantzakis wrote that the city, the correct pronunciation of which is a test of proper Castilian (Vye-YAH-dohleeth), "is like a fallen princess whose lovers all have died, and so she has had to take to industry and commerce in order to survive."

Alastair Boyd, who wrote a book detailing the artistic and cultural treasures of Castile, confessed to being "prejudiced against Valladolid for years," but pointed out that there are few places in Spain without some redeeming qualities, Valladolid included. Still, he said, "it is difficult to give a coherent account of a no longer coherent city." In many Spanish cities, the great treasures are set like jewels in a necklace of old and restored buildings that accentuate an overall atmosphere of antiquity. In Valladolid the necklace is broken by modern high-rises; incongruity and incoherence reign, and the jewels—many of which are less than crown jewels at that—are tossed around the city. Be aware, too, that the majority of the sights here are architectural; during the War of Independence Napoleon's troops stole, burned, or wantonly hacked up a great number of artworks in the interiors of churches and other buildings. But if you are seriously interested in Spanish history, architecture, art, and culture, many of Valladolid's remaining treasures are well worth searching out.

Semana Santa (Holy Week) is a very big attraction in Valladolid, and the processions, during which many pieces from Valladolid's excellent sculpture museum, the Museo Nacional de Escultura, are carried through the streets, are much more somber and serious even than those of Andalusia. The big fiesta in Valladolid is San Mateo in September, featuring major bullfights.

Seeing Valladolid

The old quarter, the core of Valladolid where most of the city's attractions are located, is a warren of narrow streets that twist and turn and change names every couple of blocks. Consequently, it's best to walk to the many historical and architectural monuments in this town: the Museo Nacional de Escultura in the remarkable pre-Plateresque Colegio de San Gregorio, the Isabelline-Gothic façade of the church of San Pablo, the Romanesque and Gothic church of Santa María la Antigua, the unfinished Herreran cathedral, the mixed styles of the Universidad, Columbus's house, Cervantes' house, and the multitude of low-priority sights considered important enough to be listed by the Valladolid tourist office.

Leave your car at your hotel or, if you are staying outside the city and driving in for the day, put your car in one of the car parks on the west side (one in the Plaza Mayor, and two more north of Plaza del Poniente near Río Pisuerga). Explore the old quarter on foot, then take a taxi, if you are not up for the trek, to the Museo Oriental in the southern part of town. Valladolid is also well served by train and bus service from Madrid and other major cities; both the train and bus stations are located south of Campo Grande, a park near the Museo Oriental.

To find your way around this convoluted city, it is important to choose the proper maps. The tourist-office brochure map has Río Pisuerga on the top of the page; a popular commercial Spanish guidebook series, *Editorial Everest,* whose map is handy because it has more streets labeled, has the Pisuerga on the bottom of the page; and the map in *Michelin Spain* (the "Green Guide") has it on the left, or western, side of town, where it should be.

Using the 16th-century arcaded **Plaza Mayor**—facing a rather undistinguished city hall—as a reference point on your map, you can then decide which of the monuments you want to visit. You might start out in the morning with the cathedral (to the east); then—detouring past a number of buildings of primarily architectural interest near the cathedral—head to the Museo Nacional de Escultura in the Colegio de San Gregorio and the nearby church of San Pablo, and finish at the church of San Benito before returning to the Plaza Mayor and the many *tapas* bars in the area.

Staying in Valladolid

We recommend staying in Tordesillas (see below), 30 km (19 miles) southwest of Valladolid, to enjoy the quiet peace of the countryside, and for easy access to the considerable backcountry attractions of Valladolid province. If you choose to stay in the city, however, the most practical choice is the ► **Hotel Olid Meliá**, a modern hotel (renovated in 1991) with a parking garage. Besides providing perhaps the city's most comfortable accommodations, the Olid Meliá is located in the heart of the old city on the Plaza San Miguel, within walking distance of most of Valladolid's major attractions. The moderately priced ► **Hotel Mozart**, which opened in 1987, offers excellent service and lots of amenities for a hotel of its category, including a parking garage. In an attractive stone building with some lovely glassed-in wooden balconies (although a surfeit of white marble within), the Mozart is very conveniently located just three blocks south of the Plaza Mayor and three short blocks north of such top restaurants as Mesón Cervantes, Mesón Panero, and Portobello.

The other hotel choices are the venerable ► **Hotel Felipe IV**, the functional ► **Hotel Meliá Parque** (also renovated in 1991), and the new, moderately priced ► **Hotel Lasa**, all located in southern Valladolid near the Campo Grande, the bus and train stations, and the Museo Oriental—several blocks from the old quarter, but closer to the top restaurants. (Be careful in Campo Grande and around the bus and train stations, especially at night. Some muggings have been reported of late.)

The Cathedral/University Area

THE CATHEDRAL

From the south side of the Plaza Mayor, walk east for a few blocks to reach the cathedral, which was originally intended to be one of the largest churches in the world. Construction started on this yet-unfinished edifice in the early 16th century, but more than 50 years passed before Juan de Herrera, the architect of El Escorial and many other outstanding buildings in Spain, got the project going in earnest—and put the Herreran stamp on it. But Herrera's design was only partially completed—the western façade and the tower—before construction languished again, this time until the 18th century, when Alberto Churriguera, with his unique vision of Baroque, added the portion of the façade above the main portal, which, strangely enough, meshes very well with Herrera's austere style.

This church sorely needs a second tower (four were originally planned) for symmetry. And although the building was never finished—the original Latin cross floor plan never even reached the crossing—it is nonetheless quite beautiful. The high altar, carved in 1572 by Juan de Juni, who is well represented in the Museo Nacional de Escultura (see below), was originally made for the church of Santa María la Antigua.

Because work on the cathedral was stopped, several sections of the early collegiate church that stood on the site remained intact. The fine **Museo Diocesano** is installed in part of the old church, within which there are also Mudejar designs, Romanesque tombs, and Gothic doors in the chapel of San Llorente. The sacristy contains one of Toledan silversmith Juan de Arfe's major pieces, a huge four-tiered silver monstrance from the late 16th century.

THE UNIVERSITY

Southeast from the cathedral is the **Universidad de Valladolid**, whose Baroque façade surrounding the main portal was designed by Narciso Tomé in 1715. As Alastair Boyd points out, during this period Spanish architects such as Tomé, who created the Transparente in Toledo, and the Churrigueras, with their wildly extravagant altarpieces, were still relatively sober in their decoration of exteriors. Such artists were in transition, still restrained by the power, weight, and conservatism of Herrera's influence, but in the end, as florid Gothic gave way to Plateresque in Spain, what was once confined to altarpieces, as Boyd puts it, "moved cheerfully outwards from the *retablos* to the façades." Spanish decoration would eventually degenerate into Rococo, but not right away. The façade of the Universidad de Valladolid would like to take off, but it is anchored firmly by four unadorned columns set on square pedestals to the no-nonsense, conservative building it decorates.

SOUTH OF THE UNIVERSITY

Around the corner, to the southeast of the Universidad, the Colegio de Santa Cruz is a representative example of the late-15th-century Renaissance style of Enrique de Egas. Just northeast, along Calle del Cardenal Mendoza, which becomes Calle de Colón, is the site of Christopher Columbus's house. Columbus died in Valladolid a broken man. "If I had stolen the Indies and given them to the Moors," he said, "Spain could not have shown me greater enmity." The house where he died, in 1506, was demolished in the 1960s but later completely rebuilt to house the Columbus museum, **Casa de Colón**, whose most interesting displays are the maps of the great admiral's three voyages and some artifacts from his New World discoveries.

NORTH OF THE CATHEDRAL

Just behind the cathedral to the north is the early-14th-century Gothic **Iglesia de Santa María la Antigua**, with a Romanesque portico and an exceptional 11th-century Romanesque tower. This *conjunto* (ensemble) works beautifully, making Santa María la Antigua one of the finest buildings in the city. A block northwest is the early-17th-century **Iglesia de Nuestra Señora de las Angustias** (Our Lady of Anguish), which contains Juan de Juni's celebrated *Virgen de los Cuchillos* (Virgin of the Knives), a polychrome statue of the Virgin Mary clutching her breast, into which enough silver daggers have been plunged to cause anguish indeed.

The Colegio de San Gregorio Area

Northeast of the Plaza Mayor, and just two blocks northeast of the Olid Meliá, two of Valladolid's main attractions face the Plaza de San Pablo: the Colegio de San Gregorio, the remarkable, incredibly ornate (Jan Morris called it "almost edible"), late-15th-century Isabelline-Gothic building in which the Museo Nacional de Escultura is housed and, next to it, the equally ornate Isabelline church of San Pablo.

Both these pre-Renaissance buildings are often called Plateresque, but they are not. They preceded the Plateresque and obviously contributed to its development, but they were executed by foreign architects and stonemasons inspired—according to Professor Denning of Trinity College in Dublin—by the kind of decoration then commonly used on the title pages of books and by the woodcarvings done for the altarpieces of the period. It is to these arts, not to the silver work that inspired Plateresque decoration, that we owe the remarkable style of these two structures.

IGLESIA DE SAN PABLO

The 15th-century Iglesia de San Pablo, which preceded San Gregorio and is even more detailed (if that is possible), was added to in the early 17th century by the duke of Lerma, whose coat of arms can be seen on the façade. The French looted and destroyed the original interior during the War of Independence, but a striking pair of Isabelline doorways remains in the since-restored church.

COLEGIO DE SAN GREGORIO

The Colegio de San Gregorio, commissioned by the prelate of Palencia, Bishop Alonso de Burgos, confessor to Queen Isabella, was built between 1488 and 1496. The façade, like that of San Pablo, looks like a giant, florid Gothic altarpiece, except that the figures, including the huge heraldic emblems of Castile and León, are largely secular. The delicacy and intricacy of much of the stonework, obviously an exceptionally laborious accomplishment, is amazing. San Gregorio's architect was Juan Guas, but the decoration of the façade has been attributed variously to others: to Enrique de Egas; to Simón de Colonia, who planned the splendid Cartuja de Miraflores and Capilla del Condestable in Burgos and designed the façade of San Pablo; and to the great Gil de Siloé, believed to have been a native of Antwerp, who worked on both Miraflores and the cathedral in Burgos with Simón and is believed to have worked on the church at Aranda de Duero with him as well. Many experts opt for a collaboration among these foreign artists, for, as Sacheverell Sitwell wrote, "It is the 'Espagnolade' of a foreigner, as much so as the drawings of Gustave Doré or the music of *Carmen*."

The great patio of San Gregorio is exceptionally rich. Beautifully turned barley-sugar columns support a second-floor gallery of archways filled with profusely decorated, intricately carved stone balconies, each with three short columns supporting a double-arched, heavily decorated panel. Running below the gargoyle-studded roofline is a frieze decorated with a repeated yoke-and-arrow (the symbol of Isabella and Ferdinand) motif that is broken at each corner by the coat of arms of the unified kingdoms of Castile, León, and Aragón.

MUSEO NACIONAL DE ESCULTURA

The Museo Nacional de Escultura (National Museum of Sculpture) in San Gregorio is filled with polychrome wood statues (many with meticulously detailed bleeding wounds); complete tableaux representing biblical scenes; Holy Week processional *pasos* (floats); altarpieces; paintings; and even an entire set of carved wooden choir stalls, done by Gil de Siloé, Alonso Berruguete, Juan de Juni, Gregorio Fernández, Pedro de Mena, and others. All the pieces are beautifully displayed and well lighted.

One of the masterpieces in the museum's collection is the early-16th-century altarpiece by Alonso Berruguete, who

Alastair Boyd claims was "the only inspired artist of the Spanish Renaissance." Berruguete spent five years working in Florence and was greatly influenced by Michelangelo (he was mentioned in the master's letters), Leonardo da Vinci (he may have been in Florence when Leonardo was painting the *Mona Lisa*), and Raphael. He returned to Spain to become the greatest Spanish sculptor of the 16th century.

Originally built for Valladolid's church of San Benito, Berruguete's retable, now dismantled and displayed in three rooms on the ground floor of the museum, measured more than 50 feet high. Other Berruguete works on display include another exceptional altarpiece, taken from the Convento de la Mejorada in Olmedo, two superb sculptures, *San Sebastián* and *The Sacrifice of Isaac,* and a fine Nativity painting.

The sculptor Juan de Juni, from Champagne, whose work can also be seen in Valladolid's cathedral and in the church of Nuestra Señora de las Angustias, is represented in this museum by one of his most highly regarded works, *The Entombment of Christ,* and also by a good John the Baptist. Gregorio Fernández, who in the early 17th century carried Juni's illusionism even further by using human teeth, glass eyes, and graphically depicted bleeding wounds to get his point across, is very well represented here, but a little bit of Fernández goes a long way. His *Cristo Yacente* (Christ Reclining) is just one of a number of profusely bleeding Cristos in various postures—reclining, in pietà tableaux, and hanging from the Cross—done by this prolific artist that are scattered throughout Valladolid.

Other notable works in the museum are Pedro de Mena's fine 17th-century statue of Mary Magdalene; the bronze statues of the duke and duchess of Lerma kneeling (whose models were done by Pompeo Leoni and cast by Juan de Arfe); and the richly detailed, carved wooden choir stalls by Diego de Siloé, son of Gil de Siloé and creator of the great golden staircase in the Burgos cathedral. There are also two fine Hispano-Flemish paintings from the 15th century: one of San Jerónimo, which was in the Convento de la Mejorada in Olmedo, and the other of Santiago, dressed as a pilgrim with his staff and a scallop shell on his hat, and San Andrés, with an X-shaped Saint Andrew's cross.

AROUND THE COLEGIO

There are several other buildings of interest in the Colegio de San Gregorio area. Also facing the Plaza de San Pablo is the **Palacio de Pimentel**, where Philip II was born. Around the corner, northeast of San Gregorio, is the **Casa del Sol**, which has a minor 16th-century Plateresque façade. Also in this area are the Palacio de Vivero (rebuilt in the 16th century), where Ferdinand and Isabella were married in 1469, and the home of the 19th-century poet and playwright José Zorrilla, author of *Don Juan Tenorio*. Southwest of the Plaza de San Pablo, past the Plaza de San Miguel, you may notice the massive façade of the 15th-century **Iglesia de San Benito**. From San Benito it's only a couple of blocks southwest to the Plaza de Poniente, and south to the Plaza Mayor.

South of the Plaza Mayor

South of the Plaza Mayor is Calle de Santiago, the major shopping street of Valladolid, with its own special twist, a place called **Las Francesas**, which has a variety of good shops surrounding the cloister of an old nunnery. The church of Santiago, also on this street, contains a fine retable by Alonso Berruguete. At the southern end of Calle de Santiago is the Plaza de Zorrilla, which forms the northern tip of the triangular-shaped **Campo Grande**, an oasis of trees, fountains, flower gardens, and pleasant walkways. Located at the southern end of the park, the convent of the Order of the Philippines houses the interesting **Museo Oriental**, which has a fine collection put together by Augustinian missionaries stationed in the Far East.

CASA DE CERVANTES

Two and a half blocks east of Plaza de Zorrilla, at Calle del Rastro 7, is the Casa de Cervantes. For three years during the brief period when Valladolid was the capital of Spain (1601 to 1606) under Philip III (the city bribed the duke of Lerma, the royal favorite, with 400,000 ducats to move the court from Madrid), Miguel de Cervantes Saavedra lived in this house. In his biography of Cervantes, William Byron describes what the building was like in those days: "...one of five new houses jerry-built by a small-bore speculator hoping to cash in on an influx of riffraff into the city. It was an instant slum." Cervantes, along with more than 20 of his relatives, friends, and perhaps a down-at-heels servant or two, crowded into 13 rooms above an old tavern that was the hangout for butchers from the nearby slaughterhouse.

Don't expect to be moved by the spirit of the great writer in today's contrived surroundings, however; the house is more interesting as a refurbished 17th-century dwelling, certainly in better shape now than it was in those days, than as a Cervantes museum. Besides, by the time Cervantes moved here, *Don Quixote* was already finished and in the hands of his publisher, Francisco de Robles, who had moved to Valladolid from Madrid to be close to the real money around the supremely corrupt duke of Lerma and the court of Philip

III. Cervantes was arrested in this house after the mysterious death of a nobleman who had been wounded in the dangerous streets of this quarter. Cervantes and his family helped the injured man into their apartments, where he died two days later, and when no one could put a finger on his assailant, Cervantes and several members of his family were arrested, albeit briefly, thus adding Valladolid to the list of jails—Algiers, Castro del Río, and Seville—that the great writer had graced with his presence.

Dining in Valladolid

Many restaurants in Valladolid are closed one evening a week, usually Sunday. Reservations are not vital at most restaurants, but it is a good idea to have your hotel concierge book a table for you nonetheless.

Mesón La Fragua, Paseo de Zorrilla 10 (just west of Campo Grande), widely considered the best restaurant in the province, strikes a balance between refined versions of authentic Castilian dishes and modern cuisine, served in a beautifully and expensively decorated Castilian atmosphere. Here you can get impeccably prepared and beautifully presented standards such as *lechazo asado* and *cochinillo asado,* as well as fresh Cantabrian fish, "grandma's" veal *morcilla,* leeks stuffed with shellfish, and oxtail cooked with *aguardiente* (brandy). Homemade tarts, chocolate truffles, and figs stuffed with nuts beckon from the dessert menu. From one of the best wine lists in Castile you can choose among the marvelous wines of the up-and-coming Ribera del Duero or, if you have a well-upholstered wallet, an older vintage of Vega Sicilia, Spain's rarest and most expensive wine, a distinguished red once praised by Winston Churchill. Tel: (9-83) 33-87-85.

Next door to Casa de Cervantes is the moderate to expensive **Mesón Cervantes**, Calle del Rastro 6, which for more than two decades has been serving typical Castilian dishes to Vallisoletanos, as the people of Valladolid are called, and to those who come looking for the spirit of the author of *Don Quixote.* Besides classic Castilian dishes such as roast suckling pig, lamb dishes, *pisto* (a dish similar to ratatouille), *menestra,* and traditional stews of the region, you can get game dishes—rabbit, partridge, venison, and wild boar—and fresh fish and shellfish from Galicia and the Cantabrian coast. Mesón Cervantes also has a good wine list that includes old vintages of Vega Sicilia. Closed in August; Tel: (9-83) 30-61-38.

Just around the corner from Mesón Cervantes, one block to the southwest, is the recently renovated **Mesón Panero**, Marina Escobar 1, where traditional Castilian and Leonese cuisine reigns supreme, especially during the gastronomic festival run by this restaurant each February. Artfully prepared dishes, often taken from old recipes, such as beans with pigeon, lamb sweetbreads with clams, stuffed pheasant, rabbit with thyme, and Castilian stew, will reward hearty appetites. Complement this classic food with a fine white wine from nearby Rueda, a local Cigales *rosado,* or a superb Ribera del Duero red from Mauro, Pesquera, or Vega Sicilia (see Peñafiel and the Red-Wine Villages, below). Tel: (9-83) 30-16-73.

A few years ago the restaurant **Santi** moved to larger quarters on Calle Correos, northwest of the Plaza Mayor, near the post office, leaving behind its charming, but tight-fitting, old tavern, which held only nine tables. Santi still serves big, reasonably priced portions of its very hearty version of Castilian home cooking, with dishes such as *menestra,* oxtail with potatoes, *merluza* (hake) in batter, and *solomillo* (steak). Closed in August; Tel: (9-83) 33-93-55. Another restaurant specializing in Castilian home cooking— *menestra,* roast lamb, and roast squab—is the moderately priced, well-regarded **La Goya**, Puente Colgante 79 (a taxi ride away, across the river southwest of Campo Grande), which also offers outdoor dining on its patio in summer. Closed in August; Tel: (9-83) 35-57-24.

If you are going through seafood withdrawal pangs out here in lamb land, **Portobello**, Marina Escobar 5, a couple of doors down from Mesón Panero and around the corner from Mesón Cervantes, is the place for fresh fish and shell-fish, which are kept alive in the restaurant's tanks and are, as elsewhere in Spain, very expensive. Tel: (9-83) 30-95-31.

Harry Debelius, a veteran journalist who has lived in Madrid for many years, succinctly described Valladolid as "Dullsville," but you may find the lively evening *tapas*-bar scene around the Plaza Mayor to your liking. Try **Taberna Pan con Tomate**, Plaza Mayor 18; or, for *tapas* and drinks alfresco, **Caballo da Troya**, a typical Castilian tavern with a terrace set in a beautiful patio, northwest of the plaza at Calle Correos 1.

Surprisingly, there are often good flamenco festivals in Valladolid, due partly to a combination of heightened national interest in this colorful Andalusian folk art and an influx of Andalusians escaping from their home region's high unemployment rate to find work in Valladolid's factories. Look for posters around town and newspaper announcements of upcoming performances. The **Casino de Castilla y León**, featuring blackjack, roulette, chemin de fer, and so on, is in Boecillo, 12 km (7½ miles) south of town on N 403, the highway to Madrid. The casino has a restaurant and a nightclub. Tel: (9-83) 55-44-11.

VALLADOLID PROVINCE

Tordesillas

A good base for exploring Valladolid—both the city and the province, which has a number of historical sites and castles—is the ▶ **Parador de Tordesillas**, a modern, comfortable building with Castilian furnishings and a swimming pool, located 30 km (18½ miles) southwest of Valladolid on N 620, the road to Salamanca, just outside of the town of Tordesillas. There is little to do here at night except have dinner and read, but that can be a blessing after traversing the broad expanses of Castile all day. Townsend Miller's entertaining novelesque history, *The Castles and the Crown,* which chronicles the rich past of this region during the 15th and 16th centuries, is an excellent scene-setter for the next day's outing. For dinner try the dining room of the parador, which serves typical regional cuisine, or the only other decent restaurant in Tordesillas, **El Torreón**, in the center of town at the junction of the Valladolid and Zamora roads (on calle Dimas Rodríguez), where you can get a good salad, lamb chops cooked on an open-hearth grill in the dining room, and a fine bottle of Ribera del Duero or Rioja. Tel: (9-83) 77-01-23.

Fortified by one of the parador's huge buffet breakfasts, you can set out in practically any direction and find a castle or historic town that figured prominently in the epoch of Ferdinand and Isabella and Charles V. You can even stay put: Tordesillas is one of the most historic towns in the region. Several crucial events in the history of Spain took place here, including the signing of the Treaty of Tordesillas (the Line of Demarcation) in 1494, arbitrated by Pope Alexander VI, which caused South America to be split between Spain and Portugal. Juana la Loca, the mad daughter of Isabella and Ferdinand, and heir to the throne, who carried the lime-covered corpse of her husband, Philip the Fair, all over Castile with her for years, was confined in the palace (now destroyed) of Tordesillas for 46 years during the 16th century. The town was one of the centers of the *comuneros* revolt against the "foreign" court of Charles V (King Carlos I), and the leaders of the uprising came here to put Juana on the throne, but she was too out of touch to be of any use to them.

CONVENTO DE SANTA CLARA

Back in the 14th century, Peter the Cruel ("cruel and sensual, more a sultan than a Christian prince," as one Spanish writer

described him)—to placate his mistress, María de Padilla, who pined for the warmth of Seville and the Moorish south—brought Moorish carpenters and masons from Seville and Toledo here to work on the palace (originally built by his father, Alfonso XI) that is now the Convento de Santa Clara. The craftsmen furnished the palace with a Mudejar façade and a spectacular ceiling that lives up to Townsend Miller's description: "a gorgeous dome of Moorish *artesonado* which burns and glitters like the star-strewn vault of some blazing Oriental night." The patio has Moorish horseshoe arches and Moorish tiles and inscriptions; and there are, of course, Moorish baths of the kind so loved by María de Padilla in Seville's Alcázar, of which this place is highly reminiscent.

All of these riches remained hidden in the cloistered convent until the beginning of this century, when special authorization was obtained for a visit by King Alfonso XIII, which led to the discovery of its treasures by the outside world and the subsequent restoration of Santa Clara. The convent sits on a hill above the Río Duero and its multi-arched medieval bridge and looks out over fields and vineyards to the south toward Medina del Campo and the Castillo de la Mota (see below). The guided tour of the convent, along with a brief walk through Tordesillas and a coffee in a bar in the arcaded Plaza Mayor, from which you can admire the Herreran tower of the church of Santa María, can be done in a pleasant hour in the morning before you set off to explore the Castilian countryside.

Wine Villages and Castle Towns

Alastair Boyd wrote, "Our slavery to the industrial civilization we have created compels us to seek space, light, air and architecture that stands properly against the sky." All around Tordesillas is castle country, where the architecture does stand out against the sky. This is the Old Castile of the harsh, treeless landscape and austere spirit, a far cry from the jasmine-perfumed pleasure gardens of the south. But the landscape is crowned by a number of impressive castles, austere churches, and other powerful evocations of an illustrious history. It can be explored in one or more day trips from your base in Tordesillas.

RUEDA WINE COUNTRY
Just south of Tordesillas is Rueda wine country. Once known for its Sherry-like fortified wines, for the last decade it has become better known for its dry white table wines. Many of the wineries in Rueda and nearby Ribera del Duero (located northeast of Tordesillas and southeast of Valladolid) are small,

family-run operations. Most are not equipped for formal tours, nor do they have English-speaking public-relations directors, slick brochures, or pristine tasting rooms, but that is part of their charm and authenticity. Obviously, you will get more out of your winery visits if you speak some Spanish.

Rueda

The town of Rueda, a few miles south of Tordesillas on N VI (the road to Medina del Campo), and its satellite towns of La Seca, Serrada, and Nava del Rey, form the heart of the Rueda wine district. You can drop in on one of several stores in Rueda or stop at a bodega (the best times for visitors are usually from 10:00 A.M. to noon and from 4:00 P.M. to 6:00 P.M. on weekdays) to sample some of Spain's best white wines. At the northern edge of Rueda on N VI is a large modern bodega, **Vinos Blancos de Castilla**, where Marqués de Riscal, the famous Rioja producer, makes a good Rueda white. At the southern edge of town on the same highway is **Vinos Sanz**, where one of the region's most innovative wine makers, Antonio Sanz, makes a wide range of white, rosé, red, and fortified wines, including his own Rueda Superior white, a good red called Almirante, and the highly rated Cabernet Sauvignon of Marqués de Griñón, whose grapes come from an estate near Toledo. Sanz has a tasting room where you can also buy wines.

If you speak Spanish, try to arrange a visit to the winery of **Angel Rodríguez**, 6 km (4 miles) east of Rueda at La Seca. (In the center of Rueda there are clearly marked road signs to La Seca; once there you will have to ask someone to direct you to the winery.) It's advisable to call ahead; Tel: (9-83) 86-81-17. Don't be put off by the unassuming entrance to the bodega at Calle Torcida 14—this is an artisan family winery, not a slick commercial enterprise. The underground caves where Angel Rodríguez makes his excellent Martinsancho white wines are beautifully rustic, the kind of place you rarely get a chance to see. To give you a taste of wine, Señor Rodríguez simply plucks a quill from a hole in one of the big barrels coopered down here many years ago, and catches the arching green-gold liquid in a glass.

MEDINA DEL CAMPO

South of Rueda on N VI lies the great medieval market town of Castile, Medina del Campo, whose huge 15th-century Mudejar **Castillo de la Mota**, in which Cesare Borgia was once imprisoned, and in which Queen Isabella I is popularly believed to have died (she actually died in a house next door to Medina's *ayuntamiento* on the Plaza Mayor), is one of the most impressive castles in Spain. For a brief period in the 16th century Medina was the financial capital of Spain, and it was said that "When the bank of Medina trembled, the whole world of finance got the shakes." Much of the town's wealth was built on wool and textiles, and it was one of the greatest market towns in Europe during the early 16th century. During the *comuneros* revolt the town was torched and most of it burned to the ground. It was rebuilt—and to this day retains the largest sheep market in the country—but never regained the status of its glory days when the Ruiz family were the most powerful bankers in Spain.

The arcaded **Plaza de España**, the town's *plaza mayor,* still captures the spirit of old Medina. Facing the plaza are several noble houses, the 16th-century collegiate church of San Antolín, the *ayuntamiento* (town hall) in the Casas Consistorales (the house built over the archway next door to it is where Isabella died), and the old *matadero* (slaughter-house). The town is at its liveliest on Sunday, which is market day in Medina—an ideal time to visit. All the shops and even the banks are open (they close on Thursdays here). Medina also hosts several animated and colorful live-stock fairs each year.

You can contemplate Medina's former glories over lunch or dinner at **Monaco**, Plaza de España 26, a new, moderately priced restaurant looking out on the square. Try the *pimientos rellenos* (stuffed peppers), lamb (of course), and perhaps a Martivillí Rueda white or Yllera Tinto, a well-regarded non–*denominación de origen* wine made by a local producer. Tel: (9-83) 81-02-95.

OLMEDO

East of Medina is the historic town of Olmedo, immortalized in Lope de Vegas's play *El Caballero de Olmedo.* Several important battles were fought here, including the pivotal battle in 1445 for control of Castile that pitted the armies of Juan II of Castile (father of Isabella I) and his powerful favorite, Alvaro de Luna, against the forces of the infantes de Aragón. Castile's forces carried the day, ensuring that Castile, not Catalan Aragón, would be the dominant force in Spain. The town still has sections of its old walls, remnants of Romanesque and Mudejar architecture in the 13th-century churches of San Andrés and San Miguel, and the Convento de la Mejorada, where Isabella I spent the last spring of her life in 1504, and where Berruguete did the fine altarpiece that is now in Valladolid.

North of Tordesillas

Another day's tour of this part of Old Castile can take you north of Tordesillas, and within a few miles of Valladolid, to the castle towns of Simancas, Torrelobatón, and

Fuensaldaña, all of which have their well-preserved castles standing "properly against the sky."

SIMANCAS

Simancas, 19 km (12 miles) northeast of Tordesillas and 11 km (7 miles) southwest of Valladolid on N 620, was a Roman town and because of its strategic situation at the confluence of the ríos Pisuerga and Duero has seen a lot of history since. In 939 forces led by Ramiro II of León and Count Fernán González of Castile won a decisive battle over Abd ar-Rahman III here, even capturing the caliph's personal illuminated copy of the Koran.

A superb, ancient 17-arch bridge, albeit a narrow one, still carries Simancas's traffic over the Pisuerga. The watch-tower on the bridge was the dividing line between the Christian and Moorish kingdoms for a while in the 11th century. The **Castillo de Simancas**, built by the Moors in the ninth century, reconstructed in the 13th century and again in the 15th, became the national archives under Philip II and now houses more than 30 million documents dating from the reigns of Ferdinand and Isabella through 1808, when Napoleon had many of them carted off to Paris. Most of the documents not destroyed (countless numbers were used to build fires or merely thrown away) were returned a few years later, and the rest found their way back here in 1942, returned by Marshal Pétain, then premier of Vichy France (and under whom Franco served in Morocco). The collection includes the marriage contracts of Ferdinand and Isabella and of Philip II and Mary Tudor, as well as the document appointing Columbus admiral, and an incredible wealth of papers bearing the signatures of many of Spain's greatest figures.

TORRELOBATON

The 14th-century **Castillo de Torrelobatón**, north of Torde-sillas on C 611 (the road to Medina de Ríoseco), was the last stronghold of the *comuneros* before their defeat in 1521 at Villalar, 16 km (10 miles) to the southeast. This castle, with its well-restored walls, square donjon (inner tower), and round towers, is simple in design, dignified and stately. It can be seen for miles across the wheat fields, dominating the small village below its towers. A few miles northeast of Torre-lobatón, on a secondary road that leads to Fuensaldaña, is Wamba, the site of a 13th-century church, the **Iglesia de Santa María**, that contains the remains of an important tenth-century Mozarabic church with horseshoe arches. Within the church is the tomb of Recceswinth, the Visigothic king of Spain who died here in 672 and was succeeded by Wamba, who took his oath on the dead king's tomb.

FUENSALDAÑA

The beautiful 15th-century **Castillo de Fuensaldaña**, with its imposing keep, located 20 km (12 miles) northeast of Wamba along the same road (and only 8 km/5 miles northwest of Valladolid), was built by Alfonso Pérez de Vivero, treasurer of Juan II of Castile, who so provoked the royal favorite, Alvaro de Luna, that Luna tossed him headfirst off a tower in Burgos. Luna was beheaded for the crime in Valladolid.

Fuensaldaña also has two restaurants, **Bodega la Nieta** and **Bodega la Sorbona**, both with dining rooms dug into caves in the hill and both serving typical Castilian dishes such as *embutidos* (charcuterie), stews, lamb chops, and grilled steaks. You might want to range a few miles beyond Fuensaldaña to the northeast to **Cigales**, where you can sample the town's excellent rosé wines in a bar near the huge Renaissance church designed by Juan de Herrera.

Peñafiel and the Red-Wine Villages

The area to the east and southeast of Valladolid (still within reach of the Parador de Tordesillas, discussed above) is some of the finest wine-producing country in Spain.

TUDELA DE DUERO

Tudela de Duero, 14 km (9 miles) southeast of Valladolid, just off N 122, has nothing of architectural interest except a 16th-century church, but it does have one of the great new wineries in Spain, **Bodegas Mauro**, located on the town's main street at Calle de Cervantes 12, at the western end of town not far from the river. The winery, which is unusual in having both underground and second-floor aging rooms, is installed in an ancient house remodeled especially for the purpose by one of the winery's partners, Luciano Suárez. Suárez is an architect who specializes in restoring historic buildings and is so good at it that he has been entrusted with the restoration of some of Spain's greatest architectural treasures, including the splendid Monasterio Santo Domingo de Silos (see the Ribero de Burgos Wine Country section, below).

Mauro's red wines, while not technically from the Ribera del Duero *denominación de origen* (Tudela is just outside the boundary), are some of the best wines of this region. To arrange a visit to Bodegas Mauro, it is best to call ahead; Tel: (9-83) 68-02-65. If you are coming from the east, stop at the bodega's roadside sales office, just down the road from the Vega Sicilia winery at Quintanilla de Onésimo, 20 km (12½ miles) east of Tudela on N 122.

In Tudela de Duero there is an exceptional, unheralded

restaurant, **Mesón 2, 39**, at Antonio Machado 39, that serves excellent regional cuisine. Start with superb home-cured olives; if you are here in springtime you can then order the *espárragos de Tudela* (these are even better than the exceptional asparagus of the other Tudela in Navarra). Have *chuletillas de cordero* (baby lamb chops) with potatoes and fried green peppers as a main course and finish with Tudela strawberries followed by coffee and one of the house *aguardientes,* in which pineapple, cherries, peaches, or other fruits have been marinated. Try a bottle of Mauro, the excellent 1986 if available, or Vega Sicilia Valbuena with your meal. Tel: (9-83) 52-07-34.

VEGA SICILIA

Vega Sicilia (founded 1864), where Spain's most exotic and expensive wine is made, is officially in the municipality of Valbuena de Duero, but the winery itself is just east of Quintanilla de Onésimo, 35 km (22 miles) east of Valladolid on N 122. For decades Vega Sicilia has enjoyed a legendary niche in the world pantheon of wines (it is claimed that Winston Churchill mistook it for a fine Bordeaux; it does have some Cabernet Sauvignon in it), and it can be found on the wine lists of Spain's greatest restaurants, but truthfully, relatively few people have had much experience with the wine, due to its scarcity and its extraordinarily high price. Mariano García, Vega Sicilia's talented young wine maker, has the perfect countenance for Spain's most aristocratic wine: His striking features make him a living replica of a *siglo de oro* Castilian grandee, straight out of a painting in the Prado.

Vega Sicilia makes three red wines: Valbuena third year, Valbuena fifth year, and Vega Sicilia "Unico," which has been known to spend up to 23 years in barrel. The wines are tremendous, powerful, and deeply colored; they finish with long, deep, spicy flavors that smooth out with food. Call ahead—except in August, when the winery is closed—to arrange a visit; Tel: (9-83) 68-01-47.

SANTA MARIA DE VALBUENA

Just northeast and across the Río Duero from the Vega Sicilia winery, next to the small, modern farm village of San Bernardo, is the 12th-century Cistercian **Abadía de Santa María de Valbuena**. This was once a very important church, as you can see by its size. It may also have been extremely important to the viticulture of this region; it is suspected that the Cistercians, who also founded the great Clos de Vougeot in Burgundy, brought cuttings of the supernal Burgundian red-wine grape, Pinot Noir, to this region, and that the grape became acclimatized over the centuries into what is now

Tinto Fino, the main grape of the Ribera del Duero and the source of Vega Sicilia, Mauro, Pesquera, Pedrosa, and the other great red wines of this region.

PESQUERA DE DUERO

Continuing a few kilometers east, you will soon reach Pesquera de Duero, home of one of the brightest new stars on the Spanish wine scene, **Pesquera**. Since Robert Parker, an influential American wine writer, compared Pesquera's red wines to Château Petrus a few years ago, this modest winery has rocketed to fame, and the owner, Alejandro Fernández, now travels the world promoting his wines. He regularly sells substantial orders of Pesquera to his old friend Julio Iglesias—not bad for a man who started out in his own machine shop, inventing farm tools and other implements, many of which he now uses in the winery. Ask Señor Fernández to show you the old Roman-style wine-press, where his first vintages were made.

To visit Pesquera, call or write ahead to: Bodegas Alejandro Fernández, 47315 Pesquera de Duero (Valladolid); Tel: (9-83) 88-10-27. From the United States you may arrange a visit to Pesquera or several other top Ribera del Duero wineries by contacting Classical Wines from Spain, 4000 Aurora Avenue North, Suite 222, Seattle, Washington 98103; Tel: (206) 547-0255. This importer is a major discoverer of fine small producers in Spain. (Note: It is absolutely imperative that you confirm your visit to any of these wineries by telephone the day before.)

PEÑAFIEL

The town of Peñafiel, 56 km (35 miles) east of Valladolid on the way to Aranda de Duero and just a few miles southeast of Pesquera de Duero (note the ancient bridge over the Duero just north of Peñafiel), is the only town of real touristic merit on the way to Aranda (see below) from Valladolid. The long, narrow, whitish-gray 14th-century **Castillo de Peñafiel**, perched on the hill above the town, is like a battleship in the sky, sailing through the clouds. The castle, whose origins date to the tenth century, is one of the best preserved and most impressive remnants of Spain's military power during the centuries-long drive to push the Moors out of the Iberian Peninsula. It is at its most spectacular in early evening, when the golden rays of the setting sun intensify the drama of the mighty fortress standing out against the sky, as a herd of sheep grazes on the hill beneath it.

Peñafiel is a fascinating and lively old market town with loads of atmosphere. In addition to the castle, the town has a number of impressive old churches (especially notable is the 14th-century **Iglesia de San Pablo**, with an exceptional Mudejar apse) and ancient buildings scattered along its steep, narrow streets. The Plaza del Coso, an unpaved square plaza surrounded by three-story balconied houses with shuttered, multipaned windows, still serves as the town bullring. Along Río Duratón, which flows through town and meets the Duero here, are inhabited millhouses that generate electricity from the rushing waters and have their own little gardens and cherry trees along the river. The stone *zarceras* (ventilation chimneys), which issue from underground wine caves burrowed into the hill (see Ribera de Burgos Wine Country, below, for more on these structures), are a prominent feature in Peñafiel. Here the *zarceras* dot the castle hill, which is a warren of undergound bodegas, and some even project from the steep streets.

Asador Mauro (no relation to Bodegas Mauro in Tudela de Duero), on Calle Atarazanas, one of the high streets leading to the castle (ask someone how to find it), is among the best *asadores* (roast houses) in the region, although open for lunch only. The brick oven is in the dining room, so you are right in the middle of the action, experiencing the sight, sound, and delicious smell of lamb as it is roasted for you. A salad, a plate of local cheese and *chorizo,* a quarter of roast baby lamb, a pitcher of Asador Mauro's house wine—perhaps one of the best house wines in the world—from a local producer, and a clay pot of *cuajada* (a mild, custard-like sheep's curd, sweetened to taste with wild honey) for dessert is the repast here, and the object of many a pilgrimage; Tel: (9-83) 88-08-16. Since adequate accommodations are not available in Peñafiel, you should continue east to Aranda de Duero (covered below) or north to Burgos for the night.

PALENCIA PROVINCE

The province of Palencia is one of the least visited in Spain. Ostensibly, there is little here of major historic or architectural interest except a few spots on the Camino de Santiago and the seventh-century Visigothic church of San Juan de Baños, in Baños de Cerrato. However, to diligent travellers bent on discovering the undersung and little explored, Palencia, with its tranquil back roads, ancient churches of the Campos Góticos (Fields of the Goths), little-known medieval towns, and sleepy brown villages, offers rewards of the spirit not always found in the more heavily touristed areas that command the most publicity.

North to Palencia City

DUEÑAS
Dueñas, northeast of Valladolid just off N 620, only 17 km (10 miles) south of Palencia, is a reasonably well preserved village that retains some of its medieval walls and gates. Although Isabella and Ferdinand first met in the Palacio de Vivero in Valladolid, and were married there, the local tradition is that they were secretly married here in Dueñas—to outwit political enemies who were willing to go to great lengths to prevent their union—before the public ceremony in Valladolid. During the turbulent political period just after their marriage they lived here for a short time, held court here, and had their first child, Isabella. While in Dueñas take a look at the 13th-century **Iglesia de Santa María de la Asunción**, which retains some vestiges of its Romanesque roots and contains late-15th-century Isabelline tombs, a 16th-century Gothic altarpiece, and a tower from the late 16th century.

BAÑOS DE CERRATO
A few miles north of Dueñas, and just south of Palencia, is Baños de Cerrato (look for signs on the east side of the road) and the little seventh-century **Iglesia de San Juan de Baños**. To find the church, follow the signs in town, turn right after you cross the railway, and continue on the road to the end of the village, where the church sits at the edge of a field. You will probably have to track down the priest, who lives nearby, to be let into the church. San Juan de Baños, built by the same King Recceswinth whose tomb is at Wamba (see Wine Villages and Castle Towns, above), is one of the most important Visigothic monuments in Spain. The modified horseshoe arches in the church may predate the arrival of the Moorish horseshoe arch in Spain. The arches rest on Roman columns taken, like much of the stone for the church, from an earlier Roman temple that may have been located on this site.

The City of Palencia

Palencia, the provincial capital (population 76,000), is located 47 km (29 miles) northeast of Valladolid on N 611 (take N 620 north to N 611 north). The city sits on the banks of the little Río Carrión surrounded by the vast high plain and great wheat field known as the "Granary of Castile," the **Tierra de Campos**, which is also shared by the provinces of Valladolid, León, and Zamora. (On clear days from a hill near **Autilla del Pino**, 18 km/11 miles southwest of Palencia, you can see more than 30 miles in all directions out over the Tierra de Campos).

Because most of the province is a plain, the buildings in this region, even church towers and castles, do not soar like buildings in other parts of Spain; perhaps they didn't need the height to detect the approach of an enemy. This is true even in the capital, which tends to have an odd overall horizontal feel that seems reflected in its earthbound, conservative inhabitants.

THE CATHEDRAL

Palencia's Gothic cathedral, in the western part of town, is known as "La Bella Desconocida," roughly meaning "the little-known jewel." It was built during the 14th to 16th centuries and was decorated by some of the greatest artists and craftsmen working in Castile at the time. Like most cathedrals in Castile, this one incorporates a number of architectural and artistic styles: Visigothic, Romanesque, Gothic, Flamboyant Gothic, Isabelline, Renaissance, and Baroque all in the same place. The cathedral has an 11th-century Romanesque chapel—reached by an Isabelline stairway—housing a fine seventh-century Visigothic chamber that is all that remains of the original church that stood on this spot, and is believed to be the crypt of the martyred San Antolín, whose remains were brought here from Toulouse by King Wamba in 673.

The early-16th-century main altarpiece of gilded wood by the sculptor and woodcarver Felipe de Vigarni, who did the carvings, and Juan de Flandes, who painted the 12 truly exceptional Flemish-style panels, is quite spectacular. Vigarni carved more than two dozen separate figures to fill most of the golden-painted niches in the retable; then, for whatever reason, Juan de Flandes was commissioned to paint scenes from the life of Christ for the center niches on each side and along the bottom of the piece. The colorful Flemish paintings provide a counterpoint to all that gold and breathe life into what would have been an impressive, but monotonous, procession of polychrome figures. Among other treasures in the cathedral are the impressive *trascoro* by the great collaborators Simón de Colonia and Gil de Siloé; a fine triptych by Juan de Flandes; works by Alonso Berruguete, Diego de Siloé, and El Greco; and a number of late-15th- and early-16th-century tapestries commissioned by Bishop Fonseca. Many parts of this cathedral, especially the side chapels, are very dimly lit; ask the custodian to light them for you.

AROUND IN PALENCIA

Palencia has several other churches dating from the 11th century to the 15th century, including the 11th- to 13th-century Romanesque **Iglesia de San Miguel** (four blocks south of the cathedral, a block inland of the Río Carrión), whose handsome restored tower is crenellated like a castle tower and has interesting Gothic windows in the belfry; a lovely ancient **stone bridge** across the Río Carrión that is Roman in origin; and a bustling vehicle-free shopping street, the Calle Mayor—but there is nothing to detain you here for more than a few hours. Just off the Plaza Mayor, where there is a modern monument to Alonso Berruguete, who was born in nearby Paredes de Nava, is the **Peña** gourmet shop, where you can buy the ingredients for a fine picnic. Señor Peña has an excellent selection of cheeses, including the rare *cabrales* from Asturias; some superb *chorizo* sausages and mountain hams; a selection of pâtés and tinned delicacies from all over Spain; and a good selection of wines.

DINING IN PALENCIA

The **Taberna Plaza Mayor** on the Plaza Mayor is a lively tavern offering a good selection of typical Castilian food in a casual *tapas*-bar atmosphere. Two other well-regarded restaurants are **Casa Damián**, Ignacio Martínez de Azcoitia 9 (the street behind the *ayuntamiento,* northeast of the Plaza Mayor), and **Lorenzo**, Avenida Casado del Alisal 10 (one block east and two blocks north of Damián). The two are owned by brothers and serve conservative, old-style Castilian *comida casera* (home cooking) learned from their mother. Their menus feature scrambled-egg dishes, stuffed peppers, *cuarto asado* (quarters of roast lamb), and *menestra* (held in particularly high regard at Casa Damián). On the wine lists are selections from the province of Valladolid: Rueda, Cigales, Ribera del Duero, and the excellent non–*denominación de origen* red wines Mauro and Yllera. Casa Damián is closed from late July to late August; Tel: (9-79) 74-46-28. Lorenzo closes from early September to early October; Tel: (9-79) 74-35-45.

STAYING IN PALENCIA

The best accommodations in the Palencia city area are located several miles from the city. On N 611, 12 km (12½ miles) north of Palencia at Monzón de Campos, is a quiet, inexpensive, ten-room hotel in the renovated ▶ **Castillo de Monzón**, a tenth-century castle with Romanesque touches. Located on a hill with views of the Tierra de Campos countryside, this charming hotel is the property of the government of Palencia, which makes it a rare find—for it is essentially a provincial parador, a little-known category of hotels not listed in the national system of paradores. The hotel is decorated with Castilian furnishings evocative of this region's austere past. Rooms are small but comfortable. Write or phone ahead, though, because it is sometimes entirely booked by Spanish tour groups (see the Accommodations Reference at the end of the chapter).

North of Palencia City

Frómista, 20 km (12 miles) north of Monzón de Campos on N 611, and Carrión de los Condes, 20 km northwest of Frómista via a secondary road, are two major shrines on the Camino de Santiago with important Romanesque churches (Carrión is about 85 km/53 miles west of Burgos on N 120).

James A. Michener wrote of Spain's Romanesque monuments in *Iberia:* "There is something perpetually clean and honorable about the best Romanesque, and when I see it my whole being responds." Edwin Mullins called them "squat brick churches rubbed by the wind."

FROMISTA

Frómista's 11th-century **Iglesia de San Martín** was founded by the widow of Sancho the Great of Navarra and taken over by the monks of Cluny in the early 12th century. Although a little less wind-rubbed than some Romanesque churches on the Camino de Santiago because of an extensive restoration at the turn of the century, San Martín is nonetheless an impressive example of Romanesque architecture. An extraordinary feature of this church is its 300-odd corbels, each with a different stone carving. In the evening light the church takes on a warm golden-brown color that, as Walter Starkie described it, "harmonizes with the golden wheat piled up on the threshing floors and the all-pervading brown immensity of Castile and Visigothic Tierra de Campos." Frómista also has a 15th-century Gothic church, **Iglesia de San Pedro**, and a late Gothic and Plateresque church, **Iglesia de Santa María del Castillo**, whose 16th-century retable contains 29 Hispano-Flemish panels.

VILLALCAZAR DE SIRGA

Between Frómista and Carrión de los Condes is the village of Villalcázar de Sirga, also known as Villasirga, whose 13th-century Templar church, the **Iglesia de Santa María la Blanca**, contains an image of the Virgin that was celebrated in the Middle Ages for purportedly curing pilgrims who were still ill even after a visit to Santiago de Compostela. Because of these miraculous cures, this simple brick-and-adobe village for a brief moment presumed to rival the fabled Galician destination, the tomb of Santiago Matamoros (Saint James the Moorslayer) at Santiago. But even with the great medieval king Alfonso X, El Sabio (The Wise), trumpeting the miracles of this Virgin of Villalcázar de Sirga in the *Cantigas*—his collection of 400 poems written in Gallego, the Galician language—in the end pilgrims were not inclined to trudge from all over Europe to stop short of their ultimate goal of Santiago de Compostela and exchange homage to the saint and Moorslayer for that of the poet-king's Virgin. Alfonso X had good reason to sing the praises of this Virgin, since she watched over the remains of his dead brother Philip, whom he had killed, and Philip's second wife, Leonor Ruiz de Castro. Their painted Romanesque sarcophagi in this church are masterpieces of medieval art.

CARRION DE LOS CONDES

Carrión de los Condes, 20 km (12 miles) northwest of Frómista, and just a few miles beyond Villasirga, was the home of the infamous infantes de Carrión, who, legend says, married El Cid's daughters, sponged off their famous father-in-law, then carried their wives off from Valencia, beat them, stripped them, and abandoned them in a forest. It was also the site of the annual tribute of 100 virgins to the Moors, which provoked the battle of Clavijo in La Rioja. Carrión is now a properous town with several noteworthy Romanesque monuments, including the 12th-century **Iglesia de Santiago**, whose frieze of an earthly band of presumably local artisans (a cobbler, a potter, a cook), musicians, and knights is in refreshing contrast to the usual collection of apostles and angels found on such buildings, and is a match for the greatest Romanesque stone carvings along the entire Camino de Santiago.

Other interesting churches in Carrión are the **Iglesia de Santa María del Camino**, also 12th-century Romanesque, with a façade containing stone carvings of what may be Mithraic bulls, and the Benedictine **Monasterio de San Zoilo** (now a seminary), originally built in the 11th century, with a 16th-century Renaissance cloister, in the arcades of which are vaulted ceilings decorated with some exceptional Plateresque stone carvings by Juan de Badajoz and his disciples.

ARANDA DE DUERO AND SOUTHERN BURGOS
Aranda de Duero

Aranda de Duero's importance stems from its location at a crossroads: It lies on N I, 156 km (97 miles) north of Madrid, and 83 km (52 miles) south of Burgos. Aranda is also on the east–west Soria–Valladolid road (N 122), which runs down the Duero river valley for most of its length; Soria is 114 km

(71 miles) to the east of Aranda, and Valladolid lies 93 km (58 miles) to the west.

At first glance Aranda de Duero seems a dull place, nearly bereft of monuments of interest—the superb 15th-century Isabelline façade of the **Iglesia de Santa María** and the narrow streets and charming **Plaza Mayor** of the 15th- and 16th-century old quarter are the exceptions—but as a base for any extensive exploration of southern Burgos province and the Ribera del Duero it is a practical choice. And for those who truly love roast lamb, Aranda has half a dozen superb *asadores* that have made the town a gastronomic legend.

DINING IN ARANDA

"Aranda de Duero, Vino y Cordero," the sign says at the entrance to the town, and what incredible *vino* and *cordero* (lamb) it is. Every *asador* in Aranda has a brick oven for roasting lamb and baking bread (of course, the bread oven came first), and every restaurant has its source of excellent Ribera del Duero house wine, which is served in pitchers. If you want to try a bottled wine from Aranda itself, **Torremilanos** is a very nice red wine. Call María Pilar Pérez, the English-speaking owner, to arrange a visit to Torremilanos's impressive new winery at the outskirts of Aranda; Tel: (9-47) 50-13-81.

Most Aranda *asadores* have their brick ovens near the entrance, where they exude irresistibly appetizing aromas as one crockery platter after another, laden with quarters of lamb, is pulled from the ovens with a wooden paddle. The *lechazo asado* (roast suckling lamb) comes out with a crackling crisp skin, and the meat is so tender and moist that it falls off the bone. A typical meal starts with grilled *chorizo* sausage, *morcilla con arroz* (blood sausage stuffed with rice), and *queso de Burgos* (cheese), followed by a salad, and then the main event, the lamb.

If you have time for only one meal in Aranda, have it at **Rafael Corrales**, Calle Carrequemada 2, a tiny, reasonably priced family-run *asador* founded at the turn of the century. Their homemade *chorizo* and roast quarter of lamb are supreme; except for salad, a slab of Castilian bread, and a pitcher of Ribera del Duero wine, that is all they serve at the picnic tables in their cozy upstairs dining rooms. Corrales is just off Avenida de Castilla in the center of Aranda, where half a dozen colorful taverns and *asadores* are located. Tel: (9-47) 50-02-77.

Casa Florencio, Calle Isilla 14 (two blocks west of Corrales), another good, moderately priced choice for roast lamb, also offers excellent baby lamb chops, roast suckling pig, roasted red peppers, braised *chorizo,* and superb *morcilla con arroz,* along with a good range of Ribera wines such as Torremilanos, Valduero, Protos, and Pedrosa. Tel: (9-47) 50-02-30. **Mesón de la Villa**, Plaza Mayor 3 (just through the archway, west of the Río Duero bridge, in downtown Aranda), also serves excellent roast lamb but is nationally known for its classic Castilian cuisine. Owner-chef Seri Bermejo, one of the finest cooks in Spain, re-creates many long-forgotten Castilian classics from centuries-old recipes—always with the best seasonal ingredients available—and other signature, market-cuisine dishes. Her affable husband, Eugenio Herrero, runs the beautifully decorated dining room filled with Castilian antiques, furniture, and paintings, and oversees the restaurant's cavernous wine cellar. While you may prefer the simplicity of Aranda's *asadores* most days, there is no denying that Mesón de la Villa is one of the greatest restaurants of Castile-León. Closed from October 12 to October 30; Tel; (9-47) 50-10-25.

STAYING IN ARANDA

Aranda's few hotels, even the convenient ▶ Hotel Los **Bronces** (out past the bullring at the northern end of Avenida de Castilla), are generally clean, have plenty of hot water, and are not expensive, but there's no guarantee of tasteful decor or firm mattresses (ask for a *tabla*—a bedboard—if your bed is too soft). However, Aranda's central location and its *asadores* for the evening meal more than compensate for the lackluster hotels, so consider forgoing the ultimate in creature comforts for a couple of days and get into the spirit of Old Castile by making Aranda your base for excursions into the highly rewarding, little-known areas around this city. (If you are willing to drive the extra hour each way to and from Burgos, you can make your base in the capital for these excursions.)

Ribera de Burgos Wine Country

From Aranda you can easily explore the Ribera de Burgos wine villages (which are within the Ribera del Duero *denominación*), located north and west of the city. (The areas discussed in this section can also be tied in with the Ribera del Duero wineries discussed above in Valladolid province.) You will enjoy meandering through this picturesque section of Castilian landscape, which is studded with small, unspoiled backcountry villages such as La Aguilera, Gumiel de Mercado, Sotillo de la Ribera, La Horra, Roa de Duero, and Pedrosa de Duero—places where tourists are practically unknown and where you can taste the area's excellent wines in cooperatives, family wineries, and local bars.

The best time to visit this region is in the spring, when the wheat fields are green and ablaze with flaming red poppies and the roads are trimmed with splendid wildflowers of just about every hue. You can make a nice loop of the area beginning just west of Aranda and just north of the main road to Palencia (C 619) on the well-paved secondary road that branches off to the northwest, following road signs toward La Aguilera, Gumiel de Mercado, and Sotillo de la Ribera, at which point you turn southwest to La Horra and Roa, then west to Pedrosa and Guzmán. In our coverage we point out some of the highlights, rather than describing the entire route.

LA HORRA

Stop at La Horra to visit **Bodegas Balbás**, the winery of Victor Balbás; Tel: (9-47) 54-10-52. Balbás and his son, Juanjo, are dedicated *cosecheros* (small grape growers who produce wines from their own grapes), making some of the Ribera's most delicious wines—dark, rich reds and beautiful ruby rosés. Balbás recently built a new winery a few hundred yards from the southern edge of the village (down a side street off La Horra's main street—ask for directions). At the winery ask to see the rustic man-made caves where they age their wines. Those strange chimney-like rock formations above the Balbás caves are man-made ventilation shafts called *zarceras*. The villages in this region have hundreds of *zarceras* sprouting from the hills, which are honeycombed with caves that were carved out for aging wines and, in some villages, cheeses.

PEDROSA DE DUERO

The **Pérez Pascuas** brothers—Adolfo, Benjamín, and Manolo—run a clean, well-maintained winery in Pedrosa de Duero; Tel: (9-47) 54-04-99. Their wines are made of grapes grown almost entirely in their impeccably tended vineyards within the municipality of Pedrosa. In this cooler upland region the three brothers, exceptionally dedicated viticulturists, produce some of the Ribera del Duero's most beautifully balanced red wines, lighter in color and style than any of the wines from the warmer Valladolid district. Because of their tawny-edged color, soft fruit, and distinctive nose, these wines are more reminiscent of Burgundy than any in the valley.

ROA DE DUERO

There are two choices for lunch in this region. You can buy food for a picnic at local stores, in morning markets, and at the Páramo de Guzmán cheese shop in Roa de Duero (see below), and accompany it all with a bottle of Ribera del Duero wine, perhaps purchased at one of the bodegas; or you can eat out in Roa de Duero, 6 km (4 miles) east of Pedrosa. (Another option for lunch if you are heading west to Peñafiel is the Mesón Mauro, described above in the Valladolid Province section.)

Roa is a picturesque village perched on a hill overlooking the Río Duero, where a locally esteemed restaurant of somewhat garish decoration but sound kitchen, **Chuleta**, Avenida de la Paz 7, specializes in *lechazo asado,* grilled meats, and grilled fish. It also offers good *almejas a la marinera* (clams), *puerros vinagreta* (leeks vinaigrette), and *alubias con chorizo* (beans with sausage). Try a bottle of the seldom-encountered Rauda Viejo or the house *clarete,* both from the Roa cooperative; Tel: (9-47) 54-03-12.

In newly excavated, extensive underground cellars nearby in Roa (and in some old caves in his hometown of Guzmán), Ambrosio Molinos and his wife, Asunción, close friends of the Pérez Pascuas brothers, age their excellent *queso de Burgos,* Páramo de Guzmán, one of the most highly prized cheeses in Spain. Made from the milk of purebred *churra* sheep, the Molinos's cheeses are unpasteurized (but made under absolutely safe, carefully monitored conditions) and are aged from three to six months. The Molinos sell their non-pasteurized cheeses as they come from the caves or immersed in high-quality olive oil to keep them fresh for several months. They also package them in tins, so that it is now possible to take home an authentic *queso de Burgos.* (If you don't make the trip to Roa, look for them in round, gray one- and two-kilogram tins all around Castile and in gourmet shops all over Spain.) The Páramo de Guzmán caves are located on the ring road that skirts Roa to the north and continues to Pedrosa de Duero. Last year the Molinos family opened a new shop and tasting room at the caves, called **Páramo de Guzmán**, with Castilian decor, picnic tables, and a *chimenea* (fireplace) for roasting lamb chops. Ambrosia Molinas is a big supporter of Ribera del Duero wines, so along with his cheeses, you can find many different types of local *vino* for sale here.

Roa is the town where the powerful regent of Spain Cardinal Cisneros, Queen Isabel's top adviser and the guiding light behind Toledo's cathedral, died in 1517, some think after he received a letter from Charles V relieving him—by then he was an ailing octogenarian—of the position he had filled so honorably and so well. Roa also has a fine 16th-century Plateresque church, La Colegiata, facing the town square.

The return east to Aranda de Duero from Roa is a short, easy, unhurried drive on good country roads. If you are continuing west to Valladolid and Tordesillas, the leisurely afternoon's drive down the Duero valley offers sightseeing, wine tasting (see the Peñafiel and the Red-Wine Villages section, above), and coffee in a village bar as diversions along the way.

Northeast from Aranda

Another excellent day trip from Aranda (or from Burgos, perhaps with a stop for lunch in Aranda) is the loop to the northeast through Peñaranda de Duero, Santo Domingo de Silos, Covarrubias, Lerma, and back to Aranda (or north to Burgos).

PEÑARANDA DE DUERO

Peñaranda de Duero, a few miles east of Aranda on C 111, is a picturesque old walled town with a castle and a photogenic, arcaded Plaza Mayor with timbered houses. Along the western side of the plaza is one of the greatest Renaissance palaces of Spain, the **Palacio de los Condes de Miranda**, which incorporates a number of architectural and decorative influences, including Moorish, Gothic, Plateresque, and Italian. Just across the square is the 16th-century **Iglesia de Santa Ana**, with an undistinguished 17th-century Italianate portal, and in the center of the plaza is a fine Gothic *rollo,* the spot where edicts were read.

Ask someone to direct you to **La Botica**, the town pharmacy, the second oldest in Spain, which is still functioning and has been in the same family since the 18th century. It is run by Señor José Jimeno, who, for a small admission fee to his museum, will show you his collection of more than 200 Talavera ceramic pharmaceutical *botes* (canisters) dating from the 18th century.

Peñaranda is a lovely and unspoiled town, a great place for tarrying over a late-morning coffee at one of the little outdoor cafés just north of the plaza. The village priest will probably stop by to inquire about your nationality and ask what you think of his town.

NORTH TOWARD SANTO DOMINGO DE SILOS

Driving north on paved country roads, you pass the village and the Dominican monastery/school of **Caleruega**, the birthplace of the founder of the Dominican order, Santo Domingo de Guzmán, in the 12th century. (Santo Domingo de Guzmán, Santo Domingo de Silos—see below—and Santo Domingo de la Calzada—see La Rioja—are three different saints.) Between Caleruega and Santo Domingo de Silos is some spectacular scenery, including the **Paso de la Yecla**, a scary narrow gorge that is about a half-mile long, several hundred feet deep, and in some places little more than a yard wide. You can walk the length of the Yecla canyon near the bottom on a narrow concrete walkway with a slender, barely adequate, steel-pipe handrail, which is all that keeps you from falling into the cold, clear pools of the tiny Mataviejas stream below. If you are careful, it is great fun.

SANTO DOMINGO DE SILOS

The 11th-century two-story cloister of the **Monasterio de Santo Domingo de Silos**, northeast of Caleruega, is one of the great jewels of Romanesque art in Spain; more than one writer has described it as the most beautiful Romanesque cloister in the world. Rows of double columns on the lower level are crowned by exquisite 11th-century stone capitals carved by at least three unknown, Eastern-inspired artists— each of whose style is distinguishable from the others. The capitals feature gryphons, winged horses, birdlike creatures with human faces, and strange otherworldly plants and flowers. Some experts believe the artists were Persians, because the Persian Muslim sect permitted the depiction of the human form, something seldom found in Mudejar art.

The Doubt of Saint Thomas, one of eight magnificent Romanesque stone carvings depicting scenes from the life of Christ in relief on the cloister's corner piers, alone is worth the trip here. Walter Starkie, whose writing drew great inspiration from Santo Domingo de Silos, summarizes the cloister and those eight great carvings as "a gigantic panorama of the 11th century, created by artists who had combined harmoniously the ornamental devices of Byzantium and the East with those of Visigothic Spain."

The monastery's other attractions are considerable: the upper cloister's capitals, dating from the 12th century; the *artesonado* ceilings painted in the 14th century; the 13th-century sepulcher of Santo Domingo, resting on the backs of three very Oriental-looking lions. The monastery **museum** has a beautiful small collection of religious artifacts such as a Mozarabic chalice and a walking stick that once belonged to the saint, a beautiful Limoges-like enamel reliquary believed to be from the 12th century, and a tenth- or 11th-century Mozarabic breviary made from some of the earliest paper in Spain. The old *botica* (pharmacy), dating from 1705, has hundreds of fine ceramic jars like those in Peñaranda. In the evening, the haunting sounds of Gregorian chant, rising and falling from the throats of the Benedictine brothers seated in the choir, carry throughout the candlelit church.

If you wish to stay overnight in Santo Domingo, there is a good hotel and restaurant, ▶ **Hotel Tres Coronas de Silos**, in a fine 18th-century stone house located on the little Plaza Mayor and overlooking the monastery. Decorated with rustic dark wood and wrought-iron trappings, and furnished with antiques and period furniture reproductions, Tres Coronas is reminiscent of a parador. The hotel has a cozy bar and a restaurant serving *tapas,* roast goat, baby lamb chops, and good Ribera del Duero wines. Tel: (9-47) 38-07-27.

COVARRUBIAS

A short distance northwest of Silos is Covarrubias, an almost perfectly preserved village with centuries-old half-timbered houses. Nestled in the Arlanza valley, and looking like an age-old settlement in perfect harmony with its natural surroundings, Covarrubias is a find.

In the early tenth century this small town was the powerful base of Count Fernán González, a figure even more important in Castile than El Cid, since by hook or by crook he managed to forge the nascent county of Castile by continually playing the Moors and the Kingdom of León off one another. As J. Vicens Vives wrote in *Approaches to the History of Spain,* this was "a transcendental moment in Peninsular affairs in which Castile actually made her appearance in history," the period when "Castile forged her warrior temperament, her will to command, and her ambition to achieve a great destiny." The *Poema de Fernán González,* a famous 13th-century work, possibly written by a monk at the monastery of San Pedro de Arlanza (east of Covarrubias; see below), glorifies the exploits of this storied knight of Castile.

Around in Covarrubias

The main sights in Covarrubias, all of which are well marked, include the tenth-century **Torre de Doña Urraca,** claimed by some to be haunted by the ghost of Urraca, who was imprisoned here by her father, the legendary Fernán; a 16th-century town gate; a superb Plaza Mayor; and a number of churches of merit, including **La Colegiata,** which now houses the tomb of Fernán González, whose remains were brought here from the monastery of San Pedro de Arlanza. Built on the ruins of former Visigothic and Romanesque churches, the church we see now dates primarily from the 15th century, although the cloister is 16th century. Apart from the impressive tombs of Fernán González and his wife, there are some 40 other tombs in this church, including that of an abbot designed by Juan de Colonia. The church also contains a sacristy with some important documents from early Castile, a wooden pipe organ that is highly esteemed for its rich tone, and a superb piece by Gil de Siloé, the *Tríptico de Covarrubias,* whose centerpiece is a truly exceptional *Adoration of the Magi* in polychrome wood.

Staying and Dining in Covarrubias

Covarrubias also has a good hotel and restaurant, the ▶ **Parador Colaborador Arlanza**, decorated in old Castilian style. The restaurant serves typical regional cuisine, and on special occasions offers a medieval menu. Closed December to March; Tel: (9-47) 40-30-25. **Galín**, Plaza Doña Urraca 4, a better choice than the hotel restaurant, serves inexpensive *comida casera* (home-cooked food) such as the famous *olla podrida* (rotten pot stew; Sundays only, not in summer), roast lamb, and stewed rabbit, plus their own homemade wine (there is a little-known wine area here, the Ribera de Arlanza). Closed during the first three weeks of September; Tel: (9-47) 40-30-15.

EAST FROM COVARRUBIAS

If you wish to expend a little extra effort to capture the true spirit of this corner of Castile—which incorporates Visigothic, Romanesque, and Renaissance architecture and has a pronounced feel of the old Spain of El Cid and Fernán González—we recommend an hour-long side trip through rugged juniper- and pine-covered hills to Quintanillas de las Viñas. Drive east from Covarrubias on C 110 to the 11th-century Romanesque (rebuilt in the 15th century) **Monasterio de San Pedro de Arlanza**, whose dramatic ruins on the banks of the Río Arlanza not only inspire contemplation but also offer an excellent site for a picnic. Eagles soar on the wind currents above this once-powerful abbey. The approach from the west overlooks San Pedro—now roofless and open to the elements—offering a bird's-eye view of the floor plan of this medieval monastery. San Pedro de Arlanza was the original resting place of Fernán González.

QUINTILLANA DE LAS VIÑAS

Turn north at Hortigüela and follow the Burgos–Soria highway (N 234) a few miles until you see signs for Quintanilla de las Viñas. In the village is a house with a "Turismo" sign, where you have to pick up the official guide, who will accompany you to the village church with the keys to let you in.

The church is said to be seventh-century Visigothic, but parts of it are definitely later, from at least the tenth century. Regardless of its imprecise lineage, this is still one of the oldest churches in Spain, and it has some exceptionally rare stone carvings of bulls, lions, peacocks, pheasants, and other animals and birds, which decorate several rows of stone blocks high on the apse of the church. The simple block lines of the church contrast with the restrained but rich stone carvings and evoke a spirituality so sadly missing in the huge, heavy buildings you will encounter in Lerma, the last stop before returning to Aranda or Burgos.

LERMA

Travel a few miles farther north on N 234 to Cuevas de San Clemente, then turn left and head southwest following the road signs to Mecerreyes and to Puentedura, where you catch C 110 west along the north bank of Río Arlanza to meet highway N I at Lerma, a town that dates to at least the eighth century, though it is now dominated by buildings from a much later period.

From this northern approach especially, Lerma's massive 16th- and 17th-century Renaissance buildings brooding on the hill overlooking the Arlanza are impressive, as is the ancient bridge east of the main road. Lerma's entrance is an archway guarded by two fortified 12th-century towers that are all that remain of its ancient fortifications. Some people find the Herreran-style buildings inside the town as oppressive architecturally as the man who built them, and his family, were politically. This was the virtual fiefdom of Philip III's corrupt *privado* (favorite) and the de facto ruler of Spain, the duke of Lerma. Alastair Boyd described the town of Lerma's attractions as "hollow grandeurs" and observed that "Lerma was built in all its essentials on the ill-gotten gains of one man and has had no real *raison d'être* since." However, Spaniards consider the duke's huge stone palace (located on the broad main plaza at the top of the hill) to be one of their most important pieces of 17th-century civil architecture. And because of the town's historic and quintessentially Castilian atmosphere (and convenient location on the main road), most travellers will find Lerma a rewarding stop.

The huge **Iglesia Colegiata de San Pedro**, riding high on a hill overlooking the Arlanza, dates to 1606 and contains the impressive tomb of the duke's uncle, Archbishop Cristobal de Rojas, who, like many of Lerma's relatives and friends, was appointed to one of the highest and most lucrative posts in the land. This tomb was designed by Pompeo Leoni and Juan de Arfe, the same pair who did Lerma's funerary monument, now in the Museo Nacional de Escultura in Valladolid. Other signs of the duke in Lerma are the two huge coats of arms that plaster the façade of the church of San Blas and resemble the ones on the church of San Pablo in Valladolid.

For lunch in Lerma try **Casa Antón**, Calvo Sotelo 5 (in the upper portion of the old quarter near the duke's palace), a century-old *asador* where you can dine on grilled lamb; Tel: (9-47) 17-03-62.

Because Lerma is roughly equidistant between Aranda, 44 km (27 miles) south, and Burgos, 37 km (23 miles) north, it is an easy drive on N I to either city.

BURGOS

Culturally and historically, Burgos is an important city. Its strategic location at the junction of the route from France to

Madrid and the east–west Camino de Santiago virtually assured this old Castilian town of a prominent place in the history of the country. Spread out along a valley of the pretty little Río Arlanzón, Burgos is located 80 km (50 miles) north of Aranda de Duero, and 240 km (149 miles) north of Madrid. It is also easily accessible on good roads (highway N 620) from Valladolid (122 km/76 miles) and Palencia (88 km/55 miles) to the southwest. Vitoria is 114 km (71 miles) northeast on A 1, and Santander and Bilbao lie on the coast to the north and the northeast.

Because of its location, its significance in the history of Spain, its grand Gothic cathedral, and its fame as the hometown of El Cid, Burgos has long been an essential stop for serious travellers in Spain. However, Alexandre Dumas, Hans Christian Andersen, James A. Michener, and almost every other writer who has ever set foot in the country—like most travellers—either paused at Burgos just long enough to see the cathedral, pay their respects to El Cid, and have lunch, or allowed a mere day or two here to satisfy stronger pangs of cultural curiosity. Hemingway would stop for a bullfight or to lunch on fresh trout, and he always had the "delicate Burgos cheese" that he so fondly remembered having brought back to Gertrude Stein in Paris, "when I'd come home from Spain in the old days third-class on the train."

It's a shame that most of those famous writers didn't stay longer, because Burgos is one of the finest cities in Spain, and its people are among the noblest of Spaniards. Even though you *can* see most of the sights in a couple of days, Burgos is a place where you could easily spend a week or that you could use as a base for a month. Burgos's charm, its easy-paced lifestyle, and the beauty of its old city along the north bank of the Arlanzón are reminiscent of one of those fine small cities in the Loire Valley, and its soul, albeit a distinctly Castilian and less outwardly demonstrative one, is on a par with that of Seville. With a population of a little more than 150,000, most of whose members seem to cling to conservative Castilian values, the town is not yet overrun by the impossible traffic, rampant crime, and drugs that have plagued other cities. (Of course, no place is immune to car break-ins, petty thievery, and occasional muggings, and even though there is less danger in Burgos than in many places, it is still wise to exercise normal precautions.)

Burgos does have, however, a reputation for extreme weather. The old Spanish adage "nine months of winter, three months of hell" has long been the standard description of the area's weather, and the winter weather will be cold, brisk, and bracing, but no more so than that of New York or Edinburgh, and with less humidity.

Many writers have taken at face value the "three months of hell" portion of the old adage, but summer in Burgos is not as bad as is often claimed. It is hot during the day, but the wonderful outdoor cafés under shade trees along the Espolón, the tree-lined *paseos* along the river, and the shade of buildings in the narrow streets diminish the effects of the heat. Burgos is some 2,900 feet above sea level, so many summer nights are lovely and cool; usually a jacket or sweater is needed for comfort, even in July. Late June, when the Fiesta de San Pedro y San Pablo takes place, is an ideal time to visit, but May, September, and October are also very good months.

The Legendary El Cid

Burgos came into being in 882, some 160 years after the first invasion of Spain by the Moors, or as one historian put it, "unhampered by a past of someone else's making." It became the first capital of nascent Castile, then but a county. Burgos was originally, and remains today, uniquely Castilian. And in no figure is Burgos and the essence of Castile better personified than the 11th-century hero El Cid Campeador (from the Arabic for "lord," and in Spanish roughly meaning "champion among warriors").

On his legendary horse, Babieca, El Cid rides across the pages of Spanish history, at times a ruthless soldier of fortune but ultimately a great hero, a patriot, and one of the most exemplary family men in history. At the church of Santa Agueda, west of the cathedral, El Cid made King Alfonso VI of Castile swear three times before the populace of Burgos that he, Alfonso, had had no part in the murder of the king's older brother, Sancho. El Cid then pledged his allegiance to Alfonso, but, having publicly humiliated the king, his fate was sealed. Alfonso ultimately banished him from Castile, and the great warrior had to sell his services to Moor and Christian alike for many years. Finally, El Cid tricked some Burgos moneylenders into funding his assault on the great Moorish city of Valencia by leaving as security a locked chest filled with stones and sand, claiming that it was actually loaded with treasure. He conquered and held Valencia for a number of years, eventually repaying his debt to the moneylenders and redeeming his chest of stones. El Cid's beautiful wife, Doña Jimena, herself the stuff of legend, finally brought the great warrior back to his beloved Castile in death, his corpse dressed in battle gear and seated on the noble Babieca, so the legend goes. El Cid's exploits were the basis of the great epic poem of the 12th century, *El Cantar de Mío Cid,* and he became the national hero of Spain.

EL CID IN BURGOS

Here in Burgos physical reminders of the real-life Cid, whose name was Rodrigo Díaz de Vivar, mingle with the air of romantic legend that surrounds his life. His image on the Arco de Santa María; the fine equestrian statue standing in a square just north of the Puente de San Pablo; the statues of Doña Jimena and other notables of the epoch lining the San Pablo bridge; the repository of the bones of El Cid and Jimena beneath a plain stone in the cathedral; the line of measure, said to be the length of La Tizona (his famous sword), on a wall of the cathedral; and the coffer (also in the cathedral) with which he supposedly tricked the money-lenders—all infuse the city with a magical sense of his presence. You can also make an excursion into the nearby countryside to San Pedro de Cardeña, the monastery where Doña Jimena and her children resided during El Cid's long periods of exile from Castile. All these reminders of El Cid are not, for the most part, sentimental or contrived, but it is the medieval ambience of Burgos that all these remnants combine to evoke that will stay with you—longer than the remembrance of the icons themselves.

Seeing Burgos

Once you get past Burgos's cocoon of dingy industrial buildings and nondescript modern high-rise apartments, you will find the inner core of the city—beautifully restored and vibrant—to be one of the finest in Spain. The ruins of a once-mighty castle crown the hill above the city, and the airy, filigreed, steel-gray spires of the magnificent cathedral rise majestically to the sky. The sights of cultural and historic interest are easily visited because the historic core of Burgos is so compact and walkable. The great Gothic cathedral, the history-steeped Casa del Cordón, and many other sights are all linked in a relatively short semicircle just north of the river.

The historic-artistic *conjunto* (ensemble) of the old center city, whose recent building code prevents construction of any structure more than three stories high, is full of charm. With the cathedral and the other historic buildings as backdrop, the old quarter has many attractions: nice little shops; the lively alleylike market street, San Lorenzo; the Plaza Mayor; a wonderful river (though the Arlanzón makes some modest trout streams look like raging torrents); and a splendid tree-shaded esplanade, the Paseo del Espolón. Sidewalk cafés, such as the venerable Café Pinedo along the Espolón and those around the Plaza Mayor, are wonderful for watching the people parade while you sip coffee or a frosty glass of beer accompanied by a dish of fine green olives cured with anchovies in the brine.

Staying in Burgos

Before starting a tour of Burgos, you need to consider your accommodation options, since hotel location is vital for getting the most out of this city. Considering the charm of old Burgos, it is unfortunate that the town's best hotel—and one of the finest in Spain—the luxurious ▶ **Hotel Landa Palace**, which also has the best restaurant, is a few kilometers south of town on the busy N I highway. The Landa Palace, a Relais & Châteaux hotel, is sumptuously decorated with period furniture, tapestries, and wrought-iron fixtures. It is incorporated into a 14th-century tower that was brought here stone by stone, reconstructed, and embellished with Gothic stonework. The Landa Palace also has a heated swimming pool with Gothic vaulting and other special touches such as marble baths. Of course, there is a hefty tariff for such opulence.

Old Burgos is such a special and romantic city that leisurely walks to and from a centrally located hotel really ought to be an integral part of the total experience, so you might prefer to drink in the atmosphere of old Burgos by staying in the city. The recently renovated ▶ **Hotel Fernán González**, a charming hotel decorated with period furniture, is located on the south bank of the Arlanzón, directly across from the Espolón and the medieval precincts. As you walk out from the Fernán González, you have the choice of heading either a block east along the river to the Puente de San Pablo or a block west to the Puente de Santa María. Either way, you will be able to contemplate the unfolding panorama of old Burgos, reinforcing the notion that you are indeed in a very special town.

The expensive, centrally located ▶ **NH Condestable** has recently been remodeled and is more comfortable now, but feels sterile with its ultramodern furnishings. Nonetheless, it remains one of Burgos's classic hotels and is just inland from the river's north bank. The very pleasant and friendly, moderately priced ▶ **Hotel Residencia Cordón** has neat, comfortable, modern rooms with uninspired decor, but is in a good location on a side street a few doors west of the Casa del Cordón. The pricey ▶ **Hotel del Cid**, whose restaurant (see below) re-creates the atmosphere of an old Castilian inn, has rooms beautifully decorated with antiques, elegant chairs and tables, and brass beds. Ask for one of the rooms that overlook the western façade of the cathedral.

Around in Old Burgos

The great Gothic cathedral of Burgos (see below) will take at least half a day to see properly. If you are going to be here only for a day, we suggest you leave it for the afternoon (it's open 4:00 P.M. to 7:00 P.M., in addition to morning hours), and dedicate your morning to exploring the outdoor sights of Burgos while the city is bustling with life.

Start at the **Puente de San Pablo** (also called the Vía Cidiana, after El Cid), which is flanked with eight 20th-century stone statues of major figures in El Cid's life, including Doña Jimena, El Cid's son, and his Moorish friend Avengalvón. Just north of the bridge is the excellent statue—completed in 1955 by the sculptor Juan Cristobal—of a luxuriantly bearded Cid dressed in chain-mail armor, his huge sword, La Tizona, pointing toward the enemy, and his cape flying behind him as he charges into battle astride his mighty horse.

CASA DEL CORDON

Behind the statue of El Cid, less than a block to the north on the right, is a pedestrian street leading into the fine Plaza de Calvo Sotelo, where the Casa del Cordón and three restaurants (see below) are located. The Casa del Cordón, a recently restored Renaissance building now occupied by a bank, is so called because of the thick Franciscan cord carved in stone above the portal. The coats of arms above the doorway belong to the palace's original owners, the high constable of Castile, Don Pedro Hernández de Velasco, and his wife, Doña Mencia, whose splendid tombs are in the equally splendid Capilla del Condestable, which they had built in the cathedral.

Isabella and Ferdinand received Columbus in this house in 1497 after he returned from his second voyage to the New World, and a number of Spanish monarchs, including Charles V, lived here at one time or another. Perhaps the most important event that occurred in this house was the death of a foreign prince, Philip the Fair, who was bent on usurping the throne of Spain from his supposedly mad wife, Juana la Loca, the daughter of Isabella and Ferdinand. After playing a hard game of *pelota* (handball or jai alai) with a Basque guard, Philip caught a chill (though some say he was poisoned) and died within a week. Juana then set out from here on a peripatetic journey across Castile with Philip's coffin, which she was to open a number of times before the handsome young libertine prince's body would finally end up in the royal chapel in Granada. Philip and Juana's son became the Holy Roman emperor Charles V and King Carlos I of Spain and subsequently locked his mother up in the palace of Tordesillas, where she was to remain for 46 years.

OTHER SIGHTS IN THE OLD TOWN

Calle de la Puebla leads from the northeastern corner of the Plaza del Calvo Sotelo, past the hotel Cordón and east a few blocks to a Camino de Santiago stop, the 14th-century Capilla de San Lesmes and, nearby, the old ruined monastery of San Juan. The Plateresque cloisters there now house the **Museo de Marceliano Santa María** (1866–1952), a distinguished Burgos Impressionist artist whose paintings are in much the same style as those of his contemporaries Sorolla and Zuloaga. But these are secondary destinations, for those who are here for more than a day.

In that category, too, are the fine 13th- and 14th-century Iglesia de San Gil, northwest of the Casa del Cordón; the 12th-century Moorish Arco de San Esteban and a section of old walls located just west of San Gil; and the recently restored 13th-century Iglesia de San Esteban, with its tiny 14th-century cloister, just south of the arch. The early-15th-century **Iglesia de San Nicolás**, has an exceptional early-16th-century reredos in alabaster by Simón de Colonia, just northwest of the cathedral on Calle Fernán González. Southwest of the cathedral, and not to be missed by devotees of El Cid, is the **Iglesia de Santa Agueda**, where the great Campeador made Alfonso VI swear his innocence (see above).

From the ruined **castillo** (perhaps Castile owes its name to this one) crowning the hill above Burgos there are excellent views of the cathedral, the town, and the valley. There are several other historic landmarks flavoring the historic *olla* (stew pot) of Burgos, worthy of perhaps a snapshot and a cursory inspection as you stroll the streets of the old quarter. Just below the castle hill, along Calle Doña Jimena, are the 16th-century Arco de Fernán González, built under Philip II; the Solar del Cid, a monolithic trio of monuments marking the site of El Cid's ancestral home; and the 14th-century Arco de San Martín, one of the original gates of the old city.

As you descend the steep streets from the Arco de San Martín along Santa Agueda you will come to the cathedral.

The Cathedral

Some visitors to the great Gothic cathedral of Burgos approve of its exterior, but find its interior broken up too much by the choir, obstructing the kinds of vistas that you get at the cathedrals of Seville and Toledo. The cathedral is also hemmed in by the buildings that huddle around it, so views of this massive edifice are more encumbered than those of the cathedrals at Seville and Santiago. The rose window is lovely, but all of León's stained glass adds up to greater magnificence. Despite these shortcomings, this is still one of the greatest religious structures in Spain, and to those interested in religious art and history, the cathedral of Burgos offers a wealth of both and a profusion of artistic detail matched by few buildings in Spain.

Work on the cathedral began in 1221 and continued for another 300 years, so it incorporates a number of architectural styles. The cathedral's dominant exterior feature, the lacy Gothic spires that soar almost 300 feet into the Burgos sky and give the city a Germanic air, were built in the mid-15th century by Juan de Colonia (Johan of Cologne), father of Simón, and are believed to have been inspired by the original plans for the cathedral of Cologne. Because the cathedral's exterior is so rich in sculpture and decoration, and so that you can better understand some of the peculiarities of its interior, we recommend that you walk the multilevel circuit of the exterior first.

THE EXTERIOR

Begin at the western door, the **Puerta de Santa María**, which is the main entrance. The façade's lower third is pierced by three massive arched doorways, but it is rather plainly decorated due to a poorly handled 18th-century attempt at restoration that stripped it of much of its sculpture. The upper portion of the façade, Juan de Colonia's Gothic masterpiece, seems to gather its strength from the lower third to propel its airy towers into the sky. Ribbed pinnacles and filigree bell towers flank a massive rose window topped by a florid twin-arched Gothic gallery with eight statues of the kings of Castile and a stone balustrade spelling "*Pulchra est et Decora.*"

Left of the main door, a stairway leads up past the church of San Nicolás to Calle Fernán González. Walk east along the cathedral to the 13th-century **Puerta de la Coronería**, or Puerta Alta, on the northern arm of the transept. As with much of the exterior stone carving on this and other churches, Puerta de la Coronería (now almost always closed) is showing the ravages of modern-day pollution, which is melting away the delicate carvings in soft stone that withstood the pounding of rain and wind for centuries.

Continuing east on Fernán González, you'll see to your right the multispired, three-story, octagonal **lantern tower**, richly decorated with balustrades, stained-glass windows, and stone carvings. The original lantern, built by Juan de Colonia in the mid-15th century, collapsed and was replaced in the mid-16th century with this one by Juan de Vallejo. Left of the lantern is the buttressed 13th-century apse, which is the oldest part of the church, and left of the apse is a third set of spires and tall stained-glass windows, this time crowning the

Capilla del Condestable, executed by Simón de Colonia in the late 15th century. While profusely decorated with crocketed spires, balustrades, and florid Gothic trimmings, the Capilla de Condestable's tower is still almost subdued in comparison to Vallejo's wedding-cake style, which must have given the Churrigueras plenty of inspiration.

Down a flight of steps is the **Puerta de la Pellejería**, so named because it led to the old tanners' district once located here. This richly decorated 16th-century Plateresque doorway by Francisco de Colonia (grandson of Juan de Colonia) is also suffering from decay. The figure of Saint John in a cauldron of boiling oil, underneath which a kneeling figure fans the flames with a bellows, seems almost comical now.

Calle Diego Porcelos leads past the cloister on the east side of the church to Calle de la Paloma, and the **Puerta del Sarmental**, considered the most exceptional of the great church's doorways. The Sarmental façade has the monumental doorway with a frieze of the 12 Apostles, a multitude of carved figures decorating the archivolts, and a tympanum featuring Christ presiding over the four evangelists, each seated at a desk taking down the word of the Lord. Above this is a huge rose window, then another florid Gothic screen guarded by 13 stone angels, topped with a balustrade and flanked by crocketed spires similar to those on the western face.

THE INTERIOR

The Sarmental door is at the center of the cathedral, so we recommend that you return to the western façade and start your tour of the interior there, at the main door, the Puerta de Santa María. As you enter this door, look high up to your left for the cathedral's amusing version of a cuckoo clock— the 16th-century mechanical figure, thought to be German, of Papamoscas (the flycatcher), whose mouth pops open to mark the hours. In the first chapel on the right is the famous *Cristo de Burgos,* a terrifyingly graphic depiction of Christ on the Cross. Curiously, the statue is dressed in a skirt and its feet rest on a pile of ostrich eggs. It is claimed that the statue was the work of Nicodemus; reports of pilgrims date it to at least the 15th century.

The choir, as in many Spanish churches, does break up the sweep of the nave, but it is a fine example consisting of 103 walnut stalls beautifully carved by Felipe de Vigarni in the early 16th century. Enclosed by a huge early-17th-century *reja* (wrought-iron grille), the choir contains the tomb of the cathedral's founder, Bishop Mauricio. In the center of the transept, beneath the lantern, is the plain stone that covers the remains of El Cid and Jimena. Four huge, richly decorated columns support the lantern and its splendid dome, whose eight-pointed star superimposed on another eight-pointed star is thought to have been inspired by the beautiful, intricate Mudejar ceilings seen in many parts of Spain. North of El Cid's tomb is the magnificent, gilded wrought-iron double staircase, the **Escalera Dorada** (Golden Staircase), designed by Diego de Siloé in 1519. It leads to the Puerta de la Coronería, now covered by tapestries.

The *capilla mayor* (main chapel) has a massive, multiniched 16th-century altar by Rodrigo de la Haya and his brother Martín. But here it is the *trasaltar*, the back wall in the ambulatory behind the main altar, that is worth your attention. In the early 16th century Felipe de Vigarni carved three of the panels in stone, including his famous *Calvary*.

Capilla de Condestable

The jewel of the cathedral's interior is the octagonal Capilla del Condestable, located behind the main altar. This exceptional chapel is the combined work of great German, Flemish, and Burgundian artists, and their sons, of the late 15th and early 16th centuries. It was begun in 1482 in florid Gothic style to house the tombs of Pedro Hernández de Velasco, the constable of Castile, and his wife (the owners of the Casa del Cordón), and it was variously worked on by several consummate artists until well into the 16th century. The architect was Simón de Colonia, son of the cathedral's master builder. Gil de Siloé, whom Alastair Boyd calls "the last great Gothic carver," did the stone carving in the balustraded Gothic archways above and alongside the altar, and probably the two huge *escudos* (coats of arms) on either side of the main altar. Felipe de Vigarni and Diego de Siloé collaborated on the superb main altarpiece and a Plateresque side altar, and Vigarni carved the splendid tombs of the constable and his wife in Atapuerca marble. Cristobal Andino forged the superb grille guarding the entrance to the chapel in 1523.

There is much more to see in the cathedral: the 13th-century **cloisters** of the original church; El Cofre del Cid, the coffer that El Cid gave to the moneylenders, in the Corpus Christi chapel; another fine retable by Gil de Siloé in the Capilla de la Concepción, which was built by Simón de Colonia; and the overblown chapel of Santa Tecla by Alberto de Churriguera, who must have seen Juan de Vallejo's fine lantern, decided to outdo Vallejo, and fell into a morass of vulgar excess instead.

The Plaza Mayor and the Espolón

East of the cathedral is the Plaza Mayor, a pear-shaped area surrounded by an arcade surmounted by three- and four-story buildings with interesting, often beautiful façades. These buildings house cafés and pastry shops as well as all sorts of stores. Around the Plaza Mayor is a network of lively, narrow shopping streets, such as **Calle San Lorenzo**, on the north side of the plaza. Colorful San Lorenzo is filled with specialty food shops offering a variety of regional foodstuffs. Fishmongers, butchers, greengrocers, bakeries, *tapas* bars, street vendors, and street musicians vie for your attention, and if all this becomes a bit too much, you can step into the fine Baroque church of San Lorenzo for a respite.

On the south side of the plaza is the 18th-century *ayuntamiento* (city hall) by Ventura Rodríguez, the architect who built the façade of Pamplona's cathedral. Beneath the *ayuntamiento* are some archways leading to the Espolón. On the columns, note the high-water marks from floods of the normally tame Arlanzón.

The **Paseo del Espolón** is the great pedestrian artery of Burgos, the communal living room of the city at leisure and one of the greatest streets of Spain. Along the northeastern side of this white stone-paved concourse, sidewalk cafés are arrayed beneath a canopy of trees that run in multiple rows the length of the Espolón and provide shade for the entire walkway. During siesta and in the early evening the cafés are filled with Burgaleses catching up on the latest gossip and observing the peregrinations of their fellow citizens. Children play in the garden that occupies the southern portion of the Espolón, frolicking around the topiary, statues, fountains, and fine wrought-iron bandstand, while lovers stroll along the balcony overlooking the Arlanzón. The Espolón is not just Spain, but Europe, at its best and most civilized.

At the western end of the Espolón is a multiturreted, fairy-tale archway, the **Arco de Santa María**, one of the most wonderful public monuments in Spain; it's even more wonderful when seen from the south bank of the Arlanzón at night, when the archway and the spires of the cathedral rising dramatically behind it are lighted. Originally a gate in the 11th-century town walls—parts of which are still visible inside the current gate and were once covered with intricately carved Moorish inscriptions—the current façade dates to the 1530s, when it was constructed by the people of Burgos to appease Charles V for their part in the *comuneros* revolt. The six main figures on the façade just above the archway are Charles V and the great heroes of Castile: El Cid, Count Fernán González, the early Castilian magistrates Laín Calvo and Nuño Rasura, and Diego Porcelos, the man credited with founding Burgos. Porcelos, legend has it, got his name because he was born one of septuplets, just like *porcillos* (piglets) are.

Walking along the esplanade on the south bank of the

Arlanzón, you get fine views of the houses facing the Espolón, the Arco de Santa María, and the spires of the cathedral. The Hotel Fernán González is nearby—just south across the avenue at the head of Calle Calera. South of the Fernán González, just around the corner on Calle Miranda, is the 16th-century **Casa de Miranda**, which now houses a small museum of archaeology. Besides the interesting two-story Renaissance patio of the mansion, items of interest in the museum include Roman sculpture and mosaics taken from the archaeological site at nearby Clunia, Visigothic sarcophagi, examples of Moorish and Mudejar art, and one of Gil de Siloé's finest pieces, the late-15th-century tomb of Juan de Padilla, one of Queen Isabella's favorite squires, who was killed during the siege of Granada (not the Juan de Padilla who led the *comuneros* revolt).

Dining in Burgos

Burgos has a wide range of restaurants, few of which are exceptional, but most of which offer good typical Castilian dishes such as *alubias con chorizo y morcilla* (white beans with *chorizo* and blood sausage), *cordero asado, chuletillas de cordero* (baby lamb chops), *menestra,* and grilled fish.

Burgos's most highly rated restaurant is the **Hostal Landa**, the very expensive, colorful, and elegant dining room of the Hotel Landa Palace, where you can eat first-rate versions of Castilian classics as well as such dishes as asparagus in puff pastry, smoked salmon, warm salad of duck livers, veal with foie gras, and *rodaballo en papillote* (turbot cooked in parchment). Tel: (9-47) 20-63-43.

The **Fernán González**, a sophisticated, elegant restaurant built by the owners of the Hotel Fernán González in a lovely adjoining house, is a relative newcomer and a welcome addition to the Burgos culinary scene. White vaulted ceilings arch gracefully over the second-floor dining rooms and a ground-floor sitting room/foyer, decorated with antiques, where guests can sip an aperitif before dinner and listen to a pianist playing classical pieces and popular tunes on a grand piano in the center of the room. To whet your appetite you can peruse a beautiful table display of regional produce— thyme, asparagus, pears in red wine, bottled chestnuts, jars of young green garlic shoots, pots of *chorizo* preserved in olive oil, and wines from the proprietors' own wineries in the Ribera del Duero and La Rioja. In the beautiful dining room overlooking the foyer, elegantly presented classic dishes such as *alubias de Ibeas* (black beans), *arroz con conejo y caracoles* (rice with rabbit and snails), *lubina a la sal* (sea bass baked in rock salt), and lamb roasted in a wood-burning oven, alternate with such creative offerings as ragout of artichokes and *cigalas,* shellfish lasagna, venison in Valduero wine sauce, squab in Armagnac, and figs in puff pastry. Try Rincón de las Navas Rioja or Valduero *rosado* or *tinto* from the García family's bodegas in Ribera del Duero. Tel: (9-47) 20-94-41.

Mesón del Cid, Plaza de Santa María 8, is located just west of the cathedral in a restored 15th-century house that was once the shop of one of Spain's earliest printers, Maestro Fadrique Alemán de Basilea, a disciple of Johann Gutenberg. The first edition of Fernando de Rojas's picaresque novel *La Celestina,* said to be the first European novel, was printed here in 1499. This colorful restaurant is decorated like an old Castilian tavern, and the waitresses wear traditional regional costumes. The upstairs dining room has a superb view of the western face of the cathedral. María Luisa de Alzaga, one of the owners, supervises the dining room with a keen eye and takes your order personally. Often derived from old Castilian family recipes, specialties here include *setas a la plancha con ajo* (grilled, garlicky mushrooms), *sopa de Doña Jimena* (a type of *sopa castellana*), *morcilla con arroz, alubias de Ibeas, berenjenas* (eggplant stuffed with *bacalao*), and baby lamb stewed with mushrooms. With this very hearty, delicious food, ask for the bright, fruity *vino joven* from Viña Pedrosa to be served *fresco* (cool). Tel: (9-47) 20-87-15.

Casa Ojeda, Calle de Vitoria 5, just one block east of El Cid's statue, has been a Burgos institution for three-quarters of a century, and has recently undergone its own renaissance, upgrading both the quality and the range of its food—and ratcheting up the prices as well. A wood-fueled brick oven turns out classic *cordero asado* along with such dishes as *alubias con chorizos y morcilla, merluza en salsa verde con kokotxas* (hake and and the supernal hake "cheeks" in a garlic and parsley sauce), and quail in Armagnac sauce. Casa Ojeda also has a popular bar that seems to be frequented by most of the well-heeled of Burgos, a gourmet shop with an excellent selection of Spanish delicacies—both fresh and in cans and jars for taking home—and a pleasant sidewalk café at the rear entrance facing the Casa del Cordón and the Plaza de Calvo Sotelo; Tel: (9-47) 20-90-52.

Also on the Plaza de Calvo Sotelo (at number 2) is the good, inexpensive restaurant **Polvorilla,** a Burgos favorite, especially popular with the bullfight crowd, who flock here during the Fiesta de San Pablo y San Pedro in late June. You can have a glass of good, cold Sköl dark beer on tap or one of the half-dozen regional wines offered by the glass to accompany a plate of delicious boiled shrimp at the downstairs bar, where Juanjo Santillana, one of the owners, holds court. Upstairs, where the dining room looks out on the

Plaza del Cordón, Juanjo's 83-year-old mother-in-law, Irene del Pozo, turns out delicious typical meals of *ensalada mixta, alubias con chorizo y morcilla, almejás a la marinera, chuletillas de cordero, cuajada* for dessert, and good *vino*. Closed for three weeks in both April and September; Tel: (9-47) 20-39-83.

La Posada, Plaza de Santo Domingo de Guzmán 18, just west of the Plaza de Calvo Sotelo and just north of the Espolón, has replaced the Asador Ribera del Duero. Decorated in an attractive taurine motif, La Posada is a colorful place to stop for a beer or a Rioja *rosado* from Sonsierra and *tapas* of olives with anchovies or roasted red peppers in olive oil. In the upstairs dining room La Posada features inexpensive daily luncheon specials such as *cocido madrileño* on Tuesdays, *rabo con patatas* (oxtail with potatoes) on Wednesdays, and *alubias blancas con almejas* (white beans with clams) on Sundays. The rest of the menu is a limited, pricier *asador* menu of grilled fish, steaks, and lamb. Tel: (9-47) 20-45-78.

Another popular place, just south of the Puente de San Pablo, at San Pablo 3, is **Don Jamón**, which is packed every evening with Burgaleses sampling such exceptional *embutidos* as *chorizo, morcilla, jamón* (ham), and *lomo* (pork loin); and the *queso de Burgos* made by Ambrosio Molinos called Páramo de Guzmán (see the Ribera de Burgos Wine Country section, above). At first glance Don Jamón seems an upscale tavern with the ubiquitous *jamones serranos* hanging from the ceiling and autographed photographs of matadors, but look closer and you will see jars of foie gras with truffles from France, framed wine labels, a humidor filled with fine Cuban cigars, and beautiful Villeroy & Boch coffee cups. In the back room is an upscale dining room where each table is set with different fine china. You can dine on such typical dishes as *cogollitos de Tudela con bonito y anchoas* (tender Tudela lettuce hearts with tuna and anchovies) and a whole *rodaballo* grilled and dressed with oil, garlic, and vinegar, or such sophisticated fare as salmon and avocado salad, free-range chicken, and sweetbreads. The owner has thousands of dollars worth of expensive old wines behind glass in the bar, but the cases are not temperature controlled, so it is best to stick with younger local Ribera del Duero wines here, rather than splurging on an expensive old Rioja *reserva*. Closed in August; Tel: (9-47) 26-00-36.

Outside the Center of Burgos

Three other religious monuments of extraordinary historical and artistic significance, and one of great interest to students of the Camino de Santiago, are located within a few miles of the center of Burgos: the Cistercian convent of Las Huelgas Reales; the Carthusian monastery called La Cartuja de Miraflores; the monastery of San Pedro de Cardeña; and the Hospital del Rey, a pilgrims' hospice on the Camino de Santiago.

HOSPITAL DEL REY
The Hospital del Rey, 3 km (2 miles) west of the old quarter, just south of N 620 at the end of El Parral park, was founded in the 12th century by Alfonso VIII as a pilgrims' hospice, and was under the auspices of the powerful convent of Las Huelgas (see below). The nuns' largesse gave the hospice an exalted reputation among the tired, thirsty, and hungry pilgrims walking the Camino de Santiago. All pilgrims who could show some proof of their status were allowed to remain at the hospice for two days and were given an ample ration of bread, meat, chickpeas, and wine (half a liter) each day. The main entrance to the hospice is the 16th-century Plateresque Puerta de los Romeros (Pilgrims' Gate), decorated with scallop shells, coats of arms, and a seated *Virgin with Child*. The 16th-century Plateresque façade of the hospital shows another version of Santiago Matamoros wielding a sword, while his horse tramples the infidel underfoot. There is also a magnificent door with exceptional woodcarvings depicting Santiago with a pilgrim praying to him, the angel of the Lord tearing through evil demons, and a wonderful grouping of pilgrims: one, barefoot and in rags, is obviously sick (and probably a robbery victim), carries a water gourd, and leans heavily on a staff that is nothing more than a tree limb; a small boy seeks aid from his father; and a woman nurses her baby. The Burgos campus of the University of Valladolid law school now occupies part of what once was the hospital.

Just to the right of the façade of Hospital del Rey is the tile-decorated **Asador La Gloria**, Puerta de los Romeros 1, where you can stop for a snack of grilled *chorizo* and beer or a lunch of salad and lamb roasted in the brick oven at the entrance. Tel: (9-47) 20-59-50.

LAS HUELGAS REALES
Las Huelgas Reales (literally, "royal leisure time," from its origins as a royal retreat), located only a mile southwest of the center of Burgos (go west on N 620 and watch for signs to the left after the Puente de Castella), is another of Castile's great medieval treasures. Las Huelgas was founded in 1187 by Alfonso VIII and his wife, Eleanor of Aquitaine, daughter of England's King Henry II and sister of Richard the Lion-Hearted. It became a Cistercian abbey and a pantheon for Alfonso and Eleanor and more than 50 members of the royal families of Castile. The fine 13th-century wooden statue of

Santiago in the Mudejar chapel here has an articulated right arm that holds a sword. Manipulated from below a platform, the arm of Santiago moved to bestow knighthood on several kings of Castile, including Ferdinand III, who legend says had the statue made so that he would not have to be knighted by someone of lower station.

Under the protection of the royal families of Castile, Las Huelgas became one of the most powerful religious institutions in Spain. The predominant architectural style of the convent is the austere transitional Gothic of the 12th- and 13th-century Cistercians, which can be seen in other churches along the Camino de Santiago, with plenty of Romanesque touches as well. Among the attractions here are the 13th-century tower in which Peter the Cruel is thought to have been born, the 12th-century Romanesque *claustrillos* (small cloisters), and a 13th- to 15th-century Gothic cloister with Mudejar vaulting. The convent is rich in tapestries, wood-carvings, and royal tombs. What is claimed to be a Moorish standard captured at the battle of Las Navas de Tolosa in 1212, but in reality is probably one of the flaps of the caliph's tent—the tent itself was sent to Pope Innocent III in Rome—is also displayed here. Of particular interest at Las Huelgas is the **Museo de Telas**, with its collection of clothing worn during the 13th century, especially the cap, tunic, and belt found in the tomb of the infante Don Fernando de la Cerda.

LA CARTUJA DE MIRAFLORES

The 15th-century monastery La Cartuja de Miraflores, 3 km (2 miles) east of Burgos on the road running along the south bank of the Arlanzón, was built by King Juan II of Castile, father of Queen Isabella, on the site of the former hunting lodge and palace of his father, Enrique III. This rather severe building, decorated only by some 16th-century Plateresque trim along the roofline and a florid Gothic doorway, was begun in 1454 by Juan de Colonia, architect of the Burgos cathedral, and completed by his son Simón in 1488 under the direction of Isabella, for the purpose of housing the tombs of her father, mother, and brother.

These tombs and the superb retable of the main altar are masterworks of the great Flemish sculptor and woodcarver Gil de Siloé. Many experts consider his funeral monument of King Juan II and his wife, Isabella of Portugal, intricately and elaborately carved in exquisite detail, to be one of the finest tombs in existence, and that of their son, Prince Alfonso, not far behind. The former is of white marble, probably taken from the Atapuerca quarries located near Santovenia, east of Burgos. It is laid out in the pattern of an eight-pointed star thought to have been inspired by the wooden Mudejar doors at Las Huelgas, but the pattern is common in this area. (It can be seen in the great dome of the Burgos cathedral, surrounding the *escudo* of Castile and León on the tomb of Princess Blanca of Portugal at Las Huelgas, and in many other places.) The superb reclining statues of Juan and Isabella are surrounded by exceptional carved biblical figures, some of which have had their heads lopped off by vandals.

The alabaster funeral monument to a kneeling young Alfonso is elaborately and intricately tooled. Alastair Boyd wrote of it: "Gothic carving has reached its highest pitch of ripeness and, dabbling with the revival of pagan themes, trembles on the brink of decadence—from which it is just restrained in this case by the precision of the master." The master, Siloé, has placed his own image in the lower left-hand portion of this tableau; he's the one wearing pince-nez glasses.

The altarpiece of polychrome wood, made from 1496 to 1499 by Siloé and Diego de la Cruz, departs from the traditional compartmentalized pattern for retables that dominates most altarpiece designs in Spain. Siloé used a series of round medallion shapes to set his scenes apart, including the great centerpiece featuring the Crucifixion. The artists' renditions of the Last Supper and of Santiago dressed as a pilgrim are particularly appealing, but most of the scenes in this magnificent work are worth studying. The gilt on the altar was supposedly crafted by Diego de la Cruz with the first gold brought by Columbus from the New World.

After the three stupendous Gil de Siloé monuments, the rest of the church is an anticlimax, but there are also a good 17th-century statue of San Bruno by the Portuguese artist Manuel Perreira, fine late Gothic choir stalls carved around 1489 by Martín Sanchez, some Plateresque choir stalls by Simón de Bueras, an Annunciation by Pedro Berruguete, and a triptych attributed to Juan de Flandes. For an unusual souvenir, buy a rosary, redolent of the super-pressed roses the monks use to make the beads.

MONASTERIO DE SAN PEDRO DE CARDEÑA

Except for patches of yellow broom, the last few miles to the monastery of San Pedro de Cardeña, located 7 km (4 miles) southeast of La Cartuja de Miraflores, are barren. There are no buildings or other obvious signs of modern life within a two-mile radius of the monastery, and even though the 11th-century Romanesque tower and part of the cloister of the martyrs are all that remain from the time of El Cid (most of the monastery is of the 15th century), the natural setting—a little oak- and ilex-covered valley—is just as El Cid saw it. To those steeped in the history of El Cid, there is a pervasive and powerful sense of his presence; he crossed this same ground to say goodbye to Jimena and his children, who were staying at San Pedro; then, as the bells tolled from the fine Romanesque tower, he rode off with heavy heart from his family and his beloved Castile into exile. Years later, after he had conquered Valencia, Jimena brought El Cid's body back on his horse, Babieca, for interment here.

For centuries San Pedro de Cardeña was the resting place of El Cid and Jimena, and it still is the resting place of Babieca, who is even honored with a stone monolith. After Bonaparte's troops profaned the tomb of El Cid and Jimena, which is still on display in a chapel here, and destroyed, defaced, or carried off many objects connected with El Cid, the bones of the couple were transported to Burgos by the French in 1808 and kept on the Espolón. In 1921, with the king of Spain as witness, the remains were moved to the Burgos cathedral. The walls of the monastery chapel where El Cid once lay are decorated with the coats of arms of 26 personages of El Cid's retinue.

The origins of San Pedro de Cardeña are believed to be Visigothic, but nothing of that epoch remains. Some 200 monks were said to have been massacred here by the Moors in 834, and it is to the memory of this event that the fine 11th-century cloister is dedicated. Ironically, the archways of this cloister are painted with alternating bands of red and white, calling to mind the striped archways of the Mezquita in Córdoba.

From juice purchased in La Rioja, the Cistercian monks at San Pedro make a white, a rosé, and a very good red wine, called Valdevegon, in a rustic old bodega on the premises, and they also make a chartreuse-like liqueur called La Tizona, named after El Cid's famous sword. These can be purchased in the monastery's gift shop.

The Camino de Santiago around Burgos

Burgos, León, and, of course, Santiago are considered the greatest pilgrimage cities on the Camino de Santiago. In Burgos province there are two major shrines.

IGLESIA DE SAN JUAN DE ORTEGA

The church of San Juan de Ortega is located 21 km (13 miles) east of Burgos on N 120, just off the Logroño–Burgos road and through the village of Santovenia. San Juan de Ortega, who lived from 1080 to 1163, was a disciple of Santo Domingo de la Calzada. San Juan built a Romanesque church dedicated to San Nicolás de Bari to serve pilgrims travelling through this desolate, bandit-infested stretch of the Camino de Santiago, thus providing a much-needed safe haven, the last stop before Burgos. San Juan's tomb is a superb Romanesque sarcophagus, and there are several fine Romanesque capitals here.

WEST TO OLMILLOS

The other shrine is Castrojeriz, about 45 km (28 miles) west of Burgos. To get there take N 120 about 20 km (12 miles) west to the Sasamón/Olmillos de Sasamón crossroads. It is well worth your time to detour a mile or so north to see the 13th-century **Iglesia de Sasamón**, another pilgrims' church with a fine door and an exceptional doorway that resembles the Puerta del Sarmental of the Burgos cathedral. Returning south to N 120 you will see Olmillos and its ruined, photogenic 15th-century castle. Follow N 120 west for 5 km (3 miles), turn south at Villasandino, and take the Palencia road about 15 km (9 miles) to Castrojeriz, which Michener imagined as being in medieval times "a magnificent settlement rising in the sky."

CASTROJERIZ

Castrojeriz is a decrepit, but still very interesting, old town now, with a ruined castle on a hill above town, the ruins of the 14th-century monastery of San Antón, the 13th-century Romanesque-Gothic collegiate church of Santa María del Manzano, the church of Santo Domingo, which has some fine 16th-century tapestries, and the church of San Juan, a 15th- to 16th-century church that has a 13th-century tower. Castrojeriz needs a face-lift, but its old buildings emit a sense of the past that lingers long after the images of many restored towns of tourist-poster quality have faded.

Ensconced in a renovated mill in Castrojeriz, **El Mesón**, Cordón 1, is a very reasonably priced country restaurant run by friendly and accommodating people. The bar area still preserves the old stone walls of the original mill and the bright, airy dining room is a warm, convivial place decorated with Castilian furniture and with a big fireplace at one end. These are pleasant surroundings in which to while away the afternoon over a lunch of such Spanish dishes as an excellent salad of good lettuce, ripe tomatoes, onion, and anchovy-cured olives; a fresh local trout cooked with a piece of *jamón serrano;* baby lamb chops served with pimientos; a dessert of ice cream served in a hollowed-out lemon; and either the house's homemade (slightly sweet) *rosado* or a bottle of Viña Pedrosa's *vino joven.* Tel: (9-47) 37-74-00.

Some 30 km (18 miles) west of Castrojeriz is Frómista (see the Palencia section, above), the next major stop on the Camino de Santiago.

GETTING AROUND

Salamanca–Zamora–León

To take in the countryside and the cities in this region travellers are well advised to rent a car. If you are travelling from Madrid, take N VI/A 6 northwest to Villacastín, then take N 501 west through Avila to Salamanca. The 200-km (125-mile) trip takes about two hours. From Salamanca N 630 leads to Zamora, about 60 km (36 miles) north, and León, about 200 km (125 miles) farther along. Salamanca, Valladolid, and Burgos are linked by a major highway, the N 620/E 3. There is frequent bus service along these major highways, too, especially to Madrid, two and a half to three hours from Salamanca.

The closest airport to these cities is in Valladolid. Rail service is spotty in the region, but there are nine trains a day between Salamanca and Valladolid, with connections to Burgos. From León there are trains to Burgos, Barcelona, Madrid (one Talgo express daily that takes about four hours), and Oviedo, to the north.

Valladolid–Palencia–Burgos

Burgos and Valladolid are fairly well served by trains and buses to and from each other and Madrid, Salamanca, León, Palencia, and other cities. Valladolid has a small airport, with daily service to and from Madrid. Most major car-rental companies have offices in Vallodolid. Unless you enjoy travelling in the provinces by buses that often run just once a day in each direction, the only practical way to explore this area is by car. Both Valladolid and Burgos have good city-bus service and a reliable fleet of taxis.

An excellent approach to this region is to head northwest from Madrid on N VI/A 6 to Valladolid province, and stay in either Valladolid or Tordesillas, from which you can explore the recommended sights of the Duero river valley, then perhaps visit Palencia, Frómista, and Carrión de los Condes. This area can also be seen using Burgos as a base. The eastern Duero valley, Peñaranda, Santo Domingo de Silos, and the rest of southern Burgos province are most convenient from Aranda de Duero, but many people will prefer the more cosmopolitan attractions of Burgos as a base. For those with little time, this trip can be done in a few days, but this region's attractions really call for a week or more.

ACCOMMODATIONS REFERENCE

The hotel rates listed below are projected rates for 1994, for double room, double occupancy, in pesetas. We strongly recommend that you confirm the price when making reservations.

When dialing telephone numbers in Spain from outside the country, drop the 9 in the area code.

Old Castile West

▶ **Camping Al-bereka.** 37624 **La Alberca.** Tel: (9-23) 41-51-95.

▶ **Gran Hotel.** Plaza del Poeta Iglesias 5, 37001 **Salamanca.** Tel: (9-23) 21-35-00; Fax: 21-35-01. 17,600 pts.

▶ **Hostal Inés.** Avenida de la Constitución 64, 24850 **Boñar.** Tel: (9-87) 73-50-86. 2,500 pts.

▶ **Hotel Las Batuecas.** Carretera de Las Batuecas, 37624 **La Alberca.** Tel: (9-23) 41-51-88 or 41-51-94; Fax: 41-50-55. 6,500 pts.

▶ **Hotel Gaudí.** Plaza Ingeniero Eduardo de Castro 6, 24700 **Astorga.** Tel: (9-87) 61-56-54; Fax: 61-50-40. 10,000 pts.

▶ **Hotel Monterrey.** Calle del Azafranal 21, 37001 **Salamanca.** Tel. and Fax: (9-23) 21-44-00. 16,500 pts.

▶ **Hotel Presa.** Avenida de Valcayo, 24900 **Riaño.** Tel: (9-87) 74-06-37. 7,000 pts.

▶ **Hotel Riosol.** Avenida de Palencia 3, 24001 **León.** Tel: (9-87) 21-66-50; Fax: 21-69-97. 9,500 pts.

▶ **Parador Enrique II.** Plaza del Castillo 1, 37500 **Ciudad Rodrigo.** Tel: (9-23) 46-01-50; Fax: 46-04-04. 12,500 pts.

▶ **Parador Hostal de San Marcos.** Plaza de San Marcos 7, 24001 **León.** Tel: (9-87) 23-73-00; Fax: 23-34-58. 16,000 pts.

▶ **Parador de Salamanca.** Teso de la Feria 2, 37008 **Salamanca.** Tel: (9-23) 26-87-00; Fax: 21-54-38. 13,000 pts.

▶ **Parador de Turismo Condes de Alba y Aliste.** Plaza de Viriato 5, 49001 **Zamora.** Tel: (9-80) 51-44-97; Fax: 53-00-63. 12,000 pts.

Old Castile East

▶ **Castillo de Monzón.** Carretera de Santander, km 11, 34410 **Monzón de Campos.** Tel: (9-88) 80-80-75. 9,000 pts.

▶ **Hotel Los Bronces.** Carretera de Madrid–Irún km 160, 09400 **Aranda de Duero.** Tel: (9-47) 50-08-50; Fax: 50-24-04. 6,950 pts.

▶ **Hotel del Cid.** Plaza Santa María 8, 09003 **Burgos.** Tel: (9-47) 20-87-15; Fax: 26-94-60. 13,000 pts.

▶ **Hotel Felipe IV.** Calle Gamazo 16, 47004 **Valladolid.** Tel: (9-83) 30-70-00; Fax: 30-86-87. 10,825–12,975 pts.

▶ **Hotel Fernán González.** Calle Calera 17, 09002 **Burgos.** Tel: (9-47) 20-94-41; Fax: 27-21-41. 9,775 pts.

▶ **Hotel Landa Palace.** Carretera de Madrid–Irún 235, 09000 **Burgos.** Tel: (9-47) 20-63-43; Fax: 26-46-76. 28,000 pts.

▶ **Hotel Lasa.** Acera de Recoletos 21, 47004 **Valladolid.** Tel: (9-83) 39-02-55; Fax: 30-25-61. 12,000 pts.

▶ **Hotel Meliá Parque.** Calle Joaquín García Morato 17,

47007 **Valladolid**. Tel: (9-83) 47-01-00; Fax: 47-50-29. 11,000 pts.

▶ **Hotel Mozart**. Menéndez Pelayo 7, 47001 **Valladolid**. Tel: (9-83) 29-77-77; Fax: 29-21-90. 11,600 pts.

▶ **Hotel Olid Meliá**. Plaza San Miguel 10, 47003 **Valladolid**. Tel: (9-83) 35-72-00; Fax: 33-68-28. 12,750 pts.

▶ **Hotel Residencia Cordón**. Calle La Puebla 6, 09004 **Burgos**. Tel: (9-47) 26-50-00; Fax: 20-02-69. 9,500 pts.

▶ **Hotel Tres Coronas de Silos**. Plaza Mayor 6, 09610 **Santo Domingo de Silos**. Tel: (9-47) 38-07-27. 7,900 pts.

▶ **NH Condestable**. Calle de Vitoria 8, 09004 **Burgos**. Tel: (9-47) 26-71-25; Fax: 20-46-45. 14,500 pts.

▶ **Parador Colaborador Arlanza**. Plaza Mayor 11, 09346 **Covarrubias**. Tel: (9-47) 40-30-25; Fax: 40-63-59. 8,200 pts.

▶ **Parador de Tordesillas**. Carretera de Salamanca (N 620), km 153, 47100 **Tordesillas**. Tel: (9-83) 77-00-51; Fax: 77-10-13. 10,000 pts.

ASTURIAS AND GALICIA

By Mike Jackson
with Robert Levine

Mike Jackson, based in New York, is a writer-producer of television documentaries who has travelled much of the world, from South America to Africa to Europe, Eastern Europe, the Pacific, and the Far East, but Spain, especially northern Spain, is where he returns every chance he gets. Robert Levine is a New York–based music and travel writer.

Think green. When you think Spain, you usually think white: white buildings, white heat—even the famous Spanish light. That's southern Spain, the land that seemed like an extension of North Africa to the Moors. This is northwestern Spain, the Spain of Asturias and Galicia, the region that attracted Celts more than two thousand years ago because it felt so much like home. Here is mile after mile after mile of lush verdancy that soothes the eye and refreshes the spirit. (The green comes, like everything else, with a price. Galicians claim that rain-free days are limited to 30 per year in their region, but then Galicia is just about the only region in Spain that does not suffer summer browning.)

The surprises Asturias and Galicia hold for the traveller are numerous: magnificent wilderness; some of the most beautiful—and least crowded—beaches in Europe; one of Christendom's three most devout pilgrimages, culminating at one of the great cathedrals of the world; small cities with charming old quarters and collections of antiquity; mighty rivers; and mountain vistas that seem the stuff of Valkyrian

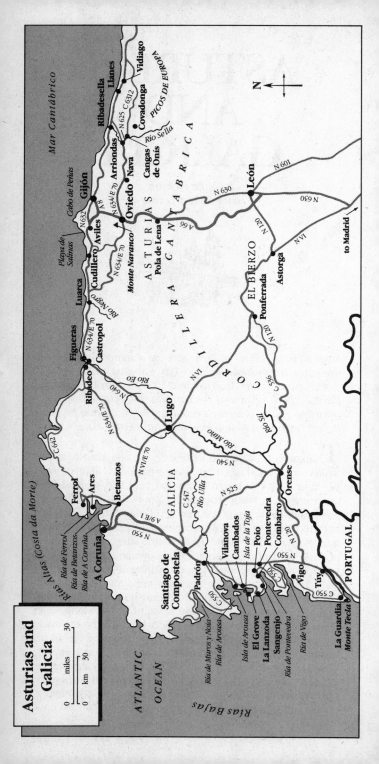

legend. Not the least of the attractions is how little these regions have been touched by mass tourism.

Asturias covers the northern coast of Spain just above León, stretching west from Cantabria to the Río Eo. West of Asturias, across the Eo, is Galicia, with the Atlantic Ocean on its western shore and Portugal to the south. Galicia's economy is centered on small-scale agriculture, Asturias's on minerals. Both regions have long coastlines with commensurate fishing industries.

The people here have a tradition of fierce independence from would-be invaders. This spirit receives no little support from the terrain, as the Moors learned in the eighth century when they failed to defeat the legendary Asturian hero Pelayo (see Covadonga, below) ten years after their successful conquest of Spain below the Cordillera Cantábrica, the huge mountain range that arcs through northern Spain. A land cut by savagely deep ravines and dominated by towering peaks lends much advantage to the defender. Beginning with the reign of Pelayo's son-in-law and successor, Alfonso I, Asturians, led by one Alfonso after another, were in the forefront of the most fervently desired of Spanish missions, the Reconquest. Early in the tenth century, Alfonso III retook neighboring León to the south; 200 years later, Alfonso VIII, called Alfonso the Noble, won a decisive victory against Islam, in 1212, at Las Navas de Tolosa in Andalusia. The Moors hung on in Granada until the very year Columbus sailed off in search of his fortune.

The regional culture, particularly in Galicia, smacks less of flamenco, bullfighting, and castanets than of the spirit of the Celtic lands these northern reaches physically resemble. At festivals dancers perform jigs to the highland wail of bagpipes. The food and drink of these regions also have the flavors of the north. Asturias makes excellent use of its extensive apple orchards with *sidra,* a tart, heady, and popular cider sometimes poured from a bottle slung over the waiter's shoulder. Galicia's hearty seafood dishes are found on the menus of exclusive Madrid restaurants, and both regions produce large quantities of cheese.

The jewel in Galicia's crown, one of the reasons this part of Spain—indeed, of the world—cannot be missed, is Santiago de Compostela. A town, a Christian mecca, a museum, and a place for great seafood and wine as well, this endpoint of pilgrims' journeys along the Camino de Santiago during the Middle Ages is a most memorable place, one that you surely should experience. North and west of Santiago, Galicia's Atlantic coastline is sliced by *rías*—fjordlike inlets on the Atlantic believed to have been formed when whole valleys caved in and were buried by the sea thousands of years ago.

The Asturias and Galicia area is wild, rugged Spain, a place with a cornerstone of Western civilization at its heart.

MAJOR INTEREST

Asturias
Los Picos de Europa
Hiking, camping, fishing along the upper Río Cares
Prehistoric cave paintings at Tito Bustillo
Oviedo's cathedral and old town
Hill and coastal towns and scenery
Picturesque fishing village of Luarca

Galicia
Food, wine, and festivals
Camino de Santiago
The Roman and Medieval city of Lugo

Santiago de Compostela
The cathedral of Santiago
Hostal de los Reyes Católicos
Shopping for jet jewelry
Dining on seafood

A Coruña's marina and old town
The *rías* (fjords) on the Atlantic coast
Pontevedra's charming old town
Islands of Arousa and La Toja

ASTURIAS

Set on Spain's northern coastline between the highlands of the Cordillera Cantábrica and the Mar Cantábrico, north of León, Asturias is a province whose geography fluctuates between highs and lows. High limestone cliffs swoop down to broad and densely populated beaches and secluded coves. Some coastal areas, such as Gijón, offer dramatic rock formations as well as sandy inlets. In rural areas farmers make their living in much the same way their ancestors did long ago. Much of the landscape is covered with apple orchards, cornfields (invariably providing fodder), and pig farms. Nothing could contrast much more to a pig farm than the cosmopolitan capital, Oviedo, whose cultural life is sophisticated and whose pace is decidedly 20th century.

Beneath the Asturian greenery lies the mineral wealth (coal, zinc, lead, manganese, iron) that accounts, directly and indirectly, for the employment of most Asturians. Coal, first exploited by the Romans in the second century B.C. and now contributing to the smog of Oviedo, is in great abundance and fuels a state-of-the-art heavy industry of steel mills and shipbuilding that in turn has attracted other large-scale manufacturing. Asturian *carbón,* particularly the hard, lustrous anthracite, is expensive to extract, and currently local miners are feeling competition from far-off Australia. But Asturian miners, like miners the world over, by the nature of their work must possess a stubborn courage just to survive, as they proved during the 1934 workers' revolt, when they took the city of Oviedo. Fighting lasted for ten days and many buildings in the city, including the university and cathedral, were severely damaged. (Two years later, many other fine structures in Oviedo were battered in the Spanish Civil War.) The tenacity exhibited by the miners is a quality that has long been associated with the Asturian character.

Asturias was the last territory of ancient Hispania to submit to Romanization, in 19 B.C. It was also the kingdom that fought most valiantly against Islam; it was populated in the eighth century by Visigoths who fled the Moors in Toledo and then began the 700-year struggle for reconquest. Remains of the ancient fortifications can still be seen.

Asturias has many examples of an unusual type of pre-Romanesque architecture called Ramiresque, after King Ramiro I (842–850). It is a style you might expect from a no-nonsense people: The buildings, made of limestone, are of small proportions with completely vaulted interiors. When they are decorated, it is with simple reliefs of human and animal figures. There are about 60 of these structures dispersed throughout the region (a few are discussed below).

Besides the contrasts in landscape and culture and the unusual architectural types, there are other Asturian pleasures to look for: the spectacular regional cheeses, such as *cabrales* (a ferocious blue cheese made from goat's milk) and *gamondedo* (a milder, soft blue cheese); the thirst-quenching *sidra;* and hearty regional cuisine, including such dishes as *fabada* (stewed beans), *pote asturiano* (beef-and-vegetable stew), *merluza a la sidra* (hake poached in cider), and *pulpo guisado* (stewed octopus)—all treats to be found nowhere else.

Asturias can be reached in leisurely fashion along the coast from San Vicente de la Barquera, to the east in Cantabria, on N 634/E 70, and then N 632 through Ribadesella to Gijón and Oviedo; or from León, to the south, on N 621 through the staggering Los Picos de Europa to the quiet retreat of the upper Río Cares. A quicker route goes due north of León on N 630, 115 km (71 miles), straight to the Asturian capital, Oviedo. Eastbound from Galicia the coast road, N 634/E 70, is the main route in the region, passing through Ribadeo, Luarca (when approached from the upper, local road Luarca looks like a scale-model fishing village), and Cudillero, to Avilés and Gijón, just northeast of Oviedo.

EASTERN ASTURIAS

The eastern end of Asturias, squeezed in between Los Picos de Europa and the Mar Cantábrico, is mountainous and secluded—and an easy drive from the coastal resort towns of both Asturias and Cantabria and not much more than two hours from Burgos in the south.

Our tour of eastern Asturias starts near the Cantabrian border, just a few kilometers inland, at Panes, 24 km (15 miles) southwest of Cantabria's San Vicente de la Barquera, by way of N 634/E 70 west and N 621 south. We cover much of the natural beauty and wonders of this mountainous, untrammeled area, with its trout streams, hiking trails, historical towns, and traces of prehistoric settlement, as we work our way westward to the capital city, Oviedo.

The Upper Río Cares

The **Río Cares** flows down from Los Picos de Europa, turning eastward from Las Arenas de Cabrales to Panes, in the very eastern tip of Asturias, near the Cantabrian border, where it meets the Río Deva. If you like the outdoors, fishing, hiking, backpacking—or perhaps just strolling along a riverbank enjoying the air and spectacular scenery—this could be the place for you.

The Río Cares, a beautiful, fast-running river, is a favorite of trout and salmon fishermen from far and wide. Río Cares salmon spend the first two years of their lives here gathering strength in order to head downriver into the Atlantic and on to deep water off Greenland. Five years later, they return from the ocean and swim upriver to the very spot where they were born to spawn and die. And fishermen return to the Cares every year, too, from March to the end of July, hoping to hook even a single salmon as it fights its way upstream. Local fishermen, who have all year long to study these waters, bait with *quisquilla,* a crayfish the size of a large grasshopper. A 13-pound salmon can be sliced into at least 40,000 pesetas worth of steaks on local restaurant tables, so fishing gets very earnest around here.

For those who don't fish, the Río Cares area has lots to offer as well. There are miles of paths along the riverbank and occasional footbridges spanning the river. Hiking trails delve deep into **Los Picos de Europa**, where there are refuge shelters and the occasional jeep track, but no roads and very few people. Experienced alpinists will find real challenge from the peaks (some capped with snow year-round) in this rough, wild mountain region—not very far from gentle green meadows where a child can safely chase butterflies. The river leaves the mountains south of the town of Las Arenas de Cabrales (which local folks usually abbreviate to "Arenas"). You can also drive into the peaks at Covadonga, an historic sanctuary in a beautiful wooded pocket under Los Picos west of the Río Cares.

NISERIAS

You can't find it on a map, which is one of the good things about Nisérias. About all there is here is an old mill that was converted into a hotel and restaurant, Casa Don Julián, in the early 1950s. Nisérias is about 18 km (12 miles) west of the village of Panes (which is on N 621). Go west on AS 114 (C 6312 on some maps) less than a mile beyond Trescares, which *is* on the map, although just barely. You'll see a sign for Nisérias, but it is the big letters of Casa Don Julián that stand out.

Casa Don Julián

The Río Cares runs by the front door of the ▶ **Casa Don Julián**, and some of the salmon makes its way to the *casa*'s tables, just one good reason to make this inexpensive hotel your headquarters for visits to some of the area's attractions. There is nothing fancy about Casa Don Julián, and once you've stayed and eaten here you'll hope, too, that it remains just as it is.

Casa Don Julián is three or four buildings across the road from each other. The rustic bar and taproom are on one side, and when you register for a room (small, monastic affairs, some with baths) you step up to the bar and sign in with bearded Ricardo Lopez Gonzalo, Don Julián's older son, or with the lovely Señora Gonzalo. (The management is now in the hands of the founder's grown children, but Don Julián leaves no doubt as to who is really in charge.) If it's early evening and fishing season there will be several people at the bar telling lies, except for the one whose 15-pound salmon is on a measuring board on a front table. Behind the bar about 20 different kinds of local cheese are on display, including *peñamellera, vidiago, cabrales, beyos,* and *cabra.* (Cheese around here is like maple syrup in Vermont—hard to avoid.) There's a stove at the end of the bar with Chinese checkers and a couple of game boards stacked ready for action. The bar is a great place to return to at the end of a day of hiking, fishing, or driving up and down the mountains.

Across the road is the *comedor* (dining room), in a bigger building with a view of a mill pond and the river, managed by Don Julián's younger son. It's a rather large restaurant, very popular with local Asturians and Cantabrians. In season, the menu includes *trucha* (trout) and *salmón,* grilled, very tasty, and certainly very fresh. Other recommended dishes are *patatas rellenas* (roast potatoes stuffed with ground pork and a piquant sauce) and the *menestra,* vegetable stew, which is actually vegetable stew with meat. The recorded music could use a little attention (it sounds as if Herb Alpert and his brass band are trapped in the Matamoros bus station). After dinner take your coffee at a table outside. Keep your toes out of the roadway. The air is filled with the sound of waters rushing somewhere, but you're allowed to sit and contemplate the starry night and not rush anywhere.

LAS ARENAS DE CABRALES

Las Arenas de Cabrales (*queso cabrales,* the region's strong blue goat's-milk cheese, is made here), about 12 km (7 miles) west of Nisérias on AS 114/C 6312, is a quiet village geared to serve the camper, hiker, fisherman, or relaxed traveller. The ► **Hotel Picos de Europa**, on the main street, is a small and well-run inn offering more of the traditional creature comforts than you'll get at Casa Don Julián, if not the setting; it has a swimming pool in addition to a bar and *comedor,* and even if you don't stay, it is a good place for lunch or dinner. Across the street is the **Alimentación Gonzalo Supermercado**, where you can stock up on provisions for a trek or a picnic. The four González women, ranging from 16 to 60, deal out with good cheer many kinds of cheese, *chorizo, bortilla* (a milder *chorizo* without garlic), and baguettes, as well as canned goods and household supplies.

SOUTH TO LOS PICOS

Río Cares bends to the south at Las Arenas de Cabrales, and AS 264 (O 204 on some maps) parallels it for about 4 km (2½ miles) to road's end at Puente Poncebos, where the **Garganta del Cares** (Cares Gorge) begins. From this point forward requires a four-wheel-drive, all-terrain vehicle is required (rentals are available in the area). If you came to hike you can park your car here and take one of two trails: the trail along the gorge down to its southern end at Caín, five and a half miles distant, and on to Posado de Valdeón, another three and a half miles past Caín; or the trail east through a draw in the massif toward Bulnes, a tiny cluster of houses surrounded by Los Picos de Europa. There are mountain shelters in several locations along the second trail where you can bunk overnight.

The Upper Río Sella

Another of northern Spain's great rivers, the Río Sella, rises south of Asturias in the province of León, carves an incredible six-mile defile, the **Desfiladero de los Beyos**, through the Cordillera Cantábrica, runs under the ancient Puente Romano (Roman Bridge) at Cangas de Onís, and empties into the Mar Cantábrico at Ribadesella (which means "bank of the Sella").

CANGAS DE ONIS

Cangas de Onís is a small and dusty industrial city about 27 km (17 miles) west of Arenas de Cabrales on AS 114/C 6312 without a great deal to offer except for the pleasant surprise of the high arching span of the **Puente Romano**, just upstream from the modern bridge on the main road. Although it's called the Roman Bridge, it may, in truth, have been built in the Middle Ages to a Roman design; that could mean that it's not more than about 1,100 or 1,200 years old. Some evenings during salmon season two or three fishermen will be casting into the white water from the bridge footing in the middle of the river while a crowd of townspeople leans against the modern bridge ready to cheer—or jeer. At the western end of the modern bridge there is a bar and café named **Puente Román**, a working-class place with a large parking area in front, good for a snack or a beverage. Cangas's **Capilla de Santa Cruz** was built around Asturias's only dolmen, but the chapel is generally closed, so you must go to the *ayuntamiento* (town hall) to get someone to let you in.

COVADONGA

About 4 km (2½ miles) east of Cangas is the turnoff to **Santuario Covadonga**, which is 7 km (4 miles) farther south along AS 262/O 220. There's not a town of Covadonga as such, just the sanctuary, which is quite a complex all by itself. This is the site where the Asturian hero Pelayo made his back-against-the-wall stand around 720, and achieved what is recognized as the first defeat of the invading Moors. Pelayo became the first king of the Asturias, ruling from Cangas de Onís. He and his family are buried in Covadonga's Cueva Santa, near a revered statue of the protector of Asturias, the Virgen Santina.

There is a parking lot just below the plaza on which stands Covadonga's large basilica (built in 1918) and its small adjacent museum. A crown encrusted with a thousand diamonds catches the eye in the basilica, and in the museum, a diamond-encrusted cross. On one side of the plaza is a large building recently renovated to accommodate *cantantes* (singers), in this case boy sopranos who starting at age eight go to school and live here while singing in choral groups at church functions. (Until, that is, their voices change and they are expelled—at which point, presumably, they move on to lower voices and higher education.) From the plaza there are truly stunning views of sheer rock faces and mountain greenery that diminish all the imposing masonry.

Down from the parking lot, next to a gloomy pile of a hotel, is a tunnel leading to the grotto where Pelayo took his last (successful) stand. Now called the **Cueva Santa**, it is dedicated to the Virgen Santina, whose statue graces the altar. Pelayo and Alfonso I are buried here.

LAGO DE ENOL AND LAGO DE LA ERCINA

Lago de Enol and Lago de la Ercina, two halcyon lakes high in the mountains, are about 12 km (7½ miles) southeast of Covadonga. Do not turn from the sanctuary entrance onto the main road but continue past the souvenir stands packed cheek-by-jowl on your right and up the mountain (and up and up and up some more). This road, best travelled on a weekday, is a mild adventure with more hairpins than straights, rewarding you with green alpine meadows and magnificent vistas. Serious bicyclists—one might even say dedicated—will occasionally pass you going up.

The two lakes are more than 4,000 feet high, near the snow line. Lago de Enol sits in a basin surrounded by meadows populated by several velvety brown Jersey cows either born here or parachuted in. These are lovely surroundings for a picnic. The road ends at Lago de la Ercina in a national park and animal reserve (no hunting), the Parque Nacional de la Montaña de Covadonga.

TITO BUSTILLO

The Paleolithic period, or Old Stone Age, stretches from about 40,000 B.C. to the dawn of recorded history, about 10,000 B.C. Evidence of that age and culture has been found in caves in the vast stretch of land from the Dordogne river valley in southwestern France to Cantabria and Asturias, where there are more than 20 such caves in addition to the famous Altamira Caves at Santillana del Mar (see the Cantabria chapter). Nothing in Spain can match Altamira's astonishing display; however, if you can't wait the three months Altamira requires for an advance reservation and want to get some sense of prehistoric art, then attend the caves at Tito Bustillo.

Take N 625 7 km (4 miles) west from Cangas, turn right onto N 634/E 70 (where the trucks are in charge), and continue north 15 km (9 miles) to **Ribadesella**, on the sea at the mouth of the Río Sella. There take N 632 through town, with its buff buildings draped with drying laundry that look like Franco-era worker housing, to a bridge that recrosses the estuary. Turn left at the "Cuevas" sign and drive less than half a mile to the white marble buildings marking the entrance to Tito Bustillo.

Guides conduct small groups along a muddy path (watch your step) within a large tube of a cavern (you feel vaguely like the Seven Dwarfs whistling off to work). The first drawings, reached after a walk of 15 minutes through, around, over, and under stalactites and stalagmites, are a bit of a disappointment, difficult to discern even with the helpful, informed guide repeatedly outlining the drawings with a dim flashlight. The last site, though, past waterfalls, is remarkable and moving: Somebody with an observant eye and an adroit hand used charcoal and manganese oxide to produce an accurate drawing of a horse here—14,000 years ago. You can see that the artist even used a bulge in the rock to give fullness to the horse's body. Above that drawing is one of a horse's head in profile, eye closed, looking as if he's enjoying something tasty. This drawing could be from a Picasso sketchpad. It has grace and power and anatomical accuracy and the look of something dashed off a moment before by an expert hand. You can see the descendants of that horse today in pastures and on mountain slopes, sometimes running wild, across Asturias and Galicia.

EAST ALONG THE COAST

There is more evidence of ancient human creativity along the coastline east of Ribadesella. Near the village of Vidiago, 35 km (22 miles) east of Ribadesella on N 632 (8 km/5 miles past the coastal town of Llanes), is the Celtic idol **Peña Tu**, a Bronze Age monolith whose meaning has not yet been explained. (There are signs showing the way to Peña Tu.) Ten kilometers (6 miles) farther east, near the Cantabrian border, is the turnoff for the **Cuevas del Pindal**, with more Paleolithic animal drawings.

CENTRAL ASTURIAS
Oviedo

From the perspective of a few miles distance, the first view of Oviedo, overhung with a layer of industrial pollution, is somewhat disagreeable. The city of nearly 200,000 occupies a basin surrounded by low hills, a classic configuration for blocking ventilating winds and entrapping smog. Ugly images of other cities obscured by industrial haze spring to mind. Not to worry: The Asturian kings, beginning with Alfonso II, El Casto (The Chaste), early in the ninth century, chose to rule from Oviedo, and clearly they knew what they were doing.

The capital city of Asturias is near the region's center, 438 km (272 miles) northwest of Madrid, 115 km (71 miles) due north of León on N 630, and 28 km (17 miles) south of coastal Gijón (via A 8 and A 66), both its rival and partner in commercial expansion. From Cangas de Onís it is 65 km (40 miles) due west on N 634/E 70.

The smog emanates from heavy industry that sprang up, initially, around the extensive coal sources south of the city. Iron smelting has been joined by textiles, manufacturing, and exploitation of other nearby mineral resources. Once there was gold nearby, too, but the Romans took care of that early on. A large, vibrant, and cosmopolitan city has emerged that somehow manages to keep industry and commerce from overwhelming an extensive cultural heritage. Oviedo is a nice surprise.

PARKING AND GETTING ORIENTED IN OVIEDO

If you're visiting the city for the day, and are driving, you'll be happier if you garage your car or park it on the street (get a *tiquete* from the meter on the block). Look for a spot or a garage near the **Campo de San Francisco**, a lovely, wooded city park near the *centro ciudad* (city center) and a good starting point for touring the areas most likely to be of interest. The *campo*—the "lungs" of the city—is where all Oviedans go for their *paseo* among the fountains, kiosks, and flowers. This is a great city park: Clean, safe, and pretty, it's a good place for wandering, jogging, or sitting on a bench and watching the crowd, or the swans in the pond.

A useful map, available at news kiosks and stationery stores, is the Karlan *Asturias Mapa Turístico,* which has Asturias on one side and city plans of Gijón and Oviedo on the other. With a couple of exceptions, most of what is interesting about old Oviedo is east of Campo de San Francisco. We start with the area around the cathedral and the Museo Arqueológico, and then visit Monte Naranco, a short car or taxi ride outside the city proper, the location of two interesting examples of pre-Romanesque architecture. The city's two deluxe hotels and some good restaurants and shops are also within an easy walk of the Campo de San Francisco.

THE CATHEDRAL

From the eastern corner of the Campo de San Francisco the cathedral's 260-foot spire (two towers were called for in the original design, but only one was completed) is an easy target. Go east from the park across Calle Uria, the city's major thoroughfare, through the Plaza de la Escandalera, with its huge fountain, and along Calle de San Francisco to Plaza de Alfonso II El Casto. The cathedral, known as **Sancta Ovetensis**, is Late, or Flamboyant, Gothic ("flamboyant," as in flame-like, in reference to the design's patterns of undulating curves). The original church here was built in the eighth century, then destroyed by the Moors; rebuilding began in the 14th century and ended 200 years later. The sooty surface is testimony to several centuries of success in the Oviedan coal mines and iron smelters.

The cathedral has three entrances, each a different height, and a beautiful tower, which the 19th-century essayist Leopoldo Alas called a "poem in stone." These give the building an intriguing asymmetry. Directly inside, on the left, is the 17th-century chapel of Santa Eulalia; its Churrigueresque, ever-so-slightly kitschy shrine containing the saint's remains is an offbeat introduction. The 16th-century retable above the main altar is a masterpiece of carved intricacy, quite magnificent. Almost 40 feet by 40 feet, it's made up of five sections, each comprised of five scenes from the life of Christ. The piece contains the occasional anachronism—one of the saints, for example, is wearing glasses. Off in the northern corner of the church is the burial place of the Asturian kings, whose remains are housed in a 12th-century marble-lidded sarcophagus.

The **Cámara Santa** (Holy Chamber), up a few steps in the south transept, is a small room with a barred entrance containing a large silver reliquary. The original structure of the Cámara Santa was built by Alfonso II early in the ninth century to keep relics out of the hands of the Moors then sweeping through southern Spain. The relics, including gold, silver, and jewels, were carried by Christian forces retreating to safe haven in Asturias behind the barrier of the Cordillera Cantábrica. The chamber was destroyed by an explosion during the workers' strike of 1934, although the jewel casket and portal survived, and was subsequently restored. In 1977 some of the valuables were stolen in what can only be termed a daring robbery. They were eventually recovered and everything is back in place and all seems to be quiet now.

A church **museum** on the upper floors displays carvings and statues of modest interest. On the third floor, though, the display of the 19th-century *conjunto de salón* (salon ensemble) of one Doña Josefina Valsera includes a wonderful round metal table, about 40 inches in diameter, inlaid with enameled portraits of family members, decorated with cupids, swagged by a heavy metal rope, and supported on metal goat's feet. Just around the corner you'll have an eyeball-to-eyeball encounter with a life-size, crucified San Sebastián shot through with dozens of arrows; the piece is attributed to Antonio Borga (1661–1730).

Take the stairs through the door at the left rear of the third floor down to the interior of the 12th-century, Romanesque *claustro* (cloister). An unmarked crypt in an arched vault off the cloister may be the most interesting place of all, imbued with a sense of mystery. The only object is a simple stone slab on an unadorned stone base.

Before you leave Sancto Ovetensis behind, sit for a moment on the rim of the fountain at the far end of the Plaza de Alfonso II, listen to the water, and take another look at the cathedral. There are not many to equal it.

THE MUSEO ARQUEOLOGICO

Oviedo's Museo Arqueológico is around the rear of the cathedral, at the southern end, on Calle de San Vicente. It is housed in the city's oldest building, the former Monasterio de San Vicente, founded in 781. Although the monastery has been restored many times over the centuries, most recently in the 1700s, part of the original building is still visible. The cloister, a tranquil refuge from modern Oviedo, was begun in the mid-16th century, but 200 years passed before its completion. It was worth the wait.

The museum contains three floors of local antiquities, some quite interesting, although the building itself may be its own best feature. On the *bajo* (lower) floor of the cloister are the 14th-century stone sarcophagi of the Asturian kings, their likenesses on the lids, faithful dogs lying at their feet. The loyal squire of one king stands at the alert, ready with battle armor. There are also ninth-century tablets on this floor. The *entreplanta* (second floor) has, among other items, Roman coins with the likeness of the second-century emperor Marcus Aurelius Antoninus and others. The *sala romana*, room III, has a large section of a handsome second-century terrazzo floor on display, a mosaic of fishes and urns and birds. *Claustro alto*, the third floor, wraps around the entire court with a beautiful view of the cloister interior and the cathedral tower.

Opposite the Museo Arqueológico is the **Plaza de Feijóo** and the entrance to the city university's Department of Philology, Psychology, and Education, within the College of Philosophy. Students hang out in the sunshine between classes around the statue of the Dominican priest Feijóo, who was a great teacher at the Universidad de Oviedo, or just down the street at **Café Feijóo**, Calle de San Vicente 18.

IGLESIA DE SANTULLANO

Also in this northeastern section of the old town, about a 15-minute walk away (head downhill from the cathedral area along Calle de Martínez Vigil to Plaza de Santullano), is the ninth-century San Julián de los Prados, contracted familiarly to Santullano. The church is important to local heritage because it is considered the most ambitious project by an ambitious leader, Alfonso II, who reigned over Asturias from 791 to 842 and made Oviedo his capital. He was a vital force against the Moors, reaching out for support from Frankish emperors Charlemagne and Louis I, providing safe haven for the holy relics of Toledo, and building the first church on the site of the famous cathedral at Santiago de Compostela. His Santullano is a princely blend of Roman and Visigothic styles. Inside are the remains of frescoes, one depicting the construction of the church itself.

LUNCHING AND SHOPPING
NEAR THE CATHEDRAL

If your blood-sugar level has dropped, try **Coconut**, off the south end of Plaza de Alfonso II at Calle de Eusebio González Abascal 7. Coconut has soft drinks and beer, but it mainly has a lot of terrific little candies—kisses, licorice sticks, and gum drops and jelly beans of all kinds.

Or you could skip Coconut and save the calories for lunch at **Restaurante El Cobalto**, Calle Jovellanos 4, on the north side of the cathedral next to the Gran Hotel España. El Cobalto is a simple, dignified place with white tablecloths and good, courteous service. They serve a very flavorsome *sopa de pescado* with a delicious baguette wrapped in tissue from the Integral Pandería & Confitería. From the *pescados* (fish) menu try *merluza a la sidra* (hake in Asturian cider) or *calamares en su tinta* (braised squid in a sauce of squid ink, garlic, and olive oil). Tel: (9-8) 522-0151.

Across the street from El Cobalto is a very interesting leather shop, **Escanda**, Calle Jovellanos 5. Escanda displays stylish, extremely well made bags, purses, cases, and leather goods of original design. The name of the shop reflects the philosophy of its owner, Felipe Prieto: "*Escanda*," he explains, "is a kind of primitive Asturian wheat, now rare and considered without value, when it is something precious from the past that should not be allowed to die out." Señor Prieto feels that craft skills and craftspeople are held in a similar light—endangered species in desperate need of encouragement and support. This craftsman was drawn to leather as a boy when he became fascinated by American Indians and decided to try to make a pair of moccasins. Señor Prieto learned his craft well enough to be commissioned, some years ago, to re-create the sandals worn by Saint Peter (European size 37, quite small) for Pope John Paul (size 45). Señor Prieto said of Saint Peter's footgear, having carefully researched the matter, that "they were actually very deluxe sandals." Saint Peter's sandals aren't available but a lot of other elegant items are. Wrapping includes a stalk of *escanda*.

The east end of Calle Jovellanos, beginning at Calle de Pelayo, is a large commercial promenade with many shops, outdoor cafés, a camera store, and a stationery store— Librería de Papelería—at Calle de Pelayo 7, that occasionally has the previous week's editions of some English-language newsmagazines.

STAYING IN OVIEDO

Northwest of the park is the quite extraordinary ▶ **Hotel de la Reconquista** (go north on Calle Marqués de Pidal, then left on Calle Gil de Jaz). Even if you are not staying there, stop by for a drink at the bar off the reception area. When you walk through the front door, you'll know you're in good hands. The lobby is a great, open space of hushed elegance, a kind of interior patio with a *mezzo* balcony high up along the entire perimeter of the room. Formerly a royal hospital, the Reconquista is a labyrinth of hallways and stairways, thoroughly deluxe, with gracious yet modern rooms. All in all, a wonderful place. Bring *muchas pesetas*.

Oviedo's other deluxe hotel is of a quite different style. The mirrored, polished, gleaming ▶ **Gran Hotel España**, at Calle Jovellanos 2, looks less impressive outside than within, but is very Euro-chic, with a staff to match. The Gran Hotel may not be in quite the same class as the Hotel de la Reconquista, on the other side of Campo de San Francisco, but little is.

DINING IN OVIEDO

A good spot for a before-dinner aperitif, or an after-dinner *aguardiente,* is **Café Riego**, Plaza de Riego 2, opposite the 17th-century, properly sober façade of the university's Facultad de Derecho (law school). Southwest of the cathedral, near the Plaza Mayor, Café Riego (an appropriate name for a watering hole—*riego* means watering or irrigation) is a popular hangout for the hip and the young, who follow a casual but stylish dress code. Inside it gets crowded and noisy and ebullient, so people spill out onto the small plaza talking, sipping *tinto* or *cerveza* (beer), lounging around the pedestal of the plaza's statue. It's a very attractive place to be on a summer's early evening. Next door is a big newspaper and magazine store, **La Palma Librería**, Calle de Ramón Cajal 2. Those young lawyers have to keep up, you know.

On Calle Trascorrales, just off the north end of the **Plaza Mayor**, which is south of the cathedral and east of Campo de Grande, there are several good restaurants, and Fernando Martín owns three of them. Señor Martín spent 12 years learning the business in Switzerland so that he could return to his home town and make good. There are **La Bocamar** and **Trascorrales**, both with simple interiors as well as casual, pleasant outdoor settings under big umbrellas. For La Bocamar, Tel: (9-8) 522-9739; for Trascorrales, Tel; (9-8) 522-2441. Together with **El Raitán**, they form a triumvirate on a knoll at the end of Calle Trascorrales. El Raitán, at number 6, is solid and rustic, with dark hewn timbers and a cozy, snug Swiss-chalet feel; Tel: (9-8) 521-4218. El Raitán has no menu as such. There is, however, a prix-fixe meal with, it's safe to say, an emphasis on protein: 12, count them, 12 meat courses (actually 11 meat and one *pollo*), each different, served on skewers (the best advice is to eat just a little of each), beginning with *chorizo criollos* (sausage with Creole sauce), then *lomo de cerdo* (pork tenderloin), *jabalí* (wild boar), *entrecôte* (rib steak), *conejo* (rabbit) . . . *ad cholesterolum*. Side dishes also keep appearing: potato gratinée, potatoes French fried, potato salad, pimientos, a powerful, pungent Roquefort sauce to pour over everything, lettuce, tomatoes, condiments of many colors. It is very well prepared, very tasty, served with prompt good cheer.

Not far from Calle Trascorrales, just south of Plaza Mayor on Plaza del Fontán, is the **Palacio de Duque del Parque**, which houses an impressive El Greco, one of the last surviving paintings from a series on the Apostles.

Closer to the park, on Calle de San Francisco, the street that leads from the park to the cathedral, is **Casa Fermín** (number 8), which serves traditional Asturian cuisine and has a spectacular wine cellar. Try their *caldereta,* a fish stew, or, if you're in the mood for meat, the *morcilla* (Asturian blood sausage), with beans or in a stew. Tel: (9-8) 521-6452. **Babilonia**, an exotic, Arabic-looking *fromagerie* at Calle Asturias 16 (around the corner from the Hotel de la Reconquista), serves an entire meal of local cheeses and pâtés. **La Goleta**, Calle Covadonga 32 (cross Calle Uria from the east end of the park onto Calle Millias Nacionales; Covadonga is the second street), also serves traditional regional specialties; Tel: (9-8) 521-3847.

MONTE NARANCO

Monte Naranco is, to risk oversimplifying, one thing to Oviedans and another to visitors. There's a large and popular city-operated *deportivo* (sports) complex at the top of the low mountain, complete with a small *fútbol* stadium, gymnasium, and giant indoor pool, that draws in the locals. In the main building you'll find a cafeteria with a long terrace graced by cool breezes and a panoramic view of Oviedo spread across the valley below. Just below the crest are what most visitors go up the mountain to see, the churches of Santa María del Naranco and San Miguel de Lillo.

Monte Naranco is about 5 km (3 miles) west of the city and can be reached by taxi. If you're driving: From Campo de San Francisco, take Marqués de Pidal northwest across Independencia, cross over the railway complex on Viaducto Ingeniero Marquina, and make an *immediate* left turn onto Avenida San de Enol. Stay on that until it ends at Avenida de los Monumentos, turn, and within a couple of kilometers you'll find yourself in a semi-rural area and climbing up Monte Naranco. Perched on a couple of the steep curves are several bars and cafés popular with Oviedans. Santa María del Naranco will appear shortly on the left.

Santa Maria del Naranco

Built in 848, Santa María del Naranco is believed to have been the entrance hall of the palace of King Ramiro I. A definitive example of Ramiresque architecture, it was a totally unorthodox structure for its time, with its adornments placed where they were needed for structural purposes rather than simply for decorative value. The building was considered somber, its minimal decoration making it appear somewhat Oriental to the Spanish. Demolished in the 15th century, it was put back together by, unfortunately, a rather blundering builder, so that it now seems haphazard. Inside, be sure to see the painting of the Holy Family and the angel playing a flute, very early examples of Spanish art.

San Miguel de Lillo

San Miguel de Lillo may have been the palace's chapel. Although it was badly damaged in the 13th century, there remain grotesque carvings on the pillars and around the doors that are unequaled in their peculiarity.

Monte Naranco also has an amphitheater cut right into the mountain. Every September the theater comes alive with all kinds of cultural events, from opera to bullfights to the Día de las Américas (Americas Day) festival on September 19.

SOUTH OF OVIEDO

If you are travelling south of Oviedo on N 630, watch for signs for **Santa Cristina de Lena** (36 km/20 miles south of Oviedo, past Pola de Lena). This small ninth-century structure is perfectly preserved and the view from the hill upon which it is perched is spectacular. The woman in the house at the foot of the hill has the key and will accompany you.

COASTAL ASTURIAS
Gijón

The trip from Oviedo northeast to the central coastal city of
Gijón is only about 30 km (19 miles). Gijón is on a very large
bay dominated by the cliff of Santa Catalina, site of the
original settlement. The largest city in Asturias (almost
300,000 inhabitants) and the most important industrial center after Bilbao in northern Spain, Gijón is a crowded, dirty
manufacturing city that, unlike Oviedo, has not elected, or
has been unable, to protect its heritage. To be fair, many
more contributions were made to Oviedo over the centuries, whereas Gijón's earlier history is primarily that of
fishing village.

Hardly anything remains of the Roman, Visigothic, or
Moorish cultures that, at one point or another, took up
residence in Gijón. In the eighth century the Asturian kings
called this town home, and in 1588 what little was left of the
Armada settled here. Until the 19th century Gijón was primarily a fishing town, but with the advent of increased
commerce with South America and of the railroad lines,
which were opened in 1860, the port became a major
gateway for mineral export. Most of the activity in Gijón still
centers around the port. The city was practically demolished
during the Spanish Civil War, but it has been rebuilt and is
now almost entirely modern. Gijón has some good beaches
and today considers itself a seaside resort.

ARRIVING IN GIJON
Entering this very energetic city that is tearing up streets,
tearing down buildings, and just generally making life tough
for the first-time visitor is an adventure. If you're headed for
the Parador el Molino Viejo, look for black-and-yellow "El
Molino Parador" signs from the A-8 superhighway; you can
also follow signs for the Estadio (Stadium) de el Molinon,
which is near the parador. The ideal route is along Avenida
de Oviedo, around the rotunda to Avenida de la Constitución, and right onto Carretera de la Costa. The Parque
de Isabel la Católica is at the east end of the city's huge
beachfront, Playa de San Lorenzo, with the parador at the
south end of the park.

AROUND IN GIJON
Gijón's **Playa de San Lorenzo** is a large, curving sandy beach
that attracts thousands of mostly Spanish vacationers every
year. The tides are gentle and the weather, at least in summer, is reliable. Bars and somewhat seedy nightclubs line

the side streets near the beach, and there's something decidedly downmarket about the whole scene.

What is interesting, and old, in Gijón is handily concentrated on Santa Catalina, the knob that sticks out into the bay at the west end of Playa de San Lorenzo. **Cimadevilla** (town summit), at the edge of the knob, is the picturesque old fishermen's quarter, whose narrow streets are cow-path derivative using essentially demented cows. Don't try to figure out this cramped district with its tilting buildings—just go with the flow. There are quite a few tiny bars to help you along.

Slightly inland, toward the city center and fronting the Plaza del Marqués, are the two oldest buildings in Gijón, both of which have been allowed to fall into terrible condition: the Iglesia de San Juan Bautista (begun in the 15th century and finished in the 18th) and the 16th-century Palacio del Conde de Revillagigedo.

Gaspar Melchor de Jovellanos, the poet, activist, and encyclopedist, was born in Gijón in 1744. There's a monument to him on the Plaza del Seis de Agosto, a few blocks south of Plaza Mayor, which is near the entrance to Cimadevilla. Just north of Plaza Mayor, on Plaza Jovellanos, there's a museum in the house in which he was born. The main reason for going there is to arrange to see what little is left of some **Roman baths** found under the Cimadevilla barrio; ask the person in charge of the museum to arrange for your visit.

STAYING AND DINING IN GIJON

▶ **Parador Molino Viejo** (Old Mill), which really was an old mill, offers the best accommodations in Gijón. Located in the beautiful, bird-filled Parque de Isabel la Católica, it is a fine place to stop and relax as you're travelling through the province. If you would prefer a hotel right on the bay, the ▶ **Príncipe de Asturias**, Calle Manso 2, near the bay end of the *parque,* is a good choice.

Asturian cooking is at its best and most authentic in Gijón. Try the *pulpo* or grilled salmon at **Casa Victor**, Calle El Carmen 11 (due south several blocks from the Plaza del Marqués), which has a good wine list, too; Tel: (9-8) 535-0093. Another dozen blocks south of Casa Victor, **El Retiro**, Calle Begoña 28, on the west side of the Jardines Begoña, serves a delicious *merluza a la cazuela* (hake stew); Tel: (9-8) 535-0030.

The Western Coastline

It's about 150 km (93 miles) west from Gijón to Ribadeo, on the west bank of the Río Eo in Galicia. It is a lovely scenic drive along N 634, close to the coast, hilly and curvy, up and down one inviting valley after another. Look for *horreos* along here, the stone sheds on stilts that keep grain away from the damp. Among the many little coastal villages lining the coast is **Salinas**, with a pretty fir-lined beach.

LUARCA

Luarca, 107 km (66 miles) west of Gijón at the mouth of the Río Negro, was once an important whaling capital. The town is built on several hills, and the whitewashed, slate-roofed houses are a charming sight, adding to the town's quaint, un-calculated appeal. For a postcard view of Luarca, exit from the main road to the local road about 3 km (1½ miles) east of town. You'll arrive at the harbor side, on a cliff between the sea and the port, for a high-angle perspective that makes the town look like a toy village with its seven bridges spanning the Río Negro. There's a fair amount of romance in Luarca—a castle in ruins; a cemetry situated in a setting that is positively Gaelic; a lighthouse; docks dotted with cafés and bars—and it's all easy and pleasant to cover on foot. The small local beach is not on the sea but on the harbor, less than a quarter-mile from the wharf.

Staying and Dining in Luarca

The wharf reflects that Luarca, with a population of about 21,000, is as much working fishing port as it is resort. **Café Glacé**, facing the harbor, is a fishermen's favorite. If you don't want to hang out with the guys, try the **Cambaral Terraza Bar**, a little farther along, at Paseo del Muelle 16, a pleasant, open place of rattan and blond furniture catering to families and serving both beer and chocolate to meet their needs, and open for breakfast. The ▶ **Hotel Báltico & Restaurant**, Paseo del Muelle 1, is a small place, quite adequate for a night or two. On the town's main plaza, a short distance from the wharf, is the ▶ **Hotel Gayoso**, about the same class accommodation as the Baltico, though twice the size. Luarca is a good place for a snack or lunch or to stop over for a night.

WEST TO RIBADEO

Back on N 634, where the donkey-powered, two-wheeled hay wagons compete for right of way with the 18-wheelers, it's 45 km (28 miles) to Ribadeo. On the east bank of the Río Eo is the small fishing village of **Figueras**, and a reasonably priced restaurant, **Peñalba**, Calle el Puerto, serving excellent river fish; the fish stew is particularly good. Tel: (9-8) 562-3760. Across the river (and the Galician border) in Ribadeo is the ▶ **Parador de Ribadeo**, Calle Amador Fernández, with a fine restaurant and panoramic views of the enormous Eo delta with the wooded mountains of Galicia for a backdrop.

GALICIA

Were it not for Santiago de Compostela, Galicia might be one of the least-known and least-travelled regions in Spain. Some of Galicia's provinces are virtually untouched by tourism. Unlike the rest of the country in both appearance and attitude, Galicia looks somewhat like Ireland. The landscape is lush and green, thick with pine and eucalyptus. You will be hard put to find here the sun-drenched look of Spanish villages to the south. The fjord-like *rías* (estuaries) provide a spectacular coastline, and the Rías Bajas (lower estuaries) of the south hold one of Spain's best-kept secrets: some of the most splendid beaches in Europe.

Galicia's people—Gallegos, as they're called in Spanish—are different from other Spaniards and seem a race apart. The rest of their countrymen sometimes see them as provincial, a little backward. Their industriousness seems to lack the high-tech energy of the Catalans, and their nightlife definitely lacks the sophistication of Madrid or Seville. They love poetry, music, land, and family, and are fascinated with death, witchcraft, and superstition. They are thoughtful, maybe a little evasive, yet they're willing to accept outsiders gracefully. They treat visitors like family, yet they will fight each other brutally over a piece of land—indeed, they worship land.

Perhaps many of these traits came from the Celts, who conquered the area in about 1000 B.C. and stayed in control until A.D. 137. This may explain why the people seem to have so much in common with the Irish and the Scots. They even play a bagpipe-like instrument called a *gaita*.

The Galician dialect is close to Portuguese, with a *soupçon* of French tones. Over the years the Gallegos have had to fight to keep their language. Today Galician is taught as the primary language in the region's schools, and road and street signs have begun to be converted from Castilian. The two look enough alike not to confuse visitors, however; for example, the Spanish *La Coruña* is in Galician *A Coruña*.

The Food of Galicia

The hallmark of Galician cuisine is seafood: *merluza* (hake), *cigalas* (prawns), *camarones* (small shrimp), *chipirones* (little squid), *langostinos* (crayfish—a bit of an effort to eat, but delicious), *almejas* (clams—very tiny and sweet and served in a broth), *vieiras* (scallops), *percebes* (goose barnacles—a great delicacy), as well as trout and local fish of all kinds, prepared in casseroles or broiled or steamed. Seafood is also rolled into delicious crêpes, or "pies," called *empanadas*.

In the colder seasons, the fabulous local meat is served; game and rabbit are Galician specialties. Try the local dish *caldo gallego,* prepared with ham and turnip tops; the ham is cooked with pork sausages and whole boiled potatoes and served en casserole. Local turnips and small peppers are especially good in season.

Gallegos, like Asturians, are cheesemakers *par excellence.* You can have an entire lunch of local cheeses made from goat's milk and sheep's milk. There are soft, semi-soft, and hard varieties, all of which are ripened naturally and without preservatives. Try the breast-shaped *tetilla*—it's mild and smooth—and some of the region's intoxicating blue cheeses. And to make all of these cheeses even more satisfying, eat them with homemade peasant bread.

For sweet desserts the locals make what they describe as a "humble" pancake pastry known as *filoa,* wonderful with custard. (By humble, they apparently mean it isn't one of those fancy French subtleties.) The Gallegos also make great almond and sponge cakes, not to be found in the rest of the country.

Follow your dessert with an *aguardiente,* a by-product of the wine-making process used as an after-dinner *digestif,* or a brandy (try the cherry). Brandy lovers will be tempted by the *queimada,* a local after-feast custom involving burning the brandy and adding sugar and lemon peel to it. Drink it fast; it's strong, but what a nice effect!

The Wines of Galicia

Of Galicia's four provinces, La Coruña, Lugo, Orense, and Pontevedra, only the last two are major wine producers, with three DOs (*denominaciones de origen*): Ribeiro, Valde-orras, and the newly created Rías Baixas (Pontevedra), where Albariño, Galicia's greatest wine, is made.

ALBARIÑO

Albariño is rapidly being recognized as Spain's long-awaited white-wine star. It is certainly the most interesting, and probably the best, white wine Spain makes, and prices are rising as rapidly as Albariño's prestige. The traditional growing area for Albariño is around the town of Cambados, on the Atlantic coast in western Pontevedra province, and near Túy, along the Río Miño, on the Portuguese border. To be called Albariño, the wine must be made from 100 percent Albariño grapes; not all wine from Rías Baixas is Albariño.

Albariño is dry and elegant, has a very lively acidity, and a pretty, flowery nose, reminiscent of fine Alsace Riesling, the German grape that many Gallegos believe was the ancestor of Albariño. Traditionally it has been made in small lots by artisan producers, some of whom have become local legends. Production has been limited, so most Albariño never left its native province and usually didn't even bear a label. Recently, however, several firms have begun making Albariño on a larger scale, so it is now possible to find these superb wines in fine restaurants and shops all over Spain. For those who can afford the prices being asked, Albariño is all the rage. Albariño goes beautifully with the rich variety of Galician seafood. Some particularly good Albariños to try are Martín Codax, Morgadío, Fillaboa, Lagar de Cervera, Valdamor, and Condes de Albarei. The white wine of Santiago Ruiz of El Rosal (Pontevedra) has only 70 percent Albariño grapes, so its designation is Rías Baixas, not Albariño, but it is still a superb wine.

RIBEIRO

Because Galicia produces much less wine than it consumes, its Ribeiro (Orense) is in high demand. Ribeiro's best wines are young, fresh, fruity, *pétillant* white wines similar to the *vinhos verdes* of Portugal. The wines are made from Treixadura, Jerez (Palomino), Macabeo, Godello, and a host of other indigenous grapes. The vines are trained on wires supported by stone posts. Try O Pazo.

VALDEORRAS

Valdeorras (Orense) is centered around El Barco de Valdeorras in the Sil River valley of mountainous eastern Orense. Although rainy, as is the rest of Galicia, the climate here is moderated by the weather of continental Spain, so the vines get a good deal of sun. The picturesque trellised vineyards are terraced on steep slate hills, which provide good drainage. The Godello grape (related to the Verdejo of Rueda, in Valladolid) makes the best Valdeorras white wines, which are fresh, medium- to full-bodied, and quite aromatic. The reds—light, cherry-colored, fruity wines—are made from Garnacha and Mencia grapes. In 1983 only 5,000 bottles of Valdeorras wine were exported, but experts believe that Valdeorras has great potential.

—*Gerry Dawes*

Festivals in Galicia

There is strong religious feeling in Galicia, and every parish church in the region holds an annual festival in honor of its patron saint. Because there are almost 4,000 parish churches, chances are you're going to come upon a festival no matter when you visit. Typically on these feast days, after mass the town's main square fills with townspeople strolling, showing off their finery, and stopping to gossip with their neighbors. There may be live bands, usually playing loud, but not very good, rock music, and several vendors selling crafts, providing you with a fine opportunity to shop for gifts (prices are often negotiable).

Some well-known festivals are Los Maios, celebrated in May to honor the arrival of spring, and Magosto, on November 11, when chestnuts are roasted and new wine is tasted. Another of interest is La Rapa das Bestas, the festival of the branding of wild horses. Galicians also celebrate Carnival, an age-old tradition here. But their most important festival is the feast day of Saint James (Santiago) on July 25, celebrated with fireworks in the main square of Santiago de Compostela. When this day falls on a Sunday, a Holy Year is designated; it is only during Holy Years that the Santiago cathedral's Puerta Santa (the rear door) is opened.

Check with a local travel agent or the Tourist Office of Spain for details concerning dates and locales of the various Galician festivals.

The Camino de Santiago

There was no Santiago de Compostela before 813, therefore no Camino de Santiago (Way of Saint James). Both came into being because that year, it is said, Pelayo, a religious hermit, saw a brilliant star appear above a wooded field that overlay an ancient Roman burying ground in what is now present-day Santiago. Pelayo told Bishop Theodomirus about the star, and the bishop investigated and unearthed a tomb. It was decided that the tomb contained the remains of Saint James, the first Apostle to attain martyrdom, with his beheading in Jerusalem at the behest of King Herod Agrippa. The revelation could not have come at a more propitious time. Spanish Christians had been fleeing the Moors for nearly a hundred years and desperately needed a rallying symbol. Santiago (Saint James) got the honor, along with a full complement of medieval armor and a sword, after he was sighted in 844 at the battle of Clavijo, south of Logroño, swinging his mighty sword, cleaving Moors by the thousands. He became Santiago Matamoros (Saint James the Moorslayer) and the patron saint of Spain. Santiago de Compostela became a shrine. It was an era when many despaired, so they went in search of hope, every year, by the hundreds of thousands, from all across Europe, throughout all of Christendom—as many as two million pilgrims each year by 1300—forging the Camino de Santiago as they walked.

The remains of Santiago were hidden away from the raiding Sir Francis Drake after the defeat of the Spanish Armada in 1589. They were lost, yet again, for centuries. Finally, in the 19th century, Cardinal Miguel Paya y Rico organized a successful hunt for them. Pope León XIII had the relics examined and declared them authentic in 1884, issuing a papal bull on July 25, the date Pelayo had seen the star.

Many of Santiago's medieval pilgrims walked for seven months to reach their goal; some rode horseback. Anybody rich enough could be carried—and entertained by roistering jesters. The uniform of the day for the foot pilgrim was a heavy woollen cloak with a linen undershirt, broad-brimmed hat with the front brim turned up, a sturdy hiking staff with a gourd of water or wine tied to it, and two pairs of thick-soled sandals, because one pair would wear out. Once in Spain there were two choices of route, both designed to circumvent the Cordillera Cantábrica. One stayed close to the northern coastline and the other, more popular route entered Spain through the Roncesvalles pass in the Pyrenees. This second, called the "French Way," stretched 500 miles, spanning Pamplona, Logroño, Santo Domingo de la Calzada, Burgos, Sahagún, León, Astorga, Ponferrada, Sarriá, and finally Santiago, all of which prospered by providing food, shelter, medical treatment, and other services. The last stop before entering Santiago was Lavacolla, which means "Wash-tail," called so because of its stream where the pilgrim could attempt to scrape away a seven-month stink. Of course, this was not a one-way walk. For the walk home, though, the traveller got to fasten the symbol of a successful pilgrimage, a scallop shell, on that upturned hat brim.

FOLLOWING THE CAMINO TODAY
Every year a few thousand people, quite a few of them elderly, still make some part of the journey. This thousand-year-old footpath is still well marked, often by the shell that is the symbol of the pilgrimage (the whole shell resembling prayerful hands). Certification is granted by officials at the cathedral in Santiago to those who cover the last 200 km (120 miles)—which pass through very beautiful scenery—on foot or on bicycle. If you decide to make the trek, start out by wearing the scallop shell, as most do these days; it draws attention and aid. Get certified and you're entitled to three meals a day for three days at one of the premier hotels in all the world, the Hostal de los Reyes Católicos, adjacent to Santiago's cathedral (you have to eat with the help,

though). That's the deal that was struck when the *hostal,* which had long served wealthy travellers, was converted into a state enterprise in the 1950s.

Nowadays, you can reach the pilgrim's goal in 55 minutes on a direct flight from Madrid. You'll miss out on all that pain but you'll also miss out on how it feels when the pain stops and you finally arrive, the hard way, in Santiago. As a compromise, you could take a week and drive a close parallel to the "French Way" and see just about everything. Wear a shell.

The hiker or biker will find *The Road to Santiago,* by Michael Jacobs (published in the United States by Chronicle), useful, as well as a map called "El Camino de Santiago," showing details of each section of the route, published in Spain by Anaya Touring in just about every language but English.

In this book we cover lengths of the Camino del Santiago in several chapters. If you wish to follow it, starting in the east, near France, consult the Aragón, Basque Country, and Navarra chapters; then, moving westward, La Rioja and Old Castile (Burgos and León); and finally Galicia, where the trail picks up at Lugo and ends at Santiago de Compostela.

EASTERN GALICIA

One of the pilgrims' last major stops before reaching Santiago was Lugo, about 105 km (65 miles) due east of their goal. If you're coming from Asturias, to the east, or up from León (some 228 km/141 miles southeast in Old Castile), this might be your first big stop in Galicia. Pilgrims were relieved to see Lugo's fortifications—it meant safety from the disagreeable elements they would encounter, both human and natural. Most people in this century prefer to see Lugo as a day trip from Santiago; it is a one-and-a-half-hour drive on C 547 and N 640.

If you've been driving westward along the Asturian coast, then take N 640 southwest from Ribadeo along the Río Eo and through dramatically beautiful scenery about 90 km (55 miles) to Lugo. The road is not in the best shape—even though sections are being improved—so allow extra time. While this region is not true wilderness, it is remote and rugged terrain—high mountains and deep ravines filled with giant eucalyptus and fir trees—and there are only a very few villages. This is simply a wonderful scenic drive. "Shotgun" farming is the agricultural method of choice here: The slopes are so steep they have to be seeded with a shotgun.

About 33 km (20 miles) south of Ribadeo, turn east at A Pontenova onto AS 24, and continue for 9 km (5½ miles), back into Asturias, to **Taramundi**, a remote mountain village of artisans, that, as part of a plan by the regional government to bring attention to the area and ease the economic plight of local people, is being showcased as a traditional town of the region. (You can also reach Taramundi from Vegadeo, just south of Ribadeo, at the head of the Eo delta on AS 24.) There is a hotel with a dining room in Taramundi, ▶ **Hotel la Rectoral**, on Calle La Villa.

Lugo

Located in the province of the same name, Lugo seems a city of stones. The first glance is overwhelming—one and a half miles of **Roman walls**, 20 feet thick and 35 feet high, wrap around the town. Walk them for a clear perspective of the old Roman town. The Plaza de España was the amphitheater and the Plaza de Campo was the site of the forum. There are 50 watchtowers and ten iron and wooden gates cut into the walls. The most interesting of these gates is the **Puerta de Miño** (now known as the Puerta del Carmen), one of the oldest, located on the western side of the city. The thickness of the walls and the size of the stones here suggest that this gate was one of the city's real strongholds.

THE OLD TOWN

Another of the ten gates, Santiago, the southwestern one, opens onto the Plaza de Pio XII, site of the **cathedral**. Built to the design of the one in Santiago de Compostela, Lugo's cathedral is of both Romanesque and Gothic design, having taken six centuries to build (it was completed in 1768). The cathedral houses the relics of San Froilán, Lugo's patron saint. Visit the Capilla de Nuestra Señora de los Ojos Grandes (Chapel of the Wide-Eyed Virgin) in the eastern end of the cathedral to see the polychrome alabaster sculpture of the Virgin dating from the 12th century. It was believed that her intercession in many of the battles of the Christian Reconquest made victory over the Moors possible.

You should also pay a visit to the **Museo Provincial**, on the ground floor of the provincial palace on Calle San Marcos, which also encompasses the church of San Francisco, next door. The museum's collection of Roman coins, sarcophagi, and other ancient items is impressive. The **Iglesia de Santo Domingo**, at the center of the old city, dates from the 13th century but nevertheless has a Romanesque-style façade.

STAYING AND DINING IN LUGO

Lugo, undervisited and underrated, gives you an opportunity to see a well-preserved medieval stronghold and the finest example of Roman military architecture in Spain (you can ignore the modern, built-up sections outside the walls). If you should decide to stay overnight in Lugo, the ▶ **Gran Hotel Lugo**—equipped with a swimming pool—will make you comfortable. It's located outside the walls in the town's residential section, five minutes south from the center. A good, reasonably priced place to eat, particularly for stews and other such hearty fare, is **Verruga**, at Cruz 12. Tel: (9-82) 22-98-55. At **Alberto**, Cruz 4, you'll find high prices for superb delicacies such as *revuelto de salmón con angulas* (salmon and baby-eel omelet) and other fish dishes in a charmingly rustic setting. Tel: (9-82) 22-83-10.

SANTIAGO DE COMPOSTELA

Ancient cities were usually born of concrete need in response to specific geography—they sprang up around a natural harbor with easy access to the sea, or a great and navigable river, or on militarily strategic high ground—the cultural attachments came later. Santiago de Compostela grew up on belief and hope—and a bit of theater.

If your image of religious shrines is of places of solemn mien and hushed voice, then you may want to rethink your position after seeing Santiago. There are a vigor and a vitality about this city of 83,000, due in part to the ongoing pull of the Saint James phenomenon and the magnificent cathedral that attracts so many visitors, foreign and domestic. But a major university is also located here, and the 32,000-strong student body adds an exuberance that helps excise such modifiers as "musty" and "stagnant" from the Santiago vocabulary.

Not only does the city have a great cathedral, it has, right next door, one of the world's great hotels, once and still a place of kings, looking onto a plaza that is both heart and core of Santiago. Gabriel García Márques wrote of it: "The city imposes itself immediately, complete and timeless, as if one has been born there. I had always believed, and continue to believe, really, that there is no more beautiful square than the one in Siena. The only place that made me doubt its authority as the most beautiful square is the one in Santiago de Compostela. Its poise and its youthful air prohibit you from even thinking about its venerable age; instead, it looks as if it had been built the day before by someone who had lost their sense of time."

For believers and poets, the "Compostela" in Santiago's full name derives from the Latin for "starry field," in recognition of the sighting by Pelayo the hermit. Crass nay-sayers and other intellectuals incline toward *compostela* being a corruption of *compostum,* Latin for burying ground. Pope Urban II probably opted for the first version when, late in the 11th century, as it was becoming a major destination for pilgrims, he gave the city an official name, Santiago de Compostela.

ARRIVING IN SANTIAGO

Known as "the Jerusalem of the West," Santiago de Compostela now stands as an exquisite, living monument—with a few worldly delights as well. You'll spend most of your time in the old town, but you'll have to pass through the new town to get to it. The new part of Santiago is like any modern city, with department stores, restaurants, and traffic problems. But when you arrive at the cathedral plaza in the heart of the old town, you'll understand the reason for your pilgrimage.

Santiago is about 600 km (370 miles) northwest of Madrid. A Coruña, capital of Galicia, is 73 km (45 miles) due north on the *autopista* A 9. Lugo is a dogleg east and north, 105 km (65 miles), on C 547 and N 640.

As you are driving into Santiago, look for the black-and-white parador signs. They will, of course, disappear just when you need them most, in which case, you will switch to the *catedral* signs. Santiago's two greatest monuments, the cathedral and the Hostal de los Reyes Católicos, occupy high ground, so think up. When you arrive at the plaza, your instincts tell you not to drive up to the front of the cathedral or the *hostal,* but, in fact, you can: Park, register, and your car goes to a garage halfway down the slope on the west side of the parador.

The Plaza de Obradoiro

The cathedral's huge square, Plaza de Obradoiro, also known as the Plaza de España or the Gran Plaza del Hospital, is flanked on all four sides by magnificent buildings. On its south side is the **Colegio de San Jerónimo**, which now houses the Institute of Galician Studies and the university rectory. The building dates from the 17th century, but its handsome Romanesque-style door is from 1490. The west side of the square houses the former **Palacio de Rajoy**. Its striking 18th-century Neoclassical façade, carved by sculptors José Gambino and José Antonio Ferreiro (both also contributed to Santiago's church of San Martín Pinario), depicts the battle of Clavijo, the legendary ninth-century clash between Christian and Moor at which Saint James made his famous appearance. The building itself was designed by the French architect Charles Lemaur, and is decidedly French-looking. The square's north side is occupied by the luxurious Hostal de los Reyes Católicos (more on this below).

The Cathedral of Santiago

You won't even notice the plaza's other buildings at first, for on the east side of the square is the 17th- and 18th-century wildly Baroque façade of the cathedral of Santiago, with its twin towers rising almost as high as the sky. The stunning building shines gold in the afternoon sun (the plaza's name, *obradoiro,* which means "work of gold," refers to the front of the cathedral). This phenomenon is caused by a certain type of lichen, built up over several centuries, reflecting the setting sun.

Although there is some Plateresque work on the church's outer façade, it is noteworthy how little this style is used in Galicia as a whole (a magnificent exception is the portal of the Hostal de los Reyes Católicos, discussed below). The Gallegos are rugged individualists, and their stonecutters held stubbornly to the styles they knew. Throughout the Galician countryside, Romanesque architecture dominates in the region's 500 or so churches. The Plateresque style of architecture and ornament was considered alien to the local stonecutters.

The cathedral's **Pórtico de la Gloria** is what the pilgrims of the Middle Ages saw first, and it is no exaggeration to say that it is one of the greatest achievements in Romanesque sculpture in the world. The *pórtico,* executed from 1168 to 1188 by a master known only as Mateo, is actually three doorways, adorned with handsome statues carved out of stone. The faces are those of human beings who actually lived at the time. Below the left tympanum is a carving of the prophet Daniel—don't miss his famous smile. On the central pillar you'll notice five indentations; your fingers will fit perfectly into them. This is where weary pilgrims first rested their hands after their arduous journey. There's something about putting your hand in the same place where Saint Francis laid his that sets the spine tingling. At the foot of the columns is Mateo's self-portrait, kneeling and facing the sepulcher, pointing to himself, perhaps indicating his responsibility for the work you're viewing. Pilgrims knock their heads three times against his upon entering, in the hope of gaining some of his wisdom.

The church's centerpiece is the statue of a seated Saint James atop the main altar at the head of the central nave. It can be reached from behind by a staircase on either side—pilgrims go up the stairs for a moment, probably all too brief, to embrace the figure from the rear. Beneath the retable is a narrow passageway that leads down a few steps to the crypt built into the foundation in the ninth-century church that preceded the cathedral. Here the pilgrim pauses for a moment before the small, dimly lit crypt with its reliquary, a silver casket containing the remains of the saint and his disciples.

The building's high-vaulted interior creates an other-worldly feel. A gigantic censer called a *botafumeiro* hangs over the transept in front of the altar. On holidays it scents the entire church; eight men are required to swing it. The *botafumeiro* was built on such a scale in an attempt to stifle the stench rising from a cathedral filled with pilgrims just in from seven months on the *camino*. (Apparently the dip at Lavacolla didn't quite do the trick.)

The chapels lining the aisles are adorned with rich altars, tombs of Spanish kings, and various works of art. The **reliquary chapel**, located off the right nave just inside the cathedral and entered through a Plateresque door, contains valuable busts, urns, and statues. The **treasury**, entered the same way but a bit farther toward the church's center, contains gold, silver, and bronze crucifixes from various centuries, statues of Saint James, and jewelry. Don't miss the bust of Santiago Alfeo, from the 14th century, encrusted with semiprecious stones, cameos, and engravings. The ornate, silver four-foot-high processional monstrance, dating from 1546, is carried through the streets during Holy Week.

Upstairs, in the *sala capitular* (chapter house), you'll find Flemish tapestries from the 17th century and a dozen from the 19th century that were based on Goya cartoons of Spanish life in the late 18th century. The view from the balcony here is matchless: A glimpse of the square below, the town's spires, and the impressive skyline will stay in your memory—but take your camera anyway. Downstairs is the cloister, built in a mixture of Renaissance and Gothic styles, and diagonally across is the entrance to the library, where the *botafumeiro* is displayed when it is not hanging in the church.

When you leave the cathedral you'll find endless pleasure in exploring its other façades and doors. Make sure to see the **Puerta de las Platerías**, a handsome, double-arched Romanesque doorway, and note the carvings of King David and the creation of Adam and Eve. Four scenes from Christ's Passion decorate the right tympanum; the left, showing the Temptation and the Woman Taken in Adultery, dates from around 1100.

The squares surrounding the cathedral, too, are ancient and picturesque. Leave yourself more than a couple of hours just to see the cathedral and its surroundings, although you will probably return to it often during your stay.

Hostal de los Reyes Católicos

Churches, sanctuaries, inns, and hospitals sprang up along the pilgrims' route to Santiago during the Middle Ages. Many of them, like the ► **Hostal de los Reyes Católicos**, exist today in other forms, to welcome the modern-day traveller. The Hostal de los Reyes Católicos was built early in the 16th century by the Reyes Católicos, Isabella and Ferdinand, to lodge weary pilgrims. Later it served as a hospital for the monarchs and the nobility. Now it is an exquisite, finely furnished hotel, with four inner courtyards (named for Matthew, Mark, Luke, and John) and its own chapel, in which concerts and exhibitions are held. The building is a combination of Late Gothic, Renaissance, and Baroque. The Plateresque entrance, prodigiously carved and crowned by a frieze of figures, contrasts with the bare stone walls of the rest of the façade.

Stay at this magnificent hotel, which is right on the Plaza de Obradoiro, if you possibly can. Double rooms are currently about 23,000 pesetas a night during high season, and 16,000 off season, which isn't too bad, considering what you get here vis-à-vis similarly priced rooms in London, Paris, or New York. In any event, a stay here is worth saving up for. If you are planning to visit in July, you might have to book a year ahead, because Saint James's Day is July 25, and the celebrations, including fireworks in the square, normally bring thousands of pilgrims as well as just plain tourists. At other times of the year, however, there are usually vacancies. (See Staying and Dining in Santiago, below, if you are unable to get a room at the Hostal de los Reyes Católicos.)

The lobby of the Hostal de los Reyes Católicos is filled with antiques, as are some of the bedrooms. Paintings decorate the hallways and rooms, which, all recently refurbished, are dignified and quiet. Many rooms have casement windows that open onto a courtyard. Walking through the courtyards of Matthew, Mark, Luke, and John in the cool of early morning, when it is utterly quiet except for the sound of birds and the muted tinkle of fountains, is a wonderful way to start the day.

There are two restaurants in the hotel, one casual, the other superb if pricey. The latter has vaulted ceilings and looks medieval, and one of its specialties is the Spanish version of *coquille Saint Jacques,* which got its name from the pilgrim's symbol, the scallop shell. The hotel also has a very pleasant bar in its antiques-filled lobby/living room. Patrons sit on fine couches and chairs and wait for their table in one of the hotel's two restaurants, or just enjoy a drink before seeking dinner elsewhere.

Don't miss the hotel's buffet-style breakfast. The table is a true groaning board: fruit, fish, cheese (many varieties available only within the region), homemade peasant breads, cereal, eggs, pancakes, and on and on—and above all, the heavenly, full-roasted Spanish coffee with steamed cream.

The place to end a day or evening in Santiago is on the

stone bench that spans the front of the Hostal de los Reyes Católicos. During the day the Plaza del Obradoiro is a very lively place—children running around playing children's games, teachers trying to hold a rehearsal for some sort of event, people crawling all over the cathedral with their video cameras, and university students, probably with hangovers, running for class. Once in a while, one or two weary and dirty people appear carrying long staves, usually wearing a scallop shell on a leather thong. They stand and look at the front of the huge façade for a long time; then they move inside. There's something, a lot of things, going on here all day long.

At night, though, it is quiet. Behind the stone bench looms the dark bulk of the *hostal*. The front of the cathedral is lighted. A car pulls up and two parents and their kids scramble out, and they all look up at the big building without saying anything. Then they all get back in the car and drive off. Sometimes the moon is out, full, over the south tower. Sometimes rain begins to fall softly.

Around in Santiago

THE CATHEDRAL AREA

The rear of the cathedral faces Plaza de la Quintana; farther east is the **Iglesia de San Félix de Solovio** (in Galician, "Félix" is "Fiz"), which dates back to the sixth century. It was rebuilt in the twelfth, and the Romanesque façade remains. This church and the **Monasterio de San Pelayo de Antealtares** share an ancient wall that closes off one side of the Plaza de la Quintana.

The huge **Monasterio de San Martín Pinario**, just to the north, overlooks the Plaza de la Immaculada. It was founded in 899 by Benedictine monks and for many hundreds of years was the most powerful monastery in Galicia, with 39 other priorates dependent on it; it is now a seminary. The main altar is impressive, a Late Baroque creation by the 18th-century architects who designed the façade of the cathedral. Sculptors Gambino and Ferreiro contributed here as well, depicting the life of San Martín. There are three cloisters and a handsome Baroque fountain in the monastery.

The **Convento de San Francisco**, which is said to have been founded by Saint Francis of Assisi when he came to Santiago on his pilgrimage in 1214, is located a long block north of the cathedral (to the left as you face the cathedral). The front courtyard of the monastery's church has a 20th-century statue of Saint Francis, the work of Francisco Asdrey, a native of Santiago. The contrast—seven centuries—is fascinating.

SANTA MARIA DEL SAR

Less than a mile outside Santiago de Compostela, in the middle of a very green valley on the banks of the Río Sar, is the 12th-century **Iglesia Colegiata de Santa María del Sar**. Although the church seems to be always closed, the sacristan lives in the house behind the church, and if you look pious, interested, or generous enough he'll let you in. The columns of this tiny Romanesque jewel are visibly slanted, and the effect is eerie. There's an ongoing debate as to whether shifts in the soil over the centuries have caused the peculiar angle or whether the columns were constructed that way. The lovely cloister has carvings that are by either master Mateo (the cathedral's stone carver) or one of his students.

The church can be reached by highway N 525, the city perimeter road, also known as the Circunvalación and as Avenida Juan 23 (Xöan 23, in Galician). Heading south on the east side of the city, you will see a marker for Santa María del Sar, with a right-hand arrow, followed by an exit for a local street: *Don't* take that one; take the next, a *very* sudden sharp right turn, then loop back underneath the Circunvalación and you'll find yourself heading eastbound across the Río Sar. (Hey, you could walk, you know.) The church will be on your right.

SHOPPING IN THE OLD TOWN

You don't have to worry about getting lost in the old quarter of Santiago, which is centered on the cathedral and is quite compact. Just let yourself wander in and out of the attractive, cobblestoned, arcaded maze of jet (petrified coal) jewelers, *tascas* (taverns), silversmiths, and cheese, souvenir, and *aguardiente* shops. Sooner or later you'll come upon a familiar fountain, plaza, or church. Try the area south of the cathedral plaza along **Rúa del Villar** and **Rúa Nueva** (also called Nova); *rúa* is Galician for "street." Wicker *mimbre* (baskets), wicker chairs, and woven handbags made by local craftspeople can be found at **Cantón del Toral 2**, at the foot of Rúa Nueva. The large bookstore a couple of doors away occasionally has English-language publications including the *International Herald-Tribune*. **Pepecillo**, the tailor at Rúa Nueva 28, has exotic ties and shirts. Señor Pepecillo will make to your measure a traditional Spanish cloak (*capa*) for about 75,000 pesetas. **Sargadelos**, Rúa Nueva 16, sells designer ceramics and ceramic art.

La tuna should be in full stroll by now. *La tuna* refers to the groups of student minstrels in red-slashed, black Renaissance velvet who walk about the old quarter playing mandolins and singing the songs of old Spain. They seem to come equipped with their own groupies.

On the other side of the cathedral, running east from the

Plaza de la Inmaculada, is Calle Azabachería. *Azabache* is Spanish for jet, and smiths on Calle Azabachería have been selling objects crafted from jet to visitors since the Middle Ages. **Regueria**, at number 9, has a good selection of jet and silver jewelry and small ceramics as well; **Obradoiro**, number 12, has jet in silver settings, ceramics, and carved stone figures about 30 inches high inspired by ancient church artifacts. There's a cheerful *señora* with a shop at Calle Azabachería 17, who is very informative about such *digestivos* as *aguardiente, oñejo de hierbas,* and *aguardiente blanco,* which are stored in various ceramic jugs (chill them in a freezer before serving). She'll demonstrate *aguardiente*'s properties as a hand lotion, too. She also sells *tarta de Santiago* (a sweet cake) and very good Galician *quesos* (cheeses), in assorted forms, including the ever-popular breast shape.

Staying, Dining, and Nightlife in Santiago

The Hostal de los Reyes Católicos (see above) is the only place you should consider staying in Santiago de Compostela if you want to see the best of this town. If you don't reserve there, for whatever reason, try the moderately priced ▶ **Hotel Compostela**, Calle Hórreo 1, a five-minute walk to the cathedral. The ▶ **Hotel Araguaney**, Alfredo Brañas 5, is smaller but more polished than the Compostela and is about a ten-minute walk south from the cathedral. Both are good hotels central to the goings on.

Two of the city's finest restaurants can be found on Rúa Nueva: **Retablo**, at number 13, and **Don Gaiferos**, at number 23. Don Gaiferos, housed in a 15th-century building with stone walls and high, vaulted ceilings, specializes in seafood and is the more stylish of the two (although dress is casual). For Retablo, Tel: (9-81) 56-59-50; for Don Gaiferos, Tel: (9-81) 58-38-94. Just a street away is **El Franco**, Calle Franco 28, a typical city *tasca* with plenty of local color.

The best restaurant in town is **Casa Vilas**, Avenida de Rosalía de Castro 88; Tel: (9-81) 59-10-00 (closed Sundays). (They also own **Anexo Vilas**, Avenida de Villagarcía 21; closed Mondays). Casa Vilas is a 20- or 25-minute walk west from the cathedral area. Walk through the park along the popular **Paseo de la Herradura**, a perfect lookout point for the town. In the park is a statue of the late-19th-century poet Rosalía de Castro, a native of Galicia, whose works focus on human suffering and on such issues as the departure of many Gallegos for the New World at the end of the last century. If you catch a glimpse of the city from the Herradura, you'll realize what a showplace it is. As the sun catches on the sandstone spires, it seems as if the city is ablaze. Santiago is a city with a spirit and a soul.

Casa Vilas is one of those places whose excellence is apparent from the moment you enter. The restaurant and the people working there exude a feeling of relaxed self-confidence. It may seem a mite pricey, depending on how you feel about *percebes* (goose barnacles) at 12,000 pesetas a serving. *Mejillones* (mussels), however, are compliments of the house. The *pulpo feria,* chunks of octopus in piquant pimiento sauce, is delicious; other dishes on the menu are *merluza a la gallega* (Galician hake), *bacalao a la gallega* (codfish Galician style), *lacón con grelos* (pork shoulder with turnip greens, sausage, and potatoes, simmered in water), *perdiz estofado* (stewed partridge), and *conejo al ajillo* (rabbit with garlic). If you're travelling about Galicia, you may want to ask your waiter for the booklet *Amigos de la Cocina Gallega,* an alliance of restaurants in the same league as Casa Vilas.

Want to dance off dinner? Head for the Hotel Peregrino, also on Avenida de Rosalía de Castro, whose disco, **Black,** is the hippest in town, popular with university students; Tel: (9-81) 52-18-50. If you aren't up to getting down try **Duque,** Santiago de Chile 13–15, where they slow things down a bit. If you've been wondering where else the students hang out, and can't stand not knowing, try **Rúa de Raiña,** at the southern end of the cathedral plaza and around the corner. *La tuna,* out of uniform, is sure to be in full cry here. Students are rolling in and out (sometimes literally) of bars and thronging the street. And so they will be, until the wee small hours of the morning.

WESTERN GALICIA

If you'd like to explore farther into this lush region, a good way to do it is to head north to A Coruña, on the Atlantic coast, and then circle counterclockwise along the coast, taking in the famous *rías,* down to Pontevedra and the islands, and following this with a last look at the region at Túy and La Guardia—just across the border from Portugal.

Along the way you'll notice squat, odd-looking structures, known as *horreos* or *cabazas,* that serve as granaries. They invariably have a cross on top, and some of them also have pyramids or various symbols of luck and fertility. These buildings are peculiar to Galicia. No one quite knows their origin or their original purpose. For the last few hundred years or so they have been used to store wheat and corn. Some experts believe that the *horreos* were first built by

Celts as dwelling places, becoming storehouses for grain as their inhabitants moved into more comfortable dwellings. In Orense province in southern Galicia the granaries are always rectangular and raised on stilts four feet off the ground. These are known as *cabeceiros;* many believe that they were built by the Swabians (or Suevi), a Germanic migratory tribe that briefly controlled Galicia (as well as northern Portugal) after the Romans.

Some *horreos* are primitive. Others, located on the acreage of *pazos* (houses of noblemen), are grand enough to house a family of four. In the province of Lugo the granaries are always covered with slate; around Santiago they are covered with granite rubble. When you see them you will know you are definitely in Galicia.

A Coruña

The most visible attraction of this friendly, pretty port city situated around a giant marina is the stone lighthouse known as **Torre de Hércules** (Tower of Hercules). A Coruña, in the very northwestern corner of Spain (about 70 km/42 miles north of Santiago de Compostela on either the N 550 or A 9/E 1), dates back to the second century, and the lighthouse survives from that era, the only Roman lighthouse still on active duty. (The upper part of the lighthouse, the tower, is not Roman, and is said to have been built by a Portuguese architect. It was restored in the 1790s.) The entire structure is more than 300 feet high; its beacon can be seen 40 miles out to sea. There was a giant oil spill off the coast here in late 1992.

This is a quaint, peaceful town, with a lovely old quarter. Begin by walking along the Avenida de la Marina past the anchored fishing boats. Stoneworkers were as prevalent in old Galicia as whalers were in Melville's New England, and you'll see their handiwork in the old arcade that still stands here. There's a local fish auction at the fishermen's market, but you have to arrive early in the morning to get its full impact. Jutting out into the harbor from the **Jardín de San Carlos** is an 18th-century fort, the **Castillo de San Antón**, which houses an archaeological museum.

When you're hungry, stop at the fanciest restaurant (and inn, if you're thinking of staying) in town: ▶ **Hotel Atlántico**, located at Jardines de Méndez Núñez 2. Make sure to get a seat looking out over the marina. Try the crêpes or any of the seafood.

Excursions from A Coruña

Consider taking a drive along the coast northeast of A Coruña to see some of Galicia's famous *rías*, firths (or

estuaries) cutting deep into the land. The northern *rías,* the
Rías Altas, are located on a fragment of coast ominously
nicknamed Costa da Morte (Coast of Death). But don't be
put off. It's your basic Galician flare for the mystical at work
here. These waters are never dangerous, just rougher than
those in the south. The towns here are quiet, not resorts,
with single-dwelling houses, each with a garden and tilled
lands. These beaches are much less populated than those in
the south (discussed below), and are good for nice solitary
walks.

South from Santiago

A little village south of Santiago de Compostela holds yet
another chapter in the story of Saint James, the Apostle who
carried Christ's doctrine to Spain. In the Book of Isaiah, Saint
Jerome wrote that one Apostle went to India, another to
Greece, and a third, James, to Spain. It was upon his return
to Jerusalem that James was executed by Herod Agrippa in
A.D. 44. It is believed that his disciples, Teodoro and
Atanasio, returned the body of James to Spain in a rudder-
less stone boat that found its way up an inland waterway
from the sea. (Nobody knows how the martyr's remains
were gotten to the field miles away to the north where
Pelayo the hermit, 800 years later, marveled at a brilliant
star.)

The inland waterway that bore the stone boat was the Río
Sar, and the boat finally stopped at **Padrón**, 20 km (12 miles)
south of Santiago on A 9 or N 550. A small 16th-century
church next to an old bridge over the Sar marks the boat's
destination. You can stop at Padrón on your way to Pontevedra, or on your way to the beaches of the Rías Bajas
(Padrón is at the head of the Ría de Arousa). At the Padrón
exit from the A 9, turn right on N 550 and continue to the
rotunda at the entrance to the town. Turn right at the sandy
plaza lined by huge oaks to the church at the end of the
plaza.

Behind folding doors that front the lower half of the altar
is the stone pier that moored the stone boat. The pier has an
inscription, *no ori eses dsp,* the meaning of which remains
unclear. The young priest of the church will open the altar
panel and tell you the entire story, in Spanish, of the stone
boat. For luck, you can also toss a coin into the cup-like
depression in the top of the pier.

If the priest is not in the church, ask the woman, or her
husband, at the Boga Boga café across the street to find
him. The priest, who is young and skinny, will come running because he doesn't get many opportunities to tell his

story and he really appreciates the accompanying tip and a chance to sell postcards of the pier.

Pontevedra

Pontevedra is about 57 km (35 miles) south of Santiago at the head of the Ría de Pontevedra on the Atlantic coast. A city of about 55,000, Pontevedra was once a major port but its harbor silted up, as have the harbors of many of the other towns on the *rías,* and the city fell on hard times until a fairly recent recovery as an industrial and mining center. The rise in success has brought a rise in smog, with an accompanying odor that on windless days can be quite offensive. Having said that, there are some interesting places to visit in Pontevedra, and a very nice parador.

THE OLD TOWN

Pontevedra's compact *zona antigua* (old town) is full of charm, very walkable (no map needed), and filled with old mansions sporting coats of arms.

The **Basílica Menor de Santa María**, a national monument also called the Sailor's Basilica, is located in the section where fishermen lived, looking out over the Ría de Pontevedra. Built in the 16th century by the sailors' guild, the basilica boasts a stunning Plateresque door by Cornelius de Holanda, handsome Baroque altars, and finely sculpted statues.

The **Museo Provincial**, housed in two Baroque buildings on the Plaza de Leña, has a large collection of prehistoric gold and siver work, exhibits about local history, and paintings from Spain's Golden Age to the present. Just south of the museum is the **Iglesia de San Francisco**, a 13th-century building with a fine rose window and interesting tombs in front of the apse. The **Iglesia de la Peregrina**, a bizarre round building with odd-looking towers is south of San Francisco. Within is the statue of the town's patroness, the Virgen Peregrina. A short walk west are the ruins of the convent and church of **Santo Domingo**, a highly evocative shell with a spooky collection of stone crosses, prehistoric objects, and Gothic crypts.

STAYING AND DINING IN PONTEVEDRA

The ▶ **Parador Casa de Barón**, Calle Maceda, occupies an elegant 18th-century manor house in the center of the old part of town. It fits very nicely into the essentially unaltered antiquity of the old quarter without skipping any amenities. For lunch or dinner, try **O Merlo**, Calle Santa María 4, also in the old quarter; Tel: (9-86) 84-43-43.

Excursions from Pontevedra

THE RIAS BAJAS

Excursions along the coast are a big draw for visitors to this area. The *rías* of Galicia's southwestern coast, the Rías Bajas, have beautiful, warm beaches, many of which are protected by islands, such as Arousa. Although the waters are calm, the *rías* also make for some interesting experiences sunbathing. When you stretch out at noon, say, you have no way of knowing how high the tide will have risen by 2:00 P.M.—so keep your eye on the water level, and protect your camera in case you have to wade back to your car. Four *rías* make up the Rías Bajas: Ría de Muros y Noia, just west of Santiago; Ría de Arousa, to its south; Ría de Pontevedra; and Ría de Vigo.

The *rías* also make for lovely, scenic drives. Along the north shore of **Ría de Muros y Noia**, for instance, there is a succession of pretty coves and beaches, small villages with balconies of hanging flowers, and, in the late afternoon, dramatic light from skies that are half pale blue, half dark violet. Beaches and seaside towns usually have a sophisticated feel; there's a pleasant tug here between that urbane sophistication and the farmer in rough clothes trying to get his dairy cows out of a field of yellow *tujo* and purple *uce*. *Uce* resembles sagebrush; *tujo* is Old World gorse, a spiny shrub with a tough, thick trunk difficult to cut through or uproot that can reach heights of eight feet. It's a problem for the farmer, but lucky us, it provides a panorama of yellow and purple and splashes of green, spread across the hillsides of the *ría* under a violet sky.

ISLA DE AROUSA

The Isla de Arousa, serviced by frequent ferry service from Vilanova (also called Villanueva), northwest of Pontevedra, has some fine, sheltered beaches. It's the largest island in Galicia and close to the mainland beaches. Most of its 5,000 inhabitants are fishermen, and the sportfishing is excellent here.

ISLA DE LA TOJA

If all-in-one resorts are to your liking, the Isla de la Toja (A Toxa) is recommended. It's up the coast from Pontevedra, just south of the Isla de Arousa. If you take C 550 you'll pass the Neoclassical monastery of San Juan de Poio, a series of beaches including the up-and-coming summer resorts of Sangenjo (Sanxento in Galician—all the signs will read that way) and El Grove. From El Grove there's a bridge to La Toja.

La Toja is an island resort paradise: There are golf, tennis, swimming, a spa, a casino, exquisite landscaping, fine dining, and plenty of very modern atmosphere. Although there are other places to stay on the island, if you're going to do it, do it right and stay at the ▶ **Gran Hotel de la Toja**.

SOUTH TO PORTUGAL
Finally, we end our coverage of Galicia with three towns near the Spanish-Portuguese border. If your travels on C 550 should take you south along the coast from Pontevedra rather than north, you'll come to the mouth of the Río Miño (Minho in Portuguese) and the town of **La Guardia**, a typical small fishing port sitting practically in the Atlantic. A kilometer south is **Monte Tecla**, which, along with phenomenal views, offers a small **museum** with fascinating pre-Roman relics. Parts of walls, huts, possible cooking implements, and other odds and ends trace the history of Galicia from the year 2000 B.C. onward.

To the northeast of La Guardia, along the Miño, is **Túy** (Tui), right on the Portuguese border; it is here that you cross the 1,000-foot-long bridge into Portugal (Valença). Túy has an overwhelming fortress-like, primitive **cathedral** dating from the 11th to the 13th centuries. The carvings on the choir stalls are fascinating, and the cloister, from the 15th century, is nicely atmospheric. Two other churches here, Santo Domingo and San Bartolomé, have been declared national monuments.

And the next thing you know, you're in Portugal.

GETTING AROUND
Travel within Asturias and Galicia is most easily done by automobile. There is a good network of roads, from the *autopistas* that link Santiago de Compostela with A Coruña and Oviedo with Gijón to the charming, winding roads of the coastal regions.

Santiago de Compostela is served by a major airport, 11 km (7 miles) east on C 547. There are many domestic flights to Santiago, as well as international service from London and other European cities. Trains from Madrid to Santiago take up to 12 hours. There's frequent and speedy train service between Santiago and A Coruña, only about an hour away.

In Asturias the hub is Oviedo, with train service to Madrid (seven to eight hours), Barcelona (thirteen hours), and, most conveniently, frequent service to León, which takes two to three hours.

For information on the excursion train El Transcantábrico, and on fishing and hunting in the Cordillera Cantábrica, consult the Getting Around section of the Cantabria chapter.

ACCOMMODATIONS REFERENCE

The hotel rates listed below are projected rates for 1994, for double room, double occupancy, in pesetas. We strongly recommend that you confirm the price when making reservations.

When dialing telephone numbers in Spain from outside the country, drop the 9 in the area code.

► **Casa Don Julián. Nisérias,** 33578 Llanes. Tel: (9-8) 541-4179. 6,000 pts.

► **Gran Hotel España.** Calle Jovellanos 2, 33003 **Oviedo.** Tel: (9-8) 522-0596; Fax: 522-0596. 15,800 pts.

► **Gran Hotel Lugo.** Avenida Ramón Ferreiro 21, 27002 **Lugo.** Tel: (9-82) 22-41-52; Fax: 24-16-60. 13,500 pts.

► **Gran Hotel de la Toja. Isla de la Toja,** 36991 Pontevedra. Tel: (9-86) 73-00-25; Fax: 73-12-01. 23,000 pts.

► **Hostal de los Reyes Católicos.** Plaza de España 1, 15705 **Santiago de Compostela.** Tel: (9-81) 58-22-00; Fax: 56-30-94. 16,000–23,000 pts.

► **Hotel Araguaney.** Alfredo Brañas 5, 15701 **Santiago de Compostela.** Tel: (9-81) 59-59-00; Fax: 59-02-87. 22,000 pts.

► **Hotel Atlántico.** Jardines de Méndez Núñez 2, 15006 **A Coruña.** Tel: (9-81) 22-65-00; Fax: 20-10-71. 14,300 pts.

► **Hotel Báltico & Restaurant.** Paseo del Muelle 1, 33700 **Luarca.** Tel: (9-8) 564-0991. 10,000 pts.

► **Hotel Compostela.** Calle Hórreo 1, 15702 **Santiago de Compostela.** Tel: (9-81) 58-57-00; Fax: 56-32-69. 13,000 pts.

► **Hotel Gayoso.** Paseo de Gómez 3, 33700 **Luarca.** Tel: (9-8) 564-0050; Fax: 547-0271. 12,000 pts.

► **Hotel Picos de Europa.** 33554 **Arenas de Cabralés.** Tel: (9-8) 584-5491; Fax: 584-5495. 7,500–9,000 pts.

► **Hotel de la Reconquista.** Gil de Jaz 16, 33004 **Oviedo.** Tel: (9-8) 524-1100; Fax: 524-1166. 23,500 pts.

► **Hotel la Rectoral.** Calle La Villa, 33775 **Taramundi.** Tel: (9-8) 564-6760; Fax: 564-6777. 12,500 pts.

► **Parador Casa de Barón.** Calle Maceda, 36002 **Pontevedra.** Tel: (9-86) 85-58-00; Fax: 85-21-95. 8,500–11,000 pts.

► **Parador Molino Viejo.** Parque Isabel la Católica, 33204 **Gijón.** Tel: (9-8) 537-0511; Fax: 537-0233. 12,000 pts.

► **Parador de Ribadeo.** Calle Amador Fernández, 27700 **Ribadeo.** Tel: (9-82) 11-08-25; Fax: 11-03-46. 11,000 pts.

► **Príncipe de Asturias.** Calle Manso 2, 33203 **Gijón.** Tel: (9-8) 536-7111; Fax: 533-4741. 14,000 pts.

CANTABRIA

By Mike Jackson
with Robert Levine

On maps Cantabria looks like a tight fit, wedged in along the north coast of Spain between Asturias to the west and the Basque Country to the east. But whatever Cantabria may be denied in area it makes up for in height, living up to its alter ego (and other name), La Montaña. The Cordillera Cantábrica is a swath of high-mountain wilderness, one of the few remaining in Europe—and it is just a couple hours' drive from some of the best beaches in Europe.

The "Spanish character" is supposed to be at its most pure on the northern side of the Cordillera Cantábrica, because the Moors essentially failed to occupy this area. Their lack of drive has been attributed by some to that of a desert people at odds with a northern seacoast climate. Perhaps the climate was to blame in part, but that overlooks just how formidable it was to travel in and out of Cantabria before the 19th century brought in the railroad. Even today the drive north along, say, N 621 into Cantabria from León provides vivid evidence of La Montaña's tenacity, as you drop dramatically down the Sierra Collaín into the Valle de Cereceda (this is a wonderful, accessible mountain drive with one incredible vista after another). Cantabria was also little threatened by seaborne invasion by the Moors (or the Romans, never much of a factor here), given the fundamentally rockbound coastline relieved only by a few golden strands.

Isolation produces insulation. Villages, customs, churches are very much now as they have been for hundreds of years, except along the north coast, where there is frenetic development in the quest to capture the *mariposa de playa* (beach butterfly). Santander, on the north coast, is both center of industry and capital of the province; inland, rains generated by the Atlantic produce lush pastures ideally suited for grazing dairy cows, of which there is one for nearly every man, woman, and child in the province. (This makes it

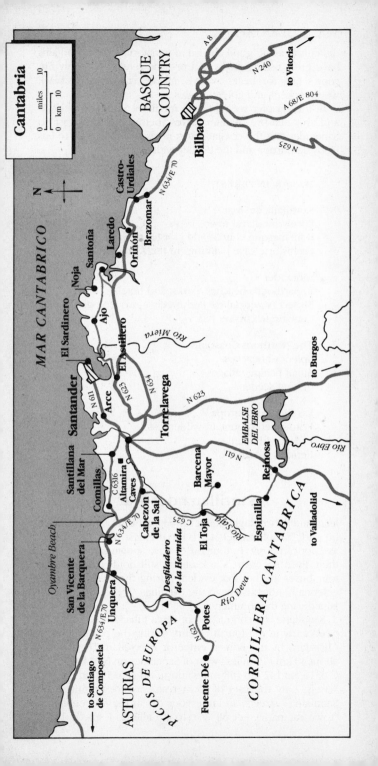

difficult to avoid good cheese in Cantabria.) The mountains have great fishing rivers and provide refuge, probably Europe's last, for bears, wolves, grouse (*capercaille*), black woodpeckers, and golden eagles.

In this chapter we start with medieval Santillana del Mar and the nearby Altamira Caves, before heading east to Santander and the coastal resort areas and then west to Los Picos de Europa and the border with Asturias.

MAJOR INTEREST

Santillana del Mar
Lovely medieval town
Romanesque church and cloister of Santa Juliana
Prehistoric cave paintings in the Altamira Caves

Santander
El Sardinero beaches, parks, and hotels
Museo Provincial de Prehistoria y Arqueología
Cantabrian cuisine

The Northern Coastline
Splendid beaches
Small fishing villages
Coastal scenery

Las Picos de Europa
Untouched mountain wilderness
La Hermida defile
Remote villages

Santillana del Mar

Jean-Paul Sartre might better have kept his mouth shut when he said, "Santillana del Mar is the prettiest village in Spain," as a lot of people in tour buses have shown up here since then. Even so, Sartre's assessment still holds true, and the tour buses are not that evident during the week—and are essentially nonexistent in the evenings. Try to avoid Santillana during the summer.

Santillana is a contraction of Santa Juliana, who was martyred early in the fourth century during the persecution of Christians by the Roman emperor Diocletian. The town is about 30 km (19 miles) west of Santander on N 611/EC 70 to C 6316, or 142 km (88 miles) north on N 623 from Burgos. Wisely, only the cars of town residents are permitted on Santillana's streets, so leave your car in the *aparcamiento* (town car park), left off C 6316 at Calle de Jesús de Tagle.

STAYING IN SANTILLANA DEL MAR

Most of Santillana's hotels are located near the car park. If you're staying at the ▶ **Parador Gil Blás**, Plaza de Ramón Pelayo 11, an excellent idea in any event, then turn right at the intersection of C 6316 and Calle de Jesús de Tagle, and left at the fork. Gil Blas is a hero of Spanish fiction whose birthplace was 18th-century Santillana del Mar, and his name is borrowed to good effect. The cobblestones of the street continue uninterrupted into the ground floor of a beautiful old country manor. After you register at the desk your car must be moved to the parking lot opposite the parador and up the slope in front of the *annexo*. The annex is pleasant enough but for the real thing request rooms in the main house. The ones at the rear overlook a patio that is especially lovely in early morning light.

On beyond the parador is ▶ **Hotel Altamira**, Calle Cantón 1, at the north end of the plaza. This 17th-century stone mansion is both charming and moderate in price, with 30 rooms, a garden, and a good restaurant. Another choice near the entrance to town is ▶ **Hotel Los Infantes**, Avenida Le Dorat 1, at the intersection of C 6316 and Calle de Jesús de Tagle. It has 30 rooms, is moderately priced, and feels rather like a ski lodge. Opposite the *aparcamiento,* spaced around the perimeter of the municipal park, are several small, moderately priced hotels: ▶ **Hotel Los Angeles**, 25 rooms; ▶ **Hotel Los Hidalgos**, 26 rooms (closed November to March); ▶ **Hotel Conde Duque**, 14 rooms; and ▶ **Hotel Las Cuevas**, 40 rooms. Finally, there is ▶ **Camping Santillana**, which has earned the government's "first category" rating, immediately west of the town limits on C 6316, through a large archway on the right. Camping Santillana is a large, modern facility with a bar and restaurant that caters to tents and caravans (RVs)—bring your own or rent one on the premises—and has a large swimming pool and is open year-round for nearby winter sports.

Many visitors headquarter in Santillana and make forays to the Altamira Caves (for which you must book three months in advance; see below), the beaches, Santander, and the mountains.

AROUND IN SANTILLANA

The whole town has the look of a history page (and has been declared a national monument). The houses, with their eaves and balconies, provide a glimpse into the past, and all the streets are cobblestone. You'll see coats of arms carved out of stone above many doorways, remnants of feudal times, when the town was a playground for the rich. Many wealthy Castilian and Basque families still own places in Santillana, the original money having come from fortunes made in the New World in the 16th and 17th centuries. (Santillana became particularly fashionable with the Madrid nobility when cholera swept the Basque Country resort town of San Sebastián a couple of hundred years ago.) Santillana is a small place, and the interesting sights can be seen in a day and on foot. We make a loose loop starting and ending at the *aparcamiento* on Calle de Jesús de Tagle.

At the corner, the 16th-century **Covento de Regina Coeli** houses the **Museo Diocesano**, featuring religious art. This former Dominican convent now belongs to the Clarisa order, and nuns still live here. The museum is sophisticated, well lit, and contains some real treasures: a 14th-century bronze cross, some naïve Romanesque sculptures, a Norman cross, and a 14th-century polychrome wooden sepulcher. Most of the objects, including paintings and sculptures, were collected throughout the Cantabrian region by the diocese from abandoned churches. These include the carved wood statues of saints from the 17th and 18th centuries along the walls of the attractive cloister. Note particularly, left of the entry, the 17th-century *Inmaculada* holding the *Infante* that is taller than the others, with more sophisticated carving. Save your ticket from the museum. It gains admittance to the Colegiata de Santa Juliana in the Plaza de las Arenas. Fresh cookies are available every day next door at the convent of Clarisa nuns.

On the other side of C 6316, Calle de Jesús de Tagle becomes Calle de Santo Domingo. You may have to wait for a passing herd of cows en route to pasture before you can cross. The farmers here have traditionally settled in town rather than in the countryside, living with their families between the animals stabled on the ground floor and the chickens kept on the roof. You're likely to come upon a herdsman watering his cows at an ancient stone trough next to a pool where townswomen wash their laundry.

At Calle de Santo Domingo 5 is the **Mesón de la Villa**, a good place for a light snack or breakfast (they serve hot chocolate and *churros*—those dangerously good fried dough sticks sprinkled with granulated sugar); in the summertime tables are set up in the garden. If you'd like to sample a local delicacy, *bizcocho,* a slightly eggier verson of angel food cake, the **Casa Quevedo**, at Calle del Río 8, is a good place to find it. And if you're looking for local souvenirs and gifts, the dishes and ashtrays made of glass enclosing crushed glass as a base are a good bet.

Stay right at the fork and onto Calle de la Carrera, which changes names several times between here and the Plaza de las Arenas. Houses and buildings along here span the 12th to the 18th century. Some of them are being renovated and are closed; the 15th-century **Torre de los Velarde**, at the corner of Calle de las Lindas (Street of the Beauties) is one. Others may be in good repair, but you have to hunt for (and tip) the caretaker in order to look around inside. One such is **La Casa de Leonor de la Vega**, whose handsome doorway stands under a pink Romanesque arch, the 15th-century house of the mother of the first marqués of Santillana, who was the town's first magistrate as well. Farther along, at Calle del Río 4, there is a huge stone *escudo* over the entry of the 18th-century **Casa de los Villa**. The size of the shield, which is way out of proportion to the size of the house, and the two huge knights supporting the Villa family coat-of-arms, gives the house its nickname, Casa de los Hombrones (House of the Giants). Its installation was an attempt by the Villa family to outdo the competition and smacks of 19th-century robber barons showing off new wealth.

PLAZA DE LAS ARENAS

Calle del Río opens onto Plaza de las Arenas. Mind the stone water trough on your left, and the German artist making extremely (perhaps obsessively) detailed renderings of the Colegiata de Santa Juliana in brown ink. He prices his work by the length of time it takes him, so at 400 pesetas per hour, the three-by-five-inch drawings cost 2,500 to 4,500 pesetas. The large sheets require 200 hours. Opposite the horse trough, next to the German artist, is a small food and gift shop, **Casa del Queso** (House of Cheese), at Calle del Río 3. Most of the shops in Santillana are at tour-bus souvenir level; Casa del Queso is an exception, a minimalist little shop with typical products of the region, such as honey liqueur, jars of *chorizo, queso de cabrales* (the region's pungent goat cheese) in olive oil, strawberries and nuts in honey, and boxes of Sanbars (if Sanbar ever decides to distribute in North America, they'll drive Twinkies to the wall). These treasures are wrapped in attractive packaging that is also practical for the suitcase.

Fanned around the perimeter of the square are several interesting sites: Where Calle del Río joins the plaza are the attached, and stylish, palaces of the Cossíos and Quevedos, two important Santillana families. Opposite, on the west side of the square, is the **Antigua Casa de los Abades**, the dwelling of the Archduchess Margaret of Austria.

Colegiata de Santa Juliana

On the north end of the square is the Colegiata de Santa Juliana, built in the 12th and 13th centuries. It is Romanesque in part, but the proportions seem askew, and it looks a bit like the result of a competition between two committees. Entry is around to the left side of the church and along a walkway bordering a pasture with grazing cows. Inside is an elaborate altar decked out in silver, created by a team of 17th-century Spanish, Mexican, and Flemish silversmiths. If you ask the sacristan (and tip him), he'll remove the silver panel and show you a rare Romanesque stone panel on the altar with vividly carved portraits of Matthew, Mark, Luke, and John. Santa Juliana's sepulcher, carved in the 15th century, is located in the central nave, and there is a statue of her in a niche above the church's entrance. The church is protected in front by a metal grate that looks like a piece of torture equipment but was actually designed to keep cows from wandering into the building.

The church opens onto a **cloister** whose garden is surrounded by columns that aren't uniform, as though each stoneworker had been encouraged to follow his muse in stone. Examine the columns to see the plantlike, abstract designs and carvings of such scenes as Christ and six Apostles, the Baptism, the decapitation of John the Baptist, and Daniel in the lion's den. There are also carvings of knights piercing demons and other nightmarish images.

Around Santa Juliana

Tucked away, east of the church, is the **Palacio de los Velarde**, the 15th-century Gothic palace of the marqués de Santillana. The marqués (1398–1458) was a soldier, politician, poet, and writer of the Spanish Renaissance who was greatly influenced by Dante, and the palace is the very soul of Spanish-Italian elegance.

Near the marqués's palace is the open-front workshop of A. Hernández, **Muebles de Estilo Español** (furniture in the Spanish style), Plaza de las Arenas 10. The work goes on right before your eyes as raw wood is transformed, via paper patterns hanging on the wall, into the heavy, florid *estilo español*. On display are finished headboards, children's chairs, chests, and very ornately carved grandfather clock cases. Señor Hernández cares not, however, to have his picture taken while working.

Around the corner from the plaza on Calle de Racial, you'll witness how some residents of Santillana still mix farm and village life interchangeably. Those are the drying pelts of several *zorros* (foxes) nailed to the street wall. A bit of everything is going on here: little screened boxes of colorful birds in the pigeon loft on the wall, a crowing rooster, a mynah whistling and jeering. There is a small stand with a sign: *bizcochos y leche* (sponge cake and milk). Other nearby houses have open spaces beneath for sheltering cows. You'll see cattle being brought in from the fields in the evening to spend the night reclining in straw splendor.

PLAZA DE RAMON PELAYO

Just beyond is Plaza de Ramón Pelayo. At the entrance to the square, on the left, is the garden entrance to Hotel Altamira, whose restaurant is a good place for lunch or a snack. Across from the hotel is the handsome **Torre de Merino** (Magistrate's Tower), the judicial quarters of the first marqués of Santillana (whose mother's house is on Calle del Río, above). The magistrate served as the king's representative. In off hours, try the white button underneath a small metal hood on the door. If you're lucky the caretaker will be there to let you look around, for a small fee. The Torre de Merino was built at the start of the 14th century. In the 18th century a spacious residence was added. Set into the tower's walls are both narrow shooting windows and windows with arched tops dating to the early Middle Ages, when the towers were feudal houses. Later they were incorporated into new houses in which the servants lived on the lower floors and the lords on the upper levels.

Diagonally across the square from the Torre del Merino is a palace with an attached 16th-century tower that once belonged to the daughter of Queen Isabella II. Together the two buildings now house an art center, the **Santillana Foundation**. The buildings, recently renovated, are handsome, and the 16th-century patio is quiet and restful. Though the foundation is open all year, the summer season has the greatest number of exhibitions, mostly the work of local painters.

On the same side of the plaza, just beyond the art center, is the 18th-century *ayuntamiento* (town hall). Farther along is the local post office. Post mail through the drop in the window labelled *buzón*.

EVENING IN SANTILLANA

Back across the Plaza de Ramón Pelayo is the **Restaurant Castillo** for a *café* or a go at the slot machine or what-have-you. The Castillo is a long bar owned by a short man with the voice of one tall and large. In the evening the bar vibrates with infectious energy when the place is packed with townspeople cheering—and betting on—hot players at the tabletop *fútbol* game.

Next door is the parador, a good place to end a tour of the town and to have lunch or dinner or bed down for the night. The *aparcamiento* is straight on along the Plaza de Ramón Pelayo and down Calle de Santo Domingo.

Restaurant Los Blasones is also close by, and moderate in price. Turn left from the parador and left around the corner to Plaza de la Gándara. The menus for varying *prix-fixe,* four-course dinners are posted outside in several languages. An à la carte menu is also available. Inside is a place of dark wood and white tablecloths on several levels with very courteous, efficient service and good food. Try the *ensalada marisco* (seafood salad)—mostly shrimp, very fresh, with caviar sprinkled atop a creamy dressing. The energetic chef likes to make sure you're satisfied. Earlier, before the 9:00 P.M. post time, you'll see him standing in the doorway of Los Blasones, looking out with the expectant air of someone anticipating a pleasurable evening. Tel: (9-42) 81-80-70 or 84-02-07 (open from March to early December).

There can be about Santillana a wisp of the harlot. All day on weekends and through the summer the tour buses roar up and pour out the running suits, which flow through the souvenir shops like a fluorescent river. When the crowds have left, the shops have closed, and there's a light rain from a darkening sky cleansing the cobblestones and freshening the spirit, Sartre's "prettiest village in Spain" returns.

The Altamira Caves

In 1868 nine prehistoric caves in the Santillana area (just south of town) were identified, and five years later bona fide prehistoric paintings, probably from 12,000 B.C. but possibly twice that old, were found within. The most famous of these paintings is of a bison lying down, curled into the contour of the stone. This figure is so sophisticated that it made specialists consider whether or not all the artwork in the caves might be a hoax.

The ceilings of the caves are low, barely five feet high, and the figures are quite large, some over six feet. You'll find that the best way to view the polychrome paintings of animals is to lie on your back and look at the ceiling. There is just enough light and time to take a slow-speed, black-and-white picture, but you need permission to take photos, and it will cost you a few extra pesetas.

You must book *far* ahead to get a tour of the caves. Since fissures were discovered in the cave walls the number of visitors has been strictly limited. Write about three months ahead to Director, Centro de Investigación, Museo de Altamira, 39330 Santillana del Mar (Santander). Request permission to visit the caves, and tell them how many are in your party (no more than five are permitted) and the date of your visit. The tours start at 10:45 A.M. daily except holidays. If you haven't written, stop at the museum office; they keep a standby list in case there are cancellations. Note: The caves are closed from the first to the fifth of each month.

If you can't get into the Altamira Caves, you might visit the stalactite caves just 100 yards away where dripping ice formations have preserved cave drawings. They may not be as impressive as the Altamira paintings, but your chances of seeing them are far greater, and you need not make reservations. There are caves elsewhere in northern Spain, perhaps without the dramatic profusion of Altamira, but moving nonetheless—and no need to book ahead. See the Asturias and Galicia chapter for a description of the caves at Tito Bustillo, about 100 km (60 miles) to the west.

Santander

Charles V landed at Santander on his second trip to Spain, and Prince Charles (later Charles I) of England embarked for home from Santander after his visit to Madrid. Neither would recognize it today. On February 15, 1941, a fire fanned by the strong winds of a tornado destroyed more than 40 city blocks. The damaged area has been almost totally rebuilt, in line with reconstruction laws that stipulated buildings of no more than five stories. Seeing such a modern town sitting along the coastline where so much else is ancient is a very strange experience.

Santander, 395 km (237 miles) due north of Madrid, and 210 km (126 miles) west of San Sebastián, is the capital of the Cantabrian region. The city is situated on a peninsula that forms the western edge of the Bay of Santander and thrusts into the Mar Cantábrico. The principal attractions are located in the district of El Sardinero at the sea end of the city. **El Sardinero** is a necklace of beaches and hotels strung between prongs of the peninsula, and to get to its pleasures you have to drive all the way through this city of 180,000 people, and then all the way back out again, easier written than done. El Sardinero has handsome, huge beaches protected from the ocean, lovely parks, a casino, and several large beach-resort hotels. The district draws many Spanish tourists and is also popular with the French, who, come summer, show up in droves. But it *is* situated deep within an essentially unremarkable city that in turn is within an industrial belt. Don't even attempt to make the drive on a summer weekend. If you come at an off time, however, the setting will reveal why royalty once considered Santander the equal of San Sebastián among resort spas.

DRIVING INTO SANTANDER

Santander is reached from the south by A-67, a four-lane superhighway that connects from another good road, the east–west N 634/E 70. Follow the "Zona Marítima" signs (bear right), which avoid the worst of the central city and eventually bring you, after several kilometers (a couple of miles), to the **Península de la Magdalena**, on the eastern prong of the peninsula, fronted by the Playa de la Magdalena on the bay side. The opposite prong is covered by a municipal golf course—the **Campo del Golf**—and is tipped by a lighthouse at Cabo Menor (minor cape). In between are a few of the city's 13 beaches: Playa de la Concha and Primera and Segunda Playas. On the other side of Cabo Menor is Playa de Mataleñas, with the lighthouse at Cabo Mayor (major cape) beyond. Primera and Segunda, which become a single strip of sand at low tide, make up **El Sardinero**, the most popular and trendy of the beaches, with a handsome park to one side.

MIDTOWN SANTANDER
Most of the heritage of Santander having either been blown out to sea in 1941, or reduced to ashes in the subsequent firestorm (with, amazingly, no deaths), little antiquity is left to be appreciated. The **cathedral**, on Calle de Cádiz and Avenida de Alfonso XIII, near the bay at about the city's midpoint, was built in the 13th century and restorations were carried out from the 16th to the 18th centuries. Some of it miraculously survived the catastrophic fire, and the rest was restored between 1942 and 1955. The bare, rustic exterior and austere interior permit you to savor the architectural lines, both Romanesque and Gothic. The relics of San Emeterio, a third-century martyr, are preserved here.

Several blocks west, at Calle de Rubio 4, is the **Museo Municipal de Bellas Artes**, which includes the library bequeathed by the Spanish man of letters Marcelino Menéndez y Pelayo (who is buried in the cathedral). When he died in 1912 his library of some 40,000 volumes and original manuscripts of Spanish writers was given to the town. Pelayo memorabilia can also be found in his house, separated from the museum by a garden. The museum has four etchings by Goya from his bitterly realistic *Desastres de la Guerra* (Disasters of War) series, which was suppressed by Carlos IV.

PASEO DE PEREDA TO LA MAGDALENA
Over the bay, just past the cathedral, are the **Paseo de Pereda** and the Jardines de Pereda, with views of the marina and the bay. The beaches at Somo and El Puntal can be reached by ferries departing every 20 minutes from the Estación Marítima, the dock located alongside Calle de Antonio López near the intersection of Calle de Rodíguez. Estación Marítima is also the terminal for the Plymouth car ferry. There's room for a lot of Frenchmen on Somo beach, a long, flat finger of beige sand stretching over four miles. Both beaches are also accessible by land.

The Paseo de Pereda ends in the east at the Plaza Matias Montero. To the left along Calle Casimiro Sainz, at number 4, is the **Museo Provincial de Prehistoria y Arqueología**. The museum's collection contains objects as old as 15,000 years and is considered one of the most interesting of its kind in Europe. Note the cudgel, from nearby El Pendo cave, a clublike object made of antler carved with the figures of a deer and a horse.

Head back down to Plaza Matias Montero and then along the waterfront eastward to Avenida de la Reina Victoria, which, near the entrance to the Península de la Magdalena, wraps around onto the beachfront and El Sardinero. **Palacio de la Magdalena** is a royal palace built on the peninsula in 1912 by Queen Victoria Eugenia for her daughter, who was married to Alfonso XIII. The king and his English wife often summered here. In summer, classes in Hispanic subjects are taught in the old palace.

STAYING IN EL SARDINERO

The crossroads of El Sardinero is tiny Plaza de Italia, central to hotels, restaurants, the casino, and the beach. The lovely park across the street looks out upon the Mar Cantábrico and is a favorite *paseo* of Santandineros at the end of the work day. Overlooking park and beach is the Art Nouveau ("Modernist" in the Spanish lexicon) casino. Flanking the casino are several large, comfortable and relatively moderate hotels including ▶ **Hotel Rhin**, Avenida de la Reina Victoria 153, and ▶ **Hotel Sardinero**, Plaza de Italia 1. But the grandest of the grand is the ▶ **Hotel Real**, Paseo de Pérez Galdós 28, in the swank residential district near the entrance to La Magdalena. The Real (Royal) is now open year-round, with 126 rooms, some of which cost 32,000 pesetas each and every day. Costly, you bet, but the view of the bay from the terrace is unforgettable. El Sardinero is also the setting for a late-summer international festival of music, theater, and dance.

DINING AND NIGHTLIFE
IN SANTANDER

While in Santander, enjoy the marvelous Cantabrian cuisine, which tends to be a delectable mixture of the cuisines of the surrounding regions, with an emphasis on fresh seafood and desserts rich in eggs, butter, and cream. At the **Bar del Puerto**, Calle Hernán Cortés 63 (two streets inland from the Paseo de Pereda), diners can watch their dishes—ox cutlet with pimientos or clams with kidney beans, for instance—prepared on an open grill. Tel: (9-42) 21-30-01. **Rhin**, at Plaza de Italia 2, on the Primera Playa in El Sardinero, next to the casino, is another good (if pricey) bet. Their hake with scallops and cream of crab soup are recommended. Tel: (9-42) 27-30-34.

Some 12 km (7½ miles) southwest of the city (take highway N 611 to Torrelavega) is **El Molino,** on Carretera Central in Puente Arce. This restaurant weds nouvelle cuisine and traditional Cantabrian food, presenting such specialties as hake with lemon and saffron mousse, and sea bass with green pepper on grilled wild mushrooms. This is a good place to stop if you're headed out of Santander in the evening. Tel: (9-42) 57-50-55.

Santander's nightlife, attracting youthful enthusiasts, is active near the bay just west of Paseo de Pereda along Calle de Hernán Cortés and on tiny Calle Gómez Oreña.

To exit the city from El Sardinero, make the first left beyond Hotel Sardinero onto Avenida de los Castros (note the *salida de ciudad,* city exit, signs). Signs will eventually appear for the *aeropuerto* and Bilbao for eastern destinations, Burgos for southern and western.

The Northern Coastline

In several of the small towns east and west of Santander along the Cantabrian coast, with its 72 beaches, there is hot-footed development aimed at harvesting the European sun-seeker's pesetas. New hotels, restaurants, and condos, plus the renovation of existing buildings—particularly to the east—are springing up in search of the Euro- (and Yankee) dollar. The villages to the west have rather more charm and are somewhat less frenetic about development. Oddly, though, overall this stretch of resorts is little known to North American and British travellers.

EAST OF SANTANDER

Towns along the coast from Santander east to Castro-Urdiales cater to hundreds of thousands of vacationers when the European capitals empty in August. Serving this area is the much-improved, excellent N 634/E 70 along, or near, the coast from Bilbao to Torrelavega (south of Santander). Regrettably, most of the truck drivers south of Paris seem to have decided to make it their own. For the vacationing visitor, there is a much more pleasant network of far less travelled (except in summer peak) secondary roads connecting the small villages between the eastern shore of the bay of Santander and Santoña. Between Santoña and Castro-Urdiales you're just going to have to suffer the curse of the *camiones.*

Castro-Urdiales to Laredo

The eastern coastal towns draw avid fans to their sheltered locations on the lee side of the peninsula that forms the Bahía de Santander. We cover this area east to west, starting 74 km (46 miles) to the east of Santander, just west of Bilbao, at the port town of **Castro-Urdiales**. The 14th-century Gothic **Iglesia de Santa María** in Castro-Urdiales is situated on a rocky promontory almost entirely surrounded by water. The church's harmonious interior is its glory, especially the apse, with large buttresses and handsome monumental brasses.

The larger town of **Laredo**, sitting on a small bay some 20 km (12 miles) to the west, was a commercial port in the Middle Ages. Now it is probably the most heavily visited of the smaller coastal towns, with proliferating high rises and vacation houses. Frequented in large part by German and French vacationers, Laredo grows from a population of 12,500 in the off-season to more than 100,000 in summer. If you stop here, two spots to see are the lively **Playa de Salve**, a beach, and the **Iglesia de Nuestra Señora de la Asunción**, a 12th-century Romanesque-Gothic church that was the only building to survive a 1638 invasion by French corsairs.

Hotels in Laredo are small seaside places. The ► **Hotel El Ancla**, Calle González Gallego 10, is close to the beach. The slightly more elegant, although slightly more moderate in price, ► **Hotel Risco**, at Calle la Arenosa 2, is situated in the upper part of town overlooking both the town and the beaches, which are a ten-minute walk away. Laredo's main dining and nightlife venues are in the Zona Rúa Mayor, around the Rúa de San Marcial. **El Jardín de Oporto** (López Seña 16) is a good spot for local *tapas* as well as coffees from Jamaica and Brazil.

What's missing along this stretch of coast is romance. There's no feeling that you've found bucolic backcountry Spain, and the fishing ports are devoted more to efficiency than to preserving the quaint and old. The **Valle de Guriezo**, between Castro-Urdiales and Laredo, does present some very handsome scenery, and there is the occasional high-angle view of a *ría* (estuary) with several hundred yards of golden sand and a small beach town clinging to water's edge.

Santoña to Cabo de Ajo

On the other side of the bay from Laredo, watched over by a huge fort Napoleon left behind, is **Santoña**, a fishing town with some pleasant, sandy beaches and a 13th-century church, but not much in the way of shops, cafés, or atmosphere. West of town, on N 629, is a big, brand-new, relatively moderate apartment-hotel with bar and restaurant, ► **Juan de la Cosa** (named for a 15th-century seafarer and navigator), right on the Playa de Berria. It's very sleek and modern, all polished marble and glass, *très* Euro-gloss. Just beyond the pool, a line of low dunes with waving grasses and a profusion of wildflowers looks over a long, broad, level, sandy beach. This is an excellent sybaritic stopover (closed in December and January), for the night or for a meal of *ensalada de marisco* and a stroll on the beach before you push on.

West of Santoña, along quieter local roads, are the beach communities of Ajo, Isla, Ris, and most notable, Noja. The newly resurfaced SP 4141 is the east–west road that spans the peninsula between Santoña and El Astillero on the Bahía de Santander. The short, twisting and turning drive up to Noja is a pretty one, lined with *roble* trees (British oaks) on either side, past ponies grazing in acres of wildflowers. (From N 634/E 70, exit at Beranga to S 403 northbound and follow signs to Noja.) **Noja** and **Ris** are practically one, with five beaches, including the **Playa de Ris** which is, it is safe to say, one of the most beautiful beaches in Spain.

There is much building activity here, and there are many condos, small hotels, and *hostals* in the area. The ► **Hotel Montemar**, Calle Arenal 21, and ► **Hotel La Encina**, Avenida de Ris 75, are good choices, with a slight nod to the latter. Both are at the far end of Noja, close to Playa de Ris, and are open for the summer season only. There is also a camping facility nearby, ► **Camping Playa Joyel** (turn left at the Camping Playa Joyel sign on Playa de Ris), which is open from Easter to September 30. It gets a "first-category" rating, accepts caravans and tents, has a nice bar and restaurant, a swimming pool, a tennis court, and miniature golf, and is on the beach.

In nearby **Ajo**, where the building trades are currently somewhat less agitated, try **Mesón la Casuca**, Calle Benedicto Ruiz, a *restaurante marisquería* (seafood restaurant) that claims its seafood *paella* is special—and is right to do so. The Mesón also has a good bar with seafood *tapas;* outdoor dining on a pleasant terrace; and rooms for rent. Tel: (9-42) 62-10-54.

Ajo's beach, a few kilometers north of town on Cabo de Ajo, is at the end of a narrow, bumpy road through an expanse of long green grass, broken, ofttimes, only by a lone horse. At the cape (*cabo*), lush green meets white sand meets blue sea—a lovely spot in the early evening.

WEST OF SANTANDER

The two Cantabrian towns of most interest west of Santander and Santillana del Mar are Comillas and San Vicente de la Barquera. West from Santillana, C 6316 (18 km/11 miles to Comillas, 33 km/21 miles to San Vicente) stays close to the sea and winds in and out of a coastal range. Just beyond Cóbreces note several slopes studded, even carpeted, by stones and boulders—clear evidence of the difficulties in farming this land.

Comillas

Comillas is a charming village on a bluff overlooking the town's harbor and the Mar Cantábrico. King Alfonso XII found the village agreeable near the turn of the century and frequently visited the marqués of Comillas, bringing visitors and prosperity in his wake. The marqués's palace, a huge Victorian pile, is now a museum containing paintings, ancient bronzes, and archaeological objects. But the real treasure is to be found in the palace garden: El Capricho, a beach house designed by Antoni Gaudí—with the expected bizarre, intriguing details. One of the nice touches: When any window is raised, a bell in the sash tinkles.

The 1885 building, complete with green and yellow tiles in intricate sunflower motifs, Mudejar-style brickwork, and wrought-iron balconies, has recently opened as a high-priced restaurant. Even if the food happens to be second rate—though priced as if it were first rate—a visit will definitely be rewarding; Tel: (9-42) 72-03-65. If you prefer, just take a look at El Capricho and dine at the moderately priced, long-popular Fonda Colasa, on Antonio López 9. Hearty, abundant homemade soups and stews are specialties; Tel: (9-42) 72-00-01.

Stroll down to the Comillas harbor, with its commercial fishing fleet, stone piers, and stone breakwater, for a pleasant outing. There's a nice beach with a white-tile walkway and places for al fresco snacking nearby. Above the harbor—in the section called Sobre del Puerto—is the new ▶ Las Brisas Motel, quite small, with a good view of the harbor and a restaurant, a ten-minute walk from the village.

West to San Vicente de la Barquera

The drive westward along C 6316 passes some lovely scenery, including the fine beach at Oyambre, before ending at La Revilla, a tiny farm village with clumps of lilies and huge shrubs of pink and white primroses on the roadside. Take a right turn here onto N 634/E 70 for a brief taste of *camión* hell, but it's not for long. Coming down the mountain there's a wonderful view of San Vicente de la Barquera, larger and looking more like a playground than Comillas. The town is reached across a long causeway over a broad delta. When the tide goes out, San Vicentians turn out with rakes to gather clams and net shrimp, which can then be enjoyed by all at seafood bars and restaurants along Avenida Generalísimo, such as Restaurant Maruja; Tel: (9-42) 71-00-77.

San Vicente is undergoing a building boom, too, that may, or may not, complement the town's several attractive 16th- and 17th-century mansions. Past the picturesque harbor, complete with fishing fleet in *de rigueur* Spanish blue, is a steep climb to the upper town, which provides another scenic view of town, harbor, and sea. The **Iglesia de Nuestra Señora de los Angeles**, in the upper town, is a good example of the transition from Romanesque to Gothic. A good hotel up here is the ▶ **Hotel Miramar**, Paseo de la Barquera 20, with a view of everything and lunch to boot (closed December 15 to March 1).

The road west of San Vicente runs above a huge and scenic valley of farmland, grazing cattle, and vast tracts of pine trees. In the background to the south, looming over all, are Los Picos de Europa.

Los Picos de Europa

The Cordillera Cantábrica spans 300 miles of northern Spain from the Pyrenees to Cabo Finisterre on the Atlantic coast of Galicia. In all great mountain ranges there are sections that particularly draw the eye and inspire wonder. Los Picos de Europa are that magnet in the Cordillera Cantábrica.

The Picos de Europa begin some 20 miles south of Santander and extend westward for 125 miles to Oviedo in Asturias. This is part of one of the last great tracts of wilderness in Europe, familiar to Spanish hikers, campers, hunters, and fishermen, but relatively unknown to North Americans. On a sunny day you can see these mountains from the beaches, the peaks snowcapped even in summer. The highest is Torre Cerredo, topping 8,600 feet, with Peña Vieja, Santa Ana, Cortés, and Tesorero not far below. Coal and iron abound, although the excavating is not intrusive. Dramatic white-water rivers pounding through incredible gorges fuel not only a remunerative hydroelectric-power industry but the heart rates of fishermen and kayakers as well.

Late spring, summer, and early fall are the best seasons to visit Los Picos de Europa, always, of course, with the caveat about summer crowds. There is a great variety of hiking trails in Los Picos. Some of the best are south of Las Arenas de Cabrales in Asturias. Between Caín and Posado de Valdeón along the Río Cares there are trails that lead into mountain shelters west and north of Cantabria's Fuente Dé. Shelters at Collado Jermoso, La Teronosa, and Amuesa, among others, can be used for overnight stays. See the Asturias and Galicia chapter for more on this area.

ALONG THE RIO DEVA

Given the proximity, day trips to Los Picos from San Vicente or Santillana are certainly possible, although there is a good sufficiency of mountain driving, so you must figure extra time even over the decent roads. If you'd rather stay in the mountains, head south for **Fuente Dé**, at road's end, some 76 km (47 miles) from San Vicente (take N 634 west to

Unquero, then turn south on N 621), and the ▶ **Parador del Río Deva**. This is a get-away-from-it-all parador, 3,000 feet up, stashed in the Valle de Líebana between massive slopes of mountain meadow and forest and only a long stone's throw from the cable car that will take you above chamois and ibex, past eagles, and up to 6,500 feet and a now-I've-seen-them-all vista (until you get to Pico de Tres Mares, that is).

The only problem with Fuente Dé as a day trip is that the route along the Río Deva (N 621) twists and turns through mountains and meadows and valleys of such beauty that you will feel you must continually stop and look and ponder, or get out and walk around, have a picnic, and look some more. The Deva guides you over, around, even through breathtaking geology, to wit the **Desfiladero de la Hermida** (La Hermida defile), about 10 km (6 miles) south of the Asturian town of Panes. There are several dramatic gorges and defiles in these mountains, but none quite like La Hermida, 12 miles long and so deep and so narrow that you are not entirely sure the towering walls of stone on either side, innocent of any plant life whatsoever, will not finally close overhead.

ALONG THE RIO SAJA

Bárcena Mayor, a national historic site—meaning that its appearance must remain essentially the same—is another day trip to road's end in Los Picos. The town dates to the Middle Ages and is known for its woodcarvers. Take N 634 19 km (12 miles) south from San Vicente to Cabezón de la Sal (which means "head of salt mines"), then head south on C 625 along the Río Saja and through the Saja mountain reserve for another 19 km (12 miles), and turn left near El Tojo onto a shiny new stretch of blacktop along the Río Lodar, a quiet stream with an occasional trout fisherman. **Bárcena Mayor** is just a couple of miles distant; no vehicles are allowed in the town, so leave your car in the large parking lot at the end of the road and walk a quarter-mile into the village.

Bárcena Mayor is a pretty place with carved wooden balconies and pots of flowers, although its monumentalization does give it an unavoidably careful look. People here farm or carve wood or both. They keep cows in the open-faced stalls beneath their houses or woodworking shops. Note the household and farm items stored in some of the niches in the rock face on the bluff overhanging the cobblestone streets. For the moment there are only a couple of gift shops and a small bar-café, and children are offered tours of the village on guided horseback rides. But the government is spending a lot of money here so you can bet that commercialization is coming at full gallop. On the way back to the parking lot, notice the handsome retaining wall alongside the walkway. The Spanish really know what to do with a boulder or two.

On the road to Bárcena Mayor there is a turnoff over a little bridge across the Río Lardo 4 km (2½ miles) from the main road. Its green-and-white sign discloses a *mesón* (tavern), and it leads to Los Tojos, a working farm hamlet just 2 km (a mile) distant, most of it straight up. The **Mesón la Bolera** in Los Tojos is a small, pleasant place with dark, beamed-ceiling interior and a little bit of everything: sausages, some groceries, some hanging pork, an array of liquors, plus a cheerful barmaid. There's a separate *comedor* (dining room), with half a dozen tables. Its weekend menu includes, among other items, *sopa de carne, sopa de pescado, chuleta terneso* (veal cutlet), *chuletillas* (lamb chops), and for dessert *flan* or *natillas*. There are benches and tables outside overlooking grazing cows and an impressive vista of the valley below. Other customers are villagers, farmers, maybe a few fellow travellers, but no tour buses; Tel: (9-42) 70-60-35.

THE SAJA AREA TO PICO DE TRES MARES

At this point you may return to the coast via C 625 north or, from the Bárcena Mayor road, make a left onto C 625 and head south through the **Nacional Reserva de Saja**. There are only one or two tiny hamlets in this protected reserve of mountains, woods, and wild animals. The drive is a long, steep climb through immense tracts of beech trees along the slopes of Cueto de Frechilla and Alto del Pedraja to the peak elevation of almost 4,100 feet near Puerto de Palombera. The views along the way and at the top make it worth being in second gear much of the time. At Espinilla, 26 km (16 miles) south of the Bárcena Mayor turnoff, you can go left to Reinosa and hop on N 611, which goes north to Santander and south to Palencia, or you can make a right turn and continue upward to **Pico de Tres Mares**, more than 7,000 feet high. Take the chairlift up the "mountain of three seas," home to the headwaters of three rivers running to three seas, Atlantic, Mediterranean, Cantabrian. There is winter skiing here, at Alto Campóo and Braña Vieja.

As you head back east toward Reinosa you'll see a road to your left that leads up to a 12th-century castle, the **Castillo de Argüeso**, standing alone on a hilltop opposite the small village of Argüeso. The *castillo* is boarded up but imparts a very medieval aura, sitting above a slope of pasture grass and a few munching horses. It's a lovely spot for a picnic.

GETTING AROUND

Aviaco, the domestic network of Iberia, flies from Madrid to Santander several times a day, and from Barcelona to Santander once a day (but the flight is not direct).

You can get to Santander from Madrid by train—several departures a day—in six hours on the high-speed Talgo. There is also an overnight train from Madrid to Santander that departs Madrid at 11:30 P.M. and arrives in Santander at 8:00 A.M. the next morning. It's *possible* to get from Barcelona to Santander by train, but the route is byzantine and the trip involves lots of time, much of it waiting in stations.

The only effective way to see Cantabria once you're there is by car, which you can rent in Santander.

El Transcantábrico

There is yet another way to see Cantabria—*and* Asturias and Galicia for that matter: El Transcantábrico, a luxury train, a kind of Orient Express, that makes leisurely and comfortable passage for no more than 54 passengers between San Sebastián in the east and Santiago de Compostela in the west, taking seven days to make the trip and changing direction each week. The service, which began ten years ago, operates summers only from early June to mid-September and includes views of mountain scenery and wilderness usually seen only by eagles, ibex, and a few mountain climbers, and tours to interesting points along the way. Sleeping compartments are air-conditioned, breakfast, lunch, and dinner are served on the train, with regional dishes a speciality, there's live music, and the bar is open *all* day long. Very sybaritic, the whole thing; the price is in the sybaritic class, too— about U.S. $1,600. See a travel agent to make arrangements for El Transcantábrico.

Hunting and Fishing in the Cordillera Cantábrica

Spain has stringent regulations, particularly for big-game hunting, which include special insurance and a license from the hunter's home country. Small-game hunting is permitted nearly year-round but limited to certain days of the week. Big-game season is also restricted to certain days of the week, from approximately early October until early February for wild boar and buck deer, with narrower windows for roe deer and chamois. Each autonomous community publishes an annual open-season calendar, usually in August, and also has the authority to issue licenses and permits for use within its borders. For aid and advice, including schedules and such esoterica as official recognition of hunting trophies, contact: Spanish Hunting Federation, Avenida Reina Victoria 72-1, 28003 Madrid; Tel: (9-1) 553-8867 or 553-9017; Fax: (9-1) 534-5421.

Trucha (trout) fishing season is from the second Sunday in May through September; *salmón* season is March 1 to July 31 (only fly fishing for salmon after July 1). Regulations may differ from one province to another and it is important to contact the provincial regulatory authority. For general information on fishing, contact: Spanish Fishing Federation, Navas de Tolosa 3, 28013 Madrid; Tel: (9-1) 532-8353; Fax: 532-6538.

The Spanish government produces excellent terrain and topographical maps, useful to the visiting hiker, camper, fisherman, hunter. Local newsstands or stationery stores may have maps beyond the standard tourist editions, but you would be wise to get these maps before trekking into the wilderness. Contact: Dirección General del Instituto Geográfico Nacional, General Ibañez de Ibero 3, 28071 Madrid; Fax: (9-1) 533-1158.

ACCOMMODATIONS REFERENCE

The hotel rates listed below are projected for 1994, for double room, double occupancy, in pesetas. We strongly recommend that you confirm the price when booking.

The telephone code for this area is 9-42. When calling from outside the country, drop the 9.

▶ **Las Brisas Motel.** Mies de la Moria, Sitio del Castillo, 39520 **Comillas.** Tel: 72-20-90. 4,500–6,000 pts.

▶ **Camping Playa Joyel.** Playa de Ris, 39180 **Noja.** Tel: 63-00-81; Fax: 63-10-72.

▶ **Camping Santillana.** 39330 **Santillana del Mar.** Tel: 84-01-83.

▶ **Hotel Altamira.** Calle Cantón 1, 39330 **Santillana del Mar.** Tel: 81-80-25; Fax: 84-01-36. 9,500 pts.

▶ **Hotel El Ancla.** Calle González Gallego 10, 39770 **Laredo.** Tel: 60-55-00; Fax: 61-16-02. 11,000 pts.

▶ **Hotel Los Angeles.** Campo de Revolgo 13, 39330 **Santillana del Mar.** Tel: 81-81-40; Fax: 84-01-77. 4,000–7,000 pts.

▶ **Hotel Conde Duque.** Campo de Revolgo, 39330 **Santillana del Mar.** Tel: 81-83-36; Fax: 84-01-36. 6,500 pts.

▶ **Hotel Las Cuevas.** Avenida de Antonio Sandí. 39330 **Santillana del Mar.** Tel: 81-83-24; Fax: 81-81-85. 4,000–6,200 pts.

▶ **Hotel La Encina.** Avenida de Ris 75, 39180 **Noja.** Tel. and Fax: 63-01-41. 7,300 pts.

▶ **Hotel Los Hidalgos.** Campo de Revolgo, 39330 **Santillana del Mar.** Tel: 81-81-01; Fax: 84-01-70. 3,800–6,500 pts.

▶ **Hotel Los Infantes.** Avenida Le Dorat 1, 39330 **Santillana del Mar.** Tel: 81-81-00; Fax: 84-01-03. 6,400–11,000 pts.

▶ **Hotel Miramar.** Paseo de la Barquera 20, 39540 **San**

Vicente de la Barquera. Tel. and Fax: 71-00-75. 4,900–6,700 pts.

▶ Hotel Montemar. Calle Arenal 21, 39180 Noja. Tel: 63-03-20. 6,930 pts.

▶ Hotel Real. Paseo de Pérez Galdós 28, 39005 Santander. Tel: 27-25-50; Fax: 27-45-73. 18,000–39,000 pts.

▶ Hotel Rhin. Avenida de la Reina Victoria 153, 39005 Santander. Tel: 27-43-00; Fax: 27-86-53. 11,500 pts.

▶ Hotel Risco. Calle la Arenosa 2, Alto de Laredo, 39770 Laredo. Tel: 60-50-30; Fax 60-50-55. 7,150–9,450 pts.

▶ Hotel Sardinero. Plaza de Italia 1, 39005 Santander. Tel: 27-11-00; Fax: 27-89-43. 12,900 pts.

▶ Juan de la Cosa. Playa de Berria, 39770 Santoña. Tel: 66-12-38; Fax: 66-16-32. 8,500–10,500 pts.

▶ Parador Gil Blás. Plaza de Ramón Pelayo 11, 39330 Santillana del Mar. Tel: 81-80-00; Fax: 81-83-91. 10,000–14,000 pts.

▶ Parador del Río Deva. 39588 Fuente Dé. Tel: 73-00-01; Fax: 73-02-12. 7,500–9,000 pts.

THE BASQUE COUNTRY

By Gerry Dawes

Gerry Dawes studied at the University of Seville and lived in Spain for eight years. He now lives in New York, where he works in the wine trade and is a regular contributor to the Wine Enthusiast *and the* Wine News. *He has lectured on Spain at the Smithsonian Institution and travels in Spain frequently.*

In the central part of northern Spain are three regions (La Rioja, Navarra, and the Basque Country) comprising five provinces that have so much in common—shared mountain terrain, history, Basque heritage, cuisine, wine, music, and so on—that they are often thought of as a homogeneous region, but each shows a distinctly different personality when you delve beneath the surface. They are cousins, not siblings, and each has more than enough historical, cultural, and culinary attractions to merit special attention. For this reason, we cover them in three separate chapters, beginning with the Basque Country. Lying on Spain's northern coast between Cantabria, to the west, and Biarritz, France, to the east, the Basque Country is arguably more likely to be a gateway to this part of Spain than is La Rioja, the province to its south, or Navarra, the one to its southeast toward Aragón and, beyond that, Catalonia.

The entire area covered by the three regions, however, is one of the lesser known in Spain. Except for the Fiestas de San Fermín in the Navarrese city of Pamplona in July and the fabulous beaches of the Basque resort of San Sebastián, there is little here to draw the hordes of tourists who descend on other parts of Spain in summer. So much the better for serious travellers, who can find richly rewarding experiences in these historic and colorful regions, each of which retains its strong individual character.

The Basque Country, El País Vasco in Spanish, has a number of beautiful villages hidden away in the fresh, verdant mountains; charming fishing villages along the Bay of Biscay; some of Spain's greatest restaurants; and one of the world's most elegant seaside resorts, San Sebastián.

You may wish to complement your culinary experiences in the Basque Country with a tour of La Rioja, where you will find some of Spain's greatest wines and most glorious bodegas (wine cellars) in picturesque, historical villages surrounded by terraced vineyards. The former kingdom of Navarra, including its capital, Pamplona, is a part of Spain known well to Hemingway fans, who will enjoy as he did the running of the bulls at the Fiestas de San Fermín; superb restaurants and excellent wines; colorful, raucous fiestas with splendid folk music; trout streams; mountain villages; and sites of historical interest, including some of the greatest artistic treasures on the Camino de Santiago. (La Rioja and Navarra are covered in separate chapters.)

MAJOR INTEREST

The beach resort town of San Sebastián
Basque cuisine, especially restaurants in San
 Sebastián
The fortress town of Fuenterrabía
Bay of Biscay fishing villages
The medieval quarter of Vitoria

A carefully planned strategy is necessary for getting the most out of a visit to the Basque Country, La Rioja, and Navarra, because the area's many tough mountain roads discourage indiscriminate province hopping here. In fact, unless you are simply stopping off at San Sebastián on the way in or out of Spain from France, it is better to plan a trip to this region as a destination, not a quick drive-through.

There are several ways to approach this area by car. Entering the region from Madrid via Burgos, probably the most likely of several approaches, we recommend the *autopistas* north to Vitoria and on to San Sebastián via Bilbao. Then you can proceed to Navarra, leaving the charming backcountry of La Rioja until last, before returning to Burgos and Madrid.

If you begin in France, you can enter at Irún, visit San Sebastián, then go southwest to Vitoria (via Bilbao, if you wish), and southeast down into La Rioja via the *autopista,* then take the national routes and secondary roads northeast

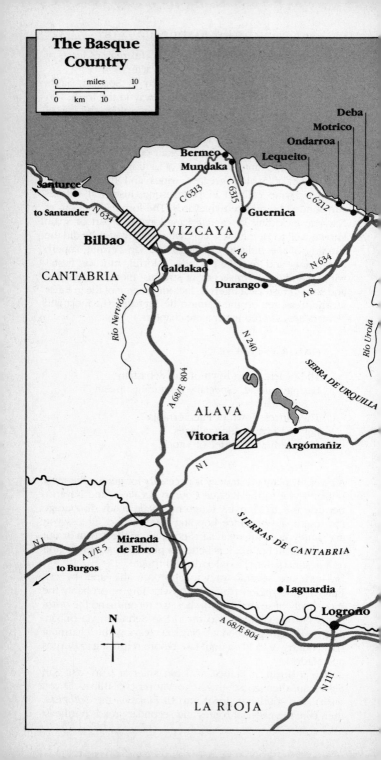

to Pamplona, then north back to your starting point at the French border.

If you are travelling in northern Spain and coming from Santander in Cantabria, you will have to do some backtracking to cover the loop of attractions in this region. If you plan to continue to Madrid after you visit this region, from Santander you should go to Bilbao and take the *autopista* to visit Vitoria, then drive down to La Rioja, on to Navarra, through the mountains to San Sebastián, then back to Bilbao, and south again on the *autopista* to Burgos and Madrid.

If you are heading to Aragón and Catalonia, you can exit the area from either Pamplona or Logroño and go east on the A 68 and A 2 *autopistas* to Zaragoza and Barcelona.

INTO THE BASQUE COUNTRY

Have you ever heard of Gipuzkoa, Bizkaia, and Araba? Probably not, because they are names in Euskera, the Basque language. Some people will know these three provinces of the Basque Country (El País Vasco in Castilian; Euskadi in the Basque language) as Guipúzcoa (Ghee-POOTH-kwah), Vizcaya, and Alava. But most people tend to identify each of the three with a city: Guipúzcoa with elegant San Sebastián by the sea; Vizcaya, to its west, with industrial Bilbao; and Alava, to the south, with Vitoria, the capital of the Basque Country.

The Basque Country is small, and for touristic purposes the principal points of interest can be covered in a few days. Usually only seasoned Spain travellers, those spending a few days on the beach at San Sebastián, true fanciers of Spanish haute cuisine, or bullfight aficionados bound for Semana Grande in Bilbao, where bulls as big as buffaloes test Spain's gutsier matadors, will stretch their itineraries to include this region.

The Basque seacoast is a series of picturesque fishing villages nestled in coves with crescent-shaped beaches, interspersed with industrial towns and graffiti-marred suburbs, but many of these villages—Guetaria, Zumaya, Zarautz, Pasajes de San Juan (Pasaia Donibane), and Fuenterrabía, all near San Sebastián, and Bermeo near Bilbao, to name the most attractive ones—are well worth a visit, especially if you have time to laze away the afternoon at a dockside fishermen's restaurant over a lunch of salad, grilled fresh fish, and *txakolí,* the local *pétillant* white wine.

A dramatic counterpoint to tawny Castile and dry Andalusia in summertime, the misty green hills of the inland Basque Country are scattered with small agricultural villages characterized by big-timbered stone houses called *caseríos,* herds of white sheep contrasting against the emerald fields, and fast-running trout streams in the valleys. The larger valley towns tend to be industrial, are often polluted, and are hotbeds of political unrest.

THE BASQUES AND THEIR LANGUAGE

The Basqués are a race of people whose roots are lost in antiquity. Some have gone as far as claiming the Vascos are the survivors of Atlantis, but wherever they came from, one thing is certain: These tough descendants of fishermen, whalers, shepherds, and mountain men are fiercely independent and proud of being Basques, and they have put every would-be subduer of their ancestral rights, from the Romans to General Franco and the present Socialist government, to the test.

Euskera, the Basques' non-Indo-European language, uses enough k's, x's, and z's to drive a printer's devil mad and at times seems designed as a linguistic labyrinth to confound outsiders. The roots of Euskera have never been traced definitively to any other tongue, though one scholar claims to have established a link between some 360 Basque words and their counterparts in Soviet Georgia, the eastern section of which is known, perhaps not coincidentally, as Iberia.

The Basque separatist movement is supported by only about 20 percent of the populace of approximately 2,500,000 Vascos, but the core of this movement is highly visible and can be extremely violent. Signs, banners, and Basque graffiti—and road signs whose Spanish equivalents of Basque names have been obliterated with spray paint—provide the traveller with an ever-lurking reminder of the volatility of the political situation, no matter how picturesque the location. All this can put a damper on your fun, the sprayed-over signs can get you lost, and in extreme situations you could be swept up in an act of political violence. Recently, however, the Basque populace seems to have gotten fed up with this situation and has staged mass peace marches to protest the violent acts of the radical minority.

Still, your chances of being caught up in political violence are far less likely than those of being robbed in New York, Rome, or Seville. Besides, San Sebastián is one of the world's loveliest, cleanest, and most elegant beach resorts. And Basque cuisine is magnificent.

Basque Cuisine

Basque cuisine is considered by all but the Catalans to be the best in Spain. It is at times supremely sophisticated; sometimes rustic, homey, and peasant-inspired; usually delicious; often served in trencherman portions; and in the best places frightfully expensive. Almost one quarter of Spain's best 100 restaurants, as rated by *Guía BMW,* the country's top gastronomic guide, are located in the Basque Country. A profusion of top-notch Basque restaurants has opened in the past decade in other regions, and the chefs at many of the best restaurants in Spain are Basques, even when the food itself is not.

Nueva cocina vasca (new Basque cuisine) began to evolve in the mid-1970s during the period when Spain's fledgling democracy was trying its wings, and, as much as the new wave in Spanish fashion, art, cinema, music, and a new morality, it is a symbol of post-Franco Spain's renaissance. Borrowing liberally from foreign influences (most notably Paul Bocuse of France), Juan Mari Arzak of the restaurant Arzak (San Sebastián), Pedro Subijana of Akelarre (San Sebastián), and Jesus María Oyarbide of Zalacaín (Madrid) caused a culinary revolution. During the first eight years (1974 to 1981) in which Spain's national gastronomy prize for best chef was awarded, it was presented to four Basques, including Arzak, Subijana, Zalacaín's chef Benjamín Urdain, and Valentina Saralegui, at Oyarbide's other Madrid restaurant, Príncipe de Viana. In the 1970s Luis Irizar ran a cooking school in Zarautz, a few kilometers from San Sebastián (the school is now in Madrid), and turned out superstar chefs such as Subijana, Karlos Arguiñano, and Ramón Roteta.

Jan Read and Maite Manjón, authors of *The Wine and Food of Spain,* quote Subijana describing *nueva cocina vasca:* ". . . the return to simple cookery and the respect for tradition and its rehabilitation. You therefore have on your menu: old dishes, some included more for nostalgic reasons than for their flavour; traditional dishes, but very carefully cooked; and finally some new ones."

The last line is where the rub comes in: "Some new ones" includes everything from perfectly cooked seafood in lovely delicate sauces to a surfeit of rich dishes made with foie gras, truffles, or sea-urchin sauce, for example. Like the "new" cuisine of any other country, new Basque cuisine has its sublime practitioners and its ridiculous imitators. Perhaps the line in the *nueva cocina vasca* credo, "traditional dishes, but very carefully cooked" is where its ultimate genius lies.

THE FOODS OF THE BASQUE COUNTRY

The best of traditional Basque cuisine is based on seafood from the sparkling cold waters of the Bay of Biscay. Fresh fish—*rodaballo* (turbot), *besugo* (sea bream), *sardinas* (sardines), and *anchoas* (anchovies)—is sprinkled with salt, and sometimes oil and lemon, and grilled over hot coals. The fish is delivered to the table whole and without sauces, fresh, natural, and sublimely delicious.

Angulas (baby eels), especially those from Aguiñaga, an estuary village a few miles west of San Sebastián, are sizzled briefly in olive oil laced with garlic and a bit of hot pepper, then served piping hot; you are provided with a bib and a wooden fork to avoid dry-cleaning bills and burned lips. *Angulas,* which are found only in Spain and France in the Bay of Biscay, are a supernal Basque delicacy, an easily acquired taste for those with caviar budgets (they can cost more than 23,000 pesetas per kilogram in the Mercado de la Brecha, but you can usually get a 100-gram *ración* for 3,000 to 4,000 pesetas in the restaurants of San Sebastián's old quarter).

Other traditional Basque Country seafood preparations are *merluza* (hake), *kokotxas* (*cocochas,* glands from the cheek of the hake, a delicacy), and *almejas en salsa verde* (clams in a sauce of garlic, parsley, and peas); *chipirones en su tinta* (squid cooked in a rich sauce made from its own ink); *txangurro* (*changurro,* spider-crab meat, cooked with onions, tomatoes, Sherry, brandy, and bread crumbs, then returned to the shell and baked), a superb dish that is often poorly done in many *típico* restaurants; and *marmitako,* a fisherman's casserole of tuna and potatoes.

With all this wealth of seafood, you would think that the lowly codfish, dried and salted at that, would take a back seat, but not in the Basque Country. Here, *bacalao* is king, a throwback of at least four centuries to when Basque fishermen roamed as far as Newfoundland to harvest cod and then preserved it in salt. Many a great Basque restaurant's reputation was made on its skill in preparing *bacalao a la vizcaina* (made with dried sweet red peppers, garlic, onion, parsley, and ham), *bacalao al pil-pil* (with garlic and chile peppers), *bacalao Club Ranero* (a hybrid of the first two), or *ajoarriero* (in tomato sauce "muleteer" style, a preparation said to have been originated by the mule drivers who transported goods, including salt cod, throughout the mountains of the Basque Country).

Traditional inland contributions to Basque cuisine include lamb, *chistorra* (thin cheroot-shaped *chorizo* sausages), *perrichicos* (tiny fingertip-size spring mushrooms), *pimientos de piquillo* (spicy peppers, usually stuffed with meat, crab, *bacalao,* or other fish), *alubias de Tolosa* (white beans cooked with *chorizo*), *truchas* (trout) and salmon from the Bidasoa river, *chuleton* (huge, thick steaks), and smoked *idiazabal,* ewe's-milk cheese from the mountains. *Cuajada,* a mild, custard-like sheep's-milk curd, sweetened to taste with wild honey, comes in a little terra-cotta pot that never seems to hold enough.

BASQUE COOKING SOCIETIES

A unique facet of the Basque culinary scene is its all-male *sociedades gastronómicas* (gastronomic societies)—more than 1,000 of them in Guipúzcoa alone, 100 of which are in San Sebastián—each with its own *txoko* (*choko,* as they call their clubhouse) consisting of a kitchen, wine cellar, and dining room. Each member of a society, which may include anyone from a political dignitary to a bus driver, takes a turn cooking his own specialties for the others. Members pay for the food, condiments, and wine they use on the honor system.

These societies date to the 19th century, and their existence goes far to explain the brilliance of Basque cuisine. The *txokos*—where the constant challenge is to come up with new variations of classic dishes and creative new dishes, and then try them out on your peers, all of whom cook—are the proving grounds on which many of the great dishes of Basque cuisine are born.

Membership in these eating and drinking societies, according to Penelope Casas, author of *The Foods and Wines of Spain,* is "a constant cause of marital friction." So drawn are some men to the art of cooking and the food, wine, and camaraderie of these clubs, they spend every evening with the boys. Recently, however, a few *sociedades gastronómicas* have opened their doors to women.

Basque Country Wines and Spirits

BASQUE COUNTRY WINE

Technically speaking, the Basque Country is an important wine producer because La Rioja Alavesa, a section of the Rioja wine district above the Río Ebro, is within its confines. But were it not for political boundaries, this region would be considered a part of Castilian Rioja, because geographically and climatologically it is. (Accordingly, we cover La Rioja Alavesa in the chapter on La Rioja.)

The other noteworthy wine district, and it is really noteworthy only to the Basques, is the maritime district around Guetaria and Zarautz that produces the green, *pétillant,* quaffable wine called *txakolí* (*chacolí*). This region recently became one of Spain's newest *denominaciones de origen.* In this rainy climate the grapes seldom get fully ripe, so *txakolí* is high in acid, which makes it a good wine with oysters and other shellfish, but, like French Muscadet, it is an acquired taste for many people. It is low in alcohol, however, so it can be drunk with relative impunity. The Basques love *txakolí* and drink copious quantities in the bars and fish restaurants of this region. The best *txakolí* is made by Txomin Echániz of Guetaria and Eizaguirre of Zarautz.

BASQUE COUNTRY CIDER

The Basques, like the Asturians, drink huge quantities of *sidra* (cider), and you will see many *sidrerías* (cider bars) in the Basque Country. San Sebastián has about 50 *sidrerías,* but the suburb of **Astigarraga**, a few miles southeast of downtown near Hernani, has several of the best ones, including the rustic Kako, Roxario, and Celaya, where the apples come from a friend's orchard. These *sidrerías,* with their huge cider vats, grills for roasting fish and meat, and long, communal tables are quite an experience. During the new cider season, which runs from January through late April or early May, you drink cider drawn straight from the big oak vats. The traditional accompaniment is an omelet with *bacalao,* followed by a huge steak or grilled fish, and lots of noise, conviviality, and *jotas* (folk songs). Before going, though, ask your hotel concierge if the local *sidrerías* are open.

Sidra is also bottled and is widely available in the bars and restaurants of the Basque Country. Sometimes a waiter or a patron will hold a bottle of *sidra* above his head in one hand and arc it into a wide-mouthed tall glass held below his waist in his other hand. This amusing and spectacular technique of pouring causes the cider to splash and fizz, releasing some of the carbon dioxide trapped in the liquid. The *sidra* is then knocked back in one gulp and the glass is passed to the next drinker. You can order a bottle of cider, however, without feeling the obligation to imitate the dexterity of the Basques in this stunt.

BASQUE COUNTRY SPIRITS

Spirits, often accompanied by the lighting of a *puro* or *habano* (usually a Cuban or Canary Islands cigar), are de rigueur after a substantial meal in the Basque Country. Among the spirits imbibed are *aguardiente de orujo* (marc or grape spirits), usually referred to as *orujo; aguardientes* (literally, "firewater") made from apples and other fruits, and similar to eau-de-vie; *anís* (anisette); *pacharán* (sloeberry- and anise-flavored *aguardiente*) from La Rioja, Navarra, and the Basque Country; and the native Basque liqueur *izarra* ("star," in Basque), made from as many as 48 different mountain herbs, flowers, and plants. All these popular drinks are usually served ice-cold in short, cylindrical glasses.

SAN SEBASTIAN

Located on a sheltered crabshell-shaped bay on the Bay of Biscay with two extraordinary beaches, San Sebastián (Donostia, in Basque) is one of the most stunningly beautiful cities in Spain, playing the role of a grand fin-de-siècle resort. It first became fashionable in the mid-19th century, when Queen Isabella II came here in the summer to bathe in the sea. Isabella's court followed, and for the next century the Spanish government made a custom of moving to San Sebastián for the summer, making it Spain's premier beach resort until the demise of *franquismo,* when most of the jet-set crowd drifted to warmer Marbella on the Costa del Sol.

Still, in August, the influx of Spaniards and French families (the city is only 20 km/12½ miles from the French border on a natural route into Spain from southern and western France) seems to double the normal population of 178,000. San Sebastián has managed to remain elegant, however, while the Costa del Sol, inundated with foreign and Spanish tourists, seems to fight a constant battle against being overwhelmed by the cheap and gaudy. Also, as the birthplace of *nueva cocina vasca* the city now draws as many food epicures to its temples of gastronomy as the Camino de Santiago once attracted religious pilgrims.

PARKING IN SAN SEBASTIAN

The parking situation in San Sebastián is not good, but if you want to see most of the attractions outside of town and visit several of the great restaurants of the Basque Country, a car is the only practical way to get around. All of the old and new sections of town on the isthmus are so-called blue zones: To park in such areas from 9:00 A.M. to 8:00 P.M., you must buy a paper parking permit, punch holes in it to show the time you parked, and place it on the dashboard so the parking police can check it. You can buy these permits at tobacco shops, from machines in some areas, such as the port, and from concierges at some hotels.

The Hotel Niza and the Bataplán discotheque mark the western boundaries of the blue zones. Beyond them you can park on the street, but unless you are fluent in Spanish and can decipher the street parking signs, and are willing to risk a break-in, we don't recommend it. Unless you are staying at the hotels María Cristina, Orly, Europa, or the Monte Igueldo, all of which have parking, we suggest you leave your car in one of the two underground car parks on the isthmus: at Plaza de Miguel de Cervantes near the Hotel de Londres y de Inglaterra or at Calle de la Reina Regente near the Hotel María Cristina. Luckily, you won't need your car to get around in the city itself. Most of the best attractions in town are easy to walk to or easily accessible by taxi.

Around in San Sebastián

San Sebastián's sheltered Bahía de la Concha, with its two beaches, is guarded by two hills, **Monte Igueldo** to the west and **Monte Urgull** to the east, and buffered from the wild Bay of Biscay by Isla de Santa Clara. Monte Igueldo's summit can be reached by car or funicular and has an amusement park. Monte Urgull has a walkway around its base and footpaths to the top, where the **Castillo de Santa Cruz de la Mota** has a marginally interesting military museum. Both hills offer superb views of the city, the bay, and the fishing port.

San Sebastián has a few historical monuments, churches, architectural points of interest, and a noteworthy museum, but you really come here for the beach, the food, and the street life. Most of old San Sebastián was destroyed by fire in the early 19th century, so don't expect to see many vestiges of the centuries-old buildings so characteristic of many other cities in Spain.

The raffish *parte vieja* (the old quarter, below Monte Urgull, rebuilt after the fire), with its lively narrow streets filled with bars, restaurants, markets, quaint (not usually touristy) shops, the fishermen's quarter, and a few older buildings of interest, more than compensates in atmosphere for what it lacks in antiquity. This area is the more typically Spanish part of San Sebastián, while the newer parts of town, especially those just south of the old quarter on the isthmus between the Playa de la Concha and Río Urumea—roughly the area between the Alameda del Boulevard (the southern limit of the old quarter) on the north and Calle San Martín near the **Catedral del Buen Pastor** on the south—where most of the chic shops and cafés are located, are more reminiscent of France. The cathedral is a late 19th-century Neo-Gothic structure with a fine steeple.

THE OLD QUARTER

The fine, arcaded **Plaza de la Constitución**, located in the center of the old quarter, is the epicenter of social life in this district. In former days bullfights were held here, but now the plaza is used for anything from folkloric festivals and flea markets to political demonstrations. The former town hall here dates from the 1830s. **Iglesia de San Vicente**, the city's oldest church, is located just north of Plaza de la Constitución, along Calle del 31 de Agosto, the only street not burned during the disastrous fire set by Anglo-Portuguese forces on August 31, 1813, and now home to some of San

Sebastián's best *tapas* bars. San Vicente is an austere early 16th-century building, in need of another tower to balance the main façade. The late 16th-century retable is the main attraction in its interior.

The municipal museum, **Museo San Telmo**, located two blocks northwest of San Vicente in the 16th-century former convent of San Telmo, contains minor paintings by El Greco and Goya, portraits by Vicente López, works by Dario de Regoyos—a Spanish Impressionist much influenced by Van Gogh—and a room of pictures by Spanish Impressionist Ignacio Zuloaga. The museum also has a section devoted to Basque culture, another to the Carlist Wars, and the enclosed cloisters hold a display of Basque funeral steles found in the region. The convent's church is decorated with 17 huge paintings by Josep Maria Sert depicting heroic, historical, and cultural scenes of San Sebastián and the province of Guipúzcoa: whaling in the Mar Cantábrico, Juan Sebastián Elcano circumnavigating the globe, Saint Ignatius Loyola, and so on. Sert was a Catalan artist who decorated the Palace of the League of Nations, the Catedral de Sant Pere in Vic (Catalonia), and the Waldorf-Astoria in New York.

Mercado de la Brecha

Follow Calle de la Pescadería east from Plaza de la Constitución to the best market in San Sebastián, Mercado de la Brecha, which has an excellent selection of seafood (upstairs in the large building to the left). By perusing the catch of the day, you will know what to order for dinner in one of San Sebastián's great restaurants. Depending on the season, you will see *nécoras,* the small, mean-looking truffle-colored crabs; big *centollo* spider crabs; *kokotxas; langostinos* (prawns); *angulas* (baby eels); *percebes* (goose barnacles); huge *cigalas* (langoustines); *almejas* (clams); *rodaballo* (turbot); and terrific-looking *lenguado* (sole). The woman who runs the Amaya fish stand does very unusual and artistic arrangements to display her fish.

Between the fish market and the market selling meat, vegetables, fruit, and cheeses in the next building to the south is a lively open-air farmer's market where vegetables such as fresh-shelled peas, tan-jacketed new potatoes, superb little black beans, and flavorful cabbages; wonderful, fresh Basque cow, goat, and sheep cheeses such as *idiazabal queso de oveja* (sheep's-milk cheese); wild honey, farmfresh brown eggs; bags of snails; flowers; and a variety of other produce from local *caseríos,* or family farms, are sold.

The Fishermen's Quarter

A couple of blocks west of the museum, at the northern end of Calle del Campanario, is the **Iglesia de Santa María**, with an 18th-century Baroque façade. To the south and west is the **Puerto Pesquero**, the fishermen's quarter, with its colorful fishing trawlers and arcaded buildings along the docks. The ground floor of almost every house along this row has an alfresco restaurant serving grilled sardines and other typical fish dishes. These restaurants are unpretentious but somewhat touristy, and they are certainly a far cry from the temples of high cuisine described below, but if you choose the restaurant carefully—look at what is being served to other patrons, and if a dish looks good, try it—you can pass a delightful, long lunch over salad, grilled fish, and a bottle of *txakolí* while watching the comings and goings in the port.

At the western end of the row of sardine restaurants is an aquarium with a seafaring museum featuring some fascinating dioramas of different ocean-fishing techniques employed by Basque fishermen, sea-fishing and boating paraphernalia, and a Basque fisherman's kitchen.

Boats leave every hour during the summer from the port for the short trip to **Isla de Santa Clara** and sightseeing tours of the bay. Tickets can be purchased at a booth located at the southern end of the port next to the yacht club.

ALONG THE BAY

San Sebastián's *ayuntamiento* (city hall), located on the bay next to the old quarter, is a huge Belle Epoque palace built in 1897 as a casino to rival Monte Carlo, Deauville, and Biarritz. The twin towers can be seen from anywhere along the esplanade; they draw the eye to this dominant building that, more than anything else in San Sebastián except the Hotel María Cristina (discussed below), leaves you with an indelible impression of fin-de-siècle style.

Just to the south following the curve of the bay is San Sebastián's splendid esplanade, the **Paseo de la Concha**, with its beautiful wrought-iron railings and lampposts. The golden sands of two of the world's finest urban beaches, the crescent-shaped **Playa de la Concha** and **Playa de Ondarreta**, separated only by a small rocky promontory, are spread out below. In peak season the beaches are very crowded but seem to absorb the mass of people until high tide, when the broad band of sand is cut so dramatically that you must either get off the beach or be prepared to emulate the proverbial tinned sardine. June, early July, and September are the best months for the beach if you want to avoid the heaviest crowds. (Note: Even in summer you will encounter occasional rainy days and cool weather; the summer climate of the Basque Coast is not perpetually cloudless like that of southern Spain.)

FESTIVALS AND SPORTING EVENTS IN SAN SEBASTIAN

San Sebastián hosts an excellent jazz festival, the Festival Internacional de Jazz de Donostia, in late July, after the one at Vitoria. In August Semana Grande is the big celebration, with regattas, spectacular fireworks, and general merrymaking, but, since the mid-1970s, no bullfights. The San Sebastián International Film Festival, a prestigious event à la Cannes, draws major international film stars to the splendid Hotel María Cristina every September.

About 10 km (6 miles) south of San Sebastián on N 240 (the San Sebastián–Tolosa–Pamplona road) is the **Hipódromo de Lasarte**, a grass racetrack where some of the finest thoroughbred racing in Spain takes place in July, August, and September, and again on Sunday mornings from mid-December to the second Sunday in February.

Doing the Chiquiteo

In San Sebastián *tapas* hopping is called *el chiquiteo,* after the short, wide-mouthed glasses known as *chiquitos* (in other Basque cities, *tapas* hopping is also called *el poteo*). The old quarter is a wonderful place to prowl in search of *tapas*. Here, in the bars along these lively, colorful streets, you can rub elbows (literally—you have to vie for space at the bar) with the people of Donostia and sample many of the traditional dishes for which the Basques, and San Sebastián in particular, lay claim to the gastronomic crown of Spain.

BARS IN THE OLD QUARTER

If you wish to do your own *tapas* tour of the old quarter, we suggest you begin at **Bar Portaletas**, Calle del Puerto 8 (just west of Plaza de la Constitución), for *banderillas* (*tapas* skewered with toothpicks) of *guindillas con anchoas y aceitunas* (small, piquant green peppers with anchovies and olives), *tortilla de patata* (Spanish omelet), *pimientos rellenos* (stuffed peppers), *jamón serrano* (cured ham), *bonito* (tuna) with mayonnaise on puff pastry, *alcachofa con bonito* (artichokes with tuna), and cold beer or *clarete* (light red or rosé wine) served in *chiquitos*. **Tamboril**, Calle de la Pescadería 2 (to the east in a corner of the Plaza de la Constitución), serves deep-fried *pimientos rellenos de carne,* delicious *boquerones en vinagre* (fresh anchovies), *guindillas,* canapés of smoked salmon, *rosado txacolí,* and excellent Rioja *tinto* from the Muga winery by the glass.

Just across the street from the farmer's market on Calle de San Juan is **Bar Gorriti,** which has a good selection of *tapas* such as kidney, eggplant, and tuna dishes, almost all of which cost only 50 pesetas per serving. West of the market, **Bar José Mari**, on Calle de Fermín Calbetón, serves a fine crab canapé, with a glass of *txacolí*. Along **Calle del 31 de Agosto**, to the north, are several of the best *tapas* bars in San Sebastián. **Bar Martínez** (at number 12) offers a wide assortment of *banderillas*. **La Cepa** (number 9, considered by many to be the best *tapas* bar in San Sebastián) serves great *jamón serrano* (the bar goes through more than 2,000 of these expensive hams every year), garlicky mushrooms sautéed with *jamón serrano,* deep-fried mussels, *angulas,* and *txacolí* poured at arm's length. You can sit down in the bar at **Restaurante Gandarias**, Calle de San Jerónimo 25 (the bar is around the corner on Calle del 31 de Agosto), and have *chorizo, cabeza de jabalí* (homemade head cheese), *callos* (tripe), and Eizaguirre *txakolí* from Zarautz.

BARS NEAR THE PASEO DE LA CONCHA

Another notable *tapas* bar, especially convenient for those staying in one of the hotels near the Paseo de la Concha, is the neighborhood bar **Ostarte**, on Calle de San Martín at the corner of Calle de Marina, near Hotels Niza, Orly, and Europa. Joni and Félix, the friendly young couple who run Ostarte, serve wonderful *tapas*. Their excellent *tortillas* (Spanish omelets, served by the slice) include one made with potatoes, red peppers, and green garlic shoots, a three-layered affair with *chorizo,* spinach, and potatoes, and a third with shrimp and garlic shoots. They serve canapés of cheese, scallions, and anchovies, of smoked trout dressed with minced onion in lemon and olive oil, and of smooth, creamy *bacalao* spread, as well as stellar, fresh homemade *chorizos*.

For early-evening aperitifs or for postprandials, try **Kabut-zia**, on the top floor of the Club Nautico (west of the *ayuntamiento* at the eastern end of Paseo de la Concha) overlooking the harbor, **Dionis**, Igentea 2 (behind the *ayuntamiento*), or the **Bataplán Bar and Discotheque**, next to Hotel Niza at the western end of Paseo de la Concha, overlooking the beach. **Basque**, a bar at Calle de Miramar 5 whose outdoor terrace café faces Plaza de Miguel de Cervantes at the eastern end of the Paseo de la Concha, is one of the most chic bars in town.

Nuevo Gran Casino de Kursaal, Calle de Zubieta 2, in the Hotel de Londres y de Inglaterra, is open from 6:00 P.M. to 2:00 A.M. (3:00 A.M. on holiday eves) for baccarat, blackjack, roulette (French and American), and other games of chance. The Kursaal also has a restaurant and bar.

Staying in San Sebastián

San Sebastián has many hotels, but only two that can be considered luxurious. Located next to the distinguished Teatro Victoria Eugenia, just south of the old quarter on a beautiful street that runs along the Río Urumea, is San Sebastián's best hotel (and one of the greatest in Spain), the ▶ **Hotel María Cristina**, Paseo de la República Argentina 4, within very easy walking distance of most of the city's best shopping and attractions. The María Cristina is a splendid Belle Epoque building whose beautifully renovated interior is a stunning, superbly elegant fin-de-siècle jewel with glittering chandeliers, beautiful thick carpeting, sumptuous furnishings, liveried doormen, and luxurious rooms that have beautiful views of the Río Urumea and the sea (from the north- and east-facing rooms). The **Gritti**, the hotel bar, one of San Sebastián's elite social spots, is at its best in the early evening. The hotel's restaurant, **Easo**, serves a sophisticated menu of Basque and international haute cuisine and on Saturday nights has a *cena musical,* with a classical pianist entertaining at dinner.

The ▶ **Hotel de Londres y de Inglaterra**, Calle de Zubieta 2, San Sebastián's other fine hotel, also takes you back in time. The lobby and furnishings in this comfortable European aristocrat exude the feel of old money and turn-of-the-century leisure. The social scene here is livelier and a little more egalitarian than that at the María Cristina, but the crowd having drinks in the lobby before lunch and, especially, before dinner is no less chic. The Londres e Inglaterra, as it is usually called, is centrally located along the Paseo de la Concha, with exceptional views of the bay.

Because space is at a premium in San Sebastián in summer, and not every traveller can afford the luxury hotels, we have selected several comfortable, if not opulent, medium-range choices in the city. The ▶ **Hotel Niza**, Calle de Zubieta 56, in a fantastic location on the Paseo de la Concha, facing the beach, still exudes Old World charm, complete with a rickety old wire-cage-and-wood elevator and a turn-of-the-century lobby furnished with antiques. The rooms facing the sea (ask for a room "*mirando al mar*") have sensational views, and have recently been given a much needed face-lift. Avoid the Niza's crowded basement pizzeria, which serves the oddest pizzas and soupiest pasta sauces we've ever tasted.

While the service is slack at the ▶ **Hotel Orly**, located on Plaza de Zaragoza just inland from the Paseo de la Concha, every room faces the sea; but only the higher floors have the views. In the same area as the Orly and the Niza is a top-notch, new, medium-range hotel choice, ▶ **Hotel Europa**,

Calle de San Martín 52, located just a block from Playa de la
Concha. Joan Domènech, a Catalan who trained at the Ritz in
Barcelona and the María Cristina here, and his wife, María
Dolores, opened this beautifully renovated Belle Epoque
building in 1990. The rooms are comfortable, well ap-
pointed, and have all the modern conveniences.

The ▶ **Hotel Monte Igueldo** is located 5 km (3 miles)
from the center of town on Monte Igueldo. Its dramatic
setting, stunning views of the bay, and free parking make it a
good choice for those who don't mind driving or taking the
funicular down to the city center. The Monte Igueldo is
decorated in the ubiquitous Scandinavian modern style, but
its rooms are reasonably priced, quite comfortable, and have
incredible vistas. Even if you are not normally an early riser,
leave your drapes open so that the light wakes you for a
daybreak peek at San Sebastián from the terrace of your
room. Few cities are as beautiful as San Sebastián seen from
here at dawn. The hotel also has a swimming pool and
access to the funicular running down to the western end of
Playa de Ondaretta.

Dining in San Sebastián

Some of the best restaurants in Spain can be found in San
Sebastián, and several of them are worthy of a gastronomic
pilgrimage, albeit an expensive one. Including tax and gratu-
ities, expect to spend 5,000 to 10,000 pesetas per person
(even more for a lavish meal in some places), depending on
your choice of wine, at many of these restaurants. When
dining in expensive restaurants here (and elsewhere in
Spain) remember this phrase, which you will see on most
menus: *El IVA (13%) no está incluido en los precios.* You
won't need a translator to tell you that the 13 percent VAT
(value-added tax) is not included in the menu prices.

Most of San Sebastian's restaurants feature many of the
traditional dishes on which the reputation of Basque cuisine
is based, but many of them also emphasize the creative,
French-influenced, and increasingly personal style of *nueva
cocina vasca,* which often reaches the pinnacle of gastronomy but sometimes borders on wretched excess. In San
Sebastián's top restaurants you will find such dishes as
grilled fresh foie gras (from Spain, as are many of the truffles
in jars marketed as "produce of France") served on a bed of
julienned zucchini; crêpes with duck confit in truffle sauce;
dwarf duck with polenta and blueberries; sautéed loin of
lamb and lamb brains with mint and lemon sauce; and a
dazzling variety of other dishes—some sublime, others con-
ceptually flawed and occasionally ridiculous.

Many of San Sebastián's best restaurants require reservations weeks in advance, and many close at different times of the year for up to a month for vacation, so write or call ahead. Most of the restaurants are closed on Sunday nights and often close one other day during the week as well, usually Mondays, but sometimes Tuesdays or Wednesdays.

Juan Mari Arzak, owner of **Arzak**, Alto de Miracruz 21, has established himself as one of the premier signature chefs of Spain, and his restaurant, with its state-of-the art kitchen in an elegantly appointed house in eastern San Sebastián, is a mecca for serious gourmets from all over Europe. Arzak is an increasingly visible star on the world gastronomic stage, and has even been given a number of prestigious awards in France. Arzak was the first restaurant in Spain to be rated three Michelin stars. It also received the highest rating in Spain's *Guía BMW,* and few people will argue if you call it the best restaurant in Spain.

Arzak is expensive, but it lives up to its reputation. Juan Mari Arzak and his wife take your order personally for such dishes as his famous *puding de krabarroka* (rockfish terrine), crêpes stuffed with *txangurro, cigalitas salteadas con ciruelas y pimiento dulce* (langoustines sautéed with prunes and sweet red peppers), roast gamecock, wild boar with sage and quince, and such superb desserts as a pastry with hot chocolate sauce served with chestnut ice cream, a light cheese soufflé with apricot cream and mandarin orange sections, and a *fromage blanc* ice cream with a sauce of red fruits. The house wines are terrific: Txomín Echañiz *txakolí,* the superb *rosado* of Julián Chivite, and Arzak's own private Rioja *reserva.* Even the Basque liqueur *pacharán* is made in-house here. Arzak's tasting menu starts at 7,500 pesetas. The restaurant is located east of San Sebastián on N I on the way to the Pasajes. It is closed from late June to early July, and in November. Tel: (9-43) 28-55-93.

Located 7½ km (5 miles) west of the center of town on Paseo del Padre Orcolaga in Barrio de Igueldo (on Monte Igueldo), **Akelarre,** named for the *akelarre*—a mythological feast and orgy involving witches, sorcerers, and satyrs that Basque folklore says takes place east of San Sebastián in the mountains of Navarra—serves first-rate *nueva cocina* and offers fine views of the Basque coast. Along with Arzak, Pedro Subijana, the chef-owner of Akelarre, is in the vanguard of *nueva cocina vasca* and he continues to vie with the maestro for the honor of having the best restaurant in San Sebastián. Subijana's food is constantly changing, depending on fresh and seasonal ingredients and his own creativity. A sampling of Akelarre's specialties includes: *morcilla* wrapped in cabbage with puréed *alubias,* skate on a bed of spinach, turbot in sea-urchin sauce, *cerceta* (dwarf duck) with polenta and blueberries, and a *menú de degu-*

stación (tasting menu) of desserts that might include a puff pastry layered with peaches and served with a cherry sauce. Akelarre closes from June 1 to 15 and for the month of December. Tel: (9-43) 21-20-52. Afterwards, at the **Ku** discotheque below the restaurant (different ownership), you can do your own version of the *akelarre* until the wee hours with *todo* San Sebastián.

Founded in 1912, **Casa Nicolasa**, at Calle de Aldamar 4, located across the street from the Mercado de la Brecha, has always been among the finest and most elegant restaurants of Guipúzcoa, serving excellent renditions of traditional northern dishes such as *menestra, txangurro,* and hook-and-line-caught *chipirones en su tinta* (squid caught in nets expel most of their ink), as well as seasonal game dishes and something Juan José Castillo, the owner, calls *orgía de postres,* an orgy of desserts. Lately Casa Nicolasa has begun to offer more *nueva cocina* dishes on its menu. Closed for three weeks in February. Tel: (9-43) 42-17-62.

Panier Fleuri, at Paseo de Marqués de Salamanca 1, just around the corner from Nicolasa on a street running along Río Urumea, moved a few years ago from its old digs in the industrial suburb of Rentería, where it had established a decades-old reputation for good food (the restaurant was recently awarded Spain's national prize for gastronomy). *Alta cocina* (haute cuisine) generally rules here, as reflected in such dishes as *cigalas* (langoustines) in puff pastry, salmon with eggplant caviar, pheasant with grapes, artichoke hearts filled with *txangurro,* and venison with chestnut purée and cranberries, all complemented by wines (some of very old vintages) from one of Spain's best cellars. A prix-fixe menu is available for about 5,000 pesetas. Closed for three weeks in June and the last two weeks of December. Tel: (9-43) 42-42-05.

West of San Sebastián on the road to the Barrio de Igueldo, **Jatetxea Rekondo**, at Paseo de Igueldo 57 (on the road up Monte de Igueldo), has the best wine cellar in Spain and one of the greatest wine lists in Europe. Ask the owner, Txomín Rekondo, to show you his superb, temperature-controlled wine cellar that holds over 100,000 bottles, including a staggering list of exceptional old Rioja *reservas* at reasonable prices and such French goodies as Château d'Yquem 1983, Clos de Vougeot 1928, and Château Lafite 1949 in magnum. Rekondo sticks to a menu of traditional dishes such as *revuelto de hongos* (scrambled eggs with forest mushrooms, for which Rekondo is particularly renowned), delicious *pimientos rellenos de bacalao,* a few excellent game dishes such as *caserío*-raised squab, and grilled meats and fish: thick steaks, lamb chops, turbot, sea bream, and so on. It is a perfect (though expensive) place to go when you want to drink a fabulous bottle and do not want elaborate sauces to combat your enjoyment of the wine. Expect to pay a minimum of 6,000 pesetas per person with a good bottle of wine. Closed in November. Tel: (9-43) 21-29-07.

The menu at one of San Sebastián's fastest-rising stars, the very popular and elegant **Urepel**, Paseo de Marqués de Salamanca 3, located next to Panier Fleuri on Río Urumea, changes daily according to what is available in the nearby Mercado de la Brecha. A creative menu, excellent service, and prices that are relatively reasonable in this town have propelled Urepel to a place among the top half-dozen restaurants in San Sebastián. Closed in July and the last two weeks in December. Tel: (9-43) 42-40-40.

In May 1993 Martín Berasategui, the young French-trained chef who is rapidly becoming a superstar of Basque cuisine, moved his exceptional restaurant, Bodegón Alejandro, from San Sebastián's old quarter to Lasarte, the suburb where the Hipódromo de Lasarte racetrack is located. Now called **Restaurante Martín Berasategui**, it is situated in Casa Loidi, an old *caserío* at Entidad Zabaleta 4 (ask your hotel concierge to help you with directions). From the dining room (or the terrace in good weather) you can look out on Berasategui's working farm with its vegetable and herb garden, orchards, and grazing cows, from which Berasategui was getting fresh vegetables, fruits, herbs, and cheeses before he moved out here. The apple-cider vinegar for the *foie-gras caliente al vinagre de sidra* (warm foie gras with cider vinegar) and the stunning apple dessert with caramel ice cream served at Bodegón Alejandro were made from apples grown at the *caserío*. Other notable dishes from Berasategui's kitchen include spider-crab, oyster, and wild asparagus soup; roast venison with blackberry sauce served with a lasagna in apple-chestnut purée; and a puff-pastry dessert with bittersweet chocolate served with hazelnut cream sauce and a bitter cocoa sorbet. After only a few years under Martín's inspired hand, Bodegón Alejandro was rated among the top three restaurants in San Sebastián, along with Arzak and Akelarre, so advance reservations are *imprescindible* (essential). At the new restaurant Berasategui offers two four-course *menús de degustación* for 2,800 and 3,800 pesetas, as well as à la carte menu selections at an average price of 4,000 to 5,000 pesetas for three courses without wine. Restaurante Martín Berasategui is closed the last two weeks of December; Tel: (9-43) 36-64-71.

At **Patxiku Kintana**, Calle de San Jerónimo 22, in the old quarter, ex-jai-alai star Patxi Kintana oversees the dining room, and his mother and wife cook excellent, traditional Basque cuisine with a personal touch: *albóndigas de jabalí* *con alubias* (wild boar meatballs with white beans), *txangurro* in puff pastry, *merluza* with clams and *kokotxas,* and *marmitako* sometimes made with salmon instead of tuna. Closed in the second half of June. Tel: (9-43) 42-63-99.

Chomín, at Avenida de la Infanta Beatriz 16, started out as a small *tapas* bar, famous for its *merluza* with clams, in the industrial town of Eibar, where some of the world's finest shotguns are made. Now Chomín is in a pretty, elegantly appointed chalet near Playa de Ondarreta and still serves the kind of down-to-earth, traditional dishes and homemade desserts that made its reputation, albeit on fancy china and alongside such haute cuisine offerings as foie gras with truffles in puff pastry and squab with foie gras. The prices, however, are more haute than down to earth; the much-heralded *merluza Chomín* costs about 4,000 pesetas. Closed in October. Tel: (9-43) 21-07-05.

In addition to these fine restaurants there are several moderately priced restaurants in the old quarter worthy of special mention. **Asador Bretxa**, Calle del General Echagüe 5 (in the basement), just east of the Mercado de la Brecha, is a popular, moderately priced *asador* (roast house) specializing in grilled seafood such as *cogote de merluza* (tenderloin of hake), *rodaballo, lenguado,* and *rape* (anglerfish), all priced according to market prices and weight. Asador Bretxa also serves traditional Basque specialties such as delicious unstuffed *pimientos de piquillo* in tomato sauce; rich, hearty, sea-flavored *sopa de pescado;* and *almejas* in a light garlic, parsley, and wine sauce. Since there is no official wine list at Bretxa and wines are served in the big *txacolí*/cider glasses, you may want to accompany this good Basque food with a simple, inexpensive Navarra *rosado,* a *txacolí,* or a *crianza* red from La Rioja. The clientele is local, the cellar atmosphere is cozy, and service is friendly, but slow; go when you have time for a leisurely lunch or dinner. Bretxa is just three blocks north of the Hotel María Cristina. Tel: (9-43) 42-05-49.

The venerable **Salduba**, at Calle de la Pescadería 6, open for more than 40 years, still serves traditional dishes such as *merluza Salduba* (hake with clams and *kokotxas*) and *pimientos rellenos de txangurro, bacalao,* or *mariscos,* and a house specialty, oxtail. Closed in November; Tel: (9-43) 42-56-27. **Casa Urbano**, at Calle del 31 de Agosto 17, has earned a loyal local following by offering beautifully grilled fish (especially *rape*), typical Basque seafood dishes such as *kokotxas en salsa verde con almejas* (hake cheeks in parsley and garlic sauce with clams), a good wine list, and reasonable prices. It is especially important to make a reservation here. Closed in the second half of June; Tel: (9-43) 42-04-34. **Itxaropena**, at Embeltrán 16, whose small dining room is in the back room of a popular *tapas* bar, is a great place to go for traditional Basque food including perfectly prepared *bacalao* dishes. Tel: (9-43) 42-45-76.

THE FISHING VILLAGES OF THE BAY OF BISCAY

East of San Sebastián

Several spots in the area stretching from San Sebastián to the French border offer excellent views of the Basque coast. **Monte Ulía**, the third hill of San Sebastián, east of the center of town, has three fine *miradores* (vantage points), including the Mirador de Ballenero (whaler), where a lookout used to watch the sea for an approaching herd.

THE PASAJES

The Pasajes, or the Pasaias, as they are known in Basque— the ports of San Juan, San Pedro, and Ancho—are located a few miles east of San Sebastián in the best-sheltered deep-water harbor between Bilbao and Bordeaux. Most of San Sebastián's commercial shipping uses the port of Ancho; San Pedro and San Juan are among the most productive deep-sea fishing ports in Spain.

Pasajes de San Juan

Pasajes de San Juan (look for signs to Pasaia Donibane, the Basque name), a picturesque fishing village and former whaling port with only one street, is one of the most beautiful towns on the Basque coast. It has all the prerequisites: pretty fishing boats, timbered houses with flower-and-laundry-bedecked balconies and coats of arms, and quayside seafood restaurants. Victor Hugo lived here in 1843 at Calle San Juan 59, now the **Museo Victor Hugo**, whose second floor has a display of models of the best-known ships built in the shipyards of the Pasajes, where the *Mari Galant* (Columbus's *Santa María*) and several ships of the Spanish Armada were constructed.

Don't take a car to San Juan in summer. The town's one-lane street, which actually tunnels through the ground floor of several houses, is a natural traffic jam, and there is only a small car park at the edge of town. Either go by bus from the center of San Sebastián (catch it on Calle de Aldamar near the Mercado de la Brecha) or drive to San Pedro and take the ferry across the inlet.

There are several reasonably priced restaurants serving great seafood in San Juan, all of them with charming glassed-in dining rooms (whose windows are left open in good weather) that look out on the inlet so you can watch the comings and goings on the waterway as you dine. After you have passed a lovely afternoon over lunch at one of these places, don't be surprised if the experience remains more vivid in your memory than a meal at one of the Basque Country's more exalted and expensive spots. At **Casa Cámara**, Calle San Juan 79, you can order *paella de mariscos* (for two, minimum), grilled fish, and traditional Basque dishes, or choose a *langosta* (rock lobster) or a *centollo* (spider crab) from holding pens hauled up from an opening in the dining room floor that leads directly to the harbor waters below. Tel: (9-43) 52-36-99. Open for more than 20 years, **Txulotxo**, Calle San Juan 82, has a pretty little dining room on the water. Renowned for his *txangurro,* the friendly chef-owner, Luis Benito, also offers such traditional dishes as *espárragos dos salsas* (white asparagus with both vinaigrette and mayonnaise), *almejas a la marinara, chipirones en su tinta,* lamb chops, and steak. Txulotxo is closed from October 15 to November 15; Tel: (9-43) 52-39-52.

FUENTERRABIA

Fuenterrabía (Hondarribia in the Basque language) is some 20 km (12½ miles) east of San Sebastián and 15 km (9 miles) east of the Pasajes. The drive on the corniche road over the heights of **Monte Jaizkíbel**, between the Pasajes and Fuenterrabía, provides the most spectacular views of the entire coast and is highly recommended as an alternative to the faster N 10 or A 1.

Overlooking the mouth of Río Bidasoa where it marks the border with France (Cabo Higuer, a few miles north of Fuenterrabía, has fine views of the French coast), Fuenterrabía was a key fortress town for centuries, and still retains substantial sections of its old ramparts. The historic **castle** was originally built in the tenth century and was reinforced six centuries later during the reign of Charles V. In 1638, during a two-month siege by French forces, the people of Fuenterrabía put up a heroic defense in this castle, an event commemorated each year on September 8 with a fiesta in honor of the town's patroness, the Virgin of Guadalupe. The castle, with its thick fortress walls and *bovedas* (vaults), has been converted into the moderately priced 16-room ▶ **Parador de Turismo El Emperador**, decorated with period furniture, antiques, suits of armor, heraldic banners, and other paraphernalia evoking a medieval atmosphere. The terrace has beautiful views of the sea and neighboring France.

If you want to stay at the parador, advance reservations are a must unless you luck into a last-minute cancellation. If you can't get into the parador, there is another exceptional hotel, the charming ▶ **Hotel Pampinot**, in a beautiful 15th-century palace in the center of old Fuenterrabía. It rivals the parador for atmosphere, but, alas, it has only eight rooms, so you may have to try the less romantic but adequate ▶ **Hotel Jauregui**, a modern 53-room hotel in the center of town.

Around in Fuenterrabía

Fuenterrabía itself is a picturesque town of steep, narrow streets lined with baronial houses embellished, like those of San Juan, with flower-covered balconies and coats of arms. The town has ten art galleries and a number of antiques shops.

The fishermen's quarter, **La Marina**, has a colorful fishing fleet, flower-bedecked houses, sidewalk seafood restaurants, and *la lonja* (fish auction). In 1660 Louis XIV of France was married by proxy to María Teresa, daughter of Philip IV, in the historic and imposing Gothic church of Santa María here, paving the way for the eventual introduction of the Bourbon dynasty into Spain. In this area, near *la lonja* and Arraunlari restaurant (see below) is the old-fashioned **Ferretería María Rosario Berrotarán**, at Kalea Domingo Egía 1, a hardware shop where you can buy great baskets, pottery cookware, and unusual kitchen utensils such as a bread knife whose wooden handle and sheath are carved in the shape of a baguette.

Dining in Fuenterrabía

Fuenterrabía has an exceptional and very expensive restaurant, **Ramón Roteta**, in the Villa Ainara on Calle Irún. Ramón Roteta is one of the early stars of *nueva cocina vasca;* he was the chef at Madrid's brilliantly successful El Amparo. His restaurant, perhaps the most elegant in Guipúzcoa—a few years ago readers of Spain's best-regarded gourmet publication voted it one of the three most elegant restaurants in the country—is in a stunningly beautiful old house with a lovely flower garden, dining terrace, and porch. Each table is set with different patterned tablecloth, silver, china, and glassware to suggest the atmosphere of a private home.

Roteta's kitchen regales the guests with such dishes as poached, country-fresh eggs with foie gras and truffles, vegetable-and-fish terrine served with olive oil infused with pimiento, oven-roasted rockfish, sole poached in *txacolí* with *cangrejos del río* (river crayfish), Bidasoa salmon filled with langoustine tails and mushrooms, and exotic desserts such as a mandarin-orange tart with rose-petal cream. The menu is complemented by an excellent wine list, liqueur selection, and, totally acceptable in fine restaurants in Spain, a good selection of properly cared-for *habanos* (Cuban cigars). Closed in February and the second half of November; Tel: (9-43) 64-16-93.

Arraunlari, on Paseo Butrón, the esplanade along the Río Bidasoa, excels at the fine Basque art of preparing fish, which is delivered directly to the restaurant by local fishermen each day. If you haven't already had *rodaballo* or *cogote de merluza,* which must be ordered for two or more people and is priced according to its weight and the prevailing market price, try it here. In addition to sparkling fresh *mariscos* (shellfish), you can try such dishes as *merluza al calvados* and *lenguado al txacolí.* Closed from December 15 to January 15; Tel: (9-43) 64-15-81.

OYARZUN

There is only one reason to stop at Oyarzun (Oiartzun), a village halfway between Fuenterrabía and San Sebastián (just two miles southeast of A 1 on your way back from Fuenterrabía), and that is a restaurant. Soaring now into the culinary heights in a province already blessed with some of Spain's greatest restaurants is family-run **Zuberoa,** in the Barrio Iturrioz (ask for directions in the village). In just a few years the Arbelaitz brothers—chef Hilario, pastry chef José María, and maître d'hôtel Eusebio—have made Zuberoa one of the top three restaurants in the province and one of the top ten in Spain. Located on its own pretty little plaza on the outskirts of Oyarzun, this beautiful restaurant is in a renovated 600-year-old *caserío* (the oldest in this area) built of local stone and timber. Twenty-five years ago this building housed both a village bar and a stable, now the main dining room. The dark wood pillars and beams, flagstone floors, antiques, and fine oil paintings on the old stone walls create a wonderful atmosphere for the superb food of Hilario Arbelaitz, one of Spain's most talented chefs. Each dish is served on beautiful china with a different pattern (usually from a different producer) for every course.

A sampling of Arbelaitz's creations might include a lovely appetizer of *cigalas* wrapped in a cabbage leaf and served with a diced tomato and chopped truffle vinaigrette (on Villeroy & Boch china); a mousse of *nécora* crab surrounded by a creamy green asparagus sauce (this on English china); *verduras salteadas,* an exquisite *menestra* made from young, tender artichokes, peas, and green and white asparagus, some of it from the *caserío*'s garden; and a hearty and delicious foie-gras dish with a garbanzo and cabbage purée. The desserts, served on local Bidasoa china, are spectacular. The voluminous wine list has among other such offerings 17 vintages of CUNE, including 1970 Imperial Gran Reserva. A *menú de degustación* is available for 7,500 pesetas. Even the bathrooms here rate a comment: They are marked simply "A" and "G," the initials for the Basque words *andrea* (women) and *gizona* (men). Zuberoa is closed in the first half of January, the first half of June, and the last half of October; Tel: (9-43) 49-12-28.

West of San Sebastián

ZARAUTZ

West of San Sebastián are three fishing and beach towns that can be visited easily in a half-day outing. Take the road along Playa de la Concha and follow the signs to the *autopista,* then follow it 17 km (10½ miles) west to Zarautz, once the summer residence of Isabella II. Here, in 1868, Isabella learned that she was no longer queen, so she left for exile in France. The town, with its beautiful mile-long beach, is still a popular summer place for aristocrats, but the villa-lined blocks between the main road and the beach offer few places to park. It can be frustrating just trying to get a look at the beach, so you may not want to get tied up here.

Zarautz does have an exceptional restaurant, **Karlos Arguiñano**, Calle Mendilauta 13, that offers first-rate traditional and modern Basque cuisine based primarily on seafood. More than a decade ago Karlos Arguiñano was a star pupil at the Zarautz cooking school run by Luis Irizar, one of the chefs responsible for the evolution of *nueva cocina vasca,* and over the years Arguiñano has become part of the vanguard of great Basque *cocina del autor,* signature cuisine. His kitchen is inventive, constantly creating new dishes from fresh, seasonal market products, redefining traditional Basque dishes, and putting a personal twist on others. Arguiñano is an elegant restaurant in a beautiful old summer house with a dining terrace and gardens facing the sea; Tel: (9-43) 13-00-00. Arguiñano recently converted the upper floors of the house into the charming and expensive ▶ **Hotel Karlos Arguiñano** with 12 rooms.

GUETARIA

Guetaria, a fishing village 9 km (5½ miles) northwest of Zarautz along a twisting coastal road, is the most picturesque and interesting town on this part of the coast. The village sits on a hill facing the port, the sea, and Isla San Antón (known locally as El Ratón because its shape resembles a crouching mouse), which is connected to the mainland by a short, man-made isthmus.

Guetaria's 13th- to 15th-century **Iglesia Parroquial de San Salvador**, built on the remains of a 12th-century church, is one of the most architecturally interesting religious monuments in the province of Guipúzcoa. A curiosity is the steep alleyway leading to the port, which passes beneath an archway that is part of the buttressing of the church. In the archway is an image of the Virgin especially venerated by village fishermen, who pass by here on their way to their boats and the rough seas of the Cantabrian coast.

Juan Sebastián Elcano, the man who brought back the battered remnants of Magellan's fleet and crew (one of the five ships and fewer than 20 of the more than 265 men who originally began the voyage limped into Sanlúcar de Barrameda three years later), thus becoming the first man to circumnavigate the globe, was from Guetaria. There is a fine statue of Elcano in the center of town.

Dining in Guetaria

Across the street from the Elcano statue is the excellent and expensive seafood restaurant **Elkano**, Calle Herrerieta 2, where the fish and *mariscos* are sparkling fresh and, when ordered *a la parilla* (grilled), are done outdoors on the grill in the front of the restaurant. Elkano is closed in November; Tel: (9-43) 83-16-14.

If you want to dine in the port area, and you probably will, since the tantalizing smell of fresh fish roasting on the outdoor grills of Guetaria's *asadores* is inescapable, **Kaia-Kaipe**, General Arnao 10 (just down the street from the archway below the San Salvador church), is the best choice if money is no object. Owned by the same family as Elkano, Kaia-Kaipe, which also specializes in impeccably fresh, expensive fish and shellfish, is decorated in an attractive maritime theme, and has a terrace that looks out on the port. The wine list is first-rate. Closed in March and the last two weeks in November; Tel: (9-43) 83-24-14. Also decorated with maritime trappings such as a fisherman's dinghy, a pilot's wheel, and fishing nets, **Talai-Pe**, on the San Antón isthmus, has dining rooms that look out over the harbor. Especially in cool weather, Talai-Pe is a good, if overpriced, choice; Tel: (9-43) 83-16-13.

In good weather you can get a salad, a splendid *rodaballo* sprinkled with lemon and oil and grilled over hot coals, and a bottle of Guetaria *txakolí* or *sidra*—both among the best in the Basque Country—at the unassuming dockside fishermen's bar **Itxas-Etxe**, served at an open-air table under the arcade; Tel: (9-43) 83-39-80. If you are ever going to try *chipirones en su tinta,* Guetaria is the place that made this squid dish famous.

ZUMAYA

Zumaya, 5 km (3 miles) west of Guetaria, at the mouth of Río Urola, is another picturesque fishing village, with a small beach in the harbor, a larger beach along the sea, a lighthouse, and a footbridge over the boat moorings of the Urola.

The main attraction in Zumaya is the **Villa Zuloaga**, just east of town, the home of Ignacio Zuloaga (1870–1945), the Basque Impressionist painter. Built on the site of a Camino de Santiago (the old northern route) pilgrims' inn called Santiago Echea, of which a 12th-century chapel and portions of the cloister remain, Villa Zuloaga is now a museum containing works of Zuloaga and works from the artist's personal collection, including several paintings by El Greco, Goya, Zurbarán, and Luis de Morales.

Just east of Villa Zuloaga is a turnoff to the right that parallels the Río Urola. About 3 km (1½ miles) along this road, near the Meagas–Cestona crossroads, is **Bedua**, a terrific traditional country restaurant that even many sophisticated diners from San Sebastián don't know about, probably because there is not so much as a sign to indicate it is there. Look to the right along the river for some old, ruined buildings, in the center of which is the *caserío* with a little boat tied up alongside. Park next to the vegetable garden and go around the building to the charming, homey dining-room-cum-bar. Thick stone walls, heavy timber supports, trestle tables, and wine barrel ends create a warm and cozy ambience, especially on a chilly day in the Basque Country. The Oriondo family, headed by José Mari at the bar, serves wonderful *revueltos de gambas y ajos tiernos* (scrambled eggs with shrimp and garlic shoots), *pimientos de Bedua rellenos de bacalao, angulas* from Río Urola, family-sized portions of grilled fish such as their exceptional garlicky, lemony *cogote de merluza*, thick steaks, vegetables from the *caserío*'s garden, homemade house wines, and cider. In good weather, you can dine outdoors at tables along the banks of the Río Urola. Tel: (9-43) 86-05-51.

SOUTH TO AZPEITIA

Those interested in Saint Ignatius Loyola (1491–1556), founder of the Jesuits, can visit the huge sanctuary of Loyola at **Azpeitia**, 16 km (10 miles) south of Zumaya. Follow N 634 a few miles west from Zumaya, then take C 6317 south, past the spa town of Cestona (Zestoa), known for its mineral waters. The ▶ **Gran Hotel Balneario de Cestona** is a fin-de-siècle spa for taking the waters for the digestion.

The **Santuario de Loyola** surrounds what is left of the former Loyola ancestral home, including the 14th-century tower where Saint Ignatius was born and years later, while recuperating from the wounds he received as a soldier defending Pamplona from a French attempt to recover Spanish Navarra, conceived the idea to form the Society of Jesus (Jesuits).

If you retrace your route back to San Sebastián through Zumaya, Guetaria, and Zarautz, you might skip the *autopista* entrance at Zarautz and follow the N 634 back to town. After Orio, whose oarsmen are the best rowers on the Basque coast, follow the picturesque road through the green hills and along the river for a pleasant re-entry into urban San Sebastián.

If instead of returning to San Sebastián you continue west along the coast road, you will pass two more typical, colorful fishing villages—**Deba**, whose Iglesia de Santa María has a noteworthy 13th-century Gothic portal and a 15th-century cloister, and **Motrico**—before entering the province of Vizcaya.

VIZCAYA PROVINCE
Coastal Villages

Vizcaya is a small province west of Guipúzcoa dominated by industrial Bilbao. **Ondarroa, Lequeito,** and **Bermeo** are the most picturesque fishing villages along the northern coast of Vizcaya, between Zumaya and Bilbao, but the big attraction is **Guernica** (southwest of Lequeito, at the junction of C 6212 and C 6315), the subject of Picasso's painting, which now hangs in the Museo Nacional Centro de Arte Reina Sofía in Madrid. On a market day in April 1937, during the Spanish Civil War, Guernica was bombed (the world's first major air raid against civilians) by General Francisco Franco's German allies. More than 2,000 people died before the *Luftwaffe* was done, and Guernica's tragedy came to symbolize the brutality of war.

Miraculously, after the terrible destruction the **Guernikako arbola**, the Tree of Guernica, long sacred to the Basques, still stood. King Ferdinand the Catholic came here in 1476 and swore to uphold the Basque *fueros* (rights) beneath the tree, and four years later Queen Isabella did the same, dressed in regional costume for the event. After that, all the kings of Castile and Spain made the trip to swear (*jurar*) beneath the venerated oak until 1876, when Vizcaya lost its *fueros* because it sided with the Carlists. Juan Carlos I, the current king of Spain, essentially renewed the custom by going to Guernica for a speech to the new Basque parliament in 1978. Grown from a cutting taken from the original oak, a descendant of the tree still stands. A piece of the old tree, said to be a thousand years old, is preserved at the Casa de Juntas (Vizcaya's assembly hall).

North of Guernica on C 6315, just a few miles southeast of colorful **Bermeo** (44 km/27½ miles northeast of Bilbao)— the most important fishing port on the Mar Cantábrico—is the pretty village of **Mundaka**, in which is the charming, inexpensive 12-room ▶ **Hotel el Puerto**, ensconced in a renovated fisherman's house overlooking the port. Just as Aguiñaga is famous for *angulas* and Guetaria for *chipirones en su tinta,* Mundaka is supposed to have the best *rodaballo;* Bermeo and other nearby villages the best tuna; Ondarroa the best *merluza;* and Santurce, a suburb of Bilbao, the best sardines. There are great waves for surfing along this coast, too.

Bilbao

Bilbao, the capital of Vizcaya since 1300, is now a large (population 385,000), modern industrial city divided by the commercial, crane-lined Río Nervión and surrounded by steep green hills. Bilbao's smoky factories account for its prosperity, but the city has been hit hard in recent years by high unemployment brought on by a steep recession, which in turn has been exacerbated by acts of terrorism.

The Basque government, however, has big plans for this Pittsburgh by the sea, and has begun sprucing up downtown along the river banks as part of a project to turn Bilbao into a major financial center. One of the centerpieces of this renaissance will be the Guggenheim Museum Bilbao, scheduled to be completed by late 1996 or early 1997.

AROUND IN BILBAO

The *casco viejo* (old quarter) of Bilbao, on the eastern bank of the Nervión, was renovated after a disastrous flood in 1983, and the results are impressive. Its narrow pedestrian-only streets are filled with bars offering the same kind of *tapas*-prowling opportunities as can be found in San Sebastián. Be aware, however, that, unlike in San Sebastián, many people here will speak to you only in Basque; they refuse to answer in Spanish.

The attractions of note in the old quarter are the much-restored **Catedral de Santiago**, originally built in the 14th century, with a Gothic cloister from 1404, and the arcaded Plaza Nueva. The **Museo de Bellas Artes** (Fine Arts Museum), in the Parque de Doña Casilda Iturriza in the new part of town, contains paintings by Velázquez, El Greco, Goya, Zurbarán, the Basque painter Regoyos, and Joaquín Sorolla, as well as Italian and Flemish artists.

BULLFIGHTS AND SPORTS IN BILBAO

Semana Grande, beginning the first Saturday after August 15, when the biggest bulls in Spain are brought to Bilbao to face Spain's bravest matadors, the majority of whom are from Andalusia or Castile, is a big event for bullfight aficionados. Tickets are not easy to come by for these important *corridas,* so if you have no luck at the *taquilla official* (ticket window) at the Plaza de Toros, and you won't pay the outrageous prices asked by scalpers, try the concierge of your hotel (ask about the surcharge) or the concierge of the Hotel Ercilla, where many of the *toreros* stay.

If you want to see something truly frightening, try to get a ticket to see a soccer match in San Mames stadium when Atletico de Bilbao is playing one of the first-division teams from Madrid.

DINING IN BILBAO

The big draw in Bilbao, however, if you are a lover of great food, is the restaurant scene. Bilbao has more than 20 highly rated restaurants. Although you may need a Basque interpreter to help you with some of the names—Gorrotxa, Goizeko-Kabi, Zortziko, and Jolastoki, to list a few—you will have no trouble remembering the dining experience, for either the exceptional quality of the cuisine or the size of *la cuenta* (the check).

Bilbao is the capital of *bacalao* (salt cod) dishes: *a la vizcaina,* made with dried sweet red peppers, garlic, onion, parsley, and ham; *al pil-pil,* with garlic and chili peppers; stuffed into peppers; put into salads; and prepared a variety of other ways. Try Demetrio and Adela Sainz's preparations of *bacalao* at **Victor**, Plaza Nueva 2, in the heart of the old quarter. Wash it down with a fine wine from Demetrio's famous wine cellar, which he is rebuilding now after the disastrous flood of 1983 washed thousands of bottles of Rioja's finest *reservas* down the Nervión, no doubt to the eternal gratitude of the sardines of Santurce downriver. Tel: (9-4) 415-1678.

Generally considered to be the greatest restaurant in Vizcaya, **Goizeko-Kabi**, at Calle Estraunza 4, will dazzle you with superlative preparations of dishes both classic and new: *pochas* with homemade *chorizo,* wild *perrichico* mushrooms with *kokotxas al pil-pil,* fresh foie gras, and langoustines with oyster and clam ravioli. You can contemplate the splendor of your meal (and the diminution of your net worth) over one of the equally splendid armagnacs, cognacs, or *aguardientes* from the restaurant's exceptional after-dinner list. Tel: (9-4) 441-5004.

At **Guria**, Gran Vía 66, you will find elements of *nueva cocina,* to be sure, but they are firmly based on the underpinnings of traditional Basque cookery, of which the owner-chef, Genaro Pildain, is a master. He is considered to be the maestro when it comes to *bacalao*. Tel: (9-4) 441-0543.

At **Zortziko**, Alameda de Mazarredo 17, the García brothers are known for their wild mushroom dishes and for Daniel's expertise with infusions and sauces made from herbs, vegetables, and fruits. The menu may include tuna carpaccio over farm tomatoes flavored with fennel, *rodaballo* with warm ginger vinaigrette, duck sausage, and a terrine of pink grapefruit with strawberry sauce. Tel: (9-4) 423-9743.

The embarrassment of culinary riches in Bilbao goes on: Hotel Ercilla's **Bermeo**, at Calle Ercilla 37, is considered by many to be the greatest hotel restaurant in Spain; Tel: (9-4) 443-8800. The owner-chef of **Gorrotxa** (at Alameda de Urquijo 30), Carmelo Gorrotxategui, is an alumnus of Goizeko-Kabi and in just over five years has brought his restaurant to within an eyelash of the top; Tel: (9-4) 443-4937. **Jolastoki**, on Avenida Leioako, draws the cream of Bilbao out to the elegant northwestern suburb of Neguri; Tel: (9-4) 469-3031. And many Bilbainos think nothing of the 10-km (6-mile) hop southeast to Galdakao to dine at **Andra-Mari**, Calle Elexalde 22, where a splendidly restored old *caserío* with terrific views overlooking the hills of Bilbao, waitresses in copies of old Basque regional costumes, a wine museum, and some of the best traditional Basque food in the province await; Tel: (9-4) 456-0005.

STAYING IN BILBAO

Bilbao's top hotels are the new, luxurious ▶ **Hotel López de Haro**; the ▶ **Hotel Villa de Bilbao**, a modern super-luxury hotel conveniently located on the Gran Vía in the newer part of town; the ▶ **Hotel Aránzazu**, a comfortable, modern, moderate-to-expensive hotel located near the Parque de Doña Casilda Iturriza in the western section of modern Bilbao; the centrally located ▶ **Hotel Ercilla**, the society epicenter of Bilbao, a favorite of seasoned travellers, the bullfight crowd, and journalists; and the ▶ **Hotel Conde Duque**, reasonably priced in an expensive town, and the best choice for those who want to be near the old quarter.

VITORIA

Vitoria, or, in Basque, Gasteiz, the prosperous capital of both El País Vasco and the province of Alava with a population of more than 200,000, is located 64 km (40 miles) south of Bilbao by way of the A 68 *autopista* and the N I or the difficult mountain route N 240. From the south (via Burgos), Vitoria is easy to reach on the A 1 *autopista* or on the heavily travelled N I, both of which come through the spectacular pass of Pancorvo, southwest of Miranda de Ebro.

AROUND IN VITORIA

Vitoria is divided into two parts, the new town and the medieval quarter. The streets of the newer sections branch off like an irregular spider's web around the picturesque core city, the **Campillo**, or *ciudad vieja* (old city), which was founded in the 12th century by King Sancho the Wise of Navarra on the site of the Basque town of Gasteiz. Tightly wrapped around the highest point in Vitoria, much of this old quarter, including portions of its 12th- and 13th-century walls, is still intact. The Campillo quarter is well worth the day you might devote to Vitoria: Its pedestrians-only streets are fascinating to explore (wear good walking shoes; the steep streets, inclines, and stairways leading up the hill will give your legs a real workout).

The Old Quarter

Imagine the bulb of a small onion cross-sectioned length-wise and you will have a good idea of the old quarter's oval layout. Wrapped in concentric lines around a core block of old buildings and tapering to a point at the north are streets with such medieval names as Herrería (ironsmith), Zapatería (cobbler), Correría (strapmaker), Cuchillería (cutler), and Pintorería (painter). In these narrow streets you will find a number of distinguished old houses and mansions (among them the 16th-century Casa del Cordón and the 15th-century Palacio de Bendaña in Calle Cuchillería), *tapas* bars, gift shops, antiques shops, horsemeat butchers, exotic spice and health-food stores, and student hangouts.

At the northern end of the Campillo (follow Calle Correría or Calle Cuchillería, which converge) are the 14th-century Gothic **Catedral de Santa María**, with an exceptional doorway, and the interesting **Museo Arqueológico**, in a balconied, brick-and-timber palace a couple of blocks northwest. South of the cathedral is the 16th-century Plateresque **Palacio de Escoriaza-Esquivel** (Fernán López de Escoriaza was physician to Henry VIII of England, his Spanish wife, Catherine of Aragón, and Charles V).

If you've food in mind, you might try the 15th-century inn, now a restaurant-cum-museum, **El Portalón**, at Calle Correría 151. The restaurant is expensive, but the food, based on traditional Basque specialties taken a step further (stuffed peppers *al gratín,* for example), is highly rated, and the antiques and old-time trappings in this spectacular house are quite special. El Portalón is known for its *menú de degustación,* a sampling of every dish on the menu. Tel: (9-45) 14-27-55.

If you are in the area at *tapas* time, try a *chorizo a la brasa* at **Tulipán de Oro**, Calle Correría 157. A sliced *chorizo* is presented on a most unusual grill: a small pottery pig with a belly full of flaming cooking alcohol. You grill your own *chorizo* to taste and eat it with chunks of bread, accompanied by bracing glasses of cold *clarete* or beer. You can even purchase a pig brazier to take home.

At the old quarter's southern end (the onion's root), you will find the 14th-century Gothic **Iglesia de San Miguel** perched above the **Plaza de la Virgen Blanca**, named for Vitoria's patroness, represented by a polychrome Madonna and Child occupying a niche at the church entrance overlooking the plaza. Just east of San Miguel, an unusual arcaded set of stairways, the **Arquillos**, leads up to the **Plaza del Machete**, where various outside administrators were made to swear on a *machete* (cutlass) to uphold the *fueros* (rights) of Vitoria, under pain of being beheaded.

The Plaza de la Virgen Blanca is surrounded by shops and fine houses with balconies enclosed by the lovely multi-paned windows characteristic of northern Spain. In the center of the plaza is the large monument built in 1923 to commemorate Wellington's decisive victory at Vitoria over Joseph Bonaparte's booty-laden troops. A good place to relax and contemplate the plaza is from a window table at the **Virgen Blanca Cafetería** (a coffeehouse and bar), in the northwestern corner of the square.

Immediately east of the Wellington monument and the Plaza de la Virgen Blanca is the late-18th-century Greco-Roman-style **Plaza de España**, a symmetrical arcaded square with balconied apartments. Just southeast of this plaza is the post office, where you can snap some amusing photographs of its patrons sticking their mail in the letter drops: the mouths of two well-polished bas-relief lions.

Just northeast of the Plaza de la Virgen Blanca at Calle Mateo B. de Moraza 9 is **Restaurante Zabala**, a typical area restaurant, very popular with the people of Vitoria and a good lunch spot. *Alubias rojas, menestra, revueltos con ajos verdes y gambas, cordero* (lamb), and the house wine, a typical young *cosechero* (grower) wine from La Rioja Alavesa, are all good here. With your *café*, sample a *licor de manzana verde* (green-apple liqueur), a Basque *pacharán* (sloeberry-flavored anisette), or *aguardiente* (marc), delicious after-dinner drinks served super-chilled; Tel: (9-45) 23-00-09.

South of the Old Town

Southwest of the Plaza de la Virgen Blanca at the end of Calle del Prado, and next to the shady, flower-filled Jardines de la Florida, is the **Catedral de María Inmaculada**, known as the

New Cathedral, a striking Neo-Gothic church (begun early in this century but consecrated only 20 years ago), whose apse resembles a giant crown.

The **Museo de Bellas Artes**, with its finely sculpted topiary gardens, is located south of the cathedral in the Palacio de Agustín on the Paseo de Fray Francisco de Vitoria. The museum has a pair of paintings by José Ribera and one by Alonso Cano. The collection of the diocese of Alava here displays polychrome religious sculpture, custodials, ecclesiastical garments, some fine triptychs, and five exceptional, highly detailed 16th-century reliquary busts of the Rhenish school.

Across from the Museo de Bellas Artes in the **Palacio de Ajuria-Enea**, at Paseo de Fray Francisco de Vitoria 3, is **La Armería** (Arms Museum), which has a fine collection of suits of armor and weapons, some dating from prehistoric times. East of the two museums, and two blocks southwest of the bullring, is Calle Heraclio Fournier, where Casa Fournier, at number 19, houses the **Museo de Naipes**, a museum of playing cards (Fournier is the foremost producer of playing cards in Spain) that date back to the 15th century.

FESTIVALS IN VITORIA

The big fiesta of Vitoria, beginning the week of August 5, is called, not surprisingly, La Fiesta de la Virgen Blanca. At 6:00 P.M. on the eve of the fiesta, an effigy of Celedonio, a mythical bon vivant dressed in Basque costume and holding onto an umbrella, descends, à la Mary Poppins, from a cable attached to the tower of the church of San Miguel across the Plaza de la Virgen Blanca high above the heads of a throng of cheering fiesta-goers, who light up huge cigars to celebrate the moment. The rest is a tamer version of Pamplona, also with top bullfights. Vitoria also hosts a well-regarded jazz festival beginning the third week in July.

DINING IN VITORIA

Since most of the best restaurants in Vitoria—Ikea, Dos Hermanas, Zaldiarán, and Olárizu—are located in the newer sections west of the old town near Avenida de Gasteiz, where most of Vitoria's finest hotels are located, you will probably want to save any *alta cocina* experience for dinner. (Note that many Vitoria restaurants close after the Virgen Blanca fiesta for the rest of August.)

Ikea, in its new location in an early-1900s mansion at Portal de Castilla 27, is now the star among Vitoria's restaurants, featuring elegantly prepared traditional fish dishes and an evolving style that leans increasingly toward *nueva cocina vasca*. Are you ready for sole stuffed with crabmeat *and* foie gras? Tel: (9-45) 14-47-47.

Now a century old, although in a new locale, **Dos Hermanas**, at Calle Madre Vedruna 10, southwest of the Plaza de Lovaina, is still considered to be one of Vitoria's finest restaurants. Dos Hermanas excels with a menu based on typical Alavesa and regional specialties (Cantabrian fish, local mushrooms, cardoons, lamb, wild boar, and so on), and dishes enhanced with those ubiquitous stars of French and modern Basque cuisine: foie gras, *magret* (breast) of duck, vegetables in puff pastry, and others. The wine cellar is extensive, with a great list of Rioja *reservas* and a special selection of wines from La Rioja Alavesa. Tel: (9-45) 13-29-34.

Elegant **Zaldiarán**, at Avenida de Gasteiz 21, and **Olárizu**, Calle del Beato Tomás de Zumárraga 54, located a few blocks north and west of Zaldiarán, are owned by the same person. Zaldiarán, while still serving highly regarded versions of classic dishes such as *pochas* and *menestra,* also features *nueva cocina vasca,* and is the more expensive of the two; Tel: (9-45) 13-48-22. Olárizu tends to lean a little more toward classical cuisine, and, like Zaldiarán, offers a *menú de degustación* so you can sample a range of dishes from the kitchen of its new chef, Iñaki Cacho; Tel: (9-45) 24-77-52.

STAYING IN VITORIA

Vitoria's best hotels are ▶ **NH Canciller Ayala**, Calle Ramón y Cajal 5, located southwest of the Campillo on the southern edge of the Jardines de la Florida, downtown Vitoria's large park, and ▶ **Hotel Gasteiz**, at Avenida de Gasteiz 45, a member of the Aranzazu chain, located on the main avenue leading in from Bilbao and the airport.

If you don't mind a short drive from the city, you may choose the ▶ **Parador de Argómaniz**, located 13 km (8 miles) east of Vitoria off N I (Madrid–Irún highway) at km 361.7 (follow signs to the parador). The parador has 54 rooms in a renovated 17th-century palace that is quiet and has fine views over the Alavesa plain. The parador restaurant, featuring regional specialties, is in an old granary.

ALAVA PROVINCE

In topography, climate, agriculture, and history, the province of Alava is part Basque, part Navarrese, part Castilian, and part Riojan. In the north are rainy, pine-clad mountains enveloped in mists. Stretching to the southwest are the wheat fields and high plains of Castile. In the seldom-visited eastern part, craggy mountains border Navarra. To the south the Sierras de Cantabria form a stunning, blue-gray backdrop for the terraced vineyards of La Rioja Alavesa along the Ebro. Scattered throughout the province are a number of isolated mountain villages waiting to be discovered by the intrepid traveller who is undaunted by winding mountain roads.

The main attraction in Alava province outside of Vitoria is the **Rioja Alavesa** wine district, with its strikingly beautiful mountain scenery and not-to-be-missed wine town of Laguardia. We cover it in the following chapter on La Rioja because, geographically, it is separated from La Rioja by only a couple of miles, while more than 30 miles of twisting mountain roads separate it from the Alava provincial capital, Vitoria.

GETTING AROUND

The Basque Country is served by the *autopista* combination A 1, A 68, A 8, which is both expensive and indirect unless you are going straight to Bilbao, but given the alternative of the truck-clogged national and regional highways, with serpentine mountain passages that often become extremely dangerous in winter, it is your best bet. Coming from France to San Sebastián is nothing; going from San Sebastián to Vitoria or Pamplona is a difficult drive over mountain roads. There are airports in Bilbao, Vitoria, and Fuenterrabía (for San Sebastián), with daily flights from Madrid. There is daily train and bus service linking all three major cities in the Basque Country to Madrid and other cities. Local bus service can get you to most of the villages in the region.

ACCOMMODATIONS REFERENCE

The hotel rates listed below are projected rates for 1994, for double room, double occupancy, in pesetas. We strongly recommend that you confirm the price when making reservations.

When dialing telephone numbers from outside the country, drop the 9 in the area code.

▶ **Gran Hotel Balneario de Cestona.** Paseo San Juan, 20740 **Cestona**. Tel. and Fax: (9-43) 14-71-40. Closed December 15 to March 15. 7,200–9,000 pts.

▶ **Hotel Aránzazu.** Rodríguez Arias 66, 48013 **Bilbao**. Tel: (9-4) 441-3100; Fax: 441-6529. 15,400 pts.

▶ **Hotel Conde Duque.** Campo de Volantín 22, 48007 **Bilbao**. Tel. and Fax: (9-4) 445-6000. 13,000 pts.

▶ **Hotel Ercilla.** Calle Ercilla 37, 48011 **Bilbao**. Tel: (9-4) 443-8800; Fax: 443-9335. 21,765 pts.

▶ **Hotel Europa.** Calle de San Martín 52, 20007 **San Sebastián**. Tel: (9-43) 47-08-80; Fax: 47-17-30. 17,600 pts.

▶ **Hotel Gasteiz.** Avenida de Gasteiz 45, 01009 **Vitoria**. Tel: (9-45) 22-81-00; Fax: 22-62-58. 15,500 pts.

▶ **Hotel Jauregui.** Calle San Pedro 28, 20280 **Fuenterrabía**. Tel: (9-43) 64-14-00; Fax: 64-44-04. 9,800 pts.

▶ **Hotel Karlos Arguiñano.** Calle Mendilauta 13, 20800 **Zarautz.** Tel: (9-43) 13-00-00; Fax: 13-34-50. 20,300–24,600 pts.

▶ **Hotel de Londres y de Inglaterra.** Calle de Zubieta 2, 20007 **San Sebastián.** Tel: (9-43) 42-69-89; Fax: 42-00-32. 16,500 pts.

▶ **Hotel López de Haro.** Obispo Orueta 2, 48008 **Bilbao.** Tel: (9-4) 423-5500; Fax: 423-4500. 29,950 pts.

▶ **Hotel María Cristina.** Paseo de la República Argentina 4, 20004 **San Sebastián.** Tel: (9-43) 42-49-00; Fax: 42-39-14. 25,000 pts.

▶ **Hotel Monte Igueldo.** Paseo del Faro 134, 20008 **San** Sebastián. Tel: (9-43) 21-02-11; Fax: 21-50-28. 15,000 pts.

▶ **Hotel Niza.** Calle de Zubieta 56, 20007 **San Sebastián.** Tel: (9-43) 42-66-63; Fax: 42-66-63. 11,650 pts.

▶ **Hotel Orly.** Plaza de Zaragoza 5, 20007 **San Sebastián.** Tel: (9-43) 46-32-00; Fax: 45-61-01. 14,500–15,950 pts.

▶ **Hotel Pampinot.** Nagusia (Mayor) 3, 20280 **Fuenter-rabía.** Tel: (9-43) 64-06-00; Fax: 64-51-28. Closed February. 17,000 pts.

▶ **Hotel el Puerto.** Portu Kalea 1, 48360 **Mundaka.** Tel: (9-4) 687-6725; Fax: 617-7064. 9,000 pts.

▶ **Hotel Villa de Bilbao.** Gran Vía 87, 48011 **Bilbao.** Tel: (9-4) 441-8150; Fax: 441-6529. 20,000 pts.

▶ **NH Canciller Ayala.** Calle de Ramón y Cajal 5, 01007 **Vitoria.** Tel: (9-45) 13-00-00; Fax: 13-35-05. 15,500 pts.

▶ **Parador de Argómaniz.** Apartado 601, 01080 **Vitoria.** 13 km (8 miles) east of Vitoria off N 1 (Madrid–Irún highway), km 361.7. Tel. and Fax: (9-45) 28-22-00. 10,500 pts.

▶ **Parador de Turismo El Emperador.** Plaza Armas del Castillo, 20280 **Fuenterrabía.** Tel: (9-43) 64-21-40; Fax: 61-21-53. 14,000 pts.

LA RIOJA

By Gerry Dawes

La Rioja, which takes its name from the Río Oja, a small tributary of the Ebro, is located some 300 km (185 miles) northeast of Madrid. It lies south of the Basque Country—Bilbao, Vitoria, and San Sebastián—and west of Navarra. Its chief city, Logroño, is 113 km (70 miles) east of Old Castile's Burgos on N 120. The region's craggy, serrated mountains form a dramatic backdrop for a trough-shaped valley scored by thousands of terraced vineyards. The famous Rioja wine-making district stretches for 80 miles along the banks of the Río Ebro, which flows southeast past Tudela, through southern Navarra, past Zaragoza in Aragón, and finally empties into the Mediterranean between Tarragona and Valencia.

Besides the obvious attractions of visiting bodegas, which range from rustic, century-old working wine museums to state-of-the-art wineries rivaling those of California, this mountain enclave offers plenty of little-known, delightful attractions to the discerning traveller. La Rioja is dotted with picturesque old villages, castles, and monasteries rich in history. The great pilgrims' road of the Middle Ages, the Camino de Santiago, passes through La Rioja, and several of the famous sites connected with it are prime attractions here.

Shopping at a leisurely pace in a provincial capital such as Logroño is much more fun than running to a big department store in Madrid at the last minute to cover everyone on your gift list. Prices are often better, and, if the selection is not as varied here, the uniquely regional quality of the choices more than compensates. In La Rioja you can buy anything from handmade *botas* (wineskins) to woven baskets, pottery, ceramics, *alpargatas* (rope-soled espadrilles made in La Rioja Baja), handmade wine cradles, and regional culinary specialties ranging from tinned *pimientos de piquillo* (spicy peppers) and tinned white asparagus to local candies. You

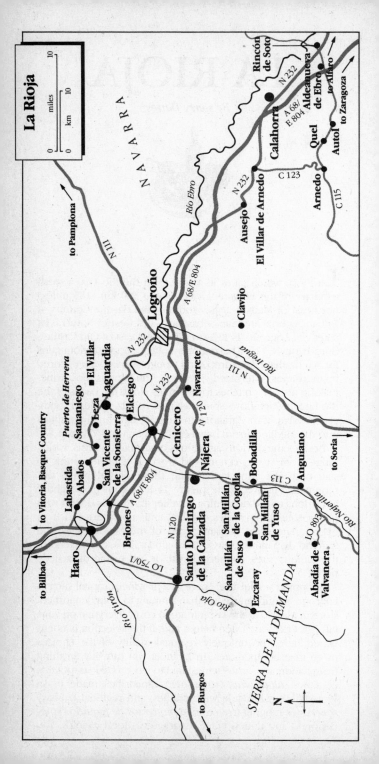

especially might want to take home a couple of La Rioja's wonderful *reserva* and *gran reserva* wines.

The Rioja area is still largely unspoiled and peaceful, the scenery is spectacular, and the mountain air is wonderful. The climate is very pleasant even in summer, except in La Rioja Baja, the area around Calahorra, which, although dry, is very hot. April through November are the best months to visit La Rioja (the grape harvest is usually in October).

MAJOR INTEREST

Spain's finest wines
Simple country food
Beautiful landscape

Logroño
Touring and shopping in the old quarter
Visiting wineries
Dining on local cuisine

The Wine Country
Haro, capital of the Rioja Alta wine district, and
other villages
The walled village of Laguardia
Local wine festivals
Visiting bodegas

The Camino de Santiago
Castle of Clavijo and the legend of Saint James
(Santiago)
Nájera's medieval history and monastery
The monasteries of southern La Rioja
Santo Domingo de la Calzada: medieval lore and
atmosphere

Hunting and fishing in the mountains of southern
La Rioja
La Rioja Baja's ancient villages and Roman heritage

The Food of La Rioja

You will find some of the best country food in Spain in La Rioja, as well as fine wines. The cuisine of La Rioja is simplicity itself, exhibiting few of the elaborate preparations so common in food of the Basque Country. Yet chances are you will remember some Rioja classics long after you have forgotten the sophisticated dishes of the region's neighbors to the north.

Trout, quail, and partridge are well-prepared in La Rioja and can be found on the menus of most restaurants; they are overshadowed, however, by two of the simplest but finest of all Spanish dishes—*pochas* (fat, tender white beans, often cooked with *chorizo* sausage and/or quail), for which a craving bordering on addiction can quickly be acquired, and *chuletillas de cordero al sarmiento* (baby lamb chops grilled over grapevine cuttings). A delicious *ensalada de lechuga, tomate, y cebollas* (lettuce, tomatoes, and onions) dressed with wine vinegar, olive oil, and sea salt, a plate of *pochas,* a brazier stacked with *chuletillas,* a pile of crisp fried potatoes, and a bottle of Rioja shared with friends can be an unforgettable experience.

Other down-to-earth regional specialties are *pimientos a la riojana* (stuffed green peppers in tomato sauce); *espárragos con mahonesa* (succulent white asparagus with homemade mayonnaise); *menestra a la riojana* (a dish made of carrots, leeks, artichokes, green beans, peas, and other vegetables cooked with ham); and *patatas a la riojana* (potatoes cooked with *chorizo* sausage). *Cordero asado* (oven-roasted lamb), *lechazo* (milk-fed baby lamb), and *cabrito asado* (roast kid) are also delicious regional offerings, as are *revueltos con ajo* (scrambled eggs with young green garlic shoots). For dessert try *melocotones en almíbar,* large, whole yellow peaches preserved in syrup.

The Wines of La Rioja

La Rioja's official *denominación de origen* is divided into three zones: La Rioja Alta, centered around the wine capital of Haro and the provincial capital, Logroño; La Rioja Alavesa, the tip of the Basque province of Alava above the Río Ebro between Haro and Logroño; and La Rioja Baja, around the old Roman city of Calahorra, southeast of Logroño and spilling over into southern Navarra.

La Rioja produces traditional-style oak-aged *blancos,* which rely upon mellowed wood flavors, austerity, stony texture, and balance for their appeal, somewhat like the white wines of the Rhône. Modern cold-fermented Rioja whites, which spend little or no time in wood, are reminiscent of Loire Valley wines.

The region yields some excellent *rosados* and *claretes,* (light red wines), but the red wines known as *vinos tintos de crianza* (*crianzas* must be aged at least one year in oak and one year in the bottle) are the backbone of the region's reputation. Some 50 firms here produce wines of such consistently high quality that many experts consider Rioja's red wines some of the best on earth.

When ordering wine in restaurants in La Rioja, it is wise to stick to the generally excellent bottles of oak-aged *crianzas, reservas,* and *gran reservas.* Some restaurants and bars in this great wine region cut corners by serving cheap wines from other regions as house wines. The chances of getting an ersatz Rioja (sometimes a spurious offering from an ill-defined area called "Alto Ebro") in this region are greater than your chances of discovering a house treasure from some little old *bodeguero* (winemaker).

The Tempranillo, a grape believed by some to be a long-acclimatized strain of Burgundy's Pinot Noir, brought to La Rioja centuries ago by the monks of Cluny and Citeaux (who built the first monasteries to help establish the Camino de Santiago), generally accounts for 70 percent or more of a typical Rioja wine. The other authorized grape varietals, Garnacha, Mazuelo, Graciano, and the white Viura, also contribute to the overall balance, harmony, flavor, and aging potential of the wine. Riojas are aged in small oak casks and in bottles for several years before being released.

Rioja *reservas* and *gran reservas* are the glory of Spanish viniculture. In quality and aging potential perhaps their only peers are the great growths of Bordeaux and Burgundy and a few special wines from Italy and California. *Reserva* wines are laid down in good years, *gran reservas* only in exceptional years. The years 1987, 1985, 1982, 1981, 1978, and 1975 are the top vintages you are likely to encounter on current wine lists, but because *reservas* are made only in good years you do not have to worry as much about getting an off year as you do in, say, Bordeaux or Burgundy.

Classic Rioja *gran reservas* from exceptional vintages are meant to reach their peak about 10 to 20 years after the harvest, and some will drink well for up to 30 or 40 years. Since many bodegas do not release their *reservas* for ten years, the wines are, in effect, cellared at the winery until they are ready to drink, aged at the bodega's expense, not the consumer's.

The producers currently making the best wines of La Rioja are CVNE (Compañía Vinícola del Norte de España), López de Heredia, Marqués de Murrieta, Bodegas Riojanas, Muga, La Rioja Alta, Marqués de Cáceres, Montecillo, La Granja Remélluri, Contino, Bodegas Olarra, Beronia, and Palacios Remondo.

VISITING WINERIES

Rioja bodegas do not see all that many foreign visitors, so most of them do not have formal tours set up; but many of them have someone on the premises who speaks English and who can take you around. Sometimes it will be the export director, a company executive, or even a family member. It is a good idea to write or call ahead. Visitors will usually get to taste the wines, which can be purchased in most wineries at bodega prices.

Consult the *Guía Vinos de España,* published by the Club

de Gourmets, for addresses, telephone numbers, names of contacts, and hours of La Rioja's bodegas. This valuable guide can be purchased in major bookstores in Spain. The ARBOR group, an association of ten high-quality wineries that includes CVNE, Marqués de Cáceres, Montecillo, and Contino, is located at Avenida del Rey Juan Carlos I 43, 26002 Logroño; Tel: (9-41) 22-53-04; Fax: 20-40-52. ARBOR can help you arrange visits to the bodegas in its association—except in August, when they are closed for vacation, as are most wineries in Europe.

EXPLORING WINE VILLAGES

The only practical way to cover the beautiful wine villages and other backcountry attractions of La Rioja is by car. The *autopista* (superhighway) A 68 follows the vineyard-lined valley of the Río Ebro, making La Rioja an easy drive from Bilbao or Vitoria to the northwest and from Zaragoza to the east. Logroño, the provincial capital, is 468 km (290 miles) from Barcelona, roughly a five-hour drive on the *autopista,* if you don't mind paying the expensive tolls. The routes from Pamplona (to the northeast) and Burgos (to the west), the picturesque N 111 and N 120, respectively, follow the historic Camino de Santiago.

To get the most from a visit to La Rioja, make Logroño your base and accomplish your sightseeing and winery visits on day trips. For extensive exploration and winery visits in western La Rioja, make Haro or Santo Domingo de la Calzada your base.

Every September 16 to 25, Logroño celebrates its San Mateo Rioja wine harvest festival, with a grape-treading contest, parades, bands, and bullfights. It's a major fiesta and a fine one.

LOGROÑO

Logroño, the capital of La Rioja, with a population of 120,000, is located on a river plain on the south bank of the Río Ebro, just south of the Basque Country. Except for its medieval core, which evolved over the centuries from the Roman city of Juliobriga, Logroño is a modern city of broad avenues and affluent-looking apartment blocks rising a few stories above smart shops, cafés, and bars. At first look the city seems to have nothing of compelling interest, other than wine, to merit a detour, but once you get to know this prosperous, efficient provincial capital it begins to grow on you. Logroño is an easy city to get in and out of, its old quarter bustles with life, and the absence of tourists is an attraction in itself.

You are not likely to suffer from acute attacks of visit-amonumentitis in Logroño. Except for seeing the cathedral of Santa María de la Redonda and the churches of Santiago el Real, Santa María de Palacio, and San Bartolomé (all of which can be done in about an hour), the main demands on your time in Logroño are winery visits, shopping, lazing over a drink in early evening at the Plaza del Espolón, and searching out good *tapas* bars in the *casco viejo,* the old quarter.

The *casco viejo,* in the north-central part of town next to the river, contains all the main historical attractions, some of Logroño's most interesting shops, and most of the city's best *tapas* bars and restaurants. The area is eminently walkable and can be reached easily on foot from the major hotels.

THE GRAN VIA TO PLAZA DEL ESPOLON

A good place to start a walking tour of Logroño is on the fine shop-lined boulevard Gran Vía del Rey Juan Carlos I (known simply as the Gran Vía), in the vicinity of the Hotel Carlton Rioja (at number 5), the city's best hotel (see below). Just east of the Carlton is a modern monument to the *labrador* that pays homage to agricultural workers, especially those who work the small vineyard plots so important to the economy of the region. Walking north from the *labrador* monument on Calle del General Vara del Rey, you will soon reach the beautiful tree-shaded **Plaza del Espolón**, which has a bandshell, fountains, kiosks, flower gardens, outdoor cafés, and a colossal equestrian statue of General Baldomero Espartero, Logroño's favorite son.

Espartero was a hero of the 19th-century Carlist Wars and one-time regent of Spain before Isabella II assumed the throne. He was heartily disliked in Catalonia, after he directed a destructive attack on Barcelona in 1843, but was much admired by Washington Irving, who travelled a great deal in Spain and was U.S. ambassador to Spain for several years. Espartero married an heiress from Logroño, eventually retired to La Rioja, and put a bodega and some vineyards that he owned at the disposal of Luciano Murrieta, one of his most trusted aides. Murrieta, who travelled to Bordeaux to study wine-making methods, patterned the new Rioja winery after the famous Bordeaux châteaux of the 1850s. He is considered the father of the Rioja wine-making style, and the bodega he founded, Marqués de Murrieta, still produces excellent wines.

THE CASCO VIEJO

From the northeastern corner of the Plaza del Espolón, walk north along Muro del Carmen to reach the first of two national monuments, **Iglesia de San Bartolomé**, a 12th- and 13th-century church with a fine Mudejar tower and an interesting, but deteriorated, early-14th-century portal depicting scenes from the life of Saint Bartholomew. A block north, on Calle del Marqués de San Nicolás, is the **Iglesia de Santa María de Palacio**, another national monument. Santa María was part of a palace given to the Knights of the Order of the Holy Sepulchre by King Alfonso VII in the early 12th century. The building's main attraction is the unusual 13th-century ogival spire, **La Aguja** (The Steeple or The Needle), considered to be one of the most beautiful in Spain.

One block north of San Nicolás, turn left (west) on Rúa Vieja (all along the Camino de Santiago are towns with medieval *rúas* that trace the old route, *rúa* being a linguistic legacy of the dominant French influence in northern Spain during that epoch) and walk two blocks to Calle de Sagasta, which crosses the Río Ebro on the Puente de Hierro (Iron Bridge). At the north end of the bridge is the turn-of-the-century Bodegas Franco-Españolas, a winery now producing some palatable but run-of-the-mill wines in a modern, facile style. You can visit the bodega weekday mornings if you call ahead; Tel: (9-41) 25-13-00.

Just west of Calle de Sagasta are the **Iglesia de Santiago el Real** and an old fountain used by Santiago pilgrims. High on the church's southern façade is the most amazing statue of Santiago Matamoros (Saint James the Moorslayer) on the entire pilgrims' route. Wearing a plumed hat and dressed in a tunic and flowing robes more suited to a bishop than a warrior, Santiago charges into the battle at Clavijo (see the Camino de Santiago section, below), wielding a large saber in one hand and holding a streaming banner in the other. The saint's huge horse tramples a multitude of Moors under his feet and exhibits what author Edwin Mullins described as "the most heroic genitalia in all Christendom, a sight to make any surviving Moor feel inadequate and run for cover."

Return to Calle de Sagasta and walk uphill (south) from the river. On the left you will find a *bota* shop, **Félix Barbero**, and the excellent roast house, Asador La Chata (see Dining in Logroño, below). At Calle Portales turn east and you will see the 15th- and 16th-century **Catedral de Santa María de la Redonda**, whose stark lines pleasingly contrast with its 18th-century main façade and fine Baroque twin towers. The **Plaza del Mercado**, in front of the cathedral, and Calle Portales, alongside it, are both arcaded and lined with shops (selling crafts and *alpargatas*) that are among the most interesting in Logroño. In a little alley, Travesía Ollería, just southeast of the cathedral, is **Baden**, a great bar for shellfish and draft beer.

West of Calle de Sagasta on Calle Portales are more shops and the Plaza de San Agustín, on which stand the rather grandiose post office and the **Palacio del Espartero**, now the

Museo Provincial de la Rioja, which features archaeological displays, revolving exhibitions of pieces from the national fine arts trust, and periodic art shows.

STAYING IN LOGROÑO

The ▶ **Hotel Carlton Rioja,** well located on the Gran Vía, is the best of the modest hostelries Logroño has to offer, and has long been the hotel preferred by the La Rioja wine trade for putting up guests. Except for the lack of porters to help with luggage, the Carlton is comfortable enough, provided you don't get a room facing the Gran Vía, which can be noisy at night. It also has a parking garage, a highly recommended asset since the parking situation along the Gran Vía is tight. Two welcome, moderately priced accommodations are the centrally located ▶ **Hotel Ciudad de Logroño,** on a plaza two blocks southwest of the Carlton, and the charming ▶ **Hotel Marqués de Vallejo,** a recently renovated former hospice in the *casco viejo* near the cathedral.

DINING IN LOGROÑO

Tapas Bars

Logroño has a number of good, small, and unpretentious restaurants and *tapas* bars, many of which are located in the old quarter. Along **Calle Laurel,** just a block northeast of Plaza del Espolón and south of Plaza de San Agustín, each bar usually has a different specialty. It seems that by 9:00 P.M. every evening half of Logroño's citizens descend on Calle Laurel to watch the peregrinations of their fellow citizens, eat *tapas,* and drink draft beer and wine. Shamefully (after all, this is La Rioja), the beer is usually better than the often mediocre house wines served on this street.

For a do-it-yourself *tapas* tour, start on Calle Laurel with *champiñones* (grilled mushrooms) or *riñones* (lamb kidneys) at **Bar Torrecilla.** At the end of Calle Laurel, on the Travesía Laurel, is **Bar Blanco y Negro,** which offers a variety of anchovy *tapas*—fried, freshly pickled in vinegar and oil, on toast, and so on. **Bar Lorenzo,** a few doors north and across the narrow *travesía,* specializes in *pinchos morunos* (grilled lamb kebabs marinated with Moorish spices) and exceptional *pimientos de piquillo* (piquant red peppers usually stuffed with meat). **La Casita,** a bar at the northern end of the *travesía,* displays on colorful ceramic platters one of Logroño's best selections of *tapas*: shrimp salad with capers, white asparagus, stuffed peppers, marinated octopus, olive salad, garlic shrimp, and pork loin with pimientos. (Note: Many of these bars close for vacation in late September, after the San Mateo festival, through the first week in October.)

Restaurants

For dinner on Calle Laurel try **El Cachetero**, a popular restaurant that is one of the best in Logroño, and charges accordingly. El Cachetero serves typical, seasonal Rioja dishes such as *pochas, cabrito asado, pimientos rellenos,* and, especially, artichoke dishes and *lenguado* (sole); Tel: (9-41) 22-84-63. A Logroño institution for *cabrito asado, cordero asado,* and *chuletón de buey* (huge steaks) is **Asador La Chata,** just off Calle de Sagasta at Calle Carnicerías 3. La Chata's oven, made from volcanic stone, turns out excellent roast meats. Your chances of hearing diners at a nearby table spontaneously singing *jotas,* the lively folk songs of northern Spain, are good; Tel: (9-41) 25-12-96.

One block south of the Río Ebro and two short blocks west of Calle de Sagasta on the main throughfare of the old quarter—Calle del Marqués de San Nicolás (also called Calle Mayor)—are two of Logroño's most highly regarded restaurants. Located in an old mansion, the famous **Mesón de la Merced,** at number 109, is large, elegant, and very expensive, with several stunningly decorated dining rooms and a magnificent wine cellar. The food, however, is over-rated and overpriced; Tel: (9-41) 22-11-66. Just across the street, at number 136, is a better choice, **Mesón del Camino,** which re-creates a medieval atmosphere in an old bodega. While under the same ownership as La Merced, Mesón Lorenzo offers a more traditional, less expensive, and less pretentious menu of Rioja specialties such as *menestra, bacalao a la riojana* (salt cod in a tomato, red pepper, onion, and garlic sauce), and *chuletillas de cordero* (baby lamb chops). Mesón Lorenzo also has a great wine list; Tel: (9-41) 20-91-30. Also in the old quarter, just steps from the Palacio del Espartero and the post office, is an inexpensive restaurant, much frequented by Logroño merchants and shopkeepers at lunchtime, the pretty **Las Cubanas,** Calle de San Agustín 17, featuring a good traditional menu of such dishes as *menestra,* rabbit stew, and stuffed peppers, and a fine house wine from La Rioja Alavesa; Tel: (9-41) 22-00-50. Another well-regarded, moderately priced restaurant on the same street is **Zubillaga,** at number 3, where you can have grilled meat and grilled fish, along with other Rioja special-ties; Tel: (9-41) 22-00-76.

BUYING WINE IN LOGROÑO

The best place to pick out a special Rioja *reserva* or two is from the huge selection at the **Palacio del Vino,** Avenida de Burgos 140 (at the western edge of Logroño on the road to Burgos), which is the commercial center for the *denom-inación de origen* of La Rioja. The Palacio del Vino offers more than 300 wines from all the bodegas in La Rioja at winery prices. **Rioja Selección**, Avenida de la República Argentina 12 (south of the Gran Vía near the Hotel Carlton Rioja), has a good selection of wines and regional food delicacies, and **Licores Espinosa**, Calle de San Agustín 13 (near the Palacio del Espartero in the *casco viejo*), has a good wine selection and a broad choice of liqueurs.

EXCURSIONS INTO LA RIOJA

Logroño makes a handy base for three immensely rewarding day-trip excursions into the little-travelled Rioja countryside. The first is a round trip northwest to Haro, taking in wineries and discovering the unspoiled villages of La Rioja Alta and La Rioja Alavesa, such as Laguardia; the second is a visit to some of the important shrines on the Camino de Santiago, including the off-the-beaten-track monasteries in the mountains of southern Rioja; and the third is a trip southeast to Calahorra and the dusty, historic villages of the fertile Rioja Baja, which is on the way to southern Navarra and then to Zaragoza in Aragón.

The Route to Haro:
Wineries and Villages

A trip to Haro, 50 km (30 miles) northwest of Logroño, will be most enjoyable if you write or call ahead to arrange one or two winery visits in the morning (see The Wines of La Rioja, above). Plan to have lunch in Haro, and allow plenty of time for the return trip through the lovely Basque villages north of the Río Ebro in La Rioja Alavesa, which, for reasons of geographical proximity, we include in this chapter rather than in the chapter on the Basque Country.

Because you are apt to be caught on a wicked hill behind a long line of trucks if you take N 232, it is wise to take the A 68 *autopista* some 20 km (12 miles) west of Logroño to **Cenicero**, where two important wineries, Marqués de Cáceres, one of La Rioja's finest new bodegas, and Bodegas Riojanas, one of its great historic wineries, are located. Notice the fine modern monument honoring La Rioja's grape harvesters on the village's main thoroughfare. Cenicero, which means "ashbin"—or, in current usage, "ashtray"—was reportedly the site of a Roman crematorium and burial ground.

Continuing northwest on N 232, you soon arrive at **Briones**, a picturesque town full of old houses emblazoned with coats of arms.

HARO

Haro is the capital of La Rioja Alta, the region's finest wine district. It is a small, charming town with a fine arcaded main square, **Plaza de la Paz**, on which stand an 18th-century town hall; a beautiful bandstand; the **Selección Vinos de Rioja**, a wineshop where you can purchase most of the greatest wines of La Rioja; and the venerable **Café Suizo**, whose terrace provides a relaxing place to watch the meanderings of the Jarreros (literally, "jugmakers"), as the people of Haro are known. The 16th-century **Iglesia de Santo Tomás** (in the old quarter, west of the Plaza de la Paz at the end of Calle Santo Tomás) has an exceptional Plateresque stone façade carved by Felipe de Vigarni to resemble the wood-carved altarpieces of the period. If you continue walking up the hill beyond Santo Tomás you will come to a little park at the top with stunning views of the mountains, vineyards, and the wineries of the Barrio de la Estación below.

Haro's Wineries

Haro has the greatest concentration of fine wineries in La Rioja, many of which are more than a century old. The best bodegas are clustered below the hill on which Haro is perched, just north of town near the convergence of the tiny Río Oja and the Río Ebro. The area, which now calls itself the Costa del Vino (Wine Coast), is traditionally known as the Barrio de Cantaranas (which means "singing frogs") and the Barrio de la Estación (railway station), for the railhead that was established here in 1880 to ship copious amounts of Rioja wine to France to be sold as Bordeaux (and under other famous names) after French vineyards were devastated by phylloxera, the vine louse. López de Heredia (founded 1877), CVNE (1879), La Rioja Alta (1890), Bodegas Bilbainas (1901), Rioja Santiago (1904), and Muga, a winery built in 1970 but employing traditional methods (they use only wooden vessels for every stage of the wine-making process, from fermentation through aging in small oak barrels), are some of the wineries located here. López de Heredia has a distinctive Art Nouveau tower and a fabulous old bodega. CVNE is perhaps the best overall winery in Spain, and La Rioja Alta and Muga should also be on anyone's short list of La Rioja's finest wineries.

The 100-year-old **Estación Enológica** (Enological Station) of Haro is installed in modern offices inside a lovely old stone building at the southwestern edge of Haro, at Bretón de los Herreros 3. The excellent, state-of-the-art **Museo del Vino de Rioja** (wine museum), is also housed in this building. The museum uses brilliant backlit transparencies, old implements, and other displays to tell the story of wine-making in this great region. It is nicely laid out for self-guided tours and the various levels are accessible by ramps and elevators, rather than stairs.

One of the best wine shops in Spain, **Juan González Muga** (no relation to the famous Muga bodega), is near the Estación Enológica, at Avenida de la Rioja 27. The colorful Señor González—who formerly held court in his shop on the Plaza de la Paz, in the store now occupied by Selección Vinos de Rioja—offers more than 2,500 wines, tinned and bottled food specialties, and liqueurs from La Rioja, Spain, and abroad, plus wine paraphernalia and books. The store is open every day.

Staying and Dining in Haro

Haro has an excellent hotel in a recently renovated 600-year-old Augustinian convent called, appropriately, ▶ **Hotel Los Augustinos** (Plaza de San Agustín 2). Like an upscale parador, Los Augustinos is decorated with antiques and period furniture reproductions. Charming and comfortable, Los Augustinos is now one of the best hotels in all of La Rioja and a fine alternative for those who enjoy village life.

Casa Terete, west of Plaza de la Paz at Calle Lucrecia Arana 17, is an obligatory stop for *cordero asado* and *cabrito asado,* roasted in the restaurant's baker's oven, and for a great lineup of *reservas.* Everyone in the wine trade who has ever visited La Rioja has had at least one meal at the scrubbed, white picnic tables upstairs at Terete. Ask someone to show you the dining room in Terete's private bodega in the ancient cellars below; Tel: (9-41) 31-00-23. The more sophisticated **Beethoven**, Calle Santo Tomás 3 (left of the town hall on the street leading to the church of Santo Tomás), with good Rioja regional dishes and a fine wine list, is also very popular, as is its sister establishment **Beethoven II**, across the street at number 8, which has excellent *tapas;* Tel: (9-41) 31-11-81 for both.

Another favorite is the small, inexpensive, and typical **La Kika**, just up the street from Beethoven. La Kika has a few tables in a luncheonette-style dining room, no menu, and no price list. The restaurant's namesake, La Kika, cooks regional home-style dishes on a cast-iron stove in her tiny kitchen from whatever ingredients are available in the market that morning. A lunch might include a plate of salad with tuna, olives, and boiled eggs thrown in; plump, white asparagus with fresh mayonnaise; a platter of grilled shrimp; clams in a delicious garlic-and-parsley sauce; a pile of baby lamb chops with fried green peppers on the side; fresh *cangrejos del río* (river crayfish); a bottle of *rosado* from the San Vicente cooperative; and *cuajada* (sheep's-milk curd) for dessert. Since La Kika is so small, it is wise to reserve ahead. Closed in September; Tel: (9-41) 31-14-47.

Haro's Wine Festival

If you are a lover of fiestas you might want to schedule your trip to coincide with Haro's **Semana del Vino** (Wine Week), which begins June 24 and culminates early in the morning on June 29 with the Battle of Wine, certainly one of the most colorful wine-related events in the world. Near the hermitage of San Felices in a glen on a mountain called Riscos de Bilibio, 6 km (3½ miles) northwest of Haro, the celebrants, backed by music from bands sponsored by various bodegas, proceed to pour, squirt, spray, and throw some 50,000 liters of young Rioja wine on, in, or around one another—while dancing the *jota*. By midmorning they manage to turn the mountain purple (and did so even before someone got the bright idea in recent years to bring in a wine-spraying helicopter to make sure everyone gets doused). The fiesta changes venue by midday, when the wine-soaked warriors parade through downtown Haro, then perform a daredevil amateur bullfight and dance in the streets until dawn. There is a professional bullfight on June 29, and throughout the week you can sample wines at displays set up by Haro's wineries in the main square.

La Rioja Alta and La Rioja Alavesa

The return trip to Logroño through the beautiful villages of La Rioja Alta and La Rioja Alavesa is best made in the afternoon with the sun at your back, when these fine old towns are beautifully illuminated in the golden light of evening. Leaving Haro via the Barrio de Cantaranas, follow the signs to **Labastida** (province of Alava), another town with heraldic emblems on many beautiful old houses, then take the clearly marked Logroño road, N 232 (this branch of N 232 runs parallel to the branch south of the Río Ebro, on which you drove into Haro).

SAN VICENTE DE LA SONSIERRA

Continue 6 km (3½ miles) southeast through scenic terrain to San Vicente de la Sonsierra (back in Rioja province), one of the most picturesque mountain towns in La Rioja. Surrounded by vineyards, San Vicente's hilltop profile incorporates a 16th-century church, a former Camino de Santiago pilgrim hospice, the remains of a castle, and ramparts from which there are stunning views of the Río Ebro, the mountains, and the terraced vineyards of the region.

San Vicente is a town of extraordinary character. During the War of Independence (Peninsular War), when the local guerrillas caught some of Napoleon's troops who had raped several townswomen, they drowned the invaders in huge vats of wine. To this day the locals will tell you that a good

wine, like the one from the excellent San Vicente cooperative, has a French touch to it. The men of this town still
practice the outlawed penance of self-flagellation during
Holy Week—using multithonged whips tipped with wax
embedded with broken glass.

In San Vicente de la Sonsierra, **Hostal Toni** (Calle Zuma-
lacárregui 27), despite the video games at its entrance, has a
good kitchen that turns out top-notch baby lamb chops *al
sarmiento, pochas,* and *ensalada.* The house wine is also
excellent here; Tel: (9-41) 33-40-01.

EAST TO LAGUARDIA

On N 232 to Abalos (also in Rioja province), barely a couple
of kilometers to the east of San Vicente, is a turnoff to the
north marked Peciña. Perhaps 3 km (2 miles) along this road
is the 12th-century Romanesque **Iglesia de Santa María de la
Piscina**, which was founded by Don Ramiro de Navarra, a
son-in-law of El Cid. Other than the beauty of the landscape,
with its rugged gray mountain walls and terraced vineyards
along the way, and the picturesque quality of the two towns'
settings, there isn't much to detain you in either Abalos or
Samaniego, the next town to the east. (Note the sign that
reads "Arabako Errioxa/Rioja Alavesa"—Basque first, then
Spanish—as you reenter the province of Alava.)

A few kilometers east of Samaniego, near Leza, is a sign
for the road to Vitoria via the mountain pass of Puerto de
Herrera. A drive of 3 km (2 miles) north along this road will
bring you to a spectacular *mirador* (lookout) called **El
Balcón de la Rioja** (The Balcony of La Rioja), from which you
can see all of La Rioja Alta, La Rioja Alavesa, and, farther off
to the south, the wild, beautiful, and sparsely populated
Sierra de la Demanda, whose peaks are often snowcapped.

LAGUARDIA

Back on the main road (N 232), continuing east from Leza,
a drive of 7 km (4 miles) will bring you to Laguardia
(called Biasteri in Basque), a strikingly picturesque wine
town. In its own way Laguardia rivals Riquewihr in Alsace,
Bernkastel in the Mosel, and Chinon in the Loire, yet,
unlike those three superb wine towns, Laguardia has not
been exploited as a tourist destination. Perched on a hilltop
some 1,200 feet above sea level, Laguardia is a completely
walled village that can be entered only through its six
medieval gates. Vehicular traffic is prohibited in the narrow
streets of the town, except for an occasional small truck
making deliveries. It is best to leave your car along the
road near the Marixa restaurant (see below), outside the
town's eastern walls. There are only a few streets inside the

walls, and you can explore the town entirely on foot in less than an hour, encountering all the major items of interest.

Within the Walls

Street life in Laguardia is particularly rich because of the traffic ban. The street becomes an extended communal parlor, "a society poised still in the attitudes that characterized us all, before the machine came to shift our rhythms," as travel writer Jan Morris observed about Spain's old ways.

In addition to its fine walls, gates, towers, and lovely views of La Rioja Alavesa's vineyards, Laguardia's architectural treasures (all within the walls) include the ruins of a tenth-century castle; a Gothic church, **Iglesia de Santa María de los Reyes**, which has an exceptional 15th-century porch richly decorated with polychrome figures; the **Iglesia de San Juan Bautista**, with 13th-century Romanesque roots; the birthplace of fabulist Félix Samaniego, a mansion that is now the Casa del Vino, the official Basque government offices and laboratory for the Alavesa wine industry; and a number of fine old houses, most of which have a wine cellar and/or stables cut into the limestone beneath them.

Laguardia's fiesta, June 27 to 29 (if you have any energy left after Haro's Battle of Wine on June 29, you might want to try Laguardia's celebration in the afternoon), features a running of the bulls, an amateur bullfight, dancing in the streets, and is famous for the custom that obliges natives of Laguardia to offer glasses of *zurracapote* (mulled wine) to strangers during fiesta.

Outside the Walls

Laguardia's two best-known wineries are Bodegas Alavesas (Carretera Elciego), producers of Solar de Samaniego, and Bodegas Palacio (Calle San Lázaro 1), which produces a fine *reserva* called Glorioso. At Calle Sancho Abarca 8, just outside the walls across the street from the village *frontón* (jai alai court), is **Restaurante Marixa**. Moderately priced, with excellent vistas of the mountains, it serves very good Rioja regional dishes such as *pochas,* lamb chops, roast goat, game dishes, potatoes with *chorizo,* and so on. Marixa also has a fine wine list with fair prices; Tel: (9-41) 10-01-65.

Just outside Laguardia's walls to the north is the **Poblado de la Hoya**, an important archaeological dig and museum on the site of an Iron Age village. One display shows a room with the scant furnishings of the age, simple pottery that is similar to that still used in La Rioja, and plain, rough garments hung on pegs; it looks as if the owner could walk in any minute from tending his flocks in the ancient Basque hills. A few kilometers farther is **El Villar**, site of the largest dolmens found in the entire Pyrenean region.

SOUTH TO ELCIEGO

Spectacular views of Laguardia can be had a short distance south of town on the road to Elciego (and on to Cenicero). On clear days, when Laguardia catches the evening light from the setting sun, it shines dramatically against the awesome backdrop of the blue-gray Cantabrian mountains. A few kilometers south of Laguardia is **Elciego**, a picturesque town that is home to Bodegas Domecq and the famous Marqués de Riscal, La Rioja's oldest winery, founded in 1860. At the southern edge of Elciego, the road to Cenicero passes through Riscal's property, so don't be surprised if you have to stop for a winery worker rolling a barrel across the road; the bodega has the right-of-way.

You can return to Logroño via Cenicero, turning east on the southern branch of N 232 there or, for a faster return, the *autopista*. If you choose to return via Laguardia on northern N 232 (15 km/9 miles), the road runs along the Río Ebro below Laguardia, affording views of old Logroño that cannot be obtained from other approaches.

The Camino de Santiago and the Monasteries of Southern Rioja

Compared to Navarra's wealth of shrines along the Camino de Santiago, La Rioja has relatively few sites, because the main route went farther north through the Basque Country for many years, until a southern road through the valley of the Río Ebro was deemed safe from Moorish attacks. What La Rioja's route lacks in number of shrines, however, it makes up in quality.

You might start your exploration with a quick excursion to the battlefield upon which Saint James is said to have appeared to aid the Christians in the Reconquest of Spain. Some 12 km (7½ miles) south of Logroño, off N 111, high in the hills overlooking the city and the Río Iregua—a stream of considerable importance to trout fishermen—stands the historic **Castle of Clavijo**, where legend tells us Saint James appeared in 844 on a mighty white stallion to turn the tide against the Moors. The Castilians had gone to war over the yearly tribute of 100 virgins demanded by the invaders from Africa. After the battle, in which Saint James supposedly killed 70,000 enemy soldiers, he became known as Santiago Matamoros (the Moorslayer), which is the way he is seen astride his mighty horse on the façade of the church of Santiago el Real in Logroño. The appearance of Santiago at Clavijo was a great boost to Castilian morale; it became the spiritual counterpoint to the arm of Muhammad that the Moors carried into battle. On one of the castle towers you can see the outline of a stylized red cross in the shape of a sword, the warrior symbol of Santiago Matamoros and the order of the Knights of Santiago.

We begin our day tour of the exceptional churches, monasteries, and shrines along La Rioja's branch of the Camino de Santiago at Nájera, 26 km (16 miles) west of Logroño via N 120. We then explore the area south and west of Nájera, ending at Santo Domingo de la Calzada. Next you have the options of returning to Logroño, staying in Santo Domingo de la Calzada, heading up to Haro (just to the north), or continuing on west to Burgos (see the Old Castile chapter).

NAJERA

Nájera was the site of a famous battle of English medieval history. The English prince Edward, known as the "Black Prince," was an ally of the Spanish king of Castile and León, Peter the Cruel, in a bloody battle (according to contemporary accounts, the Río Najerilla ran red) against Peter's half-brother, Henry of Trastamara, and Henry's French allies, led by Bertrand du Guesclin. The English troops, known as the best fighting men on earth, carried the day on a plain northeast of Nájera. In thanks, Peter presented the Black Prince with the great ruby that is the main jewel in the crown of England. It was to be a poor reward, since the treacherous Peter reneged on his other financial promises to Edward. The Black Prince was unable to pay his troops, who then rebelled against him, leading to his eventual ruin. The Battle of Nájera is also known as the Battle of Navarrete because some of the bloodiest fighting took place at the Puente de Navarrete (the bridge over the Najerilla on the road to Navarrete), not because it was fought near Navarrete, 16 km (10 miles) to the northeast.

Monasterio de Santa María la Real

The great attraction in Nájera is the Monasterio de Santa María la Real, pantheon of a number of the kings of Navarra and several members of the Castilian aristocracy of the Middle Ages. The counts of Haro, La Rioja's greatest aristocratic family, are also buried here. One of the counts, Pedro Fernández de Velasco, once threw a lavish celebration in honor of Doña Blanca de Navarra (who is buried here); the fiesta's centerpiece was a silver fountain splashing a continuous supply of Rioja wine for the celebrants.

Santa María la Real has a splendid early-15th-century Gothic **cloister**, with airy, filigree-like tracery filling the arches, and a magnificent late-15th-century choir, whose stalls are credited to Jewish wood-carvers. During the last half of July a sound-and-light show representing the history of Nájera and Santa María la Real takes place in the cloister.

THE MONASTERIES OF SAN MILLAN DE SUSO AND SAN MILLAN DE YUSO

The great monasteries of San Millán de Suso and San Millán de Yuso are located in the mountains about 20 km (12 miles) southwest of Nájera at San Millán de la Cogolla (from Nájera take C 113 south for 5 km/3 miles, then look for a road to the right with signs pointing to San Millán). In church lore, San Millán is said to have duplicated Christ's miracle of the Sermon on the Mount in the sixth century, quenching the thirst of the multitudes with a small measure of wine. The **Monasterio de San Millán de Suso** was built upon a Visigothic church founded in 537, but the building we see today is an early-tenth-century gem that was erected against a rock into which three chapels were hewn. The nave has several lovely Mozarabic horseshoe arches. Suso also houses an early tomb of San Millán, a splendid Romanesque sarcophagus carved in pale green alabaster.

It is the generally accepted belief that the written Castilian language first began to take shape here in the southern hills of La Rioja at San Millán de Suso. Early in the 13th century a Benedictine monk named Gonzalo de Berceo (Berceo is a nearby village) first decided to write his poetry in the evolving vernacular of the day, because, he claimed, he was simply not up to writing in Latin. He further discounted his effort, saying that, if nothing else, he hoped his writing would be worth "a glass of *bon vino*," then went on to create the earliest surviving literature by a known author in the Spanish language—a long metaphorical poem about the Virgin Mary.

The Augustinian **Monasterio de San Millán de Yuso** (just down the hill below Suso) is a much larger, less interesting 16th-century church, often called the Escorial of La Rioja. The great attraction of San Millán de Yuso is its **treasury**, which contains exquisite ivory carvings depicting scenes from the lives of San Millán and San Felices. Once part of a larger set, they were considered among the most beautiful carvings of their kind. Many of them were stolen, like so many of northern Spain's art treasures, by Napoleon's retreating troops as Wellington's army drove them from Spain. The remaining panels—the others are scattered among museums around the world—have been reset in a modern reliquary containing the remains of San Millán.

SOUTH TO THE ABADIA DE VALVANERA

Southeast of San Millán de la Cogolla, about 20 km (12 miles) due south of Nájera on C 113, is **Anguiano**, a small town that, every year on July 22, holds the Fiesta de Santa Magdalena, a folkloric festival featuring daring male acrobatic dancers who wear colorful skirted costumes and perform on stilts. The inexpensive seven-room ► **Hotel El Corzo**, Carretera de Lerma 12 (the main road through town), was built in 1987 mainly to accommodate the hunters and fishermen who frequent this beautiful area. The rooms offer picturesque views over the Río Najerilla, and the hotel's equally inexpensive restaurant is a good *asador* that serves home-cooked Rioja specialties; Tel: (9-41) 37-70-85.

Seventeen kilometers (11 miles) southwest of Anguiano, in the mountains off C 113, is the ► **Abadía de Valvanera**, a monastery that houses the 11th-century Romanesque statue of the Virgin of Valvanera, patroness of La Rioja and a much-venerated figure in Spain and Spanish America. Some experts say that since Queen Isabella spent eight days here praying to the Virgin during the Reconquest and subsequently bestowed an annual gift of 30,000 *maravedís* on the monastery, the claim that Columbus's ship was actually called Santa María de Valvanera has validity. The monastery has 29 moderately priced rooms for rent and a restaurant serving a dinner of monastic fare.

SANTO DOMINGO DE LA CALZADA

Return to Nájera on C 113 from Valvanera and hop on N 120 for a 21-km (13-mile) drive west to one of the most famous towns on the Camino de Santiago, Santo Domingo de la Calzada. The narrow pilgrims' road still passes through the center of the old part of town, and Santo Domingo retains many important vestiges of its medieval glory: sections of the defensive walls, including watchtowers, built during the reign of Peter the Cruel; mansions emblazoned with coats of arms; an ancient, much-renovated bridge built over the Río Glera by Santo Domingo; the pilgrims' hospital, also built by Santo Domingo; and the fine cathedral, whose bell towers dominate the profile of the town from far away.

Santo Domingo was a hermit who lived in the 11th century and devoted his life to helping travellers along the Camino de Santiago and to keeping the *calzada* (or roadbed) in a passable state of repair. Thus, the village where he lived came to be known as Santo Domingo de la Calzada.

It was in Santo Domingo that a remarkable incident in medieval Christian lore is said to have taken place. A young man and his parents making the pilgrimage to Santiago chanced to stop for the night at an inn in Santo Domingo. The innkeeper's daughter took an immediate liking to the young, weary traveller and, as one 16th-century writer put it, "would have had him medyll with her carnally," but the young man resisted her advances. She took revenge by hiding a silver wine goblet belonging to her father in the innocent's knapsack as he slept. The next morning as the boy and his parents were preparing to leave, the spurned girl reported the silver cup missing. The traveller was caught with the goods, dragged before the local magistrate, and sentenced to hang. Miraculously, though strung from the gallows, he did not die. The boy's father and mother went to the home of the judge who had sentenced him to offer the miracle as divine evidence of their son's innocence. The magistrate, who was preparing to dine on a pair of chickens, a cock and a hen, rejected the family's appeal, claiming that if the boy were blameless, those roasted chickens were alive. At that point the chickens rose and flew away.

This event is reenacted every May 12 with a white rooster and a hen, which are kept in an elaborate and colorful lighted cage high above the floor of the **Catedral de Santo Domingo de la Calzada**. Modern-day pilgrims stop at the cathedral, hoping to hear the rooster crow and to come away with a white feather as a souvenir. The cathedral, which still has some Romanesque vestiges in the apse, was completed in the Gothic style in the late 13th century, making it one of the first Gothic churches in Spain. The tower is 18th-century Baroque.

Staying and Dining in Santo Domingo de la Calzada

The ▶ **Parador de Santo Domingo de la Calzada,** next to the cathedral at Plaza del Santo 3, is installed in the restored remains of the 12th-century pilgrims' hospice and hospital, which is said to have been built by Santo Domingo himself. This is a wonderful old hospice, with vaulted ceilings, antique furniture, period decorations, suits of armor, and a stylized high-relief map of the Camino de Santiago on a stone wall. The tolling of the cathedral bells to mark the hours enhances the spirit of medieval times that this old town evokes.

The parador restaurant serves the regional cuisine of La Rioja, but **Mesón El Peregrino**, Avenida de Calahorra 21, just east of the cathedral and the parador, is just as good and considerably less expensive. El Peregrino (the pilgrim) has a big, comfortable dining room entered through a bar, where you can have *tapas* before dinner, and serves typical Rioja dishes such as *alubias* (white beans) *con chorizo, menestra,* roast lamb, and so on. The wine list offers a good selection of Riojas; Tel: (9-41) 34-02-02.

SOUTH TO EZCARAY

The best meals in this entire region are to be had at ▶ **Hostal Echaurren**, in Ezcaray, 12 km (7½ miles) south of Santo Domingo in the foothills of the wild and sparsely populated Sierra de la Demanda, a region becoming popular with hunters and skiers. In this unlikely, out-of-the-way spot, at a renovated *posada* (inn) and post house on the old coach road, Marisa Sánchez, along with her husband, Félix Paniego, runs a kitchen of such excellence that she was awarded the national gastronomy prize in 1987, joining the ranks of such celebrity chefs as Juan Mari Arzak and Pedro Subijana.

Echaurren serves the quintessential dishes of La Rioja based on regional products and taken from traditional recipes—*alubias con chorizo, menestra, chuletillas de cordero,* and *pimientos rellenos de bacalao*—along with *cogote de merluza* (a hake fillet that is superb here), homemade pâté with truffles, endive with prawns and salmon, and other outstanding creations from this talented and, until recently, little-known chef. Echaurren has a good wine list and a fine Rioja *cosechero* (vintner) house wine for 300 pesetas. Best of all, for a great restaurant Echaurren is not expensive; expect to pay about 3,000 pesetas per person, depending, of course, on what you order; Tel (9-41) 35-40-47. Hostal Echaurren also has 29 renovated rooms and a few comfortable apartments for rent that are suitable for families. The rooms are modern, functional, and comfortable. The restaurant and hotel are closed in November.

Hunting and fishing are excellent in the wild mountains of southern Rioja, especially near Ezcaray, south of San Millán de la Cogolla, and in the Rió Iregua valley. Quail, partridge, wild boar, and deer are especially plentiful, and the rivers there are well stocked with trout (check with the Tourist Office of Spain for licensing requirements and seasons).

La Rioja Baja

La Rioja Baja stretches into the southeastern part of La Rioja, around the old Roman town of Calahorra and down toward Zaragoza. In the warmer, Mediterranean-influenced climate of La Rioja Baja, vines and olive trees grow side by side. Like the Ribera Baja of neighboring Navarra, this area is known for its agricultural products, and is a center of asparagus, pimiento, and artichoke production.

SOUTHEAST FROM LOGROÑO

The Murrieta Winery

Before heading into La Rioja Baja from Logroño, try to arrange a visit to the winery and museum of **Finca Igay**, the estate of the marqués de Murrieta, which is still in the Rioja Alta zone, just 3 km (2 miles) outside Logroño on the highway to Calahorra, N 232. Call beforehand for an appointment and driving directions; Tel: (9-41) 25-81-00.

The marqués de Murrieta was responsible for establishing French wine-making techniques in La Rioja. The winery, which dates from 1872, is one of the most picturesque in La Rioja and still makes some of the region's best (and most expensive) wines. They may even send you away from the bodega's archives with one of their fine old *reserva* wines, many of which are more than 50 years old, provided you are willing to make a sizable donation to the Graham Greene Foundation, a pet project of Murrieta's owner, Vicente Cebrián (count of Creixel), to promote cultural relations between England and Spain.

ANCIENT VILLAGES SOUTH OF CALAHORRA

The first town you will encounter after the Murrieta estate on N 232 is **Ausejo**, a wine-producing town whose ruined 13th-century castle overlooks the vineyards. The hill on which Ausejo sits is a warren of underground wine cellars. Just after the harvest you can get a whiff of the fermenting wine as you explore the steep streets of the town.

Arnedo

About 7 km (4 miles) from Ausejo on N 232, at El Villar de Arnedo, turn south to Arnedo, a town that was an important crossroads during the Roman occupation and a strategic base during Moorish times. Its strange, eroded, red sandstone hills are honeycombed with man-made caves that were once inhabited. One of the most unusual restaurants in La Rioja can be found here: **Sopitas** (Carrera 4), burrowed into a hillside in what used to be an old bodega. You can sample such regional specialties as local *alcachofas* (artichokes), *espárragos blancos* (white asparagus), and *setas* (chanterelle mushrooms), and *perdices* (partridge), *codornices* (quail), and *cabrito asado*—accompanied by the stout, high-alcohol wines of La Rioja Baja; Tel: (9-41) 38-02-66.

In late September Arnedo has five days of fiesta, including *encierros* (runnings of the bulls through the streets), *gigantes y cabezudos* (giants and bigheads), bullfights, *jota*-singing competitions, and fireworks à la Pamplona; it's an authentic country-town fiesta without the tourists.

Quel and Autol

A drive of about 20 km (12½ miles) east of Arnedo on C 115 will take you through asparagus and pimiento country (you will often see rows of pimientos hung up to dry on the façades of village houses), past such strange towns as Quel, a village huddled up against a hill topped by the ruins of a once-strategic castle, and Autol, whose two odd, towerlike rocks, known as El Picuezo and La Picueza, eroded by ancient waters and the wind, are a geological curiosity. Just beyond Aldeanueva de Ebro, C 115 joins N 232, where you turn right for Alfaro, 8 km (5 miles) to the southeast.

Alfaro

In ancient times the Phoenicians had a lighthouse on the Río Ebro at **Alfaro**, now a dusty, sandstone-colored town whose official boundaries encompass almost 120 square miles, making it the third-largest municipality in Spain. The town had Celtic-Iberian roots, was named Graccurris by the Romans, and became Alfaro when the Moors took over.

Alfaro is located scant kilometers from the Navarra border, and not much farther from the provincial boundaries with Aragón and Soria. As a strategic crossroads and fortress town, it became known as the "key to Castile" during medieval times. Even today, Alfaro has far more in common with Navarrese Tudela and the villages of western Aragón than with Logroño, the provincial capital.

The best winery in this region is **Palacios Remondo**, located on N 232 at the northwestern entrance to Alfaro. Antonio Palacios, a progressive young wine maker who was trained in Bordeaux, creates a wine with considerable finesse from this warm climate, where the high-alcohol-producing Grenache is the major grape. While demolishing the remains of their ancestral home, the Palacios Remondo family found six bottles wrapped in a parchment will that was written in 1651. The winery now uses a facsimile of the parchment to wrap each bottle of its best wines, the Herencia Remondo reds. The winery's main offices are at its Logroño facility, so it is best to call ahead to arrange a visit to the bodegas in Alfaro; Tel: (9-41) 23-71-77.

▶ **Hotel Palacios** and **Tirachinas Restaurant**, Avenida Zaragoza 6, and an interesting wine museum, all owned by the Palacios family, are located next door between the winery and the bullring. The hotel is ultramodern and functional, but livable, moderately priced, and, after the parador in Calahorra, the best base around here for exploring La Rioja Baja. The Tirachinas is the place to try such local specialties as *menestra de verduras, espárragos blancos, pimientos rellenos, cabrito asado,* and *alcachofas* cooked with duck sweetbreads, all washed down with a bottle of Palacios Remondo wine; Tel: (9-41) 18-01-00.

NORTH TO CALAHORRA

After Alfaro you can head back to Logroño by way of Calahorra, 21 km (13 miles) northwest on N 232. You might make a stop near **Funes**, to see the remains of the large Roman winery there. About 10 km (6 miles) northwest of Alfaro, turn north on C 115 at Rincón de Soto; the Funes winery site is just a few hundred yards north of the Río Ebro. Funes is so near the Navarrese town of Peralta that you can easily continue north for about 10 km (6 miles) more to sample the cuisine at Atalaya, one of that region's greatest restaurants (see the Navarra chapter). In fact, you may want to tie southern Navarra and La Rioja Baja together and, depending on the direction in which you are heading, end up in either Logroño, Pamplona, or Zaragoza.

CALAHORRA

The Romans left their impact on the entire Rioja Baja area, but especially on Calahorra, the major town in the region. Roman statesman Sertorius drew the wrath of Pompey by defending the rights of the native population of Calagurris (modern Calahorra) in the first century B.C. Pompey laid siege to Calagurris, whose inhabitants held out for four years until they were reduced to cannibalism and finally starved. For their courage and stubborn refusal to surrender, the people of Calagurris became legendary (the event was known as *fames calagurritanas—fames* meaning famine, not fame) in ancient Rome. They had earlier achieved a similar notoriety with the Carthaginians, when Hannibal had besieged the town with much the same result. These events gave rise to the grisly legend of La Matrona, one of the last survivors of the Roman siege, who wandered the streets each night lighting fires all over town to trick the enemy into believing that many defenders had remained to fight. When the Romans finally entered the town, they found La Matrona gnawing on a human arm.

The great Roman rhetorician and scholar Quintilian (ca. A.D. 35–100) and the poet Prudentius (348–410) were both born at Calahorra. Almost 20 centuries later, Quintilian, who was the greatest educator of his age and the first man in Europe ever to be paid by the state for teaching, is celebrated as an *hijo del pueblo,* a true son of Calahorra. His statue stands in the center of town, and the Parador Marco Fabio Quintiliano (see below) is named after him.

The Old Town

Calahorra's old quarter, built on the original Roman site, is a lively collection of little plazas and steep labyrinthine streets, clustered on a hill above the parador. The old gate to the Roman city, the Planillo de San Andrés, still stands. The cathedral of Calahorra (Calahorra has been the site of a bishopric since the fifth century) was originally built in the 12th century but rebuilt during the 15th to 17th centuries in the Gothic style, then given a Neoclassical façade in the 18th century. Another church, Santiago, often has a family of storks residing in its belfry.

Staying and Dining in Calahorra

The ► **Parador Marco Fabio Quintiliano**, like most paradores, is comfortable enough and has the usual Castilian-type decorations, tile floors, and antiques here and there, yet this one is more sterile than most. The parador's restaurant serves good, typical Rioja fare—considering the legend of La Matrona, the many vegetarian dishes from this rich agricultural area are welcome—but, alas, for those who want to try the wines of La Rioja Baja, the restaurant's selection is paltry.

Calahorra has a few good restaurants, including **La Taberna de la Cuarta Esquina**, Cuatro Esquinas 16 (in the old quarter), which serves such dishes as scrambled eggs with green garlic shoots and eel, artichokes with clams, and fresh *pochas* in season, along with a house wine from a grower in nearby Tudelilla; Tel: (9-41) 13-43-55. Another is the homey, inexpensive, and venerable **Casa Mateo**, Calle Quintiliano 15, which is famous for its regional dishes such as the ubiquitous *menestra de verduras, pochas con chorizo,* and *conejo* (stewed rabbit). Open for lunch only; Tel: (9-41) 13-00-09.

GETTING AROUND

The usual route from Madrid to La Rioja is N I to Burgos and the four-lane toll roads A 1 and then A 68 to Logroño. For a more leisurely, picturesque entrance into Spain's greatest wine region, take N 120 from Burgos to Santo Domingo de la Calzada.

There is train and bus service to Logroño from several northern capitals, but many lines require changes. Zaragoza, Irún, Bilbao, Burgos, and Madrid (via Burgos) are served by trains to and from the Logroño RENFE station at the Plaza de Europa, located four blocks southeast of the Gran Vía del Rey Juan Carlos I (the Gran Vía) by way of Calle del General Vara del Rey and the Avenida de España, where the bus station is located. There is regular daily bus service to most of the major towns in the region.

ACCOMMODATIONS REFERENCE

The hotel rates listed below are projected rates for 1994, for double room, double occupancy, in pesetas. We strongly recommend that you confirm the price when making reservations.

The telephone area code for La Rioja is 9-41. When calling from outside the country, drop the 9.

► **Abadía de Valvanera.** Monasterio de Valvanera, 26322 **Anguiano.** Tel: 37-70-44. 4,500 pts.
► **Hostal Echaurren.** Calle Héroes del Alcázar 2, 26280 **Ezcaray.** Tel: 35-40-47; Fax: 42-71-33. 6,500 pts.

▶ **Hotel Los Augustinos**. Plaza de San Agustín 2, 26200 **Haro**. Tel: 31-13-08; Fax: 30-31-48. 12,130 pts.

▶ **Hotel Carlton Rioja**. Gran Vía del Rey Juan Carlos I 5, 26002 **Logroño**. Tel: 24-21-00; Fax: 24-35-02. 13,500 pts.

▶ **Hotel Ciudad de Logroño**. Calle Menéndez Pelayo 7, 26002 **Logroño**. Tel: 25-02-44; Fax: 25-43-90. 9,400 pts.

▶ **Hotel El Corzo**. Carretera de Lerma 12, 26322 **Anguiano**. Tel: 37-70-85. 4,000 pts.

▶ **Hotel Marqués de Vallejo**. Calle Marqués de Vallejo 8, 26001 **Logroño**. Tel: 24-83-33; Fax: 24-02-88. 6,850 pts.

▶ **Hotel Palacios**. Avenida Zaragoza 6 (N 232), 26540 **Alfaro** (La Rioja). Tel: 18-01-00; Fax: 18-36-22. 5,035 pts.

▶ **Parador Marco Fabio Quintiliano**. Era Alta, 26500 **Calahorra**. Tel: 13-03-58; Fax: 13-51-39. 11,000 pts.

▶ **Parador de Santo Domingo de la Calzada**. Plaza del Santo 3, 26250 **Santo Domingo de la Calzada**. Tel: 34-03-00; Fax: 34-03-25. 12,500 pts.

NAVARRA

By Gerry Dawes

From the green rugged Pyrenees bordering France in the north to the tawny hills and fertile river plains bordering La Rioja and Aragón in the south, Navarra has some of the most varied geography and beautiful scenery in Spain. The terrain runs the gamut from snowy peaks soaring above pine- and beech-covered slopes and pristine green valleys to wild, awesome canyons, terraced vineyards, and shimmering, heat-baked southern hills overlooking near-deserts and lush, green truck gardens irrigated by the Río Ebro. Gracing this strikingly beautiful land are a number of dramatically situated villages, important historical sites, medieval castles, and major shrines along the Camino de Santiago, the pilgrims' route to Santiago de Compostela.

For almost three centuries (1234 to 1512), Navarra (Navarre to the French) was a powerful kingdom, as French as it was Spanish, that counted the city of Bordeaux among its dominions. Basque, Roman, Visigothic, French, Aragonese, Castilian, Moorish, and Jewish influences formed the culture of this province and left behind an amazing number of superb monuments and works of art. Here the visitor will see some of the finest Romanesque and Gothic architecture in Spain.

Part of the charm of landlocked Navarra lies in its relative isolation—brought on by its mountainous terrain and the dearth of straight, fast roads for getting here. The isolation has helped keep mass tourism away from this ancient province of northern Spain, and were it not for the international fame brought to the Fiestas de San Fermín by Ernest Hemingway, Navarra would hardly be discovered at all. Yet there is so much to see in this province that you should consider it a destination, not a stopover.

Navarra's appeal goes far beyond history and architecture. Ever present as you explore the province is the enticing

thought that even some of the smaller towns have fine
restaurants where you can enjoy exceptional cuisine and
excellent wines. Travellers can also experience the culture
and crafts of the region, and explore its mountains, forests,
and waterways. Colorful folk festivals feature wonderful music, daring and often zany events, and folkloric costumes.
Concerts are often performed outdoors in such striking
settings as the Ciudadela fortress and Taconera park in
Pamplona and in the town of Olite, with a spectacular castle
as a backdrop. Those interested in regional crafts will find
leather wineskins, boots, objects crafted from alabaster (a
specialty of southern Navarra), hand-painted wood carvings
of folkloric scenes, and ceramics, including small, charming
statues of the witches of Navarrese lore. People who love
nature and the outdoors will find Navarra a paradise. Fishing, rock climbing, cave exploring, horseback riding, hiking
through the Pyrenees, mountain cycling, kayaking, and skiing in winter can all be enjoyed here, either on your own or
through an organization.

MAJOR INTEREST

Magnificent scenery
Mountain sports
Navarrese wines, cuisine, and restaurants

Pamplona
Cathedral and city hall in the old town
Fiestas de San Fermín: running of the bulls and
    bullfights
Festivales de Navarra musical performances

El Camino de Santiago
Shrines at Leyre and Sangüesa
Monastery of Roncesvalles
Puente la Reina's Romanesque bridge
Beautiful medieval town of Estella

The Pyrenees
Unspoiled mountain villages
Beautiful forests and streams
Staying in a Navarrese country house

Southern Navarra
Olite: medieval castle town
Old Moorish and Jewish quarters of Tudela

The Food and Wines of Navarra

Navarra's cuisine, restaurants, and master chefs rank among
the best in Spain. Fresh fish and shellfish from the nearby

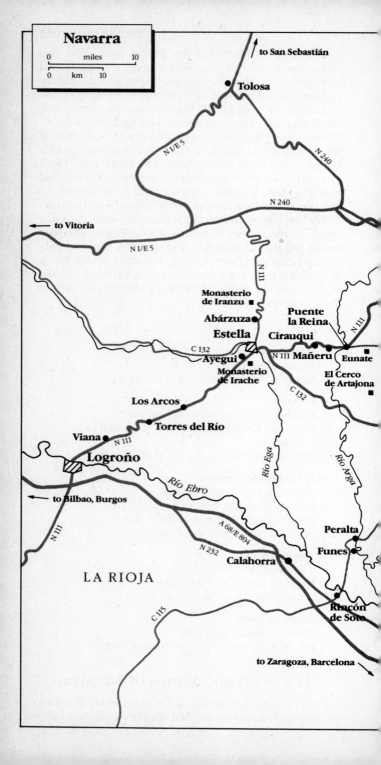

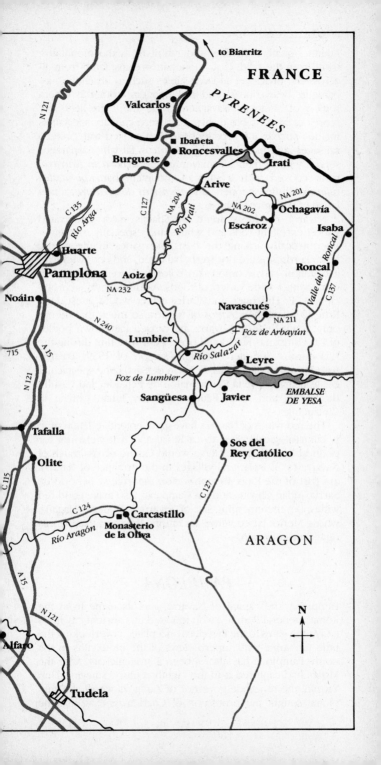

Atlantic; quail, partridge, and rabbit from the mountains; trout from the cold, clear mountain streams; lamb from all across the province; and vegetables such as artichokes, asparagus, beans, peas, and red peppers from the Ribera region of southern Navarra provide the ingredients for scores of memorable dishes. Navarrese culinary specialties include *pochas,* a legendary bean dish cooked with *chorizo* sausages and quail; *espárragos blancos,* fat white asparagus served with homemade mayonnaise; *trucha a la Navarra,* trout cooked with a slice of mountain ham; *pimientos rellenos,* stuffed peppers; and *menestra de verduras,* a mélange of young vegetables.

Navarra produces some of Spain's most underrated wines: excellent reds and whites and especially *rosados*—unequivocally among the best rosé wines in the world. Navarra *rosados* are dry, fresh, balanced, and endowed with a beautiful classic onion-skin color, and are wonderful to drink with a wide variety of foods. As Hemingway's chroniclers A. E. Hotchner and Carlos Baker would attest, Don Ernesto loved the *rosados* of Navarra so much that he not only drank them in Navarra, he carried iced-down bottles of Las Campanas Rosado all over Spain with him during the "Dangerous Summer" bullfight season of 1959. Try the *rosados* of Las Campanas; Señorío de Sarría, the spectacular estate near Puente la Reina; Malón de Echaide; and Castillo de Irache; and Gran Feudo made by Julián Chivite in Cintruénigo.

The red wines of Navarra have great potential. The region is climatologically wed to La Rioja, and if it were not for political boundaries La Rioja would extend across much of Navarra (as it is, several villages in the province of Navarra are part of the Rioja *denominación de origen*). Señorío de Sarría, Julián Chivite, and Las Campanas also make good red wines, but the emerging star of Navarra is Bodegas Magaña, whose Merlot-based wines are among the most exceptional new wines of Spain.

PAMPLONA

Pamplona, the capital of Navarra, gets its name from the Roman general Pompey, who founded this ancient city in 75 B.C. At the gates to the Pyrenees on a plateau overlooking the little Río Arga, with superb views of the mountains to the north, Pamplona has always been a strategic city. After the Moors had captured it in the eighth century, Suleyman Ibn Yaqzán, the renegade governor of Zaragoza who held Pamplona, sought the protection of Charlemagne against the emir, and offered the French king sovereignty over several northern Spanish towns. Charlemagne and his army entered Spain through the pass of Roncesvalles in 778. Suleyman rode out to meet Charlemagne, but the lieutenant he left in charge of Zaragoza seized power and refused to open the gates. Charlemagne laid siege to Zaragoza, but word of a Saxon uprising back home caused him to abandon his excursion into Spain and, as he hurried back to France, he ordered the walls of Pamplona destroyed. That decision cost the brave Roland, Charlemagne's nephew, his life, when the Basques took revenge on Charlemagne's rear guard at the pass of Roncesvalles (Roncevaux), 47 km (29 miles) northeast of Pamplona. (The legend that grew up around this incident in medieval times casts a more favorable light on Roland and Charlemagne.)

Abd ar-Rahman III, the powerful caliph of Córdoba, sacked Pamplona and destroyed its cathedral in the early tenth century. Ferdinand the Catholic finally wrested it from nearly three centuries of French rule in 1512. Ignatius of Loyola, as a soldier fighting against the French army of Jean d'Albret (Juan de Labrit in Spanish) fell on the streets of Pamplona during a battle to retake the city in 1521 (there is a pavement marker near a newspaper kiosk in front of the church of San Ignacio, on Avenida San Ignacio, to mark the spot where Ignatius was wounded). And, in 1813, during the War of Independence (Peninsular War), Wellington laid siege to the city, then drove Napoleon's troops north through the pass of Roncesvalles, and the French were out of Spain once again.

In the 20th century Pamplona owes much of its fame to Ernest Hemingway, whose glorification of Pamplona and its Fiestas de San Fermín in *The Sun Also Rises* has attracted millions of visitors to this mystical northern city for more than 60 years. The charming, sleepy old provincial capital that Hemingway discovered in the 1920s is now surrounded by modern high-rise suburbs, and the population has nearly tripled since 1950.

The Old City

Despite the veneration of the old core city by the foreign Pamplonicas who flock here every July, Pamplona is not as rich in fine old churches, museums, and distinguished medieval architecture as many other cities in Spain. And, like San Sebastián and the rest of the Basque Country, Iruña, as Pamplona is known by its large Basque population, has had more than its share of terrorism and major political problems. Nevertheless, besides the Fiestas de San Fermín, one of the world's greatest, noisiest, and most colorful parties, there is much to recommend in Pamplona, even when it is not *en fiesta*.

Pamplona makes a good base for exploring the undersung beauty, charm, and antiquity of Navarra and for sampling the cuisine of one of Spain's greatest culinary regions. It is a city of shaded streets, fountains, and plazas; interesting shops and boutiques featuring a wide variety of regional and national products; and perhaps the richest collection of good restaurants, outdoor cafés, backstreet bars, and pubs of any city its size in Spain, with the possible exception of San Sebastián.

The major items of architectural and historical interest in Pamplona are concentrated in the relatively compact, and centrally located, older part of the city and can be reached easily on foot from any of the major hotels.

THE CATHEDRAL

Standing in the northeastern corner of old Pamplona is the 14th- and 15th-century cathedral, which was built on the remains of an 11th-century Romanesque church. James Michener called the cathedral "the ugliest beautiful church in existence," describing the 18th-century Neoclassical façade by Ventura Rodríguez as "a Greco-Roman horror that makes the once gracious building look like the courthouse of Deaf Smith County, Texas." The beauty Michener refers to is the cathedral's French Gothic interior, which contains a particularly fine and elegant Gothic **cloister**.

The cathedral's other attractions are arrayed in halls surrounding the cloister. Among them are the superb alabaster tomb of Carlos III, El Noble (1387–1425), and his queen, Leonor de Trastámara, during whose reign the church was built; and the Puerta de la Preciosa, an ornate Gothic doorway of intricately carved stone. The **Museo Diocesano** displays polychrome sculptures, paintings, custodials, and religious objects from Navarrese churches, plus an unusual lectern decorated with scenes from a unicorn chase. The museum is in the former refectory and kitchens used by Augustinian monks for almost 800 years (the 11th to the 19th centuries).

Just behind the cathedral are the **ramparts**, whose remaining stone walls still mark the northern and eastern limits of the old fortress city. You can walk along substantial stretches of these old walls overlooking the Río Arga for fine views of the Pyrenees. To the west the fortress walls end at the green belt encompassing the Jardines de la Taconera and the Ciudadela (see below).

THE AYUNTAMIENTO

If the Plaza del Castillo (see below) is the heart of Pamplona, the charming *ayuntamiento* (city hall), a few blocks west of the cathedral, must be the soul. Every year on July 6 at noon thousands of people converge on the plaza in front of city hall to watch the city fathers fire the *chupinazo,* the rocket announcing the beginning of the Fiestas de San Fermín. In the afternoon the crowds return in droves to dance the *riau-riau* and watch the huge papier-mâché *gigantes y cabezudos* (giants and bigheads) lead the throng out of the plaza and through the streets for hours in the equivalent of a monumental conga line.

Even without the celebrants, the 18th-century storybook Baroque façade of the *ayuntamiento* (the rest of the building is modern) is one of Spain's most wonderful civic building fronts. The three-story structure is adorned with four pairs of matched columns on each story, each set capped by different matching capitals—one story Doric, another Ionic, and a third Corinthian. The second and third stories each have three matched sets of louvered wooden doors that open onto beautiful wrought-iron balconies decorated with pairs of gilded lions. Statues of Prudence and Justice on pedestals guard the main portal, which is an archway capped with wrought iron and another pair of gold lions. Above the third story is an attic with a clock and a balustrade flanked by two statues of Hercules. Capping the whole thing is a pair of stone lions guarding the Pamplonan coats of arms, which are topped with huge crowns; in the middle, looking like a bored Roman eunuch, is a huge statue of Fame, one arm cocked on his hip and the other holding what looks like a primitive trombone poised at his lips.

AROUND THE AYUNTAMIENTO

A couple of blocks north of the *ayuntamiento* on Calle Santo Domingo is the **Museo de Navarra**, which overlooks the corrals where the bulls are kept before the *encierro* (the running of the bulls) each morning during San Fermín. Located in a 16th-century building that once housed a charity hospital, the museum contains Roman mosaics, some distinguished Romanesque capitals from the original cloister of the cathedral, fragments from the ninth-century mosque of Tudela, and an interesting collection of medieval mural paintings taken from different churches in Navarra.

Just west of the *ayuntamiento,* at the beginning of Calle Mayor, is the **Iglesia de San Saturnino** with its Romanesque towers and a 13th-century Gothic doorway. Note the brass-lettered pavement marker in front of the church, where, as local lore has it, San Saturnino baptized 40,000 pagans from a well. One block southwest of San Saturnino, on Calle

Ansoleaga, is the Cámara de Comptos, an interesting 14th-century Gothic building that served for more than 400 years as a mint.

WEST OF THE AYUNTAMIENTO

At the western end of Calle Mayor is the Neoclassical **Iglesia de San Lorenzo**, home of the much-venerated, silver-bedecked, dark-faced statue of San Fermín. Navarra's patron saint is said to be able to descend with a cape and come to the aid of any fallen *mozo* (bull runner) in the *encierro*.

The **Jardines de la Taconera** are just west of San Lorenzo. To the south of the gardens are the restored and manicured remains of the **Ciudadela**, a 16th-century stone fortress built during the reign of Philip II (and patterned on the fortress at Antwerp). Both the Ciudadela and the Jardines de la Taconera often serve as open-air theaters in summer during the Festivales de Navarra, among Spain's finest cultural events (see below).

PLAZA DEL CASTILLO

A few short blocks southeast of the *ayuntamiento* is the arcaded Plaza del Castillo, with its shops, sidewalk cafés, park benches, shade trees, and bandstand. It is indeed the heart of Pamplona, and during San Fermín it is the place to be. Hemingway, Orson Welles, Kenneth Tynan, James Michener, and many other temporary expatriates used to hold court during fiesta at the **Bar Txoco** (pronounced "choko"), just steps from the southeastern corner of the square, where Hotel Quintana (called Hotel Montoya in *The Sun Also Rises*) was located. The late Juanito Quintana, the proprietor and Hemingway's great friend, was the prototype for Montoya, Jake Barnes's bullfight mentor. Nowadays the foreign regulars migrate to the outdoor cafés in front of Hotel Perla in the northeastern corner of the square. The venerable **Café Iruña**, across the square, still replaces its tables and chairs at fiesta time with less attractive, but more durable, outdoor furniture.

PLAZA DE TOROS

The Plaza de Toros, Pamplona's bullring, is just southeast of the Plaza del Castillo. From Bar Txoco walk south along Calle Espoz y Mina for two blocks, then look to your left. At the corner of Paseo Hemingway and Calle Amaya, in front of the bullring, is a statue of Ernest Hemingway, dedicated to him by the people of Pamplona in the 1960s. Every year on July 6 someone ties a red kerchief around Don Ernesto's neck, where it remains until the end of the fiesta.

The Fiestas de San Fermín

In 1926 Ernest Hemingway described the opening of the Fiestas de San Fermín in *The Sun Also Rises,* his immortal novel of Pamplona and the Lost Generation: "At noon on Sunday, the 6th of July, the fiesta exploded. There is no other way to describe it."

Every year at that moment mobs of people gather from all over the province of Navarra, the rest of Spain, and—since Hemingway—the world, at the *ayuntamiento* to see the *chupinazo* signaling the beginning of the Fiestas de San Fermín. As the rocket streaks into the sky above Pamplona, thousands shout *"¡Viva San Fermín!"* They then put on the red neckerchiefs that are the symbol of the fiesta, and begin singing, dancing, and doing some journeyman drinking (their apprenticeship, just as Hemingway observed more than 60 years ago, takes place in the cheaper bars of the old quarter all morning long). Within minutes the Plaza del Castillo and the streets surrounding it are filled with the cacophony of flutes, drums, horns, shouts, and exploding fireworks as the red-and-white-clad throng dances to the music of Navarra.

San Fermín is a wild, bacchanalian affair—not for the faint of heart or the abstemious—that goes on in the streets for eight days, subsiding briefly, but never fully, during the wee hours of the morning (bands begin playing in the streets at 6:00 A.M.). There are bullfights, jai alai matches, Basque woodchopping contests, *jota*-singing competitions, spectacular fireworks, a first-rate international circus and carnival, and, of course, the *encierro,* the running of the bulls. Adding an international flavor to all this are the thousands of foreigners, many of whom have not missed the fiesta in years. Everyone—from bootblacks to duchesses—joins the party.

Finally, on the night of July 14, the fiesta begins to wind down as the celebrants light candles and walk through Pamplona, alternately singing the bittersweet lament *"Pobre de mi, se han acabado las Fiestas de San Fermín"* ("Woe is me, San Fermín is over") and another song (*"Uno de enero, dos de febrero,... siete de julio, ¡San Fermín!"*—"First of January, second of February,... seventh of July, San Fermín!") that is the countdown to next year's fiesta.

The Running of the Bulls

Every morning from July 7 to July 14, brave men wearing white shirts and trousers, red sashes and neckerchiefs, and rope-soled *alpargatas* run with the fighting bulls through the streets of the city for what Hemingway called "a morning's pleasure."

DOING THE ENCIERRO

If you are young, brave, foolish, or drunk—it helps if you are all four—you may want to try the *encierro:* running the bulls. (You must also be male; women, technically, are not permitted to run, although some do get away with it.) To get an idea of the layout of the *encierro* route, which is barricaded with a double line of heavy timbers each morning before the run, start at the bottom of the hill on Calle Santo Domingo, where the bulls are corraled the night before. Walk up Santo Domingo and follow the rows of square postholes past the *ayuntamiento* to the famous canyonlike Calle Estafeta and to its end at the *teléfonos* (the main telephone office) corner, where the run doglegs left down a chute and through a narrow tunnel into the bullring. The run ends here with a mass of runners, bulls, and steers pouring in to the cheers of a packed house.

This is a dangerous stunt for "a morning's pleasure." A fighting bull can outrun a racehorse for the first 100 yards and can run the half-mile uphill *encierro* course in less than three minutes. If you begin running at the *ayuntamiento* after the bulls are released in the streets, they will pass you before you get to the bullring. In this century more than a dozen runners have been killed during the *encierro,* hundreds have been gored, and thousands more have sustained injuries serious enough to require medical attention. The greatest danger here, however, is the likelihood of being trampled by a wild-eyed sophomore from an American university. Imagine being in a crowded auditorium when someone yells "Fire!" and you find six or seven fighting bulls, several massive steers, and hundreds of hell-bent runners racing for the only exit.

If you do run the bulls, and if they come within reasonable proximity of you during the *encierro,* check the windows of local photography shops around the Plaza del Castillo's side streets afterward. Photographers stationed along the *encierro* route take dozens of snapshots each day. If you find yourself in one, you can purchase a unique personal souvenir of your San Fermín adventure.

WATCHING THE ENCIERRO

To watch the *encierro,* which begins at 8:00 A.M., you must get to the barricades by 6:00 A.M. to get a place to stand. Santo Domingo hill, the *ayuntamiento,* and the *teléfonos* dogleg near the bullring are the best places to see the action. If you get to the ticket windows by 6:30 A.M., you can buy an inexpensive ticket to see the climax of the *encierro* from a bullring seat, available only on a first-come, first-served basis. There's also wonderful music from a band parading around the ring, and an amateur bullfight, which features young heifers wreaking havoc on those foolish enough to get in their way.

Other Festivals and Events in Pamplona

BULLFIGHTS

Tickets are expensive and very difficult to come by, but a bullfight at Pamplona—for the strong at heart, at least—is an incredible experience. Only season ticket holders can get bullfight tickets ahead of time, and the same people have been buying these season tickets, called *abonos,* for years. You can try the bullring ticket windows on the day of the fight, but tickets will probably be sold out. Your next move is to check with the scalpers, who will ask a fortune depending on the location (get a seat in the shade; the sun seats are rough territory). If you are well heeled, you might ask the concierge of your hotel about ticket possibilities.

Colorful rowdy *peñas* (social clubs), each led by a noisy band and packing enough wine and food for an army, parade through the streets to the bullring each afternoon with their ribald and politically oriented cartoon banners held high. The *peñas* are fun to watch, but under no circumstances should you buy a ticket to the bullfight in *tendidos* 5 or 6, where they sit; it is a war zone. As a foreigner you will be a choice target for ice water, sacks of flour, and any leftover food and cheap wine they may throw at you.

MUSICAL PERFORMANCES

The Navarros are great music lovers and are very supportive of musicians and musical festivals. The Ronda de Otoño, in autumn, is a series of performances and art exhibitions sponsored by various Navarrese artistic groups. Pamplona's superb choral group, La Agrupación Coral de Cámara de Pamplona, is known around the world, and the colorful municipal band, La Pamplonesa, is the pride of the city. The tenor Julián Gayarre, who comes from Roncal, in the Pyrenees, and another Navarra native, Pablo Sarasate, the 19th-century virtuoso violinist who dazzled the world playing his 1724 Stradivarius, are venerated in Pamplona. Teatro Gayarre, Pamplona's principal theater, and Paseo de Sarasate, a major street, were named in honor of these great musicians.

The Festivales de Navarra

The Festivales de Navarra, which take place in August, feature sophisticated programs of music, dance, theater, and folkloric music by prestigious national and international performers. Such artists as Victoria de los Angeles, Plácido Domingo, and Montserrat Caballé, and national ballet and folkloric dance companies of Cuba, China, and Russia have appeared.

For specific information on the Festivales de Navarra and other Navarrese events, write to: Servicio de Turismo, Diputación Foral de Navarra, Arrieta 11 bis, 5°, 31002 Pamplona (Navarra).

SPORTING EVENTS

Besides bull running, which takes place not only in Pamplona but also in most Navarrese towns during their annual fiestas, the local *machos* revel in weight-lifting contests (using 200-kilogram stones), woodchopping competitions, musical chairs on horseback, and jai alai at the ubiquitous *frontón* (whose rectangular two-walled courts—sometimes a wall of the church—can be seen in every village). You can see most of these events in Pamplona and other Navarrese towns during fiesta. Outside of fiesta you can see and bet on professional jai alai every Thursday, Saturday, and Sunday, and most holidays at Frontón Euskai-Jai Berri, 6 km (4 miles) northeast of Pamplona on the Roncesvalles road, in suburban Huarte.

Staying in Pamplona

During San Fermín it is very difficult to get hotel reservations in Pamplona, and if you do manage to find a hotel room, be aware that prices are at least double what they would be outside of fiesta. Most people who do not already have connections in Pamplona rent rooms in private homes. The tourist office at Calle Duque de Ahumada 3 (around the corner from the Plaza del Castillo on the way to the bullring) will give you a list of homes with rooms for rent and provide directions. This way you get a chance to see the accommodations and the distance from the center of the action before you commit to the room. Unfortunately these rooms cannot be reserved in advance through the tourist office.

The 225-room, ultramodern ▶ Hotel Iruña Park, geared to the corporate traveller, is now Pamplona's top-rated hotel, but is a taxi ride from the center of town and a little sterile for most travellers' tastes. The ▶ Hotel Tres Reyes, located in the Jardines de la Taconera, is still the best and most conveniently located luxury hotel in Pamplona. The Tres Reyes is a full-service hotel with a garage, swimming pool, health club, shops, and a friendly and attentive staff. Every room has a balcony.

If you want comfort and many of the amenities offered by luxury hotels and don't mind ultramodern decor, the moderately priced ► **Hotel Maisonnave**, very centrally located in the old quarter southeast of the *ayuntamiento,* is one of the best all-around choices. The parking situation is bad in the narrow old streets surrounding the Maisonnave, but the hotel has a garage.

Given the inflated state of Spain's economy and the current value of the peseta, it is sad to report that hotels in the "moderate" price range can cost 10,000 to 12,000 pesetas per night. Pamplona has several choices in that category (they are much more costly during San Fermín). ► **Hotel Orhi**, located just a block south of the bullring and a few short blocks from the Plaza del Castillo, is a good, homey, moderately priced hotel with lots of repeat clientele. It can get a little noisy, though, since the wonderfully boisterous tavern and restaurant **Casa Mauleón** is located in the same building.

The bullfighters' hotel, ► **Hotel Yoldi**, a few blocks south of the Plaza del Castillo, may be aging, but it still exudes an Old World charm that is somewhat Hemingwayesque. Just off the busy traffic circle at the Plaza Príncipe de Viana, but still a comfortable walk north to the Plaza del Castillo, is the pretty, charming, 24-room ► **Hotel Avenida**. The Avenida is in a lovely renovated building with a façade enhanced by French doors that open onto balconies overlooking the plaza's lovely fountain.

The ► **Hotel Eslava**, whose owner, José Luis Eslava, used to be director of Pamplona's famous choral group, is located several blocks northeast of the center of town in a colorful part of the old quarter overlooking the ramparts and just a block from the Jardines de la Taconera. The Eslava is comfortable, cozy, and, by today's standards, a bargain.

Dining in Pamplona

If you are an aficionado of great restaurants, you will find plenty of them in Pamplona. At **Hartza**, Calle Juan de Labrit 19 (just north of the bullring), sisters Mari, Manoli, and Julia serve some of Pamplona's best food in the elegant dining rooms of a lovely renovated house decorated with antiques, oil paintings, and beamed ceilings. Hartza is famous for traditional Navarrese and Basque dishes made from seasonal ingredients. Mari or Manoli will recite the dishes of the day—*alubias de Tolosa* (red beans); baked fresh hake, turbot, or sea bream; or *almejas a la marinera* (a clam casserole). Take their suggestions and be prepared to pay 6,000 to 7,000 pesetas per person for a full dinner with wine. Tel: (9-48) 22-45-68.

The straitlaced solemnity of formal service and graceful dining at fancy, expensive restaurants runs counter to the casual, raucous atmosphere of San Fermín. The restaurants that offer such an experience are probably best left for a nonfiesta visit. **Josetxo**, Plaza Príncipe de Viana 1 (near Hotels Yoldi and Avenida), has luxurious dining rooms, impeccable service, and beautifully presented classic Navarrese dishes. Tel: (9-48) 22-20-97. **Rodero**, Arrieta 3 (southeast of the bullring, facing Parque Media Luna), features *alta cocina* (haute cuisine) that is a bit precious in concept— duck with grapefruit and honey sauce, asparagus with shellfish. Tel: (9-48) 22-80-35.

Pricey **La Olla**, Avenida de Roncesvalles 2 (half a block southwest of the main entrance to the bullring), is owned by Tito Ibarrola, a member of the family that owned Maitena, a Pamplona favorite in the 1960s and 1970s. La Olla serves a range of classic Navarrese dishes—*ajoarriero* (a salt-cod dish), *pimientos rellenos, cordero asado,* grilled fish. Tel: (9-48) 22-95-58.

Las Pocholas (also called Hostal del Rey Noble), Paseo de Sarasate 6, southwest of the Plaza del Castillo, was a favorite of Hemingway, who frequented it during the "Dangerous Summer" of 1959. Some say Las Pocholas, Pamplona's longest-established top-category restaurant, is a fading star, but for traditional dishes and specialties such as *ajoarriero con langosta* (codfish with lobster), others still swear by Las Pocholas (The Sweethearts), as the longtime owners, the Guerendiain sisters, have been known for more than 30 years. Tel: (9-48) 22-22-14.

For authentic Navarrese cooking at moderate prices, try **Casa Luis**, Calle Padre Calatayud 11 (south of Plaza Príncipe de Viana), Tel: (9-48) 23-36-75; **San Fermín**, Calle San Nicolás 44 (west of the Plaza del Castillo on a famous street with some 30 bars and restaurants), Tel: (9-48) 22-21-91; and **Shanti**, Castillo de Mayo 39 (ten blocks southeast of Plaza del Castillo near the foot of Avenida de Carlos III), Tel: (9-48) 23-10-04. The great old tavern **Casa Mauleón**, Calle Amaya 4, south of the bullring, is an obligatory stop, especially for *alubias con chorizo* (white beans with sausage), *pimientos rellenos* (stuffed peppers), the house wine, the *ambiente*— wine barrels, hustling waiters, *jota*-singing customers—and the joy of it all. Tel: (9-48) 22-84-74.

Casa Marceliano, a rowdy old tavern that was located behind the *ayuntamiento* on Calle Mercado (alongside the city market), is now closed. It was the spiritual home of many Pamplona regulars, and it used to be a favorite of both Hemingway and Michener. Mentioned in both Michener's *Iberia* and *The Drifters,* Marceliano was frequented by inveterate fiesta-goers, primarily the stout-hearted, who liked the music (impromptu *jotas;* street bands stopping at the bar), the *pochas,* the free-flowing *clarete,* and the occasional fistfight.

EASTERN NAVARRA

Navarra has some of the richest and most revered shrines on the Camino de Santiago and also has the distinction of having two branches of the great pilgrimage road within its borders. The more southerly branch enters from France via Aragón, then passes through Leyre and Sangüesa in southeastern Navarra. The other, more famous route begins at the French border at Valcarlos and comes down through the Pyrenees via Roncesvalles to Pamplona. Both routes converge at Puente la Reina, 24 km (15 miles) southwest of Pamplona, at which point the *camino* passes westward through the Navarrese towns of Mañeru, Cirauqui, Estella, Los Arcos, Torres del Río, and Viana before entering La Rioja. (For more on the Camino de Santiago, see the chapters on Aragón, La Rioja, Old Castile, and—for the object of the pilgrimage, Santiago de Compostela—Asturias and Galicia.)

In this section we cover the Camino de Santiago's southern branch, then make a loop up into the Pyrenees, returning to Pamplona along the *camino*'s northern branch.

The Camino de Santiago:
Southern Branch

Approximately 50 km (31 miles) southeast of Pamplona, by way of N 240, are Javier, Leyre, and Sangüesa—all of which are exceptionally rich in history and architecture, and the last two of which were important shrines on the Camino de Santiago.

LEYRE

The **Monasterio de San Salvador de Leyre** overlooks the huge Yesa reservoir in the dramatically beautiful Sierra de Leyre. First mentioned as a monastery in documents from A.D. 848, and claiming Visigothic roots dating to the sixth century, Leyre became the most powerful and spiritually important abbey in Navarra under the Cistercians. It counted San Sebastián in its dominions and was the pantheon of the first kings of Navarra. The primitive 11th-century Romanesque crypt and the late 11th-century naves and tower were built on the ruins of a sixth-century Visigothic church. In 1954 Benedictine monks from Santo Domingo de Silos repopulated the then-decaying monastery and restored the 17th- and 18th-century buildings for use as a hotel, the ▶ **Hospedería de Leyre**, an inexpensive, comfortable, parador-like hotel where travellers can spend a tranquil night and perhaps hear the brothers in the monastery in Gregorian chant.

JAVIER

The **Castillo de Javier**, 8 km (5 miles) southwest of Leyre, is the birthplace of Saint Francis Xavier, one of the founders of the Jesuits and the apostle to the Indies, who established missions and converted thousands to Roman Catholicism in India and Japan. The 13th-century castle was partially demolished in the 16th century by order of Cardinal Cisneros. Today the castle, while interesting, suffers a bit from the sterility of latter-day restoration. There is a sound-and-light show at the castle on summer weekends.

SANGUESA

Sangüesa, 12 km (7½ miles) southwest of Javier, is a very special town on the Camino de Santiago. Its roots can be found 5 km (3 miles) north of the present town, where it was first a Roman town known as Sancossa, then a Visigothic town, and then the Navarrese castle-fortress hill town of Rocaforte, whose ruins can still be seen there. Sangüesa's "modern" history began in 1211 when Alfonso I of Aragón, known as the Battler, granted *fueros,* or special rights and privileges, to the people of Rocaforte to get them to move down to the plain and to European merchants and craftsmen so that they would settle in this area. Alfonso also built a castle to defend Sangüesa against attacks from the Moors and to make the bridge over the Río Aragón safe for pilgrims to Santiago.

Around in Sangüesa

Sangüesa has an impresssive Romanesque church, the 12th-century Cistercian **Santa María la Real** (a national monument), located on Rúa Mayor, just across the bridge over the Río Aragón at the entrance to town. The splendid south portal is decorated in stone with a multitude of figures. Animals, birds, griffins, musicians, blacksmiths, saints, and sinners all vie for the eye's attention in this magnificent rendition of the Last Judgment by a pair of medieval artists. The church's octagonal tower and spire and odd, silo-like cylindrical staircase on the outside of the tower are a bit incongruous, rising above the splendid intricacies of the grand portal, but they are an interesting ensemble and a distinctive Sangüesa landmark.

A wealth of other monuments and mansions built by prosperous merchants graces Sangüesa, making this small town (population 4,600) an exceptionally rewarding place to visit. Two handsome mansions near Santa María la Real are the 15th-century Gothic **Palacio del Duque de Granada**, on Rúa Mayor, the original pilgrim route through the city, and the Baroque **Palacio de Vallesantoro** (now Casa de Cultura), on Calle Alfonso el Batallador, whose carved wooden eaves sport some rather grotesque but amusing figures of serpents and mythical creatures.

The **Iglesia de Santiago**, on Calle Santiago east of Rúa Mayor, is a 12th-century transitional Romanesque-Gothic church with a crenellated bell tower. The tympanum of the church's portal has a large single-stone statue of Santiago (discovered in 1965 under some floorboards in the church) standing on a large shell, his garment and hat covered with scallop shells. **San Salvador**, a 14th-century Gothic church facing the bullring on Calle Alfonso el Batallador, preserves an earlier Romanesque portal and contains a fine set of 16th-century choir stalls originally from the monastery of Leyre. Alfonso the Battler's castle, now the **Palacio del Príncipe de Viana**, on the street of the same name, was added to in the 13th century and converted into a palace in the 14th, but kept its crenellated towers, which remain today. An arcaded section of the palace done in Renaissance style is now used as the city hall.

OUTSIDE SANGUESA

There are two spectacular gorges north of Sangüesa: the **Hoz de Lumbier** on the Río Irati, just a few kilometers north of Sangüesa between the towns of Liédena and Lumbier, and the **Hoz de Arbayún** (about 4 miles long, with vertical drops of up to 400 yards), to the northeast on Río Salazar. The latter can best be seen from the Iso pass between Lumbier and Navascués.

The lovely little 12th-century **Ermita de San Adrián de Vadoluengo** is located between Sangüesa and **Sos del Rey Católico**, 13 km (8 miles) southeast of Sangüesa, across the provincial boundary into Aragón. Sos del Rey Católico, the birthplace of Ferdinand the Catholic, has excellent accommodations in the modern ▶ **Parador Fernando de Aragón**. Built on the hill next to the defensive walls of this historic town, the parador has superb views of the countryside, especially from the terrace just off the attractive, tile-decorated fourth-floor bar (take the elevator in the lobby). Although of recent construction, the parador is a distinguished building, and its massive stone walls and timbered balconies blend harmoniously with the rest of the historic buildings in Sos del Rey Católico.

The lobby is decorated with wooden benches, antiques, fine old cabinets, plush leather chairs and sofas, and a charming sculpture of Fernando as a boy. His hand is on his dagger and his face has an apprehensive look, as he appears poised to leave the safety of his mother's care and warily step out into the minefield of 15th-century politics.

As in all paradores, the restaurant offers a menu of regional cuisine, always with a few often hard-to-find dishes such as *zarrecatralla de Borja* (quail with river crayfish and snails).

The Pyrenees and the
Camino de Santiago

In this section we diverge from the Camino de Santiago to travel through part of the Pyrenees before meeting the western branch of the *camino* at Burguete near Roncesvalles. After exploring that region, we pick up the main trail again south of Pamplona at Puente la Reina.

After a night at Leyre or Sos del Rey Católico, a spectacular drive of 40 km (25 miles) to the northeast on C 137 (by way of Lumbier and Navascués) will take you into the heart of the Pyrenees, where rivers rush out of the high mountains through stands of beech trees into deep-green valleys that shelter some of the least-spoiled villages in Spain.

VALLE DEL RONCAL

The isolated Valle del Roncal is dotted with bucolic villages set against a backdrop of splendid mountain scenery. Twenty-five years ago it was not uncommon to find some Roncalese wearing the traditional dress; you can still see their colorful costumes during celebrations. Roncal has an excellent cheese, *queso Roncal,* which can be bought in shops and markets all over Navarra. The first Spanish cheese to be given an official *denominación de origen* (like wine), Roncal is reminiscent of Italian Parmesan, but milder and softer.

The great tenor Julián Gayarre (1844–1890) was from the town of **Roncal**, which also claims some of the great *jota* singers of Navarra. Gayarre's funeral monument in the village cemetery is by Mariano Benlliure (1862–1947), the Valencian sculptor who did the equestrian statue of Alfonso XII in Madrid's Parque del Retiro and the great *torero* Joselito's funeral monument in Seville.

Isaba

North of Roncal, at the eastern edge of Navarra, is the beautiful village of Isaba, located in a green valley below the rugged peaks that culminate in the **Mesa de los Tres Reyes** (Three Kings' Table), Navarra's highest mountain (7,984 feet). Every year on the first Sunday in July a colorful *romería* (pilgrimage cum picnic), where everyone dresses in regional costume, takes place at the nearby hermitage of **Idoya**. On July 13 the seven mayors of the villages of the valley turn out in typical regional dress to receive a tribute of three cows from their French neighbors from the Baretous (Bearn) valley. This event, dating from the Middle Ages, is now a fiesta drawing thousands of people to its site on the French border each year.

The government of Navarra owns the modern, but rustically decorated, 50-room ▶ **Hotel Isaba** (renovated in 1986), on the edge of town, a good base for those who want to spend quiet days exploring these beautiful mountains or skiing (no lifts) in winter. The hotel has a restaurant that serves regional dishes. A few kilometers north of Isaba in the mountain pass of Belagua is the restaurant **Venta de Juan Pito** (closed weekdays from November 1 to June 15), where you can have grilled lamb chops; Tel: (9-48) 89-30-80.

NORTHWEST TO RONCESVALLES

From Isaba it is about 60 km (37 miles) northwest on mountain roads to Roncesvalles, and light-years away from the trappings of modern life. If you have the time, the driving skills, and (most important) the good weather, you may want to take these splendidly picturesque regional roads instead of doubling back on the main roads to Pamplona (94 km/58 miles from Isaba).

Lodging in the Pyrenees

If you have decided to brave the drive into the Pyrenees you might want to stay in a *hostal* or pension in one of the mountain towns (besides Isaba, Ochagavía and Burguete have livable accommodations for the adventurous). For a unique experience in these mountains, you can stay in the country home of a Navarrese family that lets rooms to tourists, usually at very reasonable rates. Many of these private houses are the classic stone-and-timber farm and village houses called *caseríos* that are typical of Navarra and the Basque Country; they often have rooms for as many as 12 people. Meals with the family—sometimes still cooked in the *caserío*'s ancient fireplace—are usually offered with lodgings. The Navarros are legendary cooks, so you may be served dishes that surpass even the formidable output of the exceptional chefs in Navarra's formal restaurants. Many *caseríos* have stables on the ground floor, and guests sometimes get the chance to feed the livestock or milk the cows.

The government of Navarra's Servicio de Turismo publishes a booklet called *Casas Rurales* that lists private homes (with contact information) in the region, mostly located in these towns of the Navarrese Pyrenees, that rent rooms to travellers. To request a copy, write to: Servicio de Turismo, Diputación Foral de Navarra, Arrieta 11 bis, 5°, 31002 Pamplona (Navarra).

The Route Northwest

About 23 km (14 miles) west of Isaba on the mountain route, across the Portillo de Lazar pass, is **Ochagavía**, the main village of the Salazar River valley. The 15 villages of this valley retain a medieval air, and tradition has it that there are witches here. A 42-km (26-mile) drive north to Irati passes through the **Selva de Irati**, an enchanting forest of unusually tall beech trees said to be haunted by the ghost of the poisoned Navarrese queen Juana de Labrit, granddaughter of Juan de Labrit (Jean d'Albret). The road then runs down the Irati River valley—in which Hemingway fished, after hiking the considerable distance from Burguete—to the village of Arive. The more direct route from Ochagavía goes via Escaroz to Arive (25 km/15½ miles), where you can choose between turning south to Pamplona via Aoiz or continuing another 10 km (6 miles) northeast via Burguete to Roncesvalles.

NORTH OF RONCESVALLES

The western branch of the Camino de Santiago, coming from St. Jean-Pied-de-Port, crosses the French border at Valcarlos, 65 km (40 miles) northwest of Pamplona on C 135 and some 20 km (12½ miles) north of Roncesvalles. Between Valcarlos and Roncesvalles is the site of a former stop on the Camino de Santiago, the **Monasterio de San Salvador de Ibañeta**, where French pilgrims once left thousands of crosses in memory of Charlemagne and in particular of Roland, who died in these hills above Roncesvalles and was immortalized in the great, and first, French epic poem, *Chanson de Roland.* All that remains now is a modern stone monument to Roldán, as Roland is known in Spanish, and a modern hermitage that houses the bell that was tolled to guide lost pilgrims through the night and the thick fogs that often shroud the approaches to the Ibañeta pass.

Between Ibañeta and Roncesvalles (a few kilometers south) is a deep-green, mossy forest laced with icy rivulets where you can cool your wines, melons, and other picnic items for an alfresco luncheon such as the one James Michener describes in this setting in *Iberia:* "In a glade so quiet, so softly green that it seemed as if defeated knights might have slept in it the evening before, we spread our blankets and prepared the meal." These woods are a mystical place, haunted by the spirit of Roland's band and the millions of Santiago-bound pilgrims who have walked this ground.

RONCESVALLES

The monastery of Roncesvalles, which dates to the 12th century, is rather disappointing after the buildup of the legend. Fires, neglect, and overzealous and ill-advised restoration, including the unfortunate choice of a metal roof, have reduced this important monastery to a ghost of its former self. Once a proud hospital and hospice for pilgrims, renowned for its hospitality (good food, real beds, and a cobbler to mend shoes), the monastery now, as Edwin Mullins puts it in *The Pilgrimage to Santiago,* "has the feel of a run-down boarding-school of spartan character . . . an unloved, secular-looking place." Nevertheless, there are several interesting sights, such as the 13th-century Virgin of Roncesvalles, a restored Gothic **cloister**, the Gothic pantheon containing the enormous tomb of the giant king of Navarra, Sancho the Strong, and the treasury, which contains several venerated objects of colorful, but somewhat dubious, heritage.

BURGUETE

Several scenes in *The Sun Also Rises* are set in the tiny village of Burguete, 3 km (2 miles) south of Roncesvalles. Hemingway's trout-fishing expeditions to the Río Irati, east of Burguete, inspired him to write some of the best descriptive passages in literature about fishing and the camaraderie of sportsmen. In keeping with the spirit of the treasury of Roncesvalles so far as authenticity is concerned, the ▶ **Hostal Burguete**, where Hemingway stayed, will show you the piano that the Bill Gorton character supposedly played. Lift the top to see a newspaper picture of Don Ernesto and the name "E. Heminway" (sic) scratched in the wood. If you are in a romantic mood and don't mind roughing it just a bit, Hostal Burguete is still much the way it was in style and comfort, or lack thereof, when Hemingway stayed there in the 1920s. Take warm night clothes even in July.

In the *hostal*'s dining room you can order a good salad, excellent *pochas,* trout, lamb chops with potatoes, and a bottle of Navarra wine. If it is July and you have had the foresight to pick a handful of wild strawberries along the road from Roncesvalles, you can sprinkle them over ice cream for dessert. From Burguete, picturesque route C 135 twists south through several small villages to Pamplona.

WESTERN NAVARRA
Puente la Reina

The two great gateway branches of the Camino de Santiago converge 20 km (12½ miles) southwest of Pamplona on route N 111 at Puente la Reina, whose 12th-century, six-arched **Romanesque bridge** over the Río Arga may be one of the loveliest bridges in the world. The view of the bridge and village mirrored in the waters of the river on a still day is a composition of exquisite beauty. The pilgrims' way still follows its original path along the Rúa Mayor through the center of Puente la Reina, which in its day was an important market town and home to many foreign merchants, who offered fine goods from France and Italy to the steady flow of pilgrims.

The **Iglesia del Crucifijo** contains an exceptional crucifix, with an image of Christ, thought to be of German origin, his arms raised high on a Saint Andrew's cross. The 12th-century **Iglesia de Santiago** contains a superb 14th-century wooden statue of Santiago dressed as a "foot-slogger," as Walter Starkie called those pilgrims who walked the Camino de Santiago.

At the northern edge of Puente la Reina is the entrance to **Señorío de Sarría**, a huge estate resembling a feudal village. Some of the finest wines of Navarra, including a wonderful dry *rosado,* are made here. Call the winery's offices in Pamplona to arrange a visit; Tel: (9-48) 26-75-62. Just one kilometer north of town, where the two Santiago routes actually converge, is a fine modern statue of a pilgrim and the ▶ **Mesón del Peregrino**, a reasonably comfortable 15-room hotel decorated in the rustic style of a pilgrims' inn, with a swimming pool out back. Mesón del Peregrino has a sophisticated new owner, who has redecorated the hotel, upgraded the dining room, and remodeled the bedrooms. The dining room still has the same thick stone walls and stone-block floors, but the tables are beautifully set with Villeroy & Boch plates and graced with pretty flower bouquets. Such northern specialties as *cogollitas de Tudela con anchoas a la vinagreta* (lettuce hearts from Tudela with anchovies) and *rodaballo* (turbot) are excellent here and are complemented by a good selection of wines. You can also get a first-rate American-style martini here.

EXCURSIONS FROM PUENTE LA REINA

Eunate

Six kilometers (4 miles) east of Puente la Reina, near the village of Obanos, is the simple but beautiful 12th-century octagonal church of Eunate. It is thought to have been inspired by the Holy Sepulcher in Jerusalem and is closely related in style to the Vera Cruz chapel of the Knights Templar at Segovia and the church of the Holy Sepulcher at Torres del Río, between Estella and Logroño. An oddity of this church is the roofless, cloister-like structure that surrounds it.

Cirauqui

A few kilometers west of Puente la Reina on N 111 is the medieval village of **Mañeru**, and a few kilometers farther is Cirauqui. The original pilgrims' road passes through an archway at Cirauqui and up the hill to a 13th-century Romanesque church. A few feet farther on the village ends abruptly, but the cobblestone remains of the old foot trail, a uniform five meters wide (like the bridge at Puente la Reina and most of the old sections of the *camino*), head down the hill to a ruined but still walkable single-arch bridge of Roman origin, now used by the occasional foot pilgrim intent on retracing the original route and by the occasional Navarrese shepherd—wearing the traditional beret—with his flock and dog.

Estella

"Estella, la bella" goes the popular rhyme first used in the Middle Ages to describe this historic old town. And beautiful indeed is Estella's striking setting on the Río Ega, 20 km (12½ miles) west of Puente la Reina on N 111, in a valley surrounded by hills and cliffs. Many of Estella's 13,000 inhabitants are descended from rabid Carlists (a 19th-century movement, culminating in civil war in the north, to enthrone Carlos, brother of King Fernando VII, who died without a male heir in 1833). The town's streets are stacked along the hillside and graced with some of the finest medieval monuments in northern Spain.

Aymery Picaud, a 12th-century French Cluniac priest who wrote perhaps the world's first travel book—the fifth book of the *Codex Calixtinus*—a guide to the Camino de Santiago, praised Estella highly for its sweet water, good bread, excellent wine, and its "meat and fish abundant." The town became a well-used pilgrim stop in the 11th century, when *franco* (European, or Frankish) and Jewish merchants and artisans were enticed with tax-free status and special privileges (franking privileges) to help populate the area around the ancient Navarrese village of Lizarra, thus helping buttress the Christian frontier against the Moors.

AROUND IN ESTELLA

Estella still retains vestiges of this mix of cultures in its many medieval monuments, most of which are well-marked by signs. The most interesting buildings are located in the area around the Plaza de San Martín, south of the Río Ega and N 111, which was originally occupied by the *barrio franco* and the Jewish quarter. On the Plaza de San Martín is the 12th-century **Palacio de los Reyes de Navarra**, one of the oldest secular buildings in Spain. Topping a column on this building is a Romanesque capital depicting Roland slaying the giant Ferragut.

Also in this area, below the hill where a once-mighty castle stood until Philip II—afraid that it might be used against his troops by the Navarros—ordered it destroyed in 1572, is the remarkable 12th- and 13th-century **Iglesia de San Pedro de la Rúa**. San Pedro is Romanesque, with Romanesque-Gothic transitional elements and part of a lovely Romanesque cloister (the other half was destroyed when the castle walls came crashing down), where pilgrims who died in Estella were buried. Some of the beautifully carved capitals are worthy of note; four twisted columns that are highly reminiscent of the great cloister of Santo Domingo de Silos are superb.

It is the church's **north portal**, at the top of a long flight of stone steps, however, that really captures the imagination and illustrates how closely the brilliant, often warring, cultures of the Middle Ages were intertwined and how deeply they influenced one another. Here you will find the workmanship and designs of the Moriscos, the Moors living under Christian rule: Geometric, nonrepresentational design (instead of a plethora of human and mystical creatures as in Christian style) decorates the monochrome rainbow of archivolts, and a scalloped Moorish archway worthy of Córdoba caps the doorway of this important pilgrim church.

After a pogrom in the mid-13th century, the Jews rebuilt their ghetto below the eastern side of the castle hill, where it was easier to defend, and fortified it. The **Iglesia de Santa María Jus del Castillo** (Church of Saint Mary below the Castle), located east of Plaza San Martín (follow Calle Curtidores) below the castle hill, was built on the remains of what was once a synagogue.

Contrast San Pedro de la Rúa with the jewel of 12th-century Romanesque art, the doorway of the **Iglesia de San Miguel Arcangel**, across the river in the old Navarrese "Christian" quarter of the same name. Built by descendants of Lizarra natives to show up the foreigners, whom they despised because of their special privileges, San Miguel has a portal covered with scores of detailed stone carvings of symbolic religious and biblical scenes. It ranks with the portals of Sangüesa and Tudela for the excellence of its carving and profusion of characters.

Thursday is a good day to visit Estella, when the market is set up in the Plaza de los Fueros, which is located northwest of San Pedro in the most populous part of town, across the Río Ega to the northwest. In Estella's fiesta in early August, women are allowed to run with the bulls.

Also in this area in the center of Estella and northwest of Plaza de San Miguel are the venerable, reasonably priced **La Cepa**, Plaza de los Fueros 18 (on the second floor overlooking the square), regarded as the best restaurant in Estella and offering a typical Navarrese menu with some haute cuisine dishes, Tel: (9-48) 55-00-32; and **Restaurante Navarre**, located in a pretty villa southwest of Plaza de los Fueros (Gonzalo de Maeztu 16) with medieval decor and a menu of typical Navarrese and Spanish dishes such as roast suckling pig, stuffed peppers, and *merluza,* Tel: (9-48) 55-00-40.

EXCURSIONS FROM ESTELLA

Yet another worthwhile stop on the Camino de Santiago is the **Monasterio de Irache**, 3 km (2 miles) south of Estella, just off N 111 at Ayegui. Irache, believed to have its roots in the Visigothic period, was one of the earliest Benedictine monasteries and one of the first pilgrim hospitals on the Spanish portion of the road to Santiago. The massive building incorporates a blend of architectural styles accumulated over the centuries, including a 12th-century Romanesque apse, a Renaissance cloister, and a tower built in the style of Juan de Herrera, designer of El Escorial, Philip II's enormous monastery-palace complex. Facing the monastery is the Museo del Vino, a wine museum run by the Castillo de Irache winery, whose *rosado* is one of the best in Navarra.

Seven kilometers (4 miles) north of Estella, on a branch of N 111 that heads toward San Sebastián over twisting but beautiful mountain roads, is the village of Abárzuza. Just northwest of the village in the hills of the Sierra de Andia is the restored **Monasterio de Iranzu**, which was begun in the 12th century by the Cistercians and finished in the 14th century. The lovely cloister here combines fine elements of both Romanesque and Gothic styles.

If you wish to stay near Estella, the only choice is the modern, multistoried ▶ **Hotel Irache**, with a swimming pool and tennis courts, located just a kilometer west of Irache.

Toward La Rioja

Between Estella and, to the southwest, Logroño, the capital of La Rioja, there are three more towns of interest on N 111 (the main Pamplona–Logroño road) and the Camino de Santiago. **Los Arcos**, 21 km (13 miles) from Estella, has a 16th-century church, **Iglesia de la Asunción**, so crammed with Baroque gilt retables, religious statues, and paintings that almost no space is left undecorated. La Asunción's beautiful Gothic cloister, somewhat reminiscent of the cloister of Pamplona's cathedral, was built in the 15th century.

At **Torres del Río**, 7 km (4 miles) southwest, is the interesting 13th-century Romanesque **Iglesia del Santo Sepulcro** (Church of the Holy Sepulcher), similar in style to the church at Eunate (see Puente la Reina, above). The octagonal tower has an exceptional ribbed cupola forming an eight-pointed star on the ceiling.

The last stop on N 111 before Logroño is **Viana**, which is one of several towns in Navarra allowed to call their wines Rioja. Viana's 13th- and 14th-century cathedral-sized Gothic church, **Iglesia de Santa María**, is the burial place of Cesare Borgia, who was killed in a minor skirmish near Viana in 1507. Ironically, Borgia's since-profaned tomb is outside the door of the church, and the faithful step on it as they enter. The stylized 16th-century Renaissance southern portal of Santa María (by Juan de Soyaz), while Plateresque, borders on Baroque; in fact, it was the inspiration for many artists in this area during the Baroque period of the 17th and 18th centuries.

Borgia, a restaurant in Viana on Calle Serapio Urra, has earned high acclaim for its personalized cuisine, especially dishes based on fowl and game birds—duck, goose, woodcock, quail, partridge, and squab—and exceptional wine list; Tel: (9-48) 64-57-81.

SOUTHERN NAVARRA
Olite

Olite is a splendid, beautifully restored castle town straight out of a medieval fairy tale about 40 km (25 miles) due south of Pamplona (it can be reached on either the A 15 *autopista,* a toll road, or on N 121). Olite is one of those rare, compact working villages that maintains its ancient atmosphere, is not overly commercialized, and is not yet so overrun by tourism that its character has changed.

This small enclosed village can be entered only through a few ancient arched gateways; its architectural treasures are well marked and easy to find. In addition to the wonderful, multiturreted, early 15th-century **Castle of the Kings of Navarra**, Olite has two medieval churches: the 12th-century **Iglesia de San Pedro**, with an unusual missile-shaped Gothic tower from a later date, and the 13th-century **Iglesia de Santa María la Real**, with its later Gothic façade and cloister abutting the castle. In the summer some of the music programs of the Festivales de Navarra are held in the plaza, with the dramatically lit castle as a backdrop.

The ► **Parador Príncipe de Viana**, in a restored section of the castle decorated with suits of armor, period furniture, and other trappings from a bygone age, is an excellent, comfortable base for exploring Olite and the surrounding area.

Around Olite

Alternative lodgings can be found just 3 km (2 miles) north of Olite on N 121 at the modern ► **Hostal Tafalla**, which looks like a big truck stop from the outside but is a good hotel. One of its attractions is its excellent, elegant restaurant, among the best in Navarra, run by Jesús Martínez Arellano and his family, including the octogenarian matriarch, whose flower arrangements are splendid. The cuisine is sophisticated—you will see plenty of French touches— but it is based on seasonal ingredients of the region: a salad of tender young lettuce hearts from Tudela with superb prawns in a mustard vinaigrette; scrambled eggs and *perretxicos* (highly prized tiny spring mushrooms) with asparagus and truffles; local red peppers (*pimientos del pico*) stuffed with shellfish; and rabbit stuffed with young vegetables and served with mushroom ravioli. Try the superlative wines of Bodegas Magaña from nearby Tudela, whose Merlot and Merlot/Cabernet Sauvignon, made from vines brought from France in the 1970s, are among the best of Spain's new wines and go perfectly with this elegant food.

Eighteen kilometers (11 miles) northwest of Olite (11 km/7 miles northwest of Tafalla on the road to Puente la Reina) are the considerable remains of **El Cerco de Artajona**, an impressive 12th-century Templar fortress town that looks somewhat like a smaller, square-towered Avila.

MONASTERIO DE LA OLIVA

Monasterio de la Oliva, one of the earliest French Cistercian monasteries in Spain, is located 23 km (14 miles) southeast of Olite (south on N 121, east on C 124) near the village of Carcastillo. The unadorned church, with its Latin cross and pointed arches, is believed to be the earliest piece of Gothic architecture in Spain. The apse is pure 12th-century Cistercian Romanesque, and parts of the airy, delicate, almost filigreed cloister are 14th-century Gothic.

Peralta

One of Navarra's greatest restaurants, **Atalaya**, is located at Calle Dabán 11 in the town of Peralta, about 20 km (12 miles) southwest of Olite on C 115. Entered through an unassuming village bar on the ground floor, Atalaya occupies the upper floors of a building overlooking the town square. All Navarros (and many Riojans) have made the trip to Peralta to eat in Pilar Ibáñez's elegantly run dining room. The classic food of Navarra, based on fresh, seasonal, and regional ingredients—fat white asparagus from the Ribera region served with fresh homemade mayonnaise, baby lamb chops, plump stuffed red peppers, artichokes, *pochas,* partridge, trout, Cantabrian fish, and perfectly cooked fresh vegetables—alternate with rabbit in tarragon sauce and other sophisticated dishes with the chef's own personal touch. Tel: (9-48) 75-01-52.

AROUND PERALTA

To whet your appetite for Atalaya, you can do a little sightseeing in the vicinity of Peralta. Just north and west of Peralta off C 115, a few kilometers along a country road, is the 15th-century brick castle of **Marcilla**. South of Peralta on C 115—just off the road to the left a few hundred yards before the bridge over the Río Ebro crosses into La Rioja at **Rincón de Soto**—are the remains of a sizable Roman winery, complete with in-ground, stone fermentation vats. Back in Peralta you might want to taste, if not accompany a meal with, the town's powerful (15 percent alcohol) *rosado,* a gladiator's drink if ever there was one.

Tudela

Ancient Tudela, located on the Río Ebro, 54 km (34 miles) south of Olite and 94 km (58 miles) south of Pamplona, is Navarra's second city (population 25,000), after Pamplona. It is the principal town of the Ribera de Navarra, the fertile (irrigated) garden that produces white asparagus, artichokes, young green garlic shoots, pimientos, and a cornucopia of other superb vegetables and fruits that distinguish the cuisine of Navarra.

Tudela is entered by a long bridge over the Río Ebro with 17 arches, some of which date from the 13th century. The city was once ruled by the Andalusian caliphate of Córdoba, and remained under Moorish influence longer (from the eighth to the 16th centuries) than any other place in Navarra. (Moriscos, Moors converted to Christianity, were not expelled from Spain until the early 17th century.) In terms of population and culture, Tudela had the most important Moorish and Jewish quarters in the kingdom, parts of which are still preserved in the narrow, labyrinthine streets of the Morería, the old quarter, lending the air of a medieval warren to this section of town just southeast of the bridge. Benjamín de Tudela, the famous wandering Jew who travelled all over the Mediterranean region, was born here in the 12th century.

The Cathedral

Tudela's cathedral, built on the site of a former mosque (of which it retains some vestiges), is a 12th- and 13th-century Romanesque-Gothic transitional church. The fine Romanesque cloister, whose capitals are interesting though somewhat deteriorated, dates from the 12th century. The jewel of this church is the Romanesque **Last Judgment doorway**, with its profusion of stone-carved biblical figures. To photograph the entire doorway with its hundreds of carved figures, you will need an ultrawide-angle lens (20mm or wider), since it is hemmed in by other buildings crowding the narrow streets of the old quarter.

STAYING AND DINING IN TUDELA

The ▶ **Hotel Morase**, Paseo de Invierno 2, is modern, functional, reasonably comfortable, and close to the old quarter— very well situated if you plan an extensive exploration of Tudela and the surrounding countryside. Most people drive down from the Parador Príncipe de Viana, in Olite (see above). Surprisingly, the restaurants in Tudela do not uphold the culinary reputation of the region. **Mesón Julián** (Calle de la Merced 9, in the old quarter) is a typical Tudelan restaurant serving regional fare, including good local vegetable dishes such as *menestra de la Mejana* (a mélange of cooked vegetables from Tudela's La Mejana *huerta,* the irrigated garden plots along the Ebro); Tel: (9-48) 82-20-28. The restaurant in the newly renovated **Hostal Tudela**, Calle Zaragoza 56 (out near the bullring, southeast of the old quarter), offers an *asador* menu featuring grilled fish and meats and dishes with a distinctly regional slant; Tel: (9-48) 41-08-02.

GETTING AROUND

Pamplona is located 385 km (240 miles) northeast of Madrid. The most-travelled route to Pamplona by car from the capital is N I from Madrid to Burgos. From Burgos to La Rioja you can take the four-lane toll roads A 1 and A 68, which are fast but circuitous and expensive. If you prefer a more leisurely and pleasant drive, you can take N 120 from Burgos through Santo Domingo de la Calzada to Logroño, the capital of La Rioja, then N 111 through Estella to Pamplona.

From Barcelona (437 km/271 miles from Pamplona) the A 15 to A 68 combination (of recent vintage) leads right to Pamplona, by way of Zaragoza. Keep in mind, though, that the combination of expensive tolls and expensive gas makes it almost as cheap for a single person to fly from Barcelona to Pamplona.

If you are coming from San Sebastián in the north, the new version of N 240, whose work has been slowed by threats from Basque terrorists and whose construction projects have wreaked havoc with some great trout streams, still runs through scenic mountain valleys, over mountain passes, and through canyons. On some sections of the new road the trip is much faster and safer now, but less picturesque and romantic. The other roads entering Navarra—from the Basque Country to the north and west, from France to the north, from Logroño and La Rioja (and thus, from Madrid) to the southwest—are for the most part twisting mountain roads. Resign yourself to taking such drives at a slow pace, both for safety and for the exceptional number of picturesque views and sightseeing opportunities they offer. On these roads and throughout the Pyrenees of Navarra, night driving and winter driving should be undertaken with extreme caution.

Be forewarned: The parking situation in Pamplona during fiesta is chaotic, and under no circumstances should you leave anything of value in your car in Pamplona—or anywhere else in Spain, for that matter.

Pamplona has an airport at Noáin, a few kilometers south of town, which is served by daily flights from Madrid, Barcelona, and Santander. Hertz, Avis, and the Spanish car agency, Atesa, have offices in Pamplona and will arrange to deliver a car to the airport. The bus station is near the Ciudadela, only a few blocks southwest of the Plaza del Castillo. The railway station, with connections to Madrid, Irún, Zaragoza, and other major cities, is a five-minute taxi ride from the center of town. Pamplona has a good city bus system. City buses, as well as buses run by some hotels such as the Tres Reyes, provide transportation to and from the station. Taxis are also available, but hard to come by during fiesta, when the streets are often too clogged with people for taxis to be practical.

It can be very hot in Pamplona during fiesta, but it can also get very cold and rainy; the climate is Atlantic Pyrenean. Along with light summer clothing, take a warm sweater, a waterproof jacket, an umbrella, and, of course, a white shirt and white pants, if you want to look like a real Pamplonica.

Outdoor Activities in Navarra

Visitors to Navarra can find out about organized fishing, hunting, kayaking, spelunking, horseback riding, hiking, rock climbing, mountain biking, and skiing in Navarra by writing to: Servicio de Turismo, Diputación Foral de Navarra, Arrieta 11 bis, 5°, 31002 Pamplona (Navarra). A number of excellent books, pamphlets, and magazines on the province are available, as is information about towns, regions, and touring itineraries. The publication *Un Mundo Natural, Navarra,* lists the names and telephone numbers of groups and individuals who offer many of the activities listed above.

ACCOMMODATIONS REFERENCE

The hotel rates listed below are projected rates for 1994, for double room, double occupancy, in pesetas. We strongly recommend that you confirm the price when making reservations.

The telephone area code for Navarra is 9-48. When dialing from outside the country, drop the 9 in the area code.

► **Hospedería de Leyre**. Monasterio de San Salvador de Leyre, 31400 **Yesa**. Tel: 88-41-00; Fax: 88-41-37. 7,150 pts.

► **Hostal Burguete**. Unica 51, 31640 **Burguete**. Tel: 76-00-05. 3,200–4,000 pts.

► **Hostal Tafalla**. Carretera de Pamplona–Zaragoza, km 38, 31300 **Tafalla**. Tel: 70-30-00; Fax: 70-30-52. 7,000 pts.

► **Hotel Avenida**. Avenida de Zaragoza 5, 31003 **Pamplona**. Tel: 24-54-54; Fax: 23-23-23. 12,500 pts.

► **Hotel Eslava**. Plaza Virgen de la O 7, 31001 **Pamplona**. Tel: 22-22-70; Fax: 22-51-57. 9,500 pts.

► **Hotel Iruña Park**. Ronda de Ermitagaña s/n, 31008 **Pamplona**. Tel: 17-32-00; Fax: 17-23-87. 16,200 pts.

► **Hotel Irache**. Carretera de Logroño, km 43, 31200 **Estella**. Tel: 55-11-50; Fax: 55-47-54. 11,600 pts.

► **Hotel Isaba**. Carretera de Roncal s/n, 31417 **Isaba**. Tel. and Fax: 89-30-00. 9,400 pts.

► **Hotel Maisonnave**. Calle Nueva 20, 31001 **Pamplona**. Tel: 22-26-00; Fax: 22-01-66. 12,900 pts.

► **Hotel Morase**. Paseo de Invierno 2, 31500 **Tudela**. Tel: 82-17-00; Fax: 41-19-97. 10,000 pts.

► **Hotel Orhi**. Calle Leyre 7, 31002 **Pamplona**. Tel: 22-85-00; Fax: 22-83-18. 12,980 pts.

► **Hotel Tres Reyes**. Jardines de la Taconera 1, 31001 **Pamplona**. Tel: 22-66-00; Fax: 22-29-30. 17,000 pts.

► **Hotel Yoldi**. Avenida San Ignacio 11, 31002 **Pamplona**. Tel: 22-48-00; Fax: 21-20-45. 11,500 pts.

► **Mesón del Peregrino**. Carretera de Pamplona–Logroño, km 23, 31100 **Puente la Reina**. Tel: 34-00-75. 6,850 pts.

► **Parador Fernando de Aragón**. Calle Arquitecto Sainz de Vicuna, 50680 **Sos del Rey Católico** (Zaragoza). Tel: 88-80-11; Fax: 88-81-00. 9,000 pts.

► **Parador Príncipe de Viana**. Plaza de los Teobaldos 2, 31390 **Olite**. Tel: 74-00-00; Fax: 74-02-01. 11,500 pts.

ARAGÓN

By Patricia Brooks and Frank Shiell

Frank Shiell, a New York writer, is a graduate of the University of Madrid. He travels frequently throughout Spain. Patricia Brooks contributes to other sections of this guidebook.

The visitor driving from Madrid to Barcelona (or vice versa) has a rare opportunity to explore a fascinating but little-visited part of Spain—Aragón.

It isn't that Aragón is obscure. Located in the northeast, just south of the Pyrenees, the region covers about one-tenth of Spain's area—1,815 square miles. Its three provinces are, north to south, Huesca (upper Aragón), Zaragoza (the Ebro River valley), and Teruel (lower Aragón). Catalonia and Valencia are to the east, Navarra and La Rioja to the west, and Castile-León to the southwest.

Large as Aragón's land size is, the number of its inhabitants is almost inversely small, just 1.2 million, or about 3 percent of the national population. In recent decades thousands of Aragonese have left their homes and emigrated to industrial Catalonia for jobs and the promise of a better life.

Until the recent exodus, Aragón's decline had been gradual. In its time it was dominated by Rome, under Caesar Augustus, then by the Moors, and later by various Christian kings. In the 12th century the kingdom of Aragón was a power be reckoned with. Through a dynastic marriage it merged with Catalonia, and the thriving seaport of Barcelona became its capital. Its territories included Catalonia and Valencia and stretched as far south as Murcia, and it controlled the Balearics and colonized Sardinia, Naples, and Sicily.

Aragón's expansion was even greater by the 15th century, when its moment of greatest historic significance came with the union of Ferdinand of Aragón and Isabella of Castile, the Reyes Católicos (the Catholic monarchs), who shaped the subsequent history of Spain. Their daughter, Catherine of

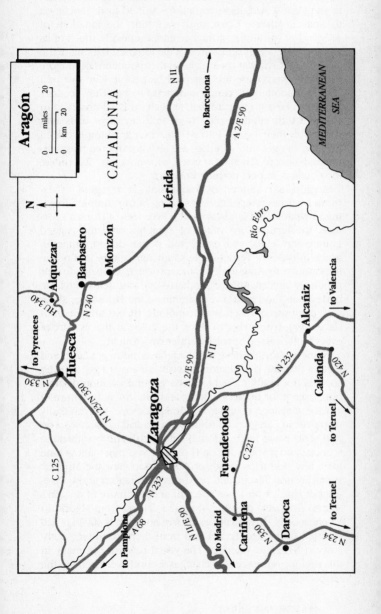

Aragón, married England's Henry VIII and gave birth to a daughter who became Queen Mary I. But after the voyages to the New World, most commerce shifted from Barcelona to Spain's Atlantic Coast, and over time the kingdom of Aragón lost most of its influence and, eventually, much of its vast territory. Much later, some of the toughest fighting of the 1936–1939 Civil War took place in the mountains of Aragón.

Today's Aragonese are reserved, as people who live in a mostly mountainous countryside tend to be. They are also known to be so obstinate that, as Richard Ford observed in the mid-19th century, they were said "to drive nails into walls with their heads, into which when anything is driven nothing can get out." Yet they are also considered trustworthy and sincere. They have been known to say, "We, unlike the Catalans, expect nothing in return."

Aragón, surrounded by mountains, is a region of extremely varied temperatures (sizzling hot in summer, freezing in winter) and landscapes: the Pyrenees of Huesca province, the fertile Ebro valley of Zaragoza, and the rugged granite-gray cliffs, red earth, and poplar-dotted, emerald-green hillsides of Teruel in the south. Agriculture is of prime importance to Aragón; Zaragoza province is Spain's major producer of corn. Miles of orchards and vast fields of wheat, barley, oats, and sunflowers dominate the landscape, along with plantings of rosemary, chamomile, thyme, and *lavanda* (lavender), from which comes the cologne that is part of every well-dressed Spanish gentleman's toilette.

Some visitors believe that Aragón is no-man's-land, and that's a pity, for it is pleasant to visit and easy to get to. Even so, it is not really thought of as a general vacation destination, except for hunters, hikers, and fishermen, but more of a place to visit on your way to someplace else. You can easily stop over in Zaragoza en route from Madrid to Barcelona on N II. This route leads through some stark and breathtaking scenery, and if your interest is piqued, you might allow time for a few side trips: south of Zaragoza to view the Mudejar sights around Teruel, and northeast of Zaragoza to the Pyrenees of Huesca, and thus you will uncover more of Aragón's secrets. It is also possible, if you're driving from Madrid to Valencia on N III, to make a side trip north on N 400 to N 420 through Cuenca to Teruel and from there continue southeast on N 234 to Valencia. The visual rewards are many in this region, as the scenery changes around every bend in the road.

MAJOR INTEREST

Zaragoza
Basílica de Nuestra Señora del Pilar

La Seo (the cathedral)
Roman walls and forum
Mercado Central de Lanuza
Museo Camón Aznar
El Tubo district
Renaissance Patio de la Infanta
Aljafería and Sástago palaces

Parque Nacional de Ordesa for hiking in the
    Pyrenees
Goya's house in Fuendetodos
Mudejar architecture of Teruel and other towns

The Food of Aragón

Aragonese cuisine is as down-to-earth as its people. A main-stay recipe is chicken, lamb, or pork prepared *chilindrón* style, meaning cooked (often sautéed or baked) with a straightforward sauce made of red peppers, tomatoes, onions, and garlic.

In mountainous upper Aragón, the people enjoy lamb or goat roasted on a spit, lamb and vegetable stew *a la pastora,* fried trout from clear Pyrenees rivers and streams, game, and so-called mountain asparagus (*espárragos montañeses*), a poetic term for calves' tails. The young lamb and kid of the mountains are superlative, especially roasted with white wine, lemon, and herbs in *ternasco asado.*

Throughout Aragón *migas* (sautéed bread crumbs) is as popular as it is in La Mancha and Castile, but with its own regional twists and variations, such as mixing the fried bread crumbs with bits of ham, *chorizo* (sausage), bacon, or black pudding, and serving them with hot chocolate or grapes.

Perdiz con chocolate (partridge with a bitter chocolate sauce) is one of Aragón's few contributions to the loftier plane of haute cuisine, but the hams of Teruel, cured in the chill winter air, are famous all over Spain. The frost of winter can be dissipated in Aragón by a number of hearty soups; two favorites are garlic soup with lemon and *sopa aragonesa,* made of liver, cheese, and toasted bread slices, baked in the oven.

Vegetables, grown in abundance, are a major part of the local diet. One of the most popular ways of serving them is in a vegetable stew called *menestra,* seasoned with diced ham and garlic. Look also for white Aragonese cabbage, *cardo silvestre* (cardoon), and *borrajas,* a distant relative of borage that has more flavor than spinach or beet greens. Fruits are also a mainstay; the region grows some of the finest peaches, apricots, plums, apples, cherries, and strawberries in Spain.

Wines of Aragón

Aragón encompasses the provinces of Zaragoza, Huesca, and Teruel—and four *denominaciones de origen* (Campo de Borja, Cariñena, Somontano, and Calatayud), whose wines are rarely encountered outside their home region, although there is growing interest in Somontano. Calatayud is a very new DO and does not yet produce wines of any significance.

Campo de Borja (Zaragoza) is a small wine region bordering on the Rioja Baja and southern Navarra. The principal grape Garnacha (Grenache) is grown in a hot, difficult microclimate, tempered somewhat by the area's proximity to the Río Ebro. The region produces powerful wines that are used mainly for blending or are consumed locally, but a wine called Duque de Sevilla can be exceptional.

Although **Cariñena** (Zaragoza) gave its name to the well-known grape, the Carignane (known as Mazuelo in Penedés and Rioja), the principal grapes of this region are the black Garnacha (Grenache) and the white Viura. Cariñena is one of the driest growing areas in Spain, a fact which accounts for the high alcohol content (14 to 15 percent) of its wines. Although robust and powerful, many wines from Cariñena become mellow and aromatic with aging (in barrel and bottle), which is a requirement (two years minimum) of this region. The brands you are most likely to encounter are Don Mendo and Monte Ducay from the San Valero Cooperative.

Somontano (Huesca) is one of Spain's newest *denominaciones de origen,* but it is scarcely known outside of Aragón. Located in the foothills of the Pyrenees, Somontano produces wines that are somewhat lighter and have better acids than the other wines of Aragón. Because of Somontano's relative isolation, several clones of grape varietals that grow here are unknown in other parts of Spain—Moristell and Parraleta, both red-wine grapes, and Alcañon, a white-wine grape. Like La Rioja and Penedés, Somontano provided large quantities of wine to the French during the phylloxera epidemic in the 19th century. Somontano is a Beaujolais-style red, which by definition will go with any dish calling for a light, fruity red wine. Look for Montesierra and Viñas del Vero, two good red wines.

—*Gerry Dawes*

ZARAGOZA

Aragón's capital city, Zaragoza, is almost in the center of the region, halfway between Madrid and Barcelona along highway N II or A 2/E 90 (and about three hours from either city by train). It is also well situated for a stopover on the route between the Basque Country and Barcelona.

Unjustly overlooked in most tourist itineraries, Zaragoza is full of pleasant, fascinating surprises and merits at least a two-night sojourn. The city spreads along the banks of the Ebro, Spain's longest river. The Ebro begins in the northern region of Cantabria and, along its route across northern Spain, flows and grows through Aragón and Catalonia before it empties into the Mediterranean near Tarragona.

Zaragozanos refer to their city as La Señora de las Cuatro Culturas (Mistress of Four Civilizations). The first of those civilizations was an ancient Iberian settlement called Sálduba, which fell in 23 B.C. to the legions of Roman emperor Caesar Augustus. Augustus changed the town's name to Caesaraugusta, and it became the third most important Roman colony on the Iberian Peninsula, after Mérida and Tarragona. The Moors conquered the flourishing city in A.D. 714 and altered its name to Sarakusta. Four centuries later (1118), Alfonso I, "El Batallador" (the Battler), and his Christian troops took over the city in the early stages of the Christian Reconquest; they pronounced its name Zaragoza (thar-a-GO-tha).

Today, Zaragoza is a bustling city (its population of 700,000 is Spain's fifth largest), with a remarkable mixture of historic, architectural, and cultural heritage much in evidence in its old sections, contrasting with its wide contemporary avenues.

In preparation for Spain's multifarious 1992 celebrations billions of pesetas were spent in Zaragoza during a much-needed, multifaceted two-year refurbishing from the underground up: installation of new water, power, and sewage infrastructures; new subterranean garages in key areas; expansion of pedestrian areas; enhancement of parks and avénues with the planting of 40,000 trees; and the restoration of dozens of historic buildings and archaeological treasures. The "old and dirty" city has become historic and sparkling.

SEEING ZARAGOZA

The ancient core of Zaragoza, known as *el casco viejo*, is built on top of the ancient Roman section, and all the sights are within easy walking distance of one another. Enclosing this core is a busy street that follows the old city walls in the form of a broad U; both arms extend northward to the right bank of the Ebro. The bottom and the right-hand (eastern) sections of this U-shaped street are called El Coso (from the Latin *cursus*, or course); the left (western) arm is called Avenida de César Augusto.

La Plaza del Pilar

When you arrive in Zaragoza, the first place to head is the Plaza del Pilar, the largest pedestrian square in Spain and one of the largest in Europe. The plaza is about a ten-minute taxi ride northeast from the city's El Portillo train station. If you arrive by car, there is a new underground parking garage extending beneath the plaza; enter from Paseo Echegaray y Caballero, which runs along the river and behind the basilica. Stairway exits emerge right inside the plaza. Most hotels are within walking distance of the plaza.

The results of Zaragoza's 1992 facelift are at their most stunning in the plaza, where refurbished architectural treasures blend (or clash, depending on one's aesthetic sense) with modern enhancements. With the completion of its invisible subterranean parking garage, the elimination of surface parking areas, and the rerouting of vehicular traffic, the square has been expanded to encompass more than 350,000 square feet, where visitors and *maños* (the affable nickname for Zaragozanos) stroll and congregate.

Dominating the plaza on the north side, with the Río Ebro behind it, is the Basílica de Nuestra Señora del Pilar, named for the holy patroness of Spain and the colossal protagonist of the city. (If you arrive in the city at 9:00 A.M., noon, or 8:00 P.M., just follow the sound of the canticle calling the faithful to mass, broadcast over loudspeakers from the basilica. A woman's voice chants "El Angelus" in Latin, alluding to the appearance of the Virgin.) Extending the entire length of the plaza's south side, a row of sixteen 50-foot-tall copper columns topped with ultra-potent spotlights now illuminates the basilica so brightly at night that it can be seen from 20 miles away.

THE BASILICA DE NUESTRA SEÑORA DEL PILAR

The extravagant Basílica del Pilar, built in the 17th century, is Spain's biggest Baroque church. It has a Neoclassical façade and is cornered by four main towers and bristles with countless spires intermingled with a dozen gigantic, mosaic-covered domes.

The center of attention in Zaragoza's gigantic basilica is the surprisingly small statue (only about three feet high) of the **Virgen del Pilar**. Legend has it that in A.D. 40 the Virgin appeared here on a pillar (hence her name) to Saint James (Santiago). Even today, the basilica is the destination of one of the two most important pilgrimages in all Spain. (The other is the cathedral in Santiago de Compostela in the northwestern region of Galicia.) Each receives hundreds of thousands of religious visitors a year.

The statue of the Virgin stands on the brown jasper pillar that has stood here, according to the faithful, since the first century, on the right side of the altar of her own chapel. Her elaborate cone-shaped dress (*manto*) is changed daily from a wardrobe that numbers in the hundreds—gold embroidered velvets and silks adorned with precious stones, each one worth a fortune. Directly behind her chapel is a small silver-rimmed oval hole through which devotees can kiss or touch an exposed part of the marble pillar.

The Virgen del Pilar appeared to Santiago on October 2 and her saint's day is October 12. On the second and twelfth days of each month her *manto* is removed to reveal the silver-covered pillar upon which she stands. October 12, also the anniversary of Christopher Columbus's arrival in the New World, is Zaragoza's most important annual celebration. Nine days of festivities (from the Saturday before October 12 to the Sunday of the following week) overwhelm the city and its visitors. Throughout Spain this holiday is known as El Día de la Hispanidad, a day celebrating the fellowship of all peoples of Hispanic heritage on both sides of the Atlantic. This joint commemoration is all the more important to the citizens of Zaragoza because Columbus took a small chunk of the Virgin's jasper pillar along with him as a good-luck charm on his history-changing journey.

Also of interest inside the basilica are two frescoes by Goya. Francisco José de Goya y Lucientes, a native of the nearby village of Fuendetodos (see below), was commissioned to paint the cupolas of the basilica. In 1771 he painted a fresco on the high vaulted ceiling of the far eastern side of the basilica above the small choir (*coreto*). Called *La Gloria,* it contains a golden triangle with the word "God" written in Hebrew. In 1780 he painted *Regina Martyrum* in the cupola in the center of the north nave. After a quarrel with the bishop, however, Goya abandoned his work and, leaving the other cupolas blank, travelled to Madrid and took up his post as court painter.

In the far left rear (northwestern) corner of the basilica, you can board an elevator for an ascent to the top of one of the four main towers. From there, a climb up quite a few spiraling stairs brings you to a wonderful view of the complicated rooftop of the basilica, the Río Ebro, and the city of Zaragoza.

AROUND IN THE PLAZA: SOUTH AND WEST

The cafés in the arcades along the south side of the plaza are a perfect place from which to observe passersby and children playing amid thousands of pigeons, and get an accurate take on Zaragoza's citizenry. Alongside the arcades, the new black-glass "cube" structure houses the **municipal tourist office**, where maps, brochures, and expert multilingual advice can be obtained. The office offers regular sightseeing walking tours in Spanish; English-language tours can be arranged in advance.

At the west end of the plaza *La Fuente de la Hispanidad,* a giant new rock-slab fountain/monument forms a semi-abstract relief map of Latin America. It commemorates Zaragoza's transatlantic cultural ties, formed because La Virgen del Pilar is also the patron saint of La Hispanidad, all Hispanic peoples. In front of the fountain, an enormous concrete sphere symbolizes a world map from the period just after the Europeans first voyaged to the Americas.

Just behind the fountain, at the edge of the *casco viejo* on Avenida de César Augusto, a remarkably intact section of the third-century **Roman walls** is now vaulted by new linear brick-and-marble sculptures and complemented by a bronze statue of Emperor Caesar Augustus. The Roman walls lead toward the river and the Puente de Santiago, in front of which stands a Mudejar tower called **Torreón de la Zuda**, the only remaining portion of the tenth-century residential palace of the Moorish governors. The tower's ground floor now houses the tourist office of the region of Aragón.

Just south of the Roman walls is the lively and lovely **Mercado Central de Lanuza**, always (except on some maps) referred to simply as Mercado Central. This public market, put up in 1904 with a flourish of Eiffel-like wrought iron, is thronged in the morning with residents who come here to shop at the myriad stalls selling fresh fish, meat, poultry, fruits, vegetables, and dairy products.

AROUND IN THE PLAZA: NORTH AND EAST

Just east of the basilica and also fronting the north side of the square is the immense, refurbished 16th-century *ayuntamiento* (city hall), not open to the public. Next to it, to the right, is the smaller yet grandiose **Lonja de Mercaderes** (also recently refurbished), a splendid example of 16th-century Aragonese Renaissance architecture. Originally a palace housing the city's mercantile center (*lonja*), it has been transformed into an important center for local, Spanish, and international art exhibitions and cultural events.

In front of La Lonja, a fountain-sculpture ensemble honors Goya, and a marble wall is inscribed with a quote of the artist, born in the province of Zaragoza, in Fuendetodos: "*La fantasía abandonada de la razón produce monstruos, pero unida a ella es la madre de las artes*" (Fantasy without reason produces monsters, but joined with it, it is the mother of the arts).

PLAZA DE LA SEO

The far eastern end of the Plaza del Pilar is called the Plaza de la Seo, on which stand side-by-side testimonies of two distinct Zaragozan eras, medieval Christian and ancient Roman.

Dating from the 12th century, Zaragoza's Catedral del Salvador, familiarly known as **La Seo**, is a synthesis of Romanesque, Mudejar, Gothic, and Churrigueresque elements. The interior is replete with religious treasures, a gold altar, and one of Spain's most important tapestry collections. However, it has been closed intermittently for restoration for more than ten years, and during the last six or seven years it has been shut continuously. The only signs of advancement in the work are its chalk-white coat of paint on the Neoclassical façade and the refurbished north wall, a spectacular 12th- to 18th-century mixture of (from the ground up) Romanesque, Gothic, Mudejar, Renaissance, Baroque, and Neoclassical styles.

In 1988, during construction of the Hotel Vía Romana (near the southeastern corner of the plaza, on Calle Don Jaime I), excavators had a surprise encounter with what turned out to be a Roman forum. The subsequently uncovered site, in front of La Seo, is about 1,000 square feet in area and evidently extends farther, below La Seo to underground parts unknown. After three years of meticulous restoration, and the extension of the plaza's granite and brick surface above it, the first- to third-century A.D. **Forum of Cesaraugusta** opened as a vast underground *in situ* archaeological museum. A temple, foundations of ancient homes, shops, and offices, as well as ceramics, artifacts, and statuary, all attest to Zaragoza's past as a flourishing Roman-era capital. The entrance to the forum is through a modernistic cuboid structure of translucent Iranian onyx that contrasts drastically with its surroundings. At press time, the forum had not yet opened permanently because of problems with seepage from the Río Ebro, which are being remedied.

El Casco Viejo

Two principal streets—Calle Don Jaime I at the eastern end of the plaza and Calle Alfonso across from the basilica—lead south from the Plaza del Pilar through the old section of Zaragoza (the *casco viejo*) to El Coso, the southern boundary. The only way to explore this compact area is on foot.

Two blocks south of the Plaza del Pilar—take Calle Don Jaime (for pedestrians, buses, and taxis only) south and turn right on Calle Espoz y Mina—is **Plaza Santa Cruz** (on the left), where local artists exhibit and sell their works on Sundays and holidays from 10:00 A.M. to 2:00 P.M. The plaza's **Café de Praga** is a popular gathering place for evening *aperitivos.* At Espoz y Mina 23 is the **Museo Camón Aznar**, housed in the Palacio de los Pardo, a splendid mid-15th-century Renaissance palace. Don't let somber exteriors fool you: Although this and other Renaissance mansions in Zaragoza, as well as many old churches, may have uninteresting brown-brick façades, their interiors can be surprisingly opulent—always make it a point to peek inside.

Aznar, who died in the 1970s, was a famous art historian considered to be the world's top authority on Goya. Included in the permanent art collection here are works by Goya and Velázquez and other masterpieces that Aznar received as gifts or was able to purchase because of his stature in the art world.

Continue west on Espoz y Mina to Calle Alfonso, turn left, and walk south for three blocks to Calle Torre Nueva. Turn right and you will come to Plaza San Felipe, on the right side of which is the immense tenth-century Mudejar tower **Torreón de la Fortea**, restored in 1992 and now housing municipal offices. On the other side of the plaza is the late-Renaissance Argillo Palace, remodeled in 1985 to house the splendid **Museo Pablo Gargallo**. A native son, born 55 miles southeast of Zaragoza in Maella, Gargallo was a contemporary and friend of Picasso. Both were born in 1881, and they later influenced each other's work. The museum's collection of more than 100 Gargallo drawings and extraordinary metal sculptures is wonderful.

EL TUBO

Return to Calle Alfonso and cross the street to enter into the labyrinth of tiny pedestrian streets known as El Tubo. Bordered by Calle Méndez Núñez on the north, and Calles Alfonso and Don Jaime on the west and east respectively, this is an earthy, ebullient old section of Zaragoza—sort of a core within the core. It is entertaining both day and (with caution) at night.

Among the countless side-by-side shops, restaurants, *tascas* (taverns), and *tapas* bars in El Tubo is a famous and fun *café cantante* (cabaret), more than 100 years old, **El Plata**. Traditional cabaret revues are performed, with *pasodoble* dancing and lyrical, piquant songs of yesteryear, as well as contemporary numbers with humorous lyrics. The more Spanish you know, the more of a kick you'll get out of it. A bit less earthy after its long-overdue remodeling job in late 1992, this place is still fun and congenial and open until the wee hours.

Modern Zaragoza

If you zigzag southward in El Tubo, you should eventually end up on Calle de los Mártires, which emerges onto El

Coso and an entirely different world of Zaragoza: the turn-of-the-century and modern quarters anchored by the broad **Plaza de España** and the elegant, tree-lined **Paseo de la Independencia**, with its fancy boutiques, department stores, restaurants, and residences.

Across El Coso and to the right (east) is the magnificent Renaissance **Casa de los Condes de Sástago**, restored in 1989. Built in the 16th century by the count of Sástago, viceroy of Aragón (whose houseguests included King Philip II), it is now a center for art exhibits and theatrical performances. The building itself is a sight to see, with its tapestries, lavishly painted ceiling in the second-floor throne room, and walls richly decorated with tiles from the Zaragozan provincial town of Muel. Windows on the right side of the façade are bordered in bright cobalt blue as a remembrance of ancient tradition and superstition in the mountains of Aragón, where until recently farmers painted blue stripes over the whitewashed walls of their stables in order to keep insects and bad spirits away from the farm animals. A section of the building houses the provincial government of Zaragoza, with a marvelous marble statue in its lobby of Saint George slaying the dragon.

La Independencia stretches about six long blocks south to the Plaza de Aragón traffic circle. Along the segment of Avenida César Augusto that runs parallel to La Independencia to the west are more good stores and cafés. (Don't be confused by the fact that the cross streets change their names as well as their personalities on the other side of La Independencia.)

A block before the Plaza de Aragón, turn left (east) from La Independencia onto Calle Joaquín Costa and walk a few blocks until you reach the small tree-shaded **Plaza de los Sitios**. Tranquil today, this was a site of bloody battles in 1808 and 1809 when Zaragozanos defended their city against Napoleon's invading troops. A statue in the center of the plaza commemorates the fallen heroes. This plaza is also the site of the **Museo de Bellas Artes**, which features Romanesque frescoes, Aragonese ceramics, and two rooms filled with Goya paintings and etchings.

To see Aragón's finest Renaissance architecture continue down Paseo de la Independencia just past Plaza de Aragón; as you approach **El Corte Inglés** department store you'll see on the left a big sleek modern bank building—Ibercaja, Aragón's most important bank. This is the last place you would expect to find a 16th-century landmark, but go inside the bank and follow the signs to **Patio de la Infanta**. The patio originally was the nucleus of a palace built in 1546 on Calle San Jorge by Gabriel Zaporta, a wealthy and extremely influential Jewish merchant banker who lent money to Holy Roman emperor

Charles V. Lavish carvings in wood, stone, and alabaster allegorize kings, emperors, and Greek gods. In the late 19th century Zaragozans regarded these treasures with indifference; a French antique dealer purchased the patio in 1902 and installed it in Paris, near Notre Dame. Later, Argentine president Perón tried to bring it to Buenos Aires, but Ibercaja came to the rescue and purchased the patio in 1958, returning it dismantled to Zaragoza where it sat in a warehouse for 25 years. Now it is on public view, within the bank building for all to admire. The patio is also an elegant setting for concerts, art exhibits, and social functions.

THE ALJAFERIA

West of the city center (just beyond where Calle Conde de Aranda runs into Avenida de Madrid, too far to walk) is one of Zaragoza's biggest surprises: the well-restored 11th-century **Aljafería**, residence of the ruling caliphs when Zaragoza was the Moorish capital of northern Spain. This astonishing example of Moorish architecture, with its elaborate geometric and intricate honeycomb fantasy designs, its arches, and its patio, fountains, pools, and orange trees, is in a way comparable to the Alhambra in Granada. In the 15th century Ferdinand and Isabella turned the second floor into their palace. Its remarkable coffered ceiling has a pineapple motif, recalling the pineapples brought back from the Americas.

La Aljafería is about a ten-minute taxi ride from the *casco viejo*. By bus, take the number 36 from the big bus stop at the far eastern end of Plaza del Pilar (in front of La Seo); the number 32 from the northern side of Plaza de España; or the number 33 from the southeastern side of Plaza de España. To return, cross the street from La Aljafería and take any of those buses back. La Aljafería is included in most city tours.

Staying and Dining in Zaragoza

The Belle Epoque ▶ **NH Gran Hotel**, inaugurated in 1929 as the Gran Hotel Zaragoza, later declared a historic monument, and totally refurbished in 1991, is the city's aristocrat of luxury hotels. If you don't stay here, it merits at least a visit for cocktails or tea in the sedate and elegant rotunda lounge, or just to see the lobby, lined with reproductions of Goya paintings. The hotel is conveniently located just off the Plaza de los Sitios.

A five-minute walk southeast from the NH Gran Hotel on Avenida de las Torres, yet centuries away, is the brand-new, ultramodern, nine-story ▶ **Hotel Boston**. Named by its Harvard-graduate Aragonese architects, this high-tech edifice is thoroughly computerized—it's referred to as "*el edificio inteligente*" (the intelligent building). Amenities in the 315 rooms include such conveniences as fax machines, computer terminals on line with Minitel and Ibertex Spanish data bases, and worldwide video conference facilities.

Zaragozanos take their cuisine seriously, as you will find at **El Coral**, the celebrated restaurant of the Hotel Boston. Aragonese master chef Manuel Cartón (previously the personal chef of former Mexican president López Portillo) creates regional specialties such as *ternasco* (roasted baby lamb) and a range of international dishes from duck *à l'orange* to Peruvian *ceviche*. Serve yourself salads and first courses from the copious buffet, order your entrée à la carte, and follow with a delicious pastry surprise. The selection of wines and *cavas* is extensive. Tel: (9-76) 59-91-92. **Los Borrachos** (named for Velázquez's painting) at Paseo de Sagasta 64, just south of Plaza de Aragón, near El Corte Inglés department store, is small, luxurious, and specializes in game, including *jabalí* (wild boar). Tel: (9-76) 27-50-36.

Txingudi (near the city university at Augustín de Quinto 4) lives up to its Basque name with fine seafood specialties, among them Cantabrian Sea *merluza* (hake) stuffed with shrimp and mushrooms and served in Champagne sauce. Prominent Zaragozanos dine in the salons or garden of this converted stately residence. The elegant, tranquil **Asador Gayarre** (Carretera Aeropuerto, km 4.3) serves typical regional entrées, from oxtail to pigeon, nouvelle style. Tel: (9-76) 34-43-86.

For traditional cuisine as well as *jota* performances, **La Venta del Cachirulo** (north of the city, Carretera de Logroño, km 1.5) is a fine restaurant serving such typical regional dishes as duck with cherries and clams with *borrajas* (a delicious vegetable native to Aragón). Tel: (9-76) 33-16-74. **Goyesco** (Calle de Manuel Lasala 44, a ten-minute taxi ride south of El Coso) prepares superb regional cuisine with great care—a salad of garden tomatoes with garlic shoots and Teruel ham, meat dishes such as their famed roasted rack of suckling lamb *a la sardalesa,* and crêpe or soufflé dessert specialties. Decor follows the theme of native son Goya, an ancestor of Goyesco's owner, with Goyaesque art and memorabilia. Tel: (9-76) 35-68-70.

The Aragonese Pyrenees

JACA

Jaca, 140 km (85 miles) north of Zaragoza on route N 330, is a convenient jumping-off point for excursions into the nearby mountains. The busy tourist office on Paseo Calvo Sotelo provides bus schedules to outlying villages and ski resorts and maps of nearby hiking trails. Those wishing to enjoy nature by day, but to return to civilization at night, can do no better than the very civilized ▶ **Gran Hotel**, located in the center of town on Paseo de la Constitucíon and boasting such amenities as a swimming pool.

Before you set out for the wilderness, though, take time to explore Jaca's 11th-century **cathedral**, one of the oldest in Spain and the first to be constructed in the Romanesque style. The grandness of this religious edifice befits Jaca, whose Christian citizenry valiantly fought off the Moors occupying their town in 761, centuries before the Moors were banished from the rest of the peninsula. Modern-day Jaca commemorates the feat with a lively procession on the first Friday of May. Jaca was also a major stop on the pilgrimage route to Santiago. Collected in the diocesan museum here are Romanesque frescoes from remote mountain villages.

EXCURSIONS FROM JACA

Some of the best hiking in the region—in fact, in all of Spain—can be found on the trails of the **Parque Nacional de Ordesa**. The main park office is just outside the village of Torla, about 60 km (37 miles) east of Jaca. The most spectacular path is the Circo Soasa, which takes you on a seven-hour circuit of the park along the ridges of dizzyingly high canyons, past waterfalls, and around the base of the Sierra de las Cutas.

Several mountain villages within an easy drive of Jaca provide a refreshing combination of Old World charm and breathtaking scenery. **Benasque**, on the eastern side of the park about 100 km (62 miles) from Jaca, is very pretty and a good base for walks along the Río Esera. **Hecho**, 50 km (31 miles) northwest of Jaca and connected by daily bus service, is surrounded by beautiful mountain scenery. What many skiers consider to be the best slopes in the Pyrenees are just 30 km (18 miles) north of Jaca in **Astun** and **Candanchú**, two neighboring resorts, with all facilities. These include, in Candanchú, a charming mountain hotel appropriately called the ▶ **Edelweiss**.

Another lovely mountain village is **Alquézar**, 44 km (27 miles) east of the rather dull little city of Huesca. Alquézar's narrow lanes open to magnificent valley views, and its 16th-century church is surrounded in part by the ruined walls of the chapel that Christians built when they recaptured the village from the Moors in the tenth century.

SOUTHERN ARAGON

Visitors are usually surprised to discover that echoes of Muslim Spain exist as far north as Aragón. The Aragonese ousted the Moorish rule in the 11th century, but were wise enough to let the huge population of industrious Moorish residents remain. From their long sojourn came the Mudejar architectural style, the work of Muslims living under Christian rule.

Aragón's most noteworthy Mudejar sights are in the southern reaches of the province. Teruel, a lovely Mudejar town, can easily be visited from Zaragoza. It's a 184-km (114-mile) drive south (via N 330 and N 234), and there are other sights along the way to break up the drive. You can also, if you are driving from Madrid, combine Teruel with a visit to the dramatic cliff-top town of Cuenca (see the Side Trips from Madrid chapter) by looping southeast on E 10 (N III) and N 400 to Cuenca, then on to Teruel via N 420, a beautiful drive that will take about three days in all.

Our coverage works its way south from Zaragoza, first visiting several towns within easy reach of the city that have interesting cultural or historical associations.

Southeast from Zaragoza

One of Aragón's famous native sons was the avant-garde film director Luis Buñuel. He was born in **Calanda**, about 100 km (68 miles) southeast of Zaragoza via N 232 almost to Alcañiz, then south on N 420 a few miles. Calanda is distinguished by a curious Holy Week custom called Los Tambores: From midnight Thursday until Saturday, teams of drummers parade the streets, drumming nonstop, even as their fingers bleed all over their drums.

Los Tambores is also celebrated in **Alcañiz**, on N 232 just south of the Calanda turnoff, a far more interesting town with an ancient history. It was known as Anitorgis to the Romans, and in 212 B.C., during the Second Punic War, the Carthaginian general Hasdrubal, brother of Hannibal, defeated the Roman Scipios here—although Rome ultimately crushed Carthage.

Alcañiz has a lovely Plaza Mayor flanked by an arcaded 14th-century *lonja* (exchange), a town hall with a Renaissance façade, and a church, Santa María, with an exuberant Baroque portal. The excellent ▶ **Parador de la Concordia** is located inside a castle with commanding views of the town, the countryside, and Río Guadalupe. Its restaurant serves excellent regional dishes.

Southwest from Zaragoza

There are two routes you can take from Zaragoza to Daroca on your way to southwestern Aragón, each involving a detour (a third route is to go straight to Daroca and to Teruel on N 330 and N 234). One is to take N 330 south 47 km (29 miles) and then C 221 east 24 km (154 miles) to **Fuendetodos**, a tiny, tranquil town where Goya was born in 1746. His modest house, open to the public, and furnishings look much as they must have during his years there. Down the street in an old country house is a new **Goya museum** that displays 80 of his etchings.

CALATAYUD

The second route is by way of Calatayud, 87 km (54 miles) southwest of Zaragoza on N II, a declining Moorish town named after its founder, Kalat Ayub, where King Ferdinand was baptized in 1461. Calatayud has several once-fine churches that seem to be slowly deteriorating, with cracks running through their entire façades. The 15th-century **Iglesia de San Andrés** is one such church, with a splendid minaret-like Mudejar brick tower; the 13th-century **Iglesia Colegiata de Santa Maria** is another. Even with cracks, Santa María is a prize, with an octagonal Mudejar brick tower and a richly ornamented, High Renaissance gray-stone portal and ornately carved wooden doors in delicate high relief. An acceptable stop for lunch in Calatayud is at **Lisboa**, on a main thoroughfare, Paseo de las Cortes de Aragón 10, where the specialties are fresh fish, roast lamb, and Aragonese wines. Tel: (9-76) 88-25-35.

Just a kilometer or two northeast of Calatayud are the excavated remains of **Bilbilis**, a Roman city on the Zaragoza–Mérida road, where the Roman poet-satirist Martial was born around A.D. 40.

From Calatayud it's a 41-km (25-mile) drive southeast on N 234 to **Daroca**, an ancient walled city with more than 100 towers and turrets. Teruel, your goal, is 98 km (61 miles) south.

The Mudejar Southwest

A profusion of Mudejar towers and brickwork is visible throughout the province of Teruel. The town of Teruel, located on a hill above the gorges of the Río Turia, makes a good base for exploring some of the natural and architectural sights in the region.

TERUEL

The unofficial capital of lower Aragón, Teruel is small enough for an easy day-long walkabout. You'll amble through narrow streets, past turn-of-the-century Modernist houses, and to a 16th-century aqueduct (Los Arcos) at the northern end of town, in the shadow of five stunning Mudejar towers dating from the 13th to 16th centuries.

Peaceful as Teruel is today, it has seen its share of tumultuous events. The town was sacked by the Romans, conquered with bloody opposition by the Moors, and captured in the Spanish Civil War, first by one side, then the other, during the freezing winter of 1937. In the end the Nationalists won, and 1,005 Republicans were executed and thrown into a common grave.

The majestic 13th-century **cathedral** is the town's focal point, with a Mudejar tower, Gothic interior, several Baroque and Churrigueresque chapels, a 15th-century altarpiece of the *Coronation of the Virgin,* a notable 16th-century wood retable by French artist Gabriel Joli, and a splendid 13th-century *artesonado* ceiling. Behind the cathedral is the **Casa de la Comunidad,** which houses an intriguing provincial museum with an excellently displayed ethnographic collection depicting Aragonese life with dioramas, ceramics, and archaeological collections.

The most impressive Mudejar towers in Teruel are those of the **Iglesia de San Martín** and the **Iglesia de San Salvador,** both dating to the 13th century, with elaborate bas-relief designs in raised brickwork and ceramic tiles in the green, black, and white Moorish style that typifies Teruel ceramic ware. You'll see the same colors in the ceramic street signs throughout town and in the bowls, vases, and plates sold at local gift shops, such as **Artesanía de la Catedral**, at Calle Joaquín Costa 7, and **Artesanía Almutazal**, Calle los Amantes 34.

The **Iglesia de San Pedro** also has an imposing Mudejar tower. Attached to the church is a funerary chapel with an alabaster relief of the ill-starred 13th-century "lovers of Teruel." These two, Isabel de Segura and Diego de Marcilla, died of grief a day apart when Isabel's father forced her to marry a rich suitor. You can see the young lovers' skeletons through the glass fronts of their tombs.

A comfortable place to stay during your visit is the modern ▶ **Parador de Teruel** on the northern outskirts of town. It makes an excellent base for trips west to Albarracín or east to El Maestrazgo. The dining room, with typical Aragonese specialties, is *the* place for lunch and dinner.

WEST TO ALBARRACIN

From Teruel you might take a day trip 39 km (24 miles) west to **Albarracín** for a rare glimpse of a Moorish-style fortified village (once an independent Moorish kingdom, named for the 11th-century chieftain who ruled it, Aben-Razin) in the heart of Aragón. The drive along the Río Guadalaviar is spectacular, twisting through mountainous terrain and hillsides tufted with golden broom and towering poplars. In places the cliffs are similar to those of the American West.

Once you reach the hilly walled village, surrounded by the river on three sides, simply wander about taking in the scenery—rose-colored houses with red-tiled roofs, over-hanging balconies with fretted woodwork, iron grilles at the windows, and coats of arms on various façades. You'll find a different perspective around each irregular corner of every winding cobbled lane. The entire village, with its unified medieval architecture and ambience, has been declared a national monument. You can climb the walls, which were built by the Moors and rise to 36 feet, for great views of the village and the surrounding countryside.

Albarracín's small Renaissance **cathedral**, with a gilded 16th-century retable in high relief and a museum with seven 16th-century Brussels tapestries and several silver treasures, is the major sight. Mostly, the town's charm lies in its irregular configurations, its spacious Plaza Mayor (where bullfights are occasionally held and Aragonese *jotas* [folk dances] are danced), the odd building shapes, the cobbled alleyways that lead up- and downhill, attractive ceramic street signs, and the ever-changing vistas.

You might lunch—on rabbit and mushroom stew accompanied by fabulous views of the valley below—or even stay overnight at the ▶ **Hotel Albarracín**, on Azagra, the dark, narrow street leading up to the loftier parts of the village. If you plan a few days of rest, or hiking or trout fishing in the Sierra de Albarracín, this is a clean, if modest, place to stay.

About 3 km (2 miles) west of Albarracín (follow the signs) are several sites with prehistoric rock paintings: El Callejón de Plou, Cueva del Navazo, and Doña Clotilde.

EAST TO EL MAESTRAZGO

You can take another day trip from Teruel east through the region of **El Maestrazgo** (named for the grand *maestres* of the Templar, the crusading order that battled the Moors on this frontier turf), an awesome, rugged, and sometimes desolate landscape hardly changed since the Middle Ages. Follow N 234 to the turnoff at La Puebla de Valverde, then go east on C 232. It's slow going along a roller-coaster mountain road, which in places makes you feel you're at the top of the world; but soon you'll reach **Mora de Rubielos**, in the lower Maestrazgo on the Río Fuenlozana, a town with a 13th-century castle (under restoration and destined to become a parador) and a 12th-century Gothic collegiate church. **Rubielos de Mora**, a walled village of 700 inhabitants, is just 14 km (8½ miles) farther. Like a Spanish version of a Cotswolds village, this one is charming, with many 17th-century mansions and houses bearing heraldic shields. Inside the 17th-century collegiate church is a magnificent 15th-century Gothic altarpiece, the colors still vivid in its many scenes from Christ's life—a work by the so-called Master of Rubielos. Rubielos has a pleasant restaurant, **Portal del Carmen**, Glorieta 2, located in one end of a 17th-century Carmelite convent; Tel: (9-74) 80-41-53.

GETTING AROUND

Aragón's only airport is in its capital city of Zaragoza, with service by Aviaco (Iberia's sister airline) from Madrid, Barcelona, and Jerez de la Frontera, and now Paris and London. It is about a 15-minute ride from the airport to the city center.

Airport taxis are plentiful; buses have no set schedules, and run according to flight arrivals and departures. Hertz, Avis, and European car-rental companies have both airport and downtown locations; arrangements can also be made at the Portillo train station (see below).

RENFE (the Spanish national railroad system), on its Madrid–Barcelona route, makes a stop at Zaragoza's Estación del Portillo in the center of the city. There is also daily train service to and from Alicante, Bilbao, Calatayud, Canfrac, Caspe, Gijón, Jaca, Lérida, Irún, Valencia, Teruel, Vigo, and A Coruña, as well as connections to Paris.

The best way to get around the old and most interesting parts of Zaragoza is by walking; in fact, in some areas, such as El Tubo, it's the only way. A car is a nuisance in the city. The best solution is to garage it while you're there. (Local taxis and buses are plentiful.) Once you set out into the region of Aragón, however, the best way to travel is by car. Roads are generally good, ranging from four-lane superhighways to narrow but well-paved two-lane roads, with the occasional bumpy, pocked road in remote areas such as El Maestrazgo.

It's important to know that with major car-rental companies, such as Avis and Hertz, the rates are about half if you make your reservations by phone from outside Spain with at least two days advance notice, rather than waiting until you are already in Spain. If you're driving one way, there is usually no drop-off charge.

ACCOMMODATIONS REFERENCE

The hotel rates listed below are projected rates for 1994, for double room, double occupancy, in pesetas. The ranges reflect low and high season rates. The high season is generally July and August, Easter, and Christmas through New Year's. We strongly recommend that you confirm the price when making reservations.

When dialing telephone numbers from outside the country, drop the 9 in the area code.

▶ **Edelweiss**. Carretera Zaragoza–Francia, km 189.4, 22889 **Candanchú** (Huesca). Tel: (9-74) 37-32-00; Fax: 37-31-76. 9,850–13,500 pts.

▶ **Gran Hotel**. Paseo de la Constitución 1, 22700 **Jaca**. Tel: (9-74) 36-09-00; Fax: 36-40-61. 10,600 pts.

▶ **Hotel Albarracín**. Azagra, 44100 **Albarracín**. Tel: (9-74) 71-00-11; Fax: 60-53-63. 12,045 pts.

▶ **Hotel Boston**. Avenida de las Torres 28, 50008 **Zaragoza**. Tel: (9-76) 59-91-92; Fax: 59-74-10. 15,000–18,000 pts.

▶ **NH Gran Hotel**. Calle Joaquín Costa 5, 50001 **Zaragoza**. Tel: (9-76) 22-19-01; Fax: 23-67-13. Rooms, 18,000 pts.; suites, 25,000–35,000 pts.

▶ **Parador de la Concordia**. Castillo de los Calatravos, 44600 **Alcañiz**. Tel: (9-74) 83-04-00; Fax: 83-03-66. 9,000–11,500 pts.

▶ **Parador de Teruel**. Apartado 67, N 234, 44080 **Teruel**. Tel: (9-74) 60-18-00; Fax: 60-86-12. 11,500 pts.

BARCELONA

By Stephen O'Shea with Patricia Brooks

Stephen O'Shea, a contributor to The Berlitz Travellers Guide to France, *travels often to Barcelona. He writes about France and Spain for numerous publications and currently resides in New York City. Patricia Brooks contributes to other sections of this guidebook.*

Over the last 15 years the word has spread: Barcelona, the booming industrial metropolis of a newly democratic Spain, is currently outstripping its rivals in urban renewal, artistic innovation, and, above all else, exuberance. A sprawling port of 1.75 million inhabitants, the City of the Counts has emerged from the inhibiting years of Franco's rule to move to center stage in Europe's cultural life. Still passionately attached to its distinct Catalan identity and language, the city teems with cosmopolitan influences, all the while displaying a local tradition that encompasses a wide breadth of museums, galleries, and public art projects, as well as a striking architectural heritage that ranges from accomplished Gothic to the inspired madness of Antoni Gaudí. Visitors in search of somnolent folklore here are in for a rude awakening. A great city too long overlooked, Barcelona has come to emulate that quintessential Catalan and bold artist, Salvador Dalí: In the packed streets, trendy night spots, and refurbished neighborhoods, the residents of Catalonia's capital are now unabashedly strutting their stuff.

MAJOR INTEREST

Neighborhoods
The Ramblas: colorful pedestrian promenade
Barri Gòtic: medieval neighborhood
Eixample: boulevards and Gaudí buildings

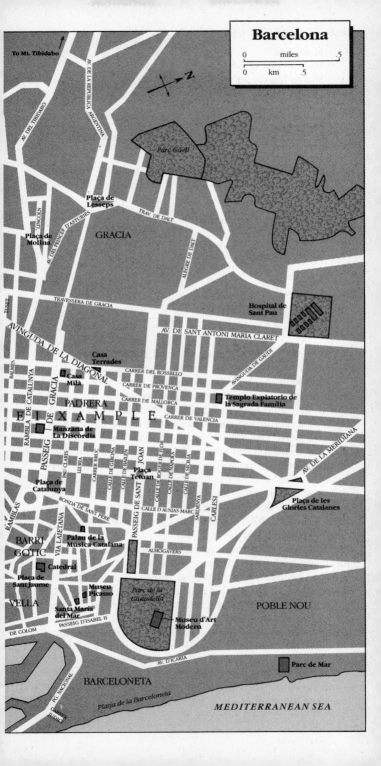

Museums
Museu d'Art de Catalunya
Museu Marés, art and curios collections
Museu Picasso
Fundació Joan Miró

Churches
Cathedral
Santa Maria del Mar
Templo Expiatorio de la Sagrada Família
Monestir de Pedralbes
Sant Pau de Camp

"Modernist" architecture
Palau de la Música Catalana
"Manzana de la Discòrdia" apartment houses
Gaudí's Casa Milà

Parks
Montjuïc
Parc Güell
Parc de la Ciutadella

At Barcelona's harborfront stands a tall column crowned by a statue of Christopher Columbus staring intently out to sea. Although there is some historical justification for the monument—after Columbus's first voyage to the New World, he sailed back to Barcelona in order to report his findings to Ferdinand and Isabella—the statue has a touch of the absurd, too, for Columbus is gazing eastward, out over the well-explored waters of the Mediterranean toward Italy. Add to that the injustice dealt to the seafaring merchants of Catalonia by the Castilian Queen Isabella, whose will specified that they be barred from the lucrative trade with the New World (a prohibition that remained in effect until 1778), and it's a wonder that Columbus is given pride of place anywhere in the city.

But that would be to underestimate the Catalan capacity for living with contradictions. Observers such as Alastair Boyd, in his *Essence of Catalonia* (now out of print), have often praised Barcelona's knack for wedding opposites in compromise, claiming that it reflects the fight in the national soul between the Catalan notions of *seny,* the common-sensical, businesslike side of a merchant people, and *rauxa,* their anarchic, Dionysian impulse to have fun. Indeed, both culture and history have made Barcelona a forum of conflicting influences that goes far beyond erecting a statue to someone whose discoveries led indirectly to a two-century economic downturn.

History and Culture

Long the most sophisticated city on the Iberian Peninsula, the most "European" in its outlook, and the most self-assured in its commercial might, for much of its history Barcelona has been a political dwarf, the capital of a stateless nation with little power over its own destiny. Despite a palpable pride in past victories, the national anthem of Catalonia—"Els Segadors" ("The Reapers")—is almost Celtic in its reminder of past disasters, having first been sung during a doomed 17th-century revolt against the Castilian ascendancy.

That long-standing conflict—Castile versus Catalonia—runs like a leitmotiv through the history of the city and provides a fillip to Catalan nationalism. Distinct from their fellow Iberians in being resolutely Mediterranean—indeed, the Catalan language is more closely related to the Provençal of France's coast than to the Castilian of Spain's interior—the Catalans, now about six million strong, have long considered themselves a people apart. Once an autonomous ally of the Kingdom of Aragón, Catalonia ruled a medieval maritime empire that overshadowed those of Genoa and Venice. The Catalan flag, four red bars on a field of yellow, dates from the 11th century and is Europe's oldest national banner. When dynastic politics of the 15th century led to the region's absorption into a Castile-dominated federation, Catalan self-government, which included a protoparliament of 100 Barcelona notables known as the Consell de Cent, went into a long eclipse.

That misfortune, however, failed to diminish national feeling, as might have happened to people less endowed with the survival schizophrenia of *seny* and *rauxa*. Instead, subject Barcelona looked upon imperial Madrid as a loutish upstart, and "provincial" Catalonia remained the most cosmopolitan of all of Spain's diverse regions, Castile included. The Catalan language, despite attempts by the Bourbons (in 1716) and Franco (in the 1940s) to stamp it out, remains a potent vehicle for regional identity. Today most official business here is conducted in Catalan, though this should not trouble visitors to Barcelona. As Catalan is a Romance language, unlike the mysterious tongue of the neighboring Basques, it abounds in cognates to French and Spanish, making menu-reading and sign-deciphering fairly easy. In addition, all Catalans can speak, however reluctantly, Castilian Spanish, and many have a good knowledge of French and English. (In this chapter we use Catalan place names, as they are more likely to be found on signs and maps.)

Added to the region's linguistic and nationalist contrasts, which many Catalans compare to Quebec's particularities within the Canadian federation, are the surprising contradictions to be found in Barcelona's urban landscape.

Known throughout Spain as the city of wily merchants and cool-headed capitalists, Barcelona is nonetheless the site of some of the wildest architectural extravagances in Europe, and has been a breeding ground for radical ideology and avant-garde art. And, in yet another contradiction, the source of Barcelona's wealth—its link to the sea— seems to have been studiously ignored in civic culture and planning until recently, when thoughtful urbanists began reclaiming the waterfront for the citizens.

Perhaps the contrast first noticed by visitors to Barcelona lies in the way the city is physically organized. Nature created the narrow plain that slopes up to the foot of the Sierra de Collcerola from the sea, but it was man who built two distinctive towns there. The oldest part of the city, called the Barri Gòtic (the Gothic Quarter), occupies a small rise once known as Monte Taber, a few hundred yards from the shore. Originally a Carthaginian settlement, founded by the Barca family of Hannibal's day, it later fell under the sway of the Romans, becoming a minor provincial town with a grandiose name, Colonia Julia Augusta Paterna Faventia Barcino. Successive waves of conquest—by the Visigoths, the Moors, the Franks—swept over the bustling port, but the Roman cyclopean walls, the remnants of which can still be seen, kept the unity of the city.

Barcelona's golden age of independence and pan-Mediterranean influence (its political reach stretched as far as Athens in the 1300s) lent the impetus to expand the city. Two successive medieval ramparts were built to contain the burgeoning town, stretching from the present-day Avinguda del Paral-lel, in the south, to the northern limit marked by the Parc de la Ciutadella. All of this is easily discernible, for the extensive Ciutat Vella (Old Town), encompassing the Barri Gòtic, the Barri Xinès, and the area north of the Via Laietana, is unmistakably preindustrial, a warren of tiny streets bordered by lines of balconies from which lush green plants hang down to seek the shafts of noonday sunlight. Yet, just a few blocks inland, the intimacy of the old town gives way to the Eixample (which means "enlargement"), an enormous grid of 19th-century boulevards laid out in a fit of rationality by Ildefons Cerdà. It's as if two cultures alien to each other happened to build on the same coastal plain, for the Eixample is as airy and expansive as the old town is cramped and quaint.

Seeing Barcelona

To make of Barcelona, it's best to visit the old town first, starting at the central Plaça de Catalunya and making your way east, or seaward, along the entertaining pedestrian thoroughfare known as Las Ramblas. (Remember, in Barcelona the sea lies to the east and the mountains to the west.) To the south of Las Ramblas, in the part of the old town that runs to the foot of the seaside prominence called Montjuïc, lies Barri Xinès, a scruffy neighborhood of sinuous streets and unpretentious charm. Just north of Las Ramblas the old town becomes a maze of small shops and busy commercial alleyways, its crowning glory the Barri Gòtic proper, containing the city's secular Gothic wonders as well as its imposing cathedral. Still farther north, across the Via Laietana, a modern boulevard with an ancient name (the Laietana were the Bronze Age people who first settled the coastal plain), stands the last third of the Ciutat Vella, its down-to-earth marketplaces and humble streets sharing pride of place with a soaring ecclesiastical masterpiece (the church of Santa Maria del Mar) and a treasure house of modern art (the Museu Picasso).

After this walk through picturesque, narrow streets, visit the Eixample, especially if you enjoy luxury shopping, bars and cafés for the well-heeled, and the turn-of-the-century fantasy of Modernist architecture. A huge grid of streets cut by the Avinguda de la Diagonal and bounded on the east (just inland from the Plaça de Catalunya) by the Gran Via de les Corts Catalanes, the Eixample stretches from the old town to the foothills of the Sierra de Collcerola.

The hills themselves hold attractions that show Barcelona's capacity to surprise: Gaudí's strange Parc Güell, the towering lookout of Mount Tibidabo, and the lovely monastery of Pedralbes. Yet the hill that will occupy you the longest stands by the seaside to the south of the old town— Montjuïc, a repository of richly endowed museums. This wooded hill also offers stunning views of Barcelona spreading from its industrial harborfront through the old town, and westward past the modern Eixample to the limits of the rugged Catalan hinterland.

A final section of our coverage is devoted to Barcelona's harbor, a long-neglected area now being opened up to pleasure-seekers from the densely populated plain. Like Christopher Columbus staring out to sea, the city now seems poised to look beyond itself, ready to receive the creative and the curious from all points of the globe. That, given the city's long history of self-sufficiency, may be Barcelona's finest contradiction.

Las Ramblas and Environs

PLAÇA DE CATALUNYA

The heart of the city, the chaotic meeting place of the Eixample and the old town, is an appropriately irregular

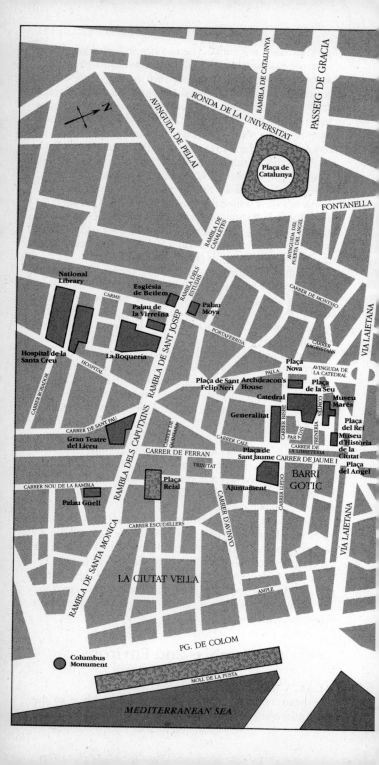

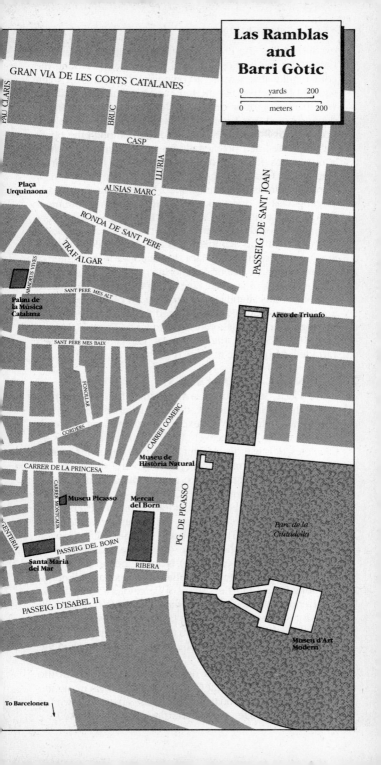

Las Ramblas and Barri Gòtic

0   yards   200

0   meters   200

GRAN VIA DE LES CORTS CATALANES

PAU CLARIS

BRUC

CASP

LLIRIA

Plaça Urquinaona

AUSIAS MARC

RONDA DE SANT PERE

PASSEIG DE SANT JOAN

TRAFALGAR

AMADEUS VIVES

Palau de la Música Catalana

SANT PERE MES ALT

Arco de Triunfo

SANT PERE MES BAIX

FONOLAR

CORDERS

CARRER COMERC

CARRER DE LA PRINCESA

Museu de Història Natural

CARRER MONTCADA

Museu Picasso

Mercat del Born

PG. DE PICASSO

Parc de la Ciutadella

GENTERIA

PASSEIG DEL BORN

RIBERA

Santa Maria del Mar

PASSEIG D'ISABEL II

Museu d'Art Modern

To Barceloneta

expanse called the Plaça de Catalunya. Remodeled several times over the past century and still pleasantly lacking the cold dignity that usually accompanies the status of main square of a metropolis, the loud and bustling *plaça* is lined with banks, outdoor cafés, and the inevitable Corte Inglés department store. Admirers of distinctive architecture will not tarry for long in this unruly square, although the opening of a café-lined promenade on its southern side, which connects Las Ramblas of the old town to the upmarket Rambla de Catalunya in the Eixample (see below), now brings hundreds of aperitif-sippers to the plaza in the early evening. Visitors brave enough to drink from the monumental fountains in Plaça de Catalunya's large, pigeon-filled central plaza are said to become honorary citizens of Barcelona. Together with Las Ramblas, a series of shaded walkways leading east from it, the Plaça de Catalunya is the center of Barcelona life. No political gathering of any importance and no outpouring of popular rage or joy takes place anywhere else but in this slightly ungainly plaza. In recent years hundreds of thousands have gathered here to celebrate the passing of dictator Generalísimo Francisco Franco (November 20, 1975) and the return of Catalan leader Josep Tarradellas from exile in Mexico (October 23, 1977).

ALONG LAS RAMBLAS

If the Plaça de Catalunya is the setting for extraordinary events in the life of the city, then Las Ramblas perform the same function for everyday existence in Barcelona. The end-to-end avenues—respectively, from west to east: Ramblas de Canaletes, dels Estudis, de Sant Josep, dels Caputxins, and de Santa Mónica—form a single thoroughfare almost a mile long that runs along the trace of a medieval rampart from the Plaça de Catalunya to the Columbus monument at the waterfront. It gives the people of Barcelona an ideal place to enact the Iberian ritual of *paseo,* the sunset stroll before the late-evening meal. This tree-lined avenue, with its wide pedestrian area in the middle (there are narrow service streets running along each side), is one of the most entertaining urban environments in southern Europe, affording opportunity for an effortless study of Barcelona society. Black-clad trendies afflicted with post-*modernismo* fashion notions jostle for space with quarreling family groups, while sailors on leave restlessly walk up from the port past the ubiquitous young couples of Barcelona, the girls in short skirts and the boys with long eyelashes.

Heading from the Plaça de Catalunya (usually from the terrace of the ever-popular **Café Bar Zurich**, which marks the spot where the traditional Barcelona *paseo* begins) down Las Ramblas, the stroller encounters flower stalls, bird-sellers, fortune-tellers, outdoor cafés, and a succession of huge book and newspaper kiosks hawking everything from the daily newspapers of Helsinki and Tokyo to elaborately erotic comic strips (a post-Franco Barcelona specialty). The booksellers and flower merchants do a particularly booming business on April 23, the feast day of Catalonia's patron saint, Jordi (George), when Catalan custom calls for lovers to exchange roses and books. Visitors will find themselves drawn again and again to the daily spectacle of the Barcelona *paseo,* for it is the best way to get a feel for the city. Las Ramblas represent, in short, what all urban planners dream of achieving when they design a pedestrian mall.

The area in and around Las Ramblas is a testament to the many faces of Barcelona: patrician, proletarian, bourgeois, revolutionary, and religious. Where the Rambla dels Estudis gives way to the Rambla de Sant Josep, evidence of the city's past prosperity can be seen in the Baroque standoff between Església de Betlem (Church of Bethlehem) to the south and the Palau (palace) Moya to the north. Farther on, past the church, is the **Palau de la Virreina**, an 18th-century mansion commissioned by the viceroy of Peru and completed by his widow, the vicereine (*virreina*). It houses a rich decorative-arts museum, showing the ingenuity of local craftsmen up to the present day, and hosts important temporary art shows. (As all major Barcelona museums and galleries do, the Virreina closes on Mondays and just after lunch on Sundays.) Also in the Virreina is the art collection of Francesc Cambó, a turn-of-the-century Catalan leader who tried to unite Barcelona business and labor in a common struggle against the central government in Madrid. Small but distinguished, the Cambó bequest includes works by Botticelli, Gainsborough, Tintoretto, and Titian.

La Boquería

But the Palau de la Virreina, a refined oasis on the Rambla de Sant Josep, is quickly forgotten in the earthy charm of its immediate neighbor, a wrought-iron market building known popularly as La Boquería. Unwilling to repeat the mistakes made by Paris and London in moving their central food markets from traditional neighborhoods, Barcelona has wisely kept its beloved Boquería in the center of town, ensuring a constant flow of voluble homemakers past the tarot-card readers in the small entranceway off Las Ramblas. Once inside, visitors may fall victim to the cornucopia of nuts and candies immediately confronting them or decide to venture farther into the din and try their luck at handling the produce before purchasing it. An excellent sampling of local color awaits those who decide to eat at **Pinocchio**, a single-counter restaurant with only ten stools, just inside the

Boquería (to get there, take the main entrance and turn right at the second aisle). Marketpeople, businessmen, and trendies gather there at all times of day.

South of La Boquería

Directly to the south, behind the clamor of La Boquería, stands the tranquil Gothic complex of the former Hospital de la Santa Creu (Holy Cross). Although no longer a hospital—its graceful 15th-century buildings, the entrances decorated with tiles, along with its quiet cloister and garden, now house an institute of Catalan studies and the national library of Catalonia—Santa Creu attests to the period when this quarter of the old city stood outside Barcelona's medieval ramparts (that is, where Las Ramblas now run) and was an area of monastic estates and charity houses. As Catalonia once straddled the Pyrenees, the great waves of monasticism sweeping France in the early Middle Ages, notably the Cluny Benedictines and the Cistercians, also affected Barcelona.

From the Santa Creu complex take Carrer Robador to Carrer de Sant Pau; turn right and continue a few blocks to find even more striking proof of this neighborhood's Christian pedigree: **Sant Pau del Camp** (St. Paul in the Fields), by common agreement the oldest church in the city, even if no one is sure exactly how old it is (a tomb inside dates from 912). What makes Sant Pau remarkable is its Romanesque **cloister** adjoining the abbot's residence, with shamrock-shaped arches, called trilobate, unique in this type of architecture and long an object of curiosity. Pablo Picasso, during his sojourn in the city, executed several studies of them, which can be seen in Barcelona's Museu Picasso.

Rambla dels Caputxins

The other giant of 20th-century art connected to Barcelona is Joan Miró. Fittingly, in executing one of his last commissioned works, a multicolored pavement mosaic at the busy meeting place of the Rambla de Sant Josep and the Rambla dels Caputxins, Miró became just another sidewalk artist on Las Ramblas. Although the promenade turns slightly seedier at this point—the area between Las Ramblas and Sant Pau del Camp (Barri Xinès) turns into a red-light district at night—the Rambla dels Caputxins covers the most interesting stretch of the walk from Plaça de Catalunya toward the seafront. It is also where the long line of sidewalk cafés begins.

Plaça Reial

Off the north side of the Rambla dels Caputxins, just below the Carrer de Ferran (the main north–south axis of the old town), stands a beautiful 19th-century square, the Plaça Reial

(Royal Square). After the Spanish state confiscated church holdings under the Disentailment Act of 1835, the disused Capuchin monastery that occupied this spot was demolished to create an arcaded enclosure dotted with palm trees, a fountain of the Three Graces, and lamp standards designed by Gaudí. Nowadays its many cafés are ideal places to wash down *tapas* in the brilliant sunshine and be horrified or bemused—depending on your view of life—by the antics of the drifters who congregate here. On weekend mornings a picturesque coin-and-stamp market is held in the Plaça Reial, although at night the conspicuously vulnerable visitor to the city should take care not to be mugged—Barcelona is, after all, a port. This warning, in fact, should be kept in mind at all times on the lower reaches of Las Ramblas, and at night in the narrow streets to the north (the Barri Gòtic) and especially to the south in the rough-and-tumble Barri Xinès.

When the 19th-century bourgeois classes of Barcelona commissioned the building of the Plaça Reial, they were responding to the wealth that industrialization and colonial trade had brought them. Along with Piedmont and Lombardy, Catalonia was the only other southern European region to experience the Industrial Revolution at the same time as areas in the north of the continent—this despite the chaos that the French occupation of Catalonia caused in the Napoleonic era. Even before the Eixample opened up the city to imaginative (and immensely profitable) real-estate development in the latter half of the 19th century, the merchants of Barcelona began creating an urban environment suited to their aspirations. Primary among these was a movement of cultural self-affirmation known as Renaixença (renaissance), a celebration of Catalan identity and urban sophistication that had long been suppressed by a centralizing Castilian monarchy. Because little sympathy for cultural life in Barcelona was ever evinced by the authorities in Madrid, the wealthy classes of the city banded together, as private Catalan businesses do even today, to subsidize the arts.

Gran Teatre del Liceu

Foremost among these institutions is the Gran Teatre del Liceu, the opera house of Barcelona, built entirely through private subscriptions. Although the façade giving onto the Rambla dels Caputxins near the Miró mosaic looks rather undistinguished, the interior of the Liceu (lyceum) is pointedly Renaissance in inspiration and has hosted many great lyric and orchestral artists since its inception in 1847. Its winter season still draws the elite of Barcelona (that is, those fortunate enough to obtain hard-to-get tickets) for elegant operatic evenings and de rigueur drinks at the pricey Café de l'Opéra. Among the 20 or so operas it presents every season, the Liceu frequently features works by Catalonia's adopted idol, Richard Wagner. The affinity between the unbridled power of the composer from Bayreuth and the ostentatious wealth of Barcelona's propertied classes was especially strong in the opening years of this century, when the latter were constructing magnificent homes throughout the city.

Palau Güell

A showy example of this building craze can be visited nearby, just a few blocks southeast from the Gran Teatre del Liceu on the narrow Carrer Nou de la Rambla. Eusebi Güell, a textile manufacturer and patron of the arts, commissioned Gaudí to construct a residence worthy of his prominent position in Barcelona society. The resulting Palau Güell is medieval in spirit, recalling the days when great lords had fortified town houses erected in the heart of the city. The municipality has since turned Güell's imposing folly into a theater museum, although the exhibits are dwarfed by the grandiose, if somewhat weirdly vegetal, ornamentation and the large central well of the house.

The fortress aspect of the Palau Güell became singularly appropriate toward the turn of the century, when the struggle between Barcelona's plutocrats and proletarians turned spectacularly violent and Las Ramblas became the scene of clashes that mixed class and regional consciousness. In a phenomenon peculiar to the region, prosperous conservatives and liberals alike opted for vocal Catalonian nationalism after growing disgusted with the bumbling foreign policy of the Madrid government, particularly the disastrous war with the United States in 1898 that led to the loss of Spain's lucrative colonial connections. Barcelona's working classes, still subjected to naked capitalism at the time (child labor was outlawed only in 1907), were interested less in political than in economic justice and felt strongly pulled toward the internationalist positions of socialism and anarchism.

The streets around Las Ramblas, now so peaceful, were witness to bloody incidents, as successive strikes degenerated into mayhem and Barcelona started the new century with the unflattering nickname of "Bomb City." In one infamous incident in 1893, an anarchist lobbed two bombs from the balcony of the Liceu, killing 20 operagoers—one device was a dud and now sits demurely on display in the city's history museum—and ensuring redoubled repression by the authorities. The darkest days occurred in 1909 after a radicalized populace refused to be conscripted to fight in Spanish-held Morocco. The popular uprising turned anticlerical and anticapitalist, with scores of buildings in the city falling prey to arson before a ferocious army was called in to suppress the revolt. Barcelona's Setmana Tràgica (Tragic Week) ended with more than 100 dead.

Thus, it should be no surprise that George Orwell could write in his memoir of the Spanish Civil War, *Homage to Catalonia:* "Barcelona is a town with a long history of street-fighting. In such places things happen quickly, the factions are ready-made, everyone knows the local geography, and when the guns begin to shoot people take their places almost as in a fire-drill." Although Orwell set down the events of 1937, his remark is evidence of Barcelona's revolutionary reputation among earlier generations. During the 1936–1939 conflict Barcelona was the strongest redoubt of Republican forces, holding out to the very end and, in defeat, suffering severe anti-Catalan measures from Francisco Franco. (In the first three days of Franco's rule in January 1939, more than 25,000 people were executed in Barcelona.) But even Orwell's tre-mendous gifts—he gives a masterful account of an interne-cine battle in Las Ramblas between Communists and anar-chists on the Republican side—sometimes falter in the face of Barcelona's sturdy irrationality: "I do not suppose I have succeeded in conveying much of the strangeness of that time. . . . I remember the fashionably-dressed woman I saw strolling. . .with a shopping-basket over her arm and leading a white poodle, while the rifles cracked and roared a street or two away."

The Barri Gòtic and Environs

PLAÇA DE LA SEU

On Sunday mornings in the Plaça de la Seu, down the monumental steps directly in front of the cathedral of Barce-lona, groups of Catalan dancers of all ages perform the *sardana.* The setting—a modern building to the west, the great front of the cathedral to the east, and remnants of the old Roman wall of Barcino to both north and south—is a reminder of both the dance's antiquity and its cherished place in contemporary Catalonian culture. Although the dance's origin is disputed—some consider it a harvest dance from pre-Christian times—there can be little doubt that the *sardana* is an expression of community. With a little knowledge of Catalan history, the visitor soon realizes that this folk tradition is not another quaint spectacle staged for the benefit of camera-toting tourists: The *sardana* has come to be a symbol of quiet resistance, of the people's will to survive as a distinct Catalan community despite repeated efforts throughout the centuries to quash the regional diver-sity of Spain. In the very recent past, Catalonia's most deter-mined adversary, Franco, understood the emotional resonance of this dance and outlawed its performance anywhere and at any time. Thus, the dancers of today are not just having fun—they're making a statement.

Across the square to the west, another source of Catalan pride—the region's architectural heritage—is on display: The **College of Catalan Architects** is housed in a modern (1960s) building covered with murals inspired by the work of Pablo Picasso. For those who, like the Catalans themselves, have an abiding interest in design and architecture, the institute's extensive bookstore, located underground, carries books in several languages and is worth a visit.

The Barri Gòtic, which serves as a backdrop to the *sardana* dancers, recalls not past struggles but past splendors. Catalonia was not always an underdog: After a picturesquely named count of Barcelona, Wilfred the Hairy (sometimes called Wilfred the Shaggy), shook off the yoke of the Carolingian Franks in the ninth century, the seafaring Catalan nation became an independent kingdom during the High Middle Ages, allied with the crown of Aragón. That time of political supremacy and power is recalled in the various museums and institutions that make up the Barri Gòtic, a complex of imposing buildings and narrow streets that, especially at night, preserves the atmosphere of the medieval city. Stretching from Plaça Nova and Plaça de la Seu to just east of Plaça de Sant Jaume, the Barri Gòtic is the oldest section of the old town. Las Ramblas are nearby to the south, as is yet another old quarter centered around Carrer de la Princesa to the north.

The Cathedral

Although its Flamboyant façade dates only from the 19th century, the cathedral, which dominates this quarter, is far older, construction having begun in 1298. The dimly lit interior, remarkable for the decorative overkill in the radiating chapels, usually buzzes with crowds of worshipers and visitors, the former drawn to the crypt of the city's patroness, Santa Eulalia, and the latter attracted to magnificently carved wooden stalls in the *coro* (chancel). It was here, in the early 16th century, that young Holy Roman Emperor Charles V (Spain's King Carlos I) tried to establish the Order of the Golden Fleece, a confraternity of such free-spending Renaissance monarchs as Henry VIII of Britain and Francis I of France. The aptly named order did not survive long, but the *coro,* by its sheer size and the richness of its wood carvings, attests to the wealth of the canons of Barcelona's cathedral.

Further proof of spiritual worldliness can be seen in the capacious **cloister** hugging the southern flank of the sanctuary. Although cloisters are usually oases of quietude suggesting the contemplative life, this enclosure is a noisy Gothic atrium frequently filled by neighborhood residents who find an ideal place to exchange gossip underneath its shaded arcades and palm trees. Adding to the occasional uproar are the raucous cries of the geese that make their home around the central fountain—settled there, it is said, in imitation of the Capitoline geese of antiquity. A cool and beautiful place to escape the hot sun of the Mediterranean summer, the cloister is the cathedral's most attractive and memorable feature. While it is true that traces of extravagant Iberian Catholicism can be found in the cloister's southwestern corner, where a chapel given over to the cult of Santa Lucia often overflows with the devout, most of the vaulted ambulatory itself, completed in 1448, seems resolutely—and loudly—down to earth.

AROUND IN THE BARRI GOTIC
Throughout this quarter be on the lookout for gargoyles, small shrines, and other hints at the antiquity of the buildings; doorways crowned by solid stone arches characteristic of Gothic domestic architecture usually deserve surreptitious entry. Inside many of these buildings, now occupied by government bodies, beautifully restored patios can be seen, with a single flight of stone stairs leading to a gallery adorned with a graceful colonnade. In one such place, hidden in the Carrer de Paradis behind the cathedral and identified as the Centre Excursionista de Catalunya, the medieval courtyard shelters four pillars from a Roman temple to Augustus.

Carrer dels Comtes de Barcelona
On the cathedral's northern flank is the narrow Carrer dels Comtes de Barcelona, which, as its name suggests, once played host to the aristocratic rulers of Barcelona. If the cathedral and the area directly south of it are reminders of the power of the medieval Catalan church, this part of the Barri Gòtic suggests the splendor of its secular elite. On this narrow street the Gothic mansion that once belonged to Barcelona's counts is now a treasure trove for art lovers, holding the collection of Frederic Marés, a 20th-century Catalan artist who combined aesthetics and eccentricity. The cellar and first two floors of the **Museu Marés** house a beautiful display of Romanesque and Gothic polychrome wood sculpture, as well as sculptural works from other periods. Room 8 on the ground floor is particularly strange for its collection of crucified Christs, displayed like so many beautiful butterflies in postures of sublime agony. On the top floor, however, fancy takes over from refinement in Marés's "sentimental" collection. Evidently a man with an inexhaustible appetite for baubles and curios from flea markets and auction rooms throughout Europe, Marés hoarded

everything from hat pins to snuffboxes. If you want to know what 18th-century binoculars look like, this is the place to go; this may be the only museum in a Gothic setting with an extensive cigar band collection.

Plaça del Rei

Less anachronistic are the attractions in the Plaça del Rei, just a few steps northeast of the rear of the cathedral. The spacious square (not to be confused with Las Ramblas's Plaça Reial), a complex of stately medieval buildings that includes a distinctive five-story tower constructed in the early 15th century, lends dignity to even the most bedraggled itinerant musician. Its western end contains the impressive **Salo del Tinell**, the grand Gothic hall in which Columbus announced his news to Ferdinand and Isabella on his first return from the New World (June 1493). An enormous chamber with remnants of martial frescoes on the wall, it looks as solid as the Barcelona counts once believed their dynasty to be. At right angles to this immense reminder of past glory is another large hall, the chapel of **Santa Agata**. Spare and evocative of medieval piety, its stone walls and carved wood ceiling are supported by the work of an earlier ruling class—the chapel sits squarely on the city walls built by the Romans.

More evidence of the Romans appears in the archaeological dig beneath **Museu de la Història de la Ciutat** (the city's history museum), located on the east side of the Plaça del Rei in the 15th-century Clariana-Padellàs house. Although frustrating because of its monolingual explanatory notes and signs, the dig gives a good idea of the extent of Roman Barcino, while the museum's upper floors show the locals' considerable pride in the medieval might of Barcelona. Maps and models are used in an instructive display that reveals how the city has changed over the centuries. Fittingly, the Clariana-Padellàs mansion offers the best evidence of these changes, having been moved stone by stone to the Plaça del Rei to save it from boulevard builders earlier in this century.

Plaça de Sant Jaume

Just as the cathedral and Plaça del Rei represent the Church and the Crown in the city's past, the Plaça de Sant Jaume, a hundred yards or so to the southeast (take Carrer del Bisbe Irurita from the cathedral), recalls another powerful element in medieval Barcelona society: the prosperous burghers and minor aristocracy. The two buildings on this remarkable square, despite their anachronistic façades, house institutions that are direct descendants of age-old councils: the **Ajuntament de Barcelona** (city hall) and the **Palau de la Generalitat** (regional government building). Parliamentary in nature, both bodies wrung concessions from successive monarchs, just as today they are the linchpin of Catalonia's autonomous status within Spain. They are also rivals for local prestige. The Ajuntament prides itself on its 14th-century chamber for the Consell de Cent, the hundred grandees who ran the city. A stunning medieval hall with a Renaissance entrance, the room is a delight to the eye: powerful arches, coffered ceiling, and chandeliers. Across the square, on its western side, the Generalitat (open to visitors only on Sunday mornings) possesses a grand staircase leading to a Gothic arcade. The building's first-floor orange-tree courtyard and medieval chapel leave the visitor convinced of Catalonia's wealth in the Middle Ages.

These two institutions stand for the stubborn Catalan tendency to refuse government by fiat. As early as 1064 prominent families forced Count Ramón Berenguer I to limit their feudal obligations under a landmark agreement known as the Usatges de Barcelona. Throughout the Middle Ages, the Consell de Cent gradually whittled away regal prerogative in matters of taxation, and the city's merchant class grew so influential that its Consulat del Mar (1258) came to govern international maritime law well into the Renaissance.

After these halcyon days of civic independence, the power of the city's merchants began to wane. Difficult, querulous subjects of the centralizing Castilian dynasty that began with the union of Ferdinand and Isabella, the burghers of Barcelona reacted with even greater alarm when that royal line eventually died out and the absolutist Louis XIV of France proposed his grandson for the vacant throne of Spain. In the ensuing War of the Spanish Succession, which drew in all of Europe, Barcelona backed the wrong horse (that is, the Hapsburg pretender) and paid dearly for it. Taking a page from his grandfather's book, Philip V, the Bourbon victor, promulgated the Decree of Nova Planta in 1716, abolishing the troublesome civic intermediaries of Catalonia as well as forbidding the use of the Catalan language in the conduct of public business. As always, Barcelona outlived its oppressors. Now, in Plaça de Sant Jaume, the celebrations of the Festa Major d'Estiu, a mid-September religious festival, have powerful Catalan nationalist overtones. In front of the Generalitat, teams from competing Catalan towns build sturdy *castells* (human pyramids) in a custom no less symbolic than the *sardana.* Whereas the dance suggests harmony, the *castell,* by its improbable, acrobatic nature, involves defiance, a trait the political bodies of Barcelona—Generalitat, Ajuntament, and their ancestors—have long displayed toward the powerful.

NORTH OF THE BARRI GOTIC

To the north of the Barri Gòtic proper, across Via Laietana, lies the final third of the old town, a surprising mix of the medieval and the modern. By exiting Plaça de Sant Jaume by Carrer de Jaume I, you leave the original Roman enclosure of Barcino. To the northeast, down the small shopping street of Carrer Argenteria, the tall octagonal towers of **Santa Maria del Mar** can be seen stretching skyward. This church, raised by the wealthy merchants of the city beside what was, in the 14th century, the harbor of Barcelona, is considered by many to be the most beautiful example of Catalan Gothic architecture in the old town. The cathedral seems cluttered when compared to its contemporary, Santa Maria. Since most of Santa Maria's decorative elements were consumed in a fire set by anarchists in 1936, you can now view the great Gothic lines of the cavernous church without devotional distractions. A stroll around the ambulatory is a peaceful respite from the liveliness of the teeming neighborhood surrounding the church.

The Born District

Directly behind Santa Maria is the Born district, a hodge-podge of cafés and bars leading north to the **Mercat del Born,** a 19th-century market building recently converted into an attractive display space for temporary exhibitions, some dealing with contemporary art. (The Parc de la Ciutadella, just beyond the Mercat del Born, is covered in The Waterfront section, below.) This anachronistic vocation for the medieval neighborhood becomes even more evident in the tiny **Carrer Montcada**, which starts to the west of Santa Maria's choir. Jammed with tourists in the summer months, the street beckons not only because of its fine Gothic town houses—Montcada was a fashionable street well into the Renaissance—but also for its art galleries (including a Maeght print gallery), crafts shops, *tapas* bars, and, yes, souvenir stalls.

The Museu Picasso

These attractions, however, are secondary to the street's principal crowd-pleaser, the Museu Picasso. In a gracious gesture to the Andalusian interloper, Catalan cultural authorities created a museum for the modern master in the 14th-century palace of Berenguer de Aguilar. As in Paris, Picasso's works marry well with medieval surroundings.

The collection, a legacy from Picasso's secretary, Jaume Sabartés, coupled with further donations by the artist, is the largest of its kind in the world. It is, however, far from comprehensive: Picasso's earliest works and the work of his old age predominate. Still, the museum is the city's fitting homage to the genius who lived in the neighborhood from 1895 to 1904. The long arm of Montmartre reached out to influence him—and eventually to pluck him away—but the memory of Barcelona was to remain with him for many years. It is said that the remembered prostitutes on Carrer d'Avinyó, which lies between Plaça de Sant Jaume and Las Ramblas, served as models for his later masterpiece *Les Demoiselles d'Avignon*.

WEST TOWARD THE EIXAMPLE

A slightly more salubrious place connected with Picasso is **Els Quatre Gats** (The Four Cats), in the neighborhood between the Barri Gòtic and the Eixample. Founded in 1897, the café is still open for business on the tiny Carrer de Montsió, east of Plaça de Catalunya by way of Avinguda del Puerta del Angel. Its creators—admirers and imitators of Montmartre's Le Chat Noir—made the café a meeting place for the young artists who sought to work away from academicism in painting and sculpture. Their frequent sojourns in Paris opened them up to the visual revolution being wrought in the French capital and, in one case, resulted in the conception of a baby whose Catalan surname would belie his Gallic upbringing: Maurice Utrillo. Yet the flowering of Barcelona's bohemia was short-lived—though a brief revival took place in the neutral city during World War I—for the very simple reason that, like Picasso, most of the group elected to move to Paris.

In a neat dovetailing of artistic movements, Els Quatre Gats is housed in the Casa Martí, an edifice designed by architect Josep Puig i Cadafalch, one of the foremost exponents of what Catalans call Modernisme. (We adopt the "Modernist" label for this turn-of-the-century movement—not to be confused with the modernists in Italy and elsewhere after World War I.) In addition to being a center of bohemia, Barcelona became a major testing ground for the explosion of architecture and decorative arts that transformed cities throughout Europe at the turn of the century. Barcelona's Modernism, a contemporary of Paris's Art Nouveau and Vienna's Secessionist movements, is the most lasting and spectacular outgrowth of the 19th-century Catalan Renaixença. Influenced as well by the Arts and Crafts school in Britain and the Gothic Revival, Modernist architects sought to create a distinctive national style that would unite fin-de-siècle aesthetics with a triumphant pride in Catalan craftsmanship. Thus, brick, ceramics, tile, and glass were lavished on the new buildings, many of which were designed by architects who doubled as political leaders—Josep Puig i Cadafalch and Lluís Domènech i Montaner are the most prominent examples. It is their buildings, along with those of the more reclusive Gaudí, that give Barcelona its extravagant architectural heritage.

Although Modernist works are usually associated with the Eixample, the old city possesses the best exemplar of the cultural politics of that time. On a side street (Amadeus Vives) north of Via Laietana rises the **Palau de la Música Catalana**, a concert hall erected in 1908 by Domènech. In keeping with the tenets of the mature Renaixença, Domènech used every traditional material Catalan craftsmen could provide to construct a Modernist masterpiece so heterogeneous and outrageous that it transcends taste. Outside, swirling, multicolored columns compete for attention with marble busts on the red-brick façade and pseudo-Moorish arches; inside, a huge bas-relief of the cavalcade of the Valkyries comes charging out of walls covered with tiles and head-size ceramic roses, as a stained-glass ceiling, complete with an enormous central bulb, spreads indirect light over the hall. The best way to see this amazing building is to attend a concert here. Even if the performance is mediocre—which is unlikely in a venue where Catalan Pau (Pablo) Casals first set the standards—the permanent spectacle of the Palau is enough to keep you in your seat.

The Eixample

When Barcelona began bursting at the seams in the middle of the 19th century, town planners were asked to submit projects for the enlargement (*eixample*) of the city. Ildefons Cerdà, winner of the contest judged by the central government in Madrid, opted for a rigid, if spacious, grid, slashed diagonally by one predictably named thoroughfare— Avinguda de la Diagonal. Although the project called for numerous green spaces, real-estate developers soon transformed the Eixample into an unrelieved residential and commercial district, possessing few trees and even fewer parks. Despite these signal disadvantages, the Eixample— especially the section directly west of the old town—has become an agreeable urban environment that exhibits the full-blown fantasy of Modernist architecture and the present-day exuberance of Catalan culture. Deceptively repetitive, like much of Manhattan, the grid nonetheless contains enough arresting sights to keep visitors blinking in disbelief.

PASSEIG DE GRACIA
Named after the now-trendy urban village to the west that it links to the Plaça de Catalunya, Passeig de Gràcia is the most prestigious avenue of the city. Where it meets Gran Via de les Corts Catalanes (just a block or so south of Barcelona's main tourist office) is where the elegance of

the Eixample really begins. Civic boosters who compare the *passeig* to the Champs-Elysées inadvertently do it a disservice—Gràcia is far more interesting. Gaudí's magnificently silly lamp standards, each one restored by private business as part of the pre-Olympic sprucing-up of the city, adorn the lower reaches of the thoroughfare, in a foretaste of the supreme architectural playfulness to be found on Gràcia between Carrer Consell de Cent and Carrer d'Aragó. Here, banks and stolid office buildings done in uninspired Victorian pastiche give way to what local punsters have labeled "La Manzana de la Discòrdia" (*manzana* means both "apple" and "block of houses" in Spanish): three apartment buildings designed by the unholy trinity of Modernist architects—Domènech, Puig, and Gaudí—standing close together on one city block. Domènech's **Casa Lleó Morera** (at number 35), its ground floor shamefully disfigured by a leather-goods store, exhibits a fanciful façade that draws its inspiration from Hispano-Moorish architecture. However compelling the exterior, the building's true appeal lies inside, where the second-floor apartments (European first floor), now occupied by the offices of a tourist board, display a riot of ceramics, woodwork, stained glass, and statuary. Although these suites are not officially open to the public, try your luck toward the end of the day (after 4:00 P.M.) by flashing this guide and saying that you'd like to take a quick peek at the place.

Farther up the block, Puig's **Casa Amatller** looks like a gabled Amsterdam edifice mysteriously transported to the Mediterranean. The families who commissioned such follies were fabulously wealthy. Many had made their fortunes in Spain's colonies and, when forced home by the Spanish-American War, were determined to make a splash in Barcelona society. Above the fireplace in the main room of the Amatller clan's apartments, an elaborate stone allegory of Europe and America makes plain the trading routes on which the family's wealth was based. Again, this building is not a museum, but the scholars studying in the art institute housed on the second floor are usually happy to show around anyone who takes an interest in the mantelpiece. Next door, the blue-green waves of ceramics on the façade of Gaudí's **Casa Batlló** can be profitably gawked at for hours—a bench has been set up for just that purpose.

Casa Milà

Gaudí's most celebrated apartment building, which art critic Robert Hughes has described indelicately—and, we must assume, intuitively—as "an elephant's erotic dream," stands a few blocks away at Passeig de Gràcia 92. The Casa Milà, nicknamed La Pedrera (the quarry), is remarkable both inside and out, stamped with the architect's flowing, organic aesthetic. Tours of the building, conducted in Catalan, Spanish, and English and held at 10:00 A.M., 11:00 A.M., noon, and 1:00 P.M. (Tuesday through Saturday), can be joined at Casa Milà's side entrance on Carrer de Provença. As these tours take a maximum of 25 Gaudí-gawkers at a time, it is wise to arrive early and buy a ticket from the gatekeeper (from 9:45 A.M. on) for a visit later in the morning. The guided exploration of Casa Milà's lobby, stairwells, and terrace is well worth the bother: However conservative the Barcelona establishment was at the turn of the century, it certainly does not show in its taste in decorators. Gaudí, a traditionalist in his Catholic faith and his regional allegiance (he refused to speak Castilian), resigned in disgust as the project neared completion because sponsors forbade him to use religious motifs in the seaweed-like outer balconies. Fearful of provoking an anticlerical populace in the wake of the Setmana Tràgica of 1909, the financial backers of Casa Milà preferred their revolutions to remain architectural.

This flamboyant creative tradition in the Eixample, Barcelona's business district, has been revived in the past two decades. In the years prior to Franco's departure, the district was the haunt of Barcelona's "divine left," the group of artists and intellectuals determined to keep abreast of developments in European and American thought—even if that meant nothing more than hopping over to Perpignan every other weekend to browse in the bookshops and attend such forbidden films as *Last Tango in Paris*. On the Avinguda de la Diagonal, editors and agents brought the work of Latin American "magical realists" to a wider European reading public, despite the cultural deep freeze into which 30 years of Franco had plunged the rest of the country. The creators of contemporary Barcelona and their camp followers, no longer a shadowy group needing divine adjectives, now comfortably coexist with businesspeople in the designer bars that dot the Eixample.

RAMBLA DE CATALUNYA

Daytime activity is concentrated around the upmarket Rambla de Catalunya, parallel to and south of Passeig de Gràcia, where collectors fresh from the galleries on Carrer Consell de Cent (a toney cross street of Gràcia that is often the scene of high-society vernissages) gather to discuss the latest works of such Barcelona artists as Miguel Barceló. An institute for the living giant of Catalan art, Antoni Tàpies, has just opened on the nearby Carrer d'Aragó between Catalunya and Gràcia. The **Fundació Tàpies**, housed in a building designed by Domènech and now adorned by a chaotic wire sculpture that locals have likened to a toilet brush, is open 11:00 A.M. to 8:00 P.M. Tuesday through Saturday and until 3:00 P.M. Sundays.

Although slightly disdainful of their fellow Iberians, the denizens of Rambla de Catalunya do not take themselves too seriously: At the eastern end of the mile-long promenade, a statue of a bull doing a passable imitation of Rodin's *The Thinker* surveys the scene; at its Diagonal end a horse in a "playmate" posture lounges suggestively on a pedestal. At the base of the latter, a discreet plaque embedded in the sidewalk carries a manifesto in Catalan and English for the continued exercise of freedom of expression.

NORTHWEST OF THE PASSEIG DE GRACIA

Beyond Avinguda de la Diagonal a few blocks to the northwest, the lure of Modernist architecture takes hold once again. The turrets and spires of Puig's **Casa Terrades**, popularly known as Casa de les Punxes (House of the Spikes), at the corner of the Diagonal and Carrer del Rosselló, foreshadows the gigantic delirium to be found half a mile or so distant: Gaudí's **Templo Expiatorio de la Sagrada Família** (Expiatory Temple of the Holy Family). By walking the few blocks north of the Diagonal to the famous structure, either along Rosselló or Provença, you get a good sense of Barcelona's enduring legacy of Modernist touches: wrought-iron balconies, curved window bays, and colorful casements. Although the neighborhood becomes distinctly less affluent than the area around Passeig de Gràcia, its buildings display ornamentation pleasing to all lovers of Modernism.

The Sagrada Família, begun in 1882, is Barcelona's postcard image to the world. Easily the most ridiculous sight on any cultural grand tour of the Mediterranean, the unfinished sanctuary, with its twin sets of four transept spires rocketing skyward, has earned mixed reviews ever since Gaudí's death in 1926 left the cathedral builders bereft of blueprints. In his later years, the great Modernist architect preferred to work in the mysticism of improvisation, thus leaving few firm indications of how he wanted construction to continue— except for a planned, but as yet unstarted, central spire that would point a whopping 500 feet into the air.

Lovers of vertigo can console themselves by scrambling on perilous walkways across the void between the wildly decorated bell towers, even if walking around the structure remains the most surefooted way to be flabbergasted. Although Orwell proclaimed the Sagrada Família "one of the most hideous buildings in the world," indulgent opinion usually sides with contemporary French journalist Paul-Jean Franceschini, who dubbed the church "Our Lady of the Smurfs." For those hooked on the excess of Modernist buildings, further enjoyment lies down Avinguda de Gaudí, which runs northwest from the Sagrada Família to the **Hospital de Sant Pau**. The latter, executed by Domènech, is remarkably multicolored and decorative, although this may escape notice after the numbing sight at the other end of the avenue.

Montjuïc and the Hills

MONTJUIC

Montjuïc—the hill "of Jove" or "of the Jews," depending on whose etymology you accept—dominates the southern quarter of the city and overlooks the harbor from a commanding height. The set piece for a burst of Barcelona-boosting, the hill played host to the successful World's Fair of 1929. That event gave the wooded prominence a clutch of varied attractions, which became even more eclectic after the 1992 Olympics passed this way. Unlike the old city it rises above, Montjuïc is verdant, calm, and, in some places, majestic. It is also home to the best art galleries in Catalonia.

Not that this could be guessed from the unfortunately pompous main approach to the hill. This ceremonial entrance begins at the Plaça de Espanya, a roaring traffic circle with a flame-topped Neo-Baroque fountain in its middle. The bombast continues with two tall red-brick campaniles that flank the beginning of the broad Avinguda de la Reina Maria Cristina, which leads in turn to a grand staircase. (Fortunately, escalators have been installed for tenderfoots.) Here, a series of fountains, the largest of which is the scene of spectacular nighttime sound-and-light shows, usher the visitor up to the Palau Nacional (National Palace). But before making the climb to this uninspiring survivor of the 1929 fair, make a small detour to the right of the central fountain. There, amid the abundant proof of the 1929 organizers' lack of a clear-cut aesthetic vision, stands the elegantly spare **German pavilion**, designed by Mies van der Rohe. Partially hidden by the bunker that served as an office of the Barcelona Olympics committee, the building (reconstructed in 1986) exemplifies what is best in Bauhaus. Hardly anyone visits this minimalist masterpiece, so the solitude necessary to appreciate its spare perfection is almost guaranteed.

Beyond the German pavilion, a hundred yards or so to the south, stands an attraction that contrasts with the cosmopolitan style of Bauhaus and celebrates all things Spanish. Constructed for the 1929 fair, **Poble Espanyol** (Spanish Village) is an amusing hodgepodge of the ersatz: Buildings in various traditional Iberian styles (Andalusian, Castilian, Galician, among others) crowd the narrow streets in an arresting display of diversity. Although it was long derided as a kitschy tourist trap by Barcelona sophisticates, the recent refurbishing of the *poble* and its pleasant outdoor jazz concerts have increased its popularity in recent years. To find out about these concerts—and any other performances in the city—pick up the *Guía del Ocio,* a weekly entertainment gazette available at newsstands.

Farther up the hill, at the top of the monumental staircase, stands the **Palau Nacional**. Despite its unprepossessing appearance, this building houses the spectacular **Museu d'Art de Catalunya**, a treasure house of painting, sculpture, and ceramics from the last 1,000 years. The gallery prides itself on the section devoted to Romanesque art, a breathtaking collection that is the largest of its kind in the world. Scores of Romanesque murals were transferred here from the Catalan countryside as a hedge against theft and deterioration in the early decades of this century, and the resulting procession of rooms with glorious, Byzantine-style devotional work makes up Barcelona's most prestigious museum. This priceless survey of religious art—murals were removed here from remote hermitages in the Catalan Pyrenees—is supplemented by a large collection of Gothic works, as well as a section devoted to the Renaissance and such masters as El Greco, Velázquez, and Zurbarán. A cultural institution of the first order, the Museu d'Art de Catalunya underwent an extensive renovation program supervised by Gae Aulenti, the innovative Italian architect who transformed a Parisian train station into the Musée d'Orsay.

For lovers of more-contemporary art, the **Fundació Joan Miró** lies farther up the hill past the Palau Nacional. Opened in 1983, this handsome white villa (designed by Catalan Josep Lluís Sert, the architect of the Maeght foundation in St-Paul-de-Vence, France) displays a representative selection of the works of Joan Miró, the Catalan artist especially revered here. Admirably organized, the collection spans all aspects of Miró's long creative life, from his early days in the international avant-garde to his final years as Olympian artist uncowed by the authorities in Madrid. A further honor to Miró can be seen near the foot of Montjuïc, just west of Plaça de Espanya, where a park has been named for him. In it stands *Donna i Ocella* (Woman and Bird), a gigantic and playful work from the artist's later years.

Aside from two small but interesting museums near Fundació Joan Miró—one, the **Museu Arqueològic**, devoted to classical archaeology (with rather uninhibited artwork from the Greco-Roman ruins of Empúries farther up the Costa Brava), the other, the **Museu Etnològic**, to ethnography and temporary anthropological exhibits—this flank of Montjuïc takes on a distinctly populist flavor. A noisy amuse-

ment park draws crowds throughout the year, as does the
Transbordador Aeri, an aerial cable car that sweeps from the
hill and out over the harbor, depositing its fearless passengers in the maritime suburb of Barceloneta (see below). For
a panoramic view of the city that is easier on the nerves, take
the *teleferic,* a more modest aerial cable car, which can be
boarded near the amusement park, 100 yards or so from the
Fundació Miró. It takes sightseers on an aerial excursion
directly over a roller coaster—a curious sensation—and up
to the summit of Montjuïc, which is crowned by a citadel that
now houses a martial museum, **Museu Militar Castell de
Montjuïc**. (If you're averse to cable cars you can always walk
up to the museum.) From the ramparts of this impeccably
restored fortress, all of Barcelona can be seen spreading out
over the coastal plain toward the tall hills in the west—a
view well worth the ascent. Also visible will be the Anella
Olímpica de Monjuïc, the great complex of sporting venues
between the Palau Nacional and the Museu Militar. It was
here that many of the most important competitions of the
1992 Olympics took place.

PARC GUELL
The city's other three hillside vantage points look back
toward the sea from the western side of town. The northern-
most is Parc Güell, a remarkable green space fashioned by
the ever-present Gaudí. (It is best reached by taxi from the
center of town or, more appropriately, from the Sagrada
Família.) Although originally commissioned to create a sub-
division of Modernist houses, Gaudí completed only two
characteristically striking—that is, weird—pavilions before
financing for the project fell through. Still, his original notions of landscaping remain: serpentine walkways supported
by columns at seemingly impossible angles, and a central
plaza—or *mirador* (lookout)—that is encircled by a magnificent, undulating bench decorated with broken tiles and
ceramics. A perennial Barcelona favorite, Parc Güell is
Gaudí's most user-friendly contribution to the city he loved.
In the architect's house, **Casa Museu Gaudí**, to the north of
the *mirador,* his curvilinear design for furniture and fixtures
can be seen in all its glory.

TIBIDABO
The most distant—and tallest—lookout over Barcelona is
the mountain of Tibidabo, which looms more than 1,500 feet
over the northern and western reaches of the city. To reach it
from Plaça de Catalunya take the subway to Avinguda del
Tibidabo, then the tramway through a neighborhood of
fanciful villas to the funicular, which runs up the wooded
slopes to the summit. (You can drive up—just head up

Carrer de Balmes and follow the signs—but that isn't nearly as much fun.) Adorned by an amusement park and a large, if graceless, church erected by a 19th-century Catalan saint, Joan Bosco, Tibidabo nonetheless takes its name from words attributed to the devil in the gospel of Saint Matthew: "Haec omnia tibi dabo si cades adoraberis me" ("All this I will give to you if you will but adore me"). Scan the mountains to the northwest for the monastery of Montserrat (see the Catalonia chapter), and, of course, look to the east for a commanding view of the city and the Mediterranean.

MONESTIR DE PEDRALBES

The last of Barcelona's scattered hill sights stands at the foot of Sierra del Collcerola, near the university district at the southwestern end of Avinguda de la Diagonal. The Monestir de Pedralbes is a highlight for any visitor interested in the art and architecture of the High Middle Ages. Best reached by taxi or by subway to Reina Elisenda station, the monastery is a well-preserved reminder of 14th-century spirituality. Among its finer elements: a vaulted chapter house, a three-story cloister, and an ornate chapel with beautiful stained glass windows. About 80 works from the fabulous Thyssen-Bornemisza art collection (see the Madrid chapter) are to be installed in the monastery in the near, though indeterminate, future. The impressive ceramics collection formerly housed in the Palau Nacional on Montjuïc is now at the **Palau de Pedralbes**, on the Diagonal. The monastery is open to the public 9:30 A.M. to 2:00 P.M., Tuesday to Sunday.

To end a visit to this section of the city, it is best to walk down to the Diagonal (where you can catch a taxi) by the Avinguda de Pedralbes. There, at the bottom on the right, stands yet another photogenic Gaudí creation: a fanciful wrought-iron gate in the shape of a dragon.

The Waterfront and
the Parc de la Ciutadella

In recent years Barcelona has been trying to repair an injustice in its urban planning: the neglect of its waterfront. Not that the port is idle—it is, in fact, one of the busiest facilities on the Mediterranean and the most active harbor in Spain. However, the citizenry of Barcelona has traditionally been denied the advantages of the city's seaside location. Once the foot of Las Ramblas was reached, the roar of trucks and the bustle of docks yielded no quarter to the pleasure seeker.

This has changed slightly: **Reials Drassanes Museu Marí-**

tim (the maritime museum) is no longer the city's best-kept secret. Housed in the most extensive medieval shipyard in Europe, just south of the Columbus monument at the waterfront end of Las Ramblas, Drassanes's magnificent vaulted halls are filled with replicas of ships that were once the pride of Barcelona. Special attention is showered on Roger de Flor, the 14th-century pirate-envoy whose tales of official banditry are relished in Catalonia with the same sly pride Englishmen reserve for Francis Drake. Flor, an adventurer who responded to Byzantium's appeals for help, ended up subduing Athens, Sardinia, and other Mediterranean lands, much to the delight and profit of the canny merchants on the Consell de Cent. Also given a place of honor are Barcelona shipwrights, who built over half the fleet that defeated the Turks at Lepanto in 1571 (the museum houses a full-size replica, glorious decoration and all, of *La Real,* the galley of Don Juan of Asturias), and Amerigo Vespucci's map of the New World.

A more far-reaching event is commemorated in the harbor across the street from Drassanes. Moored permanently at the wharf is a full-scale replica of Christopher Columbus's *Santa María.* From the wharf here, two small tour boats—called *golondrinas* (gulls)—depart every 15 minutes for a brief cruise to the end of the long breakwater that protects the central harbor of Barcelona. There is admittedly little to see on this short tour, but it is a pleasant respite from the heat and noise of the city. You can immediately pick out local residents on the cruise: Their laps are weighed down by radios and cassette players prudently removed from their cars.

Other than this flutter of history and tourism by the seaside, the waterfront of Barcelona offers few amenities to the visitor. As part of the pre-Olympic cleanup, a stretch of dockside was covered with paving stones and scattered with park benches, and Passeig de Colom, the central section of the busy coastal roadway, now runs partially below ground level, although the thunder of traffic can still be heard. A couple of restaurants (of particular interest is the **Gambrinus**—look for the giant crayfish on its roof) have been built above the highway.

BARCELONETA

Nearby, east of the old town, stands a far quieter haven, the seaside suburb of Barceloneta. In this triangular grid of narrow streets, the only sound likely to be heard is the occasional domestic spat wafting out of colorfully painted windows hung with the morning's wash. The antithesis of the Eixample, downmarket Barceloneta nonetheless used to hum with passing BMWs and Mercedes at dusk, when its excellent seafood restaurants opened for business. Most of these, unfortunately, were leveled in the spring of 1991, as part of a controversial move to clean up Barceloneta and create an upscale corniche. Citizen groups protested and the Olympic steamroller stopped. Only a handful of restaurants remain; still, the sea breezes on the new corniche (on the northern side of Barceloneta) offer a welcome respite from pollution in the city. Don't expect to be enchanted by a beautiful maritime scene, though: As in much of Barcelona, the only nature worth observing is of the human variety. (The only view worth noting is to the north, where the hotels and residences of the Olympic village stand.)

PARC DE LA CIUTADELLA

There is some beauty to be seen in the neighboring Parc de la Ciutadella, where a botanical garden and a zoo long ago replaced the citadel that gave the park its name. That fortification, bankrolled by a vengeful Philip V to make sure the anti-Catalan decrees of his Nova Planta were enforced, was built at the expense of an old quarter that once stood on the spot (Barceloneta was constructed to house the displaced). In the 19th century the city received authorization to pull down the hated symbol of Madrid rule. The World's Fair of 1888, held in the park, became a matter of civic pride, giving the people of Barcelona a chance to let other countries know of their city's eagerness to set foot on the world stage. (The occasion was not unlike the 1992 Olympics.) The Arc de Triomf (arch of triumph), celebrating victories as yet unrecorded, was duly erected on the boulevard approaching the park from the Eixample. The other vestige of that fair, apart from the park itself, is the pavilion that now houses a modest zoological museum. Far more attractive to the contemplative visitor, though, is the museum's immediate neighbor, a tranquil **conservatory**, which can be stunningly beautiful when the late afternoon light filters through the slatted roof onto the tropical vegetation within. At the eastern end of the park there is also a zoo.

Those interested in artistic development in turn-of-the-century Barcelona can visit an admirable small art museum nearby. It shares a building with the Catalan parliament. Although the parliament—the deliberative body of the Generalitat—has made noises (in the self-important manner of legislators and bureaucrats the world over) about evicting its cultural companion, the **Museu d'Art Modern** has renewed its lease in the center of Parc de la Ciutadella for the next few years at least. Its collections, which display the work of Catalan artists of the last 150 years, take on an international flavor in the rooms given over to the Barcelona bohemians of the 1890s. The portraits executed by Ramón Casas—particularly of Erik Satie in Montmartre and a very young Pablo Picasso—are touching reminders of a long-vanished avant-garde.

The Olympic Hangover

In winning, planning, and staging the 1992 Summer Olympics, Barcelona set itself a challenge. Not only would the city show itself off to the world, but it would also renew and rebuild its wide variety of attractions. The former (i.e., hosting the Games) worked out admirably; the latter remains an ongoing construction frenzy. So grandiose have been the urban improvement schemes of the last few years that many citizens doubt their city will be able to pay for its breathtaking ambitions.

Still, the scope of the projects is impressive, and visitors to Barcelona in the next few years may expect to see: a 250-meter-tall communications tower on the Tibidabo (completed); a renovated Port Vell (the old port at the foot of Las Ramblas) that will include an IMAX panoramic cinema and an aquarium and marine museum; a new conference center on a gigantic pier near the Nova Icària marina; a national theater and music museum on the Plaça de les Glories Catalanes (near the Sagrada Família); a new museum of contemporary art (still in the planning stages); botanical gardens on Montjuïc; twin skyscrapers on the waterfront (completed); and, of course, a new expressway. Along with the new stadia, hotels, and apartment buildings constructed for the Olympic sites, these projects may very well transform Barcelona in just a few years. Ildefons Cerdà, the designer of the Eixample, and Antoni Gaudí, its decorator, have good reason to be pleased with their descendants.

GETTING AROUND

For even the inexperienced traveller, finding one's way around Barcelona is relatively effortless. Those anxious over their unfamiliarity with Catalan needn't worry: It is a Latin-based language, and most of the essential words you will see on signposts and the like have unmistakable cognates in Spanish or French. Few people expect foreigners to speak Catalan—in any event, an ever-growing number of Catalans speak English, and Castilian Spanish is understood by everyone.

Arriving in the City

The airport, El Prat de Llobregat, is located along the coast south of the city, and has been expanded to handle increased passenger traffic. Cab fare to town runs to 1,500 pesetas. An inexpensive rail shuttle (about 200 pesetas), which leaves the airport every 15 minutes for the centrally located Sants train station (west of Plaça de Espanya along Carrer Tarragona), might keep you out of rush-hour traffic, but can be awkward if you're carrying a lot of luggage. From the Sants station it is a 200-peseta cab ride to the hotels near the Plaça de Catalunya and Las Ramblas. The Puente Aéreo is an hourly air-shuttle service between Madrid and Barcelona. No reservations are accepted; tickets may be bought at the airport. In addition to good air and rail connections, Barcelona can be reached—or left—by sea: Ferries, which leave from the port near the Columbus monument, link it to the Balearic Islands and a few French ports of call.

Public Transportation

Public transit in Barcelona is cheap and efficient. Tickets for both bus and subway may be purchased at kiosks and in banks. As the Eixample is sinfully easy to understand, there is no difficulty in determining bus routes from even the most cursory glance at a map. (You won't need—or be able to find—a bus in the cramped old town.) The subway, which has six lines (two of which are tram lines), is just as effortless to master. The lines are color-coded and named for their termini. A "T-2" ticket, good for ten rides, can be picked up in any station for about 560 pesetas. Call for more information about public transit; Tel: (9-3) 412-0000. The central tourist office, always useful for answering questions, is located at Gran Via de les Corts Catalanes 658, near the Carrer de Pau Clarís; Tel: (9-3) 301-7443.

Taxis

The simplest way to get around town is by taxi. Barcelona has a large fleet, which makes for very short waits for a cab. Fares are very low—300 to 400 pesetas for most rides—by New York or London standards. Distinctively black and yellow, the cabs display a green light that flashes "*lliure*" (*libre,* in Castilian) when looking for customers.

City Driving

Driving in Barcelona is much like the city itself: schizophrenic. The old town is a nightmare; the Eixample, a dream. In the latter, speeding does not seem to constitute an infraction. If you are looking for an unfamiliar street from one of the bigger avenues (for example, the Diagonal), it's best to drive down the sedate service lanes at the sides. Catalans on their broad boulevards do not suffer tentative drivers gladly. The result is a horn-honking symphony during peak hours. Sadly, like many other car-crazy cities in Spain, Barcelona is frequently blanketed in smog.

When walking around Barcelona, take care to secure cameras, purses, and wallets. Although it is not the den of thieves other Spaniards would have you believe, the city is far from angelic. Especially in the old town near the port, keep your wits about you.

ACCOMMODATIONS

The hotel rates listed below are projected rates for 1994, for double room, double occupancy, in pesetas. We strongly recommend that you confirm the price when making reservations.

The telephone area code for Barcelona is 9-3; when dialing from outside the country, drop the 9.

Las Ramblas and Barri Gòtic Area

Most hotels in the old Las Ramblas–Barri Gòtic area are conveniently sited for walking in this colorful part of town. Hotels here tend to be old, but the renovation frenzy that swept the city before the 1992 Olympics has transformed many of them completely.

A favorite of many visitors to the Barri Gòtic is the ► Hotel Colón, whose rooms have tiny balconies overlooking the cathedral, a great place to position yourself for watching the *sardana* danced in the cathedral plaza (be sure to request a room in the front.) The Colón's concierges are superior. The lounge off the lobby is a pleasant spot for tea or a drink.

Avinguda de la Catedral 7, 08002 Barcelona. Tel: 301-1404; Fax: 317-2915; in U.S., Tel: (212) 686-9213; Fax: (212) 686-0271. 37,000 pts.

Just west of the Colón is its modest relation, ► **Regencia Colón**, a useful backup choice. It lacks the closeup cathedral views, but is just a block away from the Barri Gòtic. The first hotel built in Barcelona after World War II, it isn't yet showing its age: Accoutrements have a handcrafted simplicity and are well maintained. It's peaceful at night, attractive in a low-key way, and a relative bargain.

Carrer Sagristans 13, 08002 Barcelona. Tel: 318-9858; Fax: 317-2822. 12,700 pts.

Along the lower Ramblas there are many modestly priced hotels, with much to be modest about. Others, though, were spruced up and substantially improved for the Olympics. One such choice is the ► **Hotel Oriente**, facing the entrance to the Plaça Reial. The Oriente dates back to the mid-19th century, and its handsome public rooms evoke a bygone era. Guest rooms are plain and simple. The location is handy by day but somewhat seedy at night.

Las Ramblas 45–47, 08002 Barcelona. Tel: 302-2558; Fax: 412-3819. 14,000 pts.

Also worth your attention on Las Ramblas is the beautiful,

all-new ▶ **Le Meridien Barcelona,** a couple of blocks east of Plaça de Catalunya between Carrers Pintor Fortuny and Elisabets. Formerly the rather seedy Hotel Manila and then a Ramada property, this is now a modern top-rated citadel of comfort in an extremely handy location.

Las Ramblas 111, 08002 Barcelona. Tel: 318-6200; Fax: 301-7776. 32,000 pts.

For simple digs in a convenient location, you might also consider ▶ **Hotel Suizo,** just off busy (and noisy) Via Laietana in the Barri Gòtic. Rooms are clean, modest, well kept, and moderately priced; the lounge and bar are comfortable.

Plaça del Angel 12, 08002 Barcelona. Tel: 315-4111; Fax: 315-3819. 13,500 pts.

The Eixample Area

The fashionable residential and shopping streets between Gran Via de les Corts Catalanes and Avinguda de la Diagonal have a number of hotels, giving visitors easy access to many of the city's best restaurants and shops, with the Barri Gòtic still within walking distance.

The luxurious ▶ **Hotel Ritz** looks as it must have back in 1919 when it was built in the grand Belle Epoque style, with an exuberance of crystal chandeliers, handsome carpeting, gilded mirrors, and a plethora of fresh flowers. Rooms are spacious, and many have marble fireplaces and Roman-style baths decorated with Sevillian tiles. The hotel's location on the Gran Via de les Corts Catalanes (between Carrers Lluria and Bruc), one of the busiest thoroughfares in town, puts you within an easy walk of both the Barri Gòtic and the shopping district (and makes you grateful for the double-glazed windows). There's now a health and fitness center as well as a garden restaurant, a patio bar, a piano hall for afternoon tea, and the first-rate **Diana** restaurant. The staff—from top to bottom—is obliging and well trained, and the concierges are among the best in the business. The Ritz is a member of Leading Hotels of the World.

Gran Via de les Corts Catalanes 668, 08010 Barcelona. Tel: 318-5200; Fax: 318-0148. 43,000 pts.

A block away, on the corner of the Gran Via and Carrer Bruc, is the ▶ **Gran Hotel Havana,** sparklingly renovated from a modest hotel into a real beauty. While lacking the tradition of the Ritz, it is an acceptable modern alternative. The lounge and lobby bar are compact, and the interior atrium is reminiscent of a Hyatt hotel. But guest rooms are ample enough and handsomely appointed. Many have terraces large enough for sunbathing and for dining alfresco on room service. Double-glazed windows totally erase the avenue noise. English-speaking staff members are quite helpful.

Gran Via de les Corts Catalanes 647, 08010 Barcelona. Tel: 412-1115; Fax: 412-2611. 29,000 pts.

On the same major thoroughfare is the ▶ **Avenida Palace**, around the corner from Passeig de Gràcia—a good location for anyone with shopping in mind. Built after World War II but in the grand prewar manner, with a sweeping double staircase, marble columns, and antique-style furniture, the hotel seems oddly pretentious, yet its guest rooms are sizable and comfortable, and the location is prime.

Gran Via de les Corts Catalanes 605, 08007 Barcelona. Tel: 301-9600; Fax: 318-1234. 27,200 pts.

A real find in this same area is the ▶ **Hotel Gran Via**, on the Gran Via between Passeig de Gràcia and Carrer de Pau Clarís. Housed in a former palace dating to the 19th century with an Art Nouveau staircase, the hotel has great ambience. It is also handy to both the Barri Gòtic for sightseeing and the Eixample for shopping.

Gran Via de les Corts Catalanes 642, 08007 Barcelona. Tel: 318-1900; Fax: 318-9997. 11,500 pts.

Also convenient for both shopping and sightseeing is the ▶ **Diplomatic**, which makes up in comfort what it lacks in charm. Its color-coordinated guest rooms are more attractive than the rather ostentatious glass-and-marble lobby. The location, just two blocks north of the Gran Via at Carrer Consell de Cent, is another winner, though.

Carrer de Pau Clarís 122, 08009 Barcelona. Tel: 317-3100; Fax: 318-6531. 25,000 pts.

The ▶ **Regente**, on Rambla de Catalunya at the corner of Carrer de València, is handy to both the old quarter and the bustling Eixample district. The Regente has a certain depth of character, which so many Barcelona hotels lack, no matter what the category. Public areas have a Modernist flavor, in keeping with the city's landmarks. This is no accident; the building was a private mansion from 1895 to 1964. Rooms are small, with minute balconies. There's also a pint-size rooftop with swimming pool and sun deck.

Rambla de Catalunya 76, 08008 Barcelona. Tel: 215-2570; Fax: 487-3227. 22,000 pts.

On the lively shopping street of Passeig de Gràcia, between Carrers de Mallorca and Provença, is the extremely elegant ▶ **Hotel Condes de Barcelona**, a fin-de-siècle mansion turned into a 100-room hotel. Many of the building's Modernist touches have been saved. Guest rooms are stylishly furnished, ample, and have all the usual amenities; public areas are starkly simple and modish.

Passeig de Gràcia 75, 08008 Barcelona. Tel: 487-3737; Fax: 216-0835; in U.S., Tel: (212) 686-9213; Fax: (212) 686-0271. 29,000 pts.

Another comfortable and attractive hotel, also in the center of shopping action on the busy corner of Carrer de València and Passeig de Gràcia (which might be thought of as Barcelona's equivalent of New York City's Fifth Avenue), is the ▶ **Majestic**. Despite the noisy location, double-glazed windows keep the ample front guest rooms peaceful (the back rooms are drab). A full range of amenities, including attractive furnishings and a rooftop pool, make this hostelry a considerable value.

Passeig de Gràcia 70, 08008 Barcelona. Tel: 488-1717; Fax: 488-1880. 24,900 pts.

▶ **NH Gran Hotel Calderón**, on Rambla de Catalunya between Gran Via de les Corts Catalanes and Carrer de la Diputació, couldn't be more convenient. It's also a good value for its spacious, smartly furnished, well-lit rooms; a handsome dining room with a terrific breakfast buffet; a comfortable bar; and a pool and sun terrace.

Rambla de Catalunya 26, 08007 Barcelona. Tel: 301-0000; Fax: 317-3157. 25,500 pts.

The Diagonal

This busy thoroughfare that bisects Barcelona from northeast to southwest has its share of hotels, most of which are within a short taxi ride of the city's major sights. The Diagonal has many of Barcelona's best shops and is handy to many of the better restaurants.

The first of the hotels built for the Olympics was the deluxe 290-room ▶ **Barcelona Hilton**, a silvery high rise on the Diagonal between Carrers Gandesa and Numància. Look for all the usual Hilton amenities, plus executive floors, a business center, a health club, a drugstore, and an elegant dining room with a fountain and a wall of gushing water at one end.

Avinguda de la Diagonal 589–591, 08014 Barcelona. Tel: 419-2233; Fax: 419-5003; in U.S., Tel: (800) 445-8667. 44,500 pts.

A small hotel with personality is the ▶ **Derby**, on a short, quiet, tree-shaded, semi-residential street between the Diagonal and Avinguda de Sarrià, just southwest of the Plaça Francesc Macià. Rooms are modern, well designed, and fully equipped, with a pleasing coordinated look. A few rooms on the top floor have front and rear terraces. Unlike so many Barcelona hotels, the Derby is contemporary in design without being garish. The lounge is an attractive room with comfortable chairs and original prints on the walls. An English-style pub offers Guinness on tap, along with a selection of *tapas*.

Carrer Loreto 21, 08029 Barcelona. Tel: 322-3215; Fax: 410-0862. 22,000 pts.

The comfortable ▶ **Presidente**, handily located on the

Diagonal at the corner of Carrer Muntaner, is an efficient, well-run, if somewhat characterless hotel. This modern high rise is equipped with all the essentials, though you might not think so if you judged only by the small lobby. A lounge, one flight up, offers good overviews of the busy street. The spacious guest rooms are well lighted, with attractive color-coordinated linens and decor, and there's even a swimming pool.

Avinguda de la Diagonal 570, 08021 Barcelona. Tel: 200-2111; Fax: 209-5106. 28,750 pts.

A moderately priced hotel in this area is a find indeed, and the somewhat staid ▶ **Hotel Wilson**, situated where Carrer Muntaner crosses the Diagonal (across from the Presidente), is one such place. Attractive guest rooms add to the value of this hotel.

Avinguda de la Diagonal 568, 08021 Barcelona. Tel: 209-2511; Fax: 200-8370. 14,000 pts.

Another good value is ▶ **Hotel Covadonga**, on the Diagonal just south of Plaça Francesc Macià. Fairly standard, as local hotels go, this has sizable, adequately furnished (if unexciting) rooms and a fine location.

Avinguda de la Diagonal 596, 08021 Barcelona. Tel: 209-5511; Fax: 209-5833. 11,400 pts.

One block east of the Diagonal is ▶ **Hotel Astoria**, on Carrer París between Carrers d'Aribau and d'Enric Granados. Another reasonably priced hotel, this one is comfortable and quiet with great city views from its balconies.

Carrer París 203, 08036 Barcelona. Tel: 209-8311; Fax: 202-3008. 15,500 pts.

—Patricia Brooks

DINING

Catalans have a reputation for no-nonsense hard work. But you have only to watch them in their local restaurants to discover that they play hard, too. And the prevalence of excellent restaurants in Barcelona and throughout Catalonia is argument enough that Catalans recognize the good life when they see it and can afford to enjoy it.

The Cuisine

Barcelona's geography has helped define its cuisine, which is best described as a marriage between the fruits and harvest of the southern Mediterranean landscape (tomatoes, garlic, mushrooms, olives, onions, sweet red peppers, rice, olive oil, and aromatic herbs) and the robust foods of the Pyrenees (game, freshwater fish from mountain streams, and wild mushrooms). The French are comfortable dining in Barcelona, as well they might be: It evokes memories of Provence.

Today's Catalan cooking divides fairly easily into two styles, traditional and *nueva cocina,* both owing more than a nod to France. An easy hand with seafood and fresh produce has given Catalan cooks a natural affinity for the best elements of *nouvelle cuisine* Catalan-style. Barcelona chefs often combine the techniques and ingredients of their classical cuisine with the light touch and "painterly" arrangements of the nouvelle style.

There are a few dishes that are constants—you'll find them in traditional restaurants and, with some modern adaptations, in the *nueva cocina* places as well. Rice is the base for many dishes, such as *paella a la Parellada* (made with deboned fish, shellfish, chicken, and meat). Other dishes to look for are *zarzuela marinera* (a succulent fish stew) and its variation, *opera,* in which half a lobster is added; *suquet de peix,* a sort of bouillabaise; and *brandada de bacalao* (salt cod with truffles). And be sure to sample Catalan sausages—*butifarra, salchichón,* and *longaniza,* among others—which are delicious just grilled. At many restaurants a lagniappe of *pa amb tomaquet* (toasted bread slices brushed with fresh tomato, garlic, olive oil, and salt) is served before the first course.

Dining Customs

People dine late in Barcelona, as they do in Madrid. Dinner begins generally at 9:30 P.M. or as late as 10:30 or 11:00 P.M. Lunch begins no earlier than 2:00 P.M., and may last until 4:30 or 5:00 P.M., especially at the more fashionable restaurants.

As in most cities, you can eat heartily but relatively inexpensively in Barcelona at rustic, publike neighborhood eateries, but elegant restaurants are not cheap. Barcelona restaurants tend to follow one of two divergent paths: They are either cheerfully folkloric, with whitewashed walls, lots of ceramic tiles, and rows of garlic and peppers strung from walls, or smoothly sophisticated and stylishly understated as comparable establishments in New York, London, or Paris. Their common denominator is excellent service, where a warm welcome is nothing extra, just part of a flawless professionalism. As a broad rule, the more folkloric and traditional the place, the more moderate the price.

Advance reservations are recommended for most restaurants. Barcelona's telephone area code is 9-3; drop the 9 if you are calling from outside the country.

Stylish and/or Nueva Cocina Catalana Restaurants

As in Madrid, there has been a burst of new restaurant openings in Barcelona over the past ten years. But in the rush to try the new, restaurant-goers have sometimes overlooked the tried-and-true reliables.

That may be why **Restaurante Reno**, a landmark at Carrer de Tuset 27 (an extension of Carrer d'Enric Granados, just west of the Diagonal), now offers a dual menu, with both French and *nueva cocina catalana* dishes. Reno's owner, José Juliá Bertrán, is Catalan-born, and his consistently high standards, like his father's before him, make this restaurant a pleasure to visit and return to. It's a favorite lunch place for businessmen, who undoubtedly feel at home in the handsome, wood-paneled setting so reminiscent of a private club. Try the *cazuelita de arroz con chipirones,* a light version of *paella* made with squid, or perhaps sole in puff pastry with sauce *aurore.* In keeping with the overall excellence, the restaurant also has a fine selection of Spanish and French wines. Tel: 200-9129.

Indisputably one of the city's best restaurants is **Neichel**, at Avinguda de Pedralbes 16, on the ground floor of an apartment complex near the Pedralbes monastery (north of the Diagonal between Plaça de Pio XII and Passeig de Manuel Girona). It should certainly be on any serious diner's short list of places to try in Barcelona. Alsatian chef-owner Jean-Luis Neichel, who was once chef at the excellent Hacienda el Bulli in the village of Roses on the Costa Brava, walks a delicate line between classic cooking and nouvelle presentations. His touch is as light and understated as his restaurant's quietly elegant, fresh-flower-accented pastel decor. The duck in a cassis and wild mushroom sauce is memorable, but try the prix fixe *menú de degustación* (tasting menu) to get a true sampling of Neichel's skills. And don't miss dessert, one of his hallmarks. Tel: 203-8408.

New and exquisite is **El Tragaluz**, tucked into a fashionable alley passage, Passatge de la Concepció 5, that cuts through from Passeig de Gràcia to Rambla de Catalunya (between Carrer de Provença and Carrer del Rosselló). The decor in this old mansion-turned-restaurant is stunning: high-tech architecture set off by charming wall paintings in the early Picasso style. The food of Belgian chef Pieter van de Lint marries Catalonia's finest ingredients with nouvelle techniques. There is a six-course *menú de degustación* and many à la carte dishes are superb, such as *cèps rebozados y flan de celerí con su pequeña ensalada* (deep-fried cèpes mushrooms with celery flan and a wild mushroom salad) and *bonito mi-cuit con escabeche de rossinyols* (slices of bonito tuna with Belgian endive and a pickled salad of red peppers, capers, and onion). El Tragaluz has the makings of becoming one of Barcelona's premiere restaurants. Tel: 487-0196.

Agut d'Avignon, an urbane Catalan restaurant located on five different levels in a hard-to-find cul-de-sac at Carrer de la Trinitat 3 (just east of Carrer de Ferran, on the corner of

Carrer d'Avinyó in the Barri Gòtic), is deceptive. It looks traditional, with its whitewashed walls, huge, exposed overhead beams, and rush-seated ladder-back chairs, but the rusticity has a sophisticated edge that makes it popular with local socialites and politicos. The small menu is unusual, with many dishes following the Catalan custom of combining meat or fowl with fruit, such as goose with pears or duck with figs. The fish and game dishes are especially good: mussels in a garlic cream sauce as a starter, trout Navarra-style stuffed with ham, rabbit simmered with red pepper and tomatoes. Your meal might end with a dessert of *fresas del bosque* (tiny wild strawberries) with whipped cream or of *lionesas* (little cream puffs with chocolate sauce). The wine list is heavily Spanish, with almost every wine-producing area in Spain represented. Pricey it is, as all the deluxe Barcelona restaurants are, but worth every peseta. Tel: 302-6034.

A currently popular restaurant is **Senyor Parellada**, at Carrer Argentería 37 (Argentería runs east out of Plaça del Angel, on the north side of the Barri Gòtic), which is frequented by arty upscale professionals. The capacious dining room with a skylit atrium is behind a handsome bar that has a gleaming copper-topped counter. The specialty here is seafood (this is a good place to try the Catalan *suquet de peix*), but the *xai* (baby lamb roasted with a whole garlic bulb) and veal stew are delicious, too. Tel: 315-4010.

A restaurant that's much touted in fashionable Barcelona circles and frequented by local socialites, politicians, and theater people is **Jaume de Provença**, Carrer de Provença 88 (where Provença crosses Rocafort, one block north of the Sants train station). Chef-owner Jaume Bargués adds a touch of French expertise to his *nueva cocina* dishes. His isn't flashy cooking, but it's very good, noticeably in such dishes as asparagus mousse (made with tender stalks of fresh baby asparagus) in a mousseline sauce, spinach cannelloni in Champagne sauce, turbot with prawns and saffron, and sole in a dry vermouth sauce. Not surprisingly, prices are high, but the service in the restaurant's small dining rooms and alcoves is usually flawless. A *menú de degustación* is available and is a good way to sample the restaurant's range. The fine wine list includes both Spanish and French selections. Tel: 430-0029.

Modernismo is the look at the superb **Vía Veneto**, Carrer de Ganduxer 10 (west of Plaça de Sant Gregori Taumaturg, above the Diagonal), with its color-coordinated dark-brown leather banquettes, *café au lait* wood paneling and columns, and even elegant Art Nouveau–design plates. Fortunately, the food achieves the same high standard. Specialties, a blend of French and country-style Catalan, include mussels with spinach purée; hake in Champagne sauce; fresh-pasta lasagne with mushrooms, foie gras, and basil; and roasted red peppers stuffed with seafood in a subtle garlic sauce. The four-course tasting menu is a fine value. There is a decent wine list, and the wine steward is unusually friendly and helpful. Tel: 200-7024.

Popular **Florián**, at Carrer Bertrand i Serra 20 (at the corner of Carrer Mandri, which runs one block north of Carrer de Ganduxer), melds Catalan, French, and Italian influences, creating a delectable selection of original dishes. It's a small place, but very popular because of the freshness of ingredients and the light, dexterous variations on familiar themes, as in the preparation of *angulas* (baby eels) and endive salad, hake with seaweed sauce, and tripe with *chorizo* (sausage). A well-chosen wine list tilts toward Rioja *reservas* and French selections. Tel: 212-4627.

Since one of the Costa Brava's best restaurants, **Eldorado Petit**, took up residence in Barcelona several years ago, it has more than held its own in this city. It is located in a handsome fin-de-siècle house in a residential area in western Barcelona, at Carrer Dolors Monserdá 51 (west of Passeig de la Bonanova and north of the Monestir de Pedralbes). The menu includes a panoply of wonderful traditional Catalan dishes with *nueva cocina* inventions, such as turbot in sea-urchin sauce or duck breast in vinegar-scallion sauce. Eldorado has a way with sauces and lavish desserts, and its wine cellar is well stocked. While you won't quite need a second mortgage to finance a meal here, as you might in some of Barcelona's other fashionable restaurants, it is pricey. Tel: 204-5153.

An establishment familiar to diners in Seville and Madrid is **La Dorada**, the excellent upscale Andalusian seafood house, whose Barcelona branch is at Travessera de Gràcia 44–46, between Carrers Muntaner and d'Aribau (one block west of the Diagonal). This is the place to enjoy Galician *angulas,* as well as the famous fried fish dishes of the south, among many regional marine specialties. Seafood from other regions is flown in by private plane daily. Just get your bank loan and sally forth. Tel: 200-6322.

An "in" place for shellfish is **Botafumeiro**, located in a Modernist building at Gran de Gràcia 81 (the western extension of Passeig de Gràcia), between Carrers Santa Eugenia and l'Oreneta del Cigne. Fish tanks in the entrance hall (the dining room is in the rear) tell it all: This stylish, pricey place where King Juan Carlos has been spotted specializes in seaworthy Galician dishes, such as anglerfish (*rape*) in fresh tomato sauce. The *empanadas* (meat pies) and grilled *setas* (mushrooms) are tasty, too. Tel: 218-4230.

Traditional Catalan and Other Regional Cuisine

One of the best traditional establishments in Barcelona is **Set Portes** (Seven Doors), located very near the waterfront at Passeig d'Isabel II 14 (near the entrance to the Barceloneta waterfront quarter). Year in, year out, it keeps its homey flavor and family atmosphere. In a long rambling building, its various dining rooms, with dark wood banquettes (some with small brass plaques on the back naming celebrities— Montserrat Caballé, Juan Carlos I—who have dined here), blue-and-white-tile wall paneling, and mirrors, create a pleasant backdrop for the many fine seafood standards. Try the sailor's soup, spinach fritters, *paella* fixed three different ways, *zarzuela,* or *suquet de peix.* For dessert, this might be the place to try a *crema catalana,* a richer, sweeter, eggier version of *crème caramel.* Prices are moderate for such reliable Catalan consistency. Yes, tourists come here, but so do locals, in loving twosomes or huge family outings, and the decibel level can get high at peak times. It's quieter at night and starts serving early by Barcelona standards—but taxi here. Tel: 319-3033.

Simpler, but kind of funky in its perverse plainness, is **Casa Costa,** with three floors facing the water at Carrer Balvard 125 (at Platja Sant Miguel), in Barceloneta. Chic Catalans enjoy the inverse snobbery of eating the freshest possible fish in the minimalist surroundings. The grilled shrimp with *romescu* sauce (a Tarragona specialty made with tomatoes, chili peppers, garlic, hazelnuts, and olive oil) is a house specialty and is especially tasty. Otherwise, go with the simple grilled fish. Lunch, particularly on Sundays, is the busiest time here. Tel: 319-5028.

Many traditional restaurants border the **Barri Xinès** (Chinese quarter) on Carrer Escudellers. The origins of the quarter's name are now obscure, but this run-down area east of Escudellers down to Passeig de Colom has long been seedy. It has become so unsavory and unsafe of late (because of purse-snatching) that it is best visited by cab.

A traditional and moderately priced restaurant in the Barri Xinès is **Los Caracoles** (The Snails), at Carrer Escudellers 14, just east of the lower part of Las Ramblas. It is best visited at lunchtime, as the neighborhood is safer in daylight. The restaurant has been known since 1835 for its snail dishes, *paella,* and *suquet de peix.* There's an overblown stage-set aspect to the cutsey folkloric decor, which is either off-putting or charming, depending on your sensibilities. Tel: 302-3185.

El Túnel, located just west of Passeig de Colom at Carrer Ample 33, is also in Barri Xinès territory. Its once moderate prices have escalated, but the old-time Catalan specialties, fried fish, and cannelloni are still wonderful. This is a long-time local favorite. Tel: 315-2759.

Agut, at Carrer Gignas 16, between Carrers Marquet and Simo Oller, is in the same general neighborhood. It's popular with locals for such traditional dishes as fish soup, codfish mousse, and house-made desserts. Tel: 315-1709.

Another old-timer, known for its reasonable prices and reliable fare, is **Casa Culleretes**, Carrer de Quintana 5 (the entrance is on Carrer Boquería, just off the Rambla dels Caputxins). Despite the celebrity photos lining the walls, Culleretes is a favorite of Barcelona family groups and is the place to sample such Catalan dishes as *zarzuela marinera* or *costillas de cordero* (lamb chops). Tel: 317-6485.

On a day spent roaming the Barri Gòtic, a handy place for a lunch break is **Restaurante del Tinell** (not to be confused with El Túnel, above), Calle Freneria 8, which runs northeast of the cathedral. Nothing fancy, mind you, but in a cheerful, *faux*-folkloric setting—brick floors, exposed-beam ceilings, and wrought-iron chandelier—you can enjoy a simple lunch of grilled sausages or giltfish sautéed with thyme, tomato, garlic, and onion. Service can be slow, but the old quarter grinds to a halt at midday anyway. Tel: 315-4604.

Also in the Barri Gòtic and popular with fast-track government officials is **Café de l'Academia**, Carrer Lledó 1 (a couple of blocks north of Plaça de Sant Jaume). Located in a 16th-century building that was once a stable, this is a moderately priced place for an ample Catalan-style late breakfast or lunch. Tel: 315-0026.

If you want a sea change from Catalan fare, **Guría**, at Carrer de Enamorats 97, in the northern part of the Eixample between Carrers d'Aragó and de València, is a longtime standby for traditional Basque cooking. Look for hake prepared a number of ways, *bacalao* (cod), veal chops, and other familiar northern dishes, along with a decent wine list, heavy on the Riojas. Tel: 253-1038.

Southwest of Las Ramblas, just off Avinguda del Paral·lel, is a local artists' and writers' hangout, **Can Isidre**, at Carrer les Flors 12. Among the imaginative, if pricey, specialties in this chic bistro are *ensalada de marisco* (seafood salad), *bacalao gratinado al perfume de ajos* (codfish au gratin with the essence of garlic), and *mollejas con alcachofas* (sweetbreads with artichokes). There is also a fine wine cellar. King Juan Carlos and Queen Sofía dine here, so don't be fooled by the casual appearance of the place. Tel: 441-1139.

Quick Meals

A pleasant choice for lunch while on Montjuïc is the restaurant in the **Fundació Joan Miró**. The menu is simple—mostly sandwiches and *nueva cocina* terrines—but very tasty, and the views of the city from the sunny terrace add to the enjoyment.

Restaurant Font del Gat, on Passeig de Santa Madrona halfway down Montjuïc, is another delightful lunch or light dinner stop in the area. Sit outside in the courtyard if weather permits, enjoying the grilled fish, *zarzuela,* and other Catalan specialties at this attractive, medium-priced, tree-shaded place. The restaurant is named for a fountain on the site that was designed by Puig i Cadafalch. Tel: 325-3698.

Flash-Flash Tortilleria, west of the Diagonal at Carrer la Granada del Penedès 25, is popular with the fashion and media crowd for its omelets (*tortillas*) and serves as many as 100 different kinds, as well as various salads and even some meat dishes. Tel: 237-0990.

Casa Ramón, at Passeig de Sant Joan Bosco 47 (corner of Carrer de Manuel de Falla, west of the Diagonal), is a rustic delicatessen/grill that serves delicious grilled meats, sausages, and cheeses at moderate prices. Tel: 205-7556. Also serving light lunches, sandwiches, pizzas, and snacks is **Maná Maná**, at Passeig de Gràcia 78 (at Carrer de Mallorca). Tel: 215-6387.

On the fifth floor of **El Corte Inglés** department store, Avinguda de la Diagonal 617, are several restaurants, including a self-service cafeteria. These are handy for shoppers and budget-watchers, though noisy at lunchtime. Another alternative for a light, inexpensive meal is **Treno**, next to the Hotel Cristal at Carrer de la Diputació 257, which serves good pizzas.

Even a Continental breakfast is costly at the city's better hotels. Fortunately, you can walk half a block in any direction and slip into a local bar that serves coffee and croissants. The croissants are especially crisp and tasty at **Cervecería D'Or**, on the corner of Rambla de Catalunya and Avinguda Consell de Cent. An unusual breakfast stop is **Laie**, at Carrer de Pau Clarís 85 (at Carrer Casp), a combination café-bookshop, where you can read as you eat. Laie also serves lunch and afternoon tea. Tel: 302-7310. **Mesón del Café**, at Carrer de la Llibreteria 16 (off Plaça de Sant Jaume in the Barri Gòtic), has excellent coffee and cappuccino. And if you have a yen for *churros* (fried dough; something of a rarity in Barcelona), head for **Pascual**, at Pas Sota de Muralla 7 (east of Via Laietana on the waterfront), which also has superior coffee. For homemade ice cream or a *horchata* (a thick, milky drink tasting of almonds), stop by **Gelateria Italiana Pagliotta**, at Carrer Jaume I in the Barri Gòtic.

Tapas Bars and Xampanyerías

Tapas are not a tradition in Catalan as they are in other parts of Spain, but even so there are many bars where you can enjoy them. They can tide you over until the late mealtime—or can serve as a meal. A distinctive Barcelona tradition is the *xampanyería* (Champagne bar), where the Spanish bubbly wine produced in Catalonia, *cava,* can be sampled by the glass. *Xampanyerías* are usually quite stylish places, where you can nibble *tapas* of smoked fish, patés, cheese, and even sweet tidbits as you sip.

One of the most historic places in the Barri Gòtic for *tapas* and/or a light meal is **Els Quatre Gats** (The Four Cats), set in a Modernist building designed in 1896 by Josep Puig i Cadafalch at Carrer de Montsío 3, west of the cathedral area. Picasso once exhibited in this cozy café; other artists still do. The specialties are Catalan seafood dishes, and the prix fixe meal is a bargain. But what's most special here is the *ambiente* (atmosphere). Tel: 302-4140.

A popular tri-level restaurant, **Les Ostres**, at Carrer de València 267 (near Carrer de Pau Clarís), has a terrific *tapas/cava* bar, where the noshes of choice include the raw bar and fresh seafood selections: oysters, shrimp, octopus, *angulas, berberecho* clams, and many more. Tel: 215-3035.

A favorite stop after a performance at the Palau de la Música Catalana is **La Cava del Palau**, a chic *xampanyería* at Carrer Verdaguer i Callís (a short street between Carrers Sant Pere Més Alt and Sant Pere Mitjà, just northwest of the Barri Gòtic) that starts to jump after 11:00 P.M. and continues well into the morning hours. There are dozens of regional *cavas* to sample, along with a good cheese and snack selection. Tel: 310-0938.

Cozy and casual, with rustic tables and a wide *tapas* selection is **Nou Celler**, a neighborhood *tasca* at Carrer de Princesa 16, not far from the Museu Picasso. Tel: 310-4773. A favorite with university students because of its low prices, range of *tapas* and snacks, and friendly ambience is **Alt Heidelberg** at Ronda Universitat 5 (a block east of the Gran Via de les Corts Catalanes). Tel: 318-1032. And after viewing the Templo Expiatorio de la Sagrada Família, a convenient spot for *tapas* and/or a Catalan lunch is **La Llesca**, at Avinguda de Gaudí 12. Tel: 334-6794.

—Patricia Brooks

CAFES, BARS, NIGHTLIFE

Barcelona has won a formidable reputation among Europeans over the last 15 years as a city that stays alive long into the night. Along with Berlin and—even Catalans now admit—Madrid, Barcelona is a capital of nocturnal adventures, its lively café society switching from dinner to the bars and nightclubs at about midnight.

Las Ramblas

For café life, the most compelling spot is Las Ramblas. At the **Café Bar Zurich** (Plaça de Catalunya) an ever-crowded terrace collects trendies and other people-watchers all year long, making this 1930s establishment a pillar of Catalan lounging. Of the watering holes on Las Ramblas, the most enjoyable are the **Café Viena** (Rambla dels Estudis 70), a turn-of-the-century spot, and the **Café de l'Opéra** (Rambla dels Caputxins 74), unchanged since the heyday of Modernism and Art Nouveau. Nearby, **Ambos Mundos** ranks as the Plaça Reial's best *tapas*-munching and drifter-watching place.

The Waterfront Area

The revitalized waterfront has several chic bar-restaurants, the most popular being **Gamberinus** on the Moll de la Fusta. Easily recognizable by the grinning crayfish on its roof (designed by Javier Mariscal, the same fellow who dreamed up Cobi, the mascot of the 1992 Olympics), it can be a pleasant escape from the enforced sobriety of sightseeing. Farther inland, behind the church of Santa Maria del Mar, the **Passeig del Born** has recently sprouted bars and cafés by the score. Fairly prosperous in comparison to most of its neighborhood, the gentrified Born is peppered with *xampanyerías* and relaxed establishments that peddle everything from the local *horchata de fruta* to such imported elixirs as Guinness and Jack Daniels. **Miramelindo**, as its name suggests, is a particularly good-looking bar on the Born, although a brief stroll up this street is all that's needed to find a spot suitable to your tippling aspirations.

The Eixample

The bars of the Eixample make no claim to being unpretentious. In the past decade a large number of entrepreneurs have waged what could be called the designer bar wars here. Beautifully appointed in keeping with the dictates of minimalist chic, the establishments of the Eixample try to outdo their rivals in wowing the customers. Despite their showiness, they are not frequented only by the hip—there are simply not enough trendy people to go around—but welcome adults of all ages and fashion affiliations. The wisest thing to take along on a late-night expedition to the Eixample is the *Guía del Ocio,* the weekly entertainment guide that faithfully lists the addresses of all the bars in the city. Barhopping from one designer wonderland to the next requires giving exact instructions to successive taxi drivers. (The Eixample is, quite simply, too large to stagger through on foot.)

Nick Havanna (Carrer del Roselló 208), a bar that features a pendulum, banks of videos, and glass partitions, is the dean of Eixample night spots, having launched the unrelenting struggle to be trendier-than-thou. Two blocks away, **Zsa Zsa** (Carrer del Roselló 156) recently won a design award for its unlikely combination of Oriental rugs and glass walls. As in most Barcelona bars, mixed drinks are served with more of an emphasis on drink than mix. Nearby, the **Velvet** (Carrer de Balmes 61) outshines its neighbors in studied 1950s retro-kitsch and peculiar, overdesigned lavatories.

The best bars of the **Avinguda de la Diagonal** continue to draw *pijos* (rich kids) and other assorted Barcelona night owls. **Soho** (at number 612) aims for lovers of antiseptic cool, **Boliche** (number 508) has a bowling alley, and **SiSiSi** (number 442) is for those who like to be tickled by laser beams. All are near the university district, at the southwestern end of the Diagonal.

Other perennials are **La Fira** (Carrer de Provença 171, near Nick Havanna), a warehouse filled with antique amusement-park rides and games, and **Universal** (Carrer Marià Cubí 182), a two-level affair with a mercifully relaxed upper floor. The latter, close to the Diagonal's Plaça Francesc Macià, enjoys the distinct advantage of being in a neighborhood warren of trendy bars. If you simply can't get enough of loud music and astonishing design ideas, you should ask fellow customers for the name of this week's Barcelona bar sensation.

Nightclubs and Music Halls

The three kingpins among the city's enormous nightclubs are **KGB** (Carrer Alegre de Dalt 55), **Otto Zutz** (Carrer Lincoln 15), both far west of the Diagonal, and **Zeleste** (Carrer Almogàvers 122). All are crowded and cosmopolitan after two in the morning. Zeleste, the farthest from the center—it's located in the Poble Nou district far to the north (near the 1992 Olympics development called Area Parc de Mar)—occupies a former textile factory, its layout a surprising combination of concert halls, rooftop walkways, and plush bars. Major pop groups perform here. Take a cab to get to these spectacular, far-flung night spots.

For people unattracted by glitzy nightlife, a visit to the timeless music halls in the Avinguda del Paral-lel might be the perfect antidote to the prevailing trendiness. Seedy but charming, such old-fashioned venues as **El Molino** (Carrer Vila i Vilà 99) put on cabaret-style revues, and dusty performance halls welcome flamenco and tango troupes. **La Paloma** (Carrer Tigre 27), hidden in a small street between the Paral-lel and Las Ramblas, is one of a vanishing breed: a picturesque, down-to-earth, and inexpensive European dance hall.

—*Stephen O'Shea*

SHOPS AND SHOPPING

Barcelona calls itself a city of *botiguers* (shopkeepers), and shopping here is as brisk, cosmopolitan, and exciting as in any major city. Among the inevitable individual "discoveries," you'll find the latest designs in fashion, furniture, and art, along with antiques and handcrafted items.

Fashion and Accessories

Barcelona's most fashionable shopping is in the Eixample, especially on such streets as Rambla de Catalunya and Passeig de Gràcia, the western (upper) end of Carrer Muntaner, and along the Diagonal. Here you'll find all the big international names—Yves Saint Laurent, Pierre Cardin, and the like—as well as the best of the new Barcelona boutiques, designer showrooms, and galleries. **Loewe**, famous for its high-quality (and high-priced) Spanish leather goods, is at Passeig de Gràcia 35 and Avinguda de la Diagonal 570: fabulous suits, coats, jackets, handbags, and other accessories. **Gonzalo Comella**, with fashionable clothes for men and women, is at the corner of the Diagonal (number 478) and Via Augusta. Carrer Tuset, a small street that goes west from the Diagonal, is popular with the young crowd, both for its discos and for its many small boutiques with offbeat youth fashions.

While on Passeig de Gràcia, look at **E. Furest**, at number 12–14 (also at Avinguda de la Diagonal 468), for men's custom-tailored clothing; **Mango**, number 65, for youthful women's clothes; **Adolfo Domínguez**, number 89 (also at Carrer de València 245), for men's clothing by Spain's leading new designer; **Carlos Torrents**, number 95, for stylish menswear; **Yanko**, number 100, for elegant styling in Spanish leather—handbags, shoes, belts; and **A. Gratacos**, number 108, for a wide assortment of fine fabrics.

The inveterate shopper will want to browse among the clothes and gift shops that are chockablock in the streets between Plaça de Catalunya and Fernando. **Groc**, at Rambla de Catalunya 100, is known for original clothes by Tony Miró and avant-garde jewelry by Chelo Sastre.

At the frenetically busy and bustling Plaça de Catalunya is a branch of Spain's largest department store chain, **El Corte Inglés**, and on a nearby street, Avinguda del Portal de l'Angel, is another department store, **Galerías Preciados**. **El Boulevard Rosa**, Avinguda de la Diagonal 609, consists of four floors of fashionable boutiques and shops.

Furniture and Decorative Objects

For the cutting edge in contemporary Spanish—especially Catalan—design, turn to **BD Ediciones de Diseño**, Carrer de Mallorca 291, in the Eixample, a showroom run by a group of local architects called Studio Per, featuring furniture by modern designers Javier Mariscal, Pepe Cortés, Pep Bonet, Cristian Cirici, Mireia Riera, and others. Just as intriguing are the excellent limited editions of painstakingly exact reproductions of famous works by Antoni Gaudí, Le Corbusier, Aalto, and other designers and architects of the past. Among the items reproduced are 1920s furniture by the Scottish architect Charles Rennie Mackintosh and the Italian rationalist architect Guiseppe Terragni, and rugs from designs by Cubist painter Juan Gris, Eileen Gray, and others. The showroom is in a landmark building designed by one of the most important Modernist Catalan architects, Lluís Domènech i Montaner.

Another intriguing shop is **Sala Vinçon**, Passeig de Gràcia 96, for the latest in furniture and decorative objects for the home. Savvy proprietor Fernando Amat seems always to be among the first with new functional objects and furnishings.

In the **Pesdrera** area, a little grid of streets from the Diagonal east to Carrer d'Aragó, and from Passeig de Gràcia north to Carrer de Bruc, are many new little shops with contemporary pottery, porcelain, glass, and basketware.

Art and Antiques

Along Rambla de Catalunya, Passeig de Gràcia, and Avinguda Consell de Cent are a number of art galleries with works by contemporary Catalan painters and sculptors. **Galería Joan Prats**, Rambla de Catalunya 54, is one of the better-known galleries, featuring contemporary works. **Sala Gaspar**, Avinguda Consell de Cent 323, at the corner of Carrer de Balmes, is famous for its contemporary paintings and sculpture by big-name artists. **Serie Disseny**, in the southwestern part of town at Carrer de Ganduxer 28, features small sculptures in limited editions.

Along Carrer Montcada near the Picasso museum you will find **Galería Maeght** (at number 25), a branch of the Paris atelier, with many graphics by international artists. Farther along the same street is **Galería Dalí**, with etchings and other graphics by Salvador Dalí for sale. At the **Fundació Joan Miró** on Montjuïc there is a bookshop with posters, reproductions, slides, and a good assortment of contemporary art books.

A first stop for antiques should be **Bulevar de Antiquaris**, at Passeig de Gràcia 55, a central antiques emporium with 73 dealer shops. Among them are **Cañas**, selling antique toys, and **Turn of the Century**, featuring Art Nouveau lamps. Other notable dealers are **Arturo Ramón**, Carrer de la Palla 25 (heading west from the Plaça de Sant Jaume), and **Santiago Marti**, Carrer de Provença 243 (between Rambla de Catalunya and Passeig de Gràcia).

Barcelona's oldest antiques market is held every Thursday (9:00 A.M. to 8:00 P.M.) in Plaça Nova, in front of the cathedral, but you will find antiques shops throughout the Barri Gòtic, especially on Carrer Call (leading from Plaça de Sant Jaume), Carrer de la Palla, and Carrer del Banys Nous. **Antigüedades Maria Esclasans**, Carrer de la Pietat 8 (a small street behind the cathedral), has a wide selection of *objets.*

You can uncover some fine antique jewelry in Barcelona, with good buys still available in Art Nouveau pieces. You might look at **L'Ancien Bijou**, at Passeig de Gràcia 55 in Bulevar de Antiquaris, and **Novecento**, nearby at Passeig de Gràcia 75.

Auction houses are another excellent source of antiques, not just art and vintage furniture, but books, antique ceramics, jewelry, and bibelots. Look for **Brok**, Carrer de Pau Clarís 167 (between Carrer de València and Carrer de Mallorca); **Prestige**, Carrer de València 277 (corner of Carrer de Pau Clarís); and **Subarna**, Carrer de Provença 257 (corner of Passeig de Gràcia).

Handmade Crafts and Gifts

Barcelona has one of the government-run **Artespaña** handicraft shops at Rambla de Catalunya 75, with crafts from all over Spain but especially from Catalonia. If you want a *précis* of Spanish handicrafts, a useful stop might be the **Poble Espanyol** (Spanish Village), Avinguda del Marqués de Comillas, at the northern edge of Parc de Montjuïc. Almost every region's handicrafts are for sale in shops in this exhibition area, built for the 1929 World's Fair. It's heavily patronized by tourists, and you'll find few bargains, but for the visitor with limited time for shopping it can be a gift problem-solver. Carved wooden bowls, fans, lace mantillas, regional ceramics, silk-screened tee-shirts—the range extends from tasteful to tacky. At **Estampería Castells**, on Plaça Aragonese in the Poble Espanyol, there is a nice collection of posters, prints, and hand-printed Christmas cards.

A narrow street just outside the Barri Gòtic, Carrer Montcada, has a delightful little handicraft shop: **1741**, at number 2, with a big collection of pottery.

The Barri Gòtic is a good place for serendipitous browsing through old books and maps, souvenirs, and leather, especially along Carrers Ferràn, Portaferrisa, and Freneria. Side by side on Freneria are **La Caixa de Frang**, for earthen casserole dishes, folk pottery, and well-made kitchen accessories, and **Grafiques el Tinell**, with hand-colored woodcuts and other prints made from antique blocks, as well as old maps and engravings. If you hanker for lace, either antique or modern work, **L'Arca de l'Avia**, Carrer Banys Nous 20, has exquisite tablecloths, christening clothes, nightgowns, and blouses. At

Papirum, Baixada de la Llibreteria 2, you'll find antique, handmade, and hand-colored papers and end papers.

After watching the *sardana* dancers, you may want a pair of *espadrilles,* those traditional shoes with coiled rope soles and canvas tops that Catalan men and women wear for dancing. An especially reliable shop is **La Manual Alpargatera**, Carrer d'Avinyó, just off Carrer Ferràn, which connects Plaça de Sant Jaume with Las Ramblas. The shoes are handmade, and there's a great selection from all over Catalonia.

Fine old and rare books and the art of bookbinding are Barcelona specialties. Among the best-known bookshops are **Librería Balague**, Enrique Granados 80; **Puvill**, Carrer de la Palla 29; **Diego Gómez Flores**, Carrer Banys Nous; and the bookbinder **Santiago Brugalla**, Carrer d'Aribau 7 (corner of Carrer de la Diputació).

You can browse for old (not necessarily valuable) books at the permanent stalls on Carrer de la Diputació between Carrer d'Aribau and Carrer de Balmes. For new books— bestsellers, art books—and tapes, try the just-opened New York–style bookstore called **Happy Books**, Passeig de Gràcia 77.

In a music-loving city in a music-loving country, you can expect to find many shops selling musical instruments, records, and cassettes. Some are located in Las Ramblas and Gran Via de les Corts Catalanes, others (especially guitar shops) on Carrer de Ample near the cathedral. **Joan Estruchi Pipo**, Carrer de Ample 30, is one of the best. A very complete selection of musical instruments (including classical guitars) and early and current sheet music is at **Musical Emporium**, Rambla de Canaletes 129. Record and video shops are mostly in the Eixample, especially between Plaça de Catalunya and the Diagonal. **Vidosa**, Carrer de Balmes 335–343 (west of the Diagonal, where Balmes crosses Corinto), has an extensive record, cassette, and video collection.

Markets and Food Shops

Food markets are a lively part of Barcelona life. Most fun for the visitor, whether for shopping, photographing, or just plain looking, is **La Boquería**, a vast public market on Las Ramblas (between Carrer Boquería and Carrer del Carme), that is a colorful harvest of fresh foods of all kinds. (A good *tapas* bar in the market is Bar Pinocchio.) Other public markets are **El Ninot** (on Carrer de Mallorca) and **Santa Caterina** (on Avinguda de la Catedral).

Barcelona has a number of food shops, but there's only one, **Semon**, a culinary institution at Carrer Ganduxter 31, that is the city's answer to Paris's Fauchon. Every luxury food product imaginable, domestic and imported, can be found here, along with many hot and cold dishes, baked goods, charcuterie items, cheeses, and a good wine selection. A big specialty is smoked fish (from salmon and swordfish to anchovies and trout). It's a great place for outfitting a picnic. Next door is Semon's discreet little restaurant, **L'Indret**, with only seven tables and simple but marvelous food. Tel: 201-6931.

Other good shops for food, wine, and picnic items are **Colmado Quilez**, on the Rambla de Catalunya at Carrer Consell de Cent, **El Grau Colmado**, at Consell de Cent 318, which has a vast inventory (and also a few tables in the rear for lunch), and **Mantequerias Leonesas**, Rambla de Catalunya 5, which has an unusually large deli, wine, and liquor section and a neat little bar in the rear. **La Castellana Charcutería**, at Las Ramblas 41, and **Charcutería La Pineda**, at Carrer del Pi 16 in the Barri Gòtic, are both well-stocked groceries specializing in hams, sausages, and cheeses, with *tapas* bars for sampling the wares. For herbs, spices, and an assortment of aromatic teas, try **Angel Jobal**, at Carrer de la Princesa (around the corner from the Museu Picasso on Carrer Montcada). El Corte Inglés has a vast, well-stocked supermarket, too. **Casa Vives**, Rambla de Catalunya 58, sells delectable pastries and candies, as does **Mauri**, a patisserie farther west on the same street, at number 102.

Fans of flea markets will find one, **Els Encants**, in Plaça de les Glòries Catalanes (eight blocks north of Plaça de Tetuàn on Gran Via de les Corts Catalanes) every Monday, Wednesday, Friday, and Saturday, dawn to dusk.

A **stamp-and-coin market** sets up Sunday mornings on the Plaça Reial, and also on Sundays you will find bargains in old books, stamps, coins, engravings, cassettes, videos, and myriad other goods in the **Mercat de Sant Antoni**, where Carrers Urgell and Tamarit meet.

—*Patricia Brooks*

CATALONIA

By Patricia Brooks and Ellen Hoffman

Patricia Brooks contributes to other sections of this guide-book. Ellen Hoffman is a free-lance writer whose work has appeared in the Washington Post *and the* Los Angeles Times, *among other publications. She received a prize from the Spanish government for her writing about the country.*

Geographically speaking, Catalonia is not the region it used to be. Today the region shares a border with France along the Pyrenees and occupies about 6 percent of Spain's total land area, including some 250 miles of Mediterranean coast. At its height in the 15th century the Catalan empire, allied with the kingdom of Aragón, included—in addition to the land within the borders of the modern state—Perpignan and what are now the French Pyrenees; Sicily, Sardinia, and Naples; the region of Valencia, and the Balearic Islands. The empire was defined not merely by geography, but also by the creation of such political institutions as the Consell de Cent (Council of One Hundred), a participatory system developed in the 13th century for governing its capital, Barcelona. Common language and customs were other factors uniting the kingdom.

Catalan, a 1,000-year-old Romance language whose origins can be traced to the songs and legends of the medieval troubadors, appeared as a written language in the 11th century. It has a rich literary tradition that is generally dated from the fiction and scientific works of Ramón Llull, a 12th-century Franciscan priest. It includes the public poetry contests that spurred the 19th-century "Catalan Renaissance," and the works of such 20th-century Catalans as Llorenç Villalonga, Josep M. de Sagarra, and Salvador Espriu.

In this chapter we use the Catalan, rather than the Spanish, spellings of place names, which are more common on signposts and in local guidebooks. These are followed by the Castilian names in parentheses if there is a significant difference. The chapter title, however, is the Anglicized "Catalonia," familiar to most English speakers, rather than the Catalan "Catalunya" or the Castilian "Cataluña."

Many of Spain's rulers—including the Bourbons in the 18th century and Franco in the 20th century—have denied Catalans the right to function as a political entity, to speak their language, or even to follow their own cultural traditions. Neither the loss of territory nor the repression of language and traditions, however, has diminished the core of pride and cultural identity that makes Catalonia one of the most interesting regions in Spain.

Since the end of the Franco era in 1975 the Catalan nation, as it calls itself, has been an autonomous region, or state, within the Spanish political system. Within this framework Catalans have attempted to recoup the language and cultural traditions that were forced underground for some 40 years. The selection of Barcelona as host of the 1992 Olympics was seized as an opportunity to educate both the current generation of Catalans and the rest of the world about Catalan culture and history.

The profusion of bookstores and newspaper kiosks vending Catalan-language publications (including two daily newspapers, *Avui* and *Diari de Barcelona*), the omnipresent television sets in bars and cafés with their dials set to TV-3, the Catalan-language channel—to say nothing of the thousands of adults and children who are studying the language and its literature—all testify to the renaissance of the ancient language, which 20 years ago was forbidden but is now an official language (along with Spanish) of the region.

From grandparents to young children, groups of Catalans now routinely perform the lilting Catalan national dance, the *sardana*—previously outlawed—in public squares, usually accompanied by a winds-and-brass orchestra or fife and drum. The unmistakable brilliant red and yellow stripes of the Catalan flag appear on public buildings as well as on lapel pins and bumper stickers.

The more modern Catalan artistic traditions that have nurtured such artists as cellist Pau (Pablo) Casals, opera singer Montserrat Caballé, Pablo Picasso, Joan Miró, Salvador Dalí, and architect Antoni Gaudí tend to be concentrated in the Catalonian capital, Barcelona (which we cover in a separate chapter). Even so, Catalonia outside Barcelona is a cornucopia of historical, cultural, artistic, architectural, and natural attractions. Scenically, Catalonia ranges from awesome Pyrenees peaks to sandy Mediterranean beaches, from pine-forested cliffs hugging the rugged Costa Brava to gentle vineyards of the Penedès.

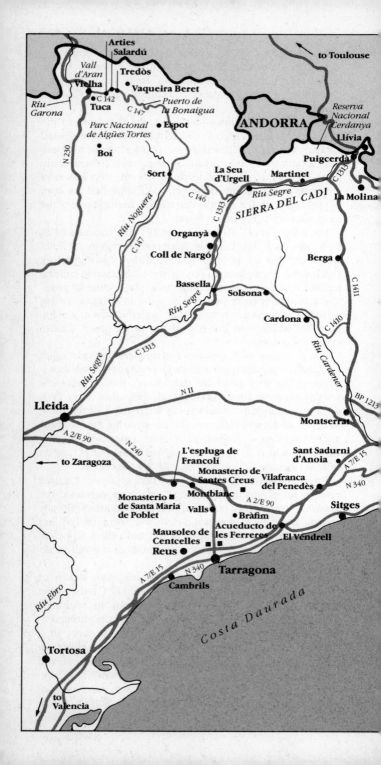

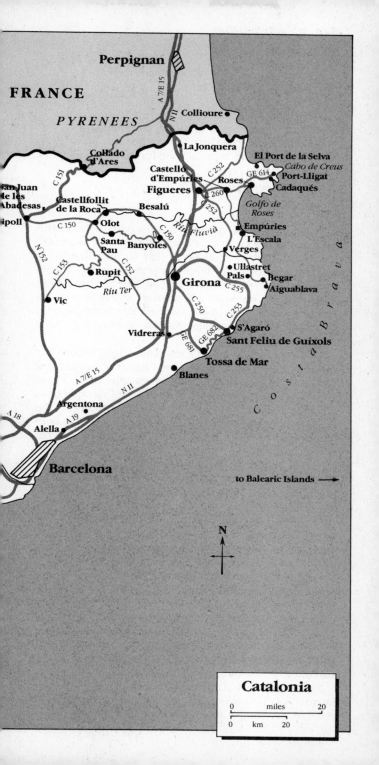

MAJOR INTEREST

Romanesque and Modernist architecture
Medieval towns and cities
Roman and Greek ruins, especially in Tarragona
Folklore and fiestas
Outdoor sports: skiing, hiking, water sports
Beach scenery and activities on the Costa Brava
Food and wine, especially the Penedès wine-
    producing region
20th-century art
The Pyrenees

The use of the word "nation" when referring to Catalonia is no accident. For Catalan nationalists—from shopkeepers to the separatists who continue to fight to sever Catalonia's political links to Spain—this is the preferred term. At times Catalonia does seem to act like an independent nation, dispatching its president and cultural officials around the globe, the former to make business deals, the latter to disseminate Catalan culture everywhere from the United States to Japan.

Catalan travelling and trading have a long history. For better or worse, Catalans have been known since medieval times—when the vibrant Jewish communities of Barcelona, Girona, and neighboring towns contributed significantly to the growth of commerce—as effective businesspeople. The economic base the Catalans built enabled the region to harness the advances of the Industrial Revolution and become, along with the Basque Country, the economic powerhouse of Spain. As one Catalan writer observed during World War I, "While the Europeans were torturing each other at Verdun, the Catalans, thanks to Spain's neutrality, devoted themselves to doing business with the contenders. In this way, vast sums of money were accumulated." This active commercial life has endowed Catalans with a cosmopolitanism reflected in, among other things, multilingualism among much of the population.

Catalonia is a land of impressive, varied natural beauty. Less than an hour outside of Barcelona on the coast you begin to encounter long, sandy beaches that give way to dramatic, umber seaside cliffs, tiny coves for swimming and picnicking, and pine forests. Inland, rocky foothills lead into imposing mountain ranges, dense forests, pristine natural parks with snowcapped mountains, or gently rolling hills covered with almond and fruit orchards.

Any trip through Catalonia illustrates the diversity and intensity of the region's historic and artistic legacy. It is possible, for example, to visit Greek and Roman ruins on the

Empordà plain, hundreds of Romanesque churches—dating back to the early days of the Catalan empire—that dot the valleys and mountains of the Pyrenees, or to make day trips from Barcelona to the large monasteries at Poblet, Montserrat, and Santes Creus. Many of the monuments of Modernist architecture—products of the turn-of-the-century movement that was the Spanish equivalent of Art Nouveau—are included in our routes below.

Barcelonans often plan excursions around famous country restaurants. The region has many, especially along the Costa Brava and in the mountains near the French border, and we bring them to your attention throughout the chapter.

Catalonians also celebrate many regional holidays and folk festivals. One involves the creation of *castellers* (human pyramids); the most famous of these can be seen during the September fiesta in the town of Valls in Tarragona province. The "dance of death" is performed by dancers in skeleton suits during the Easter processions in Verges, near the Costa Brava. There are processions of elaborately costumed "giants" and "dwarfs" in local fiesta celebrations, and bonfires are lit on the eve of San Juan, June 23, throughout the region.

The Food of Catalonia

Most gourmets consider Catalan cuisine the best in Spain, or second only by inches to Basque cooking. Geography has something to do with it: All the good, natural foods of the mountains (rabbit and other game, river trout, all kinds of sausages, a variety of wild mushrooms) are combined with the wonders of the sea (the freshest possible anchovies, sardines, mullet and other fish, lobster, shrimp, and other shellfish), along with a profusion of vegetables and fruits from Tarragona orchards and farmlands.

But credit goes also to the creativity of Catalan cooks, who have drawn on their Mediterranean heritage and proximity to France to create a distinctive, sophisticated, and exciting cuisine that stands triumphantly on its own. Like the region itself, the cooking varies from terrain to terrain: in inland Empordà and the Pyrenees, game, trout, and hearty sauces play a major role in dishes that juxtapose surprising ingredients, such as *pato con manzanas e higos* (duck with apples and figs), *oca con peras* (baby goose with pears), and *liebre con castañas* (hare with chestnuts); along the Costa Brava seafood rules in such dishes as *suquet de peix* (fish stew), *zarzuela con mariscos* (a seafood potpourri), and *llagosta i pollastre* (lobster and chicken in a hazelnut, almond, and pine-nut sauce); in Tarragona the rice dishes of Valencia have edged northward in such specialties as *arroz negro* (rice with squid and squid ink) and *arroz abanda* (rice cooked in a fish and seafood stock).

On regional menus, look for such delicious specialties as *butifarra catalana* (white sausage, served alone or in other dishes), *espinacas a la catalana* (spinach cooked with pine nuts and raisins), *escudella con castañas* (a bean, noodle, rice, spicy sausage, chestnut, and vegetable stew), *faves a la catalana* (broad beans cooked with *butifarra* sausages, pork loin, and ham), and *conejo con caracoles* (rabbit stewed with snails, herbs, and almonds). A staple is *pan con tomate* (*pa amb tomaquet* in Catalan)—slices of peasant bread rubbed with olive oil and topped with fresh tomato and a sprinkling of salt.

Catalan desserts evince similar inventiveness. Among many favorites: *mel y mató* (fresh cream cheese with honey), *crema catalana* (a richer version of flan or crême caramel, more like crême brulée), *panellets* (a sweet made of almonds, sugar, and eggs), and *menja blanc* (a pudding of ground almonds, kirsch, lemon, and cream, similar to blancmange).

The Wines of Catalonia

ALELLA

Somewhat reminiscent of Condrieu in France's Rhône Valley, Alella is a tiny *denominación de origen* (DO) whose fame comes from its white wines, which have been made in this area since the Greeks first planted vines here. Four-fifths of Alella's production is white, the best of which is made from Xarel-lo and Pansa Blanca grapes grown on granite slopes a few miles north of Barcelona, in an area rapidly being encroached upon by the city's suburbs. Alella white wines can be lovely, pale, lightly perfumed, off-dry wines of great charm. Marqués de Alella produces the region's best wines.

AMPURDAN–COSTA BRAVA

Ampurdàn–Costa Brava, on the coast southeast of Figueres, is an area in the foothills of the Pyrenees not far from the border with France. The mountains greatly influence the region's climate; the average rainfall is quite high, but the dampness is tempered by the *tramontaña,* a strong wind that blows through the region most of the year. The vineyards here produce sparkling wines, some *pétillant* whites, Vi Novell (a Beaujolais Nouveau–style red), and some powerful, low-acid, oak-aged reds of 12 to 13 percent alcohol, but 70 percent of the local wines are fruity rosés made from Garnacha and Cariñena grapes. Castillo de Perelada is the brand you are most likely to encounter in Spain. Their Blanc de Pescador white and Cazador red have their admirers. Oliveda makes a good Vi Novell.

PENEDES

Penedès, southwest of Barcelona, is one of the most important wine-producing areas in Spain. It yields some fine table wines and is one of the world's biggest producers of *méthode champenoise* sparkling wines (see below).

Excellent red, white, and rosé table wines for everyday drinking are produced at lower altitudes along the Mediterranean coast from a variety of high-quality grapes: Parellada, Macabeo (Viura), and Xarel-lo for the whites; Ull de Llebre (Tempranillo), Monastrell, Garnacha, and Cariñena for the reds. Vineyards at higher altitudes in Penedès are planted with Cabernet Sauvignon, Cabernet Franc, Pinot Noir, Chardonnay, Sauvignon Blanc, and other varietals, as well as the best native wines.

Penedès wines have won international wine competitions, and their success has had dramatic effects on wine-making in Spain, the wine consumption habits and attitudes of the Spanish consumer, and the overall image of Spanish wines abroad. Penedès might best be described as the California of Europe. The great producers of this region are Torres and Jean León.

PRIORATO

Priorato, located in the province of Tarragona, along the coast below Barcelona, is a harsh, rugged land of ancient villages and picturesque vineyards. Artisan wine-makers tend old, low-yielding vines growing on impossibly steep terrain composed of volcanic soil and slate. The grapes, usually Garnacha and Cariñena, are brought down from the vineyards by mule and burro to be crafted into massive, powerful (14 to 18 percent alcohol), black-red, oak-aged wines, some of which exhibit a lush fruit bouquet suggestive of blackberries. Look for Masiá Barril and Scala Dei.

TARRAGONA

Tarragona produces a variety of wines, most destined for export, usually in bulk. In the subregions of Campo de Tarragona and Ribera del Ebro, most of the vineyards, which in recent years have been giving way to almond and hazelnut orchards, are planted with Macabeo, Xarel-lo, and Parellada grapes that yield full-bodied white wines low in acid. Falset produces wines similar to those of Priorato from Cariñena and Garnacha grapes.

Tarragona also produces some excellent sweet dessert wines, especially Moscatels, by the *solera* system (explained in the chapter on Andalusia, in the Jerez section). But Tarragona's chief claim to fame is as the largest supplier of *vinos de misa* (altar wines) to the Catholic Church, whose standards for the preparation of these wines are far stricter than those of any *consejo regulador,* the ruling body that controls the *denominaciones.*

CAVA

The Spanish designation *cava* denotes sparkling wines made by the *méthode champenoise* in Penedès and a few other designated areas in Catalonia, La Rioja, Navarra, and Aragón. Cava is a *denominación específica* (DE), which refers to the method of producing the wine, and is subject to both the regulatory councils of the DE and of the DO in which it is located. Cavas are fermented in the bottle like French Champagne. Production is strictly controlled by law, from pressing and fermentation through disgorging, recorking, and bottling.

Cavas are produced in Brut Nature (extra dry), Brut (dry), Seco (slightly off-dry), and Semi-seco (off-dry to sweet) styles. Those labeled Cremant or Extra are generally off-dry or sweet. Some good dry *rosado* (rosé) cavas are also made. Vintage cava, like vintage Champagne, is made only in very good years.

Regulations prohibit cava producers from making or marketing under the same label any sparkling wines that are not made strictly by the *méthode champenoise*. Only cava wines can use the name "cava" on the label and place the cava symbol, a four-pointed star, on the cork.

By far the best cavas are made from Xarel-lo, Macabeo, and Parellada grapes at Sant Sadurní d'Anoia in Penedès, which accounts for 90 percent of Spain's cava production. One firm at Sant Sadurní d'Anoia is the largest producer of sparkling wines in the world.

Cavas can be found on almost every wine list in Spain. The giant cava producers Codorníu and Freixenet make a wide range of very good sparkling wines, and Mont Marcal, Mascaró, Mestres, Ferret, Roger Goulart, Raimat, Segura Viudas, and Juve et Camps (whose Ermita d'Espiells still wine is excellent) all make first-rate cavas.

SAMPLING WINES IN CATALONIA

One of the joys of visiting Catalonia is sampling cavas at one of the many *xampanerías* (Champagne bars) that have become the rage in the past few years. A visit to **Sant Sadurní d'Anoia**, the main cava-producing town, located 44 km (27 miles) west of Barcelona, for a hearty Sunday lunch is a Catalan institution. Carloads, and even busloads, of day-trippers on family, club, or company outings come out from

Barcelona for a typical Catalan feast of grilled food. Here, and in several villages around Sant Sadurní, several restaurants have *servicio barbacoa.* These grill houses, sometimes concessions at cava wineries, either charge patrons a fee for using huge grills for roasting food they have brought— sausages, lamb chops, large mushrooms, *calçots* (green onions), and eggplant, red peppers, onions, and so on, for *escalivada,* a typical Catalan dish of roasted vegetables—or they let patrons grill free of charge if they purchase the meats and/or the wine and cava from the establishment.

In addition, the restaurant usually serves full meals in a regular dining room, where you can order most of the same dishes the Catalanes are cooking in the barbecue madhouse of picnic tables and grills outside. Plates of *pa amb tomaquet,* grilled sausages, lamb chops, and rabbit with side dishes of white beans, chick-peas, grilled wild mushrooms, *ali-oli* (garlic mayonnaise), *escalivada,* and salad, all washed down with glasses of cava and *porrones* (glass beakers with drinking spouts) of red Penedès wine, will nicely duplicate the outdoor feast in slightly more tranquil surroundings. One such place, with its own palatable cava and no pretensions, except for its ability to serve prodigious amounts of home-cooked Catalan specialties, is **Canals y Munne**, Plaça Pau Casals 6, in Sant Sadurní.

If you can visit only one winery in Catalonia, make it **Codorníu** at Sant Sadurní d'Anoia. This huge cava winery, with so many miles of underground aging cellars that it has to be visited in a special train, is in a 19th-century building designed by the Catalan Modernist architect Josep Puig i Cadafalch. The main building, which contains an excellent wine museum, has been declared a national monument. Codorníu is open from Monday through Thursday, but closed at lunch.

Vilafranca del Penedès, capital of the Penedès wine district, has one of the finest wine museums in the world—and you don't have to be a wine nut to enjoy it. It is perhaps the best of several truly wonderful Catalan wine museums, including the one at the Codorníu winery and the superb collection in the Palacio de Perelada (Girona).

—*Gerry Dawes*

Seeing Catalonia

Despite the natural barriers posed by the rocky Mediterranean coast and the Pyrenees, modern highways and tunnels make it possible to tour Catalonia quite efficiently. But do keep in mind that Catalonia is too rich, large, and geographically complex to see and digest in one short trip. And you must avoid the *salida* (exit) periods (Friday and Sunday afternoons) and the holidays, especially Holy Week, Christmas, and Three Kings Day (or Epiphany, observed January 6), when monumental traffic jams on the highways around Barcelona can turn a two-hour trip into a four-, six-, or eight-hour one.

We offer three approaches to exploring some of Catalonia's most important sights:

- a route along the Costa Brava that circles inland to Figueres, Girona, and the surrounding region;
- a Romanesque route from Barcelona to the villages of the Cerdanya (an area of the Pyrenees between Spain and France), and, as an option, on to the Vall d'Aran in the Pyrenees;
- and a trip southwest of Barcelona that includes Tarragona, Lleida, the Penedès wine towns, and the monasteries. Depending on your interests and the time available, this last could be a wine or monastery trip alone, an outing along the coast, or a visit to Tarragona's Roman sites.

Each approach can originate in and/or end in Barcelona, by far the most important gateway to the region. Figueres, Girona, and access to the Costa Brava lie along route A 7, which goes north to Perpignan in France; the Pyrenees itinerary could continue on into Andorra and France below Toulouse; and Tarragona is on the way to Valencia, to the south via A 7, and near the major route (A 2) west to Zaragoza in Aragón.

THE COSTA BRAVA

The Costa Brava ("wild" or "savage" coast), a 130-mile strip of Mediterranean beaches, cliffs, coves, fishing villages, and resorts, starts at Blanes, an overbuilt tourist town (albeit with a pretty beach) about 61 km (38 miles) northeast of Barcelona, and ends at the French border. The name "Brava" refers to the rugged, sometimes rocky coastline, not to the mostly European tourists who overwhelm the former fishing villages turned high-rise resorts and beaches during the summer months. The visitor who wants to avoid the crowds and packed facilities would be advised to visit at another season. Fortunately the weather along the coast is pleasant much of the year, even when it is too cold for swimming. Our strategy is to rush through, ignore, or bypass the resort towns that have been "ruined" by tourism as we head up the most scenic part of the Costa Brava, as far as the beautiful villages of Cadaqués and Port-Lligat on the Cabo de Creus. We then loop inland to Figueres, to visit Dalí's home-museum, then head south to the medieval city of Girona, with several detours along the way. From Girona you have the option of returning to Barcelona or continuing west toward the Pyrenees. Alternatively, you can base yourself somewhere along the coast, at S'Agaró, say, or Cadaqués, and make daily excursions to the other points of interest we mention.

NORTH TO TOSSA DE MAR

To avoid traffic congestion and some of the more crowded commercial tourist resorts, take A 7 northeast from Barcelona, exit at Vidreras (exit 7), and go northeast on C 253 to just before Llagostera. There turn southeast to **Tossa de Mar**, on the coast just northeast of Blanes. Tossa de Mar is also an overbuilt resort town, but it has something more than beach: the tastefully restored narrow streets and stone houses of a 12th-century town. The **Vila Vella**, perched on a high promontory, is surrounded by a thick wall (for protection from pirates) and dominated by a round tower that overlooks the beach and sea.

SANT FELIU DE GUIXOLS

The twisting cliffside coast road to the north of Tossa de Mar offers, alternatively, vistas of the turquoise, aqua, deep-blue, and purple waters of coves and sandy beaches perfect for swimming, and garish, overdeveloped camping and resort areas that overflow with tourists during the summer.

Sant Feliu de Guíxols, 23 km (14 miles) northeast of Tossa on the coast, developed into a city in the 12th century around a Benedictine monastery, now being renovated. The town gained fame and economic strength with the discovery of the properties of cork—harvested from the local cork trees—for preserving wine. Tourism now dominates the town, which has a pleasant, tree-lined promenade along the beach and a number of good examples of Modernist architecture. The most prominent is the turn-of-the-century Casino dels Nois on the Passeig del Mar.

Sant Feliu has one of the Costa Brava's best restaurants, **Eldorado Petit**, which is affiliated with restaurants of the same name operated by the same owner in Barcelona and New York. Catalan specialties, such as the *suquet de peix* and crayfish *canalones* (ravioli) with a wild mushroom sauce, prevail on the menu of the small, attractive dining room, at Rambla Vidal 23. The *cassoulet de codornices al basílico* (quail with white beans and walnuts) is superb, as is the service. But the local secret is that the food served in the unpretentious bar on the other side of the kitchen is prepared by the same chefs at a very affordable price; at lunchtime, laborers fill the tables to dine on hearty portions of such delectable dishes as fish soup or chicken with garlic and herbs. Tel: (9-72) 32-18-18.

STAYING ON THE SOUTHERN COSTA BRAVA

At the northeastern end of town is the ► **Curhotel Hipóc-rates**, a quiet spa with regimens and therapies for disorders ranging from chronic fatigue to weight problems. Even more effective in addressing the disorders of modern life might be a stay at ► **Hostal de la Gavina** in **S'Agaró**, just a stone's throw up the coast from Sant Feliu, an elegant resort hotel with antiques-filled bedrooms, a highly regarded restaurant, mani-cured gardens, swimming pool, and magnificent views of the sea. Removed from the tourist hubbub along the beach, the hotel is part of an exclusive preserve of spacious villas se-cluded by high walls and pine forests.

Flee past the next few touristy beach towns up the coast from S'Agaró about 30 km (19 miles) to Aiguablava and the modern, clifftop ► **Parador de Aigua Blava**. The parador offers excellent views of the cliffs, the pine and cypress hillsides, and a secluded cove below—be sure to ask for a room with a balcony. Another good hotel choice in this coastal oasis is the moderately priced ► **Hotel Aigua Blava**, which faces the cove and has a pool and tennis courts. Its dining room and decor are as pleasant as the sea and hillside views. This lovely cove is a refuge from much of the commer-cialization of the Costa Brava.

NORTH TO THE EMPORDA PLAIN

From Aiguablava follow the road to Begur (about 10 km/6 miles north) and from there head inland about 7 km (4 miles) to Pals, stopping perhaps at **Sa Punta**, a restaurant with a view of Platja de Pals, for a meal of Empordàn specialties with a *nueva cocina* twist; Tel: (9-72) 66-73-76.

You are now entering the area of Catalonia known as the Empordà plain, which extends north to the French border and is anchored by the inland cities of Figueres and Girona and on the east by the coast. **Pals**, in lower Empordà, is a medieval walled village that is now a national treasure. Take a leisurely walk through tour to see the little church of San Pedro, the tawny stone Catalan houses festooned with bougainvillaea and framed by neat gardens, and a clutch of pottery shops. Many of the old houses in Pals and in Peratallada, another medieval village to the west, have been restored by Barcelonans who have snapped them up for weekend and summer homes.

About 12 km (7½ miles) northwest of Pals (take GE 650 north, GE 651 west, and GE 644 north) is **Ullastret**, the oldest Iberian ruins yet found. A small archaeological mu-

seum (at the top of a well-tended garden) displays fragments
excavated from the site. Other fragments are strewn along a
hillside walkway that leads to the museum.

Empúries

From Ullastret follow signs to Parlabà (go north and then
west) to get on C 252 heading north. (If you're driving
directly from Barcelona, take A 7 just past Girona, then C 255
east to C 252 north.) At Viladamat head east, following signs
for Empúries, which is just over a mile north of the resort
village of L'Escala. Empúries, the extensive remains of a
Roman city (Emporion), was built on a site inhabited by
early Iberian tribes, then colonized by the Greeks in 550 B.C.
as a small trading post, which eventually grew into a thriving
commercial port. The massive ruins overlook the sea and
several attractive sandy beaches fringed with pines—good
places for a picnic and a swim.

Grapes and olives were introduced to this area by the
Greeks, and Empúries conducted lively and profitable
trade—mostly in agricultural products—with Greece. The
town even minted its own money, a unit known as the *em,*
which preceded the drachma. The arrival of Roman soldiers to fight the Carthaginians during the Punic War in the
third century B.C., however, marked the decline of Greek
influence and the beginning of the influence of Roman
language and law, which became the underpinnings of
Catalan culture. By the first century A.D. the city had become Romanized, and it eventually came under the political control of Tarragona (a coastal city south of Barcelona),
capital of the Roman Empire in Spain.

Although the museum at Empúries contains Greek pottery,
coins, and other objects found on the site, most of the houses,
temples, and other structures to be seen at Empúries are
Roman. (Buy the English guidebook from the shop at the
museum entrance unless you read Castilian or Catalan.) A
posted itinerary guides the visitor past the gates of the Greek
city on the lower level—called the Cyclopean gates because
of the huge rocks from which they were constructed—and up
the hill into the grid of ancient streets of the Roman city. A
stroll through these streets, past the remains of the marketplace, a few mosaic sidewalks, the broken pillars of the forum,
and the stone walls of the shops and houses, evokes a tangible
sense of the daily life in ancient Empúries.

Cabo de Creus Peninsula

After Empúries the coast road, C 260, turns inland over the
Empordà plain to Castelló d'Empúries, site of the imposing

14th-century Gothic **Iglesia de Santa Maria**, notable for a 15th-century carved alabaster altar in its apse. From there the road swings back to the coast and the Cabo de Creus peninsula. In **Roses**, a former fishing village, now a flourishing (and crowded) resort with one of the most beautiful long, sandy beaches on this coast (small wonder it's mobbed in summer), sits at the northeastern head of the beautiful Golfo de Roses, a perfect place to catch the sunset. At this time of day the fishing docks bustle with boats arriving and slickered fishermen unloading the day's catch onto waiting trucks.

Some 17 km (11 miles) northeast of Roses, reached by a hilly, bumpy road, is **Hacienda el Bulli**, a restaurant in a hillside villa with an open terrace on a promontory overlooking the tiny bay of Montjoi. (*Bulli* means bulldog, which explains all the road signs with a sketch of a bulldog's head on the road leading to the restaurant.) Hacienda el Bulli is run by an Alsatian and specializes in haute cuisine. The food is among the best on the coast, and the views, especially from the terrace, are equally alluring, worth the roller-coaster ride from Roses. Closed October 15 to March 15. Tel: (9-72) 25-76-51. ▶ **Almadraba Park Hotel**, 4 km (2½ miles) southeast of Roses on the Playa de la Almadraba, is restful and affords water views and privacy.

CADAQUES

From Roses continue out on the peninsula to Cadaqués, a half-hour drive away over a sinuous, steep, slow-going mountain road through hillsides layered with terraces supporting pines, olive trees, and golden broom. The road affords you first a view of the sweeping Golfo de Roses and then, on the northern coast of the peninsula, which is a string of small white-sand beaches, of the tiny white houses of El Port de la Selva.

Cadaqués is an all-white fishing village turned artists' colony—Picasso, Utrillo, Duchamp, and Catalan artists Antoni Tàpies and Santiago Rusiñol have been inspired by the town's narrow streets, arcaded white houses, and its setting in a scenic horseshoe-shaped bay hugged by textured cliffs. Salvador Dalí built an elaborate residence on the adjacent nook on the seacoast, Port-Lligat.

Cadaqués has the lazy charm of a Greek island village, which may be what makes it a magnet to laid-back, bohemian-type Europeans. Good planning has kept away high-rise development, and the many chic shops and art galleries are tucked into houses throughout the labyrinthine streets of the village. The greatest local pleasure in Cadaqués is sitting at an outdoor café on the waterfront watching the passing scene. There are a few sights in town worth bestirring yourself for:

the parish church's ornate Baroque altarpiece; the **Museu Municipal de Arte Contemporáneo**, at Carrer Narcis Monturiol 15, with works by Toulouse-Lautrec and others; and a clutch of Modernist buildings, such as the 1910 Casa Serinyena, near the water. There is a small, gray-pebbled beach, but most locals prefer to make the 25-km (15-mile) excursion south to the glorious sands of the Golfo de Roses.

The modest ► **Hotel Playa Sol**, facing the water, has the best views in town and makes a good spot for inhaling the sea breezes and viewing the lively (at times downright noisy) street life. Equally pleasant is the ► **Hotel Rocamar**, with a beach, a pool, and a decent restaurant. The great views, accompanied by the scents of pines and the sea, and restful ambience more than compensate for the somewhat spartan rooms.

EXCURSIONS FROM CADAQUES

Port-Lligat, in the inlet next to Cadaqués, is a mere one-street village, remote and isolated, which is probably what attracted Salvador Dalí in the first place. You'll easily identify his white-washed house by the stone monkeys and huge sculpted eggs on the roof and the garden wrapped in fish-net. Across from the house is the ► **Hotel Port-Lligat**, an idyllic retreat, where you can swim in a delightful pool and contemplate the splendid, undeveloped coastline around you.

You can make a pleasant excursion from either Cadaqués or Port-Lligat exploring the nooks and crannies of the Cabo de Creus and visiting the **Monasterio de Sant Pere de Rodes**, an 11th-century Romanesque monastery that crowns one of the Cabo de Creus's highest peaks. (It's a 40-minute drive northwest from Cadaqués.) Only a shell of chapels and cloisters remains inside crenellated walls and Romanesque towers. The monks of Sant Pere are said to have created one of the mainstays of Empordàn cooking: *alioli,* a pungent garlic–olive oil sauce. Nearby is the castle of Sant Salvador. You can continue west from Sant Pere de Rodes to C 252 and head south to Figueres, the main city in what is known as *l'alt,* or upper, Empordà.

Figueres

From Roses it is an easy 18-km (11-mile) drive on C 260 inland to Figueres, a small, pleasant city with a major attraction: the **Teatre-Museu Dalí**, a tour-de-force that must be seen even if you don't like Dalí's work. From the small central plaza known as the Rambla, it's only a couple of blocks to Plaça Gala i Dalí and the museum, installed in a former theater that from the back resembles a pink box. The roof is adorned with rows of huge white "eggs" and its walls are dotted with what look like loaves of spiral-shaped bread. Attached is **Torre Galatea**, the building where Dalí, who was born in Figueres in 1904, was living when he died in 1989. Dalí is buried in the rotunda of the museum.

Inside the museum, every corner offers a different take on Dalí, demonstrating his wit, imagination, and sheer energy. His most famous Surrealist paintings are elsewhere, but there is ample variety here. The visitor is treated to a stunning range of artistic styles and media: a sculpted sofa that in perspective becomes ruby-red lips in a face; paintings of human figures fashioned from rocks and pebbles; an op-art painting of Lincoln; nude female mannequins, each with arms extended in a different direction, Shiva-style; Dalí's version of the Sistine Chapel; and much more. On the top floor is the Sala del Tesoro, with paintings by artists that Dalí admired, including El Greco and Urgüell. (Plans are afoot for some of the museum's works to be moved to Madrid's Museo Español de Arte Contemporáneo.) There is an interesting selection of Dalí memorabilia at **Distribucións d'Art Surrealiste**, a shop across the plaza from the museum entrance.

If you want to see where Dalí may have drawn some of his Surrealist inspiration, take a walk through the city center to view the Modernist buildings, especially the Excorxador Municipal, Casa Cusi, and Casa Salleras.

STAYING AND DINING IN FIGUERES

The ▶ **Hotel Durán**, with Dalí paintings displayed in the lobby, is centrally located and makes a good place for an overnight stay. The decor is theatrical, with "curtains" painted around each guest room door. The folklorically decorated dining room features very good regional dishes. Also noteworthy is the ▶ **Hotel Ampurdán**, located on N II on the northern outskirts of Figueres, which is so renowned for its kitchen that people drive south from France and from all over Spain just to experience such Ampurdán dishes as *platillo de oca con setas* (goose smothered in wild mushrooms), leg of lamb with anchovies, and partridge roasted with pears. The homemade sorbets are special (notably the mint, burnt almond, and Calvados), and the wine cellar is remarkable. You might try a local Ampurdán wine, such as the well-priced red Gran Recosund, vintage 1983. The hotel's guest rooms are adequate but plain, the dining room neat but unexceptional.

AROUND FIGUERES

Just 7 km (4 miles) northeast of Figueres is the medieval town of **Perelada**, popular with Catalans and other Europeans for its **Casino Castillo de Perelada**, a gambling casino ensconced in a handsomely decorated, turreted 15th-century castle. There is a museum in the castle with five guided tours a day. Each tour includes a glass of cava and a visit to the Gothic chapel and wine museum (lots of glasses and decanters, but no wine).

Girona

About 40 km (25 miles) south from Figueres and 100 km (62 miles) north of Barcelona on fast-travelling A 7, Girona is a modern city built around a medieval core, which itself was built over the Roman fortress of Gerunda. The medieval center is self-contained and of a size that allows for an interesting half-day walking tour of its dark, labyrinthine streets and important monuments.

If you enter Girona from Figueres on the slightly slower but more scenic N II, you'll see signs to the Plaça de la Independencia on the west bank of the rather murky Ríu Onyar, which divides the medieval part of the city on the east bank from the modern city on the west. Park in this area or farther south near Plaça de Catalunya, which straddles the river. Then cross to the east bank and walk north two blocks on Rambla Jacint Verdaquer. At the point where the street name changes to Rambla de la Llibertat, turn right: about three short blocks east is Plaça del VI, where the tourist office is located. Here you can pick up a map and walking-tour pamphlet of the medieval monuments and the *call* (medieval Jewish ghetto)—although Girona's sights are exceptionally well posted.

THE OLD TOWN

Start your visit to medieval Girona at the **Catedral de Santa María**. To reach it, continue north to Carrer de la Força, which was the heart of the *call*. Dark, narrow streets with barrel-vaulted arcades branch off from Carrer de la Força, the few reminders of Girona's rich Jewish heritage. From the ninth century to the 15th century the city had a large Jewish community, some of whose members were executed during the Inquisition; the rest were banished from Spain with all other Jews in 1492.

By following Força about two blocks more through the dim streets you will reach the Plaça de la Catedral, the center of the medieval town. Climb the 90 steps to the cathedral, which has the widest nave of any Gothic cathedral in the world. An admission fee entitles you to ascend the Romanesque bell tower, which offers a good view of the city; to tour the Romanesque cloister, enclosed by graceful arches adorned with carvings of animals on the capitals; and to visit the church treasury. The most unusual piece in the treasury—where most of the displays are of gilded church art and fine silver—

is the *Tapestry of the Creation,* a 12th-century embroidery with vivid, naïve representations of Adam and Eve and Noah's animals, a rare gem.

Emerging from the cathedral, descend to the plaza and turn right onto Carrer Ferràn el Catolic. A few steps ahead and on your left you'll encounter the 12th-century **Arab baths**, where you can visit the *frigidarium,* with its central pool wreathed by eight columns, and other salons for tepid, hot, and steam baths.

As you exit from the baths, take a left into the Plaça del Jurats and cross the bridge over the Ríu Galligants to visit the Benedictine monastery of Sant Pere de Galligants, in existence since 992 and now the site of the **Museu Arqueològic.** Notable Romanesque architectural features include the 11th-century door, decorated with plants and naïve creatures, and the cloister, on whose columns are sculpted New Testament stories. The museum displays prehistoric and Iberian items and finds from ancient Emporion (see the section on Empúries, above).

If you have found walking in the old quarter difficult, with all the steps and steep slopes, you'll enjoy the pleasant *level* walk by the Ríu Onyar along pedestrians-only Rambla de la Llibertat with its barrel-vaulted arcades. Trees by the river shade benches where old men in berets gather to sit and chat.

Modernist architect Rafael Masó lived in Girona. Ask the tourist office to point out the locations of his most interesting buildings. **Casa Teixidor**, on Carrer de Santa Eugenia, is one of the best known. Most are in the newer part of town, west of the river.

DINING AND STAYING IN GIRONA

For lunch, head inland from Rambla de la Llibertat to **Restaurant Cal Ros**, almost hidden along the wall behind the dim arches at Cort Real 9. It offers typical dishes, such as a country-style Spanish omelet with vegetables, in a homey dining room perfumed by a wood fire.

As an overnight choice, ▶ **Hotel Sol Girona** is the best in town, and is comfortable and convenient.

Inland around Girona

BANYOLES

If you have time before returning to Barcelona, you might drive 16 km (10 miles) northwest of Girona on C 150 to the lakeside town of Banyoles, which serves as a gateway to a series of charming small towns and, ultimately, to the rugged mountains of the Pyrenees. A circuit of the lake—which was the site of rowing and canoeing events in the 1992 Olympics—takes you to a tiny Romanesque chapel known as **Santa Maria de Porqueres**. The most notable features of this 12th-century lakeside church are the arches over the outside door and the animal carvings on the capitals of the columns inside.

BESALU

Besalú, a medieval village of stone houses and churches, with many noble 12th-century ruins, is 14 km (9 miles) northwest of Banyoles on C 150. The town also has a restored fortified Romanesque arched bridge (complete with portcullis) across the Ríu Fluvià. The best views are from the road and from the terrace of the **Café Can Quei**, which is built into the ancient stone walls in the village center. There is an interesting Romanesque church here, part of the 12th-century Benedictine monastery of Sant Pere, but it is closed to the public. Near the bridge, down a narrow lane, is an 11th-century *mikvah,* believed to be the only one remaining in Spain. This was the ritual bathing place for Jewish women and dates back to the era when Besalú had a sizable Jewish community. You can have lunch or coffee nearby at **Pont Vell 28**, an attractive restaurant on two levels with great views of the bridge; Tel: (9-72) 59-10-27. **Cúria Reial** is another good lunch stop, across from the arcaded town hall on Plaça de la Llibertat; Tel: (9-72) 59-02-63.

WEST INTO THE MOUNTAINS

From Besalú the road west enters more tortuous mountain terrain, passing through the volcanic zone of **Olot**, where ancient craters are now carpeted with forests and where the village of Castellfollit de la Roca, rising from jagged 180-foot-high basalt cliffs, makes a dramatic profile against the sky. The town of Olot is modern and industrial, with only a few Modernist buildings of interest. Two are of special note: the **Casa Sola Morales**, rebuilt in 1915 by Domènech i Montaner, with a balcony with sculptures, a loggia, and an ornamented gallery; and the Hospicio by Ventura Rodríguez, now the **Museu Comarcal de la Garrotxa**, with Modernist paintings and sculpture.

You can return to Banyoles by turning onto GE 524 at Olot and heading east, a beautiful drive past hillsides of pines and poplars. **Santa Pau** is a completely intact medieval village with houses made of reddish and black volcanic rock, 9 km (5½ miles) from Olot. Coming upon its cobbled lanes, overhanging arches, and fretted wood balconies is like entering a time warp.

From here you can choose from at least two travel strategies: One is to continue west toward Ripoll and the Pyrenees to pick up the Romanesque route (see below); another is to return to Barcelona by heading south from Olot or from Ripoll by way of Vic, also covered in the Romanesque route. If you're pressed for time, both the N II and A 7 speed southwest to Barcelona from Girona.

THE ROMANESQUE ROUTE

Along the twisting mountain roads that lead from Barcelona through the Pyrenees and eventually into France or the small republic of Andorra lies one of the richest Romanesque lodes in Europe. An isolated chapel here, a decaying hermitage there—everywhere your eyes turn is some remnant of Catalonia's Romanesque past. If your interest in the period is marginal, you may still exult in the mind-bending scenery, which changes around every turn. For the skier the Pyrenees provide another lure; for the gastronome there is the chance to experience Pyrenees Catalan cuisine firsthand.

Our route goes north from Barcelona on N 152 directly to Vic, then as far north as Puigcerdà, then northwest in the Pyrenees through La Seu d'Urgell and other towns on the way to Vielha, and back to Barcelona via Solsona, with a stop at Montserrat. To do this properly would take a minimum of five days. If you have less time, say, two to three days, you could make La Seu d'Urgell your westernmost stop in the Pyrenees; with more time (an extra two or three days) for a larger loop, you could add Lleida and Tarragona to the end of your trip, before heading northeast back to Barcelona. This route, it should be noted, often follows narrow roads along twisting, mountainous terrain where driving must be taken slowly.

VIC

Vic, which predated the Romans, is a bustling market town 67 km (42 miles) north of Barcelona. It has an arcaded main square, whose side streets have many fascinating food shops where you can buy the local specialty, *salchichón* (salami-like sausages). Vic's attractions are considerable: the late-18th-century **Catedral de Sant Pere**, built on the remains of a Romanesque church (whose crypt survives), with 20th-century sepia-toned murals throughout by Catalan artist Josep Maria Sert; a heavily restored third-century Roman temple; numerous churches; and, best of all for the art lover, the **Museu Diocesa**, a treasure house of early Catalan paintings and sculptures (Romanesque and Gothic), many of which were removed (for protection) from decaying churches in remote areas of the Pyrenees. There is a lovely alabaster retable of the Passion, a 14th-century Gothic masterwork of 21 panels on three levels by Bernat Saulet.

Staying and Dining in Vic

For lunch or dinner in Vic try **La Taula**, a stylish place across from the Roman temple, at Plaça de Don Miguel de Clariana 4, serving Catalan dishes with a *nueva cocina* flair; Tel: (9-3) 886-3229. The modern ▶ **Parador de Vic**, just 14 km (9 miles) west of town, is a tranquil place to stay, with soul-stirring views of the mountains and the Sau reservoir. If you are rushed for time, Vic is an easy day trip from Barcelona.

NORTH FROM VIC

The 33-km (20-mile) drive northeast of Vic to **Rupit** on C 153 is lovely. This stone village, cobbled from end to end, is a favorite with Barcelonans, many of whom have built country houses here. The mountain air and views are spectacular. **Hostal Estrella**, on Plaça des Bisbe Font, serves a decent lunch with even nicer views; Tel: (9-3) 856-5005.

Ripoll

Ripoll, 38 km (24 miles) due north of Vic, boasts one of the finest Romanesque architectural gems in Catalonia (albeit one that was much rebuilt in the 19th century after a devastating fire): the **Monasterio de Santa Maria**, known for its five naves and seven apsed transepts, as well as for its serenely beautiful cloister and finely sculpted 12th-century door, still miraculously intact. The nearby **Iglesia de San Pedro** has an interesting folklore museum. You can lunch or dine modestly at the ▶ **Hotel Solana del Ter**, at the edge of town; quarters are spartan but clean, in case you decide to spend the night.

Just 10 km (6 miles) northeast of Ripoll on C 151 is the **Monasterio de San Juan de las Abadesas**, a haunting place founded in the ninth century, dark and mysteriously medieval inside. Its major treasures are the 13th-century polychrome wood sculptures in the *Descent from the Cross,* which look remarkably modern. Romanesque sculpture and textiles are stunningly displayed in an adjacent museum.

THE CERDANYA REGION

The Cerdanya is the large upper valley of the Sagres river in the heart of the Catalan Pyrenees, wedged between France, Andorra, and the rest of Spain. It runs from east to west at an altitude of about 3,000 feet, is surrounded by mountain peaks reaching 9,750 feet, and has a dry and usually sunny climate. The Cerdanya was divided between Spain and France by the 1659 Treaty of the Pyrenees.

North of Ripoll beyond Ribas de Freser the N 152, becomes incredibly twisted and curving. Skiers will be tempted to head to **Puigcerdà**, a winter-sports center near the French border, 63 km (39 miles) northwest of Ripoll. There are also a golf course at Puigcerdà (Real Club de Golf de la Cerdanya) and a sports center with an ice-skating rink and an indoor swimming pool. The area is ideal for mountain hiking and trout fishing. The slate-roofed stone houses common in the Cerdanya are also common across the border in France.

Just over the border is something of a curiosity, a Spanish town completely surrounded by France—the result of a 1659 treaty error in which 33 Cerdanya villages were ceded to France, but **Llívia**, classified as a town, was not. It remains a pretty little town with narrow streets, stone houses with slate roofs, a fortified church with slits in the upper walls, and a historic apothecary shop (in business from 1415 to 1926), now a museum. If you want to spend the night, the modern ▶ **Hotel Llívia** is a comfortable place, with spectacular mountain views from all rooms, an attractive lobby, tennis courts, and an outdoor pool.

Staying and Dining in the Cerdanya Region

To savor the Cerdanya region, you might base yourself at a ski resort, such as one at the popular and well-developed town of **La Molina**, with facilities for every skill level, about 15 km (9 miles) south of Puigcerdà on N 152. The ▶ **Hotel Palace** is located at the bottom of the ski slopes, with garden, pool, and tennis facilities; the ▶ **Hotel Adserá** has a garden and pool and is handy to the slopes. One of the area's premier hotels is the ▶ **Hotel Boix**, on route C 1313 in Martinet (26 km/16 miles southwest of Puigcerdà), from which you can sally forth for daily ski or hiking excursions. If you stay at the Boix, request a room overlooking the fast-running stream next to the hotel, and plan to eat as many meals as possible in the excellent restaurant, presided over by owner-chef José María Boix.

A famous restaurant in this area, which attracts hordes of Barcelona weekenders, is **Can Borell**, known for its creative Catalan cooking. It is located at the end of a rugged corkscrew of a country road 10 km (6 miles) west, then north, of Puigcerdà, in the minuscule village of Meranges. You'll dine in a rustic, fieldstone-walled house with a fireplace and slate floors, on top-of-the-world mountain views that compete with the excellent fresh trout with almonds, wild boar, and rabbit with pear and parsnips that arrive on your plate. Don't let the autocratic host intimidate you. There are eight tiny guest rooms if you choose to spend the night.

LA SEU D'URGELL

About 50 km (31 miles) west from Puigcerdà on C 1313 is La Seu d'Urgell, a historic town west of the Cerdanya with considerable charm that makes a desirable base for daily outings. Its prospect is thrilling—located in the valley of the Ríu Segre, with the peaks of the Andorra mountains and Sierra del Cadí surrounding it. **L'Anella Olímpica** is a new riverside sports and recreation park on the Segre here that was built for the 1992 Summer Olympics white-water canoe and kayak competitions.

La Seu has a pleasant, tree-shaded *rambla* for an after-dinner stroll. But the medieval stone arcades that line the Carrer Mayor will really catch your eye—the upper stories of some ancient houses almost touch each other over the narrow, cobbled streets. The sprawling 11th- to 12th-century Romanesque **cathedral**, seat of the largest diocese in Catalonia, is eerily dark inside. Note especially the 13th-century cloister and the front façade. Next door is the **Museu Diocesa**, which contains a fascinating collection of Romanesque and Gothic art, including a very rare eighth-century copy of *Commentary on the Apocalypse,* written by a monk, Beato de Liébana.

Staying and Dining in La Seu d'Urgell

The place to stay, if you want to capture the ambience of the town, is the ▶ **Parador de la Seo de Urgell**, located diagonally across from the cathedral. This modern hotel is on the site of the old convent of Santo Domingo. A dramatic four-story-high atrium lounge, hung with plants, was built inside the tawny walls and arches of the convent's cloister. The hotel boasts a small indoor swimming pool and a dining room that serves such tasty regional dishes as *butifarra amb mongetes* (typical Catalan sausage with white beans). A good alternative choice on the outskirts of La Seu, ▶ **El Castell**, a Relais & Châteaux property, also has an excellent restaurant (and a swimming pool) and is located just below the remains of an ancient stone fortress.

If you like gustatory discoveries, plan on dinner one night at **Hostal Dolcet**, 4 km (2½ miles) east of La Seu in the tiny hamlet of Alas. It's a modest place, serving mountainous helpings of hearty local specialties at moderate prices. It's not fancy food, but such dishes as wonderfully fresh trout from the Segre and quail in a succulent brown sauce are memorable. Arrive hungry. Tel: (9-73) 35-20-16.

SOUTH TO CARDONA

Leaving La Seu d'Urgell, follow C 1313 south along the Ríu Segre through several spectacular pink and gray canyons. (Both Organyà and Coll de Nargó along the way have beautiful Romanesque churches.) Turn off at Bassella to L 301 (51 km/32 miles from La Seu), which leads you into **Solsona**, a delightful old Roman town with venerable façades sporting traces of sculpture and heraldic symbols. Solsona's special jewel is its **Museu Diocesa**, installed in an archbishop's palace around the corner from the cathedral of Santa Maria (whose chief treasure is a 12th-century statue, *Virgin of the Cloister*). In the museum you'll find Romanesque frescoes, *santos,* and paintings removed from churches all over the region.

From Solsona it's only 20 km (12 miles) east on route C 1410 to the ▶ **Parador Duques de Cardona**, situated in a medieval fortress-castle on top of a hill. If you've ever wanted to know how it feels to be a feudal lord, spend a night under the high ceilings inside the immense, thick walls—or at least stop for a fulfilling meal on the way back to Barcelona.

MONTSERRAT

Continuing southeast on C 1410, it is about 32 km (20 miles) to Manresa, an industrial town, and some 20 squiggly, curvaceous kilometers (12 miles) farther south to Montserrat. (Montserrat is also an easy day's outing from Barcelona, about 50 km/30 miles southeast.) Montserrat is actually the name of the mountains—a range of dramatic, jagged gray fingers of rock reaching upward more than 3,500 feet—that have given their name to the Benedictine **Monasterio de Montserrat**, one of Catalonia's best-known and most-visited tourist sites, especially for religious pilgrims. The remote site is spectacular—awe-inspiring, even—making it a natural spot for a hermitage.

The main attraction at Montserrat—unlike some of the other Catalan monasteries, which are renowned for their architecture—is the Romanesque statue *La Moreneta* (Black Madonna), which sits on the altar in the basilica. The Black Madonna is the patron saint of Catalonia and the object of many pilgrimages, so be prepared to encounter tour buses and crowds. The 12th-century Romanesque door survives, although much of the original church was wantonly destroyed by Napoleon's troops. Most of what stands was built in the 19th century. The Escolanía (a boys' choir) of Montserrat performs daily at church services.

In addition to the church, there is the **Museu de Montserrat**, on the Plaça de Santa Maria. One part of the museum houses a collection of artworks attributed to Caravaggio, El Greco, and other Italian, Flemish, and Spanish painters, and the modern section holds works by Picasso, Dalí, Rusiñol, and others. The cave of the Virgin—where the statue of the

Virgin was said to have been found in the year 880—can be reached by a 20-minute walk from the monastery.

Exploring the Pyrenees

The road west from La Seu to Sort, and then north over the 6,200-foot-high mountain pass **Puerto de la Bonaigua** into the Vall d'Aran and the town of Vielha, offers some of Spain's most spectacular mountain scenery. The going is slow and tortuous, on a road unpaved in some spots and often under construction in others. It snakes along the edge of steep mountains, climbing ever higher through dense pine forests toward the snowy peaks around the pass. The drive from La Seu to Sort is 53 km (33 miles) on C 146; from Sort to Vielha is another 76 km (47 miles) on C 147.

Hikers and others who savor the silent isolation of the mountains may want to schedule a few days in the **Parc Nacional de Aigües Tortes**, which has refuges for hikers and is accessible from lodgings in nearby towns, including Boí and Espot. Turn off C 147 at the road to Espot, 24 km (15 miles) north of Sort.

THE VALL D'ARAN

Approaching Bonaigua Pass, 53 km (33 miles) north of Sort, the road climbs through a landscape littered with immense boulders. The air becomes purer and more bracing and, as you arrive at the pass, the slate roofs of the houses in the **Vall d'Aran**, along Ríu Garona, suddenly come into view.

The valley, a narrow strip of towns surrounded by mountains reaching as high as 12,000 feet, was cut off by snow from the rest of Spain for more than half of each year until 1948, when a tunnel was opened to provide access from the south as an alternative to the pass. Until then the local residents—whose language, Aranese, resembles Catalan—maintained a tranquil rural existence in their gray stone houses with deeply sloped slate roofs.

Now the valley has become a modern ski center (the main ski complexes are **Vaqueira Beret**, the best in Spain, and **Tuca**), and pizza parlors and high-rise apartment buildings dot the landscape. About the only way to make contact with traditional culture is to view some of the small Romanesque churches (from the outside, because they're usually locked) in towns such as Salardú and Tredòs, or the small museum (open only in late afternoon) in **Vielha**, the capital of the region. A peaceful place to stay, with scenic views, is the ► **Parador del Valle de Arán**, 2 km (just over a mile) from Vielha.

A scrap of history may be encountered at the ► **Parador Don Gaspar de Portolá**, in Arties, a short drive east of Vielha.

The parador, built in the style of a ski lodge with sloping roof and rustic furnishings, is adjacent to the home of the Catalan explorer of the same name who served as governor of lower California in the 18th century and is credited with founding a number of missions in California. If you ask at the reception desk a staff member may show you inside the Portolá family chapel and home, which features window-like glass compartments in the walls, one housing a beehive, others designed to protect birds from winter cold.

If you prefer hiking to skiing, visit in the warmer months, when the mountain trails are open and the crowds smaller or nonexistent. The tourist office in Vielha can provide you with a trail map.

For a quick return to Barcelona or to points of interest in southern Catalonia, exit from Vielha due south through the tunnel (instead of east back through the Bonaigua Pass) in the direction of Lleida.

SOUTHERN CATALONIA

Barcelona serves as a good base for forays into the Roman and medieval precincts of southern Catalonia, as well as to the Mediterranean coast and the wine and cava country. Any of the following places can be visited on a one-day trip from Barcelona—although it would be best to stay overnight if you are going to Tarragona. As these destinations are quite close to Barcelona, choose your travel days with care; on weekends and at rush hours the highways are inevitably clogged and slow.

Penedès Wine Country

You can pass a pleasant day visiting the wineries of the Penedès. Such a visit is easy from either Barcelona or Tarragona; our route takes you from Barcelona. It is less than 45 km (28 miles) on the A 7 *autopista* west from Barcelona to **Vilafranca del Penedès**, the wine capital of Catalonia.

The **Museu dei Vi** (wine museum) in the 14th-century royal palace of the kings of Aragón provides an excellent introduction to wine making. It features a re-creation of a wine cellar and displays of huge wooden presses and other tools used to cultivate and harvest grapes and make wine. Also on display are religious art and 17th- to 19th-century ceramics. Local vintners take turns as hosts for the tasting room, where you can sample and purchase their products at the end of the museum visit. The museum is on Plaça Jaume II, a lovely spacious square on which stands the Basílica de Santa María, which has a Gothic portal, as well as a statue of

Catalan *castellers* atop one another's shoulders. The Torres vineyard just outside Vilafranca welcomes visitors for tours and tasting.

In **Sant Sadurní d'Anoia**, 11 km (7 miles) northeast of Vilafranca, every road sign seems to point to a cava-making establishment. This town, the cava capital of Spain, is a showplace of turn-of-the-century Catalan Modernist architecture. A visit to the Codorníu cava winery offers an opportunity to see the town's most important examples of the Modernist style—the family home and the cellars, with their vaulted ceilings and stained-glass windows, designed by Josep Puig i Cadafalch—as well as to observe production of the bubbly.

The Monasteries North of Tarragona

SANTES CRUES

It is easy to combine a wine tour with a visit to the area's two spectacular monasteries, but many travellers will require at least a full day to savor these two majestic complexes. Take A 7 to the turnoff 13 km (8 miles) south of Vilafranca onto A 2 west; turn north after about 20 km (12 miles) and follow the signs to the **Monasterio de Santes Crues**, which was founded in 1157 by the Cistercians. The uphill road approaching this fabulous monastery is lined with buildings that were once dependents but are now private residences. The monastery, like the one at Poblet (see below), was sacked in the 19th century. A tour reveals a Gothic cloister whose delicate columns are adorned with sculptures of flowers and animals; a cross-shaped church containing the tombs of the 13th- and 14th-century Catalan monarchs Pedro II and Jaume II and a superb rose window; a Romanesque infirmary cloister; and a cavernous wine cellar with two huge vats that still smell of wine. Pause after your tour at one of the sidewalk cafés in the lower town for a drink and an almond pastry, a local specialty.

SANTA MARIA DE POBLET

Return to A 2 and continue northeast about 20 km (12 miles) to **Montblanc**, a medieval town surrounded by thick 14th-century walls punctuated by 17 towers. The town is a pleasant place for a stroll, especially Friday mornings when there is a market in the main square.

The monumental **Monasterio de Santa Maria de Poblet** is just 15 km (9 miles) to the southwest. It was founded in 1150 by Ramón Berenguer IV after he recaptured Catalonia from the Moors. It became the home of a powerful Cistercian order and the religious center (for retreats) of the kings of

Catalonia and Aragón until 1835, when it was sacked and destroyed during an anticlerical rebellion. In 1940 the monks returned and have been restoring this magnificent property ever since. A guided tour leads you through the royal pantheon, with tombs of Catalan and Aragón kings from the 12th century, the monks' enormous dormitory, an imposing Gothic cloister, Romanesque church, the palace of King Martín the Humane, the restored library (which once had 20,000 volumes, all destroyed), and other facilities.

AROUND THE MONASTERIES

L'Espluga de Francolí, a small spa town a few minutes west of the monastery, has one of the oldest (1913) cooperative wine cellars in Catalonia, built in a Catalan Gothic style by Pere Domènech i Roura, son of Lluís Domènech i Montaner, a leader of the Modernist movement.

As you drive through the lovely, rolling landscape along N 240 you'll pass almond orchards, vineyards, olive groves, and fields bordered by wild poppies and you'll smell air perfumed with the scent of rosemary and thyme. While driving in this area and toward Tarragona, consider stopping to taste the typical *calçotada* (braised tender onions) offered at numerous roadside restaurants. The town of **Valls**, between Montblanc and Tarragona, is famous for this dish, as well as for its *castellers,* who form human pyramids at fiesta time by climbing on one another's shoulders.

Costa Daurada

The Costa Daurada, the stretch of shoreline between Barcelona and Valencia, has many places of interest even for those who don't love the beach. Between Barcelona and Tarragona, the sights mentioned can be seen in a full day's outing, but to enjoy Tarragona we recommend at least one overnight there. Tarragona makes a convenient and less stressful base than Barcelona for exploring southern Catalonia, including the above-mentioned winery and monastery tours.

SITGES

Sitges, one of the most popular and charming beach towns on the Costa Daurada, is about 40 km (24 miles) southwest of Barcelona. It has been a center of Catalan painting, music, Modernist architecture, and other arts since painter Santiago Rusiñol made it his home at the end of the 19th century, and today it attracts visitors from all over Europe, including a large number of gays.

Sitges has a lovely seaside promenade, fine beaches, and several important museums. The **Museu Cau Ferrat**, a folklorically decorated house on Carrer Fonollar, where Rusiñol lived, contains works mainly by Rusiñol, but with a sampling of El Greco, Picasso, Utrillo, and others, as well as scores of objects that Rusiñol collected from many eras. The **Museu Maricel de Mar**, next door, features Gothic religious art, and the **Museu Romàntic**, in an 18th-century manor house on Carrer San Gaudenci, has decorative arts of two centuries and an enchanting antique doll and toy collection. Near Museu Cau Ferrat, at the top of the narrow Carrer de Fonollar, is the **Mirador Miguel Utrillo**, a splendid overlook that takes in the sea, beach, and rock formations.

Sitges sponsors an annual theater festival in the spring and a horror-film festival in the fall; it is also known for its displays of "carpets" of flowers during the Corpus Christi festival in June. Modernist-style houses can be found on Carrers San Bartolomé, San Gaudenci, and Isla de Cuba.

At **El Vendrell**, about 30 km (19 miles) south of Sitges, there is a museum and archive dedicated to the Catalan musician Pau Casals, housed in his villa at Carrer Guipuzcoa 12. Casals, who summered here in the 1930s, is revered in Catalonia not only as a cellist but also as a conductor and for making music available to the general public.

Staying and Dining in Sitges

The prime place to stay in Sitges is the new deluxe ▶ **Hotel San Sebastián Playa**, whose 50 rooms overlook a small garden and swimming pool or the sandy beach. The decor is cool, blue, and elegant. The hotel has a good dining room and a sleek café, the Grand, facing the water. Another asset: It's just two short blocks from the Sitges museums. Also appealing are the ▶ **Aparthotel Mediterráneo** and the smaller ▶ **Hotel Subur Marítim**, both with swimming pools and a full range of amenities. Two private, Modernist-style residences, the ▶ **Romàntic** and ▶ **La Renaixença**, offer comfortable but simple lodgings. Some rooms have balconies, and each residence has a leafy private garden.

Among Sitges's many good restaurants is **La Fragata**, Passeig de la Ribera, where fresh seafood is served on a terrace. Tel: (9-3) 894-1086. Another fine restaurant with a view is **La Cucanya**, perched high above the sea at Racó de Santa Llucía, in Vilanova i la Geltrú, the town just south of Sitges. Tel: (9-3) 815-1934.

Tarragona

While you visit this modern seaside city, about 105 km (65 miles) southwest of Barcelona, keep in mind that Tarragona (or Tarraconensis, as it was known then) once controlled most of Roman Spain. Emperors Augustus and Hadrian found the city a restful retreat; Pliny praised the local wine;

Martial raved about its golden light. Chances are, with all the fragments of Roman columns, walls, and mosaics scattered about the old city, native son Pontius Pilate might recognize parts of it still, even though subsequent invasions by Franks, Visigoths, and Moors reduced much of Roman Tarraconensis to rubble. It is easy to understand why the Romans were attracted here in the first place: Perched on a limestone cliff some 260 feet above the sea, with miles of beach right and left, Tarragona is in a splendid natural location.

ROMAN AND MEDIEVAL TARRAGONA

While Roman remains seemingly pop up everywhere in modern, industrial Tarragona, a good way to come to grips with the city is to begin at the Roman **amphitheater**, located at the lower level of town near the beach. Three early Christians were burned alive there in A.D. 259, and the amphitheater was later used as a quarry. Within its ruins are the remains of a 12th-century church, Santa Maria del Milagro.

Just north of the amphitheater is the **Museu Arqueològic**, on Passeig de Sant Antoni, where you will find several fine Roman pavements (including one of a ferocious Medusa's head), remnants from a temple of Jupiter, many impressive marble heads and headless torsos, and other objects from local Roman sites.

Continue north a few blocks uphill to the medieval quarter of town. As you walk up the narrow Carrer Santa Ana you will pass numerous art galleries, antiques shops, and the **Museu de Arte Moderno,** which exhibits the works of local artists. The **Catedral de Santa Tecla,** the largest cathedral in Catalonia, was built on the site of a mosque, which was earlier a temple of Jupiter. Reached via a series of wide steps, the cathedral dominates the medieval quarter. The rows of gargantuan Gothic sculptures of the Apostles in niches along the portico are overwhelming. Begun in the late 11th century in Romanesque style, the cathedral incorporates the gamut of Spanish architectural styles. Note especially the 15th-century retable in the main chapel, the fine double doorway to the cloister, the cloister itself, the 52 Renaissance tapestries in the diocesan museum, and an even rarer Gothic one in the chapter house.

A must in Tarragona is a walk along the **Passeig Arqueològic,** which can be entered just north of the cathedral. This leads you, on a path shaded by cypress trees (which Catalans will tell you were a sign of hospitality in the Middle Ages), past the mammoth ancient walls reputedly built by the Scipio family, past others built by Augustus, and past even earlier Iberian ones. You'll pass six ancient gates, as well as grottoes, numerous statues, and artifacts that help bring Roman Tarraconensis alive. Entrances to the walk are at Via de L'Imperi Roma, Bojada del Rosario, and Plaça del Pallol.

MODERN TARRAGONA

Modern Tarragona centers around a long tree-shaded promenade, called Rambla Nova, that bisects the city east to west. Lined with boutiques, chic shops, and sidewalk cafés, as well as with such Modernist buildings as the convent of Las Teresianes by Bernardi Martorell and Casa Salas by Ramón Salas i Ricomà, the *rambla* is a great place for a stroll, ending at the east end at the Balcó del Mediterrani, a huge square that offers a sweeping panorama of the beach, sea, and amphitheater below (reachable by a few stairs).

STAYING AND DINING
IN TARRAGONA

The best place to stay in town is the venerable, recently remodeled ▶ **Imperial Tarraco** hotel, just above the amphitheater. The balcony of your comfortable room will give you an incredible view of both amphitheater and the sea. The ▶ **Lauria** hotel on Rambla Nova is another centrally located and comfortable place to stay, if the Imperial Tarraco is full.

For an excellent meal of fresh seafood in an unpretentious setting, descend to **Restaurant La Puda**, at Moll de Pescadors 25, across the street from the pavilion where the fishermen dock. (A siren signals the beginning of an auction of the day's catch around 3:30 or 4:00 P.M.) Good choices at La Puda include the *arrosejat,* a dish similar to a *paella,* made with noodles instead of rice; the house fish soup; and the appetizer platter of the day's fresh seafood. Tel: (9-77) 21-15-11. Another modest, rustic seaside restaurant is **Sol Ric**, at Via Augusta 227 (one of many seafood places along this sea-hugging boulevard), where on temperate evenings you can dine in the open air on *paella* or fresh red mullet in a *romesco* sauce (a local specialty made from dried sweet peppers, garlic, almonds, and olive oil). Tel: (9-77) 23-20-32. For fancier dining, local gourmets and the vintners of Penedès head southwest a few miles on N 340 to **Cambrils**, a popular resort town known for its good food. Especially notable here are **Eugenia**, Carrer Consolat de Mar 80, with a delightful terrace and garden and inventive seafood specialties, Tel: (9-77) 36-01-68; and **Can Gatell-Rodolfo**, Passeig Miramar 27, with excellent fish and rice dishes and a terrace overlooking the fishing port, Tel: (9-77) 36-01-06.

AROUND TARRAGONA

For a last glimpse of Roman Tarragona, just 4 km (2½ miles) north of town on the N 240 (toward Lleida) is the **Acueducto**

de les Ferreras, a two-tiered Roman aqueduct with 25 arches, known locally as Pont del Diablo (Devil's Bridge). If you follow the road from here to Constantí, you'll shortly (after 10 km/6 miles) come upon the **Mausoleo de Centcelles**, two pink-tiled buildings that straddle a vineyard. One has a gigantic cupola (restored by German archaeologists) and mosaic decorations, many with Christian themes. Two theories to explain the mausoleum are that Emperor Constantine had it built for his son Constans or that it was built by a fourth-century Roman patrician—no one knows for sure how it came about.

If you are driving south to Valencia, a slight detour from A 7 inland on C 235 brings you to **Tortosa** (83 km/52 miles south of Tarragona), a handy lunch stop (or overnight, if you choose) on the way.

Tortosa's attractions include the old Jewish quarter, the graceful arcaded galleries in the 14th-century bishop's palace, the unusual three-story patio in the Colegio de Sant Lluis, which Charles V founded for the schooling of Muslim converts, and 11 Modernist buildings scattered throughout the town. A medieval market has been reconstructed stone by stone in the municipal park. The real sleeper of Tortosa is its **cathedral**, begun in 1347. You enter through a 14th-century pure Gothic cloister. The cathedral interior is also Gothic, with several Baroque chapels. The prizes are the finely carved stone pulpits and a 14th-century polychrome triptych that looks as fresh as yesterday. The double ambulatory behind the main altar is rare and remarkable for its state of preservation.

The ▶ **Parador Castillo de la Zuda**, built into an old citadel at the upper western tip of town, affords marvelous views of the Ríu Ebro, plains, and mountains, and a true castlelike ambience. It has one of the better restaurants in the parador system, with fine regional cooking. The *paella valenciana* is a real winner.

Lleida

The city of **Lleida** (Lérida), capital of the Catalonian province of the same name, is a logical stopping-off point if you're going west from Tarragona to Zaragoza in Aragón. Lleida has taken its knocks through time. Local chieftains battled both Carthaginians and Romans; later, Pompey and Caesar fought between themselves over the settlement. The Moors irrigated the surrounding farmlands, but when they were driven out the city declined, and later was devastated during the War of the Spanish Succession, the War of Independence (Peninsular War) against Napoleon, and the 20th-century Spanish Civil War.

No wonder, then, that so much of old Lleida is gone, leaving a congested, industrial center. Still, like most Spanish cities, Lleida also has its treasures. You'll find some of them in the old quarter called Canyeret, a difficult area to drive in because of perilously narrow streets. Romanesque enthusiasts will rush to Plaça San José and the **Iglesia de San Lorenzo**, a 14th-century limestone delight, supposedly built on the site of a Roman temple, later a mosque. Inside are barrel-vaulted stone ceilings and four elaborately detailed retables depicting the lives of San Lorenzo and other saints. The less interesting Neoclassical new cathedral, built in the 18th century, is three blocks south.

The **Seu Vella** (Old Cathedral), which graphically demonstrates the transition from Romanesque to Gothic in its architectural style, is located on the grounds inside the fortified but decayed walls of La Zuda, the Moorish fortress on a wooded hilltop around which Lleida was built. For some 240 years (from 1707 to 1948) the cathedral was used as a military garrison, and the damage that caused is slowly being repaired. The cloister is remarkable, with towering Gothic arches and columns, pine and copper beech trees, and sweeping views of the city below. Only a few of the Zuda's walls survived a 19th-century French siege.

Fans of Modernist architecture might devote more time to Lleida than others, as there are almost a dozen buildings of interest; inquire at the tourist office for a listing. For spending the night, ▶ **Hotel Condes de Urgell II** is modern and convenient (though on a busy highway) and serves decent food. **Molí de la Nora** is a rustic restaurant with a garden, located 7 km (4 miles) outside town on Carretera Puigcerdà, the road north to La Seu d'Urgell. The kitchen has a way with fish, especially *dorada* (gilthead bream) baked in salt, served moist, delicate, and surprisingly unsalty, in a piquant sauce. Tel: (9-73) 19-00-17.

GETTING AROUND

Barcelona is the transportation center of Catalonia. It has a major international airport, El Prat de Llobregat, which is connected to London and New York by daily nonstop flights, and to other cities in the United Kingdom on a less-frequent schedule. Flights from all over Spain on Iberia and Aviaco, the domestic airline, land at El Prat. The Puente Aéreo is an hourly air-shuttle service between Madrid and Barcelona. No reservations are accepted; tickets can be bought at the airport or at a travel agency. The airports at Girona and Reus (outside Tarragona) handle cargo, not commercial passenger flights.

Catalonia may also be entered from France by train, car, or ferry. The most common point of entry by car is La

Jonquera, near Perpignan, which connects with the A 7 and N II to Barcelona. There are several other border crossings in the Pyrenees, including Puigcerdà and Collado d'Ares.

The best way to tour Catalonia is by car, although if your only destination is the Costa Brava beaches it is possible to get there using public transportation.

Catalonia's major highways fan out of Barcelona in every direction. In some cases—such as to Girona and to Tarragona—there are fast toll roads virtually paralleled by slower highways that pass through towns and carry a lot of truck traffic. Tolls on the *autopista* are extremely expensive—so expensive you can pay by credit card.

RENFE trains from the Sants station, a few blocks northwest of Barcelona's Plaça de Espanya, serve the Costa Brava north to La Jonquera at the French border and the Costa Daurada to the south. (To the north the train stops are somewhat inland, requiring bus connections to the beaches.) There is train service from Barcelona to the Pyrenees, through Vic, Ripoll, Puigcerdà, and to the French border. Other train routes include Barcelona through Lleida to Huesca in Aragón to the west; and Barcelona–Tarragona–Zaragoza (the latter also in Aragón).

There is also an extensive network of local buses that can be used to get to and around most parts of the region.

In the summer, Cruceros Costa Brava offers ferry service among various points on the coast, including Sant Feliu and Blanes.

ACCOMMODATIONS REFERENCE

The hotel rates listed below are projected rates for 1994, for double room, double occupancy, in pesetas. We strongly recommend that you confirm the price when making reservations.

When dialing telephone numbers from outside the country, drop the 9 in the area code.

Costa Brava

▶ **Almadraba Park Hotel.** Playa de Almadraba, 17480 **Roses.** Tel: (9-72) 25-65-50; Fax: 25-67-50. 9,900–12,800 pts.

▶ **Curhotel Hipócrates.** Carretera de Sant Pol 229, 17220 **Sant Feliu de Guíxols.** Tel: (9-72) 32-06-62; Fax: 32-38-04. 10,150 pts.

▶ **Hostal de la Gavina.** Plaça de Rosaleda, 17248 **S'Agaró.** Tel: (9-72) 32-11-00; Fax: 32-15-73; in U.S., Tel: (212) 856-0115; Fax: (212) 856-0193. 32,000 pts.

▶ **Hotel Aigua Blava.** Platja de Fornells, 17255 **Begur.** Tel: (9-72) 62-20-58; Fax: 62-21-12. 10,000 pts.

▶ **Hotel Ampurdán.** Carretera Madrid–Francia km 763,

17600 **Figueres.** Tel: (9-72) 50-05-62; Fax: 50-93-58. 10,500 pts.

▶ **Hotel Durán.** Lasauca 5, 17600 **Figueres.** Tel: (9-72) 50-12-50; Fax: 50-26-09. 6,600 pts.

▶ **Hotel Playa Sol.** Platja Pianch 5, 17488 **Cadaqués.** Tel: (9-72) 25-81-00; Fax: 25-80-54. 14,900 pts.

▶ **Hotel Port-Lligat. Port-Lligat,** 17488 **Cadaqués.** Tel: (9-72) 25-81-62. 5,600–7,600 pts.

▶ **Hotel Rocamar.** Virgen del Carmen, 17488 **Cadaqués.** Tel: (9-72) 25-81-50; Fax: 25-86-50. 10,400–17,000 pts.

▶ **Hotel Sol Girona.** Carrer de Barcelona 112, 17003 **Girona.** Tel: (9-72) 24-32-32; Fax: 24-32-33. 12,200 pts.

▶ **Parador de Aigua Blava.** Playa de Aiguablava, 17255 **Begur.** Tel: (9-72) 62-21-62; Fax: 62-21-66. 16,000 pts.

The Romanesque Route

▶ **El Castell.** Carretera Puigcerdà, km 129, Apartado 53, 25700 **La Seu d'Urgell.** Tel: (9-73) 35-07-04; Fax: 35-15-74; in the U.S., Tel: (212) 856-0115; Fax: (212) 856-0193. 14,000 pts.

▶ **Hotel Adserá.** 17537 **La Molina.** Tel: (9-72) 89-20-01; Fax: 89-20-25. 8,000 pts.

▶ **Hotel Boix.** Carretera Lleida–Puigcerdà (N 260), km 204, 25724 **Martinet.** Tel: (9-73) 51-50-50; Fax: 51-52-68. 13,500 pts.

▶ **Hotel Llívia.** Carretera de Puigcerdà, 17527 **Llívia.** Tel: (9-72) 89-60-00; Fax: 14-60-00. 5,550–7,800 pts.

▶ **Hotel Palace.** Avenida de Supermolina, 17537 **La Molina.** Tel: (9-72) 89-20-16. 10,759 pts.

▶ **Hotel Solana del Ter.** Carretera Barcelona Ripoll (N 152), km 140, 17500 **Ripoll.** Tel: (9-72) 70-10-62; Fax: 71-43-43. 8,800 pts.

▶ **Parador Don Gaspar de Portolá.** Afueras, Carretera de Baqueira Beret, 25599 **Arties.** Tel: (9-73) 64-08-01; Fax: 64-10-01. 10,000 pts.

▶ **Parador Duques de Cardona.** Castillo de Cardona, 08261 **Cardona.** Tel: (9-3) 869-1275; Fax: 869-1636. 8,500–10,500 pts.

▶ **Parador de la Seo de Urgell.** Santo Domingo 6, 25700 **La Seu d'Urgell.** Tel: (9-73) 35-20-00; Fax: 35-23-09. 9,000–10,500 pts.

▶ **Parador del Valle de Arán.** Carretera del Túnel (N 230), 25530 **Vielha.** Tel: (9-73) 64-01-00; Fax: 64-11-00. 9,500 pts.

▶ **Parador de Vic.** Carretera de Roda de Ter (km 14), 08500 **Vic.** Tel: (9-3) 888-7211; Fax: 888-7311. 12,000 pts.

Southern Catalonia

▶ **Aparthotel Mediterráneo.** Avenida Sofía 3, 08870 **Sitges.** Tel. and Fax: (9-3) 894-5134. 20,500 pts.

▶ **Hotel Condes de Urgell II**. Avenida de Barcelona 17, 25001 **Lleida**. Tel: (9-73) 20-23-00; Fax: 20-64-81. 11,500 pts.

▶ **Hotel San Sebastián Playa**. Port Alegre 53, 08870 **Sitges**. Tel: (9-3) 894-8676; Fax: 894-0430. 17,000 pts.

▶ **Hotel Subur Marítim**. Passeig Marítim, 08870 **Sitges**. Tel: (9-3) 894-1550; Fax: 894-0427. 14,150 pts.

▶ **Imperial Tarraco**. Passeig Palmeras, 43003 **Tarragona**. Tel: (9-77) 23-30-40; Telex: 56441; Fax: 21-65-66. 13,900 pts.

▶ **Lauria**. Rambla Nova 20, 43004 **Tarragona**. Tel: (9-77) 23-67-12; Fax: 23-67-00. 9,000 pts.

▶ **Parador Castillo de la Zuda**. 43500 **Tortosa**. Tel: (9-77) 44-44-50; Fax: 44-44-58. 11,000 pts.

▶ **La Renaixença**. Isla de Cuba 13, 08870 **Sitges**. Tel: (9-3) 894-0643; Fax: 894-8375. 7,500 pts.

▶ **Romàntic**. Sant Isidro 33, 08870 **Sitges**. Tel: (9-3) 894-8375; Fax: 894-8167. 7,800 pts.

THE BALEARIC ISLANDS

MINORCA, MAJORCA, IBIZA

By Ellen Hoffman

The Balearics are a group of islands in the western Mediterranean, south of Barcelona and east of Valencia. There are three principal islands—Minorca, Majorca, and Ibiza—as well as the tiny inhabited island of Formentera and twelve smaller, uninhabited islands, including Cabrera, which is occupied by the Spanish navy.

What attracts visitors to these islands are the turquoise and blue waters of the Mediterranean, their meteorologically benign latitudes, and their separation from the life and culture of mainland Spain (though only a half-hour away by plane). Despite the isolation geographic accident has dealt them, the islands have long received visitors both welcome and unwelcome—from Romans, Arabs, and pirates, to George Sand and Frédéric Chopin.

Three-thousand-year-old stone monuments, medieval cathedrals, and finely worked Phoenician sculptures and jewelry are only a few of the surviving clues to the rich and varied history of Minorca, Majorca, and Ibiza.

These days the great majority of visitors to the Balearics (pronounced "bahl-eh-ARE-ics") arrive from northern Europe. They head here in search of beaches and the jovial hullabaloo of pizza parlors and discotheques that inevitably spring up in resorts that cater to mass tourism.

Yet by scheduling a visit outside the high season (which is July and August, plus Easter, Christmas, and New Year's) and

535

by studying the map a bit, it is surprisingly easy to circumvent the crowds and penetrate to the islands' traditional core of natural and man-made attractions.

August—when Spaniards as well as foreigners take their vacations—is the primary vacation month in the Balearics, with crowds everywhere except on the most isolated beaches. If you don't like crowds, and your goal is to experience the "real" Balearics—as opposed to the façade constructed for tourists—avoid August. Sunny days appropriate for basking or picnicking can occur in almost any month, but for all but the most robust travellers the Mediterranean swimming season runs from late May into October. April and May—when flowers carpet the islands and the fields are green—are good months for sightseeing, as are September and much of October. Winter brings some wet, windy weather to all of the islands, but Minorca gets the brunt of it, while Ibiza remains milder.

Ideally, a visitor to the Balearics would spend several weeks exploring *each* island. **Minorca** has many archaeological sites, a wide selection of beaches, and the picturesque medieval fishing port of Ciudadela. Because Minorca is less visited than Majorca and Ibiza, it is also less developed, and services, such as transportation and historical site markers, though adequate, are somewhat less advanced.

Majorca, the largest island (about 60 miles east to west and as much as 45 miles north to south), has a major historic city—Palma—as well as two mountain ranges, including the Tramuntana in the west, which offers dramatic vistas of cliffs and sea. The island is a Mecca for artistic and literary expatriates but also has numerous resorts that cater almost exclusively to the package tourist trade, which operates all year but is most obvious during the summer.

The whitewashed villages and scenic coves and beaches of tiny **Ibiza**—only 25 miles from one end to the other—have been inundated by a wave of cosmopolitan tourists and expatriates ranging from the jet set to colorful dropouts who hawk their craftsy wares on the streets. The fortresslike Dalt Vila (Old City) serves as a backdrop to trendy nightlife in the summer (and, to a lesser degree, in the winter). But the cliffs and coves of the coast, the postage-stamp-size white towns inland, and the finely crafted jewelry and other Phoenician artifacts in the Puig des Molins museum are best savored outside the summer months, when the traffic has subsided on the island's roads, which are few and narrow.

Formentera, the fourth and smallest island on the Balearic circuit, can be reached only by boat and is known for its long, sandy, pristine beaches. It attracts day trippers, but is little developed for large-scale tourism.

When plotting your wanderings around the Balearics,

keep two things in mind: The islands are smaller than you think, and distances can be covered very rapidly. Although it's not recommended, you could probably visit every town on Ibiza or Minorca by car easily in two days. Majorca is larger, but from Palma across the island to Alcudia, on the north coast, is only about 50 km (31 miles).

Although Castilian Spanish is generally understood on the Balearic Islands, each island has its own dialect derived from Catalan. Street and highway signs may be in Castilian, the local dialect, or both—and this can be more than a bit confusing. The capital of Minorca, for example, is Mahón in Castilian and Maó in Menorquín. (We have used the local dialect and/or the names that appear on signs.) Some militant local-language-only proponents block out or destroy signs in Castilian, so it's not uncommon to encounter defaced or unreadable road markers and other signs.

MAJOR INTEREST

More than 600 miles of coastline
Seaside cliffs and mountains
Beaches—sandy, rocky, isolated, pristine
Inland rural landscapes and villages
Archaeological sites
Medieval monuments and towns
Traditional culture and food

Minorca
Prehistoric talayotic stone monuments and towns
Port of Mahón
Ciudadela, a medieval town
Beaches
View from Monte Toro

Majorca
Cathedral and Bellver castle in Palma
Tramuntana mountain range along north coast
Valldemossa: Chopin–George Sand apartment at
    monastery
Sa Calobra and Torrent de Pareis beach, gorge
Cabo de Formentor

Ibiza
Dalt Vila, the old town
Puig des Molins museum of Phoenician artifacts
Beaches and coast
Side trip to Formentera Island

The beauty and variety of the Balearic Islands' scenery—from isolated coves with crystalline waters, such as Macarelleta on Minorca, to the wild and windy pine-covered mountains of

Cabo de Formentor on Majorca—are the most compelling reasons for a visit. The islands offer endless opportunities for picnics, for hikes and excursions to beaches, forests, and archaeological monuments, and for vistas of the sea.

The Balearics are believed to have been settled about 2000 B.C. by people who arrived by sea (although no evidence of boats has been found) and lived in caves and in dwellings whose walls were constructed from the irregular gray stones that are still ubiquitous on the islands. Over time these people created the talayotic monuments, conical stone defensive towers and other megalithic remains (see below), many of which still stand on the islands.

Like other Mediterranean islands, the Balearics received waves of invaders and conquerors. Between about 500 B.C. and A.D. 1267, when they became part of the Catalan nation, the islands were occupied at various times by Phoenicians, Romans, and Arabs. During the 16th century, while the Spanish state was engaged in the colonization of the Americas, the islands were attacked by pirates and by Turks, who burned Ciudadela, then the capital of Minorca, in 1558.

For most of the 18th century Minorca was ruled by the English, who were awarded the island (as well as Gibraltar) in the Treaty of Utrecht in 1713; it was returned to Spain in 1802 as part of the Treaty of Amiens. When Spain proclaimed a new constitution and system of government after Franco's death in 1975, the Balearic island group was designated an *autonomía* (province), with its own capital and legislature in Palma, Majorca, the islands' largest city.

Since James the Conquerer (Jaume I) came from the mainland to capture Majorca from the Moors in the 13th century and founded a kingdom that embraced the islands (as well as Roussillon and Montpellier in France), Catalan language and culture have dominated daily life in the Balearics. But the perceptive visitor can still identify traces of invaders who came both before and after: in names with the prefix *Bini* or *Ben,* Arabic for "son of"; in the Roman theater and other ruins in Alcudia, Majorca; in the medieval stone towers constructed along the coasts to spot pirates cruising the Mediterranean; in the two gin factories in Minorca's port of Mahón, remnants of the British occupation of the island in the 18th century.

Medieval monuments—including the graceful cathedral that appears to be levitating above the port—abound in Palma, a city of more than 325,000 that is the capital of Majorca and of the island group. In the much smaller town of Ciudadela on Minorca many residents live in 400-year-old houses that can be identified on a map in the town museum. And the old city of Ibiza is to this day encircled by the imposing stone walls constructed in the 16th century as a defense against Turkish invaders.

The legacy of these crosscurrents of history is a common Balearic culture—distinct from that of the mainland—that also endows each island with unique traditions. Dancing and singing can be enjoyed, especially in the summer months, at hotels and plazas on all of the islands, accompanied by guitars in Minorca and by flute and drum in Ibiza. The traditional costumes of Minorca and Majorca consist of long skirts and headdresses for women and knickers for men, but Ibizan dress, said to be influenced by the proximity of North Africa, favors more voluminous skirts, dresses, and, for the men, pants, with accents of heavy gold or silver lockets and coils of necklaces. Today the visitor sees these costumes only at dancing or folkloric events.

The Food of the Balearics

The island cuisines are based on the usual Mediterranean natural ingredients, including olives and olive oil, and on such products as pork, especially the typical *sobrasada* sausage; local fish and seafood; vegetables such as eggplant and zucchini stuffed with ground meat or seafood; and figs and almonds, used as condiments.

Legend has it that mayonnaise was created in Minorca (where a Mahones—pronounced like "mayonnaise"—is a person who lives in Mahón, the capital) and discovered there by the duc de Richelieu during the brief French occupation in the 19th century. Either mayonnaise or its garlic-flavored sister, *ali-oli,* shows up commonly here as a complement to fish dishes or even as a spread for bread before the meal. Minorca is also famous for its *queso de payes* (Mahón cheese) and for its ice cream.

The spiral-shaped Majorcan pastry *ensaimada* has been adopted throughout the Balearics and can be found in any bar or cafeteria. The Mediterranean spiny lobster (*langosta*)—increasingly rare and ever more expensive—also forms the base of traditional dishes on all of the islands. Special drinks run the gamut from the Minorcan *pomada,* made of lemonade and gin and imbibed during the San Juan fiesta in June, to the *hierbas* liqueur, made of local Ibizan herbs.

The Wines of the Balearic Islands

The Balearic Islands now have an official *denominación de origen,* **Binissalem,** and more than 10,000 acres under vine, much of them in the two main wine areas of Majorca, Binissalem and Felanitx. The growers are producing some interesting red wines and *rosados* from the native Manto Negro, Callet, and Fogoneu grapes and a couple of *bodegas* are starting to make Cabernet Sauvignon. If you are visiting Majorca, try the wines of Bodegas José L. Ferrer and Herrederos de Ribas from Binissalem and the wines of Miguel Oliver from Felanitx.

—Gerry Dawes

Talayotic Monuments

Although each of the Balearic Islands has its own special places and personality, the three main islands share an unusual ancient legacy—prehistoric talayotic monuments. These distinctive stone monuments take three major forms: the *talayot,* a conical tower, perhaps used for defensive purposes; the *naveta,* a structure resembling an upside-down ship's hull, which may have been used for burials as well as for habitation; and the *taula,* a striking, T-shaped construction of two huge slabs of rock whose significance—probably religious—is still debated in archaeological circles.

While excavations on all three islands are exposing more ancient monuments all the time, **Minorca** has the largest number of accessible sites. Some pretalayotic structures date back to 2000 B.C., but the more sophisticated talayotic forms are believed to date from about 1100 B.C. until the first century A.D., when the Romans came to Minorca. The Minorcan landscape is strewn with these monuments, with the majority on the more salubrious southern half of the island, protected from the winds. Two *poblados* (towns)—Torre d'en Gaumes, on the road from Alayor to Son Bou, and Son Catlar, south of Ciudadela—offer the visitor an opportunity to view the different talayotic forms, as well as caves and the remains of other stone dwellings.

Visiting the monuments is a treat: Usually found in the fields of private farm residences, they lack waiting lines and entrance fees and, unless the farmer locks the gate at their entrance, are always accessible. Several of the most important sites, such as the *poblados* above, are indicated by purplish signs on main roads.

To visit more obscure sites, you'll need the archaeological map of Minorca (available in many shops), a keen sense of direction, a bottle of water, and a good pair of walking shoes for crossing fields and scaling stone walls. Local mores require the following courtesies: When entering private property, request permission (it will not be refused), and always close the gates you have opened (to keep the livestock from wandering away).

Proceeding from Barcelona, the closest mainland jumping-off point to the Balearics, we cover the islands from east to west; first Minorca and then Majorca, Ibiza, and, just off Ibiza, Formentera.

MINORCA

Ask a Minorcan what's special about the island and the answer will almost always be "the tranquillity." For those natives who may feel geographically—as well as socially and economically—isolated from the *movida* of modern Spain, this may be a damning assessment. But for most residents, as for visitors looking for a relaxing getaway, the tranquillity is welcome.

Of the three major islands, Minorca remains the least overrun by tourism—but, at the moment, it is also the most troubled. The traditional shoe and costume-jewelry industries have declined, and despite the outcry from environmentalists, economic need is spurring the island to the ever-increasing development of—and the subsequent pollution of—some of its loveliest natural areas. Most beach resorts on the island cater to package tours. If you want to plan your own itinerary you might consider using Mahón or Ciudadela—the two largest towns, one on each end of the island—as a base from which to make daily excursions to the more isolated areas. If you visit the island in July or August, however, reserve a car well in advance, because stocks are limited. For a summer visit, you should also book accommodations in advance. Help in finding a hotel is available from the tourist-office booth at the airport and at the Mahón tourist office.

Mahón and Ciudadela account for two-thirds of Minorca's entire population of about 68,000. All the other towns on the island are so small that you can tour each on foot in a few minutes. Mahón is close to the island's only airport and is the nucleus of the English-speaking expatriate community. Ciudadela, a 45-minute drive or an hour's bus ride to the west, has the atmosphere of a medieval city and offers access to some spectacular swimming beaches on the southern coast. The island's one major highway, the 47-km-long (29-mile) C 721, crosses the island east to west, connecting Mahón and Ciudadela, and passing through Minorca's other main towns—Alayor, Mercadal, and Ferrerias—along the way.

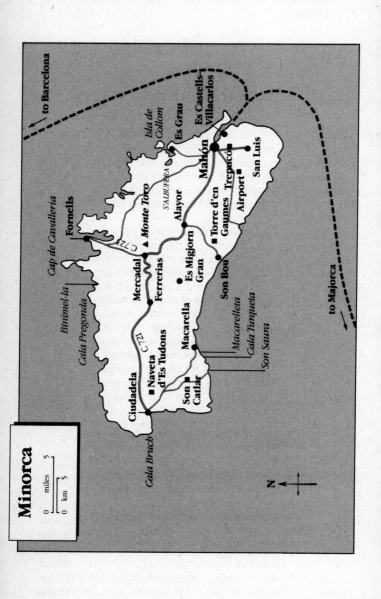

Gas stations are scarce in Minorca, but you'll find one or more along the main road just outside the large towns— Mahón, Alayor, Mercadal, Ferrerias, and Ciudadela. There are a few others a bit off the beaten track, such as one on the Mahón–Fornells road. Along with pharmacies and bakeries, gas stations on the island take turns opening on holidays and weekends. The list is disseminated each week in the local newspaper, *Menorca,* and in the English-language magazine *Roqueta,* which is published during the summer. There may be only three or four stations on the whole island open on Sundays, so check your tank before you set out.

MAHON

About 23,000 people—a third of the island's population—live in the quiet capital city of Mahón on the eastern end of Minorca. A five-minute drive from the airport, which is south of Mahón near San Luis, Mahón sprawls atop a cliff overlooking a narrow three-mile-long deep-water harbor with three islands that were formerly used as military and quarantine facilities. Mahón's port occupies the inlandmost stretch of the harbor's south bank.

Although the port of Mahón was a major commercial and strategic thoroughfare in Carthaginian and Roman times, the city retains virtually no evidence of this early history. The tone set by the neat row houses that line the web of streets in the center is more evocative of the 18th century, when the British acquired Minorca (along with Gibraltar) by the Treaty of Utrecht and moved the island's capital to Mahón from Ciudadela. Except for a seven-year interlude when the French controlled Minorca, and another 16 years when Spain reasserted its hold, the island was under British rule from 1713 until it was ceded back to Spain in 1802.

Downtown Mahón

The main Minorcan highway, C 721, which connects Mahón and Ciudadela, brings the visitor into the center of Mahón from points west of the capital. Signs for the city center lead to the **Plaça d'Explanada**, which has a parking lot, along with cafés and a park. Start your excursion at the Mahón tourist office, Plaça d'Explanada 40, where you can pick up maps and information on the island's attractions and services. From here it is possible to visit almost everything of interest in Mahón on foot in a leisurely couple of hours. Without stops to visit monuments, shop, or sip a coffee or soft drink, the walk from the plaça to the port would take only about ten minutes. (Don't try to tour the center of Mahón by car—narrow, one-way streets make this a nightmare. Leave the car at Plaça d'Explanada. You may, however, want to drive to some of the restaurants at the far eastern end of the port.)

To orient yourself for a walking tour of Mahón, remember that the Plaça d'Explanada is a plateau from which all the streets of interest run downhill to the port. Start your walking tour by descending from the Plaça d'Explanada to the east on Carrer de Ses Moreres, which a couple of blocks later, where its name changes to Carrer Doctor Orfila, near its intersection with Carrer Bastió, becomes a pedestrians-only shopping area.

Mahón offers the island's largest selection of shops and services—boutiques, banks, travel agencies, and news kiosks—all concentrated on the pedestrians-only streets. Although the shoe industry has fallen on hard times due to global competition, Minorca (especially Ciudadela) is still a major shoe-manufacturing center. Along Carrer de Ses Moreres you'll find shops selling Minorcan-made leather goods at numbers 29, 31, and 33. **Patrícia**, the shop at number 31, sells elegant, expensive shoes, handbags, skirts, and other leather goods made (and also sold) at the factory in Ciudadela. Generally less expensive shoes are sold in numerous shops in the center of town, and rope-soled sandals, *alpargatas,* can be bought not only in shoe stores but in hardware, houseware, and gift shops. On this street you'll also pass several bookstores and newsstands where you can buy the archaeological map of Minorca and books about the island.

Continuing along Carrer de Ses Moreres/Doctor Orfila (its name changes again, to Carrer Hanover), you'll come to the **Plaça de la Constitució**. Vestiges of the British domination of Minorca can be seen on the plaza in the Neoclassical façade of the **Iglesia de Santa Maria** (note the 19th-century organ with 3,000 pipes), originally begun in the 13th century and enhanced in the 18th. Another holdover from those times is an English clock, donated by Governor Sir Richard Kane, at the 17th-century *ajuntament* (town hall), also on the plaza. (Kane is perhaps best known as the governor responsible for construction of "Kane's Road," the first to cross the island from east to west, where the highway is now.)

After visiting the plaza, take the pedestrian Carrer Nou (to the right) a couple of blocks to the Plaça Reial, which has several pleasant outdoor cafés, turn left onto Carrer S'Arravaleta, and continue a block to the **Plaça del Carme**. Mahón's food market, operating from Tuesday through Saturday, is in the cloister of the Carmelite church on the plaza.

The Port

From the Plaça del Carme you can then descend the winding staircase of the **Costa de Ses Voltes** to the port. There, to the right is the Moll de Llevant, a quay lined with restaurants, bars, and yacht moorings; to the left is the Moll de Ponent (also called Anden de Poniente), another quay, which leads to the Estació Maritim, where the Trasmediterránea ferries arrive from Barcelona and Majorca, as well as to shops, restaurants, bars, and the city's two gin distilleries.

The distilleries, both a couple of minutes' walk away, are other vestiges of the British reign. One of them, **Son Xoriguer**, offers boat tours of the port and is also a good source of souvenirs and gift items, including the local gin and liqueurs and such paraphernalia as shot glasses and aprons. For information on boat tours, Tel: (9-71) 36-75-78 or 36-58-65. Also in this western area of the port are several bars and the turn-of-the-century-style **Baixamar** café, where you can get coffee, a drink, and *tapas,* and sometimes see an art show. Two branches of the shop **Lora**, at Moll de Ponent 10 and 36, sell a variety of gifts, including Minorcan-made ceramic figures of women wearing the traditional wide skirts, aprons, and head-dresses, as well as books about Minorca.

Staying and Dining
in Mahon

Within easy walking distance of the Plaça del Carme is the ▶ **Port Mahón Hotel**, an old-fashioned, English-style establishment near the center of town, providing good views of the port, as well as easy access to it on foot. In the rooms you'll find chintz bedspreads, dark wood furniture, and overstuffed armchairs. A good urban base for travellers who want to explore the eastern end of the island, it's also a short stroll away from the **American Bar**, popular with expatriates, in Plaça General Mola, and restaurants, other bars, and shops.

The ▶ **Hostal Biniali**, a 19th-century country house converted into a guest house, provides a tranquil base for visiting the island from just outside the city. The rooms, furnished with old country beds and chests, offer views of Minorca's south coast. The *hostal* has a swimming pool, garden, and restaurant. To get there, take the unnumbered road from Mahón south to San Luis, drive through the town, and turn west (right) at the traffic circle. From the circle, it's about a mile to the *hostal*.

▶ **Hotel del Almirante**, which in the 18th century was the home of the chief admiral of the British Mediterranean Squadron, is a convenient small hotel on the outskirts of

Mahón. Located on the highway that leads east from Mahón to Es Castells–Villacarlos, it's accessible by frequent bus service. You can request accommodations in the house or in a newer, poolside bungalow.

You'll find plenty of restaurants and bars on the quay along the port to the east, which continues for about a mile and is lined with dining and drinking establishments. **Jágaro**, a greenery-filled house at the eastern end of the port at Moll de Llevant 334, is a good choice for a fish or seafood meal with touches of nouvelle cuisine; Tel: (9-71) 36-23-90. Although many restaurants and bars in the port close for the winter, the restaurant at the **Club Marítimo**, a sailing club at Moll de Llevant 287, is one of the few that stay open all year; Tel: (9-71) 36-42-26.

If you want to sample traditional Minorcan cuisine, one of the best places on the island is **Pilar**, an intimate and somewhat formal restaurant that nonetheless specializes in peasant food, located at Carrer des Forn 61, in the center of town. Specialties include chicken with shrimp and the peasant soup *oliaigua,* made with tomatoes and figs; Tel: (9-71) 36-68-17.

South from Mahón

Es Castells–Villacarlos, a pretty seaside fishing village where many British expatriates live, is a ten-minute drive southeast from Mahón. Here you can dine outdoors in restaurants carved from caves formerly used to store fishermen's gear, overlooking the deep blue waters of the port and a bobbing fleet of tiny white fishing boats. You'll find a gaggle of foreign food establishments serving the likes of pizza and crêpes, but you can also dine well on fresh local fish and seafood at **Café Trebol**, in a cave next to the water on Cales Fonts.

In **Calacorb**, a tiny inlet about a ten-minute walk west of the village center (you can also drive there), Minorcans and tourists alike hold forth nightly to the accompaniment of live guitar music in the cave-bar known as **Can Pau**.

For an introduction to talayotic monuments, pay a brief visit to nearby **Trepucó**, in the countryside just south of Mahón (directions are well marked by signs). This talayotic village has a 13-foot-high *taula,* the tallest on the island, a large *talayot,* and other remains.

North from Mahón

Start an excursion to the north with a short drive that will give you an impression of the immense size of the port, as well as a view of Mahón. Go west along the Moll de Ponent to the mouth of the port, then right (east) through the steep, rocky hills—some of which are dotted with clusters of homes—that jut down into the water.

The road northwest from Mahón to Fornells, on the northern coast, leads to a bird sanctuary, fishing villages, beaches, and some of the island's best eating spots. **S'Albufera**, the only freshwater lake on the island and a protected refuge for hundreds of species of birds, can be reached by turning right on the road to the tiny fishing village of Es Grau, shortly after leaving the Mahón port, then left at the sign for the Shangri-La development. Once inside the development, keep to the right on the paved road until you see the lake below.

ES GRAU

From the coastal town of Es Grau (about 7 km/4 miles from Mahón) you can take a ten-minute motorboat trip to the **Isla de Collom**, a tiny uninhabited island with two small, sandy beaches that is visible from the shore. From the island, whose rocky terrain can also be explored on foot, you'll get a view of Minorca's cliff-lined north coast. Bring food and water. The boat, which will return to pick you up, runs only during the summer in good weather; inquire at the bar Can Bernat at Carrer de S'Arribada 18.

Unless you don't feel up to a short walk—or you want to devote your time to learning to windsurf at the school there—don't settle for the rather unappealing beach to the left as you enter Es Grau. A five- or ten-minute walk past this beach will lead you to a series of cleaner alternatives along the coast. If you hike over the cliff where the beaches end you'll find even more pristine swimming spots—always virtually empty—with views of the Isla de Collom. These spots don't have any facilities, so take food and drink along.

The North Coast

FORNELLS

Fornells, in the center of the island's north coast, reached via the road northwest from Mahón (a 22-km/14-mile drive) is a somewhat larger fishing village than Es Grau, much more popular with travellers. It is known for its seafood restaurants, its white cube-shaped fishermen's houses, and its picturesque setting on a fjord. The most famous restaurant here is **Es Plá**, Pasaje des Plá, on the water's edge, known to be a favorite of King Juan Carlos and Queen Sofía (who visit Minorca on their yacht in summertime). The specialty here is *caldereta de langosta,* a meal consisting of a rich lobster soup followed by lobster meat. Count on spending 6,000 pesetas or more per person if you choose to eat here; Tel: (9-71) 37-66-55. Locals opt for the less expensive **Can Miguel**, Paseo Marítimo, Tel: (9-71) 37-66-23; or **S'Ancora**, Gumersindo Riera 7, Tel: (9-71) 37-66-70; or **Es Cranc**, Escuelas 29 in the village center, Tel: (9-71) 37-52-42.

A sunset visit to the lighthouse of **Cap de Cavalleria**, perched high on a cliff over the sea a few miles beyond Fornells, provides a scenic aperitif for an evening of dining in Fornells or Mercadal (see below).

WEST ALONG THE COAST

Farther west along the north coast, paved roads and then a decent, marked unpaved road lead to the broad, sandy beach of **Binimel-lá**. The physically fit may tramp along the coast to the west through some of Minorca's most spectacular coastal scenery—cliffs, beaches, and coves—to **Cala Pregonda**, regarded by many natives as the most beautiful spot on the island because of the craggy, cinnamon-colored rock formations that protrude from and are reflected in the water. If you try to go to Cala Pregonda by car, you'll be stopped at the entrance by guards. But in Spain the beaches belong to the people, and hikers cannot be stopped from walking along the coast to this beach, with its crystal-clear waters. Be sure to wear sneakers or other comfortable shoes for walking on rocks and cliffs.

THE CENTER OF THE ISLAND

Miles of hand-laid stone fences; undulating hills that sprout brilliant green grasses and carpets of poppies and other flowers in the spring; white farmhouses with arched entrances; knobby bentwood gates; ancient olive groves; and grazing cows whose milk is made into the famous Minorcan cheese or ice cream—these are the charms of the interior of the island. The central towns and sights can be explored from a base in Mahón, Fornells, or Ciudadela. We cover them here, roughly from east to west, on the Mahón–Ciudadela drive.

TORRE D'EN GAUMES

Torre d'en Gaumes is the site of a talayotic town near Minorca's southern coastline. To reach the town take C 721 west of Mahón to Alayor, turn south on the road to the Son Bou resort (on the west end of town), and turn left at the sign that leads to the ruins. Because of the extensive, well-excavated network of prehistoric dwellings—a combination of caves and man-made stone walls—as well as *taulas,* this is the best place on the island to get a feeling for the form of one of these ancient towns. You can climb up some of the *taulas* to get a view of the Mediterranean to the south.

MERCADEL

Mercadal (9 km/6 miles west past Alayor), a typical Minorcan town of white houses and narrow streets that is almost in the exact center of the island, has spawned several good restaurants specializing in Minorcan food made with local products. **Ca N'Aguedet**, at Lepanto 23, in the center of town, is the most formal, with lace curtains and white table linen. It is de rigueur to enter the kitchen to check out the fresh fish or poke your nose into the *caldera* (soup pot) before making a selection. Local specialties on the menu include stuffed eggplant or squash as well as quail, partridge, and fish soup; Tel: (9-71) 37-53-91.

Ca N'Olga, a few blocks away on Carrer Na Macarrane, offers dining alfresco as well as indoors in a whitewashed Minorcan house. The creative cuisine here is more European than Minorcan, including such dishes as salmon cooked in Champagne *en papillote* and biscuit ice cream with fig conserves; Tel: (9-71) 37-54-59.

Es Molí des Recó is an informal and even boisterous restaurant housed in a windmill visible from the highway after you pass the Mercadal turnoff going west. Here the emphasis is on local dishes such as grilled rabbit served at wooden tables or on an outdoor terrace overlooking the road; Tel: (9-71) 37-53-92.

ES MIGJORN GRAN

The hamlet of Es Migjorn Gran (formerly called San Cristobál), about 6 km (3½ miles) south of Mercadal, also has a couple of good restaurants. The **Restaurant S'Engolidor**, Calle Major 3, is perhaps the best of the traditional Minorcan restaurants, featuring island products cooked in the regional style. Situated in a typical Minorcan house, it also seats diners on a flower-filled terrace in the summer. The restaurant offers the best of the island's food and ambience— along with attentive and friendly service—at moderate prices. It's closed part of the winter, however, and the schedule can be erratic; Tel: (9-71) 37-01-93.

Another good dining choice in Es Migjorn Gran is the recently opened **Restaurant Migjorn, Ca Na Pilar**, also located in a traditional house with a patio. The Minorcan-style fish soup, a rich broth with chunks of fish, is almost a meal in itself. The house dessert, a platter with several treats including chocolate-cream cake, can easily serve two. It's on the edge of town, at Carretera Migjorn–Mercadal 1, on the road to Mercadal. Tel: (9-71) 37-02-12.

MONTE TORO

Monte Toat more than 1,000 feet, is the island's highest point. It is the site of a small monastery (with a snack bar) and offers a view of the entire island if the day is at all clear. A little more than a mile away from Fornells, it can be reached via the steadily ascending main highway out of the center of Mercadal (or Fornells) in just a few minutes.

NAVETA D'ES TUDONS

The Naveta d'Es Tudons, the best-preserved megalithic monument on the island, is about 18 km (11 miles) west from Mercadal. It is also an easy drive or bike ride just 5 km (3 miles) east of Ciudadela along the main highway. Its two-level interior, believed to be a collective tomb, now bereft of urns and other remains, can be explored by anyone willing to crawl in on hands and knees.

CIUDADELA

Capital of Minorca until the British came in the 18th century, Ciudadela, at the western end of the island, retains a large portion of its medieval streets, residences, and monuments. Old women dressed in black clothing doze or peel potatoes in their doorways on the cobblestone streets of the old quarter; Sunday mass is said at a 14th-century cathedral; and visitors and residents alike stream through the narrow main street to shop in stores framed by a series of arches known as Los Arcos in Castilian and as Ses Voltes by Minorcans.

ARRIVING IN CIUDADELA

The town of Ciudadela is concentrated on a high bluff to the east of a fishing and recreational port. During the warm summer months when boaters and other visitors come to Ciudadela, the restaurants, bars, and discos, many of which are housed in the natural caves that line the south side of the port, attract a lively nighttime crowd. Ciudadela's most important historical monuments, as well as most of the shopping area, are concentrated between two plazas—the **Plaça d'Alfons III** (also known as Palmeras), the western terminus of the C 721 Mahón–Ciudadela highway, and the Plaça d'Es Borne, where the *ajuntament* (town hall) is located, reached by walking a few blocks on the pedestrian shopping street that starts on the west side of the Plaça d'Alfons III. A modest, well-kept hostelry, the ▶ **Hostal Residencia Ciudadella**, is located at Sant Eloi 10, the street that exits from the square to the south.

On the approach to Ciudadela the cross-island highway is lined with souvenir shops selling costume jewelry and leather goods. But don't let these views of Ciudadela deceive you. The old, traditional city, much of it inaccessible by car, lies inside the avenue that curves north and south from Plaça d'Alfons III, tracing the no-longer-visible walls of the old city. Although this street, known colloquially as the Contra-murada, changes its name—to the right, or north, it's Avinguda de la Constitució; to the left, it's first Avinguda el Conqueridor, then Avinguda Capità Negrete—you'll have no trouble following it because it is Ciudadela's main traffic artery.

Pedestrians should simply continue west across the Plaça d'Alfons III and enter the center of town via Carrer Carme. If you're driving, however, turn left just before you enter Plaça d'Alfons III and follow the traffic flow several blocks to the pine-tree-filled park at Plaça Colon; turn right and look for parking there or in the Plaça d'Es Borne, a little farther to the right.

The Center of Town

PLACA D'ES BORNE

Residents and tourists mingle in the main centers of Ciuda-dela life. These are the Plaça d'Es Borne (known locally as El Borne, pronounced "BOR-nay"), on which stands the *ajunta-ment;* the port below; and Los Arcos (Ses Voltes), which run along Josep Maria Quadrado between Plaça d'Es Borne and Plaça Nova (also called Plaça España). El Borne, dominated by the arched façade and turrets of the Moorish-looking *ajuntament* (built on the remains of a Moorish fort), is probably the town's most popular gathering place. For fresh seafood and fish, try **Casa Gallega**, at Plaça d'Es Borne 11; Tel: (9-71) 38-64-91. Run by Galicians from the Spanish region most famous for its seafood, this restaurant features regional treats including *pulpo a la gallega* (slices of octo-pus in spicy sauce) and the typical *empanada* (meat pie). A *paella* (the Spanish rice and seafood casserole) "for two" is enough for three diners.

During the summer, look in the plaza for Ciudadela's tourist office, located in a mobile van. Here you can get maps and lists of hotels, restaurants, and archaeological sites for the whole island.

The sidewalk along the north side of the square, atop the city's ancient ramparts, offers excellent views of the port, which is used by yachts and fishing boats alike, and is the center of the town's nightlife. The café-bar on top of the *ajuntament,* **Es Mirador del Port**, has good views of the port, the open sea to the west, and the old city wall, which is festooned with wild caper plants.

The weathered obelisk in the middle of the Plaça d'Es Borne honors those who lost their lives defending Ciudadela against a merciless attack by the Turks in 1558. On the east side of the plaza are three medieval palaces, still privately owned, which house a series of shops, bars, and an English-style tearoom, **Es Palau**, on the street level. During the summer you can visit several rooms of the **Palau Sort**, including the old kitchen and a mirror-lined salon that offers a view of El Borne. Visiting hours are limited (see the sign in front), and there is an admission fee.

Mayor Borne, the street that exits east from the square across from the *ajuntament,* leads one block past the palaces into Plaça Pio XII, where the 14th-century Gothic cathedral of **Santa Maria** is located. Built on the site of a former mosque, the cathedral has undergone various alterations, the most recent of which has endowed it with a Neoclassical façade. To the left of the cathedral's main entrance on Cal Bisbe is the **Palacio Episcopal** (bishop's palace) with a flower-adorned courtyard complete with a well, which can usually be glimpsed through the gate. At the end of the street is another palace, the Palau del Squella, owned by one of Minorca's aristocratic families, with a cameo of a woman's face carved on the façade.

THE CASCO ANTIGUO

To experience Ciudadela's **medieval quarter** to its fullest, take an immediate left turn at the Palau del Squella and then a right on Carrer Sant Miguel or Carrer Sant Sebastià, which will bring you to the narrow, convoluted streets, many of them cobblestone, of the old residential neighborhoods. The three- and four-story medieval town houses along these streets—mostly painted white or a light color on top and gray, brown, or green on the bottom—are still inhabited, and although it's illegal to keep roosters in town, you might even hear a cock crowing from a concealed interior garden. During the San Juan festival in June, which attracts visitors from all over Spain, some of the horses and riders actually prance into the hallways of these houses. Don't be concerned about losing your way in these streets. The town is very small, and anyone can direct you back to the cathedral.

Proceeding west from the cathedral on Josep Maria Quadrado, you will come to the narrow pedestrian precinct of **Los Arcos** (Ses Voltes). This arcaded strip, which leads to the colorful, café-filled **Plaça España** two blocks away, is Ciudadela's main tourist shopping area, where you can buy anything from an ice-cream cone to *alpargatas,* the locally made sandals.

If you take a right turn at Carrer del Seminari, then the first left, you will find yourself in a network of tiny streets that lead to the local food market (take the second left, then the first right). Tuesday through Saturday (the market is closed Sundays and Mondays) the locals arrive before eight in the morning to get the best of the fresh fish, seafood, and produce. Availability varies with the season, but be sure to go for fresh figs in the summer. The excellent local cheese, *queso de Mahón* (*queso de payes*), and the local *sobrasada* sausage can always be found in the butcher shops and other small shops lining the outdoor market.

On Carrer del Seminari, just past the turnoff to the market, is a 17th-century seminary with a flower-filled courtyard where a classical music concert series is presented in summer. (The tourist office can tell you where to buy tickets.) Just past the seminary the street intersects with Carrer Santissim. Turn right a few steps to **Idó**, at number 5, a shop that sells custom-made women's clothing by American designer Susan Unger, a Minorca resident. A few steps beyond, on the right, is a shop (it has no name) that sells handmade leather belts, wallets, and bags.

SHOPPING IN CIUDADELA

For more serious shopping, go through the Plaça España up to Plaça d'Alfons III, and explore the series of main streets to your right and left that border the old city. Along these streets, especially along the stretches of the Contramurada called El Conqueridor and Negrete, running south off the square, you'll find many shops, selling mostly clothing, shoes, and household goods.

Ciudadela was long a major shoe-manufacturing center, but now the industry has begun to decline. Traditionally the town has produced everything from slippers to high-fashion women's pumps and then sold them in factory stores, boutiques, and the front hallways of the families who produce them at home. If you're looking for high-quality shoes, such as some marketed under the Bally label, other places to try—besides those on El Conqueridor and Negrete—are **Torres**, on Cami de Maó (C 721), which leads east from Plaça d'Alfons III toward Mahón, and the **Patrícia** factory store (which also sells leather jackets and skirts and other leather items) on the road to Santandria south of Ciudadela.

The Port

When you've tired of touring, head for the Ciudadela port, home to a small fishing fleet and host to hundreds of yachts in the course of the summer season. It's also the major evening gathering place for everyone from international yachtsmen to punk rockers. From June until early September—but especially in August—it is thronged nightly with visitors from all over Spain and the rest of the world, as well as Ciudadela residents. Dining, barhopping, disco dancing, and people-watching are the favored activities here.

Although there may be times when you can navigate the obstacle course of traffic rules legally, driving a car into the port area is not worth the trouble. Leave it in El Borne. Once you've arrived at water's edge, the whole port area is visible. Because the area is so small, restaurants and bars located here do not have specific addresses, so if you don't see your destination, ask directions.

You can descend directly to the port from El Borne by way of the street next to the *ajuntament,* Carrer Cuesta (stopping to sample the excellent homemade ice cream—flavors include fresh fig, gin, and hazelnut—at **Sa Gelateria**, on the left side of Carrer Cuesta). Another route is via a stairway (known locally as La Escalera) that intersects with Carrer Brecha—reached by exiting El Borne on the curved street to the right of the Artistic movie theater—above the port.

From the bottom of the stairway to your left is a strip of waterside restaurants and bars where you can dine or drink inside or out. For an informal meal of fish and seafood, try the **Baleares Café**, to your right at the bottom of La Escalera. Here you can dine on a selection of *tapas*—deep-fried squid, mussels, shrimp—or a full serving of fresh fish or seafood. If pizza is more your taste, try the pies baked in a traditional wood oven at **Sa Figuera**, at the end of the port to your left.

At Carrer Brecha 16 is **Mon Bar**, a good choice for the fixed-price lunch or a meal of tasty *tapas*—try the Spanish potato omelet and the *salpicón* of seafood—prepared by Ciudadela chef Marie Marqués. The setting features a series of ancient sandstone overhead arches paired with the sleek, high-tech furniture and design often found in Barcelona but rarely in Minorca. Tel: (9-71) 48-08-98.

Although the area retains its charm—and some may prefer the tranquillity to the crowds—life in the Ciudadela port slows down considerably from October 15 until the beginning of June. Many restaurants and bars close completely; others open on weekends. It's always possible, however, to find a place to sip coffee or a glass of wine and take in the view, which reveals a long, narrow channel that meets the Mediterranean at a cliff-lined coast.

THE COAST SOUTH OF THE PORT

A nice walk out of Ciudadela's center—less than 15 minutes one way—takes you along the broad, tree-lined **Passeig de Sant Nicolau**, south of the port to the coast. Along the route you'll also pass some of Ciudadela's hotels, including the ▶ **Hotel Patricia**, at number 90–92, which serves businesspeople and other well-off travellers to Ciudadela. A sleek, modern, but small establishment, it's the only hotel of its class in town.

Once at the coast you can't miss the statue of Admiral David Farragut, son of a Ciudadela man who emigrated to the United States. His visit to his father's hometown in 1867, when he was in charge of the U.S. European Squadron, remains the inspiration for a local festival. From the coast—where a crumbling defense tower is poised on the rocky cliffs that face the island of Majorca—the fastest way to return to town is back along the Passeig de Sant Nicolau. Scenic but slower alternatives include taking a right to the Passeig del Port, which brings you to the port, or a left along a coast road dotted with cliffs and rocks, ending at the tiny and incongruously named Sa Platja Gran (Large Beach).

There are several modest, reasonably priced hotels on Sa Platja Gran and the streets nearby, including the ▶ **Hostal Mar Blava**, which has a terrace overlooking the water.

Ciudadela at Fiesta Time

A good time to experience what some would characterize as the "true" spirit of Ciudadela is during the San Juan festival, June 23 and 24, when some 100 horses and riders course through the medieval streets—even entering some houses—as they reenact ancient rites whose now-murky origins are Christian, Moorish, and pagan. As with the running of the bulls in Pamplona, the fiesta attracts thousands of revelers, many of whom participate by thrusting themselves under the prancing horses' hooves, challenging the equestrians to prove their mastery of the art.

The outdoor morning market in Ciudadela (open daily except Sundays and Mondays) is a good place to absorb local color—at fiesta time, the fishmongers sing traditional songs in voices that are anything but *sotto*—as well as to pick up picnic supplies.

Excursions from Ciudadela

The coasts north and south of Ciudadela offer picturesque vistas of high, rugged gray cliffs, roadsides lined with bright flowers in the spring, tiny coves and swimming beaches, and private summer houses nestled in rock niches at water's edge.

During the summer, excursion boats departing from the Ciudadela port tour the north or the south coast, with stops for a swim and lunch on the way. For information, inquire at the Ciudadela tourist office. Even if it's too cool for a dip, all of Minorca's coastline and beaches merit a visit for the generally clear, clean aquamarine water and the range of unusual rock formations, cliffs, and flora.

THE NORTH COAST

From Plaça d'Alfons III, where the C 721 highway enters Ciudadela, following the main road and the signs around to the right will bring you to the north coast. **Cala Bruch** is a west-coast beach of terraced rocks where you can sun and swim without getting sandy—but on windy days the surf beats on the rock walls of the cove with thundering force. Cala Bruch has a restaurant with an outdoor café that is open all day and in the evening during the summer.

THE SOUTH COAST

To explore the coast south of Ciudadela, where some of Minorca's best beaches lie, turn left (west) off the main road at the Plaça d'Alfons III and follow the Contramurada to Carrer del Sud. Turn left and continue to Carrer Alfons V; turn left again, then right a block later onto Camí de Sant Joan de Missa, which leads to the beaches.

Son Catlar, site of a talayotic town, is off this road. Turn right just past a large, imposing farmhouse and watch for an electrical tower on the right marked "Son Catlar." A few hundred feet beyond, on the left, a wall of huge, upright rock slabs runs parallel to the road. Leaving your vehicle, climb over the stone fence into the field to explore the extensive ruins of talayotic dwellings, a circular enclosure (perhaps the site of religious rites) bounded by vertical slabs of rock, and a huge talayot that looks like a heap of rocks. (For this excursion be sure to wear enclosed shoes.)

Once you return to the road, it is a five- or ten-minute drive farther south to the long, crescent-shaped beach of **Son Saura**, where a strip of pine trees behind the beach provides a refuge from the intense summer sun.

Other south-coast beaches—each located in a small, rock-bordered cove with transparent aquamarine water—include Cala En Turqueta, Es Tallaier, and Macarella. To reach these beaches, stay on the Camí de Sant Joan de Misse—past the turnoff to Son Saura—until you see the white chapel on your left and a marked turn to your right; turn, and follow the signs to the beaches. (At Macarella, if you climb over the cliff on the right you will come to **Macarelleta**, a white-sand cove frequented by nude bathers.) Good walkers or hikers should consider using the trails along these and many other coves to explore the south coast on foot.

These beaches—indeed most of the island's best beaches—are beyond the reach of public buses. You'll need either a car (a Moke or Jeep is best), a motorcycle, or a moped for the trip across a network of unmarked, unpaved, sometimes downright rocky roads that, in some cases, cross private property. Be prepared to encounter gates leading to private property on your way. Always leave gates as you find them: If open, leave open; if closed, close them behind you.

MAJORCA

The largest island in the Balearics, and by far the most visited, Majorca was the first to lure modern-day travellers and expatriates to its shores.

"One of the most beautiful landscapes in the world and one of the most unknown... tortured, bent-over, sapless trees; terrible bramble bushes, magnificent flowers, carpets of lawn and reeds; spiny caper plants," rhapsodized French novelist George Sand in *Winter in Mallorca,* based on her 1838–1839 visit here with her lover, Frédéric Chopin. The scenery alone wasn't enough to persuade the pair to stay, though. They left three months after their arrival on the island, besieged by bad weather, Chopin's tuberculosis, and the indignities inflicted by what they saw as a combination of crude peasants and haughty local society.

But other luminaries continued to arrive. One was Archduke Ludwig Salvator of Austria, who came to Majorca in 1867 at the age of 19 and became so entranced with the island that he made it his home and dedicated his life to studying its language, history, and natural environment. Another was poet Robert Graves, who came here in the 1920s, became the center of an ever-growing artists' and writers' colony, and lived here until his death in 1985.

All of these visitors chose the same area of the island— the **Tramuntana,** a mountain range that snakes along the length of Majorca's west coast around a series of tiny sandy coves, precipitous gray cliffs, olive groves, and pine forests, ending at Cabo de Formentor, a windblown ten-mile-long promontory at the northern tip of the island.

Majorca measures 45 miles from north to south and 60 miles from east to west. Its main geographical features are two large bays and the Tramuntana mountain range. The Bahía (bay) de Palma, on the southwestern side of the island, is the site of Palma, the capital city. The Bahía de Alcudia, almost directly opposite Palma on the northeastern coast, has a long beach that attracts sun-worshiping tourists from northern Europe. It is separated by a small promontory on the west

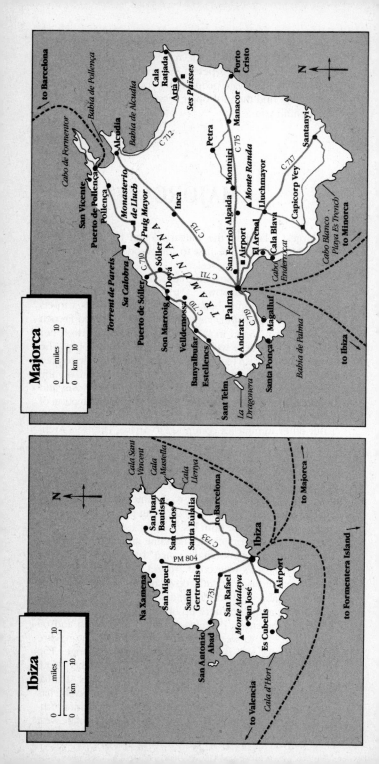

from Bahía de Pollença, another resort area. The Tramuntana, rising almost parallel to and just inland of the west coast of the island, has nine peaks more than 1,000 feet high, with Puig Mayor surpassing 4,300 feet.

The eastern side of the island is defined by a smaller mountain range, whose most scenic features are the rocky coastal cliffs where it culminates north of Artà.

The center of Majorca—for the most part, less visited by tourists than the coasts—is an almost flat agricultural area whose notable features include the Binissalem area, where Majorcan wines are produced, the industrial city of Inca, the olive groves south of Pollença, and the windmill-studded stretch from Lluchmayor to Santanyi.

Bus service connects major resorts and towns on the island, and excursion trains run several times a day between Palma and Inca and Palma and Sóller, north of Palma in the Tramuntana, but touring by car will give you much more freedom to enjoy the island's sights at your own pace as well as to explore off the beaten track.

Even though this island is considerably bigger than Minorca or Ibiza, distances are still relatively short. The route you take makes a big difference in the duration of your trip. From Palma straight across the island to Alcudia, for example, is a 55-km (34-mile) trip. (It takes more than an hour because the road goes through several towns.) But if you want to explore and savor the Tramuntana and the coast—as you should—a drive from Palma to Alcudia could take you several days with overnight stops.

Palma, which is well endowed with hotels, makes a convenient base for exploring other parts of Majorca because all the main highways emanate from the city. But unless you're especially partial to big, busy cities, we recommend that you devote a couple of days to seeing the sights and profiting from the cultural life of Palma—with a possible excursion or two to the east—and then head west or north and base yourself in Banyalbufar, Deyá, or some other destination closer to the coast and the Tramuntana. From these bases it is easy to make numerous excursions or just rest on the coast and contemplate the views of the sea and rugged cliffs.

PALMA

Like Sand and Chopin, who travelled 18 hours on a steamboat to get there, virtually all modern visitors to Majorca set foot first in Palma, the capital and—with a population of more than 325,000—the largest and most cosmopolitan city of the Balearic Islands.

Palma presents many faces to the visitor: the seaside; the

palm-lined Passeig Marítim, open to the Mediterranean's breezes; the dark, twisting streets of the centuries-old Arab and Gothic quarters that flank the modern main street, the Passeig d'Es Borne; honky-tonk nightclubs and modern apartment blocks; and the sophisticated boutiques along the arcaded Avinguda Rei Jaume III.

But what makes the city worth a stop are its medieval monuments, the two most impressive of which can be spotted by the visitor arriving by water, and often by the airplane traveller as well: the cathedral, known locally as La Seu, and the Castell de Bellver.

ARRIVING IN PALMA

The city of Palma sits above the ample bay on the southwestern end of the island, spreading inland. If you're fortunate, your landing at the airport, about a ten-minute drive east of the city, will offer views of El Jonquer, a farming area dotted with windmills (and poppies in spring), and of the cathedral. The colors and forms may remind you of the paintings of Joan Miró, the island's most famous 20th-century resident.

Entering Palma from the airport, you'll approach town from Ronda Litoral, an avenue that traces the sea (on your left) and passes below the cathedral and the Casco Antiguo, the medieval quarter (on your right) and the Parc del Mar. Just past the cathedral and other monuments, the *ronda* intersects with Avinguda Antoni Maura, to the right, and the Passeig Marítim, curving around to the left, west along the bay. If you want to park near the medieval quarter, watch for the sign for parking under the Parc del Mar to your right.

Avinguda Antoni Maura penetrates to the city center, passing the Casco Antiguo, with the cathedral and the Almudaina palace on the right, merging into the lively Passeig d'Es Borne and at Plaça Pio XII intersecting with Avinguda Rei Jaume III, a major shopping street to the west.

The **Passeig Marítim**, which continues along the water past a yacht basin, also passes by the restored 15th-century Gothic commodity exchange, Sa Llonja, and becomes a sort of tourist strip, the site of several major hotels as well as restaurants and bars. At its western end it runs below—but within sight of—the medieval Castell de Bellver, one of the city's most impressive monuments.

Castell de Bellver

Even if your stay in Palma is very limited, leave time for a visit to the hilltop castle, about a mile and a half from the city center. Because one of the main attractions of the castle is its 360-degree view of the city and its environs, this excursion is a good way to start a day of touring. Bellver can be reached

on foot, but it's a long, tiring walk, so opt for a taxi or bus if
you don't have a car.

During the 300 years in which the kings of Majorca carried out the cathedral construction started by Jaume I in
1230, they also managed (in the 14th century) to erect the
Castell de Bellver as a summer residence. From outside, the
castle appears to be a forbidding military fortress surrounded by a moat, but a step inside reveals a graceful
circular interior court open to the sky. On the first floor of
the castle there's a city museum (open every day but Sunday) featuring exhibits of ceramics and other finds from the
island's prehistoric archaeological sites. A stairway to your
right as you enter the castle leads to the roof, which offers a
view of the sea, the Palma skyline, and the hills that rise
behind the city. The castle is illuminated at night and serves
as the setting for summer concerts.

Casco Antiguo

To tour the old quarter of Palma, the Casco Antiguo, return
to the city center and turn east off Avinguda Antoni Maura,
following the signs to the **Almudaina**—a palace for the kings
of Majorca built on the site of a former Moorish fortress,
only an arch from which remains now. The Almudaina leads
onto Plaça Almoina, where you'll find the entrance to the
cathedral.

LA SEU

Situated just above the port of Palma, overlooking the sweeping Bahía de Palma, the graceful Gothic cathedral La Seu
seems to float above a forest of sailboat masts. Its impressive
dimensions are best grasped by comparison. The great nave
is larger than those of the cathedrals of Milan, Chartres,
Cologne, and Reims, as are the lateral naves, some of which
are about 90 feet high. The rose window, which has a
diameter of 17½ feet, is the largest in the world.

Inside, what is most impressive is the immense distance
from the principal entrance to the main chapel and altar—
made all the more remarkable by the unusual placement of
the choir in front by the chancel, instead of in the middle
where it would truncate the space. The chapel of the Holy
Trinity, beyond the choir, houses the tombs of Majorcan
kings Jaume II and Jaume III. A crown-shaped wrought-iron
canopy designed by Catalan architect Antoni Gaudí hangs
over the chancel. It features Christ on the cross, adorned by
the ceramic mosaics that characterize Gaudí's work, 35 bell-
shaped hanging lamps said to represent the faithful, and
representations of grain and grapes for sacrifice.

After touring the interior of the cathedral, exit onto Plaça

Almirante Moreno on the south side for a good view of the Bahía de Palma. While in this area you may also want to walk by the graceful exchange building, **Sa Llonja**, with its arched ceilings and fluted columns, facing the bay on Passeig Sagrera, just west of Avinguda Antoni Maura. The building is open to the public when there's an art exhibition.

AROUND IN THE CASCO ANTIGUO

From the cathedral it's easy—many signs mark the routes to historical monuments—to tour the Casco Antiguo on foot. A logical itinerary for a couple of hours of strolling and sight-seeing would take you east of the cathedral through the narrow streets to the **Arab baths** and their refreshing garden courtyard at Carrer Serra 13; to the church of **San Francisco** (Plaça de San Francisco 6), with its 14th-century Gothic façade, peaceful cloister, tomb of 13th-century philosopher Ramón Llull, and a statue of native son Father Junípero Serra; then through the old streets lined with imposing mansions to the inviting **Plaça Santa Eulalia**, adorned by plane trees and enlivened by cafés. This is a good place for an energizing cup of coffee or snack, as is the nearby **Xicara Xocola-tería** (a dark local bar that specializes in hot chocolate) on Carrer Morey, which intersects with the plaza to the south.

Once on Carrer Morey, it's a few steps northwest to the hoary **Almudaina arch** on Victoria Almudaina. Along with the Arab baths—both are believed to date from about the tenth century—it's the only significant remaining physical evidence of Palma's Moorish period. Continuing on Victoria Almudaina, you'll arrive shortly at Plaça Cort, dominated by the town hall. The stairway on Paseo Quintana, across the street from the town hall, descends into a labyrinth of pedestrian shopping streets offering distractions that range from the tempting chocolates in the window at **Pajarita Bonbonera**, on Carrer Sant Nicolau, to Cacharel, Stefanel, and other stylish boutiques on adjacent streets. Here, too, along the narrow Via Veri, you will find the **Centre Cultural Pelaires**, a gallery long associated with Miró, which is installed in a former convent.

Central Palma

From the Plaça Cort area it's a few minutes' walk north to **Colleció Joan March**, a small museum that contains works by Salvador Dalí, Miró, and other modern Spanish painters, at Carrer San Miguel 11.

Northwest of the Cort (turn west off the Passeig d'Es Borne at the Plaça Pio XII onto Avinguda Rei Jaume III) you'll find the city **tourist office** at number 10, sandwiched in a row of boutiques and department stores. (You can get infor-

mation about travelling in all of the Balearic Islands here.)
Places to shop include **Majorica**, at number 11, which vends
the cultured pearls for which Majorca is famous; **Galerías
Preciados** at number 15, a department store that sells everything from clothing to kitchenware; and more shoe stores—
most of whose wares are high fashion and expensive—than
you could ever imagine on one street. **Artespaña**, at Passeig
Mallorca 17, at the intersection with the western end of
Avinguda Rei Jaume III, is a good place to search for handicrafts and such home furnishings as hand-embroidered table linens.

Staying and Dining in Palma

Staying in or near Palma offers easy access to restaurants,
shopping, art galleries, and monuments. The ▶ **Hotel Saratoga**, newly renovated, has a handy central location. With
light walls, tile floors, and modern, angular furniture, the
immaculate rooms suggest a Scandinavian style; many have
balconies that overlook an ample street-level swimming
pool and terrace. On the top floor there's another pool and
a bar with views of Bellver Castle, the cathedral, and the
harbor.

The ▶ **Hotel Meliá Victoria**, a modern high-rise establishment where the rooms offer stunning, close-up views of the
port and the cathedral, sits in a protected enclave between
the Avinguda Inginiero Gabriel Roca, which traces the harbor, and Avinguda Joan Miró, near the rather seedy Plaça
Gomila. Rooms, furnished in traditional style, are spacious
and contain an ample dressing area. The hotel, which is one
of Palma's most expensive, offers such amenities as two
swimming pools, a terrace restaurant overlooking the port,
health club, business center, and free parking.

Another luxury lodging, the ▶ **Son Vida**, is located in the
hills about 5 km (3 miles) north of Palma. This 13th-century
castle-turned-hotel has opulent, high-ceilinged public salons. Guest rooms have comfortable traditional furniture
and plenty of closet and dressing space. The hotel, one of
just a handful in Spain accorded the *gran-lujo* rating, has
golf, swimming pools, restaurants, a garden, and an indoor
health club. If you stay here, request a room with a view of
Palma and the sea.

Dining options in Palma include informal, boisterous
eateries that specialize in Majorcan food; casual fish and
seafood houses; and fancy restaurants that serve fine international cuisine.

Celler Sa Premsa, a wine cellar converted into an informal restaurant, is located in the center of town at Plaça
Obispo Berenguer de Palau 8; Tel: (9-71) 72-35-29. Here

you'll rub shoulders with an animated crowd of locals who patronize it for such typical dishes as the hearty Majorcan vegetable soup, accompanied by Majorcan Binissalem wine. **Mesón de C'an Pedro**, at Rector Vives 4 in the Genova neighborhood about a ten-minute taxi ride outside of Palma, serves grilled meats—rabbit, lamb chops, chicken, and more—Majorcan soups, and the typical almond cake, in a rustic atmosphere. Guests dine at rough wooden tables; hundreds of cured hams hang from the ceiling above the bar. Tel: (9-71) 40-24-79.

For fresh fish and a view of the sea, try **Portixol**, at Sirena 27, in the small fishing enclave of Molinar, about 3 km (2 miles) east of the intersection of Ronda Litoral with Avinguda Antoni Maura in Palma. Inside the restaurant a wooden fishing boat laden with ice and suspended over a tank containing fish, lobsters, and shellfish displays some of the day's specials; Tel: (9-71) 27-18-00. (Portixol is accessible by taxi or bus; take the number 15 from Plaça de la Reina, near the cathedral.)

If you're touring in the Casco Antiguo, **El Caballito del Mar**, about a five-minute walk from the cathedral at Paseo de Sagrera 5, is a good choice for lunch. A complete à la carte seafood meal runs about 4,000 pesetas, but you can eat for less than half of that if you order the hearty Majorcan fish soup (*caldera de pescado*) and a salad; (9-71) 72-10-74.

Xoriguer, Carrer Fábrica 60, in the center of Palma, is an unpretentious restaurant that offers excellent French food and service; Tel: (9-71) 28-83-32. **Koldo Royo**, Gabriel Roca 3, is named for its chef, who serves up excellent *nueva cocina vasca* (new Basque cuisine). Examples from the menu include oysters wrapped in marinated salmon with lemon vinaigrette, baby lamb chops stuffed with sweetbreads with wild mushroom sauce; and a warm chocolate tart with cinnamon ice cream. Meals are served in a small, elegant dining room with modern paintings on pale peach walls. Be sure to request a table with a view of the sea, visible through the palm trees outside the window; Tel: (9-71) 45-70-21.

To complete an evening on the town, quaff a nightcap at **Abacanto**, a sprawling country mansion that has been converted by decorator-owner Salvador Palao into an indoor-outdoor bar where the air is perfumed by incense and the audio system plays classical music. For the privilege of sipping among the animated fountains, gilded mirrors, Baroque oil paintings and furniture, leopard-skin bar stools, live peacocks, thousands of fresh flowers, and baskets overflowing with apples, grapefruits, and other produce, you'll pay 700 pesetas for a fruit juice and twice that for a drink with alcohol. Abacanto is located in a working-class neighborhood called S'Indiotería on Camino de Son Nicolau, about a ten-minute taxi ride from central Palma; Tel: (9-71) 20-79-31.

THE WEST COAST

Nearly five million visitors arrive in Palma every year, an enormous tourist influx considering the size of the island. Many of them arrive on charter flights and most head for northeast-coast seaside resorts around the bays of Alcudia and Pollença that cater to mass tourism or to Magalluf, Santa Ponça, and other beaches on the south coast west of Palma. Probably due to the lack of large beaches, the west coast of Majorca has suffered the least from this plague of hotels, junky souvenir shops, pubs, and beer halls.

This is the area chosen by Sand, Chopin, Graves, and other discerning visitors for its scenery and tranquillity, and for the experienced traveller it probably remains the place to aim for on Majorca. Even in summer, with the exception of Valldemossa, this area remains relatively uncongested.

Distances are small on the island, and it's possible to complete a relatively satisfactory driving tour of this coast in one very long day or two shorter ones. The better way to absorb the essence of the region is to choose a hotel as a base and make leisurely forays to an appealing variety of both natural and cultural attractions. Banyalbufar, Deyá, and Cabo de Formentor are three locations—at varying distances from Palma—from which this can be accomplished.

If you stay in Deyá, the most central of these locations, you will be able to make one-day excursions to all of the points recommended here. But from Banyalbufar, the southernmost location, the drive to Formentor, at the island's northern tip is a long haul over mountainous roads—too much for one day. A compromise might be to spend a night or two in each location.

Palma to Deyá

The coastal road from Palma that goes around the knob of land protruding from the island's southwestern corner, C 719, passes through the small town of **Andratx**, with its shuttered houses, into a region of citrus groves and pine forests. A brief detour to **Sant Telm** offers a view of the transparent coastal waters washing over the rocks, and of **La Dragonera**, the rocky offshore island whose only current residents are birds and lizards. Archaeologists have found remains of a prehistoric necropolis there; historians cite it as the point from which Jaume I conquered Majorca and as a pirate refuge.

Route C 719 becomes C 710 north from Andratx toward Valldemossa, taking you through such tiny towns as Estellenchs and **Banyalbufar**, where stone houses and terraces of olive, almond, and citrus trees cling to the mountainside overlooking the sea. From its clifftop vantage point the ▶ **Hostal Mar i Vent** in Banyalbufar offers a modest, homey perch from which to contemplate the Mediterranean. A terrace and dining room with sea views, a grandfather clock in the reception hall, and salons with comfortable armchairs contribute to its atmosphere.

VALLDEMOSSA

Valldemossa, the town where Sand and Chopin spent their much-publicized winter, is all Sand said it was: with the stone houses, the graceful gardens, and the mountain views from the cells of the **Cartuja**, the Carthusian monastery (now private property) where they rented three former monks' cells in which to live.

Ironically, the town that shunned the lovers when they lived there has now become a virtual Sand-Chopin shrine. A Chopin festival is held every summer in the chapel of the Cartuja (purchase tickets from the Cartuja box office well in advance). Souvenir stands line the streets and have overflowed into virtually every room of the monastery, which serves both as a city museum and a sort of voyeur's peephole into the lives of the two famous artists. Museum exhibits include fragments of Sand's manuscripts and the preludes Chopin wrote here, as well as two of the composer's pianos and other mementos. But in the midst of all the commercialism the most affecting sight today is what most attracted Sand and Chopin 150 years ago: the tiny garden behind each cell and the view of the valley and mountain beyond.

Nearby **Port de Valldemossa** makes a pleasant excursion for lunch and some spectacular scenery. Get back on the road to Banyalbufar and drive south for about a mile, turning right at the sign for Port de Valldemossa. The road—not recommended for sufferers of vertigo—makes a steep descent down a rocky, pine-covered mountainside to the fishing village below. **Es Port**, the only local restaurant, serves a nice lunch; the Majorcan salad (chopped tomatoes, onions, and peppers) and Majorcan-style fish (baked with spinach, raisins, and pine nuts) is reasonably priced. While it's no bargain, the food is quite good, and portions are generous enough to serve two. The restaurant has a terrace overlooking the sea. Tel: (9-71) 61-20-46.

SON MARROIG

Returning to the main road and heading north, it's only a few miles beyond Valldemossa to Son Marroig, the seaside villa and garden of the Austrian archduke Ludwig Salvador, who lived on Majorca for more than 50 years, during which time he worked on an in-depth study of the island group. In the garden is an ethereal domed kiosk of white Italian marble that offers a view of the cliffs and the sea. The small museum inside the villa displays personal effects ranging from Berber rugs to Majorca seascapes by native painter Antoni Ribas, to an antique photograph of the yachts of the archduke and his cousin, the Austrian empress Elizabeth. In the summer the villa is used for a public concert series.

DEYA

The next town north is Deyá, an expatriates' colony made famous by Graves—who lived here for many years until his death in 1985—and numerous other artists and writers who have lived or visited here. This tiny mountainside town is one of the most beautiful in the Balearics, with its sand-colored houses with red-tiled roofs enlivened by cascades of flowers and vines. The houses, however, tend to be walled to guard against intrusion by the tourists who come to browse in the art galleries, quaff a beer in one of the cafés, or visit the **Deyá Archaeological Museum and Research Center,** located in town below the main road. Created by American-born William Waldren (who has conducted investigations into the island's prehistory for 40 years), the museum contains skeletons and fossils of three mammals that inhabited Majorca in the Stone Age, as well as pottery, tools, needles, and jewelry from the island's prehistoric culture. You can visit the museum most days, but call to confirm that it is open first, because the small space is staffed by rotating shifts of graduate students; Tel: (9-71) 63-90-01. For a top-side view of the town and the sea, follow the signs to the church and cemetery—a five-minute walk from the highway—where many of the tombs are adorned with pictures of the dead.

The ▶ **Hotel La Residencia** in Deyá offers a superb combination of elegance and tranquillity at a price commensurate with the quality and is one of the best lodgings in this area. Located on 30 acres of orchards and farmland, the natural stone buildings house guest rooms furnished with antiques and public rooms that serve as a gallery for local painters. With this hotel's gardens, terrace bar, swimming pool, and one of the best restaurants on the island—**El Olivo**—there's never a need to leave the grounds. Tel: (9-71) 63-90-11. The elegant restaurant is lit by tall, many-branched, forged-iron candelabras and decorated with modern paintings, wicker furniture, and a huge, ancient stone olive press. Diners, who may choose to be seated in the main dining room, a loft above, or an outdoor terrace, can order one of two tasting menus or select from an à la carte menu. The menu, which changes with the season, offers such dishes as carpaccio with Iranian caviar, sea bass, and lobster in Champagne, and plums au gratin with Armagnac *sabayon* sauce.

Deyá to Formentor

After Deyá the main road twists and turns to reveal myriad perspectives of the gray whale of a mountain, Puig Mayor, Majorca's tallest. Because of the mountains, it is difficult to gain access to the coast in this region. For a rewarding peek at the waters and the cliffs, as well as a good meal, exit from Deyá on C 710 toward Sóller and turn left at the sign for **Bens d'Avall**, where the road curves sharply to the right after kilometer 56. Signs lead to a pleasant establishment with an outdoor terrace—abloom with flowers in season—overlooking the water. The focus here is on fish and seafood of good quality at a fair price. Tel: (9-71) 63-23-81.

Back on C 710 the town of **Sóller** suddenly emerges in a valley of olive, citrus, and almond groves, and the coast appears again on the descent to **Puerto de Sóller**, a busy, picturesque port shared by fishermen and tourists and dotted with cafés. An antique orange trolley whose open-sided cars are lined with wooden benches transports visitors from the town of Sóller to the port below.

From Sóller to the northeast the road winds through about 30 tortuous kilometers (19 miles) of mountains, pine forest, and reservoirs unmarred by traces of civilization, to the turnoff for the scenic coastal area known as Sa Calobra and the Torrente de Pareis. The descent from the mountains to the coast unravels along 18 km (11 miles) of hairpin curves and plunging ramps, where the only signs of life are olive trees, large tufts of dry grasses, and grazing sheep.

After passing through a tiny space between two huge vertical rock slabs, the road runs through cork and citrus orchards to a cove called **Sa Calobra**. A café sits miraculously at the bottom. Walking to the right through two tunnels in the rock, you arrive at the **Torrente de Pareis**, a stream that emerges between the rock walls and makes its way to the sea at a confluence of smoothly pebbled beach, white sand, and translucent Mediterranean waters. During the summer the cove is the site of a concert series. For concert information, check with the Sóller tourist office at Plaça de Sa Constitució 1.

After Sa Calobra, continuing about 10 km (6 miles) north on C 710, you can visit the **Monasterio de Lluch**, just off the highway toward the coast. Lluch has been a holy site since the Virgin reputedly appeared to a shepherd here in the

13th century. It is the spiritual home of Majorcans, who come here to worship the 13th-century carved black Virgin and Child known as the *Moreneta*. (The statue is in a small chapel whose entrance is to the right of the altar of the main church.) The church—which dates from the 17th century—was rebuilt in the 19th century by several architects, including Gaudí, who was also responsible for the Stations of the Cross here.

CABO DE FORMENTOR

From Lluch it's about 20 km (12 miles) on C 710 through stark, rocky mountains to the town of Pollença and its bay. Follow the signs through town to begin your exploration of **Cabo de Formentor**, the long, narrow, feather-shaped promontory that protrudes from Majorca's north coast into the Mediterranean. The farther you drive on the twisting 19-km (12-mile) road along Formentor's mountainous spine, the narrower the road becomes and the sparser the low vegetation. At the end there's a lighthouse (with a small parking lot) and a panoramic view of the sea.

At the beginning of the cape you'll see signs for the turnoff to the ► **Hotel Formentor**, whose formal seaside gardens, pine forests, and facilities (including tennis courts, swimming pool, discotheque, and riding trails) sprawl just inland from a long strip of sandy beach. More than a hotel, this is a resort—frequented by Spanish nobility as well as political and literary figures—where most guests take the full pension and settle in for a long stay. Rooms, which are all decorated differently, contain traditional furniture; some offer views of the sea. The main dining room—which is a bit on the formal side: jacket and tie for men—serves international cuisine along the lines of rack of lamb and shrimp flambé. In summer the hotel also opens a poolside grill. Tel: (9-71) 86-53-00.

Returning to Palma

The most extensive traces of Roman civilization in Majorca are the remains of the ancient city of Pollentia, at the modern town of **Alcudia**, 8½ km (5 miles) east of Puerto de Pollença on Bahía de Pollença. For the archaeology buff who wants to see anything and everything Roman, the relatively small remains of the city and the Roman theater—as well as the **Museu Arqueològic**, which displays several large, headless statues, ceramics, and other finds from the excavations—may be worth a detour; for those who have only a passing interest, probably not.

The inland route back to Palma, C 713, while not as scenic as the coast road, is much faster and passes through pleasant citrus and olive groves and vineyards. You can stop for a meal at **Celler C'an Amer** at Pau 39 in the center of **Inca**, an industrial city known for its production of shoes and pottery. The restaurant is a former wine cellar that exudes a traditional atmosphere: Dark wooden wine casks line the walls, and strings of garlic and peppers dangle above the bar, which is popular with locals for business lunches. To pique the appetite, a pitcher of red wine, bread, and a plate of garlicky Majorcan olives are served when you arrive. To follow, you can choose traditional dishes such as *tumbet* (vegetable casserole), hearty soups, and fresh fish. Tel: (9-71) 50-12-61.

EASTERN MAJORCA

By far the most interesting and scenic region of Majorca is the Tramuntana and the cliffs, towns, coves, and forests that cling to its peaks as it weaves its way up the west coast. However, if you have time and itchy feet there are other side trips that will take you through pleasing coastal and country scenery and offer perspectives on historical figures, including medieval philosopher Ramón Llull and Father Serra.

The east coast, where the rocky cliffs, coves, and tiny beaches are endowed with considerable natural beauty, has been overdeveloped into a series of resorts for the northern European package trade; although some sights of intrinsic interest remain, tour buses, heavy traffic, high-rise hotels, and shopping centers detract from the experience considerably.

We suggest destinations in two groups: those south and southeast of Palma and those along or close to the east coast. To see all of these sights it would be best if you devoted a day each to the south and the east. However, by picking and choosing (for example, skipping La Marina and Capicorp Vey and proceeding right to Lluchmayor) you may be able to see most of these in one long day, returning to Palma at night. (Although this section is organized as a car trip, you can visit virtually all of these destinations by taking local buses from Palma or joining organized tours offered by travel agencies there.)

Southeast of Palma

An excursion southeast of Palma can take you on a scenic, roundabout route through a nature preserve, to a Bronze Age settlement, on a side trip to a beautiful stretch of beach, up a mountain to a centuries-old monastery, and finally to the home town of an 18th-century missionary responsible for the founding of two of California's largest cities.

THE SOUTH COAST

Take the airport road (C 715) east out of Palma. Just beyond the airport head south, following signs for C 717. After about a mile on C 717 turn right toward El Arenal, then pick up the unnumbered coast road toward Cala Blava. South of Cala Blava is **La Marina**, a nature preserve known for the cormorants, peregrine falcons, and many other bird species that nest on its 100-foot-high cliffs. The preserve stretches along the coast for more than 12 miles, from Cabo Enderrocat south to Cabo Blanco.

Upon reaching Cabo Blanco, take the road inland toward Lluchmayor to reach **Capicorp Vey**, a well-marked Bronze Age archaeological site, 5 km (3 miles) from the Cabo Blanco lighthouse. Here you can see several talayots—the round prehistoric towers—and the remains of numerous prehistoric stone buildings. The pottery, tools, and other finds from the excavations here are on display in the Museu Arqueològic in Barcelona.

If you're ready for a break from sightseeing, continue on the Lluchmayor road a short distance beyond Capicorp Vey and then turn east toward Salines. After a 13-km (8-mile) drive through farmland, you'll come upon markers for La Rapita and Ses Covetes, which tell you you're on the right track to reach **Es Trench**, one of Majorca's finest broad white-sand beaches. These sparkling waters and gentle waves are perfect for children; there is adequate parking about a five-minute walk from the shore.

Whether or not it's swimming season, consider a detour to Cala Santanyi and Cala Figuera, accessible by continuing past the turnoff for Es Trench to Santanyi and following signs to the coast. Cala Figuera has a picturesque port where the privileged have built Italianate villas. **Cala Santanyi** offers a sandy, protected swimming beach and **Restaurant Drac**, which serves fresh fish at reasonable prices.

NORTH TO RANDA

If you choose not to while away the afternoon on the beach, continue north on the road from Capicorp Vey for 13 km (8 miles) to its intersection with C 717, at Lluchmayor. Four kilometers (2½ miles) north of Lluchmayor, on the road to Algaida, in the town of Randa, is the **Santuario del Cura**, a Franciscan monastery perched 1,800 feet above sea level on the spine of a mountain. The monastery, with its sweeping views of much of the island (including Palma and Cabo Formentor, the island's northern tip), was used as a retreat by its founder, 13th-century Catalan philosopher Ramón Llull, author of the *Ars Magna,* one of the most renowned philosophical works in the Middle Ages. Devoted to spreading the Christian faith, Llull believed that the most effective way of doing so was to understand the language and culture of those one wished to convert. This led him to study Arabic and to travel as a missionary to the Near East and North Africa, where, it is thought, he was martyred for his beliefs. The monastery library, which, along with the church and refectory, is open to the public, contains a collection of manuscripts, music books, and prayer books of Llull's era.

PETRA

Petra, about 20 km (12 miles) northeast of Randa (take the Montuiri road northeast out of Randa, then head east on C 715 for about 14 km/9 miles, then north to Petra), is the birthplace of Father Serra, the 18th-century Franciscan missionary-explorer. Serra's expeditions up the California coast led to the founding of many missions, including those from which the cities of San Diego and San Francisco sprang.

The **Museo Junípero Serra**, the modest, thatched-roof family home, and the **Santuario de Bonany**, at which Serra preached his last sermon, can all be visited at Petra. The museum displays include a series of recent photographs and diagrams of the missions Serra founded, as well as *The First Mass in Monterey,* an oil painting depicting the friar— flanked by *conquistadores* and Native Americans—saying mass on the edge of the Pacific Ocean. The Serra sights are easily found by following the signs from the highway. The museum and the family home are on Carrer Junípero Serra, and the Santuario de Bonany is 4 km (2½ miles) southwest of the town center.

From Petra head back to the C 715, at which point you can head west, back to Palma, or continue on to Majorca's rugged east coast.

The East Coast

Majorca's east coast is lined with mountains, though these are much less grand than those on the west coast. The outstanding attractions of the east are secluded coves and beaches and several limestone caves that have been carved and shaped by the elements into fantastic forms.

THE ROAD TO ARTA

The quickest route east out of Palma is the C 715 toward Son Ferriol and Algaida. There are several interesting sights to see along the way north to Artà (78 km/48 miles from Palma) and Cala Ratjada (just beyond Artà), after which you can follow a network of roads along the east coast back to Palma. At **Manacor**, 47 km (29 miles) east of Palma (and 6 km/3½ miles east of the turnoff for the Serra sights at Petra, covered above), you can stop to buy souvenirs at a cultured-pearl factory or a woodworking factory that produces bowls and other items from native Majorcan olive wood. Both stores are on the highway as you enter town from the west.

In Manacor there is an ample collection of mosaics and sarcophagi from the now-vanished fourth-century Basílica de Son Pereto, as well as prehistoric and other artifacts, at the **Museu Arqueològic**. This museum is housed in a restored 15th-century villa (La Torre dels Enegistes) on Carretera de Son Forteza, the unmarked road that exits Manacor to the east, in the direction of the Calas de Mallorca resort.

ARTA

Continuing northeast on C 715 you'll come to **Ses Païsses**, a well-marked site of prehistoric talayots, on the east side of the highway. About a kilometer past that is Artà, a medieval village whose dominant feature is the Catalan Gothic **Iglesia de Sant Salvador**, which stands on a high hill surrounded by an imposing crenellated wall on the north side of town. From the church you can make a 25-minute drive to the Betlem hermitage, known more for its sweeping views of the coast than for its tiny chapel and shuttered living quarters. To see the view, which goes to Cabo de Formentor on the west and southwest to Colonia San Pedro, take the rocky path behind the hermitage.

CALA RATJADA

Following the C 715 northeast from Artà you'll see signs for **Cala Guya** and **Cala Mesquida**, both of which have white-sand beaches and clear, clean turquoise water. About 10 km (6 miles) northeast of Artà is Cala Ratjada, a former fishing village that is now a center of German tourism. There is good swimming at Cala Ratjada, and Cala Guya's beach can be reached from the town by a footpath.

A major attraction in this area, the **Jardines Casa March**, is an extensive sculpture garden located on the grounds of a private home. To see the sculptures by Henry Moore, Basque artist Eduardo Chillida, Rodin, and others, you must arrange an appointment by calling the local tourist office; Tel: (9-71) 56-30-33.

For serious (albeit pricey) dining in Cala Ratjada, try ► **Ses Rotges**, located in a small hotel of the same name at Carrer Rafael Blanes 21 in the center of town. French "gastronomic" cuisine with an emphasis on local fish and seafood products is how the chef characterizes the menu, which features such dishes as sole meunière, turbot soufflé, and duck *à l'orange*. Both the thatched-ceiling, stone-walled indoor dining room and the ample patio, with its white walls, palm trees, and flower beds, create a welcoming atmosphere. The ambience extends to the reasonably priced hotel rooms, which feature tile floors and wooden country furniture. Like many hotels and restaurants in Majorca's tourist areas, Ses Rotges closes for several months in winter; Tel: (9-71) 56-31-08.

SOUTH ALONG THE COAST
South of Cala Ratjada on the coast are extensive networks of limestone caves. The **Cuevas de Artà** (13 km/8 miles from Cala Ratjada) are noted for the height of the stalagmites and stalactites—one column is 72 feet high—and for the "organ" and other formations created by the action of water on the rock. Highlights of the **Cuevas del Drach** (25 km/15 miles from Cala Ratjada) include an underground auditorium that can seat more than 3,000 people and a sound-and-light show projected onto a 500-foot-long body of water named Lake Martel after the French geologist who explored the caves in the 19th century. Be prepared for long lines, traffic, and crowds if you visit the caves in the summer, as they are among Majorca's most-visited attractions.

IBIZA

Ibiza is a Mecca for the European jet set and a refuge for one of the world's largest remaining colonies of hippies, testimony to the "anything goes" social philosophy of the island. This may be reason enough for those who avoid discotheques and funky boutiques to stay away from Ibiza, even if they're tempted by the beaches and the scenic coast.

But there are some very good reasons to visit the island: to experience Ibiza city's imposing Dalt Vila, whose walls encircle an area that was populated in succession by Phoenicians, Romans, Arabs, and Christians since the seventh century B.C., and to survey the treasure trove of sculpture, ceramics, jewelry, and other finds extracted from the tombs of a Phoenician necropolis found right in the city. A drive along the small roads in the island's interior, through olive and citrus groves and tiny white towns, is another motive for a visit.

Whether viewed from land or sea, Ibiza's most prominent landmark is walled Ibiza city, nestled high above the port on the southeastern side of the island. All of Ibiza's main roads fan out from Ibiza city. A highway to the west connects it with San Antonio Abad (14 km/8½ miles away), an uncomfortably dense tourist resort on the coast. About 8 km (5 miles) south of San Antonio, Monte Atalaya, the island's highest point, rises more than 1,400 feet, overlooking a craggy coastline accented by several offshore islands—really just chunks of rock protruding from the water. Much of the island's coast-line features steep cliffs that plunge straight into the water and tiny sandy beaches, many unfortunately overdeveloped with vacation villages and such abominations as water slides.

If you're exploring Ibiza by car or moped, always keep an eye open for signs to your destination. Many roads have no name or number, but there's almost always a sign pointing to the restaurant or beach you're seeking. In August the road system can easily become overloaded, especially near the large tourist developments of Santa Eulalia (on the coast north of Ibiza city) and San Antonio Abad; the inland routes are generally less congested.

On Ibiza, as on the other Balearic Islands, the discerning visitor will want to avoid lodging in a hotel or area that caters to mass tourism. Because the island is so small—it's easy to explore by car or bus from almost any base—the main decision is whether to opt for a base in Ibiza City, where the nightlife is virtually on your doorstep, or for a more tranquil, isolated hostelry on the coast.

IBIZA CITY

The city of Ibiza wraps around the harbor. The modern quarters lie to the northeast and the older quarters, Sa Penya and **La Marina**, the water's-edge seamen's quarter dating from the 15th century—now a center of nightlife—lie to the south. Inland of La Marina the Portal de les Tables leads through the stolid 16th-century walls and gates built to shield the city from attacks by the Turks. The walls enclose the ancient Dalt Vila, the historic core of Ibiza occupied in turn by Phoenicians, Romans, Arabs, and Christians, and the area in which you'll spend most of your time here. From there it's a short walk to the even older Puig des Molins, a Phoenician necropolis where excavators have uncovered hundreds of ancient tombs.

The Dalt Vila

If it weren't so steep, a walking tour of the Dalt Vila could be accomplished in a very few minutes. But the verticality of the terrain also enhances the charm—the glimpses of the sea and the wall-to-wall white houses and shops, restaurants, and bars beckoning you to browse or pause for a drink—as you climb through the cobblestone streets to the cathedral overlooking the harbor and the archaeological site Puig des Molins. Before starting your tour of the Dalt Vila, stop at the tourist office, at Passeig Vara de Rey 13, to stock up on maps and information on restaurants, hotels, and public transportation.

The best place to start your ascent is at the **Portal de les Tables** in La Marina—one of three entrances to the quarter (and the only one you can enter by car). From here the house- and shop-lined streets zigzag up the hill to the summit of the Dalt Vila, which is dominated by the **cathedral**, a pastiche of styles with a 13th-century bell tower and a newly renovated 17th-century interior. Once you've reached the top of the Dalt Vila you'll have a fine view of Ibiza's tile rooftops, the sea, and beaches from the balustrades, reached by walking through a gate to the right of the cathedral. But there are even better views from the terrace and windows of the **Museu Arqueològic Ibiza**, at Plaça de la Catedral 3, open all day July through September, mornings only the rest of the year. This museum contains ceramics and other finds from Phoenician and prehistoric sites on Ibiza and nearby Formentera. Among its main attractions are three Roman figure sculptures. If you want to visit the cathedral and this archaeological museum, ask at the tourist office (if it is open; it has been closed for renovation).

Outside the Dalt Vila

If you have the time or interest for only one archaeological museum while in Ibiza city, definitely choose the one at **Puig des Molins**, at Via Romana 31, below the Dalt Vila in the modern city. Puig des Molins displays objects from the Phoenician necropolis on the site, which is believed to have served as a cemetery from 654 B.C. to the first century A.D. A brief guided visit to some of the estimated 400 underground tombs is included in the admission.

The museum's undisputed star attraction is a terra-cotta bust of a woman thought to be the goddess Tamit. Deeply etched reddish hair topped by a pillbox headdress sweeps back from a serene, full face with an enigmatic gaze. The thousands of reproductions of that face on postcards, posters, and in ceramic imitations sold all over the island cannot approach the beauty of the real thing.

Also among the museum's holdings is a collection of delicate ostrich eggs—most are on display in room II— painted with simple patterns of flowers, scarabs, or abstractions. Their exact significance is not known, but one theory is that they were placed in tombs as a symbol of resurrection. Room IV houses a collection of small, finely worked objects including medical instruments, tiny scarabs, gold rings and earrings, amulets representing Egyptian gods, and necklaces of multi-colored glass beads. This room also has a model of a side view of the necropolis, and many of the other museum rooms contain groupings of items found together, tomb by tomb. Hundreds of terra-cotta statues found in the tombs are also on display, of interest because they depict figures dressed in the garments, headgear, and jewelry of their time.

Other attractions in the city outside the Dalt Vila include the high-fashion, often expensive shops in La Marina and the evening handicrafts market staged by local artisans and hippies in the plaza on the **Passeig Vara de Rey**, which intersects with Carrer Ramón y Tur a couple of blocks inland from the port.

Staying and Dining in Ibiza City

Nestled on a hill a few blocks above the museum is ► **Hostal Residencia Molins Park**, a new 30-room hotel. Rooms are bright, with simple, modern furniture and balconies overlooking the city. Air-conditioning, a small swimming pool, parking, and a snack bar make the Molins Park a comfortable, convenient base for visiting the city and the island.

The ► **Royal Plaza**, a well-run and well-appointed modern hotel on Pedro Francés, a five-minute walk from the Passeig Vara de Rei, makes a good base for business and other upscale travellers. Guest and public rooms here feature opulent leather, wood, tile, and marble furnishings.

The island's best restaurants tend to be outside Ibiza city. For dining in the city, you might try one of the many outdoor eateries—possibilities range from pizza to *paella*—in the La Marina and Sa Penya neighborhoods. These meals include entertainment: watching the throngs of tourists parading by in their exotic outfits.

Another option is to ascend through the thick, ancient stone gate known as the Portal de les Tables to the quieter but still colorful **Plaça de Vila**, an inviting strip of restaurants and shops within the old walls (a good place to shop for jewelry and handcrafted leather goods). There are at least a dozen restaurants here, all offering candlelit dining rooms and outdoor dining in summer. A good choice is **La Oliva**, straight ahead and a bit up the hill to your right upon passing through the portal. The French owner offers a menu of pasta, pizza, fresh fish, and other Mediterranean dishes; Tel: (9-71) 30-57-52.

DINING OUTSIDE IBIZA CITY

Several of the island's best restaurants are located a short distance outside Ibiza City, close enough to reach by taxi if you do not have a car. One is the **Grill San Rafael**, located in a house next to the whitewashed church in the town of the same name (in the center of the island at Carretera San Antonio, km 6.7). White-haired, goateed owner Albert Campalans, who once had a chemical factory in Barcelona, "dropped out" and started up this restaurant after a visit to Ibiza 20 years ago. Approaching each table with a pad and pencil in hand, Campalans often sits down to discuss the night's menu with the guests before taking orders. The tables on the restaurant's gracious terrace overlook the lights of Ibiza City. Tel: (9-71) 19-80-56.

La Masía d'En Sord (km 1, Carretera a San Miguel, outside Ibiza City) is a huge, traditional farmhouse converted into a restaurant-gallery by artist-owner Nieves Puente. The menu is Continental, with local touches such as rabbit grilled over an open fire. Diners may sit inside on banquettes piled comfortably with pillows or at tables in the garden. The large house feels intimate because there are several small dining rooms rather than one cavernous one. The walls— on which are displayed everything from drawings of Ibizan women in traditional dress to abstract oils—bear testimony to the changing artistic moods of the owner and her daughter; Tel: (9-71) 31-02-28.

On the same road, at km 2.3, is **Ama Lur**, an elegant restaurant located in a 19th-century farmhouse, whose Basque chef creates such dishes as veal medallions with duck liver and port wine sauce, and fillets of sole with leek sauce. This is a good place to people-watch as Ibiza's bejeweled, high-fashion jet setters arrive to dine on the candlelit terrace amid palm trees and lush greenery. Unless you really limit your selection, a three-course dinner with wine at Ama Lur will cost as much as your hotel room for the night. The only disadvantage to dining here is the noise from the highway. Tel: (9-71) 31-45-54.

Nightlife on Ibiza

Ibiza's nightlife operates on several levels. But one thing all types of night spots share is late hours—many places start to get lively around midnight and stay open until dawn.

Along the streets of La Marina on the edge of the city's harbor, the action consists of barhopping and people-watching from outdoor cafés. A couple of blocks away the **Teatre Pereira** on Conde Rosselló attracts patrons with live jazz; the crowd here is relatively sedate. On the Passeig Maritim, which lines the north side of the harbor across the water from La Marina, the **casino** offers everything from roulette tables and slot machines to a nightclub and an ice-cream stand. A few doors down the street is **Keepers**, a popular late-night terrace bar.

On an island that claims to have 150 discotheques, probably the most famous and long-lasting is **Pachá**, on Paseo Marítim, behind the casino, where revelers throng to the restaurant, swimming pool, and several terrace bars, after paying a steep cover charge of 4,000 pesetas. **Amnesia**, 5 km (3 miles) from Ibiza on the road toward San Antonio, which advertises that it will bus "boys and girls" there free from that boisterous resort area, caters to a hard-core partying crowd that lasts until breakfast time on margaritas.

Ibiza night spots are constantly opening and closing and becoming "in" or "out." For information on current main attractions, check with your hotel or the tourist office.

OUT ON IBIZA ISLAND

Ibiza island's main touring attractions are beaches and coastline, the view from Monte Atalaya, and the tiny, tranquil inland towns with their bright white houses, some painted with colorful trim, and small churches with bell towers.

San Antonio on the west coast, Santa Eulalia del Río on the east, and Figueretes and d'En Bossa beaches near Ibiza City are all congested tourist areas that retain little of their traditional identity and are less deserving of the traveller's time. The only way to get a view of the craggy cliffs of Ibiza's west coast is by boat. In the summer, there are all-day excursions from the San Antonio port.

For tranquil, scenic swimming and sightseeing we recommend a tour of the east coast beaches, a drive to Na Xamena, the site of one of Ibiza's most elegant hotels, and a visit to the southwest part of the island, to the top of Monte Atalaya and the nearby beach, Cala d'Hort.

East Coast Beaches

Some of the best beaches on Ibiza can be approached only by unpaved roads through the pine groves that inspired the Greeks to call Ibiza and neighboring Formentera the Pitiüsas (pine-covered) islands. The east-side beaches, up the coast from Ibiza City, are wonderful for swimming and can also be enjoyed in cooler seasons, when you can hike and picnic along the scenic, cliff-lined coast. To visit the beaches, leave Ibiza City on the road to Santa Eulalia (about 14 km/8½ miles north).

Just off this road, a kilometer before the entrance to Santa Eulalia, is one of the island's loveliest and most unusual hostelries, ▶ **Les Terrasses**—a good choice if you seek rural tranquillity in your lodgings. Shortly after C 733 branches left toward San Juan Bautista, watch on the right for an incongruously painted bright blue rock. At the rock, turn right and drive just beyond two more blue rocks, following the small sign to the left, which takes you through the fields to Les Terrasses, a multi-terraced, six-room pension operated by former Paris model Françoise Pialoux.

The swimming pool, guest rooms, the owner's house, the sunbathing area, and the gardens spill over a series of traditional stone terraces. Guest rooms—each is decorated differently and is almost as large as a small apartment—are located in block-shaped structures with stone façades. All have wooden country furnishings, earth- and pastel-colored walls, colorful tiles, and ample bathroom facilities, such as double sinks; some have a shaded private terrace with chairs and tables.

Twice weekly Ms. Pialoux cooks and serves an outdoor dinner with offerings that range from Japanese to classical French, for about 15 guests. If you want to dine there, reserve ahead; Tel: (9-71) 33-26-43.

Most of the clientele at Les Terrasses is French, and some guests stay for weeks at a time. You may need to reserve as much as six months ahead.

To visit the local beaches, return to the main road and turn right. Continue through Santa Eulalia and follow signs to San Carlos, 6 km (3½ miles) farther. In the center of tiny **San Carlos** signs direct you to nearby beaches, all of which can be reached by roads that branch off an unnumbered coast road that edges the cliffs (and doesn't show up on maps). The first right turn from San Carlos leads to **Cala Llenya,** an ample sandy beach defined by reddish rocks at either end. Lounges, parasols, and a snack bar make this a comfortable place for swimming.

The next beach, **Cala Mastella,** is tiny and bordered by rocky cliffs. Reason enough to stop here, however, is the **Restaurant Cala Mastella.** To get there, follow the signs to **Restaurant Sa Seni** and turn right into the parking area. Leave the car and follow the path to the beach. On the left side of the beach is a path across some rocks that leads you to the open-air restaurant on the rocks right at the water's edge. This is a family business. Joan Ferrer arrives at the dock in his small white boat and lugs in a plastic bucket of fish, which the women then cook over logs in a huge open fireplace.

The menu—it never changes—is the traditional fish stew, *bullit de peix,* served in two courses to diners seated on benches at wooden picnic tables overlooking the water. First comes a brilliant yellow mélange of potato chunks and the day's catch. Next comes a huge bowl of soupy yellow rice, rather tangy and garnished with bright-red crab legs. This place may seem terribly out of the way, but it's popular and a real bargain. In the summer it's necessary to make reservations two or three days in advance for lunch (it's not open for dinner). There's no phone, so the only way to make reservations is to go there in person.

If you're a serious swimmer, go on from Cala Mastella—where the water is shallow and rocky—to a better beach. From Ferrer's restaurant you can return to the coast road and continue north toward **Cala Boix**, a brown-sand beach at which there are two summer restaurants. Nearby is **Pou d'es Lle'o**, a charming rocky cove with bright refreshing water that is, however, a mooring place for fishing boats.

Returning to the coast road again, pass up Cala Figueretas, a large, none-too-clean beach frequented by many tourists who stay in the hotels and apartments there, and continue on a mile or two to **Aigua Blava**. Here, a steep road leads to a narrow white strip of beach flanked by steep cliffs. To the right, in the summer, a beachside *chiringuito* serves reasonably priced snacks and lunches (such as fresh-grilled sardines) and offers a view of the rocky offshore island of Tagomago. A few steps through the surf around the rocks to the left bring you to an attractive sandy strip frequented by nude bathers.

To return to Ibiza City follow the road out of Aigua Blava to San Carlos.

Northeast to Na Xamena

En route to Na Xamena, on the northeastern coast, stop to visit **Balafi**, a tiny enclosed compound of a few houses and a cylindrical defense tower surrounded by a wall. The compound appears on your left, just after the San Carlos road intersects C 733, 30 km (19 miles) from Ibiza City. Leave the car at the edge of the road and take the footpath to examine this curious colony more closely, but watch out for the large, growling dogs kept by the residents to warn visitors to keep their distance.

Return to the main road and continue on to Na Xamena, for a very different but equally worthwhile view of the Ibiza coast. Follow the signs to the ► **Hotel Hacienda** in the Na Xamena development, an isolated, elegant aerie ensconced in a clifftop pine forest overlooking a pinkish rock promontory and the port of San Miguel.

You reach the hotel's beach via a zigzag wooden staircase; the waters are shared by bathers and boaters alike. It's more private at the hotel's ample pool and terrace. From your own balcony you'll have views of the sea. The traditional white architecture, complemented by greenery, makes the hotel a peaceful and beautiful choice. Its restaurant, which attracts diners from around the island, serves a good selection of fish, seafood, and meat dishes. If you value tranquillity and can afford the considerable tab, this is the place to stay on the island.

Southeastern Ibiza

From Ibiza City, take the road to San José, drive through town, and watch on your left for a road marked by several signs, including one for "Atalaia," the local name for **Monte Atalaya** and others for beaches including Cala d'Hort.

To reach the mountaintop, follow the signs, which guide you along a bumpy dirt road ascending gently through pine forests to a peak that offers panoramic views of the south and east coast and several small offshore islands. The ascent takes about 15 minutes.

When you descend from the peak, turn left and follow the signs along several unpaved, dusty roads to **Cala d'Hort**, a swimming cove ensconced between two rugged cliffs, and Isla Vedra, whose rocky nose juts out of the sea. The beach has three restaurants, all of which specialize in pricey fresh fish and seafood, including *paella*. If you prefer to lunch on sandwiches or snacks, bring them with you.

As you reach the top of the road out of Cala d'Hort, turn left onto the paved road, which will take you back to Ibiza through San José. The **Café de la Ruta**, to your left in the center of San José, is a good place for a light lunch, *tapas,* or a drink.

FORMENTERA ISLAND

Connected to the rest of Spain only by ferries and sight-seeing boats, Formentera is the smallest and flattest of the four major Balearic islands and has a population of only about 5,000.

Best known for its beaches—on which nude bathing is often acceptable—Formentera suffers from a lack of fresh water that has limited the tourist trade. Although the island is a popular destination for yachts and day trips, most of the accommodations are small hostels. A complete list is available from the tourist information center at Passeig Vara de Rey 13 in Ibiza.

On Formentera's southern coast is an excellent, long sandy beach, **Platja Mitjorn**, on which stand two large, upscale hotels that attract an international crowd: on the western end, ▶ **Formentera Playa**, and at the eastern end, ▶ **Iberotel Club La Mola**, layers of whitewashed units with luxury amenities. Nearby, on the island's highest ground, a summit called La Mola, the restaurant **El Mirador** makes a good stop for a sweeping view of the island and excellent desserts. For good swimming and a fresh-fish lunch, locals recommend **S'Illeta** beach and its one restaurant, **La Sabina**, on the western side of the narrow peninsula that juts northeast of the port.

To get to Formentera, take a ferry from Estación Marítim, at the foot of the marina in Ibiza City—both hydrofoils and boats depart almost hourly. On the west coast of Ibiza tour boats leave from San Antonio Abad. At Formentera's port of La Sabina, fleets of bicycles, mopeds, and cars stand ready for rental.

GETTING AROUND

Iberia Airlines flies from London to Palma, but this is the only scheduled air connection between an international departure point and the Balearics. Therefore most air travellers who are not taking charter flights will have to approach the islands from a point—most likely Madrid or Barcelona—on the Spanish mainland. (There is no air service to Formentera.)

The Iberia Visit Spain airpass, which allows travellers who are crossing the Atlantic on Iberia to make several stops throughout Spain for 30 days for a special low fare, allows you to stop at each of the islands (in addition to points on the mainland) if you plan the itinerary so that it's not necessary to double back on your route.

Both air and sea transportation schedules between mainland Spain and the Balearics, as well as from one island to another, change several times a year—sometimes radically. If you plan to travel during the summer, at Christmas, Easter, any Spanish holiday, or on a weekend, reserve well in advance. And although boat travel has its charms, travelling this way increases the length of your journey considerably (see below).

You can safely assume that there will be daily service on Iberia or on Aviaco, the Spanish domestic airline, from Madrid and Barcelona to Ibiza, Majorca, and Minorca. Barcelona, about a half-hour flight from each of the islands, is the closest jumping-off point. Flights from Madrid are about an hour. There are also some flights to the islands from Valencia—it's only a half-hour to Ibiza—but they do not run daily, and schedules are subject to change. Many new charter services have sprung up to serve Madrid, Geneva, Paris, and other European cities; consult a travel agent for schedules.

In planning your trip, try to reserve ahead, because flights are usually heavily booked: during the winter months (from about October to Easter) because there often are not enough flights to meet the normal demand from island residents, and during the summer months because of the influx of tourists. (To avoid delays, always book and confirm your return to the mainland well ahead of time.)

Trasmediterránea runs ferries from the mainland and among the islands two or three times a week during the winter, more often in the summer (starting in June). From Barcelona to any of the three islands directly is an eight-hour trip, sometimes overnight. The ferry—which has state-rooms as well as armchairs—carries cars and is also equipped with restaurants, bars, television, game rooms, and an outdoor pool. While the trip can be pleasant on a warm summer day, in the winter the Mediterranean can be quite rough.

The Trasmediterránea ferries also connect Minorca, Majorca, and Ibiza. The company can be reached in Barcelona at the Estación Marítima, Tel: (9-3) 317-4262, and in Valencia at Manuel Soto 15, Tel: (9-6) 367-3972.

In the islands, Trasmediterránea offices are located in Mahón (Minorca) at Nuevo Muelle Comercial, Tel: (9-71) 36-29-50; Palma (Majorca) on Passeig Muelle Viejo, Tel: (9-71) 72-67-40; and in Ibiza City (Ibiza) at Avinguda Bartolomé Vicente Ramó 2, Tel: (9-71) 30-16-50.

Another ferry company, Flebasa, offers year-round service from Denia, about halfway between Valencia and Alicante on the southern coast of Spain, to Ibiza, Majorca, and Minorca. They have offices in Denia, Tel: (9-65) 78-41-00; Madrid, Tel: (9-1) 473-2055; and Ibiza, Tel: (9-71) 34-28-21.

Each of the islands has some bus service, although it is not adequate for exploring the more isolated beaches and monuments. Bus schedules are available from local tourist offices. The tourist offices on the islands are: in Mahón, Minorca, at Plaça d'Explanada 40; in Ciudadela, Minorca, at a mobile office in Plaça d'Es Borne; in Palma, Majorca, at Avinguda Jaume III 10; in Ibiza City, at Passeig Vara de Rey 13; on Formentera Island, at Port de la Sabina. The only trains on the islands are on Majorca. There are two lines—one between Palma and Sóller, the other between Palma and Inca—which offer service several times a day from the Plaça España in Palma. Palma city bus lines are well marked and dependable.

Avis, Hertz, and Europcar (in the U.S., National) offer car rentals on all three major islands. Each island also has several—in the case of Majorca, numerous—other agencies. Sometimes the best car-rental rates, especially if you need the vehicle for a week or more, can be secured as part of a vacation package. If you'll need a car only for an occasional excursion, unless you're visiting in high season, you may get the best deal by postponing your car-rental decision until you actually arrive on one of the islands. Bicycles, motorcycles, and motorbikes are also widely available for rental, and serve well for many excursions, especially on Ibiza, Formentera, and Minorca.

ACCOMMODATIONS REFERENCE

The hotel rates listed below are projected rates for 1994, for double room, double occupancy, in pesetas. The ranges reflect low and high season rates. The high season is generally July and August, Easter, and Christmas through New Year's.

The telephone area code for the Balearic Islands is 9-71. When dialing telephone numbers from outside the country, drop the 9 in the area code.

Minorca

► **Hotel del Almirante**. Fonduco Puerto de Mahón Ctra. Villacarlos, 07720 **Es Castells**. Tel: 36-27-00; Fax: 36-27-04. 4,610–7,315 pts.

► **Hostal Biniali**. Carretera S'Uestra–Binibeca 50, **San Luis**. Tel: 15-17-24; Fax: 15-03-52. 11,900 pts.

► **Hostal Mar Blava**. Urbanización Son Oleo, 07701 **Ciudadela**. Tel: 38-00-16; Fax: 38-48-55. 3,600–4,200 pts.

► **Hostal Residencia Ciudadella**. Sant Eloy 10, 07760 **Ciudadela**. Tel: 38-34-62. 3,200–5,600 pts.

► **Hotel Patricia**. Passeig de Sant Nicolau 90–92, 07760 **Ciudadela**. Tel: 38-55-11; Fax: 48-11-20. 14,900 pts.

► **Port Mahón Hotel**. Avinguda Fort de l'Eau 13, 07701 **Mahón**. Tel: 36-26-00; Fax: 35-10-50. 18,650 pts.

Majorca

► **Hostal Mar i Vent**. Carrer Mayor 49, 07191 **Banyalbufar**. Tel: 61-80-00; Fax: 61-82-01. 6,200 pts.

► **Hotel Formentor**. Playa de Formentor, 07470 **Cabo de Formentor**. Tel: 86-53-00; Fax: 86-51-55. 28,700 pts.

► **Hotel Meliá Victoria**. Avinguda Joan Miró 21, 07014 **Palma**. Tel: 23-43-42; Fax: 45-08-24. 26,500 pts.

► **Hotel La Residencia**. Finca Son Canals, 07179 **Deyá**. Tel: 63-90-11; Fax: 63-93-70. 28,000 pts.

► **Hotel Saratoga**. Paseo Majorca 6, 07012 **Palma**. Tel: 72-72-40; Fax: 72-73-12. 10,500–12,110 pts.

► **Son Vida**. Urbanización Son Vida, 07015 **Palma**. Tel: 79-00-00; Fax: 79-00-17. 21,800–28,700 pts.

► **Ses Rotges**. Rafael Blanes 21, 07590 **Cala Ratjada**. Tel: 56-31-08; Fax: 56-43-45. 7,560 pts.

Ibiza

► **Hostal Residencia Molins Park**. Calle Joan Xico 42, 07800 **Ibiza**. Tel: 30-04-64; Fax: 39-13-29. 11,200 pts.

► **Hotel Hacienda**. Na Xamena Urbanización, 07800 **San**

Miguel. Tel: 33-30-46; Fax: 33-31-75; in the U.S., Tel: (212) 856-0115; Fax: (212) 856-0193. 27,000 pts.

► **Royal Plaza**. Carrer Pedro Francés 27, 07800 **Ibiza**. Tel: 31-00-00; Fax: 31-40-95. 16,800 pts.

► **Les Terrasses**. Carretera de Santa Eulalia, km 1, **Ibiza**. Tel: 33-26-43; Fax: 33-11-61. 13,500 pts.

Formentera

► **Formentera Playa**. 07871 **Platja Mitjorn**. Tel: 32-00-00. 10,000–12,000 pts.

► **Iberotel Club La Mola**. Apartado 23 San Francisco, 07871 **Platja Mitjorn**. Tel: 32-80-69; Fax: 32-80-69. 8,500–19,800 pts.

VALENCIA
ALICANTE AND MURCIA

By Patricia Brooks

Although Valencia is famed in song and in kitchen, it is left off the itineraries of most visitors to Spain. The country's third-largest city and capital of the Mediterranean province of the same name, Valencia is oddly uncharismatic at first sight—a huge port and major industrial-agricultural hub that fell victim to high rises and urban sprawl. A traveller driving through its flat geography may see only the ugly signs of shipping and industry, assume that's all there is, and take the turnoff skirting the city, continuing north to Tarragona and Barcelona, south to the Costa del Sol, or west to Madrid, bypassing Valencia's center completely.

Yet this would be a mistake, for Valencia has numerous things to recommend it: three rich, important museums; a cathedral with several unusual treasures; a lively covered market that is a photographer's dream; quite a number of interesting churches; streets pocketed with handsome 15th- to 19th-century mansions and public buildings; a graceful location spanning both banks (but mostly the south one) of the riverbed of the Río Turia; and more than its share of colorful history.

To cover Valencia's major sights will take two very full days, but the city has so many additional charms that grow on you—a gentle climate, a languid sidewalk-café lifestyle, gardens, fountains, unexpected outdoor sculptures, serendipitous discoveries—that even a third day can be rewarding.

Alicante, 177 km (110 miles) farther south, has fewer historical associations, but its balmy weather, seaside charm, and wide, palm-fringed seafront promenade are instant crowd pleasers. Its location as a springboard to the resorts of Benidorm, Denia, and other points both north and south along the **Costa Blanca**, as the coast here is called, doesn't hurt, either. A day or two in Alicante is time well spent.

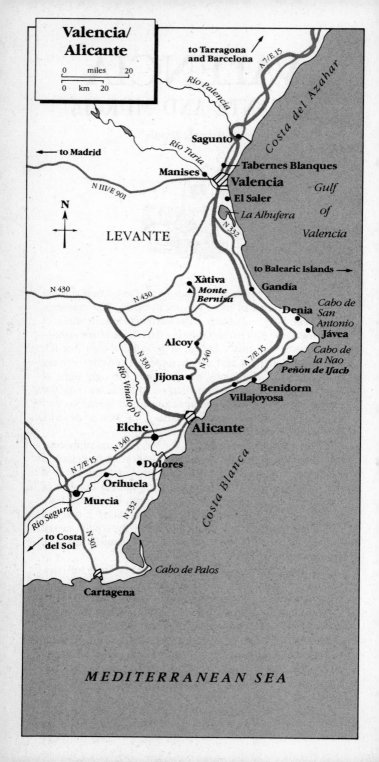

Linking the two cities, in an area sometimes called the Levante, is a coastline as different and appealing in its own way as any other in Spain. Fertile flatlands bordered by a barrier of mountains on one side and the Mediterranean on the other provide an unusual landscape. And, as elsewhere in this wildly diverse country, the scenery changes frequently as the road climbs from sand dune–protected lagoons to cypress-spiked cliffs and wild promontories high above rock-edged bays, then quickly runs down again to sandy inlets and boat-filled harbors.

Southwest of Alicante are Orihuela, a small town of considerable charm on both banks of the Río Segura, and Murcia, a large city downriver whose traffic-clogged streets sometimes discourage lingering. Yet Murcia has its attractions, including Semana Santa processions that are among the most beautiful and evocative in Spain.

MAJOR INTEREST

Diverse scenery: agricultural and coastal landscapes
Regional foods (especially *paella*)
Pre-Roman and Roman ruins at Sagunto

Valencia
Plaça de l'Ajuntament
La Seo (the cathedral)
Mercado Central, covered food market
La Lonja de la Seda (silk exchange)
Instituto Valenciano de Arte Moderno (IVAM)
Palacio del Marqués de Dos Aguas, Baroque mansion
     housing ceramics museum
Colegio del Patriarca, Renaissance building and art
     museum
Museo Provincial de Bellas Artes, important archaeo-
     logical and art collections
Fallas de Valencia festival

Around Valencia
Manises ceramics
Gandía and Xàtiva, ancient towns with rich histories
Dramatic coastal rock formations

Alicante
Charming, relaxed seaside town
Explanada de España harbor promenade
Castillo de Santa Bárbara
Museo Colección de Arte del Siglo XX

Around Alicante
Alcoy's archaeological museum and fine restaurant

Elche's ancient date-palm forest
Historic and scenic town of Orihuela

Murcia
Baroque cathedral
Museo Salzillo, sculpture

The Foods of Valencia
and the Levante

When you think of Valencia and food, one word pops into mind: *paella*. The rice-based, saffron-tinted stew known as *paella valenciana* is certainly Valencia's glory dish, and nowhere in Spain—in the entire world, for that matter—is it prepared with the same élan. The true, traditional *paella valenciana* consists of rice, small snails (usually periwinkles or sea snails), rabbit or chicken, and green vegetables—foods found in abundance in the region. Eels and land snails, also found in the area, may also be included in a true *paella valenciana*. Needless to say, there are as many *paella* variations as there are chefs, and sampling the different *paellas*—from the *Moros y Cristanos* (Moors and Christians, black beans with rice) version to those with squid, with lamb and chick-peas, with zucchini and other vegetables, and Cuban-style, with bananas and fried eggs—is part of the pleasure of a visit to this area.

It is believed that the word *paella* comes from *patella*, Latin for pan, referring to the flat round metal pan (*paellera*, in Spanish) in which the rice is cooked. Using the proper shallow, open pan is considered essential to a good *paella*, for the nature of the pan ensures even cooking and "finishing," without steaming.

In "eastern," or Levantine, cooking, *arroz* (rice)—abundant, flat-grained Valencian rice—is the base of many of the dishes served. You might encounter *arroz con costra al estilo de Elche* (rice Elche style), made with chick-peas, pork, *blanquillos* (small Levantine sausages), chicken, and the black Catalan *butifarra* pork sausage, or *arroz con pollo a la alicantina,* which consists of rice, chicken, green peppers, tomatoes, and artichokes, or *arroz abanda,* cooked in a seafood broth.

The garden of Spain, the Levante produces a harvest of fresh fruits and vegetables, widely evident in the cuisine. No vegetable is more widely used than the artichoke (*alcachofa*). A delicacy elsewhere in the world, artichokes are common in Valencia and along the coast and are often served as a first course seasoned with bits of ham—delicious! Imaginative use of vegetables, such as zucchini, eggplant, and potatoes stuffed with ground meat and enveloped by an almond (another native crop), herb, and garlic sauce, is a trademark of Valencian cuisine.

Other Levantine dishes include *cocas,* a pie made of sweet red peppers, tomatoes, anchovies, and *toyina* (salted tuna), and *pastel de Villena,* a pork loin stuffed with ham, *butifarra,* bacon, and vegetables, and then covered with a minced-meat paste and baked.

Sweets are popular in the region, too, and you'll want to look for Valencian sweet bread (*pan quemado*), Valencian *flan* (made with oranges and lemons), rice and apricot pudding, *tarta huerto del cura* (orange cream cake), and, above all, the almond-honey nougat candy of Jijona and Alicante known as *turrón,* which you will also find flavoring ice cream, sherbet, and sweet sauces. Candied almonds, available all over Spain, are especially prevalent in Valencia, Alicante, and along the coast. And don't miss the refreshing, creamy drink *horchata,* made of a tuber called *chufa,* or earth almond, which, when processed, tastes like an elusive cross between almond and coconut.

Wines of Valencia and Murcia

The warm, dry Mediterranean regions of Valencia (Valencia, Alicante, and Castellón de la Plana) and Murcia (the region south of the Valencia region) contain five *denominaciones de origen*—Alicante, Utiel-Requena, Valencia, Jumilla, and Yecla—all primarily engaged in the production of powerful bulk wines for blending. In this endeavor the Levante is second only to La Mancha. Recently a number of top producers have begun reinvesting money in their wineries and vineyards with an eye toward producing better-quality bottled wines. Modern temperature-controlled fermentation techniques have led to some improvement in the quality of a few table wines, but the region is still far from being a bastion of quality.

Alicante produces full-bodied reds and *rosados* from 90 percent Monastrell grapes. The vineyards are located in the highlands above the Mediterranean beach towns of the Costa Blanca. This area was one of the last occupied by the Moors, and so, prohibitions from the Koran aside, a sweet-tooth legacy remains in some luscious dessert wines, especially Moscatel.

Most **Utiel-Requena** (Valencia province) vineyards grow the black Bobal grape, which produces powerful red wines, but new vineyards are being planted with Tempranillo and Garnacha grapes. Because Utiel-Requena's summers are milder than those nearer the Mediterranean, the area is able to produce some good, lighter fresh *rosados*. Look for red wines from Casa lo Alto.

Valencia produces medium-bodied white table wines from Merserguera grapes, large quantities of low-acid, high-alcohol (14 to 15 percent) red table wines, and some delicious Moscatels. Some of the huge firms specializing in bulk wines are also making some interesting new quality wines for sale in bottles.

In **Jumilla** (Murcia) 90 percent of the vineyards grow Monastrell, which yields thick, black wines of up to 18 percent alcohol. Recently Jumilla has begun to produce some lighter, very well made, oak-aged table wines such as Castillo de Jumilla and Taja.

Yecla (Murcia), which is completely surrounded by the Jumilla and Alicante districts, makes not only traditionally robust reds from Monastrell grapes but also some big, smooth red wines and *claretes* from Monastrell and Garnacha.

A notable feature of the Levante's vineyards is their high proportion of ungrafted vines. The chalky soil and dry climate are not hospitable to aphids, so the vineyards in the Levante were not destroyed during the phylloxera epidemic at the turn of the century.

—*Gerry Dawes*

EN ROUTE TO VALENCIA

Valencia is just a 35-minute plane ride from Madrid, but, as everywhere in Spain, driving is the ideal way to go. From Madrid, Valencia is a 356-km (221-mile) drive over the excellent highway N III. An idyllic stopover can be made at the Parador Marqués de Villena in Alarcón (see the La Mancha chapter). You might also break the trip at **Requena**, just off highway N III, 70 km (44 miles) east of Alarcón, to see the castle ruins and two fine churches: El Salvador, with an Isabelline doorway and Baroque interior, and Santa María, with a Gothic portal and attractive *azulejos* (glazed tiles).

You can also drive south from Barcelona or Tarragona (105 km/65 miles southwest of Barcelona), which is the route we cover here. Along the 259-km (161-mile) drive south of Tarragona (via the superfast, and supercostly, *autopista* A 7/E 15), the route eventually leads over terrain you won't encounter elsewhere in Spain—flat as the proverbial pancake, with wet, languid marshlands and incredibly fertile soil. This is the Levante, with the level fields and farms of **La Huerta**, which means "the vegetable garden" and refers to the region's irrigated cropland.

The Costa del Azahar

It was the Romans who built the elaborate irrigation systems (developed further by the Moors) that have made La Huerta into the most productive land in Spain. La Huerta consists of field after field of artichokes, tomatoes, and melons, and orchards of apricot, fig, and almond trees. Most dominant are the orange trees, stretching in orderly rows farther than the eye can see and giving the section of Mediterranean landscape from just south of Tarragona to Jávea its name—the Costa del Azahar (Orange Blossom Coast).

Allow time as you drive south to Valencia for a few interesting stops along the way. About 48 km (30 miles) south of Tortosa (see the Catalonia chapter) is the small coastal town of **Benicarló**. Near the beach at the edge of town is the modern ▶ **Parador Costa del Azahar**, an attractive lunch stop (and place to stay), with good regional seafood and rice dishes and a swimming pool and beach where you might have a preprandial dip; Tel: (9-64) 47-01-00.

SAGUNTO

Farther along, about 25 km (16 miles) north of the city of Valencia, you will encounter Sagunto, which is about where La Huerta begins in the north. It was in this area that the Carthaginian general Hannibal was wounded during the eight-month siege in 218 B.C. that triggered the start of the Second Punic War. When the Carthaginians attacked the little seaport the natives sought help from Rome, but it never came. Rather than surrender, so the legend goes, the women, children, and elderly threw themselves into a furnace, while the men resisted bravely but hopelessly and were all eventually killed. Follow the winding road that leads from the Plaça Mayor up behind the town to the **Castillo de Sagunto** to see castle walls and Iberian, Carthaginian, and Roman ruins and to enjoy some splendid views of La Huerta and the sea. Halfway up the hill is the town's surprisingly well-preserved **Roman theater** (currently being restored), where 8,000 spectators once sat. Park your car here and walk up to the castle gate.

For a meal in Sagunto, try **L'Armeler**, at Calle Castillo 44, known for its *tarta de cebolla* (onion tart) and Valencian rice dishes; Tel: (9-6) 266-4382.

THE CITY OF VALENCIA

Valencia city has seen more than a little bit of history since the Romans founded it around 138 B.C. on the site of a former Greek colony. The Romans, and later the Visigoths, Moors, and Christians, set their sights on this strategic port city and its agricultural riches, but it was El Cid (Rodrigo Díaz de Vivar) who provided its most romantic legends. After a 20-month siege, the famous warrior entered Valencia in 1094, wrested the city from the Moors (who had held it for more than 300 years), and ruled it until his death in 1099. The Moors returned, however, in 1102, and held this rich port again until 1238, when Jaime el Conquistador (James the Conqueror) of Aragón seized it once and for all.

The 15th century was Valencia's heyday, a period of great commercial success and a flowering of the arts. As you stroll through the old city, you'll see numerous remnants of the Flamboyant Gothic style that was so popular then. Valencian painters Jacomart (Jaime Bacó), the Osonas (father and son), Juan Reixach, and Luis Dalmau all flourished at this time (you'll see their work in the Museo Provincial de Bellas Artes, covered below), as did artisans who brought the crafts of ceramics, gold- and silversmithing, wrought-iron mongering, and embroidery to a pinnacle of artistic development. Their mastery is evident in their works in churches and public buildings throughout Valencia.

In later years, history left its scars on Valencia. The city was on the losing side all too often: in the War of the Spanish Succession, early in the 18th century, and a hundred years later, when it suffered serious reprisals after rebelling from and then losing to Napoleon's forces under Marshal Suchet in 1812. In the Spanish Civil War, Valencia was the last outpost of the Catalonian Republican (leftist) forces, finally falling (after Madrid) to Franco's troops on March 30, 1939, and suffering extensive damage.

SEEING VALENCIA

Modern Valencia, victim of high rises, exhaust fumes, and general urban sprawl, does not, at first glance, inspire lingering. But your feelings begin to change once you reach the inner core of this flat-as-a-tortilla city straddling the Río Turia, whose bed stretches east to the port of El Grao and the Mediterranean. Parts of the old center are dotted with tree-shaded plazas and enough architectural surprises to delight any traveller. Summer here is incredibly humid, but it is made bearable by Valencia's exuberant street life, outdoor cafés, bars, and open-air restaurants.

The city of Valencia has begun to convert its street and place names back to their original Valencian-language (similar to Catalan) names. We have used the names that now appear on signs; if the old name was significantly different, we have put it in parentheses. This conversion is not complete, so some names are Valencian, while others remain Castilian.

The Old City Center

Large as Valencia is, its old center, south of the river, is manageable and forms a loose semicircle bounded by a tree-lined street on the west, south, and southeast—whose name changes from Calle Guillén de Castro to Játiva and then to Colón—and by the river on the north. Within this area is a labyrinth of streets lined with old palaces, houses, and government and commercial buildings that echo with the city's cultural and political history and accomplishments. This is the area where you will spend most of your time—with a brief foray north across the river. The center can be traversed on foot (or by taxi).

PLAÇA DE L'AJUNTAMENT SOUTH TO PLAZA DE TOROS

Plaça de l'Ajuntament (formerly called Plaza del País Valenciano) is a vast, bustling square (really a triangle) that is a center of Valencian life, similar to New York City's Times Square of yore (before the grime and crime), with cafés, shops, and wall-to-wall people. The sidewalks are red and yellow fish-scale-shaped tiles (the colors of the Valencian flag), and the monumental 19th-century *ajuntament* (city hall) occupies an entire block. The large street leading southwest of the plaza is Avenida Marqués de Sotelo. Following it two blocks brings you to the Modernist railway station, **Estación del Norte**, whose waiting room is worth a peek, to see the decorative mosaic tiles on the walls, niches, and arched ceiling. The **Cervecería Valenciana**, next to the station at the corner of Játira and Bailén, is a lively *tapas* bar with considerable ambience. A visitor interested in bullfight lore and memorabilia might walk east to the next block to the **Plaza de Toros** and, next to it, on Pasaje Dr. Serra, into the **Museo Taurino**, one of Spain's oldest and most complete bullfight museums. In season (March through mid-October), you can see a bullfight in the Plaza de Toros. Get tickets at the plaza or ask the concierge at your hotel.

NORTH OF PLAÇA DE L'AJUNTAMENT

Heading north from Plaça de l'Ajuntament up Calle de San Vicente Mártir, you will pass, on the right, the 14th-century **Iglesia de San Martín**, with an admirable bronze Gothic statue of Saint Martin on the façade. Then it is just a short block farther north to the **Plaça de Reina**, a large and lively square facing the southern door of the cathedral. As you enter the square, notice the two fanciful Modernist buildings at both corners, where Calle de San Vicente Mártir meets the plaza. The southwestern side of the plaza is called Plaça de Santa Catalina, and there you'll find the **Iglesia de Santa**

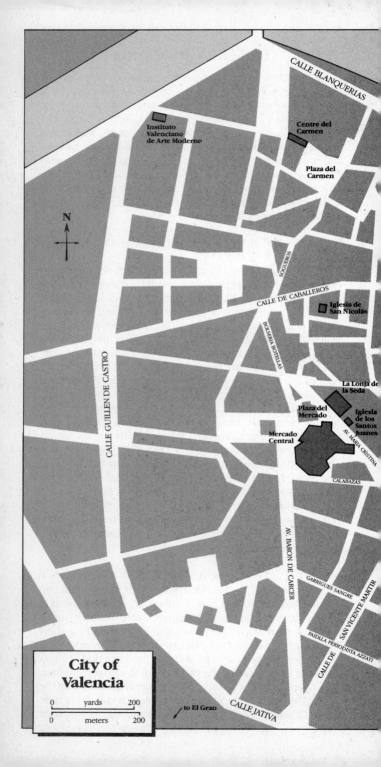

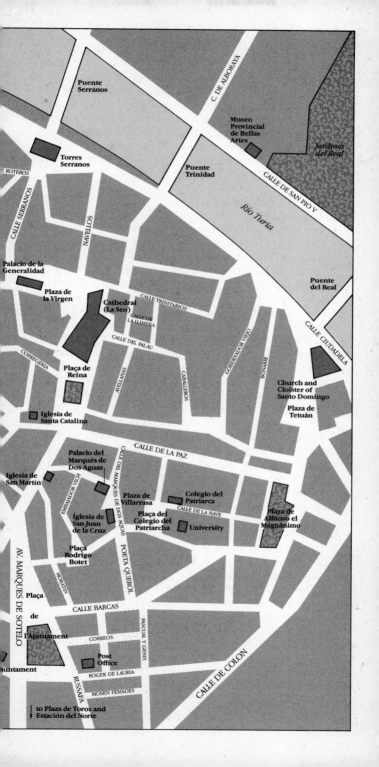

Catalina and, on the left, its adjoining 17th-century hexagonal Baroque tower of golden stone. If you're thirsty, pause along Plaça de Santa Catalina at a *horchateria* and try a *horchata* (one of Spain's many Moorish legacies), a cool, creamy drink with the consistency of a milk shake, made of crushed ice and *chufa,* that is most refreshing on a Valencian summer day. **Horchateria El Siglo** and **Horchateria de Santa Catalina** are both old reliables. Those with a sweet tooth might stop at **Turrones Ramos**, also on the plaza, for some *turrón* or marzipan.

THE CATHEDRAL

As you walk around the exterior of the cathedral, known as **La Seo**, which was constructed from 1262 to 1482, note how it evolved in that time, as styles changed, from Romanesque (southern door, Porta del Palau) to Gothic (northern, Apostle Door). Its Baroque façade came later, in the 18th century. The Baroque interior elements have been largely peeled away, leaving Gothic as the dominant style, with some Renaissance chapels. The cathedral's site is much older than the cathedral; first there was a temple of Diana here, then a Visigothic church, followed by a Moorish mosque. The tall, Flamboyant Gothic octagonal tower on the southwestern corner is the **Micalet**, or more formally, the Torre del Miguelete, so named because the bell inside the tower chimed for the first time on Michaelmas Day 1418. For centuries, the chimes functioned as "alarm clocks," reminding La Huerta farmers when to irrigate their fields. Every Thursday the Tribunal de los Acequieros (Court of the Waters) meets on the cathedral steps, as it has since at least the tenth century, to settle irrigation disputes. No oaths are taken or records kept, but the decisions of the eight judges are irrevocable.

Inside the cathedral, stop to see the **Capilla del Santo Cáliz** (chapel of the Holy Grail) in the south aisle (the first right after entering); its Flamboyant Gothic stone tracery is as delicate as feathers. Behind the chapel's altar in a glass-protected Gothic niche is a small (six inches high), deep violet agate cup reputed to be the legendary Holy Grail, the chalice Christ used at the Last Supper. According to Valencian legend, the grail was carried to Spain in the fourth century and protected in the monastery of San Juan de la Peña in the Pyrenees for 11 centuries, until it was given to the Valencian cathedral by the king of Aragón. Not everyone is impressed. V. S. Pritchett described the cup as "a disappointing object that might have come from Tiffany's."

Pass through the Holy Grail chapel to reach the **cathedral museum**, which contains many fine polychrome religious sculptures, two large Goya paintings, a Ribera, a dark and murky Zurbarán in need of cleaning, and other paintings.

While in the cathedral, look also at the *capilla mayor* (main chapel)—its 15th-century high altar with side panels painted by students of Leonardo da Vinci; the alabaster windows in the splendid Flamboyant Gothic lantern; and the fine 17th-century choir stalls, among other gems.

WEST OF THE CATHEDRAL

Leaving the cathedral by the northern door, you'll enter the eastern side of the **Plaza de la Virgen**, a cynosure of the city's open-air life, graced with an elaborate 19th-century fountain, in the center of which is a reclining, bronze Neoclassical Colossus ringed by obsequious bronze nymphets. The plaza, with its pink-and-gray marble pavement, old-fashioned gas streetlights, rows of fragrant orange trees, and sidewalk cafés, invites lingering. Have coffee or a *horchata* at **Café-Heladería El Micalet** and watch the hyperactivity on this pigeon-and-people-filled square. Across the plaza from the cafés you'll see the **Capilla de Nuestra Señora de los Desamparados** (Chapel of Our Lady of the Helpless), connected to the cathedral by a vaulted covered bridge. The chapel's exterior is classic Renaissance, its interior lavishly decorated.

Half a block west on Calle de Caballeros is the grand 15th-to 16th-century Gothic **Palacio de la Generalidad**, sometimes called La Audiencia, where the Valencia *cortes* (parliament) used to meet and general taxes were collected. Peek inside to admire the coffered ceiling and the *azulejo* frieze around the grand council chamber and the *artesonado* (wood-inlaid) ceilings in the attached 17th-century tower. There are a number of fine old manors and Gothic patios on Calle de Caballeros. Four short blocks farther west is the **Iglesia de San Nicolás**, one of the city's oldest churches, redone in exuberant Churrigueresque style, and a repository of Valencian art and treasures, the most notable being the altarpiece by Juan de Juanes in the chapel to the left of the main entrance.

PLAZA DEL MERCADO

Just four blocks south of San Nicolás is another cluster of Valencia's treasures, in the noisy, bustling Plaza del Mercado. The pulse of Valencian life, the plaza was once the scene of exhibitions, bullfights, even executions, but is now a great, bubbling marketplace. The centerpiece of all the action is the covered food market, the **Mercado Central**, which looks like a 19th-century *modernismo* fantasy of vividly colored tiles and glass-domed cupolas; it was actually built in 1928 on the site of an earlier market. There are some 1,300 market stalls arranged in two separate sections: the produce and meat section under a dome decorated with orange tiles, above which sprouts a bronze cockatoo weathervane, and the seafood section beneath a fish weathervane, whose interior tile designs are scallop shells.

Across from the market on the north is the **Iglesia de los Santos Juanes** (the Saints John), with an effusive Churrigueresque façade. The interior was badly damaged during the Spanish Civil War but has been somewhat restored.

On the northeastern side of the plaza is **La Lonja de la Seda** (Silk Exchange), a remarkable 15th-century, gargoyle-ornamented Flamboyant Gothic edifice with tower, built on the site of a Moorish *alcázar* (fortress). You can climb the tower for first-rate views of the city; be sure also to see the Lonja's 15th-century sculpted ceiling in the Salón del Consulado del Mar (Maritime Court), the orange-tree court, and the curved slender columns of the high-ceilinged great hall.

NORTH OF THE CATHEDRAL
There are several more sights of interest in the northern part of the old town. If you follow Calle Serranos north from Calle de Caballeros, you'll come to the **Torres Serranos** (just south of the Puente Serranos), a fortified 14th-century gate, restored in this century, which you can climb for a fine view of the city. If you walk west on Calle Roteros, which runs west off Calle Serranos, you'll come to Plaza del Carmen and the **Centre del Carme**, a 13th-century Carmelite convent, with well-restored 14th-century Gothic and 16th-century Renaissance cloisters, refectory, and chapter house, that was converted in 1989 by the **Instituto Valenciano de Arte Moderno** (IVAM) to form three spacious exhibition halls featuring changing exhibits of international art. Five short blocks farther west is the main building of IVAM, the dramatic and spacious **Julio González Center**, nine exhibition halls and galleries named for the contemporary Spanish artist whose works are the nucleus of IVAM's permanent collection. The IVAM bookshop has an excellent collection of contemporary Spanish art books. The center faces the river on Calle Guillén de Castro and has an agreeable café attached. You can sit on its terrace, enjoy a *paella* or a snack, sip a beer or coffee, and watch the local art scene roll by.

From there, you can head south and then east through a honeycomb of streets that will eventually bring you back to the Plaza del Mercado.

SOUTHEAST OF THE CATHEDRAL
Another grouping of handsome buildings is clustered southeast of the cathedral; take Calle de la Paz east of Plaza de Reina, then Calle del Marqués de Dos Aguas south. "Unique" is a treacherous word, but the 18th-century Baroque man-

sion called the **Palacio del Marqués de Dos Aguas** (Palace of the Marqués of Two Waters), facing Calle de la Abadía de San Martín, deserves it for its remarkably sensuous three-dimensional portal. A Baroque *fantasía* in creamy alabaster carved by Ignacio Vergara, the door bears two crouching giants pouring water from amphorae to illustrate the marqués's name. Sadly, the frescoes that Vergara painted all over the façade have recently been covered over.

The *palacio*'s splendidly ornate rooms now form a handsome backdrop for the collection of the **Museo Nacional de Cerámica**. This is no small collection, but three floors and some 5,000 pieces of mostly Spanish ceramics from Iberian times to Picasso. You don't have to have a passion for pottery to make this a stop on your visit to Valencia. Note the 13th-century Paterna and 14th-century Manises lusterware, the delightful all-tile (including the stove and chimney) kitchen covered with culinary scenes (top floor), the Picasso gallery (top floor), the magnificent double stairway lined with ceramic panels, and the gilded glory of an 18th-century coach that Vergara created for the Dos Aguas family (ground floor). A room on the top floor is devoted to artifacts of the Valencian novelist Vicente Blasco Ibáñez.

Next door, but facing Calle Poeta Querol (an extension of Calle del Marqués de Dos Aguas) is the **Iglesia de San Juan de la Cruz** (sometimes called San Andrés), a 17th-century brick building with Baroque portal and white-and-gilded Baroque interior faced with ceramic tiles. Due east of the church is the **Plaça del Colegio del Patriarca**, on which sit the Colegio del Patriarca and the old university, directly across from it (the university's library contains a copy of the first book of any consequence printed in Spain, *Les Trobes*).

The 16th- to 17th-century **Colegio del Patriarca** (built as a seminary) has a graceful Renaissance patio with two columned tiers and a museum with some choice works by Caravaggio, Rogier Van der Weyden, Juan de Juanes, El Greco, Francisco de Ribalta, Dirk Bouts, and many 15th- to 17th-century Valencian artists, as well as some excellent Brussels tapestries. There are also six fine 16th-century Flemish tapestries in the Colegio's Capilla de la Concepción. In the southwestern corner of the Colegio is the church of **Corpus Christi**, richly ornamented with frescoes and a splendid Last Supper by Ribalta above the main altar.

Calle de la Nave, a small street between the Colegio and the 19th-century university building, leads east to the imposing orange-tree-lined **Plaza de Alfonso el Magnánimo**, the center of which is occupied by a triumphant equestrian bronze statue of El Cid, the work of American sculptor Anna Hyatt Huntington. Several blocks north, the mammoth **Igle-**

sia de **Santo Domingo** dominates the riverside at Plaza de Tetuán. Saint Vincent Ferrer took his vows as a Dominican in the Capilla del Capitullo.

Outside the Old City

While most of Valencia's attractions are on the south side of the river, there is at least one to lure you over to the other side, where university, government, and commercial buildings dominate: the Museo Provincial de Bellas Artes (Provincial Museum of Fine Arts). It is closest to the Puente Trinidad, which crosses the river north of the cathedral, but if you like to walk, cross over the **Puente del Real** (southeast of Puente Trinidad), a delightful 17th-century bridge with tiny religious shrines built into niches midway. At the end of the bridge, turn left (north) and stroll alongside the **Jardines del Real**, the city's largest park, with formal gardens, an abundance of roses, walkways favored by lovers, and a small zoo in the center. Another bridge, the 16th-century **Puente del Mar**, two bridges to the southeast, has even more ornate shrines in its niches and is also a pleasure to walk across (though farther still from the museum).

MUSEO PROVINCIAL DE BELLAS ARTES

If you follow the edge of the gardens, a long block brings you to the Museo Provincial de Bellas Artes. Inside this Baroque former convent is one of Spain's most important museums, with four floors and more than 50 rooms of treasures. At the entrance level are many Iberian, Roman, and Moorish archaeological finds, such as a large Roman mosaic floor from the second to fourth centuries, as well as 16th- to 17th-century polychrome religious sculptures. The second floor is the most exhilarating, with gallery after gallery full of choice medieval, Renaissance, and 15th- to 19th-century paintings.

The richness of the 15th-century school of Valencian primitives typified by Jacomart and Reixach is a surprise for most visitors. Valencia's three most famous painters—José Ribera, Ribalta, and Bartolomé Esteban Murillo—are also well represented. In room 30 is a stunning triptych, *Los Improperios* (The Mocking of Christ), by Hieronymus Bosch; one room is a harvest of Goya paintings and drawings; and next door to that a Velázquez self-portrait hangs in solitary seclusion in an alcove. The museum also has works by El Greco, Juan de Juanes, and scores of others.

Staying in Valencia

Valencia has a number of hotels, but no truly deluxe ones. A convenient choice is the ► **Astoria Palace**, a stately, comfortable place on Plaça Rodrigo Botet, a delightful, quiet, tree-shaded plaza just two blocks north of Plaça de l'Ajuntament, close enough to walk to virtually everything you'll want to see. The Astoria Palace is the best hotel in the center of town; the rooms are comfortable, with full amenities, if somewhat small baths, and double-glazed windows to keep out the street noises.

Just off the Plaça de l'Ajuntament on Calle Barcas is the ▶ Hotel Reina Victoria, whose public rooms have a Neoclassical elegance. There is a good restaurant with local specialties and a friendly place for drinks, Bar Inglés. The wrought-iron balconies of some guest rooms overlook the beautiful plaza.

More modest but equally central choices are the ▶ Hotel Inglés, across the street from the Museo Nacional de Cerámica on Calle del Marqués de Dos Aguas, with large, plain rooms; and the ▶ Bristol, an old-fashioned hotel with compact rooms near the church of San Martín, just off Calle de San Vicente Mártir. The Cervecería Madrid, on Calle Abadía de San Martín, in front of the Bristol, is a popular and atmospheric *tapas* bar.

On the other side of the river (near the Puente de Aragón), just a block from the stunning Palau de la Música, is the new ▶ Hotel Meliá Valencia, a comfortable high-rise hotel with a swimming pool on the terrace and other modern amenities you can expect from the Meliá chain.

If you'd rather be away from city noise, just 10 km (6 miles) south of the city are two other options: the ▶ Sidi Saler Palace, a large, modern resort hotel with many amenities—garden, pool, tennis, and beach—that help compensate for the hotel's lack of charm; and ▶ Parador de El Saler, a modern member of the government-run parador chain, with large, comfortable rooms and beach, pool, and golf course. Both are right on beautiful El Saler beach (reachable by way of a brief stretch of *autopista* along the coastal road) and are geared for the holiday traveller. If you plan to visit Valencia for Fallas (the city's noisy annual festival in March; see below), either of these two modern, somewhat impersonal hotels would assure more sleep than one in the city. The windswept beach, bordered by the pine woods of La Dehesa, is relatively peaceful and uncrowded.

Dining in Valencia

Arguably the best restaurant in Valencia, at least in the old center, is La Hacienda, at Avenida Navarro Reverter 12, southeast of Plaza Porta de la Mar, which is just east of Plaza de Alfonso el Magnánimo. In a small, romantic dining room that looks like the *sala* of a *hacienda,* you might dine by candlelight on *merluza con salsa de chipirones* (hake in squid sauce), *filete de ganso con salsa de grosellas negras* (goose in black-currant sauce), or superb *paella* while listening to a parakeet chatter in the glass-enclosed garden facing you. Besides the elegant *nueva cocina*–style food, there's a good wine list, strong on Riojas. Tel: (9-6) 373-1859.

Close by, at number 16, is **Derby**, another upscale place to eat; Tel: (9-6) 334-8602. A few blocks southeast is the wide boulevard Gran Vía del Marqués del Turia, which changes to Gran Vía de Germanías as it goes westward. At number 49 you will find **Ma Cuina**, a Basque restaurant with wonderful (if pricey) seafood; Tel: (9-6) 341-7799. Less costly is the **Taberna Vasca**, adjoining it, where you can munch on a terrific *tapas* selection while sipping beer or wine. Brand new and serving excellent Valencian specialties is **Galbis**, Calle Marvá 28–30, just west of the railroad station; Tel: (9-6) 380-9473. Famous for its fabulous *paella* (and a favorite of Hemingway) is the huge, bustling **La Pepica**, at Calle Neptuno 6, on the Playa del Levante at the city's port, El Grao, southeast of the old city; Tel: (9-6) 371-0366.

More budget-conscious meals and great *tapas* can be sought on Calle Mosén Femades, a narrow pedestrian street just south of the Plaça de l'Ajuntament. **Gran Taberna Río-Sil**, at number 10, and **Alcázar**, at number 11, both offer acceptable *paella valenciana* at modest prices in rustic tavern settings; Tel: (9-6) 352-9764 for Gran Taberna Río Sil, 352-9575 for Alcázar. **El Palacio de la Bellota**, down the street at number 7, is a *taberna* known for its varied *tapas* and lively atmosphere; Tel: (9-6) 351-4994. For an ample, inexpensive lunch or dinner, try **Ateneo**, on the Plaça de l'Ajuntament. The menu includes excellent *paella* and other rice-based dishes and fish, such as sea bass with fennel, served in either a casual or a more formal setting. Ateneo's major drawback: a not-always-ingratiating staff; Tel: (9-6) 352-1612. Across the plaza is a handy, inexpensive place for a quick *bocadillo* (sandwich) or some *tapas,* **Barrachina**, a block-long glorified deli/sidewalk café that opens early and closes late.

Shopping in Valencia

While in Valencia, you will see many examples of the attractive blue-and-white pottery of **Manises**, a village whose metallic lusterware was famous in Moorish times. You can find the distinctive blue-and-white Manises plates, bowls, platters, and pitchers in many shops in Valencia, or you can make the very short drive 8 km (5 miles) west of town, along Avenida del Cid (reached by driving southwest on Calle de San Vicente Mártir through the Plaça de España), to Manises to browse at the various pottery factory showrooms. Another Valencian product is the internationally known Lladró porcelain ware. You can buy the famous Lladró figurines at many Valencian shops, such as **Ceramicas Lladró** at Calle Poeta Querol 9, or you can visit the Lladró factory, on Calle de Mayo 32, in **Tabernes Blanques**, just 5 km (3 miles) north of town on N 340, if you make arrangements in advance; Tel: (9-6) 185-0177.

A branch of the government-run shop **Artespaña**, selling many fine regional handicrafts, is on Calle de la Paz 7 (corner of Calle del Marqués de Dos Aguas), east of the Plaza de Reina. Another craft shop of interest is **Bombay**, offering art and crafts from Jesuit missions of Asia and South America, located at Calle del Marqués de Dos Aguas 5. A branch of the fine leather-goods store **Loewe** is a few doors south, opposite Hotel Inglés (at the corner of Calle Libreros). This neighborhood has many fine shops and boutiques; some of the best are on the Plaça del Colegio del Patriarca (Armani, Rosas Rosa, and Flash). Three blocks east is a big branch of the department store **El Corte Inglés**, facing the Plaza de Alfonso el Magnánimo. Another department store, **Cortfiel**, occupies the block of Avenida Marqués de Sotelo that faces the railway station.

A good place to browse for antiques is east of the cathedral, a warren of tiny streets north of Calle del Palau, leading into Calle de la Llimera, where there are shops and a Sunday-morning flea market that spills around corners from block to block. **Antigüedades Marco-Polo** is a fine shop at Calle de la Llimera 5. There is another Sunday flea and flower market in Plaça de Lope de Vega, a tiny square near the Plaza del Mercado, just opposite La Lonja de la Seda.

Festivals in Valencia

The liveliest time to visit Valencia is during the explosive (literally) **Fallas de Valencia**, March 15 to 19, held in honor of San José (Saint Joseph), the patron saint of carpenters and other artisans. Started in the Middle Ages when the carpenters celebrated the feast day of San José by burning their wood shavings, Fallas (which comes from the Latin word for torch) is one of the major festivals in Spain today, a citywide extravaganza, with gigantic wood, cloth, and papier-mâché *ninots* (caricatures) displayed in satirical, mocking floats or tableaux visible at every street corner and plaza. After a series of seemingly nonstop parades, fairs, dances, bull-fights, performances by bands of musicians (as many as 4,000 in all), and fireworks comes the finale: At midnight of the final night of the Fallas, the *ninots* are strung with firecrackers and set afire. Anyone with sensitive ears might choose another time to visit and be content to see some of the most colorful *ninot* heads at the **Fallas Museu**, Plaza de Monteolivete 4, southeast of the old city center. Each year the most inspired, prize-winning *ninots* are rescued from cremation and put on permanent display here.

The **Palau de la Música**, a dazzling new contemporary building on Paseo de la Almeda, across the river southeast of the old city center near the Puente de Aragón, presents classical music concerts and operas; Tel (9-6) 360-3212.

THE ROUTE TO ALICANTE

South of Valencia city, on the road to Alicante, you'll pass through an area called **La Albufera**, mile after mile of lagoons and watery rice fields fed by Ríos Turia and Acequia Real and the source of the rice for much of that delicious *paella*. Albufera is known for its vast stretch of sandy beach.

GANDIA

Farther along this coastal road, 68 km (42 miles) south of Valencia, is Gandía, the little town that was the duchy of the Borgia family (Borja in Spanish), whose members include the infamous Pope Alexander VI, father of Cesare and Lucrezia and grandfather of Spain's San Francisco Borja (who was born in Gandía). The former **Borja Palacio de los Duques**, located on Calle Sant Duc (just off the eastern end of the long esplanade Passeig de les Germanies), is now a Jesuit college; but anyone interested in viewing the ornate rooms, state apartments with coffered ceilings and marble floors, a small museum, and the Patio de Armas (a special beauty, lined with coats of arms) can take an hour-long tour. Gandía also boasts miles of golden-sand beaches, the most productive and fertile *huertas,* and a good, and expensive, restaurant, **La Gamba**, Playa de Gandía, east of town on the Nazaret–Oliva road, serving excellent fish and *abanda* (rice-in-broth) dishes and a curious local specialty, spaghetti *paella;* Tel: (9-6) 284-1310.

XATIVA

About 30 km (19 miles) inland from Gandía, on the northern side of Monte Bernisa, which is covered with towering cypress trees, is Xàtiva, birthplace of two 15th-century popes (Calixtus III and Alexander VI) and the 17th-century painter José Ribera. Named Xàtiva by the Moors, who lost it to Jaime el Conquistador in 1244, the town was old even when the Romans developed it from Phoenician origins. Castle walls and ramparts dominate the mountain peaks, and the tree-shaded town is a delight to wander, to see the many old mansions and fountains along Calle Moncada and the 16th-century **Iglesia Colegiata** (Collegiate Church). A cluster of well-preserved 14th- and 15th-century paintings by Valencian primitives can be viewed in the Romanesque **Ermita de Sant Feliú**, tucked into a hillside below the **castillo**. The foundations of the imposing, well-defined ruins of the *castillo* are Iberian and Roman. Cesare Borgia was once imprisoned within the *castillo*. The vistas from here are sensational, stretching all the way to the Mediterranean.

SOUTH FROM XATIVA

From Xàtiva there are two approaches to Alicante: via the inland road (N 340) south through Alcoy, a slower but more scenic route, or by going back east to Gandía, then continuing south on the coast-hugging *autopista* A 7/E 15. This latter drive is scenic, too, and fast (though costly), skirting most of the high-rise development horror of the sea resorts along the way. After Denia, whose ancient origins and history have long been obscured by tourist hotels and condos, the A 7/E 15 dips deeply down to **Jávea**, a town sheltered between two capes, Cabo de San Antonio and Cabo de la Nao. This is a convenient place to stop for lunch, at the modern, resortlike ▶ **Parador de la Costa Blanca**, which serves decent, if unexciting, regional meals. It is also a good place, if need be, to spend the night. Right at the water's edge, this four-story parador is better from the inside looking out. The views from the large bedrooms—of the sea, the canal, and a well-manicured garden full of palm trees—are lovely.

Some 12 km (7½ miles) farther southeast is one of the coastline's most dramatic sights: the 1,089-foot-high **Peñón de Ifach**, a huge rock formation jutting from the sea with two fine-sand beaches just below it. After a series of scalloped turns in the road you'll pass overdeveloped Benidorm, with a long, heavenly beach (if you can find it through the canyons of concrete high rises). Then, 11 km (7 miles) farther, you will reach **Villajoyosa**, which, despite being a resort, still retains the feeling of an old Spanish town. A delightful, dazzlingly white Moorish-style hotel, ▶ **El Montíboli**, built on a hillside overlooking the sea, is an excellent, if dear, choice for those who want to linger a bit on this coast. Quietly luxurious, it has a fine restaurant, access to the beach, golf, and riding stables. Alicante is just a short distance south, as the gulls fly.

ALICANTE

Alicante telegraphs charm the minute you catch sight of its 2,100-foot-long **Explanada de España**, a palm-lined promenade paved with black, red, and white mosaic tiles that follows the harbor. A breezily balmy climate most of the year (even in winter) and skies as clear and blue as a Murillo heaven add considerably to Alicante's natural appeal. Its level location, embraced between two hills and spread before a wide bay and natural harbor, makes it an ideal port, which it has been since Roman times.

There are few reminders today that Alicante was once the major stronghold of the Kingdom of Valencia. It is a city that is simply pleasant to be in: Join the families and lovers strolling along the Explanada at twilight, sip a *fino* at a sidewalk café, stop for tea or ice cream at **Slika**, a tiny tearoom on Rambla Méndez Núñez, or stroll along old-fashioned Calle Mayor, with its marble sidewalks lined with fancy candy shops. Then ride the elevator from the Paseo de Gomís (above the Playa del Postiguet, just northeast of the Explanada) to the top of rambling **Castillo de Santa Bárbara** for breathtaking views of the town beach below and the sea, harbor, and surrounding countryside. The castle dates from the 13th to the 16th centuries, but is believed to have Carthaginian foundations. In short, Alicante is as much a city of the senses as you'll find in Spain. The surprise is that in spite of the foreigners who have "captured" this coast, Alicante remains essentially a Spanish town.

Near the elevator entrance, on Calle de Villavieja (diagonally across from the church of Santa María on Plaza de Santa María), is the Casa de la Asegurada, a 1685 granary that now houses the **Museo Colección de Arte del Siglo XX** (Museum of 20th-Century Art), sometimes called the Museo de la Asegurada after the building. The museum's large collection belonged to the late Eusebio Sempere, a post–World War II painter of abstract art who was an Alicante native, though a Madrid resident. On three floors you'll find works by Miró, Dalí, Picasso, Antonio Saura, Antoni Tàpies, César Manrique, Sempere, and other Spanish painters and sculptors, along with such international artists as Jean Arp, Georges Braque, Victor Vasarely, Wassily Kandinsky, Rufino Tamayo, Alexander Calder, and Francis Bacon. A few blocks west, on Plaza de Ayuntamiento, is the *ayuntamiento* (town hall), built between 1696 and 1760 in the Baroque style, with Churrigueresque pillars flanking the main entrance.

Mostly, though, Alicante is to be enjoyed passively, the pause that refreshes on a whirlwind sightseeing tour. If you're in town on a Sunday, there's a band concert at noon in the bandshell on the Explanada. The city's big festival is held on June 23, Saint John's Day. This is a day of parades, street dancing, and fireworks, ending not with a whimper but a bang: a *nit de foc* (night of fire), when caricatures in wood and paper are torched in spectacular bonfires.

DINING AND STAYING IN ALICANTE

In the upstairs dining room of **Delfín**, at Explanada de España 12, you can dine on trout pie (the house specialty), baked bass, or other fresh seafood, finishing perhaps with ice cream topped with a flourish of *turrón de Jijona* (nougat sauce), while enjoying views of the Explanada and the harbor; Tel: (9-6) 520-6603. Another excellent dining choice is **Dársena**, overlooking the marina next to the Regatta Club, at Muelle del Puerto. *Paella*—in 30 different versions—is Darsena's specialty along with seafood; Tel: (9-6) 520-7399.

For your stay in Alicante, consider the convenient ▶ **Tryp Gran Sol**, a handy high rise in the center of town, one block from the Explanada and the harbor, with comfortable rooms and great views from the snack bar on top. (Parking is a problem here, however.) More modest choices, just as handy, are the small, well-maintained ▶ **Hotel Palas**, at the edge of the Explanada, and the newly renovated, also small, ▶ **NH Cristal**, at Calle Lopez Torregrosa 9.

Excursions from Alicante

JIJONA

Jijona, where so much of the best *turrón* is made, is just a few kilometers northwest of Alicante on N 340, so it's no wonder Alicante is rife with candy shops. Many of the *turrón* factories are open to visitors.

ALCOY

Alcoy, about 40 km (25 miles) north of Alicante on N 340, is a small town known for its annual *Moros y Cristianos* (Moors and Christians) celebration around Saint George's Day (April 23), when two armies of "Moors" and "Christians" slug it out in mock combat, until "Saint George" intervenes at the end to help the Christians triumph. There are many such mock battles in towns in this area, so wracked throughout the Reconquest by real conflicts. Alcoy's fiesta is the most famous, perhaps because Alcoy residents believe they won their battle against the Moors in 1276 only because of the saint's intercession.

While in Alcoy, have a look at the **Museo Arqueológico**'s sizable collection of Iberian pottery and Greek artifacts, and then stop to see the attractive 18th-century tiles in the churches of Santa María and Santo Sepulchro. And don't miss the local specialty, *peladillas*—sugared almonds.

Alcoy's contemporary claim to fame is **Venta del Pilar**, a delightful restaurant ensconced in a 200-year-old country house at Carretera de Valencia 118. Good regional dishes, lots of fresh seafood, and the house specialty—almond, orange, and chestnut tarts—make this a worthy meal stop. Tel: (9-6) 559-2325.

ELCHE

A pleasant day trip can be made southwest of Alicante to palm-forested Elche (about 24 km/15 miles on N 340), a Moorish-looking town of flat-roofed, white-washed houses that straddles both sides of the Río Vinalopó. Elche has the unenviable luck to be one of the hottest places in Spain, a fate assuaged by the oasis-like effect of all those swaying palm trees that surround the town on three sides. Dates are the major crop, as is evident from the number of shops and stalls selling the local product as well as baskets made from palm fronds. The *ramilletes* (fronds) hung from houses all over Spain after Palm Sunday originate in Elche.

Elche's main attraction, **Palmeral de Europa**, just east of town, is a date-palm forest of more than 100,000 trees—the only date-producing palms in Europe—believed to have been planted by the Phoenicians but cultivated by the Moors. A walk through the forest can take about two hours and is best done in early morning before the heat rises. Afterward there should be time before lunch to visit the **Basílica de Santa María**, a much-restored 17th-century church with a Baroque façade and portal by Nicolás de Bari. The church, in the town center near the river, is the setting of an annual 13th-century mystery play called *La Festa,* about the Assumption of the Virgin, held in mid-August. Tickets are available from the local tourist office, ten days in advance; Tel: (9-6) 545-2747. Elche's **Museo de Arte Contemporáneo**, at Plaza Raval (about a dozen blocks south of the basilica), has works by Picasso, Miró, Tàpies, and others. A block north of the basilica there is an archaeological museum in the 14th-century **Palacio Altamira**, a castlelike structure.

Plan to lunch at the notable **Els Capellans**, a restaurant in the ▶ **Hotel Huerto del Cura**, a 5-minute drive east of the Plaza Mayor at Porta de la Morera 14. Surrounded by palm trees, overlooking a garden and swimming pool, you might lunch on *arroz con costra,* an Elche specialty of rice with white sausage, chicken, rabbit, and two other types of sausage. The hotel, a member of the Best Western chain and as tranquil as a parador, makes an appealing overnight choice, with simple modern rooms and some individual cottages among the palms.

Two kilometers (about a mile) south of Elche on the secondary road to Dolores is **La Alcudia de Elche**, an excavation site where the famous *Dama de Elche* was unearthed in 1897. This mysterious, evocative bust of a woman is believed to be Iberian, dating from the fifth or fourth century B.C. The original is in the Museo Arqueológico Nacional in Madrid, but you can see a copy, along with other Iberian and Roman artifacts, in a small museum at La Alcudia.

SOUTH TO MURCIA

ORIHUELA

Some 35 km (22 miles) southwest of Elche on N 340 (or on the faster A 7/E 15, which along this route is toll-free) is Orihuela, a surprising town along the Río Segura, with palm groves, orange and lemon trees, gardens, palaces, and treasure-studded churches, whose history dates back to Roman times.

Your first stop should be the Oficina Municipal de Turismo, at Calle Francisco Díe, to pick up a map. The office is lodged in a former palace that also houses a museum of 19th-century upper-class Spanish life and an archaeological museum. You might pause for coffee next door in **El Jardín del Palacio**, in a palm-shaded garden. From there, map in hand, you can easily walk from sight to sight all over town. Walking is advised, as the streets are narrow and parking is difficult.

Some of Orihuela's prizes are found in the 14th- to 15th-century cathedral, **El Salvador** (mostly Gothic, with Baroque chapels): a marvelous 18th-century metal *rejas* (grille) with fine details, a 13th-century cloister, and a museum that contains a Velázquez painting, *Tentación de Santo Tomás de Aquino* (The Temptation of St. Thomas Aquinas), paintings by Ribera and Luis de Morales, and many fine artifacts.

From the cathedral it's a ten-minute walk to the **Colegio de Santo Domingo**, formerly Orihuela's university (defunct since the 19th century), now a school. Its elaborate Renaissance façade gives just a hint of what's inside, namely an extraordinarily ornate Baroque church, whose barrel-vaulted ceiling is a fiesta of painted angels and cherubs, two splendid two-story-high Renaissance cloisters, and a refectory whose walls are lined with tiled scenes of people, animals, and the sea.

Murcia

Although it is the capital of a province of the same name, Murcia is not widely viewed as a tourist center. Yet it has several worthy sights, and can be a nice break on the drive from Valencia to the Costa del Sol. Movie fans might note that many so-called spaghetti westerns and epic movies made in Spain in the past 10 to 20 years were filmed in the rough-hewn cliffs and hillsides of the Murcian countryside, parts of which resemble the American Southwest. Yet the city itself is the center of a fertile valley fed by the Río Segura.

Just a 25-minute drive south from Orihuela (24 km/15 miles on N 340 or A 7/E 15), Murcia is a city of 300,000 situated appealingly along the banks of the Río Segura, which is edged with gardens. Recently revitalized after decades of decline, it has a lively inner core (despite traffic-clogged streets) dominated by its enormous cathedral, several pedestrian shopping streets, and tiny tree-accented plazas.

THE CATHEDRAL

The cathedral, located on the Plaza Apóstoles (just two blocks north of the riverside street Avenida Teniente Flomesta), has one of the most famous Baroque façades in Spain. The tower can be climbed for a far-reaching view of the city and its surroundings. Inside, the 16th-century Capilla de los Vélez has remarkable star vaulting and lavish Platlike-esque ornamentation. In the cathedral museum, besides a number of finely carved religious sculptures, altarpieces, and paintings, there is a 1677 silver monstrance (carried in the Corpus Christi procession) with three tiers of finely sculpted scenes made in Toledo by Antonio Pérez de Montalto. The museum also contains works by Francisco Salzillo, a local artist who in the 18th century created lifelike polychrome wood sculptures called *pasos,* which are used each year in the Semana Santa processions—making Murcia's among the most moving of these Holy Week events. Most of the sculptor's finest work may be viewed at the **Museo Salzillo**. Eight *pasos* used during Semana Santa are on display, giving you a pretty good idea of what Semana Santa is like, if you're unable to see it in progress. The museum is all the way across town from the cathedral (and most likely your hotel) on the west side, at Avenida San Andrés Garcia Alix, and is best reached by cab, as parking is a problem.

DINING AND STAYING IN MURCIA

Murcia has more than spiritual claims to fame. A major pedestrian thoroughfare, **Calle de la Trapería**, extending north from the cathedral, has outdoor cafés, many handsome shops and boutiques, and a florid 19th-century building called the Casino, which was really a club (take a look at its ornate Arabesque ceiling and details). One block east of the cathedral is a neat bar, **Señorío de Jomelsu** (corner of Calle San Antonio and Calle Alejandro Seiquer I de la Cierva).

A very good place to stay, an easy walk southeast of the cathedral toward the river, is ▶ **Hotel Arco de San Juan**, with a pleasant lounge, cheerful breakfast room, and comfortable, if compact, modern rooms. It's practically next door to **Rincón de Pepe**, located at Calle Apóstoles 34. This large restaurant is a Murcia institution, with an appetite-whetting display of lobster, prawns, and other seafood near the entrance; many regional dishes; and an excellent wine list. Leek mousse, roasted red peppers with garlic, and duck with orange are among many specialties. Tel: (9-68) 21-22-39. A nicely appointed hotel by the same name, ▶ **Rincón de Pepe**, is next door. Behind the Hotel Arcos de San Juan, on Calle General Magallo, are several budget-stretching, peas-in-a-pod restaurants with *tapas* bars. One of them, **La Parranda**, has tables outside in warm weather. Another comfortable hotel is the ▶ **Hotel Meliá Siete Coronas**, a very modern high rise with river views just three or four blocks to the east.

GETTING AROUND

The speedy *autopista* A 7/E 15 consists of 622 km (386 miles) of superhighway, running from Girona in Catalonia in the northeast all the way south to Alicante. The luxurious Ter train follows the coast from Port-Bou, at the eastern tip of Catalonia, down to Murcia. Long-distance motor-coach lines also make a regular coastal run. In addition, there are daily flights from Madrid and Barcelona to Valencia and Alicante. Still, the best way to sightsee and explore the countryside is by car.

ACCOMMODATIONS REFERENCE

The hotel rates listed below are projected rates for 1994, for double rooms, double occupancy, in pesetas. We strongly recommend that you confirm the price when making reservations.

When dialing telephone numbers from outside the country, drop the 9 in the area code.

▶ **Astoria Palace.** Plaça Rodrigo Botet 5, 46002 **Valencia.** Tel: (9-6) 352-6737; Fax: 352-8078. 19,200 pts.

▶ **Bristol.** Abadía San Martín 3, 46002 **Valencia.** Tel: (9-6) 352-1176. 6,600 pts.

▶ **Hotel Arco de San Juan.** Plaza de Ceballos 10, 30003 **Murcia.** Tel: (9-68) 21-04-55; Fax: 22-08-09. 14,200 pts.

▶ **Hotel Huerto del Cura.** Porta de la Morera 14, 03203 **Elche.** Tel: (9-6) 545-8040; Fax: 542-1910. 14,000 pts.

▶ **Hotel Inglés.** Calle del Marqués de Dos Aguas 6, 46002 **Valencia.** Tel: (9-6) 351-6426; Fax: 394-0251. 13,750 pts.

▶ **Hotel Meliá Siete Coronas.** Paseo de Garay 5, 30003 **Murcia.** Tel: (9-6) 821-7771; Fax: 22-12-94. 15,500 pts.

▶ **Hotel Meliá Valencia.** Avenida Baleares 2, 46023 **Valencia.** Tel: (9-6) 360-7300; Fax: 360-8921. 19,950 pts.

▶ **Hotel Palas.** Cervantes 5, Plaza del Mar, 03002 **Alicante.** Tel: (9-6) 520-6751; Fax: 514-0120. 7,875–9,415 pts.

► **Hotel Reina Victoria.** Calle Barcas 4, 46002 **Valencia.** Tel: (9-6) 352-0487; Fax: 352-0487. 15,400–18,600 pts.

► **El Montíboli.** Partida Montíboli, Carretera N 332, 03570 **Villajoyosa.** Tel: (9-6) 589-0250; Fax: 589-3857. 10,900–18,300 pts.

► **NH Cristal.** Calle Lopez Torregrosa 9, 03002 **Alicante.** Tel: (9-6) 514-3659; Fax: 520-6696. 10,500 pts.

► **Parador Costa del Azahar.** Avenida del Papa Luna 3, 12580 **Benicarló.** Tel: (9-64) 47-01-00; Fax: 47-09-34. 9,000–11,000 pts.

► **Parador de la Costa Blanca.** Playa del Arenal 2, 03730 **Jávea.** Tel: (9-6) 579-0200; Fax: 579-0308. 14,500 pts.

► **Parador de El Saler.** Avenida de los Pinares 151, Carretera Saler, km 16, 46012 **Valencia.** Tel: (9-6) 161-1186; Fax: 162-7016. 14,000–15,000 pts.

► **Rincón de Pepe.** Apóstoles 32, 30001 **Murcia.** Tel: (9-68) 21-22-39; Fax: 22-17-44. 14,000–16,000 pts.

► **Sidi Saler Palace.** Playa del Saler, 46012 **Valencia.** Tel: (9-6) 161-0411; Fax: 161-0838. 17,000–24,000 pts.

► **Tryp Gran Sol.** Avenida Méndez Núñez 3, 03002 **Alicante.** Tel: (9-6) 520-3000; Fax: 521-1439. 11,700–12,275 pts.

LA MANCHA

By Patricia Brooks

Many regions of Spain have clear-cut identities. There is a unity of sorts to Andalusia, to Catalonia, to Galicia. But La Mancha, the region spread out more or less south and east of Madrid, exists in the shadow of Castile like an appendage, so it is probably natural that it now has a new name, the hyphenated Castilla–La Mancha. As such, it is Spain's largest region, encompassing five provinces (Albacete, Ciudad Real, Cuenca, Guadalajara, and Toledo), an area that sweeps from Toledo south to Ciudad Real and Almagro, southeast to Albacete, east to Cuenca, and northeast past Guadalajara to Sigüenza.

The image many visitors have of La Mancha is of a parched, arid landscape, and indeed the name in Arabic—*Manxa*—means "dry earth." That is just the broad stroke of the La Mancha picture, however. Olive trees, grapevines, blood-red wild poppies, fields of wheat and purple-blooming saffron, mountains that are home to wild boar, bear, deer, and roebuck, a natural park, and shimmering lagoons are also part of La Mancha. So are the many towns and villages, sleepy and off the beaten track, that nonetheless shelter some extraordinary sights. Toledo and Cuenca, skirting the edges of La Mancha, are famous, but most visitors aren't aware of the marvels that loom behind the names Almagro, Sigüenza, Pastrana, and Viso del Marqués. Like almost every other region in Spain, La Mancha has its share of mysteries and surprises.

La Mancha, being so vast, is a difficult region to address in one sweep, so our coverage takes the region one area at a time. You may then plan your itinerary according to the discrete areas you most want to see. We start south of Madrid in Toledo, with its Moorish, Jewish, and Christian influences so well recorded by El Greco. From here we go down into the southwestern portion of La Mancha to Almagro, which maintains the look of its 16th-century heyday, to Viso del Marqués, with its breathtaking Renaissance palace, and on to other

615

nearby towns and villages. From here we go to Cuenca, southeast of Madrid, with its cliff-hanging Casas Colgadas and sweeping views. Cuenca puts you in a position to explore the Roman ruins at Saelices and Valeria and the castles of Alarcón and Belmonte on your way southeast to Albacete and the hill town of Chinchilla del Monte-Aragón. We next cover Pastrana, just east of Madrid, with a store of artistic works in its Gothic church, and lastly we go to Sigüenza, in the northeastern corner of La Mancha, a thoroughly medieval town full of treasures.

MAJOR INTEREST

Rugged landscape, dotted with windmills and castles
Land of Cervantes's Don Quixote
Foods of La Mancha: game, river fish

Toledo
Moorish, Jewish, and Christian imprints
Paintings of El Greco
Iglesia de Santo Tomé's El Greco masterpiece
Museo de Santa Cruz: art of El Greco and contemporaries
Military history in the Alcázar
Gothic cathedral's architecture and art treasures
Casa y Museo de El Greco
Sinagoga de El Tránsito and its Museo Sefardí
Medieval Sinagoga de Santa María la Blanca

El Greco paintings at the Hospital de la Caridad in Illescas
Pottery shops of Talavera de la Reina

Southwestern La Mancha
Almagro's graceful Plaza Mayor and 16th-century theater Corral de Comedias
Italianate Renaissance palace in Viso del Marqués

Cuenca
Magnificent views from upper town
Cliff-hanging Casas Colgadas and their Museo de Arte Abstracto and restaurant
Early Gothic cathedral
Fine diocesan museum
Rock formations at Ciudad Encantada

Southeastern La Mancha
Quintessential Spanish castles at Alarcón and Belmonte
Roman ruins at Saelices and Valeria
Classic Manchegan villages
Enchanting hill town of Chinchilla de Monte-Aragón

Northeastern La Mancha
Gothic tapestries in Pastrana's Iglesia Colegiata
Medieval town of Sigüenza's castle-fortress and
treasure-filled cathedral

A Man of La Mancha

Few writers have put their stamp on an entire region as
thoroughly as Miguel de Cervantes did on La Mancha.
Cervantes didn't invent his terrain, as William Faulkner did
Yoknapatawpha County, but instead peopled a real terra
cognita—an austere yet beautiful land with a harsh climate
and clear, crisp air—with his own unforgettable characters.
"Toda la espaciosa y triste España" ("All the space and
sadness of Spain") is how native son Luis de León described La Mancha. You have only to drive through the
craggy landscape, punctuated by an occasional castle and
windmill, to realize this *had* to be the land of Don Quixote
and Sancho Panza. Ever since Cervantes created these characters, they have represented La Mancha's (and Spain's)
extremes: Quixote, the idealistic, ascetic dreamer; Panza,
the earthy, pragmatic peasant.

Miguel de Cervantes Saavedra was born just beyond the
fringe of La Mancha, east of Madrid in Alcalá de Henares, and
nothing in his humble background, as the son of an unli-
censed itinerant doctor with seven children, presaged that
he would write one of the great novels of all time, a book
translated into more languages than any other except the
Bible. Nor did his early life suggest that he would one day be
acclaimed as the major poet of Spain's *siglo de oro* (Golden
Age; 1519–1609), a period that also included the playwrights
Lope de Vega and Pedro Calderón de la Barca.

In fact, Cervantes's soap opera of a life was marked with
ironies. Born in a university town at the height of its intellectual prestige, he was educated only in the college of life. After
58 years of struggle, poverty, and hopelessness, he created the
comic novel *The Life and Adventures of the Renowned Don
Quixote de la Mancha* (1605). This ironic tale was written in
prison (tradition tells us), when Cervantes was in the depths
of despair. Before the author could complete the second part
and begin to enjoy his life, a false version by an unidentified
rogue was sprung upon the public, forcing Cervantes to rush
the real sequel to print in 1615. He died a year later. Perhaps
the final irony is that Spain's decline, set in motion partly by
the defeat of the Armada in 1588, was under way when its
greatest novel was published, and that this work, the first
modern novel, influenced England—through such writers as
Henry Fielding, Tobias Smollett, Sir Walter Scott, and Charles
Dickens—in ways that Philip II's military power never could.

The Food of La Mancha

The impoverished image *Don Quixote* evokes of La Mancha is not noticeable at the region's tables today. Because of the abundance of game in the mountains and fish in the streams and rivers, pheasant, partridge, hare, trout, and river crab are commonly served.

While dishes here lack the grace and subtlety of those of certain other regions, they certainly are abundant and hearty; regional specialties include *pisto manchego* (a tasty and firmer, denser form of ratatouille), *gazpacho manchego* (a chilled soup with hare, partridge, ham, and chicken), *sopa de ajo* (garlic soup), *cordero a la caldereta* (lamb ragout), *perdiz* (partridge) served *estofada* (stewed) or *escabechada* (preserved or pickled), *cabrito asado con ajillos* (roast kid with garlic), and *cangrejos asados a la plancha* (grilled crab).

Variations of a dish mentioned in *Don Quixote,* the *olla podrida* ("rotten pot"), consist of a heavy, one-dish stew of meat and vegetables simmered together in a special, wide-mouthed pot called an *olla.* This is a Manchego (that is, of La Mancha) staple whose antecedent is an ancient Jewish dish known as *adafina.* A Toledan version, made with lamb, is called *chanfana. Migas pastor,* or savory sautéed bread crumbs (much better than it sounds), is as popular and widely enjoyed in La Mancha as in Castile.

Manchego cheese, *queso manchego,* now widely produced elsewhere in Spain as well, is unquestionably the king of Spanish table cheeses; it is milder than Cheddar, with a similar but smoother texture.

Alajú, a popular Arab-accented dessert, is made of rosemary-scented honey, walnuts, and bread crumbs; *melindres* (honey fritters) from the village of Yepes (between Toledo and Aranjuez) are also enjoyed in Toledo. *Churros,* crisp, golden fingers of fried dough, are enjoyed throughout the region, as they are in Castile, at breakfast or as a mid-morning snack, sprinkled with sugar or dunked in hot chocolate.

The Wines of La Mancha

The land of Don Quixote is the largest *denominación de origen* in Spain, with more than a million acres of vines. Even though La Mancha is better known for its reds and *claretes,* 90 percent of the grapes grown here are Airén, a white-wine grape. Manchegan red wines are made by fermenting Airén musts with the red wine grapes Cencibel (the Tempranillo of La Rioja) and Garnacha in huge earthenware vats called *tinajas* or, increasingly, in temperature-controlled stainless-steel vats. Most La Mancha wine is sold in bulk for blending, to be used for sangría or as house wines in the cafés of Madrid.

Valdepeñas is located in southern La Mancha just north of Despeñaperros, the mountainous entrance to Andalusia. In the 19th century Alexandre Dumas wrote, "at last we enjoyed the real Valdepeñas, sharp yet exciting to the palate." Ernest Hemingway swore that Valdepeñas produced the world's best house wines, and Frank Prial of the *New York Times* once wrote that it was "probably the best jug wine in the world."

As ubiquitous in the bars and restaurants of Spain as Beaujolais is in France, Valdepeñas has become almost a generic name synonymous with pleasant, light-red house wine, so much so that very little of what is served as Valdepeñas is authentic. (Don't be surprised if your red Valdepeñas arrives chilled; the Spanish often prefer it that way.) Genuine Valdepeñas is an excellent young *clarete*-style wine made from the white grape Airén mixed with a minimum of 20 percent Cencibel. Some estate-bottled Valdepeñas are made from 100 percent Cencibel and age as nicely as a *petit château* Bordeaux. If you want to try real Valdepeñas, you will have to buy it by the bottle. Look for Señorio de los Llanos, Viña Albalí, and Marqués de Gastañaga.

Castilla–La Mancha has two other *denominación de origen* wine regions, Almansa and Mentrida, which produce undistinguished wines used mostly for blending, but Castillo de Almansa *tinto* is an exception to the rule.

—*Gerry Dawes*

TOLEDO

Toledo can be visited in a day trip from Madrid, and is easily reached by car or bus in less than two hours (70 km/43 miles south via N 401). Express train is even quicker, and sets you down at a charming, faux-Moorish railway station that lays the table for your Toledo feast.

But a mere day in Toledo would be as sacrilegious as allotting only one day to Bath or Florence or any other city filled with treasures that need to be savored slowly. Toledo, *the* city to choose if you have only one option outside Madrid, is perched above, and seemingly stitched into, a rough-hewn bluff that is surrounded on three sides by the deep gorge of the Río Tajo (Tejo in Portuguese), which flows westward across Spain and Portugal, past Lisbon and into the Atlantic.

Cervantes called Toledo "that rocky gravity, glory of Spain and light of her cities." Playwright Tirso de Molina (1584–1648) described his native city as "the heart of Spain." But it

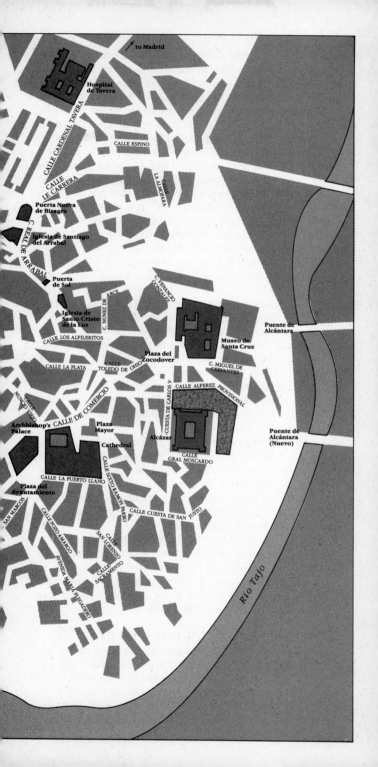

was El Greco, Toledo's adopted son, who captured it best—on canvas—and his *View of Toledo* is as recognizable today as when he painted it more than 400 years ago. Tan buildings gleam golden in the sunshine, their red terra-cotta roofs spilling almost on top of one another on streets that twist, curve, and fold back on themselves, spiraling ever upward, giving this former Castilian capital its high profile by day.

But by night Toledo assumes a completely different persona—one more reason you should spend at least one night here, preferably two, and ideally three or four. Soft amber lights, highlighting the town's most famous buildings, cast a glow on Toledo's twisting, corkscrew, cobbled passageways and narrow streets, evoking a spirit so hidden, eerie, and medieval that it can best be captured only before the tour buses clamber into town and after the daytime crowds leave (a strong argument for staying overnight). It is nighttime when Toledo's many legends and ghost stories seem especially believable.

Toledo is one of those rare cities that is even more than the sum of its parts, and its parts—a profusion of churches, museums, ancient portals, gardens hidden behind solid sheltering walls, tiny plazas, historic bridges—are spectacular. The entire town has been declared a national treasure, and all its new buildings must conform outwardly to the style of those from the 12th to the 15th century. This restriction produces a harmonious whole and gives Toledo a rare unity, though its history is much more diverse than its golden profile suggests.

Two themes are interwoven throughout Toledo; following them can form the guidelines for your visit. First there are the loose threads of the 12th through the 15th centuries, the city's golden era, when Muslims, Jews, and Christians coexisted more or less harmoniously, creating a cultural and artistic climate unparalleled elsewhere in Spain at any time and rare anywhere in the world.

Then there is the Toledo of El Greco, who left behind—in churches, museums, and the cathedral—a legacy of works that can keep you roaming for several days through the hilly but compact town, seeking them out. Both Toledo themes often overlap—in the cathedral, for example—so that you can enjoy them almost simultaneously.

MOORISH AND JEWISH TOLEDO

Toledo's superb location, nestled above a bend of the Río Tajo, shielded by protective hills, made it a natural site for, first, the seat of the Visigothic kings after the collapse of Rome, then the Muslim emirs, and finally the kings of León and Castile, who designated Toledo their capital after the Christian Reconquest. The city is a textural overlay of cultures. The Romans provided the name, Toletum, and left remains of a **Roman circus** in the public gardens just north of town.

Visigoths left even more, according to the Moors, who routed them in 711 and then extolled the architectural treasures they left behind. But as conquerors are wont to do, the Moors first destroyed them, then incorporated Visigothic elements into their own buildings, such as the capitals in the minuscule tenth-century mosque that later became the 12th-century Romanesque church of Santo Cristo de la Luz.

The Moors spent four centuries in Toledo—only half as much time as they spent in most of southern Spain. They left their imprint all over town, in the local predilection for the use of brick in walls, the underpinnings of many churches, several bridges, and the town gates.

When the rule of the Moors ended, many artisans, builders, and scholars remained in Toledo. Most Moorish traces in the city date from the post-Moor period, the 12th through the 15th centuries, when the architectural and decorative style known as Mudejar, traditional Moorish work done by Muslims living under Christian rule, developed. ("Mozarabic," a similar style, refers to Christian work executed in the Moorish style.)

In ecumenical times, before the Inquisition changed Spain's sociopolitical climate, Jews were part of Toledo's glory. The remains of their time here, before the 1492 expulsion of the Jews from Spain, can be found in such places as the Mudejar-style Sinagoga del Tránsito, which houses a Sephardic-culture museum, and around the Judería, the old Jewish quarter.

EL GRECO'S TOLEDO

It has been more than 400 years since Doménikos Theotokópoulos (1541–1614) arrived in Toledo, but his legacy remains everywhere. The Cretan-born painter, dubbed El Greco (The Greek), had studied with Titian and absorbed the works of Michelangelo in Rome and then wandered the Mediterranean region. He "found himself," so to speak, in this prosperous Castilian hill town, where he hoped to benefit from Hapsburg patronage. But Philip II didn't like El Greco's startling new style, derived from Italian and Byzantine influences, and the king never hung the single altarpiece he commissioned.

El Greco found other patrons among the city's nobility and clergy, and he spent the last 35 years of his life in Toledo, painting most of his finest pictures. It is appropriate, then, that part of the inscription on his tombstone reads: "Crete gave him life, and Toledo his brushes." When he arrived the city of 55,000 inhabitants was in its prime. It had been Charles V's "Imperial City" (1519–1558), and was (and still is) the seat of the primate of Spain. After Philip II made Madrid the capital of Spain in 1561, Toledo declined; by the time Alexandre Dumas visited in 1846 there were fewer than 12,000 residents. Today's tourism has brought it nearly to its 15th-century level.

Arriving in Toledo

If you drive south from Madrid on N 401, you might break the drive with a stop in **Illescas**, a little town just off the road at about the halfway point (36 km/22 miles south of Madrid). El Greco fans will especially want to see the five paintings at the modest convent church of **Hospital de la Caridad**. *San Ildefonso* is an acknowledged masterpiece, but two other knockouts are in the sacristy to the left of the altar: the soaring *Coronation of the Virgin* and the *Nativity,* in which the child in the manger is viewed through the surprising perspective of a cow's horns.

As you approach Toledo, just before the main gate into town, the **Puerta Nueva de Bisagra** (New Bisagra Gate, "new" as in 16th-century), you will notice on the right side of the road the **Hospital de Tavera**, a 16th-century Renaissance complex built by Cardinal Juan de Tavera. In the complex is the **Museum of the Duchess of Lerma**, in which there are 20 marvelous paintings by El Greco (especially notable is his *Holy Family*), works by Zurbarán, Tintoretto, and Titian, and José Ribera's bizarre *Bearded Woman,* based on a real person.

INSIDE THE WALLS

Diagonally across from the Puerta Nueva de Bisagra is an **Oficina de Turismo**, where you can pick up a map of the city. Toledo is a city of such twists, turns, steps, and drop-offs that even the best map can only give you approximations of where the sights are.

A couple of blocks west of the New Bisagra Gate is the Old Bisagra Gate, known as **Puerta de Alfonso VI**, dating back to the ninth century. It was through these Moorish arches that King Alfonso VI and El Cid passed in their 1085 conquest of the city. The Hostal del Cardenal (described below) is next door. Just inside the gate, up a short but steep hill, is **Iglesia de Santiago del Arrabal**, a magnificent Mudejar-style church where Vicente Ferrer, who was later made a saint, preached conversion of the Jews so vociferously that his followers reportedly threw those Jews who failed to convert to Christianity off nearby cliffs.

AROUND THE PUERTA DEL SOL

The best, in fact the only, way to get about Toledo is on foot or, if you can find one, by taxi. Parking is extremely tight, and your first mission should be to park your car for the duration of your visit (unless you are staying outside of the old town). The best parking place is a vast lot just above and to the left of the **Puerta del Sol** (with a 12th-century Mudejar gatehouse), which you will soon come to at the top of the winding hill from the Puerta Nueva de Bisagra.

Below the car park, up a hill from the Puerta del Sol, is the 12th-century Romanesque **Iglesia de Santo Cristo de la Luz**. Also known as the Mezquita (Mosque) Cristo de la Luz, it was built upon a minute-size 10th-century mosque, believed to be one of the first Moorish buildings in Spain and probably built on a Visigothic site. A custodian will let you enter the iron gate surrounding the minuscule church so you can peer inside to see the horseshoe arches and still-bright Romanesque fresco remains on the walls. He may then lead you through a tiny garden to the top of the Puerta del Sol gatehouse, from which you will have commanding views of the countryside.

The Alcázar Area

PLAZA DEL ZOCODOVER

From the parking lot near Puerta del Sol, you can walk along Calle Venancio González up to the Plaza del Zocodover, known locally as the Zoco. A perpetual beehive of activity, the square was described by Cervantes (who once lodged nearby) in his book *Novelas Ejemplares*. At dusk the Zoco is the liveliest scene in town, where the nightly *paseo,* or walkabout, takes place, and the town's residents are out in full force.

The name "Zocodover" is derived from the Arab words *sük ed-dawabb* (horse market), and this introduces you to the first of Toledo's many Moorish influences. While in the Zoco you might pause for coffee or a drink at one of the surrounding bars or sidewalk cafés, then sample the favorite Toledan sweet, *mazapán,* a sweeter version of marzipan—another Moorish gift, which remains a local cottage industry. You can buy some at the Santo Tomé pastry shop in the Zoco. An indication of changing times: There is now a McDonald's on the southern corner of the square.

MUSEO DE SANTA CRUZ

An important, but often overlooked, trove of mostly 16th- and 17th-century Spanish art can be found at the Museo de Santa Cruz, just a block east of the Plaza del Zocodover through the

Moorish arch along Calle Miguel de Cervantes. The museum is housed in a former hospital, with rich Plateresque ornamentation and Mudejar *artesonado* ceilings. It was the creation of architect Enrique de Egas, who built the royal chapel in Granada, and Alonso de Covarrubias.

In addition to 22 El Greco paintings (including the splendid *Veronica, Immaculate Conception,* and *Assumption*), the museum contains paintings by Goya, Veronese, and Ribera; 16th-century Flemish tapestries; a fine altarpiece by Pedro Berruguete; primitive sculptures and paintings; and a room full of Holy Roman Emperor Charles V's artifacts. An enormous two-story-high damask and gold-threaded banner from the battle of Lepanto (1571) adorns the entire end wall of one hall. In the attached cloister you'll find a marvelous caprice of Plateresque "embroidered" stone arches, as well as a small archaeological museum and a gallery of ceramics and *azulejos* (glazed tiles).

THE ALCAZAR

From the Zoco it is a short walk up Cuesta del Alcázar to the *alcázar,* the highest point in town, facing the river on the east. The *alcázar* is worth visiting both for its history and for the magnificence of its Renaissance architecture. The original Moorish fortress (which El Cid once commanded) was built on the site of a Roman fort and later converted (by Alonso de Covarrubias, finished by Juan de Herrera) to a royal palace for Charles V. The fortress was damaged and restored several times, and during an eight-week siege in 1936 the building was virtually leveled by Republican troops. The defending Nationalist commander, Colonel Moscardo, refused to surrender the *alcázar* even in exchange for the freedom of his captured son. This dramatic story is retold in many military exhibits (which include the commander's shrapnel-riddled office and cellars where 600 women and children lived during the siege) displayed in the rebuilt *alcázar,* which now looks as it did in Charles V's era. Aficionados of Spanish and/ or military history will be fascinated by the numerous weapons (including an inlaid sword of Boabdil, who surrendered Granada to the Reyes Católicos, Ferdinand and Isabella) and military uniforms.

The Cathedral

Returning to the Zoco and following Calle de Comercio (off the west side of the square) uphill and down, you will arrive shortly at the cathedral, which faces the Hapsburgian city hall across the Plaza del Ayuntamiento. Built in installments (1227–1493) on the site of the city's great mosque, which in turn had been constructed over a Visigothic church, the cathedral demonstrates the rich layering of Toledo's cultural influences. Only one tower of the original plan was built: It is half-Moorish, in the style of the Giralda in Seville, with similar elegance. The second tower (finished in the 17th century) has a dome designed by El Greco's son. Thus in these two towers can be seen the two most powerful imprints to be found throughout Toledo: those of the Moors and El Greco.

The cathedral is considered the second finest Gothic masterpiece in Spain, after the cathedral of Burgos. Though conceived in the French Gothic style, by the time it was finished it had become convincingly Spanish, with many Flamboyant and Plateresque touches. A Spanish proverb, with which few would argue, says, "Toledo has the richest of our cathedrals, Oviedo the holiest, Salamanca the strongest, León the most beautiful." Among many notable architectural elements of the Toledo cathedral are the three Gothic doorways on the western façade; the elaborately decorated central doorway, Puerta del Perdón, by Juan Alemán; the Gothic Puerta de los Leones on the southern side; the *sala capitular,* with its fine paneled ceiling; and the north tower, with its famous *campana gorda* (fat bell). Enter the cathedral through the cloister, to the left of the main façade, just beneath the "bridge" that links the cathedral to the 18th-century archbishop's palace on its left.

Inside, the cathedral is unusually well lighted, making it easy to see its innumerable treasures. A walk through, without visiting the sacristy and the treasury, will take at least an hour—there is that much to see. There are 22 side chapels, including the **Mozarabic Chapel** (the last in the rear, next to the Puerta del Perdón), where a Mozarabic Mass is still celebrated every Sunday. In the *capilla mayor* (main chapel) is a magnificent Plateresque *reja* (grille) and a gilded Gothic retable with four tiers of life-size figures in New Testament scenes. Covarrubias's Plateresque Capilla de los Reyes Nuevos (New Kings Chapel) contains the tombs of Henry III and his wife, Catherine of Lancaster, daughter of England's John of Gaunt. The walnut *sillerías* (choir stalls) have superbly carved figures and scenes by the talented German immigrant Rodrigo Alemán.

Behind the main chapel is 18th-century sculptor Narciso Tomé's *Transparente,* an island of angels and life-size figures surrounding a Madonna and Child and a Last Supper. A focal point of the treasury is a ten-foot-high, 400-pound **monstrance** by Enrique de Arfe (1506–1562) that is a triumph of silver and precious gems, filigree angels, bells, flowers, and turrets. In the sacristy, look for El Greco's *Disrobing of Christ*

(1579) over the altar, Goya's *Betrayal of Christ* (1788), 16 paintings of the Apostles by El Greco, and paintings by Titian, Rubens, Van Dyck, and others.

For lovers of pageantry, Toledo is *the* place to be during the feast of Corpus Christi in late spring (the date varies, depending on when Easter falls). Gold-threaded tapestries are hung on the cathedral's exterior walls, the streets are strewn with wild thyme, and marchers in medieval costumes toss rose petals along the procession path. The centerpiece of the procession is the Arfe monstrance. When it is returned to the cathedral, jubilant explosions of rockets and a rendition of the national anthem punctuate the event. Spanish celebrations are never desultory.

West of the Cathedral

Wend your way from the Plaza del Ayuntamiento to Calle de El Salvador, which leads into the tiny **Plaza de El Salvador** and then joins the delightful pedestrian thoroughfare called Calle Santo Tomé. **Mayke Cafetería-Heladería** on the plaza is a good place for an ice-cream or coffee-and-pastry pick-me-up. Browse through Calle Santo Tomé's pottery shops while walking two short blocks west to the **Iglesia de Santo Tomé**. There you'll see an El Greco masterpiece, *El Entierro del Conde de Orgaz* (The Burial of the Count of Orgaz). This superlative painting joins the natural and supernatural worlds on a single canvas. It includes portraits of several of El Greco's contemporaries: Philip II, though alive at the time, looks down from heaven, and Cervantes, Lope de Vega, and the artist himself are in the crowd of onlookers. Note the Mudejar influences in Santo Tomé's tower.

CASA Y MUSEO DE EL GRECO

Just south of Santo Tomé on the Plaza de los Alamillos del Tránsito is the Casa y Museo de El Greco (El Greco House and Museum), a much-rebuilt 16th-century house, whose period furniture and wood-paneled rooms form an appropriate backdrop for the 20 paintings displayed. Among them is the magnetic *View of Toledo*. The private chapel of the house has a Mudejar-style ceiling encrusted with stars. The name is a bit misleading; El Greco actually lived in 24 rooms of the long-gone palace of the marqués de Villena, which once occupied the site, with the same sweeping view of the Río Tajo. The Casa y Museo de El Greco and the cathedral are two of the most visited of Toledo's sights.

SINAGOGA DE EL TRANSITO

The third of Toledo's most popular sights is the Sinagoga de El Tránsito (1366), just southwest of the El Greco house on

Paseo de El Tránsito. It is a small, handsome building, decorated in Mudejar designs with polychromed stuccowork and Hebrew wall inscriptions that praise God, King Peter the Cruel, and Samuel Ha-Levi (the king's treasurer and the synagogue's founder). Levi was later tortured and killed by the king, and there are those who insist the red-bearded financier still haunts the area where he once lived. (El Greco's house is on land that was part of Levi's estate.) The synagogue became a church, El Tránsito, after the Jewish expulsion in 1492 (a royal decree that was officially rescinded in 1992). Part of El Tránsito is the **Museo Sefardí**, which houses maps, tombs, and memorabilia from Sephardic Jewish life in medieval Spain.

SINAGOGA DE SANTA MARIA LA BLANCA

Two blocks northwest on Paseo de El Tránsito (it becomes Calle de los Reyes Católicos), which once was the old **Judería** (Jewish quarter), is the Sinagoga de Santa María la Blanca (1180). This tiny architectural gem, whose restored interior is a forest of 24 richly ornamented octagonal columns and Arabic arches, was seized by Vicente Ferrer's followers in 1405 and underwent numerous metamorphoses. Viewed in juxtaposition with El Tránsito, it offers an even deeper insight into the medieval Jewish world. It is also a coming together of Toledo's three religious (and architectural) threads: Muslim, Jewish, and Christian.

MONASTERIO DE SAN JUAN DE LOS REYES

In the next block north on the same street is another of Toledo's treasures, the majestic Isabelline Iglesia de San Juan de los Reyes, part of a Franciscan monastery that was built by the Reyes Católicos after their victory over the Portuguese at Toro (before the conquest of Granada). They intended it to be their burial place (but later opted for Granada), and the escutcheons and symbols of Aragón and Castile are evident throughout. The northwestern façade was begun by Covarrubias in 1553 and finally finished in 1610. Note the chains along the outside walls facing Calle de los Reyes Católicos; they were taken off Christian prisoners of the Moors who were released by Ferdinand and Isabella's army. The two-story cloister with its garden full of orange trees, cypress, and bamboo is a lovely example of Flamboyant Gothic.

Just across the street from the entrance to the church is a small new café, **Scorpions**, a comfortable place to relax over coffee, a drink, or a light lunch before continuing your walking tour.

IGLESIA DE SANTO DOMINGO EL ANTIGUO

If you head north on Calle Pintor Matias Moreno, turn west on Calle Colegio de Doncellas, then quickly north again on Calle Santa Leocadia, you'll arrive after two blocks at the tiny Plaza de Santo Domingo el Antiguo and the church of the same name. Inside the church, above the Neoclassic altar, are six El Greco paintings (only two, those of the two Saint Johns, are originals). There is another El Greco original, to the right of the main altar, *Resurrection of Christ*. All the works here were painted in 1577–1579, and were a part of the artist's first commission after arriving in Toledo.

Other treasures in the three rooms behind the main church include a 16th-century Flemish painting, a Visigothic column, and various 14th-century naïve sculptures. El Greco is buried in the crypt, his wooden casket visible through a glass-covered opening on the floor at the rear of the church.

THE PLAZA DE SAN ROMAN AREA

If you now zigzag your way south and east you'll shortly come to Plaza de San Román. On its south side is the tiny 13th-century **Iglesia de San Román**, a former mosque with red-and-white-striped Moorish columns and arches and Romanesque frescoes, which houses the **Museo de los Concilios y de la Cultura Visigoda**. In addition to many Visigothic fragments, columns, and incised stones, the church-museum has an Arabic tower and horseshoe arches and a 16th-century cupola by Covarrubias.

A few more quick turns southwest (down Calle San Clemente to Calle San Pedro Mártir to the Plaza de Valdecaleros, then on to Calle de las Bulas) brings you to Toledo's newest sight, the **Museo Arte Contemporaneo**, with contemporary painting and sculpture. Of greater interest than some of the exhibits is the house itself, a 16th-century mansion with handsome Moorish elements in the plasterwork, arches, and exposed beam ceilings.

Staying and Dining in Toledo

Considering its wealth of sights and the hordes of tourists who come to see them, Toledo is surprisingly short of first-rate restaurants. (It has a number of ordinary ones, with almost identical menus, clustered throughout the inner city.) Three of its best are in hotels that also make excellent overnight choices. The most romantic and historic of these borders the northern end of the city, making it easy to park your car and travel around in Toledo by foot (or taxi, if need be). ▶ **Hostal del Cardenal**, built into the city walls, is an

18th-century archbishop's palace with serviceable rooms, a restful, bird-filled garden on two levels with reflecting pools, chestnuts, lilacs, roses, and shade trees, and a scenic location next to the historic Puerta de Alfonso VI (the Old Bisagra Gate). Its restaurant (operated by the owners of Botín in Madrid) has wonderfully hearty game specialties such as *perdiz* (partridge), venison ragout, and wild boar. The three-course menu of the day, including wine, is an exceptional value.

Nearby, just outside the Puerta Nueva de Bisagra on the road to Madrid, is a lovely small hotel, the ▶ **María Cristina**. Once a 15th-century church (Hospital San Lázaro), it has been handsomely restored, and its Imperial Suite is the dome of the original church. Other rooms, less lavishly decorated, are also attractive and serviceable. The restaurant, **El Abside** (The Apse), inside the central arch, is decorated in Mudejar style and features regional and international dishes.

If you don't mind driving (or taxiing) across the river, the ▶ **Parador Conde de Orgaz**, located on Cerro del Emperador (Emperor's Hill), is especially pleasant for lunch, during which you'll have a broad view of Toledo from the terrace. Try such regional dishes as *sopa de ajo* (garlic soup) and roast lamb here. Constructed in the old Toledo style, this brick-and-glass hotel has comfortable rooms, a large lounge, a patio, and a competent restaurant. Another reasonable hotel choice is the modern, high-rise ▶ **Hotel Beatriz**, some 2 km (a mile or so) from town on the road northwest to Avila. A swimming pool, tennis courts, and large, comfortable, if impersonal, rooms are among its assets. Its restaurant, Anticuario, offers a variety of solid Castilian fare.

If you don't want to leave the heart of old Toledo, there is a well-situated new hotel in town, the ▶ **Hotel Pintor El Greco**, a small place (33 rooms) with clean, comfortable, unpretentious, but neatly furnished rooms. It is located in the old Judería, near the El Greco house and the two synagogues.

Also in the center of things is the old, recently refurbished ▶ **Hotel Carlos V**, just a block from the Zoco and next door to Toledo's main youth attraction, a nonstop discotheque. The rooms in the Carlos V are small but well equipped with new furniture, amenities, and reasonably good insulation from the pulsating music next door.

For dinner you might try **Venta de Aires**, Paseo del Circo Romano 35, at the edge of town, a Toledo landmark with a nice garden in summer and a rustic ambience. The hearty regional dishes are a fine value. Tel: (9-25) 22-05-45.

Shopping in Toledo

Shopping in Toledo runs the gamut from touristic junk to respectable crafts, both of which are often bunched together in the same souvenir shops. The most famous Toledo craft, an Arab legacy, is damascene ware—steel knives, scissors, plates, and platters etched with silver, gold, or copper thread, made by hand with great precision. Shop carefully, or you may end up with a machine-made product in tin and inferior metals. The famous Toledo knives, prized for many centuries, have been trivialized to letter openers. There are two dozen or more authentic damascene workshops in Toledo, but finding their output isn't always easy. The Provincial Delegation of Tourism, at Plaza del Zocodover 11, and at Puerta Nueva de Bisagra, Paseo de Madrid, can direct you to reliable sources.

TALAVERA DE LA REINA

You will also find many shops full of the famous hand-painted Talavera ceramics in Toledo, especially along Calle Santo Tomé. But if you have a serious interest, and the time, head for the source, Talavera de la Reina, a pottery-producing town about 83 km (51 miles) northwest of Toledo, on N 403 to E 4/N V, or the more scenic C 502 along the Río Tajo. (If you are driving from Madrid to Extremadura, Talavera is directly on the route.) In Talavera you can browse through many ceramic studios and workshops where the famous decorative ware, which is now made in yellow, blue, and green, has been produced for eight centuries. The largest producer is **Artesanía Talaverana**, Avenida de Portugal 32, in Talavera. Talavera's **Museo de Ruiz de Luna**, at Plaza General Primo de Rivera 5, has ceramics dating back four centuries.

While in Talavera, you might stop for lunch at the admirable, handsomely appointed **Anticuario** on the main road through town, Avenida de Madrid 5; Tel: (9-25) 80-76-00. It's in the Hotel Beatriz, diagonally across from the **Basílica de Nuestra Señora del Prado**, which is decorated with many fine blue-and-white *azulejos* both inside and along the façade. The church is right next to the town bullring, where one of the great *toreros* of all time, Joselito, was killed in 1920. There is a bronze bust of him in the peaceful little park-promenade outside the church.

SOUTHWESTERN LA MANCHA

Travelling southeast from Toledo on N 401 (on the way to the main Madrid–Jaén highway, E 5), stop briefly at **Orgaz** (34 km/21 miles south of Toledo), where Doña Ximena, the wife of El Cid, was born, to see the impressively restored 14th-century castle of the Pérez de Guzmán family and the last work of Alberto Churriguera, a one-towered, unfinished 18th-century granite church. A country road (TO 231/232) leads southeast to Consuegra (36 km/22 miles from Orgaz), where most Spanish saffron is harvested; ten windmills profiled on a hilltop make a dramatic (and photogenic) sight.

Six kilometers (4 miles) east of Consuegra the E 5/N IV heads south 53 km (33 miles) to **Manzanares**, where you'll find the modern **Parador de Manzanares**, a good place to break your drive with a hearty La Mancha lunch of game, *migas pastor,* and local cheeses and wines; Tel: (9-26) 61-04-00. At **Valdepeñas**, 30 km (19 miles) farther south, the various bodegas and cellars might tempt you to stop to sample the region's light, refreshing red wine (see The Wines of La Mancha, above).

Almagro

Almagro, 34 km (21 miles) northwest of Valdepeñas on C 415, is often bypassed because it is off the main north–south highway, but is one of the smaller joys of La Mancha. The cheek-by-jowl abundance of handsome mansions, churches, and chapels may surprise the casual visitor, as 20th-century Almagro seems the proverbial "town that time forgot." But in its heyday, the 16th century, it was a bustling commercial center where the king's banker, Jakobo Fucar (also known as Fugger and a member of a well-known family of financiers), kept his storehouses of silver and mercury, which were mined at Almadén, to the west in Extremadura.

Almagro was a religious center as well, with convents established by all the major religious orders of the Catholic Church. In 1574, under a royal grant from Philip II, the University of Almagro was established in the **Monasterio del Nuestra Señora del Rosario** (Our Lady of the Rosary); it flourished until 1828. You can see its façade at the corner of Ronda de Santa Domingo and Calle de Colegio.

But Almagro's glory days began even earlier. From the early years of the Muslim invasion of Spain, the small Roman town was one of those frontier outposts that passed back and forth from Christians to Moors until it became a stronghold of the powerful and prosperous Order of the Knights of Calatrava. In 1214, two years before the knights made it their official seat, the town was settled by 70 noble Christian families at the order of the archbishop of Toledo. By the time Alfonso X, El Sabio (the Wise), convened his parliament here in 1273, Almagro was thriving.

AROUND IN ALMAGRO

Almagro is so small you can easily see its main sights on foot. The best bet is to park your car at the ▶ **Parador de Almagro**, on the main road at the southwestern edge of town. The parador is the best place to dine in town and to stay if you are making the drive from Madrid to Granada. Just two blocks south of the Plaza Mayor and the center of town, the parador, rebuilt from the old convent of San Francisco, is one of the most handsome in the government-run chain. Built around 16 patios, each with its own character, the complex now boasts fountains, gardens, large rooms (simply decorated with antiques, tapestries, and crafts), and a swimming pool. Castilian garlic soup, rabbit in wine sauce, white beans with quail, ragout of spring lamb *manchego,* and hake with cider are some of the excellent specialties served in its restaurant.

Amid a cluster of graceful Renaissance and Plateresque façades, colleges, convents, churches, and cobbled streets the main attraction in Almagro is the oblong **Plaza Mayor**. Lined lengthwise with block-long Flemish-style, glassed-in arcades, the plaza is the best spot to find the intricate, traditional lacework Almagro is famous for. (Also try **Pablo**, a shop nearby, at Mayor de Cornicieros 12, for local lacework as well as La Mancha pottery.)

On the south side of the plaza is a restored 16th-century theater, **El Corral de Comedias** (entrance at number 17). Built with a stage at one end and two-story stalls around an open, cobbled courtyard (reminiscent of Elizabethan theaters of the same era), the Corral evokes images of Lope de Vega and Pedro Calderón de la Barca. In fact, their plays are still performed in this national monument during a festival of classical drama and comedy held annually the last two weeks of September. For information, contact: Oficina de Turismo y Festivales, Calle Mayor de Carnicería 5, 13270 Almagro; Tel: (9-26) 86-07-17. Across the plaza is a small **Museo del Teatro**. Stroll up Calle Nuestra Señora de las Nieves (between Plaza Mayor and Plaza de Santo Domingo) to admire some very fancy palatial façades in the Barrio Noble. The **Antiguo Convento de Calatrava** (also called La Asunción), at the eastern edge of town on Camino de Calatrava, has a splendid Renaissance carved-stone stairway and two-story Plateresque cloister.

Excursions from Almagro

Almagro's parador makes a good base for exploring the immediate area, including the Don Quixote villages of La Mancha. Keep in mind, of course, that following the good Don's "trail" is like pursuing Romeo and Juliet in Italy; they are fictional characters and events. One place where fiction and reality blend is **Argamasilla de Alba**, 39 km (24 miles) northeast of Manzanares. It was here that Cervantes was imprisoned and reputedly began writing *Don Quixote*. The rebuilt prison can be seen at the whitewashed, cave-like Cueva de Medrano, on Calle de Cervantes 7 (ask at number 8 for the key). In the local parish church is a painting of Don Rodrígo de Pacheco, a local bigwig believed to have been the inspiration for the "knight of the rueful countenance."

CIUDAD REAL

Ciudad Real, 26 km (16 miles) northwest of Almagro, may have been "the seat of the god of smiles" to Cervantes, but today it is relatively inconsequential to travellers. A few sights of interest include the 14th-century Puerta de Toledo, an old Mudejar-style town gate at the north end of town joining Ronda de Toledo; a notable Gothic cathedral with fine choir stalls on Paseo del Prado in the center of town; and the Gothic church of San Pedro, six blocks southeast of the cathedral on Cuchillería Lanza, with Mudejar and Gothic doorways, a Flamboyant Gothic rose window, and a Baroque retable.

A very good (and reasonably priced) meal can be had at **Miami Park**, Ronda de Ciruela 48, at the southern edge of town, an old-fashioned restaurant featuring such regional dishes as *pisto manchego;* Tel: (9-26) 22-20-43.

VISO DEL MARQUES

Far more interesting than Ciudad Real is the little-known Viso del Marqués, about 32 km (20 miles) south of Valdepeñas on E 25/N IV, and 6 km (4 miles) west; make the turnoff at Almuradiel. Unless you are heading south to Andalusia through the dramatic, narrow mountain gorge called Desfiladero de Despeñaperros (which translates as "overthrow of the dogs"), where bandits once ambushed travellers, your best bet for seeing Viso del Marqués is to make it a half-day trip from Almagro (almost an hour's drive—53 km/33 miles—on back roads).

Palacio del Marqués de Santa Cruz

The centerpiece of the minute village of Viso del Marqués is an Italianate Renaissance palace (1564–1585) built for Alvaro de Bazán, marqués de Santa Cruz, an intrepid naval commander under Philip II. The palace would be a dazzler anywhere, but sitting as it does on this isolated patch of the dusty La Mancha plain it seems all the more remarkable. Of course, Viso wasn't always so remote; it was once on the main north–south route.

The palace is believed to be the work of a Genoese painter-architect, Giovanni Battista Castello, who worked on

El Escorial, but its origins are still enigmatic. Regardless, it is a full-fledged Renaissance beauty with proportions that take the breath away: Doric columns, elegant patios and court-yards, a magnificent barrel-vaulted stairwell, and, through-out, lavishly decorated walls, ceilings, and archways embel-lished with themes that illustrate the marqués's brilliant career and successful battles. The Spanish still debate whether the outcome of the Armada in 1588 would have been different had he lived to take command.

Unfortunately, for all its charms Viso del Marqués lacks a good restaurant. If you want lunch, you'll have to go back to Almagro or east to Almuradiel for some roast lamb or *pisto manchego* at **Los Podencos**, in the Hotel Podencos, Carre-tera de Andalucía (N IV), km 232; Tel: (9-26) 33-90-00.

CUENCA AND SOUTHEASTERN LA MANCHA

The 164-km (102-mile) drive east of Madrid to the hilltop town of Cuenca is mile after mile of dry Castilian landscape. Take N III southeast 81 km (50 miles) to Tarancón, at which point you can continue east on N 400 to Cuenca, or take a short excursion southeast (21 km/13 miles on N III) to **Saelices** to see the Roman amphitheater, columns, and other remains of Segóbriga, once an important Roman town and the capital of Celtic Iberia. There is a small museum that offers an overview of the site.

Cuenca

The 83-km (52-mile) drive east from Tarancón to Cuenca is like a lunar landscape. Then suddenly you are confronted with a grove of giant poplars and cypresses, etched against ocher bluffs, and the silhouette of a town at the top.

Cuenca is literally a cliff-hanger. Houses, some dating back to the 12th century, are sculpted into and dramatically overhang the cliffs above a deep gorge. Some 600 feet below, the Ríos Júcar (HOO-cahr) and Huécar (WAY-cahr) converge near the newer, lower part of town. The Júcar flows on toward Valencia; the Huécar ends at Cuenca's feet.

Like many Castilian hill towns, Cuenca consists of a busy but dull modern lower town and a vintage upper town, this one with a cathedral, two museums, and many ancient build-ings. Cuenca made an ideal lookout, as the Moors discovered in the ninth century. From the top you can see for miles into Castile, yet the cliffs themselves act as a natural fortress, with the rivers forming a moat on three sides. No wonder the earlier Romans and Visigoths valued it, too.

In the 12th century Muslims and Christians had a tug-of-war over Cuenca, alternately capturing and losing it. In 1177, after a nine-month siege, the Christian king Alfonso VIII, borrowing a strategy from *The Odyssey,* supposedly sent two supporters, crouching and covered by sheepskins, past the Muslim gatekeeper. Once inside they slew the guard and opened the gate to Alfonso's army. From then on the town was a Christian outpost and it later became the headquarters of the Knights of Santiago. In honor of Alfonso's ingenuity, Conquenses, as Cuenca people call themselves, still burn a light at night at Cuenca's lower gate.

THE UPPER TOWN

To explore Cuenca's upper town, drive up the corkscrew road through the 18th-century gate (supporting the town hall above it), and park in the small Plaza Mayor just below the cathedral. The ideal way to see all the narrow streets and overhanging vistas of this area is on foot.

The Casas Colgadas

What brings most outsiders to Cuenca these days are the Casas Colgadas, three adjoining 15th-century houses whose balconies are cantilevered on the steepest cliff above the Río Huécar (east of the Plaza Mayor). In the early 1960s an affluent Madrid painter, Fernando Zobel, persuaded Cuenca authorities to let him convert the picturesque but decaying buildings (which once functioned as the town hall) into a museum to house his modern collection, in exchange for renovating the buildings.

With impeccable taste Zobel and fellow artists Gustavo Tornér (a Cuenca native) and Gerardo Rueda, all members of the 1960s new wave of Spanish artists, peeled away plaster (discovering a hidden Gothic stairway and arches in the process), whitewashed the interior walls, and turned two of the attached buildings into the stunning **Museo de Arte Abstracto**, a showcase for Antoni Tàpies, Luis Feito, Eduardo Chillida, Manolo Millares, Antonio Saura, and some 60 other artists of the post–Picasso-Miró generation.

Zobel died in 1984, but the museum's future is secure because it is now part of the Madrid-based Fundación Juan March. Attracted by the museum and Cuenca's windswept prospect, many Madrid artists have made some of the ancient upper-town buildings their weekend homes as a respite from the hot, dry Castilian summers. Winter here is another story—a chiller.

In the third building is a charming restaurant, **Mesón Casas Colgadas**, the best in town by far, where local specialties include *trucha figón* (trout from the Júcar), Huécar *cangrejos* (crabs), grilled wild mushrooms, *conejo escabechado* (pickled rabbit), and excellent desserts such as *alajú* and *helado con nueces cantonesas* (ice cream with walnuts). The Spanish enjoy a postprandial digestive; try the local *resoli* (coffee liqueur with orange and cinnamon); Tel: (9-69) 22-35-09. (Another restaurant in the lower town, **Figón de Pedro**, Calle de Cervantes 13, has the same ownership and similar menu but lacks the vista; Tel: 9-69/22-68-21.)

Balconies in both the restaurant and the museum have stunning views of the river below and the textured, craggy cliffs on the opposite side. Down the hill a short distance north of the Casas Colgadas is the San Pablo footbridge, a scary, shaky passage over the Huécar that leads to the convent of San Pablo on the opposite cliff.

THE PLAZA MAYOR AREA

In the years since the museum opened, Cuenca has metamorphosed from a withered town to an increasingly prosperous one. Even the early Gothic **cathedral** in the Plaza Mayor has been scrubbed down. Don't be put off by its eclectic exterior; the interior is light enough in the morning to reveal some fine treasures, including rare (for Spain) Anglo-Norman influences in the nave (1208–1250). Also special are several superb *rejas* (grilles) by Hernando de Arenas, a local 16th-century master; a Madonna by sculptor Pedro de Mena; a treasury with a lovely Baroque ceiling; and an ornate Plateresque portal leading to the *sala capitular* (chapter house).

Around the corner from the cathedral (to the right if you are facing the cathedral), on the way to the Museo de Arte Abstracto, is a new sight in Cuenca: the **Museo Diocesano**, installed in a 16th-century archbishop's palace, with numerous treasures from Cuenca churches and the cathedral handsomely displayed without an inch of clutter. A first-rate painting by Gérard David of the Crucifixion, two fine El Greco paintings, a choice Byzantine diptych of the Virgin Mary, and numerous *santos* (wooden statues of saints), altar rugs, and tapestries are among the surprises.

Semana Santa (Holy Week), celebrated with elaborate processions in many Spanish cities, is at its most awesome in Cuenca, as candle-carrying multitudes slowly wend their way up the narrow lanes along the cliffside, looking in the darkness like elongated ribbons of flickering lights.

Just below the Plaza Mayor is another likable restaurant, with views facing across the valleys in the opposite direction from those of Mesón Casas Colgadas. It is **Los Arcos**, and while it doesn't measure up to the Mesón, it has splendid vistas and serves decent *pisto manchego, gazpacho pastor,* and other regional dishes; Tel: (9-69) 21-38-06.

STAYING IN CUENCA

If you choose to stay in Cuenca your best bet is ▶ **Hotel Cueva del Fraile**, a restored 16th-century monastery. Although 7 km (4½ miles) outside Cuenca, it is worth the drive for the mountain views, pleasant rustic Spanish flavor, tennis courts, and swimming pool. A distant second, at the edge of the lower town, is ▶ **Hotel Torremangana**, whose amenities are fewer than its four-star designation would suggest. Nevertheless, it is the best hotel in central Cuenca, with modestly furnished, serviceable rooms.

The 62-room ▶ **Parador de Cuenca**, in a 16th-century convent perched on a hilltop above Cuenca, opened in July 1993. The parador's restaurant serves typical Cuencan cuisine and regional wines, and facilities include a swimming pool and tennis court.

LA CIUDAD ENCANTADA

It is a scenic, twisting mountain drive 35 km (22 miles) north of Cuenca to Ciudad Encantada (Enchanted City), a series of spectacular rock formations that you can walk through, under, and around. Such names as El Tobogán (a roller-coaster walk through a narrow passage of steep boulders), Hongo (mushroom), Las Barcas (ships), and Elefante y Cocodrilo (elephant and crocodile) telegraph the shapes of the boulders. It's an eerie, wonderful sight—but you have to enjoy walking.

Southeastern La Mancha

From Cuenca you are in a fine position for a foray into the southeastern reaches of La Mancha. Head south on N 320 32 km (20 miles) and then west 14 km (9 miles) at the sign for **Valeria**, which has Roman ruins as well as dramatic gorges and canyons carved out by the Río Gritos.

ALARCON

Alarcón, just off N III, the main Madrid–Valencia highway, is about 85 km (53 miles) south of Cuenca by way of N 320 south and N III west. It makes a perfect overnight or lunch stop. Built on a rocky ledge that rises from a Río Júcar gorge, Alarcón boasts the quintessential Spanish castle, a 14th-century fortress, now turned into a premier, though off-the-track, parador, the ▶ **Parador Marqués de Villena**. Its dining room has some of the best regional dishes in the area, including a local specialty, a spicy pâté called *morteruelo*. The village also has five churches, four of which are in a mostly ruined state; the fifth is the well-restored 13th- to 15th-century church of **La Trinidad**.

BELMONTE

Another castle, considered one of the most typical in Spain, is at Belmonte 33 km (20 miles) northwest on N III/E 101, and 36 km (22 miles) south on N 420 from Alarcón. Built in 1456 for Juan Pacheco, the marqués de Villena, the hexagonal castle is dramatically sited. It was abandoned, then restored in the 19th century, and is now open to view. The furnishings are long gone, but the Mudéjar ceilings are worth seeing. Fray Luis de León (1527–1591), scholar-poet-professor at the University of Salamanca, was born in the village.

SOUTHWEST OF BELMONTE

Should you continue southwest on N 420 you'll pass through **Mota del Cuervo** (16 km/10 miles from Belmonte), a classic Manchegan village noted for its Quixote-style windmills. About 12 km (7½ miles) west of Mota del Cuervo (north on N 301, southwest on TO 104) is **El Toboso**, a tiny village where Don Quixote's Dulcinea supposedly lived. The **Museo Casa Dulcinea del Toboso** is an interesting example of a prosperous 17th-century Manchegan homestead, but has little (if anything) to do with the fictional Dulcinea.

ALBACETE

At Mota del Cuervo you can get on N 301 and head southeast to Albacete (108 km/67 miles). A good place to break your journey is on the outskirts of Albacete at the comfortable and modern ▶ **Parador de La Mancha**. Albacete has its attractions too: the Museo de Albacete (with interesting archaeological finds), lodged in a stunning modern building facing the Abelardo Sanchez park, and a restaurant, **Nuestro Bar**, Calle Alcalde Conangla 102, with delicious dishes, a charming setting, and bargain prices (for Spain); Tel: (9-67) 22-72-15.

Just 14 km (9 miles) southeast of Albacete is **Chinchilla de Monte Aragón**, an enchanting hill town (definitely worth your while) with a restored 15th-century castle, a delightful main square (Plaza de la Mancha), and a Gothic-Renaissance church (Santa María del Salvador).

From Albacete N 301 continues on to Murcia, on the Mediterranean coast (see the Valencia chapter).

NORTHEASTERN LA MANCHA
Pastrana

Like most Spanish towns, Pastrana, 98 km (61 miles) east of Madrid (via N II northeast to Guadalajara and then N 320/C 200 south) and some 130 km (80 miles) from Cuenca (west on N 400, then north on C 200, the road to Guadalajara), has its share of serendipitous artistic surprises. Pastrana's real finds are inside the **Iglesia Colegiata**, a small Gothic church with a Romanesque portal. It would be sufficient to discover the imposing retable with ten paintings by Juan de Borgoña, the fine choir stalls, and the tomb of the powerful and mysterious Ana Mendoza de la Cerda, known as the one-eyed princess of Eboli. But that's merely a prelude.

In the treasury, through doors with artful bas-reliefs, there are rooms full of reliquaries, *santos,* antique chests, silver and gold chalices, and vestments. But the raison d'être of a visit consists of four richly detailed **Gothic tapestries**, some of which date to the 15th century. In sweeping form, they depict the 1471 conquest of Tangier and Arzila in Morocco by Alfonso V of Portugal (El Africano), and are thought to be the work of the great Portuguese artist Nuno Gonçalves. They were supposedly a gift of Philip II to Ana Mendoza, who bequeathed them to Pastrana.

Siguenza

Sigüenza, 131 km (81 miles) northeast of Madrid on N II and C 204 (117 km/73 miles from Pastrana by way of N 320/C 200 north to N II), is the northeastern outpost of Castilla–La Mancha and is often overlooked (more's the pity) by foreign visitors, unless they are en route from Madrid to Zaragoza and Barcelona via **Guadalajara**. The last, badly bombed during the Civil War, is worth a very quick stop largely for its **Palacio del Infantado**, the Plateresque palace (1461–1492) of the Mendozas, with a totally restored diamond-pointed façade and graceful patio with a double gallery of columns.

Sigüenza is something else: a thoroughly medieval town on the Río Henares, with sloping streets that climb in layers up to a castle-fortress, which evolved from a Visigothic castle to a Moorish *alcazaba* (fortified residence). Since 1124, after the Christians captured Sigüenza, the castle has been much rebuilt and has served as a bishop's residence (Ferdinand, Isabella, and Juana la Loca were among its royal visitors), and now, finally, as a hostelry, ▶ **Parador Castillo de Sigüenza**. Luxurious as paradores go, Sigüenza's spacious rooms, with either courtyard or mountain view, and its grand public *salas* have kept their historic character, which is further enhanced by antiques and paintings and ceramics from times past. An interior grilled window in the parador overlooks the inside of the castle's nicely decorated Romanesque chapel.

THE LOWER TOWN

From the parador, a five-minute walk downhill on cobbled Calle Mayor brings you to the lower town and the graceful, though restored, Plaza Mayor, surrounded by porticoes and balconies. Much of the lower town has an old-fashioned 1950s look, but time has not, despite appearances, stood still here: Sigüenza was a Nationalist stronghold throughout the Civil War and sustained considerable damage. It is worth a walk along the side streets to see the intriguing façades of various early churches (in varying states of repair).

The Cathedral

On one side of the Plaza Major rises the **Catedral de Santa María**. The cathedral was begun in 1150 but was considerably altered in the 13th century and later. Its Romanesque-Gothic-Renaissance façade has a French flavor; its interior is completely Spanish. An expansive sweep of elongated Gothic arches with towering vaulted ceilings is delightful, and so are the beautiful 13th-century rose window, an ornate Neoclassical 16th-century retable above the main altar, a multi-tiered lacy valentine of an altarpiece (called Retablo de Santa Librada, after Sigüenza's patron saint), and many intriguing side chapels. As in many Spanish cathedrals, there is little light—to see the numerous and eclectic delights here, you need to look for the custodian in charge of light and keys.

To the right of the main altar is the 16th-century chapel of the Arce family, with its pièce de résistance, a delicately sculpted reclining alabaster figure of a youthful knight, dreamily lounging through eternity. He is El Doncel (The Young Knight) de Sigüenza, Martín Vázquez de Arce, Queen Isabella's page, who was killed in 1486 at the gates of Granada.

The cathedral's tour de force is inside the 16th-century **Sacrista de las Cabezas** (Sacristy of the Heads): the work of Plateresque architect Alonso de Covarrubias. Carved in high relief on medallions that completely cover the barrel-vaulted ceiling are 300 heads of bishops, scholars, soldiers, and other notables. Like a Chinese treasure box, the sacristy opens into the **Capilla Espíritu Sanctu**, with its *Annunciation* by El Greco, Titian's *Descent from the Cross,* and other paintings. From the late-Gothic cloisters you enter a salon of tapestries, with so many 17th-century Flemish tapestries that they have to be hung from rods like carpets displayed in a showroom. The cathedral, like Sigüenza's many other churches and monuments, has a blue-and-white ceramic plaque attached to its façade delineating the major treasures inside, a helpful précis for visitors in a hurry.

Museo Diocesano

Diagonally across from the cathedral is the Museo Diocesano, lodged in a Neoclassical 18th-century building. Its prize is Francisco Zurbarán's *Inmaculada,* painted with great clarity. Unfortunately, many of the museum's vast assemblage of Romanesque sculptures have been crudely repainted, and the museum looks as though it is in need of funds for upkeep.

SHOPPING AND DINING IN SIGUENZA
Artesanía de Sigüenza, Calle Mayor 17 (the long street leading up from the cathedral to the parador), is a tiny shop with attractive local crafts, mirrors, ceramics, and wooden chests. A modest local gathering place, **Hostal-Restaurante El Doncel**, Paseo de la Almeda 3, serves solid regional dishes such as *migas castellanas* (bread crumbs, ham, *chorizo,* and fried egg) and *cabrito asado con ajillo* (roast kid with garlic); Tel: (9-49) 39-00-01. For more stylish, and pricier, dining (in alcoves ringed by antique stone arches), the best choice in town is the parador. Try the *cabrito asado en cazuela* (in casserole), and save room for a special honeyed dessert cake, *borrachitos seguntinos.*

ATIENZA
Save time if possible for a side trip to Atienza, 31 km (19 miles) northwest on C 114. This walled Castilian village, once a Moorish stronghold liberated by El Cid, boasts a ruined castle, a medieval Plaza Mayor, and seven churches with Romanesque remains. The church of the Trinidad contains a Rococo chapel, a gift of Philip V.

GETTING AROUND
There is frequent train service (15 trains a day) from Madrid's Atocha station to Toledo, a one-and-a-half-hour trip, and good bus service from the main Madrid station. From Madrid to Cuenca is a three-hour train (five a day) or bus (four daily) ride; Sigüenza is on the Madrid–Zaragoza train route, with ten trains a day, taking one and a half to two and a half hours. To visit the other towns requires changing at major junctions, such as Toledo, Ciudad Real, or Cuenca. You *can* get there from here—but it takes time. As elsewhere in Spain, there are discoveries to be made at every bend in the road, so a car is unquestionably the way to go if at all possible.

RENFE (the Spanish national railway system) operates two weekend excursion train-and-bus tours in summer (through September): La Mancha (which includes several villages, Almagro, and an overnight in Valdepeñas) and Ciudad Encantada de Cuenca, as well as a one-day (Saturdays, Sundays, and holidays) guided tour to Sigüenza called Doncel de Sigüenza.

ACCOMMODATIONS REFERENCE

The hotel rates listed below are projected rates for 1994, for double room, double occupancy, in pesetas. We strongly recommend that you confirm the price when making reservations.

When dialing telephone numbers from outside the country, drop the 9 in the area code.

▶ **Hostal del Cardenal.** Plazoleta de Alfonso VI, Paseo de Recaredo 24, 45003 **Toledo.** Tel: (9-25) 22-49-00; Fax: 22-29-91. 9,250 pts.

▶ **Hotel Beatriz.** Carretera Avila, 45005 **Toledo.** Tel: (9-25) 22-22-11; Fax: 21-58-65. 13,900 pts.

▶ **Hotel Carlos V.** Trastamara 1, 45001 **Toledo.** Tel: (9-25) 22-21-00; Fax: 22-21-05. 9,000 pts.

▶ **Hotel Cueva del Fraile.** Carretera Cuenca–Buenache, km 7, Hoz del Huécar, 16001 **Cuenca.** Tel: (9-69) 21-15-71; Fax: 21-15-73. 10,400 pts.

▶ **Hotel Pintor El Greco.** Alamillos del Tránsito 13, 45002 **Toledo.** Tel: (9-25) 21-42-50; Fax: 21-58-19. 8,500 pts.

▶ **Hotel Torremangana.** Calle San Ignacio de Loyola 9, 16002 **Cuenca.** Tel: (9-69) 22-33-51; Fax: 22-96-71. 17,500 pts.

▶ **María Cristina Hotel.** Marqués de Mendigorría 1, 45003 **Toledo.** Tel: (9-25) 21-32-02; Fax: 21-69-54. 9,830 pts.

▶ **Parador de Almagro.** Ronda de San Francisco 31, 13270 **Almagro.** Tel: (9-26) 86-01-00; Fax: 86-01-50. 9,000–11,000 pts.

▶ **Parador Castillo de Sigüenza.** Plaza del Castillo, 19250 **Sigüenza.** Tel: (9-49) 39-01-00; Fax: 39-13-64. 10,000–11,500 pts.

▶ **Parador Conde de Orgaz.** Cerro del Emperador, 45000 **Toledo.** Tel: (9-25) 22-18-50; Fax: 22-51-66. 14,500 pts.

▶ **Parador de Cuenca.** Paseo Hoz de Huécar s/n, 16001 **Cuenca.** Tel: (9-69) 23-23-20; Fax: (9-69) 23-25-34. 14,500 pts.

▶ **Parador de La Mancha.** Carretera Nacional 301, km 260, 02006 **Albacete.** Tel: (9-67) 22-94-50; Fax: 22-60-92. 10,000–10,500 pts.

▶ **Parador Marqués de Villena.** Avenida Amigos de los Castillos 3, 16213 **Alarcón.** Tel: (9-69) 33-13-50; Fax: 33-11-07. 14,000 pts.

EXTREMA-DURA

By Carla Hunt

Carla Hunt is a freelance writer and contributor of articles to North American and international newspapers and magazines. She travels regularly on the Iberian Peninsula.

According to a recent survey, there are 6,591 storks' nests in 31 of Spain's 50 provinces. A large number of these nests—perched atop church steeples, belfries, spires, towers, turrets, and domes—are in the two provinces that make up Extremadura: Cáceres has 1,687 and Badajoz has 1,333.

Extremadura (which means "land beyond the Río Duero") is the vast, beautiful, and little-visited region called "the cradle of the *conquistadores*" that lies southwest of Madrid along the Portuguese border: This area produced seven of the most famed explorers/conquerors of the Americas. Extremadura cannot lay claim to Christopher Columbus, but the area's native sons do include Hernán Cortés, who marched through Mexico; Francisco Pizarro, who brought down Peru's Inca Empire; Pedro de Alvarado, who did the same to the Maya of Guatemala; Pedro de Valdivia, who founded Santiago but was unable to master the Mapuche Indians of Chile; Vasco Núñez de Balboa, the first European to sight the Pacific Ocean; Francisco de Orellana, the first navigator of the Amazon; and Hernando de Soto, who sailed the Mississippi River and conquered Florida.

The roots of this phenomenon lie almost literally in the soil of Extremadura. The ancestors of these 16th-century *conquistadores* and of today's rather stolid Extremeños were the veterans of the legions of Emperor Caesar Augustus, who in 23 B.C. gave them land around Mérida to farm upon their retirement from active duty. During the Middle Ages the sons of Extremadura filled the ranks of such Christian corps as the Knights Templar, the Knights of Santiago, and the Knights of

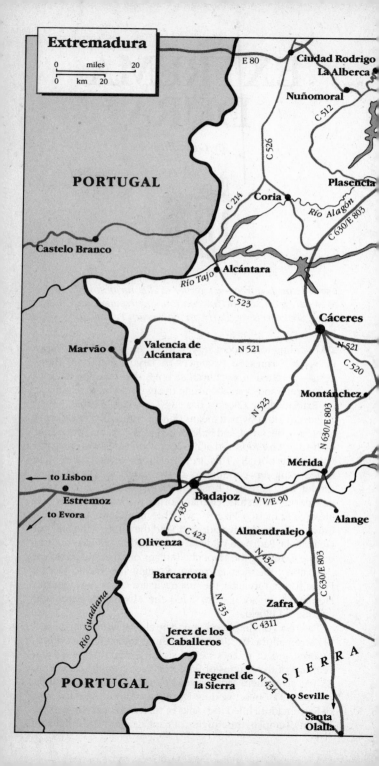

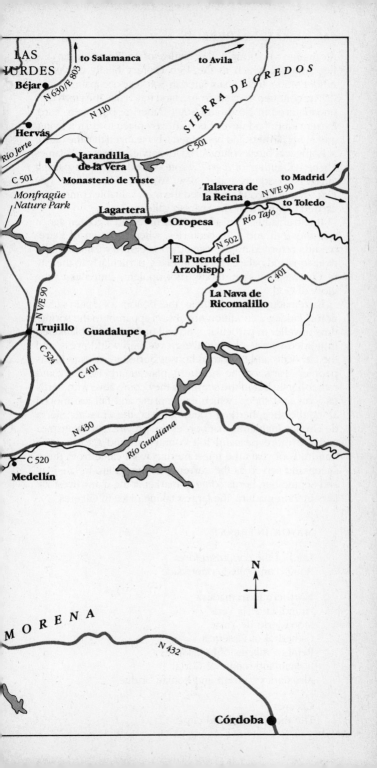

Alcántara, who fought the battles of La Reconquista (the Reconquest), which in the 15th century finally drove the infidel Moors from Spain after an 800-year occupation.

The conquerors came from a land much like the lands they encountered in North and South America: big, open, hard. Extremadura had never been an easy place to earn a living, and many farmers and herdsmen who realized that the future at home was bleak volunteered for service overseas. As James Michener, author of *Iberia*, wrote, "Uneducated, despairing villagers conquered the New World [where] their raw Extremaduran courage proved the most valuable commodity carried westward by the Spanish galleons."

If Extremadura could be said to have had a golden age, it was the 16th and 17th centuries, when the men of Extremadura returned home, using their acquired wealth to build mansions and palaces for themselves, particularly in the city of Cáceres, and rich, though not opulent, churches to the glory of God.

Extremadura still sits near the bottom of Spain's economic ladder, a condition not always apparent to the springtime traveller in particular, who will find the fields blanketed in golden wheat, silvery olive groves, and wildflowers, and the city walls and balconied houses buried in roses as big as peonies. Parts of the northern plateau are forested and rather harsh, but in the summers they come alive with herds of goats and sheep, which each spring and fall are moved along the sheepherding route between the dramatic Sierra de Gredos highlands that border the province of Salamanca and the more peaceful hill country around Cáceres. For hundreds of years the finest merino wool came from these sheep and served as the currency of the realm. In late May and September, herds come to market at the many livestock fairs in Extremadura, the largest taking place in Cáceres.

MAJOR INTEREST

Land of the *conquistadores*
Rough, unspoiled countryside

Northern Extremadura
Jarandilla de la Vera
Monasterio de Yuste
Cathedral of Plasencia
Remote villages of Las Hurdes
Roman and medieval Coria
Alcántara's convent and Roman bridge

Cáceres
The monumental old city

Casa de las Veletas archaeological and ethnographic
museum

Trujillo
The Pizarro family palace
The beautiful Plaza Mayor
Arab fortress

Guadalupe
Franciscan monastery

Mérida
Roman theater complex
Museum of Roman art and artifacts

Medellín, Cortés's hometown
Olivenza's Portuguese architecture

Zafra
Castle of the dukes of Feria

Jerez de los Caballeros
Castle of the Templars
San Bartolomé church

The regional tourist office has borrowed a page from ancient Gaul and divided Extremadura into three parts. The northern region, roughly angled from the Trujillo/Plasencia/Guadalupe axis north to the rather inaccessible mountain area of Las Hurdes, which lies south of Salamanca, is called "green Extremadura." Natives of Las Hurdes may surprise you if you head that far north: They are blond and blue-eyed, reminders of their Celtic and Visigothic ancestors. They are also tough, dour, and rather less friendly than Extremadurans to the south. In fact, *adiós* (good-bye) is hello in this part of the country.

The second division, between the Cáceres/Trujillo parallel and Mérida, to the south, and stretching to the western border with Portugal, is an extensive rolling plain—the so-called "route of the discoverers"—linking the hometowns of most of the *conquistadores*. Herein lie the most interesting sights, from remnants of a Roman past when this area was called Lusitania to outposts of Moorish occupation. The southern part of Extremadura is designated "the route of the little white towns," a term seemingly borrowed from neighboring Andalusia, which has more white towns of greater interest and is served by better roads. However, the southern Extremadurans do whitewash their houses and share the sunny dispositions of their southern, Mediterranean-bound countrymen.

Extremadura sits on La Meseta, Spain's immense central plateau—a mountain-rimmed, rocky and dry, partially forested and wonderfully spacious land, sizzling in summer and freezing in winter, that stretches from the far north to the Andalusian border. In this particular corner, seemingly adrift in all that open space, there are monumental things to see. To get the best effect, view them against the spring and fall landscapes.

Among Extremadura's pleasures are its sharp cheeses, Montánchez ham and sausages, wild game in season, codfish dishes, and gazpacho. You don't come to Extremadura for a gourmet experience, however. You come for a grand and unspoiled countryside and for history as recorded in the remembrances of things past: cave paintings from Paleolithic times (as yet not very accessible), stone dolmens from the Celts, Roman ruins, Mudejar architecture, Romanesque and Gothic churches, hilltop fortresses, quaint medieval villages, and walled towns.

You should also come with a dictionary—English is most definitely not spoken here. In exchange for the benefits of travelling without crowds and enjoying a most interesting and enchanting region, you have the drawbacks of little material in English at the tourist offices, and generally few English-speaking guides available to show you around. (Guests at the region's paradores will find that concierges usually have one or two on call.)

You will also find in touring Extremadura that many sights and historic buildings are *cerrado* (closed). The reason given locally is that many treasures have been stolen from historic civic and religious buildings. This can be frustrating for the visitor. Sometimes the only way to see a church is to be there for mass, or to happen upon it on a religious holiday, local saint's day, or to peek in during the confirmation and wedding seasons in May and June. In tiny villages, often a neighbor has the key to the church—the word for "key" is *llave;* "open" is *abierto*.

The Wines of Extremadura

Extremadura is a harsh and dry land, and it is tempting to say that Cortés and the rest of the *conquistadores* left home in search of better food and wine. Most of the area's wine production, centered at the town of Almendralejo (which has an interesting bullring decorated in ceramics and iron work), south of Mérida, is distilled into alcohol or sold in bulk to the wineless provinces of the Cantabrian coast. **Tierra de Barros** (Badajoz), which takes its name from the clay earth used to make pottery in this region, is Extremadura's only *denominación de origen*. Located in the western foothills near the Portuguese border, it has long been known by aficionados of regional wines for its powerful, deep-colored reds. Although in the past much of the produce of this area has been distilled to make grape spirits, many bodegas are starting to produce high-quality table wines. Lar de Barros is a noteworthy red wine, made from a blend of Tempranillo, Graciano, and Garnacha grapes.

There are a few other artisan wines, such as Cañamero and Montánchez (Cáceres), that are much admired locally. Cañamero is often cloudy, which its admirers say proves it is unfiltered, thereby giving it character. Montánchez can seldom be found outside the spectacular village of the same name, about 50 km (30 miles) southeast of Cáceres on C 520. Isolated and ancient, **Montánchez** is resplendent with stunning views and a charming statue of the Virgin in the tiny ceramic-lined hermitage chapel that shares the perch above the village with massive crumbling fortification walls and toppled Roman temple columns. All this makes the trip out to sample its wine and legendary mountain hams well worth the trouble: The ascent by car is steep and spectacular.

Marqués de Cáceres, an excellent Rioja that can be found all across Spain, is not, as suggested by its name, from the Extremaduran town of Cáceres.

—Gerry Dawes

Travelling in Extremadura

We start our coverage of Extremadura in the north, taking the route from Madrid to Oropesa and turning north via Jarandilla to Plasencia, Alcántara, and Coria in Cáceres province. (Alternately, you can come directly south to this region from Salamanca). Then we head south to the city of Cáceres, before heading east to Trujillo and Guadalupe, after which we work our way farther south to Mérida, Zafra, and Jerez de los Caballeros. We wind up our coverage of the area at Olivenza, south of Badajoz near the Portuguese border.

Driving off the beaten path in Extremadura is time-consuming but not rugged. Unless you are heading, say, down to the Roman baths tucked away in the village of Alange, south of Mérida, even the two-lane roads are fairly well paved, and there is little traffic. And if you ensure yourself a good night's sleep and a decent meal by planning your trip around Extremadura's half-dozen excellent and historic paradores, you will have quite a comfortable journey.

Extremadura fits naturally and most quickly into the travel corridor between Madrid and Lisbon. The N V/E 90, the most direct and well-paved route, will deliver you directly to Trujillo or Mérida for several days of sightseeing before you continue on your way to Portugal. You can also visit Extremadura most directly on three other routes: on a wide swing between Madrid and Seville, cutting on and off the north–south route through central Extremadura (N 630/E

803); on a round trip from Seville, also entering the province on N 630; from Portugal, taking the main road (N 4) east from Lisbon.

THE ROUTE FROM MADRID

If you do drive to Extremadura from Madrid, break up the drive with a stop in **Talavera de la Reina**, on the edge of La Mancha (110 km/68 miles from Madrid), to see the historic pottery exhibits at the **Museo de Ruiz de Luna** or to lunch at **Un Alto en el Camino**, at km 119 (Plaza General Primo de Rivera 5, closed Tuesdays); Tel: (9-25) 80-41-07. Continuing toward Oropesa, turn off the highway at the signs for **El Puente del Arzobispo**, a town whose pottery is as interesting as that of Talavera, if less well known. A mile west of Oropesa is **Lagartera**, famous for its lovely lace.

Oropesa, 14 km (9 miles) north of El Puente del Arzobispo and 33 km (20 miles) west of Talavera, is accessible to the Sierra de Gredos, an area popular with hunters. The ▶ **Parador Virrey de Toledo**, in the town's 14th-century castle, will make special arrangements for hunting parties. The parador was reopened in the fall of 1992 after a long renovation. Its kitchen has earned much praise in the past.

NORTHERN EXTREMADURA
The Plasencia Area

Just west of Oropesa is the Extremadura border, to the north is the Sierra de Gredos, and to the northwest is the wonderful Parador Carlos V in Jarandilla de la Vera, which will also serve the hunter well and presents an appropriately historical introduction to Extremadura's rich past.

JARANDILLA DE LA VERA

To get to Jarandilla, turn off N V/E 90 at Oropesa and drive northwest through the lovely farmlands of the Tiétar river valley, past fruit orchards and half-timbered houses, to route C 501, and continue west to Jarandilla. This is a very pretty area, white with cherry blossoms in spring and terraced with vineyards and tobacco fields. The area's brick, somewhat Moorish-looking storage barns house drying tobacco leaves. Jarandilla's 15th-century castle, briefly the dwelling of Holy Roman Emperor Charles V (Spain's King Carlos I), while he awaited the completion of his rooms in the nearby Monasterio de Yuste, is now converted into the ▶ **Parador Carlos V**. The food is very good at the parador, especially the fresh game in season.

Just past Jarandilla de la Vera (a mile from the picturesque village of Cuacos), a small, well-marked road leads to the **Monasterio de Yuste**, located on a forested preserve. After four decades commanding the Hapsburg Empire, the great Charles V retired here in his final years, painfully burdened by severe attacks of gout. In his apartments, maintained as they were when he died in 1558, visitors taking the tour of the monastery will find his wooden gout chair among the original furnishings. The paintings and priceless tapestries, however, have gone elsewhere.

PLASENCIA

From Jarandilla it's less than an hour's drive (55 km/34 miles) west on C 501 to Plasencia, a pleasant, well-preserved town that you can easily tour on foot. You can leave your car near the old quarter and the arcaded **Plaza Mayor**, whose clock tower features a life-size figure that rings the hourly chimes. For centuries, there has been a weekly market in the plaza, and the rural tradition continues on Tuesdays.

You will find Plasencia's streets lined with aristocratic palaces bearing heraldic signs and iron balconies on their façades, as well as a splendid medieval bridge with six sturdy arches spanning the Río Jerte.

The Cathedral

Plasencia's outstanding cathedral complex is actually two churches joined by a common wall. The first building was started in the 13th century and the second (designed by Enrique Egas) added in the 16th century, but neither was ever completed. In the older church, which has a peculiar Moorish-style dome, you will find a 13th-century statue of the Virgin of La Paloma in the San Pablo chapel (once the chapter house) and a lovely Romanesque-Gothic cloister with finely worked capitals. The newer, Gothic church, which serves as the cathedral, blends into the older church. Its tall columns reach right up into the ribs of the vault, an impressive sight. In addition to an altarpiece decorated with statues by the 17th-century sculptor Gregorio Fernández, there are 16th-century choir stalls carved by Rodrigo Alemán.

Staying and Dining in Plasencia

For a sampling of regional cuisine in Plasencia, try the best restaurant in town—the ▶ **Alfonso VIII**, in the hotel of the same name. From the outside, the Alfonso, centrally located at Avenida Alfonso VIII 34, is no charmer; inside, however, it is more welcoming, if rather ordinary, and its 57 rooms are air-conditioned. (Parking is available at the hotel.)

Las Hurdes

Travellers who truly want to get off the beaten path can head north from Plasencia to the Las Hurdes region of Extremadura, whose villages of crooked, half-timbered houses are set amidst grandly scaled scenery. Regional folktales tell of rampaging demons, and the region's poverty was the subject of Luis Buñuel's 1932 film *Land without Bread*. Although Spain's building boom has extended to include some new dams, schools, and roads in this area, it is still one of the most isolated corners of the country, and finding your way around requires a good map (and perhaps a visit to the tourist office in Plasencia on Plaza San Martín).

Hervás, a pretty village where a large Jewish community prospered under the protection of the Knights Templar, is about 42 km (26 miles) north of Plasencia just off N 630. It has a well-preserved *aljama* (Jewish quarter), complete with synagogue. Nineteen kilometers (12 miles) north of Hervás is the region's largest town, **Béjar** (roughly halfway between Plasencia and Salamanca), which has one of the few hotels in Las Hurdes, ▶ **Hotel Colón**, Calle Colón 42, a comfortable place with a restaurant.

A longer excursion from Plasencia might include a drive north some 75 km (47 miles) along C 512 to the picturesque villages of **Nuñomoral, Fragosa**, and **El Gasco** (off the paved road beyond Fragosa), where the Miacera Gorge falls tumble down a 180-foot drop. Continue on to visit **Huetre**, which may seem the most remote village of all, for its inhabitants still wear traditional dress.

West of Plasencia

CORIA

Seventy-seven kilometers (48 miles) west of Plasencia (take N 630/E 803 south, then turn north on C 526), and due north of Cáceres, is Coria, overlooking the valley of the Río Alagón, a tributary of the grander Río Tajo. The town is surrounded by solid Roman walls; its bridge also dates from Roman times, while the dramatic castle and cathedral are medieval. The cathedral's Gothic edifice is rather interesting, embellished with elegant Plateresque decoration and topped by a Baroque tower. Inside, the single aisle has decorative ribbed vaulting above and stone-slab flooring carved with family crests covering the tombs of those buried below.

ALCANTARA

Alcántara, about a 70-km (43-mile) drive southwest of Coria (go north on C 526, turn south on C 214, and follow the signs), close to the Portuguese border, sits high above an even more dramatic bridge, built in A.D. 105 to span the Tajo. Cross this bridge to climb the steep road into the once-fortified town where the Knights of Alcántara, one of the great orders of chivalry in Spain, presided. They played a major role in the Reconquest (during which they were called the Knights of San Julián Pereiro until they changed their name to Alcántara after defending the city against the Moors in the 13th century). The knights were also active in the wars with Portugal and even in those of independence against France. The castle of the knights is now in ruins, as is their 16th-century church. Have a look at the convent of **San Benito**, with its newly restored Plateresque façade.

The favorite local dish in Alcántara is partridge, but there is nary a restaurant to recommend in town. (When you are on the road in Extremadura, picnic food can play an important role in your midday meal.) But there's a relatively broad spectrum of restaurants in Cáceres, 62 km (39 miles) southeast via C 523 and N 521.

CENTRAL EXTREMADURA

Cáceres

To reach Cáceres, capital of its own province and the most important city in Extremadura, directly from Madrid take N V/E 90 west from Madrid to Trujillo, then N 521 west (a journey of 308 km/191 miles in all). If you are coming from Plasencia, Cáceres is 84 km (52 miles) south on N 630.

Cáceres is a treasure trove of historic buildings, most of which are enclosed within well-preserved walls dating from Roman, Moorish, and medieval times; 12 of the original towers protecting the enclosure still stand, many now crowned with enormous storks' nests. The city was founded by the Romans in 28 B.C., but the name goes back only as far as the Moorish Almohad conquest, when it was called Qazris.

The ancient walled city extends up the hill from the Plaza del General Mola, which has parking spaces in the center and lots of little cafés and shops under its surrounding arcades. These shops sell traditional handicrafts, such as embroidery and the colorful straw bonnets decorated with wool and mirrors that were once worn for special occasions. The really fancy hats are authentic and interesting souvenirs (if you don't find one on this square, look in the gift shops **Acebo** and **Jacinta González** on Plaza San Jorge, a square within the walls dominated by the Iglesia de San Francisco Javier).

Before entering the walls, stop at the **tourist office** (to the left of the main stairs) for a map. Then pass through the main gate and turn left toward the Plaza de Santa María.

WITHIN THE WALLS

There is a certain sameness (or unity, depending on your aesthetic sense) to the palaces, manor houses, and religious buildings of golden stone and pale brick that flank the narrow streets and tiny plazas of Cáceres. Yet many of the manor houses, built with wealth acquired during the conquest of the Americas, are distinguished by the owners' coats of arms over the doors and by particularly beautiful courtyards. The most elegant square in the city is the **Plaza de Santa María**, flanked by a bishop's palace and the fine 16th-century Gothic **Iglesia de Santa María**, which has a lovely carved cedar reredos and whose floor tombstones cover the graves of members of the city's most illustrious families. Just off the square is the Casa de los Golfines de Abajo, a palace that hosted the Reyes Católicos (Ferdinand and Isabella) on their visits to Cáceres; its Gothic-Moorish façade is one of the town's most outstanding.

Near the walls below the Plaza de Santa María is the **Casa de Toledo-Moctezuma**, once owned by Juan Cano de Saavedra, who accompanied Hernán Cortés to Mexico and eventually married Princess Tecuixpo Ixlaxochitl, daughter of the defeated Aztec emperor Montezuma (Moctezuma in Spanish). Also near the plaza is the **Casa del Mono** (Monkey House), at Calle Olmos and Cuesta de Aldana, which houses a museum of provincial paintings, sculpture, and religious art.

Leave the Plaza de Santa María area and wend your way upward to the **Plaza de San Mateo**, near the top of the old town. The Plaza de San Mateo was once the Moorish center of town, and its Gothic church, the **Iglesia de San Mateo**, standing tall at the highest point of the city, was built in the 14th century on the site of a former mosque. On the same plaza is the **Palacio de las Cigüeñas** (Storks' Palace), the only palace left in town with a fortified tower. (In the 15th century Queen Isabella got so fed up with the constant feuding among the families of Cáceres that she ordered all the other towers knocked down.)

Most notable on this square is the **Casa de las Veletas** (House of Weather Vanes), which incorporates part of the Moorish *alcázar*. Beneath Veletas you descend by a stone staircase into a splendid cistern whose grand brick Moorish arches reflect in the waters. The Veletas houses an excellent museum. Artifacts in the archaeological section date to prehistoric times, when local inhabitants were painting caves and hunting with Stone Age weapons. More current displays are from the Arab and medieval periods. In the ethnographic section, colorful dioramas document historical costumes and customs of Extremadura. The small house museums such as this one, and a few churches, give visitors their only opportunity to view the interiors of Cáceres.

STAYING AND DINING IN CACERES

Quite close to the Plaza de San Mateo, at Calle Ancha 6, is the ▶ Parador de Cáceres, which occupies the premises of a 14th-century mansion with a big square tower, iron balconies, and various coats of arms on the walls, including that of Diego de Ulloa, who was the commander of the city at the time the tower and palace were first used. The interior of this elegant inn is hung with medieval trappings such as old tapestries and suits of armor. Public areas, as well as the 27 guest rooms, are grouped around a central courtyard.

The parador now has competition for classy, charming accommodations in Cáceres: the brand-new ▶ Meliá Cáceres, whose 86 rooms occupy the former Castillo Ogvendo, on the small Plaza de San Juan, just outside the city walls. The Occidental chain has just opened the deluxe ▶ Hotel Quinto Centenario, a modern hotel with a pool and tennis courts, located just out of town on the road to Salamanca. In the commercial part of Cáceres, accommodations are good and comfortable at the ▶ Alcántara and the ▶ Extremadura, which cater to business travellers. Both are on Avenida Virgen de Guadalupe, and the Alcántara has a pool amidst its gardens.

The parador's restaurant, which features regional specialties, is now considered the best in town, although the Atrio, in the commercial district at Avenida de España 30, won an award as the best restaurant of Extremadura in 1989 for such dishes as sole stuffed with salmon and topped with saffron sauce, and warm tarts of banana and chocolate cream; its wine cellar is also pretty good for the area; Tel: (9-27) 24-29-28. If you'd like to dine in a former residential palace, try the excellent El Figón de Eustaquio, at Plaza de San Juan 12, which lists air-cured ham and local river trout among its specialties; Tel: (9-27) 24-81-94. El Palacio de los Vinos, right next door to the parador, at Calle Ancha 4, is a convenient and less costly alternative for wine and *tapas* or a full dinner; Tel: (9-27) 21-08-59. Less expensive restaurants and cafés are grouped around Plaza del General Mola, near the tourist office.

HERMITA DE LA VIRGEN DE LA MONTAÑA

Before you leave Cáceres, take a quick trip just southeast of the city to the Hermita de la Virgen de la Montaña, the hilltop sanctuary of the city's patron saint, the Mountain Virgin, who shares the site with an enormous statue of Christ. At the end of April, just after the festival of Saint George, who is honored in Cáceres with a parade of costumed Christians and Moors, the faithful make a pilgrimage to the lovely chapel of the Mountain Virgin. From the hermitage you can take a last look at Cáceres, as its vantage point gives you a bird's-eye view of the town.

Trujillo

A 49-km (30-mile) drive east of Cáceres along a good straight road (N 521), set atop a granite hill just off the N V/E 90 (the highway from Madrid), is Trujillo, which has been inhabited in turn by Celts, Romans, Moors, and Christians. Within its ancient walls is a precious legacy of palaces, churches, noble mansions, monuments, dozens of towers, and a hilltop castle.

THE PLAZA MAYOR

Life revolves around the old town and the Plaza Mayor, one of Spain's most beautiful squares, which is particularly enjoyable in the evening light. The plaza, on which you can park your car, is oddly shaped, with many levels connected by wide flights of stairs. The centerpiece of the square is the great bronze equestrian statue of native son Francisco Pizarro, cast in 1927 by American sculptors Mary Harriman and Charles Runsey, who provided both rider and horse with hats. (There is a twin statue in Lima, Peru.)

Trujillo was the birthplace of the Pizarros, whose family palace, the **Palacio de la Conquista**, on the Plaza Mayor, was built by Hernando Pizarro with riches from the New World. Both Pizarro brothers sailed for the Americas, but it is Francisco who is "credited" with the destruction of the Inca Empire in Peru. He married an Inca princess, killed the local ruler, took possession of his capital, appropriated his riches, and was in turn murdered himself. His brother Hernando fared better, marrying his half-Inca niece and returning to Trujillo to live royally ever after as the marqués de la Conquista. Other history-making Trujillo natives are Francisco de Orellana, the first explorer of the Amazon; Francisco de la Casas, who accompanied Cortés to Mexico and founded the city of Trujillo in Honduras; and Diego García de Paredes, founder of Trujillo in Venezuela. Hundreds of other Trujillanos joined in the Americas expeditions, and many Latin American towns (as well as at least one dictator) bear their names.

Other buildings of note on the Plaza Mayor are the **Palacio de los Duques de San Carlos**, which is now a convent, and the **Iglesia de San Martín**, whose 18th-century organ is still in use.

INSIDE THE WALLS

Off the square you pass through one of seven entrance gates into the old walled city, an ideal place to wander up and down narrow, stony streets. The Gothic **Iglesia de Santa María**, on Plaza de Santa María in the center of the walled city, is the pantheon of Trujillo's great *conquistadores*. The seats used by Ferdinand and Isabella when they infrequently attended Mass here are still in place beneath the rose window. Walk far enough uphill and you'll come to a massive crenellated wall, reinforced by big square towers and a 12th-century Arab fortress called **El Castillo**. Above the keep stands the 16th-century statue of the Virgen de la Victoria, patron saint of the city.

Visitors to Trujillo at midday on Saturdays and Sundays can enjoy a close-up look at the 15th-century former Franciscan **Convento de la Coria**, when it opens its doors to the public from 11:30 A.M. to 2:00 P.M. The convent is within the city walls, forming part of them, and stands alongside one of the original city gates. The Xavier de Salas family foundation sponsored restoration work on the premises, which are used for exhibitions and education projects. The views of the valley from the second floor show the harshness of a land that traditionally drove its young men to make their fortunes elsewhere, such as the Americas. Ask for directions to La Coria at the tourist office on the Plaza Mayor.

STAYING AND DINING IN TRUJILLO

The ▶ **Parador de Trujillo**, occupying part of the restored 16th-century convent of Santa Clara, may persuade you to stay longer than you had planned. The parador is about a five-minute walk along a cobbled street to the right off the Plaza Mayor, although if you're driving you'll take a longer route, as directed by signs. Many of the 46 rooms, now with canopied beds and marble baths, were once nuns' cells; the Renaissance cloister, with its gardens and fruit trees, is delightful. Breakfast is served in the old refectory; the vaulted dining room was once a chapel. The specialty of the house is *caldereta extremeña,* a savory stew made with either baby lamb or kid.

Meals are less expensive at the **Hostal Pizarro**, on the Plaza Mayor. The food here is hearty, made with fresh produce, but the house wine should be avoided.

Guadalupe

An 80-km (50-mile) drive east of Trujillo (southeast on C 524 and northeast on C 401), tucked in the folds of the Sierra de Guadalupe, is the pilgrimage site of Guadalupe. Guadalupe can also be reached directly from Madrid, by way of N V/E 90 to Talavera de la Reina and N 430 south to La Nava de Ricomalillo, at which point signs indicate the way to Guadalupe. Be forewarned: Although the road has recently been upgraded, this is a tough drive through the mountains. Be very cautious in poor weather.

Away from the storybook Monasterio de Guadalupe, the village of Guadalupe is quaint and quiet, with twisting little streets lined with stone houses whose tiny balconies are buried in flowers. Shops sell utilitarian and decorative wares in copper and brass, crafted in Guadalupe.

THE MONASTERIO DE GUADALUPE

The spectacular centerpiece and raison d'être of the town is the Franciscan Monasterio de Guadalupe. It was founded in the 14th century to house the Virgin of Guadalupe's statue, said to have been carved by Saint Luke, which was discovered by a shepherd shortly before Alfonso XI won his victory over the Moors in 1340. The king built this majestic Flamboyant Gothic shrine for the Hieronymite order of monks in the Virgin's honor, and over the years the Virgin became (and still is) the object of international pilgrimages. The *conquistadores* took their Extremaduran saint with them and founded namesake churches of Our Lady of Guadalupe in the Americas.

The feast day of the Virgin of Guadalupe, October 12, is dedicated to all Spanish-speaking people. To this day the faithful make the pilgrimage from miles around to pay their respects to the Virgin—by car, on foot, and on horseback, some of them spending two or more days on the road. An even grander gathering of pilgrims comes over the hills to this mountain sanctuary on September 8, El Día de Extremadura. Hotel space is at a premium for the September fête.

The monastery continued to be embellished by royalty and the faithful through the 18th century. It was abandoned in the 19th century but taken over and restored by Franciscans following the Spanish Civil War (1936–1939). It is now full of art treasures. Guided tours (45 minutes long, which is too short, so do it twice) are the only way to see the treasury rooms and the Mudejar cloisters, which close every day between 1:00 and 3:30 P.M.. The tour includes visits to the chapter house, with its splendid collection of illuminated books and Zurbarán paintings; the embroidery museum, with superb vestments and reliquaries; and the gold and white sacristy, with its eight major Zurbarán paintings of notable people associated with the monastery. Above the altar in the little chapel of Saint Jerome in the sacristy is one of Zurbarán's most famous works, *The Apotheosis of Saint Jerome,* actually hung in the space for which it was created.

The climax of the tour is a look at the Camarín, a chamber where the Virgin sits on an enamel throne, a tiny, richly dressed figure with a little black face. Christopher Columbus made a vow to this Virgin during a crossing to the New World and later travelled to Guadalupe to give thanks. Her reported miraculous powers attracted great wealth to the monastery from various *conquistadores,* royalty, and other admirers throughout the centuries.

SHOPPING, DINING, AND STAYING IN GUADALUPE

Guadalupe is known for its pottery, which has distinctive colors, and its copperware. There are many small artisans' shops around the monastery square where such local wares can be purchased. Several cafés on the square serve up coffee with honey-and-almond sweets called *muegados,* offering the best seats in the house for a frontal view of one of Spain's most important shrines to the Virgin Mary.

Some of Guadalupe's hotels are in historic buildings that attract sightseers as well as guests. Across from the monastery is the ▶ **Parador Guadalupe**, a 16th-century hospital-convent with a pool, gardens, and a patio full of lemon trees. A fine alternative is the ▶ **Hospedería del Real Monasterio**, which actually occupies a part of the Franciscan monastery and was once the hospital for pilgrims coming to venerate the statue of the Virgin of Guadalupe. The hotel's bar is in the Gothic cloister. Both hotels are charmingly furnished with historic reproductions; the Hospedería has a very good restaurant.

Mérida

To see the best of Roman Spain you must visit Mérida, on the Río Guadiana about 70 km (44 miles) due south of Cáceres on N 630. (It's also an easy drive from Trujillo, 88 km/55 miles southwest on N V/E 90.)

Mérida's history began in 23 B.C. when the emperor Augustus authorized the veterans of his fifth and tenth legions to retire from active service and take farms in the area. A bridge—the longest bridge of that period built in Spain—was built over the Río Guadiana, and Mérida became a primary link in communications between Seville to the south and Salamanca to the north. In imperial times the city was known as Augusta Emerita, and it became the capital of Lusitania, Rome's vast province on the Iberian Peninsula.

ARRIVING IN MERIDA

Mérida presents its most romantic face to those who arrive from the south, from Zafra or Seville, on the N 630/E 803, which crosses the Roman bridge over the Guadiana, bringing you immediately to the Moorish citadel. Coming in from the north on N 630 or N V/E 90, you leave the main highway, which continues to Badajoz, and pick your way through not overly attractive modern Mérida. Let the arrow-shaped signs guide you to the ▶ **Parador Vía de la Plata**, on Plaza de la Constitución, not only a lovely place to stay but a good place to have a drink and get directions and a map to the Roman ruins and other monuments that are scattered all over the city.

THE ROMAN RUINS

The Romans left a lavish legacy of monuments in Mérida, but they're rather far-flung, and you'll want to visit them by car. Drive northwest along Avenida Extremadura to the shell of the immense **Circus Maximus**, where the Lusitanians held chariot races and which was periodically flooded for the staging of naval battles. Then head south to the main theater and amphitheater.

The **Roman theater** is the gem of the remains, sitting incongruously close to modern Mérida. The theater was built in 24 B.C. by the Roman statesman Agrippa, with seating for 6,000. On the rebuilt stage statues of the gods stand once more in their niches among the columns; the chorus area is some 60 feet in diameter. The theater's rear wall is a long, two-story façade with 32 marble columns bearing Corinthian capitals on tall bases. Behind this are the marble-floored actors' rooms. The neighboring amphitheater once seated 15,000 spectators, who crowded in to witness chariot races and gladiator contests. The theater and amphitheater make up one of the most beautiful Roman complexes in Spain.

Behind the stage is a colonnade under which audiences gathered during intermission—as they still do today during the annual International Festival of Classical Drama. Greek and Roman comedies and tragedies, as well as ballet and symphony concerts, are presented from the last week in June to the first week in August. If you wish to attend, reserve tickets through your hotel when you book hotel reservations.

Near the Roman theater complex is the relatively new (opened in 1986) **Museo Nacional de Arte Romano**, housing some 32,000 pieces of Roman art and artifacts. Constructed especially for the collection, which is housed on three open levels, the museum is a monumental work with pale brick vaulted interiors, designed by Rafael Moneo, former chairman of the department of architecture at Harvard University's Graduate School of Design. In the process of construction, a Roman road was unearthed and incorporated into the building's basement. Many of the objects in the collection were stored for centuries in the old church of Santa Clara, and others were gathered from other corners of Spain. The huge mosaics set into walls and floors are the most exquisite displays, but the statuary, religious pieces, coins, jewelry, and everyday objects are all excellent. The museum is open 10:00 A.M. to 2:00 P.M. and 4:00 to 7:00 P.M.; closed Sundays.

Below the main archaeological area, just north of the museum, is the **Casa Romana del Anfiteatro**, a rich villa from the end of the first century, whose mosaic floor depicting people crushing grapes with their feet is surprisingly well preserved. South of the theater (next to the bullring) is another ancient house, the **Casa Romano del Mitraeo**, a first-century building with brilliant mosaic floors portraying the river gods worshiped by the cult of Mithras.

THE OLD TOWN

A landmark from Mérida's Moorish days is the **Alcazaba** (citadel), west of the Roman ruins at the end of the 60-arch Roman bridge that crosses the Río Guadiana at the southern entrance to the city. A square building, much longer than a football field on each side, it was originally built by the Moors and was last used by the Knights of Santiago. Much of the material used in construction came from Roman and Visigothic structures destroyed during the Muslim occupation. The castle has an interesting *aljibe* (water cistern), which over the centuries supplied Romans, Visigoths, and Moors.

Just north of the Alcazaba is Mérida's lively main square, the **Plaza España**, lined with cafés. (You may notice that the street running up the west side of the Alcazaba toward the square is named for an unlikely hero in this town of gladiators and conquerors: John Lennon.) The new **Museo de Arte Visigodo** is just north of the square; it contains archaeological and architectural remnants from the city's inhabitants between the Romans and the Moors.

From the Christian period, the 13th-century **Iglesia de Santa Eulalia**, located north of the Plaza de España on Avenida Extremadura, is a Romanesque structure that also recycled the stonework of previous occupiers. The church is dedicated to the child martyr Eulalia, who according to legend was cooked in an oven on the site for spitting in the eye of a pagan priest. In front of the church is the little **temple of Mars**, locally called the oven of Santa Eulalia.

STAYING AND DINING IN MERIDA

The ► **Parador Vía de la Plata** merits a visit even if you are not staying there. This inn on the Plaza de la Constitución, just south of Santa Eulalia, was once a convent that had been built on the site of a palace that housed the Pretorian Guard in Roman times. The historical mix shows in the decor, which incorporates many antiquities in its furnishings and is rather Andalusian in feeling. Rooms have elegant amenities such as embroidered pillows on the bedsteads and balconies over the convent garden. The food, stressing regional cuisine, is among the best offered by the paradores.

Another good hotel with a history is the ► **Hotel Emperatriz**, right on the main square, the Plaza de España. It occupies a 16th-century seignorial mansion with a central patio garden. Just outside of town (on the road to Madrid) is the big, modern, comfortable ► **Hotel Las Lomas**. The hotel is a good alternative if the parador is full, and its pool is welcome in summer. Two particularly good restaurants in Mérida are the **Nicolás**, at Calle Félix Valverde Lillo 13, and **Rufino**, Plaza Santa Clara 1. Both serve regional specialties such as lamb, Montánchez sausages, and Extremaduran soups and stews. For reservations for Nicolás, Tel: (9-24) 31-20-01; for Rufino, Tel: (9-24) 31-19-30. Both are closed on Sundays (never a good day in Mérida for dining out or sightseeing tours).

Mérida Environs

ALANGE

Alange is a little spa town—one of three in the region—about a 35-minute drive south of Mérida (take N 630/E 803, the road toward Seville, then follow the signs) to which people come for a long list of cures. The waters, rich in calcium, magnesium, and sodium bicarbonate, bubble up from ancient springs. Today's patrons drink from, bathe in, and spray themselves with the same waters—in the same actual baths—enjoyed by the Romans. There are two large indoor pools, covered with cupolas and resembling the public baths in Istanbul (without the fine mosaics, however). The spa occupies a small Arab castle that became a retreat for the Knights of Santiago. Taking the cure for a day in a spa that is a historical landmark is rather fun; however, non-Spanish-speaking participants may have a hard time following the prescribed recipes and treatments.

MEDELLIN

Don't consider going to Medellín, some 40 km (25 miles) due east of Mérida, for any reason other than that Hernán

Cortés, *conquistador* par excellence and conqueror of Mexico, came from here. His family was of the minor nobility, but as a younger son, he received no inheritance. After studying law, he joined the army and later departed for the New World. There, with his Extremaduran training and a handful of men, he brought down the Aztec empire and claimed Mexican lands and riches for Spain. His tall bronze statue standing in the village square, with plaques listing his Mexican victories, leaves little doubt that here was a man of singular arrogance and, undoubtedly, exceptional courage.

There is little else of note to see in tiny, whitewashed Medellín, except the 17th-century bridge over the Río Guadiana and the crumbling castle on the hill above town. It is hard to find anyone who knows its history, although clearly it dates to the Middle Ages. The main church—like many in Extremadura—opens only for services and doesn't seem to follow a schedule except on Sundays.

BADAJOZ

Badajoz (62 km/39 miles west of Mérida) is worth mentioning if only because it is the last major stop in Spain on the main route from Madrid (and Mérida) to Estremoz, Evora, and Lisbon in Portugal. The city occupies a hill on the left bank of the Río Guadiana, 6½ km (4 miles) from the Portuguese border. The bridge over the river, **Puente de Palmas**, was designed in 1596 by Juan de Herrera (Philip II's favorite architect, who was responsible for such works as El Escorial and the cathedral at Valladolid) and was built on Roman foundations. It is rather grand—1,909 feet long with 32 arches. There are substantial remains of Moorish occupation dotting the surrounding hills.

In town, look for the **Museo Arqueológico**, housed in the *alcázar,* which is to the right as you face the Puente de Palmas overlooking the river. The *alcázar* (locally called "*el castillo*") is also riverside and exhibits Roman statues, elaborate mosaics, Visigothic and Islamic artifacts, and cases of stone carvings, silver jewelry, coins, medical instruments, and pottery. Afterward, stop by the **Catedral de San Juan**, dating from the 13th century, to see several paintings by Zurbarán and Ribera. Off the Plaza de San Juan, at Calle Meléndez Valdés 32, is the **Museo Provincial de Bellas Artes**, which has some fine 17th-century Flemish tapestries and paintings by Extremaduran artists.

The best hotel in Badajoz is the ▶ **Gran Hotel Zurbarán**. Renovated top to toe in 1991, it's big (215 rooms) and offers gardens, a pool, and car parking. The hotel restaurant, **Los Monjes**, offers good provincial dishes. Galician cuisine is served at the restaurant **La Toja**, at Avenida de Elvas 22; Tel: (9-24) 23-74-77.

OLIVENZA

Among the dozens of little towns to explore in Extremadura, one of the few whose reminders of things past are not Moorish or even Spanish is Olivenza. Its historical outlook is toward Portugal. In the 13th century the town was given to Beatrice of Castile by her brother on the occasion of her marriage to Infante Don Afonso of Portugal; it was subsequently ruled by Afonso's son, Dinis. In 1607 it was occupied by the Spanish, and in 1801 it was ceded to Spain during the War of the Oranges. Wellington fought bloody battles on the same ground in 1811.

Just a few miles from the Portuguese border (25 km/15 miles south of Badajoz by way of C 436), and surrounded by olive grove country, Olivenza may be a part of Spain, but it has a very Portuguese look. The tell-tale signs—the elegant, twisting columns that were hallmark architecture during the reign of Portugal's Manuel I at the end of the 15th century—dominate the Baroque **Iglesia de Santa María Magdalena**. The church, on the Plaza de Santa María del Castillo, is said to have been designed by Diego and Francisco de Arruda, designers of the Hieronymite monastery and Belém tower in Lisbon.

Down a street to the right of the square is the Hospital de la Caridad (also known as Casa de la Misericórdia), whose glorious little chapel is covered in blue and white Portuguese tiles (*azulejos*). Spain has declared the town a national treasure and installed the **Museo Municipal Gonzáles-Santana**, the Extremaduran ethnographic museum, in the keep of the town's huge 13th- to 14th-century castle. The museum houses exhibits on local customs, methods of agriculture, and crafts such as ceramics, embroidery, and ironwork. There are also some archaeological artifacts. It is open Saturdays and Sundays; closed in September.

SOUTHERN EXTREMADURA
Zafra

Rather Andalusian in character, Zafra, 63 km (39 miles) due south of Mérida just off N 630/E 803 (the road toward Seville), is the belle of southern Extremadura. Known as Zafar under the Moors, it was the seat of the dukes of Feria, the first of whom, in 1437, built a fortified *alcázar* (castle) with six great round towers. Cortés lived there briefly as protégé of the duke of Feria. The massive stone structure, right in town, has been converted into the ▶ **Parador Hernán Cortés**, complete with its own chapel bearing a splendid golden cupola and a *sala dorada* with a richly carved gold ceiling. The central marble patio is thought to have been designed by Herrera. You can park at the parador and walk to every place of interest in town; it's almost next door to the old-town plazas.

Zafra owes its fortified look to the military orders of Santiago and Alcántara, and its artistic legacy to the Ferias, who were as wealthy as they were cultured. The old town is centered on the 18th-century **Plaza Grande** and the 14th-century **Plaza Chica**. These are lovely, arcaded squares, with low white houses and ironwork balconies ablaze with flowers. Just between the two plazas is a granite *vara* (column), which served to measure the length of livestock in the Middle Ages when Zafra was a major market town. The city is still known for its cattle fairs, the most important of which is the Feria de San Miguel, held during the first week of October.

Among the religious sites in town is the **Iglesia Colegiata de la Candelaria**, built by a duke of Feria in 1546 and located on Calle Sevilla just down from the Plaza de España. Inside the church are an altarpiece executed by Zurbarán in a side chapel and one by José Churriguera on the main altar. Continue walking along Sevilla, through Plaza José Antonio, to Avenida General Mola and the 15th-century **Convento de Santa Clara**. This church houses the alabaster tombs of Lorenzo Suárez de Figueroa, who was the town's benefactor and the first duke of Feria, and his wife.

STAYING, DINING, AND SHOPPING IN ZAFRA

The Parador Hernán Cortés (see above) is by far the best place to stay in Zafra. Across from the parador are two artisan stores with good selections of pottery, baskets, and other crafts that show the Andalusian influence. A short walk from the parador, just outside the wall that forms the parador entrance, is a second good hotel, the low-rise ► **Hotel Huerta Honda**, which is built around a central patio with a pool. The rooms are comfortable and modern. The hotel restaurant serves excellent food and has a good wine selection. The parador restaurant is also good.

Jerez de los Caballeros

As you drive west from Zafra (route C 4311) through the rolling hills of the Sierra del Castellar, after some 40 km (25 miles) you will see the Baroque towers of Jerez de los Caballeros rising out of the Ardila plain. A visit to Jerez is of interest primarily to those committed to following in the footsteps of the *conquistadores*. This old market town has the distinction of being the birthplace of Vasco Núñez de Balboa, who crossed the Isthmus of Panama and claimed the Pacific Ocean for Spain. His house is at Calle Capitán Cortés

12. Hernando de Soto, the first European to explore the Mississippi River, was born in the nearby town of Barcarrota; he also lived in Jerez, in a whitewashed house at Hernando de Soto 1. Anyone in town can lead you to it, although it's not open to the public.

AROUND IN JEREZ

The rectangular 13th-century **Castle of the Templars** is perched on the rocks above the town. In the 14th century, the *caballeros* (knights) did battle for their lives, and lost, in the Torre Sangrienta (Bloody Tower). Their order was officially dissolved and the town handed over to the Knights of Santiago, who built many noble mansions, churches, and convents in Jerez. Next to the castle is Santa María, a Baroque church built on a former Visigothic site.

The Plaza de España, in the center of town, is dominated by the massive and richly decorated **Torre de San Miguel**, the tower of the church of the same name. Its outstanding exterior—more interesting than the interior—features two Neoclassical doorways, one carved in granite and the other in white marble.

Another notable tower crowns the **Iglesia de San Bartolomé**; not unlike the Giralda in Seville, it is richly covered with polychrome tiles to match the blue and gold of the church below. Located in the upper part of town, the church houses a magnificent 16th-century tomb containing the remains of Don Vasco de Jerez and his wife. Jerez, a descendant of the Knights Templar who recaptured the town from the Moors, was deeded the town by Alfonso IX of León after the victory. The baptistery, a 15th-century Gothic-style chapel, is the oldest part of the church. San Bartolomé is the town's patron saint. His feast day, August 24, is marked with festivities and processions. (Holy Week is also celebrated fervently here, with processions of floats, carved images, and marching brotherhoods.)

OUTSIDE JEREZ

The history of the Jerez de los Caballeros area goes much further back than the age of the *conquistadores*—all the way to prehistoric times, in fact, as evidenced by the megalithic **Dolmen de Toniñuelo**, 5 km (3 miles) northwest of town (follow the road sign) in a pasture known as La Granja (the farm). Solar symbols carved on the monument suggest its builders were sun-worshipers.

GETTING AROUND

The best way to navigate Extremadura is by car—in fact, it's about the only way. There is air service via Air Sur from

Madrid and Seville to Badajoz, which offers little of interest and is not even a well-located center from which to visit the regional highlights. You could, however, fly into Badajoz and rent a car at the airport to visit southern Extremadura. Long-term car rentals are best done in Madrid or Seville—prices are very high in Extremadura—or, better yet, booked as part of a fly-drive package when you buy your airline tickets.

The Spanish railway (RENFE) has train service to Plasencia, Cáceres, Mérida, and Zafra on the Madrid–Seville line. Additionally, RENFE operates escorted overnight trips on summer weekends from Madrid to both Mérida and Cáceres, which provide rather nice and inexpensive excursions for a sampling of either city. The programs include rail transport, sightseeing, some meals, and a choice of accommodations. Excursions can be booked at RENFE offices or travel agencies in Madrid.

Most visitors come to Extremadura by road, into the northern area from Madrid and into the southern from Seville. There are many new roads in the region, and the going is just fine when driving on the major red roads and secondary green ones indicated on road maps. Those marked in yellow usually mean rough riding.

The most direct route to the northern half of Extremadura (province of Cáceres) is N V/E 90, which leads from Madrid to Trujillo, just 49 km (30½ miles) east of the town of Cáceres. The direct route from Salamanca, N 630, goes to Plasencia (132 km/82 miles) and Cáceres (80 km/50 miles farther). A beautiful approach into Extremadura from the north is on C 526 from Ciudad Rodrigo (province of Salamanca) to Coria and on to Plasencia or Cáceres. The roads off the main highways into the northern region twist and turn a bit but are well marked and easy to follow.

If you are coming to Extremadura from the south, the N 630/E 803 runs from Seville to Zafra, Mérida, Cáceres, and Plasencia. If you turn off the highway some 70 km (44 miles) north of Seville, just past Santa Olalla, onto C 434, take that to Fregenal de la Sierra, and then take N 435 north, you will arrive at Jerez de los Caballeros. This long drive, some 80 km (50 miles) of which is on secondary roads, is pretty, but don't count on going farther than Zafra (30 km/19 miles east of Jerez) the first night. There is also a good road (N 432) directly from Córdoba to Zafra.

The Alentejo province of Portugal, just across Extremadura's western border, offers additional access to the region. The main road comes from Lisbon via the very rewarding town of Estremoz into Badajoz, Spain, which is well worth a detour; go straight to Mérida. Farther north, cars can cross the border at Valencia de Alcántara, Spain (due east of

Castelo de Vide, Portugal), en route to Cáceres. The last hill town in Portugal on this route, Marvão, is an excellent place to stay the night, or at least to have lunch, at the small *pousada* (parador); it provides a perfect view of the plain of Spain.

ACCOMMODATIONS REFERENCE

The hotel rates listed below are projected rates for 1994, for double room, double occupancy, in pesetas. We strongly recommend that you confirm the price when making reservations.

When dialing telephone numbers from outside the country, drop the 9 in the area code.

▶ **Alcántara**. Avenida Virgen de Guadalupe 14, 10001 **Cáceres**. Tel: (9-27) 22-89-00; Fax: 22-87-68. 9,800 pts.

▶ **Alfonso VIII**. Avenida Alfonso VIII 34, 10600 **Plasencia**. Tel: (9-27) 41-02-50; Fax: 41-80-42. 13,000 pts.

▶ **Extremadura**. Avenida Virgen de Guadalupe 5, 10001 **Cáceres**. Tel: (9-27) 22-16-04; Fax: 21-10-95. 8,500 pts.

▶ **Gran Hotel Zurbarán**. Paseo de Castelar, 06001 **Badajoz**. Tel: (9-24) 22-37-41; Fax: 22-01-42. 14,500 pts.

▶ **Hospedería del Real Monasterio**. Plaza Juan Carlos I, 10140 **Guadalupe**. Tel: (9-27) 36-70-00; Fax: 36-71-77. 6,200 pts.

▶ **Hotel Colón**. Calle Colón 42, 37700 **Béjar**. Tel: (9-23) 40-06-50; Fax: 21-35-00. 7,150 pts.

▶ **Hotel Emperatriz**. Plaza de España 19, 06800 **Mérida**. Tel: (9-24) 31-31-11; Fax: 30-03-76. 8,425 pts.

▶ **Hotel Huerta Honda**. Calle López Asme 30, 06300 **Zafra**. Tel: (9-24) 55-41-00; Fax: 55-08-00. 11,900 pts.

▶ **Hotel Las Lomas**. Carretera Madrid (N V), km 338, 06800 **Mérida**. Tel: (9-24) 31-10-11; Fax: 30-08-41. 14,950 pts.

▶ **Hotel Quinto Centenario**. Avenida Virgen de Guadalupe 18, 10001 **Cáceres**. Tel: (9-27) 21-68-68; Fax: 22-25-73; in U.S., Tel: (800) 843-3311. 13,000 pts.

▶ **Meliá Cáceres**. Plaza de San Juan 11, 10001 **Cáceres**. Tel: (9-27) 21-58-00; Fax: 21-40-70; in U.S., Tel: (800) 336-3542. 12,500 pts.

▶ **Parador de Cáceres**. Calle Ancha 6, 10003 **Cáceres**. Tel: (9-27) 21-17-59; Fax: 21-17-29. 12,500 pts.

▶ **Parador Carlos V**. Carretera de Plasencia, 10450, **Jarandilla de la Vera**. Tel: (9-27) 56-01-17; Fax: 56-00-88. 10,000–12,000 pts.

▶ **Parador Guadalupe**. Calle Marqués de la Romana 12, 10140 **Guadalupe**. Tel: (9-27) 36-70-75; Fax: 36-70-76. 11,000 pts.

▶ **Parador Hernán Cortés**. Plaza Corazón de María 7, 06300 **Zafra**. Tel: (9-24) 55-45-40; Fax: 55-10-18. 13,000 pts.

► **Parador de Trujillo**. Plaza de Santa Clara, 10200 **Trujillo**. Tel: (9-27) 32-13-50; Fax: 32-13-16. 13,000 pts.

► **Parador Vía de la Plata**. Plaza de la Constitución 3, 06800 **Mérida**. Tel: (9-24) 31-38-00; Fax: 31-92-08. 16,000 pts.

► **Parador Virrey de Toledo**. Plaza del Palacio 1, **Oropesa** (Toledo). Tel: (9-25) 43-00-00; Fax: 43-07-77. 12,000 pts.

ANDALUSIA

By Robert Packard

Robert Packard has written many articles about Spain. His work has been published in the travel sections of The New York Times *and* The Philadelphia Inquirer *and in* Connoisseur *and* Travel & Leisure *magazines. He is also the author of* Refractions: Writers and Places *(1990). A resident of New York City and Maine, he visits Spain frequently.*

"**F**or half the world the image of Spain is the image of Andalusia," wrote Jan Morris. Yet, although the language is that of Spain, Andalusia's climate and culture are distinctive—the fires are banked differently. Andalusia (pronounced on-da-loo-THEE-a in Spanish) occupies the entire southern portion of the Iberian Peninsula, an area almost as large as Portugal—and the rest of Spain often finds Andalusia hard to take: too much sunshine, goes the claim, and too little attention paid to the hard currency of life.

The landscape of this Andalusian world includes extensive Mediterranean and Atlantic seacoasts. The terrain—"in variety, strangeness and grandeur, the Spanish landscape is unequalled in Europe," in the words of V. S. Pritchett—boasts mountain areas as diverse as the Baetic range, dotted with white Moorish hill towns; the snowcapped Sierra Nevada, with Spain's highest continental peak, near Granada; and the wild Alpujarras immediately to their south. Scattered about Andalusia like so many architectural jewels are the mosque at Córdoba, the Alhambra at Granada, and the cathedral at Seville.

All those stereotypical "Spanish" images come to life in Andalusia: flamenco, bullfighting, Sherry bodegas, beach cabanas, gazpacho, horse breeding, religious rituals, Gypsy music, and fiestas that take over entire communities. Andalusia has forests of dark pine, embankments of sheer rock, flowers of tropical radiance, wildlife sanctuaries, streets

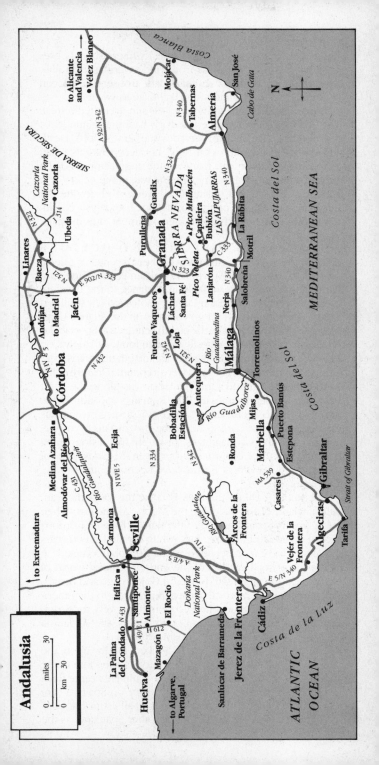

lined with orange and lemon trees, whitewashed houses with inner courtyards, black-iron window grilles, mantillas, long flounced dresses, skintight dark trousers, Cordoban brimmed hats, fans, guitars, and a climate to swear by.

But Andalusia is not some mindless sun-drenched retreat. The real world intrudes. A particularly haunting reminder of the intransigence of fate pervades the atmosphere. Death still comes in the afternoon here, hooded penitents recall unspeakable acts in the name of the Inquisition, and the darkness may carry the spine-tingling wail of the *saeta*—that lament of the faithful during Holy Week. And despite the international high life on the Costa del Sol, Andalusia continues to have one of the highest unemployment rates in Spain.

ANDALUSIA'S HISTORY AND CULTURE

Since prehistoric times Andalusia has been a center of culture on the Iberian Peninsula. The Phoenician/Punic (Carthaginian) culture was of inestimable importance to the development of pre-Roman Iberian culture (so called) in southern Spain. The Phoenicians set up colonies on the Atlantic Coast near present-day Málaga in the eighth century B.C. Spectacular Phoenician bronze statuettes have been found at Huelva, on the coast near Portugal. Imports of art and other artifacts from Greece and the Greek colonies were a common feature of life in the Phoenician and Carthaginian towns along the coast here from very early times until the Roman occupation. In the fifth and fourth centuries B.C. there was a very prosperous Carthaginian city at Gadir (Cádiz); the Phoenicians from Tyre, ancestors of the Carthaginians, probably had a flourishing base at Gadir three centuries earlier. Even the oldest parts of the Puerta de Sevilla at Seville have been attributed to the Carthaginians.

The Romans called the area Baetica; the Visigoths, Vandalusia (land of the Vandals); the Moors, Al-Andalus. When for 600 years Spain was part of the Roman Empire, Córdoba served as an administrative hub; when for almost 800 years the Moors were a presence in Spain, Córdoba became one of the intellectual capitals of the entire medieval world of Europe; during Spain's all-powerful Golden Age and Renaissance, Seville was by royal decree the gateway to the Americas. And now, at a time when economic recovery for Spain, as a member of the European Community, is vital, Andalusia leads the country in annual tourism revenue.

The rest of Spain has rarely looked kindly upon the people of Andalusia, and foreign observers often join in the abuse. One of the milder derogatory comments came from George Borrow, the classic English writer on Spain, a century and a half ago: "The Andalusians, in all estimable traits of character are ... as far below the other Spaniards as the country they inhabit is superior in beauty and fertility to the other provinces of Spain." But Andalusians tolerate the disapproval of others: They attribute it to ungovernable envy.

"Andalusia is *sol y sombra* both—sun on one side of the street, shadow on the other: a mirror both of Spain's delight and of her poverty," wrote Jan Morris. But Andalusia does not fall so easily into bullring classification. For Spaniards the *sombra* is both the more desirable and the more expensive of seats; it is the *gringos* who want to sit in the sun.

MAJOR INTEREST:
SEVILLE – CORDOBA - GRANADA TRIANGLE

Seville
Cathedral, Patio de los Naranjos, and Giralda
The Alcázar and its garden
Archivo General de Indias
Baroque Hospital de la Caridad
Exploring the Barrio de Santa Cruz
Casa de Pilatos
Museo de Bellas Artes
Parque de María Luisa
Itálica and the Museo Arqueológico Provincial
Tapas hopping
Festivals

Córdoba
Rich Arabic heritage
The Mezquita-Catedral
The Roman bridge
Cordoban leather
La Judería (the Jewish quarter)
The Medina Azahara

The Andalusian Northeast
Renaissance architecture in Ubeda
Baeza's 11th-century buildings
Cazorla National Park
Guadix's cave dwellings
Late Neolithic cave drawings and early Renaissance
    castle in Vélez Blanco

Granada
The Alcazaba
The Alhambra
The Palace of Charles V
The Generalife gardens
The cathedral and the royal chapel
La Cartuja monastery
The Sierra Nevada
Las Alpujarras

MAJOR INTEREST: ANDALUSIAN COAST

Northern Costa de la Luz
Doñana National Park
Palos de la Frontera

Jerez de la Frontera
Sherry bodegas

Cádiz

The White Towns
Arcos de la Frontera
Ronda

Málaga
The cathedral
The Alcazaba
The Roman amphitheater
Picasso in Málaga
Museo de Bellas Artes

The Costa del Sol east to the Costa Blanca
Nerja's paleolithic caves
White towns of Frigiliana and Salobreña
Almería's *alcázar*
The Cabo de Gata
Spaghetti Westerns
Arabic Mojácar

The Costa del Sol west to the Costa de la Luz
White towns of Mijas and Casares
Fashionable Marbella
Gibraltar
Baelo Claudio, ancient Roman fishing town
Classic white town of Vejér de la Frontera

ANDALUSIAN MUSIC AND DANCE

Music and dance seem indigenous to Andalusia. Even the most ardent northerner will acknowledge that flamenco developed principally in the region of Andalusia. The roots of *cante* (Spanish song) lie in stylistic traits common to Arabic, Jewish, Byzantine, and even Hindu music: the repetition of a single note and the use of pitches not found in Western scales. Certainly Andalusia has been the chosen home of Arabs, Jews, Byzantines, and Gypsies of Indian heritage. The *soleares* and other song forms are said to have sprung from the Triana Gypsy quarter of Seville. Even the names of songs and dances evoke Andalusia: *rondeña* (Ronda), *malagueña* (Málaga), *granadinas* (Granada). Beneath the haunting surface of all that Spanish music lies a strain of melancholy, a characteristic motif that links it forever, say the Andalusians, to their region.

In the 1840s *cafés cantantes* began to open in Seville, Cádiz, Jerez, and other Andalusian cities, creating a home for performances of flamenco song and dance as well as flamenco guitar playing. Purists will tell you that most of today's public presentations are on a degraded commercial level and that the art of flamenco is rarely honored in its true sense. Finding performances of first-rate flamenco dancers, singers, and guitarists is difficult, but even those of a secondary level can provide a festive evening. Ask your hotel concierge for recommendations. There is a varied selection of flamenco clubs in Granada's Sacramonte section, in the villages around Córdoba, and among Seville's flamenco "halls" or cabarets. During the summer Cádiz, Jerez, and Seville have flamenco competitions. Jerez offers a summer course on flamenco art, organized by the Cátedra de Flamencología. Many of the nightclubs in the Costa del Sol's Torremolinos and Marbella area offer flamenco shows.

The Food of Andalusia

In the past, the food of Andalusia has been maligned by tourists, famous travellers such as Richard Ford, and foreign and Spanish food writers alike. Andalusian cooking suffered from the effects of the poverty that never seemed to have been completely eradicated; in bad times cheap grades of olive oil were often blended with other inferior oils and reused to the point of being rancid, and since almost everything in Andalusia is prepared with olive oil, the food was only as good as the oil. Squeamish American and British tourists on cheap package tours, who were usually none too enamored of the taste of olive oil and garlic to begin with, helped create a demand for the bland, underseasoned, so-called Continental cuisine encountered in many hotel dining rooms and restaurants that cater to tourists. And many foreign food writers, forgetting the cardinal rule of travel—"When in Rome, do as the Romans do"—too often sought the glories of Andalusian cuisine in white-tablecloth restaurants where they were not likely to be moved by the sights, sounds, smells, and tastes that could be encountered in those days in the homey restaurants where the real cooking was taking place. Even Spanish writers, especially those from the media capitals of the north, usually looked down upon the laid-back, unsophisticated dining experiences of the south.

MALAGA

To those who know the food of the south, however, Andalusian cuisine has offered quite a different picture, especially in the past two decades or so. Málaga's delicacies include crisp, delicately fried *chanquetes* (tiny fish) at a beach-front bar in the old fishermen's barrio of El Palo; exceptional *arroz abanda* (a variation of paella in which the rice is cooked in the seafood stock and served separately) eaten alfresco at **Antonio Martín**, Hemingway's old hangout along the harbor seawall; *sardinas* grilled over a fire on the beach at **Fuengirola**; and one of the greatest of all Mediterranean folk dishes—*gazpacho malagueño* or *ajo blanco,* a cold white gazpacho of almonds, garlic, vinegar, bread, water, and olive oil, to which a few green grapes are added when it is served, creating an exquisite juxtaposition of flavors and a vibrant combination of the essential staples of Andalusian Moorish cuisine.

SEVILLE

You can sample a kaleidoscope of colorful Andalusian dishes in Seville by joining the local folks in *el tapeo*—meandering through a series of *tapas* bars for an evening. Some of the tidbits you may encounter include: *huevos de codornices aliñados* (marinated quail's eggs), *jamón serrano* (cured ham), *queso manchego* (ewe's-milk cheese), *boquerones* (a type of anchovy) *en vinagre, caracoles en su salsa* (snails in sauce), and *espinacas con garbanzos* (spinach and chick peas). In Seville *tapas* are washed down with red wine, iced Sherry, or beer.

Other local specialties to try in Seville are gazpacho and *pescaito frito* (crisp fried fish), which the Andaluces know how to prepare as well as anyone in the world. You can buy deep-fried squid, baby sole, whiting, and shark—sold by kilo weight and wrapped up in rough, semi-absorbent paper—and olives and homemade potato chips at a *freidura,* a traditional type of take-out fish stand. Drink glasses of cool, *red* Valdepeñas with this simple meal.

CADIZ

In Cádiz province, make a pilgrimage to Sanlúcar de Barrameda to munch on crunchy, exquisitely sea-flavored fresh *langostinos de Sanlúcar* (prawns), as expensive as caviar and just as divine; followed by a great seafood salad, *salpicón de mariscos;* then a variety of fried fish, such as *pijotas, acedias, boquerones, salmonetes,* and *cazón en adobo;* and, with luck, *calamares rellenos,* large stuffed squid, sliced and served cold with fresh mayonnaise. Wash it all down with cold glasses of the same exquisite, tangy, sea-laced Manzanilla, from icy half-bottles, that you sipped while sitting on an old upturned fisherman's dinghy on the beach as you watched one of the world's most glorious sunsets where the Río Guadalquivir empties into the Atlantic.

You can also drive over to the center of Puerto de Santa María to a *cocedero de mariscos,* point to a variety of already boiled shellfish, buy it by the kilo, take it to the outdoor café in front, spread out your feast on brown paper, and order pitchers of beer or bottles of Osborne's Fino Quinta. And around Jerez de la Frontera, especially on the road to Sanlúcar, are legendary roadside restaurants called *ventas,* such as **Venta Antonio** and **Venta Los Naranjos**, where the seafood and iced Sherry make an unforgettable combination.

In the untouristy city of Cádiz there are great seafood restaurants, such as **El Faro**, where you can order more of the exceptional bounty of this region. Try superb seafood soups—*caldillo de perro, sopa al cuarto de hora,* and *sopa de mariscos*—in glassed-in restaurants such as **El Anteojo**, looking out over the sparkling bay.

THE OTHER PROVINCES

You will eat well if you follow the locals in Málaga, Seville, and Cádiz, and you will even find fancy restaurants of recent vintage with top Castilian, Catalan, Basque, and foreign chefs. But in the other five provinces of Andalusia—Huelva, Córdoba, Jaén, Granada, and Almería—the haute cuisine pickings are much slimmer.

In the province of **Huelva**, bordering Portugal, you'll find more terrific Atlantic seafood, Spain's finest cured ham, *jamón de Jabugo,* and great strawberries; in **Córdoba**, meat stews such as *estofado de rabo de toro* (oxtail stew), *salmorejo* (a thick *gazpacho* dish), and *flamenquines* (a breaded, deep-fried ham-and-cheese roll); and in **Jaén** province, *pipirrana jaenera,* a delicious cold salad of chopped tomato, green peppers, hard-boiled eggs, ham, and tuna. In **Granada**, thin slices of the Sierra Nevada–cured *jamones* of Trevélez (some of the best ham in Spain) and *habas con jamón,* the same ham cooked in cubes with the local crunchy fresh broad beans from Granada's fertile plain, are excellent dishes. The famed *tortilla de Sacromonte,* originally an omelet of brains and testicles, will usually be done in a "sanitized" version with ham, peas, and kidneys, but neither version will replace the Alhambra as your greatest positive image of Granada. **Almería's** subtropical climate made it into the year-round truck garden of Europe, and from its Mediterranean coast, the sea provides the same supply of fresh fish that the Málaga and Granada coastal regions are known for. Given the variety of vegetables, fruits, and seafood available here, we may one day hear of a "new Almería cuisine" à la California.

—*Gerry Dawes*

The Wines of Andalusia

Andalusia is home to four *denominaciones de origen*—Condado de Huelva, Málaga, Montilla-Moriles, and Jerez-Xeres-Sherry—all primarily engaged in producing fortified wines. The wines of Jerez-Xeres-Sherry are covered in the Jerez de la Frontera section of the Andalusian Coast part of this chapter.

Condado de Huelva wines are the descendants of the wines of Lepe mentioned by Chaucer in "The Pardoner's Tale." Huelva's Atlantic climate produces light dry wines of the *fino* and *amontillado* family from the native Zalema grape and the Palomino of Jerez, but here these *solera*-system wines are called *condado pálido* (pale). *Condados viejos* (old) can run the spectrum from dry to sweet. Some light, fresh, dry white table wines are also made from Zalema grapes.

Mentioned in literature since Roman times, **Málaga** wines come from mountain vineyards north and east of the capital of the famous Costa del Sol. Málaga is an intensely sweet, rich, raisiny, walnut-colored wine made from Pedro Ximénez and Moscatel grapes. The wines of Málaga improve with age almost indefinitely. Lagrima, which Richard Ford called "ruby tears," is a rare Málaga made from the essence of sun-concentrated grapes pressed by their own weight. Sip Málaga or pour it over ice cream. Like cream Sherry, it goes exceptionally well with coffee. For those with a sweet tooth, Scholtz Hermanos or López Hermanos are brands to look for.

Considered by the late Frank Schoonmaker, an American wine expert, to be "one of the best aperitif wines in the world," **Montilla-Moriles** wines come from the hill country near Córdoba. In the heat of Córdoba's scorching summer the Pedro Ximénez grape achieves wines of 15½ percent alcohol naturally, so Montilla *finos* are not generally fortified with grape spirits. Consequently, they are lighter, finer, and more delicate than many Sherries, and greatly admired in many parts of Andalusia. Montilla wines are fermented in huge earthenware *tinajas* and then enter a *solera* system (see the Sherry section under Jerez, below). Montilla produces a range of *finos, amontillados* (a name derived from Montilla), *olorosos,* and creams, plus incredibly rich Pedro Ximénez wines. Look for Alvear Fino.

—*Gerry Dawes*

Holy Week in Andalusia

Celebrations of Semana Santa (Holy Week), from Palm Sunday to Easter, lead all other spectacles in Spain. Not surprisingly, those in Andalusia top those of the rest of the country. Seville, in turn, outdoes her Andalusian neighbors. In almost every community, no matter how small, there are observances that recall the trials of Christ and the tears of the Virgin.

Holy Week processions profoundly alter the routine of daily life, and you will find that travel is radically changed with respect to freedom of movement, business hours (or days!) for shops, restaurants, and offices of all kinds, and securing hotel reservations. But Holy Week is a major aspect of Spain's culture, and regardless of your religious or ethnic background, you will witness a unique and extravagant spectacle.

Many Andalusian cities and towns have distinctive Holy Week rituals: In **Arcos de la Frontera** there is a running of the bulls on Easter Sunday; in **Málaga** (a close second in pageantry to Seville) parishioners go directly from Easter Mass to the season's first *corrida* in the bullring; in **Córdoba** a full symphony orchestra and chorus occupy the cathedral within the mosque on Good Friday; in **Granada** the ladies dress in black, with mantillas and jewelry, and walk along with the religious floats.

Every day of Holy Week is marked by regalia of different colors. On Palm Sunday everywhere the church ornaments are draped in black, and parishioners take home blessed palm branches to adorn every balcony. The sound of "thunder" fills the **Seville** cathedral on Wednesday, and again on Saturday, when every bell in the city is tolled. No city in Spain surpasses Seville when it comes to processions; there may be 30 or more in a 24-hour period. *Pasos* (floats) carry startlingly lifelike polychrome figures depicting the scenes of the Passion: the Last Supper, the Garden of Olives, the Descent from the Cross. Many processioners wear long robes and *capuchones* (pointed hoods that cover their faces except for two eye slits), evoking the Spanish Inquisition and, for Americans, the Ku Klux Klan. Many, barefoot as a testament to humility and suffering, carry yard-long candles; some carry crosses to atone for sins.

The streets are darkened; melancholy wails of the *saeta* rend the air. The Christ figures are disturbingly realistic, with bloody wounds and expressions of intense agony. Each parish displays its particular Virgin, crowned, extravagantly garbed and bejeweled, but always with crystal tears on her sanctified, innocent cheeks.

Hotel reservations for Holy Week must be made well in advance (at least a year in Seville), and rates everywhere are substantially higher—but the extra expense is money well spent. Holy Week in Andalusia has no equal: It is an extraordinary fusion of religious intensity, civic competitiveness, atavistic ritual, and high drama.

Bullfighting in Andalusia

Once an activity of the upper classes, bullfighting evolved from such lofty social beginnings to become a popular spectacle. For centuries the nobility bred the bulls, then fought them in front of the king and his court. But with the advent of the Bourbon dynasty in the 18th century and Philip V's disdain for the activity, bullfighting became what is surely one of Spain's great expressions of popular enthusiasm.

The first professional bullfighter is said to have been Andalusian, Pedro Romero of Ronda, who in the late 1700s reputedly killed more than 5,000 bulls without any injury to himself. An inscription in the Ronda bullring museum states that in 1771, at the age of 17, he killed his first bull.

Bullfighting was then at its most primitive: The object was simply to kill the bull. Today the spectacle is a pageant, with so many intricate appurtenances that it has become an art form. As in life, a bullfight has spectators who sit in the torrid sun (*sol*) and those who sit in the cool shade (*sombra*); seats in the sun are (surprise!) cheaper and more numerous. The bullfight season in Spain opens in March and ends on October 12. Virtually every town in Andalusia, celebrating local fiestas, offers at least one seasonal bullfight in its own bullring. *Corridas* (bullfights) are generally scheduled for Sundays; tickets are best obtained through your hotel, but they can be bought at the bullring itself.

TRAVELLING IN ANDALUSIA

Andalusia's immense size—it's just a bit smaller than Portugal—seems at first glance to hinder a coherent plan for visiting major points of interest, but in fact the eight provinces (Huelva, Cádiz, Seville, Córdoba, Jaén, Granada, Málaga, and Almería) are readily accessible by car over mostly first-rate, if sometimes mountainous, roads. And the road signs are excellent. But if you do get lost, the worst tactic is to produce a map, an artifact that will stimulate avid interest and no recognition. The name of the nearest large town on your route, on the other hand, spoken in a vigorous tone, invariably results in directional assistance, sometimes accompanied by an offer of personal guidance. Málaga has the largest international airport in Andalusia, and Seville has doubled the size of its air facilities. Trains connect all but inland mountain towns. Bus service, varying from ultramodern to primitive, is available everywhere.

In this chapter we start with the Seville–Córdoba–Granada triangle, for which Seville is the air gateway. Córdoba is a possible—though very rushed—day trip from Seville by train; Granada, though linked to Seville by rail, is not. East of Córdoba and north of Granada, on the way to Madrid, are the historic towns of northeastern Andalusia, among them Jaén and Ubeda. South of Granada—and usually visible from town—are the peaks of the Sierra Nevada.

The second main area of Andalusia that we cover is the coast: south along the Atlantic and the Mediterranean, which are separated by Gibraltar. We start at the Costa de la Luz, southwest of Seville, with Jerez de la Frontera and Cádiz, and then go to nearby Doñana National Park and other places on the Atlantic to the west, toward Portugal's Algarve. After that we move east of Jerez inland through the Moorish white towns, starting with Arcos de la Frontera and ending at Ronda. If you are continuing east to Granada, your next stop might be the inland resort of La Bobadilla.

Málaga is next, due south of La Bobadilla (and of Córdoba, farther to the north). Málaga is the central city—and the major air gateway—of the Mediterranean Costa del Sol. After Málaga we go east along the coast to Almería and the Costa Blanca, the less-developed part of the coast, then west through the famous resorts of Torremolinos and Marbella, and on past Gibraltar to the eastern end of the Costa de la Luz, on the Atlantic, nearly as far as Cádiz and Jerez.

Choosing a Base

While we cover almost the whole of Andalusia, some travellers may prefer to concentrate on a particular area of this vast region. Using Seville as a base, for example, you can make leisurely day-long visits by car or train to Jerez and Cádiz, or by car to Doñana National Park. The Moorish white towns of southwestern Andalusia are so splendid that while a day trip by car from Seville is possible, a better alternative is to make Jerez, Arcos de la Frontera, or Ronda a base for a two-day jaunt to these infrequently visited spots.

Granada is also a fine locale for side trips. If you find the snow-peaked Sierra Nevada an irresistible aspect of the Alhambra panorama, you can drive in slightly over an hour to the peaks themselves, lunch at the parador, and, depending on the season, ski or hike. If you like remote mountain towns and don't mind the narrow roads, a visit to the wild Alpujarras (south of Granada on N 323, then east by way of Lanjarón) will delight you. Stay overnight at Bubión.

Although many travellers visit the Jaén–Baeza–Ubeda triangle of northeastern Andalusia as a side trip on the Madrid–Costa del Sol drive, the towns are several inconvenient hours from Granada; however, if you stay overnight at the parador in Ubeda, a day trip to the beautiful Cazorla National Park is a splendid possibility.

Visitors to the Mediterranean coast will be happier with a base outside of bustling Málaga, with Nerja to the east and Mijas to the west as alternatives. Farther east, the Costa del

Sol and Costa Blanca offer stunning beauty without the international party crowds; Salobreña and Almería can serve as bases for trips along this quiet coastline.

THE SEVILLE – CORDOBA – GRANADA TRIANGLE

SEVILLE

While Andalusia may not be an accurate image of most of Spain, Seville certainly seems to epitomize Andalusia. Seville makes an effort to play the starring role in every Andalusian production. Other Andalusian cities look upon Seville as one who grabs the best parts and then graciously asks for assistance. Observers are fond of playing a *yin* and *yang* game with Seville and neighboring Córdoba, 100 km (62 miles) up the Río Guadalquivir. Seville emerges as flirtatious, beguiling, theatrical, and given on occasion to the kind of exaggerated piety that foreshadows unrestrained revelry. Córdoba, in contrast, comes off as handsome, unaffected, intellectual, and sere to the point of aridity.

Even the most sanguine Sevillano would acknowledge that the annual *pasos* and penitents of Holy Week (mile after mile of floats of religious figures accompanied by funeral dirges wailed in the candlelit darkness), followed by the annual *feria* (fair week) of dancing, costumes, horses, bulls, music, song, and not a little *vino,* represent a more than passing flair for public display. Civic reticence has never been a Sevillian attribute, and nature has bedecked the city appropriately: The streets and boulevards are lined with orange trees, the parks lush with exotic blooms, the hours of sunshine unsurpassed.

THE SHAPING OF SEVILLE

Unlikely as it seems, the spirit that pervades and motivates Seville today stems from the city's victory over the Moors in 1248. For Seville, the Reconquest was quite simply a triumph of Christ over Muhammad; the Catholic Church ultimately conferred sainthood on the conqueror, Ferdinand III, who chose to live in Seville. Seville's gigantic Gothic cathedral, its obsession with Christian ritual, its uninhibited expressions of grief and joy—all are, in nature, lineal from the Reconquest.

In the flush of Spain's Golden Age, Seville became the

country's leading city. The Río Guadalquivir (more navigable then than today) brought, by royal decree, America's wealth to her docks. Under Philip II in the 16th century, Seville had worldwide political importance, reflecting its overseas trade monopoly as Spain's most important port. The city's subsequent fall from prominence mirrors the decline of Spain itself after the Renaissance. No industries were created; banking and commerce fell into the hands of foreigners; war debts ruined the economy.

Seville came to know dark days: four years of occupation by the French during the Napoleonic Wars and a period as a Fascist base during the Spanish Civil War. But on the positive side, the inauguration of the annual *feria* in 1847 heralded the touristic invasion of Seville, and the Ibero-American Exposition of 1929 brought worldwide attention to the city.

SEVILLE TODAY

For today's visitors a cautionary note, struck with some insistence, warns that petty crime in Seville is on a par with that in Rome and Naples; you are advised to keep a firm grip on handbags and wallets and leave nothing in your car. Drivers should know that all rental cars are instantly recognizable (by license plates and stickers) as such by thieves. Don't drive in the city with handbags and other valuables on display—cars are sometimes broken into even while stopped for traffic lights. Garage your car at night. Travellers are recognizable when on foot as well (clothes, camera, demeanor), and you should be especially alert during the long siesta hours, when visitors are likely to be walking about and most citizens are off the streets.

Seville sometimes seems to be producing a long-running theatrical hit, starring itself—it's a city that has taken hold of its destiny with just the right instinct and lack of reticence that attracts an enthusiastic audience. "I can't remember," wrote *Newsweek* photographer Peter Turnley about Seville, "a city where so many people were happy about the place they live in."

AROUND IN SEVILLE

For visitors, Seville's main focus of interest, centering around the cathedral, lies immediately east of Río Guadalquivir where it is crossed by the Puente de San Telmo. Just four blocks northeast of the bridge, with its guardian Torre del Oro (reputedly a former warehouse for New World gold—hence its name, Tower of Gold—now a maritime museum), stands the enormous cathedral. Within the cathedral compound, the 322-foot-high Giralda tower (which you can spy from almost anywhere in this beautiful, level-surfaced city) serves as a beacon.

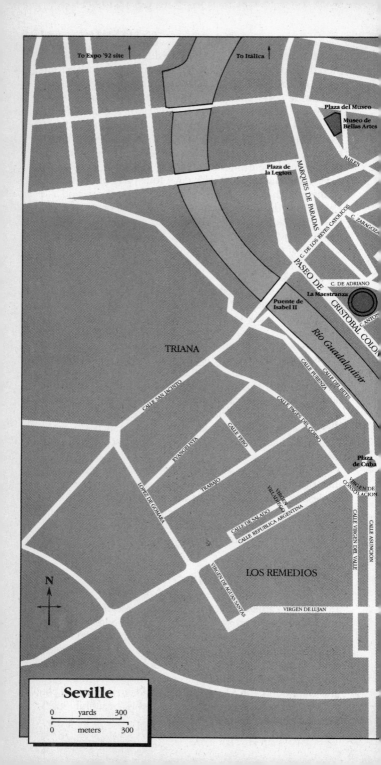

To the east of the cathedral lies the delightful old Barrio de Santa Cruz, with its shops, restaurants (often open-air, in the quarter's little plazas), and *tapas* bars. South of the cathedral, across the plaza, is the entrance to the Alcázar and its gardens beyond; opposite the cathedral's southern face is the Renaissance building of the Archivo General de Indias, and behind that the Museo de Arte Contemporaneo. Three blocks south, on Calle San Fernando, are the Alfonso XIII hotel and the university; south of them begin the extensive gardens of the Parque de María Luisa.

Some blocks northwest of the Puente de San Telmo in this compact urban area, facing the river, is the bullring, La Maestranza (Plaza de Toros); the Hospital de la Caridad is three blocks northeast of the bridge on Calle General Temprado. Three blocks north of the cathedral's western doorway on Avenida de la Constitución (Avenidas José Antonio and Queipo de Llano on many older maps) is the Plaza Nueva, the *ayuntamiento* (city hall), and the shopping district. Across the bridge, on the west bank, stretches the Barrio de Triana, with its Gypsy heritage.

The Cathedral Area

THE CATHEDRAL

The builders of Seville's enormous cathedral, begun in 1402, declared their intention of creating a structure so large that men would look at it and think them mad. They succeeded. Underlying their probably apocryphal assertion is a singular concern with how God would look at it. Their building, hardly accidentally, renders man insignificant: The edifice has five naves, each the size of a city street; the main altar stands at a huge crossing; the reredos, an ornamental screen behind the altar, is the largest in all Christendom. The immensity of the interior is said to be outdone in Europe only by St. Peter's in Rome and St. Paul's in London.

Built on the ruins of Seville's great mosque, which in turn had replaced a Visigothic church (and it, probably, a Roman temple), the cathedral faces west. The great main doors—today in sad need of cleaning—open only for ceremonial occasions; the public enters from an eastern door (there are nine portals in all) leading into the altar area of the building.

The Royal Chapel

Near the entrance is the royal chapel, the crown and axis of a series of radiating chapels. Here, on the altar, is the silver and gold catafalque of Saint Ferdinand, the conqueror of Seville. Above it, surrounded by surprisingly muscular cherubs, stands the Virgin, smiling faintly and holding in her arms a doll-like Child, richly robed and crowned. She leaves this chapel every August 15 (Feast of the Assumption) and is carried through the city before adoring throngs; Ferdinand even took this 13th-century Romanesque figure with him into battle. The chapel has a stunning Renaissance dome, rimmed in a series of martyr's heads in decreasing circles toward its distant center. The tombs, adorned with sculptures of the dead, on either side of the pews, look toward the altar: On the left is buried Alfonso X (Ferdinand's son), young and handsome; opposite him is his mother, Beatrice, who appears not only beautiful but considerably younger than her son. Both marble heads are adorned with gold crowns.

The Interior

One way to grasp the daunting architectural space within the cathedral is to walk to the extreme western end of the interior and turn around. Before you loom massive column shafts, supporting huge arches, rising to a distant ceiling. The stone floor is bare. Light shines through the Flemish stained-glass windows. One single aisle is as large as the entire nave and choir of Westminster Abbey.

From this principal doorway (Puerta Mayor), you see that two immense enclosures break the long axis of the building (384 feet). The first is the *coro* (choir), now undergoing extensive restoration, almost directly in the center of the nave, with a superb grille by Francisco de Salamanca; the choir stalls, with more than 100 seats, are splendidly carved. Travel writer Jan Morris has suggested that in Spanish cathedrals the *coro* provides the intellectual focus of the whole building.

The Chapels

Beyond this choir area, at the extreme eastern point of the nave, is the *capilla mayor* (chapel), the centerpiece of the entire cathedral. On three sides are gilded 16th-century screens. A huge late-Gothic retable (75 feet high) has more than 1,000 figures grouped in scenes from the lives of Jesus and Mary. This altarpiece was designed by Pieter Dancart, a late 15th-century Flemish sculptor; the side wings were added later.

The cathedral has more than a dozen chapels lining its northern and southern sides. Most of them have ceiling-high protective iron grilles, and many of them are so dark that their interiors, often coated with layers of dust, are impenetrable. One exception is the San Antonio chapel, or baptistery, on the north side, with Bartolomé Esteban Murillo's *San Antonio de Padua* and *Christ's Baptism*. Near the entrance to the Patio de los Naranjos (more on it below) is

Alonso Cano's *Mary,* at the altar of the Virgin of Bethlehem. On the south side, the San José chapel has paintings by Juan de Valdés Leal and Lucas Jordan, and in the San Hermenegildo chapel is a stunning Gothic alabaster tomb by Lorenzo Mercadente: The stone head of the mitered deceased rests on three alabaster cushions that seem to be sinking under the weight.

The transept contains a monument to Columbus, supported by four giant figures, and beyond it in the **Sacristía de los Cálices** is a treasure trove of paintings by Murillo, Goya, Cano, Francisco Pacheco del Río, Valdés Leal, and Titian (a chart identifies the paintings). Next door, as it were, is the **Sacristía Mayor,** decorated in exuberant Plateresque style with a wonderful dome and beautiful stone carving, which houses the cathedral treasures, mostly from the 16th century, of silver, bronze, and ivory.

PATIO DE LOS NARANJOS

The spacious open-air Patio de los Naranjos (Court of Orange Trees) extends along the entire northern face of the cathedral. Once the purification court of the former mosque, it has been altered little. In the center of the quadrangle stands an octagonal alabaster fountain basin said to have come from the original Visigothic church; from it radiates a patterned grid of 66 orange trees. A beautiful, horseshoe-shaped Moorish archway leads to this courtyard or patio from Calle Alemanes (no access). Today the patio has a patterned brick floor with four knee-high marble fountains at the corners. When the trees are in blossom or laden with fruit the court is a tranquil retreat just a step away from the unremitting human flow that inundates the interior of the cathedral.

THE GIRALDA

Sevillanos are enormously attached to the Giralda, the slender 322-foot-high tower directly adjacent to the eastern corner of the cathedral. Built as a minaret in 1184, with disciplined Arabic decorative motifs in its yellow brick and stone paneling, it was amended four centuries later by Hernán Ruiz. He added a belfry (with 24 deafening bells) and capped it with a weather vane. For the people of today's Seville the Giralda rings out the time, signals the weather, and serves as a beacon, as indeed it does for visitors, often orienting those lost in a maze of medieval streets. It looks not unlike an outsize early Italian Renaissance campanile.

You can ascend the Giralda along a ramp that winds upward as it follows the interior of the rectangular carapace. Through slits in the walls, which give some light to your progress, you can view increasingly rewarding panoramas of

Seville. A warning posted to the effect that persons should not ascend singly lest they succumb to suicidal impulses casts a chill often exacerbated at the top by the explosive clamor of the bells every quarter-hour, but the view from the summit is a knockout.

To the south, beyond the flat-roofed nave of the enormous cathedral, with its triple flying buttresses, are the Alcázar and the Parque de María Luisa. To the west, along with the Río Guadalquivir and its bridges, lies a city of white, highlighted by that splendid Seville landmark, La Maestranza, and, across the river, the Triana district, then modern high-rise apartments and the hills in the distance. In the immediate foreground to the north lies the old city, with the distant suburbs and the oil refineries beyond. Close-by, to the east, is the Santa Cruz quarter, a labyrinth of passageways, beyond which rises modern Seville, with its tall buildings in startling contrast.

THE ALCAZAR

Only a few steps south of the cathedral across the Plaza del Triunfo stands the extensive royal palace known as the Alcázar, the residence of Spanish kings for almost seven centuries. It was built by Peter the Cruel, who ruled Castile and León from 1350 to 1369. Originally a 12th-century Arabic Almohaden fortress, this fascinating building has undergone many architectural transformations; it even incorporates stylistic elements as recent as the 19th century. (Part of the building dates from reconstruction after the earthquake of 1744.) Nevertheless, the overall impression suggests the strength and delicacy of Mudejar (Moorish artisans and styles under Christian rule) architecture. The influence of Granada's Alhambra is unmistakable—in the courtyards, in the arches and the stucco ornamentation, in the ceilings and fenestration—copied with flair and imagination.

The Alcázar contains superb Flemish tapestries of the 17th and 18th centuries; tilework of rare beauty from the 14th century; and, beyond the marvelously decorative ambassador's hall, a frieze of portraits of Spanish rulers dating from the time of Philip II. Visitors are particularly taken by the harem, or living quarters (guides tell the same joke about eunuchs to each successive tour group), where the capitals of the columns are mostly from Córdoba and its nearby palace, Medina Azahara. Within this huge Alcázar complex are Christian altars, a display of exquisite Spanish fans, and 12 Flemish tapestries depicting the 1535 Tunisian campaign of Emperor Charles V.

Visitors are likely to leave Seville's Alcázar (usually through a stable-like area housing antique carriages) with a confused chronological sense of its architectural and decorative components. But even with this striking lack of conformity and continuity—and the sometimes jarring incongruities—the Alcázar offers many individual rewards of artistry.

THE JARDINES DEL ALCAZAR

Before exiting the Alcázar structure, however, you can pass directly to the **Jardines del Alcázar**, so extensive that several hours can be spent under their seductive spell. They incorporate as many stylistically diverse elements as the fortress-palace itself: Moorish, Renaissance, 19th century, and contemporary. The landscape architecture here gives a new meaning to the word "eclectic." A grotto wall—part colonnade, part unsightly stone incrustations—divides the garden. On the formal side is a large pool with a jarring orange-colored background wall; throughout the garden are fountains and the welcome sound and sight, dear to the Moors, of falling water; in the center is a mid-16th-century gazebo, a creation of Charles V, with superb tiling.

The sound of Seville's traffic comes from beyond the high crenellated brick walls. On the informal side of the gardens are long walkways and an abundance of blooms, fruit trees, and palms. The climate of Seville is such that flowers are gloriously in bloom here in all seasons. These Alcázar gardens recall, as well, the Generalife gardens of the Alhambra (although the latter have the crushing advantage of location), but the feline population of Seville's gardens outranks that of Granada's by as many as two to one. Some of the ponds in the Seville gardens are occupied by goldfish, others by ducks, prosaic creatures unthinkable in the elegant ambience of the Alhambra.

ARCHIVO GENERAL DE INDIAS

This impressive Renaissance building, between the Alcázar and the cathedral, was designed by El Escorial architect Juan de Herrera. Sometimes called the Casa Lonja (Exchange House), the archive now holds documents, maps, and charts pertaining to the Americas, and as such it is the repository for Spain in her role as discoverer and empire-builder. The building, infrequently visited by travellers, has an inner courtyard with Doric and Ionic columns and is a place of consuming interest.

Lining the salon walls of this marble-floored edifice are priceless documents behind protective grilles. A plaque states that on January 1, 1660, the painting and drawing academy founded by Murillo began its activities in these precincts. Displays on view include copies of letters from Columbus to his son, from Cervantes asking for a job, and from George Washington in 1789 regarding a commercial treaty with the chiefs of the Choctaw nation, as well as priceless original maps.

The archive is open daily; after signing in, visitors are free to examine the exhibits.

HOSPITAL DE LA CARIDAD

Just two blocks west of the Archivo General, on Calle General Temprado, is the Hospital de la Caridad, a Baroque charity hospital (seat of a brotherhood, but in this case with an actual hospital off its courtyard). While the hospital is of little interest to the visitor, the attached church, commissioned in 1661 by Don Miguel de Manara, reputedly a Don Juan figure, has some magnificent paintings. The church and the courtyard (with its narrative-pictorial glazed tiles) share a theme: the transitory nature of life and the quality of mercy it presupposes. Two superb allegorical paintings by Valdés Leal face each other across the church entranceways. The artist's subject is grim mortality: On the face of one painting he has written *in ictu oculi* ("in the blink of an eye"). Close examination of either work is not for the faint of heart. You are more likely to be reassured by the six huge Murillo canvases that adorn the church walls, each representing biblical acts of mercy. Murillo's style and flesh tones evoke a gentle and even sentimental radiance.

Above the altar stretches an extraordinary work by Pedro Roldán called *The Burial of Christ,* created in 1673. The background is a painting depicting the scene of the Crucifixion, and extending out over the altar area stretches a three-dimensional, life-size sculpted body being borne away.

Despite the dominant motif of charity (*caridad*), the overpoweringly unpalatable columns (of a twisted Baroque gold design) that frame the altar are a reminder that glitter was once synonymous with glorification.

The Barrio de Santa Cruz

No district in Seville has more native flavor than the Barrio de Santa Cruz, and it provides a refreshing break from peering at paintings and admiring architecture. This former Jewish quarter begins just east of the cathedral area. Many of its streets are narrow enough to be confined to pedestrians only, and in any event a car would be a hindrance in finding your way through this labyrinthine maze. This is an area for meandering about on individual voyages of discovery.

Almost all the white three-story buildings here have flowers in window boxes, flowers at doorsteps, and flowers and plants in courtyards glimpsed through black-grilled gateways. Little seems to have changed since George Borrow wrote, in 1843, "Nothing is more calculated to interest the stranger as he wanders through Seville than a view of these courts obtained from the street through the iron-grated door. Oft have I stopped to observe them, and as often sighed that my fate did not permit me to reside in such an Eden for the remainder of my days." Such inner courtyards usually have a central fountain and, beyond the abundance of greenery and the ubiquitous geraniums, a dado of Moorish tiles. In summer such a retreat, covered with an awning, serves as a family living room.

The *barrio* today is an odd mixture of fashionable neighborhood, tourist lure (not yet a trap), artisans' shops, low-income dwellings, restaurants, and *tapas* bars. Somehow it has managed, like the Jewish quarter of Córdoba, to retain its distinctive air. (Once more, we must strike a cautionary note: In such secluded areas it pays to be careful about camera straps, shoulder bags, and other "detachable" personal items.)

In the Barrio de Santa Cruz you have a chance to stroll at will, to stare, to pause, to enjoy a drink and *tapas,* to balance the cultural weight of the city's historic sites with a welcome sense of leisure and freedom from itineraries. The elegant narrow streets are cool, comparatively speaking; the little squares are shaded by orange trees and small palms; many of the iron grilles are exquisitely wrought; the artisans' workshops are often stimulating to visit. And what passerby can resist the temptation to peer innocently through the entrance of a particularly beautiful flower-filled patio?

North of the Cathedral Area

Three blocks up Avenida de la Constitución, which runs along the west side of the cathedral, is the Plaza Nueva, the *ayuntamiento* (city hall), and the shopping district, which is centered on the pedestrians-only street Calle Sierpes. To the northwest of Plaza Nueva is Seville's fine-arts museum, the Museo de Bellas Artes, featuring a good collection of works by many of Spain's greatest artists. Northeast of Plaza Nueva is Casa de Pilatos, a 15th-century palace full of Roman artifacts and artwork. A pleasurable morning excursion could include both the Casa de Pilatos and the Museo de Bellas Artes, a short taxi ride away from each other.

CASA DE PILATOS

The Casa de Pilatos, a superb Renaissance palace built in 1480 by Pedro Enríques de Ribera, is ostensibly fashioned in the style of the Roman villa of Pontius Pilate. The house, with its grand central patio and adjacent gardens of lemon and orange trees, features particularly fine examples of luster-ware tiles. Gothic, Renaissance, and rather pronounced

Mudejar styles have been incorporated in a way that transfigures the Roman model, and somehow the integration works handsomely. The two-story mansion—it has one of the very few domed stairways in Spain—is furnished with countless Roman artifacts: statues, busts, helmets, reclining figures. Some of the elaborate Mudejar ceilings are intricately worked in gold. The Gothic chapel has heavy Mudejar stucco and beautiful *azulejos* (glazed tiles).

The house, on Calle Aguilas, once the center of Seville, was at that time the starting point for the annual Holy Week processions. The patio fountain, centered on a tiled surface and enclosed by a gallery of marble pillars supporting Roman arches, suggests the cool spaciousness of symmetrical design that characterizes the Spanish Renaissance at its best.

MUSEO DE BELLAS ARTES

Housed in a 17th-century monastery with beautiful interior courtyards on the Plaza del Museo, the fine arts museum is about half a mile northwest of the cathedral. Specializing in the Golden Age–Renaissance period of Spain, the museum places emphasis on Seville's illustrious native artists. Murillo is the star here; room 7 alone has 20 of his works, his luminous floating style perhaps best exemplified by his colossal *Inmaculada Concepción*. In contrast, El Greco's small, intimate portrait of his son, *Portrait of Jorge Manuel,* captures the haunting intensity of his genius. Diego Velázquez, who was born in Seville but made his career in Madrid, has scant exposure in the museum; several canvases by his father-in-law and teacher, Francisco Pacheco, mostly accentuate Pacheco's limitations. José Ribera, Alonso Cano, Valdés Leal, and especially Francisco Zurbarán round out the museum's collection.

Despite the museum's seemingly endless and extensive renovations, a visit here is disarmingly low-key and casually rewards the patron with a view of treasures. Seville's role in great Spanish art remains unquestioned.

South of the Cathedral Area

THE UNIVERSITY

Seville's 18th-century university is the largest building in Spain after El Escorial; it is said to have more than 100 courtyards. Once a cigar factory and exchange house, it served as the setting of Bizet's *Carmen* and is said to have employed 10,000 cigar makers.

The building, across Calle San Fernando from and south of the Alcázar gardens (San Fernando itself has bookshops and, at its eastern end, a comfortable *tapas* bar), has corridors the length of football fields, down which stride a prodigious number of students. The coffee shop has the cigarette-butts-and-peanut-shells overtones of a *tapas* bar, and the classrooms are archaic. What matters here is serious academic pursuit. You get a tangible sense of the youthful energy of Spain today, and the lack of physical amenities provides a sharp and instructive physical contrast with American and English universities.

PARQUE DE MARIA LUISA

"We drove through the Parque de María Luisa and down the Paseo de las Delicias, names that breathe or whisper of the tall acacias, the roses, camellias, and orange trees, of what must be the most beautiful park in Europe," wrote Sacheverell Sitwell. The Parque de María Luisa, running for many acres along the banks of the Río Guadalquivir south of the Alcázar and then the university, was laid out by the French garden designer J. C. N. Forestier in the 19th century. It was initially English in design, but today its style is distinctly Spanish, with fountains, avenues, tiled benches, and romantic sweeps.

A half-day visit to this beautiful park gives you a sense of the pleasure Sevillanos, who use the park extensively, take in their seductive city. Huge acacia trees with clusters of white or yellow flowers contrast dramatically with the languorous palm trees and the fragrant pines. Luxuriant roses, in a dazzling range of sizes and colors, complement flower-beds that become splashes of blue and white, orange and yellow, mauve and deep purple, and here and there an explosive blaze of red. The many fountains throughout the park, in tiles of various shades of blue, ocher, and green, intensify the lure of light and color and bring a refreshing sense of coolness to the hot summer months. Somehow these fountains seem particularly "Spanish," lending the park its dominant decorative motif through this extensive use of *azulejos*. If a public park can be opulent, the María Luisa, with its ponds, swans, gazebos, and murmuring doves, surely qualifies.

The 1929 Ibero-American Exposition brought great changes to the garden area: A huge semicircular palace, the **Palacio Español**, fronted by handsome arcades, surveys a kind of moat with bridges under which pass countless small boats manned by what V. S. Pritchett called "congenitally incompetent rowers." At the southern end of the Parque de María Luisa are two large structures: the Museo de Arte y Costumbres Populares, and the Museo Arqueológico Provincial (for the latter, see below).

Seville is particularly rich in open park spaces; the abundance of flowers and softly shaded areas casts an almost irresistible spell over most visitors, and the entire population of the city seems to spend part of each weekend in its parks and gardens.

THE MUSEO ARQUEOLOGICO PROVINCIAL

The Museo Arqueológico Provincial, in the southern reaches of the Parque de María Luisa, contains most of the objects and artifacts from the ancient Roman town of Itálica, which is just 9 km/6 miles out of the city on N 630.

The handsome museum, in a large and well-lighted Renaissance pavilion, presents the exhibits chronologically. "Roman cities . . . liked to represent their gods copied from the original Greeks," reads a plaque in Spanish (there are no identifications in other languages); nearby statues of Mercury and Hermes attest to this close artistic connection. Particularly interesting are the magnificent mosaic floors, including one from the third century A.D. depicting Bacchus, and a number of stunning mosaics mounted on walls. Busts, funerary inscriptions, numerous amphorae, Roman glass, urns, and other objects, mostly from Itálica, strengthen the collection. A large-scale wall map shows the location and extent of Iberian cities under Roman jurisdiction during the 600 years of occupation.

A display of decorative terra-cotta figures from rooftop drainage gutters reaffirms Roman ingenuity in combining the practical with the aesthetically pleasing. In room XXVI of the museum, a display of elaborate Visigothic jewelry of the post-Roman period is a kind of Andalusian counterpart to the Visigothic jeweled votive crown in Madrid's Museo Arqueológico Nacional. There is also a picture display of the excavations at **Munigua**, north of Carmona (some 40 km/25 miles from Seville), where archaeological work is currently in progress.

Itálica

The birthplace of two Roman emperors, Itálica was clearly a provincial city of substance. Its ruins are easily reached today from Seville by local bus, which leaves every half-hour from Calle Marqués de Paradas, three blocks north of Calle de los Reyes Católicos. At Itálica are the impressive remains of an enormous amphitheater (said to have seated 40,000) and the grid of an urban complex, the streets clearly outlined, the floors of some of the buildings showing artful and imaginative mosaics. But the city is dead, moribund as only an archaeological dig site can be; the objects signifying the lives and artistries and energies of its former dwellers have been moved elsewhere. Smack in the middle of the nearby contemporary town of **Santiponce** stand the ruins of another Roman theater, and archaeological work is still going on in the outskirts of town.

Staying in Seville

Seville has a number of international-style hotels indistinguishable from their fellows, most of which are a bit removed from the cathedral-Giralda area. The most satisfying accommodation is in this locality, where no transportation other than your feet is needed.

The monarch of Seville's hotels, as it has been for most of this century, is the *gran-luxe* and decidedly pricey ▶ **Hotel Alfonso XIII**, where even the maids have maids. Occupying the most central and expensive real estate in the city, south of the Alcázar gardens and just west of the university at Calle San Fernando 2, the Alfonso sits there imperturbably, indifferent to its architectural façade—which comes close to parody. It is hard to determine precisely what the architects had in mind in this marriage of pseudo-Moorish and Edwardian. The hotel has a huge open central court (it was built before Seville summers were rendered bearable by air conditioning). The two small elevators have mirrored walls, brocaded benches, carpeted floors, three doors to close before they function, and young, uniformed attendants to ensure that they do. The newly refurbished three floors above the lobby/dining-salon/bar area are connected by carpeted stairways whose side walls are enticingly covered with decorative tiles, making walking or taking the lift a difficult choice.

Once you enter the spacious bedrooms or suites, all is comfort and modernity, from air conditioning to minibars to huge marbled bathrooms. The windows look out beyond the tops of orange trees to the swimming pool below and the muted traffic of Seville in the distance. Having a drink in the inner courtyard downstairs is an event in itself. The dining room goes well beyond conventional hotel fare and service.

Also centrally located is the ▶ **Doña María**, a superior 64-room hotel (with no dining room), just east of the Giralda on Calle Don Remondo. The decorating hand has been unrestrained in some of the rooms, but otherwise the Doña María is ideal for travellers who want to avoid tour groups and conventions. The hotel has a rooftop swimming pool.

The ▶ **Inglaterra** is another well-located and highly rated hotel, facing the *ayuntamiento*'s Plateresque façade from across the Plaza Nueva. The terrace dining room overlooks the Plaza Nueva, a central gathering place for many Seville festivals. An added boon is garage space here in midtown Seville. The hotel's 120 rooms were recently modernized,

and all are air-conditioned and comfortably, if unexcep-
tionally, furnished. Rooms that face the Plaza Nueva can be
noisy.

▶ **Las Casas de la Judería** is a cluster of 35 deluxe suites
hidden in the heart of the Barrio de Santa Cruz in what was
once the palatial residence of the 17th-century duke of Béjar.
The handsomely appointed suites—from one to three bedrooms—have fully equipped kitchens, living rooms, and
decoratively tiled bathrooms. Las Casas has a large underground garage, although the complex itself is difficult to
locate except by taxi. If you are driving in, enter the *barrio*
on Calle Mateos Gago, opposite the Giralda entrance, turn
right at Calle Fabiola, and proceed to Calle Santa María la
Blanca. Here is the narrow alleyway, Callejón de Dos Hermanas, that leads to the apartments: a real find.

Convenient to La Maestranza (the bullring) on Calle de
Canalejas, the ▶ **Tryp Colón** offers uncommon comfort and
perhaps the best hotel service in town. Built for the 1929
Ibero-American Exposition, the Colón has been completely
refurbished and once again ranks among Seville's select few
highly rated hotels.

STAYING IN CARMONA

Some 38 km (24 miles) east of Seville, on the newly widened
highway to Córdoba, the town of **Carmona**—Roman walls,
Moorish fortifications, whitewashed houses—has a wonderful parador, the ▶ **Parador Alcázar del Rey Don Pedro**, in
the hillside Moorish castle that Peter the Cruel took over as
his palace. A recent stunning addition to the Carmona hotel
roster is the 30-room (20 of which are suites) ▶ **Casa de
Carmona** in the 16th-century palace of the Lasso de la Vega
family. The rooms are luxuriously and decoratively furnished, making the hotel one of those "discoveries" that
discriminating travellers like to keep secret. Carmona is just
16 km (10 miles) from Seville's greatly expanded international airport, and 24 km (15 miles) from the new Santa Justa
railway station, which serves all Seville's rail travel.

Dining in Seville

TAPAS

Locals claim that the *tapas* custom began in Seville. Certainly
it is a long-entrenched habit in this city to stop at a favorite
bar, nibble a few tasty tidbits (called *raciones* here, as the
portion is a bit larger) with a glass of Sherry, move on to
another bar for its specialty, and finally sit down to lunch or
dinner. As the locals eat late (2:30 P.M. for lunch, 10:30 to
11:00 P.M. for dinner, although restaurants open earlier for

tourists), the *tapas* custom is a delightful way to stave off hunger and see a different side of the city at the same time.

Tapas Bars in the Triana Quarter

Many of Seville's liveliest *tapas* bars are on the west side of the Río Guadalquivir in the **Triana** area (traditionally the Gypsy quarter, but now cluttered with bars and small cafés). **Calle Salado** (which runs parallel to the street that runs directly off the Puente de San Telmo, Avenida de la República Argentina), on the block between Calles Virgen de Villadiego and Virgen de Consolación, is jammed with *tapas* bars where the youngish patrons frequently burst into spontaneous steps of flamenco or the *sevillano*. **Calle Betis**, a good restaurant street running along the west bank of the river between the Puente de San Telmo and Puente de Isabel II, also has a number of bustling *tapas* bars. One of the most rollicking is **Kiosco Las Flores**, Calle Betis 1, at the foot of Puente de Isabel II, popular for its *gambas fritas* (fried shrimp) and *coquinas* (clams in garlic). With most of its tables outside, spilling up the steps of the bridge, it's a great spot for people-watching until late hours. **La Albariza**, Calle Betis 6, serving terrific *jamón serrano,* has a charming rustic look, with tiles, white-washed walls, and wine-keg tables. **Taberna Sol y Sombra**, just outside of Triana, north of Puente de Isabel II at Calle de Castilla 151, is a favorite of bullfight aficionados for its old *torero* posters and memorabilia as much as for the garlicky shrimp, garlicky beef tenderloin (*puntillitas*), and *jamón de Jabugo.*

Tapas Bars in the Cathedral Area

On the east side of the river, **Casa Robles**, just north of the cathedral at Calle Alvarez Quintero 58, has delicious *planchas setas,* grilled with herbs, garlic, and olive oil. Several choice spots in the Barrio Santa Cruz are: **Casa Román**, facing Plaza de los Venerables (off the northeast corner of the Alcázar), known for its variety of sausages and cured hams (which hang from the ceiling); **Hostería del Laurel** (next door on the same tiny plaza), hung with hams, drying herbs, and strands of red peppers, and serving excellent ham, *tortillas,* and *cola de toro* (braised oxtails), with a decent restaurant in the rear as well (try the *paella*); and **Bar Modesto**, Calle Cano y Cueto 5, near Plaza de Santa Cruz, featuring *coquinas* and *fritura Modesta* fried squid and vegetables) amidst a good variety of *tapas*.

RESTAURANTS

Seville's restaurant scene has expanded considerably in recent years, though the pickings are still meager by big-city standards.

The city's newest, and arguably its best, restaurant is **Taberna del Alabardero**, at Calle Zaragoza 20 (a block west of Plaza Nueva). Part of a group of restaurants run by Father Luis de Lezama (others are in Madrid, Puerto Banus–Marbella, and Washington, D.C.), this branch is located in a restored 18th-century, three-story mansion, where a local poet-dramatist (Juan Antonio Cavetany y González Nandín) was born in 1861. On the ground floor is a charming bar in an open-air atrium; upstairs are three elegant dining rooms, with classical plasterwork on the ceilings. The *nueva cocina* food—a wonderful duck paté, roasted peppers stuffed with shrimp, mushrooms, and spinach in a pimiento sauce, chicken stuffed with foie gras and truffles—is elegant, too, if pricey. A *menú de degustación* (tasting menu) offers a sampling of a variety of dishes. Reservations are a must; Tel: 456-0637. The mansion also has seven handsome and expensive suites for overnight.

Also new and popular with local trend-setters is **Parabere**, Calle Narciso Campillo 4 (northwest of the cathedral area between Calle de las Reyes Católicos and La Maestranza). This tiny, funky place in a converted warehouse does a parody of the high-tech look and has a young chef doing *nueva cocina* Andalusian style. Dishes to try include the gazpacho, chicken *escabeche,* shrimp soup with curry, and broccoli with wild mushrooms and ham in a garlicky cream sauce. Tel: 456-0903.

San Marco, Calle de la Cuna 6 (off Laraña, on a street east of and parallel to Calle Sierpes) is located inside the former mansion of the countess of Lebrija, with a skylight, beamed ceilings, rose-colored walls, marble floors, Roman busts in niches, and an airy ambience. The food is a blend of *nueva cocina vasca,* Italian, and some Sevillian, with homemade pastas, memorable fish dishes, sole soufflé, duck with olives, and cream of pheasant soup on the menu. Desserts are sybaritic, and there is also, as one might expect in a place of this quality, an excellent wine list. Tel: 421-2440.

The best (if perhaps most expensive) place in town for seafood, and a favorite with local businesspeople, is **La Dorada**, at Calle Virgen de Aguas Santas 6 (south off Avenida de la República Argentina, in the Triana quarter). The assorted fish, fried as only Andalusians can do it—greaseless, crisp, delicious—is wonderful. The house specialty is *dorada a la sal* (whole gilthead fish baked in a rock-salt crust, which is chipped off at tableside, leaving a moist, meaty fish), and the fish stew and Andalusian *langostinos* (prawns) are also excellent. La Dorada has branches in Madrid and Barcelona. Tel: 445-5100.

In the same area is **Rincón de Curro**, Calle Virgen de Luján 45, popular with local old-timers. Traditional dark wood paneling, low ceilings, and colored glass windows are a drab but comfortable backdrop for *casuela de mariscos y pescados* (seafood casserole), *arroz marinera* (rice and seafood), and the hearty oxtail stew, among many standard dishes. Tel: 445-0238.

Besides the *tapas* bars mentioned above, Calle Betis also has a number of inexpensive restaurants. **Pizzería San Marco**, Calle Betis 68, is attractive, with Roman arches and ceiling, good pizza, and light meals. Tel: 428-0310. Diagonally across the street is **Río Grande**, with breathtaking river views from its terrace and plain glassed-in main dining area. In reserving, insist on this room; the views of the Giralda, Torre d'Oro, and other Seville landmarks across the way are spectacular at lunch, and even more so at dinner when they are lighted. The Andalusian fare is typical, if unexceptional—gazpacho, shrimp with saffron rice, fried fish platters—but it's the Río Guadalquivir views you're paying for. Tel: 427-3956.

Egaña Oriza, Calle San Fernando 41 (at the edge of the Alcázar garden wall) is one of the prettiest, most stylish restaurants in Seville, just a block from the Hotel Alfonso XIII. Stunningly decorated with billowy banners hanging from high ceilings, its huge glass windows face the Alcázar's brick wall and parapets. The menu, mostly composed of contemporary Basque dishes, includes such wonderful choices as *ajo* soup (garlic, almonds, and white grapes), warm vegetable terrine in a spinach sauce, goose fillets with sweet corn, and duck leg with *cepes*. The handsome bar serves elegant (if pricey) *tapas*. Tel: 422-7254.

La Albahaca, Plaza de Santa Cruz 12, offers the visitor a real Andalusian experience. Tucked into the Barrio de Santa Cruz in a whitewashed Sevillan mansion, with old *azulejos* as wainscoting, the restaurant has three intimate, antiques-furnished dining rooms, all different. The food is *nueva cocina Andalucia,* which means such dishes as *caldito de Sevilla* (rice soup with chicken, ham, and mint), pumpkin soup, lamb roasted with thyme, and whole sole with orange sauce. Desserts are decadently good. Tel: 422-0714.

In an old brick building set back through a cobbled entryway at Calle Argote de Molina 26 (a cul-de-sac near the cathedral) is **Mesón Don Raimundo**, long popular for its funky, eclectic decor (mounted elk heads, strands of garlic, ceramic plates, copper pots, and Madonna statues), reasonable prices, and original dishes. There are Andalusian specialties such as *frito misto de pescaditos* (small fried fish) and *choco con uvas* (cuttlefish with grapes), many game dishes in season (rabbit, partridge, or venison casserole with Sherry), and unusual Arab-influenced dishes (gazpacho with smoked ham, garlic, and pine nuts; clams with pine nuts), and remarkable Arab-accented desserts such as prunes in honey, figs and dates in cream and syrup, and whipped cream studded with toasted pine nuts. Tel: 422-3355.

Very handy after sightseeing is **Figón del Cabildo**, located at the edge of the crescent-shaped Plaza del Cabildo, entered through Pasaje de los Seises, a narrow passageway off Avenida de la Constitución, just west of the cathedral. (A sign in the passage states that the renowned 16th-century silver craftsman, Enrique de Arfe—father of Antonio and grandfather of Juan—once had his workshop here.) The lively ground-floor bar, with a beamed ceiling and gleaming copper kettles hung over a brick hearth, has terrific *tapas*. The "rusticated" upstairs dining room, festooned with palms and potted plants, features many local and some Continental dishes. Try the peppers stuffed with shellfish or calf's liver and spinach in a pine-nut-studded brown sauce. Tel: 422-0117.

Also convenient and popular with locals is **Enrique Becerra**, at Calle Gamazo 2, a short zigzag walk south of Plaza Nueva. The tiny entrance bar is always packed with regulars, there for the company and the great variety of *tapas*. A small dining room with a dark beamed ceiling beyond the bar is rather characterless but homey, and the food, though not inexpensive, is of high quality, relying on fresh local ingredients. As a starter, try the crisp deep-fried fresh anchovies with a layer of smoked salmon inside. Entrees such as red snapper in saffron, shark in fresh marinara sauce, or sea bass *à l'orange* are all good choices, and for dessert try the flan-like *pudding de naranja amarga,* made with orange marmalade from a local convent, or *manzana frita con salsa de crema de guindas* (fried apple slices in a cream sauce made with a local cherry liqueur). Tel: 421-3049.

—*Patricia Brooks*

Bars and Flamenco Clubs
in Seville

In a city that rarely dines before 10:00 P.M., nighttime activities tend to begin around midnight. The entire **Triana** area, on the west bank of the Río Guadalquivir between the San Telmo and the Isabel II bridges (across from the Torre del Oro and La Maestranza), is taken over nightly by Seville's younger set. Bars, discos, and restaurants vie with sidewalk gatherings to produce a scene of party-time activity, especially on weekends. Triana is not for the conservative fun seeker.

A great escape for night owls is **Bar Abades**, Calle Abades 13B (off Calle Mateos Gagos, across from the cathedral), open until 4:30 A.M. It's the "in" spot for Seville's artistic and under-40 crowd, a private house turned club (no markings outside), with comfortable chairs and couches, plants and flowers everywhere, a bar, and classical music played at medium-high volume: not a disco, not a nightclub, not a restaurant. You go there late in the evening for conversation, drink, and the sense of getting away from it all.

Tablaos (tableaux), locations where flamenco entertainment is offered, sometimes geared to the tourist trade and rather scorned by purists, include **El Patio Sevillano**, next to La Maestranza at Paseo de Cristóbal Colón 11, which usually features a number of shows during the evening; Tel: (9-5) 421-4120. **Los Gallos**, at Plaza de Santa Cruz 11, offers two shows, one at 9:00 P.M. and one from 11:00 P.M. "till dawn." Los Gallos claims to offer the purest flamenco singing and dancing, and many celebrated flamenco artists have performed here; reservations, Tel: (9-5) 421-6981.

Flamenco purists should check the schedule at the tourist office at Avenida de la Constitución 24 (Tel: 9-5-422-1404), then head for the town of **Los Palacios y Villafranca**, about 24 km (15 miles) south of Seville off N IV. **El Pozo de las Penas** is a flamenco society with its own small showplace where some of the leading (and finest) flamenco singers and musicans perform on the small stage for an appreciative audience.

Discos and jazz clubs with live entertainment are best discovered through on-the-spot schedules available at hotel front desks.

Shopping in Seville

Long known for its fans, mantillas, and ceramics, Seville also has other things to interest serious shoppers: high-fashion clothes for men and women, leather items, antiques, guitars and other musical instruments, recorded flamenco music, and jams and pastries.

SHOPS IN THE CALLE SIERPES AREA

The best-known shopping area in town is Calle Sierpes, the famous pedestrian shopping street that begins at Plaza Nueva and winds north for five blocks to Larana, and the streets leading off it and several streets parallel with it (including Calles Cuna and Velázquez).

While Calle Sierpes has many touristy souvenir shops, there are some shops of greater interest on the street. **Blasfor** (at number 33) features Lladró porcelain figurines, elegant mantillas and fans, and other gifts. **Maguedano** (number 40) has a wide selection of hats of Andalusia and elsewhere in Spain. **Zadi** (number 48) is an agent for Lladró and also has a good selection of fans. **Casa Damas**, across the street at number 61, sells guitars and other instruments and recordings of Spanish music. **Segundo Antigüedades** (number 89) is known for its fine antiques. There are two excellent bookshops on Calle Sierpes, **Pascual Lazaro Papelería & Librería** (number 2–4) and **Librería San Pablo** (number 57), with coffee-table books on Spain, posters, and a variety of religious triptychs and other artifacts.

If you want to take a break from shopping, you can enjoy a coffee and pastry at the sidewalk café in front of **La Campana Confitería**, a wonderful pastry shop at the corner of Sierpes and Larana, or at **Ochoa** (number 45), a combination pastry shop, tearoom, and café.

For *feria* costumes, jewelry, and accessories, there are a number of shops along Calle Cuna, parallel to Sierpes to the east, such as **Azahares** (at number 4), **Boutique Raquel** (number 51), and, on the side street Cerrajeria (between Cuna and Sierpes), at number 65, **Trajes Sevillanos**.

Also parallel to Sierpes (to the west) is Calle Velázquez, which has many chic boutiques, including **Mango** (at number 7); **Massimo Dutti** (number 12, corner of Calle Rioja), with great-looking men's clothes; **Asunción** (number 30), for trendy sportswear; and a branch of **C & A** department store at the point where Velázquez becomes Tetuan. On Tetuan, look for **Yanko** (at number 6) and **Mapro's** (number 3) for better men's clothes. **El Corte Ingles** has a large store at Plaza Duque de la Victoria (just north of Velázquez). Two blocks to the west, at Plaza de la Concordia 2, there's a branch of the government-run shop **Artespaña**, selling handcrafts from Andalusia and other parts of Spain.

For leather goods—purses, belts, clothes, accessories— nothing tops **Loewe** at Plaza Nueva 12. But if you ride and want hand-made riding boots, saddles, crops, and other leather goods made the Andalusian way, pay a visit to **Guarnicionería San Pablo** on Calle Bailén (just northwest of Plaza Nueva near the Magdalen church), a tiny shop crammed with leather goods.

SHOPS IN THE BARRIO DE SANTA CRUZ

While shops in the Barrio de Santa Cruz are largely tourist magnets, there are exceptions. The best shopping for antiques in Seville is along the *barrio*'s Calle Mateos Gago, in such shops as **Alberto Linares** (at number 5) and **A. Linares Muñoz** (number 8). **Renacimiento** (number 27) has antique books.

On Pasaje de Vila, **Fernán Caballero** (number 13) has watercolors and stationery, and **Populart** (number 4) sells antique ceramics. **Meye Maier** (number 12) is a small boutique specializing in handmade bed linens, lingerie, and shirts made of linen, cotton, or silk. Along the short street Pasaje Andreu are three intriguing handcraft shops: **Vasijas**, with ceramics; **Arje**, with contemporary glass, ceramics, and antique furniture; and **Mascaras Moreno**, which makes imaginative carnival masks in leather and papier-mâché.

SHOPS IN THE CATHEDRAL AREA

Another shopping area of interest is the Plaza del Cabildo, a tiny complex reached via a narrow passageway from Avenida de la Constitución (across from the cathedral). There you'll find **Antigüedades Lola Ortega**, an antiques shop; **Petrus**, for clothes; **Editorial Hiares**, for books; **Nomismática Pliego**, for stamps and coins. A coin and stamp market is held on the plaza every Sunday morning.

In the middle of the crescent-shaped building on the Plaza del Cabildo is **El Torno**, a tiny shop with fretted brown wood shutters, where you can buy hand-made baby clothes and sweaters, jams, marmalade made from bitter Seville oranges, and various kinds of tortes, almond cookies, *empanadas,* and cakes, all made by the nuns of various Seville and local Andalusian convents.

For more conventional sweets, try **Confitería Filella**, on the ground floor of a magnificent faux-Arabic building at the corner of Avenida de la Constitución and Fernández y González (across from the *ayuntamiento*). It has a fine selection of pastries and also sells packaged candies for gifts.

SHOPPING IN CONVENTS

You can visit the city's many convents for their edible specialties. These include the **Convento de San Leandro**, Plaza de San Ildefonso 1 (northeast of the cathedral), originator of the famous *yemas de San Leandro* (sweets made of egg yolks and sugar); **Convento de Santa Paula**, Calle Santa Paula 11 (at the northeastern edge of town), for marmalades, jams, and bitter-orange sweets; and **Convento de Santa Inés**, Calle Doña María Coronel 5 (a few blocks north of San Leandro), for *bollitos* (little cakes) and coffee cakes. These are cloistered convents, so the drill is to ring a bell and wait for a nun to appear or a voice to ask what you want. There is usually a list (in Spanish) of sweets available and prices. You place your order, and in a few minutes, a "lazy Susan" against the wall spins around, you put your money in it, it spins again, and there is your order all boxed to take away. Inquire at the tourist office for convent hours. Generally speaking, most are open from 9:00 A.M. to 1:00 P.M. weekdays.

ALAMEDA DE HERCULES
On Sundays a huge outdoor market is set up along Alameda de Hércules, north of the Calle Sierpes area, with stands and stalls selling antique and used objects, as well as new costume jewelry, tapes, records, gifts, and handicrafts. People-watching is a big part of the lively scene. Go early—things close up by 3:00 P.M.

—Patricia Brooks

Festivals in Seville

No one should visit Seville during either Holy Week or the April Fair (usually from April 18 to April 23, except when these dates conflict with Easter, in which case the fair takes place a week later) unless the express objective of the visit is to be among the celebrants. During these two periods the city is completely given over to celebration, the one somber, the other boisterous. Hotel rates zoom, restaurants are jammed, and streets are impassable.

During Semana Santa (Holy Week), processions of more than 50 brotherhoods take place in every section of the city. Groups of men, sometimes numbering 40 or more, carry on their shoulders *pasos* (floats) with religious figures, elaborately conceived and adorned with flowers. The streets are usually darkened and the *pasos* are accompanied by penitents dressed in long robes and pointed hoods and carrying tall, lighted candles. Dirges and *saetas*—mournful hymns based on flamenco music—fill the air, and fife and drum corps provide the musical accompaniment.

The April Fair (Feria de Abril) is an explosion of dancing—flamenco and *sevillana* in particular—wine drinking, bull-fighting, parades of horses and carriages, floodlights, fireworks, picnics, and parties. Men wear leather chaps with scarlet cummerbunds, short jackets, and broad-brimmed hats; the women are spectacularly costumed in full-skirted flamenco dresses, often with vivid polka dots; flowers adorn their hair. The fair began as a rural livestock gathering in 1848, and, while cattle-dealing still goes on, such relatively mundane activities are secondary in this rush of festive excitement and riotous color.

THE 1992 WORLD'S FAIR
The aftermath of Expo '92, the International Exposition or World's Fair, leaves Seville in a position that makes most other Spanish cities groan with envy: Seville now has world-class air, rail, and highway facilities. Seven new bridges and an opera house have become permanent parts of the cityscape. Hotel and restaurant facilities are at top level, and the city is

geared to handle countless travellers. Once again Seville took a chance, grabbed the ring, and stole the spotlight.

From its instigation, the World's Fair site was planned to be used thereafter for cultural and sporting activities. A science and technology center for the purposes of education, research, and technological development now functions as a natural outcome of Expo's infrastructure.

CORDOBA

Contemporary Córdoba, 128 km (80 miles) east-northeast of Seville, may not capture the heart of the casual visitor; the mind is a more likely target. This was, after all, the home of Seneca, Averroës, and Maimonides, and it remains a place where Muslim architecture and decoration vie with their Christian counterparts. But Córdoba in the late 20th century seems content to coast on its illustrious past, an inviting prospect for the visitor (except that in summer the city is a cauldron). Córdoba cannot compare with Seville or Granada in diversity of sights, accommodations, and activities. Romanticists say that underneath modern Córdoba lies a Moorish city, and beneath that a Roman one; realists reply that the surface is what the traveller encounters.

The Arabic Heritage

That Cordoban surface has a mosque fit to dazzle the world, an Arabic-Jewish quarter of a richly evocative flavor, and, just 7 km (4½ miles) away, the ruins of a palace, the Medina Azahara, that may once have been unequaled in splendor and opulence.

At the time of the Roman Empire, Augustus chose Córdoba as the capital of the province of Baetica (Andalusia). The importance of Córdoba declined under the Visigoths, but the Arabs, who captured the city in 711, made it the capital of Moorish Spain in 756. Córdoba became a caliphate in 929 at a time when Muslim Spain was the most advanced country in Europe. In the tenth century Córdoba was the continent's largest, wealthiest, and most cultured city.

Moorish Córdoba was a center for science in the Middle Ages: Medicine, botany, chemistry, physics, mathematics, astronomy, geography, and Greek philosophy could be studied there. Algebra and spherical trigonometry were almost entirely inventions of the Arabs, who had also introduced Arabic numerals (more precisely, Hindu-Arabic numerals), vastly more adaptable to mathematics than the Roman ones. Astrolabes, predecessors of sextants inherited by the Muslims from the Greeks, were used for navigational, astrological, and

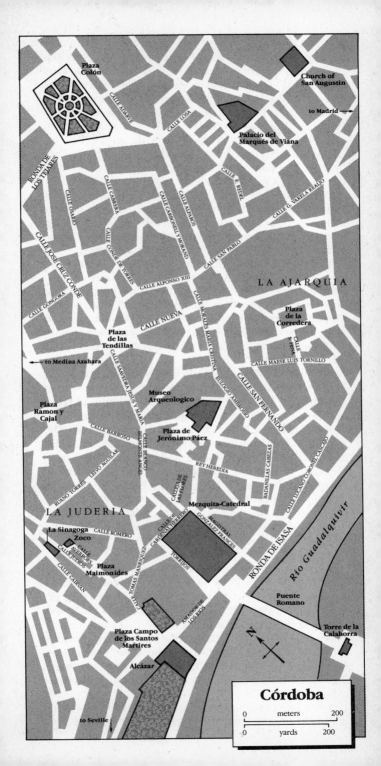

Plaza
Colón

Church of
San Augustin

CALLE ADARVE

CALLE LOSA

to Madrid →

Palacio del
Marqués de Viana

RONDA DE
LOS TEJARES

CALLE OSARIO

CALLE CABRERA

CALLE CARBONELL Y MORAND

CALLE ALFAROS

CALLE E. REPISO

CALLE CONDE DE TORRES

CALLE G. VARELA REALIO

CALLE JOSÉ CRUZ CONDE

CALLE SAN PABLO

CALLE ALFONSO XIII

LA AJARQUIA

CALLE GONGORA

CALLE NUEVA

Plaza
de la
Corredera

CALLE MORALES MARIA CRISTINA

Plaza
de las
Tendillas

CALLE
S. PENA

CALLE MAESE LUIS TORNILLO

← to Medina Azahara

EULOGIO AMBROSIO

CALLE SAAVEDRA JESÚS Y MARÍA

CALLE SAN FERNANDO

Museo
Arqueologico

Pláza
Ramon y
Cajal

CALLE BARROSO

Plaza de
Jerónimo Páez

CALLE BLANCO

BELMONTE ANGEL

RUANO TORRES LEIVO AGUILAR

REY HEREDIA

BADANILLAS CABEZAS

CALLE LUCANO CORONEL CASCAO

LA JUDERIA

CALLE ROMERO

CALLE DE
LAS FLORES

Mezquita-Catedral

Río Guadalquivir

La Sinagoga
Zoco

CALLE
AVERROES

CALLE DE
CARDENAL HERRERO

MAGISTRAL
GONZALEZ FRANCES

CALLE JUDIOS

Plaza
Maimonides

TORRIJOS

RONDA DE ISASA

CALLE CAIRAN

Puente
Romano

CALLE TOMAS MANRIQUEZ

Plaza Campo
de los Santos
Martires

AMADOR DE
LOS RIOS

N

Torre de la
Calahorra

Alcázar

to Seville →

Córdoba

| 0 | meters | 200 |
| 0 | yards | 200 |

timekeeping purposes (a 1080 A.D. brass astrolabe from Arabic Spain is currently a treasured holding of the Nürnberg museum); it is entertaining to speculate whether the Age of Discovery would have unfolded when it did, and from where, if the Arabs had not brought this instrument to the Iberian Peninsula. Córdoba probably had the first real European university in the sense in which we use the term today.

The Arabs changed the sound and the look of Spain. They brought into Europe many musical instruments, including the *shawm* (a forerunner of the oboe), kettle drums, the lute, and the oval guitar; they gave to Spanish music the exotic quality that identifies it today. They introduced paper to Europe, making possible the development of printing. Some say that Córdoba inaugurated European glassmaking, and certainly glass was widely used in Moorish Spain.

The Moors' high level of civilization rested squarely on agriculture. They used waterwheels and dug carefully engineered irrigation ditches. (From the Roman bridge in Córdoba today you can spot an Arab mill 100 yards downstream.) Flowing water was crucial to the Moors for ritual cleansing, to provide aesthetic delight in parks and gardens, and to ensure sufficient produce from fields and orchards to sustain a large urban population.

Christians living in Moorish Córdoba were initially allowed to retain some churches and use their own schools and libraries, but as the Reconquest in the north of Spain bit ever deeper into the peninsula, Latin was banned and Christian children in the city attended Arabic schools. The Jews, who had been fiercely persecuted by the Visigoths, flourished under Moorish rule, and many emigrated from the East to settle in Córdoba. As a center of Hebrew learning in the Middle Ages, the city boasted a Talmudic school renowned throughout Europe. Arabic was the official language, but bilingualism in Arabic and Hispano-Roman dialect (the Spanish linguistic equivalent of Middle English) was the norm among the educated classes of all religions.

The city was the birthplace of many celebrated figures: the rhetorician Seneca (55 B.C.–A.D. 39) and his son, Lucius (4 B.C.–A.D. 65); the poet Lucan (39–63); the writers Juan de Mena (1411–1456) and Luis de Góngora (1561–1627); and the painters Pablo de Céspedes (1538–1608) and Juan de Valdés Leal (1631–1691). But it is the philosophers Averroës (in Arabic, Ibn-Rushd; 1126–1198) and Moses Maimonides (1135–1204), both born in Córdoba, who epitomize the importance of the city, and Moorish Andalusia, to Western culture.

It was largely through Andalusia that Aristotle was introduced to Christian Europe. Averroës—at one time the chief judge of Córdoba—was the commentator on the texts of Aristotle and other Greeks that had been assembled and transmitted across North Africa by the scholars of the Arab world (many of whom were Jews and other peoples). When, after Averroës's death, his commentaries were translated into Latin, there occurred a great burst of interest in philosophy in the West. The major problem of how to reconcile the rational aspects of the resurfaced Greek thought with revealed Christian tenets absorbed Peter Abelard, Duns Scotus, Thomas Aquinas, and other celebrated doctors of the church. Averroës's commentaries were part of European university curricula for centuries following his death. Maimonides was concerned with Aristotle as well. All three cultures, in fact—Jewish, Christian, Arabic—shared the common problem of reconciling their individual religious laws with Aristotelian thought.

Arab schools of thought in medieval Spain were not necessarily those at the apex of Arab civilization as a whole, but they, and the rest of Arab culture in Spain, were truly dazzling in relation to the Christian West of the time—which they so greatly influenced.

By the time Córdoba fell to the Christians, its place in the European, the Arabic, and the Spanish sun had faded. The conqueror Ferdinand II found Córdoba in 1236 no longer "the capital of a flourishing, civilized state, but a decayed provincial town." The baton had long since passed to Seville, which when captured a mere 12 years later by Ferdinand III of Castile would in turn lose its leading role in Muslim culture to Granada, which remained preeminent for slightly more than 200 years.

AROUND IN CORDOBA

Although Córdoba is a relatively large Andalusian city (population 300,000), the area of interest to visitors is compact and can be covered easily on foot. The Mezquita-Catedral (Mosque-Cathedral) and the Alcázar are on the north bank of the Río Guadalquivir (known as the Baetis to the Romans and now no longer navigable), near a sharp bend in the river. A few blocks west, the Paseo de la Victoria (which becomes the Avenida de Cervantes) runs directly north (about 20 blocks) to the railway station. The old town, to the east of these boulevards, contains La Judería (the ancient Jewish section), the Museo Arqueológico, La Sinagoga, the Palacio de Marqués de Viana, the Plaza de Toros, the Zoco—an open-air marketplace with shops selling leather and silver filigree—a dozen churches and monasteries (Romanesque-Gothic, Baroque, Neoclassical), and, of course, restaurants and hotels. The Mezquita-Catedral is directly north of the old Roman bridge; the Alcázar is a block to the west on the riverbank.

Strolling around this exceptional city, with its strong Moorish character, gives you a sense of Córdoba's outstanding historic and cultural background; it seems little changed from its medieval-Renaissance days. The best approach is to walk from the Roman bridge to the Mezquita-Catedral, through the Jewish quarter, and up to the Palacio de Marqués de Viana.

Throughout the entire month of May the city of Córdoba is bedecked with flowers. The city's parks and squares, private patios and balconies, boulevards and alleyways are all adorned with floral arrangements of spectacular color and diversity (prizes are given for outstanding displays). This is a fine time to visit the city.

The Mezquita-Catedral

The term "unforgettable," shredded of meaning by travel chroniclers, needs resuscitation here. No visitor will forget the Mezquita-Catedral (Mosque-Cathedral) in Córdoba. But the exterior of the enormous building is forbiddingly bleak. One of the first acts of the Christians after they conquered Córdoba was to stone up the entrance doors that ranged alongside the building (and gave light and shadow to the interior rows of columns). Today you enter the mosque from the **Patio de los Naranjos** (Court of Orange Trees), usually by way of the Puerta del Pérdon (Pardon Door), to come upon a forest of more than 800 pillars dividing the rectangular building (which is slightly smaller in size than St. Peter's in Rome) into 19 north-to-south and 29 east-to-west aisles. These pillars of marble, jasper, porphyry, and breccia support two tiers of arches with alternating *voussoirs* (wedge-shaped or tapered pieces forming an arch) of white stone and red brick.

The building's columns and arches inspire a kind of visual exuberance, their delicacy and strength exalting the senses. The double arches produce a lighter and airier effect than single arches could have achieved. The limits of space are deliberately obscured so that you experience it as something fluid, limitless, and mysterious.

THE MOSQUE

The mosque is a capsule art history of Andalusia: Carthaginian and Roman pillars, Visigothic columns with fleur-de-lis carvings, Byzantine pillars from Constantinople. It occupies land that once held a Roman temple of Janus, later replaced by the Visigothic Christian church of St. Vincent. Begun in 785 by Emir Abd ar-Rahman I, the original mosque rectangle was enlarged three times, doubling the size of the building.

Columns used for interior pillars came from Carthage as well as from Roman and Visigothic buildings in France and Spain. Since their height varied, some columns were buried below floor level, while others were raised on added bases and topped with Corinthian capitals. The arches trace the famous horseshoe curve.

The mosaic tiles and marble that once covered the floor and interior walls are gone, but in front of the *mihrab* (prayer niche) the original mosaics remain, gleaming with a delicate and luminous splendor. The *mihrab,* a sacrosanct place indicating the direction of Mecca, is domed over with a single great block of white marble carved in the form of a shell. The dome is supported on star-shaped vaulting with openings through which light floods in. The niche is chained off, preventing the observer from getting a full view of its magnificence.

THE CATHEDRAL

No one who enters the mosque can be unaware that a large Christian cathedral stands within its confines. The inserted cathedral, primarily Plateresque, replaced 63 columns of the mosque. Built in the 16th century, the cathedral has its own rather eclectic architectural distinction, but its superimposition on the artistic singularity of the mosque is an aesthetic desecration. Emperor Charles V (who built the Renaissance palace in the Moors' Alhambra complex at Granada) is said to have remarked (in a suspiciously apocryphal quote that varies with each telling) that the builders of the cathedral had destroyed something unique in order to construct something that might have been erected anywhere. It is only fair to point out that the Moors themselves (after buying it) razed the Visigothic church in order to build the mosque, and we probably should be grateful that the Christians, in the fervor of the Reconquest, did not destroy the mosque entirely. Fortunately, what remains of the mosque encompasses sufficient space so that the intrusion—not only the cathedral but shrines and artifacts—can be disregarded if scarcely ignored.

Around the Mezquita-Catedral

THE PUENTE ROMANO

This bridge, which crosses the Río Guadalquivir at the foot of the Mezquita-Catedral, was built by the Romans, refurbished by the Moors, and recently had a much-needed traffic light installed at its northern end. The heavily travelled bridge has 16 arches, although the river that flows beneath it today is a pitiful remnant of the original waterway; a herd of cows regularly grazes part of the riverbed most of the year.

The pedestrian walk on the Roman bridge is so narrow that people cannot pass one another without stepping into the roadway, where vehicles are usually whizzing by; halfway across the bridge is a shrine whose candles are often lit even at high noon. The bridge itself, in inimitable Roman style, is no-nonsense, solid, and substantial, its durability somehow reassuring in a Cordoban world of historical evanescence.

At the southern end of the bridge, across the river from the Mezquita-Catedral, stands the **Torre de la Calahorra**, built in 1369 to guard the "entrance" to Córdoba. Today the tower is a historical museum, a dividing line—according to a plaque—"between east and west."

Walking back across the bridge toward the city, you get a strong sense of the history and the glory that once defined Córdoba. Directly ahead is a monumental arch erected by Philip II and said to have been designed by Juan de Herrera (the architect of El Escorial). Slightly to the left is the great medieval mosque from whose roof rises the incongruous Renaissance cathedral. Farther left, overlooking the river, is the extensive 14th-century **Alcázar**, with its fine collection of Roman mosaics. The beautiful, adjoining cypress gardens, with their tranquil pools and fountains, date back to Arabic times, as does a vegetable garden, cultivated to this day. Beyond stretches the maze of tiled roofs and white walls of the old Judería.

CALLEJA DE LAS FLORES: CORDOBAN LEATHER

Just a few hundred feet from the northeastern corner of the Mezquita-Catedral's Patio de los Naranjos is Calleja de las Flores (flower alley), a charming, if self-conscious, cobbled passageway whose white walls, flower-bedecked doorways, window boxes, and inner courtyards end in a little courtyard offering a splendid view of the cathedral belfry, which replaced the minaret of the mosque. Halfway along this absurdly narrow alleyway, pale green tiles set flush with the wall advise passersby in Spanish, English, French, Hebrew, Arabic, German, and Japanese that through an adjacent door is the **Meryan** shop and factory, specializing in fine leathers.

The Meryan shop sells embossed leather at reasonable prices, one of the few places left in Spain where leather is embossed, not simply stamped. This intricate and demanding art goes back to the time of the Moors, when the name Córdoba became synonymous with fine leatherwork. The influence of Córdoba and its art is even reflected in other languages: cordovan and cordwainer in English, *cordonnier* (shoemaker) in French, *cordewainer* in Flemish. Although the Moors first introduced hand-tooled and embossed leather to Spain, it was not until after the Reconquest in the 15th century that this Cordoban art flourished. Throughout Europe Cordoban leather, often studded with silver and gold ornaments and painted with embossed designs (called *quadamecil*), was treasured for chair coverings, chests, bedsteads, screens, and frames. In castles and churches large panels of embossed leather often hung as ornamental wall coverings.

Not everything in the Meryan shop is crafted there, and the shop has handsome jewel boxes, attaché cases, and book and folio covers as well as furniture. The proprietors will gladly show you their products, displayed in rooms once used as inner courtyards.

Visitors shopping for leather goods in Córdoba should be wary of the Zoco, at Calles Judíos and Averroës, where vendors sometimes sell "embossed" Spanish bags imported from Morocco and machine-stamped billfolds ground out in the factories of Madrid.

La Judería

The Jewish quarter, spread out north of the Mezquita-Catedral and the Alcázar, will remind you that Córdoba's Jewish population lived in economic and cultural harmony with the Moors, to their mutual benefit. On Calle Judíos, north of the Alcázar, near a monument to the physician and philosopher Moses Maimonides, is a tiny 14th-century synagogue, known as **La Sinagoga**, whose Mudejar interior has the traditional women's balcony. The synagogue is as modest in size as the Mezquita-Catedral is overwhelming. So close to the Mezquita-Catedral, the building's architectural reticence disguises its historical significance. A block or so away, on the far side of the crenellated city wall, stands a monument to Maimonides's contemporary, Averroës.

The narrow, twisting streets of the extensive Jewish quarter are delightful to explore, as glimpses of courtyards and shaded interiors succeed one another. The inevitable contrast with Seville's analogous area, the Barrio de Santa Cruz, is striking: Here in Córdoba the atmosphere is secretive, reclusive—despite the often blinding whiteness of the walls. Seville's area seems, by comparison, open and free of arcana. Here in Córdoba some of the alleyways turn back on themselves as the city slopes down to the riverbank, and it is easy literally to lose yourself in the fascinating maze. The labyrinth seems to be deserted—but unexpectedly a door opens, a pedestrian turns a corner, a dog yawns as it stretches in the warm sunlight.

Northeast of the Mezquita-Catedral

MUSEO ARQUEOLOGICO

Several blocks northeast of the Mezquita-Catedral is the Museo Arqueológico, housed in a Renaissance palace built on an old Roman foundation on the Plaza de Jerónimo Páez. The museum has artifacts from the Roman, Visigothic, Moorish, and Spanish Renaissance periods. The rooms are light and spacious and contain what some declare to be the best ceramics collection in the world, as well as the largest collection of lead sarcophagi extant. A visit offers a vivid glimpse of Spain's history. Visitors would do well to check in advance for hours and days when the museum is open; call the local tourist office, Tel: (9-57) 47-12-35.

PALACIO DEL MARQUES DE VIANA

The extensive Palacio del Marqués de Viana, a short taxi ride northeast of the Mezquita-Catedral (two blocks west of the church of San Agustín and a few blocks southeast of the railway station and Plaza Colón), was acquired as a museum in 1981. The charm of the palace lies in its numerous courtyards, which range from the classically formal colonnaded fountain area to a communal neighborhood court complete with potted plants, washtubs, and resident cats.

The palace is located in a densely populated area, but within its precincts quiet and calm prevail as you meander from flower-filled courtyards to one planted with boxwood as old as the 17th-century palace itself. Visitors can also visit the furnished rooms on the second floor, but only in the company of a guide; there are paintings by Jan Brueghels and Jacob Jordaens, Goya tapestries, Mudejar ceilings, fabulous Moorish rugs, tiled walls, rare *azulejos,* and a library of rare books. Of unusual interest in the entranceway area is the old coach room, with its ancient carriages, livery, and equestrian appurtenances. The tourist office (see the Museo Arqueológico, above) can provide the *palacio*'s hours.

Staying and Dining in Córdoba

Córdoba has limited hotel accommodations. ▶ **Parador de la Arruzafa**, large and uncharacteristically conventional in style and appointments for a parador (it has a swimming pool, for example), is north of the city limits, and you'll need a car to get there. The ▶ **Hotel Meliá Córdoba** is comfortable, unexceptional, and within walking distance of the Mezquita-Catedral.

The ▶ **Hotel Adarve**, facing the eastern side of the Mezquita-Catedral, is strikingly handsome, if a little overdressed, and gives one a sense of well-being; the ► **Hotel Maimón-ides**, on the northwestern side, is unpretentious and entirely adequate. Both these hotels are residential (no dining room, but breakfast served). The Adarve has a large garage.

El Caballo Rojo, at Calle de Cardenal Herrero 28, on the Mezquita-Catedral's northern boundary, is a delightful, atmospheric restaurant that pampers guests with good food and service, beginning with a dry Sherry *fino* and hors d'oeuvres on the house. The menu is extensive and imaginative, with an emphasis on seafood. Specialties include a snow-white Andalusian gazpacho made with almonds and a touch of garlic, and *rape mudéjar,* fresh anglerfish prepared with raisins, pine nuts, and Montilla (a wine of Córdoba). The restaurant extends for several rooms on the second floor, and its location is supremely convenient to the Mezquita-Catedral. Tel: (9-57) 47-53-75.

El Churrasco, in the heart of La Judería, has a striking interior, with a striped awning overhead to ward off the rays of the courtyard sun. Specialties are *churrasco* (grilled-meat dishes). Located at Calle Romero 16 (just northwest of the Mezquita-Catedral), it's popular and convenient to Córdoba's sites; Tel: (9-57) 29-08-19.

The Medina Azahara

Seven kilometers (4 miles) west of Córdoba, off route C 431, is a remarkable sight: the ruins of the Medina Azahara palace, which dates from 936, when Abd ar-Rahman III undertook to construct not only a royal residence but an entire city for his favorite wife, Zahara. Today this vast ruin gives only a suggestion of how magnificent the completed complex must have been: The Medina Azahara had hanging gardens, aviaries, zoos, streams, courts and kiosks, bejeweled gold fountains, and quicksilver (mercury) pools. Less than a century after its completion, it was attacked, burned, and pillaged by Muslim dissenters.

Visiting the site today is at once depressing—an Ozymandias-like capsule lesson on the ephemeral—and magnificent. The remnants of the palace lack the lacelike mural designs, the ground alabaster, and the stucco of Granada's Alhambra. Instead, the Medina Azahara is monumental, with giant blocks of marble intricately carved and said to have once been imbedded with jewels.

THE ANDALUSIAN NORTHEAST

An area of Andalusia frequently bypassed by travellers is the northeastern province of Jaén, east of Córdoba and north of

Granada. The city of Jaén, now on the main Granada–Madrid highway (N 323), is beautifully situated among vast symmetrical olive groves. A short way northeast of Jaén on N 321, which passes through agriculturally lush and peaceful countryside, are Ubeda and Baeza, two towns of exceptional interest scant miles apart, and a game preserve, Cazorla, outstanding among Spain's ten national parks. Both Baeza and Ubeda were prosperous Moorish towns—Baeza was a *taifas* (small kingdom) capital—that served as early bases for the Reconquest campaigns of Andalusia. During the Renaissance they became cities of remarkable architectural distinction, and the later shifting of campaign focus left their stunning structures almost untouched. Cazorla, infrequently visited, can be a lovely break from sightseeing, especially for sports-minded and nature-loving travellers.

These towns warrant a visit for their own sakes, but they also can be thought of as an optional side trip of a day or two from Córdoba or Granada, or as a rewarding pause on the route south to the Costa del Sol. Another choice is to make the loop through the area a side trip on the way from Córdoba to Granada. Take N IV/E 25 east from Córdoba for 108 km (67 miles) to Bailén, then continue east on N 322 for 40 km (25 miles) to reach Ubeda. Baeza is just 9 km (5½ miles) southwest on N 321. To get to Cazorla drive 10 km (6 miles) east of Ubeda on N 322, then 47 km (29 miles) southeast on J 314 and C 328. Jaén is 48 km (30 miles) southwest of Baeza on N 321, and Granada is 94 km (58 miles) south of Jaén on E 103/N 323.

In Almería province northeast of Granada are the small city of Guadix, boasting an admixture of Moorish and Renaissance monuments with communities whose dwellings are carved in natural outcroppings of porous stone, and the small town of Vélez Blanco, which has both a rare Renaissance castle and a grotto with prehistoric drawings. These towns are best visited from Granada: Guadix is 58 km (36 miles) northeast on N 342/E 26, and Velez Blanco is 116 km (72 miles) farther on the same road, plus another 5 km (3 miles) or so north on a country road.

Ubeda

One single irregularly shaped plaza in Ubeda, Plaza Vázquez de Molina, contains the most splendid assemblage of Renaissance buildings in all of Spain. Their façades are a uniform gold or sand color (the Spanish call it impure white), and their disciplined lines convey the elegance and simplicity characteristic of Renaissance architecture at its best. Just beyond the plaza are structures within two or three blocks of one another that elsewhere would have individual stellar prominence.

Why does Ubeda have this wealth of Renaissance architecture? The Spanish have an expression, "*irse por los cerros de Ubeda.*" Literally, it means "to go by way of the hills of Ubeda," but its popular meaning is "getting off the track" in conversation or just generally wasting time. Ubeda, along with its handsome neighbor Baeza, is no longer on the route to anywhere. Ubeda was once a direct-line connection between Andalusia and northern Spain. But the establishment of commercial routes by way of the city of Jaén, to the southwest, and the loss of political-military strategic position as both Córdoba and Seville fell to the Reconquest forces, meant that Ubeda ended up off the track despite her great Renaissance structures. Ironically, this also meant that no political or commercial forces felt the need to disrupt or alter them.

There are at least ten exceptional buildings in Ubeda, variations on a Renaissance theme, serenely confident in their uniformity of line but varying in all sorts of unexpected and sometimes witty quirks of design. To start your tour of Ubeda's architecture, go first to the tourist office in the Plaza de los Caídos for a small brochure, "The Map and Monuments of Ubeda," that offers invaluable line drawings and thumbnail sketches of the most outstanding buildings. The nucleus of masterworks in this small (population 30,000) town of narrow streets is Ubeda's old western section, the **Zona Monumental y Artesanía**. Excellent directional signs from N 321 through the more modern section of Ubeda lead you to the focal point, Plaza Vázquez de Molina.

PLAZA VAZQUEZ DE MOLINA

Two of the plaza's buildings have long Florentine Renaissance façades. One of them is the Parador Condestable Dávalos, a 16th-century palace (renovated in the 17th century) that belonged to Fernando Ortega, dean of Málaga. The other is the **Palacio de las Cadenas** (Palace of the Chains), designed by Andrés de Vandaelvira, with the Corinthian order on the ground floor and the Ionic above it. A third building, also by Vandaelvira, is some distance from this treasure trove of Renaissance structures: the **Hospital de Santiago**, on Calle de Obispo Cabos, several towers of which have recently had their tile work renovated. The Hospital has the disciplined severity of El Escorial without the grandiosity.

Of the churches in Ubeda, the first in rank is probably the plaza's **Capilla del Salvador**, designed by Vandaelvira and Diego de Siloé. The southern doorway of this chapel was "inspired" by Pedro Machuca, architect of Charles V's Renaissance palace at the Alhambra. Directly adjacent to El Salvador's apse is its Hospital de Ancianos ("the Salvador ancients"), strikingly beautiful with its double-tiered classic columns. Also on Plaza Vázquez de Molina is the **Iglesia de Santa María de los Reales Alcázares**, with an extraordinary and oddly shaped cloister.

ELSEWHERE IN THE ZONA MONUMENTAL

On Plaza Ayuntamiento, a building to regard with pleasure and edification is the late-16th-century **Ayuntamiento** (city hall), with its double loggia: three arches supporting pairs of Corinthian columns, above which is an open façade with six arches. This is a building on which infinite craftsmanship has been lavished. The **Palacio de Vela de los Cobos**, tucked into the corner of the narrow Calle María de Molina, just to the north, is the mid-16th-century mansion of the magistrate of Ubeda. It is a delight to observe, and its unobtrusive single white marble column at the corner balcony wittily mirrors those of the upper-floor balcony-colonnade; the building has stonecutters' marks on all its blocks. A few blocks north on Plaza Primero de Mayo is the **Iglesia de San Pablo**, a building that manages to incorporate a Gothic arched doorway within a Renaissance structure of distinction.

Of private dwellings in Ubeda, the **Casa de las Torres**, three blocks east of Plaza Vázquez de Molina at the corner of Calle Condestable Dávalos, is a Plateresque extravagance of the early 16th century, a detailed decorative morass that verges on the ludicrously excessive but manages to achieve balance.

STAYING, DINING, AND SHOPPING IN UBEDA

The hands-down place to stay and eat in Ubeda is the ▶ **Parador Condestable Dávalos**, on the Plaza Vázquez de Molina. One of the oldest of Spain's paradores (opened in 1930), it has a wonderful glass-enclosed courtyard, regal stairways, and high carved ceilings. The service in the dining room may be the best in all of Spain's paradores.

A restaurant thought well of by Spanish patrons is **Cusco**, at Explanada 8 (Parque de Vandelvira), serving an international cuisine at moderate prices. The menu offers garlic and celery soup or gazpacho as a first course, followed by fresh fish, chops, or partridge, and traditional desserts such as *flan* or mocha mousse. Tel: (9-53) 75-34-13.

Rugs made from plaited esparto grass have been a Ubedan Muslim tradition since the 11th century. The ones at the shop of **Pedro Blanco**, Calle Real 47, have original designs and shapes.

Baeza

Baeza, only 9 km (5½ miles) southwest of Ubeda on the way to Jaén, has half the population and suffers quite unfairly from the attention paid to its renowned neighbor. It suffers, too, from a lack of hotel accommodations and restaurants, and visitors usually come over from Ubeda for a quick look at the glories of Baeza and just as quickly depart.

Baeza was once a Roman town, then a prosperous Visigothic city, next the capital of a *taifas* (kingdom) under the Moors, and eventually the first town in Andalusia to fall to (or be rescued by) the Christian Reconquest forces. For a time thereafter, Baeza and Ubeda served as marshaling points for Reconquest forces in their drive south to recapture the rest of Andalusia. A printing press was established here in 1551, and a university was founded in 1595, but, like Ubeda, Baeza became a byway and eventually developed into its current mold: a quiet town in a rich agricultural area, surrounded by miles of olive groves marching in all directions of the compass.

But this peaceful town of 15,000 has some superb buildings. Along the narrow, winding, almost empty streets are 16th-century structures of rare quality. You may notice that Baeza's buildings and monuments are strikingly lacking in military fortifications: Queen Isabella had all those torn down in 1476 to end a kind of Guelph–Ghibelline, Montague–Capulet internecine struggle here between the noble families of Benavides and Carvajales.

PLAZA DE LOS LEONES

The **tourist office** of Baeza—in a building constructed in the early part of the 16th century on the Plaza de los Leones (Lions' Square)—may well have the most distinguished housing of any in Spain. Its Plateresque façade has a small projecting balcony from which the first Mass is said to have been offered after the Reconquest. Once the old civil court, it has six notaries' doorways on the ground floor. Above the doorways are medallions, and the windows of the second floor have railings and pediments.

In the center of the Plaza de los Leones is a fountain with ancient lion figures said to have been taken from the ruins of a Roman town. The statue has a tall, garbed female figure, whose lineage is reputed to be Iberian-Roman and whose likeness is that of the wife of Hannibal. This square also has a Renaissance building variously called the Old Butcher Shop, the Abattoir, and, usually, the **Carnicería**, with a gallery on its upper floor featuring a magnificent coat of arms of Charles V. As if this were not enough, the square has two monumental archways, unevenly crenella-ted, one of which, the arch of Villalar, was erected in 1526.

AROUND THE PLAZA DE LOS LEONES

Baeza has a small Romanesque church, **Iglesia de Santa Cruz**, so perfect an example of its architectural type that it could serve as a model. Just east of the Plaza de los Leones, it was constructed after the Reconquest in 1227 and has a Gothic chapel with mural frescoes. Opposite this church, the **Palacio de Jabalquinto** on the Cuesta de San Felipe, one of Baeza's great houses or palaces, is a stunner, with its Isa-belline façade, whose surprising chromatic effect is the result of the symmetrical designs etched in stone of dia-mond heads and heraldic pine cones. Flanking this façade are two elegant torch-shaped columns that rise to become small balconies. The interior of the building has a relatively simple patio with two lions at the foot of the Baroque stairway. Adjacent to the *palacio* is the old university, with its spacious patio, which became a high school in the late 19th century.

The **Catedral de Baeza**, constructed on the site of an old mosque a short walk south of the Palacio de Jabalquinto, has a 13th-century "moon" doorway, a 14th-century rose win-dow, and a monumental iron grille by Bartolomé. Just along-side the cathedral is the **Casa Consistoriales**, an elegant building with two beautiful Gothic windows and, on the door, the royal coat of arms of Juana and Philip, parents of Charles V.

The **Ayuntamiento** (city hall), north of the Plaza de los Leones off the Plaza del Pópulo, is an original and unexpected example of Andalusian Plateresque. Philip II's coat of arms is between the balconies on the upper floor. Facing the plaza is the former corn exchange, with a classic façade of five arches that are repeated on the second floor, both with Doric capi-tals. A visitor begins to wonder what Renaissance Baeza may have been like at a time when the butcher shop and the corn exchange were deemed worthy of being housed in architec-tural works of art.

Walking around in Baeza is a delight; the town is quiet and unpretentious, yet endowed with buildings and monuments of distinction. A few outsiders, succumbing to Baeza's charm, have settled here, but this small foreign enclave strives to underplay the town's rare characteristics so as to keep this jewel of a place to themselves. Like its neighbor Ubeda, however, Baeza is scalding hot in midsummer, and its mid-winter can be severe.

A very pleasant place to sample Andalusian fare here is the **Juanito** restaurant, on Paseo Arca del Agua; Tel: (9-53) 74-00-40. Air-conditioned, and thought by gourmets to offer the

best food in Jaén province, it boasts a good selection of
vintage wines. This moderately priced restaurant takes advantage of the prolific produce, game, and meats of the region.

Cazorla

Cazorla is the name of both a town and a national park. The
town, 65 km (40 miles) east of Jaén on country roads (57 km/
35 miles from Ubeda; see above), has a population of 10,250.
Its white houses with umber-tiled roofs have as a backdrop a
mammoth rock outcropping topped by the ruins of a Moorish castle and an ancient tower. The old town, clinging to this
projection, seems not to have changed much since its days as
a Moorish settlement; the new town, sprawling far below it,
is very much part of the 20th century. The town has two
castles, the Moorish one on the heights, the Castillo de la
Yedra below. Cazorla was once a practically impregnable
Moorish stronghold, and historians claim that "more than
thirty castles had to be conquered" to achieve Christian
Reconquest victory in 1248. The old town has three main
squares; the Plaza de Santa María has a Renaissance fountain
whose waters are said to come from the Río Cerezuelo
flowing beneath the square.

   Everything about the precipitously hilly town of Cazorla is
modest, except its dramatic location. Food and lodging can be
had in the town, but no hotels or restaurants are geared for
travellers. All the more reason to assure the visitor that this
hidden-away mountain town has that uncommon stamp of
authenticity: The Moorish past and the Spanish present coexist gracefully.

Cazorla National Park

This national park in northeastern Jaén province was established in 1960. Twenty kilometers (12 miles) northeast of the
town of Cazorla, it encompasses a rectangular-shaped area
whose mountains surround a deep, fertile valley. This valley
is the source of Spain's great Río Guadalquivir, which gives
life to Córdoba and Seville and empties into the Atlantic in
the Cádiz-Jerez marshland of Coto Doñana.

   The park is carefully supervised by ICONA (Institute for the
Conservation of Nature), and you must pass through a supervised gateway to enter. At the gateway, ask for directions to the
visitors' center, about 32 km (20 miles) farther into the heart
of the park. Here, in a modern building by a parking lot, are
slide shows, a diorama, and detailed maps. The park is magnificent: rich in wildlife and scenically beautiful. The roads,
however, although paved, are not for the timid, as they are

often cut into the rock above precipitous drops and have many sharp turns.

The wild mountains, peaked with whitish-gray stone, have vast tracts of pine trees. Within the park is the ► **Parador El Adelantado**, a base for hikers, sportsmen, and vacationers. From the front terrace and garden of the parador you can look out on a valley that rises up to the leveled stone perimeter far above. This vista resembles those in Bryce Canyon and Zion national parks in Utah, in the United States.

A day's hike from the parador follows a path directly behind the building that climbs perhaps 1,000 feet, levels off on a narrow but well-defined hiking trail, and carries you along on the top of the mountains, affording exceptional locations for photographing, picnicking, botanizing, and snoozing. One fork of the trail leads eventually down to the town of Cazorla; through a vent in the rocks you can see all the way below to the acres of olive trees lined up like a gigantic army on parade.

Permits for big-game (mountain goat, deer, buck) hunting during an autumn/winter season must be requested from ICONA; contact the Jaén tourist office, Tel: (9-53) 22-27-37. Wild boar can be hunted year round, but a special permit is required. Trout streams offer abundant opportunities for record catches. Bird-watchers are likely to run out of numbers here; of special interest is the rarely observable eagle owl; the tawny owl can be spotted with some frequency. Among animals, the ibex (*Capra Hispanica*), with its large, backward-curving horns, is a prized sight. Botanists will find an exceptional variety of trees, shrubs, and wildflowers; a tiny and extremely rare species of violet called the Andalusian edelweiss is found only in these parts. The scent permeating the woodland areas in this world of nature may persuade you not to return to civilization.

Jaén

The city of Jaén (population 103,000), the capital of Andalusia's northern province of the same name, is on the direct route between Madrid and the Costa del Sol by way of Granada. The city has the classic Andalusian history, having been inhabited by the Carthaginians, the Romans, the Visigoths, and the Moors, under whom it became a *taifas* capital. On its eastern side are miles of olive trees in formal rows; to the west rises Santa Catalina hill, on top of which is a castle built by the Arab king Alhamar and reconstructed in 1246 by Ferdinand III. The ► **Parador Castillo de Santa Catalina** is adjacent, with a transcendent vista of the Sierra Morena and the surrounding countryside from its many rooms with terraces. Modern architects used materials from the ancient castle ruins to build the parador, with majestic results. The French General Charles de Gaulle once stayed in a suite there on a state visit. The dining room is positively baronial: The parador's restaurant serves unexceptional meals there in exceptional surroundings. The accommodations, however, are the best in town.

Surprisingly, Jaén has less of interest than you might suspect considering its background. The streets are narrow, it is difficult to get around, and the 1525 design of the entrance to the huge cathedral by Vandaelvira succeeds in dwarfing its surroundings at the expense of aesthetics. The cathedral has superb choir stalls from the 15th and 16th centuries; in the chapter chapel there is an altarpiece by Pedro Machuca, Charles V's architect.

An extensive area of 11th-century **Arab baths** lies under the Renaissance **Palacio de Villardompardo**, on the Plaza Luisa de Marillac. Cold, warm, and hot rooms, a central pool, complex heating devices, beautiful chandeliers, and tiling cover an area so large that the baths are considered the most important in Spain. Call the provincial administration for information on available visiting times (Tel: 9-53-26-21-11) or call the baths directly (Tel: 9-53-22-33-59).

Jaén has two good restaurants. **La Fontana**, at Calle Arquitecto Berges 23, offers a variety of shellfish; Tel: (9-53) 22-88-36. **Los Mariscos**, at Calle Nueva 2, specializes in Spanish cuisine; Tel: (9-53) 25-32-06.

Guadix

About 57 km (35 miles) northeast of Granada on N 342, the ancient town of Guadix has monuments whose origins are both Arabic (fortification walls and the Alcazaba) and Reconquest (palaces, churches, and the cathedral). Guadix was a prosperous Roman colony and later an important Visigothic bishopric. The Moors occupied the town until 1489, and the Alcazaba dates from that century. The magnificent cathedral was begun in 1510 and completed 275 years later; its Gothic interior was significantly altered by Diego de Siloé, whose classical hand is also seen in the cathedral of Granada. In front of the Guadix cathedral is the arcaded Renaissance Plaza Mayor, largely rebuilt after the Spanish Civil War of the mid-1930s.

THE CAVE DWELLINGS

Although Guadix shares with Granada a vista of the snow-capped Sierra Nevada peaks in the distant background, its outcroppings of tufa, a soft, porous stone, are of more immediate interest. In the northern section of the city and in the neighboring town of Purullena, only 7 km (4 miles) away, troglodyte dwellings have been carved in the stone. Many of these dwellings have every modern appurtenance and are quite extensive. Protected from the elements, rent-free, always ripe for expansion, outfitted with chimneys, electricity, and the inevitable television, these so-called primitive dwellings are infinitely superior to slum dwellings in most large metropolitan centers.

A sizable Gypsy population adds flavor to both the cave-dwelling area and the open-air markets. Both Guadix and Purullena are famous for ceramics, and innumerable stalls display these wares. In Purullena, look for Arab-inspired pottery made with the red clay found in the area; **Miguel Cabrerizo**, Barrio Alto, has a good selection of red earthenware. In Guadix, the shop of **Ortiz Garrido**, Calle Cañada Ojeda 2, has glazed ceramics.

Vélez Blanco

In the far northeastern corner of Almería province, the little white town of Vélez Blanco offers two sterling reasons to take a slight detour off N 342 at the town of Vélez-rubio and drive some 8 km (5 miles) north on C 321 to the mountaintop on whose sides Vélez-Blanco is built. On an ancient site perches an enormous early-16th-century **castle**, one of the first buildings in Spain with an Italian Renaissance façade. To reach it by car you spiral up corkscrew streets while trying to ignore the vast panoramic view that is unfolding and praying that no vehicle is approaching in the opposite direction. From the outside, the castle is one of the most impressive in Spain: massive, turreted, crenellated, with a flying buttress–like bridge leading from one escarpment to another. Wandering through its vast rooms (all of which have huge open fireplaces), climbing to the top of its tallest tower, measuring the thickness of its great stone walls, you are struck forcibly by one obvious fact: the place is empty of its contents. The castle's interior, its magnificent courtyard and Renaissance bronze door, is not in Vélez Blanco but on Manhattan's Fifth Avenue, reconstructed in the Metropolitan Museum of Art. Undoubtedly more people see the castle's interior there than if it had remained in the backwater of Almería, but a sense of violation remains, not precisely equal to that of the pillaging of the Elgin Marbles from the Parthenon, but the analogy comes to mind.

Vélez Blanco's other outstanding sight is the **Cueva de los Letreros** (Cave of the Markings). A sign off C 321 directs you to a dust track, which turns to the left and then to the right, at which point you must leave your car. Halfway up the cliff, reached by concrete steps, is a prehistoric *abrigo* (rock shelter). You can just barely make out the sketches and paintings of human figures and animals that are said to date from 4,000 B.C. In recent years many people have thrown water on the paintings to bring out their color. The current state of the paintings is sad evidence of the frequency of this practice.

GRANADA

Granada is Andalusia's most rakish city, with a mock-sixties look to many of its pedestrians, perhaps because of the Gypsy population and a large tribe of nomadic young backpackers. Granada's mid-city traffic is horrendous (and you can't bypass the central city), but signs here are well posted: high enough that the truck ahead of you does not obscure your vision and cause you to head for Motril when your destination is Madrid.

For most travellers Granada means the Alhambra, and indeed, the city itself, despite its illustrious historic background, has a limited number of compelling attractions. Had Granada not been the last great stronghold of the Moors, causing Ferdinand and Isabella to mark it as the site of Reconquest triumph and the unification of Spain, culturally it would be ranked as a conventional Andalusian city. Should you be passing through Granada with the Alhambra as your only stop, follow signs for the cathedral area; here you will find clear signs leading you to the Plaza Nueva, where you make a sharp right uphill turn onto an unlikely looking narrow street to reach the Alhambra promontory.

AROUND IN GRANADA

Much of Granada's urban activity centers around a high traffic density point, the Plaza de Isabel la Católica, where Calle de los Reyes Católicos meets Gran Vía de Colón. Two blocks north of the plaza on Gran Vía is the entrance to the royal chapel; behind it (one entrance is on Calle de la Carcel) rises the enormous cathedral. The colorful, touristy Plaza de Bibarrambla and the Alcaicería (Silk Exchange) are a block west of the cathedral. Here you are likely to encounter Granadians from every walk of life and visitors of every nationality. The tackiest of souvenirs are on display here, as well as some fine embroidery, silver, ceramics, and brass.

Two blocks south of this atmospheric locale, Calle de los Reyes Católicos runs west to the Puerta Real, an area of traditional cafés and pastry shops. Stores in the vicinity offer an enormous variety of wares for visitors, including mantillas, shawls, leather goods, blue and green "grenadine" pottery, fans, silver filigree, dolls, woven bedspreads, and lacework.

Between Gran Vía and Calle Elvira, a street running parallel to it one block east, are some inexpensive restaurants serving savory food. East of Calle Elvira on Calle de los Reyes Católicos is the Plaza Nueva and beyond it the hillside **Albaicín** quarter, which faces the Alhambra across the puny Río Darro. White Moorish houses, some of them tiny, some opulent with high, white-walled enclosures, together with former mosques converted to churches during the Baroque period, mark this locale as the place where Moors continued to live even after the Reconquest. Walking east along the riverbank on the Carrera del Darro, you'll come to the archaeological museum, known as **Casa Castril**, on your left. Strollers will find beautiful views of the Alhambra from unexpected turns in the narrow, twisting streets of the Albaicín. If you continue east you'll reach the **Sacramonte** with its Gypsy caves, which you can see from the Alcazaba's ramparts and towers. These cave dwellings, used today by Gypsies only for putting on tourist entertainments, served as dwellings until 1963 when serious flooding compelled the Granada authorities to move the Gypsies to the suburb of La Chana.

Just three blocks east of the Plaza de Isabel la Católica is the inconspicuous Cuesta de Gomerez, leading south from the Plaza Nueva. This busy thoroughfare, lined with shops, climbs a steep slope to the Puerta de las Granadas, the archway-entrance to the extensive grounds of the Alhambra. Climbing upward, the road continues through deeply shaded elm woods, planted at Wellington's instigation, to the Alhambra promontory, where signs lead you on to the entrance of the Alcazaba-Alhambra compound. Your ticket of admission, purchased at the administration building, includes a visit to the Generalife gardens.

The Alcazaba

Travellers climbing to the summit of the Alcazaba fortress watchtower on the Alhambra promontory are forewarned: They are about to be dazzled by what awaits them. "Nothing in life," a nearby plaque reads, "nothing, is sadder than to be blind in Granada." It's all miraculously here, just as Washington Irving, the brochures, the photographs, the travel books, and all those other travellers promised.

"There is notoriously nothing more to be said on the subject," as Henry James observed of Venice. White Granada spreads out far below you; to the northeast are the Sacromonte hills, honeycombed by Gypsy caves, and a ravine. The full sweep of the Alhambra is to the east—its buildings,

towers, gardens, and the great defensive wall. And in the
distance to the southeast is the snow-clad Sierra Nevada. As if
this were not enough, at sunset nature often loses control
and indulges in a display that defines hyperbolic excess.

On this great promontory above Granada, it is not hard to
distinguish between the Alcazaba (fortress) on the "prow" of
the promontory, dating back to the ninth century, and, behind it, the Casa Real, or Alhambra, a series of palaces
constructed without any preconceived plan by two Moorish
leaders, Yusuf I (1333–1354) and Muhammad V (1354–
1391). The Alcazaba is considerably less showy than the
Alhambra, but from a standpoint of provenance it is much
closer to its original structure than the Alhambra is.

This ancient fortress has a no-nonsense look of authenticity. It was erected for military purposes, and is entirely independent of the palaces of luxury and refinement on the
eastern part of the promontory. These reddish brick and
stone façades rise from a base formed by a screen of ramparts.
Remnants of small houses, a workshop, a bakery, and a cistern, as well as dungeons for the Christian captives, are
evidence that the Alcazaba once housed a small settlement.
There's something thoroughly utilitarian about it all, a point
to keep in mind when touring the palaces; here, outside on
these battlements, we see the Moors as fighters and conquerors, tough, ruthless, and determined. Without them the Alhambra would not exist.

The Alhambra

The Alhambra is not a building but a generic term that is
used today to describe the entire hilltop settlement—except
the Alcazaba and the Generalife gardens—that includes private dwellings, shops, a small post office, a hostel, a Catholic
church, a Franciscan convent converted into a parador
(more on that below), a restaurant, a mammoth 16th-century
Renaissance palace, and an administration that handles more
than a million visitors annually.

In retrospect, the Alhambra is different from what the
traveller anticipates, as adulthood is different from the way we
perceive it as children. It is richer, less comprehensive, and
more rewarding. "Architecturally the Alhambra Palace has
little merit," writes A. C. Calvert in *Southern Spain*. "It is
impossible to trace any order in the distribution of its parts.
There is nothing imposing about the edifice, nothing stately.
Its great charm lies in its decoration, which is wonderful and,
in its own line, beyond all praise." On the other hand Jan
Morris sees the Alhambra as "foppish within, tremendous on
the outside," and V. S. Pritchett claims that "except for its
massive and splendid outer walls and gates, which are the

main beauty of the place, the Alhambra is a gay and flimsy construction."

We owe the revival of interest in Arabic Spain and in the Alhambra to Irving, Chateaubriand, Victor Hugo, and Théophile Gautier. But, as H. V. Morton observes in *A Stranger in Spain,* "Anyone who has read [Richard] Ford's grim account of the decay of the Alhambra will wonder how much of the present building is genuine and how much is restoration." The Arabic scholar James Dickie claims that "what confronts us now is but a remnant, the end-product of an uninterrupted process of metamorphosis over five centuries. It were unfair not to add that it was the much-derided Romantics who saved the Alhambra. Through the fame their writings conferred on it, the Alhambra became a household word in every language."

To those of us who visit it today, the Alhambra, however dubious its provenance, rewards us with an insight into the magnificence of Moorish architecture and decoration. What we see now may be a pale, and often inaccurate, reflection of what once was here, but enough remains to inspire us.

THE CASA REAL

The focal point for most travellers is the 25 or so palace interiors and courtyards. You enter at the Mexuar, a former council chamber, and in a vaguely predetermined order pass through the Hall of the Ambassadors, the Court of the Myrtle Trees, the Hall of the Two Sisters, the Court of the Lions with its two adjacent rooms, the Royal Baths on a lower level, and the Daraxa Garden with its *mirador* overlooking the escarpments.

How authentic is all of this? When Washington Irving arrived in 1829 for his three-month stay, the Alhambra had suffered years of neglect and decay. "The palace of the King," he wrote, had become "the nesting place of the beggar." The Alhambra, guarded by a handful of invalid soldiers garrisoned nearby, was a riot of unconventional tenancy. Whenever a tower fell to decay, wrote Irving, it was seized by "some tatterdemalion family who become joint tenants with the bats and owls of its golden halls and hang their rags, those standards of poverty, out of its windows and loopholes." Various eccentrics and one confined maniac were among the cast of characters.

The walls, the ceilings, and the floors (the numerous palace courtyards are open to the sky) bore scars from both the elements and the French military occupation of the buildings during the War of Independence (Peninsular War) in the early part of the century. When he was not immersing himself in the romantic sensibility of an imagined past, Irving observed that

the "beautiful reliefs . . . and Arabic inscriptions" were frequently "scrawled over" and the Alhambra was at the mercy of
"the pilferings of the tasteful traveler."

But as hordes of travellers follow one another through the
Alhambra today, the palace looks as fresh and inviting as if
the Moors had departed just the previous weekend. The
overwhelming impression is one of opulence of imagination, design, and craftsmanship.

Three materials predominate: plaster, wood, and tile. Frag-
ile plaster, often in stucco form, was used so extensively that it
seems evident that aesthetic satisfaction of the moment was of
more interest to the Moors than posthumous architectural
recognition. Wood was used as a decorative counterpoint to
plaster: the **Hall of the Ambassadors**, a perfect square with
some 150 designs stamped in the plaster, has an intricately
carved 60-foot-high domed cedar ceiling. Tiles are set in walls
to frame doorways and serve as dadoes to decorate the lower
part of a wall. Green, black, ocher, and white tiles predominate in the royal baths, adorning the walls and alcoves in
geometric patterns.

You pass through the much photographed and beautifully
proportioned **Court of the Myrtle Trees** and enter the pièce
de résistance, the **Court of the Lions**. This rectangular court
has a fountain at its midpoint, supported on the backs of 12
grotesque lions. On close examination (but not too close;
they were recently roped off), the lions turn out to be
caricatures of savage beasts. Their teeth are bared in bur-
lesque grins, their tails neatly wrapped around their left
hindquarters. They are stripped of any dignity by water jets
spurting from their mouths.

To the north is the Hall of the Two Sisters; to the west, the
Mocarabes Gallery; to the south, the **Abencerrajes Gallery**.
Here you are invited to kneel at the pool to catch the
reflection of the entire Court of the Lions. The marble
flooring reputedly still carries the bloodstains of some be-
headings that took place here.

The palace rooms are stripped bare. The carvings and
tracery of the walls and ceilings are mostly bone white;
remnants of the original blues and reds and golds are rarely
discernible. As with the Parthenon, contemporary viewers
get an erroneous sense of the original aesthetic. The palace's
lamps, colored glass, furniture, rugs, draperies, the play of
interior hues are gone. The tenants have left; the house is
empty.

Most of us move unthinkingly back and forth from these
chaste interiors to courtyards lush with floral exuberance
and the sparkling play of fountains. Such contrast was unknown to the Moors. For them, balance was all.

WASHINGTON IRVING'S QUARTERS

Washington Irving lived for three months in 1829 in a suite of rooms built by Charles V overlooking the Daraxa Garden. Were he to awaken in these apartments today, he would find himself, much as his character Rip Van Winkle did, in a familiar world whose properties have somehow altered. The condition of this suite in Irving's time reinforced his romanticized view of the Alhambra. The "ruined" apartments had windows "dismantled and open to the weather," and the ceilings were "broken in many places."

These rooms have been refurbished, renovated, and reconstituted. They look like a fashionable decorator's idea of a literary lair. The walls, once "scrawled over with the insignificant names of aspiring travelers," are now pristine. The carved ceilings and the tile floors are in mint condition. A desk stands apparently ready for Irving to write upon, along with silk-embroidered chairs for the comfort of his guests and a spinet for musical enjoyment. On the walls his portrait hangs near those of Ferdinand and Isabella. Beyond the windows, Irving's citron and orange trees have yielded to regal cypress rising from the garden, whose center fountain is surrounded by ten geometric planting areas.

A plaque on the door advises in Spanish that "Washington Irving wrote in these rooms his Tales of the Alhambra in the year 1829." At most, Irving wrote here a handful of the chapters that make up his book, published three years later. The door to Irving's quarters is locked, however, and the metamorphosed rooms are inaccessible, apparently awaiting Irving's return.

THE PALACE OF CHARLES V

The Emperor Charles V's immense Renaissance palace in the midst of the Alhambra is as incongruous as the Christian cathedral built with his compliance in the center of the Córdoba mosque. On the one hand the intrusions are aesthetically and culturally offensive, but on the other they call attention to the fact that Reconquest frenzy did not destroy such Moorish treasures in its wake.

Charles employed Pedro Machuca, a Spaniard who had studied in Italy under Michelangelo, as his architect in 1526. This square building, begun by Machuca in the 1530s and completed in the 20th century, has a great interior circular court open to the sky; the court has 24 double-tiered Ionic columns, and the ceilings of the colonnades are of carved cedar. The exterior of the lower surface of the building is rusticated masonry as in a Florentine Medici palace.

Unlike Córdoba's cathedral, which is superimposed on its

mosque, this is not a religious intrusion but a cultural-political statement on contrasting styles and the power they reflect. This massive palace has a cleanness of line, of symmetry, and of proportion that represents the best of late-Renaissance architecture. On its own terms it is an admirable structure: uncompromising, meticulously crafted, handsome.

The Generalife

Gardens contribute significantly to the splendor of the Alhambra. Beyond the palaces themselves, the Jardines del Partal extend from the southern embankment of the Río Darro up a series of terraces marked off by stone steps. Pools, fountains, and an opulent abundance of flowers make these gardens a place of beauty.

But the great formal garden of the Alhambra promontory is the Generalife (hen-er-al-EE-fay). This long, rectangular garden is cut into the hillside at a right angle to the Alhambra complex, separated from it by the terraced Río Darro ravine. The Generalife, a term derived from the Arabic *Gennat-Alarif,* meaning "garden of the architect," is widely considered to be one of Europe's great gardens. Three elements win it such recognition: the vistas offered from the vantage points of colonnades, balconies, and promontories; the extensive use of fountains and pools; and the plantings of trees and flowers in a climate that ensures blooms throughout the year.

Only the belvedere and the guardhouse beyond belong to Moorish times; the rest consists of Christian reconstructions and additions. The Generalife was privately owned for some years, tenanted by Spanish nobility (the marquéses de Campotojar). The plantings are contemporary, the pools and fountains extensively realigned, and, apart from some ancient trees, the Generalife is a modern re-creation of an ancient design.

The Cathedral and
the Royal Chapel

Below the Alhambra promontory stands the huge cathedral designed by Diego de Siloé in 1528. But Alonso Cano is responsible for the façade, with its three tall arcades. Cano's paintings are here as well, and in the rotunda are twin facing panels, a medallion by Cano, and figures of the Reyes Católicos at prayer by Cano's illustrious pupil Pedro de Mena. The cathedral, with five naves and nine chapels, generally gets bad reviews from art historians, however, who have described it as "pretentious" and "the saddest of wasted opportunities."

The royal chapel, right next to the cathedral, was built by Ferdinand and Isabella to hold their mausoleums and later those of their daughter, Juana la Loca (the Mad), and her husband, Philip the Fair. The chapel is an unmitigated tribute to the monarchs in the light of the glorious culminating victory of Christianity after nearly eight centuries of Moorish presence. This Renaissance chapel was designed by Enrique Egas, and the beautiful wrought-iron grille that closes off the transept was created by master Bartolomé.

Four supine figures lie in state, those of Ferdinand and Isabella carved in white marble by Domenico Fancelli, those of Juana and Philip by Bartolomé Ordóñez. In the sacristy are Ferdinand's sword, Isabella's scepter, and a collection of Isabella's fabulous art holdings, significantly non-Spanish, including works by Hans Memling, Rogier van der Weyden, Il Perugino, Pedro Berruguete, and Sandro Botticelli. The high altar retable has Renaissance groups and figures against a background of scrollwork and grotesques.

A chilling reminder of mortality as the ultimate equalizer are the four stark sarcophagi under the magnificent tomb itself (you walk down a flight of stairs to gaze at them).

Ferdinand and Isabella, who are known as Los Reyes Católicos (the Catholic monarchs), have become such legendary figures of glory in Spain that we have to remind ourselves that they represent more than just a royal couple who had a signal victory over the Moors. Under them, in 1479, Spain for the first time became a united country: Castile and Aragón were now one, at least politically. And the defeat of King Boabdil at Granada in 1492 signaled the end of nearly 800 years of Moorish occupation in Spain. For Christians this victory symbolized the triumph of Christ over Muhammad. Columbus's voyage to the New World in the same year was the beginning of a Golden Age of wealth and international power for Spain.

Largely forgotten is Isabella's installation of the Inquisition, first in Castile and then on the entire peninsula. She appointed Tomás de Torquemada as grand inquisitor in 1483, who then began systematic persecution of Moors, Jews, and, later, Protestants. In 1492, Jews in Spain were given three choices: emigration, persecution, or conversion. Most left Spain, a grievous loss of skills and intellect that was to rebound to the country's disadvantage over the following centuries.

Monasterio de la Cartuja

In the northern section of Granada (due north of the Alhambra promontory) the Carthusian monastery, known as La Cartuja, has in its church what is sometimes called a Christian response to the Alhambra's decoration. It is hardly that, but the unrestrained, exuberant Baroque stucco work on the walls and domed ceilings, almost entirely in white with opalescent and silver decorative motifs, sets them off against doors and cedar furnishings. The cloisters of the monastery are unadorned and peaceably inviting; here, as everywhere in Granada, the city's glory is the abundance and beauty of its flowers, with roses, in particular, of exquisite color and shape and impressive size.

Staying and Dining in Granada

By almost any standard, the ▶ **Parador de San Francisco**, in a renovated convent right on the Alhambra promontory that was the location of Queen Isabella's original entombment, is the best bet for lodging and dining in Granada. Its terrace looks out on the Generalife garden, and the interior of the inn reflects decorative paradores at their best. Its popularity is such that reservations must be made many months in advance.

Nearby, not on the promontory, but close enough to be removed from the bustle of the downtown area, is the venerable ▶ **Alhambra Palace**, with first-class service and rooms. The Alhambra Palace has something of a parking problem, but it is handled with admirable dispatch. The view of the city from the bar terrace is worth the price of several drinks. It's likely to be noisy in public rooms on weekends, when local celebratory functions take place.

Down in the city proper, the ▶ **Meliá Granada Hotel** with 221 rooms and a heated swimming pool, just five blocks east of the Plaza de Isabel la Católica, and the ▶ **Hotel Luz Granada** with 173 rooms, some of which have views of the Alhambra and the Sierra Nevada, on Avenida de la Constitución, which leads to both N 432 (Córdoba) and N 342 west (Málaga), are modern and geared to handle many guests.

You will find it simpler to take a taxi to most restaurants in downtown Granada, which is crisscrossed by a labyrinth of streets that follow no perceptible pattern and reflect the Roman-Visigothic-Moorish heritage. **Baroca**, west of the cathedral area, at Calle Pedro Antonio de Alarcón 34, pleases many customers with both international and Granadian cooking; Tel: (9-58) 26-50-61 (closed Sundays and the month of August). **Alacena de las Monjas**, just south of Plaza de Isabel la Católica, at Plaza Padre Suárez 5, specializes in regional foods—you may find Sierra Nevada cured ham from Trevélez and Sacramonte omelets on the menu; Tel: (9-58) 22-40-28. **Cunini**, near the northwestern corner of the cathedral on Plaza Pescadería, is known for its seafood; the shellfish is brought up daily from Motril; Tel: (9-58) 25-07-

77. On the southern side of the Alhambra hill, at Plaza Torres Bermejas 3, the **Carmen de San Miquel** has a panoramic view from its fountain-adorned patio. Its offerings include local specialties as part of its larger international menu; Tel: (9-58) 22-67-23. For lunch, a number of small and inevitably crowded restaurants in the Alhambra vicinity, most notably down the road from the Alhambra Palace hotel, have their menus and prices conveniently posted.

THE SIERRA NEVADA

The snowcapped peaks that serve as a backdrop to the Alhambra promontory are a little more than an hour's drive southeast from Granada, uphill all the way. The road (GR 420) rises to an altitude of 11,148 feet on what signs declare to be the highest route in Europe. This is Andalusia's ski center, providing some of the best skiing in Spain, even in midsummer at the highest elevations. A cluster of inns and seasonal hotels, such as the ▶ Meliá Sierra Nevada and the ▶ Meliá Sol y Nieve, in the ski resort town of Pradollano, as well as the comfortable, all-seasons ▶ Parador Sierra Nevada, about a mile beyond, provide accommodations. An excursion into the Sierra can also be a day trip from Granada.

When the road is open to the summit, you can get close to the Veleta and Mulhacén peaks, the highest in continental Spain. Some of the vistas in the quiet of the Sierra peaks are uncommonly fine, and there is something intriguing about their proximity to semitropical Granada, often a very hot place in midsummer. In nonwinter months these mountains, with their northern exposure, are rather desolate above the timberline, and there is a decided out-of-season look to the terrain. But hikes for the hearty and a parador menu that emphasizes local dishes make the Sierra Nevada inviting.

Las Alpujarras

Anyone rash enough to predict the 21st-century travel "find" in Spain might well choose Las Alpujarras, a mountain range extending southward from the Sierra Nevada to the Mediterranean. Some of the white Moorish villages in this stunning location already show telltale signs of impending touristic invasion: a low-key hippie visitation, a smattering of expatriate artists and writers, a vacation home tucked here and there in the crags, neo-boutiques, handicraft stalls, and cafés whose few outside tables are now referred to as "terraces."

Gerald Brenan, author of the most celebrated book on the Alpujarras, *South from Granada,* lived in Yegen, by his own account an unprepossessing town near the border of Almería province. Virginia Woolf, one of his visitors, was advised by Lytton Strachey, an earlier guest, not to make the trip. He was said to have declared in a high-pitched voice, "It was death."

To this day this "wild" part of Andalusia remains relatively untrod, attracting only the determined and the intrepid. What may keep it this way is its accessibility by mountain roads so narrow, winding, and precipitous that they are unlikely to be altered to accommodate touristic traffic.

A visit to a high Alpujarran town, such as Pampaneira, Bubión, or Capileira, affords a glimpse of Andalusia off the usual tourist routes. The most tortuous roads remaining in Spain will put the driver's temperament to the test, calling for utter composure (and a minimum of advice from passengers). But gratification that far exceeds mere relief in survival awaits in the grandeur and drama of the scenery. The mountains are as steep as the valleys are deep. The peaks are snowcapped well into June; the valleys are verdant, dark sluiceways for cold rushing water. The air is fresh, redolent of pine and honeysuckle.

THE MOORS IN LAS ALPUJARRAS

After the Christian Reconquest victory in Granada in 1492 many Muslims retreated to these mountains, and it was not until 1568, after several uprisings, that they were finally expelled from the area. They left behind them, as they had done along the banks of the Río Guadalquivir, a hydraulic system that enabled them to transform the slopes into croplands and orchards. They cultivated mulberries to support silkworms, and the silks made here were very highly acclaimed. The Moors' ingenuity can still be discerned on the western banks of the gorges (facing the sun), where planting terraces step up the steep inclines. (The eastern banks, almost always shaded, have little vegetation on their rocky slopes.)

The architecture of the small white Alpujarran houses, built clustered together, remains Arabic (essentially Berber) in concept and design: flat-roofed, starkly white, with rounded chimneys capped to keep out the snow. There are no inviting entrances or courtyard patios; both climate (the villages are virtually snowbound in winter) and politics dictated dwellings protective of their occupants. From a distance these towns resemble the white towns of southwestern Andalusia (see below), but here the mountains are substantially higher—indeed, Trevélez, an Alpujarran town famous for its hams, is the highest village in continental Spain—and once in them, you see that the towns are reclusive compounds of security in a world of stark and demanding beauty. You don't take a walk in the Alpujarras, you climb or descend.

INTO LAS ALPUJARRAS

To get to Las Alpujarras, drive 40 km (25 miles) south of Granada on N 323 (which continues south to meet N 340, the Costa del Sol highway), then turn east onto C 333/332. Follow C 333/332 past Lanjarón, a resort spa whose bottled water is sold throughout Spain, and just before the town of Orjiva, bear left to follow the Poqueira gorge (no route number here, just follow directional signs), which leads ever upward to three of the most enticing Alpujarran towns, Pampaneira, Bubión, and Capileira, in ascending order. They are all white and all within sight of one another.

Pampaneira, the largest, has flower-bedecked cobbled streets, and a small museum dedicated to the customs of the area. **Bubión** has a modest and inviting village compound for travellers built a few years ago in the style of the white Berber houses of the region. The compound has 24 houses of different sizes, well equipped and comfortably furnished, with fireplaces to ward off the evening chill, and a main dining room in the lodge for appetizing meals. Reservations can be made for these travellers' houses by writing or phoning the ► **Villa Turística de Bubión** (see the Accommodations Reference at the end of the chapter). Immediately north of Bubión is **Capileira**, whose houses are built almost on top of one another so that the terrace of one forms the roof of another. There is a small museum here named for Pedro de Alarcón (author of *The Three Cornered Hat*, 1874), who wrote of his journey to the Alpujarras in *Viaje a la Alpujarra* (untranslated). Capileira is slowly being discovered and could become the next decade's Mijas (see the Costa del Sol section).

Artisans in these towns have carried on the textile traditions launched by the Moors with their silkworm farming. They use hand looms to produce typical woollen blankets and rugs, the best known of which are the *mota alpujarrena* (Alpujarran thread) rugs made on wooden looms with a long metal shuttle. From other looms come plain or striped fabrics in vivid colors combined with white. The designs have an exhilarating mixture of Muslim and Christian origin: geometric shapes, animals, plants. Products handmade from the cloth, including bags, ponchos, capes, quilts, and knot rugs, are often on display in the towns; two outlets are the shop of **Nade Fabreau** on the main road in Bubión and that of **Mercedes Carrascosa and Paqui Tovar** on Calle el Cerrillo in Pampaneira.

THE
ANDALUSIAN COAST

Northern Costa de la Luz

Just 100 km (62 miles) southwest of Seville, where the Río Guadalquivir empties into the Atlantic on the northern Costa de la Luz, is the **Doñana National Park**, a 173,000-acre park containing a mind-numbing diversity of wildlife. This is a spectacular area of beaches, lagoons, and marshes, forests of juniper, pine, and cork oak, and shifting sand dunes. A short listing of animals and birds could not begin to suggest the diversity of sightings: A single ornithologist is said to have spotted 1,891 birds of 35 different species in one afternoon. The animals range from lynx to wild boar to weasels and dormice.

From Seville, the best way to reach the park is to turn off the Seville–Huelva highway (N 431) at La Palma del Condado onto a local road leading to Almonte and El Rocio. The park's information office is several miles beyond El Rocio on the right. The office has a 12-minute introductory slide presentation on Doñana's geological history, in Spanish. Visitors are not permitted to tour the park proper on their own: Four-hour safari tours leave twice daily from the park's reception area, about 11 km (7 miles) beyond the information office, at 8:30 A.M. and 5:00 P.M. from June through September and at 3:00 P.M. the rest of the year; reservations should be made at least one week in advance; Tel: (9-59) 430-0432.

Northwest of the park toward Huelva, at **Mazagón**, is the 23-room ▶ **Parador Cristóbal Colón**, which makes a handy base for exploring the area. Built on the edge of high dunes, surrounded by acres of pines and scented lavender, and lulled by the distant roar of coastal waves, the parador is one of those tranquil spots whose location you swear you will never reveal to anyone. The rooms are comfortably furnished; glass doors lead directly to the east side of the large swimming pool, around which tables and deck chairs are set next to the outdoor bar. The dining room on the second floor of the reception building offers views of the gardens and the sea. Try the **Las Dunas** restaurant at Mazagón for its *paellas* and fresh Atlantic catch.

Using the Parador Cristóbal Colón as your base, you can almost completely avoid Huelva, an uninviting industrial city,

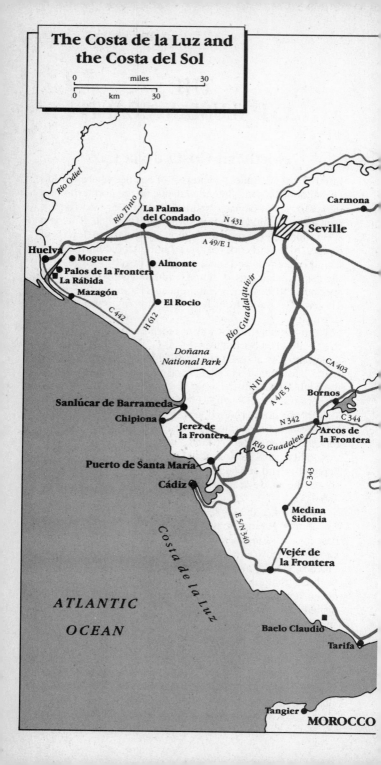

The Costa de la Luz and the Costa del Sol

0   miles   30
0   km   30

Río Odiel

Río Tinto

La Palma del Condado

N 431

Carmona

A 49/E 1

Seville

Huelva

Moguer

Almonte

Palos de la Frontera

La Rábida

Mazagón

El Rocío

C 442

H 612

Río Guadalquivir

Doñana National Park

CA 403

N IV

A 4/E 5

Bornos

Sanlúcar de Barrameda

Chipiona

Jerez de la Frontera

N 342

C 344

Arcos de la Frontera

Río Guadalete

Puerto de Santa María

C 343

Cádiz

Medina Sidonia

E 5/N 340

Vejér de la Frontera

ATLANTIC

OCEAN

Costa de la Luz

Baelo Claudio

Tarifa

Tangier

MOROCCO

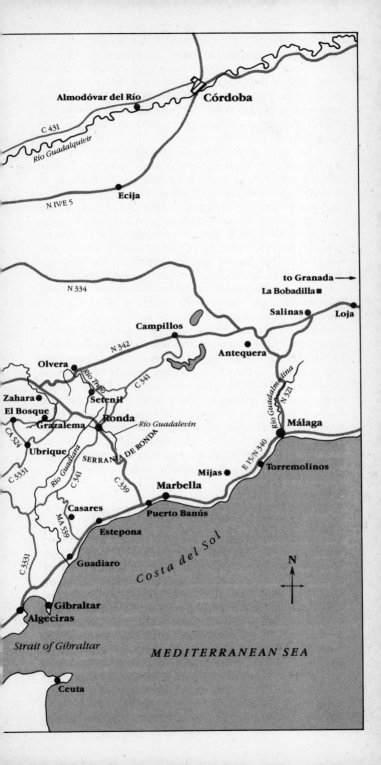

while visiting Palos de la Frontera, La Rábida, and Moguer. These towns, a stone's throw from one another, lie at the joint delta of the Odiel and Tinto rivers, which became a principal anchorage for the *conquistadores*. Thanks to the intervention of Juan Pérez, the prior of the little port of La Rábida, the Reyes Católicos, Ferdinand and Isabella, gave Columbus the necessary backing.

In the wake of the 1992 commemoration of the 500th anniversary of Columbus's voyages to the Americas, a splendid side trip can be made from Mazagón to **Palos de la Frontera**, on the Tinto estuary, some 12 km (7½ miles) to the northwest, from whose harbor Columbus sailed on August 3, 1492. Shifting coastal shorelines have long silted up the harbor of Palos de la Frontera, but the sense of history remains. Hernán Cortés, conqueror of Mexico, set out from this port in 1528, and by the 16th century the Río Tinto was the main point of departure for Spain's explorations to the Americas. A memorial to Columbus (by Gertrude Vanderbilt Whitney) and the 14th-century church of St. George are among the sights of historic interest here.

Following the Río Tinto seaward, you'll come to the monastery where Columbus stayed at **La Rábida**, southwest of Palos de la Frontera. The monastery is open to the public, and a small museum here contains models of the three celebrated ships of Columbus's first voyage, as well as navigation charts and old books. The port of **Moguer**, north of Palos de la Frontera, considered by some to be one of the most dazzling all-white Andalusian towns, was another harbor (now silted up) used by the *conquistadores*. It is also the birthplace of Nobel Prize–winning poet Juan Ramón Jiménez, whose interesting house you can visit.

JEREZ DE LA FRONTERA

Near the mouth of the Río Guadalete, less than two hours southwest of Seville by *autopista* (A 4 or N IV/E 25), the essentially flat town of Jerez physically resembles other towns and cities of southern Andalusia: The buildings are white with tiled roofs, the parks are filled with tropical plants and blooms, and the streets, lined with orange and lemon trees, are infuriatingly hard to maneuver (they follow an arcane traffic system based on the "disappearing/recurring one-way" school of urban design). With a population of more than 175,000, Jerez is really a small city. It shares its proud "de la Frontera" cognomen with other Andalusian localities—Arcos, Vejér, Chiclana, Jimena, Castellar, Conil—as witness to its role in the Christian Reconquest.

But Jerez is different from its neighbors. It has the distinction of being internationally famous as the home and source of Sherry. Centuries of Sherry and brandy production by English and Spanish companies here have resulted in an aristocracy whose large ranches, alongside the vast vineyards, provide lush areas for horse breeding. Breeding, in fact, is the key to Jerez. Family lines with inherited wealth, equestrian lines of purity and distinction, plant lines in soil cultivated to take advantage of unique natural conditions— all create in Jerez an atmosphere in which lineage is quality.

AROUND IN JEREZ

Jerez itself has a proud genealogy. The Romans called it Asta Regia. The Visigoths fought fiercely against the Moors for the area in 711. The Christian Reconquest forces captured the walled, fortified town from the Moors in 1264.

A remnant of the Moorish period in Jerez is the *alcázar,* with a late 12th-century octagonal tower. Among the town's distinguished churches is the **Iglesia de San Dionisio**, a couple of blocks north of the *alcázar* on the Plaza de la Asunción, near the center of town. San Dionisio has a Gothic-Mudejar tower, a fine patio, and a High Rococo retable; the side entrance to the church has a startling Christ figure with an expression of infinite despair. The **Casa del Cabildo Vieja** (an archaeological museum–library), also on the Plaza de la Asunción, has a Renaissance façade and contains some unexpected treasures. Among the numerous Roman artifacts are two carved heads, one of a querulous old man, his face acidulous with exasperation, and the other a young girl, whose youthful sweetness is embellished by her intricately woven and braided hair. The most remarkable artifact is a Greek helmet attributed to the seventh century B.C., found in the nearby riverbed.

The Jerez September wine festival begins at the **Iglesia Colegiata de Santa María,** just north of the *alcázar,* with the new grapes carried on a silver platter by the queen of the fiesta and held high in baskets by the ladies of her court, all wearing brightly colored Andalusian garb. The festival also includes a livestock fair, a horse auction, and flamenco dancing. The entire city seems to be in costume.

But it is the countryside around Jerez that brought it fame and that will delight the visitor. In the spring the verdant fields are ablaze with wildflowers of every hue. The half-hour drive from Jerez east to Arcos de la Frontera (see The White Towns, below) is a visual treat.

The rare soil of the Sherry vineyards is almost snow white in spring, when it absorbs the rains like a sponge, and then it hardens into a glasslike armor in the blazing heat of summer, deflecting the beating rays, while the vines' lengthy roots feed from the reserves of moisture lying beneath the crust. The ranches, for breeding both horses and bulls, seem to stretch like endless blankets of deep green. From a distance the huge black bulls look prehistoric. The horses here are among the finest in Europe, and in this aristocratic locale polo fields are as common as tennis courts.

At the annual horse show (Feria del Caballo), held in late April or early May, Jerez shows its purebred *cartujanos* in racing, dressage, and carriage competitions. The city, strung with lights and decorations, is adorned with millions of spring flowers. The streets are filled with riders of horses, women and men alike, wearing Cordoban hats, vests, formal shirts, and chaps. Carriages are drawn by two, four, or six horses, their harnesses decorated with garlands of blossoms. Seated within are young women in colorful flamenco dresses. In the formal jumping competitions the riders wear black boots, white breeches, red coats, white ties, and black headgear.

DINING AND STAYING IN JEREZ

Jerez has three good restaurants, the cuisine in all of them taking advantage of the city's proximity to the sea: **El Bosque**, at Avenida de Alcade Alvaro Domecq 26, in a park-like setting, specializes in regional dishes, Tel: (9-56) 30-33-33; **Gaitán**, Calle Gaitán 3, recently renovated, has a diversified menu, Tel: (9-56) 34-58-59; and **La Mesa Redonda**, Calle Manuel de la Quintana 3, centrally located near the Plaza del Caballo, has a limited but excellent menu, Tel: (9-56) 34-00-69. The 120-room ► **Hotel Jerez** is in the residential section of the city, near El Bosque, and is surrounded by tropical gardens. It is comfortable and air-conditioned (especially nice in this city of torrid summer temperatures) and has a swimming pool and a good restaurant.

Just 12 km (7½ miles) southwest of Jerez, in the coastal Sherry town of Puerto de Santa María, is the superb ► **Hotel Monasterio de San Miguel**, an 18th-century monastic building that has been converted into an elegant 150-room hostelry with every amenity.

Sherry

Jerez-Xeres-Sherry claims (Rioja disputes it) to be Spain's oldest *denominación de origen* (DO), the Spanish equivalent of France's *appellation contrôlée*. Jerez de la Frontera, **Puerto de Santa María**, and **Sanlúcar de Barrameda**, at the mouth of the Río Guadalquivir to the northwest, the three great Sherry towns, form what is known as the golden triangle, which encompasses the greatest vineyards of the region.

THE SOLERA SYSTEM

Sherries are not vintaged wines; they are made by an expensive, labor-intensive process, the *solera* system, which ensures continuity of style and quality in the various types of wines offered by each *bodega*. A solera is a complicated network of barrels for blending and aging Sherries until they are ready to be bottled and sold (Sherries are never bottled until the bodega receives an order).

For each style of wine to be made, rows (called *escalas,* or scales) of 500-liter American oak casks are set up. The bottom row, or last escala, contains the oldest and finest Sherry and is called the solera, a word that derives from *suelo,* Spanish for floor. The other rows are called *criaderas* (nurseries) and are identified by their row number (1, 2, 3, etc.).

Wine for shipment is always drawn from the oldest row of casks, the solera. To maintain quality, usually no more than one-third (and often less) of the wine is taken from the solera scale in any one year. The solera scale is replenished with an equal amount of wine from criadera row 1; 1 is replenished from criadera 2; and so on until the last row is reached. The last row is replenished from wine of the *añada* (current year). This complex, costly fractional blending process (known as "running the scales") requires great expertise and much manual labor. By the time each añada's wine has completed its several-year journey through the scales of the solera system, it will have taken on the noble characteristics of the older wines in the system.

ALMACENISTAS

Until recently, only the most dedicated aficionados of fine Sherry, usually armed with knowledge acquired in Spain or in England, had a chance of acquiring a bottle of classic Sherry in good shape. Fortunately for lovers of fine Sherries, the Sherry producers of Jerez are waking up to the fact that the market may be much more receptive to the real thing than to offerings primarily designed to cater to the sweet tooth of mass-market Sherry drinkers.

The Jerez firm of **Emilio Lustau** is the undisputed star of this budding Sherry renaissance. Many of the best wines in the Lustau line come from *almacenistas,* usually professional people or shopkeepers, who invest in small bodegas for modest profit but primarily because of their love of Sherry. The custom has been for the large Jerez bodegas to go to these small holders when they have a small order, usually from a British or Dutch importer, for fine amontillado or old oloroso, or when they need some wine from a special *solera* to give character to a blend needed for a larger order.

The 1/17, 1/28, and similar notations seen on the labels of some of the *almacenista* Sherries denote the number of barrels (1 through 17, 1 through 28) in a particular solera. A small lot of wine (say, 25 cases) is drawn from the solera and bottled for sale; then the solera is replenished from other barrels in the system. These numbers can be taken as an indication of the relative rarity of the wine, but if a particular wine sells out, a new lot with the same characteristics and quality will sometimes be available from the solera. The trick to maintaining quality in these small soleras is to take only small amounts no more than two or three times per year. An almacenista's stock in trade is quality wines with an average age of two decades or more; there are no shortcuts when it comes to aging. A dedicated almacenista will never allow the quality of his solera to be diluted by selling too much wine in any given year.

Until Lustau got the idea to bottle the better wines of the almacenistas (who had been selling wines to Lustau for the private-label Sherries that make up the bulk of the firm's business in the United Kingdom), such names as Cayetano del Pino, Rosario Benítez Girón, Hijos (sons) de Julio Coveñas, and Viuda (widow) de Antonio Borrego could be found only in obscure tomes. As it turns out, these almacen-istas, most of whom come from Sanlúcar de Barrameda, not Jerez, were the true guardians of great strains of classic unblended amontillados and olorosos. Even though the large bodegas will sometimes show important visitors a dazzling sample from a limited "family" solera, they seldom have enough of these old treasures to market commercially (Domecq's Sibarita and Venerable are exceptions). Be fore-warned, however, that these are not Aunt Lizzie's sweet little sipping wines; they are concentrated wines. A little bit goes a long way, so if you are a fancier of Bristol Cream or Dry Sack on the rocks, you may not find these wines your *copita de Jerez*.

TYPES OF SHERRY

The finest, most delicate wines of the Jerez DO—the dry manzanillas, finos, and amontillados—come from Palomino grapes grown in a white, chalky soil known as *albariza* in vineyards located between Jerez and Sanlúcar. These wines of the fino family are made possible by a unique type of yeast known in the Sherry country as *flor* (flower), which grows in a cream-colored layer on the surface of the wine in barrel. The layer of yeast cells prevents air from reaching the wine, thus protecting the wine from oxidation during the long periods it spends in wood. Flor also consumes any sugar left in the wine and contributes a pleasant, yeasty quality to the wine.

In some wines, primarily from lesser-quality vineyards, the flor is weak or does not grow at all. These wines are destined to become olorosos, which are coarser and less delicate than wines of the fino family. Olorosos are fortified by adding brandy, which raises the alcohol levels to the 18- to 23-percent range. Olorosos are often sweetened with wine made from Pedro Ximénez grapes, which have been sunned on straw mats to concentrate their sugars and flavors. This blending technique is used to produce sweetened olorosos and cream Sherries. Pedro Ximénez, or PX, as it is often called, and Moscatel are also used to produce intensely sweet dessert wines of the same names.

Manzanilla
Each bodega makes several different types of Sherry. Many wine experts consider manzanilla the world's greatest aperitif wine. It is a very light, dry, ethereal Sherry that comes only from the wonderful town of Sanlúcar de Barrameda, whose gentle ocean breeze is credited with giving manzanilla its distinctive tangy, taste-of-the-sea quality. The best way to experience manzanilla is to go down to Bajo de Guia beach at day's end, buy a bottle of iced manzanilla at one of the fishermen's restaurants, and watch the sun sink slowly into the sea. The Sanluqueños say that if you ever have a glass of manzanilla at sunset on Bajo de Guia, you will never drink another glass of manzanilla anywhere in the world without seeing the Sanlúcar sunset in the glass. Manzanilla is especially good with Sanlúcar's sensational fresh shellfish, and it goes beautifully with a wide variety of seafood and *tapas*.

Manzanilla Fina
Manzanilla fina, at 15½ to 16 percent alcohol, is lower in alcohol than any other type of Sherry. Hidalgo's La Gitana is splendid. More full bodied and slightly higher in alcohol are the *manzanillas pasadas,* or aged manzanillas. Barbadillo Solear, San León, La Guita, and La Goya are superb *pasadas*.

Fino
Fino, the most popular type of dry Sherry, is a light, fresh, pale-gold wine that, while more full bodied than manzanilla, can be crisp and quite delicate. Its bouquet is slightly reminiscent of almonds. The lightest and most elegant finos come from Sanlúcar de Barrameda and Puerto de Santa María; the more powerful full-bodied ones are aged in Jerez. Because they are fortified wines, they usually contain 16 to 18 percent alcohol. Try Valdespino's rich, full-bodied Inocente, the ubiquitous González-Byass Tío Pepe, Domecq La Ina, the light Osborne Fino Quinta, La Riva Tres Palmas

(rare), Diez-Mérito Don Zoilo, and the finos of Emilio Lustau. If you happen into a small bodega or tavern with its own Sherry or barrels, ask for the *fino de casa,* house fino. Drink it with shellfish, *tapas,* hors d'oeuvres, and appetizers with vinaigrette.

Amontillados

Amontillados are aged finos. In their natural state they are totally dry, gold to amber in color, and have a racy, pungent bouquet and a long, complex, nutty finish. At 17 to 20 percent, they are higher in alcohol, more full bodied, and richer than the lighter finos, and can be enjoyed with fried foods, fish, almonds, olives, and *tapas* that require a less delicate wine than fino or manzanilla. They are the classic accompaniment to soups and are splendid with powerful cheeses. Many commercial brands are slightly sweetened, and therefore not authentic amontillados. Try one of the sublime almacenista amontillados of Emilio Lustau if you want to experience the real thing.

Palo Cortado

Palo cortado is a very rare, fine, full-bodied Sherry with the nose of an amontillado, and the color, body, and alcohol content (17 to 23 percent) of an oloroso. Since most firms, as Spanish-wine expert Jan Read points out, "concoct" these wines by blending amontillado and oloroso, authentic palo cortados are hard to find, but well worth the trouble. Again, you should seek out a palo cortado from one of Lustau's almacenistas. Sip it by itself to admire its perfection and complexity.

Oloroso

Oloroso, which means "fragrant" in Spanish, is an aromatic, full-bodied (17 to 24 percent alcohol), dry to medium-dry, mahogany-colored Sherry that is rich and mellow, with flavors reminiscent of walnuts. It goes best with a dish of nuts and a good book in front of a fireplace in cool weather. Many of the Lustau almacenista olorosos are wonderful for wine connoisseurs, but they are too concentrated and powerful for the palates of many casual wine drinkers, who should be able to satisfy their desires for a dryish oloroso with Domecq's lovely Río Viejo.

Cream Sherry and Other Dessert Wines

A cream Sherry is an oloroso sweetened with Pedro Ximénez. Creams can be full, rich wines, and can be particularly good when the oloroso is very fine and judiciously sweetened. They are sipping wines with power (18 to 24 percent alcohol). Try them with desserts; pour a little over ice cream. Creams can be especially good alongside a cup of strong Spanish coffee. For those who prefer their olorosos sweetened, González-Byass Apostoles, Diez-Mérito Don Zoilo Very Rare Sweet, and Sandeman Royal Corregidor are excellent.

Several other excellent dessert wines are made in the Sherry district. Old East India is a unique dessert wine made from Sherry that is aged in casks left in the blazing Jerez sun to simulate the ancient way of making it, which was by lashing it to the decks of ships on a round trip to the Indies.

Incredibly rich, unctuous, and often achingly sweet, pure Pedro Ximénez wines are like liquid raisins. The best, like Lustau's San Emilio, are bursting with ripe, concentrated fruit, coffee, and chocolate flavors. There are also some excellent Moscatels from the beach resort of Chipiona, just below Sanlúcar.

VISITING SHERRY BODEGAS

Many of the large bodegas have tours for English-speaking guests. Small family-owned bodegas will arrange for your visit if you call or write in advance. Most bodegas receive visitors on weekdays, usually from 9:00 A.M. to 2:00 P.M., and all bodegas are closed for the month of August. The tourist office in Jerez, on Calle Alameda Cristina, opposite the church of Santo Domingo, has information about many bodegas; Tel: (9-56) 33-11-50.

Jerez de la Frontera Bodegas

The splendid old bodegas of **Pedro Domecq**, parts of which date to the foundation of the firm in the early 18th century, are an absolute must for wine lovers and travellers. Among the winery's best wines are Fino La Ina, Río Viejo Oloroso, and Sibarita Palo Cortado. Visitors are welcome weekdays from 10:30 A.M. to 12:30 P.M.

Calle San Ildefonso 3, 11404 Jerez de la Frontera (Cádiz). Tel: (9-56) 33-18-00; Fax: 31-26-17.

González-Byass, creator of Tío Pepe, is an ultra-modern, state-of-the-art winery at the southwestern edge of Jerez. Within the winery's walls there are wonderful old bodegas dating from the early 19th century and incorporating whitewashed, bougainvillaea-canopied Andalusian streets. You will be charmed by the tale of the drunken mouse and awed by the circular bodega designed by Gustave Eiffel. Visitors' hours are 11:00 A.M. to 1:00 P.M. weekdays; the bodega is closed July and August.

Manuel María González 12, 11403 Jerez de la Frontera (Cádiz). Tel: (9-56) 34-00-00; Fax: 33-20-87.

Contact Manuel Arcila to arrange a visit to **Emilio Lustau**, the marketer of the exceptional almacenista limited-production, unblended Sherries that are the quintessence of great Sherry.

Plaza del Cubo 4, 11403 Jerez de la Frontera (Cádiz). Tel: (9-56) 34-15-97.

El Puerto de Santa Maria Bodegas

Osborne, producer of the delicious Fino Quinta, has a lovely bodega in a charming town. Open for visits 9:00 A.M. to 2:00 P.M. weekdays.

Fernán Caballero 3, 11500 Puerto de Santa María (Cádiz). Tel: (9-56) 85-51-11; Fax: 85-34-02.

Sanlúcar de Barrameda Bodegas

Vinícola Hidalgo y Cia is a small family bodega with a 19th-century air. Call ahead to arrange a visit, and ask for the urbane, English-speaking Javier Hidalgo. La Gitana Manzanilla is one of their best wines. Open 10:00 A.M. to 2:00 P.M. for visitors.

Banda de la Playa 24, 11540 Sanlúcar de Barrameda (Cádiz). Tel: (9-56) 36-05-39; Fax: 35-38-44.

—*Gerry Dawes*

CADIZ

"Cádiz," wrote Lord Byron to his mother in 1809, "sweet Cádiz, is the most delightful town I ever beheld, very different from our English cities in every respect except cleanliness (and it is as clean as London), but still beautiful, and full of the finest women in Spain, the Cádiz belles being the Lancashire witches of their land."

"I have quite forgotten to say a word about Cádiz," wrote Benjamin Disraeli to *his* mother in 1830, "which is charming! Brilliant beyond description. 'Fair Florence' is a very dingy affair compared to it. The white houses and the green jalousies sparkle in the sun."

Cádiz today is a good deal less than brilliant, and delightful is not the first adjective that comes to mind. Seen from the water, Cádiz is a strip of whitish buildings on a finger of land five miles long and only a mile wide extending into the sea on the Costa de la Luz, southwest of Jerez. On one side the waves of the Atlantic crash against the protective seawall; on the other is one of Europe's great natural harbors. Seen from the mainland across the bay formed by its spit of land, in the right light (which falls upon it with surprising frequency) Cádiz looks as if it is rising out of the water.

But up close you find that time has not dealt kindly with this beldam. The seawall and the beachfront are tacky, the houses weatherbeaten, the traffic impossible, the weight of

20th-century industry and commerce pressed upon it so heavily that Cádiz emerges flattened and bereft of its fabled charm. But Cádiz has its defenders, who regard it as delightful, lively, and unaffected by tourism.

Anyone would acknowledge that Cádiz has a rich history. With 3,000 candles on its birthday cake, Cádiz is one of the oldest inhabited cities in the Western world. Variously called Gadir by the Phoenicians, possibly as early as 1100 B.C., Gaderia by the Greeks in 500 B.C., and Gades by the Romans, the city became the wealthiest port in Europe with the discovery of the Americas. This wealth made Cádiz a target, particularly for the British: Drake, Essex, Howard at the time of the Armada, Nelson at the time of the Napoleonic Wars. Perhaps Cádiz's finest hour came during the French attack in 1812, when Spanish patriots convened the *cortes* (parliament), promulgating a liberal constitution that lasted until Ferdinand VII repudiated it, in 1814.

THE OLD CITY

The old city, seedy now—even in Richard Ford's time (the 1840s) the cathedral was described by him as "a stranded wreck on a quicksand"—is separated at the promontory's narrowest point by the Puertas de Tierra from the utterly uninviting contemporary industrial beachfront area. The **Museo Provincial de Bellas Artes** (fine-arts museum), on Plaza Generalísimo Franco, has in its collection 21 fine paintings by Zurbarán. The **Hospital de Nuestra Señora del Carmen**, on Calle de Obispo Calvo, has El Greco's *Ecstasy of Saint Francis* in its chapel and an 18th-century ceramic Stations of the Cross on its patio.

For lovers of seafood, the restaurant **El Faro**, facing the Atlantic near the old cathedral, offers the widest variety of the day's catch. The management claims their fish have "never made the acquaintance of the refrigerator"; Tel: (9-56) 21-10-68. The ▶ **Hotel Atlántico**, facing the sea on the Parque Genovés, at the extreme western tip of the promontory, has a garden and swimming pool; its restaurant offers better than usual hotel fare, and at lunchtime there is an extensive buffet.

We cover the eastern part of the Costa de la Luz, beyond Cádiz and around to Algeciras, Gibraltar, and the beginning of the Mediterranean Costa del Sol, at the end of this chapter, following the Costa del Sol section.

THE WHITE TOWNS

"The route of the white towns" sounds like a public relations slogan inspired by "Follow the Yellow Brick Road," but it provides its own magic in a roughly triangular area of southwestern Andalusia. Two sides of this inverted triangle follow the Atlantic and Mediterranean coastlines to form an apex at Tarifa on the Strait of Gibraltar; the third side traces the inland route through the mountains from Arcos de la Frontera east to Ronda. Many of these towns seem untouched in their dramatic settings, as if they were still part of the medieval Moorish world.

Only a traveller with a heart of granite and an eye of glass could remain indifferent to what unfolds while driving these narrow, winding, and almost empty mountain roads. Every few miles a town comes into view, etched white against a rocky embankment or dark green vegetation. The towns, down to the last one, were built by the Moors. The streets are narrow, the houses face inward to their courtyards, the roofs are tiled. And every house is whitewashed.

Many white towns look best from a distance. They are a pleasure to visit, but, like jewels, they benefit from their settings. These white towns have made no concessions to tourism. They rarely offer accommodations except to commercial travellers and sportsmen; in most of them the local bar also serves as the place to eat. They have few buildings of architectural distinction; their Christian churches are modest. They seem sufficient unto themselves.

Their dominant element remains their whiteness. Ablaze in the sunlight, spectral at night under moonlit skies, ashen beneath the stars, they look like spring-cleaned North African towns, freshly washed and somehow transported to Mediterranean Europe.

VISITING THE WHITE TOWNS

A good way to make these towns part of a coherent travel plan is to concentrate on the northern base of the inverted triangle. On this inland route, running eastward very roughly between Arcos de la Frontera and Ronda, the diversified landscape includes vineyards, pine forests, citrus farms, ranches, valley streams, olive groves, mountains both jagged and rounded, and a seven-mile-long lake. Rounding a curve, you spy a white town in the distance, and it seems unreal: the setting theatrically conceived, the brilliance suspiciously unblemished.

Either Arcos de la Frontera, on the western end, or Ronda, on the east, could serve as a base for white-town exploration. Ronda is too big (population 32,000) to be considered a representative white town, but Arcos has all the appropriate qualities.

Arcos de la Frontera

Half an hour's drive northeast from Jerez, through country-side that in spring has poppies flaming along the roadside, past vineyards and wheat fields and ranches, Arcos first appears as a strip of white atop a narrow rock promontory that falls 500 feet to the Río Guadalete.

Arcos separates the traveller from the tourist. The town provides no amusements, no shopping, no restaurants, no bars other than the undifferentiated basic type. In Arcos there is nothing to do. But for the traveller, Arcos offers a hidden world. The Spanish essayist and journalist J. M. Ruiz Azorín called the town "the most beautiful in all Spain." Even discounting chauvinism, Arcos is something of a knockout.

AROUND IN ARCOS

Arcos looks like a huge ship cresting a green sea, its hull a stone-gray, its superstructure the church towers. On three sides of the town the promontory drops to the river. You enter by way of the fourth, the passage so narrow that it becomes a single ascending street. Soon only one vehicle can proceed in either direction, and that must pass under the eaves of a flying buttress at the rear of the church of Santa María de la Asunción.

Upon entering the town, turn right onto the Plaza de España, the town square. On one side is the **Iglesia de Santa María de la Asunción**, whose façade is a blend of Roman-esque, Gothic, and Mudejar, and whose interior has choir stalls and a main altar in the Andalusian Baroque style, a painting of the Immaculate Conception by Francisco de Ricci, and a Virgin of Bethlehem attributed to Alonso Cano. On another side of the square is the massive medieval **castle** of the dukes of Osuna; on the third side is the Parador Casa del Corregidor (see below). Running the full length of the fourth side is a balcony.

This balcony is given an unprintable name by the locals in recognition of the fact that everyone utters the same exple-tive when standing transfixed at the edge of the precipitous escarpment, looking far below at the green farmland by the banks of the river, with its two bridges, and beyond that to acres of vineyards, olive groves, ranches, and, on the distant horizon, the notched lines of peaks of the Serranía de Ronda. Within view, at the southern end of the promontory, is the **Iglesia de San Pedro**, on the site of a Moorish fortress. The church has a 16th-century tower you can climb for a transcendent visit, after requesting the key from the church caretaker.

STAYING IN ARCOS

The recently refurbished, handsome 18th-century ► **Para-dor Casa del Corregidor** (ironically, at one time in its checkered history, a home for the poor) makes a splendid base for a white-town tour of a few days. Many of the individual rooms have balconies (which lack privacy) over-looking that transcendent view, and the public rooms are styled in a manner uniquely Spanish: beautiful, glazed-tile floors, carved wooden doorways and furniture, a command-ing staircase, whitewash-white walls, beamed ceilings, and colorful handwoven draperies with a thread of scarlet in them. In many respects this parador epitomizes the sterling objectives of Spain's chain of inns for the material and aesthetic well-being of travellers.

A 17th-century ranch not far from Arcos, ► **Cortijo Faín**, offers exceptionally fine accommodations for travellers lucky enough to combine their love for beautiful furnishings with a relative disregard for expense. This Andalusian ranch sur-rounded by hills covered with olive trees has eight luxurious suites and a swimming pool fed from sparkling spring water. As a guest here you can ramble in the countryside, go horse-back riding, or join a hunting party. While you savor the Andalusian ranch life, you may begin to lose the impression that you are a guest—and feel like lord or lady of the manor. Whether you dine in your own suite or in the dining room, you will enjoy the impeccable service that stems from Cortijo Faín's mastery of the kind of understated elegance that refuses to call attention to itself. To reach Cortijo Faín, follow N 342 northeast for about a kilometer (half a mile), then take C 344 (El Bosque road) for approximately 3 km (2 miles) to the Algar road; the ranch is on the left.

Bornos

The first white town on N 342 northeast of Arcos is Bornos, fronting a ten-mile-long reservoir. Bornos is one of those places that suffers in retrospect; after visits to other white towns, Bornos seems less inviting than it did initially. At its center is the 17th-century **Palacio de los Ribera**, whose courtyard, with double-tiered arches of Renaissance propor-tions, now houses what is unfortunately the busiest place in town, the community welfare office.

Zahara de los Membrillos

From Bornos to Zahara de los Membrillos the landscape becomes increasingly mountainous. Deep valleys of brick-colored earth and rocky peaks replace the earlier flat terrain. Route N 342 follows a pine-bordered stream; you catch a first tantalizing glimpse of Zahara through a cut in the hills. Its white dwellings stand etched against the rocky projection on whose side they rise. If you visit only one white town, Zahara might well be your choice.

The town's one street zigzags back and forth as you climb the rock face to the small town plaza. From there you can walk up to the Moorish tower at the summit. The tower itself is dark and moldy, but on this summit a 360-degree perspective of quite spectacular beauty takes in the sweep of the wheat fields, meadows, and vineyards, all encircled by a perimeter of mountains. Church bells ring out the hour. An eagle soars, leisurely searching for prey. The roofs of the houses are rust-colored, a striking contrast against the white walls. The occasional donkey is still tethered outside a window. Around you are enough wildflowers to boggle a botanist: pink, purple, yellow, bright red, and blue. Among them grow strands of wheat whose seed has been blown here by the Atlantic winds, cacti with giant leaves, and thistles.

With a population of 2,000, Zahara is neither a village nor a full-fledged town. Arabic to its roots, it was a formidable Moorish stronghold (each October a celebration is held to commemorate the 15th-century Christian Reconquest), and to this day it exemplifies the Moorish-Spanish blend that characterizes the best of the white towns. It is not easy to leave.

Grazalema

But when you do leave Zahara de los Membrillos, think before turning onto the inviting, well-paved road whose signs direct you to Grazalema. That route turns out to be an invitation to torture, cutting back and forth upward and crossing a mile-high peak aptly called Puerto de las Palomas (Pass of the Doves). Minor car trouble up here becomes a major headache. We recommend driving from Zahara to the original turnoff point and taking C 339 to Grazalema.

Grazalema, one of the oldest of the white towns, was called Lacidula by the Romans. Some 3,716 feet above sea level, Grazalema is built on two levels, its parallel streets extending from one end of the town to the other. The white houses have bright flowers in pots affixed to the outside walls; the patios and balconies are alive with basil, scarlet geraniums, and carnations. One church, the Iglesia de San Juan, has a Moorish arch incorporated into its structure. Immediately behind the houses rise rock projections. Just outside the town is the Pinzapar forest, nearly 300 acres of a rare species of pine.

Grazalema has attracted many admirers. In *The Wonders*

of Spain, Yves Bottineau wrote that Grazalema "follows the slope of the hills, the tiled roofs of the churches and houses matching the color of the rockface, so that it seems as if earth, men, and town lived in a kind of symbiosis." For centuries Grazalema blankets were carried by the highwaymen of the Serranía de Ronda, and today these blankets are still woven here on large looms. Baskets, mats, and blinds made from esparto grass also are crafted in Grazalema.

Ubrique and El Bosque

Ubrique, south of the Arcos–Ronda axis about 25 km (15 miles) southwest of Grazalema, is a prosperous white town with a population of 17,000. The mammoth rocky promontories in the background, formidable to observe, seem protective rather than threatening. The town is given over to leather crafts. Small factories and shops are open to visitors, and you can observe the cutting and stamping procedures; some handwork by leather artisans is performed here as well. A picnic on a rocky ledge outside Ubrique (the shops of Ubrique have all the wine, cheese, bread, pastries, and succulent fresh fruit you could desire) offers a view of this white town, dramatically situated, immaculate, its streets lined with orange trees.

Some 17 km (11 miles) northwest of Ubrique on CA 524 is El Bosque (which means "the woods"), a town well named: a quiet, bosky retreat whose tranquillity is complemented by the modesty of its surrounding hills and plains. El Bosque (population 2,000) has the southernmost trout preserve in Europe, an ancient bullring, a modern swimming pool, and a handsome inn, ► **Las Truchas**. This inn (at which only Spanish is spoken) could serve as an alternative to the Arcos parador as a base for white-town explorations.

Olvera

From a certain point along N 342, northeast of Grazalema and Zahara, you see the façade of the rather large town of Olvera spread horizontally along the side of the mountain. It is a photographer's best shot. Once in Olvera it is easy to forget that a brochure calls it "a concert of limestone and rock high on a cliff which is presided over by a silhouette of a rocky castle." Like Grazalema, Olvera was once the refuge of bandits and cutthroats because of its remoteness. Today, it is a town dedicated to livestock.

If you wander along the alleys behind Olvera's church, in what the citizens call the Arab quarter, you come upon an extraordinary number of dogs, vaguely greyhound in origin. Pedestrians routinely step over them. The dogs have a world-weary air incongruously at odds with their skinny frames. Like Olvera itself, they look better from a distance. And from such a perspective Olvera looks very good indeed, even ravishing, framed by the dark green countryside. That's the way to view it.

Setenil

Just south of Olvera on the road southeast toward Ronda (passing through the town of Torre Alháquime), is Setenil, more a geological sport than a representative white town. It is built within a mountain that has been sliced through, century after century, by the waters of a branch of the Río Trejo. Thus, after ascending the mountain to reach the town, you descend into it. Many of the houses are built into the rocks that serve as bridges over the streets themselves. The housefronts are whitewashed, the windowsills flower-bedecked, but the roofs are monstrous rock slabs. Some streets are partly covered over with rock. More bizarre than unusual, more eccentric than inviting, Setenil's freakish attractions offer examples of local adaptation to the idiosyncrasies of nature.

Ronda

Ronda is a paradox, a town on the edge of a thousand-foot cliff, separated from the Mediterranean coastline by mountains that rise 3,652 feet from sea level, famous as a bandit hideout, the very definition of geographic inaccessibility. Nevertheless, Ronda seems to have been visited by every traveller to southern Spain since the time of the Romans. It is about 19 km (12 miles) south of Setenil, and 31 km (19 miles) east of Grazalema.

Writers have dealt with Ronda so extensively that the subject of its spectacular location has been stripped of the last bromide. The great ravine—you can scarcely avoid an attack of vertigo as you look into its depths—is spanned by three bridges, one built by the Romans, another by the Moors, and a "new" one, finished in the 1780s.

Benjamin Disraeli travelled from Gibraltar to Ronda on horseback in 1830. He characterized Ronda's setting as "a savage mountain district, abounding in the most beautiful scenery and bugs! There are a number of little villages in this Sierra, entirely inhabited by robbers and smugglers." Bug-ridden, bandit-infested Ronda seemed to Disraeli the quintessence of romantic Andalusia.

THE OLD TOWN

Today's Ronda is divided by the ravine. Most compelling is the older south side, away from the restaurants, souvenir stands, and shops. Once across the new bridge, turn left down the steep Calle Mario de Parades and you come upon the **Casa del Rey Moro**, a Moorish palace said variously to date from the 11th century to the 16th century. The houses on the steep, curved streets here could be considered mansions. Ronda is that most unlikely of white towns, one with a heritage of elegance quite apart from its strategic military position. An example of that elegance, to the right beyond the Casa del Rey Moro, is the Renaissance façade of the **Palacio de Marqués de Salvatierra** (open to visitors), whose interior is an antique-lover's dream. The *palacio* offers fine views from its triple terrace.

Turning back up the hill from here, on the Calle de Mario de Salvatierra, you come upon the **Iglesia de Santa María**, built by order of the Reyes Católicos, Ferdinand and Isabella, on the site of an old mosque. The church is a beautiful example of late Gothic art, furnished with two excellent Baroque altarpieces. Arab traces are preserved in the *mihrab* (the sacred niche in the mosque wall that faces Mecca), with its stucco decorations, and in two horseshoe arches.

THE MODERN TOWN

On the other side of the ravine stands Ronda's small bullring, of classic proportions, the **Plaza de Toros de la Real Maestranza de Caballería de Ronda**. Ronda claims that it is the oldest bullring in Spain. The bullring's most obvious architectural distinction—a perfect circular shape—is achieved with a harmonious two-tiered exterior of 68 stone (rather than the usual wood) columns, spaced about eight feet apart. Ronda's bullring looks remarkably harmonious: the right size, the right proportions, the right panache. King Juan Carlos said it best on the occasion of a recent visit to Ronda's bullring: "The celebration of bullfighting is not open for debate: It is part of our tradition and of our culture."

The bullring has a museum with a fascinating collection of *taurino* memorabilia, including suits-of-light—the elaborate, colorful costumes—worn by many famous bullfighters. Pictures, clippings, letters, swords, and footwear are all on display. Many photographs highlight the exhibit: Hemingway is here, of course, with Antonio Ordóñez and Luis Miguel Dominguin, as is Orson Welles, whose ashes were buried at his request at his nearby country place of Ordóñez (northeast of Ronda, toward Campillos).

DINING AND STAYING IN RONDA

The best restaurant in Ronda is the **Don Miguel**, Calle Villanueva 4, overhanging the northwestern side of the ravine. Specialties include partridge, pheasant, and desserts made by the cloistered Carmelite nuns (who sell their products at Plaza Merced 2). Tel: (9-5) 287-1090. Many of Ronda's other restaurants—all with menus and prices conspicuously posted—find it hard to compete with Don Miguel's location.

Ronda's famous old hotel, the ► **Reina Victoria**, perched on the edge of the gorge, is largely given over to groups, but a room with a balcony facing that view makes other matters irrelevant. The room once occupied by Rainer Maria Rilke, a fervent admirer of Ronda, has been preserved (or re-created) by the management. A very pleasant and modest hotel on a side street, the ► **Hotel Polo**, is spanking clean and well run.

East toward Granada

If you choose to head to Granada from Ronda, the first leg of your journey will be the 60-km (38-mile) drive northeast to Campillos. This drive rivals any in Spain for the beauty and tranquillity of its pastoral mountain landscape. The road is not much travelled and it has nothing of great drama, just mile after mile of hills and streams and meadows, of trees and wildflowers and vineyards and orchards. Here is the best of Spain in the serenity of its singular countryside.

LA BOBADILLA

At Campillos C 341 meets N 342, which runs east to Granada (about 130 km/82 miles away). About 60 km (38 miles) past Campillos is ► **La Bobadilla**, a luxurious resort, pure (in the sense that it has no disguises) and simple (in its dedication to the sybaritic). Ignore the signs for the town called La Bobadilla and the railroad junction Bobadilla Estación, about 15 km (9 miles) past Campillos, both of which are unrelated to the resort. Turn left for La Bobadilla resort at Salinas, about 25 km (15 miles) past Antequera and the turnoff south to Málaga.

La Bobadilla, which has been called Spain's finest hotel, covers an area almost exactly equal to that of Gibraltar. In the conventional sense, this hotel complex has no rooms. It has, instead, 35 suites, each differently styled, all of them elegant and containing every conceivable amenity. The suites, which range in size and level of luxuriousness, have around-the-clock room service, balconies, and fireplaces, and some have private gardens.

Breakfast at La Bobadilla (if you don't partake of a buffet that practically redefines the word) is set for you at a table in your quarters. The hotel has two restaurants, one of which, **La Finca** (*finca* means ranch or plantation), is superb, serving international cuisine. Swimming pools, hunting, horseback riding, tennis, a fitness club are all here to keep you in the physical condition needed to savor the self-indulgence of this Lucullan life.

(La Bobadilla has nothing historically to do with Boabdil, the young Moorish king who surrendered Granada to Ferdinand and Isabella. *His* civic commemoration is the town of Suspiro del Moro [sigh of the Moor], south of Granada on N 323, where his mother's apocryphal admonition that he shed tears like a woman for what he should have defended like a man suggests the kind of relationship that has made psychoanalysis a lucrative profession.)

When you can bear to tear yourself away from La Bobadilla, take a slight detour off N 342 at Láchar (some 20 km/12 miles before Granada), and head northeast to the little town of **Fuente Vaqueros**, where Federico García Lorca was born. Lorca's home is now a small museum containing memorabilia and even a geranium grown from the seeds of a plant that the poet's mother always kept in her classroom. It's a short distance but a far cry from La Bobadilla to Fuente Vaqueros, a humbling return to reality.

A little way past Láchar on N 342, just west of Granada, the town of **Santa Fé** is the place where Ferdinand and Isabella encamped while conducting their siege of Granada.

THE COSTA DEL SOL

The Costa del Sol covers approximately 190 miles of Mediterranean coastline. The largest city on this seafront, Málaga, with a population of more than half a million, serves as a dividing line for travellers. To Málaga's east is an extensive undeveloped and sparsely populated area, but from Málaga southwest to Algeciras and the Strait of Gibraltar, the coastline has been so overdeveloped that it has become unrecognizable from what it was a scant 50 years ago.

Gone forever from the western Costa del Sol are the quaint little Andalusian fishing villages and ports, gone are the hidden coves and bathing beaches. Here to stay are the high rises, the vast complexes of pseudo-towns and tourist villages, of restaurants, bars, fast-food outlets, gasoline stations, and vendors of souvenirs. A good many of the permanent residents of the Costa del Sol come from England, Scandinavia, France, and Germany, having first tried out the place on vacation. In the ports are yachts and sailing craft flying the flags of many nations. Supermarkets the size of city blocks are frequented by clients whose common denominator is that they don't speak Spanish.

"Hideous, vulgar, and gimcrack are the new tourist towns of Andalusia," wrote Jan Morris, "where Spanish speculators have allied themselves with hordes of shady foreigners to develop the Costa del Sol: forgotten are the old instincts of form and balance, the organic strength of Spanish architecture, the sense of frank and decorous resignation. All is flash and easy profit."

The Costa del Sol is no longer nationally identifiable; it has become indistinguishable from similar touristic desecrations of the Mediterranean coast in France and Italy, Yugoslavia and Greece. Fortunately, from time to time you can turn off the highway—N 340, which has more accidents than any comparable roadway in all of Spain and is the country's least pleasant thoroughfare—and, in a space of only a few miles, find Andalusia once more.

MALAGA

Málaga is one of those cities whose contemporary reputation rests mostly on its past accomplishments. Málaga's harbor once made it the cynosure of each succeeding epoch's commercial and military eye: The Iberians settled here, as did the Carthaginians, the Greeks, the Romans, and the Visigoths, before Málaga became a major Moorish center. After the Reconquest, the town's great cathedral, begun in 1528, replaced its central mosque. But during the time of Spain's American empire, the Atlantic ports of Cádiz and Seville (via the Río Guadalquivir) gained precedence over Málaga's Mediterranean harbor.

Today's Málaga tends to get mixed reviews from visitors. There are those who find it a delightful town with a laid-back feeling, its orange-tree-lined streets, picturesque harbor, and horse-drawn carriages lending just the right air of insouciance for casual sightseeing. Others see the city with its population of half a million, most of them living in what seem to be endless sprawling outreaches, as Marseilles-like tough; it does have one of Spain's highest rates of crime and unemployment. (Just as in Seville, when you wander about some of Málaga's beautiful parks and ancient side streets you should keep an eye on your valuables.)

But almost every visitor agrees that the small central area around the cathedral splendidly combines the historical significance of Málaga's illustrious past with the present blessings of its climate and site. At the turn of the century, well before the development of the Costa del Sol, Málaga was a favored vacation spot, especially for the British. But it is often unjustly overlooked by today's travellers, who see it more as a transportation base from which to light out for some Mediterranean resort.

The Old Town

Running due south through the center of the city, the Río Guadalmedina empties into the sea immediately west of the great harbor. The Paseo del Parque, an esplanade with tropical trees and colorful blooms, divides the harbor area from the city proper. Just three blocks north of the *paseo* stands the cathedral, the center of ancient Málaga. A few blocks directly east of the cathedral are the Alcazaba and the ruins of the Roman amphitheater, and behind them to the northeast is the **Gibalfaro** hill, with its castle offering panoramic views of the cityscape. Three blocks west of the cathedral is Málaga's main shopping area, centered on Calle del Marqués de Larios.

THE CATHEDRAL

As is customary in Andalusia, an enormous Christian cathedral replaced the great mosque of the city after the Reconquest. Begun in the 16th century, the Málaga cathedral, with its steeple still unfinished, has gigantic Corinthian columns that rise to meet cupolas with a particularly Malagan touch— palm fronds, shells, and what appear to be anchors etched on the vast ceiling. But despite its size, the interior of the cathedral is simple, with three naves and chapels, as well as the royal chapel through whose windows the Málaga sunlight penetrates. Pedro de la Mena, who was recently given a giant retrospective in the cathedral, created some wonderful choir stalls here.

THE ALCAZABA

This 11th-century Moorish fortress, built on the foundations of a Roman amphitheater, has been much restored, but enough remains of the commanding original structure, with its view of Málaga's harbor, seacoast, and mountain backdrop, to suggest something of the city's former military, political, and geographical advantages. In this entirely Moorish setting is a museum containing some outstanding Iberian artifacts, as well as some fine Roman statuary and household articles. The site is improved by a phenomenon typical of Málaga: an abundance of flowers—bougainvillaea and giant roses in particular—that seem to grow wherever there is a square foot of soil.

What remains of the seating section of the **Roman amphitheater** stands to the north of the Alcazaba, within the confines of its entranceway. A model of this theater in the fortress museum suggests that it may well have seated 20,000 people.

PICASSO IN MALAGA

At Málaga's Plaza de la Merced 15 (off the north end of the short Calle Alcazabilla, between the cathedral and the Alcazaba), a house plaque erected in 1961 on the occasion of an homage to Velázquez reads simply: "Picasso was born in this house on October 25, 1881." The house is one of six in a double row of houses that makes up the entire north side of this inviting, well-proportioned urban square. Five stories high, they are comfortable, architecturally harmonious dwellings of the middle class that look more French than Spanish. From this bourgeois background came the 20th century's most revolutionary artist.

Just two blocks away, in the **Museo de Bellas Artes** (at Calle Agustín 6), one room (XVIII) is given over to Málaga's expatriate native son. Picasso is sparingly represented here in oil by *Pair of Ancients* and *Man with a Shawl,* two representative paintings completed when he was 14 and 15 years old, respectively. The latter is signed P. Ruiz Picasso. Otherwise, the collection consists of his lithographs from the 1940s and 1950s.

This museum, housed in a former Moorish palace, has rather too many "anonymous," "school of," and "workshop" works on display, but to its credit there are two paintings by Luis de Morales, one by Ribera, a Murillo, and a fine "school of" Zurbarán, as well as some interesting early Iberian artifacts. It is no discredit to the Museo de Bellas Artes to say that it suggests why Picasso left Málaga: There is enough here to inspire—but not to gratify.

Staying and Dining in Málaga

Atop the Gibalfaro (the commanding hill by the harbor, on the northwestern side of the Alcazaba), the ► **Parador de Málaga-Gibralfaro** has very limited accommodations (12 rooms) but offers a sense of seclusion and, of course, that view. The terraced restaurant serves excellent meals (white gazpacho and fish freshly caught from Málaga's seacoast). One disadvantage of staying here is that the city is scarcely accessible except by car.

In the center of the city, the ► **Málaga Palacio**, with a rooftop pool, is a large (228 rooms), efficient hostelry, close to practically everything: the cathedral, the Alcazaba, the Museo de Bellas Artes, the airport bus stop, an indoor parking garage, and the port itself.

Some 9½ km (6 miles) west of downtown on the way to Torremolinos (turn left at the international airport exit on the Cádiz highway), directly on the rather sad beach (but with two pools), is the ► **Hotel Guadalmar**, comfortable, unpretentious, noisy on weekends with local celebratory functions, fine for children, and just a three-minute taxi ride from the airport. But without a car you will be stuck in Guadalmar-land.

Directly opposite the Museo de Bellas Artes (although you enter from a narrow side street) is **Tormes**, a modest and entirely gratifying restaurant that is a good place for lunch; you are likely to be the only non-Malaganian on hand in this well-patronized establishment; Tel: (9-5) 222-2063. The **Café de Paris**, on the Paseo Marítimo facing the Malagueta beach, on the other hand, is a rather elegant place to dine, offering a widely diversified menu; reservations, Tel: (9-5) 222-5043. In the same menu category are the **Figón de Bonilla**, also in the Paseo Marítimo area, Tel: (9-5) 222-3223; and **La Taberna del Pintor**, which specializes in roasted meats, Tel: (9-5) 221-5315. All three offer the famous cured ham *jamón de Jabugo*.

THE COSTA DEL SOL
EAST OF MALAGA

Although most travellers concentrate on the Mediterranean coastline running west of Málaga to the Strait of Gibraltar as the ever-desirable Costa del Sol, the 218-km (135-mile) seacoast stretching from Málaga east to Almería (the Costa del Sol officially ends at La Rábita on the border of the provinces of Málaga and Almería) offers relatively less development and a more tranquil pace. From a scenic point of view, the drive east on N 340 from Málaga to the city of Almería wins hands down, as it keeps the sea in resplendent view almost all the way. This stretch of the aptly named "coast of the sun" has its own share of urban development and seafront complexes for vacationers in the immediate eastern proximity of Málaga, but these multicultural, international playgrounds thin out as you progress eastward and enter a coastal area that bespeaks Spain. The most beautiful stretch of road—east *or* west—on the entire Costa del Sol runs for 23 km (15 miles) between Nerja (52 km/32 miles east of Málaga) and Almuñecar. Here the coastal highway (N 340) winds and twists around jagged capes, swoops down beside surf-splashed coves, and climbs to offer panoramic views of the seacoast and the mesmerizing blue of the Mediterranean. As a backdrop, the Sierra de Cuesta provides the appropriate touch to this sun-drenched world, its slopes alternating between slices of sheer gray granite and clusters of dark green pines.

Nerja

The town of Nerja, which has been something of an English enclave since the 1950s, faces the sea on a cliff called the **Balcón de Europa** (Balcony of Europe). Nerja's internationally famous **caves**, on the eastern extremity of the town, include an exhibit of Paleolithic discoveries and a path through deep interiors, dense with stalagmites and stalactites, that takes on a surreal aspect as the interior lighting permeates this eerie world. Indeed, the caves are somewhat theatrically tarted up, as the English point out, and summer concerts and ballet performances are offered in the vast chambers. For current schedules, check with the parador's front desk (see below) or with the tourist office at Calle Puerta del Mar 2; Tel: (9-5) 252-1531.

The best place to stay in Nerja is the ▶ **Parador de Nerja**, which faces the Mediterranean and has an elevator to take you down to a beach of fine white sand. The terraced rooms overlook the gardens, the swimming pool, and the sea beyond; the spacious dining room has a bay of windows facing the coastline. Excellent meals here are attentively served. This parador will please the most demanding traveller.

Perhaps the best place to dine in Nerja is the **Rey Alfonso**, Plaza Balcón de Europa, which is air-conditioned, has marvelous views of the sea, and serves an international cuisine. The pineapple flambé lights up the night; Tel: (9-5) 252-0958.

Frigiliana

Six kilometers (4 miles) north of Nerja on MA 105 is the astonishingly pretty white town of Frigiliana. Many recent English expatriates who respond enthusiastically to this coast's climate—the direct antithesis of their own—have put down roots here. Despite this invasion the houses invoke their Arabic origins, and every last wall is whitewashed in blinding uniformity. The contrast with the steep green hills accentuates the town's hilltop setting and makes Frigiliana a sight to remember. The Moorish-Mudejar quarter, restored painstakingly to its original architectural state, won a national prize for preservation of Andalusian villages in 1988. In the Iglesia de San Antonio, a Mudejar coffered ceiling complements the Baroque style of the building.

Salobreña

About 40 km (25 miles) east along the coast from Nerja, just before Motril, you come upon the town of Salobreña on the right, a circle of white rising up from flat land by the sea. The town is crowned by a Moorish castle, the air is redolent of jasmine, the sugarcane reaches to the shore.

Just outside the town, at km 326 on N 340, is the ▶ **Hotel Salobreña**, with moderate prices, a swimming pool, and a view of the castle at night that makes it appear to be floating on water. This is a modest retreat, likely to be overlooked by travellers scurrying by, an ideal spot for those who find comfort more gratifying than cosmopolitanism.

ALMERIA AND THE COSTA BLANCA

East of Salobreña and Motril (from which you can climb directly north to Granada on N 323; see the Alpujarras section, above), the coastal landscape along N 340 begins to change as you enter Almería province at La Rábita. The countryside becomes increasingly dry and wracked and soon begins to resemble the surface of an arid planet in outer space. A curious phenomenon meets the traveller: On both sides of the highway are acres and acres of plastic sheeting covering plants and fruits, an affront to the eye but the economic salvation of a section of Andalusia formerly devastated by poverty. The plastic prevents evaporation of moisture from the soil, bringing something like an agricultural miracle to coastal Almería. You pass by open trucks laden with produce: grapes, melons, flowers, vegetables, and oranges.

Almería

About 26 km (16 miles) past La Rábita, N 340 cuts inland for some 20 km (12 miles) before it joins the coast again to arrive at the unprepossessing city of Almería, the capital of the province. Despite its population of more than 150,000, Almería has a small-town feel, and the rest of Spain regards it as if it were on the far side of Mars. V. S. Pritchett likened Almería to one of Chekhov's bright but fading Black Sea towns: "a hot little seaport cooped into a hole below the coastal range." That range is rock of a dark ocher hue, utterly without vegetation.

Almería, like Málaga, was a Republican (leftist) town in the Spanish Civil War, as indeed were all Spanish ports, with their enlightened perceptions of the world outside of Spain. Almería has renamed one of its main streets Federico García Lorca, after the Spanish poet assassinated by the Fascists during the war; another is named after Pablo Picasso, whose painting *Guernica* has become a symbol of war's brutality.

AROUND IN ALMERIA

Now fronted by harbor appurtenances and stretches of unappetizing beach, the city of Almería was in Moorish times of historic and cultural importance. In 1031 Almería, then an important maritime center, became the capital of a principality, rivaled, it is said, only by Seville. Almería prospered both in commerce and the arts. An old Spanish saying (voiced largely in Almería) claims that Granada was but a farm when Almería was Almería.

A remnant of those times, the **alcázar**, towers above the city; you can reach it by a rocky path leading off Calle Almanzor. The Moorish stronghold has three levels. The first is a luxuriant park-like area of flowers and shrubs. The second level was formerly made up of small palaces, prisons, baths, and the like, but is barren today. From it you can admire the panoramic view while drinking mint tea served by attendants in Arab costume who stand by an enormous tent that seems Berber in provenance. The third level is a tower now bearing the arms of Charles V. Looking down on the city, you can observe the poor western district of La Chanca, built under an arid mountain overhang; the area is considered picturesque by artists and tourists, considerably less so by its poverty-stricken inhabitants, who are gradually abandoning it.

Gerald Brenan called Almería "the dead little town, so charming in its animated immobility," and if you stroll up and down the city's wonderfully old-fashioned main drag, the Paseo de Almería, you will find a Spain soon to disappear forever. Spain's great department-store chains ignore Almería, but what in American small towns are called general stores are still in existence here, offering not only an incredible miscellany of products but prices that went out of style in the 1970s along with friendly and considerate service. The sidewalk cafés are modest in every sense, and sitting in one of them, savoring some ice-cream confection, one feels contemporary stress and tension give way to the leisurely pace of a forgotten coastal town.

At the western end of the Paseo de Almería in a little plaza called Puerta de Purchena, the **Imperial Restaurant**, which has for some years specialized in seafood, is a homey, unassuming spot where you can count on acceptable but not exceptional food. The restaurant is air-conditioned and dogs are allowed; Tel: (9-50) 23-17-40.

Immediately to the left off N 340 as you enter the city is the ▶ **Gran Hotel Almería**, comfortable and, unless some local group is offering a function in the public rooms, quiet and routinely acceptable. It has an underground garage and a swimming pool. Remodeled in 1982, it is the city's best hotel choice among limited competition.

Cabo de Gata

The stretch of Spain's Mediterranean seacoast that parallels the African coast ends at Cabo de Gata, the eastern geological counterpart of the Rock of Gibraltar. Just 22 km (14 miles) east of the city of Almería, Cabo de Gata is a rockbound mountainous cape, a location likely to attract any traveller with an eye for the unconventional and for spectacular scenic topography. While not quite undiscovered, Cabo de Gata is decidedly remote.

Follow N 332 from the city of Almería east to the airport, and shortly beyond that bear right at directional signs for Cabo de Gata. First you will pass long stretches of beautiful beaches just beyond the road, but they end abruptly as the rugged, barren mountains fall directly into the sea. Here a narrow but well-paved road ascends circuitously, providing increasingly eye-popping views at every turn. At the top of one of these summits is a lighthouse complex with parking facilities; farther on is a privately owned circular tower (once a navigational lookout) whose current white-bearded, bikini-clad owner declares that he lives in a sun-drenched world where rain never falls to mar his unparalleled vista. Vertigo-inducing views soar on all sides of this parched peninsula of sand-colored cliffs. Looking out across the sea, you can scarcely discern the horizon as the color of the sky blends with that of the sparkling water.

SAN JOSE

Beyond the lighthouse the paved road becomes a gravel track that you can follow (the area has national park supervision) for perhaps 8 km (5 miles) in a treeless, uninhabited, volcanic landscape until you reach the little town of San José. An easier way to reach San José, by paved road, is to follow a clearly marked directional sign on the left as you initially approach the Cabo de Gata area; the distance from that point to San José is 25 km (15 miles). Either way, San José is worth achieving. The small community of white houses, some with red-tiled roofs, faces a long, curving beach of finely grained sand at each end of which rise sentinels of barren rock. The water is crystal clear, and the abundance of marine flora and fauna draws aficionados of underwater swimming, scuba diving, photography, and, of course, fishing.

The Cabo de Gata is one of those travel secrets that has been passed to many people, attracting particularly Germans and Scandinavians, as well as remnants of the hippie generation and nudists of every nationality. But vast stretches of it are devoid not only of humanity but of vegetation, except for a springtime dusting of purple wildflowers. For travellers who respond to the unusual in landscape and environment, the Cabo de Gata awaits.

The Costa Blanca North of Almería

From Cabo de Gata the coastline turns sharply northward, eventually creating a gigantic inverted U with Spain on the west, France's Côte d'Azur at the rounded base, and Italy on the east. What little shoreline is left to Andalusia here is known as the Costa Blanca (locally, the Costa Cálida, "Hot Coast"), a mountainous coast accessible only by local dirt roads leading to innumerable beach areas in coves and inlets.

Route N 340 turns inward at Almería on its way to the Almería-Murcia provincial border and almost immediately enters countryside that is wracked and sere, the very embodiment of aridity. In the vicinity of the town of **Tabernas** (about 32 km/20 miles north of Almería), this desolate landscape has been taken over by the motion picture industry; it's labeled "Mini Hollywood" on some maps. Much of *Lawrence of Arabia* was shot here, and the sets of Clint Eastwood's *A Fistful of Dollars* have become the permanent fixtures for innumerable "spaghetti Westerns" to gratify an apparently insatiable European appetite for the genre. The ruins of the castle where Ferdinand and Isabella stayed during the siege of Almería are part of the Tabernas landscape, but the town is almost wholly given over to filmmaking and its corollary: tours of the sets and staged fights and shootouts on a Western main street complete with saloon, run-down hotel, sheriff's office, and a tree with a hanging noose. Most of the local actors have no need for makeup; they look as tough as the climate in which they were bred.

The landscape around Tabernas, barren of vegetation, has found another, and more enduring, use for its desolation. The largest center in Europe for the harnessing of solar energy has been established here; for this purpose the climate is perfect. A little to the north of Tabernas is the Central Solar, where rows of solar panels have been set up in these desert surroundings (the Central Solar doesn't encourage visitors).

Mojácar

About 92 km (58 miles) north of Almería on N 340 (60 km/ 37 miles past Tabernas), several side roads leading east direct you to Mojácar, about 16 km (10 miles) away on the coast. Mojácar is really two places: a dramatic white Moorish town atop a mountain rising out of the plain, and a contemporary beach resort 3 km (2 miles) from town.

The town is a beauty, with narrow twisting streets and small open plazas for residential breathing space. You leave your car in a parking space and climb on foot between white Moorish houses that lead to a large "balcony" plaza overlooking the countryside and the sea. You have to keep your wits about you to separate what is authentic in Mojácar from what has been meticulously created by the many foreign settlers here to emulate and reflect the Arabic heritage of a town that reluctantly swore allegiance to Ferdinand and Isabella in 1492. Mojácar is filled with shops and bars and boutiques and cafés and tourists. Everyone you meet tells you how much more authentic Mojácar was only a few years ago, yet everyone keeps coming back. The best time to visit is in the early spring or late fall, when relative tranquillity replaces the frenetic scene that draws too many travellers.

On the Mojácar beachfront is the attractive ► **Parador de Mojácar**, whose spacious and comfortable terraced rooms face a swimming pool and its surrounding gardens. The parador serves palatable meals, but the entire beachfront area as well as the hilltop town has a multitude of restaurants of every caliber, most of them featuring seafood. **Palacio**, Plaza del Caño, in the town, serves various roast dishes and baked fish; Tel: (9-50) 47-82-79. **Tito's**, on the beach (Playa de las Ventanicas) offers a wide variety of freshly caught fish and a specialty of sole with almonds; Tel: (9-50) 47-87-11.

THE COSTA DEL SOL WEST OF MALAGA
Torremolinos

Torremolinos, just 13 km (8 miles) down the coast from Málaga, is the classic example of what went wrong with the Costa del Sol. Once a simple fishing town with a pleasant beach, today it frequently looks as if it were in the throes of preparing for a rock concert. Not a square inch of real estate remains vacant. Torremolinos is where contemporary international youth hang out when they don't have quite enough on the ball to go elsewhere. A good many visitors to Torremolinos, however, find precisely what they are seeking.

For those who want to be close by, but still far enough away to play tennis and golf in a more tranquil seaside atmosphere, the ► **Parador de Málaga del Golf**, 9 km (6 miles) west of Málaga and 4 km (2½ miles) east of Torremolinos, is both comfortable and handsome; the dining service is better than adequate.

Mijas

About 30 km (19 miles) southwest of Málaga on the coastal
highway, N 340 (which is called the Carretera de Cádiz and
runs all the way to Cádiz, on the Costa de la Luz), a road to
the right leads to the mountain town of Mijas. This hilltop
white town, some 9 km (6 miles) from the seacoast, was
discovered by travellers many decades ago, but it remains a
charmer.

As in the French Riviera's Vence, which it resembles
somewhat, its streets are mostly given over to shops, outdoor cafés, and restaurants. But Mijas is brighter and livelier, and the nearby hills are starkly Spanish, not verdant
French. Mijas and Vence share the same nearby sea—in
both cases with scarcely acceptable beaches and discolored
water at the shoreline.

Like many spots in this section of the Costa del Sol, Mijas
has a colony of British vacationers and expatriates. English is
routinely spoken here, and many of the bar-cafés list quick-
service dishes, all of which seem to end with "... and chips."
One Mijas restaurant in the central plaza advertises "pub
food."

Near the summit of the town alongside the bullring is a
splendid *mirador* (lookout), but even if you turned your
back to the brilliant Mediterranean panorama your eyes
would light upon the white church wall, the tiled roofs, and
behind them the mountain peaks.

DINING AND STAYING IN THE
MIJAS AREA

Mijas is fun to visit, one of those towns in which the sense of
holiday permeates the atmosphere. In the center of the
town, at Plaza Constitución 13, is **El Mirlo Blanco**, a pleasant
family restaurant where Basque cuisine is well prepared
with top-quality produce; Tel: (9-5) 248-5700. The ► **Hotel
Mijas**, on the left just before you enter the main plaza of the
town, offers very comfortable, thoroughly satisfactory accommodation. Ask for a room with a view—it will be slightly
more expensive but worth it. This hotel has an outside
swimming pool, as does virtually every hotel on the Costa
del Sol, as well as an indoor pool, tennis court, horseback
riding, and golf nearby.

Just 4 km (2½ miles) farther west of the Mijas turnoff
along the Cádiz highway, another turnoff to the right leads to
Mijas-Golf, a splendid location with two 18-hole courses
designed by Robert Trent Jones. The ► **Hotel Byblos Andaluz** is a luxurious spot catering to fashionable Europeans
here, none of whom looks as if he or she requires the

services of the health spa that is an inconspicuous but elaborate part of this hotel's makeup.

The Byblos is an elegant, expensive hotel run with grace and efficiency, and guests expect, and get, the ultimate in service and comfort. Luncheon is an elaborate poolside buffet; three restaurants serve dinner, one of them French haute cuisine. Encircled by rounded hills and blessed with Mediterranean breezes, the Byblos, facing those emerald fairways, has the Costa del Sol's ultimate luxury: quiet.

Marbella

Marbella, 56 km (35 miles) southwest of Málaga, about halfway to Gibraltar, is the Costa del Sol's most fashionable resort. Most of Marbella's numerous luxurious estates and villas are hidden from sight. Available to everyone's eye, however, is the stunning array of yachts and sailing craft that crowd the harbor, their suntanned crews and owners looking as if clouds were forbidden to appear on their personal horizons. Here, and at **Puerto Banús**, just to the west, come people who are unavoidably referred to as rich and famous.

STAYING AND DINING IN MARBELLA

The Costa del Sol now has the largest influx of Arabs since the time of the Reconquest, and Marbella has become the playground of countless Saudis and other Middle Easterners. This means new mosques, lavish shops, luxurious hotels, and extravagant restaurants to cater to their desires. Thus the number of expensive venues here far outweighs more reasonably priced locales. The ► **Marbella Club**, a hotel west of the town, known for its celebrity clientele, has first-class everything. Among its numerous amenities, the club has a private beach. Other super-deluxe Marbella hotels are ► **Los Monteros**, near the Marbella Club, known as the most expensive hotel in Marbella, and the ► **Puente Romano**, on the coastal highway close to Puerto Banús.

In choosing a place to dine, you will find that the **Don Leone**, Muelle Ribera 45, on the Puerto Banús harborfront, serves wonderful Italian food on its terrace; Tel: (9-5) 281-1716. The finest restaurants on the Costa del Sol, all of them with high tabs, are in the Marbella area (reservations suggested for all). They include **La Fonda**, on Marbella's Plaza Santo Cristo, owned by Madrid's famous restaurant Horcher, Tel: (9-5) 277-2512; the Belgian-run **La Hacienda**, Carretera de Cádiz, km 193, in Hacienda las Chapas, Tel: (9-5) 283-1116; and **La Meridiana**, near Puerto Banús, on Camino de la Cruz, Tel: (9-5) 277-6190.

The Road to Gibraltar

As you continue west along the Cádiz highway toward Algeciras and the Gibraltar area, the surroundings become industrialized and decidedly nonresortlike. A startling reminder of the exceptional quality of the locations along this coastline before exploitative developers took over can be found in **Casares**, a white town just 14 km (9 miles) off N 340. Look for the turnoff to the right a few miles beyond Estepona. The uphill road runs through unpopulated farm country, with unexpected turns ending in an explosive view of Casares standing on the summit of a rock promontory, the town topped by a church steeple and a crumbling castle.

In the background of this beautiful Moorish town lies the Mediterranean; in the foreground green hills extend to the base of the village escarpment. The Costa del Sol of Torremolinos and Marbella is a million miles away; Casares is Ur-Andalusian to the core of its Moorish-Reconquest being. Going to Casares just to gaze at its splendid setting is the travel equivalent of pausing to smell the roses.

Some 10 km (6 miles) south of the Casares turnoff at Guadiaro is the ▶ **Hotel Sotogrande**, set between the beach and the Sierra Almenara on the 4,000-acre Sotogrande *urbanización*. The hotel is a sports-lover's haven: Polo, tennis, two golf courses, a yachting marina, swimming pool, disco, and a wide sandy beach are part of the deal. Some rooms at the hotel have private patios with views of Gibraltar across the way. The Sotogrande *urbanización* is a residential development whose houses and condos are, in the main, occupied by well-heeled foreigners.

GIBRALTAR

Gibraltar offers you that most unexpected travel sight: It looks exactly as you had imagined. This limestone rock at the junction of the Mediterranean and the Atlantic has been occupied by Phoenicians, Romans, Visigoths, Moors, and Spanish, until 1704, when it became a British colony, which it remains. A passport and valid car insurance (all Spanish rental cars must have it) are compulsory for a visit, however brief. Visitors usually seek out St. Michael's cave, whose five passages are filled with impressive stalactites and stalagmites. Apes roam freely along the Upper Rock; the main street's shops offer goods from around the world.

STAYING IN THE GIBRALTAR AREA

Algeciras, on the western side of the Bahía de Algeciras (Gibraltar forms the eastern side of the bay), has little to offer the traveller except a wonderfully atmospheric turn-of-the-century hotel, the ▶ **Reina Cristina**, on a hill at the western end of the city. It's the kind of hotel in which some rooms still have wood-burning fireplaces, service and attention to detail still count, and the restaurant is better than conventional. To the spacious gardens come local wedding parties to have their pictures taken against the hotel's *grande dame* background (wags have suggested a wedding of Andalusian hotels, with Seville's Alfonso XIII as groom, the Reina Cristina as the bride, and Ronda's Reina Victoria as matron of honor). But Algeciras is a gray, materialistic, charmless city, despite its views of Gibraltar and Africa's distant mountains. Ferries connecting Algeciras with Ceuta and Tangier account for more than a million passengers yearly.

SOUTHERN COSTA DE LA LUZ

The stretch of Atlantic coastline running from Algeciras-Tarifa, the southern tip of Spain, northwest to Huelva and the Portuguese border is called the Costa de la Luz, a name honored more in guidebooks and maps than in actual use. The differences between this coastline and its Mediterranean counterpart are immediately discernible. Here there seems always to be a stiff wind, and the beaches, mostly deserted and of much finer sand and greater width than those of the Costa del Sol, have few towns and villages in their immediate vicinity. On weekends and holidays they are crowded with picnickers, but in general tourism has set foot very lightly in this area.

In this section we cover the Costa de la Luz from Tarifa west to Vejér de la Frontera, on the way to Cádiz—which is covered in the Northern Costa de la Luz section, at the beginning of the Andalusian Coast part of the chapter.

Baelo Claudio

Just 20 km (13 miles) west of **Tarifa**—from whose port you can look across to Morocco's Atlas mountain range and on clear days pick out white dwellings there—are the extensive remnants of the Roman fishing town Baelo Claudio. You turn left off N 340 and drive a short distance to the coast. There, next to a parking lot for a dozen cars, behind a wire fence, are the ruins of what was once a prosperous Roman town. Founded in the first century A.D. and forgotten for most of the past 15 centuries, Baelo Claudio has unusually well-preserved ruins and few visitors—and is neglected by almost all guide and reference books. The archaeological work, in any real sense, has only just begun.

In Roman times in this town, fish (in the spring, tuna swarm into the Strait of Gibraltar and enter the Mediterranean to spawn) were cut up, salted, stacked in layers in tanks of brine, and in about three weeks were ready for shipping throughout the Roman world. A Roman delicacy called *garum* was a specialty of Baelo Claudio: a fish paste of crushed flesh and roe steeped in smaller tanks, then left in containers in a warm room to evaporate the brine. When the paste cooled, it was sealed in jars and exported to gourmets all over the Mediterranean world. Many of the concrete vats are still here in the "factory" of Baelo Claudio.

This vigorous Roman town, a municipality with what historians estimate was a seasonal population of some 20,000 to 30,000 residents, had all the requisite amenities for urban civilization: a basilica, a forum, a temple, and a theater, as well as baths and less conspicuous elements to make the town function efficiently—water supply and drainage, roadways, and industrial and residential zoning.

Baelo Claudio was discovered by archaeologists in 1917, but funding has made only sporadic work possible; at the moment no such work is being carried on. But what the visitor gets is a superb sense of the layout of the town, its streets and theater, stone walls, arches, and columns. You can see that the basilica was once a rectangular building with a broad nave ending in an apse, flanked by colonnaded aisles, and probably used as a courtroom and public hall. There is even a monument plaque, erected in the second century in honor of a young man, Quintas Pupio Urbicos, apparently the mayor.

Adjacent to the ruins are a few modest contemporary houses and a cafeteria-bar. Here you can apply for admission to the fenced-in Roman area: It is closed Sunday afternoons and Mondays; otherwise it is open from 10:00 A.M. to 1:15 P.M. and from 4:00 to 6:15 P.M.

Vejér de la Frontera

Vejér de la Frontera is a gem. Halfway between Tarifa and Cádiz, built on a commanding bluff, Vejér—even from a great distance—has that unmistakable, classic white town panache. As the road climbs up to this town, it looks better with every twist and turn.

Within the town, the narrow, sharply angled, steeply inclined streets run through banks of white walls, punctuated by black window grilles and doorways leading to courtyards. "Vejér de la Frontera [is] perhaps the most spectacular of all Spanish villages," wrote Jan Morris.

Vejér is whitewashed to within an inch of its civic wellbeing. It sits atop these commanding ramparts looking out over miles of Andalusian countryside (it is about 16 km/10 miles inland from the Atlantic coastline). The remains of an Arab fortress share a dominant position with the church of San Salvador, built on the foundations of a mosque. The Jewish quarter, still well preserved, is located near the Paseo de las Corbijadas, on one side of the ramparts.

Tourism as such is unknown to Vejér. Over the years, travellers have visited and admired the town, but lack of accommodations made for brief stays. Recently, however, a 17th-century monastery has been converted into the ▶ **Hotel Hospedería del Convento de San Francisco** (referred to on some signs as Hotel Convento). The hotel has what must be Spain's single most inconvenient and uninviting entranceway: flush on the sidewalk of the minute plaza on which four narrow streets converge. There is no place to park, turn, unload your baggage, or do anything but drive back to the ramparts and return on foot to register.

Nor is the front-desk "lobby" especially inviting, but once on the second floor you know that you have come upon a real find. The monastery's large rooms have been converted handsomely into lounges and a refectory-like dining hall. The bedrooms, former cells, modernized and with adjacent bathrooms, are models of how to take advantage of the best of an ancient and noble building. The hand-carved furniture throughout the hotel was made in Valencia; the headboards reflect the angle of the high, arched ceilings.

From Vejér it is 52 km (33 miles) northwest to Cádiz, and from Cádiz and Jerez, to its north, it is a straight shot north to Seville on the *autopista*. Or, from Jerez, you can loop to the east through the white towns and back down to the Costa del Sol via Ronda.

GETTING AROUND

The best way to travel around Andalusia is by car, although train and/or bus service is available to and from most major locations. Highways and road surfaces in Andalusia are, with rare exceptions, superb. *Autovías,* or turnpikes (which do not charge tolls), abound, and the 1992 fair in Seville resulted in an intensive upgrading of all automotive transportation. The *only* way to travel to some sections of Andalusia, such as the route of the Moorish white towns and the entire wild Alpujarras range, is by car. Andalusia's two major airports are in Málaga (the larger) and Seville; Córdoba, Granada, and Jerez have smaller airports, mostly for domestic flights. Car-rental offices are at all airports, in all major cities, and in every resort on the Costa del Sol.

The best way to see Andalusia's principal cities is on foot. The areas of particular interest for travellers in Seville, Córdoba, Granada, and Málaga are remarkably concentrated for pedestrian viewing.

For travellers who enjoy luxurious train journeys, the **Andalusian Express** (Al-Andaluz) offers three- and six-day trips within Andalusia, stopping at three principal cities: Seville, Córdoba, and Granada. The elegant train combines the glamour of the Orient Express with the decor of the 1920s in the salon, the bar, and the dining cars; the sleeping accommodations and shower facilities are entirely modern. While travelling from city to city, the Andalusian Express offers passengers bar service, games, videos, and, in the evenings, live musical entertainment and dancing. Branches of the Tourist Office of Spain have information on this train, as do most travel agents.

Seville

A great virtue of Seville is that, as in Florence, almost everything of major interest to the traveller is within a ten-block area. A car can be a liability, and some areas—like the Barrio de Santa Cruz—have many narrow one-way or pedestrians-only streets. Both Seville and Florence, although they bear no physical resemblance to each other, reflect the predominantly Renaissance period of their cultural backgrounds, with a great cathedral as the nucleus. Seville's summer heat is as severe as that of Florence, and although air-conditioning is everywhere, July and August can be punishing.

Seville now has one central railway station, Santa Justa, on the eastern boundary of the city. The greatly expanded international airport, a few miles east of the city on the road to Córdoba, is served by both taxis (about 1,000 pesetas to the city center) and buses (about 200 pesetas). Within the city taxis are plentiful and reasonably priced; drivers are courteous and knowledgeable but rarely speak English. Traffic jams in the narrow streets of old Seville can cause the meter to rise sharply.

Córdoba

Córdoba is on the main highway (N IV) between Madrid and Seville-Cádiz. By car or rail, you can see much of Córdoba on a day trip from Seville (about two hours one way) or an overnight trip from Granada or Málaga (three to four hours), arriving in Córdoba at lunchtime and returning the next afternoon. The old city is best seen on foot, and in fact many of the fascinating narrow streets leading down to the river are impassable by car. Taxis are plentiful and reasonable; horse-drawn carriages are fun to go about in (check on the fare beforehand—perhaps 1,800 pesetas). If you park your car south of the Roman bridge, be sure to lock it and take all valuables with you. Parking garages are available near the mosque. Córdoba has a small domestic airport to the west of the city on N 431. The city is blazing hot in midsummer, lovely in spring and fall, moderate but chilly at night in midwinter. Directly north of the city on N 432 are fine camping and hiking areas in the scenic Sierra Morena.

Granada

Granada is 430 km (270 miles) directly south of Madrid on N IV and N 323. You can continue south from Granada on N 323 to Motril on the Mediterranean (about an hour) or go west on N 342 and veer south past Loja on N 321 for Málaga (about an hour and three-quarters) and the more frequented parts of the Costa del Sol. Granada to Córdoba on N 432 is 166 km (103 miles) and takes about three hours over an indifferent road; from Granada to Seville on N 342, turning north at Antequera on N 334, is 256 km (160 miles) and takes perhaps four hours.

Granada's small airport is west of the city at Santa Fé; airport buses leave from the Plaza de Isabel la Católica; a taxi will cost about 1,000 pesetas, but check with the driver before you set out. The railway station is off Avenida de la Constitución on the Avenida Andaluces; trains connect Granada with all the major cities of Andalusia. Granada's bus station is on Camino de Ronda, on the west side of the city; there is an extensive local bus system.

You can drive your car from the lower city up to the Alhambra compound, but, in general, if your hotel is not on the Alhambra promontory, you are better off using the city's moderately priced taxis, both to go up to the Alhambra and to get around within Granada itself. We live in a world in which almost everyone speaks a little English, but taxi drivers are often the exception; you can avoid misdirections by writing out your destination beforehand. Granada's midtown traffic at rush hour is often anarchic and frustratingly slow.

Walking about the central city is a delight. You *can* walk up to the Alhambra from the Plaza Nueva, but it's a long haul, and the entire Alcazaba–Alhambra–Generalife complex must then be visited on foot. If your legs are in good shape, walking back down into the city is pleasurable, and you can visit the house of Spanish composer Manuel de Falla, now a small museum, on Antequeruela Alta on the way down. Like all Andalusian cities, Granada is torrid and often hazy in midsummer, the time that, ironically, draws the most visitors. Spring in Granada is justly famed for its profusion of beautiful flowers and shrubs; winter can be rainy—with the occasional quirky snowfall—but on sunny days Granada is clear and sparkling.

Málaga

Traffic is heavy in downtown Málaga, and parking is limited; the garage next to the Málaga Palacio hotel in the cathedral quarter is a good bet. The central area of Málaga is best seen on foot. Take a taxi up to the Gibalfaro, but you should negotiate the fare (roughly 700 pesetas), which includes waiting time, beforehand. The international airport is 8 km (5 miles) west of the city on the Málaga–Cádiz highway. Taxis run about 1,000 pesetas from the city to the airport; buses to the airport leave from Calle Abades between the cathedral and the Málaga Palacio.

Local train service runs between Málaga and Fuengirola, to the west, on the Costa del Sol, passing through Torre-molinos and Benalmadena; trains run every half-hour from 6:00 A.M. to 10:00 P.M. These "commuter" trains also stop at both the national and the international terminals of the airport. The Málaga terminal for this train is alongside the principal RENFE railway station on Calle Cuarteles, several blocks west of the Río Guadalmedina in the harbor area. Trains connect Málaga with all the principal cities of Spain. Several ship companies have regular service to Melía; for information call Transmediterránea; Tel: (9-5) 222-4393.

ACCOMMODATIONS REFERENCE

Prices quoted below are projected daily rates for 1994 for double room, double occupancy, in pesetas. Prices are subject to change and primarily suggest price categories. We strongly recommend that you confirm prices when making reservations.

When dialing telephone numbers from outside of Spain, drop the 9 in the area code.

Seville
Rates for all Seville lodgings increase substantially during Holy Week and feria *celebrations.*

The telephone code for the Seville area is 9-5.

▶ **Casa de Carmona**. Plaza de Lasso 1, 41410 **Carmona**. Tel: 414-3300; Fax: 414-3752. 19,000 pts.

▶ **Doña María**. Calle Don Remondo 19, 41004 **Seville**. Tel: 422-4990; Fax: 421-9546. 16,000 pts.

▶ **Hotel Alfonso XIII**. Calle San Fernando 2, 41004 **Seville**. Tel: 422-2850; Fax: 421-6033. 38,000 pts.

▶ **Inglaterra**. Plaza Nueva 7, 41001 **Seville**. Tel: 422-4970; Fax: 456-1336. 23,000 pts.

▶ **Las Casas de la Judería**. Callejón de Dos Hermanas, Plaza de Santa María la Blanca, 41004 **Seville**. Tel: 441-5150; Fax: 442-2170. One-bedroom apartment, 9,500–16,500 pts.

▶ **Parador Alcázar del Rey Don Pedro**. 41410 **Carmona**. Tel: 414-1010; Fax: 414-1712. 16,000 pts.

▶ **Tryp Colón**. Calle de Canalejas 1, 41001 **Seville**. Tel: 422-2900; Fax: 422-0938. 31,000 pts.

Córdoba
The telephone code for the Córdoba area is 9-57.

▶ **Hotel Adarve.** Magistral González Frances 15, 14003 **Córdoba.** Tel: 48-11-02; Fax: 47-46-77. 18,600 pts.

▶ **Hotel Maimónides.** Torrijos 4, 14003 **Córdoba.** Tel: 47-15-00; Fax: 48-38-03. 15,000 pts.

▶ **Hotel Meliá Córdoba.** Jardines de la Victoria, 14004 **Córdoba.** Tel: 29-80-66; Fax: 29-81-47. 16,750 pts.

▶ **Parador de la Arruzafa.** Avenida de la Arruzafa, 14012 **Córdoba.** Tel: 27-59-00; Fax: 28-04-09. 15,000 pts.

The Andalusian Northeast
The telephone code for this area is 9-53.

▶ **Parador Castillo de Santa Catalina.** 23002 **Jaén.** Tel: 26-44-11; Fax: 22-39-30. 13,000 pts.

▶ **Parador Condestable Dávalos.** Plaza Vázquez de Molina 1, 23400 **Ubeda.** Tel: 75-03-45; Fax: 75-12-59. 14,000 pts.

▶ **Parador El Adelantado.** Sierra de Cazorla. Tel: 72-10-75; Fax: 72-13-03. 10,500 pts.

Granada/Sierra Nevada
The telephone code for this area is 9-58.

▶ **Alhambra Palace.** Peña Partida 2, 18009 **Granada.** Tel: 22-14-68; Fax: 22-64-04; in U.S., Tel: (212) 686-9213; Fax: (212) 686-0271. 17,600 pts.

▶ **Hotel Luz Granada.** Avenida de la Constitución 18, 18012 **Granada.** Tel: 20-40-61; Fax: 29-31-50. 16,800 pts.

▶ **Meliá Granada Hotel.** Angel Ganivet 7, 18009 **Granada.** Tel: 22-74-00; Fax: 22-74-03. 16,750 pts.

▶ **Meliá Sierra Nevada.** 18196 **Sierra Nevada–Pradollano.** Tel: 48-04-00; Fax: 40-04-58. (Open winter only.) 19,000 pts.

▶ **Meliá Sol y Nieve.** 18196 **Sierra Nevada–Pradollano.** Tel: 48-03-00; Fax: 48-08-54. (Open winter only.) 14,500 pts.

▶ **Parador de San Francisco.** Recento de la Alhambra, 18009 **Granada.** Tel: 22-14-40; Fax: 22-22-64. 22,000 pts.

▶ **Parador Sierra Nevada.** Carretera Sierra Nevada, km 35, 18196 **Sierra Nevada.** Tel: 48-02-00; Fax: 48-02-12. 9,000 pts.

▶ **Villa Turística de Bubión.** Alpujarras, 18412 **Bubión.** Tel: 76-31-11; Fax: 76-31-36. 9,500 pts.

Costa de la Luz
▶ **Hotel Atlántico.** Avenida Duque de Nájera 9, 11002 **Cádiz.** Tel: (9-56) 22-69-05; Fax: 21-45-82. 12,500 pts.

▶ **Hotel Jerez.** Avenida de Alcalde Alvaro Domecq 35, 11405 **Jerez de la Frontera.** Tel: (9-56) 30-06-00; Fax: 30-50-01. 23,000 pts.

▶ **Hotel Monasterio de San Miguel.** Larga 27, 11500 **Puerto de Santa María.** Tel: (9-56) 54-04-40; Fax: 54-26-04. 17,000 pts.

▶ **Parador Cristóbal Colón.** Carretera a Matalascañas, 21130 **Mazagón.** Tel: (9-59) 37-60-00; Fax: 37-62-28. 14,000 pts.

The White Towns

▶ **La Bobadilla.** Apartado 52, 18300 **Loja.** Tel: (9-58) 32-18-61; Fax: 32-18-10; in U.S., Tel: (212) 686-9213; Fax: (212) 686-0271. 28,800 pts.

▶ **Cortijo Faín.** Carretera de Algar, km 3, 11630 **Arcos de la Frontera.** Tel: (9-56) 70-11-67; Fax: 70-11-67. 10,000 pts.

▶ **Hotel Polo.** Mariano Souvirón 8, 29400 **Ronda.** Tel: (9-52) 87-24-47. 8,500 pts.

▶ **Parador Casa del Corregidor.** Plaza de Cabildo, 11630 **Arcos de la Frontera.** Tel: (9-56) 70-05-00; Fax: 70-11-16. 13,000 pts.

▶ **Reina Victoria.** Doctor Fleming 25, **Ronda.** Tel: (9-5) 287-1240; Fax: 87-10-75. 12,000 pts.

▶ **Las Truchas.** Avenida Diputación 1, 11670 **El Bosque.** Tel: (9-56) 71-60-61. 6,240 pts.

Málaga

The telephone code for the Málaga area is 9-5.

▶ **Hotel Guadalmar.** Carretera Cádiz, km 238–239, Urbanización Guadalmar, 29006 **Málaga.** Tel: 223-1703; Telex: 77099. 10,950–15,950 pts.

▶ **Málaga Palacio.** Cortina del Muelle 1, 29015 **Málaga.** Tel. and Fax: 221-5185. 17,350 pts.

▶ **Parador de Málaga-Gibralfaro.** Monte de Gibalfaro, 29016 **Málaga.** Tel: 222-1903; Fax: 222-1902. 11,500–15,300 pts.

Costa del Sol East of Málaga and Costa Blanca

▶ **Gran Hotel Almería.** Avenida Reina Regente 8, 04001 **Almería.** Tel: (9-50) 23-80-11; Fax: 27-06-91. 16,800 pts.

▶ **Hotel Salobreña.** Carretera 340, km 326, **Salobreña.** Tel: (9-58) 61-02-61; Fax: 61-01-01. 6,050–7,650 pts.

▶ **Parador de Nerja.** Calle Almuñecar 8, 29780 **Nerja.** Tel: (9-52) 52-00-50; Fax: 52-19-97. 13,500 pts.

▶ **Parador de Mojácar.** Playa de Mojácar, 04638 **Mojácar.** Tel: (9-50) 47-82-50; Fax: 47-81-83. 10,500 pts.

Costa del Sol West of Málaga

▶ **Hotel Byblos Andaluz.** 29650 **Mijas-Golf.** Tel: (9-5) 247-3050; Fax: 247-6783; in U.S., Tel: (800) 223-6800. 45,000 pts.

▶ **Hotel Hospedería del Convento de San Francisco.** La Plazuela 6, 11150 **Vejér de la Frontera.** Tel: (9-56) 45-10-01; Fax: 45-10-04. 10,000 pts.

▶ **Hotel Mijas.** Urbanización Tamisa, 29650 **Mijas.** Tel: (9-5) 248-5800; Fax: 248-5825. 12,350 pts.

▶ **Hotel Sotogrande.** Carretera Nacional 340, km 131,

Guadiaro (San Roque). Tel: (9-56) 79-21-00; Telex: 78171. 15,500–18,500 pts.

▶ **Los Monteros.** Urbanización Los Monteros, Carretera de Cádiz, km 187, 29600 **Marbella.** Tel: (9-5) 277-1700; Fax: 282-5846. 36,000 pts.

▶ **Marbella Club.** Carretera Cádiz, km 178, 29600 **Marbella.** Tel: (9-52) 77-13-00; Fax: 82-98-84. 35,500 pts.

▶ **Parador de Málaga del Golf.** Apartado 324, 29080 **Málaga.** Tel: 237-2072; Fax: 238-2141. 12,500–14,000 pts.

▶ **Puente Romano.** Carretera Cádiz, km 177.6, 29600 **Marbella.** Tel: (9-5) 277-0100; Fax: 277-5766; in U.S., Tel: (800) 223-6800. 33,000 pts.

▶ **Reina Cristina.** Paseo de la Conferencia, 11207 **Algeciras.** Tel: (9-56) 60-26-22; Fax: 60-33-23. 15,000 pts.

THE CANARY ISLANDS

By Patricia Brooks

For northern Europeans the Canaries are their islands in the sun, their winter getaway destination, the fastest escape route (via a short plane ride) to winter warmth. But these seven Spanish islands forming part of an archipelago spanning some 300 nautical miles in the North Atlantic, some 850 miles southwest of Cádiz, Spain, 300 miles south of Portugal's Madeira, and only 70 miles from the coast of Africa (southern Morocco), have all the familiarity of, say, Siberia to most other travellers.

Yet the Canaries—or the Fortunate Isles, as they were once called—have been known since ancient Greeks, Romans, and other early sea voyagers landed here. Ptolemy, Plutarch, and Pliny the Elder wrote about them. Pliny, in recording a journey here, explained the origin of the group's name: "Canaria, so called from the multitude of dogs of great size." The dogs, or *canis,* are long gone, but the name, adopted by conquering Spaniards centuries later, remains.

Today any winter visitor can understand why the Canaries were dubbed the Fortunate Isles. Temperatures make no wild swings, but hover year-round between 65 and 86 degrees Fahrenheit. Thus the islands—especially Grand Canary, Lanzarote, and Tenerife—are strong and steady magnets for vacationing Europeans. An added bonus: Unlike many other island vacation spots, the Canaries are considerably less expensive than the mainland.

CHOOSING AN ISLAND

It is believed that in pre-Spanish days each island was a kingdom unto itself, and that there was no interchange among them—not so much as a fishing boat. Even today,

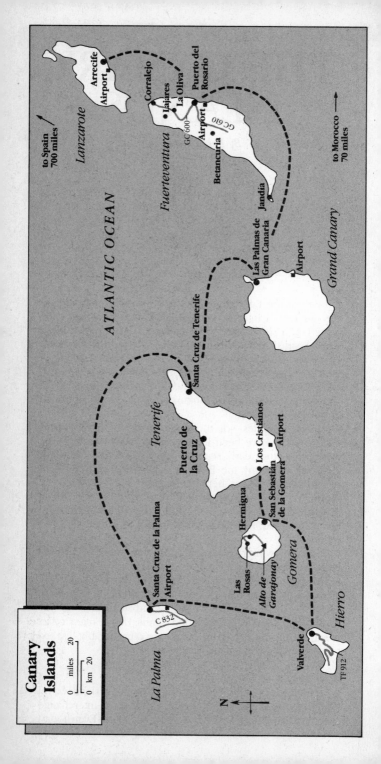

when island-hopping is easy, many vacationers tend to pick one island, apply suntan lotion, and stay put.

A pity, for each of these volcanic islands has its own personality. If you've seen one, you most definitely haven't seen them all. Tiny Gomera's misty green-terraced mountains are as different from Lanzarote's black volcanic fields as those are from the wide, white-sand beaches of Grand Canary and the acres of banana plantations of Tenerife. Island-hopping, by plane or ferry, can only contribute to the richness of experience.

In planning a visit, you should first decide whether it is to be a total getaway or a mix-and-match trip blending sight-seeing with sunbathing, swimming, and sports. If you choose a getaway vacation more decisions are required, for the islands that will provide you with a true getaway, **Hierro** and **La Palma**, are rustic, with minimal infrastructures, while the formerly secluded island of **Fuerteventura** has recently undergone a burst of touristic development. On all three the climate is desirable and the terrain agreeable.

If you want more of a balance between leisure and sights, consider Gomera, Lanzarote, Tenerife, or Grand Canary. On balance, **Tenerife** and **Lanzarote** offer the best matchup between sightseeing and playtime. **Gomera** is a lovely clump of green-tufted mountains dropped into the ocean, but the tourist facilities are limited, and the best accommodations are to be found in a very pleasant parador perched above the harbor. At the opposite extreme is **Grand Canary**, 90 percent of which is given over to tourist development, at the expense of the island's true attractions.

Carnival, a movable feast just before Lent begins, is celebrated in the Canaries as nowhere else in Spain. In Santa Cruz and Puerto de la Cruz on Tenerife and Las Palmas on Grand Canary it is an explosive, raucous, fun-loving, weeklong Brazilian-style celebration, marked by fireworks, brass bands, folk dances, and parades of costumed celebrants snaking through the streets to musical accompaniment. Everything comes to a climax on Shrove (or Fat) Tuesday, just before Ash Wednesday and the beginning of Lent.

MAJOR INTEREST

Unusual volcanic landscapes, especially on Lanzarote and Tenerife

Miles of sandy beaches and coves, acres of banana plantations on Grand Canary and Tenerife

Carnival celebrations

Fresh seafood and Canarian food specialties

Lanzarote
Arrecife's Museo Internacional de Arte
    Contemporaneo
Costa Teguise resorts and beaches
Route of the Volcanoes
Jameos del Agua volcanic cave
Mirador del Río and other scenic lookouts

Tenerife
Pico del Teide mountain and national park
Typical 17th-century Canarian houses in La Orotava
Santa Cruz de Tenerife
La Laguna, oldest town on the island
Puerto de la Cruz's waterfront promenade
The dragon tree of Icod de los Vinos

Gomera
San Sebastián de la Gomera
Tour of mountains and small villages

Grand Canary
Golden beaches in the south
Barrio Vegueta, the old quarter of Las Palmas
Interior mountain area

The getaway islands of **Hierro**, **La Palma**, and
    Fuerteventura

In this era of renewed ethnic consciousness and regional
autonomy in Spain, you hear frequent mention in the Canaries of the Guanches. These mysterious people, whose origins are in the Stone Age, were the only occupants of the
islands when the Spaniards arrived. No one is absolutely
sure of their origins, except that they were fair-skinned and
are thought to have come from North Africa. Their bone
structure suggests they were of the same racial type as Cro-
Magnon man. Similarities in the few Guanche words extant
and the Berber language suggest that Guanches may have
been Berbers who strayed the short distance west of the
North African coast to the islands and then stayed there,
never travelling even as far as the next island. Curiously, no
excavation has ever unearthed anything resembling a boat
on any of the islands. Originally, the term Guanche was
applied only to inhabitants of Tenerife, the last holdouts
against the Spaniards, but it is now used for the natives of all
seven islands.

Nowadays Canarians look and speak like most other Spaniards. Their customs and traditions, after 500 years, have
become totally absorbed into Spain's. What remains of the
Guanches today can be found mostly in a few indigenous
dishes, such as *gofio* (a type of heavy corn-and-wheat bread),

puchero (a Canarian stew), *garbanzo compuesto* (chick-pea stew), *mojo* (a spicy red or green sauce made of oil, vinegar, garlic, coriander, peppers, and cumin used to season meat and fish), and *papas arrugadas* (potatoes cooked in their skins in seawater to form a salt crust).

The Wines of the Canary Islands

The Canary Islands produce several types of wine, but have no *denominación de origen* and export little wine, even to the Spanish mainland. However, the wines of the Canary Islands, especially the Malvasia, have been known since the 16th century and are mentioned by Shakespeare and Voltaire and in accounts of the exploits of Sir Francis Drake. Recently, though, the island of Tenerife has begun to produce some inexpensive red wines from grapes called Listán Negro and Negramoll. El Lomo, La Isleta, Balcón Canario, and Viña Flores are all palatable *tintos,* but perhaps the most interesting wines carry the brand name Viña Norte. The wines of Viña Norte are made by a group of 80 different small producers, each of whom puts his own name on the label of the wine he produced.

The wines of the Canaries are made under some of the most impossible, but interesting, winemaking conditions in the world. The vines are ungrafted because the phylloxera aphid cannot live in the volcanic soil of these vineyards; there is little rain, so vines must get their water from dew absorbed by porous volcanic stones. Since strong, hot winds can blow from Africa, each vine must be planted in a yard-deep pit or protected individually by a stone wall. Vineyard work and winemaking here are very labor-intensive, and the whole process, from the strikingly picturesque vineyards to the old-fashioned harvesting techniques (the grapes are still pressed by treading), is fascinating.

—*Gerry Dawes*

Spain and the Islands

Spain didn't get around to conquering the Canaries until the 15th century. Of course, Spain wasn't Spain, as such, until Ferdinand and Isabella united their kingdoms and finally defeated the Moors in a more widely noted 15th-century event. Arabs had stumbled on the islands in the 12th century; a Genoese navigator, Lanzarotto Malocello, stopped in Lanzarote in the early 14th century and left the island his name but nothing else. Some French ships were driven to the islands by a gale in 1334, and the Portuguese came close— but didn't find the islands—at about the same time.

It was in 1402 that Spanish forces, led by Frenchman Jean de Béthencourt, stepped ashore at Lanzarote, the first island to be taken. For much of the 15th century the islands were claimed and reclaimed by Spain and Portugal. Spanish sovereignty was finally established by a treaty between Portugal and Castile in 1479, but it was not until 1496 that the locals on Tenerife were conquered. To Spain, the islands were a bulwark against, and a possible springboard to, North Africa, and, later, a way of protecting Spanish ships from Barbary pirates.

The islands remained backward for centuries after, with few amenities to encourage the rare foreigner who found his way here. All that changed radically in the mid-1970s when tourists, hungry for new and accessible all-weather vacation sites, discovered the shimmering sand beaches of Grand Canary, and its rapid development began pell-mell.

The Canaries make up two provinces of Spain. Clustered in the western province are the islands of Tenerife, Gomera, Hierro, and La Palma, with Santa Cruz de Tenerife as the capital. The eastern province, closer to Africa, consists of Grand Canary, Fuerteventura, and Lanzarote, with Las Palmas de Gran Canaria, on Grand Canary, as the provincial capital.

In our coverage we discuss the islands in order of interest (though not necessarily popularity), rather than geographically.

LANZAROTE

If you have to choose just one Canary to visit, for sheer uniqueness it should be Lanzarote (Lan-zah-ROE-tay), the fourth-largest and most easterly island. Much of this 313-square-mile mountainous, treeless, and nearly rain-free "island of the moon"—as it has been called because of its eerie landscape—is almost a minimalist study in black and white (and a bit of green): one-story white houses with kelly-green doors set against black volcanic soil, from which shoots of green plants emerge. Many of the beaches, especially those along the flat northeastern coast, are covered with fine black sand. (Most of the golden-sand beaches are at Puerto del Carmen and Playa Blanca, both in the island's southern end. The rugged, mountainous northern, northwestern, and western shores of Lanzarote are too dangerous for swimming.) Grapes are grown in the carefully cultivated *picón* (volcanic pebbles), and the vines twist like snakes along the ground instead of growing upright. Camels and donkeys are still used to cultivate the fields.

In contrast with the touristic overdevelopment of Grand

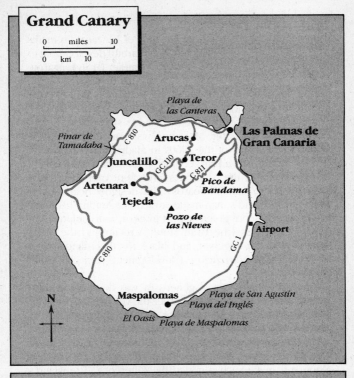

Grand Canary

0 miles 10

0 km 10

Playa de las Canteras

Las Palmas de Gran Canaria

C 810

Arucas

Pinar de Tamadaba

GC 110

Teror

Juncalillo

C 811

Pico de Bandama

Artenara

Tejeda

▲ *Pozo de las Nieves*

■ **Airport**

C 810

GC 1

N

Maspalomas

Playa de San Agustín

Playa del Inglés

El Oasis

Playa de Maspalomas

N

Isla Graciosa

Conchas

Caleta del Sebo

Mirador del Río

Cueva de los Verdes

Haría

Jameos del Agua

Arrieta

GC 700

Guatiza

Teguise

GC 710

Montañas del Fuego Parque Nacional de Timanfaya

Islote de Hilario

Tahiche

San Bartolomé

Costa Teguise

Yaiza

GC 720

Arrecife

Airport

Puerto del Carmen

Playa Blanca

Lanzarote

0 miles 10

0 km 10

Canary and patches of Tenerife, most of Lanzarote remains relatively pristine. The island owes its careful development to one man, César Manrique. You can't wander far in Lanzarote without hearing his name or seeing his handprints, so to speak, wherever aesthetics are involved, whether it's the prevention of random construction or preservation of the whitewashed houses that are the island's signature.

Trained as a painter, Manrique was part of the Spanish abstract movement of the 1960s in Madrid, but in 1968 he returned home to Lanzarote. Since then he has been unofficial custodian of the island's environment (persuading the government to ban billboards) and designer-beautifier of most of the island's man-made attractions. Among his many credits are the cool green airport interior, wall sculptures in two major hotels (the Gran Hotel Arrecife and the Meliá Salinas in Costa Teguise), and plans for the island's most elite tourist *urbanización* (development project), Costa Teguise.

Manrique's latest act of generosity was donating his dramatic modern home, with under-the-volcano rooms and rich color schemes, to the state. Ask for directions at the Meliá Salina hotel on the Costa Teguise. His is a rare legacy, and one can only wonder what will happen to the island when he is gone. There are few places where one person alone can make such a noticeable difference. The island's small size (population 50,000) has probably made this possible.

Visitors to Lanzarote tend to be well-travelled, upscale Europeans and Middle Easterners in search of something a bit different mixed with their sunshine-and-sea cocktail. Jordan's King Hussein and the actor Omar Sharif are among the international set with vacation houses on the island.

SETTING OUT ON THE ISLAND

Lanzarote, for sightseeing purposes, divides rather neatly into north and south, each different from the other, and a day for each gives ample time to cover the major sights. Although it is possible to scoot from north to south in a single day—the excellent roads are wide and under-trafficked—you would miss the pleasure of frequent stops for vistas and photographs.

Most visitors to Lanzarote arrive by air. The airport is 5 km (3 miles) south of the capital city and ferry port, Arrecife (Are-uh-SEE-fay), near the center of the east coast. Your first order of business should be to pick up a rental car (essential for touring the island) and then head for Arrecife or one of the coastal tourist developments, which have become small villages in themselves.

Southern Lanzarote

ARRECIFE

If your purpose is a quick here-today, gone-tomorrow once-over of the island, you might base yourself in Arrecife, a slightly scruffy, dusty port, noticeably lacking in sidewalks and charm. It does boast one good hotel, however, the ▶ **Gran Hotel Arrecife Playa**, centrally located downtown, facing the water, with a huge swimming pool, right next door to the town beach of golden sand. The lobby displays art by Manrique, and guest rooms are ample, with sea views.

Whether you choose to stay in Arrecife or not, you won't want to miss the wonderful **Museo Internacional de Arte Contemporaneo**, Manrique's collection of Spanish abstract paintings and sculptures, installed in the 18th-century fort, **Castillo de San José**, one of two sturdy fortresses guarding the Arrecife harbor. Included are works of Antoni Tàpies, José Guerrero, Francisco Ferreras, Manolo Millares, Fernando Zobel, and others of the Spanish abstract school, as well as artists from Germany, France, Argentina, and the United States. The fort's interior provides handsome gallery space: The stone walls and floors, arched ceilings, and staircases make an intriguing contrast with the art.

There's a second reason to visit the museum: **Restaurante San José**. Located on the lower level of the fort, the restaurant has wide windows that wrap around the sea side of the building, so that diners have a full harbor view while they enjoy *paella* (rice and seafood stew), grilled *mero* fish stuffed with ham, or other fresh seafood; Tel: (9-28) 81-23-21.

In the town's other fortress, the 16th-century **Castillo de San Gabriel**, located on an offshore island linked to the mainland by a bridge, there is a museum of archaeology and anthropology.

COSTA TEGUISE

The poshest and most exclusive development on the island is the well-run resort and burgeoning community called Costa Teguise. After the 7-km (4½-mile) drive northeast of Arrecife through a pancake-flat, arid beige landscape, you will suddenly come upon a "created community," clustered near the water's edge, of condominiums for rent, a golf course, shops, *supermercados,* restaurants, entertainment facilities, avenues bordered with palm trees and greenery, a black-sand beach, and two excellent hotels.

The edge goes to the more established hotel, the ▶ **Meliá Salinas**, which is considered *the* place to stay on the island. It is the quintessential resort hotel: large, with a tree-filled atrium, well-kept palm-fringed grounds, an imaginative saltwater swimming pool designed by Manrique with volcanic bridges you can swim under, many sports facilities, and an attractive restaurant. All guest rooms have flower-bedecked terraces overlooking the pool, a sandy beach, and the ocean. Discreet topless sunning around the pool is not discouraged.

A short walk away is the newer ▶ **Teguise Playa Hotel**, a comfortable establishment facing the ocean, which also has an atrium lobby. The rooms have balconies with ocean views, and myriad sports facilities are available. Either accommodation makes a comfortable launching pad for exploring the island.

PUERTO DEL CARMEN

Less pricey and just as convenient are the resort hotels in the other major tourist development on Lanzarote, the more built-up and crowded **Puerto del Carmen**, about 11 km (7 miles) southwest of Arrecife. Here the hands-down hotel choice is ▶ **Los Fariones**, a well-appointed high rise with many amenities: golf, tennis, a garden, a heated swimming pool, a sheltered private beach, and spacious, well-decorated rooms. Puerto del Carmen, like Costa Teguise, is a created-for-tourism community of shops, restaurants, and hotels, but with better natural tawny beaches, bigger, noisier crowds, and more congestion. These developments, like comparable ones on the Costa del Sol on the mainland, have such support systems that a vacation here can be totally self-contained.

THE VOLCANO AREA

What created the stark black landscape of Lanzarote was not one but several volcanic eruptions. The first occurred in the Timanfaya area, on the island's western coast, in 1730; 30 craters exploded from the earth simultaneously, sending out plumes of flame that continued for 19 days. One-third of the island, including 11 villages, was buried. New eruptions continued for six years, until the molten lava was layered 33 feet deep and covered 77 square miles. More eruptions followed in 1824, covering still more terrain, and even today you are aware of roiling life beneath the black lava on the **Montañas del Fuego** (Mountains of Fire), as the peaks in the Timanfaya area are called. All told, there are some 300 volcanoes, most of them extinct, on the island.

Parque Nacional de Timanfaya

Part of that old volcanic zone is now a 125-square-mile national park called Parque Nacional de Timanfaya, about 31 km (19 miles) from Arrecife on the southwestern part of the island (take GC 720 west from Arrecife to Yaiza, then take the road north to the park). It isn't just tourists who are intrigued by the 30 famed cones and fields of rubblelike lava; American astronauts heading for the moon used the lava landscape to preview what they might face on their moonwalks.

A few miles north of Yaiza you can arrange a 15-minute camel ride partway up a mountain slope. The reward for the jolting, swaying, disagreeable ride, as several camels are tethered bumpingly together, is a head-on view of a crater. After paying a relatively steep entrance fee at the park, continue along a well-kept one-way road through treeless fields and hillsides of black, gray, and rust-brown lava, devoid of any sign of flora or fauna, to **Islote de Hilario**. At this central point, you may park your car and board a free bus for a one-hour tour across desolate craters, through just over 10 km (6 miles) of the dramatic and eerie Ruta de los Volcanes (Route of the Volcanoes), where impassable clumps and surrealistic swirls of chocolate-colored lava lie motionless, like something in a Dalí painting. There's a recorded commentary (in several languages) to keep you apprised of what you are seeing.

Afterwards, back at Islote de Hilario, guides demonstrate the still-active nature of the seemingly sleeping volcano by throwing cold water into a pipe in the volcano, which causes geysers of steam to spurt forth instantly. Then they poke mounds of brush into another hole 20 inches deep to demonstrate the flash fire that quickly erupts. The temperature underground reaches 400 degrees Fahrenheit, and the gravelly earth is burning-hot to the touch. Later you may lunch—on meats or chicken grilled over an open hearth fueled by the volcano's heat—at **El Diablo**, an attractive circular restaurant whose wide windows overlook the silent, lava-encrusted slopes and valleys.

Yaiza

Upon leaving the park, it's worth your while to stop at Yaiza, a small Arabic-looking town with white buildings whose approach road is lined with vivid orange-blossomed cacti. Many foreign artists have settled in the town's dazzling all-white houses. **Galería Yaiza**, which sells local modern art and photographs, is located in one of these houses on the main street through town.

At the edge of town, at El Barranco 3, is **La Era**, one of the island's prettiest restaurants, more notable for its setting in an authentic old Canarian country house than for its hearty, somewhat rustic cooking. Three tiny, white-walled dining rooms filled with attractive ceramics, baskets, and plants open onto a bougainvillea-festooned, whitewashed courtyard. Try the Canarian specialties. Tel: (9-28) 83-00-16.

Northern Lanzarote

THE EASTERN COAST

To explore the northern part of Lanzarote, take the main road north from Arrecife to Tahiche, and then follow its eastern branch toward Guatiza and Arrieta. Just beyond Arrieta the road branches again; take the secondary road to the right (east) toward two of the major (and well-posted) sights in this part of the island, Jameos del Agua and Cueva de los Verdes. As you drive along the easy-to-follow route you will notice fields of cacti and vineyards protected by low volcanic-stone walls. Because there is so little rainfall, and not a single river on the island, the grapevines are grafted to prickly pear cactus, allowing the vines to survive on the cacti's stored moisture. The north, with its patches of cultivated green fields and more than a few palm trees dotted along the roadside, is a contrast to the parched and blackened southwest.

Cueva de los Verdes consists of four miles of connecting underground caves formed when lava streams cooled and hardened into passages. The natives often hid from Turks and Barbary pirates in these caves, which can be safely explored without a guide. The variety of lagoons and stalactites is fascinating.

Jameos del Agua, nearby, is a remarkable natural sight that was converted by Manrique into a tasteful and intriguing tourist attraction. On several levels of a *jameo* (volcanic cave) are a nightclub with dance floor, a free-form swimming pool edged by palm trees, a garden of oleander and cacti, and a seawater lagoon in which live thousands of sightless white crabs (*Munidopsis polimorpha*) unique to Lanzarote.

THE NORTHERN TIP

Return to the main highway heading north: At the northern tip of the island is the **Mirador del Río** (*mirador* means "lookout"), a small whitewashed building nestled into the top of the cliff overlooking the tiny **Isla Graciosa** across the narrow sea inlet called El Río. Once a hideout for pirates, Isla Graciosa was supposedly the inspiration for Robert Louis Stevenson's *Treasure Island*. (Some Lanzarote hotels offer excursions to Isla Graciosa and its powdery white-sand beaches, Conchas and Caleta del Sebo.)

The views are spectacular from the *mirador:* You can sit inside a very attractive bar, sip a *café con leche* (coffee with milk), admire the view through enormous windows, and watch hawks swoop and hang gliders dip along the craggy cliffs. You have the same view outside along a walkway protected by a guard rail. Upstairs in the *mirador* is a tiny shop with a small but good selection of guidebooks, Canarian dolls, and other handicrafts.

THE WESTERN COAST
Head south from the *mirador* on the twisty, curving road that loops through the mountains along the western side of the island to **Haría**, a scenic town of low-slung houses, whose glistening whiteness, punctuated by garlands of purple and fuchsia bougainvillea, has a North African cast. In the modern church are works by two Canarian sculptors: an Assumption of the Virgin by Luján Pérez and a Christ by Borges Linares. From the **Mirador de Haría**, 3 km (2 miles) south of town, there are grand views of the Atlantic, the coastline, and the valley. From Haría the road continues to Teguise, where you will pick up the road south to Tahiche and Arrecife.

TENERIFE

Like Lanzarote, Tenerife (Ten-er-EE-fay) was bypassed by Columbus, although as he sailed from Gomera to Grand Canary on his first voyage to the Americas he noted flames spouting from Tenerife's Pico del Teide. With the wisdom of one familiar with volcanoes, he reassured his frightened Spanish crew that it was a function of nature, not a judgment from God.

Centuries later, Spanish philosopher and writer Miguel de Unamuno described Tenerife and its dominant volcano this way: "And there in the distance ... stood the island of Tenerife, like a celestial vision, dominated by that gigantic watchtower of Spain, the peak of Teide. . . . One would have said that the island was suspended in the sky."

As the largest Canary, Tenerife has a terrain that is all things to almost all visitors. As the old saw goes about the weather (wait a minute, it will change), five miles up a road, the botanical profile of Tenerife might shift from subtropical to temperate, then, within miles, back again. You will find plantings at home in both warm and cold climates. Wildflower fanciers can have a field day on Tenerife, which boasts almost 1,000 species of wild flowering plants, about 270 of which are found only in the Canaries.

THE ISLAND'S TERRAIN
This 792-square-mile, ladle-shaped island climbs from sea level to more than 12,000 feet, its terrain changing endlessly, from lush foliage and palm-edged plantings to a stark lunar landscape. There are no lakes on the island, though there are several small rivers running off the mountains, and rain

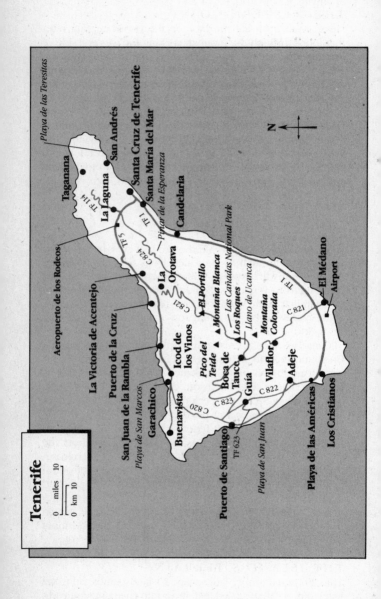

falls infrequently. The island's northern knob of land, the
ladle's handle, rises from sea level to some 1,300 feet. It has
a climate like that of Egypt and is the domain of banana
plantations and the dragon tree, a curious, spiky-branched,
cactus-like tree found only in the Canaries that seems to
"perspire" a bloodlike resin. Dante knew of the tree, and it
was used in the Middle Ages to treat leprosy. The middle of
the island, dominated by a mountain range culminating in
the Pico del Teide, has a landscape similar to that of the
American West, though adorned with lava formations. Its
climate is like that of Italy and southern France. Grapes,
maize, and tomatoes are cultivated at lower elevations;
above 3,300 feet heather, gorse, Scotch broom, and pine
predominate. The southern and southeastern parts of the
island, the bottom of the ladle's bowl, are flat and edged in
golden-sand beaches; any monotony of terrain is broken up
by the sight of mountains looming in the distance. No matter
where you are on the island, you are aware of the presence
of the Pico del Teide, which Herodotus called "a column in
the sky."

CHOOSING A BASE

Tenerife has three major destinations, all on different parts of
the island. There are basically two groups of European sunseekers who come here. The Germans and Scandinavians,
individually and in tour groups, tend to head north (where
the ladle's handle joins the bowl) to the area first developed
for tourism. The magnet is the bustling, overbuilt coastal town
of **Puerto de la Cruz**, built above scenic volcanic rock formations, with a black-sand beach. It is a springboard to some of
the island's most diverse scenery. The second group, mostly
British (especially families in search of a getaway "do-
nothing" holiday), prefers the isolation of the creamy sand
beaches and sprawling seaside developments that have
sprung up in recent years in **Playa de las Américas** and **Los
Cristianos** at the southern tip of the island (the bottom of the
ladle), where you catch the ferry to Gomera. These developments are worlds unto themselves.

Those who don't fit in either category might prefer as a
base the lively, less "touristy" port city of **Santa Cruz de
Tenerife** (usually shortened to Santa Cruz), on the northeastern coast of the island, where there are more sightseeing
opportunities. Santa Cruz is a real Canarian city, with a life
and beat of its own apart from tourism.

To reach any of the three you should rent a car, easily
picked up at Reina Sofía airport, which is located just outside
of El Médano, in the south. An *autopista,* TF 1, runs along the
coast from Los Cristianos north to Santa María del Mar, just
below Santa Cruz, where it becomes an even faster super-

highway, TF 5, that curves inland and continues down along the north coast as far as Puerto de la Cruz.

Staying on Tenerife

SANTA CRUZ DE TENERIFE

Far and away the most discreetly elegant hotel on the island is the ▶ **Mencey**, in Santa Cruz. The name meant king or ruler in Guanche times, and the Ciga-run hotel is indeed regal, having recently undergone a costly renovation. Spacious, deluxe rooms with balconies overlook either the superbly groomed garden, palm-sheltered grounds, and swimming pool, or the city and harbor. The Mencey also boasts one of the island's finest Continental restaurants. To enjoy the beach, however, you have to drive about 7 km (4 miles) along the northeast coast to Playa de las Teresitas (see Santa Cruz de Tenerife, below).

PUERTO DE LA CRUZ

Puerto de la Cruz, west of Santa Cruz on the opposite shore, is literally cheek-by-jowl with high-rise hotels in all prices and categories. They line the hills that ring the little fishing port and stretch right down to the seaside promenade that curves around the black rocky ledges above the swirling sea. The most secluded deluxe choice is the ▶ **Meliá Botánico**, cresting a hilltop above town. The hotel is spacious, set on lavish grounds dotted with lush plantings, a swimming pool, and tennis courts overlooking the town and the water.

Although the hotel is a quiet sanctuary, the town below is chockablock with shops, restaurants, nightclubs, bars, discos, and a casino catering to the masses of northern European tourists who flock here. Smack in the middle of the action is the ▶ **Monopol Hotel**, which, although a bit noisy, has several things going for it: more moderate prices, balconies almost literally over the water, a plant-filled atrium-lobby, a swimming pool, and considerable charm.

PLAYA DE LAS AMERICAS

Should you choose the southern tip of Tenerife as a home base, once again you have dozens of accommodation choices, all large high rises. Many are self-contained resorts geared to sun-lovers and lotus-eaters, where you merely collapse by the pool or beach for days on end. Most such places are long on service and convenience, shorter on charm. ▶ **La Siesta Hotel** near Playa de las Américas is a block from the gorgeous beach and comes equipped with two swimming pools, tennis courts, gardens, and the comforts—but not the solitude—of home.

Pico del Teide

Looming above the triangular island is Pico del Teide, the highest peak in all of Spain, at 12,198 feet, located in the center of the ladle. Teide is a volcano and has a crater 47 miles in circumference, 7½ miles across. Past eruptions have left a fantastic colorscape, ranging from whites, reds, and yellows to blues and blacks. Surrounding Teide are various other mountain peaks, all of which are more than 6,000 feet high but are dwarfed by Teide itself. That Teide dominates the island is evident even in the island's name: *Tenerife* means snowcapped mountain in Guanche.

DRIVING INTO THE PARQUE NACIONAL DEL TEIDE

To reach the foot of Pico del Teide and Las Cañadas, a plateau formed by the collapse of an ancient crater, you can approach from the north (via route C 821), the northeast (route C 824), the southeast (via the southern end of C 821) or, least likely, the west (C 820 south to C 822, then east along C 823). No matter which route you start on, you will end up driving through the park on C 821, crossing terrain that changes in color and character and ranges from valley to mountain pass (*cañadas* means "ravines").

The most scenically dramatic route is the one that begins at La Orotava, a north-central hill town a few miles inland from Puerto de la Cruz, at the northern end of route C 821, and continues through the park to route C 823 and ends on C 822, which parallels the island's western coast. Or you can begin at La Orotava and choose another exit route. All of the drives provide awe-inspiring vistas. (Here we cover the route into the park from La Orotava, and describe the other three routes as exits from the park, below.)

LA OROTAVA

If you are starting at La Orotava, stop first at the **Mirador de Humboldt**, less than a mile north of town, a grand lookout over the sweeping Orotava valley named for Alexander Humboldt, the famous German naturalist and explorer. La Orotava is an interesting town in its own right, with an 18th-century Baroque church, **Iglesia de la Concepción**, and for the typical Canarian houses along Calle de San Francisco. Most notable of a group of 17th-century houses with fretted wooden balconies is **Casa de los Balcones**, which now contains an **Artespaña** handicraft showroom. (Curiously, most of the embroideries in the Artespaña are from China.) You'll see similar pine balconies all across the island, but few as elaborate and old as these.

During the Feast of Corpus Christi the ground of the

entire Plaza del Ayuntamiento in La Orotava is decorated with fresh flowers and an enormous colored-sand-and-stone painting depicting the feast, made from the variegated sands of Mount Teide.

SOUTH TO THE MOUNTAINS

Continuing south from La Orotava, the well-marked road zigzags upward, past banana plantations, to a mountain pass called **El Portillo de la Villa** (33 km/20 miles, at the intersection with route C 824). Eleven kilometers (7 miles) farther, past Montaña Blanca, on the Las Cañadas plateau is the cable car to Teide's summit (operational on days when there is no wind). If you're feeling adventurous you can walk from the summit terminal at 11,664 feet to the crater's edge, a 45-minute scramble over loose volcanic rubble and past sulfurous smoke holes. Once there, you will get views that extend all over the island, and on very clear days—which are the norm on Tenerife—you can see the forms of Gomera, La Palma, and Grand Canary in the distance.

Five kilometers (3 miles) west of the cable-car station you can take a coffee or lunch break at the ▶ **Parador de Las Cañadas del Teide**, a comfortable rustic lodge that is part of the national parador system. Its handsome dining room, with a fire glowing in the hearth much of the year, is a good place to try such Canarian specialties as *cocido canario* (a stew of chunks of beef, corn cobs, squash, cabbage, green beans, potatoes, carrots, and zucchini, served in gargantuan portions) or *rancho canario* (a thick vegetable soup made with *gofio*). The parador also has a few modest guest rooms and a heated outdoor swimming pool. Next to the parador is a small hermitage dedicated to the Virgen de las Nieves (Virgin of the Snows). After lunch you might hike through a landscape that looks like the American West, on which cactus and sagebrush grow. Strewn about are enormous lava boulders called Los Roques and smaller stones, called Los Azulejos, that glisten and gleam like the lustrous ceramic tiles for which they are named. Just beyond is the **Llano de Ucana**, a vast, isolated plain.

EXITING THE PARK

When you are ready to leave the Pico del Teide area, you have three options for your return drive (a fourth would be to go back the same way you came in, to La Orotava), all of which provide a varied and spectacular landscape. You might continue southwest, then south, on C 821, which takes you on twisting mountain roads through a towering pine forest and over a steep mountain pass, veers around the red-earth face of the Montaña Colorada, and leads down, down, down past fields of grape vines to the pleasant town of

Vilaflor, a spa with the highest elevation of any town on the island. Much of the bottled water sold on Tenerife comes from Vilaflor, as does a sweet, fresh goat cheese. There is a pleasant, Belgian-run inn at the edge of town, **Tajinaste**, where you can lunch on quiche on the sun-drenched terrace or even spend the night in a simple guest room (no reservations). Tel: (9-22) 70-90-49.

A second route out of the park takes you back to El Portillo and then northeast on C 824 for 58 km (36 miles) to the *autopista* at the outskirts of La Laguna, a university town of considerable interest (discussed below). This curvaceous road, with several observation points along the way, leads through a majestic forest of pines and eucalyptus called **Pinar de la Esperanza.** An obelisk in **Las Raíces** (which means "the roots") in La Esperanza marks the place where Francisco Franco and other army officers met in June 1936 to plot the revolt that sparked the Spanish Civil War.

Still another way out of the park is to continue southwest on C 821 until it intersects C 823 at Boca de Tauce, then head north on C 823 through the wildly dramatic black-stone terrain of Malpaís ("Badland," also known as the Valle de la Santidad). Route C 823 turns into C 822, which meets the circumferential route, C 820, just north of Puerto de Santiago on the west coast. The disadvantage of this route is that it requires a lot of extra time, as you must circle most of the island to return to your base.

Santa Cruz de Tenerife

Compared to the fast-expanding touristic developments of Los Cristianos and Playa de las Américas on the southwestern coast and of Puerto de la Cruz on the north shore, with all their high-rise hotels, Santa Cruz, the main ferry port, seems old and settled. Today Santa Cruz looks like many a provincial Spanish city, full of bustle and business, but in fact it was a capital-come-lately, not emerging as a major city until the 18th century.

The area around the main **Plaza de la Candelaria**, just inland of Plaza de España and the harbor, is the liveliest part of town. For a pleasant repast, stop at one of the outdoor cafés here and watch the passersby (always an enjoyable pastime in Spain). The **Museo Arqueológico**, containing many Guanche artifacts, is nearby, on the Plaza de España (enter on Avenida de Bravo Murillo).

The **Castillo de Paso Alto**, a former fortress that is now a military museum, is north of the center of town. Uniforms, weapons, and the cannon called El Tigre (The Tiger), which cost Admiral Horatio Nelson both his right arm and the battle when he attacked castle and town on July 24, 1797, are on display.

The wonderful Mencey hotel (see Staying on Tenerife, above) is northwest of the town center, across Rambla del General Franco from the lushly planted **Parque Municipal García Sanabriá**, inside which are a number of sculptures by contemporary Spanish artists, such as Amadeo Gabino. Ambling along the *rambla* you will encounter many large sculptures, including a bronze work by Henry Moore. Note the handsome 19th- and early-20th-century mansions lining the north side of the *rambla;* many are now foreign consulates.

You will notice in Santa Cruz, and elsewhere in the Canaries, avenues bearing the names of Generalísimo Franco, José Antonio Primo de Rivera, Calvo Sotelo, and other Falangist heroes—a reminder that these conservative islands and nearby (then) Spanish Morocco were Franco's launching pad for the Nationalist revolution that began the Spanish Civil War in 1936.

AROUND SANTA CRUZ

Seven kilometers (4½ miles) northeast of Santa Cruz along the coast is **Playa de las Teresitas**, a lovely expanse of white-sand beach. The sand was imported from the Sahara and is in stark contrast with other beaches on the north coast, which are volcanic black sand. Near the beach is the village of **San Andrés**, where there are three or four simple but very good seafood restaurants. The best is **Restaurante Don Antonio**, Calle Duque 19, whose grilled sole is supreme. (Be sure to ask for the piquant *mojo* sauce to go with it.)

The Northern Coast

LA LAGUNA

Just south of Santa Cruz, the fast *autopista* TF 5 arcs across the handle of the ladle and then heads down the island's northern coastline. Right in the middle of the ladle, about 10 km (6 miles) from Santa Cruz, is La Laguna (about 10 km/6 miles from Santa Cruz), the oldest town on the island and once its capital. Its focal point is the **Plaza del Adelantado**, which is flanked by an old quarter of 17th- and 18th-century mansions. You'll also find the cathedral of **Nuestra Señora de los Remedios**, built in the Neoclassical style, nearby. The 16th-century church of La Concepción, on Calle de la Carrera, has a finely carved wood pulpit and choir.

PUERTO DE LA CRUZ

Puerto de la Cruz, no longer the sleepy little fishing village it was just 20 years ago, is 24 km (15 miles) farther southwest on the *autopista* from La Laguna. Upon approaching Puerta de la Cruz, stop at the **Jardín Botánico** (botanical garden), perched above the town on five acres of hillside (across from the Botánico Sol Hotel, on Carretera del Botánico). The gardens, started in 1788 in the spirit of scientific inquiry at the official request of King Carlos III, are a sheltered, refreshing oasis of greenery, fountains, pools, and shaded walkways, alive with the chirps of birds that make their homes in the towering, ancient trees. There are more than 4,000 exotic plants from all over the world, orchid houses, such rare trees as the Argentine *ombu,* with its curious rocklike roots, a bizarre rubber plant almost 200 years old, and local candelabra cactus, Canarian pines, and dragon trees.

Once in town (parking is a terrible problem, so leave your car above the town center) be prepared for the crowds of fellow visitors clogging the **Avenida de Colón**, the waterfront promenade where everyone congregates to stroll, shop, meet friends, and observe the passing scene. As you amble along, you will pass **Lago de Martiánez**, a fantasy of a park built into a ledge of black-lava rocks that jut into the water. Created by Lanzarote artist César Manrique, the eight-acre park consists of white paths bordered with flowers leading around a series of sculpted, sea-fed swimming pools, an artificial lake with five islands, a restaurant, a gigantic nightclub, an understated disco open all night, and a Manrique sculpture, *Homage to the Sea.* Plaza del Charco, the town's main square (inland to the west), is another favorite local gathering place.

Dining in Puerto de la Cruz

You never have to search for a place to eat in Puerto de la Cruz: You are surrounded by them. Full of plants and character is **Mi Vaca y Yo**, where you'll find fresh grilled seafood at moderate prices; Tel: (9-22) 38-52-47. It is at Cruz Verde 3, one of the small streets just off Avenida de Colón that is something of a "restaurant row." Also good, if somewhat pricier, is **Magnolia**, above the town center at Carretera del Botánico 5, serving many delicious Catalan specialties; Tel: (9-22) 38-56-14. More deluxe still is **Chiripa**, in centrally located Urbanización San Fernando, which combines Spanish dishes with Canarian specialties and maintains a fine wine cellar; Tel: (9-22) 38-14-50.

WEST OF PUERTO DE LA CRUZ

Icod de los Vinos

Twenty-three kilometers (14 miles) west of Puerto de la Cruz on the coastal road, C 820, is Icod de los Vinos, a hillside village above the Atlantic noted for its 1,000-year-old dragon tree, once believed to have medicinal properties. A remarkable sight, it has a thick trunk that seems to be many trunks melded together, and spiky cactuslike branches forming an umbrella overhead. Up a side street from the tree is the **Iglesia de San Marcos**, parts of which were built in the 15th century, with a Renaissance portal, a carving by Pedro de Mena, and a gilded Baroque retable. The church faces the peaceful, tree-shaded Parque San Lorenzo de Caceras, which leads up a few steps to a plaza framed with old, traditional pine-balconied Canarian houses.

Just below Icod de los Vinos is **Playa de San Marcos**, a black-sand beach enclosed in a natural harbor. You can enjoy the freshest of grilled sole (and other fish), served with delicious salt-encrusted potatoes (*papas arrugadas*), for an extremely modest price at **Bodegón San Marcos**, right on the beach; Tel: (9-22) 81-04-77.

Garachico

If you continue west along the pleasantly curvaceous coastal drive you will come to Garachico, an almost totally unspoiled town facing a huge rock in the ocean known simply as Roque de Garachico. If you have forgone lunch at San Marcos, you have a second chance in Garachico at an attractive upstairs restaurant, **Isla Baja**, which overlooks the waterfront promenade and serves a delicious *paella valenciana;* Tel: (9-22) 83-00-08.

There's nothing too special about Garachico, which was the capital of Tenerife until devastated by a volcanic eruption in 1716, but there is a craft shop installed in the waterfront fort, **Castillo de San Miguel**, where the Canarian lace and embroideries are very reasonably priced. From the fort you can walk over a series of connected black volcanic ledges just above the ocean, which splashes just enough water over the rocks to let you know it's there; ladders attached to several of the rocks lead down into the water, making this the local equivalent of a swimming hole.

Buenavista

A few miles west of Garachico is Buenavista, an attractively laid out 16th-century village. The town church has a sculpture of Saint Francis by Alonso Cano as well as some splendid altarpieces and Mudejar coffered ceilings.

GOMERA

The tiny (146 square miles), round, mountainous island of Gomera, just west of Tenerife, sometimes seems ephemeral, as mist hangs like a veil over its vibrant green terraced mountains and valleys planted with banana groves and grape-vines. Few volcanic traces remain on Gomera; unusually verdant for the Canaries, it is like a little emerald amidst its craggy neighbors.

TOURING GOMERA

The most convenient (and quickest) way to see Gomera is by day tour from Tenerife, departing from the ferry dock at Los Cristianos in the southwest and arriving 40 minutes later in the photogenic, snug harbor of **San Sebastián de la Gomera**, the capital, on the southeastern coast. It is easy (and advisable) to book your trip in advance through your Tenerife hotel's concierge. The tour operator then arranges to pick you up at your hotel or a designated spot and take you to the ferry.

While it is possible to rent a car and drive up into Gomera's mountains and **Parque Nacional de Garajonay** pinelands by yourself, the turns are so frequent and the steep drops so precipitous that to enjoy the heart-stopping views it is just as well to leave the driving to another and join the local bus tour. The tour usually goes up to a tiny hamlet called **Las Rosas**, overhanging a cliff, where you have lunch, and then continues to **Hermigua**, a delightful village of whitewashed houses. The 16th-century **Convento de Santo Domingo** has a Baroque altarpiece and Mudejar ceiling. Dominating the island is the 4,879-foot-high peak, Alto de Garajonay.

AROUND IN SAN SEBASTIAN

There is ample time once back at sea level in San Sebastián to walk to the town's few significant landmarks. Columbus shuttled between Gomera and Grand Canary, taking on supplies, before setting off from San Sebastián on September 6, 1492, to cross the Atlantic. He heard Mass in the **Iglesia de la Asunción** before sailing, and in the inner courtyard of the customhouse is a well from which he supposedly drew his water supply for the voyage. A good dinner (or lunch) stop is at the ► **Parador Conde de la Gomera**, on the hill, known as Lomo de la Horca (which means "gallows ridge"), overlooking the town and harbor.

If you are tempted by the do-nothing peacefulness of Gomera—the relative absence of foreigners and lack of nightlife and sightseeing agenda—the parador is certainly the place to stay for its tranquillity, superb hilltop vistas, gardens, and welcome swimming pool. Stay a while and you might even hear some of the islanders' special whistling language called *silbo,* developed in centuries past, when the Gomerians used this complicated form of whistling to communicate with each other over the mountain ridges. A few *silbadores* still practice the art today.

GRAND CANARY

The third largest island, at 592 square miles, Grand Canary, more or less in the center of the Canaries group, resembles a giant clam shell. Scenically, Grand Canary has some of the variety of Tenerife, with an interior volcanic and mountainous core, deep ravines, valleys of banana groves, and a southern shore lined with sandy beaches. Dominating the interior is Pozo de las Nieves, an often snowcapped 6,394-foot-high peak.

The island's natural beauty, however, has attracted the crowds and much of its coastline has the characterless, overbuilt appearance of seaside destinations the world over.

Staying on Grand Canary

The international airport, Aeropuerto de Gran Canaria, on the east coast, is just about equidistant from Las Palmas (25 km/15 miles north) and the southern beaches (30 km/19 miles south). Pick up a rental car at the airport for the drive (you will need it for sightseeing).

THE SOUTH SHORE

Grand Canary's south shore is a succession of long golden-sand beaches, most notably Playa de San Agustín, Playa del Inglés, Playa de Maspalomas, and El Oasis. The beaches are so beautiful and the vast sand dunes so inviting that it was probably inevitable that when development began, this area would be the magnet for the "tourist cities" that have been subsequently built up: streets lined with high-rise hotels, condominiums, stores, restaurants, pubs, churches, everything necessary to keep a vacationing population happy and eager for a return visit—very much like the Costa del Sol on the Spanish mainland. That Europeans love these developments can be attested to by the herds of tour groups, families, and singles who pile off charters from Britain, Scandinavia, Germany, and the Netherlands every day throughout the winter months. In fact, the climate is so congenial that many expatriates from the north have made Grand Canary (Tenerife, too) home.

Developed as the area is, it is the logical place to stay if you wish to combine a bit of sun, ocean, and recreation with your sightseeing. The best address is the ▶ **Iberotel Maspalomas Oasis**, a large deluxe resort hotel with a grand beach and many sports facilities and amenities, all attended to on spacious, well-kept grounds. **Maspalomas**, not many years ago just a breathtakingly beautiful beach with mammoth sand dunes, a palm oasis, and saltwater lagoon, is now a sizable tourist city.

Another luxurious property, a few miles northeast of Maspalomas, is the ▶ **Meliá Tamarindos** resort hotel, facing another gorgeous beach, **Playa de San Agustín**. The hotel has lovely gardens, large rooms facing the ocean, a sports center, and everything necessary to keep you pampered and satisfied.

LAS PALMAS DE GRAN CANARIA

Las Palmas de Gran Canaria (Las Palmas for short), the capital, a duty-free port, and the largest population center in the Canaries (approximately 300,000), is some 55 km (34 miles) north of Maspalomas, at the island's northeastern tip. It too is crammed with hotels in various categories, but the city's commercial center has become so crowded with stores and shops that it doesn't offer much solitude for reclusive visitors. It does swing, however.

If you opt to stay in Las Palmas you might try the modern ▶ **Hotel Reina Isabel** on Calle Alfredo L. Jones, just off the waterfront Paseo de las Canteras in the Puerto de la Luz quarter. The hotel faces Playa de las Canteras (a superb 16-mile-long tawny-sand beach sheltered by a low reef) and offers every imaginable luxury, including a heated swimming pool, a sauna, and an excellent restaurant. More moderately priced, but also convenient, is the old-time, pseudo-Moorish ▶ **Hotel Santa Catalina**, in the very pretty Parque Doramas, straddling the oldest part of the city and part of the new. In the park is Pueblo Canario, a compound where Canarian folk dances and songs are performed in costume in the open air every Sunday (11:45 A.M. to 1:15 P.M.) and Thursday (5:30 to 7:00 P.M.).

Las Palmas

PUERTO DE LA LUZ

Sprawling Las Palmas has two main centers, the modern hodge-podge known as Puerto de la Luz and the older Barrio Vegueta (or Vegueta Triana), to the southwest. Much of Puerto de la Luz is commercial and industrial, but dominating its touristic center is the fantastically long Playa de las Canteras and a promenade, the tile-surfaced **Paseo de las Canteras**, that shadows it, lined by hotels, cafés, tourist shops, boutiques, and restaurants. Unfortunately, this beach and promenade are victims of their own success: The beach is almost too crowded for swimming or even tanning, and the promenade at dusk seems as heavily trafficked as Times Square or Shaftesbury Avenue.

BARRIO VEGUETA

Barrio Vegueta, which dates back to the Spanish conquest, has been nearly swallowed up by larger modern neighborhoods, yet from a sightseer's point of view it is infinitely more compelling. When Columbus landed, on August 25, 1492, in search of a replacement for his damaged caravel, Vegueta *was* the city. Its narrow streets, lined with faded pastel houses, lead onto a beautiful, elongated square, **Plaza de Santa Ana**. On one side is an imposing 19th-century town hall. Opposite is the Gothic **cathedral**, parts of which were built in the 15th century, though the façade is Neoclassical. Inside are a Baroque altar and, in the treasury, a 16th-century monstrance attributed to Benvenuto Cellini. Two appealing little squares south of the Plaza de Santa Ana are worth a look: **Plaza del Espíritu Santo** and **Plaza de Santo Domingo**.

Around the corner from the cathedral, at Calle Colón 1, is the **Casa de Colón**, where Columbus stayed, briefly, in 1502. The house was built for the first Spanish governors and is interesting in itself, with open courtyards and rooms with wooden Mudejar ceilings. While there isn't much there to remind you of Columbus personally, there are fascinating exhibits relating to his voyages, as well as nautical artifacts of the 15th and 16th centuries: maps, ship models, cannons, navigation instruments, and banners.

SHOPPING IN LAS PALMAS

The big attraction of Las Palmas is shopping. As a duty-free port, the city is a bargain-hunter's paradise, with goods from all over the world. (You will have more success if you know a particular item's value at home, because not everything is a bargain.) Especially prevalent are Indian, Arab, and Oriental shops with clothes, fabrics, brand-name electronics, cameras, perfumes, and jewelry. Negotiating the price is expected. **Artesanía Canaria Taguguy**, Calle Armas 1, across from Casa de Colón in the Barrio Vegueta, sells local baskets, pottery, and other crafts. The nearby **Museo Canario**, south of the cathedral, is worth checking out for its Guanche artifacts and idols.

DINING IN LAS PALMAS

Plan to dine at **El Acuario**, in the Puerto de la Luz section, at Plaza de la Victoria 3, considered the island's finest restaurant. The accent is French and the seafood marvelous, and the prices, although on the elevated side, are lower than on the mainland; Tel: (9-28) 27-34-32. The restaurant **Julio**, north of

Puerto de la Luz, at Calle la Naval 132, is also pricey, but has excellent seafood; Tel: (9-28) 46-01-39.

Excursions from Las Palmas

INTO THE MOUNTAINS

It is Grand Canary's mountainous interior that shows off the island's diverse and most spectacular landscape. One route inland is the tortuous C 811, which goes southwest from Las Palmas. As you climb ever upward, the vegetation and terrain change dramatically. If you turn off to the left at Monte Coello you will reach **Pico de Bandama**, where at the Bandama Mirador you can peer into the mountain's huge volcanic crater, now green with planted crops. You might even practice your putting at the Golf Club of Grand Canary, poised on the crater's edge (ask at your hotel about arrangements for golf).

Returning to C 811, after another 25 km (16 miles) or so, climbing still farther upward, past clusters of golden broom and pine forests, you reach **Cruz de Tejeda**, a mountain pass some 4,747 feet high. The village of **Tejeda**, the most elevated on the island, is set in another crater, which Unamuno—who knew the Canaries well, having been exiled to Fuerteventura after the 1923 coup d'état of Primo de Rivera—described as a "petrified tempest; a tempest of fire and lava, rather than of water." Pause at Tejeda for lunch at the government-run **Parador Cruz de Tejeda**, a rustic retreat (no overnight accommodations, however) set among almond orchards with spectacular views of Roque Nublo, a jagged basalt spire, and the snowcapped Pozo de las Nieves.

From Tejeda follow the signposts northwest to **Artenara**, a village on the edge of a precipice, and **Juncalillo**, a troglodyte village whose inhabitants live in well-maintained caves formed by the cooling and hardening of lava streams. From Juncalillo you may continue westward to **Pinar de Tamadaba**, the stately survivor of a pine forest that once covered the island. At Tamadaba you can walk through the forest to a precipitous cliff, from whose top you'll have a splendid view all along the west coast—you may even spot Pico del Teide on Tenerife.

WEST OF LAS PALMAS

Another day, another breathtaking drive: This one leads from Las Palmas 22 km (13½ miles) west and inland to **Arucas**, a pretty little town near a volcanic cone called **Montaña de Arucas**. From Arucas, the tortuous road goes south 10 km (6 miles) through a valley of banana plantations to **Teror**, a cool summer resort in the interior, bordered by pine woods and ringed with mountains. Teror is home to the Virgen del Pino (Virgin of the Pines), patroness of Grand Canary. The statue, reportedly found in the branches of a local pine tree in the 15th century, now resides in the Baroque basilica of **Nuestra Señora del Pino**. Islanders make a gift-bearing pilgrimage to the shrine on September 8, the day of the Festival de la Virgen del Pino.

THE GETAWAY ISLANDS

While Hierro, La Palma, and Fuerteventura are less visited than the other islands, each has something to recommend it.

HIERRO
Tiny Hierro, the smallest, southwesternmost Canary, covers 107 square miles and has just 7,000 inhabitants. Its terrain is wooded and mountainous, with cliffs dropping into the sea. A dearth of beaches discourages the mass tourism that has afflicted the larger islands, but Hierro holds great appeal for naturalists. Especially interesting are the age-old *lajiales,* lava formations in eerie, lifelike shapes. Hierro is also the last habitat of the Salmas lizard, a huge species near extinction. If you wish to commune with nature, bird-watch, and practice your Spanish (the locals are known for their pure Castilian), a good place to base yourself is at the ► **Parador de la Isla de Hierro**, which has a swimming pool and most conveniences.

LA PALMA
Verdant, V-shaped La Palma (281 square miles), also on the western side of the Canaries group, north of Hierro and Gomera, is another natural wonderland, with grottoes, gorges, lush vegetation, giant ferns, pine and banana groves, vineyards, several fine beaches, and houses with the distinctive Canarian wooden balconies. A large volcanic crater (17 miles in circumference), the **Caldera de Taburiente** (known as the Caldron), caps the center of the island.

La Palma's major city and capital, **Santa Cruz de la Palma**, on the east coast, perches like an amphitheater on a steep slope at the edge of another crater, La Caldereta. A modest but comfortable base for exploring this not-yet-exploited island is the ► **Parador de Santa Cruz de la Palma**, in the capital, a short distance from the airport.

FUERTEVENTURA
Of the three "getaway" islands, only Fuerteventura, the second-largest Canary island and the closest to Africa, is

undergoing major tourist development. Travellers who revel in its miles of fabulous sandy shoreline and its clear waters, ideal for snorkeling and diving, say it's high time; lovers of solitude, who fear the island is heading down the over-building trail that has plagued Grand Canary, say it's a pity. For now, Fuerteventura is frequented almost exclusively by Germans, who constitute more than 90 percent of its visitors.

New hotels continue to go up, mostly at Corralejo in the north and Punta de Jandía at the southern tip, but there is still a lot of untrampled beach left, and the leaf-shaped island is a fisherman's paradise because it is separated from North Africa by a surging strait that is a favorite racing territory for tuna and swordfish.

The attractive, distinctively Canarian-looking ▶ **Parador de Fuerteventura** is on Playa Blanca, a lovely beach on the northeastern coast just 2 km (about a mile) from the capital, Puerto del Rosario, and 6 km (4 miles) north of the airport. Using the parador as a base, you can rent a car and head out to discover beaches, and visit La Oliva, inland and to the north, where there are many beautiful mansions.

Farther north, by way of the Route of the Windmills, is **Lajares**, where fine needlework is made. The old capital, **Betancuria**, located in a small volcano in the center of the island, has some handsome old buildings. Another comfortable place on Fuerteventura is ▶ **Iberotel Tres Islas Sol**, a pleasant hotel at Playa de Corralejo, on the northern tip of the island.

GETTING AROUND

It is approximately two hours by air from Madrid to Tenerife (though it's only an hour on your watch because of the time-zone change) via Iberia or its sister airline, Aviaco, with six flights a day in summer, five a day the rest of the year. Flights from Madrid to Grand Canary are almost as frequent (five a day), and take only a few minutes longer. There are also direct, if fewer, flights from Madrid to Lanzarote (twice a week, Friday and Sunday, more in summer). To La Palma, Hierro, and Fuerteventura, there are daily flights from Madrid (via Tenerife or Grand Canary) in summer, flights twice a week at other times of year.

From Barcelona there are daily nonstop flights in summer (three times a week in the off-season) to Tenerife and Grand Canary, frequent flights to Fuerteventura and La Palma (via Grand Canary or Tenerife), and a nonstop flight on Sundays to Lanzarote.

From London's Heathrow, there are daily Iberia flights to Tenerife and Grand Canary; from New York, there is a daily Iberia flight (via Madrid) to both islands.

Once in the Canaries, you can hop via Iberia, Aviaco, or Air Binter to every island except Gomera, which has no airport.

We strongly recommend that you double-check current air schedules before finalizing your plans, as they do change from season to season.

Transmediterránea has frequent ferry service (depending on the season), from Cádiz, in Andalusia, to Santa Cruz, Tenerife; to Arrecife, Lanzarote; to Puerto del Rosario, Fuerteventura; and to Las Palmas, Grand Canary. There is daily jet-foil service between Santa Cruz, on Tenerife, and Las Palmas, on Grand Canary, which takes less than an hour. Less frequent service is available between Grand Canary and Lanzarote, with a stop at Fuerteventura. There is also service from Tenerife to the island of La Palma and from there to Hierro. Ferries for Gomera leave twice daily, at 10:00 A.M. and 6:00 P.M., from Los Cristianos, Tenerife. From Santa Cruz, Tenerife, it takes six hours by boat to Lanzarote (30 minutes by air). The central office of Transmediterránea is in Madrid, at Calle Pedro Muñoz Seca 2; Tel: (9-1) 556-1025.

Once you are on an island, the best, most expeditious way to travel is by car. Numerous car-rental agencies have offices at the Lanzarote, Tenerife, and Grand Canary airports. Roads on the three islands have excellent two-lane asphalt surfaces; back roads are less well surfaced. Tenerife and Grand Canary also boast fast-moving *autopistas*.

ACCOMMODATIONS REFERENCE

The hotel rates listed below are projected rates for 1994, for double room, double occupancy, in pesetas. We strongly recommend that you confirm the price when making reservations.

When dialing telephone numbers from outside the country, drop the 9 in the area code.

Lanzarote

▶ **Los Fariones**. Acatife 2, Urbanización Playa Blanca, 35600 **Puerto del Carmen**, Lanzarote. Tel: (9-28) 51-01-75; Fax: 51-02-02. 11,500 pts.

▶ **Gran Hotel Arrecife Playa**. Avenida Mancomunidad 11, 35500 **Arrecife**, Lanzarote. Tel: (9-28) 81-12-50; Fax: 81-42-59. 9,900–10,890 pts.

▶ **Meliá Salinas**. Playa de las Cucharas, 35509 NE **Costa Teguise**, Lanzarote. Tel: (9-28) 59-00-40; Fax: 59-03-90; in U.S., Tel: (212) 686-9213. 26,000 pts.

▶ **Teguise Playa Hotel**. Parcela 225, 35509 **Urbanización Costa Teguise** (Playa El Jablillo), Lanzarote. Tel: (9-28) 59-06-54; Fax: 59-02-39; in U.S. and Canada, Tel: (800) 843-3311. 12,000–14,000 pts.

Tenerife

▶ **Meliá Botánico**. Calle Richard J. Yeoward, 38400 **Puerto de la Cruz**, Tenerife. Tel: (9-22) 38-14-00; Fax: 38-15-04; in U.S., Tel: (212) 686-9213; Fax: (212) 686-0271. 19,500–24,500 pts.

▶ **Mencey**. Calle Dr. José Naveiras 38, 38001 **Santa Cruz de Tenerife**, Tenerife. Tel: (9-22) 27-67-00; Fax: 28-00-17; in U.S., Tel: (800) 221-2340; Fax: (212) 421-5929; in Canada, Tel: (800) 955-2442. 23,000 pts.

▶ **Monopol Hotel**. Calle Quintana 15, 38400 **Puerto de la Cruz**, Tenerife. Tel: (9-22) 38-46-11; Fax: 37-03-10. 5,200–7,400 pts.

▶ **Parador de Las Cañadas del Teide**. Apartado 15, Orotava, 38300, **Las Cañadas del Teide**, Tenerife. Tel: (9-22) 38-64-15; Fax: 23-25-03. 7,000 pts.

▶ **La Siesta Hotel**. Avenida Marítima, 38660 **Arona**, Tenerife. Tel: (9-22) 79-23-20; Fax: 79-22-20; in U.S. and Canada, Tel: (800) 843-3311. 10,800 pts.

Gomera

▶ **Parador Conde de la Gomera**. Balcón de la Villa y Puerto, Apartado 21, San Sebastián de la Gomera, 38800 Gomera. Tel: (9-22) 87-11-00; Fax: 87-11-16. 14,000 pts.

Grand Canary

▶ **Hotel Reina Isabel**. Calle Alfredo L. Jones 40, 35008 **Las Palmas**, Grand Canary. Tel: (9-28) 26-01-00; Fax: 27-45-58. 12,500 pts.

▶ **Hotel Santa Catalina**. Parque Doramas, 35005 **Las Palmas**, Grand Canary. Tel: (9-28) 24-30-40; Fax: 24-27-64. 19,350 pts.

▶ **Iberotel Maspalomas Oasis**. Playa de Maspalomas, 35106 **Maspalomas**, Grand Canary. Tel: (9-28) 14-14-48; Fax: 14-11-92. 18,800–49,200 pts.

▶ **Meliá Tamarindos**. Las Retamas 3, 35100 **Playa de San Agustín**, Grand Canary. Tel: (9-28) 76-26-00; Fax: 76-22-64. 26,000 pts.

Hierro

▶ **Parador de la Isla de Hierro**. Las Playas, 38900 **Valverde**, Hierro. Tel: (9-22) 55-80-36; Fax: 55-80-86. 9,000 pts.

La Palma

▶ **Parador de Santa Cruz de la Palma**. Avenida Marítima 34, 38700 **Santa Cruz de la Palma**, La Palma. Tel: (9-22) 41-23-40; Fax: 41-18-56. 8,500 pts.

Fuerteventura

► **Iberotel Tres Islas Sol**. Playa de Corralejo, 35627 **Corralejo**, Fuerteventura. Tel: (9-28) 86-60-00; Fax: 86-61-50. 22,400 pts.

► **Parador de Fuerteventura**. Playa Blanca 45, 35600 **Puerto del Rosario**, Fuerteventura. Tel: (9-28) 85-11-50; Fax: 85-11-58. 9,500 pts.

CHRONOLOGY OF THE HISTORY OF SPAIN

Prehistory

Weapons and charred bones from elephant hunters' camps indicate that Paleolithic people lived in Spain perhaps half a million years ago. The earliest human remains have been uncovered on the Meseta (the high plateau covering much of central Spain) not far from present-day Madrid. In addition, two prehistoric settlements dating from 200,000 B.C. have been found at Gibraltar.

Paleolithic people left caves on the Iberian Peninsula decorated with remarkable paintings of the "cold-weather" animals they hunted: deer, bison, horses, and wild boar. These masterpieces, thought to be more than 12,000 years old, cover the ceilings of stone caves, such as those at **Altamira** (near Santander, on the Bay of Biscay in northern Spain), and have a surprising technical perfection. Bones of animals found on the floors of the caves suggest that the paintings were part of a ritual.

Other cave paintings, showing matchsticklike figures using bows and arrows, have been found near Valencia. These narrative scenes of human beings date from 4000 to 3000 B.C.

The Iberians and the Celts

Spain's earliest well-documented peoples were as distinctive as the regions they occupied. Probably migrating from North Africa across the Strait of Gibraltar between the 13th and 6th centuries B.C., the Iberians first settled along the Andalusian coast; then some moved inland beyond the Sierra Morena. The southern Iberians appear to have lived in walled cities; they mined the copper deposits near Almería and buried their dead in elaborate cave tombs. Some 40 miles west of Granada, constructions from about 2500 B.C. take the form of funerary chambers beneath tumuli (mounds). These cromlechs are on the outskirts of the town of Antequera. The northern people known as the Basques probably antedate the Iberians, but their origins remain unknown.

Through the rough northern passes of the Pyrenees in about 900 B.C. came Celts from western Europe. Speaking an Indo-European language—the puzzling Basque language is not Indo-European—the fair-skinned Celts tended sheep on the vast plains, built forts, and hired themselves out as mercenaries.

Throughout its early history seafaring peoples came to Spain: the Phoenicians, the Greeks, and later the Carthaginians (Carthage began as a Phoenician colony in North Africa). The Phoenicians established a trade center at Cádiz (then Gadir) in about 1100 B.C.; the location offered easy access to both the Mediterranean and the Atlantic coastlines of Europe. In the seventh century B.C. the Greeks began colonizing Iberia, establishing a lively and profitable trade in the south. They are said to have introduced what are today regarded as prototypical Spanish staples: the olive and the grape. They may also have brought some form of bullfighting or bullbaiting.

But it was the Carthaginians who first actually gained control over much of the Iberian Peninsula. Using their strategic position on the North African coast, they invaded Iberia in the sixth century B.C. The Greek historian Polybius (second century B.C.) claimed that by the fourth century Carthage had established a protectorate over all the Iberian tribes. The sculptured polychrome stone head known as *La Dama de Elche* dates from this period; it is the pride of Madrid's Museo Arqueológico Nacional.

Much later (Flaubert's novel *Salammbô* evokes this period), Carthage, in the person of Hamilcar Barca and his son Hannibal, stung by defeat in the First Punic War against Rome in 241 B.C., led huge armies (and those celebrated elephants) on tortuous expeditions that were to end in another defeat in 206 B.C., when Carthage was forced to relinquish the entire Iberian Peninsula to Rome. (But the Barca family name endures as the root of the name Barcelona.)

The Romans

Some 600 years of Roman rule (206 B.C.–A.D. 410) gave Spain a network of roads for military and mercantile purposes, a collection of seaports with docks and lighthouses, and a pattern of proven methods for mining, agriculture, and trade. Roman law gave Spain concrete evidence that order and prosperity resulted from disciplined administration. And, not least, Rome gave Spain its language.

Spain gave Rome minerals, raw materials, and olive oil, esteemed the finest in the ancient world (used for eating, cooking, lighting, and as a substitute for soap). Spain also gave Rome two emperors, Trajan and Hadrian, both born in Itálica (now Santiponce, near Seville). Born in Spain as well were the rhetorician Quintilian, the epigrammatist Martial, and the poet Lucan. Lucan's uncle, Seneca, and Seneca's father (the Elder) were both born in Córdoba. The younger Seneca was the leading intellectual figure in Nero's Rome and an influential politician, and in Renaissance times he was considered a model for dramatists.

Rome's cultural gift to Spain was the homogeneity of aesthetics and practicality. The coupling of architectural styles and engineering skill characterizes the aqueducts of Segovia (still in use), Tarragona, and Mérida. The Roman bridges— today often equipped with traffic lights—with their graceful curved arches and buttresses to stem tides and floods at Córdoba, Salamanca, and Mérida might all have been designed by the same talented professional. Roman theaters took advantage—as did those of the Greeks before them—of the natural geographical contours, as at Mérida and Tarragona. The mosaics at Itálica and Empúries trace delicate decorative motifs for such utilitarian elements as floors and walls. Even the dead were well catalogued and handsomely commemorated, as attested to by the extensive, class-conscious cemetery at **Carmona**, between Seville and Córdoba.

The ruins of an entire Roman town, now being excavated at **Baelo Claudio** (south of Cádiz on the Costa de la Luz), testify to the municipal role of law, religion, and the arts in a town that was in fact a stinking coastal fish-factory center (even the vats survive).

- **210 B.C.**: Rome's Scipio Africanus captures Carthago Nova (New Carthage, now Cartagena) and forces the Carthaginians out of Gadir (Cádiz) into North Africa.
- **206 B.C.**: Romans occupy most of the Iberian Peninsula despite continued local opposition. Spain becomes the first vast area assimilated by the Romans; Hispania, as the Romans called Spain, is divided into two great provinces—west of the Ebro, and east of that river.
- **181 B.C.**: Rome induces Iberian cities to pay taxes and provide auxiliaries for the imperial forces.
- **135 B.C.**: Iberian rebels establish a stronghold settlement at **Numantia**, near the Río Duero; in 133 B.C., after eight months of resistance against the Romans, the Numantians set their city and themselves afire; the Romans rebuild Numantia, whose ruins today near Soria, northeast of Madrid, trace a typical Roman provincial town.
- **72 B.C.**: Pompey the Great is sent to Spain to defeat the rebellious Sertorious and returns to Rome boasting that he has conquered 876 cities.

- **45 B.C.**: The struggle between Julius Caesar and the faction of Pompey culminates in the battle of Munda (near Córdoba), with Caesar emerging victorious. Caesar is assassinated the next year.
- **19 B.C.**: The emperor Augustus defeats all tribal opposition in Spain and divides the Iberian Peninsula into three provinces: Baetica (southern Spain), rich and populous, with its capital at Córdoba; Lusitania (roughly modern Portugal), sparsely inhabited but rich in minerals, with its capital at Mérida in present-day Extremadura; and Tarraconensis (all of northern and central Spain), with its capital at Tarragona on the Mediterranean coast.
- **A.D.74**: Full Roman citizenship is granted to all Iberians under the Edict of Vespasian.
- **93–138**: Successive Roman emperors, Trajan and Hadrian, are born in Itálica, near Seville. Itálica's amphitheater, the fourth largest in the Roman world, is built to hold 30,000 spectators.
- **212**: *Civis Romanus sum:* Every freeborn subject in the empire is granted Roman citizenship by the Edict of Caracalla.
- **319**: After a lengthy period of dealing with refractory Christian groups, Christianity having reputedly been introduced to Spain by Saint James (Santiago) and a visit by Saint Paul circa 65, Rome recognizes the Catholic Church as a legal institution, sharing rights with other religions.
- **410**: The Visigoths sack Rome and by 500 dominate Spain.

The Visigoths

Despite three centuries in which they ruled the Iberian Peninsula, the Visigoths are generally given short shrift by historians of Spain. They are likely to be grouped with those "barbarian hordes from the north," such as the Vandals, who invaded England, France, and Italy in the wake of the fall of the Roman Empire and gave their name to Andalusia. In general, however, the Visigoths, who displaced these earlier Germanic hordes, except in western Iberia, preserved the Roman administrative organization they found in Spain.

The small stone Arian-Christian Visigothic churches had geometric decorative motifs, anticipating their Moorish successors in Spain with arches shaped like horseshoes. Today, Madrid's Museo Arqueológico Nacional has on display a magnificent jeweled votive crown that attests to the Visigoths' predilection for, and talent for creating, sumptuous jewelry. The Gothic language brought by the Visigoths to Iberia was soon subsumed by the Latin-speaking population, while Greek survived as a literary language among the cultivated.

- **505**: The Visigoths establish supremacy on the Iberian Peninsula.
- **554**: The Visigoths make Toledo their capital; ultimately church councils here will become the main force in Visigothic government.
- **568–586**: The reign of King Leovigild unites the peninsula; he subjugates the Basques, amalgamates the previously independent kingdom of Galicia, and recovers Baetica from the Byzantines, who have controlled it since the emperor Justinian (483–565) sent an army to win back Spain for Rome.
- **578**: Saint Leander is named archbishop of Seville; he and his successor, Saint Isidore (560–636), bring Spain much cultural distinction in Europe.
- **584**: King Leovigild's son, Recared, introduces a codified law and a workable tax system modeled on Roman precedents. Converted to Catholicism, Recared oversees the religious unification of Spain, fusing the Visigothic and Hispano-Roman populations.
- **613**: King Sisebut drafts anti-Semitic legislation compelling all Jews in Spain to be baptized or be banished from the peninsula.
- **711**: King Roderick is routed by an army of 12,000 Berbers from North Africa. In three years these so-called Moors establish control in almost all parts of the peninsula.

The Moors

Claims that the Moors "occupied" Spain for almost 800 years are misleading on two counts. Over that period the Moors were a steadily decreasing presence as the Christian Reconquest pushed southward; ultimately only Andalusia was under Muslim rule, and for the final two and a half centuries Moorish Granada stood alone. But it is incorrect to speak of the Moors in Spain as if they were somehow on a prolonged visit: They were a significant presence in Spain for twice as long as America has been "occupied" by Europeans. For eight centuries there were Muslim Spaniards and Christian Spaniards and Jewish Spaniards.

The Moors called their Iberian domain "al-Andalus." As the Reconquest progressed, the geographical area applicable to this term contracted to the region of southern Spain (in modern usage Andalusia), where the Arabs had their last stronghold.

As a Muslim caliphate, Córdoba became the cultural center of western Europe. Two Cordoban contemporaries, Averroës (1126–1198) and Moses Maimonides (1135–1204), exemplified that cultural dominance. Averroës brought the teachings of Aristotle to the West and was himself a physicist, an astrologer, a mathematician, a doctor, and a philosopher. Maimonides, the famed Jewish scholar, was a doctor, a theologian, and a philosopher.

"The greatest calamity that ever happened to Spain was its expulsion of the Moors," wrote Samuel Prime in *The Alhambra and the Kremlin*. (The 1492 expulsion of the Jews was to have a similar deleterious effect on Spain's economic and cultural future.)

The Moors gave the Iberian Peninsula a heritage of decorative and architectural distinction. Stylistic characteristics of the Islamic art tradition can be seen in the three great Moorish cities of Andalusia, all of which flourished at different times: in Córdoba (fl. 756–1010) in the horseshoe-shaped arch (said to be of Visigoth origin) of the resplendent Mosque; in Seville (fl. 1010–1248) in the Giralda tower, then a minaret, with its brick construction and wide bands of decorative relief; and in Granada (fl. 1248–1492) in the Alhambra in the use of stucco and ceramics, proportioned fenestration and door panels, and stalactite ceilings. Muslim architecture in Córdoba seems to have been patterned on buildings in Syria, while that of Granada's Alhambra is more in accordance with the Maghreb (Tunisia, Algeria, and Morocco). Long after the Christian Reconquest faded from memory, Moorish artisans employed by Spaniards continued in the Islamic artistic (Mudejar) tradition.

Christians referred to the mixture of Berbers and Arabs by the generic term "Moors," but it was the Arabs who established the most enlightened state in all of Europe by the year 1000. The Arabs inherited the great learning of the Greek Classical world, much of which was stored in the libraries of Alexandria. They brought it to Spain, where translators rendered the texts into Arabic, building up an unparalleled European body of knowledge concerning astronomy, geometry, botany, medicine, and agriculture.

- **711**: Muslims from North Africa annihilate the Visigoth forces; soon the Moors occupy the entire Iberian Peninsula.
- **722**: Spanish resistance begins at Covadonga (on the northern Atlantic coast), marking the opening of the 800-year Christian War of Reconquest.
- **756–1031**: *The Umayyad dynasty.* Founded by Prince Abdal-Rahman, who established an independent emirate (not subject to Damascene control) at Córdoba, the Umayyads rule al-Andalus for almost three centuries.
- **785**: Emir Abd-al-Rahman I begins construction of Córdoba's Mezquita (Great Mosque).
- **778**: Charlemagne invades Spain; he is defeated by the

Moors at Zaragoza but keeps Navarra and the "Spanish March," which becomes Catalonia.

- **929**: The emirate at Córdoba is raised to a caliphate by Abd-al-Rahman III.
- **936**: Abd-al-Rahman III begins construction of a vast, opulent palace complex, Medina Azahara, now a ruin on the outskirts of Córdoba.
- **961–976**: The reign of al-Hakem II; Córdoba reaches heights of prominence as the wealthiest, most populated, and most cultured European city.
- **976–1008**: Al-Mansur, a Umayyad chamberlain, takes over power from the caliph's young son. This period is known as the Amarid dictatorship.
- **1009**: Medina Azahara destroyed during rebellion in Córdoba.
- **1031**: Division of the caliphate into *tarifa* (faction) kingdoms, thus ending Umayyad dynasty.
- **1085**: Toledo is captured by Alfonso VI, vitalizing the Reconquest drive.
- **1090–1145**: *The Almoravid period.* The Almoravides, fierce warriors from the Moroccan desert (the capital of this sect was Marrakech), capture Córdoba, Seville, Granada, and Valencia.
- **1094**: El Cid (Rodrigo Díaz de Vivar), the prototypical Castilian chivalric warrior (who sometimes fought under the Muslim banner), conquers Valencia; the 12th-century anonymous *Cantar de Mío Cid* later becomes the foremost Spanish epic.
- **1145–1223**: *The Almohad period.* The Almohades defeat their rivals the Almoravides in Morocco, invade Spain, and for a time make Seville their capital.
- **1184**: A minaret, later converted to the Giralda tower, is built in Seville by the Almohades.
- **1195**: Victory at the battle of Alarcos (in La Mancha) of Almohad horsemen over Spanish Christian forces pushes the lines of the Reconquest back north to the Río Tajo.
- **1212**: The battle of Las Navas de Tolosa. Alfonso VIII, with united forces, achieves victory over the Almohades, now limited to Andalusian territory. (Every Spanish schoolchild knows this date.)
- **1235–1492**: *The Nasrid dynasty.* Confined to Granada and the Tarifa–Almería coastline, the Nasrid dynasty founded by Mohammed-Ibn-Nasr, forms an alliance with Christian Spain. This often uneasy coexistence, lasting more than two centuries, made possible the creation of the great Granadian monuments of Muslim Spain.
- **1236**: Córdoba surrenders to Ferdinand III of Castile.
- **1248**: Seville surrenders to Ferdinand, who is later canonized.

- **1300:** Juan Ruiz writes *Libro de Buen Amor,* a fusion of minstrelsy and learned verse, earning him later comparison with Chaucer and Boccaccio.
- **1334–1391:** The palaces of the Alhambra at Granada are built under the reigns of Yusuf I and Muhammad V.
- **1469:** Ferdinand of Aragón marries Isabella of Castile.
- **1478:** The Inquisition, set up by papal bull from Pope Sixtus IV, gives Spain ecclesiastical powers (with secret proceedings not subject to appeals to Rome) to deal with the supposedly evil influence of Jews and *conversos* (converted Muslims and Jews). Historically, the Inquisition played a crucial role in Spain's subsequent decline as a world power.
- **1483:** All Jews are ordered to leave southern Spain.
- **1487:** Málaga is taken by Christian forces.
- **1492:** *January:* Moorish king Boabdil surrenders Granada to Ferdinand and Isabella; the Reconquest of the peninsula is completed. *March:* Expulsion of all Jews who refuse to be baptized (some 150,000), many of whom go to either the Low Countries or the Levant. (These Sephardic Jews have in some instances preserved their Castilian speech, known as Ladino.) An estimated 300,000 *conversos* remain in Spain. *October:* Columbus claims newly discovered lands overseas to the west for the Spanish Crown.
- **1494:** Pope Alexander VI publishes a bull dividing the New World between Spain and Portugal.

The Golden Empire

In the 16th and 17th centuries Spain was the most powerful country in the Western world. With vast territories in the Americas and the wealth they produced, and with the European Hapsburgian inheritance (Sicily, Naples, Milan, Sardinia, the Netherlands, Burgundy), Spain was an economic and political force of the first rank. The architecture, painting, literature, and sculpture of the period reflect Spain's self-awareness as a preeminent power.

Two antithetical Renaissance architectural styles—the Plateresque and the Classical—neatly suggest extremes of the Spanish character. The former, an exuberantly elaborate sculptured tracing, is possibly best seen in the entrance façade at the University of Salamanca. The second style, coolly severe and disciplined, was chosen by Holy Roman Emperor Charles V (King Carlos I) for his palace at the Alhambra and by his son, Philip II, who found in Juan de Herrera the perfect architect for his massive monastery-palace El Escorial. A rare example of this style in a private residence still exists in mint condition in a palace built by the Marqués de Santa Cruz at Viso del Marqués in La Mancha. Madrid's formal Plaza Mayor, built by Juan Gómez de Mora in the late 16th century, shows the Classical style at its urban best.

Literature in the Spanish Renaissance was crowned by *Don Quixote de la Mancha,* and Miguel de Cervantes's timeless classic reflects the national ethos as well as elusive reality. Cervantes, who died the same year as Shakespeare, shared fame in his lifetime with Lope de Vega (1562–1635), whose plays are the cornerstone of today's Spanish theater. Pedro Calderón de la Barca's (1600–1681) play *La Vida Es Sueño* (Life Is a Dream) may be his most honored work. Luis de Góngora y Argote (1561–1627), whose poetic style, relying on antithesis and parallelism, is the most individual of his era, contrasts sharply with his illustrious predecessor, Garcilaso de la Vega (1503–1536), a poet who is to the Spanish Renaissance what Spenser is to Elizabethan England. The picaresque novel, with its hero travelling from one adventure to another, is best represented by (in addition to *Don Quixote*) the anonymous *Lazarillo de Tormes* (1554) and Mateo Alemán's *Guzmán de Alfarache* (1599).

Tirso de Molina's (d. 1648) seminal drama *Don Juan* was to inspire more than 40 writers, poets, and composers, among them Molière, Byron, Goldoni, Mozart, Shaw, and Brecht, as well as José Zorrilla's drama *Don Juan Tenorio.*

Only two Spanish artists during the Golden Age were well known outside Spain, Bartolomé Esteban Murillo (1617–1682) and José Ribera (1588–1652); international recognition of El Greco (Doménikos Theotokópoulos, 1541–1614), Diego Velázquez (1599–1660), and Francisco Zurbarán (1598–1664) began only in the 19th century. Most early Spanish Renaissance painters confined themselves to richly colored and often mystically sentimentalized religious scenes, or to portraits of the nobility. Velázquez, painting almost nothing but secular subjects, is a masterly exception.

Gothic carving developed a purely Spanish style, the Isabelline, with fantastic lacelike surfaces. The interiors of Spanish Renaissance churches offer exquisite carving in both wood and alabaster, particularly in choir stalls, mausoleums, and retables. Crafts of the Renaissance included tapestries, embroideries, embossed leather work, and wrought-iron work in patios and on the ubiquitous balconies. Massive furniture decorated with wood carving filled Renaissance rooms.

- **1508**: Garci Rodríguez de Montalvo publishes the first novel of chivalry, *Amadís de Gaula.*

- **1512:** Ferdinand V annexes the kingdom of Navarra, completing the unification of Spain.
- **1513:** Juan Ponce de León discovers Florida; Vasco Núñez de Balboa sights the Pacific Ocean.
- **1516:** Carlos I (Charles V of the Holy Roman Empire) becomes the first ruling Hapsburg king in Spain.
- **1519:** Hernán Cortés begins the conquest of Mexico.
- **1526:** Pedro Machuca designs Charles V's palace at the Alhambra.
- **1533:** Francisco Pizarro conquers the Inca Empire in Peru.
- **1540:** The Society of Jesus (Jesuits) receives the approval of Pope Paul III; Francis Xavier is one of six members.
- **1554:** The anonymous *Lazarillo de Tormes* introduces the picaresque novel to world literature.
- **1556:** Philip II assumes the throne after the abdication of his father, Charles V, who goes off to live at a monastery in Yuste (Extremadura).
- **1562:** Saint Teresa of Avila begins writing her spiritual autobiography; Philip II's palace-monastery-museum complex, El Escorial, is begun.
- **1580:** Philip II unites Portugal with Spain.
- **1586:** El Greco paints *El Entierro del Conde de Orgaz* (Burial of the Count of Orgaz) in Toledo.
- **1588:** The defeat of the Spanish Armada by the British fleet heralds Spain's decline as a world power.
- **1600:** El Greco paints his *Saint Jerome,* now in the Frick Collection, New York City.
- **1605:** Cervantes publishes *Don Quixote.*
- **1607:** Philip III makes Madrid the nation's official capital.
- **1609:** Lope de Vega writes *The New Art of Writing Plays.* A soldier-priest, the dramatist later claims to have created more than 1,500 works, making Spanish dramatic comedy his province.
- **1624:** Velázquez paints an unadorned portrait of Philip IV.
- **1631:** Francisco Zurbarán paints *Apotheosis of Saint Thomas Aquinas.*
- **1640:** Portugal regains independence from Spain.
- **1656:** Velázquez paints *Las Meninas* (The Maids-in-Waiting), his most celebrated work.
- **1665–1700:** The reign of Carlos II.
- **1678:** Murillo paints the prototypical Madonna in his *Concepción Inmaculada* (Immaculate Conception).
- **1689:** José Churriguera, architect and sculptor, designs his first great work, a catafalque for Queen María Luisa. This ornate variation on the Baroque style—Churrigueresque—is best seen in the sacristy of La Cartuja (the Carthusian monastery) in Granada.

Bourbon Spain

In a century that marked Spain's subjugation to foreign influence—the Bourbons were, after all, French, and Italy also exerted a strong cultural influence—Goya (Francisco José de Goya y Lucientes, 1746–1828) emerges as the great exception in that age of mediocrity and lack of originality. He became court painter in 1786 under Carlos III. His earlier work had centered on popular scenes—bright, free, and charming—and now he offered paintings of notables that were realistic and often unrestrainedly candid. In the years 1790 to 1800 he produced his *Los Caprichos* (The Caprices), a series of engravings laced with social satire. A later series, *Los Desastres de la Guerra* (The Disasters of War), depicts scenes of horror and black despair reflecting the realities of the War of Independence (discussed below).

In music, the *zarzuela* continued the popular Spanish operetta tradition. Italian opera and Italian singers enjoyed court favor under Philip V and Ferdinand VI.

Despite the efforts of reformers in all fields, the 18th century was one of continued cultural decline following the collapse of the Hapsburg economy. Attempts to improve agriculture, stimulate commerce and industry, and establish a better educational system met with limited success. Even Spain's writers seemed drained of originality and expressive power.

- **1700**: Philip V founds the Bourbon dynasty in Spain. His accession to the throne leads to the beginning of the War of the Spanish Succession, against Britain and Austria, in 1701.
- **1704**: Gibraltar is taken by the British.
- **1713**: War of the Spanish Succession ends with the recognition of Philip as king of Spain. By the Treaty of Utrecht, however, Spain cedes Gibraltar to the British and loses its Italian possessions—Sicily and Sardinia—as well as Luxembourg and Flanders.
- **1714**: Philip V opens El Escorial's royal library, said to contain 200,000 volumes, to the public.
- **1746**: Ferdinand VI takes the throne.
- **1752**: Ferdinand VI founds the academy of San Fernando in Madrid for artists.
- **1759–1788**: Carlos III takes the throne and launches an extensive public works program, completes work on the royal palace in Madrid, and builds the Prado.
- **1786**: Goya paints a portrait of Carlos III as a beak-nosed hunter with dog and musket.
- **1788**: Carlos IV takes the throne.

- **1793**: After Louis XVI of France is guillotined, Spain declares war on France.
- **1800**: Goya paints *Family of Charles IV* (now in the Prado), a depiction of a powerful, bedizened, ridiculous, yet majestic family.

Napoleonic Spain and the War of Independence

Goya captured the horror and passion of the War of Independence (Peninsular War) in *The Third of May, 1808,* depicting in blazing colors the execution by firing squad of citizens of Madrid who had protested the French presence in Spain.

- **1804**: Napoleon is crowned emperor.
- **1805**: Spain joins with France in a war against England. The Spanish navy, out of Cádiz, is defeated at the battle of Trafalgar.
- **1808**: Napoleon invades Spain and declares his brother, Joseph Bonaparte, king, forcing both Carlos IV and his son, Ferdinand VII, to renounce rights to the Spanish throne. On May 2, the War of Independence (Peninsular War) begins. The Spanish army of 27,000 soldiers is victorious over the French at Bailén. Napoleon takes personal command; British campaigns against the French are led by the duke of Wellington.
- **1809**: The French (who now have close to 400,000 men in Spain) occupy Andalusia, except for Cádiz.
- **1812**: Liberals at Cádiz draft a constitution abolishing the Inquisition, censorship, and serfdom, and making the monarch subordinate to the wishes of the *cortes* (parliament). Wellington is victorious at the siege of Ciudad Rodrigo.
- **1814**: Napoleon recalls the French troops; the War of Independence ends; Ferdinand VII takes the throne and repudiates the constitution. During the decade 1810–1820 most of Spain's South American territories gain their independence.

The 19th Century

Despite the fact that Spain was relatively barren aesthetically, French composers born during this century turned to it for inspiration (Maurice Ravel for *Boléro;* Georges Bizet for *Carmen;* Edouard Lalo for his *Symphonie Espagnole;* Emmanuel Chabrier for his *España*), and Spanish composers established themselves internationally: Isaac Albéniz

(*Iberia*), Enrique Granados (*Goyescas*), Joaquín Turina (*Seville Symphony*), and Manuel de Falla (*La Vida Breve*).

The three Carlist wars that followed the death of the conservative Ferdinand and the claims of Don Carlos, his brother, as legitimate successor were fundamentally civil wars between liberals and conservatives. The former advocated constitutional government without church interference, and the latter favored an alliance between church and state. In 1875 the Bourbon Alfonso XII, as constitutional monarch, oversaw a period of social and political reforms. But the Spanish-American War late in the century ended with Spain granting independence to Cuba, ceding Puerto Rico to the United States, and selling the Philippines to the United States for $20 million. Spain as an international power had ceased to exist. "Never was a century more disastrous to a nation than the nineteenth century was to Spain," wrote Jan Morris.

- **1814–1833:** Ferdinand VII rules as absolute monarch.
- **1821:** Spain accepts the independence of Mexico.
- **1833–1868:** The reign of Isabella II.
- **1833–1874:** Three Carlist wars in which church-supported royalists fight liberal constitutionalists.
- **1870–1873:** The reign of Amadeus, chosen by the *cortes* as constitutional monarch. He abdicates in 1873.
- **1873–1875:** The first Spanish republic is established.
- **1883:** Antoni Gaudí begins building his Barcelona church, La Sagrada Família.
- **1886–1902:** After the death of Alfonso XII, Queen María Christina is regent for her son, Alfonso XIII.
- **1898:** The Spanish-American War.

The 20th Century to the Civil War

Celebrated Spanish cultural figures born into this period of crisis in the nation's self-confidence at the turn of the century include Pablo Picasso (1881–1973), who was born in Málaga, lived most of his life in France, and dominated the world of 20th-century art; José Ortega y Gasset (1883–1955), philosopher, writer, and statesman, best known for *Revolt of the Masses* (1930); Miguel de Unamuno (1864–1936), one of the "Generation of '98," whose *Tragic Sense of Life* is his philosophical credo; Juan Ramón Jiménez (1881–1958), poet and author of the children's classic *Platero y Yo;* Antonio Machado (1875–1939), poet of strength and reflective simplicity and an interpreter of the Castilian landscape; Federico García Lorca (1899–1936), the dramatist and poet whose Civil War assassination gave him a mythic aura; Joan Miró (1893–1983), painter, sculptor, engraver; Juan Gris (1887–1927), celebrated artist member of expatriate group in Paris; architect Antoni Gaudí (1852–1926); and artist Salvador Dalí (1904–1989) and Luis Buñuel (1900–1983), Spain's finest film director, who collaborated on two surrealist films, *Un Chien Andalou* and *L'Age d'Or*.

- **1902**: An anarchic union formed in Barcelona proposes general strikes instead of political action; Alfonso XIII assumes the throne at the age of 16.
- **1909**: A general strike is called in Catalonia; Spain is temporarily placed under martial law.
- **1912**: A railway strike is broken militarily by liberal prime minister José Canalejas, later assassinated.
- **1914–1918**: Spain maintains neutrality in World War I.
- **1917**: Violent strikes in northern Spain.
- **1923**: Barcelona army rebellion; Alfonso XIII approves General Miguel Primo de Rivera's military dictatorship; the constitution is suspended.
- **1926**: Treaty with Italy; Spain adopts fascist administrative policies.
- **1930**: Primo de Rivera resigns after economic failures.
- **1931**: April elections force Alfonso XIII to leave Spain; second republic proclaimed; liberal constitutionalists installed.
- **1932**: The Agrarian Reform Act expropriates large tracts of land.
- **1933**: Elections find Spain split between leftist liberals and the newly founded fascist Falange party under José Antonio, son of the late dictator Miguel Primo de Rivera.

The Civil War and the Franco Regime

Picasso's *Guernica* speaks for this searing period in Spain's history. The bombing by German planes of the ancient Basque town of Guernica on April 26, 1937, a market day, and the ensuing deaths of more than 2,000 civilians, became the ominous herald of our time. The world saw itself at the mercy of aerial expeditions of destruction.

Picasso submitted the painting to the 1937 Paris world's fair in response to his commission from the Spanish government. *Guernica* is not in itself a painting of a war scene. There is no battle, no opposing forces. Figures in the painting include six human beings and three animals, a table, a horseshoe, a sword, a flower, an arrow and a spear (both broken), and a gas lamp. *Guernica* has no single meaning; it evokes the neurosis of a war-torn age.

Picasso explicitly denied permission for the work to enter Spain until a "stable, democratic government" was installed there. In Picasso's view this did not occur in his lifetime. (He died in 1973, Franco two years later.) In 1981, on the hundredth anniversary of Picasso's birth, *Guernica* was moved from New York's Museum of Modern Art to Spain, where it was placed in the Casón del Buen Retiro of Madrid's Prado. It is now in Madrid's Museo Nacional Centro de Arte Reina Sofía.

Factional fighting in the Spanish Civil War pitted the Right, known as the Nationalists or Rebels (supported by Fascist Italy, Nazi Germany, the members of Spain's Falange party, the church, landowners, industrialists, conservatives, and the military) against the Left, known as the Republicans or Loyalists (supported by the Soviet Union, the International Brigades from Europe and America, the proletariat, anarchists, syndicalists, and intellectuals). Factions often quarreled among themselves, and both sides committed atrocities. One million casualties resulted.

- **1936**: Army revolt in Spanish Morocco; General Francisco Franco lands in Spain from Morocco, and Civil War breaks out; the battle of Madrid; government moves to Valencia; Franco is proclaimed *generalísimo* and insurgent head of state; José Antonio Primo de Rivera is imprisoned by the government; Federico García Lorca is shot by Falangists.
- **1937**: Guernica is bombed. Picasso's masterly *Guernica* engenders strong support from the Republican (Left) side; Nationalists (insurgents, the Right) gain control of much of northeastern Spain.
- **1937–1938**: The Republican government moves to Barcelona; battle of the Ebro, with the loss of 150,000 Republicans to the rebel Nationalists.
- **1939**: In January Barcelona falls to Franco's forces, aided by German tanks and planes; a vast number of refugees leave Spain for France; the Civil War ends; England and France recognize the Franco regime; Spain's population is reduced by nearly a million through Civil War deaths and emigration.
- **1939–1945**: Spain is nonbelligerent in World War II but supplies aid to the Axis powers in the early part of the war.
- **1946–1947**: Spain is excluded from both the United Nations and NATO as well as from Marshall Plan aid.
- **1953**: Spain signs a treaty with the United States, authorizing U.S. military bases on Spanish soil in exchange for $226 million in aid.
- **1955**: The United Nations admits Spain; revitalization as well as slackening of dictatorial restrictions begins in industry, housing, social security, and education.
- **1967**: The Religious Liberty Act loosens the grip of the Catholic Church.
- **1968**: The Press Act somewhat lessens press censorship.

- **1969**: Juan Carlos, grandson of Alfonso XIII, is proclaimed heir to the throne.
- **1975**: Franco dies; Juan Carlos I becomes king of Spain.

Spain Today

Since Franco's death in 1975 Spain has undergone a political and cultural transformation. The individual citizen of Spain today lives in a world in which freedom of expression and conduct prevails. The ability of the Catholic Church to maintain the illegality of divorce, birth control, adultery, homosexuality, and abortion has been broken. Women's rights, only a few decades old, are now taken for granted. The increasing influx of tourists has given Spain a billion-dollar yearly source of income, and the manners and morals of the visitors have affected the land they chose to visit.

Spain's classic figurative separation from the rest of Europe is now a thing of the past; Spain is an active member of the community of great nations, and the Spanish people have recovered from a civil and political illness that seemed almost terminal. The vaunted pride of the individual Spaniard, once thought a matter of ethnic inheritance, is now a characteristic justified by the courage and energy expended in the last 20 years.

In the past year Spain played host to the world, sponsoring both Expo '92 in Seville and the Summer Olympics in Barcelona. After a decline from Golden Age stature to rock-bottom despair and economic decrepitude, Spain has made a stunning comeback. Ironically, the emphasis on Spain's quincentennial celebration of her *anno mirabilis* shifted in subtle fashion from discovery (as Columbus lost public-relations clout) to recovery (the world media focused on Spain's current prestige).

- **1976**: Juan Carlos appoints Adolfo Suárez González prime minister.
- **1977**: First post-Franco elections; establishment of the ministry of culture.
- **1978**: Spain approves a new national constitution.
- **1981**: Suárez resigns; coup d'état is attempted by the Civil Guards in parliament, but Juan Carlos is successful in dealing with the insurgents; Leopoldo Calvo Sotela y Bustelo becomes prime minister, aligning Spain with NATO.
- **1982**: Felipe González is elected prime minister as the Socialist party wins elections; Spain joins NATO.
- **1986**: Spain joins the European Economic Community.
- **1988**: One-day general strike protests the inequity of

business-boom benefits and workers' salaries; the unemployment rate of 18 percent is the highest in Europe.

- **1989**: Spain assumes the presidency of the European Community; Camilo José Cela wins the Nobel Prize for literature; Felipe González is reelected prime minister.
- **1991**: Madrid serves as site of November Mid-East Peace Conference attended by world leaders.
- **1992**: Universal Exposition (EXPO '92) in Seville, April 20 through October 12; Sefarad '92 (homage to Sephardic Jews expelled in 1492) in Toledo, May; Summer Olympics (XXV Olympiad) in Barcelona, July 25 through August 9; Madrid serves as 1992 Cultural Capital of Europe.
- **1993**: The infrastructure left in place after Expo '92 and the Olympics is another step toward Spain's emergence as a leading travel venue.

—Robert Packard

INDEX

Abacanto, 564
Abadía de Santa María de Valbuena, 222
Abadía de Valvanera, 384, 390
Abelardo Linares, 121
Abencerrajes Gallery, 733
Abolengo, 176
El Abside, 633
Acebo, 200
Acebo Gift Shop, 657
Acosta, 120
El Acuario, 810
Acueducto de les Ferreras, 529
Acueducto Romano, 141
Adolfo Domínguez, 493
Adonias, 191
A. Gratacos, 493
La Aguja, 372
Agut, 488
Agut d'Avignon, 484
Aigua Blava, 581
Ajo, 318
Ajuntament de Barcelona, 462
Akelarre, 344
Alacena de las Monjas, 737
Alambique, 83, 125
Alameda de Hercules, 709
Alange, 666
Alaraz, 177
Alarcón, 641
Alava Province, 362
Albacete, 642
La Albahaca, 704
Albaicín, 730
Albariño, 283
La Albariza, 702
Albarracín, 441
Alba de Tormes, 177
Albatros, 175
La Alberca, 182
Alberto, 289
Alberto Linares, 707
La Albufera, 606
La Albufera Restaurant, 111

Alcalá de Henares, 149
Alcañiz, 439
Alcántara, 656
Alcántara Hotel, 659, 672
Alcazaba: Granada, 730; Málaga, 764; Mérida, 665
Alcázar: Segovia, 143; Seville, 693; Toledo, 628
Alcázar Restaurant, 604
Alcoy, 609
Alcudia, 569
La Alcudia de Elche, 610
Alella, 504
Alfaro, 388
Alfonso VIII Hotel, 655, 672
Algeciras, 775
Alhambra, 731
Alhambra Palace, 737, 782
Alicante, 23, 587, 588 (map), 591, 607
Alimentación Gonzalo Supermercado, 268
A. Linares Muñoz, 707
Aljafería, 436
Alkalde, 106
El Almacén, 140
Almadraba Park Hotel, 512, 532
Almagro, 21, 635
Almanza, 201
Almería, 768
Almudaina, 561
Las Alpujarras, 738
Alquézar, 438
Altamira Caves, 18, 312
Alt Heidelberg, 490
Un Alto en el Camino, 654
Ama Lur, 578
Ambos Mundos, 491
American Bar, 545
Amnesia, 579
El Amparo, 106
Ampurdàn–Costa Brava, 504
L'Ancien Bijou, 495
Al Andalus, 116

Andalusia, 22, 674, 675 (map)
Andalusian Express, 29, 779
Andra-Mari, 358
Andratx, 565
L'Anella Olímpica, 521
Anexo Vilas, 296
Angél Collado, 121
Angel Jobal, 497
Angel Rodríguez, 218
Anguiano, 383
Annapurna, 111
El Anteojo, 681
Anticuario, 634
Antigua Casa de los Abades, 309
Antigua Casa Sobrino de Botín, 102
Antigüedades Lola Ortega, 708
Antigüedades Marco-Polo, 605
Antigüedades Maria Esclasans, 495
Antiguo Convento de Calatrava, 636
Antolin Palomino Olalla, 121
Antonio Martín, 680
Aparthotel Mediterráneo, 527, 533
Aragón, 21, 424, 425 (map)
Aranda de Duero, 20, 229, 230 (map)
Aranjuez, 21, 126, 150
Ararat, 121
L'Arca de l'Avia, 495
Archivo General de Indias, 694
Archy, 115
Arco de Cuchilleros, 77
El Arco de los Cuchilleros Gift Shop, 120
Los Arcos: Minorca, 552; Navarra, 417
Arco de Santa María, 249
Arcos de la Frontera, 755
Los Arcos Restaurant, 640

Las Arenas de Cabrales, 268
Arévalo, 140
Argamasilla de Alba, 637
Arje, 708
L'Armeler, 593
La Armería, 361
Armería Real, 82
Armino, 176
Arnedo, 387
Arquillos, 360
Arraunlari, 351
Arrecife, 793
Artà, 573
Artenara, 811
Artesania, 145
Artesanía Almutazal, 441
Artesanía Canaria Taguguy, 810
Artesanía de la Catedral, 441
Artesanía de Sigüenza, 645
Artesanía Talaverana, 634
Artespaña: Barcelona, 495; Madrid, 119; La Orotava, 801; Palma, 563; Seville, 707; Valencia, 605
Arturo Ramón, 494
Arucas, 811
Arzak, 344
Asador Bretxa, 347
Asador La Chata, 374
Asador Gayarre, 437
Asador La Gloria, 253
Asador Mauro, 224
Astigarraga, 335
Astorga, 198
Astoria Palace, 602, 613
Astun, 438
Asturias, 18, 261, 262 (map)
Asunción, 707
Atalaya, 419
Ateneo, 604
Atienza, 645
Atrio, 659
Auditorio Nacional de Música, 116
Ausejo, 387
Autilla del Pino, 225
Autol, 387
Avenida de Colón, 805
Avenida Palace Hotel, 480
Avila, 21, 126, 135
Ayuntamiento: Baeza, 724; León, 190; Pamplona, 399
Azahares, 707
Azpeitia, 354

Babilonia, 277
Badajoz, 667

Baden, 372
Baelo Claudio, 776
Baeza, 723
Baixamar, 545
Balafi, 581
Balcón de Europa, 767
El Balcón de la Rioja, 379
Baleares Café, 554
Balearic Islands, 24, 535; maps: 542, 558
Balmoral, 115
El Balneario, 114
Baños de Cerrato, 225
Banyalbufar, 566
Banyoles, 516
Bar Abades, 705
Bar Blanco y Negro, 373
Barcelona, 23, 445, 446 (map)
Barcelona Hilton, 481
Barceloneta, 474
Bárcena Mayor, 321
Bar Chivani, 195
Bar Gallego, 101
Bar Gorriti, 340
Bar José Mari, 341
Bar Lorenzo, 373
Bar Martínez, 341
Bar Modesto, 702
Baroca, 737
Bar los Pelayos, 191
Bar Portaletas, 340
Bar del Puerto, 315
Barrachina, 604
Barri Gòtic, 452 (map), 459
Barrio de Salamanca, 88, 118
Barrio de Santa Cruz, 695
Barrio Vegueta, 810
Barri Xinès, 487
Barros, 139
Bar Torrecilla, 373
Bar Txoco, 400
Basílica Menor de Santa María, 300
Basílica de Nuestra Señora del Pilar, 430
Basílica de Nuestra Señora del Prado, 634
La Basílica Restaurant, 104
Basílica de San Isidoro, 191
Basílica de Santa María, 610
Basílica de San Vicente, 138
Basque Bar, 341
Basque Country, 16, 326, 328 (map)
Bataplán Bar and Discotheque, 341

Las Batuecas, 183
BD Ediciones de Diseño, 493
BD Madrid, 122
Bedua, 354
Beethoven, 377
Beethoven II, 377
Béjar: Extremadura, 656; Old Castile, 183
Belagua, 95, 109
Bellas Artes Gallery, 194
Bellman, 112
Belmonte, 642
Benasque, 438
Benicarló, 593
Bens d'Avall, 568
Berlin, 121
Bermeo, 355, 356
Bermeo Restaurant, 358
Besalú, 517
Betancuria, 813
La Biblioteca, 109
La Bicha, 195
El Bierzo, 163
The Big Apple, 176
Bilbao, 356
Bilbilis, 440
Binimel-lá, 548
Binissalem, 539
Black, 297
Blasfor, 706
La Bobadilla, 761, 783
La Bocamar, 277
Bodega la Nieta, 221
Bodegas Balbás, 233
Bodegas Mauro, 221
Bodega la Sorbòna, 221
El Bodegón, 201
Bodegón San Marcos, 806
La Bola, 83
Boliche, 492
Bombay, 605
Boñar, 203
La Boquería, 455, 496
Borgia, 418
Borja Palacio de los Duques, 606
Born District, 464
Bornos, 756
Los Borrachos, 437
El Bosque, 758
El Bosque Restaurant, 746
Botafumeiro, 486
La Botica, 235
El Boulevard Rosa, 493
Boutique Raquel, 707
La Bouza, 177
Briones, 375
Las Brisas Motel, 319, 324
Bristol, 603, 613
Brok, 495
Bubión, 740

Buenavista, 806
Bulevar de Antiquaris, 494
Burgos, 20, 230 (map), 239
Burguete, 413

C & A, 707
El Caballito del Mar, 564
El Caballo Rojo, 719
Caballo da Troya, 214
Cabo de Creus Peninsula, 511
Cabo de Formentor, 569
Cabo de Gata, 770
Cabo Mayor, 110
Cáceres, 21, 657
El Cachetero, 374
Cadaqués, 512
Cádiz, 752
Cádiz Province, 680
Café de l'Academia, 488
Café Bar El Globo, 113
Café Bar Zurich, 454, 491
Café Can Quei, 517
Café Castellana, 113
Café Central, 116
Café de Chinitas, 116
Café Círculo de Bellas Artes, 113
Café Comercial, 114
Café Espejo, 113
Café Feijóo, 274
Café Gijón, 87, 113, 114
Café Glacé, 281
Café-Heladería El Micalet, 599
Café Iruña, 400
Café Maravillas, 116
Café del Mercado, 124
Café de l'Opéra, 491
Café de Oriente, 83, 103, 113
Café de Paris, 766
Café de Praga, 433
Café Riego, 276
Café de la Ruta, 582
Café Suizo, 376
Café del Teatro Carlos III, 134
Café Trebol, 546
Café Victoria, 194
Café Viena: Barcelona, 491; Madrid, 113
Café Viva Madrid, 101, 115
La Caixa de Frang, 495
Cala Boix, 581
Cala Bruch, 556
Calacorb, 546
Cala Guya, 573
Calahorra, 389
Cala d'Hort, 582
Cala Llenya, 580
Cala Mastella, 580

Cala Mesquida, 573
Calanda, 439
Cala Pregonda, 548
Cala Ratjada, 573
Cala Santanyi, 571
Calatayud, 440
Caldera de Taburiente, 812
Caleruega, 235
Calle de Alcalá, 59
Calle de la Cava Baja, 78
Calleja de las Flores, 716
Calle Laurel, 373
Calle de Preciados, 75
Calle San Lorenzo, 249
Calle de Serrano, 88
Calle Victoria, 75
Cambaral Terraza Bar, 281
Cambrils, 529
Camino de Santiago, 19, 256, 285, 381, 407
La Campana Confitería, 707
Campero, 176
El Campillo, 186
Campillo Quarter, 359
Camping Al-bereka, 182, 259
Camping Playa Joyel, 318, 324
Camping Santillana, 307, 324
Campo de Borja, 428
Campo del Golf, 314
Campo Grande, 212
Campo de Moro, 82
Campo de San Francisco, 272
Ca N'Aguedet, 549
Canals y Munne, 507
Ca Na Pilar, 549
Canary Islands, 24, 785, 786 (map)
Cañas, 494
Can Borell, 520
Candanchú, 438
El Candil Viejo, 175
Cangas de Onis, 269
Can Gatell-Rodolfo, 529
Can Isidre, 488
Can Miguel, 548
Ca N'Olga, 549
Can Pau, 546
Cantabria, 17, 304, 305 (map)
Cantón del Toral 2, 295
Cap de Cavalleria, 548
Els Capellans, 610
Capicorp Vey, 571
Capileira, 740
Capilla de Condestable, 248

Capilla Espíritu Sanctu, 644
Capilla de Nuestra Señora de los Desamparados, 599
Capilla del Obispo, 77
Capilla de la Piedad, 142
Capilla del Salvador, 721
Capilla de San Andrés, 78
Capilla de Santa Cruz, 269
Capilla del Santo Cáliz, 598
El Capricho, 319
Los Caracoles, 487
Cariñena, 428
Carlos Torrents, 493
Las Carmelitas Descalzas, 177
Carmen de San Miquel, 738
Carmona, 701, 819
Carnicería, 723
Carrer dels Comtes de Barcelona, 461
Carrer Montcada, 464
Carrión de los Condes, 229
Cartuja, 566
La Cartuja de Miraflores, 254
Casa Amatller, 467
Casa Antón, 239
Casa de los Balcones, 801
Casa Batlló, 467
Casa de los Botines, 190
Casa del Cabildo Vieja, 745
Casa Cámara, 349
Casa de Campo, 82
Casa de Carmona, 701, 781
Casa Castril, 730
Casa de Cervantes, 212
Casa Ciriaco, 103
Casa de Cisneros, 77
Casa de Colón: Las Palmas, 810; Valladolid, 209
Casa de la Comunidad, 441
Casa de las Conchas, 168
Casa de los Condes de Sástago, 435
Casa Consistoriales, 724
Casa del Cordón, 244
Casa Costa, 487
Casa Culleretes, 488
Casa Damas, 707
Casa Damián, 227
Casa de Diego, 121
Casa Don Julián, 267, 303
Casa Fermín, 277

Casa Florencio, 231
Casa Gallega, 551
Casa Julián de Tolosa, 103
Casa Juvenal, 181
Casa del Labrador, 152
La Casa de Leonor de la Vega, 309
La Casa del Libro, 123
Casa Lleó Morera, 467
Casa de Lope de Vega, 74
Casa Lucio, 78, 102
Casa Luis, 406
Casa Mateo, 390
Casa Mauleón, 405, 406
Casa Milà, 467
Casa Mira, 125
Casa de Miranda, 250
Casa del Mono, 658
Casa y Museo de El Greco, 630
Casa Museu Gaudí, 472
Casa Nicolasa, 345
Casa Ojeda, 251
Casa Pablo, 152
Casa Paco, 78
Casa Palacios, 101
Casa de los Picos, 142
Casa de Pilatos, 696
Casa Pozo, 191
Casa del Queso, 309
Casa Quevedo, 308
Casa Ramón, 489
Casares, 775
Casa del Rey Moro, 760
Casa Real, 732
Casa Robles, 702
Casa Román, 702
Casa Romana del Anfiteatro, 665
Casa Romano del Mitraeo, 665
Casas Colgadas, 639
Casa de las Siete Chimeneas, 62
Las Casas de la Judería, 701, 781
Casa del Sol, 211
Casa Sola Morales, 517
Casa Teixidor, 516
Casa Terete, 377
Casa Terrades, 469
Casa de Toledo-Moctezuma, 658
Casa de las Torres, 722
Casa Urbano, 347
Casa de las Veletas, 658
Casa Victor, 280
Casa Vilas, 296
Casa de la Villa (Madrid), 77
Casa de los Villa (Santillana del Mar), 309
Casa Vives, 497
Casa Yustas, 121

Casco Antiguo: Ciudadela, 552; Palma, 561
Casco Viejo: Logroño, 371; Zaragoza, 433
Casino de Castilla y León, 214
Casino Castillo de Perelada, 514
La Casita, 373
Casita de Arriba, 134
Casita del Príncipe, 134
Casón del Buen Retiro, 69
El Castell, 521, 533
La Castellana Charcutería, 497
Castellana Inter-Continental, 95, 115
Castell de Bellver, 560
Castillo de Argüeso, 322
Castillo de Fuensaldaña, 221
Castillo de Javier, 408
Castillo de Monzón, 227, 259
Castillo de la Mota, 218
Castillo de Paso Alto, 803
Castillo de Peñafiel, 223
Castillo de los Polvazares, 199
Castillo de Sagunto, 593
Castillo de San Antón, 298
Castillo de San Gabriel, 793
Castillo de San José, 793
Castillo de San Miguel, 806
Castillo de Santa Bárbara, 608
Castillo de Santa Cruz de la Mota, 337
Castillo de Simancas, 220
Castillo de Torrelobatón, 220
Castle of Clavijo, 381
Castle of the Kings of Navarra, 418
Castle of the Templars, 670
Castrojeriz, 257
Castro-Urdiales, 317
Cat, 119
Catalonia, 23, 498, 500 (map)
Catedral de Baeza, 724
Catedral del Buen Pastor (San Sebastián), 337
Catedral de María Inmaculada (Vitoria), 360
Catedral Nueva (Salamanca), 170
Catedral de San Isidro (Madrid), 78

Catedral de San Juan (Badajoz), 667
Catedral de Santa María: Girona, 515; Sigüenza, 644; Vitoria, 359
Catedral de Santa María de la Redonda (Logroño), 372
Catedral de Santa Tecla (Tarragona), 528
Catedral de Santiago (Bilbao), 356
Catedral de Santo Domingo de la Calzada, 385
Catedral de Sant Pere (Vic), 518
Catedral Vieja (Salamanca), 170
Cathedral: Albarracín, 442; Avila, 139; Barcelona, 460; Burgos, 245; Ciudad Rodrigo, 181; Córdoba, 715; Cuenca, 640; Granada, 735; Ibiza City, 577; Jaca, 438; León, 193; Málaga, 764; Murcia, 612; Oviedo, 272; Palencia, 226; Las Palmas, 810; Pamplona, 398; Plasencia, 655; Segovia, 142; La Seu d'Urgell, 521; Seville, 690; Teruel, 441; Toledo, 628; Tortosa, 530; Tudela, 420; Valencia, 598; Valladolid, 207; Zamora, 184
Cathedral of Santiago (Santiago de Compostela), 291
Cats, 115
El Caudillo Rosa, 176
La Cava del Palau, 490
Cazorla, 725
Cazorla National Park, 725
Celler C'an Amer, 570
Celler Sa Premsa, 563
El Cenador del Prado, 104
Cenicero, 375
Centre del Carme, 600
Centre Cultural Pelaires, 562
Centro de Anticuarios Lagasca, 122
Centro de Arte y Antigüedades, 122
Centro Cultural de la Villa, 87, 116
La Cepa: Estella, 416; San Sebastián, 341
Ceramicas Lladró, 605

La Cerámica de Talavera, 119
El Cerco de Artajona, 419
Cerdanya, 519
Cervecería Alemana, 101, 115
Cervecería Madrid, 603
Cervecería Natur Bier, 101
Cervecería D'Or, 489
Cervecería Santa Ana, 101
Cervecería Santa Bárbara, 86
Cervecería Valenciana, 595
Charcutería La Pineda, 497
Charlot, 125
Charolés, 134
La Chata, 101
Chez Victor, 176
Chinchilla de Monte Aragón, 642
Chinchón, 21, 152
Chiripa, 805
Chocolatería San Ginés, 113
Chomín, 347
El Chotis, 78
Chuleta, 234
El Churrasco, 719
Cigales, 164, 221
Cimadevilla, 280
Cirauqui, 414
Círculo de Bellas Artes, 94, 114
Circus Maximus, 664
Ciudadela, 550
La Ciudad Encantada, 641
Ciudad Real, 21, 637
Ciudad Rodrigo, 177
Ciudad Universitaria, 85
Club Marítimo, 546
Coca, 145
Cock, 114
Coconut, 275
Codorníu, 507
La Colegiata, 237
Colegiata de Santa Juliana, 309
Colegio de Anaya, 169
Colegio del Arzobispo M. Fonseca, 168
Colegio de Calatrava, 169
Colegio Mayor de San Ildefonso, 149
Colegio del Patriarca, 601
Colegio de San Gregorio, 209
Colegio de San Jerónimo, 290

Colegio de Santo Domingo, 611
Colleció Joan March, 562
College of Catalan Architects, 460
Colmado Quilez, 497
Comillas, 319
Compañía Nacional de Teatro Clásico, 116
Compludo, 201
Condado de Huelva, 682
Confitería Filella, 708
Convento de las Agustinas, 140
Convento de la Coria, 661
Convento de la Encarnación: Avila, 137; Madrid, 83
Convento de Nuestra Señora de Gracia, 137
Convento de San Esteban, 169
Convento de San Francisco, 294
Convento de San José, 137
Convento de San Leandro, 708
Convento de Santa Clara: Valladolid, 215; Zafra, 669
Convento de Santa Inés, 708
Convento de Santa Paula, 708
Convento de Santa Teresa, 137
Convento de Santo Domingo, 807
Copacabana, 140
El Coral, 437
Córdoba, 22, 686, 710, 711 (map)
Coria, 656
Corpus Christi, 601
El Corral de Comedias, 636
El Corte Inglés: Barcelona, 489, 493; Madrid, 121, 123; Seville, 707; Valencia City, 605; Zaragoza, 435
Cortfiel, 605
Cortijo Faín, 756, 783
A Coruña, 298
Costa del Azahar, 593
Costa Blanca, 587, 768
Costa Brava, 24, 508
Costa Daurada, 526
Costa de la Luz, 742 (map), 782
Costa de Ses Voltes, 545
Costa del Sol, 22, 742 (map), 762

Costa Teguise, 793
Court of the Lions, 733
Court of the Myrtle Trees, 733
Covadonga, 269
Covarrubias, 237
Covento de Regina Coeli, 308
Los Cristianos, 799
Cristina de J'osh, 124
Cruz de Ferro, 200
Cruz de Tejeda, 811
Cuartel Conde Duque, 117
Los Cuatro Postes, 136
Las Cubanas, 374
La Cucanya, 527
Cuenca, 638
Cuenllas, 124
La Cueva, 134
Cueva de los Letreros, 728
Cueva Santa, 270
Cuevas de Artà, 574
Cuevas del Drach, 574
Cuevas del Pindal, 271
Cueva de los Verdes, 796
Cunini, 737
Curhotel Hipócrates, 510, 532
Cúria Reial, 517
Cusco, 722

Dalt Vila, 575
La Dama de Elche, 87
Daroca, 440
Dársena, 609
Deba, 355
Delfín, 608
Derby Hotel, 481
Derby Restaurant, 604
Desfiladero de los Beyos, 269
Desfiladero de la Hermida, 321
Deyá, 567
Deyá Archaeological Museum and Research Center, 567
El Diablo, 795
Diana, 479
Diego Gómez Flores, 496
Dionis, 341
Diplomatic, 480
Distribuciones d'Art Surrealiste, 514
Dolmen de Toniñuelo, 670
Dom Lope, 147
Doña María, 700, 781
Doñana National Park, 741
Don Gaiferos, 296
Don Jamón, 252

Don Julián, 181
Don Leone, 774
Don Miguel, 760
Don Sancho, 176
La Dorada: Barcelona, 486; Madrid, 109; Seville, 703
Dos Hermanas, 362
La Dragonera, 565
Dueñas, 225
Las Dunas, 741
Duque Discotheque, 297
Duque Restaurant, 144
Durán, 122

Easo, 342
Edelweiss Hotel, 438, 444
Edelweiss Restaurant, 112
Editorial Hiares, 708
E. Furest, 493
Egaña Oriza, 704
Eixample, 466
Ekseption, 121
Elche, 610
Elciego, 381
Eldorado Petit: Barcelona, 486; Sant Feliu de Guíxols, 509
Elígeme, 116
Elkano, 353
Embalse de Riaño, 203
Embassy, 112, 113, 115
Emilio Lustau, 747, 751
Empúries, 511
Els Encants, 497
Enrique Becerra, 705
La Era, 795
L'Ermitage, 122
Ermita de San Adrián de Vadoluengo, 409
Ermita de San Antonio de la Florida, 82
Ermita de San Segundo, 138
Ermita de Sant Feliú, 607
Escalera Dorada, 248
Escanda, 275
Es Castells–Villacarlos, 546
El Escorial, 21, 126, 131
Es Cranc, 548
Escuelas Menores, 173
Es Grau, 547
Es Migjorn Gran, 549
Es Mirador del Port, 551
Es Molí des Recó, 549
Es Palau, 552
Es Plá, 547
L'Espluga de Francolí, 526
Es Port, 566
Estación Enológica, 376
Estación del Norte, 595

Estampería Castells, 495
Estella, 415
Esterra, 176
Estiarte, 122
Es Trench, 571
Eugenia, 529
Eunate, 414
Explanada de España, 607
Extremadura, 21, 647, 648 (map)
Extremadura Hotel, 659, 672

Fábrica de Muebles, 183
Fallas Museu, 605
Fallas de Valencia, 605
Los Fariones, 794, 814
El Faro, 681, 753
Félix Barbero, 372
Félix Manzanero, 121
Fernán Caballero, 707
Fernán González, 250
Ferpal, 124
Ferretería María Rosario Berrotarán, 350
Festivales de Navarra, 403
Fiestas de San Fermín, 401
Figón de Bonilla, 766
Figón del Cabildo, 705
El Figón de Eustaquio, 659
Figón de Pedro, 640
Figueras, 281
Figueres, 513
Filatelia Casa del Sello, 123
La Finca, 761
Finca Igay, 386
La Fira, 492
Flash-Flash Tortilleria, 489
Florián, 486
La Flor Valenciana, 139
El Fogón de Santa Teresa, 140
La Fonda, 774
Fonda Colasa, 319
La Fontana, 727
Formentera Island, 582
Formentera Playa, 582, 586
Fornells, 547
Fortuny, 109
Forum de Cesaraugusta, 433
La Fragata, 527
Fragosa, 656
Las Francesas, 212
El Franco, 296
Frigiliana, 767
Friki, 119
Frómista, 228

Fuendetodos, 440
Fuengirola, 680
Fuensaldaña, 221
Fuente de la Cibeles, 59
Fuente Dé, 320
Fuente de Neptuno, 73
Fuenterrabía, 349
Fuente Vaqueros, 762
Fuerteventura, 787, 812
Fundació Joan Miró, 471, 488, 494
Fundación Caja de Pensiones, 88
Fundación Juan March, 88, 122
Fundació Tàpies, 468
Funes, 388
De Funy, 111

Los Gabrieles, 101
Gaitán, 746
Galbis, 604
Galería Dalí, 494
Galería Joan Prats, 494
Galería Maeght, 494
La Galería del Prado, 124
Galerías Piquer, 122
Galerías Preciados: Barcelona, 493; Madrid, 123; Palma, 563
Galerías Ribera, 122
Galería Yaiza, 795
Los Galetos, 112
Galiano Residencia, 97
Galicia, 18, 261, 262 (map), 282
Galín, 238
El Gallego, 100
Los Gallos, 706
La Gamba, 606
Gamberinus, 474, 491
La Gamella, 105
Gandía, 606
Garachico, 806
Garganta del Cares, 268
El Gasco, 656
Gaviria Palace, 113
Gelateria Italiana Pagliotta, 489
Generalife, 735
Gibalfaro, 764
Gibraltar, 775
Gijón, 279
Giralda, 692
Girona, 515
Goizeko-Kabi, 357
La Goleta, 277
Gomera, 787, 806
González-Byass, 751
Gonzalo Comella, 493
Gorrotxa, 358
La Goya, 214
Goyesco, 437
Grafiques el Tinell, 495
Grajal, 202

Granada, 22, 686, 729
El Gran Café, 194
Grand Canary, 787, 791 (map), 808
Gran Hotel: Jaca, 438, 444; Salamanca, 175, 259
Gran Hotel Almería, 769, 783
Gran Hotel Arrecife Playa, 793, 814
Gran Hotel Balneario de Cestona, 354, 363
Gran Hotel España, 276, 303
Gran Hotel Havana, 479
Gran Hotel Lugo, 289, 303
Gran Hotel de la Toja, 302, 303
Gran Hotel Zurbarán, 667, 672
La Granja de San Ildefonso, 146
Gran Taberna Río-Sil, 604
Gran Teatre del Liceu, 457
Gran Vía, 371
El Grau Colmado, 497
Grazalema, 757
Grill Neptuno, 106
Grill San Rafael, 578
Gritti, 342
Groc, 493
Guadalajara, 643
Guadalupe, 662
Guadix, 727
La Guardia, 302
Guarnicionería San Pablo, 707
Guernica, 355
Guetaria, 352
Guria: Barcelona, 488; Bilbao, 357

La Hacienda: Marbella, 774; Valencia, 603
Hacienda el Bulli, 512
Hall of the Ambassadors, 733
Happy Books, 496
Haría, 797
Haro, 376
Hartza, 405
Hecho, 438
Hermigua, 807
Hermita de la Virgen de la Montaña, 660
Herrera y Ollero, 120
Hervás, 656
Hierro, 787, 812
Hijos de García Tenorio, 120

Hipódromo de Lasarte, 340
Hispano, 114
Holiday Inn Madrid, 96
Horchatería de Santa Catalina, 598
Horchatería El Siglo, 598
Horcher, 105
Horno de San Gil, 103
La Horra, 233
Hospedería de Leyre, 407, 423
Hospedería del Real Monasterio, 663, 672
Hospital de la Caridad: Seville, 695; Toledo, 626
Hospital de Nuestra Señora del Carmen, 753
Hospital del Rey, 253
Hospital de Santiago, 721
Hospital de Sant Pau, 470
Hospital de Tavera, 626
Hostal Biniali, 545, 585
Hostal Burguete, 413, 423
Hostal del Cardenal, 632, 646
Hostal Delfina, 97
Hostal Dolcet, 521
Hostal Echaurren, 385, 390
Hostal Estrella, 519
Hostal de la Gavina, 510, 532
Hostal Inés, 203, 259
Hostal Landa, 250
Hostal Mar Blava, 555, 585
Hostal Mar i Vent, 566, 585
Hostal Pizarro, 661
Hostal Residencia Ciudadella, 550, 585
Hostal Residencia Molins Park, 577, 585
Hostal-Restaurante El Doncel, 645
Hostal de los Reyes Católicos, 292, 293, 303
Hostal Santa María de El Paular, 147, 154
Hostal Tafalla, 418, 423
Hostal Toni, 379
Hostal Tudela, 421
Hostería del Laurel, 702
Hostería Nacional del Estudiante, 150
Hostería Pintor Zuloaga, 148
Hotel Adarve, 718, 782
Hotel Adserá, 520, 533
Hotel Aigua Blava, 510, 532

Hotel Albarracín, 442, 444
Hotel Alfonso XIII, 700, 781
Hotel del Almirante, 545, 585
Hotel Altamira, 307, 324
Hotel Ampurdán, 514, 532
Hotel El Ancla, 317, 324
Hotel Los Angeles, 307, 324
Hotel Araguaney, 296, 303
Hotel Aránzazu, 358, 363
Hotel Arco de San Juan, 612, 613
Hotel Arosa, 94
Hotel Astoria, 482
Hotel Asturias, 96
Hotel Atlántico: A Coruña, 298, 303; Cádiz, 753, 782
Hotel Los Augustinos, 377, 391
Hotel Avenida, 405, 423
Hotel Báltico & Restaurant, 281, 303
Hotel Las Batuecas, 183, 259
Hotel Beatriz, 633, 646
Hotel Boix, 520, 533
Hotel Boston, 436, 444
Hotel Los Bronces, 232, 259
Hotel Byblos Andaluz, 773, 783
Hotel Carlos V: Madrid, 97; Toledo, 633, 646
Hotel Carlton Rioja, 373, 391
Hotel del Cid, 243, 259
Hotel Ciudad de Logroño, 373, 391
Hotel Colón: Barcelona, 478; Béjar, 656, 672
Hotel Compostela, 296, 303
Hotel Conde Duque: Bilbao, 358, 363; Santillana del Mar, 307, 324
Hotel Condes de Barcelona, 480
Hotel Condes de Urgell II, 531, 534
Hotel El Corzo, 384, 391
Hotel Covadonga, 482
Hotel Cuatro Postes, 136
Hotel Cueva del Fraile, 641, 646
Hotel Las Cuevas, 307, 324
Hotel Durán, 514, 533
Hotel Emperatriz, 666, 672

Hotel La Encina, 318, 324
Hotel Ercilla, 358, 363
Hotel Eslava, 405, 423
Hotel Eurobuilding, 96
Hotel Europa, 342, 363
Hotel Felipe IV, 207, 259
Hotel Fernán González, 243, 259
Hotel Formentor, 569, 585
Hotel Gasteiz, 362, 363
Hotel Gaudí, 199, 259
Hotel Gayoso, 281, 303
Hotel Gran Via, 480
Hotel Guadalmar, 765, 783
Hotel Hacienda, 581, 585
Hotel Los Hidalgos, 307, 324
Hotel Hospedería del Convento de San Francisco, 778, 783
Hotel Huerta Honda, 669, 672
Hotel Huerto del Cura, 610, 613
Hotel Los Infantes, 307, 324
Hotel Inglés, 603, 613
Hotel Irache, 417, 423
Hotel Iruña Park, 404, 423
Hotel Isaba, 411, 423
Hotel Jauregui, 350, 363
Hotel Jerez, 746, 782
Hotel Karlos Arguiñano, 352, 364
Hotel Landa Palace, 243, 259
Hotel Lasa, 207, 259
Hotel Llívia, 520, 533
Hotel Las Lomas, 666, 672
Hotel de Londres y de Inglaterra, 342, 364
Hotel López de Haro, 358, 364
Hotel Luz Granada, 737, 782
Hotel Maimónides, 719, 782
Hotel Maisonnave, 405, 423
Hotel María Cristina, 342, 364
Hotel Marqués de Vallejo, 373, 391
Hotel Meliá Castilla, 96, 115
Hotel Meliá Córdoba, 718, 782
Hotel Meliá Parque, 207, 259
Hotel Meliá Siete Coronas, 613

Hotel Meliá Valencia, 603, 613
Hotel Meliá Victoria, 563, 585
Hotel Miguel Angel, 95
Hotel Mijas, 773, 783
Hotel Miramar, 320, 324
Hotel Monasterio de San Miguel, 746, 782
Hotel Monte Igueldo, 343, 364
Hotel Montemar, 318, 325
Hotel Monterrey, 175, 259
Hotel Morase, 421, 423
Hotel Mozart, 207, 260
Hotel Niza, 342, 364
Hotel Olid Meliá, 207, 260
Hotel Orhi, 405, 423
Hotel Oriente, 478
Hotel Orly, 342, 364
Hotel Palace, 520, 533
Hotel Palacios, 388, 391
Hotel Palas, 609, 613
Hotel Pampinot, 350, 364
Hotel Patricia, 554, 585
Hotel Picos de Europa, 268, 303
Hotel Pintor El Greco, 633, 646
Hotel Playa Sol, 513, 533
Hotel Polo, 761, 783
Hotel Port-Lligat, 513, 533
Hotel Presa, 203, 259
Hotel Puerta de Toledo, 97
Hotel el Puerto, 356, 364
Hotel Quinto Centenario, 659, 672
Hotel Real, 315, 325
Hotel de la Reconquista, 276, 303
Hotel la Rectoral, 288, 303
Hotel Reina Isabel, 809, 815
Hotel Reina Victoria: Madrid, 93; Valencia, 603, 614
Hotel La Residencia, 567, 585
Hotel Residencia Cordón, 243, 260
Hotel Rhin, 315, 325
Hotel Riosol, 189, 259
Hotel Risco, 317, 325
Hotel Ritz: Barcelona, 479; Madrid, 73, 92, 105, 115
Hotel Rocamar, 513, 533
Hotel Salobreña, 768, 783

Hotel San Sebastián Playa, 527, 534
Hotel Santa Catalina, 809, 815
Hotel Santo Mauro, 94
Hotel Saratoga, 563, 585
Hotel Sardinero, 315, 325
Hotel Las Sirenas, 145, 154
Hotel Solana del Ter, 519, 533
Hotel Sol Girona, 516, 533
Hotel Sotogrande, 775, 783
Hotel Subur Marítim, 527, 534
Hotel Suecia, 94
Hotel Suizo, 479
Hotel Torremangana, 641, 646
Hotel Tres Coronas de Silos, 236, 260
Hotel Tres Reyes, 404, 423
Hotel Tryp Rex, 97
Hotel Tryp Washington, 97
Hotel Villa de Bilbao, 358, 364
Hotel Villa Magna, 94, 115
Hotel Villa Real, 93
Hotel Wellington, 95, 118
Hotel Wilson, 482
Hotel Yoldi, 405, 423
Hoz de Arbayún, 409
Hoz de Lumbier, 409
Las Huelgas Reales, 253
La Huerta, 592
Huetre, 656
Las Hurdes, 656

Iberotel Club La Mola, 582, 586
Iberotel Maspalomas Oasis, 808, 815
Iberotel Tres Islas Sol, 813, 816
Ibiza, 24, 535, 558 (map), 574
Ibiza City, 575
Icod de los Vinos, 805
Idó, 553
Idoya, 410
Iglesia de la Asunción: Los Arcos, 417; San Sebastián, 807
Iglesia Colegiata: Pastrana, 643; Xàtiva, 606
Iglesia Colegiata de la Candelaria, 669
Iglesia Colegiata de San Pedro, 239

Iglesia Colegiata de Santa Maria: Calatayud, 440; Jerez, 745

Iglesia Colegiata de Santa María del Sar, 295

Iglesia de la Concepción, 801

Iglesia del Crucifijo, 414

Iglesia de la Magdalena, 184

Iglesia de Nuestra Señora de los Angeles, 320

Iglesia de Nuestra Señora de las Angustias, 209

Iglesia de Nuestra Señora de la Asunción, 317

Iglesia Parroquial de San Salvador, 352

Iglesia de la Peregrina, 300

Iglesia de San Andrés, 440

Iglesia de San Bartolomé: Jerez de los Caballeros, 670; Logroño, 371

Iglesia de San Benito, 212

Iglesia de San Cipriano, 184

Iglesia de San Dionisio, 745

Iglesia de San Esteban: Astorga, 198; Segovia, 143

Iglesia de San Félix de Solovio, 294

Iglesia de San Francisco, 300

Iglesia de San Ginés, 84

Iglesia de San Ildefonso, 184

Iglesia de San Jerónimo el Real, 69

Iglesia de San José, 62

Iglesia de San Juan, 137

Iglesia de San Juan de Baños, 225

Iglesia de San Juan Bautista, 380

Iglesia de San Juan de la Cruz, 601

Iglesia de San Juan de Ortega, 256

Iglesia de San Lorenzo: Lleida, 531; Pamplona; 400; Sahagún, 202

Iglesia de San Marcos, 806

Iglesia de San Martín: Frómista, 228; Segovia, 142; Teruel, 441;

Trujillo, 661; Valencia, 595

Iglesia de San Mateo, 658

Iglesia de San Miguel: Palencia, 227; Vitoria, 360

Iglesia de San Miguel Arcangel, 416

Iglesia de San Millán, 144

Iglesia de San Nicolás: Avila, 138; Burgos, 245; Valencia, 599

Iglesia de San Nicolás de Bari, 140

Iglesia de San Pablo: Peñafiel, 224; Ubeda, 722; Valladolid, 209

Iglesia de San Pedro: Arcos de la Frontera, 755; Avila, 138; Frómista, 228; Olite, 418; Ripoll, 519; Teruel, 441

Iglesia de San Pedro de la Nave, 186

Iglesia de San Pedro de la Rúa, 416

Iglesia de San Pedro el Viejo, 78

Iglesia de San Quirce, 143

Iglesia de San Román, 632

Iglesia de San Salvador, 441

Iglesia de San Saturnino, 399

Iglesia de Santa Agueda, 245

Iglesia de Santa Ana, 235

Iglesia de Santa Catalina, 595

Iglesia de Santa Cruz, 724

Iglesia de Santa Eulalia, 665

Iglesia de Santa María: Aranda de Duero, 231; Astorga, 198; Cáceres, 659; Castelló d'Empúries, 512; Castro-Urdiales, 317; Mahón, 544; Ronda, 760; San Sebastián, 338; Trujillo, 661; Viana, 418; Wamba, 220

Iglesia de Santa María la Antigua, 209

Iglesia de Santa María de la Asunción: Arcos de la Frontera, 755; Dueñas, 225

Iglesia de Santa María la Blanca, 228

Iglesia de Santa María del Camino, 229

Iglesia de Santa María del Castillo, 228

Iglesia de Santa María Jus del Castillo, 416

Iglesia de Santa María Magdalena, 668

Iglesia de Santa María de Palacio, 372

Iglesia de Santa María de la Piscina, 379

Iglesia de Santa María la Real, 418

Iglesia de Santa María de los Reales Alcázares, 722

Iglesia de Santa María de los Reyes, 380

Iglesia de Santiago: Avila, 138; Carrión de los Condes, 229; Puente la Reina, 414; Sangüesa, 409

Iglesia de Santiago del Arrabal, 626

Iglesia de Santiago el Real, 372

Iglesia de San Tirso, 202

Iglesia de Santo Cristo de la Luz, 627

Iglesia de Santo Domingo: Lugo, 288; Valencia, 601

Iglesia de Santo Domingo el Antiguo, 632

Iglesia del Santo Sepulcro, 417

Iglesia de los Santos Juanes, 600

Iglesia de Santo Tomás, 376

Iglesia de Santo Tomé, 630

Iglesia de Sant Salvador, 573

Iglesia de Santullano, 275

Iglesia de San Vicente, 337

Iglesia de Sasamón, 257

Iglesia de la Trinidad, 143

Ikea, 361

Illescas, 626

IMBIS, 168

Imperial Restaurant, 769

Imperial Tarraco, 529, 534

Inca, 570

L'Indret, 497

Inglaterra, 700, 781

Instituto Valenciano de Arte Moderno, 600

Irizar, 104

Isaba, 410
Isla de Arousa, 301
Isla Baja, 806
Isla de Collom, 547
Isla-Graciosa, 796
Isla de Santa Clara, 339
Isla de la Toja, 301
Islote de Hilario, 795
Itálica, 699
Itxaropena, 347
Itxas-Etxe, 353

Jaca, 437
Jacinta González, 657
Jaén, 726
Jágaro, 546
Jameos del Agua, 796
Jarandilla de la Vera, 654
Jardín Botánico (Madrid), 71
Jardines del Alcázar (Seville), 694
Jardines Casa March, 573
Jardines del Real (Valencia), 602
Jardines de la Taconera, 400
El Jardín de Oporto, 317
El Jardín del Palacio, 611
Jardín del Principe, 152
Jardín de San Carlos, 298
Jatetxea Rekondo, 345
Jaume de Provença, 485
Jávea, 607
Javier, 408
Jerez de los Caballeros, 669
Jerez de la Frontera, 22, 744
Jesús Riano, 124
Jijona, 609
Jiménez de Jamuz, 201
Joan Estruchi Pipo, 496
Jockey, 108
Jolastoki, 358
Josetxo, 406
Joy Eslava, 115
Juan de la Cosa, 317, 325
Juan González Muga, 377
Juanito, 724
Judería: Córdoba, 717; Toledo, 631
Julio, 810
Julio González Center, 600
Jumilla, 592
Juncalillo, 811

Kabutzia, 341
Kaia-Kaipe, 353
Karlos Arguiñano, 352
Keepers, 579
KGB, 492
La Kika, 377
Kiosco Las Flores, 702

Koldo Royo, 564
Ku, 345

Labastida, 378
Lagartera, 654
Lago de Enol, 270
Lago de la Ercina, 270
Lago de Martiánez, 805
Laguardia, 379
La Laguna, 804
Laie, 489
Lajares, 813
Lanzarote, 787, 790, 791 (map)
Laredo, 317
Lauria, 529, 534
León, 20, 186, 196 (map)
Lequeito, 355
Lerma, 238
Lerranz, 101
Leyre, 407
Lhardy, 103
Librería Balague, 496
Librería San Pablo, 707
Licores Espinosa, 375
Lisboa, 440
Lladró, 120
Llano de Ucana, 802
Lleida, 530
La Llesca, 490
Llívia, 520
Loewe: Barcelona, 493; Madrid, 120; Seville, 707; Valencia, 605
Logroño, 19, 370
Lonja de Mercaderes, 432
La Lonja de la Seda, 600
Lora, 545
Lorenzo, 227
Luarca, 281
Luarqués, 104
Lúculo, 108
Lugo, 288
Luis Bardon Mesa, 122
Lumbrales, 177
La Luna, 172

Macarelleta, 556
Macotera, 177
Ma Cuina, 604
Madrid, 20, 47; maps: 48, 128
Madrigal de las Altas Torres, 140
El Maestrazgo, 442
Magnolia, 805
Maguedano, 706
Mahón, 543
Majestic, 481
Majorca, 24, 535, 557, 558 (map)
Majorica, 563
Málaga, 22, 679, 682, 763

Málaga Palacio, 765, 783
Mallorca Delicatessen, 112, 125
Manacor, 572
Maná Maná, 489
La Mancha, 21, 615, 616 (map)
Mañeru, 414
Mango: Barcelona, 493; Seville, 707
Manises, 604
Mantequerias Leonesas, 497
La Manual Alpargatera, 496
Manzanares, 635
Mapro's, 707
Marbella, 774
Marbella Club, 774, 784
Marcilla, 420
María Cristina Hotel, 633, 646
La Marina: Fuenterrabía, 350; Ibiza City, 575; Palma, 571
Los Mariscos, 727
Marketing Ahead, 32
Marks & Spencer, 123
Martín de Yeltes, 177
Mascaras Moreno, 708
La Masía d'En Sord, 578
Maspalomas, 809
Massimo Dutti, 707
Mauri, 497
Mausoleo de Centcelles, 530
Mayke Cafetería-Heladería, 630
Mazagón, 741
Medellín, 666
Medina Azahara, 719
Medina del Campo, 218
Meliá Botánico, 800, 815
Meliá Cáceres, 659, 672
Meliá Granada Hotel, 737, 782
Meliá Salinas, 793, 814
Meliá Sierra Nevada, 738, 782
Meliá Sol y Nieve, 738, 782
Meliá Tamarindos, 809, 815
Mencey, 800, 815
El Mentidero de la Villa, 108
Mercadel, 549
Mercado de la Brecha, 338
Mercado Central (Valencia), 599
Mercado Central de Lanuza, 432
Mercado de la Puerta de Toledo, 80, 123

Mercat del Born, 464
Mercat de Sant Antoni, 497
Mercedes Carrascosa and Paqui Tovar, 740
Mercería Guerrero, 194
Mérida, 22, 663
La Meridiana, 774
Le Meridien Barcelona, 479
Meryan, 716
La Mesa Redonda, 746
Mesa de los Tres Reyes, 410
La Meseta, 159
El Mesón, 257
Mesón la Bolera, 322
Mesón del Café, 489
Mesón del Camino, 374
Mesón de Cándido, 144
Mesón de C'an Pedro, 564
Mesón Casas Colgadas, 639
Mesón la Casuca, 318
Mesón Cervantes, 213
Mesón de Champiñón, 101
Mesón del Cid, 251
Mesón Don Raimundo, 704
Mesón La Fragua, 213
Mesón los Gallegos, 101
Mesón de la Guitarra, 101
Mesón José María, 144
Mesón Julián, 421
Mesón la Magdalena, 199
Mesón de la Merced, 374
Mesón Panero, 213
Mesón del Peregrino (Puente La Reina), 414, 423
Mesón El Peregrino (Santo Domingo de la Calzada), 385
Mesón Trasta María, 147
Mesón 2, 39, 222
Mesón de la Villa: Aranda de Duero, 232; Santillana del Mar, 308
Mesón de la Virreina, 153
Meye Maier, 707
Mezquita-Catedral, 714
Miami Park, 637
Micalet, 598
Miguel Cabrerizo, 728
Mijas, 773
Mijas-Golf, 773
Minorca, 24, 535, 540, 541, 542 (map)
El Mirador, 583
Mirador de Haría, 797

Mirador de Humboldt, 801
Mirador Miguel Utrillo, 527
Mirador del Río, 796
Miramelindo, 491
Miranda del Castañar, 182
El Mirlo Blanco, 773
Mi Vaca y Yo, 805
Moda Shopping, 124
Mogarraz, 183
Moguer, 744
Mojácar, 771
La Molina, 520
El Molino Club, 492
El Molino de la Losa, 140
Molí de la Nora, 531
El Molino Restaurant, 316
Monaco, 219
Monasterio de la Cartuja, 736
Monasterio de Guadalupe, 662
Monasterio de Irache, 417
Monasterio de Iranzu, 417
Monasterio de Lluch, 568
Monasterio de Montserrat, 522
Monasterio del Nuestra Señora del Rosario, 635
Monasterio de la Oliva, 419
Monasterio del Parral, 144
Monasterio de El Paular, 147
Monasterio de San Juan de las Abadesas, 519
Monasterio de San Juan de los Reyes, 631
Monasterio de San Martín Pinario, 294
Monasterio de San Millán de Suso, 383
Monasterio de San Millán de Yuso, 383
Monasterio de San Pedro de Arlanza, 238
Monasterio de San Pedro de Cardeña, 255
Monasterio de San Pedro de las Dueñas, 202
Monasterio de San Pelayo de Antealtares, 294
Monasterio de San Salvador de Ibañeta, 412
Monasterio de San Salvador de Leyre, 407

Monasterio de Santa Maria, 519
Monasterio de Santa Maria de Poblet, 525
Monasterio de Santa María la Real, 382
Monasterio de Santes Crues, 525
Monasterio de Santo Domingo de Silos, 236
Monasterio de Sant Pere de Rodes, 513
Monasterio de San Zoilo, 229
Monasterio de Yuste, 655
Mon Bar, 554
Monestir de Pedralbes, 473
Los Monjes, 667
Monopol Hotel, 800, 815
Montaña de Arucas, 811
Montañas del Fuego, 794
Montánchez, 653
Montblanc, 525
Monte Atalaya, 582
Monte Igueldo, 337
Monte Jaizkíbel, 349
Monte Naranco, 277
Monte de Piedad, 122
Los Monteros, 774, 784
Monte Tecla, 302
Monte Toro, 550
Monte Ulía, 348
Monte Urgull, 337
El Montíboli, 607, 614
Montilla-Moriles, 682
Montjuïc, 470
Montserrat, 522
Mora de Rubielos, 442
Mota del Cuervo, 642
Motrico, 355
Al-Mounia, 111
Mozarabic Chapel, 629
Muebles Artesanos, 149
Muebles de Estilo Español, 310
Multiplaza, 176
Mundaka, 356
Munigua, 699
Murallas de Avila, 154
Murcia, 22, 587, 611
Museo de América, 85
Museo Arqueológico: Alcoy, 609; Badajoz, 667; Córdoba, 718; León, 188; Oviedo, 274; Santa Cruz de Tenerife, 803; Vitoria, 359
Museo Arqueológico Nacional (Madrid), 87
Museo Arqueólogico Provincial (Seville), 699
Museo de Arte Abstracto (Cuenca), 639

Museo de Arte Contemporáneo (Elche), 610
Museo Arte Contemporaneo (Toledo), 632
Museo de Artes Decorativas (Madrid), 70
Museo de Arte Visigodo, 665
Museo de Bellas Artes: Bilbao, 356; Málaga, 765; Seville, 697; Vitoria, 361; Zaragoza, 435
Museo Camón Aznar, 434
Museo Canario, 810
Museo de Carruajes, 82
Museo Casa Dulcinea del Toboso, 642
Museo Cerralbo, 85
Museo Colección de Arte del Siglo XX, 608
Museo de los Concilios y de la Cultura Visigoda, 632
Museo Diocesano: Cuenca, 640; León, 193; Pamplona, 398; Sigüenza, 644; Valladolid, 208
Museo del Ejército (Madrid), 70
Museo Internacional de Arte Contemporaneo (Arrecife), 793
Museo del Jamón, 125
Museo Junípero Serra, 572
Museo Lázaro Galdiano, 88
Museo de Marceliano Santa María, 245
Museo Municipal (Madrid), 86
Museo Municipal de Bellas Artes (Santander), 314
Museo Municipal Gonzáles-Santana, 668
Museo Nacional de Arte Romano, 664
Museo Nacional Centro de Arte Reina Sofía, 71, 120
Museo Nacional de Cerámica, 601
Museo Nacional de Escultura, 210
Museo Nacional de Etnología, 72
Museo de Naipes, 361
Museo de Navarra, 399
Museo Oriental, 212
Museo Pablo Gargallo, 434
Museo del Prado, 62

Museo Provincial: Lugo, 288; Pontevedra, 300
Museo Provincial de Bellas Artes: Badajoz, 667; Cádiz, 753; Valencia, 602
Museo Provincial de Prehistoria y Arqueología, 314
Museo Provincial de la Rioja, 373
Museo Románico, 86
Museo de Ruiz de Luna, 634, 654
Museo Salzillo, 612
Museo de Santa Cruz, 627
Museo San Telmo, 338
Museo Sefardí, 631
Museo Sorolla, 89
Museo Taurino, 595
Museo del Teatro, 636
Museo de Telas, 254
Museo Thyssen-Bornemisza, 73
Museo Victor Hugo, 348
Museo del Vino de Rioja, 376
Museu Arqueològic: Alcudia, 569; Barcelona, 471; Girona, 516; Manacor, 573; Tarragona, 528
Museu Arqueològic Ibiza, 526
Museu d'Art de Catalunya, 471
Museu de Arte Moderno (Tarragona), 528
Museu d'Art Modern (Barcelona), 475
Museu Cau Ferrat, 526
Museu Comarcal de la Garrotxa, 517
Museu Diocesa: La Seu d'Urgell, 521; Solsona, 522; Vic, 518
Museu Etnològic (Barcelona), 471
Museu de la Història de la Ciutat, 462
Museu Marés, 461
Museu Maricel de Mar, 527
Museum of the Duchess of Lerma, 626
Museu Militar Castell de Montjuïc, 472
Museu de Montserrat, 522
Museu Municipal de Arte Contemporáneo (Cadaqués), 513
Museu Picasso, 464
Museu Romàntic, 527

Museu dei Vi, 524
Musical Emporium, 496

Nacional Reserva de Saja, 322
Nade Fabreau, 740
Nájera, 382
Nancy Niños, 119
De Natura, 148
Navarra, 19, 392, 394 (map)
Navatejera, 201
Naveta d'Es Tudons, 550
Neichel, 484
Nerja, 767
NH Canciller Ayala, 362, 364
NH Condestable (Burgos), 243, 260
NH Cristal (Alicante), 609, 614
NH Gran Hotel (Zaragoza), 436, 444
NH Gran Hotel Calderón (Barcelona), 481
NH Zurbano (Madrid), 95
Nick Havanna, 491
Nicolás, 666
El Ninot, 496
Niserias, 267
Noja, 318
Nomismática Pliego, 708
Nou Celler, 490
Novecento, 495
Novedades EDI, 189
Nuestra Señora del Pino, 812
Nuestra Señora de los Remedios, 804
Nuestro Bar, 642
Nuevas Galerías, 122
Nuevo Gran Casino de Kursaal, 341
Numantia, 819
Nuñomoral, 656

Obradoiro, 296
Ochagavía, 411
Ochoa, 707
Olárizu, 362
Old Castile, 20, 155, 156 (map)
Olite, 418
La Oliva, 577
Olivenza, 668
El Olivo, 567
La Olla, 406
La Olma, 148
Olmedo, 219
Olot, 517
Olvera, 758
O Merlo, 300
Ondarroa, 355
O'Pazo, 110

Orgaz, 634
Orihuela, 611
Oropesa, 654
La Orotava, 801
Ortiz Garrido, 728
Osborne, 752
Ostarte, 341
Les Ostres, 490
Otto Zutz, 492
Oviedo, 18, 271
Oyarzun, 351

El Pabellón del Espejo, 113
Pablo, 636
Pachá, 579
Padrón, 299
Pajarita Bonbonera, 562
El Pajaro Azul, 145
Palace of Charles V, 734
Palace Hotel, 74, 93, 115
Palacio de Ajuria-Enea, 361
Palacio Altamira, 610
El Palacio de la Bellota, 604
Palacio de las Cadenas, 721
Palacio de las Cigüeñas, 658
Palacio de los Condes de Miranda, 235
Palacio de la Conquista, 660
Palacio de las Cortes, 74
Palacio de Cristal, 71
Palacio del Duque de Granada, 408
Palacio de Duque del Parque, 277
Palacio de los Duques de San Carlos, 661
Palacio del Duque de Uceda, 77
Palacio Episcopal, 552
Palacio de Escoriaza-Esquivel, 359
Palacio Español, 698
Palacio del Espartero, 372
Palacio de la General-idad, 599
Palacio de los Guz-manes, 190
Palacio del Infantado, 643
Palacio de Jabalquinto, 724
Palacio de Liria, 85
Palacio de la Magdalena, 315
Palacio del Marqués de Dos Aguas, 601
Palacio de Marqués de Salvatierra, 760

Palacio del Marqués de Santa Cruz, 637
Palacio del Marqués de Viana, 718
Palacio de Monterrey, 168
Palacio Obispo, 198
Palacio de Pimentel, 211
Palacio del Príncipe de Viana, 409
Palacio de Rajoy, 290
Palacio Real: Aranjuez, 151; Madrid, 80
Palacio Real District, 60 (map), 79
Palacio Restaurant, 772
Palacio de los Reyes de Navarra, 415
Palacio de los Ribera, 756
Palacio de la Salina, 169
Palacio de Santa Cruz, 77
Palacios Remondo, 388
Los Palacios y Villafranca, 706
Palacio Valderrábanos, 139, 154
Palacio de Vallesantoro, 408
Palacio de Vela de los Cobos, 722
Palacio de los Velarde, 310
Palacio de Velázquez, 71
Palacio de Villardom-pardo, 727
Palacio del Vino, 374
El Palacio de los Vinos, 659
Palau de la Generalitat, 462
Palau Güell, 458
Palau de la Música (Va-lencia), 606
Palau de la Música Catalana, 466
Palau Nacional (Barce-lona), 471
Palau de Pedralbes, 473
Palau Sort, 552
Palau de la Virreina, 455
Palencia Province, 216 (map), 224
Palencia City, 225
Palma, 559
La Palma Island, 787, 812
La Palma Librería, 276
Las Palmas de Gran Canaria, 809
Palmeral de Europa, 610
La Paloma, 492
Palos de la Frontera, 744
Pals, 510

Pampaneira, 740
Pamplona, 19, 396
Panier Fleuri, 345
Papirum, 496
Parabere, 703
Paradís Madrid, 104
Paradiso, 145
Parador El Adelantado, 726, 782
Parador de Aigua Blava, 510, 533
Parador Alcázar del Rey Don Pedro, 701, 781
Parador de Almagro, 636, 646
Parador de Argómaniz, 362, 364
Parador de la Arruzafa, 718, 782
Parador de Cáceres, 659, 672
Parador de Las Cañadas del Teide, 802, 815
Parador Carlos V, 654, 672
Parador Casa de Barón, 300, 303
Parador Casa del Corregidor, 756, 783
Parador Castillo de Santa Catalina, 726, 782
Parador Castillo de Sigüenza, 643, 646
Parador Castillo de la Zuda, 530, 534
Parador de Chinchón, 152, 154
Parador Colaborador Arlanza, 237, 260
Parador de la Concordia, 439, 444
Parador Conde de la Go-mera, 807, 815
Parador Conde de Orgaz, 633, 646
Parador Condestable Dávalos, 722, 782
Parador Costa del Azahar, 593, 614
Parador de la Costa Blanca, 607, 614
Parador Cristóbal Colón, 741, 783
Parador Cruz de Tejeda, 811
Parador de Cuenca, 641, 646
Parador Don Gaspar de Portolá, 523, 533
Parador Duques de Cardona, 522, 533
Parador Enrique II, 180, 259
Parador Fernando de Ara-gón, 409, 423

Parador de Fuerteventura, 813, 816
Parador Gil Blás, 307, 325
Parador Guadalupe, 663, 672
Parador Hernán Cortés, 668, 672
Parador Hostal de San Marcos, 187, 259
Parador de la Isla de Hierro, 812, 815
Parador de Málaga-Gibralfaro, 765, 783
Parador de Málaga del Golf, 772, 784
Parador de La Mancha, 642, 646
Parador de Manzanares, 635
Parador Marco Fabio Quintiliano, 390, 391
Parador Marqués de Villena, 641, 646
Parador de Mojácar, 772, 783
Parador Molino Viejo, 280, 303
Parador de Nerja, 767, 783
Parador Príncipe de Viana, 418, 423
Parador Raimundo de Borgoña, 139, 154
Parador de Ribadeo, 281, 303
Parador del Río Deva, 321, 325
Parador de Salamanca, 174, 259
Parador de El Saler, 603, 614
Parador de San Francisco, 737, 782
Parador de Santa Cruz de la Palma, 812, 815
Parador de Santo Domingo de la Calzada, 385, 391
Parador de Segovia, 145, 154
Parador de la Seo de Urgell, 521, 533
Parador Sierra Nevada, 738, 782
Parador de Teruel, 441, 444
Parador de Tordesillas, 215, 260
Parador de Trujillo, 661, 673
Parador de Turismo Condes de Alba y Aliste, 184, 259
Parador de Turismo El Emperador, 349, 364

Parador del Valle de Arán, 523, 533
Parador Vía de la Plata, 664, 666, 673
Parador de Vic, 519, 533
Parador Virrey de Toledo, 654, 673
Páramo de Guzmán, 234
Paraninfo de Luis de León, 172
Parc de la Ciutadella, 475
Parc Güell, 472
Parc Nacional de Aigües Tortes, 523
Parque de María Luisa, 698
Parque Municipal García Sanabriá, 804
Parque Nacional de Garajonay, 807
Parque Nacional de Ordesa, 438
Parque Nacional de Timanfaya, 794
Parque del Retiro, 70
La Parranda, 613
Pasajes de San Juan, 348
Pascual, 489
Pascual Lazaro Papelería & Librería, 707
Paseo de las Canteras, 809
Paseo de la Castellana, 59
Paseo de la Concha, 339
Paseo del Espolón, 249
Paseo de la Herradura, 296
Paseo de la Independencia, 435
Paseo de Pereda, 314
Paseo del Prado, 62
Paso de la Yecla, 235
Passeig Arqueològic, 528
Passeig del Born, 491
Passeig de Gràcia, 466
Passeig Marítim, 560
Passeig de Sant Nicolau, 554
Pastrana, 642
Patio de las Escuelas, 173
Patio de la Infanta, 435
Patio de los Naranjos: Córdoba, 714; Seville, 692
El Patio Sevillano, 706
Patrícia: Ciudadela, 553; Mahón, 544
Patxiku Kintana, 346
La Pecera, 114
Pedraza de la Sierra, 148
Pedro Blanco, 722
Pedro Domecq, 751
Pedrosa de Duero, 233
Peña, 227

Peñafiel, 221
Peñalba, 281
Peñaranda de Duero, 235
Peña Tu, 271
Penedes, 505, 524
Península de la Magdalena, 313
Peñón de Ifach, 607
Pepecillo, 295
La Pepica, 604
Peralta, 419
Perelada, 514
Pérez Pascuas, 233
El Pescador, 107
Pesquera, 223
Pesquera de Duero, 223
Petra, 572
Petrosiam Café, 113
Petrus, 708
Pico de Bandama, 811
Picos de Europa, 18, 266, 320
Pico del Teide, 801
Pico de Tres Mares, 322
Pilar, 546
Pinar de la Esperanza, 803
Pinar de Tamadaba, 811
Pinocchio, 455
Piquio, 140
Pizzería San Marco, 704
Plaça de l'Ajuntament, 595
Plaça d'Alfons III, 550
Plaça del Carme, 544
Plaça de Catalunya, 451
Plaça del Colegio del Patriarca, 601
Plaça de la Constitució, 544
Plaça d'Es Borne, 551
Plaça España, 552
Plaça d'Explanada, 543
Plaça del Rei, 462
Plaça Reial, 456
Plaça de Reina, 595
Plaça Santa Eulalia, 562
Plaça de Sant Jaume, 462
Plaça de la Seu, 459
Plaça de Vila, 577
Plasencia, 655
El Plata, 434
Platja Mitjorn, 582
Playa de las Américas, 799, 800
Playa de la Concha, 339
Playa de Ondarreta, 339
Playa de Ris, 318
Playa de Salve, 317
Playa de San Agustín, 809
Playa de San Lorenzo, 279
Playa de San Marcos, 806

Playa de las Teresitas, 804
Plaza del Adelantado, 804
Plaza de Alfonso el Magnánimo, 601
Plaza de las Arenas, 309
Plaza de la Armería, 81
Plaza del Azoguejo, 141, 142
Plaza de la Candelaria, 803
Plaza de Cánovas del Castillo, 73
Plaza de Carlos V, 72
Plaza de los Carros, 78
Plaza del Castillo, 400
Plaza de Cervantes, 149
Plaza de la Cibeles, 59
Plaza de Colón, 87
Plaza de la Constitución, 337
Plaza de las Cortes, 74
Plaza de la Encarnación, 83
Plaza de España: Madrid, 85; Medina del Campo, 219; Vitoria, 360; Zaragoza, 435
Plaza del Espíritu Santo, 810
Plaza del Espolón, 371
Plaza de Feijóo, 274
Plaza de la Independencia (Madrid), 70
Plaza de la Lealtad, 73
Plaza de los Leones, 723
Plaza del Machete, 360
Plaza Mayor: Almagro, 636; Aranda de Duero, 231; Burgos, 248; Chinchón, 153; Ciudad Rodrigo, 181; Cuenca, 641; Madrid, 54, 76; Pedraza de la Sierra, 148; Salamanca, 166; Trujillo, 660; Valladolid, 207
Plaza del Mercado: Logroño, 372; Valencia, 599
Plaza de Obradoiro, 290
Plaza de Oriente, 83
Plaza de la Paja, 77
Plaza de la Paz, 376
Plaza del Pilar, 430
Plaza de Ramón Pelayo, 311
La Plaza Restaurant, 112
Plaza de El Salvador, 630
Plaza de San Marcelo, 190
Plaza de San Martín, 195
Plaza de San Mateo, 658
Plaza de San Román, 632

Plaza de Santa Ana, 810
Plaza de Santa Bárbara, 86
Plaza Santa Cruz, 433
Plaza de Santa María, 658
Plaza de Santo Domingo: León, 190; Las Palmas de Gran Canaria, 810
Plaza de la Seo, 433
Plaza de los Sitios, 435
Plaza de Toros: Pamplona, 400; Valencia, 595
Plaza de Toros de la Real Maestranza de Caballería de Ronda, 760
Plaza Vázquez de Molina, 721
Plaza de las Ventas, 117
Plaza de la Villa, 77
Plaza de la Virgen, 599
Plaza de la Virgen Blanca, 360
Plaza del Zocodover, 627
Poblado de la Hoya, 380
Poble Espanyol, 470, 495
Las Pocholas, 406
Los Podencos, 638
Polvorilla, 251
Pontevedra, 300
Pont Vell 28, 517
Populart, 707
Portal del Carmen, 443
El Portalón, 359
Portal de les Tables, 576
Pórtico de la Gloria, 291
El Portillo de la Villa, 802
Portixol, 564
Port-Lligat, 513
Port Mahón Hotel, 545, 585
Portobello, 214
Port de Valldemossa, 566
La Posada, 252
La Posada de Don Mariano, 148, 154
Posada de la Villa, 102
Pou d'es Lle'o, 581
Del Pozo, 125
El Pozo de las Penas, 706
Presidente, 481
Prestige, 495
Principal, 191
Príncipe de Asturias, 280, 303
Príncipe de Viana, 110
Priorato, 505
Puente Aéreo, 121
El Puente del Arzobispo, 654
Puente del Mar, 602
Puente de Palmas, 667
Puente del Real, 602
Puente la Reina, 413
Puente Román, 269
Puente Romano: Cór-

doba, 715; Salamanca, 174
Puente Romano Hotel, 774, 784
Puente de San Pablo, 244
Puente de Segovia, 80
Puerta de Alcalá, 70
Puerta de Alfonso VI, 626
Puerta de la Coronería, 246
Puerta de Miño, 288
Puerta de Moros, 78
Puerta Nueva de Bisagra, 626
Puerta de la Pellejería, 247
Puerta de las Platerías, 292
Puerta de Santa María, 246
Puerta del Sarmental, 247
Puerta del Sol: Madrid, 75; Toledo, 627
Puerta de Toledo, 79
Puerto Banús, 774
Puerto de la Bonaigua, 523
Puerto del Carmen, 794
Puerto de la Cruz, 799, 800, 804
Puerto de la Luz, 809
Puerto Pesquero, 339
Puerto de Santa María, 746, 752
Puerto de Sóller, 568
Puigcerdà, 520
Puig des Molins, 576
Puvill, 496
The Pyrenees, 410, 437
Els Quatre Gats, 465, 490

Quel, 387
Quintillana de las Viñas, 238

La Rábida, 744
El Racimo de Oro, 195
Rafael Corrales, 231
Las Raíces, 803
El Raitán, 277
Rambla dels Caputxins, 456
Rambla de Catalunya, 468
Las Ramblas, 451, 452 (map)
Ramírez, 121
Ramón Montero, 122
Ramón Roteta, 350
La Rana Verde, 152
El Rancho Chico, 195
Rascafría, 147
El Rastro, 79, 123

Real Academia de Bellas Artes de San Fernando, 75
Real Monasterio de las Descalzas Reales, 84
Real Monasterio de Santo Tomás, 138
Regencia Colón, 478
Regente, 480
Regueria, 296
Reials Drassanes Museu Marítim, 473
Reina Cristina, 775, 784
Reina Victoria, 761, 783
Renacimiento, 707
La Renaixença, 527, 534
Requena, 592
Restaurant Los Blasones, 311
Restaurant Cala Mastella, 580
Restaurant Cal Ros, 516
Restaurant Castillo, 311
Restaurant Drac, 571
Restaurante Berceo, 107
Restaurante El Cobalto, 275
Restaurante Don Antonio, 804
Restaurante Gandarias, 341
Restaurante Marixa, 380
Restaurante Martín Berasategui, 346
Restaurante Navarre, 416
Restaurante Reno, 484
Restaurante San José, 793
Restaurante Teheran, 112
Restaurante del Tinell, 488
Restaurante Zabala, 360
Restaurant Font del Gat, 489
Restaurant Maruja, 319
Restaurant Mayton, 181
Restaurant Migjorn, 549
Restaurant La Puda, 529
Restaurant Sa Seni, 580
Restaurant S'Engolidor, 549
Retablo, 296
El Retiro, 280
Rey Alfonso, 767
Rey Don Sancho: León, 189; Zamora, 185
Rhin, 315
Ría de Muros y Noia, 301
Rías Altas, 299
Rías Bajas, 301
Ribadesella, 271
Ribeiro, 284
Ribera de Burgos, 232
Ribera de Curtidores, 79
Ribera del Duero, 162
Rincón de la Cava, 101

Rincón de Curro, 703
Rincón de Pepe, 612, 613, 614
Rincón de Soto, 420
Río Cares, 266
Riofrío, 146
Río Grande, 704
La Rioja, 19, 365, 366 (map)
Rioja Alavesa, 363, 378
La Rioja Alta, 378
La Rioja Baja, 386
Rioja Selección, 375
Ripoll, 519
Ris, 318
Roa de Duero, 233
Robata, 112
Robliza de Cojos, 177
El Rodeo, 181
Rodero, 406
Romàntic, 527, 534
Roncal, 410
Roncesvalles, 412
Ronda, 759
Las Rosas, 807
Roses, 512
Royal Plaza Hotel, 577, 586
Rúa Nueva, 295
Rúa de Raíña, 297
Rúa del Villar, 295
Rubielos de Mora, 442
Rueda, 163, 217
El Ruedo, 195
Rufino, 666
Running of the Bulls, 401
Rupit, 519

La Sabina, 583
Sa Calobra, 568
Sacha, 110
Sacramonte, 730
Sacrista de las Cabezas, 644
Sacristía de los Cálices, 692
Sacristía Mayor, 692
Saelices, 638
Sa Figuera, 554
S'Agaró, 510
Sa Gelateria, 554
Sagunto, 593
Sabagún, 202
Sala Fabergé, 122
Sala Gaspar, 494
Salamanca, 20, 164, 178 (map)
Sala Vinçon, 494
S'Albufera, 547
Salduba, 347
Salinas, 281
Sa Llonja, 562
Salobreña, 767
Salo del Tinell, 462

El Salvador, 611
San Andrés, 804
San Andrés Church, 138
San Benito, 657
San Bruno, 147
San Carlos, 580
S'Ancora, 548
Sancta Ovetensis Cathedral, 273
San Fermín, 406
San Francisco, 562
San Francisco el Grande, 80
Sangüesa, 408
San José, 770
San José Optica y Radio, 189
Sanlúcar de Barrameda, 746
San Marco, 703
San Miguel de Lillo, 278
San Pedro de la Nave, 186
San Salvador, 409
San Sebastián, 17, 336
San Sebastián de la Gomera, 807
Santa Agata Chapel, 462
Santa Catalina de Somoza, 200
Santa Caterina Market, 496
Santa Cristina de Lena, 278
Santa Cruz de la Palma, 812
Santa Cruz de Tenerife, 799, 800, 803
Santa Fé, 762
Santa Maria, 552
Santa Maria del Mar, 464
Santa Maria del Naranco, 278
Santa Maria de Poblet, 525
Santa Maria de Porqueres, 517
Santa María la Real, 408
Santa María la Real de Nieva, 145
Santa María de Sandoval, 201
Santa María del Sar, 295
Santa María de Valbuena, 222
Santander, 17, 313
Santa Pau, 517
Santes Crues, 525
Sant Feliu de Guíxols, 509
Santi, 214
Santiago Brugalla, 496
Santiago de Compostela, 19, 289
Santiago Marti, 494

Santillana Foundation, 311
Santillana del Mar, 17, 306
Santiponce, 700
Santo Domingo de la Calzada, 384
Santo Domingo Church, 300
Santo Domingo de Silos, 236
Santoña, 317
Sant Pau del Camp, 456
Sant Sadurní d'Anoia, 506, 525
Sant Telm, 565
Santuario de Bonany, 572
Santuario Covadonga, 269
Santuario del Cura, 571
Santuario de Loyola, 354
San Vicente de la Barquera, 319
San Vicente de la Sonsierra, 378
Sa Punta, 510
El Sardinero, 313, 314
Sargadelos, 295
Sayat Nova, 111
Scala Meliá Castilla, 116
Scorpions, 631
Segovia, 20, 126, 141
Segundo Antigüedades, 707
Selección Vinos de Rioja, 376
Selva de Irati, 412
Semón: Barcelona, 496; Madrid, 125
Señorío de Bertiz, 110
Señorío de Jomelsu, 612
Señorío de Sarría, 414
Senyor Parellada, 485
La Seo: Valencia, 598; Zaragoza, 433
Sepúlveda, 149
Serafín, 185
Serie Disseny, 494
Seseña Capas, 120
Ses Païsses, 573
Ses Rotges, 573, 585
Setenil, 759
Set Portes, 487
La Seu (Palma), 561
La Seu d'Urgell, 521
Seu Vella, 531
1741, 495
Seville, 22, 680, 686, 688 (map)
Shanti, 406
Sidi Saler Palace, 603, 614
Sierra Nevada, 738

Sierra de la Peña de Francia, 182
La Siesta Hotel, 800, 815
Sigüenza, 643
S'Illeta, 583
La Sinagoga, 717
Sinagoga de Santa María la Blanca, 631
Sinagoga de El Tránsito, 630
SiSiSi, 492
Sitges, 526
Sky, 176
Slika, 608
Soho, 492
Sóller, 568
Sol Ric, 529
Solsona, 522
Somontano, 428
Son Catlar, 556
Son Marroig, 566
Son Saura, 556
Son Vida, 563, 585
Son Xoriguer, 545
Sopitas, 387
Sos del Rey Católico, 409
Sotheby's, 122
Subarna, 495
Supermercado Tandy, 181
El Sur, 114

Taberna del Alabardero, 703
La Taberna de la Cuarta Esquina, 390
Taberna Pan con Tomate, 214
La Taberna del Pintor, 766
Taberna Plaza Mayor, 227
Tabernas, 771
Taberna Sol y Sombra, 702
Taberna Vasca, 604
Tabernes Blanques, 605
Tafetán Taller Textil, 124
Tajinaste, 803
Talai-Pe, 353
Talavera de la Reina, 634, 654
Talgo, 27
Tamboril, 340
Taramundi, 288
Tarifa, 776
Tarragona, 23, 505, 527
La Taula, 519
Teatre-Museu Dalí, 513
Teatre Pereira, 578
Teatriz, 107
Teatro de la Comédia, 116
Teatro Español, 116
Teatro Lírico Nacional de la Zarzuela, 116

Teatro Nacional María Guererro, 116
Teatro Real, 83
Teguise Playa Hotel, 794, 814
Tejeda, 811
Temple of Mars, 665
Templo Expiatorio de la Sagrada Família, 469
Tenerife, 787, 797, 798 (map)
Teror, 812
Les Terrasses, 579, 586
Teruel, 440
Tibidabo, 472
La Tierra, 119
Tierra de Barros, 652
Tierra de Campos, 225
Tirachinas Restaurant, 388
Tito Bustillo, 270
Tito's, 772
El Tizón, 195
El Toboso, 642
La Toja: Badajoz, 667; Madrid, 100
Toledo, 21, 621, 622 (map)
Tordesillas, 215
Tormes, 766
El Torno, 708
Toro, 163
Torre de la Calahorra, 716
Torre del Clavero, 169
Torre de Doña Urraca, 237
Torre Galatea, 514
Torre d'en Gaumes, 548
Torre de Hércules, 298
Torre de los Lujanes, 77
Torre de Merino, 311
Torremilanos, 231
Torremolinos, 772
Torrente de Pareis, 568
El Torreón, 215
Torreón de la Fortea, 434
Torreón de la Zuda, 432
Torres, 553
Torre de San Miguel, 670
Torres del Río, 417
Torres Serranos, 600
Torre de los Velarde, 308
Tortosa, 530
Tossa de Mar, 509
El Tragaluz, 484
Trajes Sevillanos, 707
Tramuntana, 557
El Transcantábrico, 30, 323
Trascorrales, 277
Trea, 120
Trena de la Fresa, 151, 153

Treno, 489
Trepucó, 546
Tres Zetas, 119
Triana, 702, 705
La Trinidad, 641
La Trucha (Madrid), 101
Las Truchas (El Bosque), 758, 783
Trujillo, 21, 660
Tryp Colón, 701, 781
Tryp Gran Sol, 609, 614
El Tubo, 434
Tuca, 523
Tudela, 19, 420
Tudela de Duero, 221
Tulipán de Oro, 360
El Túnel, 487
Turn of the Century, 494
Turner Librería, 123
Turrones Ramos, 598
Túy, 302
Txingudi, 437
Txulotxo, 349

Ubeda, 720
Ubrique, 758
Ullastret, 510
Universal, 492
Universidad de Salamanca, 171
Universidad de Valladolid, 208
Urepel, 346
Utiel-Requena, 591

La Vaguada, 124
Valdeorras, 284
Valdepeñas, 621, 635
Valencia City, 593, 596 (map)
Valencia Province, 23, 587, 588 (map), 592
Valeria, 641
Valladolid City, 20, 204
Valladolid Province, 215, 216 (map)

Vall d'Aran, 523
Valldemossa, 566
Valle de los Caídos, 135
Valle de Guriezo, 317
Valle del Roncal, 410
Valls, 526
Vaqueira Beret, 523
Vasijas, 708
Vega Sicilia, 222
Vejér de la Frontera, 777
Vélez Blanco, 728
Velvet, 492
El Vendrell, 527
Venta de Aires, 633
Venta Antonio, 681
Venta del Batán, 118
La Venta del Cachirulo, 437
Venta de Juan Pito, 411
Venta Los Naranjos, 681
Venta del Pilar, 609
Venus Droguería & Perfumería, 176
La Vera Cruz, 144
Verruga, 289
Viana, 417
Vía Veneto, 485
Vic, 518
Victor, 357
Victoria Palace Hotel, 135, 154
Vidosa, 496
Vielha, 523
Vilaflor, 803
Vilafranca del Penedès, 524
Vila Vella, 509
Villajoyosa, 607
Villalcázar de Sirga, 228
El Villar, 380
Villar de Ciervo, 177
Villa Turística de Bubión, 740, 782
Villa Zuloaga, 354
Vinícola Hidalgo y Cia, 752

Vinos Blancos de Castilla, 218
Vinos Sanz, 218
La Violeta, 125
Virgen Blanca Cafetería, 360
Virgen del Pilar, 430
Viridiána, 106
Viso del Marqués, 637
Vista Alegre, 101
Vitoria, 358
Vizcaya Province, 355

Washington Irving's Quarters (Alhambra), 734

Xàtiva, 606
Xicara Xocolatería, 562
Xoriguer, 564

Yaiza, 795
Yanko: Barcelona, 493; Seville, 707
El Yantar de Pedraza, 148
Yecla, 592

Zadi, 706
Zafra, 668
Zahara de los Membrillos, 756
Zalacaín, 107
Zaldiarán, 362
Zambra, 116
Zamora, 20, 183
Zaragoza, 21, 428
Zarautz, 352
Zeleste, 492
Zortziko, 358
Zsa Zsa, 492
Zuberoa, 351
Zubillaga, 374
Zumaya, 353